ANGER AND HONSBERGER
LAW OF REAL PROPERTY

VOLUME 1

ANGER AND HONSBERGER
LAW OF REAL PROPERTY

SECOND EDITION

BY

A. H. OOSTERHOFF

AND

W. B. RAYNER

of the Faculty of Law, The University of Western Ontario
and of the Ontario Bar

VOLUME 1

1985

CANADA LAW BOOK INC.

240 EDWARD STREET, AURORA, ONTARIO

Canadian Cataloguing in Publication Data

Anger, Harry D., 1888-1953
    Anger and Honsberger : law of real property

Includes index.
First ed. had title: Canadian law of real property.
ISBN 0-88804-026-1

1. Real property — Canada. I. Honsberger, John D.
(John David). II. Oosterhoff, A. H. III. Rayner,
W. B. (Wesley B.). IV. Title. V. Title: Law of
real property. VI. Title: Canadian law of real
property.

KE625.A765 1985   346.7104'3   C85-098408-4

For
Sandra and Lois

PREFACE

In the twenty-five years since the first edition of this work appeared, much has happened in the law of real property, both in statute and case law. Apart from law review articles and case comments, however, *Anger and Honsberger* has remained the only comprehensive text on the Canadian law of real property. Because of the many changes in the law, the publisher was convinced that a new edition was warranted and, indeed, overdue.

In taking on the second edition of this work, we took the opportunity to completely revise, rewrite and reorganize the first edition. Thus, although the basic purpose of the work remains the same, namely a comprehensive text on the Canadian common law of real property, much has been added, with the result that the work is now approximately twice the size of the original.

We have divided the work into ten Parts for convenience and to make it more accessible to the reader. In the result, the first six Parts are devoted to basic principles of real property, and the remaining four Parts deal with the practical application of those principles.

In Part I a new introductory chapter and a chapter on the historical background of the Canadian law of real property have been added. Part II begins with an introductory chapter on tenures and estates, followed by separate chapters on each of the estates. The chapter on perpetuities has been moved into Part III, following chapters on invalid conditions and limitations and future interests. Part IV comprises chapters on trusts, settled estates and powers. In Part V, the chapter on co-ownership remains and a new chapter on matrimonial property has been added, consequent upon the statutory matrimonial property law reforms in all of the provinces in the past decade.

Part VI has been divided into several discrete chapters on incorporeal rights and similar interests, and separate chapters on boundaries and public rights over land have been added.

Part VII contains three entirely new chapters on contracts for the sale of land, conveyancing and remedies, while Part VIII contains eleven chapters on title, including new ones on capacity, registration and examination of title.

Parts IX and X are entirely new. The former contains two chapters on planning and other land use controls, while the latter contains an exhaustive treatment of condominiums, divided into three chapters.

vii

In discussing the law we have endeavoured to state not only the general principles, but also the divergences that appear from jurisdiction to jurisdiction. Thus, all relevant provincial statutes and cases are referred to and, where appropriate, commented upon. Moreover, the historical development of the law is traced when necessary for a proper understanding of the present position. In addition, comparative references to other jurisdictions are made where appropriate.

We are indebted to many persons and organizations for their assistance. In the first place, a number of persons have contributed chapters to the work and we wish to thank them for their outstanding contributions. These persons are Mr. John D. Honsberger, Q.C., the surviving editor of the first edition, who contributed chapters 18, 19 and 20; Mr. Bradley N. McLellan, of Weir & Foulds, Toronto, who contributed chapter 22; Messrs Peter D. Quinn and A. Costin, of McCarthy and McCarthy, Toronto, who did chapter 23; Professors Arnold S. Weinrib and Ralph E. Scane, Q.C., of the Faculty of Law, University of Toronto, who did chapters 25 and 30, respectively; and Mr. Alvin B. Rosenberg, Q.C., now Mr. Justice Rosenberg, and Mr. Howard Kirshenbaum, formerly of Rosenberg, Smith, Paton and Hyman, Toronto, who contributed chapters 38, 39 and 40. Mr. McLellan wishes to thank his research assistant, Martha McKinnon, and his secretaries, Bonny Bracken, Brigitte Hurrell and Liisa MacMurchy.

We are also indebted to the Faculty of Law, The University of Western Ontario, and the Ontario Law Foundation for making funds available to hire research assistants over the years. We want to thank our research assistants for all the valuable work they performed, namely, Linda C. Henry, David J. Goar, Michael D. Sharpe, Michael R. G. Best, David N. Beavis, David J. McKee, Joseph J. Neal, T. George Reczulski, Clive O. Llewellyn, David G. Wentzell, Andrej F. Markes, James R. Adams, and Sandra S. Cowan and, especially, Peter J. Thorup and Margaret Grottenthaler.

We are especially indebted to our secretaries, Jean Fisher, Joyce Pirt and Frances Sweitzer, and to our word processor operators, Victoria Vieau, Teresa Bourne and Jean Tasker, for their careful work in typing and retyping the manuscript.

A work of this magnitude cannot be written overnight and, as we progressed, we had to cope with new cases, texts, statutes and statute revisions. We are grateful to the staff at Canada Law Book for their willingness to incorporate the necessary revisions in the text, frequently after the type had been set, and for their extensive assistance throughout. In particular, we would like to thank Mrs. Fiona Miner and Mr. Marvin Goldstein and especially Mrs. Elizabeth Edwards for her cheerful co-operation and help throughout, and Mr. Alan Marks for his encouragement and invaluable assistance.

Finally, we wish to record our indebtedness to Mrs. Sandra M. S. Oosterhoff for her outstanding work in preparing the index.

It has been said that the law of land in countries under the Common Law of England is a "rubbish heap" which has been accumulating for hundreds of years, and is based upon feudal doctrines which no one (except professors in law schools) understands — and rather with the implication that even professors do not thoroughly understand them or all understand them the same way. It is our hope that, instead of adding to the "rubbish heap", we have explained the intricacies of the law of real property in such a manner as to make it more accessible to the profession.

We have stated the law as of July 30, 1984.

A. H. OOSTERHOFF
W. B. RAYNER

London, Ontario

October, 1984

PREFACE TO THE FIRST EDITION

Dr. Falconbridge once wrote that, "It has been said that a preface serves two chief purposes. Firstly, it enables the author to offer some reasonable excuse for having written the book at all, thus satisfying *pro tanto* the reader's natural curiosity on this point. Secondly, it gives the author an opportunity to make his own work the object of some discreet praise, thinly disguised under the form of an explanation of the supposed scope of the book, combined with the expression of a pious hope that its contents will prove useful to its readers, if readers there be."

In this book Mr. Justice Anger and I have attempted to state broadly the law of real property in the common law provinces and territories of Canada. In addition to the usual topics customarily found in a book on this branch of law, there are chapters on fixtures, mechanics' liens, titles and sections in other chapters on other related subjects not strictly considered to be a part of the law of real property. This book has been written for the practising lawyer to give him a convenient reference to the rules and principles of law. To this end the plan has been to state the law — case law and statute — and in order to assist the reader who does not have convenient access to the many series of reports, the fact situations of many of the cases cited have been briefly mentioned. It has not been feasible and is beyond the scope of the book to give at any length a criticism or analysis of the law.

The manuscript of the first eleven chapters, except for a few sections, was substantially completed by Mr. Justice Anger prior to his death. At the request of the publisher, I completed the manuscript. The task was greater than I anticipated and I feel that for a number of reasons the book does not measure up to all that Mr. Justice Anger would have wished. I nevertheless express "the pious hope that its contents will prove useful to its readers, if readers there be".

I cannot conclude without expressing my appreciation of the editorial staff of the publisher and in particular Miss Rose Lancaster. The condition of the manuscript and the shocking extent of galley corrections would have dismayed anyone else. In no small measure the publication of this book has depended upon the patience and perseverance of Miss Lancaster and her staff.

J.D.H.

Thornhill, Ontario

January, 1959

SUMMARY OF CONTENTS

VOLUMES 1 and 2

(For complete Tables of Contents, see Volume 1, page xv and Volume 2, p. ix)

VOLUME 1

SUMMARY OF CONTENTS

VOLUME 2

TABLE OF CONTENTS VOLUME 1

TABLE OF CONTENTS

TABLE OF CONTENTS

CHAPTER 16. MATRIMONIAL PROPERTY

LIST OF WORKS COMMONLY CITED

In this work a number of texts and other authorities, because they are cited so frequently, are referred to in abbreviated form. In the following list the words preceding the colon indicate the abbreviation used, and the full title is set out after the colon.

A.L.P.: *American Law of Property*, 1952.

Armour, *Devolution*: Edward Douglas Armour, K.C., *Essays on the Devolution of Land upon the Personal Representative and Statutory Powers Relating Thereto*, 1903.

Armour, *Real Property*: Edward Douglas Armour, K.C., *A Treatise of The Law of Real Property*, 2nd ed., 1916.

Armour, *Title*: Edward Douglas Armour, K.C., *A Treatise on the Investigation of Titles to Real Property in Ontario*, 4th ed., 1925.

Bl. Comm.: Sir William Blackstone, *Commentaries on the Law of England*, 15th ed., by E. Christian, 1809 (first ed. published, 1765).

Challis: H. W. Challis, *The Law of Real Property*, 3rd ed. by C. Sweet, 1911.

Cheshire: *Cheshire's Modern Law of Real Property*, 12th ed. by E. H. Burn, 1976.

Co. Litt.: *Coke upon Littleton*, 19th ed., with notes by F. Hargrave and C. Buttler, 1832.

Digby: K. E. Digby, *Introduction to the History of Law of Real Property*, 5th ed. by K. E. Digby and Wm. Harrison, 1897.

Farwell: *A Concise Treatise on Powers*, 3rd ed. by C. J. W. Farwell and F. K. Archer, 1916.

Fearne: Charles Fearne, *An Essay on the Learning of Contingent Remainders and Executory Devises*, 10th ed., by C. Butler, 1844. Vol. 2: Josiah W. Smith, *An Original View of Executory Interests*.

Gilbert: *Gilbert on Uses and Trusts*, 3rd ed. by E. B. Sugden, 1811.

Gray: J. C. Gray, *The Rule Against Perpetuities*, 4th ed. by R. Gray, 1942.

Hanbury and Maudsley: *Modern Equity*, 11th ed. by Ronald Harling Maudsley and Jill E. Martin, 1981.

Holdsworth: Sir W. S. Holdsworth, *A History of English Law*, 1903-1952.

Jarman: Thomas Jarman, *A Treatise on Wills*, 8th ed. by R. W. Jennings and J. C. Harper, 1951.

Laskin: Bora Laskin, *Cases and Notes on Land Law*, 1958.

Lewin: *Lewin on Trusts*, 16th ed., 1964, by W. J. Mobray.

Lewis: W. D. Lewis, *The Law of Perpetuity*, 1843.

Litt: *Littleton's Tenures.*

Maitland, Equity: F. W. Maitland, *Equity*, rev. ed. by J. W. Brunyate, 1936.

Maudsley: Ronald H. Maudsley, *The Modern Law of Perpetuities*, 1979.

Megarry and Wade: The Hon. Sir Robert Megarry and H. W. R. Wade, *The Law of Real Property*, 4th ed., 1975.

Morris and Leach: J. H. C. Morris and W. Barton Leach, *The Rule Against Perpetuities*, 2nd ed., 1962, with Supplement, 1964.

Plucknett: Theodore F. T. Plucknett, *A Concise History of the Common Law*, 5th ed., 1956.

Pollock and Maitland: Sir F. Pollock and F. W. Maitland, *History of English Law Before the time of Edward I*, 2nd ed., 1898.

Preston: Richard Preston, *An Elementary Treatise on Estates*, 2nd ed., 1820-1827.

Restatement, Property: American Law Institute, *Restatement of the Law of Property*, 1936.

Sanders: F. W. Sanders, *Uses and Trusts*, 5th ed. by G. W. Sanders and J. Warner, 1844.

Scott: A. W. Scott, *The Law of Trusts*, 3rd ed., 1967.

Simes and Smith: Lewis M. Simes and Allan F. Smith, *The Law of Future Interests*, 2nd ed., 1956.

Sugden, *Powers*: E. B. Sugden, *A Practical Treatise on Powers*, 8th ed. 1861.

Theobald: Sir Henry Studdy Theobald, K.C., *The Law of Wills*, 13th ed. by Stephen Cretney and Gerald Dworkin, 1971.

Thompson: *Real Property*, Latest Replacement, by John S. Grimes.

Underhill: *Underhill's Law Relating to Trusts & Trustees*, 13th ed., 1979, by David J. Hayton.

Waters: D. W. M. Waters, *Law of Trusts in Canada*, 1974.

Williams: Joshua Williams, *Principles of the Law of Real Property*, 23rd ed. by T. C. Williams, 1920. (The 24th edition of this work was published after the 1925 English property law reforms and is thus not as useful in a treatise on Canadian real property law.)

TABLE OF CASES

Table of Cases

TABLE OF CASES

TABLE OF CASES

TABLE OF CASES

PAGE

TABLE OF CASES

TABLE OF CASES

TABLE OF CASES

PAGE

TABLE OF CASES

cl

TABLE OF CASES

TABLE OF CASES

TABLE OF CASES

TABLE OF CASES

clxiii

TABLE OF CASES

clxvii

PAGE

TABLE OF CASES

TABLE OF CASES

TABLE OF CASES

TABLE OF CASES

TABLE OF CASES

TABLE OF CASES

TABLE OF CASES

TABLE OF CASES

TABLE OF CASES

TABLE OF CASES

TABLE OF CASES

TABLE OF CASES

TABLE OF CASES

TABLE OF CASES

ccxli

TABLE OF CASES

ccxliii

TABLE OF CASES

PAGE

TABLE OF CASES

TABLE OF CASES

ccxlvii

TABLE OF CASES

ccli

TABLE OF CASES

TABLE OF CASES

TABLE OF STATUTES

CANADA

ALBERTA

TABLE OF STATUTES

TABLE OF STATUTES
BRITISH COLUMBIA

cclxi

TABLE OF STATUTES

TABLE OF STATUTES

NEW BRUNSWICK

NORTHWEST TERRITORIES

TABLE OF STATUTES

TABLE OF STATUTES

ONTARIO

TABLE OF STATUTES

QUEBEC

Table of Statutes

SASKATCHEWAN

TABLE OF STATUTES

TABLE OF STATUTES

UNITED STATES

PART I

INTRODUCTION

CONTENTS OF PART I

CHAPTER 1

INTRODUCTION TO THE LAW OF REAL PROPERTY

101. SCOPE OF THE TREATISE

A treatise on the law of real property is concerned with land law and with anything pertaining to land. However, many aspects of personal property will inevitably be dealt with incidentally in that many of the rules of the law of real property are similar to or identical with those of the law of personal property. Thus, for example, the law of trusts and future interests encompasses both real and personal property. Nevertheless, for traditional and practical reasons, the emphasis in this work will be on the law of real property. Although leaseholds are regarded as personal property in the common law, traditionally they are dealt with in a work of real property and the law of landlord and tenant is, therefore, included in this treatise.

Even with the restriction to land law, it is necessary to further limit the subject-matter dealt with in this work. There are certain areas of law such as the law of mortgages and of mechanics' liens which are generally regarded as separate and distinct and in which acknowledged texts exist. For reasons of space these subjects are, therefore, dealt with more cursorily here. Other areas of the law such as municipal and other taxation and expropriation, although they undoubtedly affect the rights of a landowner greatly, can only be dealt with incidentally in a work of this nature by reason of their magnitude and because in any event they are distinctive subjects in their own right.

Apart from these exclusions, however, a traditional treatment of the law of real property has been followed. The first Part of the book commences with an introductory chapter which discusses the concept of property, defines common terms and gives a classification of property. Because the Canadian law of real property is based so closely on English law, it was thought useful to give an outline of the historical background of the Canadian law in the next chapter. To some extent this material will be duplicated in later chapters. However, an initial overview is not out of place. The first Part concludes with a chapter on the reception of English law in Canada.

Part II consists of a traditional treatment of the law of tenures and estates, and includes chapters on each of the several estates. Part III moves on to a discussion of future interests, using that term in a broad sense. There is an introductory chapter on conditions and conditional limitations, followed by chapters on future interests as such and perpetuities. Part IV in turn deals with the law of trusts, settlements and powers.

Part V consists of chapters on co-ownership and matrimonial property, including a discussion of recent matrimonial property law reform legislation. Part VI is concerned with incorporeal interests, rights over land and restrictions on land. It includes chapters on covenants and licences, incorporeal hereditaments, boundaries, public rights over land and fixtures.

Parts VII and VIII concern various aspects of conveyancing. Part VII deals specifically with the law of vendor and purchaser and includes chapters on contracts for the sale of land, conveyancing and remedies available to vendors and purchasers. Part VIII deals with the title to land and includes materials on capacity to hold interests in land, the acquisition of title, various types of title, the extinguishment of title, recording and registration, examination of title, mortgages and other encumbrances. The latter topic includes the subject of mechanics' liens.

Parts IX and X treat two relatively modern topics in real property law. Part IX concerns public control of land use through planning and environmental restrictions. Part X deals with the subject of strata titles and examines the common law strata title, co-operatives and condominiums.

In presenting the material the modern law has been emphasized. However, it will be apparent that much of the modern law of real property cannot be understood without a knowledge of its antecedents. Where necessary, therefore, a discussion of the earlier law is included. This blend of old and new is a feature of the development of Anglo-Canadian real property law.

102. THE CONCEPT OF PROPERTY

It is important in a treatise on the law of real property to consider at the outset what is meant by the idea of property although it is not intended to enter in detail upon a discussion of the question, "What is property?". As a philosophical exercise that can be highly rewarding but on a more practical level the question loses much of its force. Nevertheless, it is desirable to come to a workable definition of terms and to reject others for the purposes of this work.

It is not surprising that the concept of property, one of the most basic in society, has tended to vary with the prevailing philosophy of the day in particular societies. Thus Blackstone defined property as the "sole and despotic dominion which one man claims and exercises over the external things of the world, in total exclusion of the right of any other individual in the universe", which dominion was given him by God in creation.[1] Similarly, in the political philosophy of Locke, of the framers of the American Constitution and of the French Declaration of the Rights of Man of 1789, the right of property was regarded as an inalienable natural right of the individual, free from interference by others and by the state.[2] By contrast, Jeremy Bentham held the view that property is only a creature of the law and not a natural right. As he said: "Property and law are born together, and die together. Before laws were made, there was no property; take away laws, and property ceases."[3] A slightly different emphasis is found in the following definition of Professor Cohen, which combines both the elements of the will of the individual and the protection afforded by the state:

> ... that is property to which the following label can be attached:
> To the world:
> Keep off X unless you have my permission, which I may grant or withhold.
> Signed: Private citizen.
> Endorsed: The state.[4]

In modern western societies the property right is no longer regarded as absolute if, indeed, it ever was. It is now circumscribed by numerous regulations and restrictions imposed by the state, such as those regulating land use, those imposing environmental controls and those prohibiting the disinheritance of the family. Similarly, the right of the state to tax private wealth and to expropriate (for compensation) is a recognized feature of modern societies. Moreover, the modern industrial state does not regard property as being restricted to the control of material things but to encompass the whole field of economic interests. The result is (in theory at least) that the property right benefits the community as a whole instead of only the privileged few.[5]

At the extreme of the political spectrum is the Marxist state which shares with modern western states the awareness that property is of controlling significance in society.[6] In the communist states, however, this has led to the abolition of the private right of property and its replacement with the public right.

The term "property" may also be defined differently for different purposes. Thus, for economists property is any relationship that has an exchange value. And sociologists will define the word in terms of societal relationships and

---

§102
[1] 2 Bl. Comm., pp. 2-3.

[2] Friedmann, *Law in a Changing Society*, 2nd ed. (New York, Columbia University Press, 1972), p. 93; *cf.* Kruse, *The Right of Property* (London, Oxford University Press, 1939), pp. 7-8.

[3] Bentham, "Principles of the Civil Code" in *Theory of Legislation*, vol. 1 (Dumont, ed.; Hildreth, trans., Boston, Weeks, Jordan & Co., 1840), p. 112.

[4] Cohen, "Dialogue on Private Property", 9 Rutgers L. Rev. 357 (1954), at p. 374.

[5] Friedmann, *op. cit.*, p. 117. *Cf.* Macpherson, *Property: Mainstream and Critical Positions* (Toronto, University Press, 1978), ch. 1; Reich, "The New Property", 73 Yale L.J. 733 (1964).

[6] Friedmann, *op. cit.*, pp. 93-4.

values so that property becomes a "complex system of recognized rights and duties with reference to the control of valuable objects ... linked with basic economic processes ... validated by traditional beliefs, attitudes and values and sanctioned in custom and in law".[7]

All this, while useful, is not directly important in defining the term "property" for the purpose of this work. For it is not primarily the philosophical, sociological or economic implications of such a definition that are relevant for that purpose, but the narrow legal ones. It is to those that attention is now given.

The term "property" is used in a wide variety of meanings.[8] It may refer to a person's physical assets, to his real property, or to the totality of his wealth which consists of physical objects and various incorporeal rights which he is entitled to exercise, such as debts due to him, rights in a trust fund, stocks, patent rights, and so on. Thus it may refer to physical objects and to rights. It may also refer to the legal relations between persons and such objects and rights. It is in the latter sense that the term is used in this work.[9]

That this usage is appropriate is apparent from a knowledge of land law. English common law is unique in that it recognizes no absolute or allodial ownership of lands. Instead it recognizes estates or interests in land. While the same is not true of personal property in that a person is said to "own" a physical object or to "have" an incorporeal right, nevertheless in these cases too it is the legal relations which a person has towards such objects or rights that are of importance.

It is, therefore, the content of the property right, namely, the several rights, privileges, powers and immunities which comprise it, that is of significance in law and not the physical thing or right itself. The physical objects or rights may, after all, be multifarious, while the powers or rights are definite. They are: (1) the power to exploit the object or right, (2) the power to alienate it and (3) the power to pledge it for credit.[10] This simple generic list can be broken down further to give a list of specific powers, rights, privileges and immunities with respect to property. Property, therefore, is not just a single right, but a bundle of rights or powers.[11]

Moreover, the property right may be fragmented into various interests, some of which are independent of each other, while others are derivative. But they exist side by side. Thus, for example, the property right may be split into successive interests such as a life estate followed by a remainder or reversionary

---

[7]Hallowell, "The Nature and Function of Property as a Social Institution", 1 J. Leg. & Polit. Sc. 115 (1943), quoted in Powell, *The Law of Real Property*, revd ed. (St. Paul, West Pub. Co., 1969), §7.

[8]See, *e.g.*, Noyes, *The Institution of Property* (1936), especially ch. 5.

[9]*Cf. Restatement, Property*, p. 3.

[10]*Ibid.*, para. 5. *Cf.* Kruse, *op. cit., supra*, footnote 2, pp. 107 *et seq.*

[11]Kahn-Freund, Introduction to K. Renner, *The Institutions of Private Laws and their Social Function* (London and Boston, Routledge and Kegan Paul, 1949), p. 19; Hording, "Free Man Versus His Government", 5 *Southern Methodist Studies in Jurisprudence* (Dallas, So. Methodist University, 1958), p. 51; Noyes, *op. cit.*, p. 359.

interest. In no wise are these dependent on each other except in this sense that the remainderman or reversioner may not be able to enjoy his property in possession until the termination of the life estate. Contrarily, a mortgagee has a derivative property right. It derives from the act of the mortgagor conveying property to him or charging property in his favour. It is true that the mortgagee may acquire absolute title if the mortgagor should default, but until then his rights depend on those of the mortgagor.

103. OWNERSHIP, TITLE AND POSSESSION

The term *ownership* with regard to land is a lay term which has crept into the law, having its origin in the civil law concept of *dominium*. The latter term denotes allodial ownership.[1] In this text the term "ownership" is used to refer not to the physical object, but to the interests which a person may have in it. A person does not, therefore, own Blackacre. Instead he owns the fee simple estate or some other interest in Blackacre.

Moreover, inasmuch as the property right consists of a bundle of rights, the owner of an interest has a multitude of rights, powers, privileges and immunities. Thus, if X is said to own the fee simple in Blackacre, he not only has the right to use it, live on it, farm and recover minerals from it, he may also sell it in whole or in part, he may mortgage it, he may lease out the agricultural or mineral rights or both, he may grant a right of way over it, he may protect it from trespass and nuisance, and he may dispose of it by will or let it pass on his intestacy. And this is but a small part of the list of incidents of ownership.

The word *title* is often used as a synonym for ownership. In many cases this causes no difficulty. However, there are instances in which the meanings are not coterminous. For example, a distinction can and is drawn between the legal title to property and the beneficial ownership of it in cases where the ownership is split up.[2] Nor is it sufficient to define "title" in terms of facts the proof of which will enable a person to recover possession of a thing.[3] Even if one takes the "thing" to refer to both physical objects and rights, it is often the case that a person has no right to possession, but yet has title. This is so, for example, where one has a fee simple estate in remainder. Such a person has title to the estate, but he does not have possession, nor will he until all prior estates have determined. Generally, however, the terms "title" and "ownership" may be used interchangeably unless one wants to draw distinctions of the type referred to.

Possession is a further proprietary concept. In certain circumstances it may be said that a person who is in possession of land has a property interest in it

---

§103
[1]Lawson, *Introduction to the Law of Property* (Oxford, Clarendon Press, 1958), p. 87.
[2]A typical example is the case of a trustee who usually holds the legal title while the beneficiaries under the trust have the beneficial or equitable ownership. The distinction between these two is discussed at greater length in §105, *infra*.
[3]Lawson, *op. cit.*, p. 35.

and is thus the owner of it. He may not be the absolute owner, in that another person has a better right than he. For example, a person, A, who possesses land adverse to the interest of the person who has the registered title, B, is owner of the land with a qualified title. B is also an owner. However, he may lose his title and A may acquire an absolute title by reason of the operation of the law of adverse possession and of the statutes of limitation.[4]

Possession is not a necessary concomitant of ownership, however. For example, a mortgagee is not normally in possession of land and a person having a future estate in land must wait for the expiration of the prior estate before he is entitled to possession.

Moreover, possession may be *actual* or *constructive*. These two are otherwise respectively known as possession *in deed* and *in law*. Actual possession is self-explanatory and coincides in meaning with the lay concept of possession. Constructive possession is used in certain cases to accord a property right to a person even though he does not actually possess the whole or even part of the land or other object claimed by him. Thus, for example, in law a person has constructive possession of all land to which he has registered title,[5] except to the extent someone else occupies it adversely.[6] And a person who takes possession of land under a defective title is accorded constructive possession of the whole, while a mere trespasser is able to gain title only to the land over which he has pedal possession, that is, the land actually occupied by him.[7] Similarly, in the case of a gratuitous bailment,[8] the bailee is in actual possession while the bailor, the owner of the bailed chattel, is regarded as being in constructive possession of it in that he is always entitled to its immediate return on demand.

Of importance for this discussion is that these several concepts are all proprietary in nature. In other words, they are all aspects of the concept of property.

104. CLASSIFICATION

The first classification of property results from the common law distinction between *real* and *personal* property. In many jurisdictions this distinction is no longer of great importance. For example, in England its relevance has practically disappeared since the great property law reforms of 1925.[1] In many respects, the same can be said of the common law jurisdictions of Canada. For

---

[4]See, *e.g.*, *Limitations Act*, R.S.O. 1980, c. 240, ss. 4, 15.
[5]*Charbonneau v. McCusker* (1910), 22 O.L.R. 46 (Div. Ct.); *Earle v. Walker*, [1972] 1 O.R. 96, 22 D.L.R. (3d) 284 (C.A.).
[6]*Homestake Holdings Corp. v. Booth*, [1972] 1 O.R. 808, 24 D.L.R. (3d) 280 (C.A.).
[7]*Wood v. Le Blanc* (1904), 34 S.C.R. 627; *Walker v. Russell*, [1966] 1 O.R. 197, 53 D.L.R. (2d) 509 (H.C.J.); *Chittick v. Gilmore* (1974), 50 D.L.R. (3d) 414, 9 N.B.R. (2d) 38 (S.C.App. Div.).
[8]As where one person lends his lawn mower to his neighbour and no consideration passes.
§104
[1]Cheshire, pp. 8, 94.

example, the old rule that real property descended to the heir-at-law or devolved upon the devisee, while personal property passed to the personal representatives, has long been abolished. Today realty and personalty both vest in the personal representatives for the benefit of those entitled by will or for distribution among the next of kin of the deceased on an intestacy, and the real property is treated as if it were personalty for that purpose.[2] Nevertheless, many differences persist. This is particularly true with respect to the different manner of acquisition, investigation of title and alienation of the two forms of property. In general it may be said that these differences inevitably exist because of the physical differences between them.

The common law distinction between real and personal property differs from the civil law distinction between immovables and movables. The two sets of terms are largely, but not entirely, coterminous in meaning. The differences are of concern in the conflict of laws. Basically, the term "immovables" comprises land and anything affixed thereto or part thereof. Real property may be similarly defined. However, there is this main difference that real property does not include leaseholds. This is due to an accident of history.

At common law an action to recover land, if successful, resulted in the recovery of the res itself.[3] On the other hand, if the thing itself was not recoverable as of right, but only damages in lieu, the action was regarded as personal. Perhaps not surprisingly, the procedural labels came in due course to be applied to the objects which were the subject of the actions to recover them. Hence real property was recoverable in a real action. All other property became known as personal property.[4]

Leaseholds were originally not part of the feudal system of landholding, being regarded rather as mere personal contracts.[5] As a result, a tenant could not originally recover his term, but was only entitled to compensation if he was dispossessed. Leaseholds are, therefore, regarded as personal property. However, since they clearly have much to do with land they are classified as *chattels real* to distinguish them from *pure personalty*.[6] It is traditional for a

---

[2]See, *e.g.*, *Estates Administration Act*, R.S.O. 1980, c. 143, s. 2.
[3]That is, more precisely, the interest in the land. See §102, *supra*.
[4]Plucknett, p. 376.
[5]It has been shown that one reason why the lease was not included in the feudal system of landholding was that it was used as a speculative form of investment to avoid the church's prohibition against usury and as such was not worthy of protection by the real actions as was the interest of the freeholder: Plucknett, *op cit.*, pp. 572-3. Moreover, later it was advantageous to retain it outside the feudal scheme of estates since the term, being personalty, could be bequeathed by testament, whereas freeholds were not devisable until the *Statute of Wills*, 32 Hen. 8, c. 1 (1540) : Cheshire, p. 38.
[6]The term "pure personalty" in this context means all chattels other than leaseholds. It is not used to distinguish pure personalty from "impure personalty", otherwise known as "personalty savouring of realty". The latter terms were used in the old law of charitable uses to describe a fund consisting of the proceeds of the sale of real estate. Charities were formerly unable to accept such an interest. See Oosterhoff, "The Law of Mortmain: An Historical and Comparative Review", 27 U. of T. L.J. 257 (1977), at p. 286.

treatise on real property to deal with the law of landlord and tenant because of the close relationship between the two and the subject is therefore treated in this book in some detail.

Personal property can be further subdivided into *choses in possession* and *choses in action*. The former are physical objects capable of being in one's possession. The latter are not material things at all but rather rights which a person has that can only be enforced by an action at law. Examples of choses in action are: debts, shares, bonds, patent rights, copyright, and interests in a trust fund.

One area of overlap between real and personal property is the law of *fixtures*. Fixtures are chattels which are so affixed to the land as to become a part of it. Pursuant to the maxim *quicquid plantatur solo, solo cedit*, such chattels then lose the character of chattels. The effect is that they will pass on a conveyance of the land unless they are expressly excepted.[7] The question whether a chattel is indeed so affixed as to become a fixture is often a difficult one. It is a question of law, the answer to which depends upon an examination of the degree and the object of the annexation. In that respect the relationship of the parties may play an important role. For example, as between a vendor and purchaser, it is more readily assumed that the vendor of the freehold has affixed certain chattels than, as between a landlord and tenant, that the tenant has done so. Accordingly, the tenant is usually given the right to remove his trade fixtures.[8] In many jurisdictions the interests of security holders before affixation is protected.[9] The subject of fixtures is dealt with fully later in this work.[10]

The next distinction in real property is between *corporeal* and *incorporeal hereditaments*. An hereditament was an object, the interest in which originally descended to the heir-at-law instead of devolving upon the next of kin on an intestacy. As has been noted,[11] this distinction no longer exists, so that the continued use of the term is an anachronism. Corporeal hereditaments include land and all things that are affixed to land such as buildings, fixtures, trees and minerals. Incorporeal hereditaments are intangibles; they are rights which were regarded as real property rather than personalty because of their close affinity with land, being rights over or in respect of land. Incorporeal hereditaments are capable of being held for an estate or interest in the same way that land may be. The main examples and the only ones of any relevance in modern Canadian law are easements, *profits à prendre* and rent charges.[12]

It has been pointed out that the distinction between corporeal and incorporeal

---

[7]*Stack v. T. Eaton Co.* (1902), 4 O.L.R. 335 (Div. Ct.).
[8]*Ibid.*
[9]See, *e.g.*, *Personal Property Security Act*, R.S.O. 1980, c. 375, ss. 36, 39, 54.
[10]*Infra*, ch. 21.
[11]*Supra*, at footnote 2.
[12]Blackstone describes ten such interests, 2 Bl. Comm., c. 3, *viz.*, advowsons, tithes, commons, ways, offices, dignities, franchises, annuities, rents and corodies. The latter are rights to receive victuals for maintenance.

hereditaments is meaningless and confusing in that, in law, a property interest is only a right of ownership which, as a right, is incorporeal, never corporeal, although the object of the right may be either corporeal or incorporeal.[13] However, the distinction is one that remains in common usage and is, for that reason, retained here.

105.   FRAGMENTATION OF OWNERSHIP

The fact that the property right is not a unitary one has already been adverted to.[1] In Anglo-Canadian real property law fragmentation of the property right in several ways is thus possible. The three main ones are on the basis of time, between legal and equitable ownership and by co-ownership. A fourth one on the basis of tenure is no longer significant but its historical importance will be traced later.[2]

Division on the basis of time takes place by virtue of the doctrine of *estates*. As has been noted, the common law did not recognize allodial ownership of land. Rather it recognized estates and other interests in land.[3] These will be described in greater detail later in this work.[4] For the moment it will suffice to describe them briefly. An estate is an abstract concept distinct from the land itself. In essence, the word describes the rights a person may have in land for a period of time. The quantum of the estate thus varies with time. The largest estate possible is the *fee simple*. In theory it may last forever, being passed on by transfer or succession. It ends only when the owner of it dies intestate without an heir. In that event it passes to the Crown.[5] It may be carved up into lesser estates, namely, the *fee tail*, which lasts only so long as the direct descendants of the original tenant in tail survive, and the *life estate*, which lasts for the duration of the life specified. These three estates are known as estates of *freehold* and they are thus distinguishable from *leaseholds*. The latter are regarded in law as inferior to freeholds although in practice a long-term lease may subsist for a longer period of time.

These several estates may exist in *possession*, in *remainder*, or in *reversion*. The first of these terms is self-explanatory. When X is entitled to an immediate life estate he is entitled to enjoy it in possession. An estate in remainder is created when a person is given an estate but he is not entitled to possession until the expiration of a prior estate created by the same instrument. An estate in reversion is the estate retained by the grantor when he conveys away

---

[13]Austin, *Lectures on Jurisprudence*, 5th ed. by Robert Campbell, vol. 1 (London, J. Murray, 1885), p. 372. Contrast Challis, pp. 48 *et seq.*

§105

[1]*Supra*, §102.

[2]*Infra*, §§204-7, 401-3.

[3]*Supra*, §§102, 103.

[4]*Infra*, §§209-209.2, 405.

[5]Under the doctrine of escheat. Modern statutes have either superseded that doctrine or regulate the procedure for recovering the property. See, *e.g.*, *Escheats Act*, R.S.O. 1980, c. 142, s. 2; *Succession Law Reform Act*, R.S.O. 1980, c. 488, s. 47(7).

a lesser estate. Thus, in a conveyance by G to "A for life and then to B in fee tail", A has a life estate in possession, B has an estate in fee tail in remainder and G retains an estate in fee simple in reversion. Moreover, these estates are said to be *vested* in that they are presently existing, even though the owners are not all immediately entitled to possession. Vested thus normally means "vested in interest" and not "vested in possession". All estates are perforce vested. Other interests may exist in land which are not vested, such as contingent remainders and executory interests. In these the owner is unable to take as yet because he is unascertained or unborn, or because some condition precedent is not satisfied. These will be discussed in detail later.[6]

The division of the property interest between *legal* and *equitable* interests is due to the development side by side of the common law and equity. Legal interests are those which would have been recognized by courts of law before the fusion of the courts of law and equity. Equitable interests are those recognized in courts of equity. The separate development came about in this way. Over a period of time the procedures and remedies available in the common law courts established during the reigns of the early Norman kings, the Courts of Exchequer, Common Pleas and King's Bench, ossified into a rigid and limited system with the result that in many cases justice was denied to litigants. They began to appeal to the King in whom resided a residuum of justice. In due course such appeals were heard by the Chancellor who was usually a cleric and often the only learned man in the King's Council. The Court of Chancery thus took form and the Chancellor developed a body of rules which became known as equity.[7] Of particular interest for the present discussion is the Chancellor's enforcement of the use, the ancestor of the trust.[8] The use was interest conveyed to the use or benefit of another, the *cestui que use*. The common law took no notice of the use since it lacked the procedures to enforce it and regarded it as repugnant to the conveyance to the feoffee. It looked only to the feoffee to uses and protected his interest. The feoffee had usually promised the grantor to hold the property for the benefit of the *cestui que use* and when that promise was not honoured the *cestui que use* complained to the Chancellor who would hold the feoffee conscience-bound to his promise. The effect of his action was that, although the feoffee's title was respected at law, that is, in the common law courts, the interest of the *cestui que use* was protected by the Chancellor, in the court of equity, thus giving rise to two separate estates or interests in the same land, a legal and an equitable one.

While the courts of common law and equity are now fused in virtually all jurisdictions, the separate rules of law and equity remain in force. They are now enforced in one court and by statute, in the case of conflict, the rules of equity are made to prevail.[9] Thus, the distinction between legal and equitable

---

[6]*Infra*, ch. 10.
[7]Plucknett, pp. 178-81.
[8]The development of the use and its purposes is treated in detail later. See §§213-17, 1003.2, *infra*.
[9]See, *e.g.*, *Courts of Justice Act, 1984* (Ont.), c. 11, s. 109.

interests still maintains. The principal modern examples of such interests arise under the trust and the mortgage. The trustee normally holds the legal estate or title, the beneficiary, the equitable estate. Similarly, the mortgagee holds the legal estate while the mortgagor holds the equitable estate, called the equity of redemption.[10]

A final method of division of property is through a form of *co-ownership*. It is possible not only to convey an estate in land to one person; an estate or interest may be conveyed to two or more persons in co-ownership. A number of forms of co-ownership exist of which only two remain of practical importance, namely, joint tenancy and tenancy in common. Co-ownership will be discussed in detail later in this work.[11]

---

[10]This is somewhat of an over-simplification in that in both cases an equitable estate might be placed in trust or mortgaged in which case the trustee or mortgagee will hold an equitable title. However, the principle of the fragmentation of the title between the trustee and the beneficiary and between the mortgagee and mortgagor still operates.
[11]*Infra*, ch. 15.

CHAPTER 2

HISTORICAL BACKGROUND OF THE
CANADIAN LAW OF REAL PROPERTY

201. SCOPE OF THIS CHAPTER

Inasmuch as the Canadian law of real property is based largely on the law of England and since many of its principles derive from the feudal system, it is appropriate at this point to discuss the origins and development of the law of real property. It is clearly impossible in the space of a chapter to discuss this history in detail and, therefore, the following is only an outline. To the extent that historical rules remain relevant to the present law they will be dealt with more explicitly in subsequent chapters.[1]

The material is restricted to English law and is treated more or less chronologically. It also deals briefly with developments in English real property law since the Canadian colonies became independent. Special reference to the great property law reforms of 1925 is made. In addition, there is a brief essay on alienability in the common law. The reception of English law in Canada and its subsequent development is dealt with in more detail in the next chapter.

202. THE ENGLISH COMMON LAW

The term "common law" takes on different meanings in different contexts. Originally it referred to the body of law developed by the King's courts after the Norman Conquest in distinction from local customs, some of which survived for a time. Later the distinction was drawn between judge-made law and legislation, a distinction that is still frequently made. The term is also used to distinguish the body of judge-made law from the body of law known as equity which developed in the Court of Chancery to avoid the rigours of the common law. Sometimes the common law is held to include much of the early statute law.[1] And it is in that sense that the term is often used in Canadian jurisprudence. Indeed, the several statutes which introduced English law into the Canadian provinces have lumped all three types, that is, judge-made law, early

---

§201
[1]For an excellent outline of much of this history see 1 A.L.P., Part 1, chs. 1, 2.
§202
[1]See generally Megarry and Wade, pp. 7, 8.

statutes and equity, together as the "laws of England".[2] For the purposes of this survey the term is used to denote both the judge-made law and the early statutes, but it excludes equity.

The period in question extends for four centuries from the Conquest in 1066.[3] In it the common law was established, especially during the reign of Henry II when most of the common law institutions were founded. It was nurtured during successive reigns. Outstanding among these was the reign of Edward I[4] when many important statutes were passed that channelled the development of the law of property. These included *De Viris Religiosis*,[5] which attempted to prohibit alienations in mortmain, *De Donis Conditionalibus*,[6] which introduced the estate in fee tail and *Quia Emptores*,[7] which forbade alienation by subinfeudation.

The development of real property law can be said to fall into three distinctive chronological time periods:

There is first the period of the common law, comprising judge-made law and the early statutes.

Second came the development of equity.

Third, there is the period of statutory reforms which still continues.[8]

The three periods overlap to some extent but each represents society's answer to changing social needs. The law of real property, although more fixed than most, has thus steadily developed in accordance with the requirements of a changing society.

203. FEUDALISM

The early period of the common law was characterized by the feudal system. It is this system which shaped the early British land law and which still explains many of its archaic terms and peculiarities.

The essence of feudalism was that it involved a personal relationship of subordination between lord and man in which the man did homage and swore fealty to his lord. The personal relationship in turn involved a proprietary relationship, called tenure, whereby the man held land of the lord. This dual relationship required the lord to give protection to the man while the man was required, by virtue of his oath of allegiance, to give protection, service and reverence to his lord. The service required of the man usually included the

---

[2]See, *e.g.*, the *Property and Civil Rights Act*, S.U.C. 1792, c. 1, s. 3.
[3]Although some of the antecedents of the common law are to be found in Anglo-Saxon law they are insignificant compared to the great body of law developed by the Normans. Some Anglo-Saxon customs undoubtedly survived as local customs while others were incorporated into the common law. For a discussion of the Anglo-Saxon roots of the common law, see Digby, especially ch. 1.
[4]1272-1307.
[5]7 Edw. 1, Stat. 2, c. 13 (1279).
[6]Statute of Westminster II, 13 Edw. 1, c. 1 (1285).
[7]18 Edw. 1, cc. 1-3 (1290).
[8]Cheshire, p. 9.

duty to bear arms and was a burden on the land so that the lord might recoup the land if the service was not rendered. Moreover, it has been pointed out that the personal and proprietary relationships formed the basis for a system of military organization that was necessary in a time of weak central government. In that sense, therefore, feudalism formed the basis of public order and government in the Middle Ages.[1] Of special importance to land law is the proprietary relationship, the system of tenure. This is described in the next section.

Feudalism was not introduced into England by William the Conqueror. Some forms of it existed in Anglo-Saxon society. It is generally agreed, however, that William and his successors introduced many continental ideas on the subject and shaped and refined the concept until England became the most highly organized feudal state in Europe.[2]

William took the view that since his claims to the throne of England had been resisted by the English landowners, he became entitled to all the land as a result of his conquest. On this theory it was possible for him to allow those English landowners who recognized him to redeem their lands and to distribute other lands to his Norman followers.[3] The result was that all men in England thereafter held their lands of the King either mediately or immediately by the principle of tenure.

Tenure thus described the quality upon which land was held. Another and more important doctrine, the doctrine of estates, describes the quantity of land or the duration for which it was held.

204. TENURE

Tenure denotes the feudal relationship which subsisted between the lord and his tenants,[1] and describes the feudal services for which the land was held.[2] Under the feudal system tenure was universal, so that all land was held of a superior lord. More than that, however, the land was held of the King as ultimate lord either directly or indirectly through other lords.[3] Allodial landholding whereby a person might hold land absolutely was thus impossible.

Feudal society was arranged in a kind of pyramid. At the top was the King as *lord paramount*. Immediately below him were the tenants in chief, or *in capite*, of which there were about 1,500 at the time of the Domesday Book in 1086.[4] Except for the land retained by the King, the whole of England was divided among them. The tenants in chief, instead of continuing to hold

---

§203
[1]Plucknett, pp. 506 *et seq.*
[2]*Ibid.*, p. 517.
[3]Cheshire, p. 13.
§204
[1]*A.-G. Ont. v. Mercer* (1883), 8 App. Cas. 767 at p. 772.
[2]The word "tenure" derives from the Latin *tenere*, to hold.
[3]2 Pollock and Maitland, p. 232.
[4]Megarry and Wade, p. 14.

all the land themselves would parcel it out among their followers, not by way of alienation, but by the process of subinfeudation. The latter process created a new tenurial relationship between the tenants in chief and those below them. Those tenants in turn might again divide the lands by the same process until at last one reached the persons who actually farmed the land, the tenants *in demesne*. The intermediate owners were called *mesne*, that is, intermediate, lords. They held the land not in demesne, but in service, since they were entitled to the services of those below them. The lands actually retained by them were called *seigneuries*.

The services due by feudal tenants varied greatly. Usually, however, the tenants *in capite* held in military service of the King and the tenants in demesne would hold for a money rent or for agricultural services. Mesne lords might hold for either or both types of service or upon a personal service to their immediate lord.

The service due by the tenant to his immediate lord was *intrinsec*, for it was agreed to between the parties and within the scope of their bargain. However, services that had been reserved by the parties higher in the feudal scheme were *forinsec* to those lower down, for they were foreign to the agreement between the latter.[5] But all the services were a charge on the land, so that, for example, if a tenant *in capite* failed to render his services due to the King, the King could take action to recover them. He usually did this by distraining the chattels of the tenant who was in actual possession of the land as a result of subinfeudation.[6] The tenant who was thus sorely used could proceed by the writ of *mesne* against his lord to seek indemnity.[7]

205. TYPES OF TENURE

The kinds of services that could be reserved were many. In course of time they became differentiated into the several types of tenure which were first classified as such by Littleton about 1481.[1] The main division is between free[2] and unfree tenures. While there was no logical reason for it, there was a direct relationship between free tenures, estates of freehold and a free man's political status, so that a free man invariably held an estate of freehold by one of the forms of free tenure.[3] Another kind of tenure, leasehold tenure, developed subsequently in the 15th century. It was never part of the feudal system of tenure although it partook of many of its characteristics.[4]

---

[5]1 Pollock and Maitland, p. 237.
[6]*Warner v. Sampson*, [1959] 1 Q.B. 297 (C.A.), at p. 312, *per* Denning, L.J.
[7]1 Pollock and Maitland, p. 238.
§205
[1]Litt., ss. 95-171.
[2]Also called common law or frank tenure: Challis, p. 6.
[3]*Ibid.*, p. 7.
[4]See §209.2, *infra*.

205.1 Free Tenure

Free tenure comprised spiritual tenure, known as *frankalmoign*, or free alms, and lay tenure. The latter could in turn be divided into tenure in chivalry and in socage. Tenure in chivalry comprised *grand serjeanty* and knight service.

(a) Frankalmoign

Frankalmoign involved a grant of land in return for no definite or specific services.[1] There was, however, implied a general obligation to say prayers and masses for the souls of the donor and his heirs. The grant of land could only be made to an ecclesiastical corporation and, if alienated, the tenure was converted into socage tenure since frankalmoign could subsist only between the grantor and the original grantee.[2] After *Quia Emptores*[3] only the Crown was able to create this tenure.[4]

(b) Grant serjeanty

This type of tenure could subsist only between the King and his tenants in chief. The services due to the King were personal in nature and were of an honourable kind. A sergeant might, for example, be required "to carry the banner of the King, or his lance, or to lead his army, or to be his marshall, or to carry his sword before him on his coronation, or to be his sewer at his coronation, or his carver, or his butler, or to be one of his chamberlains of the receipt of his exchequer, or to do other like services".[5]

A related tenure, *petit serjeanty*, might subsist between the King and lesser tenants. The services required were military but were not to be performed by the tenant in person. The tenant might be required, for example, to supply the King with a small article relating to war such as a sword.[6] While this tenure was technically military, it was more like socage and was usually so treated.[7]

(c) Knight service

This was the most important form of tenure after the Conquest for it was the means whereby William assured the defence of the realm. Virtually all the tenants in chief held their land by this tenure and they were required under it to supply a fixed number of knights for forty days each year. As a method for raising an army the system had its limitations as is obvious from the fact that commencing about 100 years after the Conquest it became standard practice to commute the service into money payments called *scutage* or *escuage*. A century

---

§205.1
[1]If a specific ecclesiastical service was annexed to the grant, the tenure was known as *divine service*: Litt., s. 137.
[2]*Ibid.*, s. 139.
[3]18 Edw. 1, cc. 1-3 (1290).
[4]Litt., s. 140.
[5]*Ibid.*, s. 153.
[6]Co. Litt. 108.a.
[7]3 Holdsworth, p. 51.

later the substituted payments were no longer adequate for the purpose of maintaining an army either and were thereafter no longer collected in most cases.[8] Knight service retained its importance, however, because of the incidents attached to it, which were of great financial importance to the feudal lords and to the King.[9]

(d) Socage

Originally the tenure of free and common socage comprised every type of free tenure that was not military or spiritual. Hence it was the great residual tenure. With the decline of the military tenures it became the most important type. It had the advantage that its incidents were less onerous than those of knight service, being subject only to aids and relief. Its distinguishing feature was that the services were definite and ascertained. Usually they were agricultural in nature. In the course of time these were also commuted to a money payment known as *quit rents*. With the gradual devaluation of money over the years the money payments were often no longer collected.[10]

(e) Other kinds of free tenure

There were a number of other, minor, types of tenure and others of local importance only, such as *homage ancestral* in chivalry and in socage and special forms of socage such as *gavelkind* and *burgage tenure* of which *borough English* was one form. None of these had any lasting significance.[11]

205.2 Unfree Tenures

The main unfree tenure was villeinage. There was a variation of it called *customary freehold* which was of minor significance.[1] The villein was a serf or unfree tenant on the feudal manor. And this is what distinguishes the unfree tenant from the free. The tenant of a free tenure could seek redress in the common law courts, whereas the villein was dependent upon the will of the lord of the manor for justice, which was dispensed in the manorial court according to the custom of the manor.[2] Moreover, in the case of free tenures the services were "certain" or definite, while for the villein they were "uncertain" in that they depended upon the lord's will.[3] The villein's duties consisted of working his lord's demesne at the direction of the lord or the lord's steward.

By the 15th century the agricultural services were generally commuted into

---

[8]1 Pollock and Maitland, p. 311.
[9]The incidents are described in §206, *infra*.
[10]Cheshire, pp. 22-3.
[11]For a discussion of these forms of tenure see Challis, pp. 8 *et seq.*; Megarry and Wade, pp. 20-2.
§205.2
[1]For a description of this tenure see Megarry and Wade, p. 28.
[2]*Iveagh v. Martin*, [1961] 1 Q.B. 232 at p. 261, *per* Paull, J.
[3]1 Pollock and Maitland, p. 371.

a money payment.[4] At about the same time villeinage came to be called *copyhold*. The term refers to the record of the tenant's title. While the villein theoretically held at the will of the lord, in practice his rights were protected by manorial custom, recognized and enforced in the court of the manor. A record of all transactions respecting the land was kept by the court. These records were called the rolls of the court. Upon a sale of an interest the buyer would obtain a copy of the particular roll in which the transaction was recorded. His title thus depended upon a copy of the court roll or, more simply, his tenure was copyhold.

By the end of the 15th century the copyholder's rights had developed to such an extent that his interest was virtually equal to that of the tenant who held in free and common socage. And his rights were thereafter protected by the common law courts.[5]

206. INCIDENTS OF TENURE

The incidents of military tenure were the most extensive of all the forms of tenure and some of the incidents formed a part of the other forms of tenure as well. The incidents survived despite the decline of knight service because, except for homage and fealty,[1] they became of increasing importance to the feudal lords as a source of money. These several incidents are outlined below.

206.1 Relief and Primer Seisin

In the early stages of feudal land law, the land did not pass automatically from father to eldest son on the former's death. The tenant had a life estate in the land at most and the lord was under no obligation to accept his eldest son in his stead. The privilege of succeeding to his father's rights cost the son a sum of money called relief. Later, even though the principle of primogeniture had been established, the right of the lord to relief continued.[1]

In the case of his tenants in chief, the King was entitled not only to the relief but also to the right of *primer seisin*, that is, the right to take possession until the tenant made homage and paid the relief and the result was that the King was able to reap a year's profit from the land.[2]

Relief and primer seisin applied only to heirs of full age.[3] All feudal tenures were subject to them.[4]

---

[4]3 Holdsworth, p. 204.
[5]Cheshire, p. 26.
§206
    [1]Homage was the ceremony by which the tenant bound himself under oath to become the lord's man. Fealty encompassed the tenant's duty to faithfully perform his feudal services in accordance with his oath of fealty.
§206.1
[1]2 Bl. Comm., p. 65.
[2]Megarry and Wade, p. 17.
[3]2 Bl. Comm., pp. 66-7.
[4]*Ibid.*, p. 65.

206.2 Wardship and Marriage

Where a tenant died leaving an infant heir (that is, under age 21, if male, or under age 14, if female)[1] the lord became entitled to possession of the land. He was entitled to all the profits and was not accountable to the heir. In return he had to support, protect and educate the heir. This wardship presumably compensated the lord for the tenant's inability by reason of age or sex to carry out his or her feudal services.[2] Prior to *Magna Carta* the lord was entitled to a further half year's rent when the ward attained the age of majority, at which time he was entitled to sue for *livery* or *ousterlemain* in order to obtain possession of his land. This right was limited to the King by *Magna Carta*, however.[3]

Marriage consisted of a lord's right to choose a spouse for his ward. Should the tenant refuse an appropriate marriage, the lord was entitled to fine him the value of the marriage. And if an infant tenant married without his lord's consent the lord became entitled to double the value of the marriage.[4]

Only tenure by knight service and grand serjeanty were subject to wardship and marriage. Socage tenure was subject to the related, but much less severe, incident of guardianship.[5]

206.3 Aids

Aids were sums of money which the lord could exact of his tenants in certain circumstances. After *Magna Carta*[1] these were restricted to three, namely, the ransom of the lord, the knighting of his eldest son (*aide pur faire fitz chevalier*) and the marriage of his eldest daughter (*aide pur file marier*).

Tenure by knight service and socage were subject to aids but grand serjeanty was subject only to the aid payable to ransom the lord.[2]

206.4 Escheat

Escheat as an incident of feudal tenure has survived until modern times. It occurred whenever the tenancy terminated. It was a principle of feudal law that someone must always be seised of the land and, since all land was held of some superior lord, when a tenancy came to an end the lord would again come into possession of the land.

---

§206.2
[1]Under 16 if the girl was not married: Litt., s. 103.
[2]Megarry and Wade, p. 17.
[3]*Magna Carta*, 17 John, c. 3 (1215).
[4]2 Bl. Comm., p. 69.
[5]3 Holdsworth, pp. 65-6.
§206.3
[1]17 John, c. 12 (1215).
[2]Co. Litt. 105.b.

Escheat was of two types, namely, *propter defectum sanguinis* and *propter delictum tenentis*. The former occurred when the tenant died without heirs. Escheat of the second type occurred when a tenant was attainted for a felony, but in this case the Crown was entitled to its right to "year, day and waste", that is, the Crown could hold the land for a year and a day and was permitted to commit waste during that time.[1] A concept related to escheat was *forfeiture*. When a person committed high treason, his lands became forfeit to the Crown rather than to the lord, because forfeiture involved a breach of allegiance. Forfeiture was not, therefore, an incident of tenure, but was a royal prerogative.[2]

207. THE DECLINE OF THE TENURIAL SYSTEM

As society became oriented more and more to a wage-earning economy, the feudal system of landholding in return for services began to fall into decline and the first important statute to hasten its end was *Quia Emptores*.[1]

Prior to this enactment the number of subtenures had greatly increased by the process of subinfeudation. By this process a tenant, instead of alienating his land outright for a capital sum, created a new tenurial relationship between himself and another whereby the other person became his tenant of the land in return for a perpetual grant or service. The new tenant might create a further subtenure and in theory the process could go on *ad infinitum*. This multiplication of subtenures was inconvenient and unprofitable to the superior lords, for if a mesne lord created a subtenancy at a small rent the incidents due to his superior lord, such as wardship, on the mesne lord's death would also be minimal.[2] Thus it was in the interests of the feudal lords to stop the spread of new tenures. They succeeded in doing so in *Quia Emptores*. This landmark of English property law accomplished two important objectives. In the first place it abolished alienation by subinfeudation and secondly, it endorsed the principle of alienation by substitution. The latter idea had been gaining currency already before the statute although not initially without opposition from the feudal lords, for it meant a deterioration of the feudal bond between lord and man if a tenant could sell his land without his lord's consent. Nevertheless, the statute confirmed this right and it has been a hallowed freedom of landowners ever since.

On an outright sale, of course, no new tenurial relationship could be created and no services could be reserved. Furthermore, the existing mesne tenures

---

§206.4
[1]Megarry and Wade, p. 18.
[2]*Ibid.*
§207
[1]18 Edw. 1, cc. 1-3 (1290). An earlier provision, *Magna Carta*, 1 Hen. 3, c. 39 (1217), had already forbidden alienations which did not leave sufficient security for the feudal services, but it was not successful in practice.
[2]1 Pollock and Maitland, p. 330.

dwindled and disappeared over a period of time. With the gradual inflationary trend the value of the original rents fell to such an extent that they were often no longer collected and, as a result, evidence of their existence disappeared in the course of time.[3] Moreover, they were barred by statute if they were uncollected for a period of twenty years.[4]

The statute did not apply to the Crown, so that the Crown could continue to create new tenures and, with the disappearance of the many mesne tenures, the result was that most land in England came to be held immediately of the Crown. This was aided also by the presumption in the case of freehold land that, where no mesne lord appears, the land is held directly of the Crown.[5] One further aspect of the fact that the statute did not bind the Crown was that, until the *Tenures Abolition Act*,[6] tenants in chief could not alienate without the consent of the Crown. In practice this amounted to them having to pay a fine.[7]

It should be noted that *Quia Emptores* only applied to the fee simple estate. Thus subtenures of estates tail and life estates could still be created.

The decline of tenures was temporarily halted by the enactment of the *Statute of Uses* in 1535.[8] At that time the feudal basis of tenure was long since lost, but the tenurial incidents formed a valuable source of income to the King and the wide employment of uses tended to dry up that source. For political reasons Henry VIII was unable to raise money by taxation and so he revived the tenurial incidents by enacting the *Statute of Uses*. The effect of the statute is discussed later in this chapter.[9]

The next step in the decline of tenures was the *Tenures Abolition Act*.[10] This Act converted all existing free lay tenures into free and common socage and provided that thereafter only tenures in socage could be created. As the Act was binding on the Crown, the restriction was absolute.

Moreover, virtually all of the onerous incidents of tenure were abolished, leaving only escheat as the main survivor, as well as the services incident to socage tenures. The Act did not, however, abolish frankalmoign, copyhold, or the honorary incidents of grand serjeanty. Frankalmoign was, however, effectively obsolete since it disappeared on the alienation of land held by this tenure.[11]

---

[3]Megarry and Wade, p. 32.
[4]*Real Property Limitation Act*, 3 & 4 Will. 4, c. 27 (1833), s. 2. Any that survive to the present day may no longer be barred since they do not appear to be covered by the *Limitation Act*, 2 & 3 Geo. 6, c. 21 (1939): Megarry and Wade, pp. 792, 1018-19.
[5]Williams, p. 58.
[6]12 Car. 2, c. 24 (1660).
[7]The payment of a fine had been introduced by *Magna Carta*, 1 Hen. 3, c. 39 (1217), and was of general application, but it was abolished by *Quia Emptores*, except as regards the Crown.
[8]27 Hen. 8, c. 10 (1535).
[9]*Infra*, §§215-17.
[10]12 Car. 2, c. 24 (1660).
[11]Litt., s. 137.

The reduction of tenures was completed in England by the 1925 property law reforms. The *Law of Property Act, 1922* enfranchised copyhold, that is, it converted it into freehold land held by socage tenure, effective January 1, 1926.[12] At the same time special customs such as gavelkind and borough English were abolished[13] and frankalmoign was formally abolished.[14] Furthermore, *escheat propter defectum sanguinis* was abolished and replaced by a statutory right of the Crown to take the interest of a tenant who died intestate and without heirs as *bona vacantia*.[15]

Most of the incidents of copyhold tenure were abolished by the 1925 legislation, either immediately or over a period of time.[16] However, the following important rights survive: (i) the tenant's rights of common,[17] (ii) the tenant's or lord's right to mines and minerals,[18] (iii) the lord's rights in respect of fairs, markets and sporting,[19] and (iv) the tenant's or lord's liability for the maintenance of dykes, ditches, canals, sea-walls, bridges, ways, *etc.*[20]

In English land law today, therefore, only one tenure remains, free and common socage. And, except in the case of land that was formerly copyhold, intermediate lordships have virtually all disappeared. In practice, therefore, the tenant holds of the sovereign. The result is that tenure, as one of the two great doctrines of feudal land law still subsists, but it is of little practical importance.

208. SEISIN

The connecting link between tenure and the second important feudal concept, the doctrine of estates, was seisin. Seisin means possession, but it refers only to possession of an estate of freehold in land of freehold tenure. Thus, for example, a landlord will always have the seisin whereas the tenant under a lease is regarded as merely having possession.[1]

Seisin was of vital importance to the feudal system for the feudal incidents were enforceable only against the person seised of the land. Hence the idea took hold that there could never be an abeyance of seisin, for then all public and private rights pertaining to the land would also be in abeyance.[2] This

---

[12]12 & 13 Geo. 5, c. 16, ss. 128, 189 and 12th Sched., para. (1).
[13]*Administration of Estates Act, 1925*, 15 & 16 Geo. 5, c. 23, s. 45(1)(a).
[14]*Ibid.*, 2nd Sched., Pt. I. *Sed dubitante,* Cheshire, p. 86.
[15]*Ibid.*, s. 45(1)(d). Escheat for felony had already been abolished by the *Forfeiture Act*, 33 & 34 Vict., c. 23 (1870). This Act also abolished the Crown's right of forfeiture for treason.
[16]Megarry and Wade, pp. 36-7.
[17]*Law of Property Act, 1922*, 12 & 13 Geo. 5, c. 16, 12th Sched., para. (4).
[18]*Ibid.*, para. (5).
[19]*Ibid.*
[20]*Ibid.*, para. (6).
§208
[1]Litt., s. 324.
[2]Challis, p. 100.

principle in turn led to restrictions on the creation of estates. Moreover, as seisin was a fact, not a right, a person could be disseised by another who would then hold the seisin and would be regarded in law as the owner until the former owner repossessed the land by self-help or by action.

Dispossession was drastic, for the disseisor became *ipso facto*, the owner and was the only person who could deal with the land. This arose out of the form of conveyance called feoffment with livery of seisin. Originally this was the only possible form of conveyance of the immediate freehold. It consisted of a ceremony in which both the feoffor (vendor) and feoffee (purchaser) entered upon the land in the presence of witnesses. The feoffor would then physically transfer the seisin to the feoffee by handing him some symbol of the land such as a clod of earth or a twig, bidding him to enter on the land and then leaving him in possession of it. A charter of feoffment was often drawn up but it served only to confirm the actual prior transfer.[3]

Another consequence of dispossession was that dower and curtesy could not be claimed by the surviving spouse where a deceased spouse had been disseised.[4]

The significance of seisin is today much diminished by various statutory reforms which include the amendment or abolition of dower and curtesy and the modern method of conveying by grant. In some respects seisin remains relevant, however, for example, in connection with dower where it survives and, in respect of the principle that there can be no abeyance of seisin in connection with the creation of legal estates.

209. THE DOCTRINE OF ESTATES

The doctrine of estates is one of the most remarkable and enduring in the history of English land law. The term "estate" is probably derived from status, for in a landholding society the relationship one had to one's land no doubt defined one's standing in the community.[1] Later, however, the term "estate" described the quantity of a person's interest in land. The concept of the estate is unique to English law. It is an abstraction, interposed between the tenant and the land so that a person does not own the land itself absolutely or allodially as in the civil law. Indeed, he cannot own the land for the Crown owns it. Instead, he owns an estate or interest in the land.[2] Furthermore, it is the concept of seisin which links the abstract concept of the estate with the physical thing, the land. The person who has the seisin, or who is entitled to it in the future, has an estate in the land.[3] Moreover, the idea of estates, as distinct from ownership of land, makes possible the fragmentation of owner-

---

[3]Plucknett, p. 559.
[4]Megarry and Wade, p. 50.
§209
[1]A.L.P., p. 13.
[2]Cheshire, pp. 28 *et seq.*
[3]*Ibid.*

ship among different persons in succession.[4] Thus, for example, land may be granted "to A for life, then to B in tail, remainder to C in fee simple". In this example all three persons have estates in the land and they exist in the present, that is, they are capable of present ownership. The latter is a precondition of an estate. Even though the seisin rests in A only for the time being, the ownership of B and C also exists in the present.

There are several types of estate. They are classified on the basis of their quantity which varies with time.[5] Estates may be subdivided into *freehold estates* and *leasehold estates*.

209.1   Estates of Freehold

There are three estates of freehold, the fee simple, the fee tail and the life estate. The first two are estates of inheritance as indicated by the word "fee", a word which derives from "feodum", "feud" or "fief". They are capable of lasting forever. The words "simple" and "tail" define the classes of possible heirs.[1]

(a)   The fee simple

This is the largest estate known to the law and may be carved up into smaller estates. For example, the owner of a fee simple may create and give away several successive life interests and estates tail and still retain the fee simple.[2]

In its early stages, the fee simple was probably indistinguishable from the life estate in that the tenant could not alienate without the consent of his heir, nor without the consent of the lord. However, it was soon established that the heir apparent or presumptive had no claim to the land during his father's lifetime.[3] And *Quia Emptores*[4] endorsed the principle of free alienability of land without the consent of the feudal lord. Thereafter the fee simple could be aliened at will.

The estate was created by words of grant followed by the hallowed phrase "and his heirs". No other phraseology would do, any variation of it resulting in a life estate only. This rule was mitigated by later statutes. The modern statutes are discussed in a later chapter.[5]

(b)   The fee tail

Free alienability of land was a principle that was unattractive to the feudal lords who wished to have their lands remain in their families in perpetuity if possible. Early methods to achieve this end took the form of different types

---

[4]*Ibid.*, p. 33.
[5]2 Pollock and Maitland, p. 10. Hence, one may speak of the "quantum theory" of estates.
§209.1
[1]Megarry and Wade, pp. 41-2.
[2]2 Pollock and Maitland, p. 10.
[3]*D'Arundel's Case* (1225), Brac. N.B. 1054.
[4]18 Edw. 1, c. 1 (1290).
[5]*Infra*, §§502.1-2.

of conditional gift which collectively are called the conditional fee simple. A typical gift might be made to a person and his heirs provided that he have heirs of his body. If the grantee died without issue, the land would revert to the grantor. Once issue was born, however, the condition was fulfilled and he could convey the fee simple.[6] A variation of this type of estate was the *maritagium*, which was usually a gift to the donor's daughter and the heirs of her body upon a similar condition and with a similar result.[7] Another type of estate was the *liberum maritagium*, or frankmarriage, in which no feudal services were owed for three generations (that is, until the third heir entered), after which the land would revert to the donor if the heirs had died out. Otherwise it became freely alienable.[8]

These forms of conditional fee did not really achieve the desired result and thus in 1285 the Statute *De Donis Conditionalibus*[9] was passed. This statute provided that where a gift was made to a person and the heirs of his body on condition, expressed or implied, that he had heirs and on failure of which the land was to revert to the grantor, the intention of the grantor should be given effect to. The intention in the conditional type of gift clearly was that the land should remain in the family for as long as there were lineal descendants of the grantee and upon failure of his descendants that the land should revert to the grantor or his heirs.

The principle of free alienability soon reasserted itself, however, and various disentailing methods were devised to permit the tenant in tail in possession to bar the entail and to obtain a fee simple. These included the warranty, the fine and the common recovery.[10] The most effective of these, the common recovery, was confirmed by the courts in *Taltarum's Case* in 1472.[11] Both the fine and common recovery were in common use until they were replaced in the 19th century by the simple statutory method of the disentailing assurance.[12]

In order to create an estate tail at common law, words of procreation had to be used, such as, "and the heirs of his body". Statutes in the 19th century relaxed this requirement in much the same way as in the case of the fee simple.[13] The estate continues in effect in England but it has been abolished in most of the Canadian provinces.[14]

(c) The life estate

The life estate, as its name suggests, continues only for life. This might be for the life of the tenant himself or for the life of another, in which case the

---

[6]Plucknett, pp. 547 *et seq.*
[7]*Ibid.*
[8]*Ibid.*; Challis, pp. 12-13.
[9]13 Edw. 1, c. 1 (1285).
[10]Plucknett, pp. 617 *et seq.*
[11]Y.B. 12 Edw. 4, fol. 19 (1472).
[12]*Fines and Recoveries Act*, 3 & 4 Will. 4, c. 74 (1833), s. 51. This statute was copied, or adopted. in several of the Canadian provinces. See §606, *infra*.
[13]See §§605.1 (b) and 605.2 (c), *infra*.
[14]See §§607-607.1, *infra*.

interest is described as an estate *pur autre vie*. An example of the latter is a grant "to A for so long as B lives". An estate *pur autre vie* is created either expressly or when a tenant for life assigns his interest to another.[15] Life estates created by a deliberate act for the life of the tenant and *pur autre vie* are called conventional life estates.

In addition to the life estate created by the act of a person, there are the legal life estates, that is, those created by operation of law. These are curtesy and dower. Curtesy is a life estate in the real property of a married woman to which her husband is entitled after her death. Dower is a life estate in one-third of the real property of a married man to which his widow is entitled. These several interests will be described more fully later.[16]

At common law the conventional life estate could be created by express words such as, "to A for life", but a life estate was also created whenever the correct words of limitation were not used to create one of the other estates. Since the 19th century statutes which simplified those formulae, a life estate can now usually only be created by express words of limitation.

(d) Qualified freehold estates

The discussion has so far dealt with the estate in fee simple, in fee tail and for life absolute. The modern law recognizes variants of these known as the determinable estate and the estate upon condition subsequent. Their origin lies in the common law period although they were not well defined at that time.

The determinable estate is one which contains an alternative limitation so that it may determine automatically on either of two events. An example is a conveyance "to A in fee simple, so long as the property shall continue to be farmed". The estate will determine either when the land is no longer farmed, or when A dies intestate and without heirs, whichever occurs first. The estate upon condition subsequent is one which may be determined by re-entry by the grantor upon the happening of a specified event. Thus in a grant "to A in fee simple provided that he does not marry B", the grantor may re-enter to terminate the estate if A does in fact marry B. If the grantor does not re-enter, or if A does not marry B, the estate will continue until its natural determination.

Estates upon condition subsequent were known to the common law,[17] as were determinable life estates, but there is no real evidence of the existence of determinable fees simple. That lack of evidence caused a great debate as to whether one could create such an estate after *Quia Emptores*.[18] It was argued by some that one could not, for to do so would create a new subtenure between the grantor and grantee, something which that statute prohibited.[19] Others contended that the statute applied only to the fee simple absolute so that a

---

[15]Challis, p. 357.
[16]See ch. 7, *infra*.
[17]Litt., book III, c. 5.
[18]18 Edw. 1, cc. 1-3 (1290).
[19]See, *e.g.*, Gray, §§31-7; 1 Sanders, p. 17.

determinable fee simple could still be created.[20] Whatever may have been the position at common law, the modern law has recognized the existence of such estates.[21]

209.2 Leasehold Estates

As has been shown, leaseholds did not form part of the feudal land law and were not originally regarded as estates, but as personal contracts and as chattels real.[1] The tenant had no remedies against third parties. If he were dispossessed, he only had a personal right against his landlord. Moreover, the landlord, who held the seisin, could convey the land free from the interest of the tenant. In time, however, the tenant acquired various remedies against third parties, the most important of which was the action of ejectment.[2] About the 15th century, leaseholds were given the same protection as real property and came to be classed as estates.[3] At the same time, of course, the new leasehold tenure came into being, since the existence of an estate and tenure are necessary concomitants.[4]

Leasehold tenure is today the only one that is still of major significance. Indeed, it is essential in the landlord and tenant relationship.[5] While it is a non-feudal tenure, it has some of the attributes of tenure as it was understood in feudal land law. Thus, the rent payable is the service due by the tenant and is technically known as rent-service, and the landlord has the right of distress and the right to terminate the lease for breach of covenants.[6]

Leaseholds are often referred to as "estates less than freehold", for in law they are regarded as inferior to freeholds. This is so because they were not originally part of the feudal system. In fact, however, they can be much more valuable and enduring than a freehold. A long-term lease, for example, may well last much longer than a life estate or even a fee simple.

---

[20]See, e.g., Challis, pp. 437 et seq.
[21]*Hopper v. Corporation of Liverpool* (1944), 88 Sol. J. 213; *Re Tilbury West Public School Board and Hastie*, [1966] 2 O.R. 20, 55 D.L.R. (2d) 407 (H.C.J.).
§209.2
[1]§104, *supra*.
[2]*De ejectione firmae*. Originally it lay only to recover damages but later also to recover the term: Plucknett, pp. 373-4.
[3]Litt., s. 58.
[4]*Supra*, §209.
[5]But see *contra*, Landlord and Tenant Act, R.S.O. 1980, c. 232, s. 3, which provides:
    3. The relation of landlord and tenant does not depend on tenure, and a reversion in the lessor is not necessary in order to create the relation of landlord and tenant, or to make applicable the incidents by law belonging to that relation; nor is it necessary, in order to give a landlord the right of distress, that there is an agreement for that purpose between the parties.
Cases which have interpreted this section are: *Harpelle v. Carroll* (1896), 27 O.R. 240 (Q.B.); *Kennedy v. Agricultural Development Board* (1926), 59 O.L.R. 374, [1926] 4 D.L.R. 717 (S.C.). And see Scane, "The Relationship of Landlord and Tenant", *Law Society of Upper Canada Special Lectures on The Lease in Modern Business*, 1965, 1, 3-5.
[6]Megarry and Wade, p. 46.

Leaseholds are usually classified into four types, namely, the term of years, or the leasehold for a fixed term; the tenancy from year to year, or periodic tenancy; the tenancy at will and the tenancy at sufferance. As these several types will be discussed at length later,[7] some examples will suffice at this point. A term of years, despite its name, includes not only a lease for a term of one year, or five years, but also a lease for one month, or for any other fixed term. The tenancy from year to year, similarly, includes any tenancy for a fixed term, whether it be a year, a month or a week, which is renewed automatically for an identical period until it is terminated by the parties. A tenancy at will is one which continues indefinitely, but it may be terminated by either party at any time. A tenancy at sufferance is not, in fact, a tenancy at all. It arises when a tenant remains in possession or holds over after the termination of the lease.

210. INCORPOREAL INTERESTS

Apart from estates in land, the common law recognized a variety of incorporeal interests. These included advowsons, rents, easements and commons. The latter are the predecessor of the *profits à prendre* and there were several varieties of them, such as the common of pasture; the common of turbary, or the right to cut turf; the common of piscary, or the right to fish and the common of estovers, or the right to cut timber for fuel.[1] In the early history of land law there was little to distinguish them from estates in land and they were, therefore, transferable by livery of seisin. By the 15th century, however, it was recognized that the transfer of incorporeal hereditaments lay in grant only.[2] The main modern incorporeal interests are easements, *profits à prendre* and rent charges.

211. FUTURE INTERESTS AT COMMON LAW

A future interest in land is one in which the enjoyment of the land is postponed to a future time. As has been indicated, the common law severely restricted the creation of future interests.[1] With its emphasis on seisin, the common law insisted that someone must always be seised of the land. It was thus impossible for there to be a gap in the seisin. This insistence had the result that substantially all future interests possible at common law were vested estates. These estates are reversions and remainders.

A reversion is the interest which continues in the grantor after he has granted away a particular estate that is less than what he had. Thus, where G

---

[7]*Infra*, ch. 8.
§210
[1]1 A.L.P., p. 21.
[2]3 Holdsworth, pp. 98-9.
§211
[1]§208, *supra*.

conveys Blackacre "to A for life and then to B in tail", G retains the reversion in fee simple after the termination of the life estate and the estate tail. A reversion is always vested, that is, it is always a present interest and is not dependent upon the happening of some event or the fulfilment of any condition. The only aspect of it that is postponed is the right to possession.

A remainder is the interest that remains out of the grantor on the termination of a particular estate created by the same instrument. Thus, in a grant by G "to A for life, remainder to B in fee simple", B's interest is a remainder which is vested and which will come into possession when A dies. Remainders may be vested or contingent but at common law only vested remainders were possible because the contingent remainder necessarily involves an abeyance of seisin. Thus it was impossible at common law to create an estate that would commence in the future, as in a grant by G "to A in fee simple when he becomes 21", for until A was 21, there would be a gap in the seisin. On the other hand, it became established by the 15th century that a remainder which started out as contingent, but which became vested before the termination of the prior particular estate was acceptable.[2] Thus, in a grant by G "to A for life and then to B in fee simple at age 21", if B became 21 before A died, his interest, formerly contingent, would become vested and was allowed to take effect.

At common law, two further future interests probably existed, namely, the possibility of reverter and the right of re-entry for condition broken, although there is little evidence of them.[3] The possibility of reverter is the interest which remains in a grantor who creates a determinable fee simple. Thus, in a grant by G "to A in fee simple so long as London Bridge stands", G retains a possibility of reverter and the fee simple will return to him automatically when London Bridge falls down. The right of re-entry arises where a grantor creates a fee simple or other estate upon condition subsequent. Thus, in a grant by G "to A in fee simple provided he does not emigrate to Australia", G has a right of re-entry for breach of the condition. To recover the fee simple he must re-enter when the condition is broken. These two rights were not really interests in land at all. They were mere possibilities that a property interest might revest in the grantor in the future. Moreover the grantor could only reserve such interests to himself. He could not have the fee shift to a third party upon the happening of the stipulated event. These several interests will be described in detail later in this work.[4]

212. COMMON LAW CONVEYANCES[1]

The common law's obsession with seisin also placed severe constraints on the methods of transferring land. In fact, the only possible method for trans-

---

[2]1 A.L.P., p. 20.
[3]§209.1 (d), *supra*.
[4]See ch. 10, *infra*.
§212
[1]See generally, Gulliver, *Future Interests* (St. Paul, West Pub. Co., 1959), pp. 36-9.

ferring the immediate possession of it was the physical transfer by the process known as feoffment with livery of seisin.[2]

The *feoffment* was a grant of an estate with the physical delivery of it. The ceremony consisted of the parties assembling on the land with witnesses. The feoffor or grantor would then declare the terms of the grant and hand over some symbol of the land, such as a clod of earth or a twig, to the feoffee. After that the feoffor removed himself and all his chattels from the land, leaving the feoffee in possession. The latter was most important, or there would not be a change of possession in fact.[3] A charter of feoffment was often entered into as well, but it was a mere memorial of the feoffment and not its substance. It was not until the *Statute of Frauds*[4] that evidence in writing of the feoffment was required and only in the 19th century did a deed become necessary.[5]

The *grant* by deed did exist at common law but, of course, could not be used to convey the immediate freehold. It was used to convey incorporeal hereditaments and to assign remainders and reversions.

A third method of conveying land at common law was the *fine*. A fine was a *finalis concordia* or final compromise in an action commenced for the express purpose of reaching such a compromise and entering it in the court records. If one person, X, wished to transfer land to another, Y, Y would "levy a fine", that is, bring action against X and in the compromise X would acknowledge Y's right to the interest in the land. The fine was used where a feoffment was not possible, such as in the barring of entails.[6] It had the advantage, moreover, of providing a secure record of the transaction, the validity of which could not be contested after a comparatively short period of time.[7] The main disadvantage of the fine was that it barred only the issue of the tenant in tail, not the remainderman or the reversioner.

This was not the case with another collusive action, the *common recovery*. In this case the tenant in tail "suffered a recovery" by acknowledging that his title was defective and that the demandant could recover it and the demandant obtained judgment accordingly. In order to bar not only the issue but also the remainderman or the reversioner, the tenant in tail "vouched to warranty" a man of straw, who would falsely admit that he had conveyed the land with warranty to the tenant in tail and who would suffer judgment to be issued against him because of the defective title. This judgment required the straw man to give the tenant in tail land of equal value in substitution for that originally conveyed by him. The remainderman or reversioner would there-

---

[2]Maitland, "The Mystery of Seisin" (1886), 2 L.Q. Rev. 481.
[3]2 Pollock and Maitland, p. 84 .
[4]29 Car. 2, c. 3 (1677), s. 3.
[5]*Real Property Act*, 8 & 9 Vict., c. 106, s. 3 (1845).
[6]It was not possible to bar an entail by a fine under *De Donis Conditionalibus*, 13 Edw. 1, c. 1 (1285), which forbade it, but this method became possible under the *Statute of Fines*, 4 Hen. 7, c. 24 (1489), and 32 Hen. 8, c. 36 (1540).
[7]*I.e.*, five years under the *Statute of Fines*, 4 Hen. 7, c. 24 (1489).

after be entitled to it. However, since this part of the judgment was unenforceable, he was effectively barred as well.[8]

Fines and common recoveries were used also to bar dormant titles and as assurances by married women to dispose of their real property.[9]

A fifth method of conveying was the *lease and release*. The lease for a term of years, since it was not a freehold, was usually made by deed. In order to perfect his interest, the lessee did, however, have to enter on the land, for otherwise the deed gave him only an *interesse termini*, or interest in the term. Once the tenant had gone into possession, he was capable of taking a release, that is, the landlord could release the reversion to him by deed and the two interests would merge so as to give the tenant the fee simple and the seisin.[10]

Other methods of conveying, namely, the *bargain and sale* and the *covenant to stand seised*, were possible at common law, but only became significant after the development of uses and they are, therefore, dealt with later in this chapter.[11]

213. THE DEVELOPMENT OF USES

The use is a device developed early in the common law period for a variety of purposes. It originated in the Germanic Salman or Treuhand.[1] That was a person to whom property was transferred for purposes to be carried out during the life or after the death of the transferor. However, the use and its successor, the trust, are peculiar creatures of English law which evolved because of the distinction between courts of law and equity.

In the early stages of the use land might be conveyed to a person *ad opus*, that is, to the use of, another, for a variety of purposes. An early example of the use arose when crusaders left the country on their long journeys to the Holy Land. They would convey their lands to a friend to be held for the benefit or use of the crusader's family.[2] Later, in the early 13th century, the use was employed to convey lands to towns or cities to the use of the Franciscan friars who were then coming to England. By the rules of their order they were required to maintain perfect poverty and could not hold revenue-producing land, but the device of the use whereby the land was vested in another person for their benefit circumvented this difficulty.[3]

By the next century, the use was being employed much more by individuals. There were several reasons for the increase in the employment of the use, namely:

---

[8]Challis, pp. 310 *et seq.*
[9]*Ibid.*, pp. 393–6.
[10]*Ibid.*, p. 409.
[11]See §214.1, *infra.*
§213
[1]Holmes, "Early English Equity", 1 L.Q. Rev. 162 (1885), reprinted in 2 *Select Essays in Anglo-American Legal History* (1908), p. 705.
[2]Plucknett, pp. 576-7.
[3]Maitland, *Collected Papers*, vol. 1 (London, Cambridge University Press, 1911), p. 407.

(i)   to evade feudal incidents of tenure,
(ii) to evade the law of forfeiture,
(iii) to evade the *Statutes of Mortmain*,
(iv) to defeat one's creditors,
(v)   to acquire a kind of testamentary power with respect to land, and
(vi) to avoid dower and curtesy.

The way in which this was done was to convey the fee simple to a number of persons called feoffees to uses as joint tenants to the use of the grantor or some other person or corporation such as the friars. The beneficiary was called the *cestui que use*. The common law regarded the feoffees as owning the fee simple since they held the seisin. It took no notice of the *cestui que use* for it had no machinery to deal with his interest. Thus it regarded his interest as repugnant to the interest of the feoffees. However, most of the feudal incidents could not be exacted of the feoffees since they were joint tenants and, on the death of one, his interest would pass to the remaining feoffees, whose number could be increased from time to time. So also, if the *cestui que use* committed a treasonable offence, his land could not be forfeited to the Crown, since in the eyes of the law he had no land; it was held by the feoffees. The *Statutes of Mortmain* prohibited the conveyance of land to a religious or other corporation. But if the land was held by an individual to the use of a corporation, the statutes could be evaded. Similarly a creditor could no longer reach the land of his debtor if he had disposed of it to uses. Most important, by the device of the use a person could achieve a kind of testamentary power by requiring his friends, the feoffees, to carry out his instructions after his death. Thus, for example, X might enfeoff A, B and C to the use of himself for life and thereafter to hold the land for the benefit of his children.

By statute some of these efforts to evade the law and one's lawful obligations were curbed. Thus, for example, conveyances to the use of a corporation were prohibited.[4] Similarly, creditors were enabled to reach the lands of fraudulent debtors held in use.[5] However, the device itself was not attacked, presumably because it was recognized that the use had a legitimate place in society.

At this time, uses were only obligations of conscience in the feoffees. They were not enforceable by the *cestui que use*. When, however, the incidence of faithless feoffees, who would deny the use and retain the lands, increased, the *cestuis que use* began to appeal to the King's Council since they could not obtain redress in the common law courts as their interests were not recognized there. Furthermore, there remained a residuum of justice in the King that was not conferred on the common law courts. In practice, these appeals or petitions were usually dealt with by the Chancellor who was a member of the Council. The Chancellor was forced to take cognizance of the use because of the number of complaints made to him and he thus began, by subpoena, to require

---

[4]15 Ric. 2, c. 5 (1391).
[5]50 Edw. 3, c. 6 (1376).

the feoffees to honour the obligations or confidences undertaken by them in conscience. If they failed to do so they would be imprisoned.[6]

The Chancellor thus acted *in personam* by requiring feoffees to refrain from exercising rights they had at common law arising out of the seisin, because of reasons personal to themselves, which made it inequitable for them to enforce these rights. Nevertheless, in the process, the rights thus acquired by the *cestuis que use* were not only rights *in personam*, but also rights *in rem*, for equity came to regard their rights as estates and interests in land similar to those existing at law and, indeed, it recognized others which were impossible at law. There was, however, this difference that, while the common law interests were good against the whole world, the new equitable interests could not be asserted against a *bona fide* purchaser for value without notice.

214. EFFECT OF THE EMPLOYMENT OF USES

Of particular interest to subsequent history is the effect of the employment of uses on conveyancing and on the law of future interests. While these subjects will be dealt with again,[1] it is useful at this point to summarize their effects.

214.1 New Methods of Conveyancing

The use could be created by one of the common law conveyances such as the feoffment, the fine or the recovery. It could also be created without any conveyance, by the device known as the *bargain and sale*. Thus, for example, A might bargain and sell Blackacre to the use of B in fee simple. In this case A retained the seisin but transferred the use and, hence, the equitable title to B.

Another device, the *covenant to stand seised*, was used where there was a close blood relationship between the parties. Thus A who held the fee simple might, by deed, covenant to stand seised to the use of B, his son. The equitable title would in this way pass to B.

A use was also raised in equity where one person conveyed to another and no consideration was paid. It was presumed that no gift was intended in such a case and thus the feoffee was presumed to hold on a *resulting use* back to the feoffor unless consideration was proved, or a use was declared in favour of the feoffee or another.

214.2 New Types of Future Interests

At common law the types of future interests were strictly limited by the law's abhorrence of an abeyance of seisin.[1] The Chancellor was not concerned

---

[6]*Chudleigh's Case* (1590), 1 Co. Rep. 113 b at p. 121 b, 76 E.R. 261.
§214
[1]*Infra*, ch. 10.
§214.2
[1]*Supra*, §211.

with the technicalities of the common law, however, with the result that new types of future interests became possible. Thus in equity an interest could be made to commence at a future time by the employment of a springing use, as in a grant "to A and his heirs to the use of B and his heirs at age 21". Similarly, shifting and resulting uses were possible.

215. THE STATUTE OF USES

The advantages of uses were such that at the time of the Wars of the Roses much of the land in England was held in use.[1] There were serious drawbacks, however, to the employment of the use. Perhaps the most important of these was the loss of the feudal incidents to the lords and especially to the King. The King, who was always lord and never tenant, had everything to gain and nothing to lose by the abolition of the use. A series of statutes, passed to prohibit these evasions,[2] eventually culminated in the comprehensive *Statute of Uses*.[3] This statute was "forced upon an extremely unwilling parliament by an extremely strong-willed king", as Maitland says.[4] And it was designed to avoid evasion of feudal incidents and other lawful obligations.

The statute is lengthy and complex, but, stripped to its bare essentials, it says:

> Where any person stands ... seised of ... lands ... to the use ... of any other person, or ... body politick ... such person and body politick ... shall from hence forth stand ... seised ... in lawful seisin ... of ... the same lands ... in such like estates as they had ... in use ... in the same.

The effect of the statute was not to abolish uses but to give the legal title to the property to the *cestui que use*. The statute executed the use, so that, if a person formerly held an equitable estate in fee simple, he now acquired the legal fee simple. The feoffee to uses disappeared from the scene and the *cestui que use* stepped in his place. The result was that the use became a legal interest enforceable in the courts of law. Moreover, the statute applied not only to uses expressly created, but also to uses arising by operation of law, such as resulting uses.

216. EXCEPTIONS TO THE STATUTE OF USES

It soon became apparent that the statute did not apply to all uses, either by its express terms or as a result of judicial interpretation. Briefly these exceptions are the following:

(i) *Where the feoffee to uses is not seised.* The statute speaks of a feoffee

---

§215
[1] 1 Sanders, p. 17.
[2] 4 Holdsworth, pp. 443-9.
[3] 27 Hen. 8, c. 10 (1535).
[4] Maitland, p. 34.

37

being seised of land. Thus, where the use is imposed on a chattel real or on pure personalty the use is not executed.

(ii) *Where the use is an active use.* Thus, where a feoffee has active duties of management to perform, the use is not executed, for, unless the feoffee retains title, the intentions of the settlor cannot be carried out.[1]

(iii) *Where a corporation is seised to uses.* The statute refers only to a person or persons seised to uses, whereas, by contrast, it specifically includes a person or persons *or body politick* as a *cestui que use.* The reason for this omission probably is that, before the statute, the Chancellor would not enforce a use against a corporation because it had no conscience.[2] After the statute he did begin to enforce such uses, however, so that, where a corporation is the feoffee, the use is not executed.

(iv) *Where a person is seised to his own use.* The statute says that a person must be seised to the use of another. Hence, where land is conveyed to a person expressly to his own use the use is not executed. Such a conveyance was necessary to rebut the presumption of a resulting use.[3] Nevertheless, in such a case the grantee clearly had the estate at law and hence he was said to be "in by the common law and not by the Statute".[4]

(v) *Where there is a use upon a use.* Prior to the statute the Chancellor had held that where there was a grant "to A and his heirs to the use of B and his heirs to the use of C and his heirs", the second use was repugnant to the first and was thus void.[5] After the statute, in *Tyrrel's Case,*[6] the courts of common law followed that view and held that the whole estate was thus vested in B. About a century later, however, the Chancellor began to enforce the second use, so that the same result could be achieved as before the statute by the addition of one more use. This result caused Lord Hardwicke to exclaim, "by this means a statute made upon great consideration, introduced in a solemn and pompous manner, by this strict construction, has had no other effect than to add at most, three words to a conveyance".[7]

217. EFFECTS OF THE STATUTE OF USES

The *Statute of Uses* had far-reaching effects. Only a reference to the three most important consequences is made here, namely, its effect on conveyancing, on future interests and on the enactment of the *Statute of Wills.*[1]

---

§216
[1] 1 Sanders, p. 253.
[2] Challis, p. 389.
[3] *Doe d. Lloyd v. Passingham* (1827), 6 B. & C. 305 at pp. 314-16, 108 E.R. 465.
[4] Megarry and Wade, p. 159.
[5] Ames, "The Origin of Uses and Trusts", 2 *Select Essays in Anglo-American Legal History* (1908), p. 737.
[6] (1557), 2 Dy. 155a, 73 E.R. 336.
[7] *Hopkins v. Hopkins* (1738), 1 Atk. 581 at p. 591, 26 E.R. 365.
§217
[1] 32 Hen. 8, c. 1 (1540), am. 34 & 35 Hen. 8, c. 5 (1542).

217.1 Effect on Conveyancing

One of the advantages of the use before the statute was that it permitted secret conveyancing, especially by the device of the bargain and sale. In order to curb that and to prevent this method of secret conveyancing from being applied to the new legal interests, Parliament passed another piece of legislation, the *Statute of Enrolments*,[1] at the same time as the *Statute of Uses*. This enactment provided that every bargain and sale of a freehold interest must be made by indenture under seal and that it must be enrolled within six months in one of the King's Courts of Record.

Unfortunately, the statute had limited application and conveyancers were soon able to avoid it by employing other devices, notably the covenant to stand seised and the lease and release, to achieve the same result, but in secret. The covenant to stand seised has already been described.[2] It was of limited application since it could be used only for near relatives.

The lease and release has also been described.[3] However, this method was refined after the *Statute of Uses*. The lease was made by bargain and sale. In this way no entry was necessary for, under the *Statute of Uses*, the lessee was deemed to be in actual possession of the land.[4] Immediately afterward the reversioner would convey his interest to the lessee by release. In this way notoriety could be completely avoided.

The lease and release remained the main form of conveyancing until the 19th century when a simple deed of grant was made possible.[5] The *Statute of Uses* was, therefore, indirectly responsible for the modern form of conveyance.

217.2 Effect on Future Interests

The immediate effect of the statute was that it converted what were formerly equitable executory interests into legal ones. This did not result in destroying them, however. That would have been the case if they had to take effect at common law but, since the *Statute of Uses* directed that the *cestuis que use* should have the same estates at law as they had in the use, their interests, known as *legal executory interests*, were enforced. There is one important exception to this and that arises under the rule in *Purefoy v. Rogers*,[1] which provides that where an interest could take effect as a contingent remainder it must do so. Thus, in a grant "to X and his heirs to the use of A for life and then to the use of B in fee simple at age 21", B's interest can take effect as a remainder provided he become 21 before A dies. Therefore, it is not allowed

---

§217.1
[1] 27 Hen. 8, c. 16 (1535).
[2] §214.1, *supra.*
[3] §212, *supra.*
[4] Megarry and Wade, p. 166.
[5] *Real Property Act*, 8 & 9 Vict., c. 106 (1845), s. 2.
§217.2
[1] (1671), 2 Wms. Saund. 380, 85 E.R. 1181.

to take effect as a legal executory interest. On the other hand, a grant "to X and his heirs to the use of A in fee simple at age 21" cannot possibly take effect as a common law remainder and is thus allowed to take effect as a legal executory interest. Just as before the statute, springing, shifting and resulting executory interests remained possible, but they were now legal instead of equitable.

The more enduring effect of the statute was that it led to the development of the modern trust. This was because of the several exceptions to the statute discussed above.[2] Thus, in the case of the use upon a use, as in a grant "to A and his heirs to the use of B and his heirs to the use of C and his heirs", it will be recalled that only the first use was executed by the statute. In due course the second use came to be called a trust and the phrase "in trust for" was substituted for "to the use of", but there was no legal significance to this change. Similarly, B, who now had the legal estate, came to be called the trustee and C, who had the equitable fee simple, came to be called the *cestui que trust* or beneficiary. Just as before the statute, springing, shifting and resulting executory interests could be created, and, in the case of trusts, they remained equitable.

217.3 Enactment of the Statute of Wills

The *Statute of Uses* was thought to have abolished the right to devise land by means of the use. In some respects this was so. For, if A conveyed the fee simple to B "to the use of A in fee simple", the intent being that A would devise the use so that B would then hold to the use of his heirs, A's intentions were frustrated by the statute which, of course, gave A the fee simple at law. Another method, namely, where A conveyed "to B and his heirs to such uses as A should appoint by will and until and in default thereof to the use of A and his heirs" was different for, although A obtained the legal interest by the statute, the use was permitted to shift when he appointed by his will. The only difficulty was that A now held both the legal fee simple and the power to appoint and this was not thought possible, as the two would merge.[1]

These perceived difficulties were a severe blow to the landed gentry who had widely employed the use as a power to devise in order to provide for their younger children. For this reason they sought, among others, the repeal of the statute in the "Pilgrimage of Grace" in 1536.[2] Henry VIII conceded the point and thus the *Statute of Wills* was passed,[3] which permitted persons to devise all their lands in socage tenure and two-thirds of their lands held in knight service at their free will and pleasure.[4] One effect of this new freedom was the

---

[2]§216, *supra.*

§217.3
[1]It was later decided that there would not be a merger: *Sir Edward Clere's Case* (1599), 6 Co. Rep. 17 b, 77 E.R. 279.
[2]Plucknett, p. 587.
[3]32 Hen. 8, c. 1 (1540), am. 34 & 35 Hen. 8, c. 5 (1542).
[4]*Ibid.*, ss. 1, 2.

ability to create new future interests which could spring up in the future and shift upon stipulated events.[5] These are called legal executory devises and are analogous to legal executory interests, but do not need to employ a use.

218. THE STATUTE OF FRAUDS

Another statute of far-ranging effect was the *Statute of Frauds*, passed in 1677.[1] This statute was intended to prevent many fraudulent practices. In the area of real property it attempted to do so by imposing certain minimum formalities that must be observed in order to create and transfer interests in land. Thus it provided that leases and interests of freehold would be deemed to be estates at will only, unless they were put in writing and signed.[2] Similarly, the modern law relating to the execution and attestation of wills and trusts finds its origins in this Act.[3]

219. 19TH CENTURY REFORMS

The 19th century was an era of legislative and legal, as well as constitutional, reform. In two comparatively short periods of time from 1832 to 1845 and 1881 to 1890 much of the old law of property was irrevocably changed by legislation. Only the highlights can be sketched here. First of all, in the year 1833, there were the *Real Property Limitation Act*,[1] which abolished much of the old law on adverse possession; the *Fines and Recoveries Act*,[2] which abolished the old procedures of fines and common recoveries and substituted the simple device of the statutory disentailing assurance; the *Administration of Estates Act*,[3] under which creditors of a deceased person were able, for the first time, to sue the heir or devisee of real property in respect of all the deceased's debts; the *Dower Act*,[4] which to all intents abolished dower by making land freely alienable without a bar of dower, and the *Inheritance Act*,[5] which made important changes in the common law rules of descent. These were followed in 1837 by the *Wills Act*,[6] which simplified the law of wills and made the provisions applicable to real and personal property uniform, and,

---

[5]*Pells v. Brown* (1620), Cro. Jac. 590, 79 E.R. 504.
§218
[1]29 Car. 2, c. 3 (1677).
[2]*Ibid.*, s. 1.
[3]*Ibid.*, ss. 5 and 6, and 9, respectively.
§219
[1]3 & 4 Will. 4, c. 27 (1833).
[2]3 & 4 Will. 4, c. 74 (1833).
[3]3 & 4 Will. 4, c. 104 (1833).
[4]3 & 4 Will. 4, c. 105 (1833).
[5]3 & 4 Will. 4, c. 106 (1833).
[6]7 Will. 4 & 1 Vict., c. 26 (1837).

in 1845, by the *Real Property Act*,[7] which provided, *inter alia*, for the statutory grant.[8]

In the second half of the century there were the *Land Registry Act* of 1862,[9] and the *Land Transfer Act* of 1875,[10] which introduced a system of land titles. There was also the *Settled Estates Act*,[11] followed by the *Settled Land Act*,[12] which greatly simplified the law of settlements and made the settlement more responsible to social needs by vesting powers of management in the life tenant. The latter Act and the *Conveyancing Act* of the previous year,[13] which simplified conveyancing, foreshadowed and began the comprehensive law of property reforms completed in 1925. There were, however, several other important statutes during the last quarter of the century, including the *Trustee Act* of 1893,[14] which simplified the method of appointment and retirement of trustees, and the *Land Transfer Act*,[15] under which, for the first time, realty passed to the executors or administrators of a deceased person as his real and personal representatives with full powers of administration, including power to sell realty for debts.

The statutory reforms of the 19th century are important in that many of them were introduced into the Canadian provinces even after their establishment as colonies with representative government and, thus, after the date on which English law was no longer automatically received in them. This has not been true of later English legislation.

220. THE 1925 LEGISLATION AND THEREAFTER

The important and far-reaching legislation of 1925 swept away much of the old law of property and in the process made it simpler and more workable. Although not of the same significance for Canadian law as earlier English legislation, a brief summary of the reforms is in order.[1]

The 1925 legislation was preceded by two statutes, the *Law of Property Act, 1922*[2] and the *Law of Property (Amendment) Act, 1924*,[3] which made many necessary changes in the law. In 1925 these two statutes along with many others were repealed and their substance, together with modifications, was re-enacted in a series of statutes, namely, the *Settled Land Act, 1925*,[4] the

---

[7]8 & 9 Vict., c. 106 (1845).
[8]*Ibid.*, s. 2.
[9]25 & 26 Vict., c. 53 (1862).
[10]38 & 39 Vict., c. 87 (1875).
[11]40 & 41 Vict., c. 18 (1877).
[12]45 & 46 Vict., c. 38 (1882).
[13]44 & 45 Vict., c. 41 (1881).
[14]56 & 57 Vict., c. 53 (1893).
[15]60 & 61 Vict., c. 65 (1897).
§220
[1]For a more detailed summary of the legislation see Cheshire, pp. 83-112.
[2]12 & 13 Geo. 5, c. 16 (1922).
[3]15 & 16 Geo. 5, c. 5 (1924).
[4]15 & 16 Geo. 5, c. 18 (1925).

Trustee Act, 1925,[5] the *Law of Property Act, 1925*,[6] the *Land Registration Act, 1925*,[7] the *Land Charges Act, 1925*,[8] and the *Administration of Estates Act, 1925*.[9] All of these took effect on January 1, 1926.

The first major reform effected in 1925 was the reduction of the number of tenures to one, *viz.*, free and common socage. Thus, copyhold tenure was abolished as well as many of the remaining incidents of feudal tenure, save for some important rights, formerly incidents of copyholds.[10]

Secondly, the law of real property was assimilated as much as possible to the law of personalty. For example, henceforth personal property could be entailed.[11] Similarly, the old rules of descent for real property and distribution for personalty were abolished and replaced by a single set of new rules of distribution.[12]

Thirdly, a great number of feudal doctrines that were no longer relevant in the 20th century were abolished, such as the rule in *Shelley's Case*,[13] the rule in *Whitby v. Mitchell*,[14] and the common law remainder rules. The latter disappeared because under the 1925 legislation all future interests were made equitable.

Fourthly, conveyancing was much simplified. This was accomplished by the reduction of the number of possible legal estates to two, the fee simple absolute in possession and the term of years absolute.[15] All other interests are now equitable,[16] except for certain interests named in the statute.[17] The effect of this is, in the case of unregistered conveyancing, that a purchaser of land is concerned only with the title to the legal estate. Thus, for example, he is no longer concerned with powers of appointment, because these are equitable, and can dispose of the equitable interest only. Only the owner of the legal estate can convey it and on a sale the rights of third parties, being equitable, are normally overreached, that is, their rights are transferred to the purchase money. Moreover, if they cannot be overreached and, indeed, even if they can, they can be registered under the *Land Charges Act, 1925*[18] and, if so registered, give actual notice to all the world.

---

[5]15 & 16 Geo. 5, c. 19 (1925).
[6]15 & 16 Geo. 5, c. 20 (1925).
[7]15 & 16 Geo. 5, c. 21 (1925).
[8]15 & 16 Geo. 5, c. 22 (1925).
[9]15 & 16 Geo. 5, c. 23 (1925).
[10]See §207, *supra*.
[11]*Law of Property Act, 1925*, 15 & 16 Geo. 5, c. 20, s. 130(1).
[12]*Administration of Estates Act, 1925*, 15 & 16 Geo. 5, c. 23, ss. 45, 46.
[13](1581), 1 Co. Rep. 93 b, 76 E.R. 206, by *Law of Property Act, 1925*, 15 & 16 Geo. 5, c. 20, s. 131.
[14](1890), 44 Ch. D. 85, by *Law of Property Act, 1925*, 15 & 16 Geo. 5, c. 20, s. 161.
[15]*Ibid.*, s. 1(1).
[16]*Ibid.*, s. 1(3).
[17]*Ibid.*, s. 1(2). These are easements, rights, or privileges in or over land, rent charges in possession, charges by way of legal mortgage, land taxes, tithes, rent charges and similar charges not created by instruments, and rights of entry exercisable in respect of the legal term of years absolute or annexed to a legal rent charge.
[18]15 & 16 Geo. 5, c. 22 (1925).

The system of registered conveyancing, or land titles, introduced in the 19th century, was revised and strengthened by the *Land Registration Act, 1925*.[19] It is intended that this will replace unregistered conveyancing over a period of time.[20]

Since 1925 there have been further legislative reforms in real property such as the *Perpetuities and Accumulations Act 1964*,[21] but the reforms of 1925 were so comprehensive, far-reaching and effective that they continue to dominate the law of real property in England.[22]

221. ALIENABILITY IN THE COMMON LAW

In the history of the law of real property there can be discerned a continual struggle between those who wish to tie up their lands in perpetuity and those who desire free alienability of land. This can be described as a struggle between the landed classes and society in general, or as a struggle between the older generation and the younger. The tendency to want to control one's wealth and to rule beyond the grave is clearly very strong and many attempts have been made to give effect to it. Generally, the policy of the law has been to counter such attempts and to permit free alienability. The following description of the contest between the opposing forces is not intended to be exhaustive, but to show by example how the law of real property has developed out of this continuing contest.

221.1 Consent of the Heir

Prior to the Conquest it seems that land was usually freely alienable,[1] but after the Conquest and the perfection of feudalism in England general restrictions on alienation were introduced. Thus, at first the heir apparent or presumptive was considered to have an interest in the land so that it could not be disposed of without his consent.[2] In time, however, this right of the heir was lost and he came to be regarded as having only a *spes successionis*.[3] The result was that the tenant could dispose of his interest without his heir's consent. Indeed, the very existence of an heir was irrelevant.[4]

---

[19] 15 & 16 Geo. 5, c. 21 (1925).
[20] Cheshire, p. 104.
[21] C. 55 (U.K.).
[22] On the 1925 legislation see generally Cheshire, pp. 83 *et seq.*; Megarry and Wade, pp. 33 *et seq.*, 134 *et seq.*, 171 *et seq.*, 295 *et seq.*
§221.1
[1] 2 Holdsworth, p. 68.
[2] Plucknett, pp. 525 *et seq.*
[3] That is, a mere hope of succeeding to it on his ancestor's death which was "an absolutely bare possibility" that was not assignable: Challis, p. 76.
[4] Megarry and Wade, pp. 67-8.

221.2   Consent of the Feudal Lord

Originally the tenant could not alien without his lord's consent either. To have permitted it would have seriously weakened the feudal bond between lord and man. Moreover, the lord was vitally interested in ensuring that his new tenant was a suitable one.[1] However, the principle of freedom of alienation eventually took hold and it was confirmed by the Statute *Quia Emptores*[2] which permitted free alienation of land by substitution without the lord's consent.

Prior to *Quia Emptores* alienation was possible also by subinfeudation. By this method the tenant would not dispose of his land outright but would create a new tenure between himself and the grantee. Alienation by subinfeudation was possible without the consent of the superior lords but, because it tended to weaken their rights, the Statute *Quia Emptores* prohibited this method of alienation.[3]

221.3   Freedom of Testation

While alienation *inter vivos* thus became the rule, freedom of testation was not established for several centuries. It was, indeed, possible before and for a short period after the Conquest for a person to dispose of all of his real and part of his personal property by will.[1] However, soon after the Conquest the principle of primogeniture took effect. Under this principle, an interest in land could only pass on a person's intestacy to his heir. The heir was normally a person's eldest son, but if he had died, it was his eldest son, or if the eldest son had no issue, the tenant's next eldest son, or, if there was no son, the daughters took equally. This principle was a desirable one in the feudal system for it tended to preserve the feud as a single unit instead of having it distributed among the several children.[2]

This absolute restraint on the power to devise was often circumvented by the device of the use by means of which land could be conveyed for the benefit of another. By designating his heirs as the beneficiaries under the use, the grantor obtained freedom of testation indirectly.

By the *Statute of Wills*[3] the right to devise the fee simple in all socage land and in two-thirds of land held in knight service was secured. This right was

---

§221.2
[1] 1 Pollock and Maitland, p. 330.
[2] 18 Edw. 1, cc. 1-2 (1290).
[3] *Supra*, §207.
§221.3
[1] Megarry and Wade, p. 471.
[2] Plucknett, p. 528.
[3] 32 Hen. 8, c. 1 (1540), amended by 34 & 35 Hen. 8, c. 5 (1542).

later extended to all land held in military tenure,[4] to estates *pur autre vie*,[5] to copyholds[6] and to estates tail.[7]

221.4 Entails

The rise of the fee tail was a further attempt by the landed aristocracy to settle their lands in the family. Their attempts succeeded when the Statute *De Donis Conditionalibus*[1] was enacted. This statute made it possible to convey lands to a person and his lineal descendants. The principle of free alienation soon reasserted itself, however, with the introduction of warranties, fines and common recoveries. These methods, devised to bar entails, were sustained by the courts[2] and eventually culminated in the simple statutory device to bar the estate tail, the disentailing assurance.[3]

221.5 Seisin

It has been indicated that the doctrine of seisin restricted the creation of interests in land.[1] The law permitted no interest to be created the effect of which would be an abeyance of seisin. In that sense seisin acted as a restraint on alienation. The restriction was avoided by the device of the use which has already been described.[2]

221.6 Mortmain

The law of mortmain offers further evidence of the continual struggle over free alienability. The term "mortmain" denotes the conveyance of land into the dead hand of corporations, that is, bodies which never die. For a number of reasons, of which piety was undoubtedly one of the more important, land-owners often conveyed land to churches and various ecclesiastical corporations, including monastic orders. This was disadvantageous to the feudal hierarchy for they thereby lost many of their services, which depended upon a genera-tional turnover of the land. They, therefore, desired to place a restraint on the freedom of the individual to transfer land to corporations. Moreover, in an economic sense it was in the interest of society generally to keep land, a scarce

---

[4]As the result of the abolition of military tenures by the *Tenures Abolition Act*, 12 Car. 2, c. 24 (1660).
[5]*Statute of Frauds*, 29 Car. 2, c. 3 (1677), s. 12.
[6]*Preston's Act*, 55 Geo. 3, c. 192 (1815).
[7]*Law of Property Act, 1925*, 15 & 16 Geo. 5, c. 20, s. 176. See Megarry and Wade, pp. 471-2.
§221.4
[1]13 Edw. 1, c. 1 (1285).
[2]Plucknett, pp. 617-23.
[3]*Fines and Recoveries Act*, 3 & 4 Will. 4, c. 74, s. 51 (1833).
§221.5
[1]*Supra*, §218.
[2]*Supra*, §§213, 214.2.

resource, as freely alienable as possible. A long succession of statutes, beginning with *Magna Carta*[1] and *De Viris Religiosis*,[2] was thus enacted proscribing the alienation of land in mortmain. The prohibition was later extended to charitable uses generally by the *Mortmain Act*.[3] Mortmain was eventually repealed in England.[4] It was not widely adopted in the colonies, although it was received in Ontario[5] where it is still in force.[6]

221.7 Perpetuities and Accumulations

After the *Statute of Uses*[1] and the development of modern future interests,[2] it again became possible for landowners to tie up their land indefinitely. The rule against perpetuities was devised by the courts to counter this trend. It finds its origin in the *Duke of Norfolk's Case*,[3] although its precise formulation was not settled until later. The rule, which will be examined in detail later,[4] prohibits the vesting of an estate at too remote a date in the future. The period is described as twenty-one years from the death of a person or persons alive at the date of the creation of the interest. The rule has, in modern times, been codified, meliorated and clarified by statute.[5]

A related principle prohibited accumulation for the same period of time. However, that period was much shortened as a result of the controversy surrounding the will of one, Peter Thellusson. Thellusson's will directed the accumulation of the income from his property during the perpetuity period and the distribution of the capital thereafter among the male issue of his sons. It was postulated that the accumulation might last for about eighty years and produce a capital sum in the neighbourhood of one hundred million pounds![6] This was thought to be so outrageous that a statute was passed, generally called the *Thellusson Act*,[7] which introduced several possible accumulation periods which are generally restricted to twenty-one years.

---

§221.6
[1]1 Hen. 3, cc. 39, 43 (1217).
[2]7 Edw. 1, Stat. 2, c. 13 (1279).
[3]9 Geo. 2, c. 36 (1736).
[4]*Charities Act*, 8 & 9 Eliz. 2, c. 58 (1960), ss. 38(1), 48(2) and Sched. VII, Pt. II.
[5]*Doe d. Anderson v. Todd* (1846), 2 U.C.Q.B. 82.
[6]*Mortmain and Charitable Uses Act*, R.S.O. 1980, c. 297. See generally Oosterhoff, "The Law of Mortmain: An Historical and Comparative Review", 27 U. of T. L.J. 257 (1977).
§221.7
[1]27 Hen. 8, c. 10 (1535).
[2]Discussed in §217.2, *supra*.
[3](1681), 3 Ch. Cas. 1, 22 E.R. 931.
[4]*Infra*, ch. 11.
[5]See, *e.g.*, *Perpetuities and Accumulations Act 1964*, c. 55 (U.K.), and *Perpetuities Act*, R.S.O. 1980, c. 374.
[6]7 Holdsworth, pp. 228 *et seq.* In the event, only a small amount was realized due to extensive litigation and mismanagement. The estate was distributed in 1856: *ibid.*, p. 230.
[7]*Accumulations Act*, 39 & 40 Geo. 3, c. 98 (1800). For modern statutes which are based on it see *Perpetuities and Accumulations Act 1964*, c. 55 (U.K.); *Accumulations Act*, R.S.O. 1980, c. 5.

221.8 Conditions Against Alienation

In addition to these rules the courts have consistently refused to uphold all general restraints that are designed to prohibit alienation of interests in land. Thus all restrictions that effectively take away the power to alien are regarded as repugnant to the interest granted and will be held void.[1]

221.9 Settlements

A further example of encroachments upon the principle of free alienability is the settlement. A settlement is simply an arrangement by deed or will by which an interest in land is limited to persons in succession. The fee tail is an early example of a settlement. However, in attempting to satisfy the desires of the English landed aristocracy to ensure that the family land remained within the family, English lawyers developed several refinements on the early settlement. The two principal types and those that had lasting significance were the *strict settlement* and the *trust for sale*. A brief outline of these devices follows.[1]

The strict settlement took shape in the 17th century and it was designed explicitly for the purpose of maintaining the family estates as a unit. In many cases it would take the form of a marriage settlement executed a short period before the intended marriage, or of a settlement made by a father when his eldest son was about to be married. Thus, for example, a father might settle land on himself for life, remainder to his son S for life, remainder to the first and every other son of S successively in tail.

Provision was usually made in marriage settlements for the wife's pin-money and for annuities for widows. The latter were called jointures and both the provisions for pin-money and jointures were secured as rent charges. Also, provision was made for lump sum payments to younger sons, called portions.[2] The provisions for portions were usually secured by the creation of a long-term lease in favour of trustees (distinct from those of the settlement itself) on trust to raise the portions, or more simply by a trust to raise the portions. In either case the money could be raised by a mortgage, of the term, or on the estate, respectively.[3] The provisions for the widow and the younger sons took priority over the interest of the eldest son. In the case of a marriage settlement the ultimate reversion or remainder in fee simple would be in the husband.

---

§221.8
[1]See generally, Cheshire, pp. 318 *et seq.*; *infra*, §503.1 (a); ch. 9.
§221.9
[1]For further detail, reference may be made to Megarry and Wade, ch. 6, and Cheshire, pp. 71-83, 99-103 and 148 *et seq.* For a very lucid description of the strict settlement, its adverse effects on the economy and society and 19th century reforms, see Underhill, "Changes in the Law of Real Property", Council of Legal Education, *A Century of Law Reform*, 280 (1901, 1972 repr.), pp. 281-94.
[2]Megarry and Wade, pp. 385 *et seq.*
[3]*Ibid.*, pp. 387-8.

The intricacies of settlements were such that they could not have been achieved by common law methods of conveyancing, but the employment of the use and of the power of appointment made them much more flexible. These devices, for example, permitted the creation of interests, or the shifting of interests, at a future time and the provision for unspecified members of the family at a future time according as the exigencies of need made themselves apparent.[4]

Since a settlement invariably involved one or more estates tail, it might continue indefinitely. However, the law had long since permitted devices to bar entails and it was tempting for a tenant in tail to bar the estate and acquire a fee simple since it was much more valuable to him. A tenant in tail could not bar the entail until he was of full age, however. Nor could he bar the remainderman or reversioner without the consent of any prior life tenant in possession, called the protector of the settlement. If he did not get the consent he obtained only a base fee which lasted only as long as his lineal descendants survived, when the fee simple would pass to the reversioner or remainderman. The base fee was thus less valuable than a fee simple absolute.

In a settlement in which a father settles the family estates on himself for life and then on his eldest son in tail, the father is the protector and he would be loath to consent to the son barring the entail, for he is interested in maintaining the family estates inalienable. Therefore, when his son reached the age of majority, he would convince the son to accept an immediate share in the estate in the form of a lump sum, or of an annual income, in return for re-settling the property. A gentle hint that the son would not be given any money during his father's lifetime if he failed to agree would usually be sufficient to sway the son to do the right thing for the family. With the father's consent, the son could thus bar the entail, but he would immediately resettle it on his father for life, then on himself for life, and then on his first and every son in tail.

The combination of the strict settlement with the device of the resettlement thus assured the retention of the land in the family for a further generation, and the process could be repeated at the next generation when the son presumably would have acquired the necessary wisdom to see that a retention of the land was desirable and could persuade his son to resettle.

The widespread use of settlement unfortunately had adverse effects upon the social, economic and political structure of the country. In the first place, settlements tended to make land inalienable, for although in theory the chain could be broken, in practice, by the method of the resettlement, the land was kept tied up and out of commerce indefinitely, thus stagnating the economy.

Secondly, settlements were ultimately destructive of the lands and properties themselves. They were so set up that all beneficiaries had only a limited property interest, and often no powers of management were given to the life tenant in possession for the time being. In this way the land was starved of money which was needed for its maintenance.

---

[4]Cheshire, pp. 73-4.

Thirdly, the land was often encumbered with debts securing the portions of younger children.

Fourthly, there were serious difficulties in conveyancing, for a purchaser had to satisfy himself by inspection of intricate documents that he was getting a good title. Moreover, having notice of the terms of the trust, he would have to see that the application of the purchase money was carried out in accordance with the terms of the trust.

A series of statutes designed to meliorate these problems were passed, which culminated in the *Settled Estates Act*[5] and the *Settled Land Act*.[6] The first statute permitted a life tenant, with the consent of the Chancery Division, to sell, exchange, or partition the land and to grant certain leases. Leases could be made without the court's consent for a period of up to twenty-one years. The *Settled Land Act* was a much more drastic reform. In essence its purpose was to unfetter the land and make it marketable. It achieved this by vesting in the life tenant in possession wide powers of management, including powers of sale, exchange, and lease. Moreover, by the doctrine of overreaching, adopted by the Act, the interests of other beneficiaries of the settlement and of the purchaser were protected if the latter paid the purchase money to two trustees, or into court.[7] In other words, provided that the vendor was the tenant for life and provided the purchaser paid the money as provided by the Act, he took free of the interests of the other beneficiaries. Their interests were shifted to the purchase money.

The second method of settling land, the trust for sale, was simpler in operation. It was used, not primarily to keep land in the family, but to make provision for the several members of the family. In this case, land was conveyed to trustees upon trust to sell it and to hold the proceeds in trust for the beneficiaries. The transaction usually consisted of two deeds, the first, the conveyance, containing the necessary title information, while the second, the trust instrument, was concerned with the details of the trust. This facilitated conveyancing as a purchaser was concerned only with the first deed. The trust was invariably accompanied by a power of retention which entitled the trustees to sell at an opportune time. In many cases, such as a marriage settlement, they could only sell with the consent of the husband and wife or the survivor of them, after which the trustees could sell in their discretion.

The trust for sale worked because of the operation of the equitable doctrine of conversion. Under this doctrine equity regards that as done which ought to be done. Thus, under a trust for sale the land was immediately regarded as personalty, even if there was a power to postpone the sale. From a conveyancing point of view, therefore, the trust for sale was simple in that the purchaser was not concerned at all with the beneficial interests which consisted

---

[5] 40 & 41 Vict., c. 18 (1877). This Act was copied or adopted in some of the Canadian provinces. See, *e.g.*, *Settled Estates Act*, R.S.O. 1980, c. 468.
[6] 45 & 46 Vict., c. 38 (1882).
[7] *Re Mundy and Roper's Contract*, [1899] 1 Ch. 275 (C.A.), at p. 288, *per* Chitty, L.J.

of personality. They could not affect him. To put it in other words, under a trust for sale the doctrine of overreaching is automatic.

These two methods of settlement were continued by the 1925 reforms in the *Settled Land Act, 1925*[8] and the *Law of Property Act, 1925*,[9] respectively. In many respects, particularly in conveyancing, they have been much simplified. For example, with respect to settlements, it became obligatory to use two instruments, a vesting instrument and a trust instrument.[10]

A treatment of the modern English law of settlements and trusts for sale falls outside the scope of this work. Suffice it to say that their powers of management and of sale are now very much alike, but the two forms remain distinct in that, in the case of settlements, those powers reside in the life tenant, whereas in the case of the trust for sale they are vested in the trustees. The trust for sale is now the more widely used largely because the settlement, with its emphasis on keeping lands within the family, is inappropriate in view of modern tax legislation.[11]

221.10 Modern Restraints on Alienation

Today alienability of land in the sense of its generational turnover is aided and abetted by modern tax legislation which has the effect of requiring such a turnover at the death of the current owner in order to pay for succession duties and estate and other taxes.

On the other hand, the modern state does place certain restraints on alienation in pursuance of social policy. Examples of these are planning legislation which restricts the sale of land through such devices as subdivision control and zoning[1] and protection against disinheritance legislation[2] which restricts the testamentary power by requiring a testator to make adequate provision for his dependants. A further restriction on alienation that is somewhat of a hybrid, is modern legislation against racial discrimination. In that it prohibits racial discrimination in the disposition of land it restricts the landowner. However, to the extent that it widens the range of possible purchasers, the alienability of land is aided.[3]

---

[8]15 & 16 Geo. 5, c. 18 (1925).
[9]15 & 16 Geo. 5, c. 20 (1925).
[10]*Settled Land Act*, 15 & 16 Geo. 5, c. 18 (1925), ss. 4(1), 6, 8(1).
[11]Megarry and Wade, p. 384; Cheshire, p. 166.
§221.10
[1]See, *e.g.*, *Planning Act, 1983*, S.O. 1983, c. 1, ss. 34, 49.
[2]See, *e.g.*, *Succession Law Reform Act*, R.S.O. 1980, c. 488, Part V; *Inheritance (Family Provision) Act, 1938*, 1 & 2 Geo. 6, c. 45.
[3]See *Race Relations Act*, 1976, c. 74 (U.K.); *Conveyancing and Law of Property Act*, R.S.O. 1980, c. 90, s. 22.

CHAPTER 3

ORIGIN OF CANADIAN LAW

301. INTRODUCTION

All parts of Canada have been, at some time, British colonies. As such they received much of the English common law pursuant to the rules of common law respecting the establishment of English law in the colonies.[1] All the provinces and territories of Canada, with the exception of Quebec, still follow the common law tradition, that is to say, the laws are to a large extent judge-made, rather than the product of legislation. Quebec, on the other hand, is a civil

----

§301

[1] In this chapter the former British possessions in Canada and elsewhere are throughout referred to as colonies and the Parliament of Great Britain as the Imperial Parliament, even though all of Canada, at any rate, has long since become autonomous.

law jurisdiction with a tradition of codified law.[2] There is a distinction to be drawn between the English law that was received into British colonies and law that is, or was, in force in the colonies by reason of the fact that they formed part of the British Empire.[3] The latter is referred to as Imperial law in force *ex proprio vigore*. This consists of statutes passed by the Imperial Parliament with the intent, express or implied, that they be in force in one or more of the colonies. The prime example of this type are the Constitution Acts.[4] These statutes were not English statutes in that they never applied to England itself. They applied and apply only to the colonies. By contrast, laws that were in force in, and of local application to, England are referred to as English law which was received in whole or in part in the colonies.

The extent to which English law was received varies from colony to colony. It depends, for example, upon the date of reception, upon the existence of local or Imperial legislation regulating reception, and upon decisions of colonial courts respecting the reception of English law. Moreover, the mode of reception may make a difference. It depends upon whether a colony was acquired by settlement or by conquest. Furthermore, the law as received could thereafter be altered, but the method of adding to or altering such law depended upon whether or not the colony was given a local Legislature by Great Britain. By a series of British statutes the Canadian colonies were given Legislatures and subsequently Canada as a whole was given federal and provincial Legislatures which, within their respective constitutional spheres, have supreme authority to make laws subject only to the requirement that all legislation must have Royal Assent before it becomes effective, such assent being expressed by the Governor-General in the case of a federal statute and by the Lieutenant-Governor in the case of a provincial statute.

302. DATE OF RECEPTION

In many colonies local or Imperial legislation specifies the date upon which English law is received. Thus, in Upper Canada the date of introduction of English law relative to property and civil rights was fixed by statute as at October 15, 1791.[1] Alternatively, the date may be fixed by charter, as in the case of Rupert's Land.[2] In the case of conquered territories, English law could be introduced by the sovereign under the Royal Prerogative, unless he granted the inhabitants an assembly,[3] but this power may be subject to the terms of the

---

2Coté, "The Reception of English Law", 15 Alta. L. Rev. 29 (1977).
3*Ibid.*, p. 31.
4For example, 30-31 Vict., c. 3 (1867, Imp.).
§302
1*Property and Civil Rights Act*, S.U.C. 1792, c. 1, s. 3; now R.S.O. 1980, c. 395.
2The Hudson's Bay Company Charter of May 2, 1670, provided that the law of England applied to the territory, presumably as of that date.
3*Campbell v. Hall* (1774), 1 Cowp. 204, 98 E.R. 1045.

treaty under which the territories were ceded.[4] A number of colonies, of which the maritime provinces are examples, have no legislation fixing the date of reception. In their case, therefore, the date is that established by the rules of common law. That is generally assumed to be date of settlement, but this is clearly an inconvenient solution as that date can often not be fixed with certainty.[5] Probably a better date is the date when the colony received its first Legislature, since it is able from that time to effect changes in the law. The latter date received judicial sanction by a Newfoundland court.[6] However, the date of settlement, although not fixed precisely, is the judicially accepted date in New Brunswick.[7]

303. EXTENT OF RECEPTION

The extent to which English law was adopted in a colony is often difficult to determine. According to the common law rules, laws that are inherently inapplicable to the conditions of the colony are not received. What these are depends very much on the interpretation of such laws by local courts within the colony so that there are differences in this respect between the several provinces of Canada. The problems are not necessarily resolved in those colonies which have regulated reception by legislation either. Normally, they merely repeat the common law rules. Thus, for example, in Manitoba, the statute provides that the Court of Queen's Bench shall decide all matters of controversy relative to property and civil rights according to the laws of England as they existed on July 5, 1870, "so far as the same can be made applicable".[1] By contrast, the Ontario legislation provides merely that "in all matters of controversy relative to property and civil rights, resort shall be had to the laws of England as the rule for decision of the same."[2] This language is usually read, however, as being to the same effect as the common law rules, so that the inapplicable laws are excluded.[3] However, in *Keewatin Power Co. v. Town of Kenora*,[4] the Ontario Court of Appeal came to a different conclusion, and held that all the law of England relative to property and civil rights, save only that specifically excepted, was introduced into Upper Canada. The case seems to go to unnecessary lengths and is probably wrong. It has been implicitly rejected by the Supreme Court of Canada in a more recent case which held that the common law rule giving immunity to the owner of

---

[4]Coté, *op. cit.*, §301, footnote 2, pp. 43-5.
[5]*Cf. Scott v. Scott* (1970), 15 D.L.R. (3d) 374 at p. 379, 2 N.B.R. (2d) 849 at pp. 862-3 (S.C. App. Div.), *per* Hughes, J.A.
[6]*Yonge v. Blaikie* (1822), 1 Nfld. L.R. 277 at p. 283.
[7]See *Scott v. Scott, supra*, footnote 5, and see §307.3, *infra*.
§303
[1]*Queen's Bench Act*, S.M. 1874, c. 12, s. 1.
[2]*Property and Civil Rights Act*, S.U.C. 1792, c. 1, s. 3.
[3]*Doe d. Anderson v. Todd* (1846), 2 U.C.Q.B. 82 at p. 86, *per* Robinson, C.J. See also *Shea v. Choat* (1846), 2 U.C.Q.B. 211 at p. 221.
[4](1908), 16 O.L.R. 184 (C.A.).

animals which escape onto a highway does not apply in Ontario, because it is unsuitable.[5]

Apart from the law that is inherently inapplicable to a colony, the statutes themselves often exclude the application of specific legislation. Thus, for example, the Ontario statute excludes English law respecting the maintenance of the poor and respecting bankrupts.[6] Moreover, even in the absence of specific exceptions, certain laws are generally held not to be applicable to the colony. The prime example of this is revenue law;[7] another is the "laws of police", the phrase used by Blackstone[8] to designate laws regulating local government and administration, but not criminal law as such.[9]

It is generally assumed when a statute introduces the laws of England into a colony or, indeed, when they are introduced by the common law rules, that, save for the exceptions mentioned, the whole body of law and equity is introduced.[10] The difficulty with this assumption is that many colonies did not at first have courts of equity. Upper Canada is a prime example. It did not have a Court of Chancery, and hence did not apply rules of equity, until 1837.[11] It has been argued that in consequence equity was not introduced into Upper Canada at the time of its reception of English law in 1792.[12] This is unlikely, however. It is more probable that equity was introduced but that the machinery for its administration was not established until a later time.[13]

Once it has been established that the law of England has been received as of a particular date, there remains the question whether subsequent developments in English law are relevant to the developing law of the colony. The answer is simple enough in the case of statutes. Statutes enacted in England after the date of reception have no effect in the colonies.[14] It follows that when a statute that has been received in a colony is repealed in England, the repeal does not extend to the colony.[15]

The position as to the common law is more difficult. Strictly, there should be no difference, but in fact, colonial courts for a long time followed English

---

[5]*Fleming v. Atkinson* (1959), 18 D.L.R. (2d) 81, [1959] S.C.R. 513.
[6]*Property and Civil Rights Act*, S.U.C. 1792, c. 1, s. 6.
[7]*Yonge v. Blaikie* (1822), 1 Nfld. L.R. 277; *Uniacke v. Dickson* (1848), 2 N.S.R. 287 at p. 291.
[8]1 Bl. Comm. 107.
[9]Coté, *op. cit.*, §301, footnote 2, pp. 77-9.
[10]*Ibid.*, p. 57.
[11]A court having equity jurisdiction was established by the *Chancery Act*, S.U.C. 1837, c. 2.
[12]*Property and Civil Rights Act*, S.U.C. 1792, c. 1. See Falconbridge, *Banking and Bills of Exchange*, 7th ed. (Toronto, Canada Law Book, 1969), p. 448; *id.*, "Law and Equity in Upper Canada", 63 U. Pa. L. Rev. 1 (1914), reprinted 34 Can. L.T. 1130 (1914).
[13]Coté, *op. cit.*, p. 58.
[14]*Anonymous* (1722), 2 P. Wms. 75, 24 E.R. 646; *Gray v. National Trust Co.* (1915), 23 D.L.R. 608 at p. 610, 8 W.W.R. 1061 at p. 1063 (Alta. S.C.); *Garrett v. Roberts* (1884), 10 O.A.R. 650; *Kelly v. Jones* (1852), 7 N.B.R. 473 (S.C.), at p. 474.
[15]*R. v. Roblin* (1862), 21 U.C.Q.B. 352 at pp. 354-5; *Bank of Montreal v. Crowell* (1980), 109 D.L.R. (3d) 442, 37 N.S.R. (2d) 292 (S.C.T.D.).

decisions slavishly, if only for the interpretation of existing law,[16] and, indeed, it was thought that they were obliged to.[17] This is clearly not the case. Prior to the abolition of appeals to the Privy Council in a colony,[18] its courts were bound only by the decisions of that tribunal and of the House of Lords.[19] Such decisions are no longer binding in Canada.[20] Nevertheless, as has been pointed out,[21] colonial courts have not in practice applied a cut-off date with respect to the English common law and continue to apply English decisions, although with discrimination, even though the colonies are long since autonomous.

It has been suggested that the difficulty as to the reception of English statutes was caused by a misinterpretation of the common law rules and of the statutes that incorporated these rules. The early colonial courts were able to decide readily enough whether an English statute was or was not suitable for conditions in the colony at the time of settlement. However, once that decision was reached it became immutable, unless changed by legislation. This, it has been argued, is incorrect. The determination whether an English statute is applicable to a colony at any particular time should be made by a court when it is asked to deal with the question, not for all time, but for that time and place only. Conditions change and, therefore, the statute's applicability may change as well. Thus, the reception of English statute law, just like the reception of the common law, should be dealt with depending upon changing conditions in the jurisdiction.[22]

This approach was followed in a recent Nova Scotia case, *Bank of Montreal v. Crowell*.[23] In that case the question arose whether the *Fraudulent Conveyances Act*[24] was part of the law of Nova Scotia. The court reviewed a number of old cases which held that it was, but held that that did not mean that it continues to be so. Whether it is or not depends upon present conditions in the province. The court held, in fact, that the statute was still applicable in Nova Scotia because it permits a creditor to set aside a fraudulent conveyance even though the grantor was solvent at the time. The *Assignments and Preferences Act*[25] permits such a setting aside only if the grantor is insolvent.

---

[16]*Miller v. Tipling* (1918), 43 O.L.R. 88 at pp. 96-7, 43 D.L.R. 469 at pp. 476-7 (S.C. App. Div.), *per* Riddell, J.

[17]*Trimble v. Hill* (1879), 5 App. Cas. 342 (P.C.).

[18]Appeals to the Privy Council from Canadian courts were abolished as to criminal matters in 1931 and as to civil matters in 1949. See Laskin, "English Law in Canadian Courts Since the Abolition of Privy Council Appeals", 29 Cur. Leg. Prob. 1 (1976), at p. 2.

[19]*Robins v. National Trust Co. Ltd.*, [1927] A.C. 515 (P.C.).

[20]See, *e.g.*, *Fleming v. Atkinson* (1959), 18 D.L.R. (2d) 81, [1959] S.C.R. 513.

[21]Coté, *op. cit.*, p. 56; Laskin, *The British Tradition in Canadian Law* (London, Stevens, 1969), p. 3.

[22]Bouck, "Introducing English Statute Law into the Provinces: Time for a Change?", 57 Can. Bar Rev. 74 (1979).

[23]*Supra*, footnote 15.

[24]13 Eliz. 1, c. 5 (1570).

[25]R.S.N.S. 1967, c. 16.

Therefore, if the English Act were no longer applicable, there would be a serious lacuna in the law of the province.

304. REPEAL, AMENDMENT AND REFORM OF ENGLISH LAW

Once a colony was given a local Legislature it could repeal or amend any of the laws it received from England, even though the change conflicted with the law in force in England itself.[1] This did not, of course, apply to the laws of the Imperial Parliament in force *ex proprio vigore*,[2] but that disability was also removed as to most such legislation by the *Statute of Westminster*.[3]

Colonial Legislatures have often made use of this power and continue to do so. A serious problem remains, however. In many cases it is now difficult to determine whether a particular rule of English law or statute has application to a colony if it has not been ruled upon in the past. This results in an unfortunate uncertainty in the law which should have been removed long ago. Some jurisdictions have taken legislative action in this respect by enacting a local statute declaring certain English statutes to be in force or re-enacting them and declaring others not to be in force or repealing them. In most cases, however, there may be unnamed English statutes which remain unrepealed, so that the result remains unsatisfactory.

Ontario made a good effort in this respect in 1902. Based upon the work of its Statute Law Revision Council the province repealed a series of English statutes[4] and re-enacted them as chapters 322 to 342 of the Revised Statutes of Ontario, 1897. They were printed as volume III of that revision. In addition, some Imperial statutes in force *ex proprio vigore* were reprinted[5] and others listed as being in force.[6] Schedule C to the Revised Statutes of 1897 lists a small number of Imperial statutes relating to property and civil rights which appear to be in force in Ontario and which were not repealed, revised or consolidated. These fell within federal jurisdiction. Unfortunately, the Legislature did not take the opportunity to repeal all other, unnamed, English statutes. Thus the uncertainty, while meliorated, remains.

In British Columbia a number of Imperial Acts, probably thought to be in force, were printed in the Revised Statutes of 1897.[7] These included *Magna Carta*,[8] *Quia Emptores*[9] and the *Statute of Uses*.[10] In addition, a large number

---

§304
[1]*Colonial Laws Validity Act, 1865*, 28 & 29 Vict., c. 63, s. 3.
[2]*Ibid.*, s. 2.
[3]22 Geo. 5, c. 4 (1931, Imp.), reproduced in R.S.C. 1970, vol. Appendices, p. 401.
[4]By the *Statute Law Revision Act*, S.O. 1902, c. 1, the *Mortmain and Charitable Uses Act*, S.O. 1902, c. 2, and the *Imperial Statutes Act*, S.O. 1902, c. 13.
[5]R.S.O. 1897. vol. 3, pp. xxi–xxxv.
[6]*Ibid.*, pp. xliii–xlv.
[7]R.S.B.C. 1897, vol. 1, pp. xvii *et seq.*
[8]9 Hen. 3, cc. 32, 36 (1225).
[9]18 Edw. 1, c. 3 (1290).
[10]27 Hen. 8, c. 10 (1535).

of English statutes were incorporated, in whole or in part, into British Columbia statutes in the 1911 Revision.[11]

No other Canadian jurisdiction has taken such steps but a table showing which English laws have been held by the courts to be applicable or not applicable, as the case may be, in the various provinces of Canada, is extant and is a useful starting point in examining questions about reception.[12]

305. MODES OF RECEPTION OF ENGLISH LAW

Colonies could receive English law in one of three ways: by settlement, by conquest, or by treaty or cession. The common law rules governing these methods have general application to Canada, but they have been altered or superseded by local or Imperial statutes regarding reception and sometimes they have been disregarded in the sense that a colony has been treated as settled when in reality it was conquered. A possible fourth method of reception, by extension of territory, is discussed below.[1]

305.1 Colonies by Settlement

The substance of the general rule, as stated by Blackstone[1] and laid down in a sequence of cases,[2] that applies when British subjects discover and settle in an uninhabited or uncivilized country is that (a) prior to such colony being given a local Legislature, all existing English, common and statutory laws, except those inherently inapplicable to conditions in the colony, are immediately in force there, subject to the power of the Imperial Parliament to alter them and enact new laws, and (b) after the establishment of a local Legislature and its constitution, the power to enact local laws resides with it, subject to the general control of the Legislature of the mother country and its power to alter such constitution.

It should be noted that, in the case of a settled, as distinct from a conquered, colony, the sovereign's prerogative is limited to the establishment of a Legis-

---

[11]R.S.B.C. 1911, vol. 3, Table, p. 3186.
[12]Appendix C to Clement, *The Law of the Canadian Constitution*, 3rd ed. (Toronto, Carswell Co., 1916), p. 1060, revised and updated by Coté, "The Introduction of British Law Into Alberta", 3 Alta. L. Rev. 262 (1964), at pp. 278 *et seq.* See also Roberts-Wray, *Commonwealth and Colonial Law* (New York, Praeger, 1966), pp. 549 *et seq.*
§305
[1]*Infra*, §305.4.
§305.1
[1]Bl. Comm. 106.
[2]*Blankard v. Galdy* (1693), 2 Salk. 411, 91 E.R. 356; *Anonymous* (1722), 2 P. Wms. 75, 24 E.R. 646; *Campbell v. Hall* (1774), 1 Cowp. 204 at pp. 208-9, 98 E.R. 1045, *per* Lord Mansfield.

lature[3] and to the establishment of courts to administer English law.[4] The prerogative does not extend, even prior to the establishment of a local Legislature, to enacting new laws for the colony. As in England, that power resides in the sovereign in Parliament.[5]

In effect, therefore, British subjects thus forming a colony, carry with them their own laws and the sovereignty of their state, so that all who may join the community and their descendants have all the rights and obligations of British subjects, but are as subject to the Crown's prerogative rights and power of government as residents in the motherland.[6] As noted, however, no higher prerogative rights are possessed in the colony than in the motherland and, once the colony has been given a local Legislature, the prerogative right of the Crown without the concurrence of Parliament to legislate ceases and the right to make local laws passes to such Legislature within the limits of its constitution.[7]

Statutes passed by the British Parliament after the formation of a colony by settlement do not apply in the colony unless they so provide or their terms are of such general import as to clearly imply that they are to apply to all British subjects anywhere.[8] Those passed after the *Statute of Westminster*[9] would not apply to Canada.

The English law that has been held to be applicable and that held to be inherently inapplicable to the conditions in a settled colony may be conveniently found in Halsbury's Laws of England.[10] The British statutes which have been held to extend to colonies after they acquired a local Legislature, are also listed in the same work.[11] They include the *Colonial Laws Validity Act*[12] and legislation relating to fugitive offenders, evidence for foreign tribunals, admiralty courts and defences, colonial naval defence, colonial marriages, foreign enlistment, army discipline and merchant shipping.

305.2 Colonies by Conquest

In the case of a colony acquired by conquest in which there is an established system of law, the local laws in force at the time of the conquest remain in

---

[3]*Kielley v. Carson* (1842), 4 Moo. P.C. 63 at p. 85, 13 E.R. 225.
[4]*Ibid.*; *Re Lord Bishop of Natal* (1864), 3 Moo. P.C. (N.S.) 115 at p. 148, 16 E.R. 43.
[5]Coté, *op. cit.*, §301, footnote 2, pp. 48-9, and see *Phillips v. Eyre* (1871), 40 L.J.Q.B. 28 at p. 35, *per* Willes, J.
[6]*Mayor of Lyons v. East India Co.* (1836), 1 Moo. P.C. 175, 12 E.R. 782; *Advocate-General of Bengal v. Ranee Surnomoye Dossee* (1863), 2 Moo. P.C. (N.S.) 22, 15 E.R. 811; *Re Bateman's Trust* (1873), L.R. 15 Eq. 355.
[7]*Campbell v. Hall* (1774), 1 Cowp. 204, 98 E.R. 1045; *Re Lord Bishop of Natal, supra*, footnote 4.
[8]*Brook v. Brook* (1861), 9 H.L.C. 193, 11 E.R. 703; *Lauderdale Peerage* (1885), 10 App. Cas. 692 (H.L.); *A.-G. Alta. v. Huggard Assets Ltd.*, [1953] 3 D.L.R. 225, [1953] A.C. 420 (P.C.).
[9]22 Geo. 5, c. 4 (1931, Imp.), reproduced in R.S.C. 1970, vol. Appendices, p. 401.
[10]4th ed., vol. 6, §1196, pp. 589 *et seq.*
[11]§§1200-1, pp. 592 *et seq.*
[12]28 & 29 Vict., c. 63, s. 3 (1865, Imp.).

force until altered by the sovereign, who may impose such laws, British or otherwise, as he, or a Legislative Council appointed by him, may please,[1] provided that he does not exceed his own parliamentary authority or make changes that are contrary to fundamental principles, such as imposing restrictions on some of the inhabitants that are not applicable to others.[2] This is because the conquered inhabitants are to be regarded as British subjects. Hence, after a local Legislature is established with power to make laws, the prerogative right of the sovereign or his Legislative Council to make laws ceases, as in the case of the colony acquired by settlement.[3] It was under these principles that French Canada had imposed upon it English criminal and civil law by Royal Proclamation in 1763 and that, by statute in 1774, the French civil law, to which the inhabitants had been accustomed, was re-established instead. If, however, the system of law of the native population is not adequate and suitable for the requirements of European settlers, the latter may apply the English law to themselves.[4] Also, if a local law is contrary to the English religion or otherwise fundamentally bad, such as one permitting torture, it does not remain in force.[5]

305.3 Colonies by Treaty or Cession

In the case of a colony acquired by treaty or cession, the principles are the same as if it were acquired by conquest, except to the extent that the Royal Prerogative is modified and the rights of the inhabitants are preserved by the terms of the treaty.[1]

305.4 Extension of Boundaries

A fourth method by which English law may be received in a colony is by extension of boundaries.[1] Unless the statute providing for the extension provides otherwise, it is probable that the law of the old colony is simply extended to the new territory.[2] Examples of this mode of reception in Canada are the

---

§305.2

[1]*Campbell v. Hall* (1774), 1 Cowp. 204, 98 E.R. 1045; *Forbes v. Cochrane* (1824), 2 B. & C. 448, 107 E.R. 450; *Whicker v. Hume* (1858), 7 H.L.C. 124, 11 E.R. 50; *Mayor of Lyons v. East India Co.* (1836), 1 Moo. P.C. 175, 12 E.R. 782.

[2]*Campbell v. Hall, supra*; *Re Lord Bishop of Natal* (1864), 3 Moo. P.C. (N.S.) 115, 16 E.R. 43.

[3]*Campbell v. Hall, supra*.

[4]*Freeman v. Fairlie* (1828), 1 Moo. Ind. App. 305, 18 E.R. 117.

[5]*Anonymous* (1722), 2 P. Wms. 75, 24 E.R. 646; *Mostyn v. Fabrigas* (1775), 1 Cowp. 161, 98 E.R. 1021.

§305.3

[1]*Campbell v. Hall* (1774), 1 Cowp. 204, 98 E.R. 1045; *Re Adam* (1837), 1 Moo. P.C. 460, 12 E.R. 889.

§305.4

[1]Coté, *op. cit.*, §301, footnote 2, p. 52.

[2]*R. v. Jameson* (1896), 65 L.J.M.C. 218 at p. 226; *Vamvakadis v. Kirkoff* (1929), 64 O.L.R. 585 at pp. 588-9, [1930] 2 D.L.R. 877 at p. 880 (S.C. App. Div.).

extension of British Columbia into what are now the northern parts of that province in 1863, and the incorporation of Labrador into Newfoundland in 1811.

The converse of this situation occurs when a new colony is split off from the old, in which case it is probable, in the absence of legislation to the contrary, that the new colony acquires the same law as that of the former colony. Examples are the splitting off from Nova Scotia of New Brunswick in 1784 and of Prince Edward Island in 1769.

306. NEWFOUNDLAND[1]

Newfoundland, the oldest British colony, was first acquired by England by settlement or occupancy. It has been held, therefore, that it should continue to be regarded as so acquired, notwithstanding that, in the wars with France, it changed hands from time to time and was finally ceded by France to Great Britain by the *Treaty of Utrecht* in 1713.[2]

Possession of the island was taken by the British settlers in 1583, when the laws of England were introduced by the fact of settlement. In 1832 representative government was conferred. By commission or letters patent dated March 2, 1832, and by a proclamation of July 26, 1832, with accompanying instructions, a Governor was appointed and authorized to convoke a Legislative Assembly in prescribed manner, the persons so elected to be the General Assembly of the colony. The Governor, with the advice and consent of the Council and Assembly, was given full power to make laws for the island and its dependencies. Prior to 1832, the sole power to make such laws was in the British Parliament.[3] The first Legislative Assembly was held on January 1, 1833, and the cut-off date for the reception of English law was accordingly held by the courts to be the day before, that is, December 31, 1832.[4]

That part of Newfoundland known as Labrador, on the mainland, was added to the colony in 1811.[5]

In Newfoundland a special situation obtains, which affects the general law of real property in the province. In 1834, the General Assembly of Newfoundland passed the *Chattels Real Act*,[6] which provides in section 1 that all lands, tenements and hereditaments in Newfoundland which are regarded at common law as real estate shall be held to be chattels real and shall go to the executor or administrator of any person dying seised or possessed thereof, as other personal

---

§306
[1]On the reception of English law in the Canadian Territories see also the Appendix to Coté, *op. cit.*, §301, footnote 2, p. 86.
[2]*Kielley v. Carson* (1842), 4 Moo. P.C. 63, 13 E.R. 225.
[3]See the constitutional documents in the Appendix to C.S.N. 1916, vol. 1 (not reprinted in later revisions); *Newfoundland Act*, 5 & 6 Vict., c. 120 (1842, Imp.); *Kielley v. Carson, supra.*
[4]*Yonge v. Blaikie* (1822), 1 Nfld. L.R. 277 at p. 283.
[5]By 51 Geo. 3, c. 45 (1811, Imp.).
[6]S.N. 1834 (2nd Sess.), c. 18, now R.S.N. 1970, c. 36.

property now passes to the personal representatives, notwithstanding any law, usage or custom to the contrary. Section 2 provides that all rights or claims theretofore accrued in respect of any lands, tenements or hereditaments in Newfoundland and which were not already adjudicated upon, shall be determined in accordance with section 1, but the provision does not extend to any right, title or claim to any lands, tenements or hereditaments derived by descent and reduced into possession before June 12, 1834.

In 1792, the Imperial Parliament passed an Act[7] establishing the Supreme Court of Newfoundland and requiring that court to determine suits and complaints according to the law of England so far as it could be applied to suits and complaints arising in Newfoundland. Until passage of the *Chattels Real Act*, the only law respecting real property that could apply in Newfoundland was the law of England, as in the case of every other colony where British subjects settled. The *Chattels Real Act* revolutionized the position in regard to real property. Because of this Act, it was held in *Walbank v. Ellis*[8] that, as a tenant in tail had not in his lifetime barred the entail created by deed in 1777, his share of the estate passed to his heir-at-law, and in *Doe d. Evans v. Doyle, Executor*,[9] it was held that an estate tail general would have descended to the heirs of the body of the deceased were it not for the *Chattels Real Act*, but, as that Act was passed while the deceased lived, it would pass under the will of the deceased instead of to the heirs of his body.

Nevertheless, the ambit of the statute remains in doubt. Thus, it may well be that an instrument which purports to create estates and interests in land, that would be good at law were it not for the *Chattels Real Act*, will be valid. Notwithstanding the *Chattels Real Act*, statutes and decisions in Newfoundland repeatedly refer to land or interests therein.[10]

307. THE MARITIME PROVINCES

The maritime provinces were first occupied by France and were acquired from her by Great Britain by cession.

In the maritime provinces, there is no Imperial or provincial legislation defining the extent to which the law of England was introduced in the provinces upon their acquisition, so that the matter was left at large in those provinces.[1]

307.1 Nova Scotia

The peninsula comprising the present provinces of Nova Scotia and New Brunswick was first occupied by France in 1604 and was called Acadie. In the

---

[7]32 Geo. 3, c. 46 (1792, Imp.).
[8](1853), 3 Nfld. L.R. 400.
[9](1860), 4 Nfld. L.R. 432.
[10]See further as to the effect of the Act Gushue, "The Law of Real Property in Newfoundland", 4 Can. Bar Rev. 310 (1926).
§307
[1]Clement, *op. cit.*, §304, footnote 12, p. 276.

vicissitudes of the wars with France, Acadie was captured by forces from Virginia in 1610, named Nova Scotia, restored to France in 1632, recaptured in the time of Cromwell in 1654, restored to France in 1667, recaptured by the British in 1710 and finally ceded by France to Great Britain by the *Treaty of Utrecht* in 1713, the peninsula becoming the colony of Nova Scotia. Despite this history Nova Scotia and the other maritime provinces have always been considered to be settled colonies.[1]

Nova Scotia received representative government in 1758 and it dates its reception of English law from October 3rd of that year, the date its first Legislative Assembly met.[2] Lefroy is of the opinion that the date should be 1784 when New Brunswick was formed out of part of Nova Scotia.[3] However, this seems unlikely. The establishment of a Local Assembly in 1758 meant that the colony could thereafter alter the law of England as received on that date. It would seem reasonable to suppose that the law as so changed remained in force in Nova Scotia after 1784, even after the separation therefrom of New Brunswick.[4] As to the extent of the reception of English law in Nova Scotia, it has been pointed out[5] that the rules in the two provinces of Nova Scotia and New Brunswick as to what English law was introduced therein are not precisely the same. In Nova Scotia it has been held that the English common law was in force in the province except such as was obviously inconsistent with the circumstances of the colony, but that none of the English statute law was in force except such as was obviously applicable and necessary, the question as to whether a particular English statute applies being one for determination by the courts. Thus, in the leading case, *Uniacke v. Dickson*, Chief Justice Halliburton stated:[6]

> Among the colonists themselves there has generally existed a strong disposition to draw a distinction between the common and the statute law. As a code, they have been disposed to adopt the whole of the former, with the exception of such parts only as were obviously inconsistent with their new situations; whilst, far from being inclined to adopt the whole body of the statute law, they thought that such parts of them only were in force among them as were obviously applicable to, and necessary for, them.
>
> As respects the common law, any exclusion formed the exception; whereas, in the statute law, the reception formed the exception.

From a review of Nova Scotia decisions, it appears, therefore, that the

---

§307.1

[1]*Uniacke v. Dickson* (1848), 2 N.S.R. 287; *R. v. McLaughlin*; *R. v. Peabody* (1830), 1 N.B.R. 218 (S.C.), at p. 221, *per* Saunders, C.J., and Botsford, J.; Clement, *op. cit.*, §304, footnote 12, p. 276.

[2]Falconbridge, *op. cit.*, §303, footnote 12, p. 12.

[3]Lefroy, *Canadian Constitutional Law* (Toronto, Carswell Co., 1918), pp. 52-3.

[4]There is judicial authority for the year 1660: *Scott v. Scott* (1970), 15 D.L.R. (3d) 374, 2 N.B.R. (2d) 849 (S.C. App. Div.), but the date of establishment of the first assembly would appear to be the correct one in principle.

[5]Lefroy, *op. cit.*, footnote 3, p. 53.

[6](1848), 2 N.S.R. 287 at p. 289.

admission of British statutes in Nova Scotia has been the exception and that the Nova Scotia judges have deemed it to be the function of legislation, rather than judicial decision to bring into operation in the province provisions of British statutes not originally capable of having been operative, but which might be thought suitable to the changed circumstances of the colony.[7]

Pursuant to these principles the *Statute of Uses*[8] was considered to be part of the law of Nova Scotia,[9] but the *Statute of Enrolments*[10] was not, because there were no facilities for enrolment.[11] It appears, however, that most of the basic real property statutes were considered as received in the province.[12]

307.2 Cape Breton Island

Cape Breton Island was first occupied in 1629 by the English. Soon afterwards, it was captured by the French and named Ile Royale. Under the *Treaty of Utrecht* France retained the Island, but it was captured by the British in 1745, restored to France in 1748, recaptured by the British in 1768 and finally ceded by France to Great Britain by the *Treaty of Paris*, February 10, 1763, when it was united with Nova Scotia. The proclamation of 1763 authorized the Governor of Nova Scotia to call General Assemblies in Cape Breton and Prince Edward Island, then called St. John's Island, which was also annexed to Nova Scotia. By a commission to the Governor of Nova Scotia in 1784, when New Brunswick was formed into a separate colony, Cape Breton was granted a constitution consisting of a Lieutenant-Governor, Council and Assembly, subject to Nova Scotia. No Assembly was ever convened for Cape Breton and in 1820 in the commission to the Governor of Nova Scotia, the Crown annexed the Island to Nova Scotia. The annexation was held to be legal by the Privy Council.[1] By reason of its original occupation by the English, the Island was probably in the same legal position as Newfoundland, but the point seems to have lost significance on the union with Nova Scotia. In any event, the general law of Nova Scotia was extended to Cape Breton by provincial statute.[2]

307.3 New Brunswick

After the influx of United Empire Loyalists into Nova Scotia, the territory

---

[7]Clement, *op. cit.*, §304, footnote 12, pp. 279-80, and see *Bank of Montreal v. Crowell* (1980), 109 D.L.R. (3d) 442, 37 N.S.R. (2d) 292 (S.C.T.D.).
[8]27 Hen. 8, c. 10 (1535).
[9]*Shey v. Chisholm* (1853), 2 N.S.R. 52.
[10]27 Hen. 8, c. 16 (1535).
[11]*Berry v. Berry* (1882), 16 N.S.R. 66.
[12]See Clement, *op. cit.*, pp. 277-81, and see Comment, "Whence Came the Common Law into Canada", 56 Can. L.J. (N.S.) 281 (1920).
§307.2
[1]*Re Cape Breton* (1846), 5 Moo. P.C. 259, 13 E.R. 489.
[2]S.N.S. 1820-21, c. 5.

of New Brunswick was split off from it to form a separate colony in 1784[1] and it might have been argued that the new colony received that law of England which went into force in Nova Scotia on October 2, 1758, except to the extent that it was subsequently altered in that colony by judicial decision, and except for Nova Scotia statutes which were expressly declared to have no force in New Brunswick.[2] Moreover, although the first Governor of the new colony, Col. Thomas Carleton, was appointed on August 16, 1784,[3] the first elected General Assembly did not hold its first session until January 3, 1786.[4] Since in the interval the power of making law in the colony resided with the Imperial Parliament, it might have been argued that any English statute passed between those dates would go into force in New Brunswick, if applicable under the rules determining applicability, subject to alteration by subsequent local legislation. This is not the case, however. The provincial courts have instead clearly adopted the date of settlement as the date of reception. While that date has never been fixed precisely,[5] it is clear from the cases that the colony was regarded as established by discovery or settlement and not by conquest,[6] and that the first settlement occurred at the time of the Restoration of Charles II.[7] Hence, English statutes passed subsequent to that date, that is, 1660, have no application to New Brunswick, unless there is a provision to the contrary in them.[8]

The principle in New Brunswick as to whether an English Act is in force in the colony depends upon whether it is a law of local policy adapted solely to the country in which it was made, or a general regulation of property equally applicable to any country in which property is governed by the rules of English law.[9] If any distinction can be drawn between decisions in New Brunswick and Nova Scotia, it would appear to be that British statutes have been denied operative force in Nova Scotia unless clearly applicable, while in New Brunswick the tendency, at least of earlier authorities, seems to have been to admit

---

§307.3

[1]O. in C. (Imp.), dated June 18, 1784. See R.S.N.B. 1973, App. III.

[2]By S.N.B. 1791, c. 2. See now R.S.N.B. 1973, c. I-13, s. 6.

[3]See "Administration of the Government" in the foreword to the New Brunswick Statutes of 1786-1836.

[4]See the preamble to the first statute, S.N.B. 1786, c. 1.

[5]*Scott v. Scott* (1970), 15 D.L.R. (3d) 374 at p. 379, 2 N.B.R. (2d) 849 at pp. 862-3 (S.C. App. Div.), *per* Hughes, J.A.

[6]*R. v. McLaughlin*; *R. v. Peabody* (1830), 1 N.B.R. 218 (S.C.), at p. 221, *per* Saunders, C.J.

[7]*Ibid.*, *per* Botsford, J., and at pp. 221-2, *per* Chipman, J.; *Doe d. Hare v. McCall* (1827), 1 N.B.R. 90 (S.C.), at pp. 94-5, note *e*.

[8]*Ibid.*; *Boyd v. Fudge* (1964), 46 D.L.R. (2d) 679 at pp. 685-6, 50 M.P.R. 384 at pp. 389-90 (N.B.S.C. App. Div.), *per* McNair, C.J.N.B.; *Scott v. Scott*, *supra*, footnote 5, at p. 376 D.L.R., p. 859 N.B.R., *per* Bridges, C.J.N.B., and Limerick, J.A., and at p. 379 D.L.R., pp. 862-3 N.B.R., *per* Hughes, J.A.; *Velensky v. Hache* (1981), 121 D.L.R. (3d) 747 at p. 749, 33 N.B.R. (2d) 700 at p. 703 (Q.B.T.D.), *per* Stevenson, J.

[9]*A.-G. v. Stewart* (1817), 2 Mer. 143, 35 E.R. 895; *Doe d. Hanington v. McFadden* (1836), 2 N.B.R. 260.

them unless clearly inapplicable, but this distinction cannot be clearly pointed out in every case.[10]

Pursuant to these principles the *Statute of Uses*[11] was received into the colony by the leading case, *Doe d. Hanington v. McFadden*,[12] and it seems from the case that the *Statute of Enrolments*[13] was considered so received as well. Presumably the machinery of the provincial courts could be utilized for its operation.

307.4 Prince Edward Island

Prince Edward Island was discovered by France in 1534 and named Ile St. Jean, but France made no attempt to colonize it until after the *Treaty of Utrecht* in 1713. In 1758 it was captured by the British. By the *Treaty of Paris* in 1763, it was ceded to Great Britain and joined to Nova Scotia. It was made a separate colony on May 1, 1769.[1] English law was introduced by the Royal Proclamation of 1763, which extended this law to all former French possessions in North America. Its first Legislature did not meet until July 7, 1773, however.[2] Upon the separation from Nova Scotia, it appears to follow that the Island would take with it the law of England then in force in Nova Scotia, being whatever law went into force on October 2, 1758, except as altered by subsequent Nova Scotia legislation. It is arguable that any applicable English statutes passed between May 1, 1769, and July 7, 1773, would also be in force in the Island on the ground that in the interval, the power of making law in the Island resided with the Imperial Parliament and the Sovereign in Council.

308. QUEBEC

Quebec was a French colony until it was captured by the British in 1759. Under the *Treaty of Paris*, following the capture of Quebec and Montreal, New France, extending from Hudson's Bay to the Gulf of Mexico and including French Canada, was ceded to Great Britain. French law continued in the ceded territory until the King, exercising his prerogative right, issued a Proclamation on October 7, 1763, forming the ceded territory into the four provinces of Quebec, East Florida, West Florida, and Grenada and imposing on them English criminal and civil law.[1] The Quebec territory was so erroneously de-

---

[10]Clement, *op. cit.*, §304, footnote 12, p. 282.

[11]27 Hen. 8, c. 10 (1535).

[12]*Supra*, footnote 9.

[13]27 Hen. 8, c. 16 (1535).

§307.4

[1]*Kelly v. Sullivan* (1876), 1 S.C.R. 3 at p. 17.

[2]See the preamble to its third statute, S.P.E.I. 1773, c. 3, reciting those facts.

§308

[1]*Sed quaere: Wilcox v. Wilcox* (1857), 2 L.C. Jur. 1, and Report of Hey, C.J., in the Appendix, especially at p. xii; *Stuart v. Bowman* (1851), 2 L.C.R. 369, where doubts are raised as to the introduction of English law by the Proclamation of 1763. See also "Plan for Settling the Laws and Administration of Justice in the Province of Quebec" (1769), 1 L.C. Jur., Appendix, p. 25.

scribed that it did not include the greater part of the territory. It has been contended by some French-Canadian jurists that French Canada is to be regarded as acquired by treaty or cession and not by conquest. It is true that France itself was not conquered, that until the *Treaty of Paris* was signed the possibility of reconquest by France remained, that only a portion of the ceded territory was occupied by British forces during hostilities and that it is a fine point as to the territorial limits to which military conquest of strongholds extends. It appears, however, that the principle of international law adopted by Great Britain is that, even though the parent state be not conquered, conquered territory at once becomes a possession of the victorious party and a subsequent cession of it by treaty is merely a formal confirmation of title by conquest. Furthermore, as pointed out by Armour,[2] the distinction is of little practical importance because, as heretofore indicated, whether the territory be acquired by conquest or by cession, the prerogative right to impose law is the same, except as modified by the terms of the cession.

The view is held by some that the treaty preserved the religion, language, and laws of French Canada. This is not accurate. Upon the surrender of Quebec and Montreal, the terms of capitulation preserved to the inhabitants their possessions and religion, but not their laws or language. By the *Treaty of Paris*, the territory was ceded to the King of Great Britain "in the most ample manner and form, without restriction", the King agreeing "to grant the liberty of the Catholic religion to the inhabitants of Canada" and to order that they might worship according to the rites of their church "as far as the laws of Great Britain permit". Therefore, the civil law and language of the Province of Quebec were preserved by subsequent statute and not by treaty. The inhabitants of French Canada were naturally dissatisfied with the introduction of the strange English civil law and the absence of adequate provision for the use of their language essential to the understanding and due conduct of legal proceedings. Commencing with the strong representations of the sympathetic Governor James Murray, supported by the recommendations of the Attorney-General and Solicitor-General and the next Governor, Sir Guy Carleton, a sustained effort resulted in the passage of the *Quebec Act* in 1774.[3]

The *Quebec Act*, effective May 1, 1775, (a) established the Province of Quebec with corrected boundaries so enlarged as to include what later became Upper Canada; (b) provided for a Governor and Legislative Council and the making of ordinances by them; (c) provided for the revocation of the Proclamation of 1763; (d) provided that, in all matters relating to civil rights and the enjoyment of property, customs and wages, resort be had to the laws of Canada, that is, French law before the Proclamation, until varied by ordinances of the Governor and Legislative Council; (e) provided, however, that the Act was not to extend to lands then or later granted by the Crown in free and common socage and that the owner of lands or chattels could devise or

---

[2]*Real Property*, pp. 6-7.
[3]14 Geo. 3, c. 83 (1774, Imp.).

bequeath them notwithstanding any existing law or custom in the province to the contrary; (f) provided for the free exercise of their religion by the Roman Catholic inhabitants; and (g) provided for the continuance of the criminal law of England as introduced by the Proclamation of 1763.[4]

Except as modified by ordinances of the Governor and Legislative Council, the law thus introduced by the *Quebec Act* continued until 1791, when Great Britain passed the *Constitutional Act*[5] by which the Province of Quebec was separated into the two provinces of Upper and Lower Canada. The Act gave to each province a separate constitution and representative form of government consisting of a Governor, Legislative Council and a Legislative Assembly, the power to legislate being granted to the Council and Assembly subject to Royal Assent to be expressed by the Governor. Under the Act, all lands granted in Upper Canada were to be in free and common socage, as they were to be in Lower Canada also if the grantees so desired, but otherwise the Act left in force in both provinces the French law introduced by the Act of 1774 and ordinances passed under its authority.

Under the *Constitutional Act*, Lower Canada retained its French law of real property in force before the Proclamation of 1763, or established by ordinance under the *Quebec Act* of 1774, except for the provision that grantees would be entitled to grants in free and common socage if they so desired. In 1851 feudal rights and duties were abolished in Lower Canada.[6]

The two provinces were again united temporarily by the *Act of Union* of 1840,[7] but this did not have any major effect on the civil and common law in force in the two colonies. At Confederation in 1867, they were again separated into the two distinct provinces of Ontario and Quebec.

The territory of Quebec was enlarged in 1898[8] and 1912,[9] when large parts of what was formerly Rupert's Land were annexed to it. It seems to have been assumed that the law of Quebec was thereby introduced into those territories.[10]

309. ONTARIO

Until 1791, a large part of the territory now known as Ontario formed part of Quebec. As a result of settlement by English-speaking colonists in this area, particularly United Empire Loyalists, who were unaccustomed to French law, Parliament, by the *Constitutional Act* of that year,[1] divided the Province of Quebec into the two separate provinces of Upper and Lower Canada, each with its own separate Assembly.

---

[4]See *Citizens v. Parsons* (1881), 7 App. Cas. 96.
[5]31 Geo. 3, c. 31 (1791, Imp.).
[6]*An Act Respecting General Abolition of Feudal Rights and Duty*, S.L.C. 1851, c. 3.
[7]3 & 4 Vict., c. 35 (1840, Imp.). The Act is discussed in §309, *infra*.
[8]By *An Act respecting the north-western, northern and north-eastern boundaries of the province of Quebec*, S.C. 1898, c. 3.
[9]By the *Quebec Boundaries Extension Act*, S.C. 1912, c. 45.
[10]Coté, *op. cit.*, §301, footnote 2, p. 88.
§309
[1]31 Geo. 3, c. 31 (1791, Imp.).

Under the authority of this legislation English civil law was introduced into the province of Upper Canada by its first statute, the *Property and Civil Rights Act*,[2] which (a) recited that the province had been principally settled by British subjects who were unaccustomed to the French law of Canada; (b) repealed the provisions of the *Quebec Act* of 1774 which required such law to be resorted to in all controversies relating to property and civil rights and (c) declared that in such matters "resort should be had to the laws of England from and after the passing of the Act as the rule for decision of the same"[3] and that all matters relating to evidence and legal proof were to be regulated by the rules of evidence established in England on that date. The ordinances by the Governor and Legislative Council under the 1774 Act, except those necessarily repealed by the foregoing provisions, were to remain in force.

Consequently, when in 1792 the *Property and Civil Rights Act* came into force, Upper Canada acquired the whole law of real property that was then in force in England,[4] together with that established by unrepealed ordinances made under the *Quebec Act* of 1774. The law thus acquired, however, retained few of the incidents of feudal tenure, most of which had disappeared or had been abolished in 1660 by the *Tenures Abolition Act*.[5]

The introduction of English law by the statute of 1792 has generally been regarded by the courts as full and complete. That is, all English law was thus introduced, except such as was inherently inapplicable.[6] As has been noted, there is judicial authority of doubtful validity which would suggest that all English law, save that specifically excepted by the statute of 1792, was introduced.[7]

In general, it may be said that the Ontario courts have been more ready to accept English statutes than the courts of Nova Scotia.[8] Thus, for example, it was held that the *Mortmain Act*[9] formed part of the law of the province (admittedly because of a perceived legislative recognition of reception of that statute), despite the fact that English courts had held it to be inapplicable to colonial conditions.[10] None of the other provinces have adopted this legislation.[11]

---

[2]S.U.C. 1792, c. 1. See now R.S.O. 1980, c. 395.

[3]The date is October 15, 1792. See the present Act, R.S.O. 1980, c. 395, and Coté, *op. cit.*, §301, footnote 2, p. 88.

[4]*Keewatin Power Co. v. Town of Kenora* (1908), 16 O.L.R. 184 (C.A.), at p. 189.

[5]12 Car. 2, c. 24 (1660).

[6]*Doe d. Anderson v. Todd* (1846), 2 U.C.Q.B. 82 at p. 86, *per* Robinson, C.J. See also *Shea v. Choat* (1846), 2 U.C.Q.B. 211 at p. 221.

[7]See *Keewatin Power Co.*, *supra*, footnote 4.

[8]Clement, *op. cit.*, §304, footnote 12, pp. 280-1.

[9]9 Geo. 2, c. 36 (1736).

[10]*A.-G. v. Stewart* (1817), 2 Mer. 143 at pp. 157-9, 35 E.R. 895, *per* Sir William Grant, M.R.; *Whicker v. Hume* (1858), 5 H.L.R. 124, 11 E.R. 50; *Jex v. McKinney* (1889), 14 App. Cas. 77 (P.C.).

[11]See generally Oosterhoff, "The Law of Mortmain; An Historical and Comparative Review", 27 U. of T. L.J. 257 (1977), at pp. 295-9, 302 *et seq.*

As has been noted, Ontario attempted to effect a repeal and consolidation of English law received in the province, to the extent that this was within its legislative competence, by legislation in 1902.[12]

As a result of political disturbances, the Rebellion of 1837, during which the constitutions of Upper and Lower Canada were suspended and the law-making power was vested in the Governors and special Councils, and as the first step towards a national confederation that was seen to be desirable, the *Act of Union* in 1840,[13] formed, as of a date to be specified by Proclamation by the Governor-General, Upper and Lower Canada into the single Province of Canada with a single Legislative Council and a single Legislative Assembly in which each had equal representation. The Act divided each of the two former provinces into counties but did not expressly prescribe the basis of civil and criminal law that was to prevail. It did, however, provide (a) that that part of the *Constitutional Act* of 1791 which provided for the constitution of a Legislative Council and Assembly in each of the provinces of Upper and Lower Canada and for the making of laws, and the whole of the Acts which temporarily suspended the Constitution of Lower Canada, were to be repealed as of the effective date of the Proclamation, and (b) that such repeal was not to be held to revive any enactment repealed by those Acts. Thus the provisions of the *Quebec Act* of 1774 which had restored French civil law to the old province of Quebec and which had been repealed by the *Constitutional Act* in so far as they applied to the province of Upper Canada, were not revived by the *Act of Union*. The latter Act also empowered the Legislative Council and Assembly of Canada to make laws not repugnant to that Act, or to the unrepealed parts of the *Constitutional Act*, or to any Imperial Act extending to the provinces of Upper and Lower Canada, or either of them, or to the new Province of Canada. It followed that, subject to any particular law being altered by legislation of the new province, French civil law continued in the Lower Canada division, English common law continued in the Upper Canada division, and English criminal law in both divisions. Under the Act, in practice, statutes that were not to have province-wide effect, but were to apply only in Upper Canada or Lower Canada, so provided.

At Confederation in 1867 the united Province of Canada was again separated into two, the provinces of Ontario and Quebec. The boundaries of the province of Ontario were considerably extended in 1889[14] and 1912[15] when large parts of what was formerly Rupert's Land were annexed to the province. Presumably the law of the province was extended to these new areas.[16] There were minor changes in boundaries later as well.

[12]See §304, *supra*.
[13]3 & 4 Vict., c. 35 (1840, Imp.).
[14]By the *Canada (Ontario Boundary) Act, 1889*, 52 & 53 Vict., c. 28.
[15]By the *Ontario Boundaries Extension Act*, S.C. 1912, c. 40.
[16]*Vamvakadis v. Kirkoff* (1929), 64 O.L.R. 585 at pp. 588-9, [1930] 2 D.L.R. 877 at p. 880 (S.C. App. Div.).

310. THE TERRITORIES AND THE PRAIRIE PROVINCES[1]

Much of the land presently known as the provinces of Alberta, Manitoba and Saskatchewan, the Yukon Territory and the Northwest Territories, together with other lands, that is, the Hudson's Bay watershed, was granted by Charles II to the Hudson's Bay Company by charter on May 2, 1670. The charter provided that the law of England should apply in this territory which was known as Rupert's Land. It was considered as having been acquired by settlement even though French explorers and fur traders had initially penetrated parts of it.[2] English law was introduced into other parts of this area, whose waters did not drain into Hudson's Bay, when they were settled. For a long time there were no courts in these areas and a series of Imperial statutes provided for the administration of justice in the courts of neighbouring provinces, that is, British Columbia and Upper and Lower Canada.[3]

The Hudson's Bay Company introduced the law of England as of June 20, 1837, and later again as of January 1, 1864, into that part of its territory known as Assinniboia, the southern part of the present province of Manitoba.

310.1 Manitoba

The province of Manitoba was formed out of parts of the Northwest Territories in 1870 pursuant to the *Manitoba Act.*[1] This statute enacted that on the day on which the Queen in Council admitted Rupert's Land and the North-Western Territory into the Dominion, there was to be formed thereout the province of Manitoba. The Imperial Order in Council of June 23, 1870, fixed the date as of which English law went into force in the whole area as July 15, 1870. In 1874 the provincial Legislature confirmed this by passing a statute[2] which provided that: "The Court of Queen's Bench shall decide and determine all matters of controversy relative to property and civil rights according to the laws existing or established and being in England as such were, existed and stood on the 15th day of July, 1870, so far as the same can be made applicable to matters relating to property and civil rights in the province."[3]

To settle certain doubts about the introduction of English law within federal jurisdiction in Manitoba the Canadian Parliament passed *An Act Respecting Application of Laws to the Province of Manitoba,*[4] which provided that the

---

§310
[1]On the reception of English law in these areas see generally Coté, *op. cit.,* §304, footnote 12.
[2]*Sinclair v. Mulligan* (1888), 5 Man. R. 17 (C.A.); *A.-G. Alta. v. Huggard Assets Ltd.,* [1953] 3 D.L.R. 225, [1953] A.C. 420 (P.C.); *Walker v. Walker* (1919), 48 D.L.R. 1 at pp. 2-3, [1919] A.C. 947 at p. 951.
[3]Coté, *op. cit.,* footnote 1, pp. 263-4.
§310.1
[1]S.C. 1870, c. 3.
[2]*Queen's Bench Act,* S.M. 1874, c. 12; now R.S.M. 1970, c. C-280.
[3]*Ibid.,* s. 1; now s. 51(3).
[4]S.C. 1888, c. 33; now R.S.C. 1927, c. 124, s. 4 (still in force).

laws of England relating to matters within the jurisdiction of the Parliament of Canada as they existed on July 15, 1870, "were from the said day and are in force in the Province of Manitoba, in so far as the same are applicable to the said Province and in so far as the same have not been or are not hereafter repealed, altered, varied, modified or affected by any Act of the Parliament of the United Kingdom applicable to the said Province, or of the Parliament of Canada". Prior to those enactments, the law in the territory which became the province of Manitoba was the law of England on May 3, 1670, being the date of the charter of the Hudson's Bay Company.[5]

Manitoba's borders were extended in 1912 to encompass further areas of the former Hudson's Bay Company lands.[6] Presumably its laws were extended to this new territory. In any event, the law of England was also received in those areas as of July 15, 1870.[7] There were subsequent minor alterations in the boundaries.

310.2 Alberta[1]

Alberta was formed out of parts of the Northwest Territories by the *Alberta Act*,[2] effective September 1, 1905. The Act preserved the existing law in force.[3] This was, of course, the law in force in the Northwest Territories at that time.[4]

310.3 Saskatchewan

The province of Saskatchewan was formed out of the remaining southern parts of the Northwest Territories in 1905 by the *Saskatchewan Act*.[1] As in the case of Alberta, the Act preserved the existing law, that is, the law of the Northwest Territories.[2]

310.4 The Northwest Territories

Rupert's Land and the Northwest Territories, except for the parts annexed to Manitoba, Ontario and Quebec, continued under the jurisdiction of the Hudson's Bay Company until 1870. In that year the whole of the territories

---

[5]*Sinclair v. Mulligan* (1888), 5 Man. R. 17 (C.A.); *Larence v. Larence* (1911), 17 W.L.R. 197, 21 Man. R. 145.

[6]By the *Manitoba Boundaries Extension Act*, S.C. 1912, c. 32.

[7]By the *North-West Territories Act*, S.C. 1886, c. 25, s. 3.

§310.2

[1]See generally Coté, *op. cit.*, §304, footnote 12.

[2]S.C. 1905, c. 3.

[3]*Ibid.*, s. 16.

[4]See *Toll v. Canadian Pacific R. W. Co.* (1908), 8 W.L.R. 795 (Alta. S.C.), at pp. 798-9; *Magrum v. McDougal*, [1944] 4 D.L.R. 681, [1944] 3 W.W.R. 486 (Alta. S.C. App. Div.).

§310.3

[1]S.C. 1905, c. 42, effective September 1, 1905.

[2]*Ibid.*, s. 16.

were annexed to Canada. This was done pursuant to the *Rupert's Land Act*,[1] which authorized the Hudson's Bay Company to surrender its lands and the admission of this territory into Canada. Rupert's Land and the North-Western Territory, as it was then called, were so admitted on July 15, 1870, by Order in Council dated June 23, 1870.

Until February 18, 1887, the law in force in Rupert's Land was the law of England on May 3, 1670, being the date of the charter of the Hudson's Bay Company,[2] and that appears to be regarded as the situation in respect of the Northwest Territories generally.[3] However, a new date for the entire Northwest Territories was fixed by the *North-West Territories Act* of 1886,[4] which, by proclamation, went into force on February 18, 1887. This statute provided that the laws of England relating to civil and criminal matters, as they existed on July 15, 1870, were to be in force in the Territories in so far as they were applicable to the Territories. This provision still governs the present Northwest Territories.

310.5 Yukon Territory

Yukon Territory was formed out of the western part of the Northwest Territories in 1898 by federal statute.[1] This statute provided that the existing law of the Northwest Territories continued in force in the new Territory.[2]

311. BRITISH COLUMBIA[1]

The province of British Columbia was formed out of three separate colonies.[2] Vancouver Island was formed as a colony in 1849, when it was granted to the Hudson's Bay Company by the Crown on condition that it be settled. The lower mainland of British Columbia was organized as a colony in 1858.[3] The power to legislate for it was granted to the Governor of the Hudson's Bay Company. Pursuant to that power he proclaimed the law of England as of November 19, 1858, to be in force in the colony. The northern part of the mainland had also been granted to the Hudson's Bay Company. English law so

---

§310.4

[1] 31 & 32 Vict., c. 105 (1868, Imp.).

[2] *Larence v. Larence* (1911), 17 W.L.R. 197, 21 Man. R. 145.

[3] See *Sinclair v. Mulligan* (1888), 5 Man. R. 17 (C.A.); *Re Calder* (1891), 2 W.L.T. 1, but see *Connolly v. Woolrich* (1867), 11 L.C. Jur. 197.

[4] S.C. 1886, c. 25, consolidated as R.S.C. 1886, c. 50; now R.S.C. 1970, c. N-22.

§310.5

[1] *Yukon Territory Act*, S.C. 1898, c. 6; now R.S.C. 1970, c. Y-2.

[2] *Ibid.*, s. 9; now s. 22(1).

§311

[1] See generally Herbert, "A Brief History of the Introduction of English Law into British Columbia", 2 U.B.C. Leg. N. 93 (1954); Bouck, *op. cit.*, §303, footnote 22.

[2] See Coté, *op. cit.*, §301, footnote 2, pp. 91-2.

[3] 21 & 22 Vict., c. 99 (1858, Imp.).

far as applicable was declared to be in force in that area as of January 1, 1862, by Imperial Order in Council. The northern colony was annexed to the lower mainland in 1863 by an Imperial statute.[4] It is probable that the law of the southern colony was thus extended to the northern area.

In 1866 the colonies of British Columbia and Vancouver Island were amalgamated[5] and existing laws were continued.[6] By the *English Law Act*[7] the local Legislature decreed that the English law as of November 19, 1858, should apply to the whole of the colony.

Finally, in 1871, the colony was admitted into Canada. It has been pointed out that, as there is no federal legislation on the matter, the *English Law Act*, to the extent that it dealt with matters which subsequently fell within federal jurisdiction, remains in force and that, to the extent that the Act purports to legislate on these matters after Confederation, it is *ultra vires*.[8]

As has been noted, in 1897 and 1911, British Columbia reprinted and re-enacted a number of English statutes.[9]

312. CONFEDERATION[1]

The Confederation of Canada into a Dominion was effected by the *Constitution Act, 1867*.[2] It empowered the Queen in Council to declare by proclamation that, on and after a day to be therein appointed, the provinces of Canada, Nova Scotia and New Brunswick were to form one Dominion in the name of Canada. It divided the Province of Canada into the two provinces of Ontario and Quebec, the former to comprise what had formerly been the province of Upper Canada and the latter to comprise what had formerly been the province of Lower Canada. It also empowered the Queen in Council (a) to admit the colonies or provinces of Newfoundland, Prince Edward Island and British Columbia, or any of them, into the union or Dominion, upon addresses of the Houses of the Parliament of Canada and of their Legislatures asking for that action, and (b) to admit into the union or Dominion, Rupert's Land and the North-Western Territory, or either of them, upon addresses of the Houses of the Parliament of Canada. Under section 92 of the Act, the Legislative Assembly of each province was given exclusive legislative jurisdiction over property and civil rights except to the extent that those subjects were assigned exclusively to the Parliament of Canada by section 91.

---

[4]26 & 27 Vict., c. 83 (1863, Imp.).
[5]29 & 30 Vict., c. 67 (1866, Imp.).
[6]*Ibid.*, s. 5.
[7]S.B.C. 1867, No. 266; now s. 2 of the *Law and Equity Act*, R.S.B.C. 1979, c. 224.
[8]Coté, *op. cit.*, p. 92.
[9]§309, *supra*.
§312
[1]Although many of the statutes discussed below have already been referred to, the following material will provide a useful summary of Confederation statutes.
[2]30-31 Vict., c. 3 (1867, Imp.).

The *Rupert's Land Act*[3] authorized "the Governor and Company of Adventurers of England trading into Hudson's Bay" to surrender its lands, authorized the Queen in Council to admit Rupert's Land into the Dominion and empowered the Parliament of Canada to then legislate for its inhabitants. The *Manitoba Act*[4] provided that on the day on which the Queen in Council admitted Rupert's Land and the North-Western Territory into the Dominion there was to be formed thereout the province of Manitoba, the boundaries of which were described.

By Order in Council of June 23, 1870 it was ordered and declared that on July 15, 1870, Rupert's Land and the North-Western Territory were to be admitted into the Dominion.

By Order in Council of May 16, 1871, it was ordered and declared that on July 20, 1871, the province of British Columbia was to be admitted into the Dominion.

It has been held that the lands, including the mineral and other natural resources, of the seabed and subsoil seaward from the low-water mark on the coast of British Columbia to the outer limit of the territorial sea of Canada are vested in Canada.[5]

The *Constitution Act, 1871*,[6] expressly settled legal doubts that had arisen by providing that the Parliament of Canada may establish new provinces and territories forming part of the Dominion and not included in any province, may provide for courts and the passing of laws in such provinces and may legislate for any territory not included in a province.

The *Alberta Act*,[7] effective September 1, 1905, established described territory as the province of Alberta.

The *Saskatchewan Act*,[8] effective September 1, 1905, established described territory as the province of Saskatchewan.

Yukon Territory was split off from the Northwest Territories in 1898 by the *Yukon Territory Act*.[9] The civil law of the Northwest Territories and the Yukon Territory is still under the legislative jurisdiction of the Parliament of Canada, but much of the local legislation is enacted by Territorial Assemblies.

The *Statute of Westminster*[10] gave effect to the reports of the Imperial Conferences of 1926 and 1930 at Westminster, between Canada, Newfoundland, Australia, New Zealand, South Africa and the Irish Free State. It provides (a) that the *Colonial Laws Validity Act, 1865*[11] (under which any colonial law that is repugnant to any Act of the Imperial Parliament extending to the colony

---

[3] 31 & 32 Vict., c. 105 (1868, Imp.).
[4] S.C. 1870, c. 3.
[5] *Reference re Ownership of Off-Shore Mineral Rights* (1967), 65 D.L.R. (2d) 353, [1967] S.C.R. 792.
[6] 34 & 35 Vict., c. 28 (1871, Imp.).
[7] S.C. 1905, c. 3.
[8] S.C. 1905, c. 42.
[9] S.C. 1898, c. 6.
[10] 22 Geo. 5, c. 4 (1931, Imp.), reproduced in R.S.C. 1970, vol. Appendices, p. 401.
[11] 28 & 29 Vict., c. 63 (1865, Imp.).

is void to the extent of such repugnancy) shall not apply to any law made by the Parliament of a Dominion because it is repugnant to the law of England or to any future Act of the Imperial Parliament; (b) that the Parliament of a Dominion may repeal or amend any such future Imperial Act to the extent that it is part of the law of the Dominion and this provision was extended to the Legislatures of the provinces of Canada and laws made by them; (c) that no future Imperial Act shall extend to a Dominion so as to be part of its law unless the Act declares that the Dominion requested and concurred in its enactment; and (d) that the Parliament of a Dominion may make laws having extraterritorial effect. The Act provides, however, that the powers conferred by it on the Parliament of Canada and its provincial Legislatures are restricted to enactment of laws relating to matters within their competence and that the Act does not apply to the Constitution Acts or any order or regulation thereunder.

By the *Newfoundland Act, 1949*[12] Newfoundland was admitted into the Dominion.

Finally, by the *Canada Act*[13] of 1982 it was provided that no Act of the Parliament of the United Kingdom passed after the *Constitution Act, 1982*, which is Schedule B to the former Act, shall extend to Canada as part of its law. The *Constitution Act, 1982*, enacts the Canadian Charter of Rights and Freedoms, protects the rights of aboriginal peoples, provides for a commitment to promote equal opportunities, provides for a constitutional conference, incorporates an amending formula, and includes other constitutional amendments.[14] On the question of legislative authority, it is appropriate to add that when an Imperial Act confers power on a Legislative Assembly to make laws for a colony, that power is not in any sense exercised by delegation from or as agent of the Imperial Parliament but is as plenary and ample, within the prescribed limits, as the Imperial Parliament possessed and could bestow. Within such limits, the local Legislature is supreme and has the same authority as the Imperial Parliament.[15] That principle applies both to the Dominion Parliament and the Legislative Assemblies of the provinces.[16]

---

[12]12 & 13 Geo. 6, c. 22 (1949, Imp.).
[13]C. 11 (1982, U.K.), s. 2.
[14]For the background to this legislation, see *Reference re Amendment of Constitution of Canada (Nos. 1, 2 and 3)* (1981), 125 D.L.R. (3d) 1, [1981] S.C.R. 753.
[15]*Powell v. Apollo Candle Co. Ltd.* (1885), 10 App. Cas. 282 (P.C.).
[16]*Hodge v. The Queen* (1883), 9 App. Cas. 117 (P.C.).

PART II

TENURES AND ESTATES

CONTENTS OF PART II

CHAPTER 4

DOCTRINES OF TENURE AND ESTATE
IN CANADA

401. TENURE

The doctrine of tenure, one of the two most significant concepts in feudal land law (the other being the doctrine of estates), has already been described in some detail.[1] It remains in this chapter briefly to recapitulate this doctrine and to discuss its introduction and present status in Canada.[2]

The doctrine of tenure denotes the feudal relationship that subsisted between a lord and his tenants and it describes the quality upon which, or the services for which, land was held.[3] The doctrine required that all land must be held of a superior lord in the feudal hierarchy to whom the services were owed. That lord might in turn hold of another lord and so on up the feudal ladder until finally the land was held of the King as lord paramount. Thus, in feudal society all land, except that owned by the sovereign himself, was held either mediately (that is, through intermediate or mesne lords), or immediately (that is, directly) of the King.

In England, initially the growth of subtenures was immense because of the process known as subinfeudation. By this process a tenant of land, instead of selling it outright to a third person so that that person would be substituted for himself, would create a new tenancy whereby he would become lord and the

---

§401

[1] §§204-7, *supra*.

[2] For a more detailed discussion of the doctrine of tenure, see Hogg, "The Effect of Tenure on Real Property Law", 25 L.Q. Rev. 178 (1909).

[3] Plucknett, p. 517.

third person would become his tenant and would owe services to him. The large increase in tenures was inconvenient to the great lords, however, since they thereby lost many of their revenues,[4] and the process was checked by the Statute *Quia Emptores*,[5] which forbade alienation by subinfeudation.

In the course of time, many of the existing subtenures began to disappear, primarily for the following reason: A number of the old feudal services, such as the duty to supply knights for the King's army in the case of knight service, had been commuted into money payments called scutage. Over a period of time, as the value of money fell, these became insignificant and were no longer collected. Memories of intermediate lordships thus faded and were forgotten. The same occurred in the case of socage tenure where the agricultural services, at one time required, were also converted into money rents, called quit rents.

The process was accelerated by the *Tenures Abolition Act* of 1660.[6] By this statute all existing free lay tenures were converted into free and common socage and most of the remaining onerous incidents of tenure, such as wardship, relief, marriage and aids were abolished. Escheat was the important survivor. There was, therefore, little left for the intermediate lords and, as indicated, what was left of their rights was forgotten.

Since, however, under the doctrine of tenure a person must hold land of someone, the only person remaining was the King and the result in England is that most land is held directly of the Crown.

The discussion so far has ignored copyhold or unfree tenure which remained significant in England until 1925. However, it was never introduced into Canada and can thus be left out of consideration here.[7]

402. TENURE IN THE CANADIAN PROVINCES

It stands to reason, since most of the other forms of tenure had been abolished in England prior to the settlement and conquest of Canada, that socage was the only freehold tenure introduced into the Canadian provinces pursuant to the rules for reception of English law.[1] This is, indeed, the case, although the mode in which it was introduced varied from province to province. The effect is that today all land in Canada, except that owned by the Crown in right of the Dominion or of the several provinces, is held, not allodially or outright, but of the Crown in right of the Dominion or of a province. The doctrine no longer has much effect and can normally be disregarded. Vestiges of it remain, however. For example, it is still paid lip-service in the *habendum* of the standard deed which commences with the words "To have and to hold", and while it is not expressed that the grantee will hold by the tenure of free

---

[4] §207, *supra*.
[5] 18 Edw. 1, cc. 1-3 (1290).
[6] 12 Car. 2, c. 24.
[7] For a discussion of copyhold tenure, see §§205.2 and 207, *supra*.
§402
[1] See ch. 3, *supra*, for a discussion of these rules.

and common socage, that is understood. Moreover, certain characteristics of the tenure may still be significant such as the requirement that the services reserved must be certain. Thus it may be, for example, that a variable royalty that is not sanctioned by legislation offends this requirement.[2]

In addition to the freehold tenure of free and common socage, tenure by leasehold was also introduced into the Canadian provinces. This tenure is of much more recent vintage than socage. Indeed, it did not at one time form part of the feudal system at all since the leasehold estate, its concomitant, did not come into being as such until the 15th century.[3] Prior thereto, leaseholds had been regarded only as personal contracts and as chattels real. Leasehold tenure is today much more important than socage tenure, for it is essential in the landlord and tenant relationship.[4] It retains many of the characteristics of feudal tenure generally, such as rent, which is a rent-service, the right of distress and the right of the landlord to terminate the lease for breach of covenants.[5]

In addition to the tenure of free and common socage, a number of statutes relating to tenure were introduced into the Canadian provinces and Territories. Significant among these is the Statute *Quia Emptores*.[6] This statute has been described as a pillar of the law of real property. Not only did it abolish alienation by subinfeudation,[7] but more important, it confirmed the principle of alienation by substitution under which a person, when he buys land, steps into the shoes of the vendor and becomes tenant of his lord. Today all sale transactions of land still operate under this statute.

402.1 Ontario

Free and common socage was introduced into Upper Canada by the *Constitutional Act* of 1791,[1] section 43 of which provided in part "all lands which shall be hereafter granted within the said Province of Upper Canada shall be granted in free and common soccage, in like manner as lands are now holden in free and common soccage, in that part of Great Britain called England". In addition, the laws of England were introduced into Upper Canada by its first statute[2] which provided[3] that "from and after the passing of this Act, in all matters of controversy relative to property and civil rights, resort shall be had to the Laws of England, as the rule for the decision of the same".[4] This

---

[2]See, *e.g.*, *A.-G. Alta. v. Huggard Assets Ltd.*, [1951] 2 D.L.R. 305, [1951] S.C.R. 427, revd on other grounds [1953] 3 D.L.R. 225, [1953] A.C. 420 (P.C.).
[3]Litt., s. 58.
[4]But see contra, *Landlord and Tenant Act*, R.S.O. 1980, c. 232, s. 3, which provides:
   3. The relation of landlord and tenant does not depend on tenure, and a reversion in the lessor is not necessary in order to create the relation of landlord and tenant, or to make applicable the incidents by law belonging to that relation; nor is it necessary, in order to give a landlord the right of distress, that there is an agreement for that purpose between the parties.
See Scane, "The Relationship of Landlord and Tenant", *Law Society of Upper Canada Special Lectures on The Lease in Modern Business*, 1965, 1, at pp. 3-5.

(footnotes continued overleaf)

legislation has generally been construed to have introduced all laws of England into the province except such as were inherently inapplicable.[5] It would seem, therefore, that statutes such as the *Tenures Abolition Act*,[6] which abolished most of the tenures and their incidents except socage tenure, were introduced into Upper Canada. Tenures such as frankalmoign, copyhold and the honorary incidents of grand serjeanty, which were not abolished by that Act, were not introduced into the province since they were of peculiar local application to England and were not suitable to conditions in the North American colonies. Leasehold tenure, being suitable, was introduced.

Ontario went further than this, however, for in 1902 it re-enacted a number of English real property statutes, thereby allaying any doubts as to their reception. These several statutes are contained in volume III of the Revised Statutes of Ontario, 1897. They include *De Donis Conditionalibus*,[7] *Quia Emptores*[8] and the *Statute of Uses*.[9] A number of these statutes were subsequently absorbed into other legislation. The last two are still preserved as such.[10]

402.2 Quebec

Quebec, being a former colony of France, had a tenurial system too. However, by the Royal Proclamation of 1763, English law was introduced and while this was reversed by the *Quebec Act* of 1774,[1] that statute excepted lands theretofore granted in free and common socage from the repeal.[2] Moreover, the *Constitutional Act*[3] provided that:

> ... in every case where lands shall be hereafter granted within the said Province of Lower Canada, and where the grantee thereof shall desire the same to be granted in

---

[5]See generally §209.2, *supra*.
[6]18 Edw. 1, cc. 1-3 (1290).
[7]See §401, *supra*.
§402.1
[1]31 Geo. 3, c. 31 (1791, Imp.).
[2]*Property and Civil Rights Act*, S.U.C. 1792, c. 1.
[3]*Ibid.*, s. 3.
[4]The date is October 15, 1792. See now *Property and Civil Rights Act*, R.S.O. 1980, c. 395, s. 1.
[5]See, *e.g.*, *Doe d. Anderson v. Todd* (1846), 2 U.C.Q.B. 82 at p. 86, *per* Robinson, C.J.; *Shea v. Choat* (1846), 2 U.C.Q.B. 211 at p. 221; *sed contra, Keewatin Power Co. v. Town of Kenora* (1908), 16 O.L.R. 184 (C.A.). See generally §303, *supra*, on this point.
[6]12 Car. 2, c. 24 (1660).
[7]13 Edw. 1, c. 1 (1285), reprinted in *An Act respecting Real Property*, R.S.O. 1897, c. 330.
[8]18 Edw. 1, cc. 1-3 (1290), reprinted in *An Act respecting Real Property*, R.S.O. 1897, c. 330.
[9]27 Hen. 8, c. 10 (1535), reprinted as *An Act concerning Uses*, R.S.O. 1897, c. 331.
[10]See *An Act respecting Real Property* and the *Statute of Uses* in R.S.O. 1980, App. A.
§402.2
[1]14 Geo. 3, c. 83.
[2]*Ibid.*, s. 4.
[3]31 Geo. 3, c. 31, s. 43 (1791, Imp.).

free and common soccage the same shall be so granted; but subject nevertheless to such alterations, with respect to the nature and consequences of such tenure of free and common soccage, as may be established by any law or laws which may be made by his Majesty, his heirs or successors, by and with the advice and consent of the Legislative Council and Assembly of the Province.

The resulting admixture was dealt with by the courts in the manner described by the Privy Council in *St. Francis Hydro Electric Co. v. The King*[4] as follows: "It is undeniable that the decision in Quebec including the decisions on appeal to His Majesty in Council have uniformly regarded lands granted in free and common soccage as subject to the French law except as regards tenure."

The feudal or seigniorial system was abolished in that part of the united Province of Canada known as Lower Canada in 1854,[5] and the seigniory holdings were converted into holdings in *franc aleu roturier*. Moreover, a statute in 1857[6] declared:

V. The Laws which have governed lands held in Free and Common Soccage in Lower Canada in matters other than alienation, descent and rights depending upon marriage, are hereby declared to have always been the same with those which governed lands held in *franc aleu roturier*, except in so far only as it may have been otherwise provided by any Act of the Legislature of Lower Canada, or of this Province . . .

The result is that today in Quebec the land law is no longer based on tenure.[7]

402.3 Newfoundland and the Maritime Provinces

In Newfoundland and the maritime provinces the laws of England were received under the common law rules of reception for colonies acquired by settlement, which state in essence that all laws of England are received into a colony except such as are inherently inapplicable to conditions in the colony.[1] Inapplicable laws are generally those that have only peculiar and local effect in England such as the *Mortmain Act*.[2] The date as of which English law is received under the common law rules is generally thought to be the date the first Legislative Assembly meets.[3] The respective dates for the subject prov-

---

[4][1937] 2 D.L.R. 353 at p. 362, 66 Que. K.B. 374 (P.C.).
[5]*Seigniorial Act*, S.C. 1854, c. 3.
[6]*An Act for settling the Law concerning Lands held in Free and Common Soccage in Lower Canada*, S.C. 1857, c. 45, s. 5.
[7]See generally Laskin, pp. 26-7.
§402.3
[1]1 Bl. Comm. 106; *Blankard v. Galdy* (1693), 2 Salk. 411, 91 E.R. 356; *Anonymous* (1722), 2 P. Wms. 75, 24 E.R. 646; *Campbell v. Hall* (1774), 1 Cowp. 204 at pp. 208-9, 98 E.R. 1045, *per* Lord Mansfield.
[2]9 Geo. 2, c. 36 (1736). See *A.-G. v. Stewart* (1817), 2 Mer. 143 at pp. 157-9, 35 E.R. 895, *per* Sir William Grant, M.R.; *Whicker v. Hume* (1858), 7 H.L.C. 124, 11 E.R. 50; *Jex v. McKinney* (1889), 14 App. Cas. 77 (P.C.).
[3]*Yonge v. Blaikie* (1822), 1 Nfld. L.R. 277 at p. 283. See §302, *supra*.

inces are: Newfoundland, December 31, 1833;[4] Nova Scotia, October 3, 1758,[5] and Prince Edward Island, July 7, 1773.[6] However, in New Brunswick the date of reception is the Restoration of Charles II, in 1660.[7]

As of these dates the basic property law of England was well established and there can be no doubt that the colonists carried it with them. This would include such basic concepts of tenure and statutes such as *Quia Emptores*.[8] For the reasons discussed in connection with Ontario, tenures such as frankalmoign and copyhold would not have been imported since they were not suitable to conditions in these colonies.[9] Military tenure having been abolished by the *Tenures Abolition Act*,[10] only socage tenure remained and it thus became the only freehold tenure introduced into these provinces along with leasehold tenure. Although the *Tenures Abolition Act* postdates the reception of English law in New Brunswick and was, thus, not received in that province,[11] military tenure cannot be regarded as having been introduced into the province, since it was inherently inapplicable to the conditions in the province.

402.4 The Prairie Provinces and the Territories

In the prairie provinces, the Northwest Territories and Yukon Territory, English law was introduced by the Hudson's Bay Company Charter on May 2, 1670. The charter was treated as extending to all of the territory that "became known later as Rupert's Land and the North-Western Territory".[1] It provided that the company was to hold the land in "free and common socage and not *in capite* or by Knightes-service".[2] Thus, while the English law was received in these areas before the *Tenures Abolition Act* of 1660,[3] socage was the only freehold tenure introduced. Subsequent statutes introduced English law as of July 15, 1870, in distinct parts of these areas,[4] but they did not change the

---

[4]*Ibid.*, and see §306, *supra.*
[5]See §307.1, *supra.*
[6]See §307.4, *supra.*
[7]See §307.3, *supra.*
[8]18 Edw. 1, cc. 1-3 (1290).
[9]See the leading cases, *Doe d. Evans v. Doyle* (1860), 4 Nfld. L.R. 432; *Uniacke v. Dickson* (1848), 2 N.S.R. 287; *Doe d. Hanington v. McFadden* (1836), 2 N.B.R. 260.
[10]12 Car. 2, c. 24 (1660).
[11]*Scott v. Scott* (1970), 15 D.L.R. (3d) 374, 2 N.B.R. (2d) 849 (S.C. App. Div.).
§402.4
[1]*Walker v. Walker* (1919), 48 D.L.R. 1 at p. 2, [1919] A.C. 947 at p. 950, *per* Lord Haldane.
[2]*A.-G. Alta. v. Huggard Assets Ltd.*, [1953] 3 D.L.R. 225 at p. 234, [1953] A.C. 420 at p. 442 (P.C.).
[3]12 Car. 2, c. 24 (1660).
[4]As to Manitoba, by the *Queen's Bench Act*, S.M. 1874, c. 12, s. 1; as to the Northwest Territories, by the *North-West Territories Act*, S.C. 1886, c. 25, s. 3. As to the Yukon, the *Yukon Territory Act*, S.C. 1898, c. 6, s. 9, introduced the laws in force in Northwest Territories on June 13, 1898. Similarly, the provinces of Alberta and Saskatchewan received the existing law of the Northwest Territories when they were formed on September 1, 1905: *Alberta Act*, S.C. 1905, c. 3, s. 16, and *Saskatchewan Act*, S.C. 1905, c. 42, s. 16, respectively.

reception of free and common socage as the only operative freehold tenure. In any event, on the last-mentioned date, any tenures other than socage and leasehold would have been inapplicable in these colonies.

It is interesting to note, although the point is academic because of the reception statutes, that the introduction of the *Tenures Abolition Act*[5] into Alberta (and, presumably, into the other western provinces and the Territories) has been doubted. In *A.-G. Alta. v. Huggard Assets Ltd.*[6] the Supreme Court of Canada had held that it was introduced, but the Privy Council expressed doubts on the matter and opined that the Act was of purely local application.[7]

Of more importance to the concept of socage tenure was the decision in that case. The respondent company had objected to paying a variable royalty to the province of Alberta on petroleum and natural gas extracted by it from certain property in the province granted to the company's predecessor in 1913. It was argued on its behalf that the variableness of the royalty rendered it uncertain and that uncertainty was inconsistent with the concept of socage tenure. While it is certainly received law that the services incident to free and common socage must be certain,[8] their Lordships doubted that a variable royalty was uncertain in that sense,[9] but held that even if it was, it was competent to the provincial Legislature and its predecessor, the Parliament of Canada,[10] to vary the terms of the tenure and the latter had done so by enacting legislation exacting royalties for extraction of minerals.

A previous case, *West-Canadian Collieries Ltd. v. A.-G. Alta.,*[11] had held that the reservation of a royalty at a rate "as may from time to time be specified" was uncertain, but that the reservation could be validated by legislation.

402.5 British Columbia

In British Columbia English law was received as of November 19, 1858.[1]

---

[5]12 Car. 2, c. 24 (1660).
[6][1951] 2 D.L.R. 305, [1951] S.C.R. 427.
[7][1953] 3 D.L.R. 225, [1953] A.C. 420 (P.C.).
[8]Litt., s. 117; 1 Pollock and Maitland, p. 360.
[9][1953] 3 D.L.R. 225 at pp. 232-3, [1953] A.C. 420 at pp. 440-1 (P.C.).
[10]The federal government had retained certain lands and rights in mines and minerals in Alberta. Accordingly, it made the grant to the respondent company's predecessors. The Crown in right of Alberta succeeded to the rights of the Crown in right of the Dominion in such lands, mines and minerals pursuant to the Transfer Agreement of 1930: *Constitution Act, 1930,* 20 & 21 Geo. 5, c. 26 (Imp.); *Alberta Natural Resources Act,* S.C. 1930, c. 3; *Alberta Natural Resources Act,* S.A. 1930, c. 21. *Cf.* in respect of Saskatchewan: *Saskatchewan Natural Resources Act,* S.C. 1930, c. 41, and *Administration of Natural Resources (Temporary) Act,* S.S. 1930, c. 12; and in respect of Manitoba: *Manitoba Natural Resources Act,* S.C. 1930, c. 29, and *Manitoba Natural Resources Act,* S.M. 1930, c. 30.
[11][1952] 1 D.L.R. 346, 3 W.W.R. (N.S.) 1 (Alta. C.A.), affd [1953] 3 D.L.R. 145, [1953] A.C. 453 (P.C.).
§402.5
[1]*English Law Act,* S.B.C. 1867, No. 266. There were previous "in force" dates for distinct parts of the province. See §311, *supra.*

As in the case of the other provinces and Territories only socage tenure and leasehold tenure were introduced at this time since all others were inapplicable. In addition, certain English statutes relating to tenure were reprinted or re-enacted in the province, including *Quia Emptores*.[2]

403. ESCHEAT

One of the longest surviving incidents of tenure is escheat. The word "escheat" derives from middle English and the old French verb, "escheoir", meaning "to fall". In feudal times it denoted the fact that land had reverted to the lord of whom it was held when the blood of the tenant failed for want of heirs, or where it became attainted by felony so that the land was no longer inheritable. In other words, in the latter case, there was a constructive failure of heirs.[1] The commission of a felony was regarded as a breach of the tenant's oath of fealty.[2] Escheat was, therefore, of two types, known as *propter defectum sanguinis* and *propter delictum tenentis*.[3]

Escheat for felony was abolished in Canada in 1892.[4] Section 5(1)(b) of the present *Criminal Code*[5] provides:

> 5(1) Where an enactment creates an offence and authorizes a punishment to be imposed in respect thereof,
>
>   . . . . .
>
> (b) a person who is convicted of that offence is not liable to any punishment in respect thereof other than the punishment prescribed by this Act or by the enactment that creates the offence.

Thus, failure of heirs is now the only occasion upon which real property may escheat.[6] As land in Canada is now held of the Crown by the tenure of free and common socage, it will, in case of failure of heirs, escheat to the Crown. The Crown in this context is, of course, the Crown in right of the province, except as to lands retained or assumed by or under the jurisdiction of the Dominion.

---

[2]18 Edw. 1, cc. 1, 2 (1290), reprinted in R.S.B.C. 1897, p. xliii.
§403
[1]Challis, p. 34.
[2]*Warner v. Sampson*, [1959] 1 Q.B. 297 (C.A.), at p. 312, *per* Lord Denning, M.R.
[3]See §206.4, *supra*.
[4]*Criminal Code*, S.C. 1892, c. 29, s. 965.
[5]R.S.C. 1970, c. C-34.
[6]The word "heirs" in this context, of course, includes persons treated as natural-born heirs by reason of adoption or legitimacy legislation. See, *e.g.*, *Child Welfare Act*, R.S.O. 1980, c. 66, s. 86; *Children's Law Reform Act*, R.S.O. 1980, c. 68, ss. 1, 2; *Wills Act*, R.S.B.C. 1979, c. 434, s. 30; *Succession Law Reform Act*, R.S.O. 1980, c. 488, s. 1(1). Such legislation defeats the Crown's right of escheat even if it does not expressly bind the Crown: *Re Cummings*, [1938] O.R. 486, [1938] 3 D.L.R. 611 (S.C.), affd [1938] O.R. 654, [1938] 4 D.L.R. 767 (C.A.); and see *Re Hamilton Estate* (1948), 28 M.P.R. 53 (N.B.S.C.).

This is as a result of sections 108, 109 and 117 of the *Constitution Act, 1867,*[7] under which each province was given the beneficial interest in all land within its boundaries, except as stated above.[8] It follows that, except as to lands retained or assumed by the Dominion, property escheats to the Crown in right of the province.[9]

The provinces have all enacted legislation respecting escheat. In Ontario the first statute was enacted in 1877.[10] This does not mean, however, that the law of escheat as such was abrogated, for the legislation operates by its terms only after an escheat has occurred. The same applies where personal property accrues to the Crown on failure of heirs as *bona vacantia,* for several of the statutes deal with this as well. Thus, section 2(1) of the present Ontario *Escheats Act* provides:

> 2(1) Where any property *has become* the property of the Crown by reason of the person last seised thereof or entitled thereto having died intestate and without lawful heirs, or has become forfeited for any cause to the Crown, the Public Trustee may cause possession thereof to be taken in the name of the Crown, or, if possession is withheld, may cause an action to be brought for the recovery thereof, without an inquisition being first made.[11]

In most of the provinces there is comparable legislation.[12] In three, however, the legislation is slightly different.

In Alberta the property of a deceased person who dies intestate without heirs also passes to the Crown under the *Ultimate Heir Act*[13] which names the Crown in right of Alberta as ultimate heir and entitled to such property. Section 1 of the Act defines "ultimate heir" as:

> 1. In this Act, "ultimate heir" means the person entitled to take by descent or distribution the property of whatsoever nature of an intestate in the event of failure of heirs or next of kin entitled to take that property by the law in force before July 1, 1929.

Thus, under the Alberta legislation the old law of escheat has been abolished and replaced with a statutory right.

---

7 30 & 31 Vict., c. 3.
8 *St. Catharines Milling and Lumber Co. v. The Queen* (1887), 13 S.C.R. 577 at p. 599, *per* Ritchie, C.J., affd 14 App. Cas. 46 (P.C.). It follows from this that the provinces have no legislative jurisdiction over land beyond their boundaries such as the continental shelf which lies below the low-water mark. The Dominion has legislative jurisdiction there and can, for example, explore it and exploit the minerals: *Reference re Ownership of Off-shore Mineral Rights* (1967), 65 D.L.R. (2d) 353, [1967] S.C.R. 792.
9 *A.-G. Ont. v. Mercer* (1883), 8 App. Cas. 767 (P.C.).
10 *An Act to amend the Law respecting Escheats and Forfeitures,* S.O. 1877, c. 3. For the law of escheat prior to the Act, see *A.-G. Ont. v. O'Reilly* (1878), 26 Gr. 126.
11 R.S.O. 1980, c. 142 (emphasis added).
12 *Escheat Act,* R.S.B.C. 1979, c. 111; *Escheats Act,* R.S.M. 1970, c. E140; R.S.N.S. 1967, c. 91; R.S.P.E.I. 1974, c. E-9; R.S.S. 1978, c. E-11; *Escheats and Forfeitures Act,* R.S.N.B. 1973, c. E-10; *Escheat and Confiscation Act,* R.S.Q. 1964, c. 315.
13 R.S.A. 1980, c. U-1, s. 2.

In Newfoundland, the *Abandoned Lands Act*[14] provides that lands such as those granted by the Crown which remain unused and unoccupied for forty years may, on application to the Supreme Court, be declared to revert to the Crown. However, the statute provides that nothing in the Act shall prevent application of the general law relating to escheat of lands to the Crown.[15] Moreover, the *Chattels Real Act*[16] converts all land into "chattels real" so that they pass as *bona vacantia* on the death of the owner intestate and without heirs.

The Nova Scotia *Escheats Act*[17] has converted the right of escheat into a statutory right. Under section 1(b) of this statute, the Lieutenant-Governor in Council is empowered to direct the Attorney-General to take proceedings to revest in the Crown all lands of persons dying intestate and without heirs.

In Ontario, escheat is now also a statutory right, for section 47(7) of the *Succession Law Reform Act*[18] provides:

> 47(7) Where a person dies intestate in respect of property and there is no surviving spouse, issue, parent, brother, sister, nephew, niece or next of kin, the property becomes the property of the Crown, and the *Escheats Act* applies.

Parliament has also enacted similar legislation in respect of property to which the Crown in right of the Dominion becomes entitled, chiefly in respect of lands in the Territories.[19]

The subject of escheat will be dealt with more appropriately and fully in the chapter on Extinguishment of Title.[20] It is appropriate, however, at this point to deal with some general aspects of the matter.

In the first place, there is the question whether equitable interests are subject to escheat. It is arguable that they are not. Escheat, being a feudal incident, originally applied only to legal estates.[21] It followed, of course, that on the death of a sole trustee[22] or mortgagee,[23] the land escheated despite the existence of the interest of the *cestui que trust* or the equity of redemption. In this respect the law is now otherwise, for legislation generally provides that the rights of a beneficiary under a trust and of a mortgagor survive upon the death of the trustee and the mortgagee.[24] Prior to this legislation, if the beneficiary under a trust died intestate and without heirs, the trustee became entitled to the property for his own use.[25] Similarly, in the case of a mortgage, the

---

[14]R.S.N. 1970, c. 1, s. 2.
[15]*Ibid.*, s. 23.
[16]R.S.N. 1970, c. 36.
[17]R.S.N.S. 1967, c. 91.
[18]R.S.O. 1980, c. 488.
[19]*Escheats Act*, R.S.C. 1970, c. E-7.
[20]See ch. 31, *infra*.
[21]*Burgess v. Wheate* (1759), 1 Eden 177, 28 E.R. 652; Challis, pp. 37-40.
[22]Challis, p. 36.
[23]*Peachy v. Duke of Somerset* (1722), 1 Str. 447 at p. 454, 93 E.R. 626.
[24]See, *e.g.*, *Estates Administration Act*, R.S.O. 1980, c. 143, s. 7.
[25]*Burgess v. Wheate* (1759), 1 Eden 177, 28 E.R. 652.

mortgagee became entitled to the land in such circumstances subject, however, to the mortgagor's debts to the extent that they did not exceed the value of the equity of redemption.[26]

England made equitable interests subject to escheat by the *Intestates Estates Act, 1884.*[27] This legislation has also been enacted in British Columbia.[28] Moreover, the definition of "ultimate heir" in the Alberta Act,[29] as the person entitled to take the "property of whatsoever nature" of an intestate appears to cover equitable interests as well. It is doubtful that the Nova Scotia legislation deals with the problem effectively, since it refers only to the "lands" of persons dying intestate and without heirs.[30]

Where there is no legislation making equitable interests subject to escheat it is arguable that equitable interests in real property pass to the Crown as *bona vacantia.* This is by reason of devolution of estate legislation in force in several provinces which provides, *inter alia,* that all real property of a deceased person shall be administered and dealt with as if it were personalty.[31] An equitable interest in real property would thus devolve as if it were an equitable interest in a chattel real which can be the subject of *bona vacantia.*[32] It may be noted that, perhaps somewhat incongruously, the same does not apply to legal estates as a result of this legislation; escheat continues to operate in respect of them.[33]

In Newfoundland, since land is converted into chattels real by the *Chattels Real Act,*[34] presumably all such interests, whether legal or equitable, would pass as *bona vacantia* on the death of the owner intestate and without heirs.

It should also be noted that in England[35] and in British Columbia[36] the doctrine of escheat applies to incorporeal hereditaments. It did not do so at common law since these interests were not based on tenure. There appears to be no similar legislation in effect elsewhere in Canada.

Another general question that may be conveniently dealt with at this point is whether the Crown is liable on escheat for the debts of the deceased. It

---

[26]*Simpson v. Corbett* (1884), 10 O.A.R. 32 at p. 38, *per* Hagarty, C.J.O.

[27]47 & 48 Vict., c. 71, ss. 4, 7 (1884).

[28]*Escheat Act,* R.S.B.C. 1979. c. 111. s. 3.

[29]*Ultimate Heir Act,* R.S.A. 1980, c. U-1, s. 1.

[30]*Escheats Act,* R.S.N.S. 1967, c. 91, s. 1(*b*).

[31]*Estate Administration Act,* R.S.B.C. 1979, c. 114. s. 90; *Devolution of Real Property Act,* R.S.A. 1980, c. D-34, s. 2; R.S.S. 1978, c. D-27, ss. 4, 5; *Chattels Real Act,* R.S.N. 1970, c. 36. s. 2; *Real Property Act,* R.S.N.S. 1967, c. 261, s. 6(1): *Estates Administration Act,* R.S.O. 1980, c. 143, s. 2(1); *Devolution of Estates Act,* R.S.M. 1970, c. D70, s. 18 as amended by S.M. 1976. c. 69, s. 14; R.S.N.B. 1973, c. D-9, s. 3; *Probate Act,* R.S.P.E.I. 1974, c. P-19, s. 108(1); *Devolution of Real Property Ordinance,* R.O.N.W.T. 1974, c. D-5, s. 3(1); R.O.Y.T. 1971, c. D-4, s. 3(1).

[32]*Wentworth v. Humphrey* (1886), 11 App. Cas. 619 (P.C.); *Re Stone* (1936), 36 S.R. (N.S.W.) 508 at p. 518, *per* Jordan, C.J. These cases were decided under the comparable New South Wales legislation.

[33]*Trusts and Guarantee Co. v. The King* (1916), 32 D.L.R. 469 at p. 484, 54 S.C.R. 107 at p. 129, *per* Anglin, J.

[34]R.S.N. 1970, c. 36.

[35]*Intestates Estates Act, 1884,* 47 & 48 Vict., c. 71, s. 7.

[36]*Escheat Act,* R.S.B.C. 1979, c. 111, s. 3.

would seem that the Crown does take subject to registered charges such as mortgages and charges and statutory liens such as mechanics' liens,[37] but the law is by no means clear on the subject.

In the case of unsecured debts, it would appear that the Crown may not take subject to them. Thus, in *Re Hole*,[38] the court held that in such a case the death separates the assets from the liabilities and the Crown takes the assets free from the liabilities. The court assumed that the province would act fairly to the creditors and pay their claims as an act of grace. A contrary decision is *Nelson and Cranston v. National Trust Co.*,[39] where Stuart, J., stated, "an escheat to the Crown is always subject to debts".[40] The law is thus unsettled on this point and it may be that unsecured creditors have at most a "moral claim".[41] It would seem, however, that the claims of creditors should rest, not on executive grace, but on definite rights granted by legislation.

404. FORFEITURE

Strictly, forfeiture is not part of the law of tenure since it does not involve a return of the land to the superior lord. Forfeiture in feudal law occurred when a person committed high treason. This was considered to be an offence against the King and the tenant's lands were thus forfeited to the monarch.

Forfeiture for treason has been abolished in Canada.[1] Different types of forfeiture remain, however, such as forfeiture on the dissolution of a corporation, of lands held in mortmain and of lands held for charitable uses. In these cases forfeiture is to the Crown. There are other cases, such as the right to re-enter for condition broken and the right of the landlord to re-enter for breach of covenant, in which the forfeiture is to a person other than the Crown. As the law of forfeiture concerns peculiarly the termination of estates, it is dealt with in the chapter on Extinguishment of Title.[2]

405. ESTATES

The doctrine of estates has already been described in some detail[1] and thus

---

[37]*A.-G. Ont. v. Mercer* (1883), 8 App. Cas. 767 (P.C.), at p. 772, *per* Lord Selborne, L.C.
[38][1948] 4 D.L.R. 419, [1948] 2 W.W.R. 754 (Man. K.B.). The case was actually one of *bona vacantia*. See also *Re Androws* (1957), 10 D.L.R. (2d) 731, 26 W.W.R. 452 (Man. Surr. Ct.), which involved both realty and personalty.
[39](1920), 51 D.L.R. 474, [1920] 1 W.W.R. 852 (Alta. S.C. App. Div.).
[40]*Ibid.*, at p. 475 D.L.R., p. 853 W.W.R.; and see *Re Wells*, [1933] Ch. 29 (C.A.), at p. 50, *per* Lawrence, L.J.
[41]See *Escheats Act*, R.S.O. 1980, c. 142, s. 4; "Case and Comment", 27 Can. Bar Rev. 592 (1949).
§404
[1]*Criminal Code*, S.C. 1892, c. 29, s. 965; see now R.S.C. 1970, c. C-34, s. 5(1)(b).
[2]Ch. 31, *infra*.
§405
[1]See §209, *supra*.

needs only a recapitulation at this point. The concept of the estate is an abstract idea interposed between the tenant and the physical thing, the land. A person is said to own an estate or interest in the land. He does not own it allodially, that is, he does not own the land itself; the Crown has the ultimate interest in it under the doctrine of tenure.

The doctrine of estates determines the quantity of a person's ownership, not in terms of area, but in terms of time. It is on this basis that estates are classified.[2] Estates can first of all be divided into freehold and non-freehold or leasehold estates. Freehold estates in turn comprise inheritable estates and estates not of inheritance.

Estates of inheritance are two in number. The first is the fee simple estate which is the largest estate known to the law and can be said to comprise all others in the sense that the other estates can be carved out of it in such a manner that the estate itself is not exhausted. It continues until the owner dies intestate and without heirs. The second estate of inheritance is the estate in fee tail. This estate is less than the fee simple in that it continues only so long as the lineal descendants (either general, of a particular sex, or by a particular spouse) of the original tenant in tail or the grantor survive, for the estate cannot be inherited by collaterals. It has been abolished in most of the Canadian provinces.[3]

The life estate, as its name implies, is not inheritable since it continues only during the life of the tenant or some other person for whose life it is granted, except that in the latter case, where the owner of the estate dies during the lifetime of that other person, the remaining part of the estate is inheritable. This latter type is called an estate *pur autre vie*. Life estates can also be created by operation of law. Of these there are two types — dower, which is the interest a widow is entitled to for her life in one-third of her deceased husband's real property, and curtesy, which is the interest to which a widower is entitled for his life in all the undisposed real property of his deceased wife. These two legal life estates have been modified extensively by statute in several of the provinces by the so-called "homestead" legislation, and have been abolished in others, including New Brunswick, Nova Scotia, Ontario and Prince Edward Island which have replaced them with, *inter alia*, a right to possession of the matrimonial home, which the registered owner cannot defeat except with the other spouse's consent during the joint lives of husband and wife.[4] These provisions are bolstered in several of these provinces by the right of the spouses to seek an order for increased support out of the estate of a deceased spouse,[5] a

---

2 Pollock and Maitland, p. 10.
3 See §607, *infra*.
4 *Marital Property Act*, S.N.B. 1980, c. M-1.1, Part II; *Matrimonial Property Act*, S.N.S. 1980, c. 9, ss. 6-11; *Family Law Reform Act*, R.S.O. 1980, c. 152, Part III; S.P.E.I. 1978, c. 6, Part III.
5 *Succession Law Reform Act*, R.S.O. 1980, c. 488, Part V.

right of division of family assets on a breakdown of marriage[6] and mutual rights of support during marriage.[7]

Leasehold estates are regarded as being less than freeholds because they did not originally form part of the classification of estates in the feudal system. Instead, leases were regarded merely as personal contracts. They came to be treated as estates in the 15th century.[8] Although less than a freehold in law, in reality a long-term lease can be much more valuable than a fee simple estate. The four types of leasehold, namely, the term of years, the periodic tenancy, the tenancy at will and the tenancy at sufferance, have already been referred to.[9]

In addition to the estates outlined above, which may be described as estates absolute, defeasible estates known as determinable estates and estates upon condition subsequent are possible for each type.[10]

All of these estates were probably introduced into the Canadian provinces under the rules of reception discussed above.[11] There may be some doubt as to the estate tail since in the beginning there was no machinery for the barring of this estate.[12] It seems more probable, however, that the estate was introduced although the machinery to bar it came later.

It should not be thought that the estates enumerated above are inflexible and fixed in number. As in the case of tenure,[13] it is possible for the Legislature of a province to create further estates or to vary existing ones. Thus, in *Town of Lunenburg v. Municipality of Lunenburg*[14] the court had to interpret legislation which provided that on payment of certain moneys, the defendant should have "the use forever" of certain parts of a building for a court-room, judge's room and related amenities. It was held that this need not be construed as creating a fee simple since the Legislature was competent to create any interest unknown to the common law and that it had done so in this instance by creating a lease in perpetuity.

Parliament may also sanction the making of a perpetual lease which, apart from such sanction, would be impossible. Thus, in *Wotherspoon v. Canadian Pacific Ltd.*[15] the court recognized a lease in perpetuity of a railway, which was

---

[6]*Family Law Reform Act*, R.S.O. 1980, c. 152, Part I; S.P.E.I. 1978, c. 6, Part I; *Marital Property Act*, S.N.B. 1980, c. M-1·1, Part I; *Matrimonial Property Act*, S.N.S. 1980, c. 9, ss. 12 *et seq.*

[7]*Family Law Reform Act*, R.S.O. 1980, c. 152, Part II; S.P.E.I. 1978, c. 6, Part II; *Child and Family Services and Family Relations Act*, S.N.B. 1980, c. C-2.1, Part VII; *Family Maintenance Act*, S.N.S. 1980, c. 6. See further ch. 16, *infra.*

[8]Litt., s. 58.

[9]See §209.2, *supra*, and see ch. 8, *infra.*

[10]See §209.1(d), *supra.*

[11]*Supra*, ch. 3 and §402.

[12]*Re Wright and Riach* (1923), 54 O.L.R. 404 at p. 409, [1924] 2 D.L.R. 273 at p. 276 (S.C. App. Div.); *Re Estate of John Simpson* (1863), 5 N.S.R. 317 (C.A.).

[13]*A.-G. Alta. v. Huggard Assets Ltd.*, [1953] 3 D.L.R. 225 at p. 235, [1953] A.C. 420 at p. 443 (P.C.).

[14][1932] 1 D.L.R. 386, 4 M.P.R. 181 (N.S.S.C.).

[15](1979), 22 O.R. (2d) 385, 92 D.L.R. (3d) 545 (H.C.J.), vard 35 O.R. (2d) 449, 129 D.L.R. (3d) 1 (C.A.).

sanctioned by statute.[16] Except in its perpetual aspect, however, the estate was construed as conferring the normal incidents inherent in a landlord and tenant relationship.

Similarly, the City of Winnipeg was, by its Charter,[17] given possession of every street within the limits of the city while the title to the freehold remained in the Crown notwithstanding the issuance of a certificate of title to the city. In an application to determine whether the city had a sufficient interest in the street so as to be the "owner" thereof within the meaning of the *Mechanics' Lien Act*,[18] the court held that it did have a sufficient interest for that purpose, but that it was contrary to public policy for a lien to be registered against a street.[19]

Novel interests cannot be created by the parties, however. Thus, an attempt to have a contract for the installation of washers and dryers on certain premises run with the land so as to bind the purchaser and his successors in title was unsuccessful in *Re Fairhill Developments and Aberdeen Properties Ltd.*[20]

406. SEISIN

The concept of seisin as possession of an estate of freehold in land of freehold tenure and thus as the connecting link between the two basic feudal doctrines of tenure and estates has already been described.[1] It remains to dilate upon the importance of seisin in the Canadian provinces today. There can be no question that seisin was introduced as part of the law of England since it was an essential part of the basic feudal land law. Moreover, it has always been recognized in Canada as a required element.

Seisin and, especially, the ceremony known as feoffment with livery of seisin were of great importance in early colonial conveyancing. Some novel decisions were reached, however, because of different conditions in the colonies from those which obtained in the motherland. Thus, as most land in the colonies was granted by letters patent from the Crown, the status of the seisin of a grantee from the Crown was in some doubt. It was held, however, that the letters patent constituted seisin in fact and that the actual delivery of corporeal possession was not necessary in such circumstances.[2] And in a subsequent

---

[16]*An Act to confirm the lease of the Ontario and Quebec Railway to the Canadian Pacific Railway Company, and for other purposes*, S.C. 1884, c. 54; *An Act respecting the Ontario and Quebec Railway Company*, S.C. 1884, c. 61.

[17]*Winnipeg Charter*, S.M. 1956, c. 87, s. 683, since repealed and substituted by *City of Winnipeg Act*, S.M. 1971, c. 105.

[18]R.S.M. 1954, c. 157, s. 2(*d*); now R.S.M. 1970, c. M80, s. 2(*d*).

[19]*Re Shields (Trustee of Estate of Harris Construction Co. Ltd.) and City of Winnipeg* (1964), 47 D.L.R. (2d) 346, 49 W.W.R. 530 (Man. Q.B.), apld in *Alspan Wrecking Ltd. v. Dineen Construction Ltd.* (1972), 26 D.L.R. (3d) 238, [1972] S.C.R. 829.

[20][1969] 2 O.R. 267, 5 D.L.R. (3d) 118 (H.C.J.).

§406

[1]See §208, *supra*, and see generally Thorne, "Livery of Seisin", 52 L.Q. Rev. 345 (1936); Maitland, "The Mystery of Seisin", 2 L.Q. Rev. 481 (1886); Bordwell, "Seisin and Disseisin", 34 Harv. L. Rev. 592 (1920-21), at p. 717.

[2]*Weaver v. Burgess* (1871), 22 U.C.C.P. 104.

case it was held that letters patent from the Crown, being title by record, operate by way of feoffment with livery of seisin to the patentee and, as such, provide a better title than a prior title by possession.[3] The result was that, where a married woman claimed under letters patent from the Crown, her husband was entitled to curtesy out of the land afer her death without the necessity of him entering upon them.[4] Apart from that, however, actual possession is *prima facie* evidence of seisin.[5]

Livery of seisin in fact was still necessary as between subjects, however, although the requirements appear to have been less stringent than in feudal times. Thus, in one case, in order to prove livery of seisin under an unregistered deed, the grantor and grantee passed the land and the grantor declared that he had deeded it to the grantee. The grantee thereupon took hold of a part of a building on the land, said that he intended to repair it, and afterwards exercised ownership over it. The court held that in those circumstances livery of seisin was complete.[6]

By contrast, a mere indenture which purported to grant land to the grantee, "his heirs and assigns", was held not to convey the fee simple, because there had been no livery. At most the grant conveyed a term of twenty-one years.[7]

In some parts of the common law provinces there exist what are known as "French titles". These refer to lands granted by the French authorities while these areas formed part of New France. There are many such titles in and around Windsor, Ontario, where they were granted by the governor of Fort Pontchartrain (now Detroit) under the authority of the Intendant at Quebec. Although some of these titles were subsequently confirmed by letters patent from the Crown in right of Ontario, it has been held that this is not necessary because the titles were undisturbed by the English conquest. Despite their French origin, it would seem that, upon the establishment of English rule, the common law doctrines of tenure, estates and seisin were introduced automatically with respect to these lands.[8]

The *Statute of Frauds*[9] required that a feoffment be made in writing, signed by the feoffor. It did not abolish feoffment with livery of seisin, however.[10]

---

[3]*Greenlaw v. Fraser* (1874), 24 U.C.C.P. 230.
[4]*Weaver v. Burgess, supra*, footnote 2.
[5]*Re F. G. Connolly Ltd. and A.-G. N.S.* (1974), 44 D.L.R. (3d) 733, 8 N.S.R. (2d) 470 (S.C. App. Div.).
[6]*McLardy v. Flaherty* (1847), 5 N.B.R. 455 (C.A.).
[7]*McDonald v. McGillis* (1867), 26 U.C.Q.B. 458.
[8]See *Re London Life Insurance Co. and Unwin* (Urquhart, J., 1941, unreported); *Drulard v. Welsh* (1906), 11 O.L.R. 647 (Div. Ct.), revd on other grounds 14 O.L.R. 54n (C.A.). And see *Third Report of the Bureau of Archives*, Ontario, 1905, for the proceedings of the land boards and the reports of the provincial surveyors, on this matter.
[9]29 Car. 2, c. 3 (1677). The statute was received in the Canadian provinces and re-enacted in some.
[10]For a case on the applicability of the statute to the doctrine of conventional line boundaries, see *Bea v. Robinson* (1977), 18 O.R. (2d) 12, 81 D.L.R. (3d) 423 (H.C.J.). As to the question whether a deed must be not only sealed and delivered, but also signed, see *Town of Eastview v. Roman Catholic Episcopal Corp. of Ottawa* (1918), 44 O.L.R. 284, 47 D.L.R. 47 (C.A.).

Following the lead of England, which, in 1845, enacted legislation permitting the conveyance of an estate in possession by a simple grant and requiring it to be evidenced by deed,[11] a number of Canadian provinces provided for feoffment by statutory grant. The Ontario *Conveyancing and Law of Property Act*[12] based upon legislation of 1851[13] now provides:

> 2. All corporeal tenements and hereditaments, as regards the conveyance of the immediate freehold thereof, lie in grant as well as in livery.
> 3. A feoffment, otherwise than by deed, is void and no feoffment shall have any tortious operation.[14]

The effect of this legislation is that a mere deed of grant will suffice to pass a freehold estate in possession, feoffment with livery being unnecessary. And this is so, even though the deed does not use the word "grant", so long as the deed can be construed as having been intended as a deed of grant.[15]

Section 2 would appear to permit the continued use of feoffment with livery of seisin. However, section 3 requires a deed for the transfer of real property, so that there is an apparent conflict between the two. The English Act of 1845 did not require that the transfer be effected by deed, only that it be evidenced by deed, and it would thus seem that the Ontario legislation, by going further, has effectively abolished feoffment by livery.

This was not the view of the court in *Re Bouris and Button*.[16] The court there opined that section 2 does not make transfers by livery void, although it may make them obsolete, so that a freehold interest can still be transferred by livery of seisin. The report of the case does not indicate, however, whether the court considered the effect of section 3 and the case is, therefore, not decisive on the point.

In Nova Scotia both the feoffment and the livery of seisin have been abolished.[17]

It would appear that feoffment with livery of seisin is still possible in Newfoundland. In *Butt v. Humber*[18] the court considered whether a signed document, not under seal, which purported to convey land without consideration was, *inter alia*, a feoffment. It was held that it was not, as vacant possession was given. The document was not a deed, nor was any interest transferred in equity because there was no consideration. The court held, however, that the instrument was sufficient to pass title.

---

[11]*Real Property Act*, 8 & 9 Vict., c. 106, ss. 2, 3.
[12]R.S.O. 1980, c. 90, ss. 2, 3.
[13]*Simplification of the Transfer of Real Property Amendment Act*, S.C. 1851, c. 7, ss. 2, 3, repealing *Simplification of the Transfer of Real Property Act*, S.C. 1849, c. 71, s. 2, which permitted the conveyance by deed of all lands that could theretofore have been conveyed by lease and release.
[14]For similar legislation see *Property Act*, R.S.N.B. 1973, c. P-19, ss. 10(2), 11; *Real Property Act*, R.S.P.E.I. 1974, c. R-4, ss. 7, 8, 9.
[15]*Pearson v. Mulholland* (1889), 17 O.R. 502 (Q.B.).
[16](1975), 9 O.R. (2d) 305, 60 D.L.R. (3d) 233 (C.A.).
[17]*Conveyancing Act*, R.S.N.S. 1967, c. 56, s. 2(3).
[18](1976), 17 Nfld. & P.E.I.R. 92 (Nfld. S.C.T.D.).

In England the feoffment with livery as well as the other old forms of conveyance, the bargain and sale and the lease and release, have been abolished.[19] The latter two forms of conveyance, provided they are by deed, are still possible in Canadian jurisdictions which have legislation similar to Ontario's, since that legislation only deals with feoffment by livery. Both of these types of conveyance took effect under the *Statute of Uses*.[20] The bargain and sale, especially, was in common use in Ontario, as is apparent from many early titles. Provision was made by statute in 1797 for registration of conveyances by bargain and sale in the County Register Offices in lieu of enrolment,[21] but the requirement for registration was abolished in 1834,[22] at which time corporations were also made competent to use this conveyancing device.[23]

Clearly, a feoffment with livery is not possible under land titles legislation which provides for transfers in the prescribed manner, that is, by transfer in the statutory form.[24]

It should be noted that section 3 of the *Conveyancing and Law of Property Act*[25] also abolishes the common law doctrine of the *tortious* feoffment. At common law, if the owner of a limited interest enfeoffed another with the fee simple in the land, an estate in fee simple was in fact transferred, even though the feoffment was tortious.[26] Now, only such interest as the grantor owns can be conveyed.

Seisin continues to be important for dower, for at common law a widow was entitled only to dower out of her husband's lands of which he was solely seised.[27] Subsequently, dower in equitable estate was made possible.[28] Curtesy out of legal and equitable estates in possession was always possible.[29]

Seisin also remains important in the creation of future estates at law. In this respect the rule that there cannot be an abeyance of seisin and the prohibition against the creation of an estate in the future continue in full force and the statutes permitting conveyances by deed of grant do not affect this. Thus, in *Savill Brothers, Ltd. v. Bethell*[30] a conveyance of land unto and to the use of the purchaser in fee simple "except and reserving unto the vendors

---

[19]*Law of Property Act, 1925*, 15 Geo. 5, c. 20, ss. 51, 52, 207, Sch. 7.
[20]27 Hen. 8, c. 10 (1535). See §217.1, *supra*.
[21]*An Act to supply the want of Enrolment of Deeds of Bargain and Sale*, S.U.C. 1797, c. 8.
[22]*Real Property Amendment Act*, S.U.C. 1834, c. 1, s. 47.
[23]*Ibid.*, s. 46. See now *Conveyancing and Law of Property Act*, R.S.O. 1980, c. 90, s. 20.
[24]See, *e.g.*, *Land Titles Act*, R.S.O. 1980, c. 230; R.R.O. 1980, Reg. 552, s. 24; R.S.C. 1970, c. L-4, s. 78, Sch., Form I; R.S.A. 1980, c. L-5, s. 68; R.S.S. 1978, c. L-5, s. 89, Sch. 2, Form J; S.B.C. 1978, c. 25, ss. 39, 314(f); *Real Property Act*, R.S.M. 1970, c. R30, s. 82(1), Sch. C.
[25]R.S.O. 1980, c. 90.
[26]Challis, p. 138.
[27]Cameron, *A Treatise on the Law of Dower* (Toronto, Carswell & Co., 1882), p. 4.
[28]See, *e.g.*, *Dower Act*, R.S.O. 1970, c. 135, s. 3, repealed by the *Family Law Reform Act*, S.O. 1978, c. 2, s. 70(2).
[29]Megarry and Wade, p. 15.
[30][1902] 2 Ch. 523.

a piece of land not less than forty feet in width commencing . . . at the point marked 'A' on the said plan" annexed to the conveyance "and terminating at the nearest road to be made by the purchaser or his assignee on the estate so as to give access to such road from" other lands of the vendor, was held void as to the reservation of the easement. The deed operated at common law and not under the *Statute of Uses*[31] since it was to the use of the grantee himself and the reservation of the easement (which operates as a regrant in law),[32] not being fixed, was a grant *in futuro.*[33]

---

[31]27 Hen. 8, c. 10 (1535).

[32]*Doe d. Douglas v. Lock* (1835), 2 Ad. & E. 705, 111 E.R. 271; *Durham & Sunderland Ry. Co. v. Walker* (1842), 2 Q.B. 940, 114 E.R. 364.

[33]*Cf. Re Chauvin* (1920), 18 O.W.N. 178 (H.C.), in which the rule that there cannot be a fee after a fee in any common law grant was upheld.

97

CHAPTER 5

THE ESTATE IN FEE SIMPLE

501. DEFINITION

The estate in fee simple is the largest estate or interest known in law and is the most absolute in terms of the rights which it confers. It permits the owner to exercise every conceivable act of ownership upon it or with respect to it, including the right to commit waste.[1] Moreover, his rights extend, in theory at least, "up to the sky and down to the centre of the earth":[2] *cujus est solum*

---

§501
[1]Challis, p. 218.
[2]*Corbett v. Hill* (1870), L.R. 9 Eq. 671 at p. 673, *per* James, V.C.

ejus est usque ad coelum et ad inferos. Thus, for example, a contract for the sale of land includes the rights to the minerals lying beneath the surface, unless they are excepted from the sale.[3] While technically the owner holds of the Crown under the doctrine of tenure, in practice his ownership is the equivalent of the absolute dominion a person may have of a chattel, except as to the nature of the subject-matter which is indestructible.[4]

The estate is an estate of inheritance as indicated by the word "fee". That is, at common law it would descend to the heir at law of the owner. Under modern legislation the estate may be devised by will and, where the owner dies intestate, it will devolve upon his heirs. It may also be freely alienated *inter vivos.* The word "simple" indicates that at common law the estate descended to the heirs general of the owner, that is, his descendants and collateral relatives under the rule of primogeniture. An estate limited to a particular class of heirs who are descendants of the grantor is a fee tail.[5]

The estate in fee simple is of uncertain duration, a characteristic of all freehold estates. It comes to an end on the death of the owner intestate and without heirs, when it escheats to the Crown.

The rights of the owner of the fee simple may, however, be restricted. Thus, the estate may be subject to a condition, a collateral or an executory limitation, or to the terms of a trust. Moreover, it is subject to rules of public policy such as the rule against perpetuities, to restrictions such as the law of nuisance, and to modern statutory restraints, such as family disinheritance and matrimonial property legislation, environmental protection statutes, planning and zoning legislation, expropriation by the State, aeronautics legislation, and to the right of the Crown to minerals.[6]

The word "fee", as a shorthand form for fee simple, is normally taken to refer to the common law estate. It can, however, have a wider significance. Thus, in *Re Forfar and Township of East Gwillimbury,*[7] the Ontario Court of Appeal held that the word as used in the *Planning Act*[8] means such estate or interest in the land as is reasonably necessary to accomplish the purpose of the legislation, namely, to control subdivision of land. Accordingly, it held that the word was not used in its narrow legal sense, but encompassed the reservation of a power of appointment.

---

[3]*Schmit v. Montreal Trust Co.* (1969), 69 W.W.R. 521 (Sask. Q.B.); *Mastermet Cobalt Mines Ltd. v. Canadaka Mines Ltd.* (1977), 17 O.R. (2d) 212, 79 D.L.R. (3d) 743 (H.C.J.), affd 21 D.L.R. (2d) 494, 91 D.L.R. (3d) 283 (C.A.). Rights above and below the surface are discussed in §3905, *infra.*

[4]Megarry and Wade, p. 40.

[5]*Ibid.,* p. 42.

[6]For a discussion of these and other limitations on the fee simple see Baalman, "The Estate in Fee Simple", 34 A.L.J. 3 (1960); Carmichael, "Fee Simple Absolute as a Variable Research Concept", 15 National Resources J. 749 (1975).

[7][1971] 3 O.R. 337, 20 D.L.R. (3d) 377 (C.A.), affd 28 D.L.R. (3d) 512, [1972] S.C.R. v, overruling *Re Carter and Congram,* [1970] 1 O.R. 800, 9 D.L.R. (3d) 550 (H.C.J.). See also *Reference re Certain Titles to Land in Ontario,* [1973] 2 O.R. 613, 35 D.L.R. (3d) 10 (C.A.).

[8]R.S.O. 1960, c. 296, s. 26(1), as amended. Now S.O. 1983, c. 1, s. 49(3).

The reservation on a sale of land of "merchantable timber" has also been held to create a fee simple of such timber, which is inheritable and extends to all trees existing at the time of the grant which are, or should thereafter become, merchantable.[9] Since it is an estate, it is not limited in time, but may be defeated by adverse possession by the owner of the rest of the land or by another.[10] A reservation of a right to cut trees may, however, be construed as merely an incorporeal hereditament, that is, a *profit à prendre*, if that was intended.[11]

502. CREATION

The estate in fee simple is created either *inter vivos* or by will by "words of purchase" followed, although it is not necessary under some modern statutes, by "words of limitation". Words of purchase are words designating the person who receives the estate and the phrase is used to describe the recipient, not only where he acquires the estate by deed *inter vivos* for consideration, but also where it is given to him either *inter vivos* or by will. To take by purchase is thus distinguished from taking by descent which, before modern devolution of estates legislation, occurred where the heir at law of the owner succeeded to the estate on the latter's death intestate. Words of limitation are words which define the nature of the interest acquired. They are called words of limitation because it is the grantor's right to limit an estate as he sees fit, and the effect of the words is generally called a "limitation". Thus, in a grant "to A and his heirs" the words "to A" are words of purchase and the words "and his heirs" are words of limitation, which are apt to create an estate in fee simple in A.[1]

502.1 Inter Vivos Dispositions

(a) At common law

At common law, in order to create an estate in fee simple *inter vivos*, it was necessary to grant it to a person "and his heirs". Save for some immaterial exceptions,[1] this magic formula had to be used. This did not mean that the heirs

---

[9]*Smith v. Daly & Booth Lumber Ltd.*, [1949] O.R. 601, [1949] 4 D.L.R. 45 (H.C.J.).
[10]*John Austin & Sons Ltd. v. Smith* (1982), 35 O.R. (2d) 272, 132 D.L.R. (3d) 311 (C.A.).
[11]*Arkansas Fuel and Mineral Ltd. v. Dome Petroleum Ltd.* (1966), 54 D.L.R. (2d) 574, 54 W.W.R. 494 (Alta. S.C. App. Div.). For a case involving a conveyance of a *profit à prendre*, see *Cameron v. Silverglen Farms Ltd.* (1983), 144 D.L.R. (3d) 544, 58 N.S.R. (2d) 31 (S.C. App. Div.), leave to appeal to S.C.C. refused D.L.R. *loc. cit.*, 57 N.S.R. (2d) 180n.

§502
[1]See generally, Megarry and Wade, p. 52.

§502.1
[1]It was possible to create the estate by words of direct and immediate reference, as where a father granted to his son and his heirs and the son afterwards granted to the father "as fully as the father infeoffed him". Also, in some cases, no words of limitation were necessary. Thus a coparcener or joint tenant could release to another without words of limitation. See Challis, pp. 222-3.

of the grantor received an interest. Early in the common law, indeed, the heir apparent or presumptive of the owner was thought to have an interest so that the owner could not dispose of the land without his consent. This was probably a carry-over from Anglo-Saxon land law, under which the owner was also permitted to dispose of part of his land by will or post-obit gift.[2] However, by the 12th century the heir lost his veto power over *inter vivos* alienation while at the same time the owner lost his power to devise his land. This was perhaps as a result of a compromise between the tenants and the feudal lords to whom the testamentary power was anathema since it tended to weaken the feudal bond between them and their tenants,[3] or perhaps because it tended to protect the heir in that wills were often made shortly before death and were "wrung from a man from his agony" by the Church.[4] In any event, thereafter the heir no longer had an interest in the land. He had at most a *spes successionis* or hope of succeeding to it on his father's death. Wills of land were not again possible until the enactment of the *Statute of Wills* in 1540.[5] By the 13th century, therefore, the words "and his heirs" had become words of limitation.

Exactly why the words "and his heirs" were necessary to create an estate in fee simple is unclear. Once it had been determined that the heir no longer had an interest, they should have been unnecessary if there was an evident intention to create a fee simple. Nevertheless, it became fixed that no other words would suffice.[6] And while on its face the estate would seem to have to determine when the original grantee and his heirs had died, the interpretation placed upon these words was that the estate would continue so long as there were heirs of the owner for the time being.[7]

If other words were used, such as, "to A forever",[8] or "to A in fee simple",[9] only a life estate was created. Similarly, if the words, "and his heirs", were omitted, at common law only a life estate was created.[10] The word "forever" was frequently added, but it was unnecessary as the estate is, in theory, of unlimited duration, because the law does not expect a failure of heirs.[11] Similarly, the word "assigns", which was frequently added, was unnecessary.[12]

It was, however, necessary to use the plural word "heirs" because if the grant were to a person and his "heir", that word could refer only to the person

---

[2] Pollock and Maitland, pp. 321-3.
[3] 1 A.L.P., p. 77.
[4] Pollock and Maitland, p. 328.
[5] 32 Hen. 8, c. 1 (1540).
[6] 1 A.L.P., pp. 83-4.
[7] Megarry and Wade. p. 68.
[8] *Jack v. Lyons* (1879), 19 N.B.R. 336 (C.A.).
[9] *Re Gold and Rowe* (1913), 4 O.W.N. 642, 9 D.L.R. 26 (S.C.).
[10] *Re Airey* (1921), 21 O.W.N. 190 (H.C.). See to the same effect, *Millard v. Gregoire* (1913), 11 D.L.R. 539, 47 N.S.R. 78 (S.C. App. Div.), in which only the words "doth grant and convey" were used.
[11] *Pells v. Brown* (1620), Cro. Jac. 590, 79 E.R. 504.
[12] *Ahearn v. Ahearn* (1894), 1 N.B. Eq. 53.

who would be the heir at the death of the grantee, so as not to be a word of inheritance or limitation. In such a case, at common law, the grantee would get only a life estate.[13] Moreover, the grantee did not have an heir during his lifetime, for *nemo est haeres viventis*, that is, a living person has no heir.[14] He might have an heir apparent, that is, his eldest son, who will become his heir if he survives, or an heir presumptive, such as his daughter, where he has no sons and none are subsequently born or survive him.[15] On the other hand, a grant "to the heirs of A" where A was dead was good. The words were construed as meaning "to the heir of A and his heirs", giving an estate in fee simple to the person who was A's heir in fact.[16] Perhaps somewhat incongruously, a grant "to the heir of A" was thought not to have the same effect, since it lacked words of limitation and would thus give A only a life estate.[17]

It further followed from the strict rule at common law that nothing could be added to the words of limitation and, if anything were added, it was simply disregarded as repugnant. Thus a grant "to A and his heirs male" would give A a fee simple only, the word "male" being repugnant to the estate.[18]

(b) Statutory reforms

Statutes passed in the 19th century made an immense change in these rules. Following upon the *Conveyancing and Law of Property Act, 1881,*[19] the several provinces passed statutes which generally provide that in a deed it is not necessary to use the word "heirs" to convey a fee simple, but the words "in fee simple" may be used, or other words sufficiently indicating the intention and furthermore, if no words of limitation are used, a deed can pass all the estate or interest held by the grantor, unless a contrary intention appears in the deed.

Thus, the Ontario *Conveyancing and Law of Property Act*[20] provides:

> 5(1) In a conveyance, it is not necessary, in the limitation of an estate in fee simple, to use the word "heirs".
>
> (2) For the purpose of such limitation, it is sufficient in a conveyance to use the words "in fee simple" or any other words sufficiently indicating the limitation intended.
>
> (3) Where no words of limitation are used, the conveyance passes all the estate, right, title, interest, claim and demand that the conveying parties have in, to, or on the property conveyed, or expressed or intended so to be, or that they have power to convey in, to, or on the same.

---

[13]*Chambers v. Taylor* (1837), 2 My. & Cr. 376, 40 E.R. 683; *Re Davison's Settlement*; *Cattermole Davison v. Munby*, [1913] 2 Ch. 498.
[14]Co. Litt. 8 b; *Re Parsons*; *Stockley v. Parsons* (1890), 45 Ch. D. 51; *Re Green*; *Green v. Meinall*, [1911] 2 Ch. 275; *Re Cleator* (1885), 10 O.R. 326 (C.A.), at p. 334.
[15]Megarry and Wade, pp. 52-3.
[16]*Marshall v. Peascod* (1861), 2 J. & H. 73, 70 E.R. 976.
[17]*Re Davison's Settlement*, [1913] 2 Ch. 498.
[18]*Idle v. Cook* (1705), 1 P. Wms. 70 at p. 77, 24 E.R. 298.
[19]44 & 45 Vict., c. 41, s. 51 (1881).
[20]R.S.O. 1980, c. 90; first enacted as the *Conveyancing and Law of Property Act*, S.O. 1886, c. 20, s. 4.

(4) Subsection (3) applies only if and as far as a contrary intention does not appear from the conveyance, and has effect subject to the terms of the conveyance and to the provisions therein contained.

(5) This section applies only to conveyances made after the 1st day of July, 1886.[21]

The *Conveyancing Act* of Nova Scotia provides simply that: "A conveyance does not require a habendum or any special form of words, terms of art or words of limitation."[22]

It should be noted that the English Act[23] did not make provision for the absence of words of limitation as the Ontario legislation does. Thus, it was held that a conveyance "in fee" alone was not apt to create a fee simple but passed a life estate only.[24] This lacuna has now been remedied.[25] By contrast, in Ontario, a conveyance which purported to convey "all [of the grantor's] estate and interest" in the lands was held, because of section 5(3) of the Ontario Act, to be sufficient to pass the fee simple even though it did not contain words of limitation.[26] The case also held that the word "grant" is not necessary in the operative words, the word "transfer" being sufficient.

Nevertheless, the simple word "fee" is ambiguous and does not necessarily mean fee simple, as it may mean fee tail where that estate continues to exist.[27]

Although the word "assigns" has no conveyancing value, in practice the limitation is frequently to the grantee and his "heirs and assigns". The word "assigns" does not enlarge the estate which was fully created by the word "heirs", nor is it necessary in order to enable the grantee to alienate the estate, as that is his right anyway.[28]

By what is known as the rule in *Shelley's Case*,[29] if a grant be made to a person for life, with remainder to his heirs, he takes an estate in fee simple and not a mere life estate, because the word "heirs" is construed as a word of limitation and not as a word of purchase; that is, the effect of the words is to limit the estate to the grantee only, so that the interest of the heirs would only

---

[21]For similar legislation see *Property Law Act*, R.S.B.C. 1979, c. 340, s. 19; *Law of Property Act*, R.S.A. 1980, c. L-8, s. 7(1); R.S.M. 1970, c. L90, s. 4; *Property Act*, R.S.N.B. 1973, c. P-19, s. 12(3); *Conveyancing Act*, R.S.N.S. 1967, c. 56, s. 5. There appears to be no similar legislation in Prince Edward Island, the Northwest Territories and Yukon Territory. No such legislation would seem necessary in Newfoundland where the *Chattels Real Act*, R.S.N. 1970, c. 36, converts all land into chattels real. See Gushue, "The Law of Real Property in Newfoundland", 4 Can. Bar Rev. 310 (1926). However, the *Conveyancing Act*, R.S.N. 1970, c. 63, s. 19, provides that every conveyance shall by virtue of the Act pass all the estate a party has.

[22]R.S.N.S. 1967, c. 56, s. 2(2). Cf. *Property Law Act*, R.S.B.C. 1979, c. 340, s. 15(1).

[23]*Conveyancing Act, 1881*, 44 & 45 Vict., c. 41, s. 51.

[24]*Re Ethel and Mitchells and Butlers' Contract*, [1901] 1 Ch. 945.

[25]*Law of Property Act, 1925*, 15 & 16 Geo. 5, c. 20, s. 60(1).

[26]*Re Airey* (1921), 21 O.W.N. 190 (H.C.).

[27]*Re Taylor* (1916), 36 O.L.R. 116, 28 D.L.R. 488 (S.C.).

[28]*Brookman v. Smith* (1871), L.R. 6 Exch. 291, affd L.R. 7 Exch. 271; *Milman v. Lane*, [1901] 2 K.B. 745 (C.A.); *Re Woking Urban District Council (Basingstoke Canal) Act, 1911*, [1914] 1 Ch. 300; *Ahearn v. Ahearn* (1894), 1 N.B. Eq. 53.

[29](1581), 1 Co. Rep. 93 b, 76 E.R. 206.

arise through inheritance if he did not dispose of the land by deed or will, and the words are not to be regarded as directly conveying an interest to the heirs as purchasers, that is, persons who acquire an estate otherwise than by inheritance.[30]

(c) Problems of construction

It is a general rule, usually referred to as the doctrine of repugnancy, that in a deed subsequent words cannot cut down or contradict a preceding clear grant, or be repugnant thereto.[31]

In a deed, the first part, naming the grantor and grantee and defining what is granted, is called the "premises"; the words which grant an estate in the described land are called the "operative words"; and the description is usually, although not necessarily, followed by words commonly called the *habendum*, but which are really the *habendum* and *tenendum*, which run "to have and to hold unto" the grantee and his heirs. The words "to have" are the *habendum*, the words "to hold" being the *tenendum*. The *tenendum* is merely a conveyancing relic, though originally it was used to denote the tenure by which the estate was to be held, such as by military service or in free and common socage, and sometimes to denote the lord of whom the estate was to be held. Since all land is now held in free and common socage and is held of the Crown as chief lord, the entire expression that is commonly called the *habendum* is unnecessary, unless the grantee is to hold his estate for the use and benefit of another or others. If the grantee is to hold to the use of another, the *habendum* is the proper place to specify the use. The general rule can thus be expressed as follows: The *habendum* may explain, qualify, lessen or even enlarge an estate granted by the operative words, but it cannot contradict or be repugnant to them.

In *Goodtitle v. Gibbs*,[32] in which it was held that, if the grantee's interest is not limited in the premises, but is limited in the *habendum*, he takes the interest limited in the *habendum*, Abott, C.J., said:

> If no estate be mentioned in the premises, the grantee will take nothing under that part of the deed except by implication and presumption of law, but if an habendum follow, the intention of the parties as to the estate to be conveyed will be found in the habendum, and, consequently, no implication or presumption of law can be made, and if the intention so expressed be contrary to the rules of law, the intention cannot take effect, and the deed will be void. On the other hand, if an estate or interest be mentioned in the premises, the intention of the parties is shewn, and the deed may be effectual without any habendum, and if an habendum follow which is repugnant to the premises, or contrary to the rules of law, and incapable of a construction consistent with either, the habendum shall be rejected, and the deed stand good upon the premises.

---

[30]See further on this rule, §1009.6, *infra.*

[31]See generally, Williams, "The Doctrine of Repugnancy", 59 L.Q. R. 343 (1943); Russell, "The Case of the Disappearing Fee, or When is a Fee not a Fee", 53 Ill. Bar J. 334 (1964-65).

[32](1826), 5 B. & C. 709 at p. 717, 108 E.R. 264.

It was stated in *Spencer v. Registrar of Titles*[33] that "although the habendum cannot retract the gift in the premises, it may construe and explain the sense in which the words in the premises should be taken". Hence, in that case, where the grant was to a person in trust for another person, his heirs and assigns, and the *habendum* was to the grantee and his heirs, the lack of limitation of an estate in the operative words was supplied by the *habendum* so that the grantee took a fee simple in trust. Similarly, where the operative words in a deed by a tenant in tail granted land "in fee simple" which, without using the word "heirs", was insufficient by statute to convey a fee absolute and bar the entail, but the *habendum* read "to have and to hold unto the said party of the second part, his heirs and assigns, to and for his and their sole and only use forever", it was held that the operative words and the *habendum* were together sufficient to pass a fee simple and bar the entail.[34]

If the operative words, however, grant an estate in fee simple, the *habendum* cannot cut it down by repugnant words.[35] Thus, if the operative words grant to a man in fee simple and the *habendum* purports to limit the estate to the man and his wife, the *habendum* is repugnant to the operative words and the wife would take no interest.[36] Conversely, if the operative words grant a life estate and the *habendum* purports to pass a fee simple, the *habendum* is repugnant and the grantee will take only a life estate.[37]

In *McLeod v. Town of Amherst*[38] the operative words in a deed created a fee simple in the municipality, but the *habendum* contained the words "for use as a public park and for other recreational purposes". It was held that the operative part of the deed prevailed over the repugnant words in the *habendum*; further, that the words could not be construed as a trust, nor as a condition subsequent. Even if it was a condition subsequent, it offended the rule against perpetuities and would thus leave the municipality with the fee simple absolute.

On the other hand, if the operative words grant lands to a person and his heirs and the *habendum* is to him and his heirs for the life of another person, the *habendum* is not actually repugnant to, but merely qualifies, the operative words, so that the grantee and his heirs have an estate *pur autre vie*.[39]

Similarly, where land was granted to a man and his heirs and the *habendum* limited it to the grantor until marriage and thereafter to the use of the intended wife and her heirs, it was held that, after marriage, the wife took an estate in fee simple.[40]

The co-existence of a fee and a use in one person is permitted by the law, and there is no repugnance between them. Hence, if land is conveyed by a deed

[33][1906] A.C. 503 (P.C.), at p. 507.
[34]*Re Gold and Rowe* (1913), 4 O.W.N. 642, 9 D.L.R. 26 (S.C.).
[35]*Doe d. Meyers v. Marsh* (1852), 9 U.C.Q.B. 242.
[36]*Langlois v. Lesperance* (1892), 22 O.R. 682 (Ch. Div.).
[37]*Purcell v. Tully* (1906), 12 O.L.R. 5 (Div. Ct.).
[38](1973), 39 D.L.R. (3d) 146, 8 N.S.R. (2d) 504 (S.C.T.D.), affd 44 D.L.R. (3d) 723, N.S.R. *loc. cit.* p. 491 (S.C. App. Div.).
[39]*Owston v. Williams* (1858), 16 U.C.Q.B. 405.
[40]*Re Bayliss and Balfe* (1917), 38 O.L.R. 437, 35 D.L.R. 350 (H.C.).

which, in the premises, grants the land in fee simple and the *habendum* limits the estate to uses, the grantee may, in a conveyance from him, grant and appoint to the new grantee and effectually defeat his wife's inchoate right of dower.[41]

502.2 Creation by Will

(a) At common law

The strict common law rule that in a grant to a person the words "and his heirs" were necessary to pass a fee simple did not apply to wills in regard to which more latitude was allowed under the fundamental rule that the testator's intent was to be determined and given effect to. If a testator devised land showing clearly that he intended a fee simple to pass, it would pass even though he had not used the right technical words.

The reason for this greater latitude was that a testator is not presumed to be acquainted with the technicalities.[1] No strict formula was thus required in order for a fee simple to pass by will. A testator did not have to use the words "and his heirs". Words such as, "to A in fee simple", or "to A forever" would be sufficient if an intention to create a fee simple could be deduced.[2] Moreover, the onus to show such intention was on the devisee.[3] If a devise were to a person without words of limitation to show the intention, the devisee took only a life estate, for the absence of words of limitation made it impossible to infer from the rest of the will that an estate in fee simple might have been intended.[4]

(b) Statutory reforms

These rules have now been changed by legislation. Most of the Canadian statutes are based on the English *Wills Act, 1837*,[5] although similar legislation has been in effect in Ontario since 1834.[6] These statutes provide that no words of limitation are required and that a testator is presumed to dispose of the largest estate he has, unless a contrary intention is shown. This completely reversed the onus of proof.[7]

---

[41]*Re Walsh and Sovis*, [1956] O.R. 202, 2 D.L.R. (2d) 356 (H.C.J.). *Cf. Hunter v. Munn*, [1962] O.W.N. 250 (C.A.), which held that a *habendum* to uses is not repugnant to a grant in fee and may be used to subject the grant to a lesser estate, that is, a life interest in the parties.
§502.2
[1]*Brennan v. Monroe* (1841), 6 U.C.Q.B. (O.S.) 92 at p. 94.
[2]*King v. Evans* (1895), 24 S.C.R. 356 at p. 364, *per* Strong, C.J.
[3]Megarry and Wade, p. 56.
[4]*Doe d. Ford v. Bell* (1850), 6 U.C.Q.B. 527; *Dumble v. Johnson* (1866), 17 U.C.C.P. 9; *Hamilton v. Dennis* (1866), 12 Gr. 325; *Re Virtue* (1922), 22 O.W.N. 482 (H.C.).
[5]7 Wm. 4 & 1 Vict., c. 26, ss. 28, 34 (1837).
[6]*Real Property Amendment Act*, S.U.C. 1834, c. 1, s. 50.
[7]Megarry and Wade, p. 56.

The Ontario *Succession Law Reform Act*[8] now provides:

26. Except when a contrary intention appears by the will, where real property is devised to a person without words of limitation, the devise passes the fee simple or the whole of any other estate or interest that the testator had power to dispose of by will in the real property.[9]

Thus, where a testator devised his home to his daughter for her own use, it was held that, under the statute, she took a fee simple,[10] and a devise of the remainder to "lawful children" is to be construed as a remainder to "lawful children and their heirs", so as to pass a fee simple.[11]

In certain cases the words of limitation are ambiguous. Thus, in *Re Cathcart*,[12] the testator devised land in trust for his widow and daughter "for and during their lives and the life of the survivor of them in fee simple". It was held that they took the fee simple estate.

Difficulties sometimes arise when the testator uses the common law formula in the disjunctive. But in *Re Wright and Fowler*,[13] a devise to the testator's daughter "or her heirs" was held to pass the fee simple to the daughter, the disjunctive "or" being read as "and". The argument in such cases is that the testator intended to pass an estate in fee simple to the devisee with a substitutional gift to the heirs if the devisee predeceases the testator. In other words, it is argued that there is an attempt to prevent lapse, so that the words "or his heirs" should be read as words of purchase or, as they are more commonly called in this context, *words of substitution*.

This was the argument in *Re Ottewell*[14] where the testator devised land to his brother "to hold unto him, his heirs, executors and administrators absolutely and forever", and the brother predeceased the testator. The courts held that the words "heirs, executors and administrators" are terms of art, passing an absolute interest. They are, therefore, words of limitation rather than of substitution. In the result, the gift lapsed.

Where there are no words of limitation, or where there is a contrary intention in the will, however, it passes only a life estate. Thus, where land was devised

---

[8]R.S.O. 1980, c. 488.

[9]For similar legislation see: *Wills Act*, R.S.A. 1980, c. W-11, s. 26; R.S.B.C. 1979, c. 434, s. 24; R.S.M. 1970, c. W150, s. 26; R.S.N.B. 1973, c. W-9, s. 25; R.S.N.S. 1967, c. 340, s. 26; R.S.N. 1970, c. 401, s. 16; R.S.S. 1978, c. W-14, s. 25; *Probate Act*, R.S.P.E.I. 1974, c. P-19, s. 74; *Wills Ordinance*, R.O.N.W.T. 1974, c. W-3, s. 20(1); R.O.Y.T. 1971, c. W-3, s. 19(1).

[10]*Re Grafton* (1924), 26 O.W.N. 262 (H.C.).

[11]*Chandler v. Gibson* (1902), 2 O.L.R. 442 (C.A.). To the same effect, see *Re Armstrong* (1918), 15 O.W.N. 148 (H.C.); *Grant v. Fuller* (1902), 33 S.C.R. 34, "to her children if any at her death"; *Re Hammond* (1920), 18 O.W.N. 253 (H.C.).

[12](1915), 8 O.W.N. 572 (H.C.). See also *Re Traynor and Keith* (1888), 15 O.R. 469 (Ch. Div.), where a devise to the testator's daughter, "to her and her heirs but not to their assigns", was held to pass the fee simple.

[13](1916), 10 O.W.N. 299 (H.C.).

[14](1969), 7 D.L.R. (3d) 358, 70 W.W.R. 47 *sub nom. Tottrup v. Patterson* (Alta. S.C. App. Div.), affd 9 D.L.R. (3d) 313, [1970] S.C.R. 318.

to two devisees without words of limitation, but the executors were directed to sell the property after the death of the devisee, it was held that such direction showed an intent contrary to the devisees taking a fee simple and they took only life estates.[15]

The rule in *Shelley's Case*[16] relating to words of limitation in a deed applies equally to a will, so that, if a testator devises land to a person for life with remainder to his heirs, indicating that he means the whole line of heirs, the devisee will take a fee simple, regardless of the fact that the testator may add restrictions or conditions which are repugnant to an estate of inheritance and which are, therefore, void.[17]

(c) Problems of construction

As in the case of deeds, a clear gift in a will cannot be cut down by subsequent inconsistent words in the will. The general rule as stated by Middleton, J.A., in *Re Walker*,[18] is that, where a testator gives property to a person, intending him to have all the rights incident to ownership, and then adds a gift over of what remains at the death of that person, he is endeavouring to do what is impossible; his intention is plain but it cannot be given effect to. The court must endeavour to give such effect to the testator's wishes as is possible, by ascertaining which part of the testator's intention predominates and by giving effect to it, rejecting the subordinate intent as repugnant to the dominant intent. In that case, it was accordingly held that, where a testator gave all his real and personal property to his wife and by subsequent words provided that what was undisposed of by her was to be divided in a particular manner, the gift over failed and the wife took absolutely.

Under the general rule, where a testator devised property to his wife "to have and to hold to her and to her heirs and assigns forever" and went on to provide that, after her death, the property was to be divided equally between the heirs, it was held that the wife took the property absolutely in fee simple and was entitled to dispose of it by will.[19]

Where the testator gave the balance of his real and personal property to his wife for her use and benefit and provided that, at her death, she was to leave the remaining balance, if any, in a particular manner, it was held that she took an absolute estate and it was not possible to make a gift over of part of an absolute gift.[20]

---

[15]*Re Virtue* (1922), 22 O.W.N. 482 (H.C.). To the same effect, see *Wilson v. Graham* (1886), 12 O.R. 469 (Ch. Div.); *Re Richer* (1919), 460 O.L.R. 367, 50 D.L.R. 614 (S.C. App. Div.), a devise to the testator's wife, "the free use of all my estate both real and personal for her lifetime", with a gift of the unspent balance to his children after his wife's death.

[16](1581), 1 Co. Rep. 93 b, 76 E.R. 206. See §502.1 at footnote 29, *supra.*

[17]*Van Grutten v. Foxwell*, [1897] A.C. 658 (H.L.). See further §1009.6, *infra.*

[18](1924), 56 O.L.R. 517 (S.C. App. Div.).

[19]*Re Foss*, [1940] 4 D.L.R. 791, [1940] 3 W.W.R. 61 (Alta. S.C.).

[20]*Re Moore* (1925), 57 O.L.R. 530 (H.C.).

CHAP. 5 THE ESTATE IN FEE SIMPLE §502.2

Equally repugnant and to no avail was a provision, following the devise of the whole estate to the testator's wife, that what property was left at her death was to be sold and divided in a particular manner,[21] and a provision, following a devise to the testator's wife, that when she died the estate was to be divided between the couple's sons.[22]

The interposition of trustees or the postponement of enjoyment to a future time will not affect the application of the doctrine. Thus, where a devise of a house to be used and enjoyed by the devisee during her natural life and a direction that a farm was also to be given to her, was followed by a direction that the two properties were not to be sold without the reason for the sale being approved by trustees and that, in the event of sale, the properties were to be offered to persons interested in neighbouring properties because of personal associations, it was held that the testatrix intended a fee simple and not a life estate to be given and that, having given the fee simple, the stipulation that the properties were not to be sold without the consent of the trustees was inoperative.[23]

Similarly, where a testator devised real estate to a person at a future time and directed that in the meantime all the income from the property was to be applied to the donee for his benefit, it was held that the devise passed the fee simple immediately.[24]

An absolute devise of all, and not just part, of the rents and profits of land or income from land, without any gift over, passes the fee simple estate in the land to the devisee, but such devise for life passes a life estate in the land to the devisee.[25]

In Re Thomas,[26] a codicil directed that one property was to "be held by my daughter . . . who shall receive all rents and benefits during her natural life and at her decease . . . all rents shall be invested for the benefit of her heirs on their coming of age". It was held that she took a fee simple. The codicil further directed that all rents from another property were to be divided

---

[21]Re Sigman (1926), 30 O.W.N. 280 (H.C.).
[22]Re Loveless (1929), 36 O.W.N. 340 (H.C.); Wilson v. Wilson, [1944] 2 D.L.R. 729, [1944] 2 W.W.R. 412 (B.C.C.A.). Cases to the same effect are: Re Hornell, [1945] O.R. 58, [1945] 1 D.L.R. 440 (C.A.); Bartrop v. Blackstop (1957), 10 D.L.R. (2d) 192, 21 W.W.R. 241 (Sask. C.A.); Re MacInnis and Townshend (1973), 35 D.L.R. (3d) 459, 4 Nfld. & P.E.I.R. 211 (P.E.I.C.A.); Re Patton, [1971] 3 O.R. 85, 19 D.L.R. (3d) 497 (H.C.J.); Re Freedman (1974), 41 D.L.R. (3d) 122, [1974] 1 W.W.R. 577 (Man. Q.B.), noted 1 E. & T.Q. 117 (1973-74); Re McElwain and Demartini (1974), 3 O.R. (2d) 705, 46 D.L.R. (3d) 525 (Div. Ct.); Rankin v. Rankin, [1980] 6 W.W.R. 307, 4 Man. R. (2d) 209 sub nom. Re Rankin's Will; Rankin v. Rankin (Q.B.).
[23]Re McGivern, [1944] 2 D.L.R. 333, 17 M.P.R. 83 (N.B.S.C.). Cf. Re Lysiak (1975), 7 O.R. (2d) 317, 55 D.L.R. (3d) 161 (H.C.J.).
[24]Re Miller, [1957] O.W.N. 84, 8 D.L.R. (2d) 170 (C.A.).
[25]Re Vair and Doyle (1922), 23 O.W.N. 407 (H.C.); Re Thomas (1901), 2 O.L.R. 660 (H.C.J.); McKenzie v. McKenzie (1924), 56 O.L.R. 247, [1925] 1 D.L.R. 373 (H.C.); Mannox v. Greener (1872), L.R. 14 Eq. 456; Re Martin; Martin v. Martin, [1892] W.N. 120 (H.C.J.).
[26]Supra, footnote 25.

between the testator's wife and daughter equally and that, on the death of a life tenant, the property was to be sold, one-half of the proceeds to go to the wife or her heirs and the other half to be invested, the interest to go to the daughter for life and the principal to go to her heirs. It was held that the daughter took a fee simple in one-half of this other property.

In some cases another construction is possible, however. Thus, where a testator gave all his real and personal property "unto my wife . . . absolutely, and in the event of her death, to be equally divided among my children", the words "in the event of her death" were construed to mean if she died before the testator. There was thus a substitutional gift.[27]

Despite the frequent application by the courts of the doctrine of repugnancy in wills, it would seem more appropriate to attempt to ascertain the testator's intention from the whole will, in which case even an apparent absolute gift followed by a gift over can be given effect to[28] and the courts sometimes take this approach.

Thus, in *Re Shamas*,[29] a testator, by a home-drawn will, gave all he owned to his wife. He directed her to pay his debts and to raise the family. He then continued, "All will belong to my wife until the last one comes to the age of 21 years old. If my wife marries again she should have her share like the other children if not, she will keep the whole thing and see that every child gets his share when she dies." The court held that, on reading the will as a whole, the testator's intention was to give a life estate to his widow (subject to divestment on remarriage) coupled with a power to encroach, with remainder in fee to the children.[30]

In a separate category are cases in which the testator gives property to his wife during widowhood or while she remains unmarried, with or without a gift over. In this case the rule appears to be that where the gift is to the wife so long as she remains unmarried without a gift over, she receives a determinable fee simple, whereas, if the gift is to her during her widowhood, she has only a determinable life estate which ends on her remarriage or death.[31] Thus, where a testator left his whole estate to his wife absolutely as long as she may live, it was held that she took absolutely.[32]

[27]*Re Walker and Drew* (1892), 22 O.R. 332 (Q.B.). *Cf. Re Hand* (1975), 9 O.R. (2d) 346, 60 D.L.R. (3d) 402 (H.C.J.), a devise of residue to the testator's sister, "for her lifetime", with power to encroach, the sister to have as full use of the property as if it were her own, with a gift over. Held that the gift over was effective.

[28]See *Re Hornell*, [1945] O.R. 58, [1945] 1 D.L.R. 440 (C.A.), *per* Laidlaw, J.A., dissenting; Kennedy, "Gift by Will to W; At Her Death 'What Remains' to the Children", 28 Can. Bar Rev. 839 (1950).

[29][1967] 2 O.R. 275, 63 D.L.R. (2d) 300 (C.A.).

[30]See to the same effect *Re Kirk*, [1956] O.W.N. 418, 2 D.L.R. (2d) 527 (H.C.J.); *Re Lanigan*, summarized in [1979] 3 A.C.W.S. 53 (Ont. H.C.J.); *Bartrop v. Blackstock, supra*, footnote 22; *Re Huffman* (1979), 25 O.R. (2d) 521, 101 D.L.R. (3d) 365 (H.C.J.).

[31]*Re Perrie* (1910), 21 O.L.R. 100 (H.C.J.), at pp. 104-5.

[32]*Re Cooper Estate* (1921), 61 D.L.R. 315, [1921] 3 W.W.R. 76 (Sask. K.B.).

On the other hand, where a testator devised and bequeathed his realty and personalty to his widow, who was to have the "free use" of it for life, and provided that what remained "unspent" on her death was to go to the children, it was held that the widow only had a life estate in the realty, the remainder going to the children in fee simple, together with whatever remained of the personalty.[33]

Again, where a will, devising property to the widow, read, "to her the whole control of my real and personal estate as long as she lives", she was held entitled to a life estate only.[34]

A devise to a wife for "as long as she remains my widow" with a gift over in the event of her remarriage, has been held to give her a life estate only and not a fee simple defeasible upon remarriage.[35]

The will may also, in appropriate circumstances, create an estate in fee simple upon a condition subsequent. This was the result in *Re Gilbert*,[36] where the testator gave all his property to his widow, subject to a proviso that if she predeceased the testator or remarried, then the property should go to the children.

502.3 Corporations

(a) At common law

A corporation can have no heirs. Hence the use of the word "heirs" as a word of limitation is inapt in a conveyance to a corporation. This is irrelevant in the case of a corporation aggregate since it cannot die, as it consists of a number of members. Thus, words of limitation which were and are usually added to a grant to a corporation such as, "and its successors", or "and its successors and assigns", are unnecessary.[1] In the absence of words of limitation, however, it might seem that a corporation receives only a life estate. But, as a corporation aggregate never dies, the estate is effectively perpetual and, thus, like a fee

---

[33]*Re Richer* (1919), 46 O.L.R. 367, 50 D.L.R. 614 (S.C. App. Div.).

[34]*Re Turnbull Estate* (1906), 11 O.L.R. 334 (H.C.J.); *cf. Martin v. Pellan* (1954), 13 W.W.R. (N.S.) 154 (B.C.S.C.), a devise to a husband to enjoy the premises so long as he is able, held to create a life estate.

[35]*Re Branton* (1910), 20 O.L.R. 642 (H.C.J.); *Re Ferguson*, [1942] O.W.N. 115, [1942] 2 D.L.R. 332 (H.C.J.); *Re Dietrich*, [1963] O.R. 70, 36 D.L.R. (2d) 17 (H.C.J.); *Re McLean*, [1957] O.W.N. 11, 6 D.L.R. (2d) 519 (C.A.). *Cf. Re Goodwin* (1969), 3 D.L.R. (3d) 281 (Alta. S.C.), a devise to a daughter-in-law provided she does not remarry, with a gift over, is a determinable life estate. To the same effect is *Re Mulhall Estate* (1976), 21 R.F.L. 175 (B.C.S.C.), a gift to the testator's wife "so long as she remains my widow", with a gift over in the event of her remarriage, and *Re Waters* (1978), 21 O.R. (2d) 124, 89 D.L.R. (3d) 742 (H.C.J.), a devise of a house to a beneficiary "for as long as she lives, or until she re-marries, or gives to my executors and trustees a written notice that she no longer needs and desires the use of the property".

[36][1959] O.W.N. 294 (H.C.J.).

§502.3

[1]*Re Woking Urban District Council (Basingstoke Canal) Act, 1911*, [1914] 1 Ch. 300 (C.A.).

simple. On the dissolution of a corporation, its interest at common law was thought to revert to the grantor who, it was supposed, retained a possibility of reverter. However, as a corporation was permitted freely to alienate its interest, the possibility was destroyed on alienation.[2] A corporation could thus be said to have "a fee simple for the purpose of alienation, but only a determinable fee for the purpose of enjoyment".[3] Because of the supposed possibility of reverter, it seems that a restraint on alienation in a grant to a corporation was said to be valid, although it would be void if attached to a deed to an individual.[4] Modern case-law holds, however, that the property of a dissolved corporation does not revert to the grantor, but escheats to the Crown.[5]

In the case of a corporation sole, being a single incorporated person such as an archbishop, that person could die, but have a successor in office. It was thus necessary at common law, in order to convey a fee simple to a corporation sole, to add "and his successors" as words of limitation. Failure to do so created only a life estate in the incumbent.[6] A conveyance to a corporation sole "and his heirs" gave him only a fee simple in his individual capacity.[7]

Both in the case of a corporation sole and in the case of a corporation aggregate having a head, the rule at common law was that a grant was void unless the office was filled at the time of the grant. However, if the grant was made during an incumbency the estate was simply in abeyance during a subsequent vacancy.[8]

(b) Statutory reforms

The possibility of reverter in favour of the grantor of land to a corporation has been abolished by legislation. Statutes now often provide that on dissolution of a corporation its undisposed of assets are forfeit to the Crown.[9]

As to the requirement of words of limitation, it would seem that under legislation such as section 5(3) of the Ontario *Conveyancing and Law of Property Act*,[10] no words of limitation are necessary in the case of a corporation sole or aggregate since that section provides that where no words of limitation are used the conveyance passes all the estate the grantor has. The same result might not obtain under section 5(2) which permits the use of the words "in fee

---

[2]Co. Litt. 35b; Challis, pp. 35-6, 226, 467-8; Armour, *Real Property*, p. 66.

[3]Challis, p. 226.

[4]*Ibid.*

[5]*Re Jolin and Lart Investments Ltd.* (1977), 18 O.R. (2d) 161 (Dist. Ct.), and see §§502.3(b) and 1007.3, *infra.*

[6]*Paris v. Bishop of New Westminster* (1897), 5 B.C.R. 450 (S.C.). There were two exceptions to this rule, namely, for grants to the Crown and grants in frankalmoign; Megarry and Wade, p. 54.

[7]*Ibid.*, p. 55.

[8]*Ibid.*

[9]See *e.g.*, *Corporations Act*, R.S.O. 1980, c. 95, s. 322; *Business Corporations Act*, R.S.O. 1980, c. 54, s. 245; *Property of Dissolved Corporations (Vesting) Act*, R.S.N. 1970, c. 310; *Dissolved Corporations Property Act*, R.S.N.S. 1967, c. 77.

[10]R.S.O. 1980, c. 90. And see statutes collected at footnote 21 in §502.1.

simple" since those take the place of the former phrase "and his heirs". In England under the *Conveyancing and Law of Property Act, 1881*,[11] which did not have the equivalent of Ontario's section 5(3), it is thus likely that, in the case of a corporation sole, the continued use of the words, "and his successors" was necessary. In any event, even under the Ontario legislation, some indication in the deed that the corporation sole is intended to take in its corporate capacity is probably necessary to avoid the implication that he might take in his own right.

In England the matter was dealt with effectively by section 60(2) of the *Property Act, 1925*,[12] which provides that a conveyance to a corporation sole by his corporate designation without the word "successors", passes the fee simple or the whole estate the grantor has in the absence of a contrary intention. There appears to be comparable legislation only in British Columbia.[13]

Section 180(2) of the English Act of 1925[14] provides, moreover, that a grant to a corporation aggregate or sole during a vacancy in its head or office does not affect the grant, but that the interest thereby conveyed vests notwithstanding, subject to a right in the successor, or of the corporation aggregate after the appointment of its head, to disclaim it. There appears to be no similar legislation in Canada.

503. CHARACTERISTICS OF THE ESTATE

The characteristics of the estate in fee simple have already been discussed in part under the preceding headings. It remains to speak of its main characteristics, that is, its alienability and the doctrine of waste.

503.1 Alienability

The owner of an estate in fee simple has, as the main incident of the estate, the right to freely alienate the land, that is, the right to transfer it, both *inter vivos* and on death. This was not always so. Early in the common law the tenant in fee simple was restricted in alienating his estate *inter vivos* at the behest both of his feudal lord and of his heir. The former had an interest in any tenant who might be substituted for his present one or who might be added to the feudal structure by the process of subinfeudation. The heir was thought to have an interest in the land which could not be destroyed by the tenant.[1] Moreover, the tenant's early freedom to dispose of his land by will was soon abolished, with the result that land could pass on the tenant's death only to his heir by the principle of primogeniture.[2] The right to freely alienate land was

---

[11]144 & 45 Vict., c. 41, s. 51 (1881).
[12]15 & 16 Geo. 5, c. 20 (1925).
[13]*Property Law Act*, R.S.B.C. 1979, c. 340, s. 19(2).
[14]*Law of Property Act, 1925*, 15 & 16 Geo. 5, c. 20.
§503.1
[1]See §§221.1, 221.2 and 502.1(a), *supra*.
[2]See §§221.3, 502.2(a), *supra*.

assured by the Statute *Quia Emptores*[3] in 1290, however, and the tenant in fee simple reacquired the right to dispose of his land by will in 1540.[4]

(a) Inter vivos

The Statute *Quia Emptores*[5] forbade alienation by subinfeudation and removed all restraints on alienation by substitution of an estate in fee simple that had previously existed. The statute is in force in all the common law jurisdictions of Canada under the rules of reception of English law.[6] Moreover, it has been re-enacted or reprinted in some cases.[7] The statute has been described as a pillar of real property law,[8] for it still operates, whenever a person sells his land, to put the purchaser in the vendor's place.

Since 1290, the right of alienation has been an inseparable incident of an estate in fee simple. As a result, the courts have viewed with disfavour any restraints on alienation. Although these restraints arise most often in wills they may be dealt with conveniently at this point. A condition that would take away the necessary incidents of the estate, such as that the holder shall not take the profits, or shall not have the power to alienate, either generally or for a limited time, is void as being repugnant to the estate created.[9]

The reason such restraints are void is because they keep property out of commerce and tend to result in a concentration of wealth.[10] Moreover, they tend to prejudice creditors, discourage property improvements, and encourage impermanence and instability in that they limit the benefits, but not the burdens, of property ownership.[11]

Where a devise was to a person and his heirs "but not to their assigns", these added words were void and the devisee took a fee simple.[12] Also, in a devise "to my nephew . . . or his children or son" which contained a condition that it "shall not be sold, mortgaged or conveyed in any way from the descendants of said family forever", the condition was held void. Its effect was to destroy or take away the enjoyment of the fee simple given and it was thus repugnant to it.[13]

---

[3]18 Edw. 1, cc. 1-3 (1290).
[4]By the *Statute of Wills*, 32 Hen. 8, c. 1 (1540).
[5]18 Edw. 1, cc. 1-3 (1290).
[6]§402, *supra*.
[7]*An Act Respecting Real Property*, R.S.O. 1897, c. 330, s. 2, reprinted in R.S.O. 1960, App. A; *Statute of Westminster, the Third*, R.S.B.C. 1897, vol. 1, p. xliii.
[8]Maitland, *The Constitutional History of England* (Cambridge, Univ. Press, 1908), p. 20.
[9]*Blackburn v. McCallum* (1903), 33 S.C.R. 65.
[10]*Stephens v. Gulf Oil Canada Ltd.* (1975), 11 O.R. (2d) 129 at p. 156, 65 D.L.R. (3d) 193 at p. 220 (C.A.).
[11]*Laurin v. Iron Ore Co. of Canada* (1977), 82 D.L.R. (3d) 634 (Nfld. S.C.T.D.), at p. 646.
[12]*Re Traynor and Keith* (1888), 15 O.R. 469 (Ch. Div.).
[13]*Re Collier* (1966), 60 D.L.R. (2d) 70, 52 M.P.R. 211 (Nfld. S.C.). *Cf.*, to the same effect, *Doherty v. Doherty*, [1936] 2 D.L.R. 180, 10 M.P.R. 286 (N.S.S.C.); *Re Malcolm*, [1947] O.W.N. 871, [1947] 4 D.L.R. 756 (H.C.J.); *Re Woods* (1933), 13 Nfld. L.R. 109; *Re Rourke* (1946), 15 Nfld. L.R. 461; *Re Quinn Estate* (1975), 13 N.B.R. (2d) 181 (N.B.S.C.).

In *Blackburn v. McCallum*,[14] it was held that a general restraint on alienation of an estate in fee simple is void even if it is limited as to time, such as for twenty-five years from the death of the testator. This case overruled previous cases which had held that a restraint on alienation for a limited period was valid.[15] If the condition prohibits a sale or a lease except with the consent of some other, named, person, it is also void.[16] Similarly, a restraint limiting the right to sell to one person only is void.[17]

A partial restraint, however, merely prohibiting alienation to a particular class of persons, is valid, if the class is not so large that the prohibition amounts to an absolute restraint on alienation.[18]

Restraints may take the form either of options, on the one hand, or of repurchase or pre-emptive rights, or rights of first refusal on the other. An option creates an equitable interest in land which is specifically enforceable, for the optionor grants the optionee a right to compel a conveyance of the land at a future time, which right is solely within the optionee's control.[19] Absent any statutory provisions to the contrary, the other rights are merely personal and contractual and create no present interest in land. For this reason an option may be void for perpetuity, as well as being a restraint on alienation, if it is exercisable[20] beyond the perpetuity period.[21] Moreover, it is at least arguable that the property concept of restraint on alienation ought not to be applied to rights that are contractual, such as rights of first refusal, pre-emption and repurchase.[22] However, some cases do in fact apply the concept of restraint on

---

[14]*Supra*, footnote 9; *Re Rosher*; *Rosher v. Rosher* (1884), 26 Ch. D. 801; *Re Cockerill*; *Mackaness v. Percival*, [1929] 2 Ch. 131.

[15]*Hutt v. Hutt* (1911), 24 O.L.R. 574 (C.A.), and others.

[16]*McRae v. McRae* (1898), 30 O.R. 54 (Div. Ct.); *Pardee v. Humberstone Summer Resort Co. of Ontario Ltd.*, [1933] O.R. 580, [1933] 3 D.L.R. 277 (H.C.J.). A clause in a mortgage providing for acceleration of payment on a sale by the mortgagor is not a restraint on alienation: *Briar Building Holdings Ltd. v. Bow West Holdings Ltd.* (1981), 126 D.L.R. (3d) 566, 16 Alta. L.R. (2d) 42 (Q.B.). A clause entitling the mortgagee to approve an assignee of the equity of redemption is a restraint on alienation, however: *Re Bahnsen and Hazelwood*, [1960] O.W.N. 155, 23 D.L.R. (2d) 76 (C.A.).

[17]*Re Buckley* (1910), 1 O.W.N. 427 (H.C.J.), at p. 428, *per* Boyd, C.

[18]*Blackburn v. McCallum, supra*, footnote 9; *Re Macleay* (1875), L.R. 20 Eq. 186.

[19]*Stephens v. Gulf Oil Canada Ltd., supra*, footnote 10, at p. 154 O.R., p. 218 D.L.R., *per* Howland, J.A.

[20]Or if it is in fact exercised beyond the perpetuity period in jurisdictions where the period has been modified by the "wait and see" principle. See, *e.g.*, *Perpetuities Act*, R.S.O. 1980, c. 374, s. 13.

[21]*Politzer v. Metropolitan Homes Ltd.* (1975), 54 D.L.R. (3d) 376, [1976] 1 S.C.R. 363; *Canadian Long Island Petroleums Ltd. v. Irving Industries (Irving Wire Products Division) Ltd.* (1974), 50 D.L.R. (3d) 265, [1975] 2 S.C.R. 715; *Stephens v. Gulf Oil Canada Ltd.* (1975), 11 O.R. (2d) 129, 65 D.L.R. (3d) 193 (C.A.); *British Columbia Forest Products Ltd. v. Gay* (1976), 74 D.L.R. (3d) 660, 1 B.C.L.R. 265 (S.C.), affd 89 D.L.R. (3d) 80, 7 B.C.L.R. 190 (C.A.); *Laurin v. Iron Ore Co. of Canada, supra*, footnote 11; *Re McKee and National Trust Co. Ltd.* (1975), 7 O.R. (2d) 614, 56 D.L.R. (3d) 190 (C.A.).

[22]*B.C. Forest Products Ltd. v. Gay, supra*, footnote 21, 74 D.L.R. (3d) at p. 668, 1 B.C.L.R. at p. 275.

alienation to such rights,[23] but it has been suggested that an option to purchase is more objectionable as a restraint on alienation, than a pre-emptive right.[24] Whether the terms of the agreement establish an option, or a pre-emptive or other right of purchase, they may be interpreted to create either a condition, which, if repugnant to the interest granted, that is, as imposing a restraint on alienation, is void, or a covenant, which, if breached, gives rise only to a cause of action for damages. Whether one is dealing with a condition or a covenant is not always easy to ascertain, but, as a general rule, it may be said that, unless words of condition are used, or the language of the instrument otherwise clearly shows an intent on the part of the grantor to impose a condition, the restraint will be construed as a covenant and not as a condition, for the latter are not favoured in law.[25]

A restraint contained in a will must perforce be a condition, since the devisee cannot be said to have covenanted to observe the restraint; it is imposed solely by the testator.[26]

A restraint in the nature of a pre-emptive right, given by a vendor to a purchaser of part of the vendor's lands, with respect to other lands retained by the vendor, is not a condition, since the land is not the subject of a sale.[27]

However, an option and a pre-emptive or other right of purchase, especially one at a fixed price below the expected future market value, may, in certain circumstances, be construed as a condition and it would then be void as a restraint on alienation.[28]

Three recent cases, *Stephens v. Gulf Oil Canada Ltd.*,[29] *British Columbia Forest Products Ltd. v. Gay*,[30] and *Laurin v. Iron Ore Co. of Canada*,[31] take somewhat divergent approaches to these issues.

In the *Stephens* case, under an agreement, mutual pre-emptive rights were given to the purchaser of part of the vendor's land, with respect to land retained by the vendor, and to the vendor, with respect to the land sold, both at a fixed price, namely, in the case of the vendor's pre-emptive right, the purchaser's cost price. The two pre-emptive rights were construed by the

---

[23]See, *e.g.*, *Stephens v. Gulf Oil Canada Ltd.*, *supra*, footnote 21; and *Laurin v. Iron Ore Co. of Canada* (1977), 82 D.L.R. (3d) 634 (Nfld. S.C.T.D.).

[24]*Stephens v. Gulf Oil Canada Ltd.*, *supra*, footnote 21, at p. 160 O.R., p. 224 D.L.R.

[25]*Pearson v. Adams* (1912), 27 O.L.R. 87 at p. 92, 7 D.L.R. 139 at p. 144 (Div. Ct.), *per* Riddell, J., revd 28 O.L.R. 154, 12 D.L.R. 227 (C.A.), restd 50 S.C.R. 204; *Paul v. Paul* (1921), 50 O.L.R. 211, 64 D.L.R. 269 (S.C. App. Div.); *Stephens v. Gulf Oil Canada Ltd.*, *supra*, footnote 21, at pp. 158-9 O.R., pp. 222-3 D.L.R.; *B.C. Forest Products Ltd. v. Gay*, *supra*, footnote 21, at p. 670 D.L.R., pp. 277-8 B.C.L.R.

[26]*Laurin v. Iron Ore Co. of Canada*, *supra*, footnote 23, at p. 648.

[27]*Ibid.*, at p. 650; *Stephens v. Gulf Oil Canada Ltd.*, *supra*, footnote 21, at p. 161 O.R., p. 225 D.L.R.

[28]*Stephens v. Gulf Oil Canada Ltd.*, *supra*, footnote 21, at pp. 160-1 O.R., pp. 224-5 D.L.R.

[29](1975), 11 O.R. (2d) 129, 65 D.L.R. (3d) 193 (C.A.).

[30](1976), 74 D.L.R. (3d) 660, 1 B.C.L.R. 265 (S.C.), affd 89 D.L.R. (3d) 80, 7 B.C.L.R. 190 (C.A.).

[31](1977), 82 D.L.R. (3d) 634 (Nfld. S.C.T.D.).

Court of Appeal to be covenants and not conditions, because (a) the rights were not referred to in the transfer to the purchaser, nor in the charge back to the vendor, (b) the agreement did not clearly show an intention to create a conditional sale, and (c) the purchaser's pre-emptive right, being with respect to land retained by the vendor, was a covenant and, the rights being mutual, therefore, so was the vendor's pre-emptive right.

The court did not decide that the vendor's pre-emptive right was void, as was assumed in the *Gay*[32] and *Laurin*[33] cases, but merely opined in the alternative that, if the vendor's pre-emptive right were to be construed as a condition, then it would be void as a partial restraint on alienation, since it fixed a price that was well below the anticipated increase in market value. The result would then be to deter the purchaser from selling. The purchaser's pre-emptive right, being mutual, would then fail as well, even though it was clearly a covenant.[34]

In the *Gay* case, the plaintiff employer sold a house to its employee, the defendant, and his wife. Under the terms of sale, the plaintiff had a right of repurchase during a five-year period if the defendant should desire to sell, or should cease to be employed by the plaintiff, and the defendant could require the plaintiff to exercise its right to repurchase for a ten-year period. The price agreed to be paid was the original cash price plus principal repayments on any mortgages, plus improvements, less any repairs.

The trial judge held, and the Court of Appeal agreed, that these terms were covenants, not conditions (which would be void for perpetuity and, perhaps, as restraints), on the ground that there was no apparent intention to create a condition subsequent. As a covenant, the right to repurchase was not a restraint on alienation but, having been created between contracting parties,[35] it was merely a first step on the part of the defendant in the process of alienation to a known person at an agreed price.[36]

Even if the term were a restraint, it was only partial, the courts held, as it did not substantially deprive the defendants of their right to alienate, in that they would be reimbursed for all their investment. Fluctuating market conditions and, in particular, an anticipated increase in the market value due to

---

[32]*Supra*, footnote 30, at pp. 667-8 D.L.R., pp. 274-5 B.C.L.R. See 89 D.L.R. (3d) at p. 89, 7 B.C.L.R. at p. 199, *per* Bull, J.A., and at p. 96 D.L.R., pp. 206-7 B.C.L.R., *per* Hinkson, J.A.

[33]*Supra*, footnote 31, at pp. 648-9.

[34]*Supra*, footnote 29, at pp. 160-1 O.R., pp. 224-5 D.L.R.

[35]*Cf.*, on this point, the *Laurin* case, where the court suggests, at p. 649, that an option or right of first refusal granted by the owner of land after, and not in connection with, the acquisition of title, is not invalid, even though it prescribes a fixed price, or a price determined by a formula, which is below the anticipated future market value, for it is merely a covenant and not a condition.

[36]This statement is probably true only of an option. A right of first refusal, or other right to purchase, is not a step in the process of alienation, but merely a provision which describes the circumstances in which the right comes into existence. See the *Laurin* case, at p. 649.

factors other than improvements, are not to be taken into account in determining whether there was a restraint. In this respect, the courts disagreed with the *Stephens* case to the extent that it appeared to have held that an increase in the market value could convert an otherwise lawful option or right of first refusal into an unlawful one.

In the *Gay* case, the right to repurchase was held by the trial judge to be a right of first refusal rather than an option, since it created no clear vested equitable interest in the plaintiff optionee. In the circumstances, that was irrelevant, since, by statute in British Columbia, rights of first refusal and other rights of purchase had been declared, retroactively, to create equitable interests in land.[37] The Court of Appeal did not find it necessary to decide this point.

In the *Laurin* case, the defendant company also provided housing for its employees. The plaintiff bought a house from the defendant on terms that the defendant could repurchase it when the plaintiff ceased to be employed by the defendant, when the plaintiff wished to sell, and if the defendant were required to make a payment on its guarantee of the mortgage. The repurchase price was to be the amount of principal repaid on the mortgage (there being no down payment), plus the value of improvements made with the consent of the defendant, less straight-line depreciation at two per cent per annum on the original sale price.

In the opinion of the court, whether one is dealing with a covenant or condition in a deed is not so much a question of interpretation as a question of fact, which depends upon the circumstances in which the terms were made. In this case, the right to repurchase, a right of first refusal, was held to be a condition and not a covenant, because (a) it was inseparably linked to the acquisition of title, and (b) it was unreasonable as to time and price, in that the plaintiff was denied the benefit of increasing property value, and of his maintenance, and had to resell at a reducing price. In the court's view, where either, or both, criteria (a) and (b) are absent, the term should be construed as a covenant and, hence, not as a restraint.

The results in these three cases are easily reconciled, but not the reasoning. In the *Stephens* and *Gay* cases the courts appear to have followed the traditional approach of relying upon the intention of the parties to determine whether the contractual term created a covenant or a condition. In principle this is to be preferred, although the search for an elusive intent may be difficult. In the *Laurin* case, the court discarded the intent approach and looked primarily at the facts to determine, on the basis of two criteria, whether a condition or a covenant was employed. This approach would seem to lead to a more consistent result. Moreover, it would seem that the assumption in the *Gay* case, that a term between contracting parties cannot be a restraint on alienation, is incorrect. If the parties are in unequal bargaining positions, as may well be the case where an employer provides housing for his employees, the term may be

---

[37]*Laws Declaratory Act*, R.S.B.C. 1960, c. 213, s. 36A, enacted by the *Attorney-General Statutes Amendment Act*, S.B.C. 1975, c. 4, s. 10A. See now *Property Law Act*, R.S.B.C. 1979, c. 340, s. 9.

so unreasonable as to seriously impair the employee's desire or ability to sell. In that event, it should be held to be a restraint. It is, however, arguable that fluctuating market conditions ought not to enter into a determination, since they can affect both parties.

While these three cases have clarified the law of restraints on alienation to some extent, the law is still very unclear in this area. On principle, it would seem that, if restraints are bad because they tend to weaken the economic and social structure of society by keeping property out of circulation, discouraging improvements and encouraging impermanence, then they should be subject to being struck down whether they are in the form of options, pre-emptive rights, covenants or conditions, whether they were made between two contracting parties, or whether they are with respect to land retained or sold.

Whether a particular restraint is good or bad depends upon the extent of the restraint and upon changing social, political and economic conditions. Factors that should be taken into account in deciding a particular case are the reasonableness of the restraint in terms of price and the time during which it is in effect and the relative bargaining positions of the parties.

It should be noted that certain forms of conditions, such as a restraint on the use to which land may be put, may also be restraints on alienation. Such restraints, usually in the form of conditions, are not normally dealt with on this basis.

It should be noted further that options and pre-emptive and repurchase rights may, in certain circumstances, also be held void at law for restraint of trade,[38] or in equity for being oppressive and unconscionable.[39]

Conditions which are valid as imposing only a partial restraint on alienation, conditions which are void as imposing a general restraint on alienation, or are otherwise repugnant to the estate created, and conditions which are void as being contrary to public policy, uncertain, or impossible to perform, are further discussed in chapter 9.

It is clear that the Legislature has the power to impose restraints on alienation. Moreover, in *Morgan v. A.-G. P.E.I.*[40] it was held that the province has legislative competence to prohibit non-residents of the province from acquiring or holding more than a specified amount of land without permission.[41]

---

[38]*Stephens v. Gulf Oil Canada Ltd.*, *supra*, footnote 29.

[39]*Laurin v. Iron Ore Co. of Canada*, *supra*, footnote 31.

[40](1973), 42 D.L.R. (3d) 603, 5 Nfld. & P.E.I.R. 129 (P.E.I.C.A.), affd 55 D.L.R. (3d) 527, [1976] 2 S.C.R. 349.

[41]The legislation in question, *Real Property Act*, R.S.P.E.I. 1951, c. 138, s. 3(2), as re-enacted by 1972, c. 40, s. 1, now R.S.P.E.I. 1974, c. R-4, s. 3, prohibits a non-resident of the province from acquiring and holding more than ten acres of land, or land being more than five chains' shore frontage, without the consent of the Lieutenant-Governor in Council. *Cf.* the *Land Transfer Tax Act*, R.S.O. 1980, c. 231, s. 2(2), which imposes a tax of 20% of the value of the consideration for a conveyance upon its registration where the transferee is a non-resident of Canada, whereas a resident's tax is only 2/5 of one per cent up to $45,000 and 4/5 of one per cent of any excess. See also R.R.O. 1980, Reg. 879, s. 7, made under the provisions of s. 14 of the *Public*

Apart from such legislation, statutes generally provide that aliens are freely capable of acquiring and owning real estate.[42]

While it is possible to convey land to persons under a disability, such as infants, conveyances by them are void.[43] There may also be interpretational difficulties in connection with conveyances or gifts by will to illegitimate children. These are dealt with below.[44]

In a separate category are gifts to a person followed by a gift over if he dies without a will. Such gifts over are said to be void as repugnant to the first gift, on the ground that the donor cannot interfere with the law of intestate succession and alter its course.[45] This rule is an anomaly and does not really fit the doctrine of repugnancy. While it is true that at common law a person could not grant a fee after a fee, it is possible to shift the fee upon a stated contingency under a trust or will. Why should a donor not be able to do so when the contingency is the death intestate of the donee? Moreover, as has been stated,[46] if a testator may interfere with the laws of intestacy that would apply on his own death if he had not made a will, why should he not be able to do so on the death intestate of his donee?

A married man could not dispose of his estate so as to defeat his wife's dower right in jurisdictions where dower in its traditional form survived until recently, unless the estate, when acquired, was equitable and always remained so.[47] The same is true of a disposition of the homestead under homesteads legislation, which sometimes applies to both spouses.[48]

Moreover, under recent matrimonial property legislation enacted in most provinces, spouses are given mutual rights of possession in the matrimonial home which cannot be defeated except with consent.[49]

These several rights will be dealt with more fully in the chapters, "The Life Estate"[50] and "Matrimonial Property".[51]

Lands Act, R.S.O. 1980, c. 413. The regulation provides that, for one year after the registration of a subdivision plan creating summer resort locations, only persons who have resided in Ontario for the twelve preceding months may apply for a lease of a summer resort location, and, for a further year thereafter, only such a resident, a Canadian, or a landed immigrant, may apply for such a lease. See also Citizenship Act, S.C. 1974-75-76, c. 108, s. 33, am. 1976-77, c. 52, s. 128(2), and see Spencer, "The Alien Landowner in Canada", 51 Can. Bar Rev. 389 (1973).

[42]Law of Property Act, R.S.M. 1970, c. L90, ss. 2, 3; Property Act, R.S.N.B. 1973, c. P-19, s. 10; Real Property Act, R.S.N.S. 1967, c. 261, s. 1; Aliens' Real Property Act, R.S.O. 1980, c. 19. Cf. Citizenship Act, S.C. 1974-75-76, c. 108, s. 33.

[43]Jewell v. Broad (1909), 19 O.L.R. 1 (H.C.J.), affd 20 O.L.R. 176 (Div. Ct.).

[44]See §§2805.10 and 2805.11, infra.

[45]Re McIntyre (1919), 16 O.W.N. 260 (H.C.); Re Walker (1924), 56 O.L.R. 517 (S.C. App. Div.); Re Gee (1973), 41 D.L.R. (3d) 317, [1974] 2 W.W.R. 176 sub nom. Re Gee Kee (Gee John Kow) (Chee John Kow) (B.C.S.C.).

[46]Williams, "The Doctrine of Repugnancy", 58 L.Q. Rev. 343 (1943), at p. 354.

[47]See §§707-707.13, infra.

[48]See §§710.4-710.8, infra.

[49]See §§1605.1-1605.11, infra.

[50]Ch. 7, infra.

[51]Ch. 16, infra.

(b) By will

Since the *Statute of Wills*[52] in 1540, a person has been able to devise his estate in fee simple by will.[53] This right is subject to the rules against restraints on alienation already discussed, to rules of public policy such as the rule against perpetuities, and to modern legislation against disinheritance of dependants. This legislation, which is based on pioneering statutes passed in Australasia at the beginning of the 20th century, varies from province to province. Generally, however, it enables a dependant of the testator, usually defined as a spouse or infant or incapacitated older children (although often a wider class of dependants is described), to apply to the court for an order for support where adequate provision for the support of the dependants has not been made by the testator. Thus, the Ontario legislation provides:

> 58(1) Where a deceased, whether testate or intestate, has not made adequate provision for the proper support of his dependants or any of them, the court, on application, may order that such provision as it considers adequate be made out of the estate of the deceased for the proper support of the dependants or any of them.[54]

The statutes sometimes apply to intestacy as well.[55]

Moreover, a widow was entitled to dower at common law, as extended by statute, in her husband's real property in jurisdictions where dower was, until recently, still in effect,[56] unless he put her to her election in his will to take the provisions in the will in lieu of dower. Under the western "homesteads" legislation[57] the dower right is abolished[58] and replaced with a right to a life interest in the family home. The right is sometimes given to the husband as well and may accrue to a spouse on the death testate or intestate of the other spouse.

The husband's right of curtesy, a life estate in all his deceased wife's un-

---

[52]32 Hen. 8, c. 1 (1540).

[53]The statute permitted a devise of all lands held in socage tenure and of two-thirds of land held in knight service. When the latter tenure was abolished by the *Tenures Abolition Act*, 12 Car. 2, c. 24 (1660), all land formerly held under that tenure could be devised. Copyholds became devisable by *Preston's Act*, 55 Geo. 3, c. 192 (1815).

[54]*Succession Law Reform Act*, R.S.O. 1980, c. 488, s. 58. For similar legislation see: *Family Relief Act*, R.S.A. 1980, c. F-2, s. 3; R.S.N. 1970, c. 124, s. 3(1); *Wills Variation Act*, R.S.B.C. 1979, c. 435, s. 2(1); *Testators Family Maintenance Act*, R.S.M. 1970, c. T50, s. 3(1); R.S.N.B. 1973, c. T-4, s. 2(1); R.S.N.S. 1967, c. 303, s. 2(1); *Dependants of a Deceased Person Relief Act*, R.S.P.E.I. 1974, c. D-6, s. 2; *Dependants' Relief Act*, R.S.S. 1978, c. D-25, s. 4; *Dependants' Relief Ordinance*, R.O.N.W.T. 1974, c. D-4, s. 3(1); O.Y.T. 1980 (2nd), c. 6, s. 2(1). This type of legislation is dealt with more fully in ch. 28.

[55]See, *e.g.*, *Succession Law Reform Act*, R.S.O. 1980, c. 488, s. 58(1).

[56]See §707 where the statutes and their repeal are set out.

[57]The statutes are cited in §710.2, footnote 1, *infra*.

[58]*Estate Administration Act*, R.S.B.C. 1979, c. 114, s. 107; *Law of Property Act*, R.S.A. 1980, c. L-8, s. 3; R.S.M. 1970, c. L90, s. 9; *Devolution of Real Property Act*, R.S.S. 1978, c. D-27, s. 18; *Intestate Succession Act*, R.S.S. 1978, c. I-13, s. 15; *Land Titles Act*, R.S.C. 1970, c. L-4, s. 5.

disposed of real property, survived in Ontario and Prince Edward Island until recently,[59] but has now been abolished in all provinces.[60]

Certain constructional difficulties may arise in connection with persons who are illegitimate or who are adopted.[61]

(c) On intestacy

At common law after the right to devise land by will was lost, interests in land descended to the heir under the primogeniture rule. On the other hand, while a person could dispose of his personal property by testament, if he failed to do so, it was distributed among his next of kin. Today the rules of descent are otiose since the law of descent has been assimilated into that of the devolution of personal property. The rules of distribution on intestacy are set out in chapter 29.[62]

503.2 Waste as an Incident of an Estate in Fee Simple

The holder of an estate in fee simple has, as an incident of his estate, the right to exercise acts of ownership of all kinds, including the commission of waste, such as felling trees, mining and pulling down buildings.[1] Even when his estate comes to an end with an executory gift over, he is not impeachable for waste,[2] although it was held that in such a case he is in the same position as a life tenant without impeachment for waste and may not commit equitable waste, that is, wanton or malicious acts, such as destruction of houses or felling of trees left for ornament or shelter[3] and, if a will or settlement expressly prohibits waste, it will be restrained.[4]

504. DESTRUCTION OF THE ESTATE IN FEE SIMPLE

The estate in fee simple may be extinguished in a number of ways. Thus, it will come to an end when the owner dies intestate and without heirs, when it

---

[59]*Conveyancing and Law of Property Act*, R.S.O. 1980, c. 90, s. 29; *Devolution of Estates Act*, R.S.O. 1970, c. 129, s. 30(2); *Probate Act*, R.S.P.E.I. 1974, c. P-19, s. 98(1).

[60]*Estate Administration Act*, R.S.B.C. 1979, c. 114, s. 107; *Law of Property Act*, R.S.A. 1980, c. L-8, s. 4; R.S.M. 1970, c. L90, s. 10; *Married Women's Property Act*, R.S.N.B. 1973, c. M-4, s. 8; *Devolution of Real Property Act*, R.S.S. 1978, c. D-27, s. 18; *Intestate Succession Act*, R.S.S. 1978, c. I-13, s. 15; R.S.N.S. 1967, c. 153, s. 2, declaring inapplicable from September 1, 1966, the *Descent of Property Act*, R.S.N.S. 1954, c. 69, under which curtesy was retained; *Chattels Real Act*, R.S.N. 1970, c. 36; *Succession Law Reform Act*, R.S.O. 1980, c. 488, s. 48; *Land Titles Act*, R.S.C. 1970, c. L-4, s. 6; *Family Law Reform Act*, S.P.E.I. 1978, c. 6, s. 62.

[61]See §§2805.10 and 2805.11, *infra*.

[62]See §§2904-2904.6, *infra*.

§503.2

[1]*Attorney-General v. Duke of Marlborough* (1818), 3 Madd. 498, 56 E.R. 588.

[2]*Re Hanbury's Settled Estates*, [1913] 2 Ch. 357.

[3]*Turner v. Wright* (1860), 2 De G. F. & J. 234 at p. 246, 45 E.R. 612.

[4]*Blake v. Peters* (1863), 1 De G. J. & S. 345, 46 E.R. 139 (C.A.). See further §706.8, *infra*, for a more detailed discussion of the law of waste.

escheats to the Crown. Similarly, the estate is forfeit to the Crown on the dissolution of a corporation which has undisposed of assets. The estate may also be determined by adverse possession. This arises where a stranger occupies land in an open and notorious manner to the exclusion of the rightful owner. The stranger is accorded an estate in fee simple by the common law by virtue of his possession, although, for the time being, the estate of the true owner continues. If the stranger occupies the land adversely to the owner for the requisite number of years, usually ten or more, depending upon the province, the several statutes of limitation extinguish the title of the former owner, as well as his right to re-enter or to bring an action to recover possession, and the stranger's estate in fee simple is then absolute.[1] Generally, adverse possession is not possible under land titles systems of land registration.

The several ways in which title may be extinguished are discussed in chapter 31.

505. QUALIFIED FEES SIMPLE

The foregoing discussion has proceeded on the assumption that the fee simple is an absolute estate. It is possible, however, to qualify the estate in certain ways so that it will, or may, determine before its normal time, that is, before the owner of it dies intestate and without heirs. These varieties of the estate are called qualified or defeasible fees simple and, to distinguish it, the unqualified estate is sometimes referred to as the estate in fee simple absolute. There are five types of qualified fees, *viz.*, the conditional fee simple, the base fee, the determinable fee simple, the fee simple subject to a condition subsequent and the fee simple subject to an executory limitation.

505.1 The Conditional Fee Simple

The conditional fee simple is the predecessor of the fee tail. It was an estate granted to a person and the heirs of his body upon a condition, expressed or implied, that if the donee died without heirs, the estate would revert to the donor. If the donee had issue, the condition was performed and the estate became absolute and freely alienable. However, if the land was not aliened, it descended to the heirs of his body as specified in the grant.

As the estate was superseded by the fee tail there is no need to discuss it further.[1] It should be noted, however, that it survives in a few of the American states which did not receive the fee tail.[2] Moreover, this estate should not be confused with the estate upon a condition subsequent which is a quite different interest.

---

§504
[1]See, *e.g.*, *Limitations Act*, R.S.O. 1980, c. 240, ss. 4, 15. But see §3106.21.
§505.1
[1]See further §209.1 (b), *supra*, and §601, *infra*.
[2]1 A.L.P., §§211, 212; 1 *Restatement, Property*, §§68-77.

505.2 The Base Fee

A base fee means exclusively the estate in fee simple into which an estate tail is converted when the issue in tail are barred, but the persons claiming by way of remainder or reversion are not barred. In such a case, the grantee from the tenant in tail has a base fee, being an estate in fee simple which will endure as long as there are issue of the donee in tail, but when they fail, it will come to an end and pass to the person or persons entitled to the remainder or reversion.[1]

505.3 The Determinable Fee Simple

The determinable fee simple, sometimes called a fee simple on limitation or on special limitation, is an estate which will determine automatically on the happening of the event specified on the limitation. Thus, in a grant "to A in fee simple so long as London Bridge stands", the estate determines when London Bridge comes tumbling down. This is not the only occasion for its termination, however, for the estate also comes to an end on the death of the owner intestate and without heirs. Thus the words "so long as London Bridge stands" are an alternative limitation to the words "in fee simple". Moreover, the alternative may never happen, in which case the estate continues until its "natural" end. But the event must not be a certainty, such as the death of a person, or the estate will not be a fee simple.[1]

Under a determinable fee simple, the grantor has a *possibility of reverter*, that is, a possibility of acquiring a vested estate in future. This is known as a mere possibility and is not an estate or interest in land.[2]

There was much argument in the past as to whether a determinable fee simple was possible after *Quia Emptores*.[3] It was argued that the possibility of reverter created a subtenure between the grantor and grantee, which is impossible under that statute.[4] Others, however, maintained that the statute applied only to the fee simple absolute, so that determinable fees were permissible.[5] In fact, possibilities have nothing to do with the law of tenure. They are part of the law of estates, although they are not estates themselves.

In any event, determinable fees simple have now received judicial recognition. Thus, in *Hopper v. Corp. of Liverpool*[6] it was held that the estate was possible. The case appears to construe the limitation in question, which pro-

---

§505.2
[1]See §606.1, *infra*.
§505.3
[1]Megarry and Wade, p. 74.
[2]Challis, p. 83.
[3]18 Edw. 1, cc. 1-3 (1290).
[4]See, *e.g.*, Gray, *The Rule Against Perpetuities*, paras. 31-7; Sanders, *Uses*, p. 17.
[5]*E.g.*, Challis, pp. 437 *et seq.*; Powell, "Determinable Fees", 23 Col. L. Rev. 207 (1923); Farrer, "Reverter to Donor on a Determinable Fee", 50 L.Q. Rev. 33 (1934).
[6](1943), 88 Sol. Jo. 213.

vided in part "so long as the said building . . . shall be used and enjoyed for the uses and purposes of the said institution called the Lyceum . . .", as a condition subsequent. This would seem to be in error as the words used are apt to create a determinable fee simple. Similarly, in *Re Tilbury West Public School and Hastie*,[7] Grant, J., held that a grant in fee simple to the trustees of a school section "for so long as it shall be used and needed for school purposes and no longer" created a valid determinable fee simple.

While each case must depend upon an interpretation of the instrument under consideration, in general it may be said that words indicating duration, such as "so long as", "during", "while" and "until", are apt to create a determinable estate.[8]

Gifts to a person "during widowhood" and similar expressions have already been discussed.[9]

505.4 The Fee Simple upon Condition Subsequent

The fee simple upon condition subsequent is similar on its face to the determinable fee. However, it is created by the addition of a condition to a grant in fee simple, which may cut the estate short at the instance of the grantor. Thus, in a grant "to A in fee simple, provided the land is used for a school", the estate may be determined by the grantor when it is no longer so used. If the specified event does not occur the estate will determine naturally upon the death of the owner intestate and without heirs.

The estate upon condition subsequent should be distinguished from an estate subject to a condition precedent where the grantee receives nothing unless the condition is satisfied. A good example of the distinction arose in *Re Down*.[1] In that case there was a devise to the testator's son when he "arrives at age 30 years providing he stays on the farm". The age qualification was a condition precedent, the requirement that he stay on the farm was construed as a condition subsequent.

In a fee simple upon condition subsequent the grantor retains a *right of entry*, or a right of entry for condition broken. Again, this is a mere right not coupled with an interest in land and it is not an estate or interest itself.[2] As distinguished from a determinable fee, the fee upon condition subsequent does not determine automatically. The grantor must re-enter in order to bring the estate to an end. If he does not, the estate continues.[3]

Fees simple upon condition subsequent were possible at common law.

---

[7][1966] 2 O.R. 20, 55 D.L.R. (2d) 407 (H.C.J.).
[8]*Ibid.*, and see Megarry and Wade, p. 76.
[9]§502.2 (c), *supra*.
§505.4
[1][1968] 2 O.R. 16, 68 D.L.R. (2d) 30 (C.A.).
[2]*Re Taxation of University of Manitoba Lands*, [1940] 1 D.L.R. 579, [1940] 1 W.W.R. 145 (C.A.).
[3]Megarry and Wade, p. 77.

Language apt to create such an estate are words of condition, such as "on condition that", "provided that", "but if", and so on.[4]

The essential distinction between the fee simple upon condition subsequent and the determinable fee is that in the former there is a grant of the fee followed by a separate condition which may determine or defeat the estate granted, while in the latter the determining event is part of the limitation and describes the limits of the estate. The distinction has also been phrased as follows:

> If the purpose is to compel compliance with the condition by the penalty of forfeiture, an estate on condition arises, but if the intent is to give the land for a stated use, the estate to cease when that use or purpose has ended, no penalty for a breach of condition is involved, since the purpose is not to enforce performance of the condition but to convey the property for so long as it is needed for the purpose for which it is given and no longer.[5]

In *Re McKellar*[6] lands were granted to the Canadian National Railway Company. The deed recited that the lands were granted in fee, "but only so long as the said Railway Company shall continue to occupy and use the... lands for [railway] purposes ...". After the description, the deed continued, "... but upon the express condition and understanding that so soon as the said Railway Company shall cease to occupy and use the lands ... for [railway] purposes ... then the fee simple ... shall revert to the [grantor]," and the *habendum* stated that the grant was subject to the above condition. The court held that the *habendum* annexed the condition to the grant so that it conveyed a fee simple upon a condition subsequent and not a determinable fee.[7]

The distinction between determinable fees and fees upon condition subsequent is a fine one and it has, for that reason, been described as "little short of disgraceful to our jurisprudence".[8] Be that as it may, the distinction is real and important consequences flow from it, namely, in the mode of determination, in the applicability of the rule against perpetuities, in the ability to alienate the right of entry and the possibility of reverter and in the application of rules respecting the striking down of conditions for reasons of public policy and uncertainty.

505.5　Special Rules Applicable to Rights of Entry and Possibilities of Reverter

At common law the right of entry and the possibility of reverter could only be reserved to the grantor. They could pass by descent to his heirs, but could

---

[4]*Ibid.*, p. 76. See *Re North Gower Township Public School Board and Todd*, [1968] 1 O.R. 63, 65 D.L.R. (2d) 421 (C.A.).

[5]1 A.L.P., p. 97.

[6][1972] 3 O.R. 16, 27 D.L.R. (3d) 289 (H.C.J.), affd [1973] 3 O.R. 178*n*, 36 D.L.R. (3d) 202*n* (C.A.).

[7]See also *Re Essex County Roman Catholic Separate School Board and Antaya* (1978), 17 O.R. (2d) 307, 80 D.L.R. (3d) 405 (H.C.J.).

[8]*Re King's Trust* (1892), 29 L.R. Ir. 401 at p. 410, *per* Porter, M.R.

not be reserved to a stranger. Nor could they be assigned *inter vivos* or be devised by will.[1] Today they still cannot be reserved to a stranger in a common law grant, but can take effect only as legal or equitable executory interests. However, they can be assigned and devised under legislation to that effect, although there are doubts about the extent and effectiveness of such legislation. This matter is dealt with in the chapter, "Future Interests".[2]

At common law the possibility of reverter was not subject to the rule against perpetuities[3] while the right of entry was.[4] Legislation in respect of perpetuities now generally makes both interests subject to the rule. This matter is dealt with in the chapter, "Perpetuities".[5] Furthermore, since a condition appended to an estate may lead to forfeiture, the law has been jealous in its scrutiny of conditions subsequent and will readily hold them void as offending public policy, as incapable of performance, or for uncertainty. If the condition is void, the estate becomes absolute. Conversely, determinable fees are not dealt with so strictly. However, if the determining event in a determinable fee is void, for example, for uncertainty, the whole estate is void since, if the limitation is struck down, the estate is not properly limited.[6] These matters are dealt with more fully in the chapter, "Invalid Conditions and Conditional Limitations".[7]

505.6 The Fee Simple Subject to an Executory Limitation

The executory gift over is a future interest and will be treated more fully in the chapter, "Future Interests".[1] This interest, sometimes called an interest upon conditional limitation, may be created under a deed to uses, under a trust and, probably, under a modern will. Under these instruments, the common law rule that a possibility and a right of entry cannot be reserved to a stranger is inoperative. In these cases, it is thus possible to shift the fee simple from one person to another on a stated contingency. Thus, in a grant "to A in fee simple to the use of B in fee simple until X marries and then to the use of C in fee simple", B's estate will terminate if X marries. If X dies unmarried, it becomes absolute. The same result can be obtained by using words of condition, such as, "but if X marries".

---

§505.5
[1]Challis, pp. 83, 219.
[2]See § 1012, *infra*.
[3]*Re Tilbury West Public School Board and Hastie*, [1966] 2 O.R. 20, 55 D.L.R. (2d) 407 (H.C.J.). But see, *contra*, *Hopper v. Corp. of Liverpool* (1943), 88 Sol. Jo. 213.
[4]*Re North Gower Township Public School Board and Todd*, [1968] 1 O.R. 63, 65 D.L.R. (2d) 421 (C.A.).
[5]See §§1104.15, 1104.16, 1107.12, *infra*.
[6]Co. Litt. 206 a, b; *Re Greenwood; Goodhart v. Woodhead*, [1903] 1 Ch. 749.
[7]See ch. 9, *infra*, and see Megarry and Wade, pp. 77 *et seq*.
§505.6
[1]See §1011, *infra*.

CHAPTER 6

THE ESTATE IN FEE TAIL

601. DEFINITION

The estate "in fee tail", "estate tail", or "fee tail" may be defined as a free-hold estate of inheritance limited not to the grantee's heirs general, as in the case of the fee simple, but to the heirs of his body. The owner of the estate is called the *tenant in tail*, the line of heirs is called the *entail* and the land is said to be entailed. The word "tail" derives from the Norman-French *tailler*, meaning to carve or cut off. Hence, it signifies an estate that is cut out of the fee simple and it is thus a lesser estate.

602. ORIGIN AND HISTORY

As has been noted,[1] the immediate predecessor of the fee tail was the conditional fee simple which existed at common law prior to the Statute *De Donis*

§602

[1] §§209.1 (b), 505.1, *supra*.

Conditionalibus.[2] This was an estate granted to a person and the heirs of his body, either the heirs general or a particular class of heirs, such as male heirs. It was called a conditional fee because of a condition expressed or implied in the grant that, if the donee died without such heirs, the estate would revert to the donor. The estate was construed as a conditional gift in fee simple on condition that the donee had issue. As soon as he had issue, the condition was regarded as performed and the estate became absolute in the sense that it enabled him to alienate the land so as to bar the issue, or to charge the land with encumbrances that would bind the issue. This was because the birth of the issue made the donor's possible reversion more remote and it was his interest, rather than that of the issue, that was regarded as important. If the donee did not alienate the land, however, it would descend to the heirs of his body specified in the grant, upon the failure of whom it would revert to the donor. For that reason, and in order to ensure that the land would descend in the ordinary way to general heirs entitled to inherit at common law, the donees of conditional fees alienated the land as soon as they had issue and then repurchased the land so as to acquire an absolute fee simple. The construction thus put by the courts upon such conditional gifts deprived the nobility, as donors, of their reversionary rights and, in their own interests, they caused the statute *De Donis* to be passed.[3] It provided that the will of the donor, expressed in the form of the deed, should prevail, so that those to whom the land was given upon such condition should have power to alienate it, but that, after their deaths, it should remain to the specified issue upon the failure of whom, whether because no issue was born, or because the line of issue failed, the land should revert to the donor or his heir.

In construing the statute, the courts held that the donee no longer had a conditional fee simple which became absolute when he had issue but, since the statute did not create any new estate and merely preserved the fee to the issue and the reversion to the donor, they divided the estate into two parts. The part of the donee or tenant in tail came to be called a fee tail; the part of the donor, being the reversion, was the ultimate fee simple expectant upon failure of issue.

The effect of the statute clearly was to restrain the alienation of land, a concept repugnant to the current owners and to the common law. It was, therefore, not surprising that attempts were soon made to bar the entail, so as to give the tenant in tail the fee simple absolute. The two main devices developed for this purpose were the common recovery and the fine. The common recovery was sanctioned by the courts in *Taltarum's Case*.[4] This device involved a fictitious or collusive action. It was commenced by writ of right by the person who was intended to obtain the fee simple against the tenant in tail in possession, who was said to "suffer a recovery" by the action. The plaintiff would

---

[2]13 Edw. 1, c. 1 (1285).
[3]Re-enacted in Ontario by section 1 of the *Act Respecting Real Property*, R.S.O. 1897, c. 330, reprinted in R.S.O. 1950, App. A.
[4](1472), Y. B. 12 Edw. 4, fol. 19.

falsely allege that he had a superior title to the defendant. The defendant would then allege that the land had been conveyed to him in tail with warranty by a third person, X, and he would require X to "vouch the warranty", that is, to defend the action. X would default and judgment would be given to the plaintiff to recover the land and to the defendant to recover lands of equal value from X. X would be a straw man and judgment-proof. In time, the court crier was often used as the vouchee and because he was used so frequently for this purpose, he came to be called the "common vouchee". The effect of the judgment was to bar both the issue of the tenant in tail as well as the reversioner or remainderman, since it had been judicially determined that the plaintiff's title was superior to that of the tenant in tail and his grantor. Moreover, while the judgment against X for equivalent lands was never acted upon, since he was judgment-proof, it was regarded as sufficient compensation for the defendant.

Subsequently, the plaintiff would convey the land to the erstwhile tenant in tail, or, at his direction, to some third person.

It should be noted that, if the estate tail was preceded by a life estate, the consent of the life tenant, called "the protector of the settlement", was necessary in order to complete the proceedings. This was because a common recovery could be brought only against a person seised of the land. This provision was retained in subsequent estates tail legislation.[5]

The fine also involved an action, but in this case the action was settled, resulting in a "final accord" between the parties, which was entered as a judgment with the approval of the court. The practice of "levying a fine" was prohibited by De Donis itself, but was subsequently revived by statute.[6] The fine only barred the issue, however, not the reversioner or remainderman, and gave the tenant in tail only a qualified fee simple, the base fee, which would last only as long as the issue of the tenant in tail survived.[7]

The actions of fine and common recovery were not used in the Canadian colonies because, initially, there was no common bench on whose roll they could be enrolled.[8]

In the 19th century, these cumbersome devices were replaced by statute. The Fines and Recoveries Act[9] substituted the simple device of permitting a tenant in tail, with the consent of the protector, if any, to bar the entail, by conveying the land in fee simple and enrolling the deed in the High Court of Chancery.[10] This legislation was declared in force in Manitoba.[11] In other

---

[5]Plucknett, pp. 620-2.
[6]Statute of Fines, 1 Ric. 3, c. 7 (1484), re-enacted 4 Hen. 7, c. 24 (1489), 28 Hen. 8, c. 36 (1536), and 32 Hen. 8, c. 36 (1540).
[7]Plucknett, p. 619.
[8]Re Wright and Riach (1923), 54 O.L.R. 404 at p. 409, [1924] 2 D.L.R. 273 at p. 276 (S.C. App. Div.), per Riddell, J.; Re Estate of Simpson (1863), 5 N.S.R. 317 (C.A.).
[9]3 & 4 Wm. 4, c. 74 (1833).
[10]Plucknett, p. 622.
[11]See now Law of Property Act, R.S.M. 1970, c. L90, s. 30(1); infra, §607.1.

provinces, statutes modelled on the English Act were passed but these have since been repealed in most cases.[12]

The *Fines and Recoveries Act* merely confirmed the judicial antipathy to restraints on alienation, for the courts had long since declared that unbarrable entails could not be created. A condition that a tenant in tail could not suffer a common recovery or levy a fine was, therefore, void.[13] This rule was not abrogated by the Act of 1833.[14]

In England, important changes were made in the law of entails by the *Law of Property Act, 1925*,[15] the most important of which were that fees tail could thereafter exist only in equity under a trust,[16] personalty could be entailed,[17] disentailing assurances no longer had to be enrolled,[18] and the estate could be barred by will.[19]

It should be noted that, as *De Donis* applied only to freehold lands, conditional gifts analogous to the conditional fee may, presumably, still be created with respect to other hereditaments.

603. TYPES OF ESTATE TAIL

The person creating an estate tail by deed or will may limit the estate to a man and the heirs of his body, or the male or female heirs of his body, without restriction as to the wife by whom they are to be born, or he may limit it to a man and the heirs or male heirs or female heirs of his body by a particular wife. Similarly, he may limit it in any such way to a woman and the heirs of her body. Therefore, there are six classifications of estates tail known by the following names:[1]

Estate in Tail General — One unrestricted either as to sex of the issue or as to spouse, *e.g.*, "to X and the heirs of his body".

Estate in Tail Male General — One restricted to male issue but not restricted as to spouse, *e.g.*, "to A and the heirs male of his body".

Estate in Tail Female General — One restricted to female issue but not restricted as to spouse, *e.g.*, "to A and the heirs female of his body".

Estate in Tail Special — One restricted to issue of any sex by two particular spouses, *e.g.*, "to X and the heirs of his body begotten upon Y".

Estate in Tail Male Special — One restricted to male issue by two particular spouses, *e.g.*, "to X and the heirs male of his body begotten upon Y".

12See §607, *infra.*
13See, *e.g., Mildmay's Case* (1605), 6 Co. Rep. 40 a, 77 E.R. 311.
14See *Dawkins v. Lord Penrhyn* (1878), 4 App. Cas. 51 (H.L.), at p. 64.
1515 & 16 Geo. 5, c. 20 (1925).
16*Ibid.*, s. 1.
17*Ibid.*, s. 130(1).
18*Ibid.*, s. 133.
19*Ibid.*, s. 176. See Megarry and Wade, pp. 94-6.
§603
1Co. Litt. 21.

Estate in Tail Female Special — One restricted to female issue by two particular spouses, *e.g.*, "to A and the heirs female of his body begotten upon Y".

604. CHARACTERISTICS OF THE ESTATE TAIL

The two main distinguishing features of the estate tail are the rules of inheritance applicable to it and the restraints on alienation. These and others are discussed below.

604.1 Inheritance

The rules of inheritance for the fee tail were identical to the common law rules of descent applicable to the fee simple, with the obvious exception that collaterals were excluded, as were lineal ascendants. Descent was traced from the last purchaser, that is, from the original donee in tail and not from the person entitled by descent. Thus the land would descend to the heir-at-law of the original tenant in tail under the principle of primogeniture. Under this principle, males were preferred to females and the eldest son was preferred to later sons.[1]

If the estate is in *tail general*, the issue of the donee, by whatever marriage and of either sex, are capable of inheriting in succession. Elder sons and their issue inherit before younger sons and their issue, sons and their issue inherit before daughters and their issue, and daughters inherit equally among themselves, the issue of each daughter taking such daughter's share.

If the estate is in *tail male general*, only male issue claiming continuously through male issue can inherit, elder sons having priority over younger sons.

If the estate is in *tail female general*, only female issue claiming continuously through female issue can inherit.

An estate in *tail special* may be a limitation to the donee and the heirs of his or her body by a particular wife or husband, or it may be a limitation to a man and woman already married, or able lawfully to marry, and the heirs of their bodies. In the first case, the donee has an estate in tail special, and in the second case, the two donees have a joint estate in tail special. If the estate is in tail male special, or tail female special, the issue inherit under the same rules as applied, respectively, to estates in tail male general and tail female general.

It is not necessary, however, that the spouse who is to have the issue be specifically named. It is sufficient if he or she is defined as belonging to a class. Thus, where there was a devise to "Charles, if he married a fit and worthy gentlewoman, and his issue male", it was held that he took an estate in special tail male.[2] Also, a devise to a person with a provision that no person was to

---

§604.1

[1]For a more detailed discussion of the common law rules of descent, see, *infra*, §2902, and see 2 Pollock and Maitland, p. 260.
[2]*Pelham Clinton v. Duke of Newcastle*, [1902] 1 Ch. 34 (C.A.), affd [1903] A.C. 111 (H.L.).

inherit, "unless a lawful issue of a male child got by marriage with a respectable Protestant female, of proper conducted parents", was held to create an estate in special tail male.[3]

In the case of a tail special, if the named spouse predeceased the tenant in tail without leaving issue, he was thereafter known as a "tenant in tail after possibility of issue extinct", as he had effectively only a life estate. In distinction from other tenants in tail, he could not then bar the entail[4] and was liable to equitable waste.[5]

There can be a limitation for one type of estate tail followed by a remainder for another type, such as a limitation in tail male followed by a remainder in tail general, thus exhausting all possible issue.

It is thus apparent, for example, that (a) in the case of a tail male, the son of a daughter cannot inherit; (b) in the case of a tail female, the daughter of a son cannot inherit; and (c) in the case of a tail male special, if the donee in tail has only a daughter by his first wife and, upon a second marriage, has a son, neither child can inherit. Descent in the required manner must be unbroken. If the required issue are not born to the donee in tail, or if the required line of issue comes to an end, the estate reverts to the donor and his heirs, or goes over to the remaindermen.

604.2 Alienability

Because of its nature, that is, that it had to descend to a particular class of heirs, the estate was rendered inalienable by *De Donis*. A tenant in tail could alienate the land in fact, but his issue or the reversioner or remainderman could defeat the estate so created after his death,[1] so that effectively only a life estate *pur autre vie* was created.[2] As has been shown, once the estate became barrable by fine or common recovery, and subsequently by the statutory method of the disentailing assurance, the fee tail was almost as freely alienable as the fee simple.[3]

604.3 Other Characteristics

Apart from the restrictions on inheritance and alienation, the tenant in tail had virtually the same rights as a tenant in fee simple. He was not liable for

---

[3]*Magee v. Martin*, [1902] 1 I.R. 367 (C.A.).
[4]*Recoveries Act*, 32 Hen. 8, c. 31 (1540), 14 Eliz. 1, c. 8 (1572), and see also *Fines and Recoveries Act*, 3 & 4 Wm. 4, c. 74 (1833), s. 18. This provision was incorporated in the Ontario *Estates Tail Act*, R.S.O. 1950, c. 117, s. 4.
[5]See generally Megarry and Wade, pp. 97-8.
§604.2
[1]*Viz.*, by the writs of "formedon in the descender", "formedon in the remainder", and "formedon in the reverter". The first of these was provided for in *De Donis*. See 2 Pollock and Maitland, p. 28.
[2]Megarry and Wade, p. 84.
[3]*Supra*, §§209.1(b), 212.

waste of any kind[1] and could, by statute, grant long-term leases that were binding on his issue.[2] Moreover, the wife of a tenant in tail was entitled to dower in the lands and the husband of a tenant in tail to an estate by the curtesy.

With respect to impeachability for waste, it has been seen that a "tenant in tail after possibility of issue extinct" could be restrained from committing equitable or malicious waste, such as tearing down the main residence without cause.[3] Equity protected the remainderman or reversioner in such a case since, as in the case of a life estate, the reversion or remainder is certain to fall into possession.

605.　CREATION OF ESTATES TAIL

As in the case of the fee simple,[1] at common law the rules for the creation of the estate tail had to be strictly observed in the case of *inter vivos* dispositions. In the case of wills the rules were more relaxed. The rules were simplified by legislation in the 19th century.

605.1　Inter Vivos Dispositions

(a)　At common law

In order to create an estate tail by deed at common law, it was necessary to limit it to a person and the heirs of his body. The word "heirs" was essential;[1] the words "of his body" were not. Words signifying that the heirs were to issue from the body of the donee, such as "of his flesh" or "from him proceeding" were sufficient to indicate that only direct lineal descendants were intended and not heirs generally, whether lineal or collateral.[2] Thus, a limitation to the "right heirs" of a person by a particular wife, was held sufficient to create an estate tail.[3] A limitation to the grantee and his heirs, which ordinarily passes a fee simple, will be cut down to an estate tail if it provides that, in the event he

---

§604.3

[1]*Attorney-General v. Duke of Marlborough* (1818), 3 Madd. 498, 56 E.R. 588.
[2]*Statute of Leases*, 32 Hen. 8, c. 28 (1540). See Megarry and Wade, p. 93.
[3]See §604.1, at footnote 5, and see *Turner v. Wright* (1860), 2 De G. F. & J. 234, 45 E.R. 612.

§605

[1]See, *supra*, §502.1(a).

§605.1

[1]Co. Litt. 20 a, b; *Seagood v. Hone* (1634), Cro. Car. 366, 79 E.R. 920; *Wheeler v. Duke* (1832), 1 C. & M. 210, 149 E.R. 377; *Phillips v. James* (1865), 2 Dr. & Sm. 404, 62 E.R. 675, affd 3 De G. J. & S. 72, 46 E.R. 565 (C.A.).
[2]Co. Litt. 20 b; *Beresford's Case* (1607), 7 Co. Rep. 41 a, 77 E.R. 471; *Idle v. Cooke* (1705), 2 Ld. Raym. 1144 at p. 1153, 92 E.R. 257; *Jack d. Westby v. Fetherstone* (1829), 2 Hud. & B. 320 (Ir.); *Re Ley* (1912), 5 D.L.R. 1, 2 W.W.R. 790 (B.C.C.A.); *Re Wright and Riach* (1923), 54 O.L.R. 404, [1924] 2 D.L.R. 273 (S.C. App. Div.); *Re Carr and Smith*, [1950] O.R. 26, [1950] 1 D.L.R. 747 (H.C.J.).
[3]*Wright v. Vernon* (1854), 2 Drew 439, 61 E.R. 789, affd 7 H.L.C. 35, 11 E.R. 15.

should die "without heirs", there is a gift over to a person capable of being his collateral heir, because that indicates that "without heirs" means without heirs of his body.[4]

The rule in *Shelley's Case*[5] applies to any freehold estate, so that a grant to a person for life with remainder to the heirs of his body, or a similar expression signifying such heirs, will convey an estate tail to the grantee and not a mere life estate.[6]

(b) By statute

In England, these rules were very much simplified by the *Conveyancing and Law of Property Act*.[7] This legislation was adopted in the Canadian provinces. The several statutes provided in effect that, in a *deed* limiting an estate tail, it was no longer necessary to use the words "heirs of the body" or "heirs male of the body" or "heirs female of the body", it being sufficient to use the words "in tail" or "in tail male" or "in tail female", according to the intent, or to use words sufficiently indicating the limitation intended. The legislation, however, made no reference to an *estate tail special* and, to create one by deed, it would probably be necessary to adhere to the rules of common law.[8]

It should be noted that in Manitoba, which still retains the fee tail, there is no similar legislation in force with respect to the fee tail. The Manitoba statute merely provides that no words of limitation are necessary in a conveyance and that such conveyance passes all the title the grantor has unless a contrary intention is expressed.[9] This would seem to suggest that a fee tail, unless it is created by words indicating a contrary intention, must still be created by the common law formula.

605.2 Testamentary Dispositions

(a) Generally

As in the case of an estate in fee simple, the strict common law rule as to the words that must be used to create an estate tail by deed did not apply to a will (in regard to which more latitude was allowed) under the fundamental rule that the testator's intent was to be ascertained and given effect to. Consequently, a devise to a person and his "issue" would create an estate tail, unless other language in the will indicated that the word was not used in its primary sense,

---

[4]*Wall v. Wright* (1837), 1 Dr. & Wal. 1, 56 R.R. 147 (Ir.); *Re Smith's Estate* (1891), L.R. 27 Ir. 121; *Re Waugh; Waugh v. Cripps*, [1903] 1 Ch. 744.
[5](1581), 1 Co. Rep. 93 b, 76 E.R. 206.
[6]For a more detailed discussion of this rule see §1009.6, *infra*.
[7]44 & 45 Vict., c. 41 (1881), s. 51. See §502.1(b), *supra*.
[8]See, *e.g.*, *Conveyancing and Law of Property Act*, R.S.O. 1950, c. 68, s. 4.
[9]*Law of Property Act*, R.S.M. 1970, c. L90, s. 4, and see also the *Wills Act*, R.S.M. 1970, c. W150, s. 26, to the same effect.

as meaning heirs of the body,[1] and a devise to a person and "his heirs lawfully begotten" would create an estate tail.[2] Where a testator devised his property to his daughter with a gift over to his brothers and sisters "in the event of her dying without heirs", it was held that in view of the fact that the respective devisees were so related, "heirs" meant heirs of the body and the daughter took an estate tail.[3] Again, where a testator devised a farm to his son with a gift over to the rest of the "family" who survived him if the son died without leaving an "heir", it was held that the words "heir" and "family" meant heirs of the body and the son took an estate tail.[4]

However, in another case where the testator devised his farm to X as long as he lived and, if X had any "family", then the farm would become his own, it was held that as the primary meaning of "family" is "children" and not "heirs of the body", the rule that if an ulterior devisee stands related to the prior devisee in descent the word "heirs" should be construed as heirs of the body, was not applicable. Hence, X did not receive a fee tail, but a life estate and a remainder in fee simple, subject to a condition precedent that he should have family, which he did not.[5]

As in the case of a devise in fee simple, if words of limitation clearly devise an estate tail, no subsequent words of restriction, "no inference of intention, however irresistible, no declaration of it, however explicit, will have the slightest effect".[6] Thus, words empowering the devisee to vary the proportions of the heirs,[7] or a direction that if the devisee should leave no heirs of his body "the land is to be divided equally among his brothers and sisters him surviving, to hold to them and their assigns forever", would be repugnant to the estate tail granted.[8]

Since the rule in *Shelley's Case*[9] applies to the devise of any freehold estate, if a testator devises land to a person for life, with remainder to the "heirs of his body" or to his "issue" or using any other expression signifying such heirs, the devisee will take an estate tail of the general or special classification indicated by the words used. In every such case, the language of the gift that is to follow the life estate must be construed according to the ordinary rules of

---

§605.2

[1]*Roddy v. Fitzgerald* (1858), 6 H.L.C. 823, 10 E.R. 1518; *King v. Evans* (1895), 24 S.C.R. 356.

[2]*Ray v. Gould* (1857), 15 U.C.Q.B. 131. Presumably the words "in fee tail", or words of similar import, would also create a fee tail, having regard to the lenient approach to wills by the courts and by analogy to the statutory rules respecting conveyances *inter vivos*: see §605.1, footnotes 7 and 8, *supra*. If no words of limitation were used, however, a fee simple would be created, at least if the testator had such an estate to give: see statutes collected in §502.1, footnotes 19-21.

[3]*Re McDonald* (1903), 6 O.L.R. 478 (H.C.J.).

[4]*Re Thompson*, [1936] O.R. 8, [1936] 1 D.L.R. 39 (C.A.).

[5]*Re McKellar*, [1972] 3 O.R. 320, 28 D.L.R. (3d) 162 (H.C.J.).

[6]*Jordan v. Adams* (1861), 9 C.B. (N.S.) 483 at p. 499, 142 E.R. 190, *per* Cockburn, C.J.

[7]*Fleming v. McDougall* (1880), 27 Gr. 459.

[8]*Re Cleator* (1885), 10 O.R. 326.

[9](1581), 1 Co. Rep. 93 b, 76 E.R. 206. See further §1009.6, *infra*.

construction. If the language indicates that the testator used the words "heirs of the body" or "issue" or similar words in a restricted sense, meaning children, or some individual who would be the heir of the body of the devisee at the time of his death, the devisee will take only a life estate. If the language, however, indicates that the testator meant a line of lineal descendants, the rule will apply and the devisee will take an estate tail, no matter what restriction or conditions were added by the testator, for the rule is a rule of law, not one of construction, so that the intention of the testator is irrelevant. Indeed, the rule often defeats the actual intent of the testator, whose attempt to impose restrictions or conditions is contrary to law as being repugnant to the estate created.[10] The fact that the testator adds distributive words, indicating how the gift is to be distributed among the heirs, for example, that it is to go to them "share and share alike", or is "equally to be divided among them", does not take the case out of the operation of the rule.[11]

A testator may use the word "heir" as a collective name for "heirs", in which case the rule will operate. Thus, where a testator devised land to a person and "on his death to his male heir forever", it was held that the rule operated and the devisee took an estate tail.[12] In another case, a testator devised land to his son for life and after his death to his heir-at-law should he have any and if not, to his brother, and it was held that the son took a defeasible estate in fee simple or fee tail which, upon his death without such an heir, was defeated by the executory devise to the brother in fee simple.[13] If, however, a testator clearly uses the word "heir" or "heirs" as meaning "child" or "children", the rule does not apply. Thus, where a testator devised land to his son for life and, if he should leave a lawful heir or heirs, the lands were to be equally divided among them "at the death of their father", it was held that the use of the word "father" indicated that "heirs" meant children.[14]

A testator may use the word "heirs" as meaning "heirs of the body", so as to give the devisee a fee tail instead of a fee simple, and where a testator devised land to a son for life and on his death to his heirs, with a gift over if he died without leaving a child or children, it was held that the son took an estate tail, because the testator's reference to children showed that by heirs he meant heirs of the body.[15]

The word "issue" primarily means heirs of the body or lineal descendants and will be given that meaning as a word of limitation, unless the language of the will clearly shows that children are meant.[16] Where there was a devise to

---

[10]*Van Grutten v. Foxwell*, [1897] A.C. 658 (H.L.). See also *Tunis v. Passmore* (1872), 32 U.C.Q.B. 419; *Re Romanes and Smith* (1880), 8 P.R. (Ont.) 323; *Re Kendrew* (1918), 43 O.L.R. 185 (S.C. App. Div.).

[11]*Van Grutten v. Foxwell, supra; Re McTavish* (1923), 25 O.W.N. 362 (S.C.).

[12]*Silcocks v. Silcocks*, [1916] 2 Ch. 161.

[13]*Grant v. Squire* (1901), 2 O.L.R. 131 (H.C.J.).

[14]*Smith v. Smith* (1885), 8 O.R. 677 (H.C.J.).

[15]*Re Cole and Clarkson* (1921), 21 O.W.N. 88 (H.C.).

[16]*Roddy v. Fitzgerald* (1858), 6 H.L.C. 823, 10 E.R. 1518; *Re Davidson* (1926), 59 O.L.R. 643 (C.A.); *Watson v. Phillips* (1910), 2 O.W.N. 261 (H.C.J.).

a person for life and after his death to his issue "and their heirs", the addition of those words did not change the primary meaning of the word "issue" and the devisee took an estate tail under the rule in *Shelley's Case*.[17] On the other hand, where there was a devise to the testator's daughters for their lives as tenants in common, with remainder to "their respective issues in fee so that the child or children of each will take his, her or their mother's share", it was held that by "issues" the testator meant children, so that the rule did not apply and the daughters got a life estate and not an estate tail.[18]

The word "descendants" *prima facie* means heirs of the body and where a testator uses it in its primary sense and devises to a person for life with remainder to his descendants, the devisee takes an estate tail under the rule.[19]

On the other hand, the word "children" *prima facie* means the immediate offspring and where a testator does not use it in the broader sense of heirs or heirs of the body, but only uses it in its ordinary sense, as where he devises to a person for life and after his death to his children, the rule does not apply and the devisee takes only a life estate.[20] If words of division or inheritance are attached to the gift to the children, they still take as purchasers and the rule does not apply.[21]

(b) The rule in Wild's Case

A fundamental rule of construction of importance on the subject of estates tail created by will is the rule in *Wild's Case*.[22] It laid down the following three principles:

(1) If a testator devises land to A and his children, or to A and his issue, and A has no issue at the date of the will, A takes an estate tail. This is called the first branch of the rule in *Wild's Case*.

(2) If, under such a devise, A has issue at the date of the will, the words "children" or "issue" are construed as words of purchase, and not as words of limitation. Thus, A would take jointly for life with those of his children who were alive at the testator's death, the gift being a class gift. This is known as the second branch of the rule in *Wild's Case*.

(3) If a testator devises land to A for life and on his death to his children, even if A has no children at the date of the will, he takes only a life estate and the children take a remainder in fee simple, at least if the devise can be construed as comprising two gifts, with the gift to the children being post-

---

[17]*Parker v. Clarke* (1856), 6 De G. M. & G. 104 at p. 109, 43 E.R. 1169.
[18]*Re Taylor* (1916), 36 O.L.R. 116, 28 D.L.R. 488 (S.C.). See also *Montreuil v. Walker* (1911), 3 O.W.N. 166 (H.C.J.); *Re Russell* (1915), 8 O.W.N. 248 (S.C.).
[19]*Re Sutherland* (1912), 19 O.W.R. 702 (H.C.J.).
[20]*Grant v. Fuller* (1902), 33 S.C.R. 34; *Chandler v. Gibson* (1901), 2 O.L.R. 442 (C.A.); *Re Simpson*, [1928] 3 D.L.R. 773, [1928] S.C.R. 329.
[21]*Bowen v. Lewis* (1884), 9 App. Cas. 890 (H.L.); *Re Simpson, supra*. For a more detailed discussion of the rule in *Shelley's Case* see §1009.6, *infra*.
[22](1599), 6 Co. Rep. 16 b, 77 E.R. 277.

poned. Otherwise A would take a fee tail. This is called the third branch of the rule in *Wild's Case*.

These rules of construction are always subject in their operation to a contrary intent expressed in the will.[23]

The following are Canadian applications of the rule:

Where a testator devised land to a man and his wife "and to their children and children's children forever", and provided that the couple should not be at liberty to dispose of the land, "as it is my will that the same may be entailed for the benefit of their children", it was held that the couple took an estate by the entireties for their joint lives and the life of the survivor and, further, that a mortgage made by them was valid as regards their life interest.[24]

Where a testator devised land to a woman for life "and to her children, if any, at her death" and she had no children at the date of the will, it was held that she took only a life estate because the gift to the children was not immediate and the word "children" cannot be construed as a word of limitation.[25]

Where a testator devised land to a man for life, with remainder "to his first and each subsequent son successively according to seniority" and failing sons to his daughters, and the devisee died unmarried and without issue, it was held that he took only a life estate.[26]

A power of appointment given to a tenant in tail to appoint to some one or more of his children, does not prevent the operation of the rule.[27]

Since the estate tail has been abolished in most Canadian jurisdictions, the rule in *Wild's Case* now has limited application. Under the first branch, A would today probably get the fee simple,[28] or, perhaps, a life estate with remainder in fee simple to the children. The point has never been determined.[29] Today, A and his children would take the fee simple estate as tenants in common and not as joint tenants under the second branch of the rule.[30] The third branch of the rule still operates as before, except that an estate tail can no longer be raised in such circumstances.

---

[23]*Byng v. Byng* (1862), 10 H.L.C. 171 at p. 178, 11 E.R. 991, *per* Lord Cranworth.

[24]*Peterborough Real Estate Co. v. Patterson* (1888), 15 O.A.R. 751: 2nd branch.

[25]*Grant v. Fuller* (1902), 33 S.C.R. 34: 3rd branch. Contrast *Re Haig* (1925), 57 O.L.R. 129 (S.C. App. Div.). The *Haig* case failed to consider the third branch of the rule and is thus probably wrongly decided.

[26]*Re Beckstead* (1928), 62 O.L.R. 690, [1928] 4 D.L.R. 666 (S.C.): 3rd branch.

[27]*Re Smith and Love* (1920), 18 O.W.N. 181 (H.C.): 1st branch.

[28]Because the statutes abolishing the fee tail provide that a limitation that formerly would have created a fee tail shall be construed as an estate in fee simple or the greatest estate the testator had in the land. See, *e.g.*, *Conveyancing and Law of Property Act*, R.S.O. 1980, c. 90, s. 4.

[29]See Bailey, "The Law of Property Act, 1921, s. 130(2)", 6 C.L.J. 67 (1936-38); Megarry, "To A and his issue: The Law of Property Act, 1925, Section 130(2)", 9 C.L.J. 46 (1945-47); Bailey, *ibid.*, p. 185; Ross, "Real Property — Judicial Construction of 'to A and His Children' ", 75 W.Va. L. Rev. 296 (1972-73).

[30]*Conveyancing and Law of Property Act*, R.S.O. 1980, c. 90, s. 13; *Succession Law Reform Act*, R.S.O. 1980, c. 488, s. 26. There is comparable legislation in other jurisdictions.

(c) Death without issue

Prior to 19th century legislative changes, if land were devised to a person, or to a person and his heirs, with a gift over if such person should die without issue, or without having issue, or without leaving issue, the words meant an indefinite failure of issue at any time and the devisee took an estate tail.[31] This rule of construction applied only to realty, since personalty could not be entailed.[32] Moreover, while under an estate tail a gift over in default of issue did not offend the rule against perpetuities if it were vested, or certain to vest prior to the determination of the estate tail, a gift over of personalty in default of issue would offend the rule, since it might vest too remotely, namely, whenever the donee's issue died out.[33] By section 29 of the Imperial *Wills Act,*[34] and by section 28 of the corresponding Ontario Act,[35] in any devise or bequest of realty or personalty, the words "die without issue" or "die without leaving issue" or "have no issue" or other words which import a want of issue or failure of issue of any person in his lifetime or at his death, or an indefinite failure of his issue, shall be construed to mean a want or failure of issue in his lifetime or at his death and not an indefinite failure of issue, unless a contrary intention appears by the will by reason of such person having a prior estate tail, or by reason of a preceding gift which, without any implication arising from such words, is a limitation of an estate tail to him or his issue or otherwise, but the legislation provides that it does not extend to cases where words import if no issue described in a preceding gift be born, or if there be no issue who live to attain the age, or otherwise answer the description required for obtaining a vested estate by a preceding gift to such issue.

Cases decided under this legislation have held that no implication of an estate tail can arise from words in a will made or republished since the date of enactment of the legislation importing a failure of issue, unless an intention to use the words as denoting an indefinite failure of issue is very distinctly marked. The result of the legislation appears to be that the words denoting a failure of issue mean a failure at the time of death in every case, unless the words refer to a prior estate or preceding gift, or they are so clearly used to denote a failure of issue at any time as to exclude the statutory rule of construction, which only applies where there is ambiguity as to whether the words mean failure of issue in the lifetime of the person, or at death, or an indefinite failure of issue.[36]

Similar legislation was enacted in the other common law provinces and the

---

[31]*Sisson v. Ellis* (1860), 19 U.C.Q.B. 559; *Little v. Billings* (1880), 27 Gr. 353; *VanTassell v. Frederick* (1896), 27 O.R. 646 (H.C.J.).

[32]*Doe d. Ellis v. Ellis* (1808), 9 East. 382, 103 E.R. 618.

[33]*Candy v. Campbell* (1834), 2 Cl. & Fin. 421, 6 E.R. 1213; Megarry and Wade, pp. 263, 505.

[34]7 Wm. 4 & 1 Vict., c. 26 (1837).

[35]*Succession Law Reform Act,* R.S.O. 1980, c. 488.

[36]*Martin v. Chandlar* (1894), 26 O.R. 81 (Q.B.).

Territories.[37] Because of the general abolition of the estate tail, modern versions of the legislation, that is, the legislation in force in those jurisdictions which have adopted the *Uniform Wills Act*,[38] no longer make reference to the estate tail.[39]

Strangely, while in Newfoundland the estate tail has been abolished, since all real property interests in that province are converted into chattels real,[40] section 17 of the *Wills Act*[41] refers to a contrary intention appearing in the will "by reason of such person having a prior *quasi estate tail*". This is not the same as the *quasi*-entail created out of an estate *pur autre vie* as in a gift "to A and the heirs of his body for the life of Y".[42] Rather, it is an interest created in chattels real which would have been an estate tail if the property were real property.

The statutory provision has been applied to a gift over on death "without leaving male issue".[43] The statutory rule of construction, however, is to be construed strictly and confined to cases in which the word "issue", or some word having precisely that meaning, is used and does not extend to cases in which the word "heirs" is used.[44] Where the statutory provision applies, a devise, instead of giving an estate tail, now creates an estate in fee simple, with an executory devise over on the death of the devisee without issue then living.[45]

The legislation as it now stands still presents practical difficulties since the devisee cannot know until his death whether or not the gift over will take effect. This problem was rectified in England by section 10 of the *Conveyancing Act, 1882*,[46] which provided that the gift over became void as soon as the devisee had issue who attained his majority, so that the devisee's interest would become absolute at that time. This legislation was not incorporated into the Canadian statutes.

In those jurisdictions in which the estate tail has been abolished, it can, of course, no longer be raised by a contrary intention.

---

[37]*Wills Act*, R.S.A. 1980, c. W-11, s. 28; R.S.B.C. 1979, c. 434, s. 26; R.S.M. 1970, c. W150, s. 28; R.S.N. 1970, c. 401, s. 17; R.S.N.B. 1973, c. W-9, s. 27; R.S.N.S. 1967, c. 340, s. 27; *Probate Act*, R.S.P.E.I. 1974, c. P-19, s. 80; *Wills Act*, R.S.S. 1978, c. W-14, s. 28; *Wills Ordinance*, R.O.N.W.T. 1974, c. W-3, s. 21; R.O.Y.T. 1971, c. W-3, s. 20(1).

[38]*Uniform Acts of the Uniform Law Conference of Canada* (Queen's Park, Toronto, 1978), p. 53-1.

[39]See, *e.g.*, *Wills Act*, R.S.M. 1970, c. W150, s. 28; *Succession Law Reform Act*, R.S.O. 1980, c. 488, s. 28.

[40]See, *infra*, §607.

[41]R.S.N. 1970, c. 401.

[42]See Megarry and Wade, p. 102.

[43]*Re Edwards*; *Edwards v. Edwards*, [1894] 3 Ch. 644; *Upton v. Hardman* (1874), I.R. 9 Eq. 157.

[44]*Re Leach*; *Leach v. Leach*, [1912] 2 Ch. 422 at p. 428; *Re Brown and Campbell* (1898), 29 O.R. 402.

[45]*Nason v. Armstrong* (1894), 21 O.A.R. 183, revd on other grounds 25 S.C.R. 263; *Re Pettigrew* (1929), 36 O.W.N. 182 (H.C.); *Re Toll and Mills* (1919), 16 O.W.N. 215 (H.C.).

[46]45 & 46 Vict., c. 39 (1882).

605.3 Qualified Estates Tail

As in the case of the fee simple, a fee tail may be qualified as a determinable estate or as an estate upon condition subsequent. It may also be subject to a condition precedent.[1] The same principles as discussed in connection with the fee simple would apply in such a case.[2] Thus, for example, a restraint on alienation would be void.[3]

606. BARRING THE ENTAIL

The *Fines and Recoveries Act* of 1833[1] and the Canadian legislation based thereon essentially provided for two modes of barring the entail. The first and most important of these was by deed. The second was by mortgage. The estate could not be barred by will or by a mere contract.[2] In England the estate can now be barred by will.[3]

Subject to the provisions regarding the protector of the settlement, discussed below, if the tenant in tail used the method of the deed, the legislation stated that the grantee from him acquired a fee simple estate.[4]

Alternatively, he could mortgage the land, in which case the entail would also be barred and, when the mortgage was discharged, the tenant in tail would acquire the fee simple.[5] Indeed, even if the mortgage was not discharged, the mortgage operated so as to give the fee simple to the mortgagee and also to bar the entail as regards the mortgagor.[6] A tenant in tail could also acquire the land himself by the first method by conveying to a trustee for himself, or he could convey to his own use under the *Statute of Uses*.[7] As a result of subsequent legislation permitting a person to convey to himself,[8] a tenant in tail could simply bar the entail by executing a deed in favour of himself.

All instruments barring the entail had to be enrolled or recorded within six months of execution. In England, this was done in the Court of Chancery.[9]

---

§605.3
[1]Challis, p. 253.
[2]*Supra*, §§502.1(c), 502.2(c).
[3]*Re Fenner and Martin* (1927), 32 O.W.N. 212 (H.C.).
§606
[1]3 & 4 Wm. 4, c. 74 (1833) (hereafter referred to as "F.R.A.").
[2]F.R.A., s. 40; *Estates Tail Act*, R.S.O. 1950, c. 117, s. 24 (hereafter referred to as the "Ontario Act").
[3]*Law of Property Act, 1925*, 15 & 16 Geo. 5, c. 20, s. 176.
[4]F.R.A., s. 15; Ontario Act, s. 3.
[5]F.R.A., s. 21; Ontario Act, s. 7; *Re Fenner and Martin* (1927), 32 O.W.N. 212 (H.C.).
[6]*Culbertson v. McCullough* (1900), 27 O.A.R. 459.
[7]27 Hen. 8, c. 10 (1535).
[8]See, *e.g.*, *Conveyancing and Law of Property Act*, S.O. 1933, c. 9, s. 39a. The section was taken from the *Law of Property Act, 1925*, 15 Geo. 5, c. 20, s. 72(3) (U.K.). See *Re Sherrett and Gray*, [1933] O.R. 690, [1933] 3 D.L.R. 723 (H.C.J.).
[9]F.R.A., s. 41.

In Manitoba, registration in the land titles office is necessary;[10] in Ontario, registration in the registry office sufficed.[11]

606.1 The Base Fee

The legislation did require the tenant in tail to obtain the consent in writing of a person, called the "protector of the settlement" in certain cases. The consent could be endorsed on the disentailing assurance itself, or in a separate document. Normally the protector would be the owner of the prior possessory estate (or the first of such estates subsisting for the time being, if more than one),[1] but the settlor could appoint special protectors, not exceeding three, in lieu of the person who would otherwise have been the protector.[2] The disentailing assurance would effectively bar the issue and the reversioner or remainderman if the protector's consent was obtained. If there were no protector, the disentailing assurance would, of course, be sufficient by itself. The discretion of the protector to grant or refuse his consent was absolute, except that he could not enter into an agreement to withhold his consent.[3]

Where there was a protector and his consent was not obtained, only the issue were barred. The remainderman or reversioner was not. The effect, in that case, was that the grantee or mortgagee acquired only a base fee.[4] However, where a father conveyed land to his son in tail and the son, in a separate deed, reserved a life interest to his father, the father was not the protector of the estate. Accordingly, when the son disposed of the property to his wife by deed and later mortgaged it, it was held that the deed to the wife barred the entail completely and defeated the father's estate, since it was not a prior estate, and further, that even if the deed did not have the effect of barring the estate, the mortgage did.[5]

The base fee may be described as a qualified fee simple.[6] Its characteristics are that it continues only so long as the original tenant in tail or any of his issue are living and that it is followed by a reversion or a remainder.

606.2 Enlarging the Base Fee

It stands to reason that the base fee was a less desirable estate than the fee simple for although it could last a long time, it was liable to be cut short before a fee simple absolute could be cut short. It was, however, possible to enlarge the base fee into a fee simple. This would be effected by a further

---

[10]*Law of Property Act*, R.S.M. 1970, c. L90, s. 30(1).
[11]Ontario Act, s. 25.
§606.1
[1]F.R.A., s. 22; Ontario Act, s. 8.
[2]F.R.A., s. 32; Ontario Act, s. 15.
[3]F.R.A., ss. 36, 37; Ontario Act, ss. 20, 21.
[4]F.R.A., s. 34; Ontario Act, s. 18.
[5]*Re Carr and Smith*, [1950] O.R. 26, [1950] 1 D.L.R. 746 (H.C.J.).
[6]Challis, p. 325.

disentailing assurance executed by the tenant in tail, or by the person who would have been the tenant in tail if the issue had not been barred. If at the time of such assurance there was still a protector, his consent would be required.[1] If there were no longer a protector, the assurance by itself would be sufficient to enlarge the base fee.[2]

The base fee would also be enlarged into a fee simple if the owner acquired the immediate remainder or reversion in fee simple, but the statute prevented a merger in such cases,[3] so that the fee simple absolute thereby created remained free from any encumbrances on the remainder or reversion.[4] Finally, the base fee would be enlarged automatically in the hands of the owner if he remained in possession adverse to the remainderman or reversioner for ten years after the death of the protector.[5]

607. ABOLITION OF THE FEE TAIL

In most of the provinces and Territories of Canada the estate tail has been abolished. The following are the relevant statutes:

In *Alberta*, section 9 of the *Law of Property Act*[1] provides that any devise or limitation, which would therefore have created an estate tail, shall create a fee simple or the greatest estate that the testator or transferor had in the land.

In *British Columbia*, section 10(1) of the *Property Law Act*[2] provides that an estate in fee simple shall not be changed into any limited fee or fee tail, but the land, whatever form of words is used in any instrument, shall be and remain an absolute estate in the owner for the time being. Section 10(2) states that any limitation which, before June 1, 1921, would have created an estate tail transfers the fee simple or the greatest estate that the transferor had in the land.

In *Newfoundland*, real property interests are transformed into chattels real, so that the estate tail no longer exists in that province.[3]

In *New Brunswick*, section 19 of the *Property Act*[4] abolishes estates tail and provides that every estate which would hitherto have been adjudged a fee tail shall be adjudged a fee simple and, "if no valid remainder is limited thereon, shall be a fee simple absolute and may be conveyed or devised by the tenant in tail, or otherwise shall descend to his heirs as a fee simple".

---

§606.2
[1] F.R.A., s. 35; Ontario Act, s. 19.
[2] F.R.A., s. 19; Ontario Act, s. 5.
[3] F.R.A., s. 39; Ontario Act, s. 23.
[4] Megarry and Wade, p. 97.
[5] *Limitations Act*, R.S.O. 1950, c. 207, s. 30.

§607
[1] R.S.A. 1980, c. L-8.
[2] R.S.B.C. 1979, c. 340. References to estates tail that still exist are still found in some statutes, see, *e.g.*, the *Land (Settled Estate) Act*, R.S.B.C. 1979, c. 215, s. 29.
[3] *Chattels Real Act*, R.S.N. 1970, c. 36, s. 2.
[4] R.S.N.B. 1973, c. P-19.

It is interesting to speculate on the meaning of the words, "and if no valid remainder is limited thereon". Presumably, the estate would not be converted into a fee simple absolute if there were. However, an early Nova Scotia case held, with respect to the then identical Nova Scotia legislation,[5] that the legislation intended to repeal the estate tail in its entirety and that the statute therefore applied despite the existence of a valid remainder.[6] In *Ernst v. Zwicker*,[7] the Supreme Court of Canada approved this interpretation. In *Re Simpson*,[8] the court assumed that the Nova Scotia legislation was copied from a New York statute, but that only a part was taken over, which caused the difficulties in construction. It has been pointed out that the New York statute did indeed continue where the Nova Scotia legislation left off, giving the remainderman a contingent limitation in fee simple, which would vest in possession on the death of the first taker without issue.[9]

In *Nova Scotia*, section 5 of the *Real Property Act*[10] provides that all estates tail are abolished and every estate which hitherto would have been adjudged a fee tail shall hereafter be adjudged a fee simple and shall descend as such.

In *Ontario*, section 4 of the *Conveyancing and Law of Property Act*[11] provides that a limitation in a conveyance or will that before May 27, 1956, would have created an estate tail, shall be construed as an estate in fee simple or the greatest estate that the grantor or testator had in the land. The *Estates Tail Act*[12] and *De Donis* were repealed at the same time.[13]

In *Prince Edward Island*, the fee tail is effectively abolished, since, under section 17 of the *Real Property Act*,[14] a deed executed in legal form by a tenant in tail and registered in accordance with the *Registry Act*[15] extinguishes and destroys an estate tail.

In *Saskatchewan*, section 243 of the *Land Titles Act*[16] is in the same terms as section 10(1) of the British Columbia Act.[17] Section 244 provides that any limitation that theretofore would have created an estate tail, transfers the absolute ownership or the greatest estate that the transferor had.

Where a testator devised property to his nephew "to have and to hold for his own use and comfort so long as he shall live, and to his male children at his decease", it was held that the devise did not create an estate tail, but a life

---

[5]*Estates Tail Act*, R.S.N.S. 1859, c. 112, s. 1.
[6]*Re Estate of Simpson* (1863), 5 N.S.R. 317, 745 (C.A.); accord, *McKenzie v. McKenzie* (1865), 6 N.S.R. 178 (S.C.).
[7](1897), 27 S.C.R. 594.
[8]*Supra*, footnote 6.
[9]Laskin, p. 67.
[10]R.S.N.S. 1967, c. 261.
[11]R.S.O. 1980, c. 90, enacted by S.O. 1956, c. 10, s. 1.
[12]R.S.O. 1950, c. 117.
[13]By the *Estates Tail Repeal Act*, S.O. 1956, c. 19, and by S.O. 1956, c. 76, respectively.
[14]R.S.P.E.I. 1974, c. R-4.
[15]R.S.P.E.I. 1974, c. R-11.
[16]R.S.S. 1978, c. L-5.
[17]*Property Law Act*, R.S.B.C. 1979, c. 340, s. 10(1).

estate in the nephew and, by the operation of the predecessors of sections 243 and 244, it created a fee simple in his male children upon his death.[18]

In the *Northwest Territories*, section 20(2) of the *Wills Ordinance*[19] provides that any devise or limitation that would, theretofore, have created an estate tail, shall be construed to pass the fee simple or the greatest estate the testator had in the land.

In *Yukon Territory*, section 19(2) of the *Wills Ordinance*[20] makes an identical provision. *Quaere* whether in the Northwest Territories and in the Yukon the estate tail has been abolished only to the extent that it could formerly have been created by will. There appear to be no provisions respecting the creation of an estate tail by deed or transfer.

607.1 The Estate Tail in Manitoba

While there may be some surviving estates tail in Ontario and Prince Edward Island, Manitoba is the only province in which they may definitely still be created. Manitoba never enacted its own Estates Tail Act but simply incorporated the English *Fines and Recoveries Act*[1] into its law. Section 30(1) of the *Law of Property Act*[2] provides, however, that in view of the requirement of enrolment of disentailing assurances in the High Court of Chancery, registration in the land titles office for the land titles district in which the land is situate is substituted for enrolment.

608. THE ESTATE TAIL IN THE UNITED STATES

The estate tail was received as part of the common law of England in most states, although it has been held in some states that *De Donis* never became part of their law. In those, the conditional fee simple is still recognized. In many of the states in which the fee tail was introduced, it has since been abolished by converting it into a life estate with remainder over, to a fee simple absolute, or, if the fee tail was followed by a valid reversion or remainder, into a fee simple subject to a conditional limitation. In those states which retain the estate tail it can generally be barred by a statutory disentailing deed.[1]

---

[18]*Re Smith Estate*, [1947] 1 W.W.R. 997 (Sask. K.B.).
[19]R.O.N.W.T. 1974, c. W-3.
[20]R.O.Y.T. 1971, c. W-3.
§607.1
[1]3 & 4 Wm. 4, c. 74 (1833).
[2]R.S.M. 1970, c. L90.
§608
[1]See generally, Thompson, §§1868-9.

CHAPTER 7

THE LIFE ESTATE

PART II   TENURES AND ESTATES

701.   NATURE

Estates for life are freehold estates, but they are not inheritable. Thus, in feudal law as well as today, a tenant for life held and holds the seisin in the real property. Moreover, since the Statute *Quia Emptores*[1] applies only to estates in fee simple, it is theoretically possible for a life tenant to create new tenures by subinfeudation. In fact, however, when a life tenant conveys today, the grantee always takes by substitution and not by subinfeudation.[2]

As indicated by the name, life estates continue only for the duration of the life of the person named. The holder of the estate is the life tenant and his is usually the measuring life, but in the form of the estate known as the estate *pur autre vie*,[3] another person is the measuring life.

Life estates may be created by deed, lease, or will, by statute, or otherwise by operation of law.

702.   CLASSIFICATION

Estates for life are classified according to their mode of creation. Those created expressly are called *conventional life estates*, while those created by statute, or otherwise by operation of law, are called *legal life estates*.

702.1   Conventional Life Estates

These are two in number, namely:

(i) The estate for the life of the tenant, which is created by deed, lease, or will for the life of the grantee, lessee, or devisee.

(ii) The estate *pur autre vie*. This estate is also created by deed, lease, or will, but is granted to the life tenant for the duration of the life of another or others called the *cestui(s) que vie*. The estate may be created either by express grant as in a deed "to X for the life of Y" or by the assignment by the life tenant of his estate to another in which case the life tenant becomes the *cestui que vie*.

As in the case of the fee simple and the fee tail, the conventional life estate may be made defeasible by using words of duration or condition so as to create a determinable life estate or a life estate upon condition subsequent. Thus, a devise to the testator's wife "for her sole use and benefit during the remainder of her natural life or until her remarriage", with remainder over, creates a determinable life estate defeasible on the widow's remarriage.[1]

----

§701
[1] 18 Edw. 1, cc. 1-3 (1290).
[2] 1 A.L.P. §2.15, p. 24.
[3] See §§702 and 704, *infra*.
§702.1
[1] *Humble v. Fullarton* (1958), 41 M.P.R. 164 (N.B.S.C.), affd 42 M.P.R. 118 (S.C. App. Div.).

702.2 Legal Life Estates

Apart from life estates created by statute, these estates are three in number, namely:

(i) Tenancy by the curtesy, which is a husband's life estate in his deceased wife's undisposed of real property;

(ii) Dower, which is a wife's life estate in one-third of her deceased husband's real property of which he was solely seised or to which he died beneficially entitled; and

(iii) The estate of a tenant in tail after possibility of issue extinct, that is, the tenant in tail special after the named spouse predeceases him, without leaving issue of the marriage.

These several types are discussed in detail below.

703. ESTATE FOR THE LIFE OF THE TENANT

A conventional life estate for the life of the tenant may be created by deed, lease, or will.

703.1 Creation by Deed

As indicated in chapter 5, at common law a life estate was created either by using express words to that effect, or whenever the appropriate formula necessary to create an estate in fee was not used.[1] As a result of 19th century statutory reforms, today, if no words of limitation are expressed in a deed, the deed will pass all the estate or interest held by the grantor.

Thus, the Ontario *Conveyancing and Law of Property Act*[2] provides:

> 5(1) In a conveyance, it is not necessary, in the limitation of an estate in fee simple, to use the word "heirs".
>
> (2) For the purpose of such limitation, it is sufficient in a conveyance to use the words "in fee simple" or any other words sufficiently indicating the limitation intended.
>
> (3) Where no words of limitation are used, the conveyance passes all the estate, right, title, interest, claim and demand that the conveying parties have in, to, or on the property conveyed, or expressed or intended so to be, or that they have power to convey in, to, or on the same.
>
> (4) Subsection 3 applies only if and as far as the contrary intention does not appear from the conveyance, and has effect subject to the terms of the conveyance and the provisions therein contained.

---

§703.1

[1] §502.1, *supra*.

[2] R.S.O. 1980, c. 90; first enacted as the *Conveyancing and Law of Property Act*, S.O. 1886, c. 20, s. 4.

(5) This section applies only to conveyances made after the 1st day of July, 1886.[3]

Therefore, if a grantor wishes to grant a life estate only, it is necessary that he define the estate in the deed or lease. If he grants for a life without mentioning the life, it will be regarded as the life of the grantee, for an estate for a person's own life is considered to be greater than an estate for the life of another.[4]

In *Hayduk v. Waterton; Flechuk v. Waterton*[5] a father transferred land to his son, after which the son executed an encumbrance giving his father and mother a "life-rent" in the land. The son also executed a petroleum lease with his father's consent. As the term "life-rent" derives from Scottish jurisprudence, and has no precise meaning in the common law, its meaning had to be deduced from the son's intention as expressed in the document. It was held that while the term conveys the idea of a life tenancy and thus would normally include the proceeds of a royalty from the petroleum lease, since the members of the family had agreed to the father's right to royalties, the royalty payments fell due to the life tenants.

A life estate may also be granted by inadvertence. Thus in *Unrau v. Barrowman*,[6] the plaintiff's land was forfeited to the Crown for tax arrears. He remained on the land under a lease from the Crown. When the lease expired he was informed by letter that he could remain on the land so long as he remained in residence as a squatter. It was held that the plaintiff held a life estate in the land and was not a mere licensee.[7]

On the other hand, a grant to a person for "as long as he wants" was held to create a tenancy at will only,[8] and a grant to X of the use of a bedroom and bedding and board in a dwelling-house so long as he remained a resident on the lands, was held to create a mere licence.[9]

703.2 Creation by Will

In cases of wills the courts have always been more ready to try to ascertain

---

[3]For similar legislation see *Property Law Act*, R.S.B.C. 1979, c. 340, s. 19(1), (2); *Law of Property Act*, R.S.A. 1980, c. L-8, s. 7(1); R.S.M. 1970, c. L90, s. 4; *Property Act*, R.S.N.B. 1973, c. P-19, s. 12(3); *Conveyancing Act*, R.S.N.S. 1967, c. 56, s. 5. There appears to be no similar legislation in Prince Edward Island and the Northwest Territories and Yukon Territory. No such legislation would seem necessary in Newfoundland where the *Chattels Real Act*, R.S.N. 1970, c. 36, converts all land into chattels real. However, the *Conveyancing Act*, R.S.N. 1970, c. 63, s. 19, provides that every conveyance shall by virtue of the Act pass all the estate a party has.
[4]Co. Litt. 41b, 42a; *Re Coleman's Estate*, [1907] 1 I.R. 488; *Gluckstein v. Barnes*, [1900] A.C. 240 (H.L.); *Neill v. Duke of Devonshire* (1882), 8 App. Cas. 135 (H.L.), at p. 149.
[5](1968), 68 D.L.R. (2d) 562, [1968] S.C.R. 871.
[6](1966), 59 D.L.R. (2d) 168 (Sask. Q.B.).
[7]For a similar case see *Lapointe v. Cyr* (1952), 29 M.P.R. 54 (N.B.S.C.).
[8]*Humans v. Doyon*, [1945] O.W.N. 275, [1945] 2 D.L.R. 312 (C.A.). *Cf. Treadwell v. Martin* (1976), 67 D.L.R. (3d) 493, 13 N.B.R. (2d) 137 (S.C. App. Div.).
[9]*Wilkinson v. Wilson* (1894), 26 O.R. 213 (H.C.J.), and see *Re Grafton* (1924), 26 O.W.N. 262 (S.C. App. Div.).

the testator's intention than in cases of deeds. Thus, at common law an estate in fee simple might be created even though the appropriate formula was not used, provided an intention to create a fee could be deduced, the onus to show such intention being on the devisee. In the absence of words of limitation the devisee would take a life estate[1] and a life estate would also be created by express words to that effect.

As a result of 19th century statutory reforms, which provided that, unless a contrary intention appears in the will, a devise of real property without words of limitation will pass all the estate or interest that a testator has, it is now necessary for a testator carefully to describe the interest if he wishes to create only a life estate.

The Ontario *Succession Law Reform Act*[2] now provides:

> 26. Except when a contrary intention appears by the will, where real property is devised to a person without words of limitation, the devise passes the fee simple or the whole of any other estate or interest that the testator had power to dispose of by will in the real property.[3]

In all cases of ambiguity, it is the task of the court to ascertain the intention of the testator through the language he used in the light of the circumstances known to him.[4] "Speaking generally, no aid can be derived from reported decisions which do not establish a principle but simply seek to apply an established principle to a particular document."[5]

The general rule is that a clear gift cannot be cut down by subsequent repugnant words and that the court must endeavour to give such effect to the testator's wishes as is possible, by ascertaining which part of the testator's intention predominates and by giving effect to it, rejecting subordinate expressions as repugnant to the dominant intent.[6]

It is always the duty of the court to try to ascertain the testator's intention, however. Thus, where land was devised to two devisees without words of limitation but the executors were directed to sell the land after the death of the devisees, this direction was held to indicate that they were to have life estates only.[7] Similarly, where a testator left the residue of his estate to his sister and provided that, upon her death "the unused or unexpended balance

---

§703.2
[1]See §502.2, *supra*.
[2]R.S.O. 1980, c. 488.
[3]For similar legislation see *Wills Act*, R.S.A. 1980, c. W-11, s. 26; R.S.B.C. 1979, c. 434, s. 24; R.S.M. 1970, c. W150, s. 26; R.S.N.B. 1973, c. W-9, s. 25; R.S.N.S. 1967, c. 340, s. 26; R.S.N. 1970, c. 401, s. 16; R.S.S. 1978, c. W-14, s. 25; *Probate Act*, R.S.P.E.I. 1974, c. P-19, s. 74; *Wills Ordinance*, R.O.N.W.T. 1974, c. W-3, s. 20(1); R.O.Y.T. 1971, c. W-3, s. 19(1).
[4]*Re Cutter* (1916), 37 O.L.R. 42, 31 D.L.R. 382 (H.C.).
[5]*Re Walker* (1925), 56 O.L.R. 517 (S.C. App. Div.), at p. 522, *per* Middleton, J.A.
[6]*Ibid.*, and see cases collected in §502.2(c), *supra*.
[7]*Re Virtue* (1922), 22 O.W.N. 482 (H.C.).

shall revert", Boyd, C., held that the apparent gift should be cut down to a life estate.[8]

Where a testator gave his wife the free use of his real and personal estate for her life and, after her death, the balance of the estate remaining "unspent" was to go to his children, Riddell, J., held that the provision as to the balance was not repugnant to the gift of the residue and that she had only a life estate in the realty because "one spends money, not land, and the word unspent is quite inappropriate to land".[9]

A devise to a wife for "as long as she remains my widow", with a gift over in the event of her remarriage, gives her a life estate until remarriage which terminates it,[10] and it is just as perfect a life estate as if it had been given absolutely.[11] In a Saskatchewan case, however, it was held that a devise to the testator's wife for so long as she remained his widow, with a gift over on her remarriage, gave her a fee simple defeasible upon remarriage and not a life estate so defeasible.[12]

Where a testator gives a woman a life estate if she so long remains unmarried, with a gift over on her marriage, the gift over takes effect on her death if she does not marry.[13]

A will giving to the testator's widow "the whole control of my real and personal estate as long as she lives" was held to give her a life estate.[14] Similarly, where a will gave the wife property "to be at her will and disposal during her life" and directed its disposition after her death, she was held to be entitled to a life estate.[15] A devise of property for life with power of sale, however, gives the devisee a life estate only with the right to require the trustees to sell and pay over the income to the devisee.[16]

A gift of the profits of land for life passes a life estate in the land,[17] and a direction in a will that a person shall have the use or occupancy of a house or land confers a life estate on that person and is equivalent to a devise of the rents

---

[8]Re Cutter, supra, footnote 4.

[9]Re Richer (1919), 46 O.L.R. 367, 50 D.L.R. 614 (S.C. App. Div.).

[10]Re Branton (1910), 20 O.L.R. 642 (H.C.J.); Re Ferguson, [1942] O.W.N. 115, [1942] 2 D.L.R. 322 (H.C.J.); Re Perrie (1910), 21 O.L.R. 100 (H.C.J.), at pp. 104-5. Cf. Re Waters (1978), 21 O.R. (2d) 124, 89 D.L.R. (3d) 742 (H.C.J.).

[11]National Trust Co. v. Shore (1908), 16 O.L.R. 177 (H.C.J.); Re Branton, supra, footnote 10; Re Carne's Settled Estates, [1899] 1 Ch. 324.

[12]Re Jackson; Houston v. Western Trust Co., [1940] 1 D.L.R. 283, [1940] 1 W.W.R. 65 (Sask. C.A.).

[13]Re Branton, supra, footnote 10; Burgess v. Burrows (1871), 21 U.C.C.P. 426; Eaton v. Hewitt (1863), 2 Dr. & Sm. 184, 62 E.R. 591; Underhill v. Roden (1876), 2 Ch. D. 494.

[14]Re Turnbull Estate (1906), 11 O.L.R. 334 (H.C.J.).

[15]Doe d. Keeler v. Collins (1850), 7 U.C.Q.B. 519. See also Martin v. Firth and Martin (1980), 31 N.B.R. (2d) 204 (Q.B.T.D.), devise of all property to the testator's widow to have the use thereof for life and on her death the remainder to go equally to the testator's brothers and sisters, held to give a life estate to the widow with a power to appoint in her favour as necessary.

[16]Re Asp Estate, [1924] 2 W.W.R. 1089 (Man. K.B.).

[17]Re Vair and Doyle (1922), 23 O.W.N. 407 (H.C.).

and profits.[18] Similarly, a direction that a person shall have a right of residence in property during life confers a life estate in it.[19] So also, a direction that a mother and a daughter were to have a lien on property as a home during their lives, conferred a joint life estate on them.[20] Where a devise of all of the testator's real and personal estate to his sons in a fee simple was subject to the conditions that his daughters were to have the privilege of living in the homestead and being maintained out of the proceeds of the estate during their lives, it was held that they took a life estate in the homestead, the death of some not diminishing the rights of the survivors.[21] Where the testator's daughter was to live on a farm as long as she remained unmarried, she took a life estate until marriage.[22] Where a widow was to have the right to reside in a house during widowhood, she took a life estate in it during widowhood.[23] The rule extends to part of a residence and, where the testator devised to his wife a bedroom and parlour of her own choice in his dwelling-house and the use of the kitchen, yard and garden, it was held that she took a life estate in the bedroom and parlour selected by her and also in the kitchen, yard and garden.[24] In certain cases, however, only a licence will be found to have been given.[25]

Sometimes the gift of a life estate may be implied from the terms of the will. Thus, where a devise is made to B after the death of A and no estate is expressly given to A, but B is the testator's presumptive heir, it is presumed that the intention was to give a life estate to A.[26] The doctrine is based upon the supposition that the probability of an intention to benefit the person in question is so strong, a contrary intention cannot be supposed.[27] It arises in general from the presumption against intestacy and the inference to be drawn from the whole will where there is no express provision and where there is a gap in the dispositions to be filled.[28] If the will shows that the testator must have intended an interest that the will does not expressly create, the court will mould the language so as to give effect as far as possible to the intent which it thinks the testator has sufficiently shown.[29]

A will may give a life estate to a person, with power to appoint the remainder as he sees fit, or to a specified class of persons. Where a will provided, "I leave my property to my wife too [*sic*] share with the childring

---

[18]*Mannox v. Greener* (1872), L.R. 14 Eq. 456; *Coward v. Larkman* (1886), 60 L.T. 1; *Pettigrew v. Durley* (1972), 5 N.B.R. (2d) 834 (S.C.).

[19]*Fulton v. Cummings* (1874), 34 U.C.Q.B. 331.

[20]*Scouler v. Scouler* (1858), 8 U.C.C.P. 9.

[21]*Bartels v. Bartels* (1877), 42 U.C.Q.B. 22.

[22]*Judge v. Splann* (1892), 22 O.R. 409 (H.C.J.).

[23]*Shaw v. Shaw* (1920), 17 O.W.N. 458 (H.C.).

[24]*Smith v. Smith* (1889), 18 O.R. 205 (H.C.J.).

[25]*Moore v. Royal Trust Co.* (1956), 5 D.L.R. (2d) 152, [1956] S.C.R. 880.

[26]*Ralph v. Carrick* (1879), 11 Ch. D. 873 (C.A.); *Doe d. Driver v. Bowling* (1822), 5 B. & Ald. 722, 106 E.R. 1355.

[27]*Crook v. Hill* (1871), L.R. 6 Ch. 309.

[28]*Watkins v. Frederick* (1865), 11 H.L.C. 358 at p. 374, 11 E.R. 1371.

[29]*Towns v. Wentworth* (1858), 11 Moo. P.C. 526 at p. 543, 14 E.R. 794.

[*sic*] at her death as she thinks fit", it was held that she took a life estate with a power of appointment among the children, as she saw fit.[30] Where a testator directed that his wife should "remain in full possession of all my estate both personal and real and after her death one-half of my personal estate shall be divided as she may direct", it was held that she took a life estate with power of appointment.[31] If a life estate is given to a person with power of appointment by will, it does not make the gift an absolute gift that will devolve upon his personal representative if he does not exercise the power.[32]

Except under statutory powers, a tenant for life may dispose of the land only to the extent of his own interest and the recipient takes at most an estate *pur autre vie*, for the life of the tenant for life. In the case of a lease, except one authorized by statute, the lease ends with the death of the life tenant unless it is affirmed by the remaindermen.[33]

704. ESTATE PUR AUTRE VIE

An estate *pur autre vie* is an estate granted to one person, called the tenant *pur autre vie*, for the life of another person, called the *cestui que vie*, that is, he who lives. It may be granted for the concurrent lives of several persons, called the *cestuis que vie* either for their joint lives only, or also for the life of the survivor of them, but, unless it is expressly limited for joint lives, it will also be for the life of the survivor.[1]

The estate may be created by express limitation by deed or will, or by the assignment of an existing life estate, in which latter case the assignee is the tenant *pur autre vie* and the assignor is the *cestui que vie*. The estate may also be granted to a person and his heirs, although this will not extend the estate beyond the life of the *cestui que vie*.

A limitation which granted land to X for his life and for the life of his heir was construed by the court to convey two life estates to X, one for his own life and one for the life of his heir. The latter was an estate *pur autre vie*.[2]

704.1 Alienation by Tenant Pur Autre Vie

The tenant *pur autre vie* may dispose of his estate during his lifetime and, upon his death, the assignee will continue to hold for the life of the *cestui que vie*.

---

[30]*Re Wolfe and Holland* (1912), 3 O.W.N. 900, 1 D.L.R. 568 (H.C.J.); and see *Re John Tomashewsky Estate*, [1923] 1 D.L.R. 1143, [1923] 1 W.W.R. 1020 (Alta. S.C.); *Re Drew and McGowan* (1901), 1 O.L.R. 575 (H.C.J.); *Re Newton* (1912), 3 O.W.N. 948, 2 D.L.R. 576 (H.C.J.).

[31]*Henderson v. Henderson* (1922), 52 O.L.R. 440 (H.C.).

[32]*Re Estate of George F. Will*, [1923] 1 D.L.R. 741, 56 N.S.R. 95 (S.C.).

[33]*Camston Ltd. v. Volkswagen Yonge Ltd.*, [1968] 2 O.R. 65 (Co. Ct.). On dispositions authorized by statute see further §§1305.2-3.

§704
[1]*Chatfield v. Berchtoldt* (1872), L.R. 7 Ch. 192.

[2]*Re Amos; Carrier v. Price*, [1891] 3 Ch. 159.

At common law, the tenant *pur autre vie* could not devise his estate by will and, since it was not an estate of inheritance, it could not pass to his heirs by descent. On his death, however, the land did not revert to the grantor, as he had granted it for the life of the *cestui que vie*, and it did not escheat because only an entire fee simple could escheat. By reason of the rule that the freehold must never be vacant, the estate was completed by means of the doctrine of occupancy. If no one was entitled to enter into occupancy, any person who did enter into possession could hold the land during the life of the *cestui que vie* by right of occupancy and he was called the general occupant. If the grant were to the tenant *pur autre vie* and his heirs, the heir was treated as being the person nominated as occupant after the death of the tenant and was called the special occupant. If a tenant or other person were actually in possession, he became special occupant by the same title.[1] In a deed, the heir must be named to make him special occupant,[2] but in a will the intention of the testator is sufficient.[3] There may be a special occupant of an equitable estate *pur autre vie*,[4] but there cannot be a general occupant of an incorporeal hereditament.[5]

An estate *pur autre vie* may not be entailed, although a *quasi*-entail may be effected by limiting the estate to a person and the heirs of his body with remainder over, which estate may be barred otherwise than by will,[6] but, if the tenant does not alienate in his lifetime, the issue and the remaindermen in succession take as special occupants.[7] An estate *pur autre vie* may be limited by way of remainder and the remainderman, if not barred, will take as special occupant; but a *quasi*-tenant in tail in remainder expectant upon a life estate cannot, without the consent of the life tenant, defeat subsequent remainders.[8] Similarly, if an estate *pur autre vie* is given to a person and his heirs, with an executory devise over, he cannot defeat the executory devise by disposing of the estate.[9] It is submitted that a *quasi*-entail can no longer be created in jurisdictions in which estates tail have been abolished.

Since at common law an estate *pur autre vie* could not be devised by will and, if it were limited to the tenant and his heirs, went to the heir only as special occupant and not by descent, the estate was not an asset available for creditors of the deceased tenant. These common law rules were changed, however, by statute.

By the several statutes respecting wills every person may devise an estate *pur autre vie* to which he is entitled at the time of his death, whether or not

---

§704.1
[1]Challis, p. 359; *Northern v. Carnegie* (1859), 4 Drewry 587, 62 E.R. 225.
[2]*Earl of Mountcashell v. More-Smyth*, [1896] A.C. 158 (H.L.).
[3]*Re Sheppard; Sheppard v. Manning*, [1897] 2 Ch. 67.
[4]*Reynolds v. Wright* (1860), 2 De G. F. & J. 590, 45 E.R. 749.
[5]*Northen v. Carnegie, supra*, footnote 1.
[6]*Re Barber's Settled Estates* (1881), 18 Ch. D. 624.
[7]*Re Michell; Moore v. Moore*, [1892] 2 Ch. 87.
[8]*Allen v. Allen* (1842), 2 Dr. & War. 307 (Ir.).
[9]*Re Barber's Settled Estates, supra*, footnote 6.

there is any special occupant and whether it is a corporeal or incorporeal hereditament.[10]

In Alberta, the *Wills Act*[11] provides that a person may devise all real and personal property of a nature which was devisable under the law existing before the Act, which would include an estate *pur autre vie*. In Nova Scotia the *Wills Act*[12] provides that a person may devise all real property to which he is entitled at death and which, if not devised, would devolve upon his heirs and representatives. The definition of "real property" includes any estate, right, or interest in messuages, lands, rents and hereditaments, which include an estate *pur autre vie*.

In Ontario by the *Estates Administration Act*,[13] all real property vested in any person without a right in another person to take by survivorship on his death, whether testate or intestate, devolves to and becomes vested in his personal representative as trustee for the persons beneficially entitled thereto and, subject to payment of his debts and so far as it has not been disposed of by deed, will, contract or other disposition, is to be distributed as if it were personal property.[14] In the interpretation of any statute or instrument to which the deceased was a party or under which he had an interest, the personal representative is deemed to be his heir, unless a contrary intention appears, but without affecting the beneficial right to any property or the construction of any words of limitation of any estate in any deed, will or other instrument.[15] As Armour points out,[16] this does not provide for ownership of the estate between the death of the tenant *pur autre vie* and the grant of letters of administration to the personal representative, thus raising the question whether there cannot be a general occupant in the interval. Moreover, since the personal representative holds as trustee subject to payment of debts, what he really holds in trust is the surplus after payment of debts and not the land itself unless it is unnecessary to sell the land in order to pay debts.

There is similar legislation in effect in most of the other provinces.[17] In Newfoundland, the *Chattels Real Act*[18] provides that all lands, tenements and

---

[10]*Wills Act*, R.S.B.C. 1979, c. 434, s. 2(a); R.S.M. 1970, c. W150, s. 3(a); R.S.N.B. 1973, c. W-9, s. 2(a); R.S.S. 1978, c. W-14, s. 3(a); *Succession Law Reform Act*, R.S.O. 1980, c. 488, s. 2(a); *Wills Ordinance*, R.O.N.W.T. 1974, c. W-3, s. 4(a); R.O.Y.T. 1971, c. W-3, s. 4(1)(a); *Probate Act*, R.S.P.E.I. 1974, c. P-19, s. 59(1)(b).
[11]R.S.A. 1980, c. W-11, s. 3(a).
[12]R.S.N.S. 1967, c. 340, s. 2.
[13]R.S.O. 1980, c. 143.
[14]*Ibid.*, s. 2(1).
[15]*Ibid.*, s. 6.
[16]*Real Property*, pp. 89-90.
[17]*Devolution of Real Property Act*, R.S.A. 1980, c. D-34, s. 2(1); R.S.S. 1978, c. D-27, s. 4; *Estate Administration Act*, R.S.B.C. 1979, c. 114, s. 90; *Devolution of Estates Act*, R.S.M. 1970, c. D70, s. 18; R.S.N.B. 1973, c. D-9, s. 3; *Probate Act*, R.S.P.E.I. 1974, c. P-19, s. 108(1); *Real Property Act*, R.S.N.S. 1967, c. 261, s. 6(1); *Devolution of Real Property Ordinance*, R.O.N.W.T. 1974, c. D-5, s. 3(1); R.O.Y.T. 1971, c. D-4, s. 3(1).
[18]R.S.N. 1970, c. 36, s. 2. For a discussion of this statute, see Gushue, "The Law of Real Property in Newfoundland", 4 Can. Bar Rev. 310 (1926).

hereditaments in Newfoundland which are regarded at common law as real estate shall be held to be chattels real and shall go to the executor or administrator of any person dying seised or possessed thereof as personal estate now passes to the personal representatives.

704.2 Production of Cestui Que Vie

In Ontario, the *Conveyancing and Law of Property Act*[1] makes provision for proof that the *cestui que vie* still lives. If he remains out of Ontario or absents himself for seven years, so that it cannot be ascertained whether he be alive or dead, and an action is commenced by the reversioner for recovery of the estate, he is to be presumed dead unless he is proved to be alive and possession will then be given to the reversioner, his heirs or assigns.[2] A tenant who is thus evicted may later, in an action, recover possession by showing that the *cestui que vie* is living or was living at the time of the eviction, in which case the tenant, his executors, administrators or assigns may hold the estate for the remainder of the life of the *cestui que vie* and recover from the reversioner all profits received by the reversioner during the period of eviction.[3] The Supreme Court, upon application of a person entitled to an estate by way of remainder, reversion or expectancy after the death of another person, supported by affidavit that he has cause to believe that such death has occurred and is being concealed, may order the person suspected of concealing the death to produce the person believed dead and, if the latter is not produced, he is to be presumed dead and the claimant may take possession of the land.[4] Whoever was thus ousted may later, by action, recover possession of the land and of the profits received meanwhile upon proving that the person not produced was alive.[5] If the person ordered to produce another person shows to the satisfaction of the court that the latter is alive, but his appearance cannot be procured or compelled, the court may order possession of the estate to continue.[6] A person having an estate determinable upon a life who holds possession after its termination without the consent of the person next entitled is a trespasser and the next person entitled may recover the profits received during the wrongful possession.[7] There do not appear to be similar provisions in the other provinces. The Ontario provisions derive from two old English statutes,[8] however, which were not introduced into the other provinces.

---

§704.2
[1] R.S.O. 1980, c. 90.
[2] *Ibid.*, s. 46.
[3] *Ibid.*, s. 47.
[4] *Ibid.*, ss. 48, 49.
[5] *Ibid.*, s. 50.
[6] *Ibid.*, s. 51.
[7] *Ibid.*, s. 52.
[8] *Cestui Que Vie Act*, 19 Car. 2, c. 6 (1667); 6 Anne, c. 72 (1707).

705.   LIFE ESTATES CREATED BY LEASE

The general comments above on the creation of an estate for the life of the tenant[1] are applicable to life estates created by leases as well.

An estate for the life of the tenant, or an estate *pur autre vie*, may be granted by lease and the lessee has a freehold estate. A contractual lease for life at a rent does not differ from an estate for life created by a settlement. A life estate is a freehold and is subject to the rule that it may not be granted to commence in future unless it has some preceding freehold estate to support it. A lease may be granted for a term of years determinable on the death of a specified person but, even though the term is so long that it must exceed the life of that person, it is a chattel interest and is personal rather than real estate.

By the Imperial *Statute of Frauds*,[2] all leases of lands, tenements or hereditaments must be in writing, signed by the parties making them or by their agents authorized to do so, otherwise they have force and effect as leases at will only; however, section 2 excepts from the necessity of writing leases for a term not exceeding three years whereby there is reserved to the landlord a rent of two-thirds at least of the full improved value of the demised premises. The Imperial *Real Property Act*[3] further provides that a lease required by law to be in writing is void at law unless made by deed, that is, under seal.

The Imperial *Statute of Frauds* necessarily went into force in all provinces except Quebec and the Imperial *Real Property Act* necessarily went into force in Alberta, British Columbia, Manitoba, Saskatchewan and the Northwest and Yukon Territories. In various provinces there is also the following legislation:

In Ontario, by the *Statute of Frauds*[4] all leases and terms of years of all lands, tenements or hereditaments are void at law unless made by deed (that is, under seal) and that provision necessarily applies to leases for life or lives. Section 3 corresponds with section 2 of the Imperial *Statute of Frauds*.

In British Columbia, the *Statute of Frauds*[5] provides that no leases may be assigned, granted or surrendered except by deed or note in writing by the party assigning, granting or surrendering the same.

In New Brunswick, the *Statute of Frauds*[6] makes a similar provision and the *Property Act*[7] provides that leases that are required to be in writing must be under seal. In Nova Scotia, the *Statute of Frauds*[8] provides that no interest in land may be assigned, granted or surrendered except by deed or note in writing. In Prince Edward Island, the *Real Property Act*[9] provides that leases

---

§705
[1] §§703-703.2, *supra*.
[2] 29 Car. 2, c. 3, s. 1 (1676).
[3] 8 & 9 Vict., c. 106, s. 3 (1845).
[4] R.S.O. 1980, c. 481, s. 1(2).
[5] R.S.B.C. 1979, c. 393, s. 1(2).
[6] R.S.N.B. 1973, c. S-14, s. 8.
[7] R.S.N.B. 1973, c. P-19, s. 11(1).
[8] R.S.N.S. 1967, c. 290, s. 3.
[9] R.S.P.E.I. 1974, c. R-4, s. 8.

that are required by law to be in writing must be made by deed.

The equitable rights of the parties in the absence of a seal are discussed in chapter 27.[10]

A lease for the life of the lessee or the life of another should state in the *habendum* that he is to hold during his life or the life of that other but, if there is a lease for life without mentioning the life, it is deemed to be for the life of the lessee, because an estate for a man's own life is considered to be greater than an estate for the life of another and the lease is to be construed most strongly against the grantor.[11]

706. CHARACTERISTICS OF LIFE ESTATES

Inasmuch as a life estate is a freehold estate, but one not of inheritance, it differs markedly from the fee simple and the fee tail. Since it is of only limited duration and is followed by an estate or estates in remainder or reversion, it follows that the enjoyment of the life tenant must be curtailed and certain obligations imposed on him in order to protect the interests of those coming after him. These several characteristics are described in the following sections.

706.1 Right of Enjoyment

It is an inherent right of a life tenant to receive the rents and profits of the land during the life estate.

If there is a direct conveyance or devise of land to a person for a life estate so as to give him the legal estate, it follows that he is entitled to actual possession and management. Where property is devised to trustees in trust for a person for life, who, therefore, only has an equitable estate, he is ordinarily entitled to possession but the court has a discretion as to whether to give possession to the trustees or to the life tenant. Thus, where a will devising property to trustees to pay the rents and profits to a life tenant showed the testator's intent to be that the trustees were to have control and management, the court refused to give possession to the life tenant.[1] So also, where others have a claim, the court has a discretion as to giving the life tenant possession. Thus, where a will directed trustees to pay the rents and profits of a property to the testator's son for life and after his death to divide them among his children as he might direct but, in default of such direction to divide the property equally among all children, conveying to each child his share upon attaining the age of 21 years and meanwhile to apply the proceeds

---

[10]§2702, *infra*.

[11]Co. Litt. 41b, 42a; *Re Coleman's Estate*, [1907] 1 I.R. 488; *Gluckstein v. Barnes*, [1900] A.C. 240 (H.L.); *Neill v. Duke of Devonshire* (1882), 8 App. Cas. 135 (H.L.), at p. 149.

§706.1

[1]*Whiteside v. Miller* (1868), 14 Gr. 393; *Re Cunningham* (1917), 12 O.W.N. 268 (H.C.).

to support the children, the court held that the life tenant was not entitled to possession.[2] On the other hand, where a will devised property to trustees in trust to allow the testator's widow the use of it for her support during her life and, after her death, to sell the property and divide the proceeds among the testator's children who were adults, it was held that as there were no active duties imposed on the trustees, the usual incidents of a life estate, by which the life tenant may occupy the property, or let, or otherwise dispose of it as he sees fit, should be given effect to. Consequently, the widow was entitled to leave the property and let it and a lease made by the trustees without her consent was set aside and possession was directed to be given to her or to her nominee.[3]

706.2   Right to Emblements

Emblements are the produce of sown or planted land. The word "emblement" is derived from the old French *emblaement*, from the verb *emblaer* and the Latin *imbladare*, meaning to sow with corn, corn being used in the European sense of wheat and other grains.

The right to emblements is a right given by law to a person who has an estate of uncertain duration which unexpectedly comes to an end through no act or fault of his, to take growing crops which he sowed or planted. Emblements comprise only produce of a species that grows by the industry of man and that ordinarily repays the labour by which it is produced within the year in which the labour is bestowed and the right extends to only one crop of a species that yields more than one crop. The species are grains, roots, clover, potatoes and hops, but not growing grass even if produced from seed and ready to cut as hay.[1] Therefore, if a life tenant sows the land for crops which are harvested annually and dies before harvesting them, to compensate him for his labour and expenses, his personal representatives are entitled to the crops as emblements. This is because the life estate was ended by "an act of God" and it is a maxim of the law that no one is to suffer from an act of God; furthermore, husbandry is for the public benefit and should have all the security the law can give.[2] The doctrine of emblements, however, does not extend to fruit trees, grass or other natural products of the soil which are not planted annually for present profit only, but are planted for the future profit of the tenant and successive occupants.

Since the doctrine of emblements is based upon uncertain duration of the estate, it applies to a tenant *pur autre vie* who, upon the death of the *cestui*

---

[2]*Orford v. Orford* (1884), 6 O.R. 6 (H.C.J.); *Homfray v. Homfray* (1936), 51 R.C.R. 287 (S.C.).
[3]*Hefferman v. Taylor* (1888), 15 O.R. 670 (H.C.J.).
§706.2
[1]*Graves v. Weld* (1883), 5 B. & Ad. 105, 110 E.R. 731; *Haines v. Welch* (1868), L.R. 4 C.P. 91.
[2]Co. Litt. 55; 2 Bl. Comm. 122, 403; *Lawton v. Lawton* (1743), 3 Atk. 13, 26 E.R. 811.

que vie, is entitled to the crops he has sown[3] and extends to a tenant under a lease granted by a life tenant or otherwise determinable upon a life, so that, when the tenant's lease is terminated by the death of the life tenant or other person whose death terminates the lease, he is entitled to the crops he has sown.[4]

Whoever has the right to emblements has the right of entry upon the land to gather them,[5] if he shows that the crop is fit for harvesting or needs care or cultivation.[6]

The doctrine of emblements does not apply if the estate of the person who sowed the crops is ended by his own fault or act, as where his estate is forfeited for breach of a condition, or an estate at will is ended by the tenant, or where a widow who holds land during widowhood remarries.[7]

706.3 Right to Fixtures

On the death of a life tenant, his personal representatives may remove articles brought onto the premises by him and attached to the freehold by him for the more convenient or luxurious occupation of the premises, or for purposes of trade, provided that they can be removed without substantial damage to the premises. This right, as between the personal representatives and remainderman, is virtually the same as exists between landlord and tenant.[1]

706.4 Duty to Pay Taxes

As between life tenant and remainderman, the life tenant must pay all annual taxes imposed on the land,[1] but this liability is limited to an amount equal to the annual value of the land.[2] A determinable life estate is, while it exists, subject to the incidents of a life estate, so the holder of a life estate which is determinable at the option of the executor must pay the taxes.[3] If part of the land is productive and part unproductive, the life tenant of the

---

[3] *Kelly v. Webber* (1860), 3 L.T. 124.
[4] *Atkinson v. Farrell* (1912), 27 O.L.R. 204, 8 D.L.R. 582 (H.C.J.); *Graves v. Weld, supra*, footnote 1.
[5] *Kingsbury v. Collins* (1827), 4 Bing. 202, 130 E.R. 746.
[6] *Hayling v. Okey* (1853), 8 Exch. 531, 155 E.R. 1461.
[7] *Oland's Case* (1602), 5 Co. Rep. 116 a, 77 E.R. 235; *Bulwer v. Bulwer* (1819), 2 B. & Ald. 470, 106 E.R. 437; *Kingsbury v. Collins, supra*, footnote 5.
§706.3
[1] *Re De Falbe; Ward v. Taylor*, [1901] 1 Ch. 523 (C.A.), at pp. 530, 539, affd [1902] A.C. 157 *sub nom. Leigh v. Taylor* (H.L.); *Re Hulse; Beattie v. Hulse*, [1905] 1 Ch. 406; *Bain v. Brand* (1876), 1 App. Cas. 762 (H.L.), at pp. 770, 772.
§706.4
[1] *Biscoe v. Van Bearle* (1858), 6 Gr. 438; *Gray v. Hatch* (1871), 18 Gr. 72; *Re Cunningham* (1917), 12 O.W.N. 268 (H.C.); *Re Redding; Thompson v. Redding*, [1897] 1 Ch. 876.
[2] *Mayo v. Leitovski*, [1928] 1 W.W.R. 700 (Man. K.B.), at p. 702.
[3] *Re McDonald* (1919), 46 O.L.R. 358, 50 D.L.R. 658 (S.C. App. Div.).

whole cannot collect the rents of the productive part and refuse to pay the taxes on the unproductive part, for the person entitled to possession is the person to pay the yearly taxes on the property and the fund out of which taxes are ordinarily payable is the rents of the land. Hence, the life tenant cannot collect rents from one portion of the property and allow taxes to accumulate on a vacant portion,[4] or collect rents from a portion consisting of an improved farm and not pay taxes on a portion consisting of wild lands.[5] Apparently, however, if he pays a local improvement rate imposed on the inheritance, he can keep it alive as against the remainderman.[6] In a sense the life tenant is in the position of a *quasi*-trustee vis-à-vis the remainderman so that he cannot, for example, let the taxes go in arrears and then buy in at a tax sale. He will then hold in trust for the remainderman.[7] Where a testator places the duties of "upkeep and maintenance" on the trustees, the burden of paying the taxes is not shifted.[8]

706.5 Duty to Insure

A life tenant is not bound to insure[1] and as between himself and the remainderman, he cannot be charged with the premiums on a policy of fire insurance.[2] A life tenant of a settled leasehold must, however, observe all the covenants in the lease which have to be performed by the lessee for the lessor, including the covenant to insure or repair if there is one[3] and the insurance premiums are payable out of income.[4]

706.6 Duty of Life Tenant and Remainderman to Pay Encumbrances

If the estate is subject to a mortgage, the life tenant must pay the interest, but the principal, when due, is payable by the remainderman or reversioner;[1]

---

[4]*Re Denison; Waldie v. Denison* (1893), 24 O.R. 197 (H.C.J.), where a receiver of the life estate was appointed to pay the arrears of taxes out of the rents; *cf. Re May* (1914), 6 O.W.N. 29 (H.C.), at p. 30.

[5]*Biscoe v. Van Bearle, supra*, footnote 1.

[6]Armour, *Real Property*, p. 96, citing *Re Smith's Settled Estates*, [1901] 1 Ch. 689.

[7]*Mayo v. Leitovski, supra*, footnote 2.

[8]*Re Cox* (1960), 22 D.L.R. (2d) 597 (Ont. H.C.J.).

§706.5

[1]*Re Darch* (1914), 6 O.W.N. 107, 16 D.L.R. 875 (H.C.); *Re Bennett; Jones v. Bennett*, [1896] 1 Ch. 778 (C.A.), at p. 787.

[2]*Re Betty; Betty v. Attorney-General*, [1899] 1 Ch. 821 at p. 829; *Re Cunningham* (1917), 12 O.W.N. 268 (H.C.), at p. 269.

[3]*Re Betty, supra; Re Gjers; Cooper v. Gjers*, [1899] 2 Ch. 54.

[4]*Re Redding; Thompson v. Redding*, [1897] 1 Ch. 876.

§706.6

[1]*Biscoe v. Van Bearle* (1858), 6 Gr. 438; *Gray v. Hatch* (1871), 18 Gr. 72; *Reid v. Reid* (1881), 29 Gr. 372; *Marshall v. Crowther* (1874), 2 Ch. D. 199; *Kekewich v. Marker* (1851), 3 Mac. & G. 311, 42 E.R. 280; *Re James Morrison Estate* (1921), 68 D.L.R. 787 at p. 791, [1922] 3 W.W.R. 493 at pp. 496-7 (Sask. K.B.); *Re May* (1914), 6 O.W.N. 29 (H.C.).

however, this obligation of the life tenant exists only as between himself and the remainderman or reversioner and not as between himself and the mortgagee.[2] In *Reid v. Reid*[3] the rule was applied to a dowress who was held obligated to pay one-third of the interest until the mortgagee was paid. The obligation of the life tenant is not personal but is a charge on his estate and, if he fails to keep down interest, future rents and profits are liable to make good the default,[4] the proper remedy for the remainderman being an application to the court for a receiver to appropriate rents for the purpose of paying interest.[5] If several estates are included in the same settlement, the life tenant must, out of the whole rents and profits, keep down the interest on all charges.[6]

If a life tenant pays off an encumbrance, the general rule is that it is presumed that he does so for his own benefit and not for the benefit of the persons entitled in a remainder, unless the evidence shows a contrary intention.[7] The life tenant is under no obligation to prove his intent to pay off a charge for his own benefit or to make any declaration or do any act to demonstrate his intent, the simple fact of payment by him being sufficient to establish his *prima facie* right to have the charge raised out of the estate, although the smallest demonstration that he intended to discharge the estate is sufficient.[8] The burden of proving an intent to exonerate the estate lies on the remainderman[9] and evidence drawn from the form of documents may be rebutted by the personal evidence of the life tenant.[10]

Under the above presumption, when a life tenant pays off an encumbrance, he is entitled to hold it as a charge without interest against the remainderman or reversioner. Consequently, where a testator devised encumbered land to his wife for life with remainder as she might appoint and she paid off the encumbrance out of her own funds and appointed the estate to another, evidence was directed to be given as to whether the estate was of considerably greater value than the claim paid off; if so, she was to have a lien for the amount advanced by her but, if otherwise, it was intended that the appointment should be freed and discharged from the claim.[11] The presumption that the life tenant pays off the mortgage for his own benefit is not rebutted by showing that the life tenant is a parent of the remainderman.[12] In ejectment proceedings, a

---

[2]*Carrick v. Smith* (1874), 34 U.C.Q.B. 389 at p. 394; *Re Morley*; *Morley v. Saunders* (1869), L.R. 8 Eq. 594.
[3]*Supra.*
[4]*Makings v. Makings* (1860), 1 De G. F. & J. 355, 45 E.R. 396.
[5]*Baron Kensington v. Bouverie* (1859), 7 H.L.C. 557 at p. 575, 11 E.R. 222.
[6]*Frewen v. Law Life Assurance Soc.*, [1896] 2 Ch. 511; *Honywood v. Honywood*, [1902] 1 Ch. 347.
[7]*Burrell v. Earl of Egremont* (1844), 7 Beav. 205, 49 E.R. 1043; *Lord Gifford v. Lord Fitzhardinge*, [1899] 2 Ch. 32.
[8]*Macklem v. Cummings* (1859), 7 Gr. 318 at p. 321; *Baron Kensington v. Bouverie*, *supra*, footnote 5.
[9]*Re Harvey*; *Harvey v. Hobday*, [1896] 1 Ch. 137 (C.A.).
[10]*Lord Gifford v. Lord Fitzhardinge*, *supra*, footnote 7.
[11]*Macklem v. Cummings* (1859), 7 Gr. 318.
[12]*Re Harvey*; *Harvey v. Hobday*, *supra*, footnote 9.

defence by a widow and dowress who paid off a mortgage made by her husband that she was entitled to possession of the property as against her children until she should be repaid, and afterwards as dowress, was allowed.[13]

The taking of a reconveyance or discharge of a mortgage does not affect the claim of the life tenant who paid it. A testator devised mortgaged land to his son, subject to a life estate to his widow defeasible upon the son attaining his majority. The widow paid the mortgage and took a discharge of it in 1888, which she registered in 1903. The son, after attaining his majority, predeceased her, leaving a will in which he left the property to her for life, remainder to his sisters. There being no evidence that she paid off the mortgage for her own benefit, or for the benefit of those entitled to treat the principal money paid by her in discharge of the mortgage as a subsisting charge in her favour upon the mortgaged land, her right was held not to be affected by taking and registering the discharge. It was also held that, although she made no claim until 1909, when the action was brought, the *Real Property Limitations Act*[14] was no bar to her claim, as it did not begin to run until the son became of age in 1892, and continued to run until his death in 1900, but her second life estate then commenced with the obligation to pay out of the rents and profits the interest on the still subsisting charge, with the result that, through payment of interest in this way, the statute was not a bar. It was held that she was not bound to elect between retention of the charge and acceptance of the life estate under her son's will.[15]

Where the owner of land mortgaged it and then conveyed it in fee simple subject to the mortgage and to a life estate in favour of himself, it was held that the grantee, upon payment of the mortgage, was not entitled under the *Mortgage Act*[16] to an assignment of it to himself or to his nominee, as the effect of the transaction was that the grantee was to assume the liability of the mortgage debt and relieve the life estate from it and the mortgagee had notice of the equitable right of the life tenant to have his life estate relieved of the burden of payment of the mortgage; but, apparently, the grantee was entitled to have the mortgage assigned in such a way that it would remain an encumbrance upon the remainder vested in him.[17]

The same principles are applicable to other encumbrances such as an annuity charged on the land. Thus, where a testator who was seised of land in fee simple subject to a mortgage securing an annuity to his wife, devised the land for life with remainder over in fee simple, it was held that the annual payments to the widow by a life tenant were to be treated partly as payments of interest which the life tenant was bound to pay and partly as payment of principal for which the life tenant had a charge on the inheritance in the

13*Carrick v. Smith* (1874), 34 U.C.Q.B. 389, quoting *Burrell v. Earl of Egremont, supra*, footnote 7.
14R.S.O. 1887, c. 111, s. 23.
15*Currie v. Currie* (1910), 20 O.L.R. 375 (H.C.J.).
16R.S.O. 1897, c. 121, s. 2(1), (2).
17*Leitch v. Leitch* (1901), 2 O.L.R. 233 (H.C.J.).

proportion which the value of the life estate bore to the value of the reversion.[18] If a life tenant pays interest in excess of the rents and profits received by him, he may make himself an encumbrancer to the extent of the excess but, if during his life, he does not intimate that the rents and profits are insufficient or that he intends to charge the corpus with the deficiency, his legal representatives cannot set up such a charge after his death.[19]

706.7 Duty to Repair

A life tenant is not bound to repair unless the instrument creating the estate requires him to repair. As this subject is really an aspect of the law of waste, it will be dealt with in the next section. Where a testator placed the duties of "upkeep and maintenance" on the trustees, the repair duties were allocated on the basis that costs of use and enjoyment, such as gardening and snow removal, were to be borne by the life tenants, and the costs of maintenance and repair by the trustees.[1]

706.8 Waste

(a) Nature and remedies

The law of waste, which applies to lessees as well as to life tenants, is designed to protect the reversioner or remainderman from acts of the life tenant which tend to injure or despoil the land to the detriment of those who come after him.[1]

If a life tenant commits waste he is liable in damages which generally amount to the decrease in the value of the reversion, less an allowance for immediate payment.[2] In certain cases, exemplary damages may be awarded.[3] Alternatively, or in addition, an injunction may be granted to prevent threatened or apprehended waste or the repetition of waste.[4] However, as an injunction is discretionary, it may be refused where the waste is minor

---

[18]*Whitesell v. Reece* (1903), 5 O.L.R. 352 (H.C.J.), following *Yates v. Yates* (1860), 28 Beav. 637, 54 E.R. 511; *Re Dawson; Arathoon v. Dawson*, [1906] 2 Ch. 211; see also *Re Harrison; Townson v. Harrison* (1889), 43 Ch. D. 55.

[19]*Baron Kensington v. Bouverie* (1859), 7 H.L.C. 557, 11 E.R. 222.

§706.7

[1]*Re Cox* (1960), 22 D.L.R. (2d) 597 (Ont. H.C.J.).

§706.8

[1]Megarry and Wade, p. 103.

[2]*McPherson v. Giles* (1919), 45 O.L.R. 441 (H.C.).

[3]*Hiltz v. Langille* (1959), 18 D.L.R. (2d) 464 at p. 470, 42 M.P.R. 333 at p. 341 (N.S.S.C. App. Div.).

[4]*Courts of Justice Act, 1984* (Ont.), c. 11, s. 114; *Judicature Act*, R.S.A. 1980, c. J-1, s. 5(3)(c), (j); *Law of Property Act*, R.S.A. 1980, c. L-8, s. 63; *Judicature Act*, R.S.N.B. 1973, c. J-2, s. 33; R.S.N. 1970, c. 187, s. 21(m); R.S.P.E.I. 1974, c. J-3, s. 15(5); S.N.S. 1972, c. 2, s. 39(9); *Law and Equity Act*, R.S.B.C. 1979, c. 224, s. 36; *Queen's Bench Act*, R.S.M. 1970, c. C280, s. 59(3); R.S.S. 1978, c. Q-1, s. 45, para. 8.

and not likely to be repeated.[5] If the waste has resulted in a profit to the life tenant, for example, by the sale of minerals or timber, the money can be recovered by an accounting.[6] Whether waste has been committed is a question of fact and the onus is on the plaintiff to prove the damage.

Formerly, at common law, waste by a tenant by the curtesy, a dowress, or a guardian was punishable because the law itself gave them their interest,[7] but waste by a tenant for life or for years was not punishable unless provided against by the grantor, lessor or testator creating the estate, because if he wished to prevent it, his failure to so provide was his own neglect.[8]

In Ontario the *Conveyancing and Law of Property Act*[9] now provides:

> 29. A tenant by the curtesy, a dowress, a tenant for life or for years, and the guardian of the estate of an infant, are impeachable for waste and liable in damages to the person injured.
> 30. An estate for life without impeachment of waste does not confer upon the tenant for life any legal right to commit waste of the description known as equitable waste, unless an intention to confer the right expressly appears by the instrument creating the estate.
> 31. Tenants in common and joint tenants are liable to their co-tenants for waste, or, in the event of a partition, the part wasted may be assigned to the tenant committing the waste at the value thereof to be estimated as if no waste had been committed.
> 32. Lessees making or suffering waste on the demised premises without licence of the lessors are liable for the full damage so occasioned.

These sections derive respectively from the *Statute of Gloucester*,[10] the Imperial *Judicature Act*,[11] the *Statute of Westminster II*,[12] and the *Statute of Marlbridge*.[13] The *Statute of Gloucester* introduced the writ of waste and imposed triple damages on the person committing waste, but the writ of waste was abolished in Upper Canada in 1834.[14] The *Statute of Gloucester* and the *Statute of Marlbridge* were re-enacted in Ontario in the 1897 revision[15] and were then changed to their present redaction.

In British Columbia, the *Law and Equity Act*[16] provides that an estate for life without impeachment of waste does not confer on the tenant for life any legal right to commit equitable waste unless the intention to confer such right expressly appears in the instrument creating the estate. In Manitoba, the *Law*

---

[5]*Patterson v. Central Canada Loan and Savings Co.* (1898), 29 O.R. 134 (H.C.J.).
[6]*Dashwood v. Magniac*, [1891] 3 Ch. 306 (C.A.); Megarry and Wade, p. 103.
[7]*Drake v. Wigle* (1874), 24 U.C.C.P. 405 (C.A.), at p. 408.
[8]3 Holdsworth, pp. 121-2.
[9]R.S.O. 1980, c. 90.
[10]6 Edw. 1, c. 5 (1278).
[11]36 & 37 Vict., c. 66, s. 25 (1873).
[12]13 Edw. 1, c. 22 (1285).
[13]52 Hen. 3, c. 23 (1267).
[14]*Real Property Amendment Act*, S.U.C. 1834, c. 1, s. 39.
[15]R.S.O. 1897, c. 330, ss. 21, 23.
[16]R.S.B.C. 1979, c. 224, s. 12. To the same effect is the *Judicature Act*, S.N.S. 1972, c. 2, s. 39(2).

of *Property Act*[17] makes a similar provision and stipulates further that lessees making or suffering waste without licence of the lessors are liable for the full damage occasioned. In Nova Scotia, the *Dower Act*[18] provides that a dowress shall not commit or suffer waste but shall maintain buildings and fences in good repair. There are similar provisions in other provinces.[19]

(b) Types of waste

There are four types of waste, namely, ameliorating, voluntary and permissive, which subsist at law, and equitable waste.

(i) Ameliorating waste

Any act which changes the character of property is, technically, waste. Ameliorating waste is that which results in benefit and not in an injury, so that it in fact improves the inheritance. Examples of this kind are the turning of pasture land into arable land and vice versa and the conversion of run-down dwellings into modern, productive shops. Unless the character of the property is completely changed, it is unlikely that a court will award damages or grant an injunction for ameliorating waste as between a life tenant and a remainderman.[20]

(ii) Voluntary waste

Voluntary waste is the commission of an act which is injurious to the inheritance or to those entitled in remainder or reversion, either (a) by diminishing the value of the estate, such as by felling trees, mining, or destroying buildings or gardens, (b) by increasing the burden on it, or (c) by impairing evidence of title.

Old English cases held that impairment of title occurred and, hence, that waste was committed, if pasture land was turned into arable land, or arable land into woodland, or vice versa, for this changed the course of husbandry and the identity of the property and, therefore, it affected the evidence of title. This type of conduct is not today regarded as waste,[21] for it has little or no application where land is laid out in lots with a system of registration of title and, having regard to the improved means of identifying a property by maps, the supposed injury to title is now a "theoretical absurdity".[22] It is, therefore, unlikely that old English cases to the effect that a change in the

---

[17]R.S.M. 1970, c. L90, ss. 12, 13.
[18]R.S.N.S. 1967, c. 79, s. 5.
[19]*Judicature Act*, R.S.N.B. 1973, c. J-2, s. 28; R.S.N. 1970, c. 187, s. 21(*h*); *Law of Property Act*, R.S.A. 1980, c. L-8, s. 62; *Queen's Bench Act*, R.S.S. 1978, c. Q-1, s. 45, para. 2.
[20]See, *e.g.*, *Holderness v. Lang* (1886), 11 O.R. 1 (H.C.J.); *Rene v. Carling Export Brewing and Malting Co. Ltd.* (1929), 63 O.L.R. 582, [1929] 2 D.L.R. 881 (S.C. App. Div.).
[21]*Jones v. Chappell* (1875), L.R. 20 Eq. 539 at p. 541.
[22]*Doherty v. Allman* (1878), 3 App. Cas. 709 (H.L.), *per* Lord O'Hagan at p. 726 and Lord Blackburn at p. 735.

course of husbandry is waste, are applicable to Canada as between life tenant and remainderman, although they may still be of importance as between landlord and tenant for a term of years if the latter takes unauthorized liberties. When it is desired to give to the tenant for life the right to cut timber or do other acts which would otherwise be regarded as voluntary waste, it is customary to make him a life tenant "without impeachment for waste". It is not sufficient to provide that the property shall be "under the control of" the life tenant,[23] or that the life tenant shall have "full and absolute control",[24] or that the life tenant may use it "as he might deem fit".[25] If, in order to give effect to conflicting dispositions in a will, a devise in terms longer than a life estate must be cut down to a life estate, the life estate is regarded as unimpeachable for waste.[26]

A life tenant who is impeachable for waste may not commit voluntary waste, but it is not such waste unless it is in fact injurious to the inheritance either by diminishing the value of the estate, or by increasing the burden on it.[27] A tenant for life who wrongfully cuts and sells timber is not permitted to derive any benefit from his wrongful act[28] and the cut timber or its proceeds belongs to the owner of the first vested estate of inheritance.[29]

Although a life tenant who is impeachable for waste may not ordinarily fell trees, or work mines or quarries, or take things out of the soil, as he would thereby be removing parts of the inheritance itself, there are certain circumstances in which he may do those things without being guilty of waste.

It is not waste if a tenant for life cuts timber on wild land for the sole purpose of bringing it into cultivation, provided that the inheritance is not damaged and it is done in conformity with the rules of good husbandry, for it is not waste unless the inheritance is injured.[30] Although it was held in an early case that a tenant who lawfully cut timber would be guilty of waste if he sold it,[31] that case must apparently be taken as overruled by the Divisional Court in *Lewis v. Godson*,[32] holding (a) that a life tenant who cuts timber or removes stones for the purpose of sale is guilty of waste, (b) that, whether cutting trees is waste depends upon whether the act is such as a prudent farmer would do upon his own land, having regard to the land as an inheritance, and whether the cutting would diminish the value of the land,

---

[23]*Clow v. Clow* (1883), 4 O.R. 355 (H.C.J.).
[24]*Pardoe v. Pardoe* (1900), 16 T.L.R. 373, cutting timber and applying the proceeds to the life tenant's own use was held to be waste.
[25]*Currie v. Currie* (1910), 20 O.L.R. 375 (H.C.J.), cutting and selling cordwood held to be waste.
[26]*Clow v. Clow, supra,* footnote 23, at p. 357.
[27]*Doe d. Grubb v. Earl of Burlington* (1833), 5 B. & Ad. 507 at p. 516, 110 E.R. 878; *Drake v. Wigle* (1874), 24 U.C.C.P. 405; *Holderness v. Lang, supra,* footnote 20.
[28]*Seagram v. Knight* (1867), L.R. 2 Ch. 628.
[29]*Honywood v. Honywood* (1874), L.R. 18 Eq. 306 at p. 311.
[30]*Drake v. Wigle, supra,* footnote 27; *Hiltz v. Langille* (1959), 18 D.L.R. (2d) 464, 42 M.P.R. 333 (N.S.S.C. App. Div.).
[31]*Saunders v. Breakie* (1884), 5 O.R. 603 (H.C.J.).
[32](1888), 15 O.R. 252 (H.C.J.).

and (c) that a life tenant who cuts timber or removes stones for the purpose of clearing the land and bringing it under cultivation or for agricultural improvement is not guilty of waste, and if he sells the removed timber and stones, he is not guilty of waste. Armour, C.J., quoted with approval the maxim "No sale is waste if the first act is not waste."[33] Where an estate is kept for the purpose of producing saleable timber, it is not waste for the life tenant to cut it periodically, as that is regarded as a mode of cultivation to allow proper growth of other timber and as an intended annual source of revenue,[34] but, where the estate is partially cultivated it is capable of some beneficial enjoyment without cutting any growing timber and in such a case the remainderman, even if the remainder is defeasible, may bring an action for waste or seek an injunction.[35] The court may also, under statutory authority, authorize leases of privileges to cut timber or remove earth, coal, stone or mineral.[36]

A life tenant impeachable for waste may not open new mines, quarries or pits or work old, abandoned mines or pits,[37] but may work mines or pits which were previously worked for a purpose not special or limited, such as for fuel or repair for particular tenements.[38] Mines, the working of which was suspended for a temporary cause such as diminished prices, are to be regarded as opened mines.[39]

A life tenant, including one who is impeachable for waste, has been entitled since ancient times to *estovers* or *botes*, the alternative common law term for the wood that a tenant for life or for years may take from the land for repair of his house, of the implements of husbandry and of fences or hedges, and for fuel. The word "estovers" is said to be derived from the Norman French *estouviers*, in turn derived from *estouffer*, to furnish. The word "bote" is derived from the old English *botan*, to furnish, and signified repair. Estovers consist of *housebote*, for the repair of the house, *firebote*, for fuel, *ploughbote*, for the making and repair of agricultural implements, and *haybote* or *hedgebote*, for the repair of fences, but they must be reasonable and used for the actual repairs required and cannot be sold to save money for repairs,[40] so they may not be cut in advance,[41] or sold to reimburse the

---

[33]See also *Currie v. Currie, supra*, footnote 25.
[34]*Honywood v. Honywood, supra*, footnote 29; *Dashwood v. Magniac*, [1891] 3 Ch. 306 (C.A.); *Hiltz v. Langille, supra*, footnote 30.
[35]*Humble v. Fullarton* (1958), 41 M.P.R. 164 (N.B.S.C.), affd 42 M.P.R. 118 (N.B.S.C. App. Div.); *Hiltz v. Langille, supra*, footnote 30.
[36]*Settled Estates Act*, R.S.O. 1980, c. 468, s. 2(1); *Land (Settled Estates) Act*, R.S.B.C. 1979, c. 215, s. 6; *cf. Settled Estates Act*, 40 & 41 Vict., c. 18, s. 4 (1877); *Judicature Act*, R.S.A. 1980, c. J-1, s. 6(2); *Queen's Bench Act*, R.S.M. 1970, c. C280, s. 55(1).
[37]*Viner v. Vaughan* (1840), 2 Beav. 466, 48 E.R. 1262.
[38]*Elias v. Snowdon Slate Quarries Co.* (1879), 4 App. Cas. 454 (H.L.); *Earl Cowley v. Wellesley* (1866), 35 Beav. 635, 55 E.R. 1043 (gravel); *Miller v. Miller* (1872), L.R. 13 Eq. 263 (brick-field).
[39]*Greville-Nugent v. Mackenzie*, [1900] A.C. 83 (H.L.).
[40]Co. Litt. 41, 53.
[41]*Gorges v. Stanfield* (1597), Cro. Eliz. 593, 78 E.R. 836.

life tenant for outlay in repairs,[42] or sold in order to purchase other timber for repair, or exchanged for more suitable timber.[43]

The rigour of this old common law rule, however, was not applied in Ontario. In *Hixon v. Reaveley*,[44] Boyd, C., refused to grant an injunction restraining a life tenant from cutting and selling enough timber to produce sufficient money with which to repair the house, on the ground that, although the cutting down of timber without intent to repair but for sale generally is waste, if the cutting and sale are for the purpose of repair and the sale is an economical mode of making repairs, is for the benefit of all concerned, and the proceeds are applied to repairs, the cutting down and sale is not waste. He stated that the niceties of the ancient learning as to waste which obtain in England are not to be transferred without discrimination to a new and comparatively unsettled country like Ontario and that it would be repugnant to the principles of common sense that the tenant should be obliged to make repairs in the way most expensive and injurious to the estate. In regard to that case, Armour made the following comment:[45]

> It is hardly a nicety of law that permits timber suitable for repairs to be cut and used for repairs, but forbids the cutting and selling of timber unfit for repairs in order to produce money for making repairs. If there were no timber, but minerals were found, the tenant for life might on the same reasoning open a mine and sell enough ore to effect repairs, which would undoubtedly be waste. Nor is the law of England to be applied only with such discrimination as the court may think fit. In *Keewatin Power Co. v. Kenora*,[46] it was said by Moss, C.J.O., that
> "when ... it is distinctly and unequivocally declared that, in controversies relating to certain subjects, such as property and civil rights, resort should be had to the common law of England as it existed at a certain day, what warrant is there for saying that the rules of property prevailing at that time are not to be administered?"

Nevertheless, had the decision in *Hixon v. Reaveley* been different, the life tenant would have had the alternative of paying for repairs out of his own pocket or letting the house become dilapidated, the latter being permissive waste for which he would not have been liable. Also, the decision is in the same spirit as that expressed by the House of Lords in *Doherty v. Allman*[47] in regard to the ancient learning in respect of changing arable land into meadow or vice versa. It remains to be seen whether a life tenant will be held entitled to sell stone, gravel, sand, etc., in order to produce money for repairs. The court, under statutory authority, may, of course, authorize their removal in certain circumstances and subject to conditions.[48]

---

[42]*Gower v. Eyre* (1815), G. Coop. 156, 35 E.R. 514.
[43]*Simmons v. Norton* (1831), 7 Bing. 640, 131 E.R. 247.
[44](1904), 9 O.L.R. 6 (H.C.J.).
[45]*Real Property*, p. 94.
[46](1908), 16 O.L.R. 184 (C.A.), at p. 189.
[47](1878), 3 App. Cas. 709 (H.L.).
[48]See statutes collected at footnote 36, *supra*.

(iii) Permissive waste

Permissive waste is an act of omission or neglect, such as allowing buildings to fall down or to become dilapidated.

A tenant for life, whether legal or equitable, is not liable for permissive waste if the instrument creating his estate does not require him to repair.[49] This principle applies both to land settled by the instrument creating the estate and to land purchased under a direction in such instrument.[50] As between life tenant and remainderman, the cost of repairs necessary to remedy dilapidation is chargeable against the interest of the remainderman.[51] If the life tenant's estate is expressly made subject to the condition of maintaining or repairing the premises and he fails to repair, damages may be recovered after his death for such sum as is necessary to put the premises in the state of repair in which he should have left them.[52] If the settlor imposes a condition that the tenant for life shall keep the premises in repair, the obligation extends to repair dilapidations existing when the settlement came into force.[53] A direction that trustees shall pay for repairs out of rents throws the cost of ordinary repairs on income but not the cost of extraordinary repairs which would be equivalent to rebuilding.[54] An equitable tenant for life of settled leaseholds is not liable to the remainderman for permissive waste, in the absence of an express condition that he shall repair.[55] A life tenant is not liable for accidental injury, such as by fire or tempest, and is not bound to insure.[56]

(iv) Equitable waste

Equitable waste is wanton, malicious or unconscientious destruction, such as of houses or trees planted or left for purposes of ornament or shelter. It is called equitable waste because, although it is voluntary waste, courts of equity would not allow it to be committed even by a tenant who held "without impeachment for waste".

A tenant may, by express words, be allowed also to commit equitable waste, but if he has not been so authorized he may be enjoined from cutting down

---

[49]*Re Cartwright; Avis v. Newman* (1889), 41 Ch. D. 532; *Patterson v. Central Canada Loan and Savings Co.* (1898), 29 O.R. 134 (H.C.J.); *Re Parry and Hopkin*, [1900] 1 Ch. 160; *Currie v. Currie* (1910), 20 O.L.R. 375 (H.C.J.), at p. 380.

[50]*Re Freman; Dimond v. Newburn*, [1898] 1 Ch. 28.

[51]*Patterson v. Central Canada Loan and Savings Co.*, supra, footnote 49; *Currie v. Currie*, supra, footnote 49; *Re Elliot* (1917), 41 O.L.R. 276, 40 D.L.R. 649 (S.C. App. Div.); *Re Vair* (1923), 54 O.L.R. 497 (H.C.).

[52]*Woodhouse v. Walker* (1880), 5 Q.B.D. 404; *Batthyany v. Walford* (1886), 33 Ch. D. 624, affd 36 Ch. D. 269 (C.A.); *Re Williames; Andrew v. Williames* (1885), 54 L.T. 105 (C.A.); *Re Bradbrook; Lock v. Willis* (1887), 56 L.T. 106 (Ch. Div.).

[53]*Re Bradbrook*, supra, footnote 52; *Re Andrews; Andrews v. Board*, [1952] O.W.N. 163 (Surr. Ct.).

[54]*Crowe v. Crisford* (1853), 17 Beav. 507, 51 E.R. 1130.

[55]*Re Parry and Hopkin*, supra, footnote 49.

[56]*Re Darch* (1914), 6 O.W.N. 107, 16 D.L.R. 875 (H.C.).

ornamental trees, or trees that give shelter.[57] In such cases, however, the court must determine not whether such trees are in fact ornamental or give shelter, but whether they were planted or left by the owner for the time being for that purpose.[58] Furthermore, if trees were originally planted for the ornament of a house that was pulled down by the settlor without intention of rebuilding, they cease to be protected as ornamental trees.[59]

706.9 Alienability

As in the case of other estates, restraints on the alienation of life estates are frowned upon by the law and will be struck down unless they are minor. However, as the life estate is a limited one, so are the powers of alienation. Generally, the life tenant can dispose of only the interest that he has for the duration of his life. At common law it was possible for a life tenant or a lessee in possession to convey the immediate freehold estate to any person, other than the person next entitled to the freehold in possession (in which case it would be a surrender). This was called a tortious feoffment if it attempted to give more than the feoffor owned, but the land could be recovered by the rightful owner by entry, in certain cases, or by action. Tortious feoffments have been abolished by statute, however.[1] Today, a person can convey no more than the estate he owns.[2]

Thus, today, when a life tenant conveys his life estate, an estate *pur autre vie* is created for the life of the grantor. Similarly, a mortgage or other encumbrance and a lease affect only the life estate and end with the death of the life tenant.

Under settled estates legislation in effect in some provinces, it is, however, possible for a life tenant under stringent conditions to make leases which extend beyond his death. Moreover, the courts are given power under this legislation to authorize the sale, lease or encumbrance of settled estates. This subject is dealt with more fully in the chapter, "Settled Estates".[3]

707. DOWER

Dower was the estate that a wife had for her life in certain freehold estates

---

[57]*Turner v. Wright* (1860), 2 De G. F. & J. 234, 45 E.R. 612; *Ford v. Tynte* (1864), 2 De G. J. & S. 127, 46 E.R. 323 (C.A.).
[58]*Weld-Blundell v. Wolseley*, [1903] 2 Ch. 664.
[59]*Micklethwait v. Micklethwait* (1857), 1 De G. & J. 504, 44 E.R. 818 (C.A.).
§706.9
[1]*Real Property Act*, 8 & 9 Vict., c. 106, s. 4 (1845); and see *Conveyancing and Law of Property Act*, R.S.O. 1980, c. 90, s. 3. See generally Challis, pp. 405 *et seq.*
[2]*Property Law Act*, R.S.B.C. 1979, c. 340, s. 19(2); *Law of Property Act*, R.S.A. 1980, c. L-8, s. 7(1); R.S.M. 1970, c. L90, s. 4; *Conveyancing Act*, R.S.N.S. 1967, c. 56, s. 5(*a*); R.S.N. 1970, c. 63, s. 19; *Conveyancing and Law of Property Act*, R.S.O. 1980, c. 90, s. 5(3).
[3]See §§1305.2-1305.3, *infra*.

of her deceased husband. Until his death, her right was said to be inchoate.[1] During the lifetime of her husband a wife nevertheless had an interest in all his real property, except in equitable interests of which the husband never held the seisin, and that interest could not be alienated or interfered with by the husband without the wife's consent.[2] By statute, a widow was entitled to dower out of equitable interests to which the husband died beneficially entitled.

Until recently, all of the common law provinces, except Newfoundland, retained dower in one form or another. Dower has now been abolished in New Brunswick,[3] Nova Scotia,[4] Ontario[5] and Prince Edward Island,[6] however, and replaced with other rights.[7] The provisions repealing dower in these provinces do not apply "in respect to a right to dower that has vested" before the legislation came into force.[8] It is probable that the intended meaning of this exception is that, where a husband has died prior to the effective date of the statute, his widow's dower consummate is preserved. The use of the word "vest" is inexact in this context, however, for neither dower inchoate, nor dower consummate, is an interest in land, merely a possibility coupled with an interest. Only when dower is assigned by metes and bounds does it become an interest in land.[9]

In Newfoundland, there is no statute expressly dealing with dower, although there are statutes dealing with estates of intestates and homesteads. In the western provinces, the traditional dower right has been abolished and replaced with a life interest in the "homestead". Homestead legislation will be dealt with later in this chapter.[10]

It is undoubtedly true that dower today does not afford a widow the financial security it once did. There are several reasons for this, the most important being the fact that a husband's assets today are likely to consist largely of personalty and the existence of devices to defeat the wife's dower. Nevertheless, because dower has only recently been abolished, it retains its importance, especially for title purposes, and it is therefore treated at some length.

In England dower was made of little importance by the *Dower Act, 1833*,[11]

---

§707

[1]*Allan v. Rever* (1902), 4 O.L.R. 309 (H.C.J.).

[2]*Freedman v. Mason*, [1956] O.R. 849, 4 D.L.R. (2d) 576 (H.C.J.), revd on other grounds [1957] O.R. 441, 9 D.L.R. (2d) 262 (C.A.), affd 14 D.L.R. (2d) 529, [1958] S.C.R. 483.

[3]By the *Marital Property Act*, S.N.B. 1980, c. M-1.1, s. 49(1), (2).

[4]By the *Matrimonial Property Act*, S.N.S. 1980, c. 9, s. 33.

[5]By the *Family Law Reform Act*, S.O. 1978, c. 2, s. 70.

[6]By the *Family Law Reform Act*, S.P.E.I. 1978, c. 6, s. 62.

[7]See ch. 16, *infra*.

[8]*Family Law Reform Act*, S.O. 1978, c. 2, s. 70(4); S.P.E.I. 1978, c. 6, s. 62(4); *Marital Property Act*, S.N.B. 1980, c. M-1.1, s. 49(3); *Matrimonial Property Act*, S.N.S. 1980, c. 9, s. 33(4).

[9]*Freedman v. Mason*, *supra*, footnote 2, at p. 858 O.R., p. 584 D.L.R., *per* McRuer, C.J.H.C.

[10]§§710-710.15, *infra*.

[11]3 & 4 Will. 4, c. 105 (1833).

which provided that for persons who married thereafter, dower could not be claimed out of land disposed of by the husband by deed or will, or in respect of which he had made a declaration by deed or will in bar of dower. Dower was finally abolished by the *Administration of Estates Act 1925*.[12]

In New Brunswick, Nova Scotia, Ontario and Prince Edward Island the dower right was replaced by spousal rights of possession in the matrimonial home, rights to a division of assets on a breakdown of marriage and other rights.[13]

In the western provinces recent matrimonial property legislation makes provisions for similar rights, but these are invariably in addition to the homestead rights, except in the Yukon, where there is no homestead legislation.[14]

These matrimonial property rights will be discussed in chapter 16.

707.1 Dower at Common Law

Dower at common law was the right of a wife on surviving her husband to an estate for her life in one-third of the freehold estates of inheritance of which her deceased husband was solely seised at any time during the marriage and which her issue by him might possibly have inherited.[1] It was not necessary that issue be actually born to her, it being sufficient that issue capable of inheriting might have been born to her, and, in considering the possibility of issue, the law did not consider the age of the parties.[2]

To entitle the widow to dower at law it was necessary to prove the marriage. It was not necessary to prove the marriage strictly. Evidence of cohabitation and reputation was sufficient.[3]

Dower attached and could not be removed except by a release if the legal estate rested in the husband but for a moment.

The requirement that the husband be solely seised excluded a joint tenancy from dower, but not a tenancy in common because each tenant in common is separately seised of an undivided part.[4] As the surviving joint tenant takes the whole, nothing descends to the heirs of joint tenants who die,[5] but the

---

[12]15 & 16 Geo. 5, c. 23, s. 45(1) (1925).

[13]*Family Law Reform Act*, R.S.O. 1980, c. 152; S.P.E.I. 1978, c. 6; *Marital Property Act*, S.N.B. 1980, c. M-1.1; *Matrimonial Property Act*, S.N.S. 1980, c. 9.

[14]*Marital Property Act*, S.M. 1978, c. 24, s. 24; *Family Maintenance Act*, S.M. 1978, c. 25, s. 32; *Matrimonial Property Act*, R.S.A. 1980, c. M-9, s. 28; *Family Relations Act*, R.S.B.C. 1979, c. 121, ss. 55(2), 77(6); *Matrimonial Property Act*, S.S. 1979, c. M-6.1, ss. 16, 52.

§707.1
[1]2 Bl. Comm. 131.

[2]Co. Litt. 40a; Cameron, *Treatise on the Law of Dower* (Toronto, Carswell & Co., 1882), p. 4; Haskins, "The Development of Common Law Dower", 62 Harv. L. Rev. 42 (1948-49).

[3]*Phipps v. Moore* (1848), 5 U.C.Q.B. 16; *Losee v. Murray* (1865), 24 U.C.Q.B. 586.
[4]Litt., §45.
[5]*Haskill v. Fraser* (1862), 12 U.C.C.P. 383.

estate of a tenant in common descends to his heirs.[6] If the husband severed a joint tenancy, thus turning the joint tenancy into a tenancy in common, or if partition took place, dower attached to the husband's part and, if he became entitled to the whole of the joint tenancy by survivorship, dower attached to the whole.[7] At common law, because the husband must be seised, there could be no dower in a remainder or reversion to which he had not become entitled in possession at the time of his death,[8] so it was held that no dower attached to a remainder in fee expectant upon a life estate if the remainderman died or alienated the land before the death of the life tenant, because seisin of the freehold was in the life tenant and the remainder was not an estate of inheritance in possession.[9] Similarly, where property was conveyed to a husband under an agreement whereby the grantor was to be allowed to remain in possession of a specified portion for his life, it was held that the widow of the grantee had no dower in such portion during the life of the grantor.[10] If there was a lease at a rent, however, the reversion was treated as a freehold in possession to which dower attached notwithstanding the lease, because the possession of the tenant was the possession of the lessor.[11]

At common law, it was not necessary that the husband's seisin continue until his death, a temporary seisin being sufficient for the purposes of dower.[12]

707.2 Statutory Extension of Dower

At common law, the right of dower attached only to legal estates. By statute in Ontario, New Brunswick, Nova Scotia and Prince Edward Island, the right of dower was extended to equitable estates, that is, those to which the husband died beneficially entitled. Thus, the Nova Scotia *Dower Act*[1] provided:

2. Where a husband dies beneficially entitled to any interest in land in which his widow is not entitled to dower at common law, and such interest, whether wholly equitable or partly legal and partly equitable, is an estate of inheritance in possession, or equal to an estate of inheritance in possession, (other than an estate in joint tenancy), his widow shall be entitled to dower in respect to such interest.[2]

---

[6]*Ham v. Ham* (1857), 14 U.C.Q.B. 497.
[7]*Reynard v. Spence* (1841), 4 Beav. 103, 49 E.R. 277.
[8]Co. Litt. 32a.
[9]*Cumming v. Alguire* (1855), 12 U.C.Q.B. 330; *Pulker v. Evans* (1856), 13 U.C.Q.B. 546; *Leitch v. McLellan* (1883), 2 O.R. 587 (H.C.J.).
[10]*Slater v. Slater* (1870), 17 Gr. 45.
[11]*Stoughton v. Leigh* (1808), 1 Taunt. 402, 127 E.R. 889.
[12]2 Bl. Comm. 132.
§707.2
[1]R.S.N.S. 1967, c. 79, rep. 1980, c. 9, s. 33(1), hereafter referred to as the "Nova Scotia Act", or the "N.S. Act".
[2]To the same effect are: *Dower Act*, R.S.N.B. 1973, c. D-13, s. 1; R.S.O. 1970, c. 135, s. 3; R.S.P.E.I. 1974, c. D-17, s. 4. These statutes are hereafter referred to as the "New Brunswick Act", or the "N.B. Act", the "Ontario Act", or the "Ont. Act", and the "Prince Edward Island Act", or the "P.E.I. Act".

Examples of inheritable equitable estates and inheritable estates that are partly equitable and partly legal, are provided by trusts and by conveyances to uses. If land is conveyed or devised to a trustee in trust for another person and the trustee has active duties to perform, the trustee has the legal estate and the person for whom he holds the land, the *cestui que trust*, has an equitable interest only.[3] The *Statute of Uses*[4] applies only to the first of two or more non-successive uses, so if land is conveyed to and to the use of A in trust for or to the use of B, A retains the legal estate and B has only an equitable interest[5] and if the limitation is to A and his heirs to the use of B and his heirs in trust for C, B has a legal estate in fee simple in trust for C who has the equitable interest.[6] An example of an interest partly legal and partly equitable is a conveyance to the use of A and his heirs during the life of A (legal), with remainder to the use of B and his heirs in trust for A and his heirs (equitable), A thus having an estate of inheritance.[7] If a husband contracts to purchase land and dies before its conveyance to him, he had an equitable interest in the land to which he died beneficially entitled and his widow had a right of dower in the land.[8]

707.3 Momentary Seisin

Since momentary seisin was sufficient to have the right of dower attach, the seisin of a husband who took an estate in fee and immediately mortgaged it to secure a portion of the purchase price was sufficient to have dower attach.[1] Thus, where a vendor conveyed land to a purchaser who, in accordance with a prior agreement, immediately reconveyed the land to the vendor by way of mortgage, in which mortgage the purchaser's wife did not join, it was held that she was entitled to dower.[2] In such case, the dower so to be allotted had to be charged with payment of one-third of the interest of the mortgage money unless the dowress chose to pay one-third of the mortgage debt.[3] Where a husband bought land and mortgaged it, the mortgage being delivered and registered before delivery of the deed to him, it was contended that he had never had the legal estate so that his wife had no dower, but was held that the mortgagee obtained the legal estate through him and that, although he

---

[3]*Spencer v. Registrar of Titles*, [1906] A.C. 503 (P.C.); *Fair v. McCrow* (1871), 31 U.C.Q.B. 599; *Whiteside v. Miller* (1868), 14 Gr. 393.
[4]27 Hen. 8, c. 10 (1535).
[5]*Gamble v. Rees* (1850), 6 U.C.Q.B. 396.
[6]*Cooper v. Kynock* (1872), L.R. 7 Ch. 398.
[7]See *Re Michell; Moore v. Moore*, [1892] 2 Ch. 87 at p. 99.
[8]*Craig v. Templeton* (1860), 8 Gr. 483.
§707.3
[1]*Lynch v. O'Hara* (1856), 6 U.C.C.P. 259.
[2]*Potts v. Meyers* (1857), 14 U.C.Q.B. 499; *Smith v. Norton* (1861), 7 U.C.L.J. O.S. 263; *Heney v. Low* (1862), 9 Gr. 265.
[3]*Heney v. Low, supra.*

only had seisin for an instant, that was sufficient for dower to attach.[4] On the other hand, the discharge of a mortgage does not operate as a reconveyance of the legal estate until registration. Hence, where the owner of the equity of redemption gave a new mortgage which was registered before registration of the discharge of the old, the effect of the registration of the mortgage was to vest the legal estate in the new mortgagee and not in the husband who, therefore, never had a legal estate in which his wife had any inchoate right of dower.[5] The seisin of the mortgagee, however, did not entitle his widow to dower because his legal estate is subject to being divested upon satisfaction of the condition of payment of the mortgage debt.[6]

707.4　Where Husband's Estate is Defeated

Since birth of issue was not essential, dower attached even if the husband's estate was defeated for want of issue, as where land was devised to a husband with an executory devise over if he died without issue, in which case the widow had her dower, although the devise over took effect.[1] Similarly, dower was not defeated by an escheat.[2] If a husband's seisin was defeated by re-entry for breach of condition, however, his estate was gone and the right of dower ceased.[3] Similarly, the dower right was gone where the husband's determinable fee came to an end on the happening of the event specified in the limitation.[4]

707.5　Dower in Exchange of Lands

In a transaction of exchange of one property for another, the wife was not entitled to dower in both properties and had to elect to have dower in one or the other.[1] To have that result, however, the exchange had to be proved in proper technical form by deed. Hence, where it was contended that the husband had exchanged other lands for the lands in question and that the wife had elected to have her dower in the other lands, the production of the husband's ordinary deed of bargain and sale of the other lands for a money consideration and parol evidence clearly showing that the transaction was in

---

[4]*Re Irvine* (1928), 62 O.L.R. 319, [1928] 3 D.L.R. 268 (S.C. App. Div.); *Whyte v. Davey*, [1933] O.W.N. 147 (H.C.J.).

[5]*Re Tierney* (1927), 60 O.L.R. 652, [1927] 3 D.L.R. 943 (H.C.).

[6]*Ham v. Ham* (1857), 14 U.C.Q.B. 497.

§707.4

[1]*Moody v. King* (1825), 2 Bing. 447, 130 E.R. 378; *Smith v. Spencer* (1856), 4 W.R. 729.

[2]*Burgess v. Wheate*; *Attorney-General v. Wheate* (1759), 1 Eden 177 at p. 193, 28 E.R. 652.

[3]Litt., §325; Co. Litt. 201b.

[4]See generally, Haskins, "The Defeasibility of Dower", 98 U. of Pa. L. Rev. 826 (1949-50); "Recent Cases", 36 Minn. L. Rev. 280 (1951-52).

§707.5

[1]*McLellan v. Meggatt* (1850), 7 U.C.Q.B. 554; *White v. Laing* (1852), 2 U.C.C.P. 186.

fact an exchange, were insufficient to disentitle the wife to the dower claimed.[2] Similarly, parol evidence that the husband had "traded" other lands out of which the wife's dower had been satisfied, without production of deeds, was held to be insufficient,[3] as was also the production of two deeds by which the husband and the other party "conveyed" to each other, for the word "convey" does not have the same effect as "exchange".[4]

707.6 Defeating Dower by a Grant to Uses

If a husband's seisin was merely transitory, as where he was merely the grantee to uses, dower did not attach because the grant which conveyed the freehold to him immediately vested possession in the *cestui que use*, the person entitled to the use, and the grantee is merely a conduit through whom the use and possession passes in transit to the *cestui que use*.[1] This is due to the operation of the *Statute of Uses*.[2] Thus, if A granted land to B and his heirs to the use of C and his heirs, the wife of B had no dower in the land, because the grant which gave B the estate immediately took it away from him again by giving the use and possession to C.[3] The *Statute of Uses* operates whenever lands are conveyed or devised to one person in trust for, or to the use of, or for the benefit of another person, without active duties being imposed upon the grantee or devisee.[4]

Conveyancing methods, employing the *Statute of Uses*, were devised to enable a husband to defeat dower. A conveyance might be made to a third person to such uses as the husband shall appoint and, in default of and until such appointment, to the use of the husband in fee. Under such a limitation, dower would immediately attach to the husband's fee but would be divested upon the husband conveying and appointing the estate to the use of a purchaser from himself, reciting his power of appointment, in which case the *Statute of Uses*, by reason of the original conveyance, vests the fee in the purchaser free from the dower interest.[5] At one time there was a conflict of legal authority on the question whether the same thing would be accomplished if the original conveyance were to the husband in fee to such uses as he might

---

[2]*Towsley v. Smith* (1854), 12 U.C.Q.B. 555.
[3]*Stafford v. Trueman* (1857), 7 U.C.C.P. 41.
[4]*Leach v. Dennis* (1864), 24 U.C.Q.B. 129.
§707.6
[1]2 Bl. Comm. 131-2; *Sneyd v. Sneyd* (1738), 1 Atk. 442, 26 E.R. 282.
[2]27 Hen. 8, c. 10 (1535).
[3]*Smith v. Norton* (1861), 7 U.C.L.J. 263.
[4]*Fair v. McCrow* (1871), 31 U.C.Q.B. 599 ("in trust for the sole benefit of"); *Tunis v. Passmore* (1872), 32 U.C.Q.B. 419; *Re Romanes and Smith* (1880), 8 P.R. (Ont.) 323; *Re Hall and Urquhart* (1928), 35 O.W.N. 201 (H.C.); *Barker v. Greenwood* (1838), 4 M. & W. 421, 150 E.R. 1494; *Williams v. Waters* (1845), 14 M. & W. 166, 153 E.R. 434.
[5]*Re Walsh and Sovis*, [1956] O.R. 202, 2 D.L.R. (2d) 356 (H.C.J.).

appoint and, until appointment, to himself in fee.[6] It was formerly supposed that, as the grantee had, until exercise of the power, a vested estate to which dower attached, it could not be defeated by exercise of the power. The reason this was thought to be so was that a common law seisin and a use or power of appointment could not co-exist in the same estate in the same person, that the power would be merged in the fee so as to be nugatory and void, and that, for the power to have any effect, it was necessary that the conveyance be to one person to such uses as another person might appoint and, until appointment, to the use of the latter.[7] Modern cases suggested otherwise, however,[8] and it was held in Re Hazell,[9] that where a conveyance is made to a husband to such uses as he shall appoint and, in default of appointment, to himself in fee, the wife's inchoate right of dower attached immediately, subject to being defeated upon the exercise of the husband's power of appointment.

The decision in Re Hazell on this point is curious and of doubtful validity. However, it stood the test of time and was followed in several cases.[10] The decision was curious in another respect as well, for it held, by erroneous analogy to the procedure involved in the barring of an estate tail, that while the making of a mortgage by the grantee to uses does not exhaust the power to appoint, once the mortgage is discharged and the discharge is registered, the grantee to uses does not receive back the fee coupled with the power, but only the fee. The effect was that while a bar of dower by the wife of the grantee to uses was not necessary in a grant to a second person to uses, registered after the mortgage but before the discharge, a grant to a third person after the registration of the discharge did require a bar of dower by the wife of the second grantee to uses.

Because of the fact that a statutory discharge does not operate as a reconveyance until registration under the Registry Act,[11] where a discharge had been executed but not registered, the grantee to uses could continue to defeat his wife's dower by grant.[12]

In order to avoid the effects of Re Hazell, conveyancers used one of two conveyancing techniques. The first employed a release and reconveyance to uses by the mortgagee instead of a statutory discharge. The second used a "long uses" clause in which the habendum in the deed to uses spelled out in detail that a limited appointment, such as a mortgage, did not exhaust the power and that registration of a statutory discharge to the grantee or his

---

[6]See the discussion of the authorities referred to in Armour, Real Property, pp. 114-15, note (j).

[7]Ibid.

[8]See, for example, Ray v. Pung (1822), 5 B. & Ald. 561, 106 E.R. 1296; Lyster v. Kirkpatrick (1866), 26 U.C.Q.B. 217.

[9](1925), 57 O.L.R. 290, [1925] 3 D.L.R. 661 (S.C. App. Div.), following Ray v. Pung, supra, footnote 8.

[10]Re Armstrong and Brown, [1952] O.W.N. 55 (C.A.); Re Walsh and Sovis, supra, footnote 5; Re Rowe, [1957] O.R. 9, 10 D.L.R. (2d) 215 (H.C.J.).

[11]R.S.O. 1970, c. 409, s. 61, rep. & sub. 1972, c. 133, s. 24.

[12]Re Dresser, [1959] O.W.N. 103 (H.C.J.).

successor in title (if the latter also held to uses) did not exhaust the power to appoint. The second device was specifically approved.[13]

These devices were no longer required in Ontario after an amendment was made to the *Registry Act* in 1966,[14] which reversed *Re Hazell*. The amendment tacitly condones the use of a deed to uses with a power of appointment in the grantee, and it provides that a mortgage does not exhaust the power and that the grantee to uses may continue to exercise his power of appointment notwithstanding the registration of a discharge of mortgage.[15] A similar provision was earlier made for land registered under the *Land Titles Act*.[16] Without it a transfer to uses was theretofore impossible under that system of registration.

A husband could defeat his wife's dower if he held under a deed to uses, not only during his lifetime by executing a deed or mortgage in exercise of his power of appointment, but he could also do it by will, at least if his power extended to appointments made by will. Thus, where land was conveyed to a person in fee simple to hold to himself and his heirs forever to such uses as he should by deed or will appoint and, in default of appointment, to the use of himself and his heirs absolutely, and by will he gave all his property to his executors in trust to convert and divide the proceeds, it was held that the executors could sell the land free from the dower of the testator's widow because she had no claim to dower, as the will operated as an exercise of the power of appointment.[17] Of course, if a husband, having the use until he exercises the power of appointment, were to die without exercising the power, his widow would have her dower, as it would not be divested.

707.7 Dower and Mortgages

Since, under the several statutes, the husband had to die beneficially entitled to land before his widow had any right of dower, there was no inchoate right of dower in an equitable interest during his life, and he was able to defeat her dower by alienating it during his lifetime.[1] Therefore, although a wife was entitled to dower in an equity of redemption resulting from her husband having made a mortgage in which she joined to bar her dower, she was not entitled to dower in an equity of redemption which he purchased and sold in his lifetime, as the legal estate had never vested in him and he did not die beneficially entitled to the land.[2] Where a purchaser of land who had not paid

---

13*Re Morley and Kent*, [1966] 2 O.R. 368, 56 D.L.R. (2d) 679 (H.C.J.).
14Now R.S.O. 1980, c. 445, s. 59.
15See Gosse, *The Registry Act and the Land Titles Act of Ontario* (Toronto, Carswell & Co., 1967), pp. 15 *et seq.*
16Now R.S.O. 1980, c. 230, s. 92.
17*Re Osborne and Campbell* (1918), 15 O.W.N. 48, 55 D.L.R. 258 (H.C.), *per* Middleton, J.; *Re Dresser, supra*, footnote 12.
§707.7
1*Gardner v. Brown* (1890), 19 O.R. 202 (H.C.J.); *Fitzgerald v. Fitzgerald* (1903), 5 O.L.R. 279 (C.A.).
2*Re Luckhardt* (1897), 29 O.R. 111 (H.C.J.).

the purchase money or obtained a conveyance mortgaged his equitable interest, it was held that the giving of a power of sale in the mortgage operated to defeat dower, even though the power was not exercised until after the husband's death.[3]

In regard to mortgages in which the wife joined to bar dower, the Ontario Act provided that no bar of dower in a mortgage, or other instrument intended to have the effect of a mortgage or other security upon land, should have operated to bar dower to a greater extent than necessary to give full effect to the rights of the mortgagee or grantee under such instrument,[4] and that, where such land was sold under any power of sale in the instrument or under any legal process, the wife should be entitled to dower in any surplus of the purchase money remaining after satisfaction of the claim of the mortgagee or grantee to the same extent as she would have been entitled to dower if the land had not been sold, and, except where the mortgage or instrument was for purchase money of the land, the amount to which she was entitled should be calculated on the basis of the amount realized from the sale over and above the amount of the mortgage.[5] The Nova Scotia Act contained comparable provisions,[6] save that there was no exception as to purchase-money mortgages.

The provision in section 9(1) of the Ontario Act was originally enacted by the *Dower Act* of 1879,[7] which went into force on March 11, 1879, and this must be borne in mind when referring to cases decided before that date. The former rule was that if a wife barred her dower in a mortgage by her husband, his legal estate was thereby turned into an equitable estate with his wife's consent, and he could alienate it without it being necessary for her to join to bar her dower and she would have no dower unless he died beneficially entitled to the land.[8]

The new rule provided by the Act of 1879 and found in section 9(1) of the Ontario Act stipulated that the bar of dower in a mortgage is only for the purpose of the mortgage and is not a bar of dower in the remaining equity of redemption. Therefore, in such cases there could be no conveyance of the equity of redemption free from dower unless the wife joined in it.[9] Hence, where a wife barred her dower in a first mortgage and later in a second mortgage, it was held that her right of dower in the equity of redemption could not be defeated by a transfer by the husband in his lifetime.[10] Where a wife joined in a mortgage of the legal estate to bar her dower and the mortgage was paid off before her husband's assignment for the benefit of creditors (by which his interest in the land was conveyed to the assignee) but the discharge of the mortgage was not registered until after the assignment,

---

[3] *Smith v. Smith* (1852), 3 Gr. 451.
[4] Ont. Act, s. 9(1).
[5] *Ibid.*, s. 9(2).
[6] N.S. Act, ss. 6, 7.
[7] S.O. 1879, c. 22.
[8] *Beavis v. Maguire* (1882), 7 O.A.R. 704.
[9] *Pratt v. Bunnell* (1891), 21 O.R. 1 (H.C.J.).
[10] *Re Lesperance* (1927), 61 O.L.R. 94, [1927] 4 D.L.R. 391 (H.C.).

it was held that the wife's dower would accrue on her husband's death as her bar of dower in the mortgage operated only to the extent necessary to give effect to the rights of the mortgagee.[11]

The provision in section 9(2) of the Ontario Act to the effect that, upon mortgaged land being sold under power of sale or by legal process, the wife was entitled to dower out of the surplus calculated upon the amount realized from the sale and not just upon the amount realized over and above the mortgage debt was originally enacted in 1895.[12] In the case of *Pratt v. Bunnell*,[13] which was decided prior to the 1895 statute, it had been held that, on such a sale, dower was to be calculated only out of the surplus of the land or money remaining after satisfying the mortgage debt, but that view was dissented from by a later Divisional Court which held that where a mortgagee sells the land, dower was to be computed on the entire purchase price and to be paid out of the surplus remaining after satisfying the mortgage debt.[14] Hence, where a wife barred her dower in a first mortgage and later in a second mortgage, it was held that, as such bar only operates to the extent of giving full effect to the mortgages and a sale by the second mortgagee realized sufficient to pay off both mortgages, she was entitled to her dower out of the surplus calculated on the full amount realized by the sale.[15] Similarly, where the devisee of a farm subject to payment of legacies mortgaged the land, his wife joining in the mortgage to bar dower, paid the legacies and died owning the equity of redemption, it was held that she was entitled to dower computed upon the basis of the full value of the land, because the devisee received a legal estate that would have entitled his wife to dower at common law subject to the charge for legacies. Even if the legacies were unpaid when he died, his wife would have been entitled to dower computed upon the full value of the land subject to satisfying the legacies.[16] Where a deceased husband had mortgaged his legal estate with his wife joining in the mortgage to bar her dower, and the property was sold for an amount in excess of the mortgage debt, and mechanics' lien claimants and creditors claimed the surplus, it was held that she was entitled to dower calculated on the full price realized and payable out of the surplus after the mechanics' liens were satisfied.[17]

The same result obtained under section 7 of the Nova Scotia Act even though the sale occurred after the husband's death. Thus, in *Canada Permanent Trust Co. v. Morrison*,[18] a wife barred her dower in a mortgage and remained in possession after her husband's death. The property was then sold by the mortgagee and the widow's estate (she having died in the meantime) was held entitled to her dower out of the surplus, equal to one-third of the net

---

[11]*McNally v. Anderson* (1913), 4 O.W.N. 901, 9 D.L.R. 449 (H.C.).
[12]*An Act respecting Dower in Mortgaged and other Property Act*, S.O. 1895, c. 25, s. 3.
[13]*Supra*, footnote 9.
[14]*Gemmill v. Nelligan* (1895), 26 O.R. 307 (H.C.J.).
[15]*Re Lesperance*, *supra*, footnote 10.
[16]*Re Zimmerman* (1904), 7 O.L.R. 489 (H.C.J.).
[17]*Re Robinson*, [1938] O.W.N. 361, [1938] 4 D.L.R. 771 (H.C.J.).
[18](1970), 10 D.L.R. (3d) 594, 1 N.S.R. (2d) 764 (S.C. in Chambers).

rents from the property from the time of her husband's death to her own. Even if there were no forced sale but the widow barred her dower in a deed by her husband's executors, reserving her right to dower payable out of the proceeds of the sale, she would have been entitled to her dower calculated on the same basis as in the statute.[19]

Where the mortgage was for unpaid purchase money, the widow was only entitled to dower calculated on the surplus of the amount realized on the sale after first deducting the balance of the mortgage debt at the time of the death of the husband.[20]

A mortgage is one for unpaid purchase money only if it is given back to the vendor in the same right to secure unpaid purchase money. Thus, a mortgage to another to finance the purchase, or to the vendor in his individual, instead of his representative, capacity, is not a purchase-money mortgage.[21] Similarly, a mortgage given to a stranger to refinance a purchase-money mortgage is not, itself, a purchase-money mortgage.[22]

The Ontario Act provided[23] that a mortgagee or other person holding any money out of which a wife was dowable under section 9 could pay the money into court, but a widow was not entitled to take her interest in money under section 9 and, in addition, a share of the money as personal estate.[24]

The *Land Titles Act*[25] provided that where the registered owner acquired land subject to a charge and transferred it subject to that charge, or where the registered owner of land that was subject to a charge subsequently married and transferred the land subject to that charge, the wife of the owner was not entitled to dower in the land.

707.8 Exceptions to Dower Generally

By reason of the general law there were a number of instances in which dower did not arise. These were as follows:

(a) Fiduciaries

The wife of a trustee did not have a dower interest in lands of which her husband was a trustee. The reason was that, while a trustee normally has the seisin, he does not hold it for his own benefit, but for the benefit of the *cestui que trust*, who has the real interest. It was not a "fraud" on the marital rights of the wife for a husband to take title to land in the name of a trustee in order to defeat dower.[1]

---

[19]*Re Smith*, [1952] O.R. 135, [1952] 2 D.L.R. 104 (C.A.).
[20]*Re Auger* (1912), 26 O.L.R. 402, 5 D.L.R. 680 (H.C.J.).
[21]*Re Smith, supra*, footnote 19.
[22]*Re Lesperance* (1927), 61 O.L.R. 94, [1927] 4 D.L.R. 391 (H.C.).
[23]Ont. Act, s. 10.
[24]*Ibid.*, s. 11.
[25]R.S.O. 1970, c. 234, s. 132, rep. 1978, c. 7.
§707.8
[1]*Gillis v. Sewell*, [1942] 4 D.L.R. 582 (Ont. H.C.J.).

The same result obtained with the employment of fiduciaries generally and where the husband was a *quasi*-trustee. Thus, a man who before marriage contracted to sell land became a *quasi*-trustee for the purchaser and, upon his marriage, his wife was not entitled to dower in the land, unless the purchaser forfeited his rights and the husband again became seised of the land to his own use.[2] Where a widower occupied Crown lands for which he had obtained the patent and executed a bond in favour of his son, in consideration of services rendered, to the effect that the land was to be conveyed to the son on the father's death on condition that the son pay the Crown dues, which he did, and the father remarried and thereafter obtained the patent, it was held that the widow was not entitled to dower because the husband had possession only for life and held the fee in trust for the son.[3]

Similarly, where a mother gave her son certain moneys which he invested in land it was held that the son held the land in trust for the mother and thus the son's widow's dower rights were subject to that equitable lien in favour of the mother. This was so even though the son executed a declaration of trust only shortly before his death, for the declaration was mere evidence of the trust which was constituted when the money was advanced.[4]

(b) Mortgagees

Although a mortgagee was seised of the legal estate, his widow was not entitled to dower because the legal estate is subject to being divested upon the satisfaction of the condition in the mortgage of payment of the mortgage debt.[5] The same reasoning applied to a mortgage of an equity of redemption or of any other equitable interest; the wife of the mortgagee was not entitled to dower even if he died beneficially entitled to the mortgage.

On the other hand, if the mortgage is foreclosed, the mortgagee becomes the owner and his wife formerly became entitled to dower.

(c) Joint tenancies

Both at common law and under the several statutes, dower did not attach to a joint tenancy since the husband who was a joint tenant was not solely seised. This is distinct from a tenancy in common in which each tenant in common is separately seised of an undivided share.[6] It follows that if the husband severed the joint tenancy, or if it were partitioned, dower attached to his share. Similarly, if the husband became entitled to the whole interest by survivorship, dower attached to the whole.[7]

2*Gordon v. Gordon* (1864), 10 Gr. 466; *Lloyd v. Lloyd* (1843), 2 Con. & Law. 592 (Ir.).
3*Brown v. Brown* (1904), 8 O.L.R. 332 (H.C.J.).
4*Bradley v. Holden* (1958), 13 D.L.R. (2d) 684 (Ont. H.C.J.).
5*Ham v. Ham* (1857), 14 U.C.Q.B. 497.
6Litt., §45.
7*Reynard v. Spence* (1841), 4 Beav. 103, 49 E.R. 277.

§707.8 PART II TENURES AND ESTATES

(d) Partnership lands

There was no dower in land held as partnership property. Partnership property is regarded as personalty and as part of the capital assets of the partnership, available to satisfy partnership debts and thereafter for distribution among the partners according to their partnership shares, for no partner can claim specific partnership property, but is merely entitled to his share of the surplus assets after satisfaction of partnership debts.[8] This is so even if land is conveyed to one partner alone.[9] It is always a question of fact, however, as to whether particular property was acquired as a partnership asset for, under the *Partnership Act* of each of the provinces (except Quebec), co-ownership and sharing profits do not necessarily constitute a partnership or a partnership transaction.

707.9 Statutory Exceptions to Dower

In addition to exceptions arising by the general law, there were certain statutory exceptions to dower. These were as follows:

(a) Separate, unimproved parcels

There was no dower in any separate and distinct parcel of land which, at the time of the husband's alienation of it, or his death, was in a state of nature and unimproved by clearing, fencing, or otherwise, for the purpose of cultivation or occupation,[1] but this was without restriction of the right of the widow to have woodland assigned to her from which she might take firewood necessary for her use and timber for fencing the other portions of the same parcel assigned to her.[2] Moreover, under the Nova Scotia Act[3] a widow was entitled to have a reasonable allowance made for the value of such unimproved lands. Where a testator, before he died, had contracted to sell a timbered lot, it was held that the lot was not in a state of nature but was improved for the purposes of cultivation in part, so that his widow was entitled to dower in the whole lot, with the right to have assigned to her one-third of the part that was not woodland and one-third of the woodland and the right to take from the latter firewood and timber for fencing the other part.[4]

---

[8]*Darby v. Darby* (1856), 3 Drewry 495 at p. 503, 61 E.R. 992; *Conger v. Platt* (1866), 25 U.C.Q.B. 277; *Re Music Hall Block*; *Dumble v. McIntosh* (1885), 8 O.R. 225 (H.C.J.); *Re Cushing's Estate* (1895), 1 N.B. Eq. R. 102.
[9]*Selkrig v. Davies* (1814), 2 Dow. 230 at p. 242, 3 E.R. 848 (H.L.); *Phillips v. Phillips* (1832), 1 My. & K. 649, 39 E.R. 826.
§707.9
[1]Ont. Act, s. 5; N.B. Act, s. 4; N.S. Act, s. 4(1).
[2]Ont. Act, s. 5; N.B. Act, s. 4; N.S. Act, s. 4(3).
[3]N.S. Act, s. 4(2).
[4]*Re McIntyre*; *McIntyre v. London and Western Trusts Co.* (1904), 7 O.L.R. 548 (H.C.J.).

186

(b) Mining lands

There was no dower in land granted by the Crown as mining land if it were granted or conveyed to the husband and he did not die entitled to it.[5]

(c) Streets and highways

There was no dower in land dedicated by the owner for a street or public highway.[6]

(d) Where wife was of unsound mind

In Ontario, a person whose wife was of unsound mind and who was a patient in a mental institution at the time he acquired the land could convey or encumber it free of dower while his wife was so confined.[7] However, the Ontario Act also made provision for a husband to make application to the court for an order dispensing with a bar of dower in such circumstances and the court could make such an order unconditionally, or direct that the value of the dower should be paid into court or be otherwise secured and applied for the wife's benefit.[8]

(e) Where wife had not resided in province

Where a wife had not lived in the province since the marriage, the husband could sell land in Ontario free of dower.[9] However, this right existed only during the husband's lifetime. Once he died the wife's dower right became consummate and his estate could not then sell free from dower.[10]

707.10 Dower after Termination of Marriage

Since only a wife was entitled to dower, a wife who obtained a divorce or annulment from her husband by reason of his misconduct, forfeited her dower.[1]

In New Brunswick, a wife was not, since 1973, entitled to dower after the marriage had been terminated. Prior thereto her dower right was denied only where the marriage was terminated by divorce or judicial separation by reason of her adultery.[2]

---

[5]Ont. Act, s. 6.
[6]*Ibid.*, s. 7.
[7]*Ibid.*, s. 12(1).
[8]*Ibid.*, s. 13. See further §707.13, *infra*.
[9]*Ibid.*, s. 12(2).
[10]*Re Lou Night Jung* (1960), 23 D.L.R. (2d) 52 (Ont. H.C.J.).
§707.10
[1]*Frampton v. Stephens* (1882), 21 Ch. D. 164, and see *Re Williams and Ancient Order of United Workmen* (1907), 14 O.L.R. 482 (H.C.J.); *Re Hodgins* (1920), 18 O.W.N. 231 (H.C.).
[2]S.N.B. 1973, c. 31, s. 1; now N.B. Act, s. 5.

A wife was effectively precluded from claiming dower in her husband's estate if she had barred her dower in a separation agreement.[3]

707.11 Statutory Bars to Dower

The Ontario Act provided that where a wife willingly left her husband and went away and continued with her adulterer, she was barred forever from an action to demand dower, unless her husband was willingly reconciled with her and permitted her to dwell with him, in which case she was restored to her action.[1] The Nova Scotia Act contained a similar provision, but it did not provide for reconciliation.[2] Under the Prince Edward Island Act, a husband could apply to the court for an order dispensing with a bar of dower where his wife had lived apart from him in such circumstances as would disentitle her to alimony.[3] Forfeiture under these provisions occurred if the wife voluntarily lived in adultery apart from her husband, even if she left his house in consequence of his violence, or was deserted by him.[4] It was not necessary that she live continuously with one man.[5] Living the life of a prostitute caused forfeiture under this provision of the Act.[6] In England, under a similar statutory provision, it was held that the right of dower was forfeited by the wife's adultery even if she left her husband by reason of his cruelty,[7] or if her adultery was brought about by his misconduct.[8]

Where a wife lived in adultery apart from her husband she was barred not only from taking her dower, but from electing to take her preferential share and her distributive share in the real property of her husband's estate where he died intestate, for, having lost her dower right, she also lost her right to that which she might otherwise have taken in lieu.[9]

707.12 Barring Dower

In this section are considered consensual bars of dower by deed and marriage settlement, as well as the refusal of a wife to bar dower in circumstances in which it was impossible to obtain a court order dispensing with a bar of dower.

---

[3]*Re Schop*, [1948] O.W.N. 338 (H.C.J.).
§707.11
[1]Ont. Act, s. 8.
[2]N.S. Act, s. 8.
[3]P.E.I. Act, s. 7.
[4]*Woolsey v. Finch* (1869), 20 U.C.C.P. 132; *Neff v. Thompson* (1869), 20 U.C.C.P. 211.
[5]*Re S* (1907), 14 O.L.R. 536 (H.C.J.).
[6]*Ibid.*
[7]*Woodward v. Dowse* (1861), 10 C.B. (N.S.) 722, 142 E.R. 637.
[8]*Bostock v. Smith* (1864), 34 Beav. 57, 55 E.R. 553.
[9]*Re Schop*, [1948] O.W.N. 338 (H.C.J.); *MacWilliams v. MacWilliams*, [1962] O.R. 407, 32 D.L.R. (2d) 481 (C.A.).

(a) Where the wife joined in the deed

A married woman who was of sound mind could bar her dower in her husband's land by joining in the deed. The Ontario Act provided that where a wife joined in a conveyance or mortgage purporting to convey or mortgage land, or signed, other than as witness, a conveyance or mortgage by her husband, but the conveyance or mortgage contained no words purporting to release her dower or other interest in the land, it should have the same effect as if it contained a bar of dower by her.[1]

However, where a husband and wife were joint tenants of land and when they conveyed the wife signed only to bar her dower, which was, of course, unnecessary, it was held that her bar of dower did not operate as a conveyance of her interest.[2]

The Prince Edward Island Act was more restrictive. It provided that no deed or mortgage in which a married woman joined to bar dower, and no power of attorney for the purpose, was valid or effectual unless the deed or power of attorney was acknowledged by her, apart from her husband, as having been freely executed by her without compulsion by him and that she was aware of the value and contents of the deed or power of attorney, and the officer taking the acknowledgement was to endorse his certificate on the instrument, and, in order to release and convey dower or the right of dower, it was sufficient to say in an instrument "and the said A. B. doth hereby release all her right of dower".[3]

The several statutes further provided that a married woman who was under the age of majority and of sound mind could bar her dower in any land by joining with her husband in a deed or conveyance to a purchaser for value, or mortgage, or by transfer or charge, in which deed, conveyance, transfer or charge a release or bar of her dower was contained and she could similarly release her dower to any person to whom the land had been previously conveyed.[4] The *Married Women's Property Act*[5] provided that a married woman could dispose of her real or personal property in the same manner as if she were a *feme sole* without the intervention of a trustee.[6]

(b) Refusal to bar dower

Dower was a wife's primary right and it could not be taken away from her even by order of the court, except in certain special circumstances. Therefore, where a husband sold land and his wife was unwilling to bar her dower, the purchaser did not obtain a clear title and he could refuse to complete the transaction. However, where the purchaser wished to complete, the court

---

§707.12
[1] Ont. Act, s. 19.
[2] *Re Mancini and Saltzman*, [1967] 1 O.R. 319, 60 D.L.R. (2d) 402 (Dist. Ct.).
[3] P.E.I. Act, s. 12.
[4] N.B. Act, s. 6; N.S. Act, s. 14; Ont. Act, s. 20; P.E.I. Act, s. 13.
[5] R.S.O. 1970, c. 262, s. 2(1), rep. 1975, c. 41, s. 6.
[6] *Cf.* to the same effect *Married Women's Deeds Act*, R.S.N.S. 1967, c. 175, s. 2.

could in appropriate circumstances permit him to pay a portion of the purchase price, not exceeding one-third, into court to indemnify him from any future claim for dower by the wife in accordance with the practice laid down in *Re Woods and Arthur*.[7]

Under this practice, the vendor was entitled to interest on the money during the joint lives of himself and his wife and the money would be paid out to him if his wife predeceased him. If his wife survived him, she was entitled to have her dower assigned to her by metes and bounds or otherwise to have it calculated and paid to her if it could not be assigned, in which case the purchaser would receive the interest on the money in court until she died, after which the fund would be paid to the vendor's estate. Alternatively, the surviving wife could elect to take the interest on the money in court for her life and after her death the fund would be paid to her husband's estate.

It was the duty of the vendor "to ascertain *bona fide*, whether his wife was willing to bar her dower, and to induce her by any reasonable sacrifice on his own part to do so".[8] If he did not do so but deliberately failed to carry out his duty he was not entitled to cancel the agreement for his inability to satisfy the purchaser's objection to title, that is, the absence of a bar of dower, and the court would in those circumstances grant the purchaser specific performance with a *"Re Woods and Arthur* order".[9]

(c) Barring dower in a marriage settlement

Jointure was an historical method used to bar dower in present or after-acquired real property. Technically, as the word implies, it was a joint estate limited to the husband and wife, but was recognized as extending to an estate limited to the wife only. It could be legal or equitable. A legal jointure is defined as a competent livelihood of freehold to the wife of lands and tenements to take effect presently after the death of the husband for the life of the wife at least, and might be made before or after marriage.[10] When the *Statute of Uses*[11] turned uses into legal estates, so that the husband became seised of any lands of which he had the use, a wife would have had her dower in all such lands as well as her interest under a jointure if the statute had not provided against it.

In Ontario, the *Statute of Uses*[12] provides, accordingly, that where lands are conveyed to husband and wife and the heirs of the husband, or to husband and wife and the heirs of their bodies or one of their bodies, or to husband and wife for their lives or the life of the wife, or to any person or persons and their heirs and assigns to the use of the husband and wife or the use of the

---

[7](1921), 49 O.L.R. 279, 58 D.L.R. 620 (H.C.).
[8]*Kendrew v. Shewan* (1854), 4 Gr. 578 at p. 580, *per* Esten, V.C.
[9]*Freedman v. Mason*, [1957] O.R. 441, 9 D.L.R. (2d) 262 (C.A.), affd 14 D.L.R. (2d) 529, [1958] S.C.R. 483. See also "Recent Cases", 29 Minn. L. Rev. 280 (1945).
[10]Co. Litt. 36b.
[11]27 Hen. 8, c. 10 (1535).
[12]R.S.O. 1897, c. 331, reprinted in R.S.O. 1980, vol. Appendices.

wife, for the jointure of the wife, she shall not be entitled to dower in the residue of any lands that were her husband's at any time, unless he did not have the jointure, in which case she is entitled to dower.[13] It also provides that, if she is evicted from her jointure or part of it, without fraud, by lawful entry or action or by discontinuance of her husband, she is to be endowed of as much of the residue of her husband's lands of which she was before dowable as amounts to the lands from which she was evicted.[14] Finally, the statute provides that, if a wife has any land given or assured to her after marriage, for her life or otherwise in jointure, she is entitled, after the death of her husband, to refuse to take the land and to elect to have dower instead in all lands of which her husband was seised for an estate of inheritance during coverture.[15]

A jointure made before marriage under the similar Imperial statute bound the wife and barred her dower even though she was an infant and the jointure was not of the value of the dower.[16] The requisites of a jointure were that it had to take effect immediately after the death of the husband, it had to be for the wife's life at least and not for any smaller estate, such as an estate *pur autre vie*, or for years, it had to be made to herself and not to another person in trust for her and it had to be in satisfaction of her whole dower and not just part of it, although that fact need not be expressed in the deed itself.[17]

It is to be noted that the Act provides that if the jointure be made after marriage, the wife may make her election after the death of her husband, because formerly she could not consent during coverture. After the *Married Women's Property Act*,[18] however, she had the power to consent during coverture, so where a husband conveyed land in trust for his wife and she was in possession for many years, survived her husband, and did not claim dower until seven months after his death, it was held that she had to act promptly after his death and, having failed to do so, she could not elect to take dower.[19]

Dower could also be barred by equitable jointure. Any provision intended to be in lieu of dower and accepted by a wife of full age as being in satisfaction of her dower, was in equity a bar to the right of dower, whatever the provision might be and whether it was made before or after the marriage.[20]

Instead of legal jointure, another method to bar dower, being the more usual method adopted in Ontario, was that of a marriage settlement or agreement before marriage, under which the wife accepted its provisions for her in lieu of dower in present or after-acquired lands. In such case, if she

---

13*Ibid.*, s. 5.
14*Ibid.*, s. 6.
15*Ibid.*, s. 7.
16*Earl of Buckingham v. Drury* (1762), 3 Bro. P.C. 492, 1 E.R. 1454 (H.L.), also reported as *Drury v. Drury* (1762), 4 Bro. C.C. 506n, 29 E.R. 1013.
17*Gilkison v. Elliot* (1867), 27 U.C.Q.B. 95.
1845 & 46 Vict., c. 75 (1882).
19*Eves v. Booth* (1900), 27 O.A.R. 420.
20*Dyke v. Rendall* (1852), 2 De G. M. & G. 209, 42 E.R. 851.

were an adult, the inadequacy or precariousness of its provisions or their failure to materialize was immaterial, her dower being barred nevertheless. Thus, in *Dyke v. Rendall*,[21] Lord St. Leonards said:

> If the present were a jointure operating as a bar under the Statute of Uses, the case would have been governed by the 7th section of that statute, but in equity the bar rests solely on contract, and my opinion is that in this Court, if a woman, being of age, accepts a particular something in satisfaction of dower, she must take it with all its faults, and must look at the contract alone, and cannot in case of eviction come against anyone in possession of the lands, on which otherwise her dower might have attached . . .
>
> My conclusion is, that the Plaintiff has accepted in lieu of dower payment of money at least, and that she is also concluded by the acceptance of the bond, and, although the bond was not satisfied, that she has no right to resort to the lands of her husband bought after, and sold during, the marriage.

Similarly, a provision in a marriage settlement accepted by the wife in satisfaction of dower and "thirds", was held to bar her from claiming an interest on her husband's intestacy.[22]

A settlement, however, must be read as a whole in order to determine whether it was intended to bar the wife's claim against the whole of her husband's property or only against part of it.[23]

Where the widow had agreed in a marriage settlement to take a certain sum in satisfaction of her dower out of lands then or in future owned by her husband and he died intestate, beneficially owning real estate, it was held that she was not entitled to any interest in it.[24]

(d) Separation agreements

A bar of dower contained in a separation agreement was as effectual as a bar of dower contained in a deed or marriage settlement and disentitled a wife from claiming dower on her husband's death.[25]

707.13 Court Order Dispensing with Bar of Dower

(a) Generally

Under the Ontario Act, an owner of land who was married and wished to sell or mortgage the land free of dower could, in any case where he and his wife were living apart, or the whereabouts of his wife was unknown, or his wife was of unsound mind and confined as such in a hospital for mentally ill, mentally defective or epileptic persons, apply to a judge of the Supreme Court, or to a judge of the County or District Court of the county or district

---

[21]*Supra*, footnote 20, at pp. 219 and 220.
[22]*Gurly v. Gurly* (1842), 8 Cl. & Fin. 743, 8 E.R. 291 (H.L.). *Cf. Dorsey v. Dorsey* (1898), 29 O.R. 475 (H.C.J.).
[23]*Colleton v. Garth* (1833), 6 Sim. 19, 58 E.R. 502.
[24]*Toronto General Trusts Co. v. Quin* (1894), 25 O.R. 250 (H.C.J.).
[25]*Re Schop*, [1948] O.W.N. 338 (H.C.J.).

in which the owner resided or the land was situate, for an order dispensing with the concurrence of his wife for the purpose of barring her dower.[1] The order could be made in a summary way upon such evidence as to the judge seemed proper and upon notice served personally.[2] Where the judge was satisfied that notice could not be served personally, the order could be made after notice had been served upon the Public Trustee.[3]

The judge could make the order without imposing any conditions or he could, unless the wife had been living apart from the husband under such circumstances as disentitled her to dower, ascertain and state in the order the value of the dower and by the order direct that the amount thereof should be paid into court, or should remain a charge upon the land, or be secured otherwise for the benefit of the wife, or be paid or applied for her benefit as he might deem best.[4] After the making of the order, a conveyance or mortgage expressed to be free from dower was sufficient to bar her right to dower, subject to the terms of the order.[5] Section 13(6) extended the section to any case in which an agreement of sale had been made or a conveyance executed by the husband and part of the purchase money had been retained by the purchaser on account of dower, or an indemnity was given against dower, and, in any such case, any person interested in the land or in the retained purchase money or the indemnity could make the application. A wife living apart from her husband under a separation agreement by which she received maintenance was not for that reason disentitled to alimony and the section did not apply to such a case.[6] Furthermore, where the wife was not confined in a hospital for the mentally ill, but the jail surgeon of the county or district in which she resided and another medical practitioner named by the judge each certified that she was mentally ill and the judge or a judge of the Supreme Court certified that he had personally examined her and was of the opinion that she was mentally ill, the judge could make the same order as in section 13,[7] and could make similar orders in regard to other lands on that evidence and other evidence that satisfied him of her continued mental illness.[8]

There were similar provisions in the Nova Scotia and Prince Edward Island Acts[9] and in the Nova Scotia *Married Women's Deeds Act*.[10]

Furthermore, under the Ontario Act, where an owner, being at the time married, but who was living apart from his wife, or where the whereabouts of his wife were unknown, or his wife was of unsound mind and confined in a

---

§707.13
[1]Ont. Act, s. 13(1).
[2]*Ibid.*, s. 13(2).
[3]*Ibid.*, s. 13(3).
[4]*Ibid.*, s. 13(4).
[5]*Ibid.*, s. 13(5).
[6]*Re Davidson* (1929), 65 O.L.R. 19, [1930] 2 D.L.R. 84 (H.C.).
[7]Ont. Act, s. 14.
[8]*Ibid.*, s. 15.
[9]N.S. Act, ss. 9-13; P.E.I. Act, ss. 6-11.
[10]R.S.N.S. 1967, c. 175, ss. 10, 11.

hospital, conveyed or mortgaged land without his wife joining in the conveyance or mortgage, the purchaser or mortgagee, if he did not have notice that the grantor or mortgagor had a wife living at the time, could apply to a judge of the Supreme Court or a judge of the County or District Court of the county or district in which he resided, or the land was situate, for an order enabling him to convey or mortgage the land free from the dower of the wife.[11]

(b) On bankruptcy

The Ontario Act provided that where the owner of land had become bankrupt and a sale of the land was desired to wind up the estate, but his wife refused to release her dower, the trustee or assignee in bankruptcy could apply to a judge of the Supreme Court or to a judge of the County or District Court of the county or district in which the land was situate for an order enabling him to sell the land free from dower and an order could be made as in section 13.[12]

(c) On the death of the husband

The Ontario *Devolution of Estates Act*[13] provided that where the personal representative of the husband desired to sell real property free from dower, he could apply to a judge of the Supreme Court who, having regard to the interests of all parties, could order that it be sold free from the right of the dowress, in which case such right passed by the order without any conveyance or release of dower being required; and the judge could direct the payment of such lump sum out of the purchase money to the dowress as he deemed, on the principles applicable to life annuities, to be a reasonable satisfaction of her interest, or could direct payment of an annual sum, or of the interest on income derived from the purchase money and, for that purpose, could direct investment of the purchase money.

707.14 Right of Quarantine

Magna Carta[1] conferred on a widow the right of quarantine (from the French *quarante*), that is, a right to reside in her husband's house for forty days, during which time her dower was to be assigned to her. Accordingly, the Ontario Act provided that a widow was entitled to reside in her husband's chief house for forty days after his death, within which time her dower was to be assigned to her, and meanwhile she was entitled to reasonable maintenance; for her dower there was to be assigned to her one-third of all the lands of which her husband was seised during coverture except those of which he

---

[11]Ont. Act, s. 17.
[12]*Ibid.*, s. 16.
[13]R.S.O. 1970, c. 129, s. 10, now rendered otiose.
§707.14
[1]16 John, c. 7 (1215).

was seised in trust for another.[2] If she was wrongfully deprived of quarantine or dower, she was entitled to recover damages from the wrongdoer.[3]

707.15 Assignment of Dower

Upon her husband's death, apart from her quarantine, a widow was not entitled to possession of any of his real property until her dower had been assigned to her by the person entitled to the freehold, but, once it had been assigned to her, she was entitled to possession in priority to leases made by her husband during coverture without her consent.[1] The Ontario Act provided that the dowress and the tenant of the freehold could, by an instrument executed by them under seal in the presence of two witnesses, agree upon the assignment of dower, or upon a yearly or gross sum to be paid to her in lieu of dower. The instrument could be registered in the proper registry office, and entitled her to hold the land assigned to her as tenant for life against the assignor and all persons claiming through him, or to distrain or sue for the sum agreed to be paid to her by the tenant of the freehold. The registered instrument was a lien on the land for such sum and was a bar to any action for dower in the land.[2]

If the right of dower was not thus settled by agreement, the widow could sue to recover dower. The Act further provided that in estimating damages for detention of dower, or in estimating the yearly value of the land for the purpose of fixing a yearly sum of money in lieu of dower, the value of permanent improvements made after the husband alienated the land was not to be taken into account, but the damages or yearly value were to be estimated upon the state of the property at the time of his alienation or death, allowing for any general rise in the price and value of land in the locality.[3] The sheriff, after judgment and receipt by him of a writ of assignment of dower, had to appoint two resident freeholders and an Ontario land surveyor as commissioners to measure the dower.[4] It was the duty of the commissioners (a) to measure off one-third of the land mentioned in the writ, according to the nature of the land and having regard to buildings, and (b) to ascertain what permanent improvements were made by a purchaser from the husband, or after the husband's death and, if possible, award dower out of that part of the land that did not contain the improvements but, if that could not be done, they were to deduct either in quantity or value from the part assigned to the dowress the proportionate benefit she would receive from the improvements.[5] If, from peculiar circumstances such as there being a mill or factory on the

---

[2]Ont. Act, s. 1.
[3]*Ibid.*, s. 2.
§707.15
[1]*Allan v. Rever* (1902), 4 O.L.R. 309 (H.C.J.).
[2]Ont. Act, s. 21.
[3]*Ibid.*, s. 23.
[4]*Ibid.*, s. 24.
[5]*Ibid.*, s. 29(1).

land, the commissioners could not make a fair assignment of dower by metes and bounds, they were to assess and report to the sheriff a yearly sum which was as nearly as possible one-third of the clear yearly rents of the premises after deducting rates and assessments payable, and in assessing such yearly sum they were to allow and deduct for the permanent improvements.[6] That yearly sum was a lien on the land mentioned in the writ or on such portion as the commissioners might direct and was recoverable by distress or by action against the tenant of the freehold.[7] The sheriff was to return the writ with the report of the commissioners.[8] Either party could appeal from the report to a judge in court who could confirm or vary the report or refer it back to the commissioners with his directions, or he could set aside the report and appoint, or direct the sheriff to appoint, new commissioners whose report was to be treated as if no other report had been made; if misconduct or fraud on the part of the commissioners was alleged, they could be made parties and might be liable for costs and the report could be set aside, but if there was no appeal from the report, or the appeal was dismissed, the report was final and conclusive on all parties to the action for dower and a copy of the report could be registered in the proper registry office.[9] After registration, the dowress could have the sheriff directed to put her in possession of the land assigned to her and to levy all costs awarded to her.[10]

The object of the Act, in regard to the amount the widow should receive in lieu of assignment of dower, was to place her in the same position as she would have been in if it had been possible to make the assignment by metes and bounds, but subject to the qualification that she was not to have the benefit of permanent improvements made after alienation by her husband or after his death; it did not make one-third of the rental value an absolute criterion.[11]

The Nova Scotia *Dower Procedure Act*[12] provided in sections 1 to 12 for an action to recover dower and damages for its detention, a judgment for the recovery of dower, with or without damages, being enforced by a writ of seisin directed to the sheriff of the county in which the land lay. Sections 13 to 18 provided for assignment of the dower, being one-third of the lands by metes and bounds, by commissioners appointed by the sheriff; if that could not be done because of peculiar circumstances, such as there being a mill or manufactory on the land, the commissioners were to assess a yearly sum, being one-third of the clear yearly rents or profits of the premises, which yearly sum was a lien on the land recoverable by distress or action against the tenant of the freehold. The tenant of the freehold could, before action, serve upon

---

[6]*Ibid.*, s. 29(2).
[7]*Ibid.*, s. 29(4).
[8]*Ibid.*, s. 30.
[9]*Ibid.*, s. 31.
[10]*Ibid.*, s. 32.
[11]*McNally v. Anderson* (1914), 31 O.L.R. 561, 19 D.L.R. 775 (S.C. App. Div.).
[12]R.S.N.S. 1967, c. 80, rep. 1980, c. 9, s. 33(2).

the dowress a notice that he was willing to assign dower and could apply to the court for a judgment that a writ of seisin might issue.[13] The dowress and tenant of the freehold could, by instrument under seal, agree upon the assignment of dower or a yearly sum in lieu; the instrument had to be registered, was a lien on the land for the sum agreed upon, and was a bar to an action for dower.[14]

The Prince Edward Island Act provided that, where a person, having the freehold of lands subject to dower, neglected to assign to the widow her dower interest within two months after demand by her, such person could be sued by the widow for dower.[15] If she recovered judgment, damages could be allowed to her and the court could order the defendant to deliver possession of her dower interest to be determined by metes and bounds in such manner as the court might direct or, if no division could be made by metes and bounds, order the defendant to pay to her one-third of the rents or profits, or to pay the amount of the value of her dower interest as determined by the court.[16]

707.16 Limitation Periods

Where a husband had been entitled to a right of entry or action with respect to any land and his widow would have been entitled to dower in it if he had recovered possession of it, she had a right of dower in it which, however, she had to sue for or obtain within the period during which the right of entry or action might be enforced.[1]

The Ontario *Limitations Act*[2] provided that no action for dower could be brought after ten years from the death of the husband, notwithstanding any disability of the dowress or any person claiming through her.[3]

If the dowress, after the death of her husband, was in possession of the land out of which she was dowable, either alone or jointly with the heir or devisee or a person claiming by devolution from her husband, the period of ten years was to be computed from the time when her possession ceased.[4]

No arrears of dower or damages on account of arrears were recoverable for a period longer than six years before the commencement of the action.[5]

Where a mortgage was revived by a husband's acknowledgement, which was not concurred in by his wife, although she joined in the mortgage itself to bar

---

[13]*Ibid.*, s. 22.
[14]*Ibid.*, s. 23.
[15]P.E.I. Act, s. 1.
[16]*Ibid.*, s. 3.
§707.16
[1]N.B. Act, s. 2; N.S. Act, s. 3; Ont. Act, s. 4; P.E.I. Act, s. 5.
[2]R.S.O. 1980, c. 240, expected soon to be replaced by new legislation, see §3106.21.
[3]*Ibid.*, s. 25, now effete.
[4]*Ibid.*, s. 26, now effete.
[5]*Ibid.*, s. 27; *Limitation of Actions Act*, R.S.N.B. 1973, c. L-8, s. 33(2); R.S.N.S. 1967, c. 168, s. 24; *Statute of Limitations*, R.S.P.E.I. 1974, c. S-7, s. 14. These provisions are now effete.

197

her dower, the wife could invoke the *Limitations Act* in an action to enforce the mortgage, the extension of which she was not a party to.[6]

707.17 Election

Dower was the widow's primary right and it could not be taken from her except by order of the court or by forfeiture of her right by her conduct. She could, however, be put to her election by the husband in his will to choose between dower and the provision for her in the will. She might also have an election on her husband's intestacy between dower and her right to take a share in her husband's estate.

(a) Under the husband's will

A testator could put his wife to her election either expressly or by implication. The Nova Scotia Act provided that if a testator manifested an intention to dispose of his property in a manner inconsistent with his wife's dower right she had to elect between the benefits given by the will and her dower.[1] This was also the common law rule.

No difficulty arose where the testator expressly made a gift to his widow in lieu of dower. In such case, she had to elect whether to take the gift or her dower. Thus, where a testator gave his wife an annuity in lieu of dower in all of his lands, it was held that she could not have the gift and dower in any of the lands, whether or not they were devised, for "In cases of realty, the testator is deemed to have purchased the dower for the benefit of whomsoever the estate may go to, whether it passes under the will or devolves upon the heir by operation of law."[2]

The difficulty arose where the testator made a gift to his wife without expressing that it was to be in lieu of dower. In such cases,

> the general rule recognised is that it is not sufficient to collect an intention that the testator does not mean his widow to have her dower, but you must find an intention so to dispose of his estate that her claim to dower would be inconsistent with that disposition.[3]

---

[6]*Royal Bank of Canada v. Chittick*, [1965] 2 O.R. 37, 49 D.L.R. (2d) 501 (H.C.J.).
§707.17
[1]N.S. Act, s. 1.
[2]*Davidson v. Boomer* (1871), 18 Gr. 475 at p. 479, *per* Strong, V.C.
[3]Kindersley, V.C., in *Parker v. Sowerby* (1853), 1 Drewry 488 at p. 492, 61 E.R. 539, affd 4 De G. M. & G. 321, 43 E.R. 531, cited by Rose, J., in *Re George Shunk Estate* (1899), 31 O.R. 175 (H.C.J.), at pp. 176-7. In the latter case an estate consisting of realty and personality was devised, after a direction to pay debts and personal and testamentary expenses and after a specific devise of land, to executors in trust to sell and convert into money, to pay to the widow out of the proceeds a sum of money for her own use absolutely and to divide the remainder among nephews and nieces, and it was held that the widow was not put to her election but was entitled to both the bequest and dower. See also *Re Baker* (1981), 10 E.T.R. 146 (Ont. H.C.J.).

The rule was put another way as follows:

> It is not enough to say that upon the whole will it is fairly to be inferred that the testator did not intend that his widow should have her dower; in order to justify the Court in putting her to her election, it must be satisfied that there is a positive intention to exclude her from dower, either expressed or clearly implied.[4]

Hence, a mere devise to a wife of part of an estate in which she had dower did not bar her dower in the residue of the estate and, where there were separate devises, she might be barred of her dower in one but not in the other.[5]

Thus, where a testator blended his real and personal estate into a fund from which payments were to be made to his widow and other devisees and postponed division of the corpus until after the death of his wife, it was held that the wife was not bound to elect between dower and the payments, for the mere creation of a blended fund was not inconsistent with dower. It would have been inconsistent only if the benefits given under the will together with dower would have effectively defeated the testator's intention by cutting down the share of the specific devisee or by giving the widow a greater share than the testator intended.[6]

Similarly, if real and personal property were blended, not for the purpose of equal division, but in order to obtain an income out of which payments of stated amounts were to be made annually to the wife, the division of the corpus not being made until after her death, there was no inconsistency with her dower right.[7] There would have been an inconsistency if the widow were given instead a percentage of the whole net income from the fund so that it would have been clear that the payments to her depended upon the actual net revenue received from the estate from time to time.[8]

Where a testator gave a house for his wife's residence during her life and another house for the use of nephews and nieces until the youngest attained 21 years of age or married, it was held that this personal occupation by nephews and nieces, while it lasted, was inconsistent with the claim of the wife to have one-third of the house put aside for her use as dowress, that the widow accordingly had to elect as to the houses, but that the deprivation of dower for a time in part of the real estate was not sufficient to put her to her election as to the residue of the estate.[9]

Where a testator gave to his wife for life the use of the dwelling in which she resided, together with the use of the yard as enclosed, the fruit from trees and

---

[4]*Gibson v. Gibson* (1852), 1 Drewry 42 at p. 52, 61 E.R. 367; *cf. Wilson v. Wilson* (1883), 7 O.R. 177 (H.C.J.); *Rudd v. Harper* (1888), 16 O.R. 422 (H.C.J.).
[5]*Cowan v. Besserer* (1883), 5 O.R. 624 (H.C.J.).
[6]*Leys v. Toronto General Trusts Co.* (1892), 22 O.R. 603 (H.C.J.); *Re Hill*, [1951] O.R. 619, [1951] 4 D.L.R. 218 (H.C.J.).
[7]*Re Grant* (1965), 52 D.L.R. (2d) 313, [1965] S.C.R. 628, a wife who was given an annual fixed allowance and the right to reside in a house, was entitled to claim dower in respect of other real property.
[8]*Re Lynch Estate* (1975), 56 D.L.R. (3d) 510, 20 R.F.L. 237 (N.S.S.C. App. Div.); *Re Hendry*, [1931] O.R. 448, [1931] 4 D.L.R. 908 (H.C.).
[9]*Leys v. Toronto General Trusts Co.*, *supra*, footnote 6.

an annual allowance in money, so as to exclude the probability that she would require other means of support, and the rents and profits of the real estate of the testator were insufficient to satisfy the widow's claim for dower in it, it was held that she must elect between the gifts and dower.[10]

Where a testator bequeathed to his widow the annual income of his real and personal estate during her widowhood for the support of herself and the maintenance and education of all the children during their minority, a proportionate part of the income to be paid to each child on attaining majority, after making ample provision for the support of the widow during widowhood, it was held that this did not show an intention of the testator that the provision for her was to be in lieu of dower.[11]

Where a will gave land to a widow during widowhood, she received the equivalent of a life estate in the whole, which was inconsistent with a claim for a contemporaneous life estate in one-third of the land as dowress.[12]

Election was a question of fact in each case and, to hold a widow to have elected, she must have had a fair chance of exercising judgment, in full knowledge of her rights, of what she was surrendering, of what she was getting in exchange, and of the need to elect.[13]

Where, however, a widow to whom a mortgage was bequeathed by a will exercised her rights as mortgagee and took other benefits under the will, she was held to have elected to take under the will.[14]

Where a widow brought an action for the construction of her husband's will, it was held that she had thereby elected to take under the will and could not thereafter elect to take her dower in his undisposed of realty.[15]

It was held, where a testator devised all his real and personal estate to his widow during her widowhood and she entered upon the real estate and applied the personal estate to her use, that she had elected to take under the will.[16]

(b) On intestacy

On the husband's intestacy, his wife retained her dower right. It was taken

---

[10]*Becker v. Hammond* (1866), 12 Gr. 485.

[11]*Laidlaw v. Jackes* (1877), 25 Gr. 293 at p. 296, affd 27 Gr. 101.

[12]*Marriott v. McKay* (1892), 22 O.R. 320 (H.C.J.); *Re Allen* (1912), 4 O.W.N. 240, 7 D.L.R. 494 (H.C.J.). Further examples of the widow's being put to her election are found in the following cases: *McLennan v. Grant* (1868), 15 Gr. 65; *Armstrong v. Armstrong* (1874), 21 Gr. 351; *Rody v. Rody* (1881), 29 Gr. 324; *Card v. Cooley* (1884), 6 O.R. 229 (H.C.J.); *Dawson v. Fraser* (1889), 18 O.R. 496 (H.C.J.). In these cases the widow was not put to her election: *Wilson v. Wilson, supra*, footnote 4; *Rudd v. Harper, supra*, footnote 4; *Elliott v. Morris* (1896), 27 O.R. 485; *Re George Shunk Estate, supra*, footnote 3; *Carscallen v. Wallbridge* (1900), 32 O.R. 114 (H.C.J.); *Re Sexsmith* (1925), 57 O.L.R. 283 (H.C.).

[13]*Bratt v. Bratt* (1926), 30 O.W.N. 320 (H.C.); *Coleman v. Glanville* (1871), 18 Gr. 42; *Spread v. Morgan* (1865), 11 H.L.C. 588, 11 E.R. 1461.

[14]*Jones v. Shortreed* (1907), 14 O.L.R. 142 (H.C.J.).

[15]*Rudd v. Harper* (1888), 16 O.R. 422 (H.C.J.).

[16]*Westacott v. Cockerline* (1867), 13 Gr. 79.

into account in determining the widow's share of the estate for, generally speaking, she had to elect between her dower right and her right to take her statutory share of her husband's estate.

In Nova Scotia the widow was formerly entitled to elect to take dower in lieu of her statutory share. However, after 1975, she could no longer elect dower. Instead, she has a right to elect to take her husband's principal residence together with its appurtenant land and household goods and furnishings in lieu of or as part of her $50,000 preferential share.[17]

In New Brunswick the widow had to elect within six months to take her dower in lieu of her share under the *Devolution of Estates Act*,[18] otherwise she lost her dower right.

In Prince Edward Island, until 1978, when dower was abolished, the value of the widow's dower formed part of her share under the *Probate Act*,[19] but she could waive the right to dower.

Under the now repealed provisions of the Ontario *Devolution of Estates Act*,[20] a widow had to elect between taking her dower in real property of which her husband was at any time seised or to which he was beneficially entitled at the time of his death, or taking the interest given to her by the Act in her husband's undisposed of real property, and unless she so elected she was not entitled to share in his undisposed of real property. This provision applied both to the real property of an intestate husband and to real property as to which there was an intestacy under the husband's will.[21]

If the widow elected to take her share under the intestacy statutes of the several provinces, except New Brunswick's, she was entitled to a preferential share of the net estate[22] together with a distributive share in the remainder. In New Brunswick there was no preferential share, so the widow received only a distributive share. The latter varied, depending upon the number of surviving issue and next of kin, from one-third to the entire remainder.[23]

If, instead, the widow elected to take dower, she lost her preferential share

---

[17]*Intestate Succession Act*, R.S.N.S. 1967, c. 153, s. 5, rep. and sub. 1975, c. 61, ss. 1(*b*), 3.
[18]R.S.N.B. 1973, c. D-9, s. 33, now effete.
[19]R.S.P.E.I. 1974, c. P-19, s. 98, repealed by *Family Law Reform Act*, S.P.E.I. 1978, c. 6, s. 62.
[20]R.S.O. 1970, c. 129, s. 8(1), repealed by *Succession Law Reform Act*, S.O. 1977, c. 40, s. 50(1), and see *Family Law Reform Act*, R.S.O. 1980, c. 152, s. 70.
[21]*Cowan v. Allen* (1896), 26 S.C.R. 292.
[22]The lesser of the net estate or $50,000: *Intestate Succession Act*, R.S.N.S. 1967, c. 153, s. 3(1), (2), am. 1975, c. 61, s. 1(*a*); *Probate Act*, R.S.P.E.I. 1974, c. P-19, s. 89(3); *Devolution of Estates Act*, R.S.O. 1970, c. 129, s. 11, am. 1973, c. 18, s. 1, rep. S.O. 1977, c. 40, s. 50(1).
[23]One-half if one child or issue of one child survive; one-third if more than one child or issue of more than one child survive: *Devolution of Estates Act*, R.S.N.B. 1973, c. D-9, s. 22(1)-(3); *Intestate Succession Act*, R.S.N.S. 1967, c. 153, s. 3(5), (6), as renumbered 1975, c. 61, s. 1(*d*); *Probate Act*, R.S.P.E.I. 1974, c. P-19, s. 87(1)-(3). Two-thirds if no issue survive; one-half if one child or issue of one child survive; one-third if more than one child or issue of more than one child survive; all if no issue and no next of kin of the husband survive: *Devolution of Estates Act*, R.S.O. 1970, c. 129, ss. 31, 31a (added by 1973, c. 18, s. 3), now repealed and substituted by *Succession Law Reform Act*, S.O. 1977, c. 40, s. 50(1). See generally §503.1(c), *supra*.

and her distributive share in the real property of her husband's estate and received only a distributive share in the personalty.[24]

The widow's election had to be by deed or instrument in writing attested by at least one witness[25] and could, therefore, be made by her will which, as to election, spoke from the time of its execution and not from the time of her death.[26] The personal representative of the deceased could, by notice in writing, require her to make her election and, if she failed to execute and deliver a deed or other instrument of election within six months after service of the notice, she was deemed to have elected to take her dower.[27] In the absence of such a notice, there was no time limit for her election and she could elect at any time before distribution of the undisposed of real property, or the proceeds thereof if it had been sold.[28]

Whether a widow had elected was a question of fact and she was not presumed to have elected to give up her dower where the facts were consistent with ignorance and neglect. Thus, if the widow remained in possession of her husband's lands and purported to dispose of them by will, she would be presumed to have elected to take her dower and the will was of no effect.[29] In such a case the widow might be accountable to her co-heirs for receiving more than her share of the rents and profits.[30]

In *Re Carberry*[31] it was argued that a widow's witnessed signature to an affidavit of value and relationship filed for succession duty purposes which set out a scheme of distribution based on the statutory shares by reference to another's affidavit, and her signature to a letter by her solicitor which set out a similar scheme, amounted to an election, but the court held that they did not because the widow had not put her mind to an election. Similarly, her signature on a deed of expropriation in favour of a municipality did not amount to an election since it was not so intended.

Under the Ontario Act, where the widow was an infant or a mentally incompetent person, her right of election could be exercised on her behalf by the official guardian with the approval of a judge of the Supreme Court, or by some person authorized by a judge of the Supreme Court to exercise it.[32] Where the widow was a patient in an institution within the meaning of the

---

[24]*Toronto General Trusts Co. v. Quin* (1894), 25 O.R. 250 (H.C.J.).

[25]*Devolution of Estates Act*, R.S.O. 1970, c. 129, s. 8(1).

[26]*Re Ingolsby* (1890), 19 O.R. 283 (H.C.J.).

[27]*Devolution of Estates Act*, R.S.O. 1970, c. 129, s. 8(2); *Re Carberry*, [1963] 2 O.R. 462, 40 D.L.R. (2d) 40 (H.C.J.).

[28]*Baker v. Stuart* (1898), 25 O.A.R. 445.

[29]*Re Case*, [1973] 3 O.R. 50, 35 D.L.R. (3d) 683 (H.C.J.), doubting *Whitmarsh v. Whitmarsh*, [1972] 1 O.R. 536, 23 D.L.R. (3d) 520 (Co. Ct.). An earlier case, *McDonald v. McMurchy* (1924), 26 O.W.N. 210 (H.C.), which treated a widow as having elected to give up her dower because she intended to do so, must also be regarded as of doubtful authority on this point.

[30]*McDonald v. McMurchy, supra*, footnote 29.

[31]*Supra*, footnote 27.

[32]*Devolution of Estates Act*, R.S.O. 1970, c. 129, s. 8(3).

Mental Hospitals Act[33] and the Public Trustee was committee of her estate, he could exercise her right of election on her behalf.[34]

Before electing, the widow was entitled to know what the estate would produce, because her distributive share under the Act was subject to her husband's debts while her dower was not and she could not make a fair choice until she knew the comparative basis of her two interests.[35]

> Until debts are ascertained and cleared it cannot be known what the amount or value of a distributive share can be, and until that is known an election by the widow would be a farce. The Legislature meant her right of election to be of some value, a right to take what was most for her advantage.[36]

While a dower interest died with the wife, a widow's administrator was entitled to recover the value of her dower interest where she had barred her dower in a deed in the course of the administration of her husband's estate but reserved her right of election and died before the estate was fully administered.[37]

Where there was a partial intestacy, the widow's right of election might be modified. Thus, where a testator gave his real estate to his widow during her widowhood and the will contained no other provisions except to appoint executors, she took a life estate in the realty during widowhood and could not claim dower in the realty in addition to such life estate but was put to her election. If she elected against the will, she could then make the further election under the Act to take her distributive share of one-third of the land, but if she elected to take the estate given to her by the will during widowhood, her right of dower was gone and she could not then elect under the Act to take one-third of the land because her right under the Act was to take one-third of the undisposed of land in lieu of dower.[38] Similarly, where a testator by his will gave his widow $1,000 in lieu of dower, gave legacies to certain persons, including legacies to his sons on their attaining their majorities, directed his executors to convert his realty and personalty into money and invest it, there was an intestacy as to $6,000 remaining after the realty had been sold and all debts and legacies paid. The widow elected to take under the will and claimed her share of the $6,000. It was held by Middleton, J., that, as the testator had intended to prevent his widow from claiming dower in the lands

---

[33]R.S.O. 1980, c. 263.
[34]*Devolution of Estates Act*, R.S.O. 1970, c. 129, s. 8(4).
[35]*Re Rose* (1896), 17 P.R. 136.
[36]*Per* Maclennan, J.A., in *Baker v. Stuart* (1898), 25 O.A.R. 445 at p. 447.
[37]*Re Pettit Estate* (1902), 4 O.L.R. 506 (H.C.J.).
[38]*Re Allen* (1912), 4 O.W.N. 240, 7 D.L.R. 494 (H.C.J.). At the time of this case in cases of partial intestacy, the surviving spouse was not entitled to a preferential share in Ontario: *Re Harrison* (1901), 2 O.L.R. 217 (H.C.J.). Now the amount received under the will is taken into account in determining the preferential share: *Succession Law Reform Act*, R.S.O. 1980, c. 488, s. 45(3). The surviving spouse is entitled to his full preferential share in partial intestacies in Nova Scotia and Prince Edward Island: *Intestate Succession Act*, R.S.N.S. 1967, c. 153, s. 13; *Probate Act*, R.S.P.E.I. 1974, c. P-19, s. 97.

in question to the prejudice of his scheme of an immediate sale of the lands, she could not assert any claim against the lands, having elected to accept the benefit offered by the will but, the testator having died intestate as to $6,000 of the proceeds of the sale of the land not disposed of, she had the same right to share in the $6,000 as if he had by his will declared that it was to be distributed as on an intestacy. He also held that the fund was to be dealt with as if it were land and the widow could elect under the Act to take one-third of it. He also stated that, if he were wrong and the fund must be treated as personalty, she would be entitled to one-third of it.[39]

A widow's right under the Act to elect to take a distributive share of her husband's realty applied only to realty which descended upon an intestacy. Where lands were devised to a widow's husband but, if he left no issue, were to pass to his brothers, it was held that the widow had dower in the lands notwithstanding the defeasible character of the fee which vested in her husband. She, however, was not entitled to elect to take between her dower and a distributive share of the devised lands.[40]

Since a widow's right to dower was lost if she deserted her husband and committed uncondoned adultery, her right of election was also lost in such a case.[41] She had lost her dower right and, therefore, could not elect to take her preferential share and her distributive share in the real property of her husband in lieu thereof. Her right to take her distributive share in the personalty was unaffected, however, and where the husband's entire estate consisted of personalty she would have her preferential share as well.[42]

Just as a bar of dower in a deed precluded a wife from claiming dower on her husband's death in the property conveyed, so a general bar of dower contained in a separation agreement had the effect of barring her dower and ending her right of election.[43]

(c) Dower and claims for dependants' relief

When a widow made a claim against her husband's estate for relief on the grounds that he failed to make adequate provision for her future maintenance,[44] the value of her dower interest might be taken into account if she elected to take dower, especially if the legislation under which she claimed placed a maximum limit on an award such as the amount she would have

---

[39]*Re McEwen*; *McEwen v. Gray* (1911), 2 O.W.N. 945 (H.C.J.); *cf. Re Johnston*, [1968] 1 O.R. 679, 67 D.L.R. (2d) 396 (H.C.J.).
[40]*Cowan v. Allen* (1869), 26 S.C.R. 292.
[41]See §707.11, *supra*.
[42]*Re Schop*, [1948] O.W.N. 338 (H.C.J.); *MacWilliams v. MacWilliams*, [1962] O.R. 407, 32 D.L.R. (2d) 481 (C.A.).
[43]*Re Schop*, *supra*, footnote 42.
[44]Under the *Testators' Family Maintenance Act*, R.S.N.B. 1973, c. T-4; R.S.N.S. 1967, c. 303; *Dependants of a Deceased Person Relief Act*, R.S.P.E.I. 1974, c. D-6; *Dependants' Relief Act*, R.S.O. 1970, c. 126. The Ontario statute was repealed and replaced by what is now the *Succession Law Reform Act*, R.S.O. 1980, c. 488, Pt. V.

received on an intestacy.[45] Where a claim for relief was calculated on the basis of the widow's statutory share on an intestacy, she would be barred subsequently from claiming her dower as well, but the making of an application for relief did not by itself constitute an election by the widow to give up dower,[46] except, perhaps, where the will contained an express or implied election in lieu of dower.[47]

707.18 Calculation of Dower

Under the several statutes, where dower could not be assigned by metes and bounds, the value of the dower could be calculated in terms of one-third of the annual rents and profits[1] or, where the dower was dispensed with by court order, dower could be paid to the wife as interest on money in court, as an annual sum or as a lump sum.[2] In the case of a lump sum payment and where dower was due to a wife by reason of the fact that she did not bar her dower on a sale by her husband, the present value of the dower had to be calculated.[3] For many years this was determined in accordance with the life expectancy tables known as "Cameron's Tables"[4] even though they were out of date.[5] However, it was held in Re Casselman[6] that the court could take judicial notice of the fact that those tables were no longer applicable and the court used instead the 1965-67 Canadian Life Tables[7] and relied on actuarial evidence to determine the value of the dower. Furthermore, the court also held that dower should be calculated on the gross value of the property at the husband's death without any deductions for real estate commissions or legal fees.

707.19 Priority over Husband's Creditors

A wife's dower right took priority over her husband's creditors, so that a sale of land under an execution against the husband, defeated only his interest, not her dower right.[1] The widow's dower consummate (although not her

---

[45]*Dependants' Relief Act*, R.S.O. 1970, c. 126, s. 10.
[46]*Re Neiman and Borovoy*, [1954] O.W.N. 527, [1954] 2 D.L.R. 732 (C.A.); *Re Greisman*, [1954] O.W.N. 793, [1955] 1 D.L.R. 741 (Surr. Ct.); *Re Casselman* (1974), 6 O.R. (2d) 742, 54 D.L.R. (3d) 37 (C.A.).
[47]*Re Lynch Estate* (1975), 56 D.L.R. (3d) 510, 20 R.F.L. 237 (N.S.S.C. App. Div.).
§707.18
[1]See §707.15, *supra*.
[2]See §707.13, *supra*.
[3]*Re MacWilliams* (1963), 49 M.P.R. 47 (P.E.I.S.C.).
[4]In the appendices to Cameron, *Treatise on the Law of Dower* (Toronto, Carswell & Co., 1882).
[5]See, *e.g.*, *Re Smith*, [1952] O.R. 135, [1952] 2 D.L.R. 104 (C.A.); *R. v. Sonnenberg*, [1971] F.C. 95, 2 L.C.R. 298 (Fed. Ct. T.D.) (expropriation).
[6](1974), 6 O.R. (2d) 742, 54 D.L.R. (3d) 37 (C.A.).
[7]Published by Statistics Canada.
§707.19
[1]*Parent v. Drouillard*, [1937] O.W.N. 238 (H.C.J.).

inchoate right) was subject to seizure and sale at the suit of her own creditors, however.[2]

A sale of the husband's land for taxes extinguished every interest in the land, including the right of dower, but not easements. It operated as a new root of title.[3]

707.20   Powers and Duties of a Dowress

(a) Power to lease

The *Settled Estates Act*[1] confers on life tenants of settled estates certain leasing powers[2] and provided that such powers could be exercised by a dowress of unsettled land[3] and that the leases are binding on all persons entitled to subsequent estates,[4] but the widow had no exercisable rights until her dower had been first assigned to her.

(b) Waste

The *Conveyancing and Law of Property Act*[5] provides that a dowress is impeachable for waste[6] and that no life tenant without impeachment for waste may commit equitable waste unless the instrument creating the estate expressly confers the right.[7] The Nova Scotia *Dower Act*[8] provided that a dowress could not commit or suffer waste but had to maintain buildings and fences in good repair.

708. CURTESY

Curtesy was the life estate of the husband to which he was entitled in all of his wife's undisposed of real property. It has now been abolished in Prince Edward Island,[1] Ontario,[2] Nova Scotia[3] and New Brunswick.[4]

---

[2]*Execution Act*, R.S.O. 1970, c. 152, s. 28(2), repealed by *Family Law Reform Act*, S.O. 1978, c. 2, s. 70(3).

[3]*Tomlinson v. Hill* (1855), 5 Gr. 231; *Municipal Act*, R.S.O. 1980, c. 302, s. 471; *Assessment Act*, R.S.N.S. 1967, c. 14, s. 178; *Real Property Tax Act*, R.S.N.B. 1973, c. R-2, s. 14(3); R.S.P.E.I. 1974, c. R-6, s. 15(3).

§707.20

[1]R.S.O. 1980, c. 468.

[2]*Ibid.*, s. 32(1).

[3]*Ibid.*, s. 32(2), now effete.

[4]*Ibid.*, s. 33(2).

[5]R.S.O. 1980, c. 90.

[6]*Ibid.*, s. 29, now effete.

[7]*Ibid.*, s. 30.

[8]R.S.N.S. 1967, c. 79, s. 5, rep. 1980, c. 9, s. 33(1).

§708

[1]*Family Law Reform Act*, S.P.E.I. 1978, c. 6, s. 62.

[2]*Succession Law Reform Act*, R.S.O. 1980, c. 488, s. 48.

[3]*Intestate Succession Act*, R.S.N.S. 1967, c. 153, s. 2, declaring inapplicable from September 1, 1966, the *Descent of Property Act*, R.S.N.S. 1954, c. 69, under which curtesy was retained. See also *Matrimonial Property Act*, S.N.S. 1980, c. 9, s. 33(3).

[4]*Married Women's Property Act*, R.S.N.B. 1973, c. M-4, s. 8.

708.1 Curtesy at Common Law

If a married woman was seised of an estate of inheritance, her husband had, at common law, by the curtesy of England, an estate therein for his life expectant on her death, subject to his having issue by her born alive and capable of inheriting the property.[1] When he became entitled to such estate upon her death, he was called *tenant by the curtesy*.

An estate by the curtesy could exist in an equitable estate,[2] and in money theoretically converted into land.[3] It could also exist in an incorporeal hereditament, such as a rent-charge.[4] There could be an estate by the curtesy in property limited to the separate use of the wife[5] and in statutory separate property of the wife, such as under the *Married Women's Property Act*.[6]

To entitle a husband to a tenancy by the curtesy, the requisites were a valid marriage, seisin of the wife, issue capable of inheriting and death of the wife.

The marriage had to be legal but did not have to be canonized.[7]

The wife had to have seisin in deed, that is, actual seisin or possession.[8] Seisin in law, being a right to possession, was ordinarily not sufficient.[9] However, seisin in law was held to be sufficient where the nature of the wife's title was such that she could not have seisin in deed in her lifetime, such as where there was a devise to her in fee simple, or in fee tail, and she predeceased the testator leaving issue, in which case the devise took effect under the *Wills Act*[10] and her husband was entitled to an estate by the curtesy, unless she had barred the estate by her will.[11] A grant of Crown lands by letters patent conferred seisin and possession for the purpose of an estate by the curtesy.[12]

In the case of an incorporeal hereditament in gross, seisin in deed was necessary if there had been an opportunity of obtaining it but, if there was no opportunity, such as where the wife died before an instalment of a rent-charge fell due, seisin in law was sufficient.[13]

Since seisin or actual possession by the wife was necessary in the case of

---

§708.1

[1]Litt., §§35-52.

[2]*Watts v. Ball* (1708), 1 P. Wms. 108, 24 E.R. 315; *Chaplin v. Chaplin* (1733), 3 P. Wms. 229 at p. 234, 24 E.R. 1040; *Casborne v. Scarfe* (1737), 1 Atk. 603, 26 E.R. 377.

[3]*Lingen v. Sowray* (1711), 1 P. Wms. 172, 24 E.R. 343; *Chaplin v. Horner* (1712), 1 P. Wms. 483, 24 E.R. 483; *Edwards v. Countess of Warwick* (1723), 2 P. Wms. 171, 24 E.R. 687.

[4]Co. Litt. 29a.

[5]*Appleton v. Rowley* (1869), L.R. 8 Eq. 139; *Eager v. Furnivall* (1881), 17 Ch. D. 115.

[6]45 & 46 Vict., c. 75 (1882); *Hope v. Hope*, [1892] 2 Ch. 336; *Re Lambert's Estate*; *Stanton v. Lambert* (1888), 39 Ch. D. 626.

[7]*Re Murray Canal; Lawson v. Powers* (1884), 6 O.R. 685 (H.C.J.).

[8]Co. Litt. 29a; *Doe d. Andrew v. Hutton* (1804), 3 Bos. & Pul. 643, 127 E.R. 347.

[9]Co. Litt. 29a; *Parks v. Hegan*, [1903] 2 I.R. 643.

[10]7 Will. 4 & 1 Vict., c. 26 (1837).

[11]*Eager v. Furnivall, supra*, footnote 5.

[12]*Weaver v. Burgess* (1871), 22 U.C.C.P. 104.

[13]Co. Litt. 29a.

land, there could be no tenancy by the curtesy in a remainder or reversion after a freehold interest which did not fall into possession during the marriage.[14] Also, if the wife had a life estate and a reversion in fee following a contingent remainder, there was an estate by the curtesy in the reversion if the remainder did not take effect, because the life estate and reversion were united in her,[15] but there was no curtesy in the reversion if the remainder took effect.[16]

Since possession by a tenant for years was possession by the reversioner, there was an estate by the curtesy in a reversion following a term of years,[17] even though no rent was received before the wife died.[18] The wife had to be solely seised of the entirety or of an undivided share, so there was an estate by the curtesy where she was seised as tenant in common but not where she was a joint tenant.[19]

Entry by one tenant in common was entry by all for the purpose of giving an estate by the curtesy.[20]

An event which divested the wife of her estate also divested the estate by the curtesy.[21] If, however, the wife's estate was not divested in her lifetime but was merely defeated after her death by an executory devise, the husband had his estate by the curtesy. Thus, where there was a devise in trust for a girl in fee simple on her attaining the age of 21 or marrying, but a devise over if she died before attaining age 21 without leaving issue, and she married, had a child which died and then died herself before attaining age 21 without leaving issue, it was held that her husband had his estate by the curtesy.[22]

As soon as a child capable of inheriting by descent was born to the wife, the husband had a vested estate by the curtesy and it was not divested by the subsequent death of the child either before or after the death of the wife.[23] But the issue had to be capable of taking by descent, else there was no estate by the curtesy. Thus, where there was a devise to the wife in fee simple but, if she died before her husband, to her children in fee simple, and she predeceased her husband leaving issue, he had no estate by the curtesy.[24]

Where there was a devise to the wife in fee simple but, if she should die leaving issue, then to the issue and their heirs, and she died leaving issue, it was held that her husband had no estate by the curtesy.[25]

---

[14]Co. Litt. 29a; *Gibbins v. Eyden* (1869), L.R. 7 Eq. 371; *Re Gracey and Toronto Real Estate Co.* (1889), 16 O.R. 226 (H.C.J.).
[15]*Doe d. Planner v. Scudamore* (1800), 2 Bos. & Pul. 289 at p. 294, 126 E.R. 1287.
[16]*Boothby v. Vernon* (1723), 9 Mod. R. 147, 88 E.R. 368.
[17]Co. Litt. 29a.
[18]*De Grey v. Richardson* (1747), 3 Atk. 469, 26 E.R. 1069.
[19]*Palmer v. Rich*, [1897] 1 Ch. 134 at pp. 140, 141.
[20]*Sterling v. Penlington* (1739), 7 Vin. Abr. 149 at p. 150.
[21]2 Bl. Comm. 155.
[22]*Buckworth v. Thirkell* (1785), 3 Bos. & Pul. 652, 127 E.R. 351, note (a).
[23]*Paine's Case* (1587), 8 Co. Rep. 34 a, 77 E.R. 524; *Steadman v. Palling* (1746), 3 Atk. 423, 26 E.R. 1044.
[24]*Sumner v. Partridge* (1740), 2 Atk. 47, 26 E.R. 425.
[25]*Barker v. Barker* (1828), 2 Sim. 249, 57 E.R. 782; *Jones v. Davies* (1861), 7 H. & N. 507, 158 E.R. 573.

The issue had to be born alive[26] and during the marriage.[27] Therefore, it was held that, if the wife died in labour and a Caesarean operation was performed, the husband had no estate by the curtesy because, at the moment the wife died, he was not entitled as no issue had been born.[28]

The birth of issue could be either before or after the wife was entitled to the property or seised of it.[29]

An estate by the curtesy was defeated if the wife elected to relinquish the land to which the estate attached, as where she elected to take a legacy given to her by a will which disposed of her estate.[30] The right of curtesy was also defeated by a dissolution of the marriage.[31]

In general, the incidents of an estate for life are the same whether the estate arises by act of the parties or by operation of law.[32] Thus, a tenant by the curtesy had the same liability for waste as other tenants for life and he had such liability at common law before it was imposed by statute on life tenants generally. He also had to keep down charges. He had the rights of a tenant for life regarding his enjoyment of the property and, on his death, his personal representatives were entitled to emblements. A tenant by the curtesy had the statutory powers of a tenant for life of settled land in regard to leasing and sale.

708.2 Curtesy as Affected by Statute

In New Brunswick, Nova Scotia, Ontario and Prince Edward Island, tenancy by the curtesy has been abolished.[1]

In Prince Edward Island, the now repealed provisions of the *Probate Act*[2] provided that nothing in the Act affected the right to an estate by the curtesy, but the value of the estate by the curtesy was to be considered as a part of the share inherited by the husband and was to be deducted in computing the

---

[26] As to proof, see *Brock v. Kellock* (1861), 3 Giff. 58, 66 E.R. 322; *Jones v. Ricketts* (1862), 31 Beav. 130, 54 E.R. 1087.

[27] Co. Litt. 29b; *Paine's Case, supra,* footnote 23; *Basset v. Basset* (1744), 3 Atk. 203 at p. 207, 26 E.R. 918; *Goodtitle v. Newman* (1744), 3 Wils. 516, 95 E.R. 1188.

[28] *Bowles' Case, Tudor's Leading Cases on Real Property,* 4th ed., 110; Co. Litt. 29b.

[29] Co. Litt. 29b.

[30] *Lady Cavan v. Pulteney* (1795), 2 Ves. Jun. 544 at p. 560, 30 E.R. 768.

[31] *Wilkinson v. Gibson* (1867), L.R. 4 Eq. 162; *Prole v. Soady* (1868), L.R. 3 Ch. 220.

[32] 2 Bl. Comm. 122.

§708.2

[1] *Married Woman's Property Act,* R.S.N.B. 1973, c. M-4, s. 8; *Intestate Succession Act,* R.S.N.S. 1967, c. 153, s. 2; *Matrimonial Property Act,* S.N.S. 1980, c. 9, s. 33(3); *Succession Law Reform Act,* R.S.O. 1980, c. 488, s. 48; *Family Law Reform Act,* S.P.E.I. 1978, c. 6, s. 62.

[2] R.S.P.E.I. 1974, c. P-19, s. 98, repealed by *Family Law Reform Act,* S.P.E.I. 1978, c. 6, s. 62.

balance. However, the husband could waive the right and take his full preferential and distributive share under the Act.[3]

In Ontario under the now repealed provisions of the *Conveyancing and Law of Property Act*,[4] the estate in the land by the curtesy was preserved and is defined[5] to include incorporeal hereditaments and any undivided share in land. The Act provided[6] that, where a husband had issue born alive and capable of inheriting any land to which his wife was entitled in fee simple or in fee tail and he survived her, whether the issue lived or not, he was entitled, subject to the *Married Women's Property Act*,[7] to an estate for his life in such land as may not have been disposed of by her deed or will, but if he had no such issue by his wife, he was not entitled to any estate or interest in such land if he survived her, except such as may have been devised to him by her will or such as he may have become entitled to under the *Devolution of Estates Act*.[8]

Under the *Married Women's Property Act*[9] a married woman could defeat her husband's expectant estate by the curtesy by disposing of the property in her lifetime or by will in the same manner as if she were a *feme sole*.

Under the former provisions of the *Devolution of Estates Act*[10] the real and personal property, whether separate or otherwise, of a married woman, in respect of which she died intestate was to be distributed as follows: one-third to her husband if she left issue and one-half if she left no issue, and, subject thereto, it was to devolve as if her husband had predeceased her. A husband who, if the Act had not been passed, would have been entitled as tenant by the curtesy in real property of his wife, could by deed or instrument in writing, attested by at least one witness and delivered to the personal representative, if any, or, if none, deposited in the office of the Registrar of the Supreme Court in Toronto, within six months after his wife's death, elect to take such interest in the real and personal property of his wife as he would have taken if the Act had not been passed, in which case his interest was to be ascertained in all respects as if the Act had not been passed and he was entitled to no further interest thereunder.[11] Therefore, as was held in a case interpreting a similar earlier enactment,[12] unless he elected within six months after his wife's death

---

[3]The lesser of the net estate or $50,000 plus one-half of the residue if there is no issue, or one-half if one child or issue of one child survive, or one-third if more than one child or issue of more than one child survive: *ibid.*, ss. 89 and 87, respectively.

[4]R.S.O. 1970, c. 85, s. 29, repealed by the *Succession Law Reform Act*, S.O. 1977, c. 40, s. 51(1).

[5]*Conveyancing and Law of Property Act*, R.S.O. 1970, c. 85, s. 1.

[6]*Conveyancing and Law of Property Act*, R.S.O. 1970, c. 85, s. 29, rep. 1977, c. 40, s. 51(1).

[7]R.S.O. 1970, c. 262, rep. 1975, c. 41, s. 6 and S.O. 1978, c. 2, s. 82.

[8]R.S.O. 1970, c. 129.

[9]R.S.O. 1970, c. 262, s. 2, rep. 1975, c. 41, s. 6.

[10]R.S.O. 1970, c. 129, s. 30(1).

[11]*Ibid.*, s. 30(2).

[12]R.S.O. 1897, c. 127, s. 4.

210

to take an interest as tenant by the curtesy, he was entitled only to his one-third distributive share.[13]

If the husband elected to take curtesy under the Ontario legislation, he would become entitled to a life estate in all his wife's undisposed of real property and also receive all his wife's personalty by virtue of the *jus mariti*.[14] It has, however, been argued that this result obtained only if the wife left no issue her surviving and that if she did, the husband would receive his distributive share only.[15]

Formerly, under the *Devolution of Estates Act*[16] a personal representative who wished to sell, free from curtesy, any property devolving upon him, could apply to a judge of the Supreme Court who could make an order to that effect, having regard to the interests of all parties, and who could direct the payment out of the purchase money, in satisfaction of curtesy, of a gross sum deemed by him, upon the principles applicable to life annuities, to be in reasonable satisfaction of the right of curtesy, or of an annual sum or of the interest or income to be derived from the purchase money.

In Alberta, British Columbia, Manitoba and Saskatchewan, a husband's estate by the curtesy is abolished, as is a wife's right of dower, the wife and, in Alberta and Manitoba, the husband having rights in the "homestead" constituting their residence.[17]

In Newfoundland, as the *Chattels Real Act*[18] transforms real property interests into chattels real, there is no estate by the curtesy.

709. DOWER AND CURTESY IN NEWFOUNDLAND

There is no right of dower or curtesy in Newfoundland because the *Chattels Real Act*[1] transformed all lands, tenements and hereditaments in Newfoundland into chattels real, which pass to the executor or administrator of the person dying seised or possessed of them as personal property passes to the personal representatives.

Any property that the owner does not dispose of in his lifetime or by will is governed by the *Intestate Succession Act*[2] which provides that the estate

---

[13]*Chevalier v. Trepannier* (1902), 1 O.W.R. 847 (H.C.J.). Since the extension of the preferential share provision to husbands, he would also be entitled to his preferential share: see *Devolution of Estates Act*, R.S.O. 1970, c. 129, s. 12, rep. 1977, c. 40, s. 50(1). As to the right to a preferential share on a partial intestacy, see §707.17, footnote 38, *supra*.

[14]See generally *Re Lambert's Estate; Stanton v. Lambert* (1888), 39 Ch. D. 626; *Dorsey v. Dorsey* (1898), 29 O.R. 475 (H.C.J.); Oosterhoff, *Succession Law Reform in Ontario* (Toronto, Canada Law Book, 1979), p. 75.

[15]"Comment", 44 Can. Bar Rev. 346 (1966).

[16]R.S.O. 1970, c. 129, s. 10, rep. 1977, c. 40, s. 50(1).

[17]See §§710-710.15, *infra*.

[18]R.S.N. 1970, c. 36.

§709

[1]Originally passed in 1834 and now R.S.N. 1970, c. 36.

[2]R.S.N. 1970, c. 183, s. 6, rep. and re-en. 1979, c. 32, s. 44.

of a person dying intestate leaving a spouse and no issue, belongs to the surviving spouse absolutely.

If a wife has left her husband and is living in adultery at the time of his death she takes no part in the estate, and if a husband has left his wife and is living in adultery at the time of her death he takes no part in the estate.[3]

710. HOMESTEAD LEGISLATION

In the western provinces, dower and curtesy in the historical legal sense have been abolished and replaced with an equivalent life estate in certain lands of the deceased spouse, referred to as his or her "homestead". This term is variously defined in the several provinces, but generally, it includes the matrimonial home together with adjoining land.[1]

710.1 Abolition of Dower and Curtesy

Dower and curtesy have been abolished in Alberta,[1] British Columbia,[2] Manitoba,[3] the Northwest Territories,[4] the Yukon,[5] and Saskatchewan,[6] and have been replaced with a statutory right of dower, homestead right, or matrimonial property right in favour of a wife and, in Alberta, Manitoba and the Northwest Territories, in favour of a husband as well. This statutory right is hereafter referred to as the "homestead right".

710.2 Definitions

The several statutes[1] define "homestead" and "dower rights" in different ways. The Alberta Act defines "dower rights" as meaning all rights given by

---

[3]*Ibid.*, s. 18.
§710
[1]See generally Bowker, "Reform of the Law of Dower in Alberta", 1 Alta. L. Rev. 501 (1961); "Changes in the Dower Act Recommended by the Legislation Committee of the Manitoba Bar Association and Approved by Council", 34 Man. Bar News 7 (1962); Micay, "The New Dower Act: A New Estate Planning Tool", 35 Man. Bar News 255 (1964); Wakeling, "Some Recommended Changes in the Homesteads Act", 28 Sask. Bar Rev. 119 (1963); "Note", 28 Sask. Bar Rev. 49 (1963).
§710.1
[1]*Law of Property Act*, R.S.A. 1980, c. L-8, ss. 3, 4.
[2]*Estate Administration Act*, R.S.B.C. 1979, c. 114, s. 107.
[3]*Law of Property Act*, R.S.M. 1970, c. L90, ss. 9, 10.
[4]*Land Titles Act*, R.S.C. 1970, c. L-4, ss. 5, 6.
[5]*Ibid.*
[6]*Devolution of Real Property Act*, R.S.S. 1978, c. D-27, s. 18; *Intestate Succession Act*, R.S.S. 1978, c. I-13, s. 15.
§710.2
[1]*Dower Act*, R.S.A. 1980, c. D-38; R.S.M. 1970, c. D100; *Homestead Act*, R.S.B.C. 1979, c. 173; *Land (Wife Protection) Act*, R.S.B.C. 1979, c. 223; *Homesteads Act*, R.S.S. 1978, c. H-5; *Matrimonial Property Ordinance*, R.O.N.W.T. 1974, c. M-7. These several statutes are hereafter in this and the following sections referred to as "the Alta. Act", *etc.*, or, in the case of British Columbia, as "the B.C. *Homestead Act*" and "the B.C. *Land (Wife Protection) Act*". The Yukon has no similar legislation.

the Act to the spouse of a married person in respect of the homestead and property of the married person, including the right to withhold consent to a disposition, the right to damages for a wrongful disposition, the right to payment from the Assurance Fund of an unsatisfied judgment in respect of a wrongful disposition, and the right to a life estate in the homestead and in exempt personal property of a deceased married person.[2] The definition of "matrimonial property rights" in the Northwest Territories Ordinance is to the same effect.[3]

"Homestead" is defined in the Alberta Act as the parcel of land on which the dwelling-house occupied by the owner of the parcel as his or her residence is situate and which consists of not more than four adjoining lots shown on a registered plan in an urban municipality or not more than one quarter section of land in a rural municipality.[4] The definition of "residential property" in the Northwest Territories is to the same effect.[5] The Manitoba Act defines "homestead" similarly, but enlarges it to include six lots in one block shown on a registered plan in an urban municipality or not more than one quarter section plan in an urban municipality, or 360 acres in a rural municipality, appurtenant to the dwelling-house.[6] Under the Saskatchewan Act a homestead is the home and buildings of the owner and the lot or lots on which they stand, up to 160 acres.[7] In British Columbia a homestead is the parcels of land, whether leasehold, freehold or both, together with any erections or buildings thereon, that are registered as a homestead in the name of the husband and on which is situate a dwelling occupied by the husband and wife as their residence.[8] An application for entry on the register must be made before the husband's death.[9]

A residence in which a husband lives with his wife, part of which is rented to tenants, is his homestead where the primary function of the building is a home for the husband and wife.[10] A home may be a homestead where a husband built the home as a residence for his wife and children, visited it often for meals but never slept in it, since the definition of "homestead" in section 1 of the *Land (Wife Protection) Act*, which requires joint occupancy by the husband and wife, does not require joint physical occupancy.[11]

710.3   Creation of Homestead

In all of the western provinces except British Columbia the homestead is created by statute. In British Columbia, however, it is necessary for the owner

---

[2]Alta. Act, s. 1(*d*).
[3]N.W.T. Ord., s. 2(*b*).
[4]Alta. Act, s. 1(*e*).
[5]N.W.T. Ord., s. 2(*d*).
[6]Man. Act, s. 2(*e*).
[7]Sask. Act, s. 2.
[8]B.C. *Homestead Act*, s. 1; B.C. *Land (Wife Protection) Act*, s. 1.
[9]*Re Kergin* (1974), 47 D.L.R. (3d) 592, 18 R.F.L. 169 (B.C.S.C.).
[10]*Seroy v. Seroy and Komar* (1964), 48 D.L.R. (2d) 78, 50 W.W.R. 65 (Man. C.A.);
   Packer v. Packer (1959), 24 D.L.R. (2d) 411, 31 W.W.R. 22 (Man. Q.B.).
[11]*Re Gale and Gale* (1962), 33 D.L.R. (2d) 771, 39 W.W.R. 246 (B.C.C.A.).

of the property to have it registered as a homestead[1] and a wife, or a husband on her behalf, may make application to the Registrar of Titles for an entry on the register that a homestead is subject to the provisions of the British Columbia Act.[2] In most cases there can be only one homestead even where a person changes his residence,[3] but in Saskatchewan every property that has been a homestead at any time is a homestead.[4]

710.4　Extinguishment of Rights

A spouse loses his rights in a homestead where he consents in writing to the disposition of the homestead or releases his rights, or where the court by order dispenses with consent.[1]

710.5　Consent to Disposition

A person is prohibited from disposing of his homestead *inter vivos* to anyone other than his spouse unless the spouse consents to the disposition in writing.[1] Moreover, a homestead ceases to be such when the spouse has consented thereto in writing, even though the consent was in respect of an agreement of purchase and sale and the land is later recovered by the vendor spouse.[2]

In some of the provinces a special form of consent must be endorsed on or annexed to the instrument effecting the disposition;[3] in others the execution of the instrument by the spouse is sufficient.[4] The consent must be evidenced by an acknowledgement by the spouse that he or she is aware of the nature of the act.[5] In some cases the spouse may have the consent executed by an attorney as well.[6]

The Manitoba Act specifically provides that a consent to an encumbrance

---

§710.3
[1]B.C. *Homestead Act*, s. 3.
[2]*Ibid.*, B.C. *Land (Wife Protection) Act*, s. 2.
[3]Alta. Act, s. 3; N.W.T. Ord., s. 4; Man. Act, s. 4.
[4]Sask. Act, s. 2.
§710.4
[1]The fact that title to the husband's property is in the Director, the Veterans' Land Act does not defeat his wife's homestead rights.
§710.5
[1]Alta. Act, s. 2; B.C. *Land (Wife Protection) Act*, s. 3; Man. Act, s. 3; Sask. Act, s. 3; N.W.T. Ord., s. 3.
[2]Alta. Act, s. 3(2)(*b*); N.W.T. Ord., s. 4(2)(*b*); Man. Act, s. 4(1); *Onofriechuk v. Burlacu* (1959), 30 W.W.R. 282 (Man. C.A.).
[3]Alta. Act, s. 4; N.W.T. Ord., s. 5; Man. Act, ss. 5, 26; B.C. *Land (Wife Protection) Act*, ss. 3, 7; B.C. *Homestead Act*, s. 7.
[4]Sask. Act, s. 3(1).
[5]Alta. Act, s. 5; N.W.T. Ord., s. 6; Sask. Act, s. 3(1); Man. Act, s. 8; B.C. *Land (Wife Protection) Act*, s. 8.
[6]Man. Act, s. 7.

only has such effect as is necessary to give full effect to the right of the encumbrancer. Furthermore, if the homestead is sold by the mortgagee, the spouse is entitled to a one-half share of the surplus moneys arising from the sale, but the court may deny the spouse his one-half if it finds that he is separated from his spouse.[7]

Non-compliance with the legislation invalidates the mortgage of a homestead, even though the mortgage is registered on title and money is advanced under it.[8] A transfer is also void if it does not comply with the legislation, but this is subject to the rights of a purchaser for value who relies on the certificate of title in good faith and without fraud. The fact that a subsequent transferee knows that the spouse of a homestead owner was not a party to the original transfer is not fraud, for he may rely on the register, although such knowledge by a first transferee would amount to fraud.[9]

The court may in certain cases, by order, validate a defective consent.[10]

Where a person disposes of land which is not a homestead, or where his or her spouse is not entitled to homestead rights therein, the instrument effecting the disposition must be accompanied by an affidavit setting out those facts and the transferee is thereupon protected.[11]

Once a valid consent has been given, for example, to an agreement of sale, no further consent to the deed is required.[12]

The consent provisions of the several statutes are strictly construed for the benefit of the spouse having homestead rights. Thus, even though a wife was present during a lease transaction but did not sign the consent and understood little English, she is not estopped from contesting the validity of the lease.[13] Similarly, the mere signature by the wife on an agreement of sale without further compliance with the legislation, renders the agreement unenforceable,[14] and a mere verbal agreement by the wife to a sale is also ineffective.[15] This is true even though the spouses hold title to the homestead jointly, for the

---

[7]*Ibid.*, s. 11.

[8]*British American Oil Co. Ltd. v. Kos and Kos* (1963), 42 D.L.R. (2d) 426, [1964] S.C.R. 167.

[9]Sask. Act, s. 11; *Deptuch v. Kurmey* (1964), 48 W.W.R. 45 (Sask. Q.B.).

[10]Man. Act, s. 12; N.W.T. Ord., s. 6(3); Alta. Act, s. 5(3).

[11]Sask. Act, s. 7.

[12]Alta. Act, s. 6; N.W.T. Ord., s. 7; Sask. Act, s. 6; Man. Act, s. 26(1); B.C. *Land (Wife Protection) Act*, s. 10.

[13]*Guzak v. McEwan* (1965), 53 D.L.R. (2d) 55, 52 W.W.R. 335 (Sask. Q.B.). *Cf. Broersma v. Maier* (1969), 9 D.L.R. (3d) 110, 72 W.W.R. 153 (Alta. S.C.T.D.).

[14]*McColm v. Belter* (1974), 50 D.L.R. (3d) 133, [1975] 1 W.W.R. 364 (Alta. S.C. App. Div.). *Cf. Senstad v. Makus*, [1975] 4 W.W.R. 290, 20 R.F.L. 269 (Alta. S.C.T.D.), revd 69 D.L.R. (3d) 184, [1976] 6 W.W.R. 123 (S.C. App. Div.), restd 79 D.L.R. (3d) 321, 17 N.R. 361 (S.C.C.); *Westward Farms Ltd. v. Cadieux, Barnabe, Third Party; Barnabe v. Cadieux, McKague Sigmar Realty Ltd., Third Party* (1982), 138 D.L.R. (3d) 137, [1982] 5 W.W.R. 1 (Man. C.A.), leave to appeal to S.C.C. refused November 1, 1982.

[15]*Martens v. Burden and Burden* (1974), 45 D.L.R. (3d) 123, [1974] 3 W.W.R. 522 (Alta. S.C.T.D.). *Cf. Rose v. Dever* (1971), 26 D.L.R. (3d) 462, 1 N.R. 57 (Man. C.A.), affd 42 D.L.R. (3d) 160n, [1973] S.C.R. vi.

wife's interest in a homestead is not the same as her interest in the joint tenancy.[16]

Not only is an agreement which fails to comply with the statute unenforceable, damages are not normally recoverable under it against the spouse who has executed it.

In *Gostevskyh v. Klassen*[17] the appellants, a husband and wife who were joint tenants of a homestead, advertised it for sale. The respondent entered into an agreement of purchase and sale with the husband only and the wife later refused to complete. Although the respondent was awarded damages at trial in his action for specific performance or damages in lieu, the decision was reversed on appeal. The Court of Appeal held that since the legislation does not specifically authorize a spouse to appoint the other as his or her agent, both must execute a disposition of the homestead. Since that was not done, the agreement was ineffective and damages were not recoverable under it. Nor could damages be awarded against the husband for breach of an implied warranty of authority on his part that he could give his wife's consent, since the legislation does not contemplate his appointment as his wife's agent for that purpose. Even if such damages could have been awarded, they would have the result of reducing the spouses' joint estates, which is contrary to the purpose of the statute.[18]

However, where the wife represented to the purchaser that she was the sole owner of land, having acquired her husband's interest, and where the husband released his homestead interest in a separation agreement which was never executed, but a release executed during trial was registered, the wife is estopped from raising her husband's homestead right as a defence to an action for specific performance.[19]

Where a husband and his common law wife bought property as tenants in common but later changed the title to a joint tenancy, and where the wife signed a release after her husband's death, it was held that the change to a joint tenancy was void as there was no consent to it by the wife, but that the wife's release was also ineffective as it purported to affect the rights of her infant children on her husband's death.[20]

The transfer of land by a sheriff under a writ of execution is not a disposition made by a married person so as to require the spouse's consent.[21]

---

[16]*Kiehl v. Culbert*, [1972] 1 W.W.R. 234, 5 R.F.L. 330 (Sask. Dist. Ct.).

[17](1979), 106 D.L.R. (3d) 459, 21 A.R. 170 (C.A.).

[18]See also *McKenzie v. Hiscock* (1967), 65 D.L.R. (2d) 123, [1967] S.C.R. 781, and *Vandermeulen v. Wieler* (1980), 109 D.L.R. (3d) 357, [1980] 4 W.W.R. 164 (Man. Q.B.), to the same effect.

[19]*Palinko (Palinka) v. Bower*, [1975] 1 W.W.R. 756, 18 R.F.L. 62 (Alta. S.C.T.D.), revd on other grounds [1976] 4 W.W.R. 118 (S.C. App. Div.). Failure of a spouse to acknowledge consent to a sale of the homestead does not affect the validity of the sale if the spouse in fact consents to it and does not attack the validity of the consent: *McFarland v. Hauser* (1978), 88 D.L.R. (3d) 449, 23 N.R. 362 (S.C.C.).

[20]*Toth v. Kancz* (1975), 54 D.L.R. (3d) 144, [1975] W.W.D. 90 (Sask. Q.B.).

[21]"Note", 4 Alta. L. Rev. 506 (1966).

710.6   Release of Homestead Rights

In addition to executing a consent to a specific transaction, a spouse may execute a release of his or her homestead rights.[1] The parties may in writing terminate the release or the court may, in certain circumstances, order that the release be terminated.[2] A person may also, for valuable consideration, execute an agreement releasing or abandoning his or her homestead rights,[3] or contracting out of all his or her rights under the legislation.[4] An ante-nuptial agreement to waive the benefits of the legislation is not inherently contrary to public policy, but it is only effective if there is full disclosure of all material facts.[5]

710.7   Caveats

In Alberta and the Northwest Territories, where a release of homestead rights has been registered, a spouse may register a caveat before the land has been transferred and the caveat has the effect of cancelling the release.[1] In Manitoba a caveat or dower notice may be filed where a release has been terminated.[2] In Saskatchewan, a wife may file a caveat to protect her rights in the homestead.[3]

Where a person devised land to his son "subject to a life interest of my wife" and prohibited his son from selling the property to the prejudice of that life interest, the son had a sufficient interest in the land capable of supporting a homestead interest where he and his wife lived on the land for ten years, even though the son was not the registered owner, and the son's wife was entitled to file a caveat against it.[4]

A caveat filed by a creditor against a husband's homestead interest in land is ineffective where the husband subsequently released his homestead interest and divorced his wife. His interest was contingent on his surviving his wife and ceased with the release.[5]

In British Columbia, the entry on the title to a homestead by a wife

---

§710.6
[1]Alta. Act, s. 7; N.W.T. Ord., s. 8; Man. Act, s. 6(1).
[2]Man. Act, s. 6(3), (4).
[3]Alta. Act, s. 9; N.W.T. Ord., s. 10; B.C. *Land (Wife Protection) Act*, s. 11; B.C. *Homestead Act*, s. 8.
[4]Man. Act, s. 23; *Broder v. Broder*, [1973] 1 W.W.R. 669, 9 R.F.L. 308 (Man. Q.B.), affd [1973] 6 W.W.R. 191 (Man. C.A.).
[5]*Stern v. Sheps* (1966), 61 D.L.R. (2d) 343, 58 W.W.R. 612 (Man. C.A.), affd 69 D.L.R. (2d) 76, [1968] S.C.R. 834.
§710.7
[1]Alta. Act, s. 8; N.W.T. Ord., s. 9.
[2]Man. Act, ss. 6(5), 27(1).
[3]Sask. Act, s. 8.
[4]*Re Weinberger and Weinberger* (1975), 54 D.L.R. (3d) 613, 20 R.F.L. 150 (Sask. Q.B.).
[5]*Re Heiden and Huck* (1971), 21 D.L.R. (3d) 750, [1971] 5 W.W.R. 446 (Alta. S.C.T.D.).

operates like a caveat, but does not give her priority over judgment creditors. It merely protects her against a disposition by the husband of his interest without her consent.[6] In Saskatchewan a wife is given an opportunity to file a caveat where the husband becomes bankrupt.[7] Moreover, where she has filed a caveat, she is not bound by a judgment in a mortgage action unless she is joined in the action.[8]

In Saskatchewan a caveat lapses where it is determined by the court that the wife is living apart from her husband under circumstances disentitling her to alimony.[9] Furthermore, any interested person may apply to the court for an order directing that a caveat shall lapse.[10] However, a wife may file a caveat against any property that has been a homestead at any time and if she files more than one, her husband is not entitled to have all except one removed.[11]

710.8 Dispensing with Consent

In Alberta and the Northwest Territories the owner of land may apply to the court for an order dispensing with the spouse's consent where the parties are separated, where the spouse has not lived in the jurisdiction since the marriage or his or her whereabouts is unknown, where the owner has two or more homesteads, where the spouse has made an agreement for valuable consideration releasing his or her homestead rights, or where the spouse is mentally incompetent or of unsound mind, and the court may order that consent be dispensed with, with or without conditions.[1] The statutes of the other provinces contain similar provisions.[2]

An order dispensing with the consent of the spouse to the partition of the homestead may be made where the spouses are separated,[3] and the parties' conduct is not determinative of whether the court should exercise its discretion.[4] A sale of land pursuant to a partition order is not a disposition within the meaning of the statute.[5] Thus, a partition order may be made without the spouse's consent, but where the property is sold, the value of the homestead interest is to be paid to the spouse out of the purchase price in annual instalments.[6] Similarly, in British Columbia the court may order partition or sale of a

---

[6]*Gathe v. Gathe* (1972), 31 D.L.R. (3d) 702, [1973] 1 W.W.R. 234 (B.C.C.A.).
[7]Sask. Act, s. 8(3).
[8]*Ibid.*, s. 15.
[9]*Ibid.*, s. 9.
[10]*Ibid.*, s. 10.
[11]*Birkeland v. Birkeland* (1971), 20 D.L.R. (3d) 757, [1971] 5 W.W.R. 662 (Sask. Q.B.).
§710.8
[1]Alta. Act, s. 10; N.W.T. Ord., s. 11.
[2]Sask. Act, s. 3(2); B.C. *Land (Wife Protection) Act*, s. 9; Man. Act, s. 13.
[3]*McWilliam v. McWilliam* (1961), 34 W.W.R. 476 (Alta. S.C. App. Div.); *Wagner v. Wagner* (1970), 73 W.W.R. 474 (Alta. S.C.).
[4]*Dos Reis v. Dos Reis* (1979), 8 R.P.R. 56 (Man. Co. Ct.).
[5]*Wagner v. Wagner, supra*, footnote 3.
[6]*Law of Property Act*, R.S.M. 1970, c. L90, ss. 19(2), 24.

homestead worth more than $2,500, but it must have regard to the preferences of the parties and may order the purchase of other homestead property with the proceeds.[7]

710.9 Action for Damages

In Alberta and the Northwest Territories a person is liable to his or her spouse in damages if a disposition of a homestead is made without the spouse's consent.[1] Furthermore, the spouse has the right to claim payment from the Assurance Fund for any unsatisfied judgment.[2]

710.10 Life Estate to Survivor

The surviving spouse has a life estate in the homestead of the predeceased spouse which takes priority over any testamentary dispositions.[1] However, in British Columbia the estate exists only during the minority of the children or while the widow remains unmarried, but if only the widow survives she gets the homestead absolutely and if any children survive, they receive it absolutely in equal shares when the youngest attains his majority.[2]

In Saskatchewan and British Columbia the homestead vests in the personal representative in trust for the widow.[3]

In Manitoba, where the husband and wife have left their homestead and have taken up residence elsewhere without the spouse's consent to a change in homestead, the survivor may elect to treat one or the other residence as the homestead.[4] There are similar provisions in Alberta and the Northwest Territories.[5]

During the lifetime of the survivor the homestead may be disposed of with the consent of the survivor executed in the same manner as a consent to a disposition during the owner's lifetime.[6]

In Alberta and the Northwest Territories the surviving spouse is also given a life estate in the personal property of the deceased that is exempt from seizure under a writ of execution.[7]

---

[7]B.C. *Homestead Act*, s. 9.
§710.9
[1]Alta. Act, s. 11; N.W.T. Ord., s. 12.
[2]Alta. Act, s. 13; N.W.T. Ord., s. 14.
§710.10
[1]Alta. Act, s. 18; N.W.T. Ord., s. 19; Man. Act, s. 14(1); Sask. Act, s. 12; B.C. *Land (Wife Protection) Act*, s. 5; B.C. *Homestead Act*, s. 6.
[2]B.C. *Homestead Act*, s. 6.
[3]Sask. Act, s. 12; B.C. *Land (Wife Protection) Act*, s. 4.
[4]Man. Act, s. 4(4)-(6).
[5]Alta. Act, s. 19; N.W.T. Ord., s. 20.
[6]Alta. Act, s. 21; N.W.T. Ord., s. 22; Sask. Act, s. 12; Man. Act, s. 14(2).
[7]Alta. Act, s. 23; N.W.T. Ord., s. 24.

In Manitoba, where the deceased has not left the surviving spouse at least one-third of the net value of his or her real and personal property, the survivor is also entitled to the difference between such one-third and any advancements made by the deceased to the surviving spouse, together with the proceeds of insurance on the deceased's life which are payable to the surviving spouse.[8] However, this additional right does not apply where the deceased gave the surviving spouse by will, or by advancement, property, or an income, or both, above specified amounts.[9] Furthermore, the surviving spouse is required, where he or she is entitled to a share of the net estate in addition to the homestead right, to elect to take either the benefits under the Act or those under the will and, if within the specified time the surviving spouse fails to make the election, or elects to take under the will, he or she must take the benefits conferred by the will,[10] but such election does not deprive him or her of the life estate in the homestead.[11] If the surviving spouse elects to take under the Act, the benefits conferred on him or her by the will are ineffective,[12] except that a declaration in the will in respect of a policy of insurance in favour of the surviving spouse is unaffected.[13]

Similarly, where the owner of a homestead dies intestate, the surviving spouse's homestead rights are unaffected and he or she takes the life estate in addition to the statutory share.[14]

Orders made under dependants' relief legislation are often subject to the surviving spouse's homestead rights.[15]

710.11   Applicability to Mines and Minerals

The surviving spouse's homestead rights apply to mines and minerals contained in a homestead.[1]

710.12   Statutory Exceptions

In Alberta and the Northwest Territories the legislation does not apply to co-ownership where the married person is co-owner with a person other than

---

[8]Man. Act, s. 15.

[9]*Ibid.*, s. 16; "Note", 35 Man. Bar News 349 (1965).

[10]Man. Act, s. 17.

[11]*Ibid.*, s. 17(8).

[12]*Ibid.*, s. 19.

[13]*Ibid.*, s. 20.

[14]See, *e.g.*, *Intestate Succession Act*, R.S.A. 1970, c. 190, s. 14, not carried forward in R.S.A. 1980, c. I-9; *Law of Property Act*, R.S.M. 1970, c. L90, ss. 9, 10. For the shares to which spouses are entitled on an intestacy, see §503.1(c), *supra.*

[15]*Family Relief Act*, R.S.A. 1980, c. F-2, s. 4; *Testator's Family Maintenance Act*, R.S.M. 1970, c. T50, s. 22.

§710.11

[1]Alta. Act, s. 24; N.W.T. Ord., s. 25; Man. Act, s. 9.

his or her spouse, but it does apply to co-ownership between a husband and wife.[1]

In Saskatchewan the Act does not apply to transfers of land required for the construction of a railway, or a gas, oil or water pipe line, nor to an agreement granting an easement for public utility purposes,[2] and land acquired for the purpose of a public highway.[3]

710.13 Statutory Bars

Where a spouse is living separate and apart from the other in circumstances disentitling him or her to alimony, the homestead rights are lost, as is the right to file a caveat, but in some provinces the right to file a caveat and the right to give or withhold consent are lost only by order of the court.[1] This does not necessarily affect any other rights that the survivor may have in the estate, however.[2]

Upon the dissolution of marriage by divorce or a judgment of nullity, a spouse's homestead rights cease,[3] even where an action to enforce them was commenced while the marriage was subsisting, but was not concluded when the marriage was dissolved.[4]

710.14 Priority over Creditors

Generally, a spouse's homestead rights take priority over the creditors of the owner of the homestead to the extent that property is made exempt from seizure[1] and the rights continue to be protected after the death of the owner of the homestead.[2] It was held, however, that the wife's rights under British Columbia's *Wife's Protection Act* (now known as the *Land (Wife Protection) Act*[3]) were subject to the payment of debts and to foreclosure in a mortgage

---

§710.12
[1]Alta. Act, s. 25; N.W.T. Ord., s. 26.
[2]Sask. Act, s. 17.
[3]*Ibid.*, s. 18.
§710.13
[1]Alta. Act, s. 22; N.W.T. Ord., s. 23; Sask. Act, ss. 3(2), 9; Man. Act, s. 22; *Re Nixey* (1972), 31 D.L.R. (3d) 597 (Man. Q.B.); *Re Rudiak* (1958), 13 D.L.R. (2d) 566, 25 W.W.R. 38 (Alta. S.C.); *Masciuch v. Drabyk*, [1974] 5 W.W.R. 638, 18 R.F.L. 175 (Man. Surr. Ct.).
[2]*Sysiuk v Sysiuk*, [1948] 1 D.L.R. 676, [1947] 2 W.W.R. 897 (Man. C.A.).
[3]B.C. *Land (Wife Protection) Act*, s. 6.
[4]*Clark v. Clark* (1965), 55 D.L.R. (2d) 218, 54 W.W.R. 744 (Alta. S.C. App. Div.).
§710.14
[1]Sask. Act, s. 12; *Exemptions Act*, R.S.S. 1978, c. E-14, s. 2(1), para. 10; R.S.A. 1980, c. E-15, s. 1(1)(j); *Court Order Enforcement Act*, R.S.B.C. 1979, c. 75, s. 43. (The Act does not apply to lands registered under the B.C. *Homestead Act*.)
[2]*Re Mymryk and Canada Permanent Trust Co.* (1968), 67 D.L.R. (2d) 159, 63 W.W.R. 313 (Man. Q.B.).
[3]R.S.B.C. 1979, c. 223.

action.[4] Moreover, under the Saskatchewan Act the personal representatives of a creditor may make application for an order dispensing with the signature of the wife and permitting the personal representatives to deal with the land on the ground that it is not necessary for the maintenance and support of the widow, or is otherwise unnecessary.[5]

A trustee in bankruptcy cannot dispose of the homestead without the consent of the spouse, even if there is more than one homestead.[6]

Where the surviving spouse is bankrupt as well, however, his or her homestead right passes to the trustee in bankruptcy, subject to a claim for exemption.[7]

The homestead rights of a spouse must be determined in a foreclosure action and cannot be contested collaterally thereafter.[8]

710.15   General Provisions

(a) Settlement of disputes

In some of the statutes the court is given wide power to settle disputes arising under the legislation.[1]

(b) Legal disability

All of the statutes are made applicable to married persons who are minors.[2]

(c) Homestead rights and matrimonial property rights

Homestead rights are in addition to, not in substitution of, matrimonial property rights created under recent legislation in Manitoba,[3] Alberta,[4] British Columbia[5] and Saskatchewan.[6] These rights will be discussed in chapter 16.

---

[4]*Arrow Transfer Co. Ltd. v. Seear* (1969), 6 D.L.R. (3d) 347 (B.C.S.C.).
[5]Sask. Act, s. 13.
[6]*Re Stevenson* (1971), 20 D.L.R. (3d) 119, 16 C.B.R. (N.S.) 173 (Sask. Q.B.).
[7]*Re Gates and Gates* (1973), 40 D.L.R. (3d) 442, [1974] 1 W.W.R. 618 (Alta. S.C.T.D.).
[8]*Leutner v. Garbuz and Zottenburg* (1970), 14 D.L.R. (3d) 367, [1971] 1 W.W.R. 436 (Alta. S.C.).
§710.15
[1]N.W.T. Ord., s. 28; Man. Act, s. 28; B.C. *Homestead Act*, s. 9.
[2]Alta. Act, s. 26; N.W.T. Ord., s. 27; Sask. Act, s. 19; Man. Act, s. 24; B.C. *Land (Wife Protection) Act*, s. 13.
[3]*Marital Property Act*, S.M. 1978, c. 24, s. 24; *Family Maintenance Act*, S.M. 1978, c. 25, s. 32.
[4]*Matrimonial Property Act*, R.S.A. 1980, c. M-9, s. 28.
[5]*Family Relations Act*, R.S.B.C. 1979, c. 121, ss. 55(2), 77(6).
[6]*Matrimonial Property Act*, S.S. 1979, c. 17-6.1, ss. 16, 52.

711. TENANT IN TAIL AFTER POSSIBILITY OF ISSUE EXTINCT

This estate arises when the spouse of a tenant in tail special predeceases him without leaving issue, so that there is no longer any possibility of having issue by that spouse. Thus, in a gift "to X and the heirs of his body begotten upon Jane Doe", when Jane Doe predeceases X leaving no issue her surviving, X becomes a tenant in tail after possibility of issue extinct. In effect this converts the estate tail into a life estate. The result is that X is thereafter liable for equitable waste,[1] although not for voluntary waste since he remains, in name at least, a tenant in tail.[2] Moreover, he is no longer able to bar the entail.[3]

---

§711
[1]*Cooke v. Whaley* (1701), 1 Eq. Ca. Abr. 400, 21 E.R. 1132.
[2]*Williams v. Williams* (1810), 12 East. 209, 104 E.R. 81.
[3]See generally, Megarry and Wade, pp. 97-8.

CHAPTER 8

LEASEHOLDS

801. CREATION OF THE RELATIONSHIP OF LANDLORD AND TENANT

The relationship of landlord and tenant is created by a contract express or implied, by which one person who is possessed with an interest in real property, and who is called the *landlord* or *lessor*, confers on another person, called the *tenant* or *lessee*, the right to exclusive possession of the real property or some part of it for a period of time which is definite or can be made definite by either party, usually in consideration of a periodical payment of rent either in money or its equivalent. The interest in the property remaining in the landlord, being the interest of which he has not disposed, is called the *reversion*. The interest or estate which the tenant has in the land is known as the *term*.

It is important to distinguish a lease from other interests such as licences, easements or *profits à prendre* which superficially may bear some similarity to a lease. The lease creates the relationship of landlord and tenant to which certain common law incidents apply and is subject to the statutory provisions of the various Landlord and Tenant Acts.[1]

In contrast to a lease a licence does not create an interest in land but rather gives the right to use property in a manner which otherwise would be a trespass. Usually a licence based on contract is not assignable. A licence normally does not give the right of exclusive possession. The distinction between the two will turn on the intention of the parties.[2]

---

§801

[1]*University of Prince Edward Island v. President of Student's Union of University of Prince Edward Island* (1976), 70 D.L.R. (3d) 756 (P.E.I.S.C.); *Oliver v. Harvey* (1974), 49 D.L.R. (3d) 462, [1975] 2 W.W.R. 39 (Sask. Dist. Ct.); *R. v. Poulin*, [1973] 2 O.R. 875, 12 C.C.C. (2d) 49 (Prov. Ct.).

[2]For a discussion of licences see §1704.1, *infra*. See also *City Meat Market (Sault) Ltd. v. Hagen*, [1970] 1 O.R. 563, 9 D.L.R. (3d) 58 (H.C.J.), affd [1970] 3 O.R. 682, 13 D.L.R. (3d) 698 (C.A.); *Appah v. Parncliffe Investments Ltd.*, [1964] 1 W.L.R. 1064

An easement creates an interest in land and is an incorporeal hereditament. In essence the holder of the easement (the owner of the dominant tenement) has the right to compel the use or restrict the use of the land of the giver of the easement (the servient tenement) in some manner.[3] No right of exclusive possession flows to the holder of the dominant tenement under an easement.

A *profit à prendre* again is an interest in land but one which gives no right of exclusive possession. Rather, the holder of the profit is given the right to take part of, or the product from, the land of the giver. The right is assignable.[4]

The mere payment of money for the use of land does not itself create the relationship of landlord and tenant, as the agreement could constitute a licence rather than a tenancy.[5]

In Ontario, section 3 of the *Landlord and Tenant Act*[6] provides that the relation of landlord and tenant shall not depend on tenure and a reversion in the lessor shall not be necessary in order to create the relation of landlord and tenant or to make applicable the incidents by law belonging to that relation, nor shall it be necessary in order to give a landlord the right of distress that there is an agreement for that purpose between the parties. This has been called a peculiar provision.[7] Under this provision a tenant in fee simple may agree to become the tenant of another person for a stipulated time and the statute annexes to the agreement all the incidents of law belonging to the common law relation of landlord and tenant, including the incident of the landlord's right of distress.[8]

At common law, when the reversion was transferred to another by grant, it was necessary for the tenant to attorn to the new owner. It was not necessary to attorn if the reversion was transferred by devise or descent. By statute all grants or conveyances of any reversion or remainder are effectual without attornment, although the tenant is not prejudiced by a payment of rent to the grantor or by a breach of any condition for non-payment of rent before notice

---

(C.A.); *Abbeyfield (Harpenden) Society Ltd. v. Woods*, [1968] 1 W.L.R. 374 (C.A.); *Re B.A. Oil Co. and Halpert*, [1960] O.R. 71, 21 D.L.R. (2d) 110 (C.A.); *Re Texaco Ltd. and Wherry*, [1960] O.W.N. 36 (C.A.); *Re Totem Tourist Court and Skaley*, [1973] 3 O.R. 867 (Dist. Ct.); *Willoughby v. Willoughby*, [1960] O.R. 276, 23 D.L.R. (2d) 312 (C.A.); *Crane v. Morris*, [1965] 1 W.L.R. 1104 (C.A.); *R. v. Poulin*, supra.

[3]For a discussion of easements see §1802.1, *infra*.

[4]For a discussion of *profits à prendre* see §1812, *infra*. See also *Ontario-Minnesota Pulp & Paper Co. Ltd. v. Township of Atikokan*, [1963] 1 O.R. 169, 36 D.L.R. (2d) 370 (H.C.J.); *Bowaters Newfoundland Ltd. v. Pelley Enterprises Ltd.* (1973), 5 Nfld. & P.E.I.R. 233 (Nfld. S.C.), vard 12 Nfld. & P.E.I.R. 251 (C.A.).

[5]*Young v. Bank of Nova Scotia* (1915), 34 O.L.R. 176 at p. 181, 23 D.L.R. 854 at p. 858 (S.C. App. Div.); *Re Imperial Oil Ltd. and Robertson*, [1959] O.R. 655, 21 D.L.R. (2d) 535 (C.A.); *Re Can. Petrofina Ltd. and Trudell*, [1960] O.R. 82, 21 D.L.R. (2d) 569 (C.A.).

[6]R.S.O. 1980, c. 232.

[7]Armour, *Real Property*, pp. 123-6.

[8]*Kennedy v. Agricultural Development Board* (1926), 59 O.L.R. 374 at p. 377, [1926] 4 D.L.R. 717 at p. 720 (H.C.).

to him of the grant by the grantee.[9] This provision in effect creates the relationship of landlord and tenant between the new owner and the tenant.[10]

A vendor of land may attorn to and become the tenant of the purchaser. However, it has been held that a purchaser in possession under an agreement of purchase and sale which is in default, in the absence of attornment, is not an overholding tenant.[11] A mortgagor may attorn to and become the tenant of the mortgagee. However, if in a mortgage there is no real intention to create the relationship of landlord and tenant and the intent is merely to give the mortgagee a power of distress and thus priority over creditors of the mortgagor, the attornment clause will not be effective to create the relationship.[12] However, a mortgagee who has foreclosed is entitled to take proceedings under a landlord and tenant statute to eject mortgagors who refuse to give up possession.[13] Similarly, a receiver appointed by court order may be a "landlord" within the meaning of the term.[14] It has been decided that where the mortgage is by way of sublease the mortgagee as subtenant may obtain relief from forfeiture of the head lease under the applicable Landlord and Tenant Act.[15]

The relationship of landlord and tenant may be created by estoppel. If, for example, a person who has no interest in lands makes a demise to another and afterwards acquires the title, the demise is as valid as it would have been if he had title at the time he purported to make the demise. Such a demise is said to create an estate by estoppel. By acquiring the title subsequently it is said that the estoppel "is fed". The result is that the lease is valid and creates a binding estate in interest which dates back to the date of the purported demise.

802. LEASES AND AGREEMENTS TO LEASE

A document which binds the parties merely to make and accept a lease thereafter is not a lease but is an agreement for a lease. If the document contains all the material terms of letting from which nothing is to be inferred and which does not show that any further or other document is contemplated,

---

[9]*Commercial Tenancy Act*, R.S.B.C. 1979, c. 54, s. 14; *Landlord and Tenant Act*, R.S.O. 1980, c. 232, s. 62; R.S.S. 1978, c. L-6, s. 60; R.S.M. 1970, c. L70, s. 56; R.S.N.B. 1973, c. L-1, s. 46; R.S.P.E.I. 1974, c. L-7, s. 22; *Landlord and Tenant Ordinance*, R.O.N.W.T. 1974, c. L-2, s. 28; R.O.Y.T. 1971, c. L-2, s. 40.

[10]*Brydges v. Lewis* (1842), 3 Q.B. 603, 114 E.R. 639.

[11]*Smith v. Young* (1976), 17 N.S.R. (2d) 247 (S.C. App. Div.).

[12]*Hobbs, Osborne and Hobbs v. Ontario Loan & Debenture Co.* (1890), 18 S.C.R. 483 at p. 500; *Central Mortgage & Housing Corp. v. Hankins* (1962), 33 D.L.R. (2d) 727, 39 W.W.R. 144 (Alta. S.C. App. Div.); *Danforth Discount Ltd. v. Humphries Motors Ltd.*, [1965] 2 O.R. 765, 52 D.L.R. (2d) 98 (C.A.).

[13]*Foster (Wardell Estate) v. Kurytnik* (1963), 45 W.W.R. 383 (Man. Co. Ct.).

[14]*Re Clarkson Co. Ltd. and Morrison* (1975), 8 O.R. (2d) 414, 58 D.L.R. (3d) 190 (Div. Ct.).

[15]*Re Toronto-Dominion Bank and Dufferin-Lawrence Developments Ltd.* (1981), 32 O.R. (2d) 597, 122 D.L.R. (3d) 272 (C.A.).

it is essentially a lease and not an agreement for a lease.[1] Even if the document stipulates for the preparation of a subsequent formal lease, it is construed as a lease if it contains words of present demise and the essential terms of the letting.[2]

The essential terms of a lease are the amount of rent, the mode of payment, the commencement and duration of the term and the covenants.[3] With respect to rent, where a lease permits renewal and rent for the renewal term is to be fixed by arbitration,[4] or by the landlord,[5] the terms of the renewal at least with respect to rent are certain. The same holds true where rent is to be fixed by arbitration at stated intervals throughout the original term,[6] or where the lease provides for periodic adjustment through a formula based on "cost of living" divided by "cost of living index".[7] Where an oral lease is alleged, cogent evidence must be adduced fixing the commencement of the term with certainty. If such evidence is not forthcoming the claim of lease will fail.[8]

In all cases, the question whether a document operates as a lease or an agreement for a lease depends upon the intention of the parties.[9]

At common law a valid lease could be made without writing. By the *Statute of Frauds*, all leases and agreements for leases for terms exceeding three years or for terms less than three years whereby the rent reserved is less than two-thirds of the full improved value of the demised premises must be in writing.[10] Otherwise they have the effect of estates at will only,[11] but if entry is made under a lease not within the statute and the rent is paid by the year, or with reference to an aliquot part of a year, the tenant will become a tenant from year to year.

Every lease required by law to be in writing is "void at law" unless made

---

§802

[1]*Pain v. Dixon* (1922), 52 O.L.R. 347 at p. 350, [1923] 3 D.L.R. 1166 at pp. 1169-70 (H.C.).

[2]*Warman v. Faithfull* (1834), 5 B. & Ad. 1042, 110 E.R. 1078.

[3]*Chapman v. Towner* (1840), 6 M. & W. 100, 151 E.R. 338.

[4]*Re Bondi and City of Toronto*, [1968] 1 O.R. 205, 66 D.L.R. (2d) 66 (C.A.).

[5]*J. H. Samuels & Co. Ltd. v. Crown Trust Co.; Crown Trust Co. v. J. H. Samuels & Co. Ltd.* (1959), 18 D.L.R. (2d) 451, 27 W.W.R. 160 (Alta. S.C.).

[6]*Re Canada Permanent Trust Co. and Orvette Investments Ltd.* (1974), 7 O.R. (2d) 34, 54 D.L.R. (3d) 198 (H.C.J.), affd 11 O.R. (2d) 752, 67 D.L.R. (3d) 416 (C.A.).

[7]*Re Collins Cartage & Storage Co. Ltd. and McDonald* (1980), 30 O.R. (2d) 234, 116 D.L.R. (3d) 570 (C.A.).

[8]*Reinhardt v. Bast* (1966), 59 D.L.R. (2d) 746, 57 W.W.R. 757 (Sask. Q.B.).

[9]*Sidebotham v. Holland*, [1895] 1 Q.B. 378 (C.A.), at p. 385; *MacDougall v. Joncas* (1969), 2 D.L.R. (3d) 505, [1965-69] 2 N.S.R. 355 (S.C. App. Div.).

[10]*Statute of Frauds*, R.S.B.C. 1979, c. 393, s. 1; R.S.O. 1980, c. 481, ss. 1(1), 3; R.S.N.B. 1973, c. S-14, s. 7; R.S.N.S. 1967, c. 290, s. 2, and the Imperial *Statute of Frauds*, 29 Car. 2, c. 3, s. 2, in force in Alberta, Saskatchewan, Manitoba, Northwest Territories and Yukon. In British Columbia the statute does not refer to value of the rent reserved.

[11]*Tress v. Savage* (1854), 4 El. & Bl. 36, 119 E.R. 15; *Doe d. Lawson v. Coutts* (1837), 5 U.C.Q.B. 499; *White v. Nelson* (1860), 10 U.C.C.P. 158; *Caverhill v. Orvis* (1862), 12 U.C.C.P. 392.

by deed.[12] The words "void at law" are interpreted as meaning void as a lease. The instrument, however, may be valid as an agreement for a lease if it is capable of being specifically enforced by a court of equity.[13] Moreover, in Alberta the Court of Appeal has permitted an oral lease to be used as a defence by a tenant in occupation against eviction.[14]

Since the enactment of the Judicature Acts it has been held that where there is an agreement for a lease (a lease without a seal is an implied agreement for a lease) and possession has been taken under it, and if the circumstances are such that specific performance would be decreed, the right of specific performance gives the parties the legal rights and obligations of landlord and tenant.[15]

The law relating to the necessity of a lease to be in writing is summed up as follows:

> Prior to the Statute of Frauds, a demise for a term of years by parol was perfectly lawful. That statute made a writing . . . necessary. And a subsequent statute . . . required the writing to be under seal. If, however, at law, possession had been taken under the parol demise, and rent paid, the tenant was regarded as a tenant, not at will merely, as described in the Statute of Frauds, but as a tenant from year to year, upon the terms contained in the writing so far as appropriate to such a tenancy; while in equity his rights were much larger, for there the Courts would in a proper case decree specific performance, treating the parol demise, if otherwise sufficient, as an agreement for a lease, with the result that the parties were regarded in equity as landlord and tenant from the time possession was taken . . . And now, under the provisions of . . . the Judicature Act, the equitable rule prevails.[16]

In *Manchester Brewery Co. v. Coombs,*[17] Farwell, J., said:

> Although it has been suggested that the decision in *Walsh v. Lonsdale* takes away all differences between the legal and equitable estate, it, of course, does nothing of the sort, and the limits of its applicability are really somewhat narrow. It applies only to cases where there is a contract to transfer a legal title, and an act has to be justified or an action maintained by force of the legal title to which such contract relates. It involves two questions: (1.) Is there a contract of which specific performance can be obtained? (2.) If Yes, will the title acquired by such specific performance justify

---

[12]*Conveyancing and Law of Property Act,* R.S.O. 1980, c. 90, s. 9. The position is otherwise in British Columbia: see *Horse & Carriage Inn Ltd. v. Baron* (1975), 53 D.L.R. (3d) 426 (B.C.S.C.).

[13]*Parker v. Taswell* (1858), 2 De G. & J. 559, 44 E.R. 1106; *Zimbler v. Abrahams,* [1903] 1 K.B. 577 (C.A.); *Kingsworth Estate Co. Ltd. v. Anderson,* [1963] 2 Q.B. 169 (C.A.); *Warmington v. Miller,* [1973] 1 Q.B. 877 (C.A.).

[14]*Re Whissel Enterprises Ltd. and Eastcal Developments Ltd.* (1980), 116 D.L.R. (3d) 174, 25 A.R. 92 (C.A.).

[15]*Walsh v. Lonsdale* (1882), 21 Ch. D. 9 (C.A.); *Rogers v. National Drug & Chemical Co.* (1911), 23 O.L.R. 234 (H.C.J.), affd 24 O.L.R. 486 (C.A.); *Tann v. Seiberling Rubber Co. of Canada Ltd.,* [1965] 1 O.R. 157, 47 D.L.R. (2d) 194 (H.C.J.); *Pearson v. Skinner School Bus Lines (St. Thomas) Ltd.,* [1968] 2 O.R. 329, 69 D.L.R. (2d) 283 (H.C.J.); *Re Walker,* [1961] O.W.N. 4, 1 C.B.R. (N.S.) 245 (H.C.J.); *Re Pattenick and Adams Furniture Co. Ltd.,* [1970] 2 O.R. 539, 11 D.L.R. (3d) 416 (H.C.J.).

[16]*Rogers v. National Drug & Chemical Co.* (1911), 24 O.L.R. 486 (C.A.), at p. 488.

[17][1901] 2 Ch. 608 at pp. 617-18.

at law the act complained of, or support at law the action in question? It is to be treated as though before the Judicature Acts there had been, first, a suit in equity for specific performance, and then an action at law between the same parties; and the doctrine is applicable only in those cases where specific performance can be obtained between the same parties in the same court, and at the same time as the subsequent legal question falls to be determined. Thus, in *Walsh v. Lonsdale*, the landlord under an agreement for a lease for a term of seven years distrained. Distress is a legal remedy and depends on the existence at law of the relation of landlord and tenant; but the agreement between the same parties, if specifically enforced, created that relation. It was clear that such an agreement would be enforced in the same court and between the same parties: the act of distress was therefore held to be lawful.[18]

803. TYPES OF LEASEHOLDS

There are five types of leaseholds: (1) a tenancy at will; (2) a tenancy at sufferance; (3) a tenancy for a term certain; (4) a periodic tenancy, and (5) a life tenancy.

803.1 Tenancy at Will

A tenancy at will is a tenancy by which the tenant is in possession of property under an express but more often an implied agreement that the tenancy is determinable at the will of either party. It may be expressly created on the termination of a lease by authorizing the lessee to continue in possession as a tenant at will. In such a case, in the absence of a contrary intention being shown, the terms and conditions of the original lease apply to the tenancy at will so far as they are consistent with such a tenancy.[1] A tenancy at will may arise by implication in many circumstances, for example, when an intending purchaser enters into possession before the conveyance to him,[2] or where a person is given the right, upon payment of taxes, to occupy premises until a purchaser is found,[3] or if a tenant with the consent of the lessor remains in possession after the expiry of his lease.[4] In the latter case a tenancy may be implied from the payment and acceptance of rent[5] although the overriding consideration is the intention of the parties.[6] Upon the commencement of

---

[18]As to the difference between equitable rights and equitable interests see *Com'rs of Inland Revenue v. G. Angus & Co.; Same v. J. Lewis & Sons* (1889), 23 Q.B.D. 579 (C.A.).
§803.1
[1]*Morgan v. William Harrison, Ltd.*, [1907] 2 Ch. 137 (C.A.).
[2]*Howard v. Shaw* (1841), 8 M. & W. 118. 151 E.R. 973; *Liscombe Falls Gold Mining Co. v. Bishop* (1904), 35 S.C.R. 539. 25 C.L.T. 78.
[3]*East v. Clarke* (1915), 33 O.L.R. 624. 23 D.L.R. 74 (S.C. App. Div.). The position may be otherwise where one co-tenant occupies the property by agreement: *Stevens v. Skidmore*, [1931] O.R. 649, [1931] 3 D.L.R. 455 (S.C. App. Div.).
[4]*St. George Mansions v. King* (1910), 15 O.W.R. 427 (Div. Ct.); *Re Grant and Robertson* (1904), 8 O.L.R. 297 (Div. Ct.).
[5]*Ibid.*
[6]*Re Can. Petrofina Ltd. and Trudell*, [1960] O.R. 82, 21 D.L.R. (2d) 569 (C.A.).

negotiations he becomes a tenant at will; until that time he is a tenant at sufferance or an overholding tenant.[7]

Where a tenant is entitled to occupy a lease by virtue of his employment and the employment is terminated, a tenancy at will may be created.[8] However, it is not always easy to determine if a tenancy at will or licence exists.[9]

The difficulty in distinguishing between a lease and a licence has not been lessened in Ontario by Part IV of the *Landlord and Tenant Act*[10] in view of the broad definition of "tenancy agreement" contained in the Act.[11] Because the Act creates restrictions on the landlord's right to obtain possession of the premises, the Act specifically empowers the landlord to terminate a tenancy when the tenant was an employee who was provided with a rental unit for the term of his employment and when the employment relationship is ended.[12] It is not necessary that the landlord be the employer in order to use the statutory power to terminate. It is sufficient if the landlord has arranged with the employer to rent the premises for the term of the employment.[13]

803.2 Tenancy at Sufferance

A tenant at sufferance is one who, having entered on land by a lawful title, continues in possession after the title has ended without obtaining the consent of the person entitled to the land.[1]

In a residential tenancy governed by the various provincial Residential Tenancy Acts[2] an overholding tenant may be a tenant at sufferance or the tenancy may be deemed to have been renewed. The landlord cannot regain possession of the premises without going through procedures specified by the legislation even after the tenancy has been properly terminated by notice. The tenancy cannot be a periodic tenancy as no rent is accepted and cannot be considered a tenancy at will. A tenancy at sufferance cannot be created by contract but can only be created by implication of law. There can be no tenancy at sufferance against the Crown.[3]

---

[7]*Idington v. Douglas* (1903), 6 O.L.R. 266 (H.C.J.).
[8]*Reid v. Canada Tungsten Mining Corp. Ltd.*, [1974] 3 W.W.R. 469 (N.W.T.S.C.).
[9]With respect to the differences between a tenancy at will and a licence generally, see §804, *infra*.
[10]R.S.O. 1980, c. 232.
[11]*Ibid.*, s. 81(*e*).
[12]*Ibid.*, s. 110(3)(*d*). See *Re Rio Algom Ltd. and Turcotte* (1978), 20 O.R. (2d) 769, 88 D.L.R. (3d) 759 (Div. Ct.).
[13]*Re Rio Algom Ltd. and Roberts* (1979), 27 O.R. (2d) 288, 106 D.L.R. (3d) 555 (Dist. Ct.); *Re Rio Algom Ltd. and Turcotte, supra*, footnote 12.
§803.2
[1]Co. Litt. 57b.
[2]*Landlord and Tenant Act*, R.S.O. 1980, c. 232, s. 106; R.S.M. 1970, c. L70, s. 113(1), enacted 1970, c. 106, s. 3; am. 1971, c. 35, s. 21(*a*); 1980, c. 60, s. 22; R.S.A. 1980, c. L-6, s. 12; *Residential Tenancy Act*, S.B.C. 1984, c. 15, s. 7; *Residential Tenancies Act*, S.N.B. 1975, c. R-10.2, s. 21; R.S.S. 1978, c. R-22, s. 29, am. 1979, c. 69, s. 20(*e*).
[3]Co. Litt. 57b.

803.3 Tenancy for a Term Certain

The usual form of tenancy is for a term of years or a "term certain". Such a tenancy must be created by express contract and its commencement and duration must be indicated with certainty, either originally or in such a way as to be ascertainable afterwards with certainty.[1] Thus, where a head tenant under a month-to-month tenancy agrees to allow a subtenant to remain in possession for the term of the head lease, there can be no term certain.[2] On the other hand, a lease for one year whereunder the landlord has the right to terminate the lease before the expiration of the term is not uncertain, nor is the right of premature termination repugnant.[3] The tenancy will commence on its stated commencement date[4] and will automatically come to an end at the end of the term.[5] In the absence of any stipulation to the contrary, it is not necessary to serve a demand for possession or notice to quit at the end of the term.[6]

There is no limit on the length of the term provided that it is not in perpetuity. A perpetual lease is invalid at common law but can be validated by Parliament.[7] A lease may, however, contain a term providing for its perpetual renewal.[8] Thus, a lease for twenty-one years, renewable in perpetuity for further twenty-one-year terms does not offend the rule against perpetuities and is not invalid as creating an uncertain term.[9] Nor is it important that rent for the renewal periods is to be fixed by arbitration.[10] It is of course important that the lease comply with other relevant statutory provisions.[11] Moreover,

---

§803.3

[1] *Omsac Developments Ltd. v. Colebourne* (1976), 28 O.R. (2d) 455, 110 D.L.R. (3d) 766 (H.C.J.).

[2] *Re Casson and Handisyde* (1974), 3 O.R. (2d) 471 (Co. Ct.).

[3] *Atkins v. Lawrence* (1967), 62 W.W.R. 439 (Sask. C.A.).

[4] *Jones v. Royal Trust Co.* (1960), 50 M.P.R. 104 (N.B.S.C. App. Div.), where the word "from" in a tenancy "from May 1st . . ." was, from its context, deemed to include May 1st.

[5] *City of Toronto v. Ward* (1909), 18 O.L.R. 214 (C.A.).

[6] This is not the case with respect to residential tenancies governed by provincial legislation which often requires the landlord or tenant to give notice even with respect to tenancies of terms certain. Otherwise, when the term ends, the tenancy is converted into a periodic tenancy. See, for example, *Landlord and Tenant Act*, R.S.O. 1980, c. 232, s. 98; R.S.M. 1970, c. L70, s. 103, enacted 1970, c. 106, s. 3; re-enacted 1971, c. 35, s. 15; am. 1972, c. 39, s. 4; 1975, c. 37, ss. 8, 9; 1977, c. 23, s. 15; 1980, c. 60, ss. 18-20; *Residential Tenancy Act*, S.B.C. 1984, c. 15, s. 23, but see also s. 7(2), (3).

[7] *Wotherspoon v. Canadian Pacific Ltd.*; *Pope v. Canadian Pacific Ltd.* (1981), 35 O.R. (2d) 449, 129 D.L.R. (3d) 1 (C.A.).

[8] *Sevenoakes, Maidstone & Tunbridge Ry. Co. v. London, Chatham & Dover Ry. Co.* (1879), 11 Ch. D. 625.

[9] *J. E. Gibson Holdings Ltd. v. Principal Investments Ltd.* (1964), 44 D.L.R. (2d) 673, [1964] S.C.R. 424.

[10] *The Queen v. Walker*; *The Queen v. M. E. Clark & Sons Ltd.* (1970), 11 D.L.R. (3d) 173, [1970] S.C.R. 649.

[11] Such as requirements with respect to bars of dower: see *Broersma v. Maier* (1969), 9 D.L.R. (3d) 110, 72 W.W.R. 153 (Alta. S.C.).

the right of renewal will be subject to other terms of the lease such as termination clauses.[12] In Ontario a tenant is not entitled to the benefits of section 20 of the *Landlord and Tenant Act*[13] so as to obtain relief from his failure to give notice of renewal properly pursuant to the terms of the lease.[14]

803.4 Periodic Tenancy

A periodic tenancy is so called because it continues from period to period until terminated by a proper notice. A term in a lease which restricts the landlord's right to determine a periodic tenancy is not repugnant to a periodic tenancy and does not make the maximum duration of the term uncertain.[1] The usual periods are weekly, monthly, quarterly and yearly.

The nature of a tenancy from year to year is that it is a lease for a year certain with a growing interest during every year thereafter springing out of the original contract and part of it.[2] There is not, in the contemplation of the law, a recommencing or re-letting at the beginning of each year,[3] so that a tenancy from year to year is one continuous term, dating from its inception, and not a recurrence of yearly tenancies commencing anew each year.[4]

A periodic tenancy may be expressly created by the use of appropriate words as "from year to year" or "from month to month". It is more often created by the presumption of law from the fact of possession and the payment of rent periodically unless there are circumstances indicating a different intent. A tenancy may also arise by implication if the tenant remains in possession after the termination of a tenancy for a term of years or term certain. *Prima facie*, all leases for uncertain terms are leases at will. It is the reservation of an annual rent that turns them into leases from year to year.[5] A general letting for so long as both parties wish is a letting at will but, if the lessor accepts a yearly rent or rent measured by an aliquot part of a year, it is evidence of taking for a year,[6] but if the rent is on a monthly basis the court may conclude that a monthly tenancy exists.[7] Hence, tenancies from year to year have been implied by the courts when land is let from a specified date at an annual rent payable quarterly, determinable by either party on a quarter's

---

[12]*Needham and Needham v. Arthur* (1959), 22 D.L.R. (2d) 164 (B.C.C.A.).
[13]R.S.O. 1980, c. 232.
[14]*Affiliated Realty Corp. Ltd. v. Sam Berger Restaurant Ltd.* (1973), 2 O.R. (2d) 147, 42 D.L.R. (3d) 191 (H.C.J.).
§803.4
[1]*Re Midland Ry. Co.'s Agreement*; *Charles Clay & Sons Ltd. v. British Rys. Board*, [1971] Ch. 725 (C.A.).
[2]*Oxley v. James* (1844), 13 M. & W. 209 at p. 214, 153 E.R. 87, *per* Parke, B.; *Cattley v. Arnold*; *Banks v. Arnold* (1859), 1 J. & H. 651 at p. 660, 70 E.R. 905.
[3]*Gandy v. Jubber* (1865), 9 B. & S. 15 at p. 18, 122 E.R. 914.
[4]*Sherlock v. Milloy* (1893), 13 C.L.T. 370.
[5]*Roe d. Bree v. Lees* (1777), 2 Black. W. 1171, 96 E.R. 691.
[6]*Richardson v. Langridge* (1811), 4 Taunt. 128, 128 E.R. 277.
[7]*Humans v. Doyon*, [1945] O.W.N. 275, [1945] 2 D.L.R. 312 (C.A.).

notice,[8] or when there has been a letting at an annual rental payable monthly.[9] Monthly tenancies have been implied when there was an agreement to pay a specified sum per month for the use of a farm for so long as the owner would permit[10] and when there was an agreement to rent premises at a rent of $25 a month for the first three months and $35 a month thereafter.[11]

Where a tenant is allowed to hold over at the expiration of his lease, the terms on which he continues to hold are matters of evidence rather than law. If there is nothing to show a different understanding, the tenant will be considered to hold on the same terms as in his original lease.[12] It may be said that where there has been a holding over after a term for a fixed period and rent is paid and accepted, some kind of tenancy is plainly intended by the parties, and, in the absence of some express agreement as to its character, the presumption is made that the parties intend to go on as before. When the original term has been for one year or a term of years, at a yearly rental, the presumption is that the parties intend to continue with a yearly tenancy. If the original term has been a monthly tenancy at a monthly rent, then, on holding over and the payment and acceptance of rent as before, a monthly tenancy is presumed.[13]

A tenancy from year to year has been held to be created on the overholding and payment of rent after a fourteen-and-one-half-year tenancy at a yearly rental payable quarterly[14] and after a tenancy for eighteen months at a yearly rental payable quarterly.[15]

The overholding of a lease for a term of months less than a year creates a tenancy from month to month in the absence of circumstances showing a different intent by the parties.[16] Where a tenant overholds on a year's lease, it is a matter of intention whether the tenant overholds as a monthly or yearly tenant. The contemplation of the parties that a new lease would be necessary each year supports the contention of a monthly tenancy.[17]

---

[8]*King v. Eversfield*, [1897] 2 Q.B. 475 (C.A.).

[9]*United Cigar Stores Ltd. v. Buller and Hughes* (1931), 66 O.L.R. 593, [1931] 2 D.L.R. 144 (S.C. App. Div.).

[10]*Orser v. Vernon* (1864), 14 U.C.C.P. 573.

[11]*Methodist Church v. Roach* (1908), 9 W.L.R. 23 (B.C. Co. Ct.).

[12]*Mayor, Aldermen and Burgesses of Thetford v. Tyler* (1845), 8 Q.B. 95 at p. 101, 115 E.R. 810; *Henderson v. Craig* (1922), 68 D.L.R. 629, [1922] 2 W.W.R. 597 (K.B.), affd [1923] 1 D.L.R. 1174, [1923] 1 W.W.R. 306 (C.A.); *Morrow v. Greenglass* (1974), 5 O.R. (2d) 353, 50 D.L.R. (3d) 337 (C.A.).

[13]*Grumbacher v. Booster Nut Ltd.*, [1948] O.R. 945, [1949] 1 D.L.R. 157 (C.A.).

[14]*Doe d. Buddle v. Lines* (1848), 11 Q.B. 402, 116 E.R. 527; *Re Sons of England Benefit Soc. and Ezrin*, [1962] O.W.N. 42 (Co. Ct.).

[15]*Young v. Bank of Nova Scotia* (1915), 34 O.L.R. 176, 23 D.L.R. 854 (S.C. App. Div.).

[16]*MacGregor v. Defoe* (1887), 14 O.R. 87 (H.C.J.); *Eastman v. Richards* (1898), 3 Terr. L.R. 73 (N.W.T.S.C.), affd 29 S.C.R. 438 *sub nom. Eastman v. Richard & Co.*; *Grumbacher v. Booster Nut Ltd., supra*, footnote 13.

[17]*Imperial Oil Ltd. v. Murphy* (1960), 45 M.P.R. 338 (Nfld. S.C.).

803.5 Tenancy for Life

A tenancy for life is a freehold estate or tenancy but is not an estate of inheritance as is a fee simple. It is held of the immediate reversioner and reverts to him on the death of the tenant or the person for whose life the tenancy was held.

At common law unless a tenancy for life was created by deed it was void. However, equity in a proper case would decree specific performance treating the parol demise, if otherwise sufficient, as an agreement for a lease.[1]

A lease for life should state in the *habendum* for whose life the lease is made. A lease for life, without mentioning for whose life the lease is to be, is deemed to be for the life of the lessee, as an estate for a person's own life is deemed to be greater than an estate for the life of another and because a deed should be construed most strongly against the grantor. If the lessor has no power to grant a lease for the life of another such a lease will be construed as being for the life of the lessor.[2] If no reference is made to survivors, a lease for the lives of others is deemed to continue during the life of the survivor[3] but, if the lease is for a term of years on condition that named persons shall so long live, the lease ends on the death of the first named person.[4] Normally, a lease made by the holder of a life estate ends on the death of the life tenant. However, where remaindermen, aware of the terms of the lease, accept rent after the death of the life tenant, the lease will continue. The remaindermen will be taken to have confirmed the lease.[5]

A lease for life, although a tenancy at common law, may not be a tenancy within the meaning of residential tenancy legislation where that legislation defines a tenancy as being exclusive occupation for a term that may be terminated by the landlord or tenant only in accordance with the provisions of the legislation. If there is no express right of termination in the tenancy for life, the tenancy does not fall within the statutory definition.[6]

804. RIGHTS AND OBLIGATIONS OF LESSOR AND LESSEE

804.1 Right to Possession

Upon the execution of a valid lease containing an express covenant to give possession or where such a covenant may be implied by the words used, the

---

§803.5
[1]*Walsh v. Lonsdale* (1882), 21 Ch. D. 9 (C.A.).
[2]Co. Litt. 41b, 42a; *Doe d. Pritchard v. Dodd* (1833), 5 B. & Ad. 689 at p. 692, 110 E.R. 945.
[3]*Brudnel's Case* (1592), 5 Co. Rep. 9 a, 77 E.R. 61; *Doe d. Bromfield v. Smith* (1805), 6 East 530, 102 E.R. 1390.
[4]*Ibid.*
[5]*Camston Ltd. v. Volkswagen Yonge Ltd.*, [1968] 2 O.R. 65 (Co. Ct.), affd *loc. cit.* p. 68n (C.A.).
[6]*Oliver v. Harvey* (1974), 49 D.L.R. (3d) 462, [1975] 2 W.W.R. 39 (Sask. Dist. Ct.), where section 2(*l*) of the *Residential Tenancies Act*, R.S.S. 1978, c. R-22, was considered.

lessee is entitled to possession of the demised premises from the lessor, and it is the duty of the lessor to put the lessee into possession.

Until entry of the tenant on the demised premises has been made the tenant's title has not been perfected. He has, without entry, no estate in the land but only a right which is known as an *interesse termini*, except in the case of a tenancy for life or lives which is a freehold interest. As a verbal lease is a contract concerning an interest in lands within the meaning of the *Statute of Frauds*, an action for possession or for damages for the refusal to give possession cannot be maintained if possession is refused and if the lease is verbal.[1] An action may be maintained to give possession if the lease is by deed and if there are words in the lease, such as "demise" which will imply a covenant to give possession.[2]

Residential tenancies and the right to possession

Where the doctrine of *interesse termini* has been abolished, as it has with respect to residential tenancies under various provincial statutes,[3] there will be an implied covenant for quiet enjoyment in every demise, a covenant which extends to the putting of the tenant into possession at the outset of the term.[4] Moreover, an implied covenant for quiet enjoyment gives the tenant the right to maintain an action for possession if the landlord refuses to give or prevents the tenant from obtaining possession.[5] The measure of damages for refusing possession is the difference between what the tenant agreed to pay and the worth of the demise.[6]

804.2   Right to Quiet Enjoyment

The nature of a covenant for quiet enjoyment is primarily "an assurance against the consequences of a defective title, and of any disturbances thereupon",[1] together with an assurance that the enjoyment of the premises will not be substantially interfered with, or caused by the lessor, or those claiming

---

§804.1

[1] *Moore v. Kay* (1880), 5 O.A.R. 261.

[2] *Saunders v. Roe* (1867), 17 U.C.C.P. 344; *Jinks v. Edwards* (1856), 11 Ex. 775, 156 E.R. 1045.

[3] *Residential Tenancy Act*, S.B.C. 1984, c. 15, s. 48(3); *Residential Tenancies Act*, R.S.S. 1978, c. R-22, s. 14; S.N.B. 1975, c. R-10.2, s. 10; *Landlord and Tenant Act*, R.S.O. 1980, c. 232, s. 87; R.S.A. 1980, c. L-6, s. 53; R.S.M. 1970, c. L70, s. 89, enacted 1970, c. 106, s. 3; R.S.P.E.I. 1974, c. L-7, s. 93; *Landlord and Tenant (Residential Tenancies) Act*, S.N. 1973, No. 54, s. 8; *Landlord and Tenant Ordinance*, R.O.Y.T. 1971, c. L-2, s. 66, enacted 1972, c. 20, s. 1; R.O.N.W.T. 1974, c. L-2, s. 54.

[4] *Miller v. Emcer Products Ltd.*, [1956] Ch. 304 (C.A.).

[5] *Smart v. Stuart* (1837), 5 U.C.Q.B. (O.S.) 301.

[6] *Jones and Mary's Ready to Wear (No. 2) v. Caple and Seaton Holdings Ltd.* (1959), 29 W.W.R. 310 (B.C.S.C.); *Procopio v. D'Abbondanza* (1975), 8 O.R. (2d) 496, 58 D.L.R. (3d) 368 (C.A.).

§804.2

[1] *Howell v. Richards* (1809), 11 East 633 at p. 642, 103 E.R. 1150.

under him.[2] If there is substantial interference, the covenant is broken, although neither the title nor possession of the land may be otherwise affected.[3] If there is no express covenant, a covenant for quiet enjoyment on the part of the lessor will be implied, as the mere relationship of landlord and tenant is sufficient to imply the covenant.[4] Moreover, the use of the words "grant and demise" or the word "demise" will imply the covenant quite apart from the implication arising out of the relationship.[5]

The covenant may be implied by statute. For example, in Ontario the covenant is implied if the lease is made for valuable consideration.[6]

If there is an express covenant,[7] the covenant will not be implied, but in this regard the covenant for quiet possession must be distinguished from the implied obligation of the grantor not to derogate from his grant.[8]

To constitute a breach of the covenant, whether express or implied, there must be physical interference with the enjoyment of the premises. The mere interference with the comfort of the lessee is insufficient.[9] Where access to the demised premises is diminished by the landlord's acts, or others claiming under him, the covenant is breached whether the acts take place on the demised premises or otherwise.[10]

The mere challenge of the tenant's title by the landlord is not by itself a breach of the covenant, but persistent acts of intimidation by the landlord, even in the absence of any direct interference, can amount to a breach.[11] Thus, where a landlord serves a tenant with a notice to vacate after creating several scenes in the demised premises which were being used as a coffee counter, a breach was found.[12]

Where the landlord entered the premises prematurely[13] or where he refused to make structural repairs to worn-out toilets,[14] a breach was found.

The covenant protects the tenant from any disturbance of the lessor or those claiming under him except lawful re-entry but does not protect the tenant from unlawful disturbance from third parties. Thus, the covenant is not broken

---

[2]*Sanderson v. Mayor of Berwick-Upon-Tweed* (1884), 13 Q.B.D. 547 (C.A.).
[3]*Ibid.; Christin v. Dey* (1922), 52 O.L.R. 308, [1923] 3 D.L.R. 1116 (S.C. App. Div.); *Irvine Recreations Ltd. v. Gardis* (1982), 133 D.L.R. (3d) 220, 17 Sask. R. 174 (Q.B.).
[4]*Budd-Scott v. Daniell*, [1902] 2 K.B. 351; *Markham v. Paget*, [1908] 1 Ch. 697; *Geary v. Clifton Co. Ltd.* (1928), 62 O.L.R. 257, [1928] 3 D.L.R. 64 (H.C.).
[5]*Kerr v. Bearinger* (1869), 29 U.C.Q.B. 340; *Mostyn v. West Mostyn Coal & Iron Co., Ltd.* (1876), 1 C.P.D. 145; *Baynes & Co. v. Lloyd & Sons*, [1895] 2 Q.B. 610 (C.A.).
[6]*Conveyancing and Law of Property Act*, R.S.O. 1980, c. 90, s. 23.
[7]*Mostyn v. West Mostyn Coal & Iron Co., supra*, footnote 5; *Grosvenor Hotel Co. v. Hamilton*, [1894] 2 Q.B. 836 (C.A.).
[8]See §804.3, *supra*.
[9]*Browne v. Flower*, [1911] 1 Ch. 219.
[10]*Maclennan v. Royal Ins. Co.* (1876), 39 U.C.Q.B. 515; *Owen v. Gadd*, [1956] 2 Q.B. 99 (C.A.); *Andrews v. Paradise* (1725), 8 Mod. 318, 88 E.R. 228.
[11]*Kenny v. Preen*, [1963] 1 Q.B. 499 (C.A.).
[12]*Franco v. Lechman* (1962), 36 D.L.R. (2d) 357 (Alta. S.C. App. Div.).
[13]*Teske v. Eggenberger* (1963), 41 D.L.R. (2d) 520 (Alta. S.C.).
[14]*Buttimer v. Bettz* (1914), 6 W.W.R. 22 (B.C. Co. Ct.).

when holders of an invalid option from the landlord threaten to obstruct work being carried out by the tenant on the demised premises as the holders were not lawfully claiming from or under the landlord.[15] Normally, the landlord is not responsible for damage caused by independent contractors hired by him. However, if the contractor is hired to do acts which the landlord would have to do at his risk, and the acts invoke a breach of the covenant, the landlord will be liable.[16]

A purchaser of two adjoining properties, who demolishes one thus causing loss of support in the other by a tenant under an unexpired lease from the former common owner, will be liable as he is claiming through or under the landlord.[17]

The general rule is the same whether the covenant be express or implied.[18]

A breach of the covenant may be restrained by injunction if damages are not a sufficient remedy.[19]

An implied covenant for quiet enjoyment operates only during the continuance of the landlord's estate which enables him to give possession to the tenant. If the lessor's estate determines before the expiration of the term of the lease, the landlord's liability on the implied covenant ceases except as to past acts.[20]

The covenant has no reference to noise.[21]

804.3 Derogation from Grant

It has been said that common honesty underlies the maxim that a grantor cannot derogate from his grant.[1] The principle arises by implication and is based in part upon the view that the grantor intends his grant to be effective.[2]

The doctrine is limited in that it does not hinder all activities of the grantor but only certain activities on adjacent lands of the grantor. Thus, a reasonable use of adjacent premises by the landlord which simply makes the use of the demised premises more expensive is not a derogation.[3]

---

[15]*Zachariuk v. Jones; Jones v. Refectory Steak House Ltd., Zachariuk, Third Party* (1975), 54 D.L.R. (3d) 463 (B.C.S.C.).
[16]*Broben Investments Ltd. v. Cadillac Contractors & Developments Ltd.,* [1962] O.R. 207, 31 D.L.R. (2d) 402 (H.C.).
[17]*Mahas v. Canadian Imperial Bank of Commerce,* [1963] 2 O.R. 447, 40 D.L.R. (2d) 25 (H.C.J.).
[18]*Wallis v. Hands,* [1893] 2 Ch. 75; *Gilliland v. Seacoast Construction Ltd.* (1976), 15 N.B.R. (2d) 437 (N.B.S.C.).
[19]*Allport v. Securities Corp.* (1895), 64 L.J. Ch. 491; *Mahas v. Canadian Imperial Bank of Commerce, supra,* footnote 17.
[20]*Baynes & Co. v. Lloyd & Sons,* [1895] 1 Q.B. 820, affd [1895] 2 Q.B. 610 (C.A.).
[21]*Jenkins v. Jackson* (1888), 40 Ch. D. 71; *Hudson v. Cripps,* [1896] 1 Ch. 265.
§804.3
[1]*Harmer v. Jumbil (Nigeria) Tin Areas, Ltd.,* [1921] 1 Ch. 200 (C.A.), at p. 226, *per* Younger, L.J.
[2]*Bayley v. Great Western Ry. Co.* (1884), 26 Ch. D. 434 (C.A.).
[3]*O'Cedar, Ltd. v. Slough Trading Co. Ltd.,* [1927] 2 K.B. 123.

It has been said that the purpose of the doctrine is to prevent the frustration of any special purpose for which the grant is made,[4] or to prevent the premises from being rendered unfit[5] or to prevent a forfeiture.[6]

The extent of the obligation will be gathered from surrounding circumstances based on the parties' reasonable contemplation.[7]

It has been held that a derogation from grant does not occur when a landlord leases a shop in his shopping centre to a tenant carrying on business in competition with an existing tenant, as the conduct in introducing the competitor does not render the premises less fit for the purposes of carrying on business.[8] Nor will an increase in insurance premiums payable by the tenant resulting from activity carried on by the landlord on adjoining premises amount to a derogation of grant.[9]

On the other hand where the lease contained an attached plan showing ample parking for the demised premises, a substantial reduction in parking did amount to a derogation from grant.[10]

Although an express covenant for quiet enjoyment will exclude an implied covenant to the same effect, it will not exclude the principle of derogation from grant.[11]

The principle of derogation from grant has application to situations other than leases.[12]

804.4   Implied Covenant as to Fitness

At common law the tenant takes the premises subject to any defects existing at the time of letting or subsequently arising and there is no implied condition or warranty that the premises are fit for the purpose for which they were intended to be used.[1] The one exception, at common law, where such a condition is implied is the case of furnished premises used for habitation. In that case there is an implied covenant that the premises are fit for habitation.[2] The implied covenant has been extended to premises demised to be used as a

---

[4]*Pwllbach Colliery Co., Ltd. v. Woodman*, [1915] A.C. 634 (H.L.).
[5]*Browne v. Flower*, [1911] 1 Ch. 219.
[6]*Harmer v. Jumbil (Nigeria) Tin Areas, Ltd.*, [1921] 1 Ch. 200 (C.A.).
[7]*Ibid.*
[8]*Clark's-Gamble of Canada Ltd. v. Grant Park Plaza Ltd.* (1967), 64 D.L.R. (2d) 570, [1967] S.C.R. 614.
[9]*Caplan v. Acadian Machinery Ltd.* (1976), 13 O.R. (2d) 48, 70 D.L.R. (3d) 383 (Div. Ct.).
[10]*Langley's Ltd. v. Lawrence Manor Inv. Ltd.*, [1960] O.W.N. 436 (H.C.J.).
[11]*Grosvenor Hotel Co. v. Hamilton*, [1894] 2 Q.B. 836 (C.A.); *Federic v. Perpetual Investments Ltd.*, [1969] 1 O.R. 186, 2 D.L.R. (3d) 50 (H.C.J.).
[12]For a more detailed discussion of the principle, see ch. 27; see also Elliott, "Non-Derogation from Grant", 80 L.Q.R. 244 (1964).
§804.4
[1]*St. George Mansions Ltd. v. Hetherington* (1918), 42 O.L.R. 10, 41 D.L.R. 614 (S.C. App. Div.).
[2]*Davey v. Christoff* (1916), 36 O.L.R. 123, 28 D.L.R. 447 (S.C. App. Div.).

nursing home, but applies only to the state of the premises at the beginning of the lease.[3]

Apart from this exception, and the provisions of the various Residential Tenancy Acts, and in the absence of express provisions to the contrary or representations, warranties or collateral conditions,[4] rent remains payable even though the premises were unfit for occupancy at the time of letting,[5] or even though the premises were then in a dangerous or defective state,[6] or though the premises subsequently become unfit due to lack of repair[7] or fire damage.[8]

If there is an implied covenant that the premises be fit for habitation at the commencement of the tenancy, the condition must be fulfilled or the tenant can repudiate the lease.[9]

Residential tenancies and the implied covenant as to fitness

For most practical purposes the covenant has been subsumed by legislation passed with respect to residential tenancies. That legislation often requires the landlord to provide and maintain the premises in a good state of repair and fit for habitation during the tenancy.[10] This statutory duty goes well beyond the implied covenant in placing positive duties on the landlord. First, the duty arises whether the premises be furnished or unfurnished. Secondly, the duty arises at the commencement of the tenancy as does the implied covenant but the duty continues throughout the term which is not the case with the implied covenant.[11] Thirdly, the duty requires the landlord not only to keep the premises fit for habitation, but also to repair.

Because of the various provincial legislation applicable to residential tenancies, the importance of the implied covenant has become much diminished. However, in so far as the implied covenant can be applied to furnished

---

[3]*Gentz v. Dawson* (1966), 60 D.L.R. (2d) 545, 58 W.W.R. 409 (Man. Q.B.).
[4]*Crescent Motor Co. Ltd. and Pike v. North-West Tent & Awning Co. Ltd.* (1970), 72 W.W.R. 694 (Alta. Dist. Ct.).
[5]*Hart v. Windsor* (1843), 12 M. & W. 68, 152 E.R. 1114.
[6]*Cavalier v. Pope*, [1906] A.C. 428 (H.L.).
[7]*Barker v. Ferguson* (1908), 16 O.L.R. 252 (Div. Ct.).
[8]*Cyclone Woven Wire Fence Co. Ltd. v. Canada Wire & Cable Co. Ltd.* (1920), 19 O.W.N. 161 (S.C. App. Div.), affg 18 O.W.N. 103 (H.C.).
[9]*Smith v. Marrable* (1843), 11 M. & W. 5, 152 E.R. 693; *Collins v. Hopkins*, [1923] 2 K.B. 617; *Gordon v. Goodwin* (1910), 20 O.L.R. 327 (Div. Ct.); *Davey v. Christoff, supra*, footnote 2.
[10]See *Residential Tenancy Act*, S.B.C. 1984, c. 15, s. 8; *Residential Tenancies Act*, R.S.S. 1978, c. R-22, s. 20(1), stat. con. 3; S.N.B. 1975, c. R-10.2, s. 3(1); *Landlord and Tenant Act*, R.S.O. 1980, c. 232, s. 96; R.S.M. 1970, c. L70, s. 98(1), enacted 1970, c. 106, s. 3; R.S.P.E.I. 1974, c. L-7, s. 102; *Landlord and Tenant (Residential Tenancies) Act*, S.N. 1973, No. 54, s. 7(1), stat. con. 1; *Landlord and Tenant Ordinance*, R.O.N.W.T. 1974, c. L-2, s. 60(1); R.O.Y.T. 1971, c. L-2, s. 75(1), enacted 1972, c. 20. In Alberta, the *Landlord and Tenant Act*, R.S.A. 1980, c. L-6, s. 14(c), provides that the premises must be fit for habitation at the beginning of the tenancy.
[11]*Gentz v. Dawson, supra*, footnote 3.

premises that do not qualify as residential tenancies under the legislation, the covenant may still retain some utility.

804.5   Repairs and Improvements

With respect to tenancies not covered by residential tenancy legislation, in the absence of express stipulations to the contrary and except for furnished premises, a landlord is under no obligation to put the premises into repair at the commencement or during the term, and is not liable for loss or damage suffered by the tenant, his customers or guests, due to the defective condition of the premises.[1]

The covenant to repair will not be implied from a covenant by the tenant to repair, except as to wear or damage by fire or tempest. The express exceptions do not lead to the implication that the landlord is to repair such damage.[2]

If there is an express covenant to repair on the part of either the landlord or tenant, the covenantor need not renew a building worn out by age or decaying from faulty construction. Thus, if by the passage of time, it becomes impossible to repair without rebuilding, the covenantor is not liable if he refuses to rebuild.[3] However, the fact that it may be merely inconvenient or unprofitable for the covenantor to fulfil his obligation to repair is not a factor to be considered.[4] In one case, where the landlord covenanted to repair under a lease containing a fire clause which terminated the lease if repairs could not be made in sixty days, and where a fire did not destroy the premises but rendered them unfit for use, the repair covenant was held to have no application.[5] It was only applicable where the premises remained fit for use.

Where there is a general covenant to repair on the part of the tenant, the covenant will be construed to have reference to the condition of the premises at the commencement of the lease.[6] A covenant to keep and leave premises in repair is satisfied by keeping the premises in substantial repair according to their nature.[7] Where, however, the tenant covenants to keep the premises in good repair, and at the end of the tenancy to give them up in good repair, order and condition, the tenant is obliged to put the premises in that condition and cannot leave the premises in bad repair because he found them in that

---

§804.5

[1] *Lane v. Cox*, [1897] 1 Q.B. 415 (C.A.); *Bromley v. Mercer*, [1922] 2 K.B. 126 (C.A.); *Scythes & Co., Ltd. v. Gibsons Ltd.*, [1927] 2 D.L.R. 834, [1927] S.C.R. 352; *Albert v. Pelletier* (1976), 66 D.L.R. (3d) 536, 13 N.B.R. (2d) 211 (S.C. App. Div.); *Sfyras v. Kotsis* (1975), 10 O.R. (2d) 27, 62 D.L.R. (3d) 43 (Co. Ct.); *Re Trella and Anko Investments Ltd.* (1981), 122 D.L.R. (3d) 713 (Alta. Q.B.).
[2] *Arden v. Pullen* (1842), 10 M. & W. 321, 152 E.R. 492.
[3] *Torrens v. Walker*, [1906] 2 Ch. 166.
[4] *Hewitt v. Rowlands* (1924), 93 L.J.K.B. 1080 (C.A.).
[5] *Stein v. Canada Trust Co. and Dyer*, [1961] O.R. 637, 29 D.L.R. (2d) 87 (H.C.J.).
[6] *Walker v. Hatton* (1842), 10 M. & W. 249, 152 E.R. 462.
[7] *Stanley v. Towgood* (1836), 3 Bing. (N.C.) 4, 132 E.R. 310; *Vicro Investments Ltd. v. Adams Brands Ltd.*, [1963] 2 O.R. 583, 40 D.L.R. (2d) 523 (H.C.J.).

condition. Again, however, the extent of the repair is to be measured by the age and class of the premises.[8]

Where the tenant covenants to repair, he is not liable for dilapidation that results from the natural operation of time and the elements, although he must take care that the premises do not suffer more damage than the operation of time and the elements would effect.[9]

Under a covenant to repair which does not exclude liability for fire or damage by the Queen's enemies, the tenant must repair though the premises be burnt or destroyed by the Queen's enemies.[10]

The exception in a covenant to repair, "reasonable wear and tear excluded", refers to dilapidations caused by the friction of air, by exposure, and by ordinary use.[11]

The standard of repair is determined by the premises. Thus, an improvement of the neighbourhood will not raise the standard, nor a deterioration lower it.[12]

Where a landlord has covenanted to repair, he is not bound to repair until he has received from the tenant notice of want of repair.[13] However, he is not entitled to a second notice when repairs carried out under the first notice prove insufficient within a few days of the making of them.[14] Notice is not required when the landlord has demised only a part of the premises and retained under his control that part, the defective condition of which has caused the damage.[15] When there is a covenant by the landlord to repair, a licence by the tenant to allow the landlord to enter for a reasonable time for the purpose of executing the repairs is implied.[16]

The landlord cannot absolve himself of liability under his covenant by delegating the duty to repair to an independent contractor.[17]

Where the landlord is in breach of his covenant to repair, the measure of damages recoverable by the tenant is the difference in value to the tenant during the period of non-repair, after notice, between the premises in its unrepaired condition and its repaired condition if the obligations under the covenant have been met. The tenant can also recover for damages caused to his personal property,[18] and for direct losses such as loss of profit by the breach of covenant.[19] If the landlord is in breach of his covenant, there is no

---

[8]*Proudfoot v. Hart* (1890), 25 Q.B.D. 42 (C.A.).

[9]*Gutteridge v. Munyard* (1834), 7 Car. & P. 129, 173 E.R. 57; *Lister v. Lane and Nesham*, [1893] 2 Q.B. 212 (C.A.); *Sotheby v. Grundy*, [1947] 2 All E.R. 761 (K.B.D.).

[10]*Paradine v. Jane* (1647), Aleyn 26, 82 E.R. 897; *Redmond v. Dainton*, [1920] 2 K.B. 256.

[11]*Terrell v. Murray* (1901), 17 T.L.R. 570.

[12]*Anstruther-Gough-Calthorpe v. McOscar*, [1924] 1 K.B. 716 (C.A.).

[13]*Makin v. Watkinson* (1870), L.R. 6 Exch. 25; *Torrens v. Walker*, supra, footnote 3.

[14]*Adams Furniture Co. Ltd. v. Johar Investments Ltd.*, [1961] O.R. 133, 26 D.L.R. (2d) 380 (H.C.J.).

[15]*Melles & Co. v. Holme*, [1918] 2 K.B. 100; *Murphy v. Hurly*, [1922] 1 A.C. 369 (H.L.).

[16]*Saner v. Bilton* (1878), 7 Ch. D. 815.

[17]*Adams Furniture v. Johar Investments Ltd.*, supra, footnote 14.

[18]*Hewitt v. Rowlands* (1924), 93 L.J.K.B. 1080 (C.A.).

[19]*Macartney and Loma Industrial Products Ltd. v. Queen-Yonge Investments Ltd.*, [1961] O.R. 41, 25 D.L.R. (2d) 751 (H.C.J.).

duty on the tenant to repair so as to minimize loss.[20] However, in the case of minor repairs the tenant may, after the elapse of a reasonable time, after the giving of notice of non-repair, make the repairs and deduct the cost thereof from his rent.[21] A breach by the tenant of his covenant to repair permits the landlord to claim damages for diminution of the value of the reversion because of the non-repair.[22]

In the absence of an express agreement by either party, the liability of the tenant to maintain the demised premises is founded partly on the doctrine of waste and partly on an implied covenant to use the premises in a tenant-like manner. This implied covenant will be excluded if there is an express covenant to repair. In determining whether waste has been committed it must be remembered that the tenant cannot change the nature of the demised premises.[23] However, if the use is reasonable and proper given the nature and class of the property, no waste can be committed.[24] Although neither a tenant at will nor a tenant from year to year is liable for permissive waste (in the absence of a covenant to repair),[25] both are liable for voluntary waste.[26]

A tenant may deduct from rent the value of improvements if the lease specifically permits the deduction.[27] However, if the tenant otherwise carries out improvements and renovations, he is not entitled to recover their costs.[28]

It has been said that if the landlord has knowledge of defects which are a source of danger and damage to a tenant, the landlord is obligated to take reasonable care to remedy defects,[29] although there is no obligation upon the landlord to disclose defects. Consequently, at common law,[30] if a tenant finds an unfurnished house to be uninhabitable, he has no remedy unless he was induced to take it by the deceit of the landlord. This general principle has become confused by cases which have placed and removed liability on the landlord somewhat indiscriminately. Those cases dealing with access should be treated separately and are dealt with hereafter. Apart from those cases, it has been held that the landlord is under no liability for the death of the tenant caused by carbon monoxide fumes from a defective gas heater where there is

---

20*Amell v. Maloney* (1929), 64 O.L.R. 285, [1929] 4 D.L.R. 514 (S.C. App. Div.); *United Cigar Stores Ltd. v. Buller and Hughes* (1931), 66 O.L.R. 593, [1931] 2 D.L.R. 144 (S.C. App. Div.).

21*Brown v. Trustees of Toronto General Hospital* (1893), 23 O.R. 599 (H.C.J.), but see *United Cigar Stores Ltd. v. Buller, supra*, footnote 20.

22*Miles v. Marshall* (1975), 7 O.R. (2d) 544, 55 D.L.R. (3d) 664 (H.C.J.).

23*West Ham Central Charity Board v. East London Waterworks Co.*, [1900] 1 Ch. 624.

24*Saner v. Bilton, supra*, footnote 16.

25*Blackmore v. White*, [1899] 1 Q.B. 293.

26*Burchell v. Hornsby* (1808), 1 Camp. 360, 170 E.R. 985.

27*Wheeler v. Sime and Bain* (1846), 3 U.C.Q.B. 143.

28*Hiscock v. Squires* (1975), 8 Nfld. & P.E.I.R. 394 (Nfld. C.A.); *Truck Stop Ltd. v. Royalite Oil Co. Ltd.* (1970), 73 W.W.R. 521 (Sask. Q.B.), revd on other grounds [1971] 1 W.W.R. 161 (Sask. C.A.).

29*Cockburn v. Smith*, [1924] 2 K.B. 119 (C.A.); *Ellies v. Lee*, [1933] O.W.N. 468 (C.A.).

30This statement must now, of course, be read subject to the provisions of the various provincial residential tenancy legislation.

no express covenant to repair for unfurnished premises, and where the landlord is aware of the defects.[31] The same result applied to patrons of the tenant where the landlord has not contracted to repair or reserved the right to enter to make repairs. In such a case the court concluded that he has not maintained a measure of control to support liability.[32]

On the other hand the landlord has been held liable for death or injury to the tenant for noxious fumes escaping from adjacent premises occupied by him, such liability founded either on the doctrine of *Rylands and Horrocks v. Fletcher*,[33] or on the principle of derogation from grant.[34]

Where a landlord keeps control of access to the demised premises he is under a duty of care not to expose the tenant and others using the means of access to a concealed trap or danger.[35] Although it has been said that in the absence of a concealed danger or trap the landlord is not liable for damages caused by a defective condition,[36] this statement must be looked at with some caution. There now seems to be little doubt that the landlord owes his tenant a higher duty than owed to an invitee and thus must use reasonable care to keep means of access in a reasonably safe condition, even where there is no express covenant to do so.[37] The duty has been said to arise by an implied contract[38] and will apply to those uses which are subsidiary to the letting.[39] The obligation of the landlord extends to those areas of access used by the tenant but does not extend to tradesmen's entrances.[40]

Although a detailed examination of liability of the tenant or landlord to the public for injury due to non-repair is beyond the scope of this book,[41] in general it may be said that if premises are out of repair so as to constitute a nuisance to the public, and a member of the public suffers injury thereby, the tenant as occupier, and not the landlord, is *prima facie* liable for damages.[42]

---

[31]*Reid v. Union Gas Co. of Canada Ltd. and Lampel Leaseholds Ltd.*, [1961] O.R. 213, 27 D.L.R. (2d) 5 (H.C.J.).

[32]*Williams v. Emmons*, [1961] O.R. 696, 29 D.L.R. (2d) 301 (H.C.J.).

[33](1868), L.R. 3 H.L. 330.

[34]*Federic v. Perpetual Investments Ltd.*, [1969] 1 O.R. 186, 2 D.L.R. (3d) 50 (H.C.J.), and see §804.3, "Derogation from Grant", *supra.*

[35]*Fairman v. Perpetual Investment Building Society*, [1923] A.C. 74 (H.L.).

[36]*Lucy v. Bawden*, [1914] 2 K.B. 318.

[37]*Miller v. Hancock*, [1893] 2 Q.B. 177 (C.A.); *Fanjoy v. Gaston* (1981), 127 D.L.R. (3d) 163, 36 N.B.R. (2d) 226 (C.A.).

[38]*MacNeill v. Hi-Rise Developments Ltd.*, [1974] 3 W.W.R. 296 (Sask. Q.B.); *Richardson v. St. James Court Apartments Ltd.*, [1963] 1 O.R. 534, 38 D.L.R. (2d) 25 (H.C.J.), affd [1963] 2 O.R. 569n, 40 D.L.R. (2d) 297n (C.A.).

[39]*Sinclair v. Hudson Coal & Fuel Oil Ltd.*, [1966] 2 O.R. 256, 56 D.L.R. (2d) 484 (C.A.).

[40]*Holman v. Ellsmar Apartments Ltd.* (1963), 40 D.L.R. (2d) 657 (B.C.S.C.).

[41]For a detailed examination of the cases in the area and with respect to the landlord's liability to the tenant, his guests and invitees, both on and off the demised premises, see Williams, *Canadian Law of Landlord and Tenant*, 4th ed. (Toronto, Carswell, 1973), pp. 374-410.

[42]*Pretty v. Bickmore* (1873), L.R. 8 C.P. 401; *Nelson v. Liverpool Brewery Co.* (1877), 2 C.P.D. 311.

However, if the landlord has knowledge of the lack of repair which caused the injury, liability shifts to him if, either the want of repair existed at the time of the letting (based on a principle of misfeasance in letting the premises in a dangerous condition),[43] or if the danger comes from want of repair arising during the term and the landlord with notice of the want of repair fails to repair pursuant to a covenant by him to repair.[44] The basis of this principle is the avoidance of circuity of actions because to hold the tenant liable would cause him to exercise his remedy over against the landlord.

In the absence of any agreement to repair, the landlord is not liable to a stranger for personal injuries caused by the dilapidated condition of the premises where the condition does not amount to a public nuisance.[45]

Apart from the application of the principle of *Rylands v. Fletcher*,[46] and the possible application of the principle of derogation from grant, the landlord is not liable for damage caused by the escape of water or steam in the absence of negligence.[47] Similarly, the tenant is not liable to other tenants for the escape of water and steam.[48]

If the premises are damaged by fire caused by the negligence of the tenant, he will be liable and the landlord will not have waived his cause of action in tort by refusing to rebuild the premises even if he may be deemed to have waived his claim in contract.[49]

Residential tenancies and the obligation to repair

The repair obligations of the landlord and tenant with respect to residential tenancies have been much altered. In general the landlord has to provide and maintain the rented premises in a state of good repair and fit for human habitation. He must also comply with any health, safety or housing standards.[50]

---

[43]*Nelson v. Liverpool Brewery, supra*, footnote 42; *O'Leary v. Smith*, [1925] 2 D.L.R. 1022, [1925] 2 W.W.R. 81 (Man. C.A.).

[44]*Payne v. Rogers* (1794), 2 H. Bl. 350, 126 E.R. 590; *Nelson v. Liverpool Brewery Co.*, *supra*, footnote 42.

[45]*Copp v. Aldridge & Co.* (1895), 11 T.L.R. 411.

[46](1868), L.R. 3 H.L. 330.

[47]*Barker v. Ferguson* (1908), 16 O.L.R. 252 (Div. Ct.); *Blake v. Woolf*, [1898] 2 Q.B. 426; *Scythes & Co., Ltd. v. Gibsons Ltd.*, [1927] 2 D.L.R. 834, [1927] S.C.R. 352; *Hess v. Greenway* (1919), 45 O.L.R. 650, 48 D.L.R. 630 (S.C. App. Div.); *Anderson v. Oppenheimer* (1880), 5 Q.B.D. 602.

[48]*Ross v. Fedden* (1872), L.R. 7 Q.B. 661.

[49]*Canadian Imperial Bank of Commerce v. Whiteside* (1968), 2 D.L.R. (3d) 611 (Man. C.A.).

[50]See *Residential Tenancy Act*, S.B.C. 1984, c. 15, s. 8; *Residential Tenancies Act*, S.N.S. 1970, c. 13, s. 6(1), stat. con. 1; R.S.S. 1978, c. R-22, s. 20, am. 1979-80, c. 69, s. 5; 1980-81, c. 40, s. 3; S.N.B. 1975, c. R-10.2, s. 3(1); *Landlord and Tenant Act*, R.S.O. 1980, c. 232, s. 96; R.S.M. 1970, c. L70, s. 98(1), enacted 1970, c. 106, s. 3; R.S.A. 1980, c. L-6, s. 14; R.S.P.E.I. 1974, c. L-7, s. 102; *Landlord and Tenant (Residential Tenancies) Act*, S.N. 1973, No. 54, s. 7(1), stat. con. 1; *Landlord and Tenant Ordinance*, R.O.N.W.T. 1974, c. L-2, s. 60(1); R.O.Y.T. 1971, c. L-2, s. 75(1), enacted 1972, c. 20, s. 1.

His obligation to repair exists notwithstanding any agreement or waiver to the contrary, and his obligation extends to leases entered into before the coming into force of the legislation.[51] The obligation is not dependent upon notice by the tenant of non-repair and it is not lessened because the premises were in a state of non-repair at the commencement of the lease.[52] The duty to maintain the premises in repair extends not only to the part of the premises physically occupied by the tenant but also to all the common areas of the premises such as hallways, swimming pools, laundry rooms and parking spaces.[53] In other words, the expression "rented premises" to which the repair obligation attaches encompasses more than mere physical space and includes all that the tenant is entitled to under the lease.[54]

In Ontario the landlord's obligation can be enforced by summary application to the County Court[54a] and the tenant can seek thereunder an abatement of rent for non-repair,[55] and for the failure of the landlord to provide common facilities which it is his duty to provide.[56]

It has been held that the tenant can raise, as a defence on an application by the landlord to terminate the tenancy, the failure of the landlord to repair so long as the tenant has paid into court the arrears of rent claimed.[57] Payment of rental arrears into a private trust fund has been held insufficient to allow such a defence to be raised.[58]

Although the statutory obligation to repair has been deemed to create an implied covenant,[59] the effect of the breach of this covenant is uncertain. The legislation in Ontario provides that all material covenants are interdependent and that breach on one side relieves the other party of his obligations.[59a] In one case the tenant was entitled to withhold rent because of the breach, so long as the rent was paid into court,[60] while in another it was held that the covenant to repair was independent of the covenant to pay rent, and that the

---

[51]*Levin v. Active Builders Ltd.* (1973), 40 D.L.R. (3d) 299, [1973] 6 W.W.R. 279 (Man. C.A.).

[52]*Re Quann and Pajelle Investments Ltd.* (1975), 7 O.R. (2d) 769 (Co. Ct.).

[53]*Re Gagnon and Centre-Town Developments Ltd.* (1975), 10 O.R. (2d) 245 (Co. Ct.), revd on other grounds 14 O.R. (2d) 550 (Div. Ct.); *Re Quann and Pajelle Investments Ltd.*, supra, footnote 52; *Lewis v. Westa Holdings Ltd.*; *Lewis v. Perry* (1975), 8 O.R. (2d) 181 (Co. Ct.).

[54]*Pajelle Investments Ltd. v. Herbold* (1975), 62 D.L.R. (3d) 749, [1976] 2 S.C.R. 520.

[54a]*Landlord and Tenant Act*, R.S.O. 1980, c. 232, s. 96(3).

[55]*Re Victoria Park Community Homes Inc. and Buzza* (1975), 10 O.R. (2d) 251 (Co. Ct.); *Re Pajelle Investments Ltd. and Booth (No. 2)* (1975), 7 O.R. (2d) 229 (Co. Ct.); *Re Gagnon and Centre-Town Developments Ltd.* (1975), 10 O.R. (2d) 245 (Co. Ct.), revd on other grounds 14 O.R. (2d) 550 (Div. Ct.).

[56]*Pajelle Investments Ltd. v. Herbold, supra*, footnote 54.

[57]*Re Victoria Park Community Homes Inc. and Buzza, supra*, footnote 55.

[58]*Re Pajelle Investments Ltd. and Booth (No. 2), supra*, footnote 55.

[59]*Re Quann and Pajelle Investments Ltd.* (1975), 7 O.R. (2d) 769 (Co. Ct.).

[59a]*Landlord and Tenant Act*, R.S.O. 1980, c. 232, s. 89.

[60]*Ibid.*

tenant was not entitled to withhold rent except upon an application under the repair provisions of the legislation.[61] The British Columbia statute specifically provides that the court may order payment of rent into court to be applied to the costs and expenses of complying with the tenancy agreement.[62]

In Ontario, it has been held that when the tenant relies on a breach of a contractual provision to repair (as distinguished from the statutory duty to repair), the lease is not terminated. Rather, the tenant's remedy is in damages.[63]

The landlord may be liable in tort for damages suffered by the tenant resulting from a breach of the statutory duty to repair.[64] However, his duty to repair does not impose absolute liability on the landlord for damages caused by latent defects of which he was unaware.

In Nova Scotia it has been held that breach by the landlord of his statutory duty to repair gives rise to a right of action in tort in favour of the tenant and his family but that the test for liability is negligence.[65]

The landlord's duty to repair operates only during the term of the tenancy.[66]

With respect to residential tenancies the tenant has a statutory obligation to maintain ordinary cleanliness and to repair damage caused by the wilful or negligent conduct of himself or persons permitted on the premises by him.[67] This obligation differs little from the tenant's implied obligation to use the premises in a tenant-like manner. Failure of the tenant to meet this obligation may be raised by the landlord as a defence to the landlord's breach of his own duty to repair.[68]

804.6 Waste

A tenant may be liable for the tort of waste if he carries on a use which is unreasonable or improper[1] and thus causes lasting damage to the reversion or

---

[61]*Re Pajelle Investments Ltd. and Booth (No. 2)*, *supra*, footnote 55.

[62]*Residential Tenancy Act*, S.B.C. 1979, c. 15, s. 9(2)(c).

[63]*Temlas Apartments Inc. v. Desloges* (1980), 29 O.R. (2d) 30, 112 D.L.R. (3d) 185 (Div. Ct.).

[64]*Fleischmann v. Grossman Holdings Ltd.* (1976), 16 O.R. (2d) 746, 79 D.L.R. (3d) 142 (C.A.).

[65]*Gaul v. King et al.* (1979), 103 D.L.R. (3d) 233, 33 N.S.R. (2d) 60 (S.C. App. Div.); *Basset Realty Ltd. v. Lindstrom* (1979), 103 D.L.R. (3d) 654, 34 N.S.R. (2d) 361 (S.C. App. Div.).

[66]*Re Bruns and Fancher* (1977), 16 O.R. (2d) 781, 79 D.L.R. (3d) 276 (Div. Ct.).

[67]*Residential Tenancy Act*, S.B.C. 1984, c. 15, s. 8(4); *Residential Tenancies Act*, S.N.S. 1970, c. 13, s. 6(1), stat. con. 3; R.S.S. 1978, c. R-22, s. 20(1), stat. con. 6; S.N.B. 1975, c. R-10.2, s. 4(1); *Landlord and Tenant Act*, R.S.O. 1980, c. 232, s. 96(2); R.S.M. 1970, c. L70, s. 98(2), enacted 1970, c. 106, s. 3; re-enacted 1971, c. 35, s. 10; am. 1975, c. 37, s. 5(1); R.S.A. 1980, c. L-6, s. 16; R.S.P.E.I. 1974, c. L-7, s. 102(2); *Landlord and Tenant (Residential Tenancies) Act*, S.N. 1973, No. 54, s. 7(1), stat. con. 2; *Landlord and Tenant Ordinance*, R.O.N.W.T. 1974, c. L-2, s. 60(2); R.O.Y.T. 1971, c. L-2, s. 75(2), enacted 1972, c. 20, s. 1.

[68]*Policicchio v. Phoenix Ass'ce Co. of Canada* (1977), 17 O.R. (2d) 118, 79 D.L.R. (3d) 453 (Dist. Ct.).

§804.6

[1]*Saner v. Bilton* (1878), 7 Ch. D. 815.

changes the nature of the demised premises.[2] It has been held that damage by fire started by the tenant's negligent act is voluntary waste for which the tenant will be rendered liable whether he be a tenant at will[3] or a tenant from month to month.[4]

It is possible for a tenant to contract out of liability for waste.[5] Thus, where a lease required the landlord to insure against fire, and where the tenant's covenant to repair excluded damage caused by perils against which the landlord was required to insure, the tenant was not liable for waste.[6]

To a great extent, therefore, the question of waste may not be an important issue between the parties. In many cases contractual terms, and in the case of residential tenancies, statutory provisions, will obviate an inquiry into alleged acts of waste. However, the concept of waste still is of major importance when life estates are in existence.[7]

804.7 Rent

Rent is what is payable by a tenant to his landlord under a tenancy either as compensation for the use of the demised lands, or as an acknowledgment of the title of the landlord. Historically it was known as rent-service, which has been defined as being "an annual return, made by the tenant in labour, money or provisions, in retribution for the land that passes".[1]

Although rent need not necessarily be money, the rent must be certain. If the rent is not set as a stated amount, but is to fluctuate depending upon certain conditions, it is sufficient in terms of certainty that the formula by which the rent can be made certain is itself certain.[2]

At common law the landlord has the right, as an incident of the reversion, to distrain for arrears of rent. This right arises only for arrears of rent-service, and if there is no true tenancy, the landlord cannot distrain for arrears of payments, even if characterized as "rent" by the parties, in the absence of an express contractual or statutory term. If, however, there is a true tenancy there need be no reservation in the lease of an express power to distrain. Again, this

---

[2]*West Ham Central Charity Board v. East London Waterworks Co.*, [1900] 1 Ch. 624; *Phillipps v. Smith* (1845), 14 M. & W. 589, 153 E.R. 610; *Re Collins Cartage & Storage Co. Ltd. and McDonald* (1980), 30 O.R. (2d) 234, 116 D.L.R. (3d) 570 (C.A.).

[3]*Nichols v. R.A. Gill Ltd.* (1974), 5 O.R. (2d) 741, 51 D.L.R. (3d) 493 (H.C.J.).

[4]*Tudor Developments Ltd. v. Van Es* (1975), 53 D.L.R. (3d) 716, [1975] W.W.D. 74 (Alta. S.C.T.D.). See also *Balageorge v. McCulloch*, [1977] 4 W.W.R. 195 (Man. Q.B.).

[5]*Meux v. Cobley*, [1892] 2 Ch. 253.

[6]*Agnew-Surpass Shoe Stores Ltd. v. Cummer-Yonge Investments Ltd.* (1975), 55 D.L.R. (3d) 676, [1976] 2 S.C.R. 221.

[7]For a more detailed discussion of waste, and various types thereof, see ch. 7, "The Life Estate", and especially §706.8, *supra*.

§804.7

[1]*Cheshire's Modern Law of Real Property*, 12th ed. by Burn (London, Butterworths, 1976), pp. 428-9.

[2]*Ex parte Voisey; Re Knight* (1882), 21 Ch. D. 442 (C.A.).

common law right has been limited by statute. In the case of residential tenancies, in many jurisdictions it has been abolished in whole or in part,[3] while in the case of non-residential tenancies the right is governed by various sections in the provincial Acts.[4]

Where the lease provides for accelerated rent upon certain conditions, including insolvency of the tenant, the landlord may distrain for accelerated rent.[5]

If the landlord elects to forfeit the lease he loses the right to distrain,[6] as the right to forfeit and the right to distrain are mutually exclusive.[7]

It has been decided in Ontario that the landlord's distress creates a lien which is exempt from the *Personal Property Security Act*[8] and thus takes priority over a chattel mortgage.[9] It has also been held that a landlord retains the right of distress for arrears of rent accrued before a receiver is appointed under a debenture given by the tenant even though the landlord accepts rent for a subsequent period.[10] However, the right to claim priority may be lost because of the application of the doctrine of estoppel.[11]

The due date for the payment of rent will be governed by the terms of the lease. When rent falls due on a particular day the tenant has the whole of the day in which to make payment.[12] If the lease does not specify when rent is to be paid and the rent is annual, it is not payable until the end of the year.[13] Where a provincial statute permits a landlord to re-enter if the rent reserved remains unpaid for fifteen days after any of the days on which it should have

---

[3]*Residential Tenancy Act*, S.B.C. 1984, c. 15, s. 48(1); *Residential Tenancies Act*, S.N.S. 1970, c. 13, s. 4; S.N.B. 1975, c. R-10.2, s. 14; R.S.S. 1978, c. R-22, s. 13; *Landlord and Tenant Act*, R.S.O. 1980, c. 232, s. 86(1); R.S.M. 1970, c. L70, s. 88, enacted 1970, c. 106, s. 3; R.S.P.E.I. 1974, c. L-7, s. 98; *Landlord and Tenant Ordinance*, R.O.Y.T. 1971, c. L-2, s. 65(1), enacted 1972, c. 20, s. 1. As to the awarding of exemplary damages for illegal distraint under a residential tenancy see *Ozmond v. Young* (1980), 28 O.R. (2d) 225, 109 D.L.R. (3d) 304 (Div. Ct.).

[4]*Commercial Tenancy Act*, R.S.B.C. 1979, c. 54, ss. 3, 4; *Tenancies and Distress for Rent Act*, R.S.N.S. 1967, c. 302, s. 13; *Landlord and Tenant Act*, R.S.O. 1980, c. 232, s. 41; R.S.S. 1978, c. L-6, s. 20; R.S.M. 1970, c. L70, s. 30; R.S.P.E.I. 1974, c. L-7, s. 26; R.S.N.B. 1973, c. L-1, s. 21; *Landlord and Tenant Ordinance*, R.O.N.W.T. 1974, c. L-2, s. 19; R.O.Y.T. 1971, c. L-2, s. 19.

[5]*Commercial Credit Corp. Ltd. v. Harry D. Shields Ltd.* (1980), 29 O.R. (2d) 106, 112 D.L.R. (3d) 153 (H.C.J.), affd 32 O.R. (2d) 703, 122 D.L.R. (3d) 736 (C.A.).

[6]*Scarf v. Jardine* (1882), 7 App. Cas. 345 (H.L.). As to when the right is not lost, see *Cameron v. Eldorado Properties Ltd.* (1980), 113 D.L.R. (3d) 141, 22 B.C.L.R. 175 (S.C.).

[7]*Country Kitchen Ltd. v. Wabush Enterprises Ltd.* (1981), 120 D.L.R. (3d) 358, 35 Nfld. & P.E.I.R. 391 (Nfld. C.A.), and cases cited therein.

[8]R.S.O. 1980, c. 375.

[9]*Commercial Credit Corp. Ltd. v. Harry D. Shields Ltd.* (1981), 32 O.R. (2d) 703, 122 D.L.R. (3d) 736 (C.A.).

[10]*Saskatoon Credit Union Ltd. v. Parklane Investments Ltd.* (1980), 112 D.L.R. (3d) 496, 6 Sask. R. 348 (Q.B.).

[11]*Re Wilson and The Queen in right of Canada* (1979), 106 D.L.R. (3d) 645, 1 Man. R. (2d) 372 (C.A.).

[12]*Dibble v. Bowater and Morgan* (1853), 2 El. & Bl. 564, 118 E.R. 879.

[13]*McIntosh v. Leckie* (1906), 13 O.L.R. 54 (H.C.J.).

been paid,[14] it has been decided in some instances that the earliest the landlord can re-enter is the seventeenth of the month if rent is payable on the first, while in others a notice to quit was allowed to be served on the sixteenth.[15]

In *Cottam v. Smith*[16] it was decided that a landlord, by virtue of a course of conduct, may be deemed to have agreed to accept late payment of rent and thus be precluded from exercising a right of forfeiture which he may otherwise have. However, this case should be read subject to section 26 of the *Landlord and Tenant Act*,[17] which provides that where there is a waiver of a condition or covenant by the landlord in one instance, the waiver shall not be deemed or assumed to extend to any other instance or condition.

If no place for payment is specified in the lease, the tenant must seek out the landlord to pay him as he has contracted to pay him. It is not sufficient for the tenant to remain on the demised premises and plead thereafter that he was able and willing to pay while waiting for the landlord to call for rent.[18] However, over a period of time a course of conduct may establish that the landlord has agreed to accept rent at a specific location, as, for example, the demised premises.[19] If the landlord directs that the rent be paid to a specific location such as his home, he is required to be there or have some person there authorized to receive the rent.[20]

Where the landlord directs that rent be paid by post and the remittance is lost, the loss falls upon him as the post office is his agent.[21] If, however, he does not so specifically direct, the posting of the remittance is not equivalent to payment.[22] It may be difficult in some instances to determine if the landlord has authorized payment of rent by mail, and each case will turn on its facts with different conclusions reached on subtle differences in wording.[23] The authorization to remit by mail may be express or implied, and it has been

---

[14]See for example, the *Landlord and Tenant Act*, R.S.O. 1980, c. 232, s. 18(1).
[15]For a discussion of both lines of cases see *Weber v. Pennell*, [1947] O.W.N. 578 (C.A.); *Urbach v. McClarty*, [1953] O.W.N. 58, [1953] 1 D.L.R. 316 (C.A.); *Banrevi v. Larman*, [1953] O.W.N. 210, [1953] 2 D.L.R. 619 (Co. Ct.).
[16][1947] O.W.N. 880 (C.A.).
[17]R.S.O. 1980, c. 232. See also *Landlord and Tenant Act*, R.S.M. 1970, c. L70, s. 25; R.S.N.B. 1973, c. L-1, s. 17; R.S.S. 1978, c. L-6, s. 16; R.S.P.E.I. 1974, c. L-7, s. 17; *Landlord and Tenant Ordinance*, R.O.N.W.T. 1974, c. L-2, s. 15; R.O.Y.T. 1971, c. L-2, s. 15.
[18]*Haldane v. Johnson* (1853), 8 Ex. 689, 155 E.R. 1529.
[19]*Browne v. White*, [1947] 2 D.L.R. 309, [1947] 1 W.W.R. 622 (C.A.), but see *Laung v. Hum*, [1949] 1 D.L.R. 365 (N.S. Co. Ct.).
[20]*Clarke v. Kirkpatrick*, [1948] O.W.N. 406 (C.A.).
[21]*Warwicke v. Noakes* (1791), Peake 98, 170 E.R. 93.
[22]*Baker v. Lipton* (1899), 15 T.L.R. 435; *Davidovich v. Hill*, [1948] O.W.N. 201, [1948] 2 D.L.R. 613 (C.A.); *Bolton v. O'Reilly*, [1952] O.W.N. 49 (Co. Ct.); *Dennaoui v. Green Gables Fine Foods Ltd.* (1974), 47 D.L.R. (3d) 609, 19 N.S.R. (2d) 631 (S.C.T.D.).
[23]This difficulty is illustrated by a comparison of the following cases: *Mitchell-Henry v. Norwich Union Life Ins. Society Ltd.*, [1918] 1 K.B. 123, affd [1918] 2 K.B. 67 (C.A.); *Davidovich v. Hill, supra*, footnote 22.

held that very little evidence beyond a course of dealing is evidence of an implied request.[24]

Where payment of rent by post is authorized, generally, sending the remittance in the ordinary way will be appropriate, depending upon the amount. For example, a substantial amount should not be sent by treasury bills.[25] Certainly the tenant, if authorized to pay by post, must exercise due caution and may be required to register the letter.[26] It has been decided that where payment by post is authorized, payment is made when mailed, not when received.[27]

Rent is payable to the landlord or an agent expressly or impliedly authorized to receive it. After the landlord's death, rent is payable to his personal representative until the property is vested in the proper beneficiary. If there are several landlords holding as joint tenants, any one can bring an action or give a receipt[28] for the entire rent. If they hold as tenants in common all must bring an action for the entire rent, or each must sue individually for his share.[29]

Since rent is an incident of the reversion, accruing rent and future rent passes to and is payable to the assignee of the reversion, but not overdue rent which has not been expressly assigned by the landlord. In general, a tenant is not prejudiced by payment of rent to the assignor before he receives notice of the assignment from the assignee.[30] Prepayment of rent before it is due stands on a different footing. Prepayment of rent to the landlord before the due date does not protect the tenant from a claim by a mortgagee who gives notice before the due date.[31] However, if prepayment of rent predates the making of the mortgage the tenant cannot be required to pay once again to the mortgagee on demand.[32]

In many instances the lease will provide for accelerated rent upon the happening of certain conditions, the most common provisions relating to bankruptcy and insolvency. Under the provisions of the *Bankruptcy Act*,[33] the landlord is entitled to accelerated rent for a three-month period after the date

---

[24]*Mitchell-Henry v. Norwich Union Life Ins. Society Ltd., supra*, footnote 23, but see *Pennington v. Crossley & Son* (1897), 13 T.L.R. 53 (C.A.).

[25]*Ibid.*

[26]*Lastaff v. Lorenson* (1930), 38 O.W.N. 119 (S.C. App. Div.).

[27]*Burd v. Fox* (Ont. C.A.), unreported, but referred to in an article by Arnup, "Recent Cases on Rental Regulations", 25 Can. Bar Rev. 625 (1947), at p. 631; *Kraszewski v. Old*, [1948] O.W.N. 634, [1948] 4 D.L.R. 75 (C.A.).

[28]*Robinson v. Hofman* (1828), 4 Bing. 562 at p. 565, 130 E.R. 885.

[29]*Last v. Dinn* (1858), 28 L.J. Ex. 94.

[30]*Commercial Tenancy Act*, R.S.B.C. 1979, c. 54, s. 14; *Landlord and Tenant Act*, R.S.O. 1980, c. 232, s. 62(2); R.S.S. 1978, c. L-6, s. 60(2); R.S.M. 1970, c. L70, s. 56(2); R.S.P.E.I. 1974, c. L-7, s. 22(2); R.S.N.B. 1973, c. L-1, s. 46(2); *Landlord and Tenant Ordinance*, R.O.N.W.T. 1974, c. L-2, s. 28(2); R.O.Y.T. 1971, c. L-2, s. 40(2).

[31]*De Nicholls v. Saunders* (1870), L.R. 5 C.P. 588; *Cook v. Guerra* (1872), L.R. 7 C.P. 132.

[32]*Green v. Rheinberg* (1911), 104 L.T. 149 (C.A.); *Lord Ashburton v. Nocton*, [1914] 2 Ch. 211.

[33]R.S.C. 1970, c. B-3, s. 107(1)(*f*).

of the bankruptcy. However, the Act does not preclude a claim by the landlord for accelerated rent prior to the bankruptcy pursuant to the conditions in the lease even where he claims for accelerated rent under the Act.[34] The right to accelerated rent is to replace the right of distress lost to the landlord on the bankruptcy.[35]

If the rent for the balance of the term becomes due because of an acceleration clause, subject to the limitations of the *Bankruptcy Act*, the tenant is liable for the entire amount claimed so long as the clause is not characterized as a penalty clause in circumstances where the court will offer relief.[36]

If the tenant is evicted by the landlord or his agent or anyone claiming through him or by title paramount, the tenant is not liable for rent accruing due after the eviction,[37] but is liable for rent which accrued due before the eviction.[38] An eviction occurs where there is an act of grave and permanent character by the landlord or his agent done with the intention of depriving the tenant of the whole or part of the premises.

If a tenant under a verbal lease for a present demise does not enter upon the premises, an action for rent agreed to be paid cannot be maintained, as such an agreement is a contract respecting an interest in lands within the meaning of the *Statute of Frauds*,[39] unless, of course, the lease is one which may be made by parol.

805. COVENANTS

805.1 General

In order to determine the rights and liabilities of successive parties to the tenancy, it is necessary to distinguish between covenants made between the lessor and the lessee. Any covenant entered into between a lessor and lessee is binding between the two personally and their personal representatives. On an assignment of the reversion or term a covenant may be binding upon the grantee of the reversion or assignee of the term. Similarly, the benefit of a covenant may pass to these parties.[1]

---

[34]*Re Prairie Farm Power Ltd.* (1974), 49 D.L.R. (3d) 736 (Alta. S.C. in Bankruptcy); see also *Re Supreme Draperies & Awnings Ltd.* (1975), 10 O.R. (2d) 211, 62 D.L.R. (3d) 607 (S.C.). For a detailed examination of the right to claim for accelerated rent before and after bankruptcy, a subject beyond the scope of this book, see Williams, *Canadian Law of Landlord and Tenant*, 4th ed. (Toronto, Carswell, 1973), pp. 183, 260-66.

[35]*Re Sol Max Ltd.* (1975), 12 O.R. (2d) 240, 68 D.L.R. (3d) 424 (C.A.), but see *Re Greenstein* (1966), 9 C.B.R. (N.S.) 10 (Ont. S.C. in Bankruptcy).

[36]*Neon Products of Canada Ltd. v. Smith* (1961), 8 C.B.R. (N.S.) 68 (Ont. S.C.), affd *loc. cit.* (C.A.).

[37]*Ferguson v. Troop* (1890), 17 S.C.R. 527.

[38]*Fitzgerald v. Mandas* (1910), 21 O.L.R. 312 (H.C.J.), at p. 315.

[39]R.S.O. 1980, c. 481. See *Bank of Upper Canada v. Tarrant* (1860), 19 U.C.Q.B. 423; Williams, *Canadian Law of Landlord and Tenant*, supra, footnote 34, at p. 179.

§805.1

[1]The general principles enunciated above have been codified by statute. See, for example, the *Landlord and Tenant Act*, R.S.O. 1980, c. 232, ss. 4-8.

A covenant is said to run with the term, or as it is more usually put, with the land, when either the liability to perform it, or the right to take advantage of it, passes to the assignee of the tenant.[2] There are, thus, four situations to be considered, namely: (1) when the burden of the lessee's covenant runs with the land; (2) when the burden of the lessor's covenant runs with the reversion; (3) when the benefit of the lessor's covenant runs with the land, and (4) when the benefit of the lessee's covenant runs with the reversion.

805.2 Burden of Lessee's Covenant

When a covenant relates to something *in esse*, or in being, at the time of the lease, which directly concerns the land, it binds the assigns whether they are named or not.[1] Even if the thing to be done under the covenant is not to be done on the actual land demised, "yet if the thing to be done is clearly for the benefit, support, and maintenance of the subject-matter demised, the obligation to do it runs with the land".[2] It should be noted that the distinction between covenants *in esse* and *in posse* discussed immediately hereafter has been abolished for residential tenancies in most jurisdictions.[3]

Covenants of this nature which have been held to run with the land are: covenants to pay rent;[4] covenants to render services in the nature of rent;[5] covenants to allow deductions out of rent;[6] covenants to pay taxes where the covenant was made by the lessee for himself and his assigns.[7] (In Nova Scotia, it has been held that a covenant to pay taxes is a personal covenant and does not run with the land.[8] Although this last decision is a decision by five judges, it is submitted that the decision is wrong and should not be followed); covenants to insure against fire;[9] covenants to manure or to expend manure

---

[2]*Spencer's Case* (1583), 5 Co. Rep. 16 a, 77 E.R. 72.
§805.2
[1]*Spencer's Case* (1583), 5 Co. Rep. 16 a, 77 E.R. 72.
[2]*Lyle v. Smith*, [1909] 2 I.R. 58 (K.B.), at p. 65, *per* Lord O'Brian, L.C.J.
[3]*Landlord and Tenant Act*, R.S.O. 1980, c. 232, s. 90. See also R.S.P.E.I. 1974, c. L-7, s. 94; R.S.M. 1970, c. L70, s. 92, enacted 1970, c. 106, s. 3; *Landlord and Tenant (Residential Tenancies) Act*, S.N. 1973, No. 54, s. 12(2); *Residential Tenancy Act*, S.B.C. 1984, c. 15, s. 48(3); *Residential Tenancies Act*, R.S.S. 1978, c. R-22, s. 17; S.N.B. 1975, c. R-10.2, s. 12; *Landlord and Tenant Ordinance*, R.O.N.W.T. 1974, c. L-2, s. 55; R.O.Y.T. 1971, c. L-2, s. 69, enacted 1972, c. 20, s. 1.
[4]*Stevenson v. Lambard* (1802), 2 East 575, 102 E.R. 490; *Williams v. Bosanquet* (1819), 1 Brod. & B. 238, 129 E.R. 714.
[5]*Vyvyan v. Arthur* (1823), 1 B. & C. 410, 107 E.R. 152.
[6]*Baylye v. Hughes* (1629), Cro. Car. 137, 79 E.R. 720.
[7]*Wix v. Rutson*, [1899] 1 Q.B. 474; *Mackinnon v. Crafts, Lee & Gallinger* (1917), 33 D.L.R. 684, [1917] 1 W.W.R. 1402 (Alta. S.C. App. Div.).
[8]*McDuff v. McDougall* (1889), 21 N.S.R. 250 (S.C.).
[9]*Vernon v. Smith* (1821), 5 B. & Ald. 1, 106 E.R. 1094; *Douglass v. Murphy* (1858), 16 U.C.Q.B. 113.

on the farm;[10] covenants to repair;[11] a covenant to not carry on a particular trade on the demised premises;[12] a covenant to maintain a sea-wall;[13] a covenant that a named person should not be concerned in the business carried on in the demised premises.[14]

When a covenant relates to a thing in future or not in being at the time of the lease, which directly concerns or benefits the land, it binds the assigns if they are named but not otherwise.[15] It has been admitted that there is no intelligible basis in distinguishing covenants which relate to things *in esse* and things *in posse* but the distinction remains.[16]

Examples of the covenant immediately described which have been held to run with the land are covenants to erect new buildings[17] and covenants in a mining lease to build a smelting mill on waste land adjacent to the demised land.[18]

Under the provisions of sections 5 and 6 of the *Landlord and Tenant Act* of Ontario[19] the burden of the lessee's covenant runs with the reversion where the covenant is related to the land, and an assignee of the reversion may enforce a condition of re-entry or forfeiture even though that person becomes so entitled after the condition of re-entry or forfeiture becomes enforceable.

If the covenant is a personal or collateral covenant which affects merely the person and which does not affect the nature, quality or value of the thing demised or the mode of using or enjoying it, the covenant does not, apart from the equitable doctrine of notice, run with the land. This is so even if the covenant expressly extends to assigns.[20]

The following covenants have been held to be collateral covenants which do not run with the land: a covenant to pay an increased rent in respect of improvements made by the lessor;[21] a covenant in a lease of a silk mill to

---

[10]*Atkinson v. Farrell* (1912), 27 O.L.R. 204, 8 D.L.R. 582 (Div. Ct.).

[11]*Williams v. Earle* (1868), L.R. 3 Q.B. 739; *Perry v. Bank of Upper Canada* (1866), 16 U.C.C.P. 404.

[12]*Mayor of Congleton v. Pattison* (1808), 10 East 130, 103 E.R. 725.

[13]*Lyle v. Smith*, [1909] 2 I.R. 58 (K.B.).

[14]*Lewin v. American & Colonial Distributors, Ltd.*, [1945] Ch. 225.

[15]*Spencer's Case* (1583), 5 Co. Rep. 16 a, 77 E.R. 72; *Doughty v. Bowman* (1848), 11 Q.B. 444, 116 E.R. 543.

[16]*Minshull v. Oakes* (1858), 2 H. & N. 793, 157 E.R. 327.

[17]*Spencer's Case, supra,* footnote 15; *Doughty v. Bowman, supra,* footnote 15.

[18]*Sampson v. Easterby* (1829), 9 B. & C. 505, 109 E.R. 188, affd 6 Bing. 644, 130 E.R. 1429.

[19]R.S.O. 1980, c. 232. See also *Landlord and Tenant Act*, R.S.M. 1970, c. L70, ss. 4, 5; R.S.A. 1980, c. L-6, s. 19; R.S.N.B. 1973, c. L-1, s. 2; R.S.S. 1978, c. L-6, ss. 3, 4; R.S.P.E.I. 1974, c. L-7, s. 2; *Landlord and Tenant Ordinance*, R.O.N.W.T. 1974, c. L-2, s. 3; R.O.Y.T. 1971, c. L-2, s. 3. The Prince Edward Island, New Brunswick, Northwest Territories and Yukon statutes specifically provide that the right of re-entry or forfeiture is not enforceable if it has been waived or released before the assignee has become entitled but one would assume this to be the case in the other jurisdictions as well.

[20]*Mayor of Congleton v. Pattison, supra,* footnote 12.

[21]*Raymond v. Fitch* (1835), 2 C.M. & R. 588, 150 E.R. 251.

employ only a certain class of persons therein;[22] a covenant to pay taxes on premises of the lessors other than the demised premises;[23] a condition in a lease that in case any writ of execution shall be issued against the goods of the lessee, the then current year's rent shall immediately become due and payable and the term forfeited;[24] a covenant by a lessor, not mentioning assigns, to pay for buildings to be erected on the lands demised;[25] a covenant by the lessor not to build or keep any house for the sale of beer within half a mile of the demised premises;[26] a covenant that if the tenant does not exercise his right of renewal prior to the expiration of the term then the lessor will pay to him a fixed sum;[27] a covenant that the lessee shall have an option to take a lease of other property.[28]

The above rules relating to covenants which run with the land are confined to covenants annexed to the land by a lease under seal[29] or where there is a lease or agreement which operates as a lease in writing.[30] A mere assignment of a parol tenancy does not pass to the assignee the right to enforce a collateral covenant.[31] However, where an assignee goes into possession and rent is paid and received on the footing of the old tenancy, an agreement between the lessor and the assignee will be implied such that there will be a new tenancy on the terms of the old.[32]

805.3 Equitable Doctrine of Notice and Negative Covenants

Whether a covenant, including a collateral covenant, runs with the land, or whether there has been a legal assignment, an assignee who takes with notice, either actual or constructive of a negative covenant, is bound by it.[1] In effect, a negative covenant creates an equitable interest enforceable against any subsequent holder of the land except a *bona fide* purchaser for value without notice of the covenant.[2] If a covenant is partly positive and partly negative,

---

[22]*Mayor of Congleton v. Pattison, supra,* footnote 12.
[23]*Gower v. Postmaster-General* (1887), 57 L.T. 527.
[24]*Mitchell v. McCauley* (1893), 20 O.A.R. 272.
[25]*McClary v. Jackson* (1887), 13 O.R. 310 (H.C.J.).
[26]*Thomas v. Hayward* (1869), L.R. 4 Ex. 311.
[27]*Re Hunter's Lease; Giles v. Hutchings,* [1942] Ch. 124.
[28]*County Hotel & Wine Co., Ltd. v. London & North Western R. Co.,* [1918] 2 K.B. 251, affd [1921] 1 A.C. 85 (H.L.).
[29]*Elliott v. Johnson* (1866), L.R. 2 Q.B. 120 at p. 127.
[30]*Manchester Brewery Co. v. Coombs,* [1901] 2 Ch. 608 at p. 619; *Rogers v. National Drug & Chemical Co.* (1911), 23 O.L.R. 234 (H.C.J.), affd 24 O.L.R. 486 (C.A.).
[31]*Elliott v. Johnson, supra,* footnote 29.
[32]*Buckworth v. Simpson and Benner* (1835), 1 C.M. & R. 832, 149 E.R. 1317.
§805.3
[1]*Tulk v. Moxhay* (1848), 2 Ph. 774, 41 E.R. 1143; *Hayward v. Brunswick Permanent Benefit Building Society* (1881), 8 Q.B.D. 403 (C.A.); *London County Council v. Allen,* [1914] 3 K.B. 642 (C.A.).
[2]*Re Nisbet and Potts' Contract,* [1905] 1 Ch. 391, affd [1906] 1 Ch. 386 (C.A.); *Rogers v. Hosegood,* [1900] 2 Ch. 338 (C.A.).

and if it is severable, it will be enforced so far as the negative part of the covenant is concerned.[3]

In considering the question of notice one must not overlook the relevant statutory provisions requiring the registration of leases. The Ontario *Registry Act*[4] provides that every lease for a term longer than seven years shall be adjudged fraudulent and void against any subsequent purchaser or mortgagee for valuable consideration without actual notice unless the lease is registered, which is deemed to constitute notice of the lease to all persons claiming any interest in the land.

805.4 Burden of Lessor's Covenant

At common law the grantee of the reversion probably took it with the burden of any covenants made by the lessor.[1] This was also the effect of the statute of 32 Hen. VIII, c. 34 (1540), which gave lessees the like remedies against assignees of the reversion as they might have had against the lessor. Under the statute, for the burden of the covenant to run with the reversion, the lease had to be by deed.[2] If the lease is not by deed and if, after it has been assigned, rent is paid to the assignee of the lessor, an agreement to continue the tenancy on the same terms as before will be inferred.[3] However, since the Judicature Acts, the rule in *Walsh v. Lonsdale*[4] has been applied to the case of covenants running with the reversion in leases which were not by deed.[5] In order for the burden of the lessor's covenant to run with the reversion, the covenant must touch or concern the land and not be a collateral covenant.[6]

Provisions similar to 32 Hen. VIII, c. 34, are found in various provincial Landlord and Tenant Acts.[7]

Lessors' covenants which have been held to run with the reversion are:

---

[3]*Clegg v. Hands* (1890), 44 Ch. D. 503 (C.A.). The nature of the right to enforce restrictive covenants is fully discussed in *Re Nisbet and Potts' Contract, supra.*
[4]R.S.O. 1980, c. 445, ss. 65(1), (2), 69(1). See also *Cathray Realties Ltd. v. Simpson-Sears Ltd. and Wetston* (1975), 12 N.S.R. (2d) 658 (S.C.T.D.); *Maurice Demers Transport Ltd. and Demers v. Fountain Tire Distributors (Edmonton) Ltd.* (1973), 42 D.L.R. (3d) 412, [1974] 1 W.W.R. 348 (Alta. S.C. App. Div.).
§805.4
[1]*Derisley v. Custance* (1790), 4 T.R. 75, 100 E.R. 902.
[2]*Standen v. Chrismas* (1847), 10 Q.B. 135, 116 E.R. 53.
[3]*Cornish v. Stubbs* (1870), L.R. 5 C.P. 332 at p. 339.
[4](1882), 21 Ch. D. 9 (C.A.).
[5]*Rogers v. National Drug & Chemical Co.* (1911), 24 O.L.R. 486 (C.A.).
[6]*Thursby v. Plant* (1669), 1 Wms. Saund. 237, 85 E.R. 268; *Re Dollar Land Corp. Ltd. and Solomon*, [1963] 2 O.R. 269, 39 D.L.R. (2d) 221 (H.C.J.).
[7]R.S.O. 1980, c. 232, ss. 7, 8; R.S.S. 1978, c. L-6, ss. 5, 6; R.S.A. 1980, c. L-6, s. 19; R.S.M. 1970, c. L70, ss. 6, 7; R.S.N.B. 1973, c. L-1, s. 3; R.S.P.E.I. 1974, c. L-7, s. 4; R.O.N.W.T. 1974, c. L-2, s. 4; R.O.Y.T. 1971, c. L-2, s. 4.

a covenant for quiet enjoyment;[8] a covenant to renew,[9] but it has been stated that the rule that a covenant for renewal runs with the reversion is anomalous and difficult to justify;[10] a covenant to pay rates and taxes;[11] a restriction on the right to give a notice to quit for a certain specified period of time;[12] a covenant to supply water to the demised premises;[13] a covenant not to permit certain uses to be carried on on retained lands held by the lessor when the lease was entered into which would have the effect of increasing the insurance premiums of the lessee.[14]

805.5 Benefit of Lessor's Covenant

The benefit of a lessor's covenant runs with the land in favour of the assignee of the lessee. The rule used to be that the lease had to be by deed, but since the Judicature Acts the rule in *Walsh v. Lonsdale* would probably be applied so as to enable the benefit of a lessor's covenant in a parol lease to run with the land. The covenant should also touch or concern the land.[1]

805.6 Benefit of Lessee's Covenant

At common law, the benefit of a lessee's covenant did not run with the reversion except for a covenant to pay rent or to render services in the nature of rent.[1]

By the statute of 32 Hen. VIII, c. 34, the grantee and the assignees of the reversion were given the same remedies by action for non-performance of conditions, convenants or agreements contained in the indenture of lease, as the lessor himself had. However, the statute applies only when the lease is by deed and the covenant touches or concerns the land.[2]

Since the Judicature Acts the rule in *Walsh v. Lonsdale*[3] has modified the former rule. If the lessee has an agreement under which a lease by deed would have to be given and the agreement is specifically enforceable, the agreement

---

[8]*Campbell v. Lewis* (1820), 3 B. & Ald. 392, 106 E.R. 706, but see *Dewar v. Goodman*, [1908] 1 K.B. 94 (C.A.), at p. 108.

[9]*Muller v. Trafford*, [1901] 1 Ch. 54 at p. 60; *Rogers v. National Drug & Chemical Co.*, *supra*, footnote 5.

[10]*Woodall v. Clifton*, [1905] 2 Ch. 257 (C.A.).

[11]*South of England Dairies, Ltd. v. Baker*, [1906] 2 Ch. 631.

[12]*Breams Property Investment Co. v. Stroulger*, [1948] 2 K.B. 1 (C.A.).

[13]*Jourdain v. Wilson* (1821), 4 B. & Ald. 266, 106 E.R. 935.

[14]*Re Coast-to-Coast Industrial Developments Ltd. and Gorhim Holdings Ltd.* (1960), 22 D.L.R. (2d) 695 (Ont. H.C.J.).

§805.5
[1]*Spencer's Case* (1583), 5 Co. Rep. 16 a, 77 E.R. 72.

§805.6
[1]*Vyvyan v. Arthur* (1823), 1 B. & C. 410, 107 E.R. 152.

[2]*Spencer's Case* (1583), 5 Co. Rep. 16 a, 77 E.R. 72; *Stevens v. Copp* (1868), L.R. 4 Exch. 20.

[3](1882), 52 L.J. Ch. 2 (C.A.).

is treated as a lease by deed for the purpose of the statute of 32 Hen. VIII, c. 34.[4]

The benefit of the following lessees' covenants has been held to run with the reversion: a covenant prohibiting the sale of manure off a farm;[5] a covenant by a lessee of a public house agreeing to take liquor from the lessor.[6]

Several of the provincial Landlord and Tenant Acts[7] provide that upon severance of the reversion, and, notwithstanding an avoidance or cessor of the term granted as to part of the land, every condition or right of entry or other condition in the lease shall be apportioned and remain annexed to the several parts of the reversionary estate in like manner as if the land comprised in the severed part, or the land as to which the term remains subsisting, had alone originally been comprised in the lease.

805.7 Rental Scheme

Owners of neighbouring properties may have mutual rights to enforce negative covenants which the various owners or their predecessors in title entered into with a common vendor if the properties were originally laid out in a building scheme. Analogous to a building scheme, if a property is laid out upon a common rental scheme, the various lessees can enforce the negative covenants by the other lessees. A building let out as flats may constitute a rental scheme.[1] On the other hand the renting of a row of houses does not appear to constitute a rental scheme.[2] The rental of separate lock-up stores in self-contained shopping centres could be considered a rental scheme if the requisite elements exist.[3]

By analogy to a building scheme, the requisites of a rental scheme are: (1) that both the plaintiff and defendant must derive title under a common landlord; (2) that previously to renting the separate premises to which the plaintiff and defendant are respectively entitled, the landlord laid out his estate, or a definite portion thereof (including the separate premises rented by the plaintiff and defendant, respectively) for rental, subject to restrictions intended to be imposed on all premises of the estate, and which, though varying in

---

[4]*Manchester Brewery Co. v. Coombs*, [1901] 2 Ch. 608; *Rickett v. Green*, [1910] 1 K.B. 253; *Rogers v. National Drug & Chemical Co.* (1911), 23 O.L.R. 234 (H.C.J.), affd 24 O.L.R. 486 (C.A.).

[5]*Chapman v. Smith*, [1907] 2 Ch. 97.

[6]*Fleetwood v. Hull* (1889), 23 Q.B.D. 35.

[7]R.S.O. 1980, c. 232, s. 9; R.S.M. 1970, c. L70, s. 8; R.S.N.B. 1973, c. L-1, s. 4; R.S.P.E.I. 1974, c. L-7, s. 5; R.S.S. 1978, c. L-6, s. 7; R.O.N.W.T. 1974, c. L-2, s. 5; R.O.Y.T. 1971, c. L-2, s. 5.

§805.7

[1]*Newman v. Real Estate Debenture Corp., Ltd. and Flower Decorations Ltd.*, [1940] 1 All E.R. 131 (K.B.).

[2]*Ashby v. Wilson*, [1900] 1 Ch. 66.

[3]*Re Spike and Rocca Group Ltd.* (1979), 107 D.L.R. (3d) 62, 23 Nfld. & P.E.I.R. 493 (P.E.I.S.C.).

details as to particular premises, are consistent and consistent only with some general scheme of development; (3) that these restrictions were intended by the common landlord to be, and were, for the benefit of all premises intended to be rented, whether or not they were also intended to be and were for the benefit of other premises retained by the landlord, and (4) that both the plaintiff and defendant or their predecessors in title rented their premises from the common landlord upon the footing that the restrictions subject to which the leases were made were to enure to the benefit of the other premises included in the general scheme, whether or not they were also to enure for the benefit of other premises retained by the landlord.[4]

806. ASSIGNMENT AND SUBLEASE

Because of the differences in the legal relationships created by an assignment of lease on one hand, and a sublease on the other, the distinction between the two must be carefully noted. When a tenant enters into a lease with a landlord there is privity of estate[1] (and privity of contract between the two as the lease operates both as a conveyance and a contract). When the tenant assigns the lease to a third party, the assignee becomes the tenant of the landlord with resulting privity of estate between the two.[2] If there is privity of contract, all covenants are enforceable. If there is privity of estate, but not privity of contract, only those covenants which touch and concern land are enforceable, but no others.[3] If there is no privity of estate or contract, then, apart from restrictive covenants running with the land[4] and apart from the right of an assignee to enforce the benefit of the covenant in certain cases,[5] no covenants are enforceable. Thus, in the case of an assignment, covenants which touch and concern the land are enforceable between the assignee and the landlord.

A sublease creates no direct relationship between the subtenant and the landlord. Hence, there is neither privity of estate nor privity of contract between them.[6] Rather, as between the head tenant and the subtenant, the head tenant stands in the position of landlord vis-à-vis his subtenant, while retaining his position as tenant vis-à-vis his own landlord.

It has been decided that a "sublease" of the entire term operates as an assignment, not a sublease, as there is no reversionary interest left in the

---

[4]*Elliston v. Reacher*, [1908] 2 Ch. 374, affd *loc. cit.* p. 665 (C.A.); *Reid v. Bickerstaff*, [1909] 2 Ch. 305 (C.A.); *Re Wheeler* (1926), 59 O.L.R. 223, [1926] 4 D.L.R. 392 (S.C. App. Div.).

§806

[1]*Milmo v. Carreras*, [1946] 1 K.B. 306 (C.A.).

[2]Williams, *Canadian Law of Landlord and Tenant*, 4th ed. (Toronto, Carswell, 1973), p. 700, and cases cited therein.

[3]Megarry and Wade, *The Law of Real Property*, 4th ed., p. 721.

[4]*Tulk v. Moxhay* (1848), 2 Ph. 774, 41 E.R. 1143.

[5]See ch. 17, *infra*.

[6]*Lawler v. Sutherland* (1852), 9 U.C.Q.B. 205; *Re Aronovitch and Lyons Tours (Canada) Ltd.* (1973), 42 D.L.R. (3d) 701, [1974] 1 W.W.R. 678 (Man. C.A.).

original tenant to support a tenurial relationship between the tenant and the third party.[7] In other words, to create a valid sublease, notwithstanding the words used, the tenant in creating the sublease must reserve the last day of his original term.[8] However, this may not be necessary in Ontario because of a rather curious provision contained in the *Landlord and Tenant Act*.[9] Section 3 of that Act reads:

> 3. The relation of landlord and tenant does not depend on tenure, and a reversion in the lessor is not necessary in order to create the relation of landlord and tenant, or to make applicable the incidents by law belonging to that relation; nor is it necessary, in order to give a landlord the right of distress, that there is an agreement for that purpose between the parties.

The plain language of this section would lead one to assume that a tenant could create a sublease notwithstanding his failure to reserve to himself some residue of the original term.[10]

An assignment will operate at law upon the death of the lessor[11] or the lessee,[12] by legal process[13] or bankruptcy.[14] However, the area that gives rise to difficulty is an *inter vivos* transfer of the term by the tenant. It has been decided that a legal lease must be transferred by deed.[15] However, an assignment not made by deed, and thus void at law, may operate as an agreement if supported by writing or part performance.[16]

Often the lease will contain a covenant prohibiting the tenant from assigning or subletting, or parting with possession, without the consent of the landlord. Various provincial Short Forms Acts contain such a provision.[17] Such a pro-

---

[7]*Spencer's Case* (1583), 5 Co. Rep. 16 a, 77 E.R. 72; *Hicks v. Downing alias Smith v. Baker* (1696), 1 Ld. Raym. 99, 91 E.R. 962; *Milmo v. Carreras, supra*, footnote 1; *Mount Citadel Ltd. v. Ibar Developments Ltd. and two other actions* (1976), 14 O.R. (2d) 318, 73 D.L.R. (3d) 584 (H.C.J.); *Gaumont v. Luz* (1980), 111 D.L.R. (3d) 609, [1980] 5 W.W.R. 533 (Alta. C.A.).
[8]Megarry and Wade, *The Law of Real Property*, 4th ed., p. 651.
[9]R.S.O. 1980, c. 232.
[10]For an interesting, if speculative, discussion of this possibility, see Scane, "The Relationship of Landlord and Tenant", in *Law Society of Upper Canada Special Lectures on The Lease in Modern Business*, 1965, 1. See also *Kennedy v. Agricultural Development Board* (1926), 59 O.L.R. 374, [1926] 4 D.L.R. 717 (H.C.).
[11]*Doe d. Wright v. Smith* (1838), 8 Ad. & E. 255, 112 E.R. 835.
[12]*Mellows v. Low*, [1923] 1 K.B. 522 (C.A.).
[13]This means execution by a judgment creditor.
[14]*Bankruptcy Act*, R.S.C. 1970, c. B-3, s. 50(5).
[15]*Statute of Frauds*, R.S.O. 1980, c. 481, s. 2; *Cornish v. Boles* (1914), 31 O.L.R. 505, 19 D.L.R. 447 (S.C. App. Div.).
[16]*Cornish v. Boles, supra*, footnote 15. As to what constitutes a seal, see *Procopia v. D'Abbondanzo*, [1973] 3 O.R. 8, 35 D.L.R. (3d) 641 (H.C.J.), vard 8 O.R. (2d) 496, 58 D.L.R. (3d) 368 *sub nom. Procopio v. D'Abbondanza* (C.A.).
[17]*Short Forms of Leases Act*, R.S.O. 1980, c. 473; *Land Transfer Form Act*, R.S.B.C. 1979, c. 221; *Real Property Act*, R.S.P.E.I. 1974, c. R-4, Part IV; *Conveyancing Act*, R.S.N. 1970, c. 63, s. 11; R.S.N.S. 1967, c. 56; *Short Forms Act*, R.S.M. 1970, c. S120; *Land Titles Act*, R.S.A. 1980, c. L-5, s. 102; R.S.S. 1978, c. L-5, s. 123; R.S.C. 1970, c. L-4, s. 92.

vision is necessary to restrict the tenant's right to assign or sublet, as the right to assign or sublet is an incident of the tenant's estate.[18] In the absence of any express restriction on the tenant's right to assign or sublet, the landlord is not entitled to have such a restriction implied.[19]

The express covenant will be strictly construed against the landlord and hence, a covenant not to assign was held not to prohibit a subletting or parting with possession.[20]

Many of the provincial Landlord and Tenant Acts contain sections providing that, in every covenant restricting assignment or subletting without leave, leave shall not be unreasonably withheld unless the lease so specifically provides.[21] With residential tenancies, the provincial Acts in general, subject to some variation, provide that the lease cannot prohibit subletting or assignment, but may require the consent of the landlord, such consent not to be unreasonably withheld.[22]

It has been held that an equitable assignment does not breach the covenant not to assign without leave as the assignment must be one at law.[23] An assignment by operation of law is not a breach of the covenant. Rather, a voluntary act by the tenant is contemplated. Thus, the vesting in a trustee on the bankruptcy of the tenant, even where the tenant petitions, is not a breach.[24] An advertisement to assign does not amount to an assignment and thus is itself not a breach of the covenant.[25] Moreover, the covenant has been held to apply

---

[18]*Paul v. Nurse and Nurse* (1828), 8 B. & C. 486, 108 E.R. 1123; *Scala House and District Property Co. Ltd. v. Forbes*, [1973] 3 All E.R. 308 (C.A.).

[19]*Hampshire v. Wickens* (1878), 7 Ch. D. 555.

[20]*Church v. Brown* (1808), 15 Ves. Jun. 258 at p. 265, 33 E.R. 752. However, a covenant against subletting will restrict an assignment: *Greenaway v. Adams* (1806), 12 Ves. Jun. 395, 33 E.R. 149.

[21]*Landlord and Tenant Act*, R.S.M. 1970, c. L70, s. 22(1); R.S.N.B. 1973, c. L-1, s. 11(1)(a); R.S.P.E.I. 1974, c. L-7, s. 12(1)(a); R.S.S. 1978, c. L-6, s. 13; R.S.O. 1980, c. 232, s. 23(1); *Landlord and Tenant Ordinance*, R.O.N.W.T. 1974, c. L-2, s. 12(1)(a); R.O.Y.T. 1971, c. L-2, s. 12(1)(a). See also *Re Bathurst Manor Cigar Store Ltd. and Bathurst Manor Shopping Plaza Ltd.*, [1968] 2 O.R. 829 (Co. Ct.).

[22]*Residential Tenancy Act*, S.B.C. 1984, c. 15, s. 12; *Residential Tenancies Act*, S.N.B. 1975, c. R-10.2, s. 13; S.N.S. 1970, c. 13, s. 6(1), stat. con. 4; R.S.S. 1978, c. R-22, s. 20(1), stat. con. 8; *Landlord and Tenant Act*, R.S.O. 1980, c. 232, s. 91; R.S.M. 1970, c. L70, s. 93, enacted 1970, c. 106, s. 3; R.S.P.E.I. 1974, c. L-7, s. 92; *Landlord and Tenant (Residential Tenancies) Act*, S.N. 1973, No. 54, s. 7(1), stat. con. 3; *Landlord and Tenant Ordinance*, R.O.N.W.T. 1974, c. L-2, s. 56; R.O.Y.T. 1971, c. L-2, s. 70, enacted 1972, c. 20, s. 1. The right to assign or sublet comes to an end on the expiry of the lease and does not continue when the tenant remains in possession on a month-to-month basis: see *Re Lifshitz and Forest Square Apartments Ltd.* (1982), 36 O.R. (2d) 175, 134 D.L.R. (3d) 144 (Div. Ct.).

[23]*Gentle v. Faulkner*, [1900] 2 Q.B. 267 (C.A.).

[24]*Woodfall, Law of Landlord and Tenant*, 28th ed. (London, Sweet & Maxwell, 1978), 1-1203; *Re Riggs, Ex p. Lovell*, [1901] 2 K.B. 16. See also *Maleganos v. Uncle Tom's Drive-In Ltd.* (1976), 12 O.R. (2d) 477, 69 D.L.R. (3d) 365 (Co. Ct.), affd 15 O.R. (2d) 14, 74 D.L.R. (3d) 760 (Div. Ct.).

[25]*Woodfall*, 1-1191.

only to *inter vivos* transfers and does not restrict a devise of the term by the tenant.[26]

A covenant restricting the tenant's right to part with possession is not breached if the tenant retains possession while allowing a third person to use the premises, for example, by way of licence.[27] However, if the covenant restricts the area or occupation of the premises, the covenant will be considered as more than a covenant not to part with possession.[28] The concept of parting with possession requires more than the sharing of premises with another. It connotes a withdrawal from the premises in favour of another.[29] It has been held that an option given by the tenant for the remainder of a term amounted to an "assignment" even though the assignment itself would not take place until the exercise of the option.[30]

If the covenant requires written consent, oral consent will not suffice.[31] The covenant is breached even if through mistake or forgetfulness, notwithstanding the consent, if asked for, could not reasonably have been refused.[32]

The covenant runs with the land and binds assigns of the lessee. Thus, a reassignment by an assign to the original lessee made without consent is a breach of the covenant.[33]

An assignment made in breach of the covenant is effective to vest the tenant's estate in the assignee, subject to the landlord's right of entry.[34] Similarly, a sublease made in breach of the covenant vests the interest in the subtenant, subject to the landlord's right of entry.[35]

If the lease is silent as to the effect of a breach of the covenant, there is no right of entry in the landlord unless given by statute.[36] However, in the common situation the lease will provide for a right of entry for breach of the covenant. If the breach of the covenant amounts to forfeiture, the court may grant relief from forfeiture when all the circumstances are considered. In general, the tenant must show himself blameless and take all reasonable precautions either to prevent forfeiture or to rectify the situation without delay.[37]

---

[26]*Ibid.*, 1-1207.

[27]*Ibid.*, 1-1195.

[28]*Ibid.*

[29]*Stapleton Enterprises of Manitoba Ltd. v. Bramer Machine Shop Ltd.* (1977), 81 D.L.R. (3d) 717, [1978] 1 W.W.R. 297 (Man. Q.B.).

[30]*Saskatchewan Minerals v. Keyes* (1971), 23 D.L.R. (3d) 573, [1972] S.C.R. 703.

[31]*Roe d. Gregson v. Harrison* (1788), 2 T.R. 425, 100 E.R. 229 (K.B.).

[32]*Woodfall, op. cit., supra*, footnote 24, 1-1193.

[33]*Goldstein v. Sanders*, [1915] 1 Ch. 549; *Woodfall, op. cit.*, footnote 24, 1-1200.

[34]*Paul v. Nurse and Nurse* (1828), 8 B. & C. 486, 108 E.R. 1123.

[35]*Parker v. Jones*, [1910] 2 K.B. 32.

[36]*Mount Citadel Ltd. v. Ibar Developments Ltd. and two other actions* (1976), 14 O.R. (2d) 318, 73 D.L.R. (3d) 584 (H.C.J.). Similarly if there is no clause in the lease forfeiting for non-performance of covenants, an assignment in breach of the covenant will not amount to a forfeiture: *Re Kutasy and Kelly* (1978), 19 O.R. (2d) 589, 88 D.L.R. (3d) 119 (Div. Ct.).

[37]*Re Jawanda and Walji* (1975), 10 O.R. (2d) 527, 63 D.L.R. (3d) 639 (Div. Ct.); *Wakefield v. Cottingham*, [1959] O.R. 551, 19 D.L.R. (2d) 511 (C.A.); *Lam Kee Ying Sdn. Bhd. v. Lam Shes Tong trading as Lian Joo Co.*, [1975] A.C. 247 (P.C.).

Relief will be granted where the breach is capable of remedy and has been remedied.[38] Moreover, the forfeiture may be waived if the landlord accepts rent due after the breach.[39] Acceptance of rent after the bringing of an action for possession does not amount to a waiver as the bringing of the action is an irrevocable election to terminate the tenancy.[40]

Where the covenant provides that consent may not be withheld unreasonably and the landlord withholds consent unreasonably, the tenant may assign without consent as he is released from his covenant by the unreasonable refusal.[41] Several cases have concluded that the landlord must base his refusal either on the nature or personality of the assignee or the effect of the assignment on the value of the property and not merely on grounds personal to the landlord.[42] However, Lord Denning has suggested[43] that the earlier cases do not lay down any fixed principle of law, and that the reasonableness of the refusal must be tested by the circumstances of each case.[44] The onus of satisfying the landlord of the suitability of the assignee lies on the tenant.[45]

Under a commercial lease, a subtenant can apply for relief from forfeiture where the landlord is exercising a right of forfeiture.[46] Under a residential lease, since the subtenant is included in the definition of "tenant", he may seek relief from forfeiture where the landlord seeks possession.[47]

Again, under a commercial tenancy, the goods and chattels of the assignee

---

[38]*Re Vanek and Bomza; Re BP Canada Ltd. and Bomza* (1976), 14 O.R. (2d) 508, 74 D.L.R. (3d) 175 (H.C.J.).

[39]*Roe d. Gregson v. Harrison* (1788), 2 T.R. 425, 100 E.R. 229 (K.B.).

[40]*Civil Service Co-operative Society, Ltd. v. Trustee of McGrigor*, [1923] 2 Ch. 347. The bringing of the action suffices as a declaration of the landlord's intent to exercise any right of forfeiture: *Com'rs of Works v. Hull*, [1922] 1 K.B. 205.

[41]*Treloar v. Bigge* (1874), L.R. 9 Exch. 151.

[42]*Re Gibbs and Houlder Brothers & Co., Ltd.'s Lease; Houlder Brothers & Co., Ltd. v. Gibbs*, [1925] Ch. 575 (C.A.); *Bates v. Donaldson*, [1896] 2 Q.B. 241 (C.A.); *Viscount Tredegar v. Harwood*, [1929] A.C. 72 (H.L.); *Re Town Investments Ltd. Underlease*; *McLaughlin v. Town Investments Ltd.*, [1954] Ch. 301; *Premier Confectionery (London) Co., Ltd. v. London Commercial Sale Rooms, Ltd.*, [1933] Ch. 904; *Pimms, Ltd. v. Tallow Chandlers in City of London*, [1964] 2 All E.R. 145 (C.A.). See also *Coopers & Lybrand Ltd. v. William Schwartz Construction Co. Ltd.* (1980), 116 D.L.R. (3d) 450, 36 C.B.R. (N.S.) 265 (Alta. Q.B.).

[43]*Bickel v. Duke of Westminster*, [1976] 3 All E.R. 801 (C.A.), at pp. 804-5. See also *Toronto Housing Co. Ltd. v. Postal Promotions Ltd.* (1981), 34 O.R. (2d) 218, 128 D.L.R. (3d) 51 (H.C.J.), affd 140 D.L.R. (3d) 117 (C.A.); *Re Acklands Leasehold Properties Ltd. and Steehild Investments Ltd.* (1981), 127 D.L.R. (3d) 646 (Ont. C.A.).

[44]*Bickel v. Duke of Westminster, supra,* footnote 43. See also *Re Griff and Sommerset Management Services Ltd.* (1978), 19 O.R. (2d) 209, 84 D.L.R. (3d) 386 (C.A.). The court in this case preferred to be bound by earlier decisions when considering an attempt by a trustee in bankruptcy to assign a lease pursuant to section 38(2) of the *Landlord and Tenant Act*, R.S.O. 1980, c. 232.

[45]*Re FigurMagic Int'l Ltd.* (1974), 19 C.B.R. (N.S.) 92 (Ont. S.C.), leave to appeal granted on condition 19 C.B.R. (N.S.) 310.

[46]*Landlord and Tenant Act*, R.S.O. 1980, c. 232, s. 21; R.S.M. 1970, c. L70, s. 20; R.S.N.B. 1973, c. L-1, s. 15; R.S.P.E.I. 1974, c. L-7, s. 16; R.S.S. 1978, c. L-6, s. 11; *Landlord and Tenant Ordinance*, R.O.N.W.T. 1974, c. L-2, s. 47; R.O.Y.T. 1971, c. L-2, s. 59.

[47]*Re Baker and Hayward* (1977), 16 O.R. (2d) 695, 78 D.L.R. (3d) 762 (C.A.).

or subtenant on the premises are subject to distress,[48] but the subtenant may serve the landlord with a declaration stating that the original tenant has no interest in the goods distrained, setting forth the amount due as rent to the original tenant and upon payment of that amount, may discharge the goods and chattels from the distress.[49]

A breach of the covenant is not capable of remedy and the landlord need not send notice to the tenant requiring him to remedy the breach before pursuing his remedies.[50] However, such a notice is required by most provincial Landlord and Tenant Acts.[51]

The measure of damages for a breach of the covenant is that which will put the landlord in the same position as if the breach had not occurred, and the range of damages extends from nominal to special damages.[52]

807. TRANSFER OF THE REVERSION

A grant or assignment of the reversion creates the relationship of landlord and tenant between the assignee and tenant without the need for attornment by the tenant,[1] although the assignment itself must be by deed.[2] A purchaser of the reversion takes the reversion subject to the provisions of land recordation Acts which may void the lease as against the purchaser if it is unregistered. Where the lease need be registered, and it is not, acceptance of rent by the purchaser on a monthly basis does not revive the lease, but rather creates a monthly tenancy.[3]

The assignee of the reversion takes subject to the benefits and obligations of the covenants which run with the land, as there exists privity of estate between the assignee and tenant.[4] The Landlord and Tenant Acts of some provinces expressly provide that the assignee of the reversion may enforce every condition of re-entry or forfeiture even where the assignee became so

---

[48]For example, *Landlord and Tenant Act*, R.S.O. 1980, c. 232, s. 31; R.S.N.B. 1973, c. L-1, s. 34(1); R.S.M. 1970, c. L70, s. 37.

[49]For example, *Landlord and Tenant Act*, R.S.O. 1980, c. 232, s. 32.

[50]*Scala House and District Property Co. Ltd. v. Forbes*, [1973] 3 All E.R. 308 (C.A.), but see *Mount Citadel Ltd. v. Ibar Developments Ltd. and two other actions* (1976), 14 O.R. (2d) 318, 73 D.L.R. (3d) 584 (H.C.J.).

[51]As, for example, section 19(2) of the *Landlord and Tenant Act*, R.S.O. 1980, c. 232.

[52]*Swanson v. Forton*, [1949] Ch. 143 (C.A.).

§807

[1]*Landlord and Tenant Act*, R.S.O. 1980, c. 232, s. 62; R.S.M. 1970, c. L70, s. 56; R.S.N.B. 1973, c. L-1, s. 46; R.S.P.E.I. 1974, c. L-7, s. 22; R.S.S. 1978, c. L-6, s. 60; *Commercial Tenancy Act*, R.S.B.C. 1979, c. 54, s. 14; *Landlord and Tenant Ordinance*, R.O.N.W.T. 1974, c. L-2, s. 28; R.O.Y.T. 1971, c. L-2, s. 40.

[2]*Conveyancing and Law of Property Act*, R.S.O. 1980, c. 90, s. 9.

[3]*Ronan v. Derheim* (1977), 78 D.L.R. (3d) 622, 4 A.R. 192 (S.C. App. Div.).

[4]*Landlord and Tenant Act*, R.S.O. 1980, c. 232, ss. 4-8; R.S.A. 1980, c. L-6, s. 19; R.S.M. 1970, c. L70, ss. 3-7; R.S.N.B. 1973, c. L-1, ss. 2, 3; R.S.P.E.I. 1974, c. L-7, ss. 2-4; R.S.S. 1978, c. L-6, ss. 3-6; *Landlord and Tenant Ordinance*, R.O.N.W.T. 1974, c. L-2, ss. 3, 4; R.O.Y.T. 1971, c. L-2, ss. 3, 4.

entitled after the right of re-entry or forfeiture became enforceable.[5] Even where there is no privity of estate between an assignee of the reversion and the original tenant, the assignee may enforce a covenant to pay rent.[6]

808. OPTIONS AND RENEWALS

In general, an option to purchase the fee given to a tenant in a lease is enforceable in the same way as any other option.[1] It is not, in the absence of special provisions, a term of the tenancy. It may be enforced by a decree of specific performance.[2] Once the option is exercised, the tenant becomes the owner of the property in equity and subsequent default under the lease does not impair his rights as a purchaser.[3] In many instances the option will be stated to be exercisable within the term of the lease, or a part thereof, and must be exercised within the stated period.[4] Thus, where an option is said to be exercisable within the fixed term of the lease, and the tenant overholds as a monthly tenant, the option is lost at the end of the original term.[5]

It had been held that as between the original contracting parties, an option to purchase exercisable through the term of a ninety-nine-year lease does not offend the rule against perpetuities,[6] but, apart from statute, the position now appears to be that such an option does offend the rule.[7]

Whether the option may be exercisable at a time when the tenant is in default under the lease depends upon the intention of the parties. Where the option is exercisable during the term of the lease and default occurs, but where the landlord has not yet terminated the lease, the option is still exercisable.[8]

A contract to renew the lease on the same terms and conditions permits the tenant to renew, but without any further right of renewal.[9] This right is also

---

[5]*Landlord and Tenant Act*, R.S.O. 1980, c. 232, s. 6; R.S.M. 1970, c. L70, s. 5; R.S.N.B. 1973, c. L-1, s. 2(3); R.S.P.E.I. 1974, c. L-7, s. 2(3); *Landlord and Tenant Ordinance*, R.O.N.W.T. 1974, c. L-2, s. 3(3); R.O.Y.T. 1971, c. L-2, s. 3(3).
[6]*Arlesford Trading Co. Ltd. v. Servansingh*, [1971] 1 W.L.R. 1080 (C.A.).
§808
[1]See ch. 11, *infra*. The option is subject to the rule against perpetuities: *Roberts v. Hanson* (1981), 120 D.L.R. (3d) 299, 28 A.R. 271 (C.A.), leave to appeal to S.C.C. refused 38 N.R. 87n, 29 A.R. 450n.
[2]*Brown v. Moore* (1921), 62 D.L.R. 483, 62 S.C.R. 487.
[3]*Canadian Petrofina Ltd. v. Berger* (1962), 35 D.L.R. (2d) 440, [1962] S.C.R. 652.
[4]*Ibid*. In the absence of any express terms it has been suggested that the option may be exercised so long as the tenant remains in possession with the consent of the landlord: *Re Friendly and Wilkinson-Kompass Ltd.*, [1968] 2 O.R. 749 (H.C.J.) and cases cited therein, revd on other grounds [1969] 1 O.R. 611, 3 D.L.R. (3d) 343 (C.A.).
[5]*Rafael v. Crystal*, [1966] 2 O.R. 733, 58 D.L.R. (2d) 325 (H.C.J.).
[6]*Re Kennedy and Beaucage Mines Ltd.*, [1959] O.R. 625, 20 D.L.R. (2d) 1 (C.A.).
[7]*Harris v. Minister of National Revenue* (1966), 57 D.L.R. (2d) 403, [1966] S.C.R. 489.
[8]*Re Kennedy and Beaucage Mines Ltd.*, supra, footnote 6.
[9]*Re Fice and Department of Public Works of Ontario* (1921), 50 O.L.R. 501, 64 D.L.R. 535 (S.C. App. Div.).

enforceable by specific performance[10] and if not merely personal, the right runs with the land.[11] Although a subtenant under a sublease containing a right of renewal cannot compel the landlord to renew under a renewal clause in the head lease, he can compel the tenant to exercise his right of renewal in the head lease,[12] and if the tenant does exercise his right of renewal, the subtenant is entitled to enforce his right of renewal so long as the tenant holds the premises.[13]

In *Blomidon Mercury Sales Ltd. v. John Piercey's Auto Body Shop Ltd.*[14] the court concluded that where the lease does not specify when or how the option is exercisable, the lessee's remaining in possession after the expiration of the term is a valid exercise of the option.

809. TERMINATION

809.1 Notice to Terminate

In the case of commercial tenancies, the general rule determining the length of notice is fixed by common law, not statute.[1] Although there is some inconsistency in the earlier cases[2] which referred to the necessity of reasonable notice, generally, in the absence of a special agreement or statutory provision, a tenancy from year to year is determinable by a half-year's notice expiring at the end of some year of the tenancy.[3]

The notice must clearly indicate when the premises are to be vacated and must not be subject to any contingency. It need not be in any particular form

---

[10]*Ibid.*

[11]*Alexander v. Herman* (1912), 21 O.W.R. 461; *Calford Properties Ltd. v. Zeller's (Western) Ltd.*, [1972] 5 W.W.R. 714 (Alta. S.C. App. Div.).

[12]*Dental Co. of Canada Ltd. v. Sperry Rand Canada Ltd.* (1971), 17 D.L.R. (3d) 738, [1971] S.C.R. 266.

[13]*Ramey v. Fenety* (1973), 8 N.B.R. (2d) 679 (S.C.). As to the application of the doctrine of estoppel to the right of renewal, see *Kelly, Douglas & Co. Ltd. v. Ladner Shopping Centre Ltd.* (1980), 114 D.L.R. (3d) 139, 22 B.C.L.R. 343 (C.A.), leave to appeal to S.C.C. refused D.L.R. *loc. cit.*, 33 N.R. 583*n*.

[14](1981), 129 D.L.R. (3d) 630, 33 Nfld. & P.E.I.R. 462 (Nfld. S.C.T.D.).

§809.1

[1]The Landlord and Tenant Acts of Prince Edward Island (R.S.P.E.I. 1974, c. L-7, s. 19(1)(*c*)) and New Brunswick (R.S.N.B. 1973, c. L-1, s. 19(1)(*c*)) provide that subject to any express agreement to the contrary, sufficient notice to quit shall be deemed to have been given if there is given in the case of a tenancy from year to year, three months' notice ending, in the case of a tenancy originally from year to year, with an anniversary of the last day of the first year thereof, and in the case of all tenancies from year to year, with an anniversary of the last day of the original tenancy, provided that in the case of an agricultural lease, not less than six months' notice to quit shall be given. Similar legislation is found in Alberta (R.S.A. 1980, c. L-6, s. 7), the Northwest Territories (R.O.N.W.T. 1974, c. L-2, s. 17(1)(*c*)) and the Yukon (R.O.Y.T. 1971, c. L-2, s. 17(1)(*c*)).

[2]*Doe d. Martin and Jones v. Watts* (1797), 7 T.R. 83 at p. 85, 101 E.R. 866.

[3]*Sidebotham v. Holland*, [1895] 1 Q.B. 378 (C.A.); *Walker v. Oram*, [1929] 3 D.L.R. 734, [1929] 1 W.W.R. 876 (Alta. S.C.).

and errors in it will not invalidate it if the tenant is not misled. Thus, where a lease permitted both parties to terminate upon either one year's notice or three months' notice upon payment of fixed compensation, a notice by the landlord to terminate on one year's notice, while attempting to keep alive his right to terminate on three months' notice was not equivocal and ineffective.[4] Similarly, a notice to terminate upon two alternative dates, one of which was the last day of the tenancy "next following the giving of notice" was held not to be ambiguous.[5]

A notice to quit may be verbal.[6]

A contractual right to give notice to quit will be governed by the construction put on the contractual terms. Hence, a right to give notice upon sale by the landlord did not permit the purchaser to terminate the tenancy after the sale.[7]

A notice to quit must be given by or to the landlord or his agent and by or to the tenant or an agent authorized for the purpose. A servant of the tenant at his dwelling-house is his implied agent and, apart from the question of agency, a notice to quit served on the wife of the tenant at the demised premises is sufficient.

If a letter, properly directed, containing a notice to quit, is proved to have been put in the post office, it is presumed that it reached its destination at the proper time in the regular course of business of the post office and was received by the person to whom it was addressed.[8] The time of such delivery is the time of service.[9]

At common law, in the absence of special agreement, a periodic tenancy is determinable by a notice to quit equal to the length of the period and expiring at the end of a complete period.[10]

In several provinces the Landlord and Tenant Acts provide that a week's notice to quit and a month's notice to quit, respectively, ending with the week or month, are sufficient notice to determine, respectively, a weekly or monthly tenancy.[11]

A tenancy at will is determinable by either party expressly or impliedly intimating to the other his wish to put an end to the tenancy. Until that occurs, the tenant is lawfully in possession and, unless the tenancy has been otherwise

---

[4] Re Yonge-Rosedale Developments Ltd. and Levitt (1975), 9 O.R. (2d) 258 (Co. Ct.), vard 12 O.R. (2d) 129 (Div. Ct.).
[5] Municipality of Metropolitan Toronto v. Atkinson (1977), 78 D.L.R. (3d) 142, [1978] 1 S.C.R. 918.
[6] Gemeroy v. Proverbs, [1924] 3 D.L.R. 579, [1924] 2 W.W.R. 764 (Sask. C.A.).
[7] Re Marathon Grill Ltd. and Plaid Place Ltd. (1981), 119 D.L.R. (3d) 510, 45 N.S.R. (2d) 50 (S.C. App. Div.).
[8] Gresham House Estate Co. v. Rossa Grande Gold Mining Co., [1870] W.N. 119.
[9] R. v. Inhabitants of Slawstone (1852), 18 Q.B. 388, 118 E.R. 145.
[10] Eastman v. Richard & Co. (1899), 29 S.C.R. 438; Queen's Club Gardens Estates, Ltd. v. Bignell, [1924] 1 K.B. 117.
[11] R.S.O. 1980, c. 232, s. 28; R.S.A. 1980, c. L-6, ss. 5, 6; R.S.S. 1978, c. L-6, s. 18; R.S.M. 1970, c. L70, s. 27; R.S.N.B. 1973, c. L-1, s. 19; R.S.P.E.I. 1974, c. L-7, s. 19; R.O.N.W.T. 1974, c. L-2, s. 17; R.O.Y.T. 1971, c. L-2, s. 17.

determined, the landlord cannot recover possession without a previous demand of possession. Anything that amounts to a demand of possession, although not expressed in precise and formal language, is sufficient to indicate the determination of the landlord's will.[12] A landlord impliedly determines a tenancy at will when he does any act on the premises which is inconsistent with the continuance of the tenancy, such as an entry upon the land to take possession and put an end to the tenancy.[13] When acts occur upon the land which would determine a tenancy at will, the tenant is presumed to be there and to know of the acts.[14]

A tenant will impliedly determine a tenancy at will when he does an act which is inconsistent with the tenancy, as where he cuts down trees and pulls down houses or otherwise commits voluntary waste[15] and he thereby becomes a trespasser *ab initio*; that is, the tenancy is not only determined but treated as if it had never existed.[16]

Because the relation between the parties of a tenancy at will is personal, the general rule is that the death of either party determines a tenancy at will[17] and in such cases no demand of possession is necessary.

For the purpose of the *Statute of Limitations* and the barring of the landlord's right to make an entry or recover possession, a tenancy at will is deemed to have been determined at the end of one year from its commencement unless it is determined sooner.[18]

No notice is required to determine a tenancy at sufferance and the landlord may enter or the tenant leave at any time without notice.

The acceptance of rent after a notice to quit has been given and during ejectment proceedings is dangerous as it may amount to a waiver by the landlord of the notice to quit or it may create a new tenancy.[19] A landlord may, however, safely collect rent until the end of the term.[20]

In *Davenport v. The Queen*[21] the Privy Council held that "where money is paid and received as rent under a lease a mere protest that is accepted conditionally and without prejudice to the right to insist upon a prior forfeiture, cannot countervail the fact of such receipt". Such a reservation avails the

---

[12]*Doe d. Price v. Price* (1832), 9 Bing. 356, 131 E.R. 649.

[13]Co. Litt. 55b; *Woodworth v. Thomas* (1892), 25 N.S.R. 42 (S.C.).

[14]*Pinhorn v. Souster* (1853), 8 Ex. 763 at p. 770, 155 E.R. 1560.

[15]*Countess of Shrewsbury's Case* (1600), 5 Co. Rep. 13 b, 77 E.R. 68; *Kokatt v. Melidonis* (1920), 55 D.L.R. 155, [1920] 3 W.W.R. 800 (Sask. C.A.).

[16]*Pollock's Law of Torts*, 15th ed. by Landon (London, Stevens, 1951), pp. 281, 297-8.

[17]*Robertson v. Bannerman* (1858), 17 U.C.Q.B. 508; *Doe d. Green v. Higgins* (1874), 1 P.E.I.R. 466 (S.C.).

[18]See ch. 31, "Limitations", *infra*.

[19]*R. M. Ballantyne Co. Ltd. v. Olympic Knit & Sportswear Ltd.*, [1965] 2 O.R. 356, 50 D.L.R. (2d) 583 (C.A.), but see *Trustee of Estate of Royal Inns Canada Ltd. v. Bolus-Revelas-Bolus Ltd.* (1981), 33 O.R. (2d) 260, 124 D.L.R. (3d) 95 (S.C. in Bankruptcy), revd on other grounds 37 O.R. (2d) 339, 136 D.L.R. (3d) 272 (C.A.).

[20]*Toronto General Trusts Corp., Malone and McCarthy v. Sidney I. Robinson Fur Co.*, [1945] 3 W.W.R. 688 (Sask. Dist. Ct.), affd [1946] 1 W.W.R. 137 (K.B.); *Banrevi v. Larman*, [1953] O.W.N. 210, [1953] 2 D.L.R. 619 (Co. Ct.).

[21](1877), 3 App. Cas. 115 (P.C.). See also *Chernec v. Smith*, [1946] O.W.N. 513, [1946] 3 D.L.R. 765 (C.A.).

landlord nothing and is ineffective. Where a cheque in payment of rent for the month immediately after the expiry of the term of the notice to quit was accepted and held with the intention of using it for use and occupation pending an application for an order for possession and this intention was not communicated to the tenant at the time the cheque was received, it was held that the notice to quit went for nothing and the tenancy continued. The landlord, having retained the cheque with the intention of using it, must be deemed to have used it for the purpose for which it was sent.[22] These judgments should not be taken for authority that the acceptance of rent after a notice to quit for a period prior to the date of termination of the tenancy amounts to a waiver of the notice to quit.[23]

Payments made after the expiration of a notice to quit which are expressly treated by the parties as being payments for use and occupation will not create an implied tenancy even if the payments are for any periodic term, such as a month.[24] Where hearing of an application for possession was adjourned for six months, acceptance in the interval of sums equivalent to the original rent was held not to constitute waiver of the notice.[25]

In *Suwala v. Prociw*[26] a landlord brought proceedings for possession after expiration of a notice to quit. After dismissal of his application, he accepted and cashed money orders for rent accrued up to and including the month in which his application was dismissed and for the period pending the hearing of his appeal which was subsequently allowed. He retained without cashing the money orders sent for rent for the months prior to that time when the appeal was heard. It was held that the acceptance and retention of the money orders could not be regarded as evidence of a new tenancy.

Where a tenant became entitled to remain in possession after the time specified in the notice to quit, not by reason of any agreement between himself and the landlord, but by reason of certain war orders having the force of a statute and the landlord was powerless to dispossess him, it was held that the acceptance of rent during the prescribed period could not be evidence of an agreement for a new tenancy on the old terms.[27]

Residential tenancies and notice to terminate

Residential tenancies and notice requirements for termination thereof are dealt with specifically by legislation. In Ontario, the statute[28] provides that no tenancy, whether periodic or for a term certain, may be terminated by either

---

[22]*Ucci v. Livingstone*, [1946] O.W.N. 861 (C.A.); *McIntyre v. Bird*, [1946] O.W.N. 905 (C.A.); *R. M. Ballantyne Co. Ltd. v. Olympic Knit & Sportswear*, supra, footnote 19; *Central Estates (Belgravia) Ltd. v. Woolgar (No. 2)*, [1972] 1 W.L.R. 1048 (C.A.).

[23]Arnup, "Recent Cases on Rental Regulations", 25 Can. Bar Rev. 625 (1947), at p. 630; *Dobson v. Sootheran* (1887), 15 O.R. 15 (H.C.J.).

[24]*McIntyre v. Bird*, supra, footnote 22; Arnup, *op. cit.*, footnote 23, at pp. 632-3.

[25]*Sammon v. Cawley* (1919), 53 I.L.T. 224.

[26][1949] O.W.N. 33, [1949] 1 D.L.R. 340 (H.C.J.).

[27]*Burns v. Hodgson*, [1945] O.R. 876, [1946] 1 D.L.R. 510 (C.A.); *Labunda v. Sit Hing Fong* (1951), 4 W.W.R. (N.S.) 575 (B.C.S.C.).

[28]*Landlord and Tenant Act*, R.S.O. 1980, c. 232, s. 98.

landlord or tenant except in accordance with the statute, unless expressly provided otherwise by the statute. A somewhat similar provision is found in the Manitoba Act.[28a]

The British Columbia statute has several specific provisions which permit termination under a variety of circumstances.[29]

In other provinces, the legislation requires only that the requisite notice be given to terminate periodic tenancies[30] and, in some jurisdictions, the legislation[31] provides that the landlord and tenant may mutually agree upon the means of termination. The length of notice varies with the term of the periodic tenancy.[32] In Manitoba,[33] a landlord under a tenancy for a term certain must submit to the tenant a new tenancy agreement, for a year term, at least three months prior to the expiry of the original agreement. The tenant then must accept or reject the new agreement at least two months prior to the expiry of the original term. The Act permits the parties to agree to do otherwise. If the tenant fails to execute the agreement he is deemed to have given notice of his intention to terminate at the end of the fixed term. Conversely, if the landlord fails to submit the new agreement the original agreement is deemed to have been renewed for a further six months.

The Ontario and British Columbia statutes have separate notice periods if the landlord requires the premises for his personal use or the use of his family,[34] or for the purpose of demolition, extensive repairs, renovation or conversion to a non-residential use or condominium.[35] In British Columbia a sale to a purchaser who intends to use the property for his own use also allows

---

28aLandlord and Tenant Act, R.S.M. 1970, c. L70, s. 100, enacted 1970, c. 106, s. 3; am. 1971, c. 35, s. 12.

29Residential Tenancy Act, S.B.C. 1984, c. 15, s. 23.

30Residential Tenancies Act, S.N.B. 1975, c. R-10.2, s. 24; S.N.S. 1970, c. 13, s. 7, am. 1970-71, c. 74, s. 3; 1975, c. 64, s. 4; Landlord and Tenant (Residential Tenancies) Act, S.N. 1973, No. 54, s. 15; Landlord and Tenant Act, R.S.A. 1980, c. L-6, s. 4; R.S.P.E.I. 1974, c. L-7, s. 110; Landlord and Tenant Ordinance, R.O.N.W.T. 1974, c. L-2, s. 62; R.O.Y.T. 1971, c. L-2, s. 78, enacted 1972, c. 20, s. 1.

31See, for example, Residential Tenancies Act, R.S.S. 1978, c. R-22, s. 22.

32Landlord and Tenant Act, R.S.O. 1980, c. 232, ss. 100-102; R.S.A. 1980, c. L-6, ss. 6-8; R.S.M. 1970, c. L70, s. 103, enacted 1970, c. 106, s. 3; re-enacted 1971, c. 35, s. 15; am. 1972, c. 39, s. 4; 1975, c. 37, ss. 8, 9; 1977, c. 23, s. 15; 1980, c. 60, ss. 18-20; R.S.P.E.I. 1974, c. L-7, ss. 107-109, am. 1981, c. 19, s. 2; Landlord and Tenant (Residential Tenancies) Act, S.N. 1973, No. 54, s. 15; Residential Tenancy Act, S.B.C. 1984, c. 15, s. 23(1)(g); Residential Tenancies Act, S.N.S. 1970, c. 13, s. 7, am. 1970-71, c. 74, s. 3; 1975, c. 64, s. 4; S.N.B. 1975, c. R-10.2, s. 24; R.S.S. 1978, c. R-22, ss. 24-26; Landlord and Tenant Ordinance, R.O.N.W.T. 1974, c. L-2, s. 65; R.O.Y.T. 1971, c. L-2, ss. 81-83, enacted 1972, c. 20, s. 1. An unusual provision is found in the Newfoundland statute where, for the termination of a weekly tenancy, the landlord is required to give a longer period of notice than the tenant.

33R.S.M. 1970, c. L70, s. 103(7), (8), enacted 1970, c. 106, s. 3; re-enacted 1971, c. 35, s. 15; 1975, c. 37, s. 9.

34Landlord and Tenant Act, R.S.O. 1980, c. 232, s. 105; Residential Tenancy Act, S.B.C. 1984, c. 15, s. 29(3). See McInnis v. Shirlmae Enterprises Ltd. (1977), 2 B.C.L.R. 391 (Co. Ct.).

35Landlord and Tenant Act, R.S.O. 1980, c. 232, s. 107; Residential Tenancy Act, S.B.C. 1984, c. 15, s. 29(4).

termination.[35a] Where the reason for termination is the carrying out of demolition, repairs or conversion, the tenant may terminate upon a shorter period of notice. In Ontario the tenant is given a right of first refusal to relet after repair.[36] Notice need not be given where the tenant has abandoned the premises or where there has been a surrender.[37]

In some provinces the notice must be in writing, signed by the person giving notice and identifying the premises.[38] In Manitoba the landlord must give his reasons for termination.[39] Many of the provincial Acts establish procedures for the service of notice.[40]

It has been decided that a notice to terminate not given in conformity with the statutory requirement is of no effect.[41]

809.2   Application to Court

The provinces have enacted residential tenancy legislation providing a summary procedure for resolving disputes between landlord and tenant with respect to possession and termination. It is beyond the scope of this work to deal with this legislation in detail.[1] In some cases the summary procedure has

---

[35a]*Residential Tenancy Act*, S.B.C. 1984, c. 15, s. 29(2).
[36]*Landlord and Tenant Act*, R.S.O. 1980, c. 232, s. 107(3).
[37]*Ozmond v. Young* (1980), 28 O.R. (2d) 225, 109 D.L.R. (3d) 304 (Div. Ct.).
[38]*Landlord and Tenant Act*, R.S.O. 1980, c. 232, s. 99; R.S.P.E.I. 1974, c. L-7, s. 111; R.S.A. 1980, c. L-6, s. 8; *Residential Tenancy Act*, S.B.C. 1984, c. 15, s. 33(1)(*a*); *Landlord and Tenant (Residential Tenancies) Act*, S.N. 1973, No. 54, s. 15(3); *Residential Tenancies Act*, R.S.S. 1978, c. R-22, s. 22. In Manitoba, Northwest Territories and the Yukon the notice need not be in writing but verbal notice is not enforceable by the landlord: *Landlord and Tenant Act*, R.S.M. 1970, c. L70, s. 101(1), enacted 1970, c. 106, s. 3; am. 1971, c. 35, s. 13(*a*); *Landlord and Tenant Ordinance*, R.O.N.W.T. 1974, c. L-2, s. 63; R.O.Y.T. 1971, c. L-2, s. 79, enacted 1972, c. 20, s. 1.
[39]*Landlord and Tenant Act*, R.S.M. 1970, c. L70, s. 101, enacted 1970, c. 106, s. 3; am. 1971, c. 35, s. 13; 1975, c. 37, s. 6; 1977, c. 23, s. 12.1; 1980, c. 60, s. 17.
[40]*Landlord and Tenant Act*, R.S.O. 1980, c. 232, s. 123; R.S.A. 1980, c. L-6, s. 48; R.S.M. 1970, c. L70, s. 102, enacted 1970, c. 106, s. 3; am. 1971, c. 35, s. 14; 1975, c. 37, s. 7; 1977, c. 23, ss. 13, 14; R.S.P.E.I. 1974, c. L-7, ss. 112, 114; *Residential Tenancies Act*, R.S.S. 1978, c. R-22, s. 60; S.N.B. 1975, c. R-10.2, s. 25; *Landlord and Tenant (Residential Tenancies) Act*, S.N. 1973, No. 54, s. 15(4); *Landlord and Tenant Ordinance*, R.O.N.W.T. 1974, c. L-2, s. 64; R.O.Y.T. 1971, c. L-2, s. 89, enacted 1972, c. 20, s. 1.
[41]*Re Bransfield Construction Co. Ltd. and Cox*, [1973] 3 O.R. 989, 39 D.L.R. (3d) 27 (Div. Ct.).
§809.2
[1]*Landlord and Tenant Act*, R.S.A. 1980, c. L-6, ss. 41-47; R.S.M. 1970, c. L70, ss. 107 and 108, enacted 1970, c. 106, s. 3; am. 1971, c. 35, ss. 18 and 19; 1972, c. 39, ss. 6 and 7; 1975, c. 37, ss. 12 and 13; 1977, c. 23, s. 16; R.S.O. 1980, c. 232, ss. 113 *et seq.*; R.S.P.E.I. 1974, c. L-7, ss. 113-115; *Landlord and Tenant (Residential Tenancies) Act*, S.N. 1973, No. 54, s. 19; *Residential Tenancy Act*, S.B.C. 1984, c. 15, ss. 38-45; *Residential Tenancies Act*, S.N.S. 1970, c. 13, s. 10, am. 1973, c. 70, s. 2; S.N.B. 1975, c. R-10.2, ss. 27, 28; R.S.S. 1978, c. R-22, ss. 47-54; *Landlord and Tenant Ordinance*, R.O.Y.T. 1971, c. L-2, s. 86; R.O.N.W.T. 1974, c. L-2, ss. 69-74. For a detailed discussion of these statutory provisions see Williams, *Canadian Law of Landlord and Tenant*, 4th ed. (Toronto, Carswell, 1973), p. 633.

taken the form of additional administrative tribunals or agencies, such as the creation of rentalsmen, and the operation of these bodies will be dealt with later.[2] However, in general, one cannot have recourse to the summary procedure where there are involved questions of fact or questions of law in issue.[3]

809.3 Forfeiture Generally

A forfeiture may arise and the tenancy thereby determine by the breach of a condition which stipulates the cesser of the term upon the occurrence of a prescribed event, or of a covenant that is made conditional by the terms of the lease, and by the non-payment of rent in certain cases. A breach of condition on which the tenancy expressly has been made to depend gives the lessor the right to avoid a lease and re-enter without an express proviso for re-entry. The lessor can only re-enter on a breach of a covenant when the right has been expressly provided for in the lease or when the right has been given by statute. A provision in a lease requiring the lessee to do or not do a certain thing will in general be construed as a covenant unless the word "condition" in some form is used or implied.

A general rule of interpretation of forfeiture clauses is that courts will always lean towards a strict construction and, thus, plaintiffs seeking to take advantage of forfeiture should be in such a position as to claim their rights without asking any favour from any court.[1]

Where a lease contains an express proviso for re-entry or forfeiture by the lessor on certain specified grounds, the courts have held that such a proviso does not give the lessee the right to treat the lease as at an end. The lease is not void but voidable,[2] and at the option of the lessor.[3] The lease does not become void until the lessor has exercised the option or done something that shows his intention to avoid it.[4] It has been held that the mere retaking of possession does

---

[2]See §814, "Residential Tenancy Controls", infra.
[3]*New Brunswick Housing Corp. v. Finnemore* (1976), 14 N.B.R. (2d) 169 (Co. Ct.); *Re Zeghers and Santorelli* (1975), 54 D.L.R. (3d) 637 (Man. Co. Ct.); *Mirdco Holdings Ltd. v. Westfair Foods Ltd. and Wellington Management Ltd.*, [1975] W.W.D. 158 (Sask. Dist. Ct.); *Re Sam Richman Investments (London) Ltd. and Riedel* (1974), 6 O.R. (2d) 335, 52 D.L.R. (3d) 655 (H.C.J.).
§809.3
[1]*Just v. Stewart* (1913), 12 D.L.R. 65, 4 W.W.R. 780 (Man. K.B.); *René v. Carling Export Brewery & Malting Co. Ltd.* (1929), 63 O.L.R. 582, [1929] 2 D.L.R. 881 (S.C. App. Div.); *Re Clark and Mihailescu* (1974), 5 O.R. (2d) 201, 50 D.L.R. (3d) 11 (H.C.J.). See also, *Thompson v. Larsen*, [1975] W.W.D. 100 (Sask. Dist. Ct.); *Sturgess v. Gladmer Developments Ltd.*, [1975] W.W.D. 92 (Sask. Dist. Ct.).
[2]*Jardine v. A.-G. Nfld.*, [1932] A.C. 275 (P.C.).
[3]*Re J. B. Jackson Ltd. and Gettas* (1926), 58 O.L.R. 564, [1926] 2 D.L.R. 721 (S.C. App. Div.); *Linton v. Imperial Hotel Co.* (1889), 16 O.A.R. 337; *Paulson v. The King* (1915), 27 D.L.R. 145, 52 S.C.R. 317, affd 54 D.L.R. 331, [1921] 1 A.C. 271 (P.C.).
[4]*Palmer v. Mail Printing Co.* (1897), 28 O.R. 656 (H.C.J.); *Davenport v. The Queen* (1877), 3 App. Cas. 115 (P.C.); *Re Rexdale Investments Ltd. and Gibson*, [1967] 1 O.R. 251, 60 D.L.R. (2d) 193 (C.A.).

not amount to a forfeiture.[5] It has also been decided that the issuance of a writ of possession does not amount to forfeiture. Service of the writ is the important factor.[6]

A lessee cannot take advantage of his own wrong to bring about a forfeiture of the lease so as to compel the lessor to force against him the forfeiture of his lease.[7]

The right of a landlord to elect whether he will or will not exercise his right to repossess himself of the demised premises as provided in the lease may be affected by taking physical possession or by acquiring possession by means of some possessory action or proceeding. The bringing of an action in ejectment is equivalent to the ancient re-entry, and is an unequivocal exercise of the lessor's election to determine the lease.[8] The institution of summary proceedings under provincial landlord and tenant legislation for recovery of possession is also an exercise of the landlord's right to repossess. When a tenancy has been determined, any act of the landlord showing an intention to repossess the demised premises is sufficient to revest possession in him.[9]

Once a lessor has re-entered upon a forfeiture, the estate which he had at the time he granted the lease is revested in him. A sublessee or other person claiming under the lessee loses his estate as well as the lessee.[10]

Where a lessor has the right to re-enter, he is entitled to enter and take possession if he can do so without a breach of the peace, and he is not bound to bring an action of ejectment or an action for possession.[11] If the landlord forcibly re-enters he may be liable to criminal proceedings but there is no civil remedy preventing a landlord from re-entering into possession by using such force and even violence as may be necessary to overcome any resistance with which he is met.[12]

809.4 Forfeiture for Non-payment of Rent

At common law the right of re-entry for non-payment of rent was restricted to leases in which there was an express condition or proviso giving the lessor the right to re-enter and determine the tenancy for such non-payment.[1] In the

---

[5]*Gulutzan v. McColl-Frontenac Oil Co. Ltd.* (1960), 25 D.L.R. (2d) 567, 35 W.W.R. 337 (Sask. C.A.).
[6]*Canas Property Co. Ltd. v. K.L. Television Services Ltd.*, [1970] 2 All E.R. 795 (C.A.).
[7]*Paulson v. The King, supra*, footnote 3.
[8]*Re Bagshaw and O'Connor* (1918), 42 O.L.R. 466, 42 D.L.R. 596 (S.C. App. Div.).
[9]*Hey v. Moorhouse* (1839), 6 Bing. (N.C.) 52, 133 E.R. 20; *Jones v. Chapman* (1849), 2 Ex. 803, 154 E.R. 717.
[10]*Smith v. Directors of Great Western Ry. Co.* (1877), 3 App. Cas. 165 (H.L.).
[11]*Taylor v. Jermyn* (1865), 25 U.C.Q.B. 86.
[12]*Richter v. Koskey and Adler*, [1953] O.W.N. 746, [1953] 4 D.L.R. 509 (H.C.J.).
§809.4
[1]*Doe d. Dixon v. Roe* (1849), 7 C.B. 134, 137 E.R. 55.

absence of an express stipulation to the contrary as a condition precedent, at common law, to entitle a lessor to determine a lease for non-payment of rent, a formal demand of the rent was necessary.[2] In making a formal demand, it was necessary that the demand should be made: (1) by the landlord or his duly authorized agent;[3] (2) on the day the rent fell due, at such convenient hour before sunset as would give time to count the money before sunset, the demand being continued by the person remaining until, or returning at, that time. In other words, if the proviso for re-entry be on the non-payment of rent for thirty days after it becomes due, the demand must be made on the thirtieth day after the rent became due (exclusive of the day on which it became due) and not on any other day;[4] (3) on the demised premises and at the most notorious place there, as for example, the front door of a dwelling-house,[5] and (4) the demand must be for the precise sum due.

Unless the lease is governed by the relevant statutes or there be express words in the lease dispensing with a formal demand of the rent, no entry or action to recover possession can be maintained for non-payment of rent unless there has been a formal demand thereof according to the above-mentioned rules of common law which are always strictly applied.[6] The parties to the lease can, however, by contract agree to dispense with the necessity of a formal demand.[7]

It is now provided by statute that in every demise a proviso for re-entry is implied if the rent reserved shall remain unpaid for fifteen days, after any of the days on which it ought to have been paid, although no formal demand shall have been made thereof, or if there has been conviction of the tenant for keeping a disorderly house within the meaning of the Criminal Code.[8]

When the statutory provisions are utilized, they must be followed strictly.[9] If the tenant is in default for the statutory period the landlord may elect to terminate and may do so by peaceably re-entering without judicial proceedings.[10]

---

[2]Faugher v. Burley (1876), 37 U.C.Q.B. 498.

[3]Roe d. West v. Davis (1806), 7 East 363, 103 E.R. 140.

[4]Doe d. Dixon v. Roe, supra, footnote 1.

[5]Cole's Law and Practice in Ejectment (London, H. Sweet, 1857), p. 413.

[6]Faugher v. Burley, supra, footnote 2.

[7]Campbell v. Baxter (1864), 15 U.C.C.P. 42.

[8]Landlord and Tenant Act, R.S.O. 1980, c. 232, s. 18; R.S.S. 1978, c. L-6, s. 9; R.S.M. 1970, c. L70, s. 17; R.S.N.B. 1973, c. L-1, ss. 8, 9; R.S.P.E.I. 1974, c. L-7, ss. 9, 10; R.O.N.W.T. 1974, c. L-2, ss. 9, 10; R.O.Y.T. 1971, c. L-2, ss. 9, 10. The provisions in Saskatchewan, Northwest Territories and the Yukon apply when rent is unpaid for two calendar months. The Short Forms of Leases Act, R.S.O. 1980, c. 473, Sch. B, para. 12, specifically provides for entry by the lessor for non-payment of rent or non-performance of covenants without the necessity for formal demand. See also Winter v. Capilano Timber Co., Ltd., [1927] 4 D.L.R. 36, [1928] S.C.R. 1.

[9]Pridham Estates Ltd. v. Janowski (1968), 66 W.W.R. 695 (B.C. Co. Ct.).

[10]Re Rexdale Investments Ltd. and Gibson, [1967] 1 O.R. 251, 60 D.L.R. (2d) 193 (C.A.).

Residential tenancies and forfeiture for non-payment of rent

There are special statutory provisions relating to residential tenancies although the provisions are by no means uniform from province to province. In Ontario, and similarly in Manitoba,[11] upon non-payment of rent the landlord may serve notice of termination, but the notice must point out the tenant's right to avoid termination by paying the rent due. If he fails to do so after receiving the notice, the landlord may then apply to the court for a writ of possession. Even then the tenant is permitted to stop the proceedings by payment of rent and costs.[12]

In Prince Edward Island, a landlord may give thirty days' notice to terminate a monthly tenancy if rent is in arrears for more than fifteen days.[13] In Newfoundland, if rent is in arrears for more than one rent period the landlord may give notice to quit at the end of the next full rent period.[14] In Nova Scotia, if rent is in arrears for thirty days the landlord may give notice to the tenant to quit fifteen days from the date the notice is given.[15] In New Brunswick, where the tenant is in arrears, the landlord may apply to the rentalsman to request a service of a notice to quit.[16] In Saskatchewan, the landlord may apply to the rentalsman for an order of possession.[17] In British Columbia, the landlord may give notice to quit when rent is in arrears, but the tenant may within five days of the receipt of the notice pay the rent due.[18] In Alberta, the landlord may give at least fourteen days' notice of termination of the tenancy, but the tenant may pay the arrears or serve the landlord with a notice of objection, in which case the landlord may apply to court for termination.[19] In the Northwest Territories, failure of the tenant to pay rent within seven days of the date on which it was due and after demand, constitutes, at the landlord's option, termination of the tenancy, and the landlord may then apply for possession.[20] In the Yukon, the commercial tenancy provisions apply, so that if the tenant fails to pay rent within seven days from the time when due and after demand, the landlord can require the tenant to show cause before a judge why an order should not be made for delivery up of possession.[21]

---

[11]*Landlord and Tenant Act*, R.S.O. 1980, c. 232, s. 108; R.S.M. 1970, c. L70, ss. 104(1) and 111(4), enacted 1970, c. 106, s. 3; re-enacted 1971, c. 35, ss. 15 and 20; am. 1972, c. 39, ss. 5 and 10(*b*); 1974, c. 59, s. 39(1)(*a*). As to the form of the writ of possession under the Ontario statute, see *Re Municipality of Metropolitan Toronto and Bremner (No. 2)* (1980), 30 O.R. (2d) 385, 117 D.L.R. (3d) 621 (C.A.).
[12]For an application of the Ontario legislation, see *Re Dean and Grohal* (1980), 27 O.R. (2d) 643, 108 D.L.R. (3d) 510 (Div. Ct.).
[13]*Landlord and Tenant Act*, R.S.P.E.I. 1974, c. L-7, s. 108(3), enacted 1981, c. 19, s. 2.
[14]*Landlord and Tenant (Residential Tenancies) Act*, S.N. 1973, No. 54, s. 15(6).
[15]*Residential Tenancies Act*, S.N.S. 1970, c. 13, s. 7(3).
[16]*Residential Tenancies Act*, S.N.B. 1975, c. R-10.2, s. 19.
[17]*Residential Tenancies Act*, R.S.S. 1978, c. R-22, ss. 22, 47.
[18]*Residential Tenancy Act*, S.B.C. 1984, c. 15, s. 26.
[19]*Landlord and Tenant Act*, R.S.A. 1980, c. L-6, s. 23.
[20]*Landlord and Tenant Ordinance*, R.O.N.W.T. 1974, c. L-2, ss. 66, 69.
[21]*Landlord and Tenant Ordinance*, R.O.Y.T. 1971, c. L-2, s. 54.

809.5 Notice Required Before Forfeiture

In most provinces, the Landlord and Tenant Acts[1] provide that a right of re-entry or forfeiture under a proviso for a breach of any covenant or condition in the lease other than a proviso in respect of the payment of rent, shall not be enforceable by action, entry, or otherwise, unless and until the lessor serves a notice on the lessee specifying the particular breach complained of, and if the breach is capable of remedy, requiring the lessee to remedy it and in any case to make compensation in money for the breach. If the lessee fails within a reasonable time thereafter to remedy the breach, if it is capable of remedy, and to make reasonable compensation in money to the satisfaction of the lessor for the breach, the right of re-entry may be exercised.

Although the Acts give no form of notice, the notice complaining of the breach of the covenant must be sufficiently specific to enable the tenant to know with reasonable certainty what he is required to do, so that he will have an opportunity of remedying the breach before an action is brought. A more general notice of breach of a specified covenant is not sufficient. A notice by a lessor to his lessee that "you have broken the covenants for repairing the inside and outside of the houses" (describing them) contained in a specific lease was held to be insufficient.[2] The lessee is entitled to know how he is said to have broken a covenant, although the notice need not identify every defect in the condition to which attention is drawn. The right of re-entry or forfeiture arises upon neglect on the part of the lessee to remedy the condition.[3] The notice is not bad because in attempting to enumerate the specific breaches it includes some breaches which have not been committed.[4] The notice is required for breaches of both positive and negative covenants.[5]

The notice is necessary as a condition precedent to re-entry without action,[6] even where the breach is incapable of remedy[7] and to summary proceedings against overholding tenants.[8] The fact that the notice does not claim a certain sum for damages does not make it bad.[9] A notice need not ask for compen-

---

§809.5

[1] R.S.O. 1980, c. 232, s. 19(2); R.S.S. 1978, c. L-6, s. 10(2); R.S.M. 1970, c. L70, s. 18(2); R.S.N.B. 1973, c. L-1, s. 14(1); R.S.P.E.I. 1974, c. L-7, s. 15(1); R.O.N.W.T. 1974, c. L-2, s. 46(1); R.O.Y.T. 1971, c. L-2, s. 58(1). See also *Commercial Tenancy Act*, R.S.B.C. 1979, c. 54, s. 28.

[2] *McMullen v. Vannatto* (1894), 24 O.R. 625 (H.C.J.); *Fletcher v. Nokes*, [1897] 1 Ch. 271; *Re Clark and Mihailescu* (1974), 5 O.R. (2d) 201, 50 D.L.R. (3d) 11 (H.C.J.).

[3] *Jolly v. Brown*, [1914] 2 K.B. 109, affd *loc. cit.* p. 118 (C.A.), affd [1916] 1 A.C. 1 *sub nom. Fox v. Jolly* (H.L.).

[4] *Matthews v. Usher* (1899), 68 L.J.Q.B. 988, revd on other grounds [1900] 2 Q.B. 535 (C.A.).

[5] *Walters v. Wylie* (1912), 20 O.W.R. 994, 1 D.L.R. 208 (Div. Ct.).

[6] *Greenwood v. Rae* (1916), 36 O.L.R. 367, 30 D.L.R. 796 (S.C. App. Div.).

[7] *Mount Citadel Ltd. v. Ibar Developments Ltd. and two other actions* (1976), 14 O.R. (2d) 318, 73 D.L.R. (3d) 584 (H.C.J.).

[8] *Re Snure and Davis* (1902), 4 O.L.R. 82 (Div. Ct.); *Pridham Estate Ltd. v. Janowski* (1968), 66 W.W.R. 695 (B.C. Co. Ct.).

[9] *Holman v. Knox* (1912), 25 O.L.R. 588, 3 D.L.R. 207 (Div. Ct.).

sation in money if the breach is capable of remedy though it must inform the lessee what the lessor wants done.[10] A notice complaining that the tenant had not "kept the said premises well and sufficiently repaired, and the party and other walls thereof" is insufficient,[11] while a notice, giving in detail a list of repairs to be done wherever required, leaving it to the tenant to decide where the repairs should be made, has been held to be a good notice.[12]

The notice required is not to be construed as an election to exercise the right of forfeiture, but a preliminary statutory requirement for its exercise. If the lessee complies with the notice, the ground for forfeiture disappears and with it any right of re-entry.[13]

Residential tenancies and notice required before forfeiture

In Ontario, a landlord, in order to terminate a tenancy for breach of a covenant or a condition in a lease, is required to give notice of termination, specifying the act complained of and requiring rectification within seven days. In the event of non-rectification, the landlord is able to apply to the court for a writ of possession.[14] Only those breaches that fall within the statutory scheme[15] can result in the issuance of a writ.

In British Columbia, the landlord may give notice of an early termination of a tenancy where the tenant's conduct is such that the quiet enjoyment of neighbouring tenants is impaired, or where the tenant is causing extraordinary damage, or for various other reasons related to the tenant's conduct as set out in the statute.[16]

The Saskatchewan Act permits the landlord to terminate the tenancy on seven days' notice where the tenant has breached his statutory duty with respect to cleanliness, where the tenant has made improper use of the premises, or where the tenant has created, or permitted the creation of a nuisance or disturbance to other persons in the building.[17] The landlord cannot regain possession except by an order of the rentalsman,[18] and in determining the matter the rentalsman must make a just and equitable order.[19]

---

[10]*Lock v. Pearce*, [1893] 2 Ch. 271 (C.A.); *Ellis v. Breslin* (1974), 2 O.R. (2d) 532 (H.C.J.).

[11]*Re Serle; Gregory v. Searle*, [1898] 1 Ch. 652.

[12]*Matthews v. Usher*, *supra*, footnote 4.

[13]*Re J. B. Jackson Ltd. and Gettas* (1926), 58 O.L.R. 564, [1926] 2 D.L.R. 721 (S.C. App. Div.).

[14]*Landlord and Tenant Act*, R.S.O. 1980, c. 232, ss. 109, 113. As to the particulars of the notice, see *Re Berhold Investments Ltd. and Fall* (1982), 35 O.R. (2d) 338, 132 D.L.R. (3d) 481 (Div. Ct.).

[15]*Landlord and Tenant Act*, R.S.O. 1980, c. 232, s. 109(1), (5): see *Re Kay and Parkway Forest Developments* (1982), 35 O.R. (2d) 329, 133 D.L.R. (3d) 389 (Div. Ct.).

[16]*Residential Tenancy Act*, S.B.C. 1984, c. 15, s. 27: see *Re Miller and Zuchek* (1982), 132 D.L.R. (3d) 142 (B.C.C.A.).

[17]*Residential Tenancies Act*, R.S.S. 1978, c. R-22, s. 27(1).

[18]*Ibid.*, s. 27(2).

[19]*Ibid.*, s. 47; *Sturgess v. Gladmer Developments Ltd.*, [1975] W.W.D. 92 (Sask. Dist. Ct.); *Thompson v. Larsen*, [1975] W.W.D. 100 (Sask. Dist. Ct.).

In Manitoba[20] and Newfoundland[21] the landlord may terminate on five days' notice to the tenant if a statutory condition is breached.

In Alberta,[22] Prince Edward Island[23] and the Yukon[24] the landlord may apply to the court for termination and in Nova Scotia[25] an application may be made to a magistrate on five days' notice to the tenant.

In New Brunswick[26] the legislation requires the landlord to serve notice of the alleged breach on the tenant, except in the case of non-payment for rent, and if the tenant fails to comply with his obligation an application may be made to the rentalsman for termination.

There are no specific applicable provisions in the Northwest Territories.[27]

809.6   Licence to do an Act Which Otherwise Would Operate as a Forfeiture

At common law, a licence to do any act which, without a licence, would operate as a forfeiture, operated as a general waiver of the particular covenant which destroyed the covenant altogether (the rule in *Dumpor's Case*)[1] but it would appear that the rule does not apply to conditions which are capable of a continuing breach.[2]

It is now provided that a licence to do any act which, without a licence, would operate as a forfeiture, shall, unless otherwise expressed, extend only to the permission actually given, or the act specifically authorized to be done and shall not operate as a licence generally.[3]

In *Royal Trust Co. v. Bell*,[4] Beck, J., discussed this rule. He said:

> It may be, too, that the rule laid down in *Dumpor's Case*, the effect of which has been done away with by statute in England and Ontario, but not in this province, namely, that once a licence to assign has been given, the condition of forfeiture in default of a licence is exhausted, is effective equally in a case of the condition of

---

[20]*Landlord and Tenant Act*, R.S.M. 1970, c. L70, s. 98(3), (4), enacted 1971, c. 35, s. 10; am. 1972, c. 39, s. 3; 1975, c. 37, s. 5.

[21]*Landlord and Tenant (Residential Tenancies) Act*, S.N. 1973, No. 54, s. 11.

[22]*Landlord and Tenant Act*, R.S.A. 1980, c. L-6, s. 20.

[23]*Landlord and Tenant Act*, R.S.P.E.I. 1974, c. L-7, ss. 115, 116.

[24]*Landlord and Tenant Ordinance*, R.O.Y.T. 1971, c. L-2, s. 75(2), (3), enacted 1972, c. 20, s. 1.

[25]*Residential Tenancies Act*, S.N.S. 1970, c. 13, s. 10.

[26]*Residential Tenancies Act*, S.N.B. 1975, c. R-10.2, s. 5.

[27]Reference may, however, be had to the *Landlord and Tenant Ordinance*, R.O.N.W.T. 1974, c. L-2, ss. 60, 65, 69.

§809.6

[1]*Dumpor's Case* (1603), 4 Co. Rep. 119 b, 76 E.R. 1110.

[2]*Maunsell v. Hort* (1877), L.R. 1 Ir. 88 (C.A.).

[3]*Landlord and Tenant Act*, R.S.O. 1980, c. 232, s. 24; R.S.S. 1978, c. L-6, s. 14; R.S.M. 1970, c. L70, s. 23; R.S.N.B. 1973, c. L-1, s. 10; R.S.P.E.I. 1974, c. L-7, s. 11; *Law and Equity Act*, R.S.B.C. 1979, c. 224, s. 25; *Landlord and Tenant Ordinance*, R.O.N.W.T. 1974, c. L-2, s. 11; R.O.Y.T. 1971, c. L-2, s. 11.

[4](1909), 12 W.L.R. 546, 2 Alta. L.R. 425 (S.C.).

forfeiture for alterations made without leave; and that, therefore, a licence for alterations having been given by the lessor in one instance, the condition was gone.

In *Baldwin v. Wanzer*; *Baldwin v. Canadian Pacific Ry. Co.*,[5] where a lessor gave a licence to the lessee to alienate part of the demised premises, it was held that the licence did not affect a subsequent alienation without leave.

Many of the Landlord and Tenant Acts[6] further provide that where a licence has been given to one of several lessees, to assign or underlet his share or interest or to do any other act which may not be done without a licence, such licence shall not operate to extinguish the right of re-entry for a breach of a covenant by the other lessees. And where a licence is given to a lessee to assign or underlet or to do any act in respect of part of the demised premises, it shall not operate to destroy the right of re-entry for the breach of a covenant in respect of the remainder of the premises. This is a similar section to the Imperial statute, 22-23 Vict., c. 35, s. 2.

809.7   Waiver of Forfeiture

Where a forfeiture has occurred it is the option of the lessor as to whether he will take advantage of it, even where, under a proviso, the lease is declared to be wholly void. In such a case the lease is considered to be not void but voidable and notwithstanding the cause of the forfeiture, the tenancy continues until the lessor does some act which shows his intention to determine it. If the lessor elects not to take advantage of a forfeiture the forfeiture is waived. Such an election may be express or implied. An unequivocal act which shows a claim by the lessor of the existence of a tenancy after the act complained of operates as such a waiver.[1]

A forfeiture is waived and a subsisting tenancy is recognized, provided that the lessor has knowledge of a cause of forfeiture, by the lessor bringing an action for rent accrued subsequent to the breach,[2] or accepting rent accruing subsequent to the cause of forfeiture.[3] However, the receipt of rent after the right of forfeiture has accrued that was due prior to the cause of forfeiture is not a waiver,[4] and a waiver cannot be prevented by the rent being accepted

---

[5](1892), 22 O.R. 612 (H.C.J.).

[6]R.S.O. 1980, c. 232, s. 25; R.S.S. 1978, c. L-6, s. 15; R.S.M. 1970, c. L70, s. 24; R.S.N.B. 1973, c. L-1, s. 10(3); R.S.P.E.I. 1974, c. L-7, s. 11(3); R.O.N.W.T. 1974, c. L-2, s. 11(3); R.O.Y.T. 1971, c. L-2, s. 11(3).

§809.7

[1]*Straus Land Corp. Ltd. v. International Hotel Windsor Ltd.* (1919), 45 O.L.R. 145, 48 D.L.R. 519 (S.C. App. Div.); *Lippman v. Lee Yick*, [1953] O.R. 514, [1953] 3 D.L.R. 527 (H.C.J.); *Poirier v. Turkewich* (1963), 42 D.L.R. (2d) 259 (Man. Q.B.).

[2]*Dendy v. Nicholl* (1858), 4 C.B. (N.S.) 376, 140 E.R. 1130; *Gulutzan v. McColl-Frontenac Oil Co. Ltd.* (1960), 25 D.L.R. (2d) 567, 35 W.W.R. 337 (Sask. C.A.).

[3]*Davenport v. The Queen* (1877), 3 App. Cas. 115 (P.C.); *Cornish v. Boles* (1914), 31 O.L.R. 505, 19 D.L.R. 447 (S.C. App. Div.); *Capitalex Holdings Inc. v. Gartamk Investments Ltd.* (1975), 11 O.R. (2d) 578 (H.C.J.).

[4]*Dobson v. Sootheran* (1887), 15 O.R. 15 (H.C.J.).

without prejudice to the forfeiture.[5] However, the lease may contain a waiver clause designed to prevent the application of the principle of waiver, but such a clause has been held to be inapplicable to a situation where the landlord accepts rent accruing due after giving notice of forfeiture.[6] Even where the landlord has made a demand, and accepted rent through a clerical error, waiver occurs, notwithstanding that the tenant knew of the landlord's intention to forfeit.[7]

Where by a course of conduct it had been recognized that rent would be properly paid if paid any time during the first fifteen days of the month and the tenant was at all times ready, willing and able to pay the rent from the first of the month and a notice to quit was served on the sixteenth day of the month, it was held that the legal right to forfeiture was defeated by waiver.[8]

Where the act or omission which constitutes the breach of a covenant and occasions the forfeiture is of a continuing nature, there is a continually recurring cause of forfeiture and acceptance of rent or the levying of distress is only a waiver of the forfeiture down to the time the rent is received[9] or the distress is levied.[10] A demand of rent falling due after a notice to repair has expired does not operate as a waiver if there is subsequent non-repair.[11] Covenants to repair, to insure, to cultivate or to use the premises in a particular manner have been held to be continuing covenants and the omission to observe them is a continuing breach.[12] A covenant which requires the complete performance of a definite act within a specified time is not a continuing covenant.[13] Thus, a covenant to build within a specified time is not such a covenant.[14] In one case, where the breach was one which the tenant could not discontinue, *i.e.*, insolvency, waiver of the breach by the landlord became irrevocable and, thus, the lease could not be terminated in the future on that ground.[15] In the Landlord and Tenant Acts of some provinces it is provided that a waiver of the benefit of a covenant or condition in a lease shall not be deemed to

---

[5]*Davenport v. The Queen, supra,* footnote 3; *Strong v. Stinger* (1889), 61 L.T. 470.

[6]*Trustee of Estate of Royal Inns Canada Ltd. v. Bolus-Revelas-Bolus Ltd.; Bolus-Revelas-Bolus Ltd. (Third Party)* (1982), 37 O.R. (2d) 339, 136 D.L.R. (3d) 272 (C.A.).

[7]*Central Estates (Belgravia) Ltd. v. Woolgar (No. 2),* [1972] 1 W.L.R. 1048 (C.A.).

[8]*Cottam v. Smith,* [1947] O.W.N. 880 (C.A.).

[9]*Doe d. Muston v. Gladwin* (1845), 6 Q.B. 953, 115 E.R. 359; *Leighton v. Medley* (1882), 1 O.R. 207 (H.C.J.).

[10]*Thomas v. Lulham,* [1895] 2 Q.B. 400 (C.A.); *Shepherd v. Berger,* [1891] 1 Q.B. 597 (C.A.); *Doe d. Ambler v. Woodbridge* (1829), 9 B. & C. 376, 109 E.R. 140.

[11]*Penton v. Barnett,* [1898] 1 Q.B. 276 (C.A.).

[12]*Doe d. Baker v. Jones* (1850), 5 Ex. 498, 155 E.R. 218; *Coward v. Gregory* (1866), L.R. 2 C.P. 153; *Coatsworth v. Johnson* (1886), 54 L.T. 520 (C.A.); *Doe d. Ambler v. Woodbridge, supra,* footnote 10.

[13]*Morris v. Kennedy,* [1896] 2 I.R. 247 (C.A.).

[14]*Jacob v. Down,* [1900] 2 Ch. 156.

[15]*Canadian Freehold Properties Ltd., Landlord v. Tamarisk Developments Ltd., Tenant,* [1975] W.W.D. 131 (B.C. Co. Ct.).

extend to any instance or breach thereof, other than that to which it specially releases, unless a contrary intention appears.[16]

809.8 Relief from Forfeiture

There is an equitable jurisdiction in the courts to grant relief from forfeiture where there has been fraud, accident, surprise or mistake[1] or in cases where compensation can be made or where the rigid exercise of the legal right would produce a hardship or a great loss and injury where a clear mode of compensation can be discovered.[2] From very early times relief has been granted for the breach of the covenant to pay rent and relief has been granted for other breaches although the earlier cases are not quite uniform.[3] Relief, however, would not be granted by courts of equity where the breach was wilful.[4] Nor would it appear that a tenant who had committed a breach of a covenant through forgetfulness could ask to be relieved on the ground of mistake.[5] The court, however, considered it immaterial that a landlord would gain a greatly improved value if relief from forfeiture was not granted.[6]

In addition to the equitable right to relief from forfeiture the courts in certain cases have a statutory jurisdiction to grant relief from forfeiture. The Landlord and Tenant Acts of several jurisdictions[7] provide that the court has a discretionary power to grant relief on such terms as to payment of rent, costs, expenses, damages, compensation, penalty or otherwise, including the granting of an injunction to restrain any like breach in the future as the court may deem just. This statutory right can only be invoked where the lessor is proceeding by action or otherwise to enforce a right of re-entry or by forfeiture.[8] Some step taken by the landlord evidencing a clear intention to bring the tenancy to an end is required before forfeiture takes place.[9] Thus, notice

---

[16]*Landlord and Tenant Act*, R.S.O. 1980, c. 232, s. 26; R.S.S. 1978, c. L-6, s. 16; R.S.M. 1970, c. L70, s. 25; R.S.N.B. 1973, c. L-1, s. 17; R.S.P.E.I. 1974, c. L-7, s. 17; R.O.N.W.T. 1974, c. L-2, s. 15; R.O.Y.T. 1971, c. L-2, s. 15.

§809.8
[1]*Bamford v. Creasy* (1862), 3 Giff. 675, 66 E.R. 579; *Edwards v. Fairview Lodge*, [1920] 3 W.W.R. 867, 28 B.C.R. 557 (S.C.); *Highbank Lodge Trustees v. Thomas* (1976), 15 N.B.R. (2d) 47 (S.C.).
[2]*Sanders v. Pope* (1806), 12 Ves. Jun. 282, 33 E.R. 108; *Re Clark and Mihailescu* (1974), 5 O.R. (2d) 201, 50 D.L.R. (3d) 11 (H.C.J.).
[3]Woodfall, *Law of Landlord and Tenant*, 28th ed. (London, Sweet and Maxwell, 1978), 1-1920.
[4]*Hill v. Barclay* (1811), 18 Ves. Jun. 56, 34 E.R. 238.
[5]*Barrow v. Isaacs and Son*, [1891] 1 Q.B. 417; *Smith v. Wade* (1902), 1 O.W.R. 549.
[6]*Job v. Banister* (1856), 2 K. & J. 374, 69 E.R. 827.
[7]R.S.O. 1980, c. 232, s. 20; R.S.S. 1978, c. L-6, s. 10; R.S.M. 1970, c. L70, s. 19; R.S.N.B. 1973, c. L-1, s. 14; R.S.P.E.I. 1974, c. L-7, s. 15; R.O.N.W.T. 1974, c. L-2, s. 46; R.O.Y.T. 1971, c. L-2, s. 58.
[8]*Falkowski v. Wilson*, [1965] 2 O.R. 26, 49 D.L.R. (2d) 490 (H.C.J.).
[9]*Re Rexdale Investments Ltd. and Gibson*, [1967] 1 O.R. 251, 60 D.L.R. (2d) 193 (C.A.).

of termination for non-payment of taxes together with a demand for possession at a future date does not constitute a forfeiture, and the court has no jurisdiction to grant relief from forfeiture.[10] In the Ontario *Landlord and Tenant Act*[11] an action is defined to include any proceedings under Part III of the Act which deal with summary applications against overholding tenants notwithstanding the fact that the County Court judge who hears these applications presides as a *persona designata* and not as a court.[12] "Re-enter" in the sense used in the legislation in reference to relief from forfeiture means to re-enter during the term of the lease[13] and "forfeiture" implies that the tenant lost something, *viz.*, the rest of the term.[14] Therefore, where the tenancy is one from month to month and a notice is given to the tenant terminating the tenancy there is nothing to restore to the tenant, as the effect of granting relief from forfeiture is to restore the lease.[15]

The Ontario *Courts of Justice Act, 1984*[16] also gives the court power to relieve against all penalties and forfeitures and in granting such relief to impose such terms as to costs, expenses, damages, compensation and all other matters as may be deemed just.

The power of the court to relieve against a right of re-entry or forfeiture for the breach of a condition or covenant has been restricted so that there is no right for relief from forfeiture of the breach of a covenant or condition against the assigning, underletting, parting with the possession or disposing of the land leased or to a condition for forfeiture on the bankruptcy of the lessee, or on the lessee making an assignment for the benefit of creditors or on the taking in execution of the lessee's interest, or in the case of a mining lease, to a covenant or condition allowing the lessor to have access to or inspect books, accounts, etc., of the mine or the workings thereof.[17]

If there is a misunderstanding or mere inadvertence on the part of the tenant

---

[10]*Re Mostyn's (Collingwood) Ltd. and Victoria & Grey Trust Co.* (1974), 6 O.R. (2d) 721, 54 D.L.R. (3d) 16 (H.C.J.); *Re Simpson and Young & Biggin Ltd.*, [1972] 1 O.R. 103, 22 D.L.R. (3d) 291 (C.A.).

[11]R.S.O. 1980, c. 232, s. 19(1)(a).

[12]*Miller v. Davey*, [1945] O.W.N. 793 (C.A.).

[13]*Archibald v. Richardson*, [1946] O.W.N. 920 (C.A.).

[14]*Archibald v. Richardson, supra*, footnote 13; *Semotiuk v. Rogerson*, [1943] 3 D.L.R. 714, [1943] 2 W.W.R. 331 (Alta. S.C.); *Re Levy's Trusts* (1885), 30 Ch. D. 119; *Re Sumner's Settled Estates*, [1911] 1 Ch. 315; *Affiliated Realty Corp. Ltd. v. Sam Berger Restaurant Ltd.* (1973), 2 O.R. (2d) 147, 42 D.L.R. (3d) 191 (H.C.J.).

[15]*Dendy v. Evans*, [1910] 1 K.B. 263 (C.A.); *T. M. Fairclough & Sons, Ltd. v. Berliner*, [1931] 1 Ch. 60; *Archibald v. Richardson, supra*, footnote 13; *Winbaum v. Ginou*, [1947] O.R. 242, [1947] 2 D.L.R. 619 (H.C.J.).

[16](Ont.), c. 11, s. 111. For similar legislation in other provinces, see *Queen's Bench Act*, R.S.S. 1978, c. Q-1, s. 44, para. 5; R.S.M. 1970, c. C280, s. 63, Rule 7; *Judicature Act*, R.S.N.B. 1973, c. J-2, s. 26(3); *Judicature Ordinance*, R.O.N.W.T. 1974, c. J-1, s. 18(f); R.O.Y.T. 1971, c. J-1, s. 8(f); *Law and Equity Act*, R.S.B.C. 1979, c. 224, s. 21.

[17]*Landlord and Tenant Act*, R.S.O. 1980, c. 232, s. 20(7); R.S.S. 1978, c. L-6, s. 10(9); R.S.M. 1970, c. L70, s. 19(7); R.S.N.B. 1973, c. L-1, s. 14(9); R.S.P.E.I. 1974, c. L-7, s. 15(9); R.O.N.W.T. 1974, c. L-2, s. 46(9); R.O.Y.T. 1971, c. L-2, s. 58(9).

in breaching a covenant not to assign or sublet,[18] or a mere technical breach,[19] relief may be granted. It has been suggested that even if the breach is incapable of remedy, the statutory notice requirements must be followed before forfeiture will succeed.[20]

Where there is a power to grant relief it will not be exercised where the term had meanwhile expired by effluxion of time,[21] even though the lease gives an option of purchase to be exercised during the term which the lessee had attempted to exercise after the forfeiture.[22]

When a landlord has acquired the right to re-enter on the conviction of the tenant for keeping a disorderly house within the meaning of the *Criminal Code*, the court may refuse to grant relief from forfeiture depending upon the circumstances.[23]

Relief from forfeiture can only be granted on proper terms and it is only granted where compensation can be made for the breach.[24] Where the lessee had altered the premises so as to amount to waste or a breach of covenant to repair, relief from forfeiture may be granted upon payment into court of a sufficient amount to ensure the restoration of the premises at the expiration of the lease to their original condition.[25]

The scope of inquiry by the court in determining whether to grant relief from forfeiture is broad. The court can properly consider breaches of covenants other than the particular breach upon which the action for possession is founded.[26]

Where there has been non-payment of rent, the lessee is not entitled as of right to relief against forfeiture. Relief is in the discretion of the court and may be refused on collateral equitable grounds.[27] Where, however, an action is brought to enforce a right of re-entry or forfeiture for non-payment of rent and the lessee at any time before judgment pays into court all the rent in arrears

---

[18]*Re Jawanda and Walji* (1975), 10 O.R. (2d) 527, 63 D.L.R. (3d) 639 (Div. Ct.).
[19]*Maleganos v. Uncle Tom's Drive-In Ltd.* (1976), 12 O.R. (2d) 477, 69 D.L.R. (3d) 365 (Co. Ct.), affd 15 O.R. (2d) 14, 74 D.L.R. (3d) 760 (Div. Ct.), but see *Wakefield and Wakefield v. Cottingham*, [1959] O.R. 551, 19 D.L.R. (2d) 511 (C.A.).
[20]*Mount Citadel Ltd. v. Ibar Developments Ltd. and two other actions* (1976), 14 O.R. (2d) 318, 73 D.L.R. (3d) 584 (H.C.J.).
[21]*Coventry v. McLean* (1894), 21 O.A.R. 176.
[22]*Ibid.*
[23]*Inglewood Construction Co. Ltd. v. Langlois*, [1950] O.W.N. 842 (Co. Ct.); *Re Vanek and Bomza*; *Re BP Canada Ltd. and Bomza* (1976), 14 O.R. (2d) 508, 74 D.L.R. (3d) 175 (H.C.J.).
[24]*Re Abraham* (1926), 59 O.L.R. 164, [1926] 3 D.L.R. 971 (S.C. App. Div.).
[25]*Sullivan v. Dore* (1913), 25 O.W.R. 31, 13 D.L.R. 910 (S.C.).
[26]*Godfrey Estates Ltd. v. Ken Cambridge Ltd.* (1974), 5 O.R. (2d) 23, 49 D.L.R. (3d) 337 (H.C.J.); *Re Jeans West Unisex Ltd. and Hung* (1975), 9 O.R. (2d) 390, 60 D.L.R. (3d) 446 (H.C.J.).
[27]*Coventry v. McLean, supra*, footnote 21; *Lane v. Kerby* (1920), 19 O.W.N. 381 (H.C.); *Re Jeans West Unisex Ltd. and Hung, supra*, footnote 26; *Texaco Canada Ltd. v. Sloan* (1963), 60 D.L.R. (2d) 596, 45 W.W.R. 552 (Sask. Q.B.).

and the costs of the action, the proceedings in the action shall be forever stayed. In such a case it is not a question of the court granting relief; rather, the payment into court creates an absolute stay of the action.[28] In view of the fact that costs are in the discretion of the court and no amount is mentioned in the statutes, it has been held that the lessee should not be penalized if the amount paid in for costs is insufficient, providing any additional costs are paid before the judgment given becomes effective.[29]

Where the landlord has re-entered for non-payment of rent the court has an equitable jurisdiction to relieve from forfeiture.[30] Moreover, re-entry does not preclude relief from forfeiture under the provisions of landlord and tenant legislation.[30a]

In Ontario, any application, either in an action or any other proceeding, for an order for relief from forfeiture should be made by motion, notice of which should be given to the lessor unless the circumstances of the case render it impracticable.[31]

Several of the provinces have legislation providing that where a landlord is proceeding to enforce a right of entry or forfeiture, any person claiming as a subtenant any interest in the premises may apply for an order vesting the remainder of the term, or part thereof, in him upon conditions as required by the court, so long as the term so vested in him is no longer than the term remaining under the sublease.[32]

A lessee who has assigned his interest under a lease cannot seek relief from forfeiture by reason of a breach by his assignee. He has no status to do so even if he remains liable on his covenants.[33] However, a mortgagee by way of sublease may, on default of the head lessee, apply for relief from forfeiture.[34]

810.   OVERHOLDING

810.1   Right to Possession on Overholding

The landlord at the end of the term may enter into possession of the

---

[28]*Landlord and Tenant Act*, R.S.O. 1980, c. 232, s. 20(4); R.S.S. 1978, c. L-6, s. 10(6); R.S.M. 1970. c. L70, s. 19(4); R.S.P.E.I. 1974, c. L-7, s. 15(5); R.O.N.W.T. 1974, c. L-2, s. 46(5); R.O.Y.T. 1971, c. L-2, s. 58(5); *Commercial Tenancy Act*, R.S.B.C. 1979, c. 54. s. 29(3); *Kamin v. Kirby*, [1950] O.W.N. 68, [1950] 2 D.L.R. 179 (H.C.J.); *Corbett v. Hansen*, [1946] 2 W.W.R. 431 (Sask. Dist. Ct.).

[29]*Kamin v. Kirby, supra*, footnote 28; *Corbett v. Hansen, supra*, footnote 28.

[30]*Glen Eagle Manor Ltd. v. Finn's of Kerrisdale Ltd.* (1980), 116 D.L.R. (3d) 617 (B.C.S.C.).

[30a]*Re Rexdale Investments Ltd. and Gibson*, [1967] 1 O.R. 251, 60 D.L.R. (2d) 193 (C.A.); *Badley v. Badley* (1982), 138 D.L.R. (3d) 493, [1982] 5 W.W.R. 436 (Sask. C.A.).

[31]Rules of Civil Procedure, Rules 37.07, 38.07.

[32]*Landlord and Tenant Act*, R.S.O. 1980, c. 232, s. 21; R.S.M. 1970. c. L70, s. 20; R.S.N.B. 1973. c. L-1, s. 15; R.S.P.E.I. 1974, c. L-7, s. 16; R.S.S. 1978, c. L-6, s. 11; R.O.N.W.T. 1974. c. L-2, s. 47; R.O.Y.T. 1971, c. L-2. s. 59.

[33]*Re Francini and Canuck Properties Ltd.* (1982), 35 O.R. (2d) 321, 132 D.L.R. (3d) 468 (C.A.).

[34]*Re Toronto-Dominion Bank and Dufferin-Lawrence Developments Ltd.* (1981), 32 O.R. (2d) 597, 122 D.L.R. (3d) 272 (C.A.).

demised premises and may use such force and even violence as may be necessary to overcome any resistance with which it is met.[1] As a result of breaching the peace, the landlord may be liable to criminal proceedings but there is no civil action which may be taken against him.

Upon the determination of a tenancy, the landlord is entitled to the vacant possession of the demised premises and he may bring an action therefore.[2] The Landlord and Tenant Acts of most provinces provide for summary proceedings to permit a landlord to obtain an order directing an overholding tenant to deliver up possession.[3] In some provinces, as a condition precedent to the right to resort to these proceedings, the landlord must serve on the tenant a written demand of possession. The section in the Acts of these provinces is specific that a demand of possession cannot be served until after the lease has been terminated. A notice to quit and a demand of possession can, therefore, never be embodied in one document, for there is no right to serve a demand of possession until after the time fixed by the notice to quit has expired and the lease terminated thereby.

Residential tenancies and right to possession on overholding

The position with respect to overholding residential tenancies is much different and is governed by the appropriate statutes.[4]

810.2   Overholding with Consent

Until rent is paid or something said or done on the part of the landlord to indicate an intention to treat the tenant holding over as his tenant for a further term, the landlord may treat him as a trespasser and bring an action of eject-

---

§810.1
[1]*Hemmings v. Stoke Poges Golf Club, Ltd.*, [1920] 1 K.B. 720 (C.A.); *Butcher v. Poole Corp.*, [1943] K.B. 48 (C.A.); *Clifton Securities Ltd. v. Huntley*, [1948] 2 All E.R. 283 (K.B.); *Richter v. Koskey and Adler*, [1953] O.W.N. 746, [1953] 4 D.L.R. 509 (H.C.J.).
[2]*Ibbs v. Richardson* (1839), 9 Ad. & E. 849, 112 E.R. 1436. On overholding, the tenant is treated as a tenant at sufferance.
[3]*Landlord and Tenant Act*, R.S.O. 1980, c. 232, s. 76; R.S.A. 1980, c. L-6, s. 20; R.S.S. 1978, c. L-6, s. 50; R.S.M. 1970, c. L70, s. 70; R.S.N.B. 1973, c. L-1, ss. 61; 62; R.S.P.E.I. 1974, c. L-7, s. 78; *Commercial Tenancy Act*, R.S.B.C. 1979, c. 54, s. 18; *Overholding Tenants Act*, R.S.N.S. 1967, c. 219; *Landlord and Tenant Ordinance*, R.O.N.W.T. 1974, c. L-2, s. 34; R.O.Y.T. 1971, c. L-2, s. 46, and see *Stefanik v. Blazewich*, [1946] 3 D.L.R. 676, [1946] 2 W.W.R. 530 (Man. C.A.); *Re Anderson and Anderson* (1966), 57 D.L.R. (2d) 561, 56 W.W.R. 30 (B.C. Co. Ct.); *Burquitlam Co-operative Housing Ass'n v. Romund* (1976), 1 B.C.L.R. 229 (Co. Ct.); *Mirdco Holdings Ltd. v. Westfair Foods Ltd. and Wellington Management Ltd.*, [1975] W.W.D. 158 (Sask. Dist. Ct.); *Re Zeghers and Santorelli* (1975), 54 D.L.R. (3d) 637 (Man. Co. Ct.); *New Brunswick Housing Corp. v. Finnemore* (1976), 14 N.B.R. (2d) 169 (Co. Ct.).
[4]The statutory provisions have been examined in §§809.1, 809.4 and 809.5, *supra*.

ment.[1] When, however, a tenant is allowed to continue in possession after the expiration of a tenancy by agreement, the terms on which he continues to occupy are matters of evidence rather than of law.[2] If there is nothing to show a different understanding he will be considered to hold on the terms of the old lease in so far as these terms are applicable. It is also a question of intention whether the parties, when the lease provides for overholding, intend the tenant to remain under the overholding provisions or under a new lease.[3]

810.3 Action for Double Value

In British Columbia, Manitoba and Ontario, if a tenant for any term for life or years wilfully holds over after the tenancy has expired, he is liable to pay to the landlord at the rate of double the yearly value of the lands for the period so held over provided the landlord makes a demand in writing for possession, after the determination of the tenancy.[1] The right to claim double value applies where the tenant holds over knowing that he has no right to keep possession and not where the tenant claims to hold over under a fair claim or right or under a *bona fide* mistake.[2]

The legislation referred to above limits the remedy of double value to any term for life, lives or years. The statute applies to a tenancy from year to year[3] but it does not apply to a weekly tenancy[4] and it would seem that it does not apply to a monthly or quarterly tenancy.[5] Although the statute mentions both a demand and a notice in writing, it is not necessary that the demand and notice in writing should be distinct,[6] as a notice to quit constitutes in itself a demand for possession and is a sufficient notice in order to exercise the remedy.[7] The notice and demand may be served before the expiration of the

---

§810.2

[1]*Leighton v. Vanwart* (1877), 17 N.B.R. 489 (S.C.), at p. 491, *per* Allen, C.J.
[2]*Henderson v. Craig* (1922), 68 D.L.R. 629, [1922] 2 W.W.R. 597 (Man. K.B.), affd [1923] 1 D.L.R. 1174, [1923] 1 W.W.R. 306 (C.A.).
[3]*Vancouver Block Ltd. v. Wilson* (1967), 61 W.W.R. 648 (B.C.C.A.).

§810.3

[1]*Landlord and Tenant Act*, R.S.O. 1980, c. 232, s. 58; R.S.M. 1970, c. L70, s. 52; R.S.N.B. 1973, c. L-1, s. 56; R.S.P.E.I. 1974, c. L-2, s. 76; *Commercial Tenancy Act*, R.S.B.C. 1979, c. 54, s. 15; *Landlord and Tenant Ordinance*, R.O.N.W.T. 1974, c. L-2, s. 31; R.O.Y.T. 1971, c. L-2, s. 43. There is no such limiting provision in the other provinces.
[2]*Wright v. Smith* (1805), 5 Esp. 203, 170 E.R. 786; *Swinfen v. Bacon* (1861), 6 H. & N. 846, 158 E.R. 349; *Dickson Co. v. Graham* (1913), 23 O.W.R. 749, 9 D.L.R. 813 (H.C.); *Yonge-Rosedale Developments Ltd. v. Levitt* (1978), 18 O.R. (2d) 295, 82 D.L.R. (3d) 263 (H.C.J.).
[3]*Ryal v. Rich* (1808), 10 East 48, 103 E.R. 693; *Lake v. Smith* (1805), 1 Bos. & Pul. (N.R.) 174, 127 E.R. 426.
[4]*Lloyd v. Rosbee* (1810), 2 Camp. 453, 170 E.R. 1216.
[5]*Wilkinson v. Hall* (1837), 3 Bing. (N.C.) 508, 132 E.R. 506.
[6]*Wilkinson v. Colley* (1771), 5 Burr. 2694, 98 E.R. 414.
[7]*Messenger v. Armstrong* (1785), 1 T.R. 53, 99 E.R. 968.

term requiring the tenant to deliver up possession on the expiry of the term[8] or after the expiration, provided the landlord has not done any act which would create a new tenancy.[9] The notice, however, must be a valid notice to quit.[10]

The double value is computed from the end of the term if the notice was given before the term was determined[11] and from the date of serving the notice if it was given after the determination.[12]

As a claim against an overholding tenant for double the yearly value of the land is an unliquidated claim recoverable only by action pursuant to the statute, it is therefore not proveable against an estate in the hands of an assignee for creditors,[13] and double value, not being in the nature of rent but a penalty, cannot be the subject of distress.[14]

810.4 Action for Double Rent

If a tenant gives notice of his intention to quit at a time mentioned in the notice and does not deliver up possession at the time so mentioned, he is liable to pay to the landlord double the rent or sum which he would otherwise have to pay thenceforward during all the time that he continues in possession.[1] It would seem that the liability under the Ontario statute does not apply to a tenant holding over in good faith.[2]

The notice to quit given by the tenant must be valid and sufficient to determine the tenancy in order to entitle the landlord to double rent.[3] The notice may be either verbal or in writing.[4] The notice must be certain. The landlord has the same rights and remedies to recover the double rent that he had to recover the single rent.[5] Where a tenant has given notice to quit and continues in possession paying double rent, he may at any time give up possession and stop the double rent without giving a fresh notice.[6]

---

[8]*Ibid.*
[9]*Cobb v. Stokes* (1807), 8 East 358, 103 E.R. 380.
[10]*Johnstone v. Hudlestone* (1825), 4 B. & C. 922, 107 E.R. 1302.
[11]*Soulsby v. Neving* (1808), 9 East 310, 103 E.R. 592.
[12]*Cobb v. Stokes, supra,* footnote 9.
[13]*Magann v. Ferguson* (1898), 29 O.R. 235 (H.C.J.).
[14]*Soulsby v. Neving, supra,* footnote 11.
§810.4
[1]*Landlord and Tenant Act,* R.S.O. 1980, c. 232, s. 59; R.S.M. 1970, c. L70, s. 53; R.S.N.B. 1973, c. L-1, s. 57; R.S.P.E.I. 1974, c. L-7, s. 77; *Commercial Tenancy Act,* R.S.B.C. 1979, c. 54, s. 16; *Landlord and Tenant Ordinance,* R.O.N.W.T. 1974, c. L-2, s. 32; R.O.Y.T. 1971, c. L-2, s. 44.
[2]*Ord v. Public Utilities Com'n of Town of Mitchell,* [1936] O.R. 61, [1936] 1 D.L.R. 540 (H.C.J.).
[3]*Johnstone v. Hudlestone* (1825), 4 B. & C. 922, 107 E.R. 1302.
[4]*Timmins v. Rowlison* (1764), 1 Black. W. 533, 96 E.R. 309.
[5]*Ibid.*
[6]*Booth v. Macfarlane and Barbour* (1831), 1 B. & Ad. 904, 109 E.R. 1022.

810.5 Action for Use and Occupation

When a person is in possession of premises without a lease, the relationship of landlord and tenant does not exist and there is no rent payable as such. Where, however, it is shown that the plaintiff is entitled to land which the defendant occupied by permission of the plaintiff, an agreement to pay the plaintiff a reasonable compensation for such use and occupation will be implied.[1]

In a common law action for use and occupation the plaintiff must prove a contract express or implied to pay compensation for use and occupation.[2] If, however, it turned out that there was a lease, the landlord in an action for use and compensation would be nonsuited.[3] To aid the landlord the Imperial *Distress for Rent Act*[4] was passed. That Act provided that:

> 14. ... to obviate some Difficulties that many Times occur in the Recovery of Rents, where the Demises are not by Deed ... it shall and may be lawful to and for the Landlord or Landlords, where the Agreement is not by Deed, to recover a reasonable Satisfaction for the Lands, Tenements or Hereditaments, held or occupied by the Defendant or Defendants, in an Action on the Case, for the Use and Occupation of what was so held or enjoyed; and if in Evidence on the Trial of such Action any Parol Demise or any Agreement (not being by Deed) whereon a certain Rent was reserved shall appear, the Plaintiff in such Action shall not therefore be nonsuited, but may make use thereof as an Evidence of the *Quantum* of Damages to be recovered.

Except for the difference of doing away with a nonsuit, the statute does not make the action of use and occupation maintainable where it was not maintainable before, as, for example, where there is a demise under seal.[5] By reason of the date as of which English law was adopted by the provinces[6] that statute necessarily went into force in each of the provinces except Quebec. In Ontario, this statute was repealed by the *Statute Law Revision Act*.[7] However, by reason of the fusion of equity and common law with the right of a plaintiff to make alternative claims, the strict common law rule is no longer applicable, notwithstanding the repeal of the statute. It is now sufficient to set out in the statement of claim facts which entitle the plaintiff to relief and pray for any relief that the facts warrant.[8] It has been held that under a prayer for general relief, the court will now grant the appropriate relief which the facts warrant although unable to grant the specific relief claimed.[9] The liability to pay com-

---

§810.5
[1]*Zalev v. Harris* (1924), 27 O.W.N. 197 (S.C. App. Div.); *Young v. Bank of Nova Scotia* (1915), 34 O.L.R. 176, 23 D.L.R. 854 (S.C. App. Div.).
[2]*Re Crawford v. Seney* (1889), 17 O.R. 74 (H.C.J.).
[3]*Young v. Bank of Nova Scotia, supra*.
[4]11 Geo. 2, c. 19, s. 14 (1738).
[5]*Beverley v. Lincoln Gas Light & Coke Co.* (1837), 6 Ad. & E. 829, 112 E.R. 318; *McFarlane v. Buchanan* (1862), 12 U.C.C.P. 591.
[6]See ch. 1, *supra*.
[7]S.O. 1902, 2 Edw. 7, c. 1, s. 2, Schedule.
[8]*Phelps v. White* (1881), L.R. 7 Ir. 160 (C.A.).
[9]*Slater v. Canada Central Ry. Co.* (1878), 25 Gr. 363.

pensation whether under the name of rent or for use and occupation depends on possession, and where there is no possession there can be no liability to pay compensation.[10] Proof of a written agreement to take the premises for a future time is insufficient to render a defendant liable for use and occupation without proof of entry.[11] Entry by one of two or more tenants is sufficient as against all.[12] Temporary occupation only is insufficient to make the occupant liable for use and occupation.[13] Acts of ownership such as sending in a person to clean and paper rooms have been held sufficient.[14]

A lessee may still be liable for use and occupation when the lease has expired and the lessee has given up possession if the premises are in the possession of a sublessee as the lessor may refuse to accept the possession and hold the original lessee liable, for the lessor is entitled to receive the possession of the entire premises at the end of the term.[15] If a tenant holds over after expiration of his lease without any agreement for a new tenancy or without any payment of rent, so as to be a tenant at sufferance, he is liable for use and occupation while he continues in possession.[16]

810.6 Action for Mesne Profits

An action for *mesne profits* is an action of trespass brought to recover profits derived from land whilst the possession of it was improperly withheld, that is, the yearly value of the premises. *Mesne profits* are the rents and profits which a trespasser has, or might have received or made during his occupation of the premises, and which, therefore, he must pay over to the true owner as compensation for the tort which he has committed. A claim for rent is therefore liquidated, while a claim for *mesne profits* is always unliquidated.[1]

In an action to recover *mesne profits* the plaintiff must prove that he has entered into possession, that he had title during the period for which he claims, that the defendant was in possession during that period and the amount of the *mesne profits*.[2] Once the plaintiff re-enters, the period of the plaintiff's possession relates back to the time when his right of re-entry accrued.[3]

---

[10]*Newport Industrial Development Co. v. Heughan* (1928), 62 O.L.R. 364, [1928] 3 D.L.R. 547 (S.C. App. Div.), affd [1929] 3 D.L.R. 108, [1929] S.C.R. 491; *Wilkes v. Home Life Ass'n of Canada* (1904), 8 O.L.R. 91 (Div. Ct.).

[11]*Woolley v. Watling* (1837), 7 Car. & P. 610, 173 E.R. 268.

[12]*Glen v. Dungey and Farrant* (1849), 4 Ex. 61, 154 E.R. 1125.

[13]*How v. Kennett and Gough* (1835), 3 Ad. & E. 659, 111 E.R. 564.

[14]*Smith v. Twoart* (1841), 2 Man. & G. 841, 133 E.R. 984.

[15]*Lindsay v. Robertson* (1899), 30 O.R. 229 (Div. Ct.).

[16]*McFarlane v. Buchanan* (1862), 12 U.C.C.P. 591.

§810.6

[1]*Wharton's Law Lexicon*, 13th ed., p. 558; *Mayne's Treatise on Damages*, 11th ed. by Earengey (London, Sweet & Maxwell, 1946), p. 471.

[2]Williams and Yates, *Law of Ejectment*, 2nd ed. (London, Sweet & Maxwell, 1911), p. 208.

[3]*Barnett v. Earl of Guildford* (1855), 11 Ex. 19, 156 E.R. 728; *Ocean Accident & Guarantee Corp., Ltd. v. Ilford Gas Co.*, [1905] 2 K.B. 493 (C.A.).

As *mesne profits* are damages for trespass, they can only be claimed as from the date the defendant ceased to hold the demised premises as a tenant and became a trespasser. Therefore, as a rule, *mesne profits* can only be claimed from the time when the lessor does some unequivocal act evidencing his intention to determine the tenancy as by re-entry or issue of a writ.[4] Execution of a writ of possession or actual possession taken after a judgment in ejectment, entitles a plaintiff to recover damages for any period over which he can prove a right to possession as the entry when made relates back to the origin of the title, and all who occupied in the meantime by whatever title they came in are answerable to the plaintiff for their occupation.[5] In some cases, however, a lessor at will might have an action of trespass against the lessee even before the lessor enters into possession or does some equivocal act evidencing his intention to determine the tenancy. An example occurs where a lessee at will, possessor by consent, or licensee abuses his right of entry, authority or licence in a manner so inconsistent with his contract that it is deemed to amount to a determination of the contract. In such cases the lessee is deemed to be a trespasser *ab initio*; that is, the authority or justification is not only determined, but treated as if it had never existed.[6]

811. SURRENDER

811.1 Surrender and Its Effect

A surrender is the yielding or delivering up of lands or tenements and the estate a man has therein, unto another that has a higher and a greater estate in the same lands or tenements.[1] A surrender differs from a release. By a release a greater estate descends upon a lesser estate. By a surrender a lesser estate falls into a greater estate.

The surrender may be either express or implied and to give a surrender legal effect, the surrenderee must have the immediate estate in remainder or reversion expectant on the estate of the surrenderor.[2] For example, if A lets to B for five years and B lets to C for four years, C cannot surrender to A, as A has not the immediate estate in remainder or reversion expectant on the estate of the surrenderor.[3] One joint tenant cannot surrender his estate to another joint tenant but he may grant, release, or assign to him.[4] Nor can a tenancy held jointly be surrendered by one of two joint tenants in the absence of express

---

[4]*Hill and Redman's Law of Landlord and Tenant*, 16th ed., p. 539; *Elliott v. Boynton*, [1924] 1 Ch. 236 (C.A.).

[5]*Mayne on Damages, supra*, footnote 1, p. 472.

[6]*Pollock's Law of Torts*, 15th ed. by Landon (London, Stevens, 1951), pp. 281, 297-8.

§811.1

[1]*Sheppard's Touchstone of Common Assurances*, 8th ed. by Atherley (London, S. Brooke, 1826), vol. 2, p. 300.

[2]Co. Litt. 337b.

[3]Bac. Abr. (London, A. Strachan, 1832), tit. "Leases and Terms for Years", s. 2.

[4]*Sheppard's Touchstone, supra*, footnote 1, p. 303.

authority.[5] A surrender immediately divests the estate of the surrenderor and vests it in the surrenderee, for it is a conveyance at common law to the perfection of which no other act is requisite but the bare grant.[6] The concept of surrender has no application where there does not exist a landlord-tenant relationship. Thus, surrender does not apply to an agreement of lease. A party complaining of a breach of an executory contract, *i.e.*, an agreement to lease, can bring an action for damages subject to the principle of mitigation.[7]

A lessee can give title to his lessor by a surrender only to the same extent that he could give it to another person by his assignment.[8] The effect of a surrender of a term is to extinguish the interest created by the lease by means of the term merging in the reversion.[9] It does not put an end to the liability for breaches of covenants that have been previously committed, nor does it operate to destroy the rights of third parties who have acquired interests under the lease before its surrender.[10]

A surrender of a term does not affect the rights of subtenants. It operates as to subtenants as well as to third parties only as a grant subject to their rights.[11] Thus, where a tenant surrenders his lease to his landlord after subletting a part of the demised premises, the subtenant cannot be dispossessed except by determining his lease in the usual way,[12] although the subtenant had notice of the surrender,[13] or at the time of surrender the lease was liable to forfeiture,[14] and even if the lessor had no notice at the date of the surrender that a cause of forfeiture had accrued.[15]

The surrender of a lease stops rent accruing.[16] At common law where there is a lease and sublease and the former was surrendered, the liability of the subtenant on his covenant to pay rent ended because of the principle that the immediate reversion was extinguished and by reason of the rule that the covenants of, and remedies against, a tenant cease on the merger of the reversion in another estate.[17] The liability of a subtenant to pay rent on the

---

[5]*Leek and Moorlands Building Society v. Clark*, [1952] 2 Q.B. 788 (C.A.).

[6]*Sheppard's Touchstone, supra*, footnote 1, p. 301.

[7]*Windmill Place v. Apeco of Canada Ltd.* (1976), 72 D.L.R. (3d) 539, 16 N.S.R. (2d) 565 (S.C. App. Div.), affd 82 D.L.R. (3d) 1, [1978] 2 S.C.R. 385.

[8]*Walter v. Yalden*, [1902] 2 K.B. 304 at p. 310, *per* Channell, J.

[9]Co. Litt. 337b.

[10]*Williams v. Taperell* (1892), 8 T.L.R. 241; *Dalton v. Pickard*, [1926] 2 K.B. 545*n* (C.A.); *Richmond v. Savill*, [1926] 2 K.B. 530 (C.A.).

[11]*Pleasant v. Benson* (1811), 14 East 234, 104 E.R. 590.

[12]*Pleasant v. Benson, supra*, footnote 11; *Grand Western Ry. Co. v. Smith* (1876), 2 Ch. D. 235 (C.A.), vard 3 App. Cas. 165 (H.L.); *Shapiro v. Handelman*, [1947] O.R. 223, [1947] 2 D.L.R. 492 (C.A.); *Re Roanne Holdings Ltd. and Victoria Wood Development Corp. Ltd.* (1975), 8 O.R. (2d) 321, 58 D.L.R. (3d) 17 (C.A.).

[13]*Mellor v. Watkins* (1874), L.R. 9 Q.B. 400.

[14]*Grand Western Ry. Co. v. Smith, supra*, footnote 12; *Spicer v. Martin* (1888), 14 App. Cas. 12 (H.L.).

[15]*Parker v. Jones*, [1910] 2 K.B. 32.

[16]*Southwell v. Scotter* (1880), 49 L.J.Q.B. 356.

[17]*Webb v. Russell* (1789), 3 T.R. 393, 100 E.R. 639.

surrender of the head lease is now preserved by statute which provides that where the reversion expectant on a lease of land merges or is surrendered, the estate which for the time being confers as against the tenant under the lease the next vested right to the land shall, to the extent of and for preserving such incidents to and obligations on the reversion as but for the surrender or merger thereof would have subsisted, be deemed the reversion expectant on the lease.[18]

811.2 Express Surrender

An express surrender is declaratory of the intention of the surrenderor to yield up his estate. In order to effect a surrender, it is necessary that the surrenderor have a vested interest in possession or remainder, that the estate of the surrenderor be of an equivalent rank or lower, that the surrender be to the person who has the next immediate estate in remainder or reversion, that there be a privity of estate between the surrenderor and surrenderee and that the surrender be of the whole estate.

In an express surrender the usual operative words are "surrender, give or yield up"[1] but the use of the word "surrender" is not necessary.[2] The words "releases and quitclaims" have been held sufficient to surrender a term of years when the grantee has the reversion.[3] If the words used indicate an intention to effect a surrender, it is sufficient and the words used will be construed so as to give effect to that intention.[4]

811.3 Surrender by Operation of Law

A surrender of a lease by operation of law as distinguished from an express surrender is effected in two ways, (1) where a tenant accepts from a landlord a new lease or estate incompatible with the existing or original estate and (2) when the tenant delivers up possession to the landlord and the possession is accepted by the landlord.

In a surrender by operation of law, the law gives effect to the intention of the parties as appearing by their acts.[1] It has been argued that there must be

---

[18]*Landlord and Tenant Act*, R.S.O. 1980, c. 232, s. 17; R.S.M. 1970, c. L70, s. 16; R.S.S. 1978, c. L-6, s. 8; R.S.N.B. 1973, c. L-1, s. 5; R.S.P.E.I. 1974, c. L-7, s. 6; R.O.N.W.T. 1974, c. L-2, s. 6; R.O.Y.T. 1971, c. L-2, s. 6.

§811.2

[1]*Sheppard's Touchstone*, 8th ed. by Atherley (London, S. Brooke, 1826), vol. 2, p. 306.
[2]*Carleton v. Ross* (1927), 33 O.W.N. 88 (Co. Ct.), revd on other grounds *loc. cit.* p. 163 (S.C. App. Div.).
[3]*Gray v. Chamandy & Sons* (1929), 63 O.L.R. 495, [1929] 2 D.L.R. 706 (S.C. App. Div.).
[4]*Smith v. Mapleback* (1786), 1 T.R. 441, 99 E.R. 1186.

§811.3

[1]*Ferguson v. Craig*, [1954] O.W.N. 631, [1954] 4 D.L.R. 815 (H.C.J.); *Rae v. Howard* (1973), 39 D.L.R. (3d) 135, 11 N.S.R. (2d) 656 (S.C.T.D.).

a common intent to relinquish the relationship of landlord and tenant although it need not be expressly stated, and that where there is no mutual agreement to rescind the contractual obligations of a lease, the doctrine of surrender in law will not bring about such result in spite of the intention of the parties.[2] However, the Supreme Court of Canada[3] has approved the judgment of *Lyon v. Reed*,[4] which held that the doctrine of surrender by operation of law may take place independently, even in spite of intention. It would not at all alter the case to show that there was no intention to surrender the particular estate or even that there was an express intention to keep it unsurrendered. Where, however, the minds of the parties to a lease concur in the common intent of relinquishing the relationship of landlord and tenant, and execute this intent by acts which are tantamount to a stipulation to put an end thereto, there at once arises a surrender by act and operation of law.[5]

When a tenant abandons possession, it does not amount to a surrender unless the landlord accepts it with an intent to end the term[6] and the acceptance of the key is not necessarily an acceptance of the premises by way of surrender.[7]

Although the repudiation of a lease by a tenant together with the taking of possession by the landlord may amount to surrender,[8] it will not automatically so do in all cases. The landlord may take possession of the premises simply to relet the premises on the tenant's account.[9] If he does so, surrender will not occur, and the landlord will not, in so doing, prejudice his claim for damages based on breach of contract.[10] If surrender does occur, any claim for future rent is lost.[11]

---

[2]Updegraff, "The Element of Intent in Surrender by Operation of Law", 38 Harv. L. Rev. 64 (1924-25).

[3]*A.-G. Sask. v. Whiteshore Salt & Chemical Co. Ltd. and Midwest Chemicals Ltd.*, [1955] 1 D.L.R. 241, [1955] S.C.R. 43.

[4](1844), 13 M. & W. 285 at pp. 306-7, 153 E.R. 118.

[5]*A.-G. Sask. v. Whiteshore Salt & Chemical Co. Ltd. and Midwest Chemicals Ltd.*, supra, footnote 3; *Goldhar v. Universal Sections & Mouldings Ltd.*, [1963] 1 O.R. 189, 36 D.L.R. (2d) 450 (C.A.); *Trustee of Estate of Royal Inns Canada Ltd. v. Bolus-Revelas-Bolus Ltd.* (1981), 33 O.R. (2d) 260, 124 D.L.R. (3d) 95 (S.C. in Bankruptcy), where the above principle was found to be inapplicable on the facts: see 37 O.R. (2d) 339, 136 D.L.R. (3d) 272 (C.A.).

[6]*Meeker v. Spalsbury*, 66 N.J.L. 60, 48 Atl. 1026; *Shell and Stoffman Investments Ltd. v. General Office Machines Ltd.* (1961), 67 Man. R. 390 (C.A.); *Fuda v. D'Angelo* (1974), 2 O.R. (2d) 605, 43 D.L.R. (3d) 645 (H.C.J.).

[7]*Elsworth v. Brice* (1859), 18 U.C.Q.B. 441; *Ferguson v. Craig*, [1954] O.W.N. 631, [1954] 4 D.L.R. 815 (H.C.J.).

[8]*Green v. Tress* (1927), 60 O.L.R. 151, [1927] 2 D.L.R. 180 (S.C. App. Div.); *Noble Scott Ltd. v. Murray* (1925), 56 O.L.R. 595 (H.C.), affd 57 O.L.R. 248 (S.C. App. Div.); *Levesque v. J. Clark & Son Ltd.* (1972), 7 N.B.R. (2d) 478 (S.C.).

[9]*Goldhar v. Universal Sections & Mouldings Ltd.*, supra, footnote 5; *Bel-Boys Buildings Ltd. v. Clark* (1967), 62 D.L.R. (2d) 233, 59 W.W.R. 641 (Alta. S.C. App. Div.).

[10]*Highway Properties Ltd. v. Kelly, Douglas & Co. Ltd.* (1971), 17 D.L.R. (3d) 710, [1971] S.C.R. 562; *Korsman v. Bergl*, [1967] 1 O.R. 576, 61 D.L.R. (2d) 558 (C.A.); *Fuda v. D'Angelo* (1974), 2 O.R. (2d) 605, 43 D.L.R. (3d) 645 (H.C.J.).

[11]*Bel-Boys Buildings Ltd. v. Clark*, supra, footnote 9.

The surrender implied by the acceptance of a new lease by an existing tenant is based upon estoppel by act *in pais*. The law attributes the force of estoppel to certain acts of notoriety, such as livery of seisin, entry, acceptance of an estate and the like; the grant of a new lease to a stranger, with the tenants' assent, and change of possession preceding or following the lease, bring such a case within the scope of the same doctrine, which mere oral assent would not do.[12]

812. MERGER

On a surrender the landlord acquires the term whereas a merger takes place when the tenant acquires the immediate reversion.[1] In order to effect a merger it is necessary that the two estates should come to one and the same person in one and the same right.[2] If there is an intermediate estate, a merger will not take place[3] and if the intention of the parties is that the term is to be kept alive, a merger will not result if the term and reversion are held in the same person.[4] The intention need not be expressed but may be implied if it would be of advantage to the person in whom the estates become united.[5] In equity the merger of a term does not destroy restrictive covenants which are attached to it,[6] but where the covenant is for the benefit of the lessor, the merger may extinguish the covenant.[7]

813. FRUSTRATION

The doctrine of frustration developed to mitigate the old common law rule that if a person has absolutely contracted to perform certain things he cannot evade liability if performance becomes impossible.[1] The doctrine, first clearly enunciated in *Taylor v. Caldwell*,[2] requires that the parties be discharged from their obligation if the subject-matter of the contract is destroyed, if a change of law makes performance illegal or, more arguably, if a supervening event has frustrated the common venture.

---

[12]*Wallis v. Hands*, [1893] 2 Ch. 75; *Mickleborough v. Strathy* (1911), 23 O.L.R. 33 (Div. Ct.); *Lyon v. Reed* (1844), 13 M. & W. 285, 153 E.R. 118; *Badaloto v. Trebilcock* (1923), 53 O.L.R. 359, [1924] 1 D.L.R. 465 (S.C. App. Div.); *Fontainbleu Apt. Ltd. v. Hamilton*, [1962] O.W.N. 223 (Co. Ct.).

§812

[1]*Sheppard's Touchstone of Common Assurances*, 8th ed. by Atherley (London, S. Brooke, 1826), vol. 2, p. 310; Bac. Abr., vol. IV, p. 863, tit. "Leases for Years, when merged by Union with the Freehold or Fee".

[2]*Chambers v. Kingham* (1878), 10 Ch. D. 743.

[3]Bl. Comm. 177.

[4]*Capital & Counties Bank, Ltd. v. Rhodes*, [1903] 1 Ch. 631 (C.A.).

[5]*Ingle v. Vaughan Jenkins*, [1900] 2 Ch. 368.

[6]*Birmingham Joint Stock Co. v. Lea* (1877), 36 L.T. 843.

[7]*Lord Dynevor v. Tennant* (1888), 13 App. Cas. 279 (H.L.).

§813

[1]*Paradine v. Jane* (1647), Aleyn 26, 82 E.R. 897.

[2](1863), 3 B. & S. 826, 122 E.R. 309.

It has been held that the doctrine is not applicable to a demise of real property.[3] The rationale behind this conclusion is the nature of the lease, *i.e.*, that even if the demised premises be destroyed, the tenant still has an interest in the real property which is not destroyed. It would seem that the exclusion of the doctrine is based on the importance the court places on the conveyancing, as opposed to the contractual nature of the lease.

Whether the exclusion of the doctrine to leases of real property is proper and will be maintained is open to question. If the rationale behind the exclusion of the principle is based on the fact that the lessee still can acquire some interest in the real property, that rationale is open to question after the decision in *Capital Quality Homes Ltd. v. Colwyn Construction Ltd.*[4] In that case the court applied the doctrine to a purchase of land where it found that the vendor and purchaser were involved in a common venture.[5] If the doctrine is applicable where a contract creates an interest in land by way of sale, it is suggested that there is no good reason why the doctrine cannot be applicable equally to an interest in land created by a contract to lease.

It may well be that there is a further justification for the application of the doctrine to a landlord-tenant relationship. In *Highway Properties Ltd. v. Kelly, Douglas & Co. Ltd.*,[6] the Supreme Court of Canada, in considering the remedies open to a landlord upon wrongful repudiation of a lease by a tenant, commented upon the contractual, as opposed to the conveyancing nature of a lease. The decision in that case recognized this contractual nature, for Laskin, J., stated[7]:

> I approach the legal issue involved in this appeal by acknowledging the continuity of common law principle that a lease of land for a term of years under which possession is taken creates an estate in the land, and also the relation of landlord and tenant, to which the common law attaches various incidents despite the silence of the document thereon. For the purposes of the present case, no distinction need be drawn between a written lease and a written agreement for a lease. Although by covenants or by contractual terms, the parties may add to, or modify, or subtract from the common law incidents, and, indeed, may overwhelm them as well as the leasehold estate by commercial or business considerations which represent the dominant features of the transaction, the "estate" element has resisted displacement as the pivotal factor under the common law, at least as understood and administered in this country.
>
> There has, however, been some questioning of this persistent ascendancy of a concept that antedated the development of the law of contracts in English law and

---

[3] *Leightons Investment Trust, Ltd. v. Cricklewood Property & Investment Trust, Ltd.*, [1943] K.B. 493 (C.A.); *Denman v. Brise*, [1949] 1 K.B. 22 (C.A.). See also *Dunkelman v. Lister* (1927), 60 O.L.R. 158, [1927] 2 D.L.R. 219 (H.C.), affd 61 O.L.R. 89, [1927] 4 D.L.R. 612 (S.C. App. Div.).

[4] (1975), 9 O.R. (2d) 617, 61 D.L.R. (3d) 385 (C.A.).

[5] It should, however, be noted that the court refused to apply the doctrine where no such common venture existed: see *Victoria Wood Development Corp. Inc. v. Ondrey*; *Ondrey v. Victoria Wood Development Corp. Inc.* (1977), 14 O.R. (2d) 723, 74 D.L.R. (3d) 528 (H.C.J.), affd 22 O.R. (2d) 1, 92 D.L.R. (3d) 229 (C.A.).

[6] (1971), 17 D.L.R. (3d) 710, [1971] S.C.R. 562.

[7] *Ibid.*, at p. 715.

has been transformed in its social and economic aspects by urban living conditions and by commercial practice. The judgments in the House of Lords in *Cricklewood Property & Investment Trust, Ltd. v. Leighton's Investment Trust, Ltd.*, [1945] A.C. 221, are illustrative. Changes in various States of the United States have been quite pronounced, as is evident from 1 *American Law of Property* (1952), #3.11.

He concluded his judgment as follows:[8]

> There are some general considerations that support the view that I would take. It is no longer sensible to pretend that a commercial lease, such as the one before this Court, is simply a conveyance and not also a contract. It is equally untenable to persist in denying resort to the full armoury of remedies ordinarily available to redress repudiation of covenants, merely because the covenants may be associated with an estate in land. Finally, there is merit here as in other situations in avoiding multiplicity of actions that may otherwise be a concomitant of insistence that a landlord engage in instalment litigation against a repudiating tenant.

The judgment makes it clear that the court is willing to examine the contractual nature of the lease and, indeed, perhaps recognize that this aspect of the lease should be stressed rather than the conveyancing aspect. If this be so, it takes little imagination to grasp the possibility of applying the reasoning of the case to situations involving the doctrine of frustration.

Residential tenancies and frustration

In British Columbia the doctrine has, by statute, been made applicable to both commercial[9] and residential tenancies,[10] and in Manitoba,[11] Ontario,[12] Prince Edward Island,[13] New Brunswick,[14] Newfoundland,[15] Saskatchewan[16] and Yukon Territory[17] the doctrine has been made applicable to residential tenancies.

814. RESIDENTIAL TENANCY CONTROLS

Several provinces have passed residential tenancy legislation whereby a statutory tribunal is empowered to enforce the controlling legislation. In Ontario, enforcement of the provisions of the legislation has been given to a residential tenancy commission.[1] In British Columbia the legislation gave a

---

[8]*Ibid.*, at p. 721.
[9]*Commercial Tenancy Act*, R.S.B.C. 1979, c. 54, s. 33.
[10]*Residential Tenancy Act*, S.B.C. 1984, c. 15, s. 27(i).
[11]*Landlord and Tenant Act*, R.S.M. 1970, c. L70, s. 90, enacted 1970, c. 106, s. 3.
[12]*Landlord and Tenant Act*, R.S.O. 1980, c. 232, s. 88.
[13]*Landlord and Tenant Act*, R.S.P.E.I. 1974, c. L-7, s. 91(3).
[14]*Residential Tenancies Act*, S.N.B. 1975, c. R-10.2, s. 11(2).
[15]*Landlord and Tenant (Residential Tenancies) Act*, S.N. 1973, No. 54, s. 10.
[16]*Residential Tenancies Act*, R.S.S. 1978, c. R-22. s. 15.
[17]*Landlord and Tenant Ordinance*, R.O.Y.T. 1971, c. L-2, s. 67, enacted 1972, c. 20, s. 1.
§814
[1]*Residential Tenancies Act*, R.S.O. 1980, c. 452.

rentalsman similar power,[2] while in Alberta it was proposed that such power be given to a non-curial tribunal. The constitutionality of legislation which attempts to grant enforcement power to a tribunal, other than a court, has been successfully challenged.

In Alberta, the proposed legislation formed the basis of a constitutional reference whereon the Alberta Appellate Division concluded that the creation of a tribunal which could grant orders for possession and for specific performance of statutory obligations would impinge upon the federal government's right to appoint judges to those courts set out in section 96 of the *Constitution Act, 1867*.[3]

However, in British Columbia, the court concluded that power of a rentalsman to terminate a tenancy was *intra vires* provincial jurisdiction.[4] Whether this decision will survive the recent decision of the Supreme Court of Canada in *Reference Re Residential Tenancies Act*[5] is debatable.[6]

In the reference from the Court of Appeal of Ontario, the Supreme Court of Canada concluded that although the general subject-matter of landlord and tenant rights and obligations fell properly within provincial jurisdiction, it was not within the legislative competence of the provinces to empower a residential tenancy commission to make an order evicting a tenant or to make orders to both landlord and tenants to comply with their obligations imposed by the legislation. To do so would be to usurp to provincial jurisdiction the right of the federal government to appoint judges to those courts described by section 96 of the *Constitution Act, 1867*.

One difficulty flowing from this decision is the determination of just how much of the Ontario legislation may be constitutionally valid. The impugned powers of the commission recur throughout the Act. Although the general or substantive law governing the parties' relationship is within provincial jurisdiction, enforcement by way of a statutory tribunal is not. The difficulty is to

---

[2]*Residential Tenancy Act*, R.S.B.C. 1979, c. 365 rep. and replaced by the *Residential Tenancy Act*, S.B.C. 1984, c. 15, s. 61.

[3]*Reference re proposed Legislation Concerning Leased Premises and Tenancy Agreements* (1978), 89 D.L.R. (3d) 460, [1978] 6 W.W.R. 152 *sub nom. Reference re Constitutional Questions Act (Alberta)* (Alta. S.C. App. Div.).

[4]*Re Pepita and Doukas* (1979), 101 D.L.R. (3d) 577, [1980] 1 W.W.R. 240 (B.C.C.A.). As to the exercise of the rentalsman's powers, see *Re Kelsey and Williams* (1980), 115 D.L.R. (3d) 227, 24 B.C.L.R. 136 (Co. Ct.).

[5](1981), 123 D.L.R. (3d) 554, [1981] 1 S.C.R. 714.

[6]In the latter case, Mr. Justice Dickson who delivered the opinion of the court pointedly refused to express an opinion on the British Columbia decision even though the Ontario Court of Appeal, in its reasoning, drew a number of distinctions between the Ontario and the British Columbia legislation. In a subsequent decision in Nova Scotia, the Appeal Division of the Nova Scotia Supreme Court determined that certain powers conferred on the Residential Tenancies Board under the *Residential Tenancies Act*, S.N.S. 1970, c. 13, s. 11(3) as amended, were *ultra vires*: see *Re Burke and Arab; A.-G. N.S. Intervenor* (1981), 130 D.L.R. (3d) 38, 49 N.S.R. (2d) 181 (S.C. App. Div.), leave to appeal to S.C.C. granted 41 N.R. 533n, N.S.R. *loc. cit.* p. 608n. For British Columbia the question is academic with the passing of a new *Residential Tenancy Act*, S.B.C. 1984, c. 15 whereby the position of rentalsman has been done away with.

excise the tainted enforcement procedure from the valid substantive provisions when both are so closely intertwined.

The residential tenancy legislation in recent years either establishes or did establish rent controls.[7] Since administration of this legislation by provincial boards would not appear to be unconstitutional because such administration would not appear to violate section 96 of the *Constitution Act, 1867*, it is effective to control rent increases.[8]

The legislation also controls the right of the landlord to demand security deposits. The legislation in general limits the amount that may be demanded as a security deposit, requires the payment of interest thereon and seeks to ensure that the security deposit will be properly returned to the tenant.[9] It would appear that this legislation is also constitutionally valid. In general, the amount of the security deposit is limited to a month, or part of a month's rent.[10] In *Re Veltrusy Enterprises Ltd. and Gallant*[11] rent for a twelve-month period which had to be paid over the first eight months did not run afoul of the legislation.

---

[7]*Residential Tenancies Act*, R.S.O. 1980, c. 452, Part XI; *Residential Tenancy Act*, R.S.B.C. 1979, c. 365, s. 64, repealed by S.B.C. 1984, c. 15, s. 61, but the timing of rent increases is controlled by the new statute, s. 18; *Residential Rent Review Act*, S.N.B. 1975, c. R-10.1, s. 6 (expired June 30, 1979, as provided by 1978, c. 48, s. 1); *Landlord and Tenant (Residential Tenancies) Act*, S.N. 1973, No. 54, s. 20(7)(*d*); *Residential Tenancies Act*, S.N.S. 1970, c. 13, s. 11(3)(*d*); *Rent Review Act*, S.P.E.I. 1975, c. 82; *Rent Stabilization Act*, S.M. 1976, c. 3 (repealed 1980, c. 60, s. 36(*a*)).

[8]*Edison Rental Agency (1969) Ltd. v. Mudge* (1979), 101 D.L.R. (3d) 77 (Man. C.A.); *Re Burgundy Holdings Ltd. and Rent Stabilization Board* (1980), 115 D.L.R. (3d) 224 (Man. Q.B.).

[9]*Landlord and Tenant Act*, R.S.A. 1980, c. L-6, ss. 37-40; R.S.O. 1980, c. 232, ss. 84, 85; R.S.P.E.I. 1974, c. L-7, ss. 96, 97, am. 1981, c. 19, s. 1; R.S.M. 1970, c. L70, s. 84(1), enacted 1970, c. 106, s. 3; *Landlord and Tenant (Residential Tenancies) Act*, S.N. 1973, No. 54, s. 18; *Residential Tenancy Act*, S.B.C. 1984, c. 15, ss. 15, 16, 17; *Residential Tenancies Act*, S.N.B. 1975, c. R-10.2, s. 8; S.N.S. 1970, c. 13, s. 9, am. 1975, c. 64, s. 5; 1976, c. 16, s. 27; R.S.S. 1978, c. R-22, ss. 30-37, am. 1980-81, c. 40, ss. 4, 5; *Landlord and Tenant Ordinance*, R.O.N.W.T. 1974, c. L-2, ss. 50, 51; R.O.Y.T. 1971, c. L-2, ss. 63, 64, enacted 1972, c. 20, s. 1.

[10]*Ibid.*

[11](1980), 28 O.R. (2d) 349, 110 D.L.R. (3d) 100 (Co. Ct.), revd on other grounds 32 O.R. (2d) 716, 123 D.L.R. (3d) 391 (C.A.). As to the use of the deposit to have cleaning carried out, see *Re MacNeill and North American Leaseholds Ltd.* (1980), 118 D.L.R. (3d) 37 (Alta. Q.B.).

PART III
CONDITIONS AND
FUTURE INTERESTS

CONTENTS OF PART III

CHAPTER 9

INVALID CONDITIONS AND CONDITIONAL LIMITATIONS

901. CONDITIONS

An estate upon condition may be said to be an estate, the existence of which depends upon the happening or not happening of an event which will create, enlarge or defeat the estate. If the event must happen, or must not happen, e.g., the death of a named person, the estate is not conditional. Thus a grant which provides "to A for life and upon his death to B" is not conditional with respect to B as A's death is certain to occur.

A conditional estate is not a distinct species of estate but rather is a qualification of an estate, for any estate, whether freehold or less than freehold, may be subjected to a condition.

901.1 Classification

A condition is defined as a qualification or restriction annexed to an estate, whereby it is provided, that in case a particular event does or does not happen (a neutral condition), or in case the grantee does or does not do a particular

301

act (a personal condition), an estate shall be created, enlarged or defeated.[1] A condition may be either precedent or subsequent. A condition precedent is one which must be fulfilled before an estate can commence. A condition subsequent is one which either enlarges or defeats the estate already created.[2] In other words, a condition precedent is a condition of acquisition while a condition subsequent is one of retention or enlargement.

When an estate commences or takes effect it is said to be vested (from the old French *vestir* and the Latin *vestire*, "to clothe", that is, to clothe with a right). It is important to note that an estate may be said to be vested in interest, or in possession. An estate is vested in possession when the taker of the estate has the right to immediate possession whereas an estate is vested in interest when the taker of the estate, who is ascertainable, is ready to take in possession immediately upon the determination of a prior estate. Hence all estates vested in possession are, *a fortiori*, vested in interest, but not all estates vested in interest are vested in possession.

Two simple examples suffice to illustrate the difference:

A grant "to A in fee simple" vests the estate in A both in interest and possession if one assumes the grantor's estate was vested;

A grant "to A for life, remainder to B in fee simple" vests A's estate in interest and possession, but B's estate is only vested in interest as he is not able to take possession until the determination of A's prior life estate.

Thus, a condition precedent is one to be performed before an estate can vest in interest, while a condition subsequent is one to be performed after an estate has vested in interest. The event to which the condition subsequent refers need not be subsequent to the event upon which the estate comes into possession.[3]

The characterization of a condition, as being either a condition subsequent or a condition precedent is of crucial importance. For example, if a condition precedent be void, the entire grant or devise fails, whereas if a condition subsequent be void only the condition fails, thus transforming the estate granted or devised into an absolute estate.[4] The problem of characterization is not always easily resolved as no particular words are necessary to create either a condition precedent or a condition subsequent.[5] Suitable words such as "pro-

---

§901.1

[1]*Cruise's Digest of the Laws of England respecting Real Property*, 4th ed., vol. 2 (London, Saunders and Benning, 1835), p. 2.

[2]*Ibid.*, tit. 13, c. 1, s. 6.

[3]*Egerton v. Earl Brownlow* (1853), 4 H.L.C. 74, 10 E.R. 359.

[4]See §903, *infra*.

[5]*Jordan v. Dunn* (1887), 13 O.R. 267 (H.C.J.), at p. 282, affd 15 O.A.R. 744. See also *Re North Gower Twp. Public School Board and Todd*, [1968] 1 O.R. 63, 65 D.L.R. (2d) 421 (C.A.), although the problem in that case was to characterize the words as creating either a fee simple on condition subsequent or a conditional limitation. Nevertheless, the comments of Laskin, J., seem equally applicable to the characterization problem that exists when the choice is between conditions precedent or subsequent.

vided that", "so that", "under the condition that", "upon condition that" may suffice, but no precise form of words is necessary as it is sufficient that the words used were intended to have the effect of creating a condition.[6]

"Conditions are to be construed liberally according to the intention of the grantors, and in a will the intent is more especially to be regarded."[7] Thus, in a deed, whether a condition is precedent or subsequent depends not upon its position in the deed but upon its operation and the intention of the parties to be deduced from the whole instrument,[8] or, put another way, however the clauses in a deed may be arranged, the question depends upon the order of time in which the interest and nature of the transaction requires its performance.[9]

In a will, whether a condition is precedent or subsequent is a matter of construction which depends upon the intention of the testator as manifested by the will. If the condition requires something to be done over time, the tendency of the court is to construe it as a condition subsequent, a condition of retention.[10] It may be suggested that if the condition is personal to the grantee or beneficiary which requires him to do, or refrain from doing, an act for his life or a considerable period of time, logic would compel a conclusion that the condition is one of retention, not acquisition.[11]

Because of the court's bias in favour of early vesting, if the condition is capable of being construed as either a condition subsequent or a condition precedent, all other things being equal, the court will prefer the former construction.[12]

If a will contains a gift over for failure to meet the terms of the condition, the court will be influenced in favour of a condition subsequent.[13]

If the condition to be met is one that must be met before any interest is created, it is a condition precedent.[14] Thus the following have been held to be conditions precedent: a residuary gift to a charitable institution on condition that the Ontario government waive succession duties on other bequests,

---

[6]*Doe d. Henniker v. Watt* (1828), 8 B. & C. 308, 108 E.R. 1057; *Re Melville* (1886), 11 O.R. 626 at p. 631 (H.C.J.); *Re Cleghorn* (1919), 45 O.L.R. 540, 48 D.L.R. 511 (S.C. App. Div.), affd 19 O.W.N. 197 (S.C.C.).

[7]*Doe d. McGillis v. McGillivray* (1852), 9 U.C.Q.B. 9 at p. 13, *per* Robinson, D.J.

[8]*Roberts v. Brett* (1865), 11 H.L.C. 337, 11 E.R. 1363.

[9]*Jones v. Barkley* (1781), 2 Dougl. 684, 99 E.R. 434.

[10]*McKinnon v. Lundy* (1893), 24 O.R. 132 (H.C.J.), revd on another point 21 O.A.R. 560, restd 24 S.C.R. 650 *sub nom. Lundy v. Lundy*, where the condition, which required the paying off of a mortgage, was held to be a condition subsequent; see also *Re Harkin* (1925), 28 O.W.N. 494 (H.C.), where a condition requiring the devisee to pay off encumbrances was held to be a condition precedent.

[11]*Bashir v. Com'r of Lands*, [1960] 1 All E.R. 117 (P.C.); *Woodhill v. Thomas* (1889), 18 O.R. 277 (H.C.J.).

[12]*Re Greenwood; Goodhart v. Woodhead*, [1903] 1 Ch. 749 (C.A.); *Re Down*, [1968] 2 O.R. 16, 68 D.L.R. (2d) 30 (C.A.); *Duffield v. Duffield* (1829), 3 Bligh N.S. 260, 4 E.R. 1334; *Cameron v. Haszard*, [1937] 2 D.L.R. 574, [1937] S.C.R. 354; *Eastern Trust Co. v. McTague* (1963), 39 D.L.R. (2d) 743, 48 M.P.R. 134 *sub nom. Re Blanchard Estate; Quinn and Blanchard v. Eastern Trust Co.* (P.E.I.S.C.).

[13]*Re Ross* (1904), 7 O.L.R. 493 (H.C.J.); *Re Down, supra*, footnote 12.

[14]*Poirier v. Brulé* (1891), 20 S.C.R. 97.

the residuary gift failing because the government has no power to waive such payment;[15] a condition that legatees work on a farm until their legacies become due;[16] a condition that, after a period of ten years during which a son was to have income only, the estate was to go to him provided that the executors were satisfied that he had led a sober life during the period;[17] a condition that a person come to Canada and make her permanent home in Canada.[18]

On the other hand, if the condition is one of retention it is a condition subsequent and the following are illustrations thereof:

A testator devised his estate to his wife absolutely for herself, her heirs and assigns, forever, in lieu of dower, but upon the express condition that she make a will providing for his two children, and, if she failed to do so, the estate devised to her was instead to be divided equally between his two children, their heirs and assigns forever. He gave the undisposed of residue of his estate to his wife. She complied with the condition by making a will in favour of his children and it was held that she took an estate in fee simple but could not revoke the will.[19]

Where a testator devised land to his son in words passing a fee simple estate, subject to the condition that the son "shall not during his lifetime either mortgage or sell" the land devised to him, it was held that the restraint on alienation imposed by this condition was valid because there was a specific limitation as to the character of alienation and as to the time within which such alienation was not to be made.[20]

Where a testator gave his entire estate to his widow during her life but subject to a direction that if she remarried "everything shall be divided between the children", followed by a residuary clause in favour of the widow alone, it was held that she took the whole estate absolutely subject to being divested of it if she married again.[21]

A testator devised land to his wife during widowhood and, after her death, to his son on condition that he pay certain sums to the testator's other children within three years after the testator's death. The plaintiff in ejectment claimed title by sheriff's deed under an execution against the son. It was held that the condition in the will was a condition subsequent, that the son's estate was a vested remainder and saleable under execution and that it was for the defendant to show it had been divested by non-fulfilment of the condition and not for the plaintiff to show performance of it.[22]

A condition of a devise may be a condition precedent to a particular point and a condition subsequent thereafter. Thus, a testator, after giving his wife a

---

[15]*Re Reeves* (1916), 10 O.W.N. 427 (H.C.).
[16]*Oliver v. Davidson* (1882), 11 S.C.R. 166.
[17]*Re O'Grady* (1921), 19 O.W.N. 389.
[18]*Melnik v. Sawycky* (1977), 80 D.L.R. (3d) 371. [1978] 1 W.W.R. 107 (Sask. C.A.).
[19]*Re Turner; Turner v. Turner* (1902), 4 O.L.R. 578 (H.C.J.).
[20]*Re Porter* (1907), 13 O.L.R. 399 (H.C.J.).
[21]*Re Lacasse* (1913), 4 O.W.N. 986, 9 D.L.R. 831 (H.C.).
[22]*Lundy v. Maloney* (1861), 11 U.C.C.P. 143.

life estate in certain land, devised the land to her son upon the following conditions: "First, that he abstain totally from intoxicating liquor and card-playing. Second, that he be kind and obedient to his mother. Third, that he be known among his friends as an industrious man ten years after the death of his mother. Should my son Michael not fill to the letter these conditions, then he shall have no right or title to the use of the said property during or after his mother's lifetime. But I will and bequeath said half lot to my grandson J., to hold to his heirs and assigns forever." It was held that the three conditions were conditions precedent to the time of the mother's death and that the first and third conditions were conditions subsequent after the mother's death; that the first condition was valid and not too vague or indefinite for trial or adjudication by the court and, as it had been broken, the son's title failed in so far as the condition was precedent and was forfeited in so far as it was subsequent. It appeared also that the second and third conditions were valid and not too vague or indefinite for trial or adjudication of the court.[23]

901.2 Distinctions

(a) Limitations and conditional limitations

A distinction must be made between an estate granted upon a condition subsequent and an estate granted upon a determinable limitation. In both instances the estate is vested subject to defeasance but important consequences flow from the distinction. To understand the distinction it is necessary to refer to the meaning of words of limitation. "Words of limitation" specify the estate granted and measure the length of time that the estate will last. Thus the words "and his heirs" or "in fee simple" are words of limitation and measure the estate created.[1] A determinable estate has embedded within the words of limitation a condition which potentially divests the estate. On the other hand, an estate on condition subsequent does not have the condition within the limitation creating the estate, but rather, the condition subsequent is superadded to the estate granted.[2] Although certain words such as "while", "so long as", "during" and "until" are indicia of a determinable estate and although other words such as "on condition that", "if", "but if" and "if it happens" are indicia of an estate upon condition subsequent,[3] the words used are not compelling.[4] Rather, the type

---

[23]*Jordan v. Dunn* (1887), 13 O.R. 267 (H.C.J.), affd 15 O.A.R. 744.
§901.2
[1]*Goodright v. Wright* (1717), 1 P. Wms. 397, 24 E.R. 442.
[2]*Re North Gower Township Public School Board and Todd*, [1968] 1 O.R. 63, 65 D.L.R. (2d) 421 (C.A.); *Re Essex County Roman Catholic School Board and Antaya* (1977), 17 O.R. (2d) 307, 80 D.L.R. (3d) 405 (H.C.J.).
[3]Megarry and Wade, p. 76; *Re Tilbury West Public School Board and Hastie*, [1966] 2 O.R. 20, 55 D.L.R. (2d) 407 (H.C.J.), vard *loc. cit.* O.R. 511, 57 D.L.R. (2d) 519 (H.C.J.).
[4]*Re North Gower Township Public School Board and Todd, supra*, footnote 2; *Hopper v. Liverpool Corp.* (1944), 88 Sol. Jo. 213.

of estate granted must be determined by a proper construction of the deed or will as a whole.[5] In making that determination the normal rules of construction will apply, e.g., a recital will not be given an interpretation which conflicts with a granting clause in a deed.[6]

If the estate created is determinable in nature the person creating the estate retains a possibility of reverter. Upon the happening of the event determining the estate, the estate ends automatically.[7] If the estate granted is subject to a condition subsequent the person creating the estate holds a right of entry. If the event which gives rise to defeasance occurs, the estate may be ended if, and only if, the right of entry is exercised. The estate is not ended automatically as in the case of the determinable estate,[8] at least with respect to corporeal hereditaments.[9]

Since the condition subsequent may result in a forfeiture, the court, given its bias against forfeiture, will construe the condition strictly and will require certainty in the language used.[10] Moreover, certain limitations placed on the creation of conditions subsequent do not apply to determinable estates.[11]

Although there existed some confusion as to the applicability of the rule against perpetuities to the possibility of reverter remaining after the creation of a determinable estate,[12] it seems clear that, at common law, the rule was not applicable to the possibility of reverter as it remained vested in the person creating the estate.[13] On the other hand, the right of entry that arises after an estate on condition subsequent is contingent and is subject to the rule against perpetuities, as that rule existed at common law.[14] If the right of entry was void for remoteness, or indeed void for any other reason, the holder of the estate on condition subsequent held his estate absolutely, as only the condition, and not the entire estate, was struck down.[15]

At common law, in a conveyance of the fee simple, the right of re-entry for breach of a condition cannot be limited by way of remainder as the grant

---

[5]*Ibid.*

[6]*Re McKellar*, [1972] 3 O.R. 16, 27 D.L.R. (3d) 289 (H.C.J.), affd [1973] 3 O.R. 178*n*, 36 D.L.R. (3d) 202*n* (C.A.).

[7]Co. Litt. 214b; *Re Melville* (1886), 11 O.R. 626 (H.C.J.); *McKinnon v. Lundy* (1893), 24 O.R. 132 (H.C.J.), revd on other grounds 21 O.A.R. 560, restd 24 S.C.R. 650 *sub nom. Lundy v. Lundy*; *Re Machu* (1882), 21 Ch. D. 838; *Re Dugdale*; *Dugdale v. Dugdale* (1888), 38 Ch. D. 176.

[8]Challis, 219; Co. Litt. 214b, 218a; *Re Melville, supra*, footnote 7; *Re Evans's Contract*, [1920] 2 Ch. 469.

[9]*A.-G. v. Cummins*, [1906] 1 I.R. 406.

[10]*Re Tuck's Settlement Trusts*; *Public Trustee v. Tuck*, [1978] Ch. 49 (C.A.). For a more detailed discussion, see §903.3, *infra*.

[11]See §903, "Void Conditions", *infra*.

[12]*Hopper v. Liverpool Corp., supra*, footnote 4.

[13]*Re Tilbury West Public School Board and Hastie, supra*, footnote 3.

[14]*Re Essex County Roman Catholic School Board and Antaya* (1977), 17 O.R. (2d) 307, 80 D.L.R. (3d) 405 (H.C.J.), and cases discussed therein; *Re Hollis' Hospital Trustees and Hague's Contract*, [1899] 2 Ch. 540; *Pardee v. Humberstone Summer Resort Co. of Ontario, Ltd.*, [1933] O.R. 580, [1933] 3 D.L.R. 277 (H.C.J.).

[15]Co. Litt. 206a; *Re Turton*; *Whittington v. Turton*, [1926] Ch. 96.

exhausts the fee, but can only be reserved to the grantor and his heirs.[16] Before breach of the condition, the grantor actually has no reversion but only a right of entry. In *Re Melville*[17] a man conveyed land in fee simple to the municipal council of a district for the purpose of erecting a schoolhouse for the use of the district. The deed was subject to the proviso that the municipal council was to erect the schoolhouse within one year and, if it erected any other building except the schoolhouse or if it sold or transferred the land, the grantor or his heirs could re-enter and avoid the estate of the council. The council complied with the condition by building the schoolhouse before the grantor, by his will, devised his real estate to nieces. Thereafter, the successors of the council broke the condition by dealing with it otherwise than as authorized by the deed. The land having been sold, a petition was filed asking that it be declared whether the devisees under the will or the heirs of the grantor were entitled to the proceeds. It was held that a condition, as distinguished from a conditional limitation, is a means by which an estate is prematurely defeated and determined and no other estate created in its room and that the condition in this case was valid. It was further held that, under the existing *Wills Act*,[17a] the word "possibility" in section 2 included a "right of entry for condition broken" mentioned in section 10 of the Act and that a possibility is more extensive than a right of entry for condition broken. A possibility might therefore be the subject of a devise and is covered by the general word "land". Upon breach of the condition, no new estate was acquired so as to require words applicable to after-acquired estates to be found in the will. The possibility of reverter was a contingent interest that existed in the testator when his will was made. The subsequent breach of the condition gave a right of entry, by which the contingent interest might be converted into an estate of possession, and, consequently, the devisees and not the heirs were entitled to the land or to the money representing it.

Although no objection was taken in *Re Melville* that the condition offended the rule against perpetuities,[18] there is no doubt that the condition is subject to the rule against perpetuities at common law.[19]

At common law, neither the mere possibility of reverter nor the right of entry for condition broken could be conveyed or devised but descended to the heirs, though it could be released.[20]

---

[16]Littleton's Tenures, s. 347; Co. Litt. 214b, 379a; *Re Melville* (1886), 11 O.R. 626 (H.C.J.).

[17]*Supra*, footnote 16.

[17a]R.S.O. 1877, c. 106.

[18]As pointed out by Robinette, "Real Property", 9 C.E.D. (Ont.) 176.

[19]*Matheson v. Town of Mitchell* (1919), 46 O.L.R. 546, 51 D.L.R. 477 (S.C. App. Div.); *Fitzmaurice v. Board of School Trustees of Twp. of Monck*, [1949] O.W.N. 786, [1950] 1 D.L.R. 239 (H.C.J.). It should be pointed out that the *Perpetuities Act*, R.S.O. 1980, c. 374, s. 15, makes both conditions and conditional limitations, that is, the right of entry and the possibility of reverter, subject to the rule against perpetuities; for a detailed discussion, see §1103.9(1), *infra*.

[20]*Lampet's Case* (1612), 10 Co. Rep. 46 b at p. 48 a, 77 E.R. 994; *Doe d. Christmas v. Oliver* (1829), 10 B. & C. 181, 109 E.R. 418.

The *Conveyancing and Law of Property Act*[21] provides that a contingent, executory or future interest, a possibility coupled with an interest in land and a present or future right of entry upon land may be disposed of by deed. It has been pointed out that the section does not appear to authorize the conveyance of a mere possibility before breach of a condition, as such possibility is not coupled with an interest in land, and the section does not authorize conveyance of a right of entry after breach of a condition because it does not include such a right of entry.[22] Under the corresponding Imperial *Real Property Act*,[23] it was similarly held that the provision does not relate to a right to re-enter for condition broken but only to an original right where there has been a disseisin or where the party has a right to recover land and only his right of entry remains.[24]

Wills statutes similarly provide for the devisability of these interests. Thus the Ontario *Succession Law Reform Act*[25] provides in section 2:

2. A person may by will devise, bequeath or dispose of all property (whether acquired before or after making his will) to which at the time of his death he is entitled either at law or in equity, including,

. . . . .

(b) contingent, executory or other future interests in property, whether the testator is or is not ascertained as the person or one of the persons in whom those interests may respectively become vested, and whether he is entitled to them under the instrument by which they were respectively created or under a disposition of them by deed or will; and

(c) rights of entry, whether for conditions broken or otherwise.[26]

If a grant is made in fee on a condition subsequent, the grantor retains a right of entry which may be waived. This right may not be assignable as it is not, strictly, real property. The right of entry must be exercised by the person for the time being entitled to the reversion,[27] but if the grantor assigns the reversion after the breach has occurred, the assignee cannot exercise the right of entry as the right cannot be assigned.[28]

---

[21]R.S.O. 1980, c. 90, s. 10. For similar legislation in other jurisdictions see: *Property Act*, R.S.N.B. 1973, c. P-19, s. 15; *Real Property Act*, R.S.N.S. 1967, c. 261, s. 26; R.S.P.E.I. 1974, c. R-4, s. 11; *Property Law Act*, R.S.B.C. 1979, c. 340, s. 8.

[22]Robinette, "Real Property", 9 C.E.D. (Ont.) 176; *Baldwin v. Wanzer*; *Baldwin v. Canadian Pacific Ry. Co.* (1892), 22 O.R. 612 (H.C.J.).

[23]8 & 9 Vict., c. 106, s. 6 (1845).

[24]*Hunt v. Bishop* (1853), 8 Ex. 675 at p. 680, 155 E.R. 1523; *Hunt v. Remnant* (1854), 9 Ex. 635 at p. 640, 156 E.R. 271; *Crane v. Batten* (1854), 23 L.T. (O.S.) 220; *Jenkins v. Jones* (1882), 9 Q.B.D. 128 at p. 131 (C.A.); see also *Cohen v. Tannar*, [1900] 2 Q.B. 609 (C.A.), as to the same construction applying to the Imperial *Conveyancing and Law of Property Act*, 44 & 45 Vict., c. 41, s. 10 (1881).

[25]R.S.O. 1980, c. 488.

[26]To the same effect are: *Wills Act*, R.S.B.C. 1979, c. 434, s. 2; R.S.M. 1970, c. W150, s. 3; R.S.S. 1978, c. W-14, s. 3; R.S.N.B. 1973, c. W-9, s. 2; R.S.A. 1980, c. W-11, s. 3; *Wills Ordinance*, R.O.N.W.T. 1974, c. W-3, s. 4; R.O.Y.T. 1971, c. W-3, s. 4. See also *Wills Act*, R.S.N.S. 1967, c. 340, s. 2.

[27]*Doe d. Marriott v. Edwards* (1834), 5 B. & Ad. 1065, 110 E.R. 1086.

[28]Armour, *Real Property*, pp. 418-21; *Clark v. Corp. of City of Vancouver* (1903), 10 B.C.R. 31 (C.A.), affd 35 S.C.R. 121.

As has been pointed out,[29] words of express condition are not ordinarily construed as a limitation unless there is a limitation over, so that, if strict words of condition are used but if, on breach of the condition, the estate is limited to a third person and does not revert to the grantor, the words are construed as a conditional limitation and not a condition. Thus, if A grants an estate to B, on condition that he marry C within two years and, on his failing to do so, to D and his heirs, this is construed as a conditional limitation because, if it were regarded as a condition, only A or his heirs could avoid the estate by entry for breach of the condition which they might fail to do, so that D's remainder might be defeated by the neglect, but when construed as a limitation, the estate of B ceases by his breach and that of D commences, so that he may enter on the lands when the breach occurs.

It is a settled rule of construction that where a will is not clear, words are not construed as imparting a condition, particularly a condition of forfeiture, if they are fairly capable of another interpretation[30] and words expressing a condition may be treated as words of limitation.[31]

(b) Conditions and covenants

A condition that will create an estate upon condition must be distinguished from a covenant to do or abstain from doing some act. The difference in effect is that breach of a true condition may defeat an estate and give a right to re-entry, but breach of a covenant gives merely a right of action.[32] The covenant contractually binds one to performance whereas the condition does not, its breach leading to potential defeasance. Although uncommon, it is possible for a clause to operate as a covenant and a condition at one and the same time.[33]

No particular form of words is necessary to create a covenant. A deed will not be construed to create an estate upon condition unless language is used which, according to the rules of law, *ex proprio vigore*, imparts a condition or the intent of the grantor to make a conditional sale is otherwise clearly and unequivocally indicated. Conditions subsequent are not favoured in law. If it is doubtful whether a clause in a deed is a covenant or a condition, courts of law will always incline against the latter construction. The usual and proper technical words by which an estate upon condition is granted by deed are "provided", "so as" or "on condition". In grants from the Crown and in devises, a conditional estate may be created by the use of words which declare

---

[29]Armour, *op. cit.*, *supra*, footnote 28, p. 164, citing *Sheppard's Touchstone on Common Assurances*, p. 124.

[30]*Edgeworth v. Edgeworth* (1869), L.R. 4 H.L. 35 at p. 41.

[31]*Pelham Clinton v. Duke of Newcastle*, [1902] 1 Ch. 34, affd [1903] A.C. 111.

[32]*Caldy Manor Estate Ltd. v. Farrell*, [1974] 3 All E.R. 753 (C.A.); *Stephens v. Gulf Oil Canada Ltd.* (1975), 11 O.R. (2d) 129, 65 D.L.R. (3d) 193 (C.A.).

[33]*Bashir v. Com'r of Lands*, [1960] 1 All E.R. 117 (P.C.); *Pearson v. Adams* (1912), 27 O.L.R. 87, 7 D.L.R. 139 (H.C.J.), revd on other grounds 28 O.L.R. 154, 12 D.L.R. 227 (C.A.), restd 50 S.C.R. 204 at p. 209.

that it is given or devised for a certain purpose or with any particular intention, but this rule is applicable only to those grants or gifts which are purely voluntary and where there is no consideration moving the grantor or donor other than the purpose for which the estate is declared to be created. Such words do not make a condition when used in deeds of private persons.[34] Ordinarily, non-fulfilment of the purpose for which a conveyance by deed is made will not of itself defeat an estate. There is no authoritative sanction for the doctrine that a deed is to be construed as a grant on a condition subsequent solely for the reason that it contains a clause declaring the purpose for which it is intended that the granted premises will be used, where such purpose will not enure specially to the benefit of the grantor and his assigns.[35]

It has been said that a condition is created by the grantor or testator whereas a covenant is made by the grantee.[36] Thus options and rights of pre-emption have been held to be covenants,[37] not conditions, but in making this distinction the transaction must be looked at as a whole.[38]

Where the operative words of a deed create a fee simple absolute, and where the *habendum* contains words that could operate as a condition or a covenant, the court will construe the words as a covenant rather than a condition as the *habendum* cannot cut down the operative words of the grant; it may only explain those words.[39]

902. VESTING AND DIVESTING OF CONDITIONAL GIFTS

If there is doubt as to whether a condition in a will is precedent or subsequent, the court prefers to construe it as a condition subsequent, and will do so if such a construction is consistent with the will as a whole and will not construe it as a condition precedent unless the will clearly shows that it is intended to be such.[1] Therefore, the presumption as to intent is in favour of vesting at the testator's death or at the earliest moment after that date which is possible under

---

[34]*Pearson v. Adams, supra*, footnote 33, *per* Anglin, J., at p. 212 S.C.R.

[35]*Pearson v. Adams, supra*, footnote 33, 27 O.L.R. 87 at p. 93, 7 D.L.R. 139 at pp. 144-5; *Powell v. City of Vancouver* (1912), 1 W.W.R. 1022 (B.C.S.C.), affd 8 D.L.R. 24, 3 W.W.R. 108 and 161 (C.A.); *Paul v. Paul* (1921), 50 O.L.R. 211, 64 D.L.R. 269 (S.C. App. Div.).

[36]*Laurin v. Iron Ore Co. of Canada* (1977), 82 D.L.R. (3d) 634, 19 Nfld. & P.E.I.R. 111 (Nfld. S.C.T.D.).

[37]*Stephens v. Gulf Oil Canada Ltd., supra*, footnote 32.

[38]*Laurin v. Iron Ore Co. of Canada, supra*, footnote 36.

[39]*MacLeod v. Town of Amherst* (1973), 39 D.L.R. (3d) 146, 8 N.S.R. (2d) 504 (S.C.), affd 44 D.L.R. (3d) 723, 8 N.S.R. (2d) 491 (S.C. App. Div.).

§902

[1]*Egerton v. Earl Brownlow* (1853), 4 H.L.C. 1 at pp. 182-3, 10 E.R. 359; *Woodhouse v. Herrick* (1855), 1 K. & J. 352 at pp. 359-60, 69 E.R. 494; *Lady Langdale v. Briggs* (1856), 8 De G. M. & G. 391, 44 E.R. 441; *Re Greenwood; Goodhart v. Woodhead*, [1903] 1 Ch. 749 at p. 755 (C.A.); *Re Down*, [1968] 2 O.R. 16, 68 D.L.R. (2d) 30 (C.A.); *Cameron v. Haszard*, [1937] 2 D.L.R. 574, [1937] S.C.R. 354.

the terms of the will, whether the gift is of real or personal property.[2] The presumption is that the testator intended the gift to be vested, subject to being divested if necessary, rather than have it remain in suspense.[3]

The presumption is especially applied in the case of remainders, because the construction of a remainder as contingent might exclude issue by reason of the parents' dying before the vesting of the remainder.[4] It is also especially applied in the case of residuary gifts of real and personal property.[5]

If the terms of a gift can be fairly construed as merely postponing the right of possession, so as to draw a distinction between the time of vesting and the time of enjoyment, that construction is adopted if the terms of the will permit.[6]

Furthermore, in construing a will, the court leans against the divesting of vested interests,[7] and favours that construction which leads to indefeasible vesting as soon as possible.[8] Consequently, subject to the intention garnered from the whole will, divesting conditions are construed strictly[9] and, if there is a vested gift with a provision divesting it on an express contingency, the gift is held not to be divested unless that precise contingency occurs.[10]

If there is a provision revoking or divesting a gift on the failure of a condition, the condition must wholly fail or no revocation or divesting will occur.

---

[2]*Driver v. Frank* (1818), 8 Taunt. 468, 129 E.R. 465 (Ex. Ch.); *Duffield v. Duffield* (1829), 3 Bligh N.S. 260 at pp. 311, 331, 4 E.R. 1334 (H.L.); *Re Blakemore's Settlement* (1855), 20 Beav. 214 at p. 217, 52 E.R. 585; *Brocklebank v. Johnson* (1855), 20 Beav. 205, 52 E.R. 581; *Re Merricks' Trusts* (1866), L.R. 1 Eq. 551; *Radford v. Willis* (1871), 7 Ch. App. 7; *Hervey-Bathurst v. Stanley*; *Craven v. Stanley* (1876), 4 Ch. D. 251 (C.A.); *Rhodes v. Rhodes* (1882), 7 App. Cas. 192 (P.C.); *Re Wrightson*; *Battie-Wrightson v. Thomas*, [1904] 2 Ch. 95 at p. 103 (C.A.).

[3]*Hickling v. Fair*, [1899] A.C. 15 (H.L.), at pp. 30, 36, per Lord Blackburn.

[4]*Driver v. Frank* (1814), 3 M. & S. 25 at p. 37, 105 E.R. 521, affd 8 Taunt. 468, 129 E.R. 465 (Ex. Ch.); *Re Watkins*; *Maybery v. Lightfoot*, [1914] A.C. 782.

[5]*Love v. L'Estrange* (1727), 5 Brown. 59, 2 E.R. 532; *Booth v. Booth* (1799), 4 Ves. Jun. 399, 31 E.R. 203; *Pearman v. Pearman* (1864), 33 Beav. 394 at p. 396, 55 E.R. 420; *West v. West* (1863), 4 Giff. 198, 66 E.R. 677.

[6]*Montgomerie v. Woodley* (1800), 5 Ves. Jun. 522 at p. 836, 31 E.R. 714; *Bingley v. Broadhead* (1803), 8 Ves. Jun. 415, 32 E.R. 416; *Duffield v. Duffield* (1829), 1 Dow & Cl. 268 at p. 311, 6 E.R. 525 (H.L.); *Peard v. Kekewich* (1852), 15 Beav. 166 at p. 171, 51 E.R. 500; *Dennis v. Frend* (1863), 14 I. Ch. R. 271.

[7]*Maddison v. Chapman* (1858), 4 K. & J. 709 at pp. 721, 723, 70 E.R. 294; *Re Wood*; *Moore v. Bailey* (1880), 43 L.T. 730 at p. 732; *Re Roberts*; *Percival v. Roberts*, [1903] 2 Ch. 200 at p. 204.

[8]*Minors v. Battison* (1876), 1 App. Cas. 428 (H.L.); *Hervey-Bathurst v. Stanley, supra*, footnote 2; *Re Teale*; *Teale v. Teale* (1885), 53 L.T. 936 at p. 937; *Re Stark & Trim*, [1932] O.R. 263, [1932] 2 D.L.R. 603 (C.A.).

[9]*Kiallmark v. Kiallmark* (1856), 26 L.J. Ch. 1 at p. 5; *Blagrove v. Bradshaw* (1858), 4 Drewry 230 at p. 235, 62 E.R. 89.

[10]*Tarbuck v. Tarbuck* (1835), 4 L.J. Ch. 129; *Cox v. Parker* (1856), 22 Beav. 168, 52 E.R. 1072; *Potts v. Atherton* (1859), 28 L.J. Ch. 486 at p. 488; *Re Kirkbride's Trusts* (1866), L.R. 2 Eq. 400 at p. 402; *Re Pickworth*; *Snaith v. Parkinson*, [1899] 1 Ch. 642 (C.A.); *Re Searle*; *Searle v. Searle*, [1905] W.N. 86 (H.C.J.); *Parkes v. Trusts Corp. of Ontario* (1895), 26 O.R. 494 (H.C.J.), at p. 498; *Beckett v. Foy* (1855), 12 U.C.Q.B. 361; *Re Hanna* (1917), 11 O.W.N. 347 (H.C.).

Thus, where a testator directed his trustees to divide his real estate equally between his sons then living when his eldest son attained the age of 25 years at which time the share of the eldest son was to be conveyed to him but, if any of the sons died before attaining the age of 25 years without issue, the share of one so dying was to be divided equally among the survivors, and the eldest son died before attaining the age of 25 leaving a widow and infant daughter, it was held that the daughter took the land as her father's heiress subject to her mother's dower because the executory limitation did not take effect unless the double event happened, *i.e.*, the eldest son's dying before age 25 and without issue.[11]

Similarly, where a testator gave his widow a life interest in his estate and, after her death, gave the residue equally to his two brothers or, in case of their dying before his wife, the residue to be equally divided between their heirs, and the one brother died during the life of the widow and the other survived her, it was held that the share of the one who first died passed under his will as the event provided for, *i.e.*, the death of both brothers during the life of the widow, had not happened.[12]

Again, where there was a gift over if the donee died "before having children", the court refused to construe the words as meaning "without leaving issue surviving".[13]

In the case of a gift over upon several specified events connected by the word "and" and if the language is capable of having its ordinary sense, the court is not willing to construe the word "and" as "or" because the effect would be to divest a gift in an event other than the double event provided for by the testator.[14] Where there was a bequest to an infant with a gift over in the event of the infant's not surviving the testator and dying before attaining the age of 21, the court refused to construe "and" as "or". The infant took a vested interest upon surviving the testator which was not subject to divestment.[15] In *Lillie v. Willis*,[16] a testatrix devised and bequeathed all her real and personal estate to her son in fee with a gift over if he died without issue before her brother and sister. The sister died in the lifetime of the son. It was held that, as the event of the son's dying before both the brother and sister could not happen, he took an indefeasible fee simple.

Conversely, if the interest of a donee follows a life interest and is contingent only on his attaining a specified age and not on his surviving the life tenant and

---

[11]*Cook v. Noble* (1884), 5 O.R. 43 (H.C.J.).
[12]*Re Metcalfe; Metcalfe v. Metcalfe* (1900), 32 O.R. 103 (H.C.J.).
[13]*Re Breault and Grimshaw* (1918), 13 O.W.N. 387 (H.C.).
[14]*Doe d. Usher v. Jessep* (1810), 12 East. 288 at p. 293, 104 E.R. 113; *Key v. Key* (1855), 1 Jur. N.S. 372; *Coates v. Hart; Borrett v. Hart* (1863), 3 De G. J. & S. 504, 46 E.R. 731; *Malcolm v. Malcolm* (1856), 21 Beav. 225, 52 E.R. 845; *Reed v. Braithwaite* (1871), L.R. 11 Eq. 514.
[15]*Re Stamp* (1918), 14 O.W.N. 80 (H.C.).
[16](1899), 31 O.R. 198 (H.C.J.).

there is a gift over on his death before that of the life tenant or under the specified age, the word "or" is construed as "and".[17]

Similarly, if there is a devise to a person in fee simple or absolutely, with a gift over to other donees if he dies without children or under the age of 21 years, the word "or" is construed as "and" and the gift over does not take effect unless both events happen.[18]

The rule is based upon the presumed intention of the testator to benefit the children of the devisee directly or indirectly, an intention that would be defeated if the devisee were to die under age 21 leaving children and the rule were not applied.[19]

The word "and", however, may be construed to mean "or" if one member of a compound sentence is included in the other and construing it literally would render one member of the sentence unnecessary but making the change would give effect to each member. This construction is generally made in favour of vesting so as not to defeat a previously vested gift. A limitation of real estate to A during the lifetimes of B and C, without saying, "and during the lifetime of the survivor of them", gives A an estate during the lifetimes of B and C and the survivor. But a limitation for 100 years, if A and B shall so long live, is determined by the death of either, because this is a collateral condition.[20] If there is a gift to a person and, after his death, to his children, with a gift over if he dies "unmarried and without issue", the word "and" will be construed as "or" if it appears that the word "unmarried" is used in the ordinary sense of never having been married, in which case the words "and without issue" would be unnecessary.[21] Usually, however, if the word "unmarried" in such a case can be given the meaning "without leaving a spouse", it will be given that meaning, so as to give effect to all of the words.[22]

The word "and" is not changed to "or" if that would make part of the sentence imperative.[23]

Following the rule of leaning against the divesting of a vested interest, if there is a gift to a person for life and after his death to his children so expressed as to give them a vested interest whether or not they survive the parent and

---

[17]*Miles v. Dyer* (1832), 5 Sim. 435, 58 E.R. 400, and 8 Sim. 330, 59 E.R. 131, followed in *Bentley v. Meech* (1858), 25 Beav. 197, 53 E.R. 611.

[18]*Doe d. Herbert v. Selby* (1824), 2 B. & C. 926, 107 E.R. 626; *Morris v. Morris* (1853), 17 Beav. 198, 51 E.R. 1009; *Imray v. Imeson* (1872), 26 L.T. 93; *cf. Re Adam* (1922), 23 O.W.N. 96 (S.C. App. Div.), in which case there was a gift over if the donee should die before coming of age or die leaving no children.

[19]*Re Crutchley; Kidson v. Marsden*, [1912] 2 Ch. 335 at p. 337; *Grey v. Pearson* (1857), 6 H.L.C. 61, 10 E.R. 1216.

[20]*Day v. Day* (1854), Kay. 703 at p. 708, 69 E.R. 300.

[21]*Wilson v. Bayly* (1760), 3 Brown. 195, 1 E.R. 1265; *Hepworth v. Taylor* (1784), 1 Cox 112, 29 E.R. 1086; *Maberly v. Strode* (1797), 3 Ves. Jun. 450 at p. 454, 30 E.R. 1100; *Bell v. Phyn* (1802), 7 Ves. Jun. 453 at p. 459, 32 E.R. 183; *Roberts v. Lord Bishop of Kilmore*, [1902] 1 I.R. 333.

[22]*Re Sanders' Trusts* (1866), L.R. 1 Eq. 675; *Re King; Salibury v. Ridley* (1890), 62 L.T. 789; *Re Chant; Chant v. Lemon*, [1900] 2 Ch. 345 at p. 348.

[23]*Key v. Key, supra*, footnote 14; *Re Kirkbride's Trusts* (1866), L.R. 2 Eq. 400 at p. 403.

there is a gift over if the parent dies "without leaving children", these words are construed, according to the context of the will, as "without having children",[24] or as "without having had children",[25] or as "without leaving children who have attained vested interests",[26] so as not to divest the vested interests. This rule is applied where the interests of the children are to vest at their birth,[27] or are to vest at the age of 21,[28] or when the youngest attains a specified age,[29] or at age 21, or marriage,[30] or are to vest on the happening of any similar event without reference to surviving their parent.[31]

If there is a gift for life and, after the death of the life tenant, to a number of persons equally or to such of them as survive the life tenant, ordinarily this is construed as divesting only the interests of those who do not survive in favour of those who do, so that, if all die before the life tenant, their personal representatives take their shares equally.[32]

Similarly, where the gift to the survivor of a number of persons is conditional on some event, it is construed as conditional upon his surviving that event.[33]

Where, however, the will shows that the reference to survivorship means survivorship among themselves and not just survivorship of the life tenant, the rule is not applied and the survivor of them takes the gift even though none of them survive the life tenant.[34]

903. VOID CONDITIONS

Conditions may be invalid for a number of reasons, such as repugnancy, public policy, impossibility of performance, and others. In this respect a distinction is drawn between conditions precedent and conditions subsequent. The latter are more readily struck down since that will cause the estate to vest abso-

---

[24]Re Tookey's Trust; Re Bucks Ry. Co. (1852), 21 L.J. Ch. 402, 1 Drewry 264, 61 E.R. 453; Kennedy v. Sedgwick (1857), 3 K. & J. 540, 69 E.R. 1223; White v. Hill (1867), L.R. 4 Eq. 265; Re Brown's Trust (1873), L.R. 16 Eq. 239; Re Jackson's Will (1879), 13 Ch. D. 189.

[25]Marshall v. Hill (1814), 2 M. & S. 608, 105 E.R. 508; Bryden v. Willett (1869), L.R. 7 Eq. 472; Treharne v. Layton (1875), L.R. 10 Q.B. 459.

[26]Re Cobbold; Cobbold v. Lawton, [1903] 2 Ch. 299 (C.A.).

[27]Treharne v. Layton, supra, footnote 25; Re Bradbury; Wing v. Bradbury (1904), 73 L.J. Ch. 591; Re Goldney; Re Dighton (1911), 130 L.T.Jo. 484.

[28]Maitland v. Chalie (1822), 6 Madd. 243, 56 E.R. 1084; Re Thompson's Trust; Re Trustee Relief Act, 1848, Ex p. Oliver (1852), 5 De G. & S. 667, 64 E.R. 1291.

[29]Kennedy v. Sedgwick, supra, footnote 24.

[30]Casamajor v. Strode (1843), 8 Jur. (O.S.) 14.

[31]Barkworth v. Barkworth (1906), 75 L.J. Ch. 754 at p. 756.

[32]Browne v. Lord Kenyon (1818), 3 Madd. 410, 56 E.R. 556; Sturgess v. Pearson (1819), 4 Madd. 411, 56 E.R. 757; Page v. May (1857), 24 Beav. 323, 53 E.R. 382; Re Pickworth, [1899] 1 Ch. 642 (C.A.); Penny v. Com'r for Railways, [1900] A.C. 628 at p. 634 (P.C.).

[33]Clarke v. Lubbock (1842), 1 Y. & C.C.C. 492, 62 E.R. 985; Cambridge v. Rous (1858), 25 Beav. 409, 53 E.R. 693; Maddison v. Chapman (1861), 1 J. & H. 470, 70 E.R. 831; Marriott v. Abell (1869), L.R. 7 Eq. 478; Re Deacon's Trusts (1906). 95 L.T. 701.

[34]White v. Baker (1860), 2 De G. F. & J. 55, 45 E.R. 542 (C.A.).

lutely. If conditions precedent are void, however, the whole gift is void as well. That at least is the rule with respect to real property. With respect to personal property, the English cases, followed sometimes in Canada, hold that the fact that the condition is void does not necessarily render the gift void. This point is dealt with below.[1]

If the determining event arises not by way of condition, but by way of determinable limitation, then, if the determining event is void for whatever reason, such as uncertainty, the whole gift is void, just as in the case of a condition precedent, for then the estate is improperly limited.[2]

903.1 Repugnancy

A condition in a deed which is repugnant to the estate created by it is void. Where a deed in fee simple, after the *habendum*, contained a proviso that the conveyance was to be void and the estate was to revert to the grantor upon default by the grantee in performance of the covenant thereinafter contained, the covenant being that the grantee would cultivate the land during the life of the grantor for his benefit, the proviso was held to be void as being inconsistent with the grant.[1] Where a deed clearly granted an estate in fee simple and, in a subsequent provision, an attempt was made to postpone the vesting of the grantee's estate until he attained the age of 21 years, without vesting the estate in another person meanwhile, it was held that such subsequent provision was repugnant to the earlier operative words of the deed and should be disregarded.[2]

In regard to gifts in a will, the general rule is that, where there is an absolute gift of real or personal property and a condition is attached which is inconsistent with and repugnant to the gift, the condition is wholly void and the donee takes the gift free from the condition.[3] Therefore, after an absolute gift, a proviso for forfeiture in case of bankruptcy of the donee or an alienation by him is void.[4]

The most common type of condition that is repugnant to the estate granted

---

§903
[1]See §903.3, *infra*.
[2]See *Re Moore; Royal Trust Co. v. Moore*, [1954] 3 D.L.R. 407, 13 W.W.R. (N.S.) 113 (B.C.S.C.), revd [1955] 4 D.L.R. 313, 16 W.W.R. 204 (C.A.), restd in part 5 D.L.R. (2d) 152, [1956] S.C.R. 880.
§903.1
[1]*Brown v. Stuart* (1855), 12 U.C.Q.B. 510.
[2]*Eisenhauer v. Eisenhauer*, [1943] 1 D.L.R. 411, 16 M.P.R. 438 (N.S.S.C.).
[3]*Bradley v. Peixoto* (1797), 3 Ves. Jun. 324, 30 E.R. 1034; *Byng v. Lord Strafford* (1843), 5 Beav. 558 at p. 567, 49 E.R. 694; *Watkins v. Williams; Haverd v. Church* (1851), 3 Mac. & G. 622, 42 E.R. 400; *Egerton v. Earl Brownlow* (1853), 4 H.L.C. 1 at p. 181, 10 E.R. 359.
[4]*Re Machu* (1882), 21 Ch. D. 838; *Re Dugdale; Dugdale v. Dugdale* (1888), 38 Ch. D. 176; *Corbett v. Corbett* (1888), 14 P.D. 7 (C.A.); *Metcalfe v. Metcalfe* (1889), 43 Ch. D. 633.

is a restraint on alienation.[5] However, a condition making alienation mandatory may also be void as repugnant to the estate held, an incident of which is to enjoy it as well as alienate it. Consequently, where there was a condition attached to a devise in fee simple that, if the devisee did not live until the age of 21 years or, if he attained that age and had not made a will, there was to be a gift over, the condition was held to be repugnant to the estate and void.[6] Similarly, a condition attached to a devise requiring the devisee, on a sale of the land, to pay certain sums to other persons was held void as repugnant to the estate as there was no obligation to sell, no intention to benefit the other persons otherwise and it was the devisee's right as absolute owner to receive all proceeds of sale. The power of disposition by a testator extends only to the creation of those interests which are recognized by law and no others.[7]

In short, if an estate is given, an incident of the estate which cannot be directly taken away or prevented by a donor cannot be taken away indirectly by a condition which would cause the estate to revert to the donor, nor by a conditional limitation which would cause it to shift to another person.[8] The rule applies also where the estate given is merely a life estate.[9]

The jurisdiction of a court to construe a will is not ousted by a direction in a will that it is to be settled in another manner, such as by the executors or trustees or by arbitration,[10] nor is a condition that a beneficiary shall not dispute the validity of a will ordinarily construed as applying where there is a reasonable cause for litigation.[11] If a condition is couched in such language as to prevent a donee from resorting to any proceedings whatsoever concerning the gift even to secure its enjoyment, the condition is void as being repugnant to the gift.[12]

If property is given absolutely, a condition cannot be added to the gift that is inconsistent with its absolute character, so if a devise in fee simple is made upon a condition under which the estate is shorn of its necessary incidents, such as that a wife shall not have dower or that a husband shall not have curtesy, or that the devisee shall not have the profits or shall not have the power to alienate generally or for a limited time, the condition is void as repugnant to the estate created.[13]

---

[5]Because of the plethora of cases under this topic, and because of recent developments in various provincial jurisdictions this topic is dealt with separately: see §903.7, *infra*.
[6]*Holmes v. Godson* (1856), 8 De G. M. & G. 152, 44 E.R. 347.
[7]*Re Elliot; Kelly v. Elliot*, [1896] 2 Ch. 353.
[8]*Re Dugdale, supra*, footnote 4, at p. 182, *per* Kay, J.
[9]*Brandon v. Robinson* (1811), 18 Ves. Jun. 429, 34 E.R. 379; *Metcalfe v. Metcalfe, supra*, footnote 4.
[10]*Re Walton's Estate* (1856), 8 De G. M. & G. 173, 44 E.R. 356 (C.A.); *Massy v. Rogers* (1883), 11 L.R. Ir. 409.
[11]*Adams v. Adams*, [1892] 1 Ch. 369 (C.A.); *Re Williams; Williams v. Williams*, [1912] 1 Ch. 399 at p. 401.
[12]*Rhodes v. Muswell Hill Land Co.* (1861), 29 Beav. 560 at p. 563, 54 E.R. 745; *Re Williams, supra*, footnote 11.
[13]*Blackburn v. McCallum* (1903), 33 S.C.R. 65.

903.2 Devolution by Law

A condition that prohibits a course of devolution that the law directs is void. For example, the law provides how the real property of a person who dies intestate shall devolve and be inherited, and any condition in a will attempting to alter the course of devolution by operation of law is void because no person may create a new mode of devolution, so a condition that an estate in fee simple is not to be inherited is void.[1] Consequently, if land is devised in fee simple, a condition that if the devisee dies intestate there is to be a devise over to another person, is void as repugnant to the estate created.[2] A condition that is repugnant to other gifts in the will is void, so a gift over is bad which defeats or abridges an estate in fee simple by altering the course of its devolution and is to take effect at the moment of devolution or is to defeat an estate and take effect on the exercise of any rights incident to that estate, such as on partition by two or more prior donees, on an alienation,[3] or non-alienation,[4] or on an escheat,[5] or on forfeiture to the Crown.[6]

If the condition is worded so as to defeat the estate upon the mental incompetency of the donee,[7] it will be void, as the law provides for devolution upon the event, *i.e.*, mental incompetency.

Although a condition may not be attached to an estate limiting devolution by law, no such restriction exists with respect to a determinable limitation.[8] Thus, an estate determinable upon bankruptcy may be created.[9]

903.3 Public Policy

Conditions which are contrary to public policy, or are illegal or immoral are void. A condition which is contrary to public policy is one in which the state has

---

§903.2

[1]*Holmes v. Godson* (1856), 8 De G. M. & G. 152, 44 E.R. 347; *Re Wilcocks' Settlement* (1875), 1 Ch. D. 229.

[2]*Farrell v. Farrell* (1867), 26 U.C.Q.B. 652; *Kerr v. Leishman* (1860), 8 Gr. 435; *Re Babcock* (1862), 9 Gr. 427; *Re McIntyre* (1919), 16 O.W.N. 260 (H.C.); *Re Walker* (1925), 56 O.L.R. 517 (S.C. App. Div.), at p. 521.

[3]*Shaw v. Ford* (1877), 7 Ch. D. 669 at p. 674.

[4]*Re Beetlestone*; *Beetlestone v. Hall* (1907), 122 L.T.Jo. 367.

[5]*Mildmay v. Mildmay* (1601), Moore (K. B.) 632 at p. 633, 72 E.R. 805; *Carte v. Carte* (1744), 3 Atk. 174 at p. 180, 26 E.R. 902.

[6]*Re Wilcocks' Settlement* (1875), 1 Ch. D. 229.

[7]*Re Ashton*; *Ballard v. Ashton*, [1920] 2 Ch. 481; *Re Gee* (1973), 41 D.L.R. (3d) 317, [1974] 2 W.W.R. 176 *sub nom. Re Gee Kee (Gee John Kow) (Chee John Kow)* (B.C.S.C.).

[8]For the distinction between estates determinable and estates on condition subsequent, see §901.2(a), *supra*.

[9]*Re Leach*; *Leach v. Leach*, [1912] 2 Ch. 422. For the distinction between the effect of such a condition attached as a condition subsequent, see *Re Machu* (1882), 21 Ch. D. 838.

an interest in the non-performance of the condition.[1] However, since the determination as to what is contrary to public policy varies from time to time,[2] it may be difficult to determine at any given time whether the condition will be valid or void in the future.

There are several broad categories into which conditions held void for public policy fall. Perhaps the category most clearly against public policy encompasses those conditions that incite the donee to commit a crime, or other act prohibited by law,[3] or to do an act contrary to statute.[4] Included in this category are conditions that tend to incite the donee to use corruption or exert private or political party influence in a matter of state, such as in the obtaining of a title of honour.[5] Conditions that forbid a devisee from entering into the defence of the realm,[6] or forbidding performance of a public duty,[7] are void. Conditions forbidding the entering into a religious order have not been held void on the ground of public policy.[8]

Conditions which encourage disregard of marital obligations are void as contrary to public policy.[9] Thus, conditions tending to cause a future separation of the spouses are void, whether the condition is in a settlement or an agreement.[10] However, if the condition merely refers to the circumstances existing at the time of the creation of the interest and cannot influence the conduct of the parties, it is valid.[11] Thus, a gift to a married woman, already separated from her husband, with a gift over if she reconciles with her husband, is not

---

§903.3

[1]*Cooke v. Turner* (1846), 15 M. & W. 727 at p. 735, 153 E.R. 1044.

[2]*Evanturel v. Evanturel* (1874), L.R. 6 P.C. 1 at p. 29.

[3]*Mitchel v. Reynolds* (1711), 1 P. Wms. 181 at p. 189, 24 E.R. 347; *Earl of Shrewsbury v. Hope Scott* (1859), 6 Jur. 452 at p. 456.

[4]*Re Brown; Brown v. Brown* (1900), 32 O.R. 323 (H.C.J.).

[5]*Egerton v. Earl Brownlow* (1853), 4 H.L.C. 1 at pp. 69, 99, 142, 150, 163, 172 and 196, 10 E.R. 359.

[6]*Re Beard; Reversionary and General Securities Co. Ltd. v. Hall*, [1908] 1 Ch. 383; *Re Adair*, [1909] 1 I.R. 311. *Cf. Re Pape Estate*, [1946] 4 D.L.R. 700, [1946] 3 W.W.R. 8 (Alta. S.C.).

[7]*Re Morgan; Dowson v. Davey* (1910), 26 T.L.R. 398.

[8]*Re Dickson's Trust* (1850), 1 Sim. (N.S.) 37, 61 E.R. 14.

[9]*Re Nurse* (1921), 20 O.W.N. 428 (H.C.); *Re Cutter* (1916), 37 O.L.R. 42, 31 D.L.R. 382 (S.C.).

[10]*Hindley v. Marquis of Westmeath* (1827), 6 B. & C. 200, 108 E.R. 427; *Marquis of Westmeath v. Marquis of Salisbury* (1831), 5 Bligh N.S. 339, 5 E.R. 349 (H.L.); *Marquis of Westmeath v. Marchioness of Westmeath* (1830), 1 Dow & Clark 519, 6 E.R. 619 (H.L.); *Re Moore; Trafford v. Maconochie* (1888), 39 Ch. D. 116 (C.A.); *Re Morgan; Dowson v. Davey* (1910), 26 T.L.R. 398; *Cartwright v. Cartwright* (1853), 3 De G. M. & G. 982, 43 E.R. 385 (C.A.); *Re Nurse, supra*, footnote 9; *Re Fairfoull* (1973), 41 D.L.R. (3d) 152 (B.C.S.C.), reconsidered 44 D.L.R. (3d) 765 sub nom. *(No. 2)* (S.C.), affd [1974] 6 W.W.R. 471, 18 R.F.L. 165 (S.C.); *Re McBride* (1980), 27 O.R. (2d) 513, 107 D.L.R. (3d) 233 (H.C.J.), holding such a condition to be *malum prohibitum*. See critical comment by Oosterhoff in 5 E. & T.Q. 97 (1971-81).

[11]*Shewell v. Dwarris* (1858), Johns. 172, 70 E.R. 384, but see *Eastern Trust Co. v. McTague* (1963), 39 D.L.R. (2d) 743, 48 M.P.R. 134 sub nom. *Re Blanchard Estate; Quinn and Blanchard v. Eastern Trust Co.* (P.E.I.S.C.).

necessarily void.[12] Moreover, a gift to a wife so long as she cohabits with her husband, with a gift over if cohabitation ceases, is valid as a conditional limitation and not a gift defeasible on a void condition.[13] The limitation does not encourage separation but rather the converse.

Conditions contrary to parental obligations and rights are void. Thus, where a testator left his estate to his executors in trust for the benefit of his grandson until he attained the age of 21 years when the whole estate was to be given to him subject to the condition that, if the grandson, before coming of age, went to live with his father, he was to be disinherited of the whole of the estate which was to then go to the testator's son, it was held that the grandson took a vested interest in the property and that the condition was a condition subsequent which was void as contrary to law, the father having the legal right to custody of the child.[14]

Similarly, a condition requiring children not to live with their father if separated from his wife was held void,[15] as was a condition that legatees would forfeit legacies if they should live with or be in the custody or under the guardianship or control of their father.[16]

A condition preventing a child from residing with the mother was held to be void.[17]

Where the condition of a devise by a father to his infant daughter, however, was that the infant must live with a guardian named in the will and not with the mother, the condition was held valid. Blake, V.-C., quoted with approval the summary of the authorities in *Chambers, On Infants*, as follows:[18]

> "In the case of a gift to an infant coupled with the appointment of guardians other than the legal guardians, or direction for the education of the infant in a particular manner, with the express provision that the gift shall be void, if the condition be not complied with, Equity can afford no relief, but the estate must be forfeited if the father or guardian refuse to surrender his legal rights."

A condition not to interfere with the education of the testator's daughter was enforced.[19]

A condition may forbid a change of religion for an adult,[20] or may prohibit a conversion to another faith,[21] but it may not do so in the case of a child as

---

[12]*Re Charleton; Bracey v. Sherwin* (1911), 55 Sol. Jo. 330; *Re Hope Johnstone; Hope Johnstone v. Hope Johnstone*, [1904] 1 Ch. 470.

[13]*Re Hope Johnstone, supra*, footnote 12.

[14]*Clarke v. Darraugh* (1883), 5 O.R. 140 (H.C.J.).

[15]*Re Morgan, supra*, footnote 10.

[16]*Re Sandbrook; Noel v. Sandbrook*, [1912] 2 Ch. 471.

[17]*Re Thorne* (1922), 22 O.W.N. 28 (H.C.).

[18]*Davis v. McCaffrey* (1874), 21 Gr. 554 at p. 561, quoting *Chambers* at p. 181.

[19]*Colston v. Morris* (1821), 6 Madd. 89, 56 E.R. 1024.

[20]*Hodgson v. Halford* (1879), 11 Ch. D. 959.

[21]*Wainwright v. Miller*, [1897] 2 Ch. 255.

such a condition conflicts with the parents' duty to provide religious training to the child.[22]

A condition prohibiting two sisters from residing together is not void for public policy,[23] at least when the sisters are of the age of majority.

One type of condition frequently litigated is a condition in restraint of marriage. Such conditions as amount to an unreasonable general restraint are void for public policy.[24] However, there are many exceptions to this general principle.

In regard to gifts of real property, the intention to restrain marriage is not shown merely by a proviso defeating a gift on the marriage of the devisee. "Looking at the object of this will, and the fact that the testator probably thought that his property was not more than enough for these women to live upon together, his direction that the one who married should lose her share, cannot be said to be opposed to public policy."[25]

A condition restraining marriage is valid where the court can gather that the testator's object is not to promote celibacy but to induce the donee to remain single for the benefit of her children, or unless she marries a husband who is able to provide for her, or for some other reason personal to himself, or where the testator had an interest in the donee remaining unmarried.[26]

Both in England,[27] and in Canada,[28] conditions in restraint of a second marriage are not void as contrary to public policy, whether the conditions be imposed by the spouse or a third party.[29]

Partial restraints on marriage which are reasonable in the circumstances have been held valid. Thus, restraints against marrying a named person[30] or

---

[22]*Re Borwick; Borwick v. Borwick*, [1933] Ch. 657; *Re Tegg; Public Trustee v. Bryant*, [1936] 2 All E.R. 878 (Ch.). See, however, *Re Evans; Hewitt v. Edwards*, [1940] Ch. 629, where the testator's daughter converted to the proscribed faith and had her child baptised in that faith before the testator's death.

[23]*Ridgway v. Woodhouse* (1844), 7 Beav. 437 at p. 443, 49 E.R. 1134.

[24]*Lloyd v. Lloyd* (1852), 2 Sim. (N.S.) 255 at p. 263, 61 E.R. 338; *Morley v. Rennoldson*, [1895] 1 Ch. 449 (C.A.); *Re Cutter* (1916), 37 O.L.R. 42, 31 D.L.R. 382 (H.C.), but see *Re McBain* (1915), 8 O.W.N. 330 (H.C.).

[25]*Jones v. Jones* (1876), 1 Q.B.D. 279 at p. 283, *per* Blackburn, J.

[26]*Lloyd v. Lloyd, supra*, footnote 24; *Newton v. Marsden* (1862), 2 J. & H. 356 at p. 367, 70 E.R. 1094; *Allen v. Jackson* (1875), 1 Ch. D. 399 at p. 406 (C.A.); *Jones v. Jones*, *supra*, footnote 25; *Re McBain* (1915), 8 O.W.N. 330 (S.C.).

[27]*Lloyd v. Lloyd, supra*, footnote 24, at p. 263; *Newton v. Marsden, supra*, footnote 26; *Re Rutter; Donaldson v. Rutter*, [1907] 2 Ch. 592; *Allen v. Jackson* (1875), 1 Ch. D. 399 (C.A.).

[28]*Re Deller* (1903), 6 O.L.R. 711 (H.C.J.); *Cowan v. Allen* (1896), 26 S.C.R. 292 at p. 313; *Re Goodwin* (1969), 3 D.L.R. (3d) 281 (Alta. S.C.), but see *Re Tucker* (1910), 16 W.L.R. 172, 3 S.L.R. 473 (S.C.); *Re Muirhead Estate*, [1919] 2 W.W.R. 454, 12 Sask. L.R. 123 (K.B.).

[29]*Newton v. Marsden, supra*, footnote 26; *Allen v. Jackson, supra*, footnote 27.

[30]*Jarvis v. Duke* (1681), 1 Vern. 19, 23 E.R. 274; *Lester v. Garland* (1808), 15 Ves. Jun. 248, 33 E.R. 748.

persons,[31] or with one of a class of persons, whether the class be one based on occupation,[32] nationality[33] or religion,[34] are valid.

A condition forbidding marriage below a specified reasonable age has been held valid.[35]

In England, it has been held that a condition in a will forbidding marriage without the consent of a specified person is valid.[36]

A condition in restraint of marriage which, though partial in form, is of such a nature that it might amount to a total prohibition is void. Thus, a condition against a son marrying "a relation by blood" was held void by Russell, J., who said:

> No marriage with a supposed stranger in blood could be contracted except subject to the risk that should a common ancestor be traced the provision for defeasance would operate. The son could only be certain that he was marrying a blood relation, he could never be certain that he was not. A provision which by its nature produces those results is in my opinion a provision leading to the probable prohibition of marriage and is void accordingly.[37]

A gift conditional upon the donee marrying a particular person,[38] or one of a particular class of persons,[39] has been held valid.

Determinable fees, the determining event being marriage, are not so strictly limited. If the gift is until marriage, upon marriage there is nothing to carry the gift beyond marriage.[40]

In gifts of personal property, conditions precedent, such as those requiring a consent to the marriage of the legatee or forbidding the legatee from disputing the will, may be regarded as void as being made merely *in terrorem*, that is, as a mere threat to induce the legatee to comply with the condition and not to affect the bequest, unless the testator shows he was not merely making a threat by providing for a gift over, or into residue, upon non-compliance with the condition.[41] That doctrine which is derived from the civil law and adopted by courts of equity, does not apply to devises of real property.[42] In Ontario, the

---

[31]*Re Bathe; Bathe v. Public Trustee*, [1925] Ch. 377.
[32]*Jenner v. Turner* (1880), 16 Ch. D. 188.
[33]*Perrin v. Lyon* (1807), 9 East. 170, 103 E.R. 538.
[34]*Duggan v. Kelly* (1848), 10 I. Eq. R. 295 at p. 473; *Hodgson v. Halford* (1879), 11 Ch. D. 959; *In the Goods of Knox* (1889), 23 L.R. Ir. 542.
[35]*Stackpole v. Beaumont* (1796), 3 Ves. Jun. 89 at p. 97, 30 E.R. 909; *Younge v. Furse* (1857), 8 De G. M. & G. 756, 44 E.R. 581.
[36]*Aston v. Aston* (1703), 2 Vern. 452, 23 E.R. 890; *Lloyd v. Branton* (1817), 3 Mer. 108 at p. 116, 36 E.R. 42; *Re Whiting's Settlement; Whiting v. De Rutzen*, [1905] 1 Ch. 96 (C.A.).
[37]*Re Lanyon; Lanyon v. Lanyon*, [1927] 2 Ch. 264 at p. 274.
[38]*Davis v. Angel* (1862), 4 De G. F. & J. 524, 45 E.R. 1287; *Kiersey v. Flahavan*, [1905] 1 I.R. 45.
[39]*Hodgson v. Halford, supra*, footnote 34.
[40]*Morley v. Rennoldson; Morley v. Linkson* (1843), 2 Hare 570, 67 E.R. 235; *Leong v. Chye*, [1955] A.C. 648 at p. 660; *Re Goodwin* (1969), 3 D.L.R. (3d) 281 (Alta. S.C.).
[41]*Re Dickson's Trust* (1850), 1 Sim. (N.S.) 37 at p. 43, 61 E.R. 14; *Re Whiting's Settlement, supra*, footnote 36.
[42]*Jenner v. Turner* (1880), 16 Ch. D. 188 at p. 196.

doctrine was held to apply to a bequest of mixed realty and personalty.[43]

The civil law rule also applies in England to conditions precedent annexed to gifts of personalty that are *malum prohibitum*, but not to those that are *malum in se*.[44] The civil law rule has been followed in Canada, both in respect of the *in terrorem* rule and the *malum prohibitum* type of case,[45] as well as in a case involving a condition incapable of performance when the will was made.[46] The rule has been decisively rejected in Ontario, however, and the rule applicable to conditions precedent annexed to devises of real property has been approved instead, namely, that if the condition is void, the gift is also void.[47]

A condition against disputing a will or legitimacy is valid with respect to real property.[48]

Regard should be had to section 22 of the *Conveyancing and Law of Property Act*[49] which provides:

> 22. Every covenant made after the 24th day of March, 1950, that but for this section would be annexed to and run with land and that restricts the sale, ownership, occupation or use of land because of the race, creed, colour, nationality, ancestry or place of origin of any person is void and of no effect.

903.4 Uncertainty

A condition that is too uncertain for the court to ascertain its meaning is void for uncertainty.[1] It has been said that the condition must be such that "the

---

[43]*Re Hamilton* (1901), 1 O.L.R. 10 (H.C.J.). *Cf. Re Estate of Pashak*, [1923] 1 D.L.R. 1130, [1923] 1 W.W.R. 873 (Alta. S.C.), which, however, involved not a condition precedent, but a determinable interest.

[44]See, *e.g.*, *Re Piper*; *Dodd v. Piper*, [1946] 2 All E.R. 503 (Ch.); *Re Elliott*; *Lloyds Bank Ltd. v. Burton-on-Trent Hospital Management Ltd.*, [1952] Ch. 217; *Reynish v. Martin* (1746), 3 Atk. 330, 26 E.R. 991; Jarman, vol. 2, pp. 1387, 1457-8; Theobald, paras. 1582-3.

[45]*Re Hamilton, supra*, footnote 43; *Re Estate of Pashak, supra*, footnote 43; *Re Grafton*, [1933] O.W.N. 526 (H.C.J.); *McKinnon v. Lundy* (1893), 24 O.R. 132 (H.C.J.), revd on other grounds 21 O.A.R. 560, restd 24 S.C.R. 650 *sub nom. Lundy v. Lundy*; *Patton v. Toronto General Trusts Corp.*, [1930] A.C. 629, [1930] 4 D.L.R. 321 (P.C.); *Re Starr*, [1946] O.R. 252, [1946] 2 D.L.R. 489 (C.A.); *Re Curran*, [1939] O.W.N. 191, [1939] 2 D.L.R. 803n (H.C.J.); *Re Fairfoull* (1973), 41 D.L.R. (3d) 152 (B.C.S.C.), reconsidered 44 D.L.R. (3d) 765 *sub nom. (No. 2)* (S.C.), affd [1974] 6 W.W.R. 471, 18 R.F.L. 165 (S.C.); *Re McBride* (1980), 27 O.R. (2d) 513, 107 D.L.R. (3d) 233 (H.C.J.).

[46]*Re MacDonald*, [1971] 2 O.R. 577, 18 D.L.R. (3d) 521 (H.C.J.).

[47]*Re Gross*, [1937] O.W.N. 88 (C.A.); *Re Going*, [1951] O.R. 147, [1951] 2 D.L.R. 136 (C.A.). *Cf. Re Mercer*, [1953] O.W.N. 765, [1954] 1 D.L.R. 295 (H.C.J.), and see comment by Oosterhoff, 5 E. & T.Q. 97 (1979-81).

[48]*Cooke v. Turner* (1846), 15 M. & W. 727, 153 E.R. 1044; *Evanturel v. Evanturel* (1874), L.R. 6 P.C. 1.

[49]R.S.O. 1980, c. 90.

§903.4

[1]*Re Ross* (1904), 7 O.L.R. 493 (H.C.J.); *Re Borwick*; *Borwick v. Borwick*, [1933] Ch. 657; *Clayton v. Ramsden*, [1943] A.C. 320 (H.L.), condition respecting person of Jewish parentage and Jewish faith; *Re Hurshman; Mindlin v. Hurshman* (1956), 6 D.L.R. (2d)

Court can see from the beginning, precisely and distinctly, upon the happening of what event it was that the preceding vested estate was to determine".[2]

Cases dealing with conditions in the context of certainty are legion and not all are reconcilable one with the other.[3] For these reasons a single recitation of words found to be uncertain in one instance or another does not advance the inquiry very much. However, a stricter test for certainty is applied to a condition subsequent than to a condition precedent,[4] perhaps because in the former instance, if the condition is uncertain the condition only is struck down,[5] while in the latter if the condition is uncertain the entire bequest or grant fails.[6]

A distinction must be drawn between conceptual uncertainty and evidential uncertainty.[7] Where the grantor or testator has not used words of sufficient clarity the condition is conceptually uncertain and will be struck down. However, where the words used are sufficiently clear but their application is unclear

---

615 (B.C.S.C.), condition against marrying a Jew; *Re Loney Estate*, [1953] 4 D.L.R. 539, 9 W.W.R. (N.S.) 366 (Man. Q.B.), gift to promote socialism; *Re Wecke*; *Montreal Trust Co. v. Sinclair and Wecke* (1958), 15 D.L.R. (2d) 655, 26 W.W.R. 164 (Man. Q.B.), gift to nephew willing to emigrate and operate farm.

[2]*Re Down*, [1968] 2 O.R. 16 at p. 23, 68 D.L.R. (2d) 30 at p. 37 (C.A.), *per* Laskin, J.A., quoting from a passage in *Clavering v. Ellison* (1859), 7 H.L.C. 707, 11 E.R. 282.

[3]See, for example, *Fillingham v. Bromley* (1823), Turn. & R. 530, 37 E.R. 1204; *Dunne v. Dunne* (1855), 7 De G. M. & G. 207, 44 E.R. 81; *Wynne v. Fletcher* (1857), 24 Beav. 430, 53 E.R. 423; *Hamilton v. McKellar* (1878), 26 Gr. 110; *Re Switzer* (1931), 40 O.W.N. 461 (H.C.); *Clavering v. Ellison* (1859), 7 H.L.C. 707, 11 E.R. 282; *Duddy v. Gresham* (1878), 2 L.R. Ir. 442 (C.A.); *Jeffreys v. Jeffreys* (1901), 84 L.T. 417; *Re Stewart Estate*, [1920] 2 W.W.R. 352, 30 Man. R. 382 (K.B.); *Re James Morrison Estate* (1921), 68 D.L.R. 787, [1922] 3 W.W.R. 493 (K.B.); *Re Messinger* (1968), 70 D.L.R. (2d) 716, 66 W.W.R. 377 (B.C.S.C.); *Re McColgan*, [1969] 2 O.R. 152, 4 D.L.R. (3d) 572 (H.C.J.).

In the following cases, the language of a condition was held to be sufficiently clear to be valid: *Tattersall v. Howell* (1816), 2 Mer. 26, 35 E.R. 850, condition that the donee give up bad company; *Maud v. Maud* (1860), 27 Beav. 615, 54 E.R. 243, condition that the donee "follow the paths of virtue"; *Evanturel v. Evanturel* (1874), L.R. 6 P.C. 1, condition against disputing a will or disputing legitimacy; *Re Moore's Trusts*; *Lewis v. Moore* (1906), 96 L.T. 44, condition that the donee marry a person of ample means to maintain her in comfort and affluence; *Pew v. Lefferty* (1869), 16 Gr. 408, bequests conditional on the legatee continuing to be a good boy and remaining in some respectable family, otherwise a gift over; *Re Fox and South Half of Lot No. One in Tenth Concession of Downie* (1884), 8 O.R. 489 (H.C.J.), condition that a devisee "remain sober" in the opinion of the executor for five years; *Jordan v. Dunn* (1887), 13 O.R. 267 (H.C.J.), affd 15 O.A.R. 744, condition that a devisee abstain totally from intoxicating liquors, be kind and obedient to his mother and that he be known among his friends as an industrious man ten years after the death of his mother; *Re Delahey*, [1951] O.W.N. 143, [1951] 1 D.L.R. 710 (H.C.J.), gift to divest if donee becomes member of Roman Catholic Church.

[4]*Blathwayt v. Baron Cawley*, [1976] A.C. 397 (H.L.); *Re Tuck's Settlement Trusts*; *Public Trustee v. Tuck*, [1978] Ch. 49 (C.A.), wherein the distinction was criticized by Lord Denning, M.R.

[5]*Re Down, supra*, footnote 2.

[6]*Re Lysiak* (1975), 7 O.R. (2d) 317, 55 D.L.R. (3d) 161 (H.C.J.).

[7]*Re Coxen*; *McCallum v. Coxen*, [1948] Ch. 747 at pp. 761-2; *Re Gulbenkian's Settlements*, [1970] A.C. 508 (H.L.); *Re Baden's Deed Trusts*, [1971] A.C. 424 (H.L.).

because of uncertainty as to facts, the condition is evidentially uncertain and will not be struck down. The court will apply the condition as best it can on the available evidence.[8]

A condition may fail to take effect because the court declines to investigate whether there has been, or will be, compliance.[9]

903.5 Impossibility of Performance

A condition may be one which presumes a state of facts that actually does not or cannot exist. In such a case, if the intention is clear that the condition is to operate only if that state of facts exists, it does not have effect at all and the gift will take effect as if there were no condition.[1]

On the other hand, if the intention is clear that the condition is to operate in any event and the state of facts does not exist, the condition becomes impossible to perform. In that case, if performance of the condition was originally impossible or later becomes impossible by an "act of God" or circumstances which neither testator nor donee could control, the result depends upon whether the condition is precedent or subsequent; if it is a condition precedent, performance is not excused and the gift does not take effect.[2]

Performance of a condition precedent cannot be excused on the ground of impossibility of performance[3] but performance of a condition subsequent may be.[4] The impossibility, however, must be in the nature of things and a condition is not void merely because its performance is highly improbable or because it is out of the power of the donee to ensure its performance.[5] Thus, a condition requiring naturalization was not impossible of performance because a private Act of Parliament might have been obtained,[6] nor was a condition requiring use of a black gown in the pulpit impossible to perform.[7]

A donee may not be bound by a condition in a will because of some act of

---

[8]*Re Tuck's Settlement Trusts, supra,* footnote 4.

[9]*W v. B* (1849), 11 Beav. 621, 50 E.R. 957; *Cooke v. Cooke* (1864), 11 Jur. 533, 4 De G. J. & S. 704, 46 E.R. 1093; *Poole v. Bott* (1853), 11 Hare 33 at p. 39, 68 E.R. 1175.

§903.5

[1]*Yates v. University College, London* (1873), 8 Ch. App. 454 at p. 461, affd L.R. 7 H.L. 438.

[2]*Re Croxon; Croxon v. Ferrers,* [1904] 1 Ch. 252; *Egerton v. Earl Brownlow* (1853), 4 H.L.C. 1 at p. 120, 10 E.R. 359; *Priestley v. Holgate* (1857), 3 K. & J. 286, 69 E.R. 1116.

[3]*Re Greenwood; Goodhart v. Woodhead,* [1903] 1 Ch. 749 (C.A.); *Re Edwards; Lloyd v. Boyes,* [1910] 1 Ch. 541, but see *Re MacDonald,* [1971] 2 O.R. 577, 18 D.L.R. (3d) 521 (H.C.J.), and critical comment on *Re McBride* by Oosterhoff, 5 E. & T.Q. 97 (1979-81) at pp. 104-6 wherein the decision of *Re MacDonald* was adversely commented upon.

[4]*Re Forbes; Harrison v. Comis,* [1928] 3 D.L.R. 22, [1928] 1 W.W.R. 880 (K.B.).

[5]*Egerton v. Earl Brownlow, supra,* footnote 2.

[6]*Re Knox; Von Scheffler v. Shuldham,* [1912] 1 I.R. 288.

[7]*Re Robinson; Wright v. Tugwell,* [1892] 1 Ch. 95, affd [1897] 1 Ch. 85 (C.A.).

the testator or other event subsequent to the date of the will, so that the condition has been substantially performed or nullified in the testator's lifetime, or he has dispensed with the condition, or made it impossible for the donee to perform it.[8]

903.6 The Rule Against Perpetuities

Both conditions precedent and conditions subsequent are subject to the rule against perpetuities which requires the estate to take effect within a period consisting of a life, or lives in being, and twenty-one years. In the case of a condition precedent, since the estate given is contingent, if the condition violates the rule, the entire estate is defeated.[1]

However, if a condition subsequent violates the rule, only the right of entry remaining in the grantor's or testator's estate is defeated, for the estate to which the condition is attached is vested upon the grant or death of the testator and only the right of entry is contingent.[2]

Although there was some sifference of opinion on the point,[3] it now seems well settled that a determinable estate, and the possibility of reverter arising therefrom, are not subject to the rule at common law.[4] Both the estate given and the possibility of reverter are vested, the former in the grantee or beneficiary and the latter in the grantor or testator. Since the rule against perpetuities applies only to contingent interests it has no application to determinable interests.

However, modern perpetuities statutes now make not only rights of entry but also possibilities of reverter subject to the rule as modified by the statutes.[5]

---

[8]*Darley v. Langworthy* (1774), 3 Brown. 359, 1 E.R. 1369; *Smith v. Cowdery* (1825), 2 Sim. & St. 358, 57 E.R. 382; *McKinnon v. Lundy* (1893), 24 O.R. 132 (H.C.J.), revd on other grounds 21 O.A.R. 560, restd 24 S.C.R. 650 *sub nom. Lundy v. Lundy; Re Macdonald*, [1971] 2 O.R. 577, 18 D.L.R. (3d) 521 (H.C.J.).

§903.6

[1]See ch. 11, *infra.*

[2]*Re Trustees of Hollis' Hospital and Hague's Contract*, [1899] 2 Ch. 540; *Re Da Costa; Clarke v. Church of England Collegiate School of St. Peter*, [1912] 1 Ch. 337, applied in *Matheson v. Town of Mitchell* (1919), 46 O.L.R. 546, 51 D.L.R. 477 (S.C. App. Div.); *Pardee v. Humberstone Summer Resort Co. of Ontario, Ltd.*, [1933] O.R. 580, [1933] 3 D.L.R. 277 (H.C.J.); *Fitzmaurice v. Board of School Trustees of Twp. of Monck*, [1949] O.W.N. 786, [1950] 1 D.L.R. 239 (H.C.J.).

[3]*Hopper v. Corp. of Liverpool* (1944), 88 Sol. Jo. 213.

[4]*Re Tilbury West Public School Board and Hastie*, [1966] 2 O.R. 20, 55 D.L.R. (2d) 407 (H.C.J.), vard O.R. *loc. cit.* p. 511, 57 D.L.R. (2d) 519 (H.C.J.); *Re North Gower Twp. Public School Board and Todd.* [1968] 1 O.R. 63, 65 D.L.R. (2d) 421 (C.A.); *Re McKellar.* [1972] 3 O.R. 16, 27 D.L.R. (3d) 289 (H.C.J.), affd [1973] 3 O.R. 178n, 36 D.L.R. (3d) 202n (C.A.); *MacLeod v. Town of Amherst* (1973), 39 D.L.R. (3d) 146, 8 N.S.R. (2d) 504 (S.C.), affd 44 D.L.R. (3d) 723, 8 N.S.R. (2d) 491 (S.C. App. Div.); *Re Essex County Roman Catholic Separate School Board and Antaya* (1977), 17 O.R. (2d) 307, 80 D.L.R. (3d) 405 (H.C.J.).

[5]For a more detailed discussion, see §1107.12, *infra.*

903.7 Restraint on Alienation

As discussed previously,[1] since the enactment of the Statute *Quia Emptores*[2] the right of alienation has been an inseparable incident of an estate in fee simple. Thus a general restraint on alienation expressed as a condition is void, whether it be in a will[3] or a deed.[4] Hence, conditions prohibiting the donee from selling or mortgaging property,[5] or requiring the donee to keep the property for his heirs,[6] or restricting alienation to one person,[7] or prohibiting alienation without the consent of one person,[8] have been held to be invalid general restraints.

A distinction must be drawn between partial restraints on alienation, which may be valid, and general restraints. A partial restraint prohibiting alienation to a particular person, or to a particular class of persons so long as the class is not so big as to amount to a general restraint, is valid.[9]

In *Blackburn v. McCallum*,[10] Davies, J., suggested that a time limitation is necessary if a restriction on alienation of a fee simple is imposed even with respect to a class of persons, otherwise the devise might be bad as contravening the rule against perpetuities. However, where the rule against perpetuities could be violated, a condition restraining a devisee from disposing of property except to children or grandchildren of the testator was held valid because that left the devisee a comparatively large class among whom to dispose of the property.[11]

A restraint may be partial in that it prohibits alienation only to a certain group or it may prohibit alienation totally for a limited period of time. If the restraint is of the latter nature, it will be treated as a general restraint and hence will be invalid. Thus, general restraints limited to the life of the holder of the estate in fee simple,[12] or to the life of another,[13] or to a substantial

---

§903.7

[1]See §503.1, *supra*. The cases dealing with total restraints on alienation have been discussed in that chapter and the reader is referred thereto.

[2]18 Edw. 1, cc. 1, 2 (1290).

[3]*Blackburn v. McCallum* (1903), 33 S.C.R. 65.

[4]*Lario v. Walker* (1881), 28 Gr. 216.

[5]*Re Thomas and Shannon* (1898), 30 O.R. 49 (H.C.J.); *Re Shanacy and Quinlan* (1897), 28 O.R. 372 (H.C.J.); *McFarlane v. Henderson* (1908), 16 O.L.R. 172 (H.C.J.); *Re Corbit* (1905), 5 O.W.R. 239.

[6]*Re Casner* (1883), 6 O.R. 282 (H.C.J.); *Re Lane and Beacham* (1912), 23 O.W.R. 250, 7 D.L.R. 311 (H.C.); *Lario v. Walker* (1881), 28 Gr. 216; *Heddlestone v. Heddlestone* (1888), 15 O.R. 280 (H.C.J.); *Re Collier* (1966), 60 D.L.R. (2d) 70, 52 M.P.R. 211 (Nfld. S.C.).

[7]*Attwater v. Attwater* (1853), 18 Beav. 330, 52 E.R. 131; *Re Dowsett* (1926), 31 O.W.N. 353 (H.C.); *Crofts v. Beamish*, [1905] 2 I.R. 349 (C.A.).

[8]*McRae v. McRae* (1898), 30 O.R. 54 (H.C.J.); *Pardee v. Humberstone Summer Resort Co. of Ontario, Ltd.*, [1933] O.R. 580, [1933] 3 D.L.R. 277 (H.C.J.); *Rutherford v. Rispin* (1926), 59 O.L.R. 506, [1926] 4 D.L.R. 822 (H.C.).

[9]*Blackburn v. McCallum* (1903), 33 S.C.R. 65; *Re Macleay* (1875), L.R. 20 Eq. 186; *Re Rosher; Rosher v. Rosher* (1884), 26 Ch. D. 801.

[10]*Supra*, footnote 9.

[11]*Rogerson v. Campbell* (1905), 10 O.L.R. 748 (H.C.J.).

[12]*Re Carr; Carr v. Carr* (1914), 20 D.L.R. 74, 28 W.L.R. 776 (B.C.S.C.).

[13]*Re Rosher, supra*, footnote 9.

number of years after the testator's death,[14] or until a devisee reached the age of 60,[15] have been held invalid.

A partial restraint prohibiting certain methods of alienation but permitting others has been held to be valid. Where a devise in fee simple directed that the devisee should not sell or cause to be sold the devised land or any part thereof during her life, but that she was at liberty to grant it to any of her children as she thought proper, such restraint on alienation was held valid and the giving of a mortgage by the devisee was held not to be a violation of the restraint.[16] Moreover, it is to be observed that the direction also left the devisee with the power to lease, to convey to anyone other than by way of sale and to devise to anyone by will.

Where a testator devised a property to his daughter with a provision that "she shall not dispose of the same only by will and testament", it was held that she took a fee simple restricted by a condition against alienation in any way except by a testamentary instrument and that such restraint was valid.[17] In *Re Northcote*,[18] a testator devised land to his son in fee simple subject to an express condition that he should not sell or mortgage it during his life but with power to devise it to his children as he might think fit in such way as he might desire, and it was held that the condition was valid. In *Re Bell*,[19] a testator devised land equally to his three sons without power to any of them to charge or alienate it or any part of it except by will. It was held that the restraint on alienation was valid.

Similarly, in *Re Martin and Dagneau*,[20] the testator devised lands to his sons with a provision that "none of my sons will have the privilege of mortgaging or selling their lot or farm aforesaid described, but if one or more of the lots have to be sold on account of mismanagement, the executors will see that the same will remain in the Martin estate". The sons became indebted and no one in the family was in a position to purchase the lands. One son, an executor, agreed to sell his land, but it was held that this restraint on alienation was valid and that he could not make title.

Again, where a testator devised land to his son in fee simple subject to the condition that he was not to mortgage or sell it in his lifetime, a divisional court held that the restraint on alienation was valid because it was limited.[21]

It seems impossible to reconcile the foregoing decisions with the decision in *Re Shanacy and Quinlan*,[22] which held that a condition restraining devisees from selling or mortgaging was void as being an absolute restraint on alienation, although the restraint, by necessary implication, left them with the power to

---

[14]*Blackburn v. McCallum, supra*, footnote 9. For a discussion of the effect of *Blackburn* see *Hutt v. Hutt* (1911), 24 O.L.R. 574 (C.A.).
[15]*Re Huron and Erie Mortgage Corp. and Coghill* (1918), 13 O.W.N. 442 (H.C.).
[16]*Smith v. Faught* (1881), 45 U.C.Q.B. 484.
[17]*Re Winstanley* (1884). 6 O.R. 315 (H.C.J.).
[18](1889), 18 O.R. 107 (H.C.J.).
[19](1899), 30 O.R. 318 (H.C.J.).
[20](1906), 11 O L.R. 349 (H.C.J.).
[21]*Re Porter* (1907), 13 O.L.R. 399 (H.C.J.).
[22](1897), 28 O.R. 372 (H.C.J.).

devise by will, as did the restraint in those cases just mentioned. It is suggested that *Re Shanacy and Quinlan* is a decision more in harmony with English decisions, the cardinal principles of which were reiterated by the Supreme Court of Canada in *Blackburn v. McCallum*.[23] It should also be noted that most of the decisions referred to preceded the decision of the Supreme Court of Canada in *Blackburn v. McCallum*.

Following what appears to be a trend away from this cardinal principle are cases in which the restraint was against sale only. For example, where a testator devised land to his son for life and after his decease to his heirs and assigns forever with a provision that after his death the land was to be sold if his youngest child then living was of the age of 21 years, the proceeds to be divided equally between his children at the time of sale, it was held that, under the rule in *Shelley's Case*,[24] the son took a fee simple, without trust for children, but that, under the terms of the will, there was a restraint on alienation by sale, although not by mortgage.[25]

It has been held that, where a gift is absolute, a restraint on the power of leasing is void on the same principle as a restraint on alienation.[26]

A condition annexed to an estate tail that the donee should not alienate was held to be void, as a right to bar the entail was a necessary incident of the estate.[27]

Several recent decisions[28] dealing with contractually imposed conditions or covenants have already been discussed in chapter 5[29] and the reader is referred thereto.

Since the points dealt with in the foregoing cases have not gone before the Supreme Court of Canada, apart from *Blackburn v. McCallum*, it may be appropriate to note the observations of the late Mr. E. D. Armour[30] to the effect that restraints on alienation are contrary to the Statute *Quia Emptores*[31] which provides that it is lawful for every freeman to sell at his own pleasure his lands and tenements or part of them, so that the feoffee (grantee) shall hold them of the chief lord of the same fee, by such service and customs as his feoffor (grantor) held before. He cites a decision of Cozens-Hardy, J., in *Merttens v. Hill*,[32] holding that a custom of a manor to exact a fine on

---

23(1903), 33 S.C.R. 65.

24(1581), Co. Rep. 93 b, 76 E.R. 206.

25*Meyers v. Hamilton Provident and Loan Co.* (1890), 19 O.R. 358 (H.C.J.).

26*Re Rosher; Rosher v. Rosher* (1884), 26 Ch. D. 801.

27*Dawkins v. Lord Penrhyn* (1878), 4 App. Cas. 51 (H.L.), at p. 64.

28In particular, *Stephens v. Gulf Oil Canada Ltd.* (1975), 11 O.R. (2d) 129, 65 D.L.R. (3d) 193 (C.A.); *Laurin v. Iron Ore Co. of Canada* (1977), 82 D.L.R. (3d) 634, 19 Nfld. & P.E.I.R. 111 (Nfld. S.C.T.D.); *British Columbia Forest Products Ltd. v. Gay* (1976), 74 D.L.R. (3d) 660, 1 B.C.L.R. 265 (S.C.), affd 89 D.L.R. (3d) 80, 7 B.C.L.R. 190 (C.A.).

29See §503.1, *supra*.

30*Real Property*, pp. 170-1.

31In Ontario, R.S.O. 1897, c. 330, s. 2, reprinted in R.S.O. 1980, App. A.

32[1901] 1 Ch. 842 at p. 857.

alienation to one born outside the manor was repugnant to the estate and a restraint on alienation which could not stand against the statute.

904. EFFECT OF INVALIDITY

If a conveyance or devise is upon a condition precedent which is void, the conveyance or devise is also void and does not vest, but, if a conveyance or devise is upon a condition subsequent which is void, it takes effect free from the condition.[1]

If a valid condition is coupled with a void one, the whole is void. Thus, where a devise in fee simple had a condition attached that, if the devisee died "intestate or without issue", there was to be a devise over, the condition as to dying without issue being good but being bad as to dying intestate, the whole was void. Therefore, the devisee took free from the condition.[2]

905. VOIDABLE CONDITIONS

If there is a direction in a will that a donee is not to enjoy a vested gift until he attains a specified age, the court, upon application of the donee or persons claiming under him, will strike the direction from a will unless it clearly indicates that some other person is to have the enjoyment until the donee attains that age, or unless the enjoyment is so clearly taken away from the donee until he attains that age as to induce the court to hold that there is an intestacy as to the income meanwhile.[1]

906. PERFORMANCE OF CONDITIONS

In the case of a provision in a will divesting or revoking a gift made upon a condition that certain circumstances exist or will recur, the condition must be completely unfulfilled, or no revocation occurs. Thus, where a testator devised land subject to a condition that if the devisee died without issue before the death of the testator's brother and sister and the sister predeceased the testator but the brother and devisee survived him, it was held that the condition in defeasance was not fulfilled and the devise was not divested, the court declining to construe "and" as "or".[1]

§904
[1]*McKinnon v. Lundy* (1893), 24 O.R. 132 (H.C.J.), at p. 137, revd on other grounds 21 O.A.R. 560, restd 24 S.C.R. 650 *sub nom. Lundy v. Lundy*; *Jordan v. Dunn* (1887), 13 O.R. 267 (H.C.J.), at pp. 281, 282, affd 15 O.A.R. 744.
[2]*Re Babcock* (1862), 9 Gr. 427.
§905
[1]*Gosling v. Gosling* (1859), Johns. 265 at p. 272, 70 E.R. 423; *Wharton v. Masterman*, [1895] A.C. 186 (H.L.), at p. 192; *Re Thompson; Griffith v. Thompson* (1896), 44 W.R. 582; *Re Couturier; Couturier v. Shea*, [1907] 1 Ch. 470 at p. 473.
§906
[1]*Lillie v. Willis* (1899), 31 O.R. 198 (H.C.J.).

Again, where a testator gave certain bequests and provided by a codicil for their revocation if he had ineffectually ordered by his will that the proceeds of certain insurance policies be part of his estate and his order proved to be ineffectual in regard to one of the policies, it was held that no revocation occurred because the condition was that the order be ineffectual in regard to all policies and such condition had not been fulfilled.[2]

A condition attached to a devise, however, that it is to be divested and go to another person on a certain event does not fail to take effect if the devise over is ineffective for some reason, unless the will shows the intent that there is to be no divesting unless the devise over is effective. Thus, where a testator devised lands for the benefit of his wife for life, after her death for the benefit of his daughter for life and after her death to her children, but provided that, if his son returned to Toronto within five years, the executors were to hold part of the lands for the son for life and after his death divide it among his children, and the son returned within the five years, received the rents and profits and died unmarried and intestate, it was held that the failure of the executory devise to such children resulted only in a lapse of such devise which passed to the daughter under a residuary clause.[3]

Again, where a testator gave the rents and profits of his estate to his wife for life and, after her death, gave the rents and profits of his real estate to his daughter for life and, at her decease, devised the real estate to her son in fee simple but provided that, if the son died without issue before his mother, she was to have half of the real estate absolutely and the other half was to go to a named church and the son died under the age of seven years before his mother, it was held that the son took a vested estate, liable to be divested upon his death during his mother's life. It was further held that the divesting took effect even if the devise over to the church was void as being contrary to the *Statutes of Mortmain* and that, there being no residuary clause, there was an intestacy in regard to such devise over.[4]

The fact that the donee is ignorant of the condition does not excuse him from performance.[5]

The court may hold that a condition precedent or a condition subsequent has been sufficiently performed by being complied with substantially, although not literally. Thus, when, without the fault of the donee, a literal compliance with a condition becomes impossible, the *cy-près* doctrine applies and it is sufficient if the condition is complied with as nearly as is practicable.[6] The

---

[2]*Milburn v. Grayson*; *Re Walsh Estate* (1921), 60 D.L.R. 181, 62 S.C.R. 49, varg D.L.R. loc. cit. p. 182, [1920] 2 W.W.R. 518 (C.A.).

[3]*Walsh v. Fleming* (1905), 10 O.L.R. 226 (H.C.J.).

[4]*Re Archer* (1907), 14 O.L.R. 374 (H.C.J.).

[5]*Hawkes v. Baldwin* (1838), 9 Sim. 355, 59 E.R. 394; *Re Hodges' Legacy* (1873), L.R. 16 Eq. 92; *Powell v. Rawle* (1874), L.R. 18 Eq. 243; *Astley v. Earl of Essex* (1874), L.R. 18 Eq. 290; *Adams v. Gourlay* (1912), 26 O.L.R. 87 at p. 93, 4 D.L.R. 731 at p. 736 (H.C.J.).

[6]*Adams v. Gourlay*, supra, footnote 5. There have been many examples of this approach. See, for example, *Re Grenier* (1917), 12 O.W.N. 362 (H.C.), a trust for the purpose

court, however, does not usually so hold in the case of conditions which divest an estate which has become vested.[7] There may be cases in which an attempted but uncompleted performance may be held sufficient, but it is not the general rule, even if completion of performance was prevented by the death of the donee or other "act of God".[8]

If a testator has prescribed a period within which a condition is to be performed, the condition must usually be performed and the period must usually be strictly observed.[9]

If the testator does not prescribe a period and the condition is to be performed by the donee personally, not requiring action or concurrence by another person, the period for performance is the lifetime of the donee and the condition is not complied with if he dies without performing it.[10]

Thus, if a gift is conditional upon marriage with a particular person or with the consent of a particular person, the donee has his whole life in which to perform the condition.[11]

If other persons are benefited, the general rule is that a reasonable period is allowed for performance of a condition.[12] Thus, where a testator devised 100 acres to one son, for which he was to pay to the executors a sum by instalments for the benefit of another son and, in default of such payment, the

---

of placing a memorial window in a certain church and it was impossible to carry out the purpose; *Hyland v. Throckmorton* (1870), 29 U.C.Q.B. 560, where a testator devised land to his son for life and by codicil directed that, if his son "after three months after my decease" deposited a hundred pounds to be invested for a specified purpose, the land was to go to him in fee, it was held that payment within a reasonable time after three months from the testator's decease was sufficient, the court declining to construe "after" as "within"; *Jordan v. Dunn* (1887), 13 O.R. 267 (H.C.J.), affd 15 O.A.R. 744, a condition against use of intoxicating liquors did not preclude its use for medicinal purposes; *Re Quay* (1907), 14 O.L.R. 471 (H.C.J.); a condition against gambling meant gambling as a means of livelihood and not simply for amusement; *Re Sax*; *Barned v. Sax* (1893), 68 L.T. 849, a condition that donees cease to carry on a business which was sold to a company of which the donees became managing directors; *Re Arbib and Class's Contract*, [1891] 1 Ch. 601 (C.A.), a condition requiring return to England satisfied by a temporary visit; *Dawson v. Oliver-Massey* (1876), 2 Ch. D. 753, a gift on marriage if entered into with the consent of the parents, one of whom died; *Walcot v. Botfield* (1854), Kay. 534, 69 E.R. 226, a condition requiring "residence" does not imply domicile but mere personal presence at some time, and a condition requiring residence in a house for a specified period each year is enforced but does not require spending nights there.

[7]*Hervey-Bathurst v. Stanley*; *Craven v. Stanley* (1876), 4 Ch. D. 251 (C.A.), at p. 272.
[8]*Priestley v. Holgate* (1857), 3 K. & J. 286 at p. 288, 69 E.R. 1116; *Re Conington's Will* (1860), 6 Jur. N.S. 992.
[9]*Simpson v. Vickers* (1807), 14 Ves. Jun. 341, 33 E.R. 552; *Brooke v. Garrod* (1857), 2 De G. & J. 62, 44 E.R. 911; *Austin v. Tawney* (1867), 2 Ch. App. 143; *Re Glubb*; *Bamfield v. Rogers*, [1900] 1 Ch. 354 (C.A.).
[10]*Patching v. Barnett* (1881), 51 L.J. Ch. 74 (C.A.); *Re Greenwood*; *Goodhart v. Woodhead*, [1902] 2 Ch. 198 at pp. 204, 205, revd on other grounds [1903] 1 Ch. 749 (C.A.).
[11]*Johnson v. Smith* (1749), 1 Ves. Sen. 314, 27 E.R. 1053; *Beaumont v. Squire* (1852), 17 Q.B. 905 at pp. 933, 936.
[12]*Davies v. Lowndes* (1835), 1 Bing. (N.C.) 597 at p. 618, 131 E.R. 1247.

executors were to dispose of fifty acres for the benefit of the other son or convey the fifty acres to him, it was held that the devisee, although making default, with the result that the fifty acres were conveyed to the other son, was entitled to a re-conveyance of the fifty acres upon paying the principal sum and interest.[13]

A person who is entitled to a gift over in the event of non-performance by a donee may release the donee from performance,[14] but, as a rule, not to the prejudice of the rights of other persons.[15]

A court may grant relief to a donee against forfeiture under a condition precedent or condition subsequent on equitable grounds, such as, if performance of the condition was prevented by the executors,[16] or by persons interested under a gift over,[17] or under a prior gift,[18] and not by the fault of the donee,[19] or if the condition is in the nature of a penalty.[20]

In regard to infancy, the position of the infant differs according to whether a condition is precedent or subsequent. If a condition precedent is attached to a gift to an infant and can be performed by him, he is bound by it and, in case of non-performance by him, the gift does not take effect, because it was not intended to take effect unless the condition were performed.[21] In the case of a condition subsequent requiring an act of volition, however, he does not forfeit the gift by non-performance during infancy, because the gift had taken effect as intended and, being under disability, he cannot be said to refuse or neglect to perform the condition.[22]

Thus, where a testator bequeathed an annuity to his grandson, then twelve years of age and known by the testator to be a Roman Catholic and incapable of changing his religion during infancy under the law of his domicile, the annuity being upon condition that the grandson "is and proves himself to be until the date of his death of the Lutheran religion", it was held that the testator must have intended to give to the grandson a real opportunity of making the change of religion effectively and that, as he had done so within a few days after attaining his majority, he was entitled to the annuity and all arrears.[23]

A donee may be excused on grounds of public policy from performing a condition subsequent which he or she is not free to perform on account of

---

[13]*Carson v. Carson* (1858), 6 Gr. 368.
[14]*Ex parte Palmer* (1852), 5 De G. & Sm. 649, 64 E.R. 1283.
[15]*Wynne v. Fletcher* (1857), 24 Beav. 430, 53 E.R. 423.
[16]*Brooke v. Garrod* (1857), 2 De G. & J. 62, 44 E.R. 911.
[17]*Falkland (Lord) v. Bertie* (1696), 2 Vern. 333 at p. 343, 23 E.R. 814.
[18]*Hayes v. Hayes* (1674), Cas. *temp.* Finch 231.
[19]*Clarke v. Parker* (1812), 19 Ves. Jun. 1 at p. 17, 34 E.R. 419.
[20]*Priestley v. Holgate* (1857), 3 K. & J. 286 at p. 288, 69 E.R. 1116.
[21]*Doe d. Luscombe v. Yates* (1822), 5 B. & Ald. 544, 106 E.R. 1289; *Ledward v. Hassells* (1856), 2 K. & J. 370, 69 E.R. 825; *Bevan v. Mahon-Hagan* (1892), 27 L.R. Ir. 399.
[22]*Parry v. Roberts* (1871), 25 L.T. 371, 19 W.R. 1000; *Partridge v. Partridge,* [1894] 1 Ch. 351; *Re Edwards; Lloyd v. Boyes,* [1910] 1 Ch. 541.
[23]*Patton v. Toronto General Trusts Corp.,* [1930] 4 D.L.R. 321, [1930] A.C. 629 (P.C.).

marriage or public duties, as where a married woman cannot comply with a condition as to residence without separating from her husband,[24] or where a person absent on military services cannot comply with a condition as to residence,[25] or a person cannot comply with a condition by reason of his duties as a parish priest.[26]

If compliance with a condition is against good morals, the donee or devisee may be absolved from performing it.[27]

The jurisdiction of the court to construe a will is not ousted by the direction of a testator that questions of construction are to be settled in another manner, such as, by executors or trustees or by arbitration.[28] A direction that a beneficiary is to forfeit his interest if he resorts to litigation is inoperative to prevent him from seeking the aid of the court.[29]

On the other hand, a condition that a beneficiary shall not dispute the validity of a will or interfere with management of the estate on pain of forfeiture if he does so may be valid so as to cause forfeiture by litigation by him.[30] Such a condition, however, is not ordinarily construed as applying where there is a reasonable cause for litigation,[31] or as applying to defence of proceedings commenced by other persons.[32] Accordingly, an application to the court to construe a will does not come within prohibition against taking any proceedings "to set aside, cancel or modify in any manner any part of the will",[33] nor does a beneficiary who suggests that a certain course should be followed by the executors "question" a will within the meaning of a forfeiture provision.[34]

If a condition is couched in such language that it prevents a donee from resorting to any proceedings whatsoever concerning the gift, even to secure its enjoyment, the condition is void as repugnant to the gift.[35]

---

[24]*Woods v. Townley* (1853), 11 Hare. 314, 68 E.R. 1295.

[25]*Re Adair*, [1909] 1 I.R. 311.

[26]*Brannigan v. Murphy*, [1896] 1 I.R. 418.

[27]*Adams v. Gourlay* (1912), 26 O.L.R. 87, 4 D.L.R. 731 (H.C.J.).

[28]*Re Walton's Estate* (1856), 8 De G. M. & G. 173, 44 E.R. 356 (C.A.); *Massy v. Rogers* (1883), 11 L.R. Ir. 409.

[29]*Rhodes v. Muswell Hill Land Co.* (1861), 30 L.J. Ch. 509 at p. 511, 29 Beav. 560, 54 E.R. 745; *Massy v. Rogers, supra*, footnote 28.

[30]*Violett v. Brookman* (1857), 26 L.J. Ch. 308; *Adams v. Adams*, [1892] 1 Ch. 369 (C.A.).

[31]*Adams v. Adams, supra*, footnote 30, pp. 375, 377; *Re Williams; Williams v. Williams*, [1912] 1 Ch. 399 at p. 401.

[32]*Cooke v. Cholmondeley* (1849), 2 Mac. & G. 18 at p. 28, 42 E.R. 8; *Massy v. Rogers, supra*, footnote 28.

[33]*Harrison v. Harrison* (1904), 7 O.L.R. 297 (H.C.J.).

[34]*Re McIntyre* (1930), 39 O.W.N. 62 (H.C.).

[35]*Rhodes v. Muswell Hill Land Co.* (1861), 29 Beav. 560 at p. 563, 54 E.R. 745; *Re Williams; Williams v. Williams, supra*, footnote 31.

CHAPTER 10

FUTURE INTERESTS

1001.   DEFINITION AND SCOPE

A future interest is an interest in property in which the right to possession or enjoyment of the property is postponed to a future time.[1] Nevertheless, it is a presently existing interest in the property and it is thus part of the total ownership of the property. The fact that a future interest is a presently existing interest implies that it confers present, as well as future, rights and obligations. Thus, if G grants "to A for life, remainder to B in fee simple", B's interest is future in that his present enjoyment of the estate granted to him is postponed. However, during A's lifetime he does have valuable property rights, including the right to alienate his interest and the right to restrain A from committing waste.

---

§1001
[1]Simes and Smith, §1; 1 Fearne, p. 2.

Although the definition of a future interest speaks of a postponed enjoyment, it must be made clear that such enjoyment is not guaranteed. Thus, the owner of the future interest may not in fact enjoy it in possession at a future time. For example, in a grant by G "to A for life, remainder to B for life, remainder to C in fee simple", B may die before A, so that his life estate will never fall into possession. Of course, C may also die before his estate in fee simple becomes a possessory estate but, unless he dies intestate without heirs, the estate will then pass to his heirs who will eventually enjoy it in possession. Similarly, in a devise by T "to A for life, remainder to B in fee simple, but if B ceases to farm the land, then to C in fee simple", C or his heirs will never receive the land in possession unless B or his heirs cease to farm the land.

Because enjoyment is postponed in a future interest, the interest is sometimes called an "estate in expectancy". This term is somewhat misleading in that it is applied both to future interests which are vested, and to contingent interests, or interests which are not vested. Moreover, a distinction should be drawn between an estate in expectancy on the one hand and an "expectancy", a "mere expectancy", or a *spes successionis* on the other. The latter is a mere hope of a person that he will succeed to an estate or interest in land as heir or next of kin of the present owner.[2] An expectancy is not an interest in land. However, since it partakes of some of the characteristics of a future interest, it is dealt with in this chapter.[3]

The purpose of future interests is to enable the present owner of property to prescribe the time when and the conditions upon which the next generation may enjoy it. A great variety of reasons may motivate the present owner to dispose of his property in this way instead of giving it absolutely. For example, he may wish to provide for a successive enjoyment by his wife and children and will, therefore, give a life estate to her with remainder to the children. He may be concerned about a wastrel son and thus set up a protective or spendthrift trust to protect the property from the son's creditors. He may wish to make special provision for certain members of the family, for example, a person of unsound mind, with a gift over on his death. He may also be concerned about the incidence of death taxes and distribute his estate in such a way as to minimize them. All of these desires are usually effected by the use of future interests.

It will be apparent that in seeking to execute his intentions, the creator of the future interest may run afoul of the policy of the law which tends to favour free alienability of property and, thus, to disfavour restraints placed upon the power of alienation. The rules of law which prohibit restraints in alienation, the rule against perpetuities, rules prohibiting the creation of certain types of future interests, modern legislation against disinheritance of dependants, and other rules of law, have been devised to curb the desires of present owners of property to dispose of it as they see fit.[4] The law of future interests is thus concerned primarily with the creation of future interests and the restrictions

---

[2]Simes and Smith, §2.

[3]*Infra*, §1005.

[4]For a summary of the development of the policy in this respect, see §221, *supra*.

placed upon their creation and transfer and some of these restrictions are dealt with in this chapter. The rule against perpetuities is dealt with in the next chapter and other restrictions are dealt with elsewhere in this work.

1002. CLASSIFICATION OF FUTURE INTERESTS

Future interests are usually classified according to the manner in which they are created and the mode of creation is related to the historical development of future interests as described in the next five sections. The following types are discussed in this chapter:

A. Those arising at common law:
  1. Reversions
  2. Possibilities of Reverter
  3. Rights of Entry for Condition Broken
  4. Remainders
B. Those arising as a result of the *Statute of Uses*:[1]
  1. Legal Executory Interests
  2. Equitable Remainders
  3. Equitable Executory Interests, including Executory Devises

In addition to the foregoing, the following are also types of future interests: inchoate dower and curtesy initiate, escheat, the interest of the grantee under a deed in escrow, the interest of a mortgagee, and the future enjoyment of an incorporeal hereditament. The first three of these have been dealt with elsewhere[2] and will not be considered further here.[3] In fact, however, none of these interests is usually regarded as a future interest and they are, therefore, left out of the discussion in this chapter.

Certain other types of "interest", such as the bare expectancy, or *spes successionis*, and the possibility of an appointment under a power of appointment, are not in fact interests in land, but are mere possibilities. Because the bare expectancy closely resembles a future interest, however, it is dealt with in this chapter.[4]

---

§1002

[1]27 Hen. 8, c. 10 (1535).

[2]Dower: §§707-707.20; Curtesy: §§708-709; Escheat: §§403, 3102.

[3]It should be noted that dower, both inchoate and consummate, is a mere possibility coupled with an interest in land until it is assigned by metes and bounds: *Freedman v. Mason*, [1956] O.R. 849 at pp. 860-1, 4 D.L.R. (2d) 576 at p. 586 (H.C.J.), *per* McRuer, C.J.H.C., revd [1957] O.R. 441, 9 D.L.R. (2d) 262 (C.A.), affd 14 D.L.R. (2d) 529, [1958] S.C.R. 483. Hence, dower consummate, until it is assigned, is also a future interest.

[4]On the classification of future interests, see Kales, "Future Interests in Land", 22 L.Q. Rev. 250 and 383 (1906); Bingham, "Professor Kales and Common Law Remainders", 5 Mich. L. Rev. 497 (1907); "Note", 20 Harv. L. Rev. 243 (1906-7); Waggoner, "Reformulating the Structure of Estates: A Proposal for Legislative Action", 85 Harv. L. Rev. 729 (1972); Fratcher, "A Modest Proposal for Trimming the Claws of Legal Future Interests", [1972] Duke L. Rev. 517.

1003. HISTORICAL DEVELOPMENT OF FUTURE INTERESTS

The history of future interests may be divided roughly into three periods: the feudal period during which a limited number of future interests were allowed at common law; an intermediate period when uses came to be employed to overcome the rigours of the common law and in which different kinds of future interests were permitted to operate in equity; and the modern age, after the *Statute of Uses*,[1] when many of the old equitable interests were converted into valid legal interests, the trust was developed and future interests in personalty became common. An outline of this history is given in the following sections.

1003.1 Future Interests at Common Law

At common law the creation of future interests was severely restricted. The reason for this was that the common law placed great emphasis on the doctrine of seisin, which insists that someone must always be seised of the land and which prohibits a gap in the seisin.

The insistence of the common law on the sanctity of seisin meant that, with few exceptions, only vested estates could be created as future interests at common law. Moreover, because the common law would not permit a vested interest to be defeated in favour of anyone other than the grantor or his heirs, future interests such as rights of entry for condition broken and possibilities of reverter could not be limited to a stranger.

Thus, the only future interests possible at common law were the reversion, the vested remainder and the possibility of reverter and the right of entry for condition broken and the last two only if they were reserved to the grantor and his heirs.

A reversion is the interest which continues in the grantor after he has conveyed away a particular estate that is less than what he owned. A remainder is the interest that remains out of the grantor on the termination of a particular estate, created by the same instrument. Thus, in a grant "to A for life, remainder to B in tail", A has a life estate in possession, B has a vested remainder in tail and the grantor retains the reversion in fee.

A possibility of reverter is the interest that remains in the grantor when he grants a determinable fee simple. The estate will return to the grantor automatically when the estate so granted determines. A right of entry for condition broken is a right in the grantor to terminate an estate he has granted upon condition subsequent when the condition is breached.

Contingent remainders were not originally allowed because they involved the possibility of a gap in seisin. A contingent remainder is one which is limited to an unborn or unascertained person, or which is subject to a condition precedent. When the person is born or the condition is fulfilled, the remainder vests. However, by the middle of the 15th century they were allowed to take

---

§1003
[1] 27 Hen. 8, c. 10 (1535).

effect if they in fact vested during the continuance of the preceding estate.[1] Interests which purported to spring up in the future, that is, which were not supported by a vested estate preceding it, as in a grant "to A when he attains the age of 21", were not permitted, because the seisin would be in abeyance until A became 21.

These difficulties did not exist in the case of reversions and vested remainders, since these estates would fall in automatically when the preceding estates determined. Nor was there a difficulty with possibilities of reverter and rights of entry for condition broken, even though under the latter interest the grantor had to exercise his right of entry before he recovered his estate. This was not thought of as involving a gap in the seisin.

It was to overcome these and other difficulties that uses were developed.

In Manitoba common law future interests have been abolished. Such interests now take effect in equity behind a trust.[2] Hence the rules respecting legal interests discussed in this chapter have no application to that province.

1003.2   The Development of Uses

(a) Uses before the Statute of Uses

The doctrine of uses was introduced in England by the astute legal advisers of the religious houses in their long legal battle with the state to get around the *Statutes of Mortmain* which prevented corporations from holding land without a licence from the Crown. Under the system of feudal tenure, a number of profits or benefits accrued to the King as lord paramount and to lesser lords of the fee in certain circumstances, including relief, wardship, marriage, and escheat upon the death without heirs of the holder of the freehold. These profits were lost if the land was alienated to a corporation. The corporation could not have children or die and the land could not change hands by descent or otherwise, unless the corporation chose to alienate it. Corporate religious bodies acquired lands by purchase or gift to such an extent that much of the land in England was held by them. They did not wish to alienate it and the land was thus tied up in perpetuity and said to be in mortmain.

The conveyance of land in mortmain was forbidden by *Magna Carta*[1] and subsequent statutes. It was, therefore, impossible for religious institutions to acquire the legal title to land. To evade this restriction uses were introduced. This device involved a grant of land to some person to the use of the religious bodies instead of to them directly. The grantor, A, would grant the land to B, with a direction to B to permit the religious institution to have the occupation and use of the land. B's legal title was purely nominal, for the purpose of evading the provisions of the *Statutes of Mortmain*. Originally, the only way the church had of enforcing the obligation on the part of B to permit its

---

§1003.1
[1]Megarry and Wade, p. 182.
[2]*Perpetuities and Accumulations Act*, S.M. 1982-83, c. 43, s. 4.
§1003.2
[1]1 Hen. 3, cc. 39, 43 (1217), re-enacted as 9 Hen. 3, cc. 32, 36 (1225).

occupation of the land was the threat of spiritual punishment, which was generally sufficient. Eventually, the court of Chancery began enforcing these grants as a matter of equity in that court. The employment of such grants grew so extensively that in 1391 a statute[2] declared such uses to be subject to the *Statutes of Mortmain* and forfeitable as land. That disposed of the device in so far as it concerned the religious bodies, but the practice gradually became more widespread because the desirability of uses for purposes other than evading mortmain statutes had become manifest. For example, at common law, as there could be no alienation of land without the consent of the lord and livery of seisin, land could not be devised by will. If, however, the holder of an estate granted it to another to the use of the grantor and his heirs or to such uses as the grantor might appoint by his will, two major benefits flowed. The grantor could, in his lifetime, divide the use among his children whom he wished to benefit and could devise the use by his will. Furthermore, the use not being land, it was not subject to such feudal burdens as forfeiture by escheat or for treason.

The technical name that is given to the person who holds the title in a grant to uses is the feoffee or grantee to uses; the beneficiary is technically known as the *cestui que use.*

At common law, before the *Statute of Uses,*[3] the grantee or feoffee to uses was regarded as having the lawful seisin and legal estate in land. The *cestui que use* had no estate in or title to the land except for a trust or confidence for which there was no remedy at law but only in the court of Chancery.[4] In the court of Chancery, which enforced equity, however, a use was defined as a trust or confidence, not issuing out of the land, but a thing collateral that was annexed in privity of contract to the estate and person of the legal owner,[5] the effect being that the *cestui que use* was entitled to the profits and the legal owner should convey according to his directions. Originally, the *cestui que use* was not regarded in equity as having an estate in the land itself but, later, the use was treated as an equitable estate.[6]

The custom of raising uses in land grew constantly. By the end of the 14th century a large part of English land was held subject to uses, so that the legal title to the land was in one person and the beneficial title to the land in another. Titles were often in an uncertain condition as a result. The strongest objection to the prevalence of uses came from the Crown by reason of the serious encroachments upon its feudal rights as a result of the creation of equitable titles which were entirely free from the common law feudal obligations. In an attempt to meet this situation, a series of statutes was passed in the 14th and 15th centuries, culminating in the *Statute of Uses.*[7]

---

[2]"Assurance of Lands to certain Places, Persons, and Uses, shall be adjudged Mortmain", 15 Ric. 2, c. 5 (1391).
[3]27 Hen. 8, c. 10 (1535).
[4]*Chudleigh's Case* (1595), 1 Co. Rep. 120 a at p. 121 b, 76 E.R. 270.
[5]*Ibid.*; Co. Litt., 272b.
[6]*Brent's Case* (1583), 2 Leo. 14, 74 E.R. 319.
[7]27 Hen. 8, c. 10 (1535).

(b) The Statute of Uses

In 1535, the *Statute of Uses*[8] was passed to put an end to the distinction between the legal estate and beneficial interest in the land by giving the *cestui que use* the legal estate. The statute went into force in each of the provinces of Canada, except Quebec, but it was repealed as of January 1, 1926, in England by the *Law of Property Act, 1925*,[9] although it remains in force as to deeds coming into operation before that date.

In Ontario, the *Statute of Uses* was re-enacted as part of the 1897 statute revision.[10] In British Columbia the statute was also reprinted in the 1897 revision.[11]

The *Statute of Uses* did not abolish the former conveyance to uses, but merely abolished the estate of the grantee to uses, and turned the former equitable interest of the *cestui que use* into the legal interest and ownership by providing that he stand seised, for all purposes of the law, of whatever interest was limited to his use and of which the grantee to uses would otherwise be seised. The statute is thus said to execute the use because nothing remains to be done by the grantee to uses.

Under the statute, a person cannot be seised of an estate of which he could not be seised at common law but, apart from the transfer of seisin when applicable, the rules governing the creation and extent of uses remained, in general, the same. A change which was effected by the statute was that, as the legal estate never vested for a moment in the grantee to uses, it could not escheat or be forfeited by any act of his and he could neither alienate it free from the use nor alienate it at all (for since earliest times it was held that the whole estate of the grantee to uses was executed by the statute in the *cestui que use*, leaving nothing to the grantee to uses).[12] Thus, where letters patent were granted by the Crown to a father in fee simple in trust for his son, a lunatic, and his heirs and assigns, it was held that the letters patent were an assurance under the statute and created a use which, although it could not vest in the son by reason of his disability, was executed in his heir on his death, so that a deed by the heir was valid as against a deed by the grantee of the letters patent.[13]

The interests which thus were created were either legal remainders if they were vested, or legal executory interests. The latter are interests which are so limited that they do not comply with the rules pertaining to common law remainders. Hence, they might involve a gap in the seisin. However, since the statute gave the *cestui que use* the same interest at law as he had in the use,

---

[8]*Ibid.*
[9]15 & 16 Geo. 5, c. 20.
[10]R.S.O. 1897, c. 331. It is reprinted in App. A to R.S.O. 1980, Vol. 9.
[11]R.S.B.C. 1897, Vol. 1, p. xiv.
[12]*Brent's Case, supra,* footnote 6.
[13]*Doe d. Snyder v. Masters* (1851), 8 U.C.Q.B. 55.

these new future interests, which were formerly equitable, were now permitted to exist at law.[14]

The *Statute of Uses* has been called "the keystone of all modern conveyancing".[15] It is also the key to the modern trust and modern equitable future interests. This is demonstrated by the development of the following rules which govern the operation of the statute:

Rule 1: There must be a person seised to a use or trust. Therefore, an estate of freehold must be limited to the grantee to uses. Consequently, the Act does not apply to a grantee for a term of years only, although a freehold may be granted to a grantee to hold to the use of another person for a term of years.[16] The grantee of a vested remainder has sufficient seisin for the statute to operate in regard to any declared uses of the remainder.[17]

Rule 2: The *cestui que use* and the grantee to uses must be different persons for the statute to operate. This is because a grant to and to the use of the grantee gives him the legal estate at common law, not under the statute.[18] But such a declaration of a use to the grantee himself, although it is not a use which is capable of being executed by the statute, and although it has no effect upon the seisin, which would be in the grantee by the common law without it, nevertheless avails to make any subsequent use limited upon it incapable of being executed by the statute. Such a subsequent use would be a "use limited upon a use" and would take effect, if otherwise valid, as a trust.[19] If the grant declares uses in successive estates and the first use is to the grantee to uses, such as for life or a term of years, with a use in remainder, the grantee takes his use at common law and the statute executes the use in remainder.

Thus, where there was a grant to a father to have and to hold to the use of himself and his son in fee simple, it was held that father and son took as joint tenants, that the son took the entirety on the death of the father, and further, that joint tenants may be seised to a use even though they come in at different times.[20] Again, where land was conveyed to the grantee and his heirs to the use of the grantor and his heirs until his proposed marriage and thereafter to the use of his intended wife and her heirs, for her sole and separate use and benefit forever, it was held that, on marriage, the wife acquired the

---

[14]As to these interests, see §§1010-1010.3, *infra*.

[15]Williams, *Seisin of the Freehold*, p. 137. And see Barton, "The Statute of Uses and the Trust of Freeholds", 82 L.Q. Rev. 215 (1966).

[16]*Heyward's Case* (1595), 2 Co. Rep. 35 a, 76 E.R. 489; *Symson v. Turner* (1700), 1 Eq. Cas. Abr. 220, 21 E.R. 1003; Gilbert, p. 182; 1 Sanders, p. 87.

[17]1 Sanders, p. 105; and see *Haggerston v. Hanbury* (1826), 5 B. & C. 101, 108 E.R. 37, holding that where A, a tenant in tail subject to a term, conveyed to A and B in fee simple to the use of A in order to bar the entail, the deed operated to give the reversion to A as A and B were seised of the freehold.

[18]*Sammes's Case* (1609), 13 Co. Rep. 54, 77 E.R. 1464; *Doe d. Lloyd v. Passingham* (1827), 6 B. & C. 305, 108 E.R. 465; *Savill Brothers, Ltd. v. Bethell*, [1902] 2 Ch. 523 (C.A.).

[19]Challis, p. 390.

[20]*Sammes's Case, supra,* footnote 18, and see also *Doe d. Hutchinson v. Prestwidge* (1815), 4 M. & S. 178, 105 E.R. 800; *Orme's Case* (1872), L.R. 8 C.P. 281.

legal estate in fee simple.[21] Similarly, a use to a grantor and his intended wife in tail was held to be good for, whenever the contingency happened, the statute immediately executed the use into possession.[22] The rule is departed from if the circumstances require. Thus, in the case of a grant to a person to the use of himself and the heirs of his body, the statute is applied so as to divest him of his common law estate and to execute the use under the statute in the interests of the issue in tail.[23] Also, if the grant declares uses in a number of estates and the grantee's use is between other uses, as where it is a life estate preceded and followed by other estates, all uses are executed under the statute on grounds of convenience.[24] This is said to be because of "a direct impossibility or impertinency for the use to take effect by the common law".[25]

Rule 3: A use must be expressly declared or created impliedly, to take effect immediately or in the future.

An express use must be in writing under the *Statute of Frauds*[26] because it is an interest in the land.

It is immaterial whether the words "use", "confidence" or "trust" are used because the common law makes no distinction between them.[27] Any expression may be used showing an intention that one person is to hold to the use of or in trust for another.[28]

Wherever land is devised or conveyed to one person in trust for, to the use of, or for the benefit of, another person and no active duties are imposed on the grantee or devisee, the beneficiary takes the legal estate under the statute.[29] If active duties are to be performed by the trustee or grantee to uses, however, the statute does not operate. Thus, where land was devised to executors:

> ... to hold the same in trust for the use and benefit of my son William during his lifetime, and after the death of my son William in trust for his heirs, issue of his body, until the youngest of said heirs shall become of age, and then to convey it to

---

[21]*Re Bayliss and Balfe* (1917), 38 O.L.R. 437, 35 D.L.R. 350 (H.C.).

[22]*Woodliff v. Drury* (1595), Cro. Eliz. 439, 78 E.R. 679.

[23]*Sammes's Case, supra,* footnote 18.

[24]1 Sanders, p. 92, listing other exceptions to the rule.

[25]Bacon, *Reading upon the Statutes of Uses* (London, W. Stratford, 1804), p. 63; and see Challis, p. 390.

[26]29 Car. 2, c. 3 (1677).

[27]*Lord Altham v. Earl of Anglesey* (1709), Gilb. Rep. 16, 25 E.R. 12. Formerly, a distinction was drawn between uses as permanent arrangements and trusts confidences, which were regarded as mere temporary arrangements; see 1 Sanders, p. 2.

[28]*Hummerston's Case* (1575), 2 Dyer 166 a, 73 E.R. 363; *Bettuans Case* (1576), 4 Leo. 22, 74 E.R. 702.

[29]*Fair v. McCrow* (1871), 31 U.C.Q.B. 599, a devise to one person "for the sole benefit of" another person; and see *Tunis v. Passmore* (1872), 32 U.C.Q.B. 419, a devise "in trust for the only benefit of R.B." for life and after his death "in trust for" the heirs of his body, giving him an estate tail; *Barker v. Greenwood* (1838), 4 M. & W. 421 at p. 429, 150 E.R. 1494, where Parke, B., said: "[W]here the words are, 'in trust to permit and suffer A.B. to take the rents and profits,' there the use is divested out of them [the trustees], and executed in the party, the purposes of the trust not requiring that the legal estate should remain in them"; and see *William v. Waters* (1845), 14 M. & W. 166, 153 E.R. 434; *Re Hall and Urquhart* (1928), 35 O.W.N. 201 (H.C.).

said heirs the children of my said son William taking equal shares, and the child
or children of any deceased child of my said son to take their parent's share in
equal proportion,

it was held that the son took an estate for life and that the legal estate vested
in the trustees for the benefit of his heirs.[30]

Letters patent issued by the Crown come within the statute, so that where
letters patent conveyed land to a father in fee simple in trust for his son, a
lunatic, his heirs and assigns, the statute executed the use in the heir of the
son on his death and the heir's deed was held valid as against the deed of the
grantee of the letters patent.[31]

Words limiting uses receive the same construction as words of limitation
at common law.[32] Therefore, estates in uses must be created by words that
would create common law estates and are, in regard to duration, subject to
the same rules as estates created at common law.[33] Consequently, the *cestui
que use* has the same estate at law as that limited to him in the use, including
all the incidents and benefits of the legal estate.[34] As was indicated in the preceding paragraph, a freehold cannot, at common law, be limited to commence
in the future and a remainder must vest no later than the end of the preceding
estate, so there could be no desultory limitations, creating estates to arise at
intervals and not continuously.[35] Consequently, there can be no desultory
limitations of the use of a common law estate.[36] A use may be limited to take
effect in the future, either as a remainder which is subject to the rules of

---

[30]*Re Romanes and Smith* (1880), 8 P.R. (Ont.), 323 at pp. 324-5, where Proudfoot, V.C.,
said:

> When an estate is given to trustees to receive the rents and pay them to the
> beneficiary, the trustees take the legal estate to enable them to perform the trust;
> but if the estate is given to them to permit another to receive the rents the beneficial
> devisee takes the legal estate and not the trustee. This miraculous distinction, as Sir
> James Mansfield termed it, is too firmly established to be questioned: *Doe d.Leicester
> v. Biggs* (1809), 2 Taunt. 109; or, as stated by Mr. Lewin (*Trusts*, 5th ed., 247), if
> any agency be imposed on the trustee as by a limitation to the trustee to convey
> the estate, the statute of uses does not apply, and the legal estate is vested in the
> trustee. This was the case in *Doe d. Shelley v. Edlin* (1836), 4 A. & E. 582. And
> where an estate was limited to the trustee to permit a tenant for life to receive the
> rents during his life, and on his death to convey to another in fee, the legal estate
> during the life of the tenant for life is vested in him, and the remainder in the
> trustees: *Doe dem Noble v. Bolton* (1839), 11 A. & E. 188; *Adams v. Adams*, 6
> Q.B. 860.

[31]*Doe d. Snyder v. Masters* (1851), 8 U.C.Q.B. 55.

[32]Gilbert, pp. 143-309.

[33]*Corbet's Case* (1600), 1 Co. Rep. 83 b at p. 87 b, 76 E.R. 187; *Nevil v. Nevil* (1619),
1 Brownl. 152, 123 E.R. 724; *Makepiece v. Fletcher* (1734), 2 Com. 457, 92 E.R. 1158;
Tapner d. Peckham v. Merlott (1739), Willes 177, 125 E.R. 1119; 1 Sanders, pp. 122
et seq.

[34]1 Sanders, pp. 117-20.

[35]*Corbet's Case, supra,* footnote 33; *The Prince's Case* (1606), 8 Co. Rep. 1 a at pp. 13 b,
17 a, 77 E.R. 481; *Atkins v. Mountague* (1671), 1 Ch. Ca. 214, 22 E.R. 768; Challis,
p. 113.

[36]1 Sanders, p. 133; Gilbert, p. 147.

common law, or as an executory interest which is not subject to those rules.[37]

An implied use arises where a conveyance which does not declare uses is made without consideration or, if it declares uses, disposes of only part of the use that the grantor was able to declare, the use of the undisposed-of part remaining with him. Such implied uses are called resulting uses.[38]

Rule 4: A use can be conveyed only in land actually belonging to the grantor and cannot be declared in land to be acquired by him.[39]

Rule 5: The statute executes only the first declaration of a use. In interpreting the statute, the courts of common law ruled that there could be "no use upon a use" so that if land were limited to A to the use of B to the use of, or in trust for, C, the statute only executed the use to B, giving him the legal estate, and C thus retained an equitable interest in the nature of a trust, enforceable only in the court of Chancery.[40]

Thus, where land was conveyed to a trustee in fee simple to certain uses and, after their determination, to the use of the trustee in fee simple to receive the rents and profits and pay them to A, a married woman, for her separate use and, after the determination of that estate, to stand seised of the land to such uses and upon such trusts as A might by will appoint and, in default of appointment, to the use of the heirs and assigns of A, it was held that, although the construction might be otherwise in a will, the trustee took the legal estate in fee and A took an equitable estate for life with an equitable remainder to her heirs and assigns, which two estates, under the rule in *Shelley's Case*,[41] gave her the equitable estate in fee simple.[42] It was said that, notwithstanding the statute, there were three ways of creating a use or trust that would remain a creature of equity as it was before the statute: (a) where a man seised in fee limits a term of years in trust for A, for the statute could not execute it because A could not be seised of a term; (b) where lands are limited to the use of A in trust to permit B to receive the rents and profits, for the statute can only execute the first use; and (c) where lands are limited to trustees to receive and pay over rents and profits to named persons, for the lands must remain in the trustees to answer these purposes.[43]

If a conveyance is made to and to the use of the grantee and his heirs, the grantee at once acquires a fee simple at common law and not under the statute but, since a use was so declared, it prevents the statute from executing any further use imposed upon the grantee, so that if the conveyance provided that the grantee was to hold to the use of, or in trust for, any other person, such

---

[37] 1 Sanders, pp. 141 *et seq.* See further §1010.1, *infra.*
[38] See §1010.1(a), *infra.*
[39] 1 Sanders, p. 105.
[40] *Tyrrel's Case* (1557), 2 Dyer 155 a, 73 E.R. 336; *Tipping v. Cozens* (1694), 1 Ld. Raym. 33, 91 E.R. 918; *Haggerston v. Hanbury* (1826), 5 B. & C. 101, 108 E.R. 37; *Doe d. Lloyd v. Passingham* (1827), 6 B. & C. 305, 108 E.R. 465; *Gamble v. Rees* (1849), 6 U.C.Q.B. 396; 2 Bl. Comm. 335; 1 Sanders, p. 275; Gilbert, p. 347.
[41] (1581), 1 Co. Rep. 93 b, 76 E.R. 206.
[42] *Cooper v. Kynock* (1872), L.R. 7 Ch. 398.
[43] *Symson v. Turner* (1700), 1 Eq. Cas. Abr. 220, 21 E.R. 1003.

person would have only an equitable estate.[44] If there is a remainder after the use declared to the grantee, however, the remainder is executed by the statute.[45]

In a conveyance where land is limited to such uses as the husband might, by deed or will, appoint and in default of appointment to him in fee, the fee simple continues in the settlor. Dower, however, will attach at once for, if the grantee dies without exercising the power of appointment, the fee passes from the settlor to the grantee. The right to dower will be defeated by the exercise of the power by the husband in his lifetime by deed or will.[46] There is nothing repugnant to the co-existence of a power with the fee. If the granting clause of a deed contains both the words "fee simple" and words giving the right to appoint uses, the grantee may exercise the power of appointment and defeat his wife's right to dower. And this is true even if the granting clause grants to the grantee in fee simple and the *habendum* clause is to uses.[47]

The ruling of the courts of common law that the statute could only execute the first use limited to the *cestui que use* and that, if the limitation added that he was to hold to the use of, or "in trust for", some other person or persons, this second use or trust remained an equitable interest, resulted in the court of Chancery having sole jurisdiction over it as a trust or confidence. The ruling was assailed by many as absurd and even contrary to the statute. The creation of the second use was said to be in defiance of the statute. Lord Hardwicke's celebrated remark was that "a statute made upon great consideration, introduced in a solemn and pompous manner, by this strict construction, has had no other effect than to add at most, three words to a conveyance".[48] Nevertheless, the result was beneficial because it gave rise to all of our modern law respecting trusts.

The *Statute of Uses* was passed before the *Statute of Wills*[49] when lands were not generally devisable by will. The reference to wills in the statute may only have been due to the fact that a custom to devise land existed in certain places, so that it is said that the statute may not directly operate on wills. However, if a testator uses expressions that are appropriate to a conveyance

---

[44]1 Sanders, pp. 89-90; *Tipping v. Cozens, supra,* footnote 40, in which case a conveyance was made to and to the use of trustees and their heirs during the life of J in trust to preserve contingent remainders but to permit J to take the profits, and it was held that J had only an equitable interest; *Doe d. Lloyd v. Passingham, supra,* footnote 40, in which case an estate was limited to A to the use of A in trust for B and it was held, although A took the legal estate at common law and not under the statute, the second use or trust could not be executed by the statute; see also *Cooper v. Kynock, supra,* footnote 42.

[45]*Sammes's Case* (1609), 13 Co. Rep. 54, 77 E.R. 1464.

[46]*Re Rowe,* [1957] O.R. 9, 10 D.L.R. (2d) 215 (H.C.J.).

[47]*Re Hazell* (1925), 57 O.L.R. 290, [1925] 3 D.L.R. 661 (S.C. App. Div.); *Re Armstrong and Brown,* [1952] O.W.N. 55 (C.A.); *Re Walsh and Sovis,* [1956] O.R. 202, [1956] 2 D.L.R. (2d) 356 (H.C.J.); *Re Carter and Congram,* [1970] 1 O.R. 800, 9 D.L.R. (3d) 350 (H.C.J.).

[48]*Hopkins v. Hopkins* (1738), 1 Atk. 581 at p. 591, 26 E.R. 365.

[49]32 Hen. 8, c. 1 (1540).

to uses, it is an indication that he intends them to be construed as if the will were a conveyance and effect will be given to that intention.[50]

The use upon a use should be distinguished from a use after a use as in a grant "to X and his heirs, to the use of Y for life and then to the use of Z in fee". In that case both uses are executed, for X holds to the use of Y and Z successively.

It should also be noted that in order to protect contingent interests, uses must be inserted in each successive limitation. Thus, in a grant "to X and his heirs to the use of Y for life when he attains the age of 21 and then to Z when he marries after Y's death", gives Y a legal executory interest because the use is executed. Since Z's interest is not limited by a use, however, his interest would be a contingent remainder.

Rule 6: The statute does not execute a use where the seisin is given to a corporation. This is because of a peculiar collocation of words in the statute. It provides that it applies where "any person or persons" are seised to the use "of any other person or persons or body politick". The inference thus was that the words "person or persons" as used the first time did not include a "body politick" or corporation. Hence, in a conveyance "to XYZ Ltd. to the use of A", the use is not executed and A has an equitable estate in fee simple.[51] Where a corporation is the *cestui que use* and the seisin is in an individual, however, the use is executed.[52]

The statute thus created new future interests, namely, legal executory interests and, by reason of the foregoing exceptions, equitable future interests could still be created after the statute.

1003.3 Future Interests under Wills

Prior to the *Statute of Uses*[1] devises of land were not possible at common law. Landowners did employ the use, however, to achieve a measure of testation. For example, A might convey the fee simple "to B to the use of A in fee simple", which would permit A to devise the use in equity, so that B would then hold for A's heirs. Similarly, if A conveyed "to B in fee simple, to such uses as A shall appoint by will and until and in default of appointment to the use of A", A could dispose of the equitable interest by will.

Because the statute effectively gave the legal estate to the grantor, the landed gentry sought and obtained redress when the *Statute of Wills*[2] was passed. This

---

[50]1 Sanders, p. 253; Gilbert, p. 356; Challis, p. 387; Co. Litt. 272a; *Baker v. White* (1875), L.R. 20 Eq. 166 at p. 170.

[51]Sanders, p. 253.

[52]Cruise. *A Digest of the Laws of England*, 4th ed. by H. H. White (London, Saunders and Benning. 1835), i, p. 354.

§1003.3

[1]27 Hen. 8, c. 10 (1535).

[2]32 Hen. 8, c. 1 (1540).

Act permitted a person to devise his lands "at his free will and pleasure".[3] The effect of this language was that devises did not have to comply with the common law remainder rules so that new legal future interests, comparable to those arising under the *Statute of Uses*, could be created, which could spring up in the future and shift upon stipulated events.[4] These are called springing and shifting executory devises.[5]

The *Statute of Uses* does not apply to wills, so that a use does not need to be employed to achieve this result.[6]

If a trust is employed in a will, the interests created thereunder are, of course, equitable. Moreover, as a result of the statutory trust in favour of the beneficiaries, with the personal representative as trustee, constituted under modern devolution of estates legislation, today future interests arising under wills are all equitable.[7]

1003.4 Future Interests in Personalty

Today the ownership and transmission of interests in personalty is much more important than that of interests in land, since the wealth of the nation is now concentrated primarily in personalty. This presents little difficulty in so far as such interests are equitable. Interests in personal property can readily be created under a trust. Moreover, the common law restrictions on future interests would not apply to personalty in any event as they were couched in terms of interests in land. Furthermore, future interests in chattels may be created by will. In that case, the gift of a limited interest, such as for life (with a remainder over) would be regarded as giving the use of the chattel to the "life tenant" for his life.[1] If the chattel is a consumable[2] however, the testamentary gift is absolute, for clearly the chattel will, or is likely to be, used

---

[3]*Ibid.*, ss. 1, 2. Actually only two-thirds of lands held in knight service and all lands held in socage tenure were made devisable. When knight service was converted into socage tenure by the *Tenures Abolition Act*, 12 Car. 2, c. 24 (1660), all freehold land became fully devisable.

[4]*Pells v. Brown* (1620), Cro. Jac. 590, 79 E.R. 504.

[5]See §1010.2, *infra*.

[6]*Re Tanqueray-Willaume and Landau* (1882), 20 Ch. D. 465 (C.A.), at p. 478, *per* Jessel, M.R.

[7]See §1011, *infra*.

§1003.4

[1]*Hide v. Parrat* (1696), 2 Vern. 331, 23 E.R. 813; 1 Fearne, pp. 402 *et seq.*; *Hoare v. Parker* (1788), 2 T. R. 376, 100 E.R. 202; *Re Tritton* (1889), 61 L.T. 301; *Re Thynne*, [1911] 1 Ch. 282; *Osterhout v. Osterhout* (1904), 7 O.L.R. 402 (Div. Ct.) affd 8 O.L.R. 685 (C.A.); *Re Turnbull Estate* (1906), 11 O.L.R. 334 (H.C.J.); *Re McLaughlin* (1915), 8 O.W.N. 277 (H.C.); *Re Ridd Estate*, [1947] 2 W.W.R. 369 (Man. K.B.); *Re Henry*, [1969] 2 O.R. 878, 7 D.L.R. (3d) 310 (H.C.J.); *Re Bangs* (1962), 38 D.L.R. (2d) 99 (Man. Q.B.); *Re Fraser* (1974), 46 D.L.R. (3d) 358, [1974] 6 W.W.R. 560 sub nom. *Minister of Finance v. Fraser* (B.C.C.A.); Laskin, pp. 369-70.

[2]*Res quae ipso usu consumuntur.*

up during the limited ownership, so that the use and the property are the same.[3]

The exact description of the interest held by the "life tenant" and "remainderman" of a chattel under a will is uncertain. Many of the cases suggest that the "life tenant" in fact is the absolute owner, subject to a fiduciary duty to preserve the chattel for the "remainderman", who is regarded as having an executory interest.[4] This would, therefore, suggest that the "life tenant" is given the use of the property only.[5]

Apart from a will or a trust, future interests cannot be created in personal chattels by deed *inter vivos*.[6] Whether a future interest can be created by deed out of a leasehold interest does not appear to have been dealt with in England or Canada. In the United States, future interests in personal chattels and chattels real may be created by deed.[7] Apart from historical considerations, which ought not to be given undue weight today, there seems to be no reason in principle why this approach should not be followed in Canada.

1004. VESTED AND CONTINGENT INTERESTS

A future interest may be either *vested* or *contingent*. For certain types of future interests, namely, those arising under the *Statute of Uses*[1] and under wills, the term "executory" is used instead of "contingent". There is no difference between the two terms, except in the mode of creation of the interests and their susceptibility to destruction.

The term "vested" has two possible meanings, namely, "vested in possession" and "vested in interest". The latter is the commonly understood meaning in relation to future interests and it is so used here. A vested interest in this sense is either an interest that is presently being enjoyed by the owner, in which case it is also vested in possession, or one that is presently ready to fall into possession upon the natural determination of all preceding interests. Thus, in a grant by G "to A for life, remainder to B for life, remainder to C in fee simple", A's life estate is vested in interest and in possession, while B's life estate and C's estate in fee simple are both vested in interest. B's estate is vested

---

[3]*Randall v. Russell* (1817), 3 Mer. 190, 36 E.R. 73; *Cockayne v. Harrison* (1872), L.R. 13 Eq. 432 at p. 434; *Myers v. Washbrook*, [1901] 1 Q.B. 360; *Re Elliott* (1916), 10 O.W.N. 378 (H.C.); *Re Bangs, supra,* footnote 1; *Re Fraser, supra,* footnote 1, not following *Re Troupe,* [1945] 2 D.L.R. 540, [1945] 1 W.W.R. 364 (Man. K.B.); *Re Ingram Estate* (1961), 36 W.W.R. 536 (Man. Q.B.).

[4]*Re Tritton, supra,* footnote 1; *Re Thynne, supra,* footnote 1; *Re Swan,* [1915] 1 Ch. 829 at pp. 833-4; *Re Bellamy* (1883), 25 Ch. 620; *Re Henry, supra,* footnote 1.

[5]*Cf. Law of Property Act, 1925,* 15 & 16 Geo. 5, c. 20, s. 130(5), which speaks of the "usufructuary for the time being" in reference to trusts of settled chattels. See generally Oliver, "Interests for Life and Quasi-Remainders in Chattels Personal", 24 L.Q. Rev. 431 (1908).

[6]*Bennett & White (Calgary) Ltd. v. Municipal District of Sugar City (No. 5),* [1951] 4 D.L.R. 129 at p. 143, [1951] A.C. 786 at p. 812 (P.C.).

[7]1 A.L.P., §4.4; Gray, p. 749; Simes and Smith, §§11, 12.

§1004

[1]27 Hen. 8, c. 10 (1535).

in interest for the present, even though it may not fall into possession in fact, namely, if B dies before A.

Vested interests, in the context of real property, are estates in land. Contingent and executory interests are not, but may become so upon the happening of a contingency, the performance of some condition, or the ascertainment or birth of the person to whom it is limited.

An interest may thus be said to be vested if, (a) it is limited to a person who is in existence, (b) it is limited to a person who is ascertained, and (c) it is not subject to a condition precedent. An interest is contingent or executory if it does not satisfy one of these three criteria, for in that case it is not presently capable of falling into possession upon the natural determination of all preceding interests. Thus, for example, in a grant by G "to A for life, remainder to B in fee simple, provided B marries C", B's interest is contingent. It will become vested if he marries C, but, because this grant operates at common law, he must do so before A's death, otherwise his interest will fail.

1004.1   Types of Vested Interests

Vested interests are of three types, namely, absolutely vested, subject to partial divestment and subject to complete divestment.

(a)   Absolutely or indefeasibly vested interests

An example of this type would be a grant by G "to A for life, remainder to B in fee simple". In this example, B's remainder is vested absolutely.

If, however, B's interest were defeasible by an executory interest, or in some other way, it would not be vested absolutely.

Historically, any estate in remainder, if it was not defeasible by executory limitation, contingent remainder, or otherwise, was regarded as vested absolutely. Modern classifications, however, regard any remainder less than a fee simple absolute, or analogous interest in personalty to one person, as not indefeasibly vested, since the person to whom it is limited may not survive until it falls into possession.[1]

Hence, in a gift "to A for life, remainder to B for life", B's remainder is vested subject to complete divestment. Similarly, in a gift "to A for life, remainder to B's children in fee at age 21", the interest of B's children who are 21 at the date of the gift is vested, but is subject to partial divestment in favour of other children who reach that age later.

(b)   Vested subject to partial divestment or defeasance, or vested subject to open

This type applies to class gifts and may apply to powers of appointment.[2]

---

§1004.1
[1] 1 A.L.P., §§4.33, 4.35.
[2] A power of appointment may effect a partial or a complete divestment. An example is given under §1004.1(c) below. The same result obtains where a power of sale is given to the life tenant: *Doe d. Savoy v. McEachern* (1887), 26 N.B.R. 391 (S.C.).

An example would be a devise by T "to A for life, remainder to all his children who attain age 21 in fee simple". If A has a child, C, who is 21 at the time of T's death, his interest is vested. The interests of A's other children who are under 21 are contingent, but they will become vested if and when they attain the age of 21 before A's death, and C's interest will be defeated or reduced correspondingly. It should be noted that in the case of class gifts in wills the rules of construction known as the class closing rules may operate, in the absence of a contrary intention, so as to exclude potential members of the class. Thus, in the last example, children of A who are not yet 21 at his death are excluded. The rules, although developed for wills, apply as well to settlements.[3]

The class closing rules are as follows:[4]

Compound Gifts

1. *An immediate gift to a class*
An example would be a gift "to the children of A equally".

The class closes on the testator's death and only those children then living share in the gift.[5] However, if there are no children living at that time, the class remains open until it closes naturally, that is, by the death of A.[6]

2. *A postponed gift to a class*

An example would be a gift "to X for life, remainder to the children of A equally".

The class closes at the death of the life tenant and only those children then living, or the personal representatives of those who survived the testator but predeceased X, can take. But if there are no children living at that time, the class remains open to let in all after-born children of A.[7]

3. *An immediate gift to a class coupled with a condition*

An example would be a gift "to the children of A when they attain age 21".

In this case the class closes on the testator's death or as soon thereafter as one member of the class has satisfied the condition. Children alive at that time

---

[3]*Re Knapp's Settlement*, [1895] 1 Ch. 91; *Re Wernher's Settlement Trust*, [1961] 1 W.L.R. 136.

[4]The rules are set out in summary form. For further detail reference should be had to the standard texts, *e.g.*, Jarman, pp. 1659-1702; Bailey, *The Law of Wills*, 7th ed. (London, Pitman, 1973), pp. 179 *et seq.*; Hawkins and Ryder, *The Construction of Wills* by E. C. Ryder (London, Sweet & Maxwell, 1965), p. 106. The rules are summarized in *Re Chartres*, [1927] 1 Ch. 466 at pp. 471-2, and in *Re Bleckly*, [1951] Ch. 740 (C.A.), at pp. 748-50. See also Trautman, "Class Gifts of Future Interests: When is Survival Required?", 20 Vand. L. Rev. 1 (1966).

[5]*Viner v. Francis* (1789), 2 Cox 190, 30 E.R. 88.

[6]*Shepherd v. Ingram* (1764), Amb. 448, 27 E.R. 296.

[7]*Devisme v. Mello* (1782), 1 Bro. C.C. 537, 28 E.R. 1285; *Re Dawe's Trusts* (1876), 4 Ch. D. 210.

who have not yet satisfied the condition may take when they become 21, but all unborn children are excluded.[8]

4. *A postponed gift to a class coupled with a condition*

An example is a gift "to X for life, remainder to the children of A who attain age 21".

In this case the class closes at the later of the determination of the life estate and the fulfilment of the contingency by a child of A. Other living children are potential members, but unborn children are excluded. The estates of children of A who survived the testator and attained the age of 21, but predeceased X, can take.[9]

Separate Gifts

1. *An immediate gift to a class, whether or not it is coupled with a condition*
An example is a gift of "$1,000 to each of the children of A" (or, "who attain age 21").

The class closes at the testator's death, whether or not any takers or potential takers are in existence. Children who are born, but who have not yet satisfied the condition, may take when they become 21.[10]

2. *A postponed gift to a class, whether or not it is coupled with a condition*

An example is a gift "to X for life, and then to pay $100 to each of the children of A" (or, "who become 21").

The class closes at the termination of the prior interest and only those persons who are then living, or the personal representatives of those who survived the testator and whose interest vested during the life tenancy, can take, or are potential takers.[11]

(c) Vested subject to complete divestment or defeasance

This type applies to gifts defeasible under an executory gift and to powers of appointment, as well as to any remainder less than an absolute fee simple or an analogous interest in personalty to one person. Thus, in a devise "to A for life, remainder to B in fee simple, but if B leaves no issue him surviving, then to C in fee simple", B's remainder is vested but is subject to complete divestment on the stated contingency.

A devise "to A for life, remainder as A shall appoint, and in default of appointment to B in fee simple", is construed to mean, "to A for life, remainder to B in fee simple, but if A appoints, then, to the extent of such appointment, to the appointees in fee simple". Thus, B would have a vested remainder,

---

[8]*Andrews v. Partington* (1791), 3 Bro. C.C. 401, 29 E.R. 610.
[9]*Re Canney's Trusts* (1910), 101 L.T. 905; *Re Bleckly, supra,* footnote 4.
[10]*Rogers v. Mutch* (1878), 10 Ch. D. 25.
[11]*Ibid.*

subject to complete or partial divestment, depending upon the extent of the appointment.[12]

In fact, modern American writers treat the three classes of vested interests as mutually exclusive. Hence a remainder that is apparently partially defeasible may well be subject to complete divestment. Thus, a gift "to A for life, remainder to A's children at age 21", in which A is given a power to encroach on the capital, appears to give A's children a vested remainder subject to partial divestment to admit children who later qualify. In fact the remainder is subject to complete divestment because of the power to encroach. Only if the remainderman is certain to receive at least part of the interest in possession would it be regarded as subject to partial defeasance.[13]

1004.2 Importance of the Distinction between Vested and Contingent Interests

Historically, the distinction between interests that are vested and those that are contingent was critical. Contingent remainders were destructible and were not permitted to take effect unless they in fact became vested during the continuance of the prior particular estate. Moreover, a contingent remainder that purported to create a fee simple after a fee simple, or that had the effect of unnaturally defeating a preceding estate, was void. Furthermore, contingent remainders were inalienable at common law.[1]

While these rules are no longer applicable in many cases, the distinction continues to be relevant in the following respects:[2]

(i) The owner of a vested interest does not have to do anything to take his interest, while the owner of a contingent interest receives nothing if he dies before the contingency is satisfied, or if the contingency is not fulfilled.

(ii) The owner of a vested interest has the right, if he is a child, to maintenance under a trust, while the owner of a contingent interest often does not.

(iii) The owner of a vested interest is entitled to the intermediate income from a fund or to possession of land, if the income has not otherwise been disposed of, or another person has not been given a right of possession.

(iv) A vested interest may accelerate if a preceding interest is destroyed, a contingent interest may not.[3]

(v) The owner of a vested interest can command a higher price for his interest than the owner of a contingent interest.

(vi) A contingent interest may not always be alienable in law.

---

[12]*Cunningham v. Moody* (1748), 1 Ves. Sen. 174 at p. 177, 27 E.R. 965, *per* Lord Hardwicke, L.C.; *Doe d. Willis v. Martin* (1790), 4 T.R. 39 at p. 64, 100 E.R. 882.
[13]Restatement, *Property*, §157, comment c; 1 Simes and Smith, §115.
§1004.2
[1]These rules are discussed in §1009.2, *infra.*
[2]These matters are dealt with in subsequent sections of this and the next chapter.
[3]See Pritchard, "Acceleration and Contingent Remainders", 32 C.L.J. 246 (1973).

(vii) A contingent interest may still be destructible in certain cases.

(viii) Whether an interest is vested or contingent is important for the application of the rule against perpetuities.[4]

1004.3 Rules as to Vesting

(a) Introduction

Because of the serious consequences of holding a gift to be contingent, the courts tend to construe a gift as vested if possible and thus will often construe an apparent condition precedent as subsequent. Moreover, they tend to disfavour divesting of vested interests and thus will readily strike down a condition subsequent. In this section, the general rules of construction will be dealt with first, followed by a discussion of particular circumstances in which these rules are applied.

(b) General rules of construction

The following general rules of construction particularize the approach outlined above. While they are also applicable to conveyance *inter vivos*, they are extracted from cases interpreting wills and are thus couched in those terms.

Rule 1: If there is doubt as to whether a condition is precedent or subsequent, the court prefers to construe it as a condition subsequent, and will do so if such a construction is consistent with the will as a whole and will not construe it as a condition precedent unless the will clearly shows that it is intended to be such.[1]

Rule 2: The presumption as to intent is in favour of vesting at the testator's

---

[4]Much has been written on the perceived importance of the distinction. The following articles are representative: Kales, "Future Interests in Land", 22 L.Q. Rev. 250 and 383 (1906); *id.*, "A Modern Dialogue between Doctor and Student on the Distinction between Vested and Contingent Remainders", 24 L.Q. Rev. 301 (1908); *id.*, "Vested and Contingent Remainders", 8 Col. L. Rev. 245 (1908); Bingham, "Professor Kales and Common Law Remainders", 5 Mich. L. Rev. 497 (1907); Graustein, "Vested and Contingent Remainders", 20 Harv. L. Rev. 243 (1907); Foulke, "Vested and Contingent Remainders", 15 Col. L. Rev. 680 (1915); Tiffany, "Future Estates", 29 L.Q. Rev. 290 (1913); Lawler, "Classifications of Contingent Remainders", 29 Calif. L. Rev. 290 (1941); Waggoner, "Reformulating the Structure of Estates: A Proposal for Legislative Action", 85 Harv. L. Rev. 729 (1972), at p. 743; Fratcher, "A Modest Proposal for Trimming the Claws of Legal Future Interests", [1972] Duke L. Rev. 517; Rabin, "The Law Favours the Vesting of Estates. Why?", 65 Col. L. Rev. 467 (1965).
§1004.3
[1]*Duffield v. Duffield* (1829), 1 Dow & Clark 268, at p. 311, 6 E.R. 525 *per* Best, C.J.; *Egerton v. Earl Brownlow* (1853), 4 H.L.C. 1 at pp. 182-9, 10 E.R. 359; *Woodhouse v. Herrick* (1855), 1 K. & J. 352 at pp. 359-60, 69 E.R. 494; *Lady Langdale v. Briggs* (1856), 8 De G. M. & G. 391, 44 E.R. 441; *Re Greenwood*; *Goodhart v. Woodhead*, [1903] 1 Ch. 749 (C.A.), at p. 755.

death or at the earliest moment after that date as is possible under the terms of the will, especially where the property is land.[2]

Thus, where a testator devised land to his widow for life for the support of herself and the testator's children, with power to sell as she might think proper for the benefit of the estate, and after her death devised what might remain undisposed of to trustees to stand seised for the benefit of the children in equal shares and to pay each child his share on attaining his majority but, if any child died before his majority, without issue, to pay and apply his share to the survivors, it was held that the estates of the children were vested in equity upon the death of the testator, subject to the power of sale, and vested as realty because there was no trust to convert realty into personalty and the use of the words "pay" and "pay and apply" did not operate as a conversion of realty into personalty.[3]

In the case of a gift to a class, the general rule is that, in the absence of a clear intention to the contrary in the will, the members of the class are to be ascertained at the testator's death.[4] The mere fact that division is to be at the end of a life interest does not show a contrary intention and the fact that a person has a preceding life interest does not exclude him from being a member of the class.[5]

A testator devised property to his daughter and the residue of his estate to his executors in trust for his widow and daughter, with a limited power to the daughter to dispose of it by will, and then directed that, if the daughter died without surviving issue and without having made a will, the executors were to sell all the estate after the death of the widow if she survived the daughter and divide it among "my own right heirs". The daughter died unmarried before her mother, having made a will in which she had disposed of the residue. It was held that she was entitled to it as the "right heir" of the testator.[6]

If the gift to the class is not immediate, it vests in those who constitute the

---

[2]*Driver d. Frank v. Frank* (1818), 8 Taunt. 468, 129 E.R. 465 (Ex. Ch.); *Duffield v. Duffield* (1829), 3 Bligh N.S. 260 at p. 311, 4 E.R. 1334 (H.L.); *Re Blakemore's Settlement* (1855), 20 Beav. 214 at p. 217, 52 E.R. 585; *Brocklebank v. Johnson* (1855), 20 Beav. 205, 52 E.R. 581; *Re Merrick's Trusts* (1866), L.R. 1 Eq. 551; *Radford v. Willis* (1871), L.R. 7 Ch. 7; *Hervey-Bathurst v. Stanley*; *Craven v. Stanley* (1876), 4 Ch. D. 251; *Rhodes v. Rhodes* (1882), 7 App. Cas. 192; *Re Wrightson*; *Battie-Wrightson v. Thomas*, [1904] 2 Ch. 95 (C.A.), at p. 103; *Bickersteth v. Shanu*, [1936] A.C. 290, [1936] 1 W.W.R. 644 (P.C.); *Re Duffield*, [1971] 1 O.R. 515, 16 D.L.R. (3d) 7 (H.C.J.), *per* Stark, J.; *Re Taylor*, [1972] 3 O.R. 349, 28 D.L.R. (3d) 257 (H.C.J.), *per* Lacourcière, J.; *Re Down*, [1968] 2 O.R. 16, 68 D.L.R. (2d) 30 (C.A.), *per* Laskin, J.A.

[3]*McDonell v. McDonell* (1894), 24 O.R. 468 (H.C.J.).

[4]*Re Winn*; *Brook v. Whitton*, [1910] 1 Ch. 278; *Re Prast* (1927), 32 O.W.N. 107 (H.C.).

[5]*Thompson v. Smith* (1897), 27 S.C.R. 628. In that case a testator devised property to his widow and child for their joint lives and the survivor of them for life, directing that at the decease of both, the residue of his real and personal estate should be enjoyed by and go to the benefit of his lawful heirs. It was held that the child was entitled to the residue as heir.

[6]*Re Ferguson*; *Bennett v. Coatsworth* (1897), 24 O.A.R. 61.

class at the testator's death, but so as to open and let in those of the class subsequently coming into existence before the period of distribution.[7]

If words are used in a remainder to a class indicating survivorship, they refer to the period of distribution and not to the death of the testator, so only those who survive the period of distribution are entitled.[8] Thus, in *Keating v. Cassels*[9] the testator devised land to his son G and his wife and the survivor of them and, after their death, to their children, including E, the son of G by his first wife, "to have and to hold the same to the said children of the said [G] or the survivors of them, for ever, share and share alike"; E died before his father. It was held that he took nothing and the remainder vested in the two surviving children upon the death of the last life tenant. Similarly, in *Re Gardner*[10] the testator gave his real and personal estate to his widow and directed that, after her death, his whole estate was to be divided among the children of four named persons "or their heirs" and added that "should no heirs of any of the above be alive" it was to go to the "next in heirship". It was held that "children or their heirs" meant "children or their issue", that the estate was to go to all children living at the testator's death or born afterwards during the life of the widow and that their shares vested at once but, if any child died during the life of the widow leaving issue, that child's share was divested and vested in the issue.

Rule 3: The presumption is that the testator intended the gift to be vested, subject to being divested, if necessary, rather than have it remain in suspense.[11] This presumption is particularly applied to remainders, because keeping a remainder contingent might exclude issue by reason of the parents dying before the vesting of the remainder.[12] Moreover, the presumption is stronger for residuary gifts, for if the gift fails by reason of the contingency not being satisfied, there will be an intestacy.[13]

A testator devised land to his wife for life or widowhood and, after her death, to her son upon condition that he pay certain sums to the testator's other children within three years of the testator's death. It was held that the condition was a condition subsequent, and that the son took a vested remainder subject to being divested if the condition was not fulfilled.[14]

---

[7]*Hickling v. Fair*, [1899] A.C. 15 (H.L.); *Re McKee* (1921), 21 O.W.N. 270 (H.C.); *Re Smith* (1927), 61 O.L.R. 412, [1928] 1 D.L.R. 179 (S.C. App. Div.); and see *Latta v. Lowry* (1886), 11 O.R. 517 (H.C.J.); *Re Chandler* (1889), 18 O.R. 105 (H.C.J.).

[8]*Parr v. Parr* (1833), 1 My. & K. 647, 39 E.R. 826; *Re Miller* (1911), 2 O.W.N. 782 (H.C.).

[9](1865), 24 U.C.Q.B. 314.

[10](1902), 3 O.L.R. 343 (H.C.J.).

[11]*Taylor v. Graham* (1878), 3 App. Cas. 1287 at p. 1297, *per* Lord Blackburn; *Hickling v. Fair, supra,* footnote 7, at pp. 30, 36.

[12]*Driver d. Frank v. Frank* (1814), 3 M. & S. 25 at p. 37, 105 E.R. 521, affd 8 Taunt. 468, 129 E.R. 465 (Ex. Ch.); *Re Watkins; Mayberry v. Lightfoot*, [1913] 1 Ch. 376, revd [1914] A.C. 782 (H.L.).

[13]*Love v. L'Estrange* (1727), 5 Brown. 59, 2 E.R. 532; *Booth v. Booth* (1799), 4 Ves. Jun. 399, 31 E.R. 203; *Pearman v. Pearman* (1864), 33 Beav. 394 at p. 396, 55 E.R. 420; *West v. West* (1863), 4 Giff. 198, 66 E.R. 677.

[14]*Lundy v. Maloney* (1861), 11 U.C.C.P. 143.

Where a testator devised a farm to his grandson "when he arrives at twenty-one years of age", the farm to be kept in repair by the executors, with a devise over in case of death of the grandson "before receiving the share", it was held that the land vested in the grandson subject to being divested if he died before attaining age 21.[15]

Where a testator bequeathed all the rents and profits of his real and personal estate to his widow for life and, after her death, bequeathed the rents and profits of his real estate to X for life and, after her death, devised his real estate to X's son, William, in fee but, if William died without issue before his mother, the mother was to have half and the other half was to go to a church, it was held that William took a vested estate liable to be divested upon his death in the lifetime of his mother.[16]

A testator devised his real estate to his widow for life and directed that, after her death, it was to be divided equally among two brothers, a sister and the children of a deceased brother, and provided that, if either of the brothers or the sister predeceased the widow, one-quarter was to go to their heirs, executors and administrators. The sister died before the widow, leaving a son and disposed of her real and personal property by will. It was held on appeal that the sister took a vested remainder that was divested upon her death before the widow, although her heirs took her share as a designated class under the testator's will.[17]

Where there was a gift to A for life, remainder to A's children, with a gift over to the children of any child of A who might die before the period of distribution, it was held that the children of A who survived the testator took a vested remainder and that, therefore, the widow of a son of A who died before A without issue took his share, such son's share being divested only if he died before the period of distribution leaving issue.[18]

Where a testator devised lands to trustees in trust to pay the income to two daughters and a granddaughter, during the lifetime of the survivor of them and of two other persons, and provided that, if any of the legatees died before the end of that period, her share was to go to her surviving child or children, and one of them died childless during the period, it was held that she took a vested interest *pur autre vie* and, as she died childless, her interest was not divested and passed to her personal representatives.[19]

Similarly, a remainder may be vested subject to being divested if the devisee dies without issue. Thus, a testator devised land to his widow for life and after her death, to his son Philip in fee and, after devising other property to another son, directed that if any of his sons died leaving no children, the property of that son was to be divided among all his children equally. When the testator died, Philip was living and had two children. He and the widow conveyed the

---

[15]*Re Dennis* (1903), 5 O.L.R. 46 (H.C.J.).
[16]*Re Archer* (1907), 14 O.L.R. 374 (H.C.J.).
[17]*Glendenning v. Dickinson* (1910), 14 W.L.R. 419, 15 B.C.R. 354 (C.A.).
[18]*Re Smith* (1927), 61 O.L.R. 412, [1928] 1 D.L.R. 179 (S.C. App. Div.).
[19]*Re Woodward; Smith v. MacLaren*, [1945] 2 D.L.R. 497, [1945] 1 W.W.R. 722 (B.C.S.C.).

land devised to him. It was held that Philip's estate was vested but subject to being divested if he died leaving no children, which might still happen, and that, consequently, he had no title which could be forced upon an unwilling purchaser and a decree for specific performance was refused.[20]

Where a will provided for the income of a fund to be paid to A with remainder in fee to his surviving issue upon attaining the age of 21 years but, if A should die without issue, the remainder in fee was to go to B and C equally, it was held that the effect was that the remainders of B and C were vested upon the death of the testator subject to being divested upon A dying with issue, so that, when B predeceased A who died without issue, B's executors were entitled to share equally with C.[21]

Where a testator devised land to his son and, in the event of the son dying without issue, to two daughters and, if they died without issue, "her or their shares shall go" to two other persons, it was held that the remainder of the daughters was vested subject to being divested upon their death without issue and, one daughter having died without issue, her share passed to the two persons having the devise over, the devise to them not being contingent on both daughters dying without issue, as otherwise the expression "her or their" had no meaning.[22]

Where a testatrix, however, devised her real property to her husband for life or until remarriage and thereafter to three daughters equally and provided that, if the property were not sold, it was to be kept in repair and taxes and insurance paid annually and directed that, if any of the daughters married and died without children, her share was to return to the estate but, if there were children, her share was to be divided equally among them, it was held that, on the husband's death, the estate vested absolutely in the daughters, as there was no executory devise to cause a divestment.[23]

Rule 4: If the terms of a gift can be fairly construed as merely postponing the right of possession, so as to draw a distinction between the time of vesting and time of enjoyment, that construction is adopted if the terms of the will permit it.[24]

For this reason, a remainder which is limited to a person to take effect in interest at the end of the preceding estate remains a vested remainder and does not become a contingent remainder merely by the fact that actual possession of the land by him is postponed and made dependent upon certain circumstances, so that it is possible that he may never come into possession of it.[25]

---

[20]*Vanluven v. Allison* (1901), 2 O.L.R. 198 (H.C.J.).

[21]*Re Stewart,* [1939] O.R. 153, [1939] 2 D.L.R. 185 (H.C.J.).

[22]*Re Harkin,* [1940] O.W.N. 6, [1940] 1 D.L.R. 798 (S.C.).

[23]*Re Coon,* [1946] O.W.N. 113 (H.C.J.).

[24]*Montgomerie v. Woodley* (1800), 5 Ves. Jun. 522 at p. 836, 31 E.R. 714; *Bingley v. Broadhead* (1803), 8 Ves. Jun. 415, 32 E.R. 416; *Duffield v. Duffield* (1829), 1 Dow & Clark 268 at p. 311, 6 E.R. 525 (H.L.); *Peard v. Kekewich* (1852), 15 Beav. 166 at p. 171, 51 E.R. 500; *Dennis v. Frend* (1863), 14 I. Ch. R. 271.

[25]*Parkhurst v. Smith d. Dormer* (1742), Willes 327, 125 E.R. 1197, 3 Atk. 135, 26 E.R. 881 (H.L.).

Where possession by a devisee is dependent upon his attaining a particular age or surviving a particular person, the remainder is vested subject to being divested upon his death before the prescribed time. Thus, in a devise "to A for life, remainder to all her children that should be living at her death, equally amongst them if more than one, to be divided share and share alike, when and as they should respectively attain the age of twenty-four", the children had a vested interest.[26]

A testator devised his property to his wife to be held for the maintenance of his son until the son attained the age of 24 years at which time the property was to come into his possession. The testator further provided that, upon the death of his wife, the property should pass to the possession of the son to be owned by him, his heirs and assigns forever and that, if the son died before his mother, the property was to be hers for life and thereafter to be divided equally between her relatives and the testator's relatives but, if the son died leaving a wife or children, the property was to go as provided by the son's will. It was held that the will was sufficient to pass the testator's property, including the land in question, and that the son's interest was vested, to come into his possession and control at the age of 24.[27]

In the case of successive limitations, words in a gift which are in the form of a condition but which in fact merely denote that the gift is to come into possession at the determination of the preceding interest are not ordinarily construed as a condition precedent to vesting. To have that effect, the condition must involve no incident that is not essential to the determination of the preceding interest and, if a condition is added that is not connected with the preceding interest, it must be fulfilled before the gift can vest. The test of the effect of limitations of this nature is whether the words which import a contingency can be read as equivalent to "subject to the interest previously limited".[28] Therefore, the words "at the death" or "after the death" of a person do not denote that the donee must survive that person to have a vested interest, but only denote the time at which the gift is to take effect in possession.[29]

Thus, where a testator devised land to his stepson for life and provided that, after the death of the stepson, "in the event of his having a son whose name shall be Richard", the land was to go to "the said Richard", it was held that a son who was named Richard took a vested remainder even though he died in early infancy and did not survive the life tenant.[30]

---

[26]*Farmer v. Francis* (1824), 2 Bing. 151, 130 E.R. 263.
[27]*Re Cooke and Driffl* (1885), 8 O.R. 530 (H.C.J.).
[28]*Maddison v. Chapman* (1858), 4 K. & J. 709 at pp. 719, 720, 70 E.R. 294, in which case legacies payable "at the death" of a life tenant were held to be vested; *Edgeworth v. Edgeworth* (1869), L.R. 4 H.L. 35, where the words were, "in case the said *Francis Beaufort Edgeworth* should come to the possession of the said estate" and it was said (p. 41), "It is impossible to annex to an estate previously clearly given an additional condition from words which ... may be interpreted, as a description only of what must occur before the estate given to the person in remainder can arise."
[29]*Re Leckie* (1921), 20 O.W.N. 478 at p. 479 (H.C.).
[30]*Re Lishman* (1920), 19 O.W.N. 365 (H.C.).

Again, where a testator directed his real estate to be sold and the proceeds to be divided among his children, but the share of J to be placed at interest for his benefit, to be paid to him each six months and, after his death, his share was to be divided equally between A and S, two of the testator's other children, it was held that the interests of A and S were vested and that the interest of A who had assigned it before he predeceased J went to his assignee.[31]

The same rule applies to gifts to a class. Thus, where a testator devised land to A "during his and B's natural life then and after that to be given to B's children" in fee simple, it was held that the children of B in existence at the testator's death took vested remainders subject to being partly divested in favour of B's children subsequently born and that the personal representatives of any child of B dying before the period of distribution were entitled to the share of such child.[32]

Again, where a testator devised land to his son, A, during his lifetime and at his death to go to and be vested in A's son, B, "or, in case other sons should be born to my son A, then to be equally divided between all of the boys", it was held that A took a life estate only and that a remainder in fee was vested in his sons as a class, so as to let in all sons born before his death.[33]

The will, however, may show that vesting is not to take place until the end of the preceding estate and that the person entitled to the remainder must survive to such time. Thus, in *Merchants Bank of Canada v. Keefer*,[34] the testator devised property to his widow during her life or widowhood and directed that, after her death, a parcel of land was to go to his son Thomas, in fee simple "if he be then living". It was held that the son's remainder was contingent on his surviving his mother and could not vest unless he did survive her, as otherwise the words were redundant.[35]

Similarly, it was held that, under the terms of a will, the vesting of the remainder depended upon the double event of the life tenant dying and the devisee attaining majority.[36]

Rule 5: The court leans against the divesting of vested interests,[37] and

---

[31]*Martin v. Leys* (1868), 15 Gr. 114.

[32]*Latta v. Lowry* (1886), 11 O.R. 517 (H.C.J.).

[33]*Re Chandler* (1889), 18 O.R. 105 (H.C.J.).

[34](1885), 13 S.C.R. 515.

[35]The same will devised other lands to the testator's son Thomas and three other sons as tenants in common, to take effect from and after the death or second marriage of the widow, with a proviso that, if any child died without issue, before coming into possession of his share, the share was to go to the survivors; all interested persons conveyed the lands to the four sons, after which two sons died; the conveyance was confirmed by statute which declared that it was not to be affected by the two deaths and confirmed the estates of Thomas and the other surviving son as tenants in common, subject to the life estate of their mother, with the right of survivorship if either of them died without issue before their mother; Thomas survived his remaining brother, although both died without issue before their mother. It was held that he took a vested remainder in fee simple expectant upon the determination of the mother's life estate.

[36]*Evans v. Evans* (1902), 1 O.W.R. 69 (Div. Ct.).

[37]*Maddison v. Chapman* (1858), 4 K. & J. 709 at pp. 721, 723, 70 E.R. 294; *Re Wood*; *Moore v. Bailey* (1880), 43 L.T. 730 at p. 732; *Re Roberts*; *Percival v. Roberts*, [1903] 2 Ch. 200 at p. 204.

favours that construction which leads to the indefeasible vesting of property as soon as possible.[38] Consequently, divesting conditions are construed strictly[39] so that, if a provision divests a vested gift on a specified contingency, the gift is held not to be divested unless that precise contingency occurs.[40]

Thus, in *Parkes v. Trusts Corp. of Ontario*,[41] a testator devised a farm to his executors in trust for his grandson, with power to sell it and apply the proceeds for his benefit and, if he died before attaining the age of 21, they were to transfer the land, or the proceeds if it were sold, to his father. The father predeceased the son who died before attaining 21. It was held that the grandson took a vested fee simple subject to it being divested on the happening of a specified event which had become impossible so that his estate became absolute. Similarly, in *Beckett v. Foy*,[42] the testator devised certain land to his son and devised to B other land that was not fully paid for, directing that the son's land was to be held by the executors until a deed for B's land had been obtained and that the executors were to pay the money due to take up a deed, out of the rents of the real and personal estate. It was held that the son's land vested on payment for the deed to B's land, although the deed to it had not been executed. In *Re Hanna*,[43] there was a vested devise subject to it being divested if the devisee did not return from war. There was a temporary return which was held not to cause the property to vest in him absolutely.

If there is a provision revoking or divesting a gift on the failure of a condition, the condition must wholly fail or no revocation or divesting will occur. Thus, where a testator directed his trustees to divide his real estate equally between his sons then living when his eldest son attained the age of 25 years, at which time the share of the eldest son was to be conveyed to him but, if any of the sons died before attaining the age of 25 years without issue, the share of one so dying was to be divided equally among the survivors and the eldest son died before attaining the age of 25 leaving a widow and infant daughter, it was held that the daughter took the land as her father's heiress subject to her mother's dower because the executory limitation did not take effect unless the double event happened, that is, the eldest son dying before 25 and without issue.[44]

Similarly, where a testator gave his widow a life interest in his estate and, after her death, gave the residue equally to his two brothers or, in case of their dying before his wife, it was to be equally divided between their heirs, and

---

[38]*Minors v. Battison* (1876), 1 App. Cas. 428 (H.L.); *Hervey-Bathurst v. Stanley*; *Craven v. Stanley* (1876), 4 Ch. D. 251; *Re Teale*; *Teale v. Teale* (1885), 53 L.T. 936 at p. 937; *Re Stark & Trim*, [1932] O.R. 263, [1932] 2 D.L.R. 603 (C.A.).

[39]*Kiallmark v. Kiallmark* (1856), 26 L.J. Ch. 1 at p. 5; *Blagrove v. Bradshaw* (1858), 4 Drewry 230 at p. 235, 62 E.R. 89.

[40]*Tarbuck v. Tarbuck* (1835), 4 L.J. Ch. 129; *Cox v. Parker* (1856), 22 Beav. 168, 52 E.R. 1072; *Potts v. Atherton* (1859), 28 L.J. Ch. 486 at p. 488; *Re Kirkbride's Trusts* (1866), L.R. 2 Eq. 400 at p. 402; *Re Pickworth*; *Snaith v. Parkinson*, [1899] 1 Ch. 642 (C.A.); *Re Searle*; *Searle v. Searle*, [1905] W.N. 86 (H.C.J.).

[41](1895), 26 O.R. 494 (H.C.J.), at p. 498.

[42](1855), 12 U.C.Q.B. 361.

[43](1917), 11 O.W.N. 347 (H.C.).

[44]*Cook v. Noble* (1884), 5 O.R. 43 (H.C.J.).

the one brother died during the life of the widow and the other survived her, it was held that the share of the one who first died passed under his will as the event provided for, namely, the death of both brothers during the life of the widow, had not happened.[45]

Again, where there was a gift over if the donee died "before having children", the court refused to construe the words as meaning "without leaving issue surviving".[46]

In the case of a gift over upon several specified events connected by the word "and", as the language is capable of having its ordinary sense, the court is not willing to construe the word "and" as "or" because the effect would be to divest a gift in an event other than the double event provided for by the testator.[47] In Re Stamp[48] there was a bequest to an infant with a gift over in the event of the infant not surviving the testator and dying before attaining the age of 21. The court refused to construe "and" as "or". The infant took a vested interest upon surviving the testator which was not subject to be divested. In Lillie v. Willis,[49] a testatrix devised and bequeathed all her real and personal estate to her son in fee with a gift over if he died without issue before her brother and sister. The sister died in the lifetime of the son. It was held that, as the event of the son dying before both the brother and sister could not happen, he took an indefeasible fee simple.

Conversely, if the interest of a donee follows a life interest and is contingent only on his attaining a specified age and not on his surviving the life tenant and there is a gift over on his death before that of the life tenant or under the specified age, the word "or" is construed as "and".[50]

Similarly, if there is a devise to a person in fee simple or absolutely, with a gift over to other donees if he dies without children or under the age of 21 years, the word "or" is construed as "and", and the gift over does not take effect unless both events happen.[51]

The rule is based upon the presumed intention of the testator to benefit the children of the devisee directly or indirectly. His intention would be defeated if the devisee were to die under 21 leaving children and, therefore, the rule is not applied in those circumstances.[52]

---

[45]Re Metcalfe; Metcalfe v. Metcalfe (1900), 32 O.R. 103 (H.C.J.).
[46]Re Breault and Grimshaw (1918), 13 O.W.N. 387 (H.C.).
[47]Doe d. Usher v. Jessep (1810), 12 East 288 at p. 293, 104 E.R. 113; Key v. Key (1855), 1 Jur. N.S. 372; Coates v. Hart; Borrett v. Hart (1863), 3 De G. J. & S. 504, 46 E.R. 731; Malcolm v. Malcolm (1856), 21 Beav. 225, 52 E.R. 845; Reed v. Braithwaite (1871), L.R. 11 Eq. 514.
[48](1918), 14 O.W.N. 80 (H.C.).
[49](1899), 31 O.R. 198 (H.C.J.).
[50]Miles v. Dyer (1832), 5 Sim. 435, 58 E.R. 400, 8 Sim. 330, 59 E.R. 131, followed in Bentley v. Meech (1858), 25 Beav. 197, 53 E.R. 611.
[51]Doe d. Herbert v. Selby (1824), 2 B. & C. 926, 107 E.R. 626; Morris v. Morris (1853), 17 Beav. 198, 51 E.R. 1009; Imray v. Imeson (1872), 26 L.T. 93; cf. Re Adam (1922), 23 O.W.N. 96 (H.C.), in which case there was a gift over if the donee should die before coming of age or die leaving no children.
[52]Re Crutchley; Kidson v. Marsden, [1912] 2 Ch. 335 at p. 337; Grey v. Pearson (1857), 6 H.L.C. 61, 10 E.R. 1216.

The word "and" may, however, be construed to mean "or" if one member of a compound sentence is included in the other and construing it literally would render one member of the sentence unnecessary, but making the change would give effect to each member. This construction is generally made in favour of vesting so as not to defeat a previously vested gift. A limitation of real estate to A during the lifetimes of B and C without saying "and during the lifetime of the survivor of them" gives A an estate during the lifetimes of B and C and the survivor. But a limitation for 100 years, "if A and B shall so long live", is determined by the death of either, because this is a collateral condition. If there is a gift to a person and, after his death, to his children, with a gift over if he dies "unmarried and without issue", the word "and" will be construed as "or" if it appears that the word "unmarried" is used in the ordinary sense of never having been married, in which case the words "and without issue" would be unnecessary.[53] Usually, however, if the word "unmarried" in such a case can be given the meaning "without leaving a spouse", it will be given that meaning, so as to give effect to all of the words.[54]

The word "and" is not changed to "or" if that would make part of the sentence inoperative.[55]

Following the rule of leaning against the divesting of a vested interest, if there is a gift to a person for life and after his death to his children, so expressed as to give them a vested interest whether or not they survive the parent, and there is a gift over if the parent dies "without leaving children", these words are construed, according to the context of the will, as "without having children",[56] or as "without having had children",[57] or as "without leaving children who have attained vested interests"[58] so as not to divest the vested interests. This rule is applied where the interests of the children are to vest at their birth,[59] or are to vest at the age of 21,[60] or when the youngest attains that age,[61] or at 21 or marriage,[62] or are to vest on the happening of any similar

---

[53]*Wilson v. Bayly* (1760), 3 Brown. 195, 1 E.R. 1265; *Hepworth v. Taylor* (1784), 1 Cox 112, 29 E.R. 1086; *Maberley v. Strode* (1797), 3 Ves. Jun. 450 at p. 454, 30 E.R. 1100; *Bell v. Phyn* (1802), 7 Ves. Jun. 453 at p. 459, 32 E.R. 183; *Roberts v. Bishop of Kilmore*, [1902] 1 I.R. 333.

[54]*Re Sanders' Trusts* (1866), L.R. 1 Eq. 675; *Re King; Salisbury v. Ridley* (1890), 62 L.T. 789; *Re Chant; Chant v. Lemon*, [1900] 2 Ch. 345 at p. 348.

[55]*Key v. Key, supra*, footnote 47; *Re Kirkbride's Trusts* (1866), L.R. 2 Eq. 400 at p. 403.

[56]*Re Tookey's Trust; Re Bucks Ry Co.* (1852), 21 L.J. Ch. 402, 1 Drewry 264, 61 E.R. 453; *Kennedy v. Sedgwick* (1857), 3 K. & J. 540, 69 E.R. 1223; *White v. Hill* (1867), L.R. 4 Eq. 265; *Re Brown's Trust* (1873), L.R. 16 Eq. 239; *Re Jackson's Will* (1879), 13 Ch. D. 189.

[57]*Marshall v. Hill* (1814), 2 M. & S. 608, 105 E.R. 508; *Bryden v. Willett* (1869), L.R. 7 Eq. 472; *Treharne v. Layton* (1875), 10 Q.B. 459 (Ex. Ch.).

[58]*Re Cobbold; Cobbold v. Lawton*, [1903] 2 Ch. 299 (C.A.).

[59]*Treharne v. Layton, supra*, footnote 57; *Re Bradbury; Wing v. Bradbury* (1904), 73 L.J. Ch. 591; *Re Goldney; Re Dighton; Clarke v. Dighton* (1911), 130 L.T.J. 484.

[60]*Maitland v. Chalie* (1822), 6 Madd. 243, 56 E.R. 1084; *Re Thompson's Trust* (1852), 5 De G. & Sm. 667, 64 E.R. 1291.

[61]*Kennedy v. Sedgwick, supra*, footnote 56.

[62]*Casamajor v. Strode* (1843), 8 Jur. 14.

event without reference to surviving their parent.[63]

There have been suggestions in recent cases that the distinction between conditions precedent and subsequent is illogical to the extent that the same words are given a different meaning if the condition is construed as precedent than if it is construed as subsequent.[64] Moreover, there appears to be a tendency in modern cases not to strike down conditions subsequent as readily as before.[65] However, the general rules of construction set out above still represent the accepted approach.

The application of these rules differs in some respects depending upon whether the gift is one of realty, personalty, or a mixed fund of realty and personalty, or is a legacy charged on real property. The application of the rules as they affect real property is discussed below, with appropriate references to any differences as regards personalty.[66]

(c) The prima facie principle

The general principle with which construction commences is that all words importing futurity, whether conditional or merely temporal, make a gift *prima facie* contingent. Thus, where property is given to a person "if", or "provided that" a specified event occurs, the gift will be contingent, but it will also be contingent if words such as "at", or "upon" the occurrence of the event, or "when", "as", or "from and after" its occurrence are used. Hence, a gift "to A when he shall attain the age of 25 years", is *prima facie* contingent.[67] The reason that no distinction is drawn between conditional and temporal words of futurity is that the latter, in that they denote the time when the gift is to take effect, are merely the equivalent of words of condition.[68]

The general principle is equally applicable to a gift to a class, such as a gift "to A's children as and when they attain the age of 25 or marry".[69]

Since the general principle is a rule of construction, however, it yields to a contrary intent found in the instrument effecting the gift, and the courts, applying the general rules set out above, readily find such an intent. The following discussion provides instances of exceptions to the general principle.

---

[63]*Barkworth v. Barkworth* (1906), 75 L.J. Ch. 754 at p. 756.

[64]*Re Tuck's Settlement Trusts*, [1978] 2 W.L.R. 411 (C.A.), *per* Lord Denning, M.R.

[65]*Ibid.*, partial divestment if beneficiary marries a person not of Jewish blood and Jewish faith, held valid; *Blathwayt v. Baron Cawley*, [1976] A.C. 397 (H.L.), divestment if beneficiary should be, or become Roman Catholic, held valid.

[66]For a fuller treatment of these rules, reference should be had to the standard texts on wills. See, *e.g.*, Jarman, ch. 39; Hawkins and Ryder on *The Construction of Wills* by E.C. Ryder (London, Sweet & Maxwell, 1965), ch. 17; Theobald, ch. 41; *Williams Law Relating to Wills*, 4th ed., by C.H. Sherrin and R.F.D. Barlow (London, Butterworths, 1974), ch. 93; Feeney, *The Canadian Law of Wills: Construction* (Toronto, Butterworths, 1978), ch. 8.

[67]*Re Francis*, [1905] 2 Ch. 295; *Re Pfrimmer*, [1945] 3 D.L.R. 518, [1945] 2 W.W.R. 142 (Man. K.B.).

[68]*Hanson v. Graham* (1801), 6 Ves. Jun. 239 at p. 243, 31 E.R. 1030, *per* Grant, M.R.

[69]*Leake v. Robinson* (1817), 2 Mer. 363, 35 E.R. 979.

(d) Gifts over on death under age: The rule in Phipps v. Ackers

Where a gift that is *prima facie* contingent is followed by a gift over on death under age, the apparent contingency is usually construed as merely fixing the time of payment, that is, the time when the gift will fall into possession on the determination of the prior interest. The gift will then be construed as vested subject to divestment. Thus, a gift "to A when he attains the age of 25 and, if he dies under that age, to B", will give A a vested interest subject to defeasance if he dies before he reaches the age of 25.

This is known as the rule in *Phipps v. Ackers*,[70] or the rule in *Edwards v. Hammond*.[71] This rule, originally applicable only to real property, was devised to avoid the destruction of legal contingent remainders. These fail if they do not vest during the continuance of a prior particular estate.[72] Hence, by construing the apparent contingency as vested, the gift is saved.

The reason for the rule is as follows:

> ... where the devise is to a party at a given age, and the property is given over if the devisee dies under that age ... the Court has discovered an intention expressed in the will that the first devisee shall take all that the testator has to give, except what he has given to the devisee over; and, in order to give effect to that intention, has held, by force of the language of the will, that the first devise was not contingent, but vested, subject to be divested upon the happening of the event upon which the property is given over.[73]

The rule is the same whether words of condition or of time are used. Thus, in a devise "to A, *if* he attains the age of 21 and, if he dies under that age, to B", the gift to A is construed as vested subject to divestment.[74] Moreover, the rule applies equally to class gifts.[75]

Although the rule in *Phipps v. Ackers* was developed in the context of real property, and more specifically in the context of legal contingent remainders, it now applies to all remainders, whether legal or equitable, and to executory interests.[76] Moreover, the rule has been extended to gifts of personalty,[77] and to gifts of a mixed fund of realty and personalty.[78] However, in the latter case there is some doubt as to the application of the rule in the case of class gifts. The earlier authorities state that in a gift of a mixed fund of realty and

---

[70] (1842), 9 Cl. & Fin. 583, 8 E.R. 539.

[71] (1684), 3 Lev. 132, 83 E.R. 614.

[72] In a grant "to A for life, remainder to B if he attains the age of 21", the remainder in favour of B is contingent. It will be destroyed unless B reaches the specified age during A's lifetime. This rule also applies to legal executory interests: *Purefoy v. Rogers* (1671), 2 Wms. Saund. 380, 85 E.R. 1181. See §1010.3, *infra*.

[73] *Bull v. Pritchard* (1847), 5 Hare 567 at p. 571, 67 E.R. 1036, *per* Wigram, V.C.

[74] *Edwards v. Hammond, supra*, footnote 71.

[75] *Randoll v. Doe d. Roake* (1817), 5 Dow 202, 3 E.R. 1302.

[76] *Stanley v. Stanley* (1809), 16 Ves. Jun. 491, 33 E.R. 1071.

[77] *Re Heath*, [1936] Ch. 259; *Re Kilpatrick's Policies Trusts*, [1966] 1 Ch. 730 (C.A.); *Re Barton*, [1941] 3 D.L.R. 653 at p. 656, [1941] S.C.R. 426 at p. 429, *per* Kerwin, J.; *Re Johnston*, [1945] 3 D.L.R. 213, [1945] 2 W.W.R. 324 (Man. K.B.).

[78] *Whitter v. Bremridge* (1866), L.R. 2 Eq. 736.

personalty, "to the children of A when they attain 21 and, if any die under that age, their shares shall go to the others", the rule does not apply.[79] Later authorities suggest, however, that the rule applies here as well.[80]

The rule applies also where the gift over is stated to take effect in the event that the first named beneficiary dies before the specified contingency without leaving issue. In this case it makes no difference whether it be a class gift, or whether it be a gift of realty or personalty or of a mixed fund.[81] The implication in such a case is that the first named beneficiary is to take if he leaves issue, even though he dies before the specified contingency.

Furthermore, while the rule in *Phipps v. Ackers* is framed in terms of a gift over upon failure to attain a specified age, it applies also to other contingencies, such as surviving a prior life tenant.[82]

The rule may, of course, be displaced by the context of the will. Thus, if there is an additional contingency, unconnected with the determination of the prior interest, but personal to the beneficiary, as where the gift is "to A for life, and then to B if he be then living, and if B dies without issue him surviving, to X, or if B dies leaving issue, to such issue", the gift will be construed as contingent.[83]

A contrary intention is also found where the attainment of the age (or the satisfaction of such other contingency as may be specified) is made part of the description. This occurs, for example, where the gift is "to the children of A who attain 21", or "to the first child of A to attain 25", with a gift over in each case on failure to reach the specified age. In these cases, the gift is *prima facie* construed as contingent.[84] The reason is that no specific persons are named and, until the contingency is satisfied, there is no one who completely answers the description of the beneficiaries provided by the testator and, thus, the estate cannot vest in anyone.[85]

(e) Gifts over, other cases

A rule of construction similar to the rule in *Phipps v. Ackers* operates to construe a gift that is *prima facie* contingent as vested where the gift over

---

[79]*Vawdry v. Geddes* (1830), 1 Russ. & My. 203, 39 E.R. 78.

[80]See, *e.g.*, *Re Turney*, [1899] 2 Ch. 739 (C.A.).

[81]*Bland v. Williams* (1834), 3 My. & K. 411, 40 E.R. 156.

[82]*Finch v. Lane* (1870), L.R. 10 Eq. 501; "to A for life, remainder to B if B survives A, but if B predeceases A without leaving issue, then to C". B died before A, leaving issue, and it was held that B took a vested interest defeasible only if she predeceased A without leaving issue.

[83]*Merchants Bank of Canada v. Keefer* (1885), 13 S.C.R. 515. A direction to accumulate which is void in that it exceeds the permissible period does not amount to a contrary intention; *Brotherton v. I.R.C.*, [1978] 2 All E.R. 267 (C.A.).

[84]*Duffield v. Duffield* (1829), 1 Dow & Cl. 268, 6 E.R. 525; *Festing v. Allen* (1843), 12 M. & W. 279, 152 E.R. 1204; *Bull v. Pritchard* (1847), 5 Hare 567, 67 E.R. 1036; *Re Astor*, [1922] 1 Ch. 364 (C.A.).

[85]*Duffield v. Duffield, supra*, footnote 84, at p. 314, *per* Best, C.J.

takes effect, not where the first named beneficiary fails to satisfy the contingency, but where another person named in the will fails to do so. Thus, in a gift "to the children of A when they attain the age of 25, with the income to be applied to them for their maintenance and education in the meantime, but if A dies without children him surviving, then to B", the gift over has the effect of making the gift to A's first child absolutely vested.[86] The reason for this construction is that if the first gift were contingent and A had a child, but he died under 25, neither the child nor B could take, thus causing the gift to fail completely.[87]

As in the case of the rule in *Phipps v. Ackers*, however, if the age attainment is made part of the description of the beneficiary, as in a gift "to the children of A who attain 21, and if A dies without children him surviving, to B", a contrary intention is present which makes the first gift contingent.[88]

(f) The rule in Boraston's Case

The rule in *Boraston's Case*[89] also was devised to permit early vesting so as to save what would otherwise be destructible contingent remainders.

The rule is that where property is devised to a person upon the attainment of a specified age and until that time it is devised to another, the first person takes an absolutely vested estate immediately. To achieve this result, the devise is read as one to the second person for a term of years with remainder to the first, and when so read, it will take effect upon the natural determination of the preceding estate, so that the attainment of the specified age is not a condition precedent.[90]

The rule is of limited application, however. Thus, it only applies if the words importing futurity are temporal, such as, "when" the named devisee attains the specified age, or "at", "upon", or "from and after" his attaining that age. Words of condition, such as "if", have been held to import only a condition precedent; they cannot introduce a condition subsequent.[91]

Secondly, the rule applies only to real property, although it has been extended to a devise which included freeholds and leaseholds in the same gift,[92] and to a bequest of personal property which was directed to be converted into land.[93]

Thirdly, the rule applies only where the intermediate interest is limited to the time when the ulterior devisee attains the age specified. Thus, if the devise were "to A in fee when he attains 25, and until then to B for ten years", A being 20 at the time, the rule is excluded and A's interest is contingent. However,

---

[86]*Re Bevan's Trusts* (1887), 34 Ch. D. 716.
[87]Hawkins and Ryder, *supra*, footnote 66, at p. 287.
[88]*Re Edwards*, [1906] 1 Ch. 570 (C.A.).
[89](1587), 3 Co. Rep. 16 a, 76 E.R. 664.
[90]*Phipps v. Ackers* (1842), 9 Cl. & Fin. 583 at p. 591, 8 E.R. 539, *per* Tindal, C.J.
[91]*Doe d. Wheedon v. Lea* (1789), 3 T.R. 41 at p. 43, 100 E.R. 445, *per* Ashhurst, J.
[92]*James v. Lord Wynford* (1852), 1 Sm. & G. 40, 65 E.R. 18.
[93]*Snow v. Poulden* (1836), 1 Keen. 186, 48 E.R. 277.

it is not necessary that all of the intermediate income be disposed of until the ulterior devisee attains the specified age.[94]

(g) Convenience of the estate rule

The *prima facie* construction that a gift which imports words of futurity is contingent yields where the postponement of the gift is solely to let in a prior interest. Thus, in a typical example, "to A for life, and after A's death to B", B's interest is vested *a morte testatoris*. The apparent condition precedent to B's taking, that is, A's death, is not a true contingency at all but merely indicates that B's enjoyment is postponed until A's life estate has determined. The "convenience of the estate" demands that A enjoy the gift in possession first, followed by B.[95]

The same reasoning applies where the will directs that payment be made to the ulterior devisee after the death of the first devisee. This was the decision in the leading case, *Browne v. Moody*.[96] The gift in this case, stripped to its bare essentials, was a fund given "to A for life, and on the death of A to divide the corpus between B, C and D, and should any of them predecease A, leaving issue, the issue to take the parent's share". The will failed to provide for the eventuality of any of the remaindermen dying before A without issue, so that, if the gift were contingent and a remainderman predeceased A without leaving issue, it would fail as to that part. The Privy Council held the gift to be vested, however (subject to being divested if a remainderman should predecease the life tenant leaving issue), because the purpose of postponing the division of the corpus was only to permit A to enjoy the income during his lifetime. Lord Macmillan phrased the rule applicable to such cases as follows:

> ... where there is a direction to pay the income of a fund to one person during his lifetime and to divide the capital among certain other named and ascertained persons on his death, even although there are no direct words of gift either of the life interest or of the capital, the rule is that vesting of the capital takes place *a morte testatoris* in the remaindermen.[97]

The rule does not apply where there is a contrary intention, namely, where the postponement is not for the convenience of the estate, but is for a reason personal to the legatee. This occurs, for example, where the attainment of a specified age is made part of the description of the legatee, as in a gift "to A for life and after his death to his children who marry", or "who attain 21".[98] Moreover, it would appear that the rule can only apply if the postponement is

---

[94]*James v. Lord Wynford, supra,* footnote 92.
[95]*Re Jobson* (1889), 44 Ch. D. 154.
[96][1936] O.R. 422, [1936] 4 D.L.R. 1 (P.C.); followed in *Re Hooper,* [1955] 3 D.L.R. 321, [1955] S.C.R. 508; *Re MacInnes,* [1958] O.R. 592, 15 D.L.R. (2d) 684 (H.C.J.); *Re Duffield,* [1971] 1 O.R. 515, 16 D.L.R. (3d) 7 (H.C.J.); *Re Rauckman* (1969), 8 D.L.R. (3d) 494, 71 W.W.R. 73 (Sask. Q.B.).
[97]*Browne v. Moody, supra,* footnote 96, at p. 427 O.R., p. 5 D.L.R.
[98]*Re Astor,* [1922] 1 Ch. 364 (C.A.).

to a certain date, that is, one which must happen, such as the death of a life tenant.[99] Thus, postponement until marriage would not attract the rule.

The convenience of the estate rule also applies to a class gift in the following form: "to the children of A when the youngest attains the age of 21". The gift in such a case is not postponed until the youngest is 21; that is, it is not contingent upon all of the children surviving until the youngest attains the age of 21, for the postponement is merely to let in younger children, and thus, for the convenience of the estate.[100] Whether the interest of each child is contingent upon his attaining the specified age depends upon the context. If, for example, there is a gift over of a child's share in case he dies under 21, his share will be vested subject to divestment.[101]

(h) Where the gift is to "take effect" at a future time

If a testamentary gift is directed to "take effect" at a future time, for example, when the devisee attains a specified age or marries, the phrase "take effect" is *prima facie* construed as meaning "take effect in possession or enjoyment", thus giving the devisee a vested estate.[102] This interpretation is like that under the convenience of the estate rule, but it applies even though there is no postponement to a prior interest, or if there is a postponement such as a trust for sale to allow for payment of debts.[103]

(i) Postponed payment

Where the bequest directs that payment is postponed until a specified age, *prima facie*, it will be construed as vested absolutely.[104] In order for this construction to operate, however, the direction to pay must be separate and distinct from the words of gift. If it is not, the gift will be construed as contingent. Thus, a bequest "to A payable when he becomes 25", and a bequest "to the children of B to be divided among them when the youngest attains age 21", are vested absolutely, in A *a morte testatoris*, and in the children of B at that time or at birth.[105] So is a gift "to A, the income to be accumulated until he reaches the age of 25 years when the capital and accumulated income shall be

---

[99]*Browne v. Moody, supra*, footnote 96, at p. 427 O.R., p. 5 D.L.R.

[100]*Leeming v. Sherratt* (1842), 2 Hare 14, 67 E.R. 6. It may be, of course, that there is a contrary intention in the form of another contingency, as in a gift "to A for life and on her death *leaving issue*, in trust until her youngest child should attain age 21, when the estate is to be divided among the issue equally". A child of A would not take a vested interest unless he attained age 21 *and* survived his mother. On the other hand, if such a child's interest had vested, the words "without leaving issue" could have been construed as "without leaving issue who have obtained vested interests": *Re Patterson Estate* (1958), 66 Man. R. 416 (Q.B.).

[101]*Re Lodwig*, [1916] 2 Ch. 26.

[102]*Bickersteth v. Shanu*, [1936] A.C. 290, [1936] 1 W.W.R. 644 (P.C.), noted 14 Can. Bar Rev. 349 (1936); *Re Squire*, [1962] O.R. 863, 34 D.L.R. (2d) 481 (H.C.J.).

[103]*Re Paterson Estate* (1957), 22 W.W.R. 38, 65 Man. R. 127 (Q.B.).

[104]*Re Couturier; Couturier v. Shea*, [1907] 1 Ch. 470.

[105]*Re Bartholomew* (1849), 1 Mac. & G. 354, 41 E.R. 1302.

paid to him".[106] However, a bequest in the following form, "I give and bequeath the sum of $20,000 to be paid or transferred to my children when the youngest attains the age of 21", would be contingent as the gift is indistinct from the direction to pay.

Moreover, it appears that the postponement must be to a time definite, that is, one that is bound to happen, if at all, such as the attainment of a specified age. Thus, a direction to postpone payment until the marriage of the donee will not render the gift vested.[107]

It should also be noted that if a gift is held to be vested in these circumstances, and in those described in the preceding subsection, and the specified age is greater than the age of majority, the rule in *Saunders v. Vautier*[108] will operate so as to entitle the donee to call for payment as soon as he reaches the age of majority. This rule may be ousted by a gift over of the intermediate income to another person, by a gift over in the event that the primary donee dies under the specified age, thus rendering the gift vested subject to divestment, or by a clear direction in the will that the donee is not to receive the intermediate income. The rule has been abolished in Alberta, where an application must now be made to the court for consent to terminate or vary the trust.[109]

The rule of construction that a gift coupled with a separate and distinct direction postponing payment is *prima facie* vested, does not apply where the legacy is charged on land.[110]

(j) Gift of intermediate income

If the will gives the donee the capital upon an apparent contingency and also directs that the whole of the intermediate income be paid to him or applied for his benefit, the gift is *prima facie* vested.[111] It does not matter that the gift of income is defeasible,[112] or that part of the income is to be applied in payment of an annuity to another person, if the remainder is applied solely for the benefit of the original beneficiary,[113] although, if the whole of the income is given to another, the gift of the capital will be contingent.

The rule also applies where there is a trust to apply the whole income for

---

[106]*Josselyn v. Josselyn* (1837), 9 Sim. 63, 59 E.R. 281.

[107]*Atkins v. Hiccocks* (1737), 1 Atk. 500, 26 E.R. 316. But see *Re Barrow* (1980), 29 O.R. (2d) 374, 113 D.L.R. (3d) 184 (H.C.J.), affd 129 D.L.R. (3d) 767n (C.A.), leave to appeal to S.C.C. refused 41 N.R. 536n; bequest with payment postponed until person ceased to be under disability held to be vested.

[108](1841), 10 L.J. Ch. 354. See, *e.g.*, *Re Lithwick* (1975), 9 O.R. (2d) 643, 61 D.L.R. (3d) 411 (H.C.J.); *Re Squire*, [1962] O.R. 863, 34 D.L.R. (2d) 481 (H.C.J.); *Re Beresford* (1966), 57 D.L.R. (2d) 380, 56 W.W.R. 248 (B.C.S.C.).

[109]*Attorney General Statutes Amendment Act*, S.A. 1973, c. 13, s. 12.

[110]*Taylor v. Lambert* (1876), 2 Ch. D. 177.

[111]*Re Williams*, [1907] 1 Ch. 180. It should be noted that if the gift of the intermediate income is not distinct, the rule in *Saunders v. Vautier*, *supra*, footnote 108, may apply.

[112]*Re Kirkley* (1918), 87 L.J. Ch. 247.

[113]*Jones v. Mackilwain* (1826), 1 Russ. 220, 38 E.R. 86.

the benefit of the beneficiary with a discretionary power in the trustees to apply only so much as they think fit.[114]

In the case of class gifts, the rule applies if the whole of the income of the share of each member of the class is to be applied for his benefit,[115] and it appears that where there is a trust to apply the whole income from each share for the beneficiary of that share, coupled with a discretionary power to apply only so much thereof as the trustees think fit, the rule will be the same.[116]

However, if the income is not allocated to each member's share, but the trustees are given a discretionary power to apply the income from the whole fund to all or any one or more of the members of the class, the gift of the capital is not vested.[117]

The gift, if vested in these circumstances, may be vested absolutely, or vested subject to divestment. The latter construction will obtain if there is a gift over of the capital upon failure of the beneficiary to attain the specified age.[118]

Clearly, a gift of intermediate income will not lead to a construction that the gift of the capital is vested if the will discloses a contrary intention. This will arise, for example, where the gift of the income is itself contingent, that is, the income does not vest until the contingency has been satisfied, as in a gift "to A with interest at 21",[119] or in a gift "to A when he marries, together with accumulated interest".[120]

A legacy charged on land which directs that the income be paid to the legatee until the contingency is satisfied, is not within the rule and will be construed as contingent.[121]

Where the intermediate income is not given to the beneficiary, but provision is made for his maintenance out of the corpus of the estate until he attains the specified age, the gift, in the absence of a gift over, will be contingent.[122]

(k)   Gifts to survivors

Property often is given to a class of persons or to a group of named persons, and the testator wishes to make provision for the event that one or more of them

---

[114]*Re Ussher; Foster v. Ussher*, [1922] 2 Ch. 321; *Re Barton*, [1941] 3 D.L.R. 653, [1941] S.C.R. 426, noted 18 Can. Bar Rev. 653 (1940).

[115]*Re Gossling; Gossling v. Elcock*, [1903] 1 Ch. 448 (C.A.).

[116]*Fox v. Fox* (1875), L.R. 19 Eq. 286. *Cf. Re Turney; Turney v. Turney*, [1899] 2 Ch. 739 (C.A.); *Re Williams; Williams v. Williams*, [1907] 1 Ch. 180; *Re Woolf; Public Trustee v. Lazarus*, [1920] 1 Ch. 184; *Re Ussher, supra*, footnote 114; *Re Cairns Estate*, [1972] 4 W.W.R. 322 (B.C.S.C.); *Sed Dubitante, Re Wintle; Tucker v. Wintle*, [1896] 2 Ch. 711; *Re Hume; Public Trustee v. Mabey*, [1912] 1 Ch. 693. See the discussion of the conflicting decisions on this point in Hawkins and Ryder, *supra*, footnote 66, at pp. 291 *et seq.*

[117]*Re Parker; Barker v. Barker* (1880), 16 Ch. D. 44; *Fast v. Van Vliet* (1965), 49 D.L.R. (2d) 616, 51 W.W.R. 65 (Man. C.A.). *Cf. Re Cairns Estate, supra*, footnote 116.

[118]*Re Barton, supra*, footnote 114.

[119]*Re Kirkley* (1918), 87 L.J. Ch. 247.

[120]*Morgan v. Morgan* (1851), 4 De G. & Sm. 164, 64 E.R. 781.

[121]*Parker v. Hodgson* (1861), 1 Dr. & Sm. 568, 62 E.R. 495.

[122]*Re Waines*, [1947] 2 D.L.R. 746, [1947] 1 W.W.R. 880 (Alta. S.C. App. Div.).

die before they become entitled to the gift. Typically, he will phrase the gift so that it will go to the intended beneficiaries "or the survivors or survivor" of them. If nothing further is added, that is, if he does not indicate at what time they must be surviving, the *prima facie* construction is that he meant the time of distribution.[123] That time is determined in accordance with the class closing rules.[124] This means that if the gift is immediate, the beneficiaries must survive the testator in order to take; otherwise, the gift over to the survivors becomes effective. If the gift is postponed, as in a gift "to A for life, remainder to his children, or the survivors or survivor of them", the period of distribution is the death of A, so that only those children living at A's death are entitled to take.[125]

If the gift is contingent, the period of distribution is postponed until the contingency is satisfied and only those surviving at that time can take. Thus, in a gift "to A for life, remainder to the children of B who attain 25 and if B has no children, then to the survivor of C, D, and E", the period of distribution arises at the later of the death of A and the attainment of age 25 by the first child of B. The gift to the survivor of C, D, and E is contingent until all of B's children have died under age 25. Hence, if C predeceased B's only child, who died at age 20, only D or E is entitled.[126]

A contrary intention is evidenced by language in which the testator refers to a specific time of survival, such as the word "then".[127] In that case, the *prima facie* rule is ousted.

Where the will shows that the reference to survivorship means survivorship among the remaindermen themselves and not just survivorship of the life tenant, the rule is not applied and the survivor of them takes the gift even though none of them survive the life tenant.[128]

If the reference to survivorship uses the conjunctive rather than the disconjunctive, as in "the survivors *and* survivor of them", the conjunction will normally be construed as "or", except where the gift is in joint tenancy, for survivorship is a necessary incident of that form of co-ownership. In the latter

---

[123]*Cripps v. Wolcott* (1819), 4 Madd. 11, 56 E.R. 613; *Re Stillman*, [1966] 1 O.R. 113 (H.C.J.).

[124]See §1004.1(b), *supra*.

[125]*Browne v. Lord Kenyon* (1818), 3 Madd. 410, 56 E.R. 556; *Sturgess v. Pearson* (1819), 4 Madd. 411, 56 E.R. 757; *Page v. May* (1857), 24 Beav. 323, 53 E.R. 382; *Re Pickworth; Snaith v. Parkinson*, [1899] 1 Ch. 642 (C.A.); *Penny v. Com'r for Railways*, [1900] A.C. 628 at p. 634 (P.C.).

[126]*Carver v. Burgess* (1853), 18 Beav. 541, 52 E.R. 212. *Cf. Davies v. Thorns* (1849), 3 De G. & Sm. 347, 64 E.R. 510: "to such persons as A may appoint and in default of appointment to A's surviving brothers and sisters". A failed to appoint and it was held that only the brothers and sisters living at her death were entitled to share. See also *Clarke v. Lubbock* (1842), 1 Y. & C. C. C. 492, 62 E.R. 985; *Cambridge v. Rous* (1858), 25 Beav. 409, 53 E.R. 693; *Maddison v. Chapman* (1861), 1 J. & H. 470, 70 E.R. 831; *Marriott v. Abell* (1869), L.R. 7 Eq. 478; *Re Deacon's Trusts; Deacon v. Deacon* (1906), 95 L.T. 701.

[127]*Re Pickworth; Snaith v. Parkinson*, [1899] 1 Ch. 642 (C.A.).

[128]*White v. Baker* (1860), 2 De G. F. & J. 55, 45 E.R. 542.

case, therefore, the reference is construed to refer to an indefinite survivorship, so that, as each person dies, the survivors take his share among them and the last survivor will take the whole.[129]

In certain circumstances, the reference to survivorship may be construed to mean that the beneficiary must survive until his interest vests, rather than until the period of distribution. Thus, in a gift "to A for life, remainder to his children when they attain 25, and in case one dies his share shall go to the survivors", the share of each child vests when he reaches the specified age, although the period of distribution, at the earliest, is A's death. If the *prima facie* rule of construction were to operate here, it would defeat the gift to any children of A whose shares had vested, but who died before the period of distribution. Since it is unlikely that this result was intended, the reference to survivorship is thus construed as a reference to when their interests vest.[130]

Where there is a gift over to the survivors of a class of persons in the event that one member of the class dies without issue, the *prima facie* construction is that only those persons who are still living at the death of the deceased member of the class, may take.[131] It is only where a contrary intent is shown, as by a further gift over of the whole fund in the event that all members of the class die without issue, that the reference to survivors will be taken to mean a reference to the other members of the class or their issue.[132]

(l) Vesting of gifts over on death

A substitutional gift, or gift over, is often made contingent on the death of the primary legatee so that, apparently, the substitutionary legatee takes a contingent interest until that time. The gift over may be stated to take effect on the death of the first person, or on his death in circumstances specified in the will. In this type of gift the rules of construction, known as the rules in *Edwards v. Edwards*,[133] apply. The rules are as follows:

(i) Where there is an immediate gift to a person, absolutely,[134] with a gift over to another person in the event of the first person's death, *prima facie*, the gift over is construed as taking effect only in the event that the first person predeceases the testator. Thus, in a gift "to A, and if he shall die, to B", B takes a vested interest only if A predeceases the testator. If A survives the testator,

---

[129]*Stringer v. Phillips* (1730), 1 Eq. Cas. Abr. 293, 21 E.R. 1054; *Page v. May* (1857), 24 Beav. 323, 53 E.R. 382.

[130]*Bouverie v. Bouverie* (1847), 2 Ph. 349, 41 E.R. 977; *Crozier v. Fisher* (1828), 4 Russ. 398, 38 E.R. 855. *Cf. Re Taylor*, [1972] 3 O.R. 349, 28 D.L.R. (3d) 257 (H.C.J.).

[131]*Gilmour v. MacPhillamy*, [1930] A.C. 712 (P.C.); *Re James's Will Trusts; Peard v. James*, [1962] Ch. 226.

[132]*Re Friend's Settlement; Cole v. Allcot*, [1906] 1 Ch. 47.

[133](1852), 15 Beav. 357, 51 E.R. 576, *per* Lord Romilly, M.R., as restated in *O'Mahoney v. Burdett* (1874), L.R. 7 H.L. 388, *per* Lord Cairns, L.C.

[134]Or "in fee simple", in the case of land. Clearly, if the gift is "for life" only, the gift over is simply a remainder which is vested: *Re More's Trust* (1851), 10 Hare 171, 68 E.R. 885 .

his interest has vested absolutely. Hence, the words "if he shall die" are read as meaning "if he shall die before his interest vests".[135]

(ii) Where there is a postponed gift to a person absolutely with a gift over to another person in the event of the first person's death, as in a gift "to A for life, remainder to B, but if B dies, to C", *prima facie*, the gift over will take effect only if the first person dies during the lifetime of the testator,[136] or during the lifetime of the life tenant. B's interest will be vested on the death of the testator, subject to defeasance if he predeceases A; if he survives A, his interest becomes absolute.

(iii) Where there is an immediate or a postponed gift to a person, with a gift over on death coupled with an express contingency, such as a gift "to A, but if he dies without leaving children, then to B", *prima facie*, the gift over will only take effect whenever the death of the first person occurs and the contingency is satisfied.

These rules may be displaced by a contrary intention disclosed by the will. For example, if the gift is "to A for life, remainder to B, but if B dies without issue, to C", and the testator indicates by other language in the will that the remainder interest is to be paid at A's death, the contingency is referable to that time and C will take only if B predeceases A without issue.[137]

1005. SPES SUCCESSIONIS

A *spes successionis*, or hope of succession, is a person's expectation of inheriting an estate or interest in land as heir or next of kin of the holder of the estate or interest. It is not a future interest, but is treated here because, on the face of it, it appears to have some of the attributes of a future interest.

No one can be the heir of a living person for, as long as he is alive, there is no one who has the right to take by descent. While he is living, a person can only have an heir apparent or presumptive. The expectation of inheriting is not an estate or interest, either at law or in equity, and confers no title and the rule is the same where there is a limitation by will or settlement to the heir or next of kin of a living person, or to the persons who would be his heirs or next of kin if he were to die at some future time.[1] The distinction is between an interest that has arisen and one that has not arisen and may never arise, but in regard to which there is a remote possibility that the event upon which it depends will occur; the latter is not an interest or right, but is nothing more than a bare expectation of a future right. Hence, a person having nothing more

---

[135]The rule also applies where the gift is "to A if he attains the age of 21, and if he dies, to B" but then B will take only if A dies under age 21: *Home v. Pillans* (1833), 2 My. & K. 15 at p. 23, 39 E.R. 850.

[136]*Willing v. Baine* (1731), 3 P. Wms. 113, 24 E.R. 991.

[137]*Olivant v. Wright* (1875), 1 Ch. D. 346 (C.A.). *Cf. Re Roberts; Roberts v. Morgan*, [1916] 2 Ch. 42; *Re Taylor, supra*, footnote 130.

§1005

[1]*Re Parsons; Stockley v. Parsons* (1890), 45 Ch. D. 51.

than that has no right of action, such as the right to sue for preservation of the property concerned.[2] Therefore, a *spes successionis* is merely the expectation of an interest and confers no interest at all, not even contingent,[3] or in expectancy.[4]

Not being an interest, but merely an expectancy, a *spes successionis* is not capable of valid assignment at law and a purported assignment of it operates only as an agreement to assign which will not be enforced by a court of equity if it is voluntary, that is, without consideration.[5] If the assignment is for valuable consideration, however, it will be given effect as binding upon the assignor so as to apply to his interest when it comes into existence if it is of such a nature and so described in the assignment that it can be identified.[6]

1006. REVERSIONS

The first type of future interest to be considered is the reversion.

A reversion is the estate that remains in the grantor who grants by one deed, or the heirs of a testator who devises by will, a lesser vested estate or a succession of lesser vested estates than the vested estate which he has.[1] It is called a reversion because possession of the land will revert to him and his heirs at the end of the lesser estate or the last lesser estate. A reversion may be expressly reserved by the person who creates the lesser estate or estates, but it is not necessary that he do so, or even that he have an intention of creating a reversion, for it remains in him by operation of law. Thus, in a grant by G "to A for life", and in a devise by T "to A for life, remainder to B for life", G and T retain the fee simple in reversion at law. A reversion may also be equitable, as where the grantor's interest arises under a trust or is the equity of redemption.

A reversion may be transferred subsequently by deed or will, and the transferee's interest will still be called a reversion.

1006.1 Nature and Creation

While more than one remainder may be created by the same instrument, there can be only one reversion. Moreover, a reversion is always vested, for it stands ready to fall into possession whenever the lesser estates determine. It may, however, be vested absolutely or vested subject to defeasance as, for

---

[2]*Davis v. Angel* (1862), 4 De G. F. & J. 524, 45 E.R. 1287.

[3]*Allcard v. Walker*, [1896] 2 Ch. 369 at p. 380.

[4]*Re Green*; *Green v. Meinall*, [1911] 2 Ch. 275.

[5]*Meek v. Kettlewell* (1843), 1 Ph. 342, 41 E.R. 662, 13 L.J. Ch. 28; *Re Ellenborough*; *Towry Law v. Burne*, [1903] 1 Ch. 697.

[6]*Tailby v. Official Receiver* (1888), 13 App. Cas. 523 at p. 543 (H.L.); see also *Flower v. Buller* (1880), 15 Ch. D. 665; *Re Coleman*; *Henry v. Strong* (1888), 39 Ch. D. 443 (C.A.).

§1006

[1]Co. Litt. 22b; 2 Bl. Comm. 175.

example, where a contingent remainder may become vested during a prior particular estate.[1]

A reversion may be created by the owner of any estate, and the reversionary interest will be the same estate that the transferor held. Thus, for example, where G, the owner of a fee simple, grants "to A for life", he retains a fee simple in reversion. Similarly, where a life tenant grants an estate for years, he will have a reversion for life, and this is so even though the lease be for a long term, such as 999 years, for in the eyes of the law a lease is a lesser estate than a freehold.[2] A lessee who demises for a term of years less than the term he himself has, also has a reversion.

A freehold reversion after a term of years used to be called a freehold estate in possession subject to the term. The reason for this terminology is that in law the lessee does not have the seisin; the freeholder does.[3] While this is still true today, it is more usual now to speak of the landlord's reversion, whether he be a freeholder or a lessee.

A reversion arises by operation of law in the heir or heirs in cases where dower or curtesy has been assigned to the surviving spouse.[4]

It should be noted that the doctrine of tenure operates so as to create a tenurial relationship between the grantor who retains the reversion and the owner of the lesser estate.[5] The reason for this is that the Statute *Quia Emptores*,[6] which forbade alienation by subinfeudation, only applied to fees simple, not to other estates.[7] In most cases, however, this doctrine can be disregarded since no services will be reserved on the grant. As between a landlord and tenant, however, the doctrine remains of importance, for leases normally reserve a service, that is, rent, to the landlord.

A reversion may be sold at any time, it being immaterial that a life tenant of the land is alive and in possession,[8] or that a tenant or the life tenant is in possession.[9]

If rent is payable by the person in possession, it is severable from the reversion. The rent may be granted or devised by the holder of the reversion, in which case the person entitled to the rent may distrain for it in his own name.[10] The reversion may be granted or devised, reserving the rent but if it is not reserved, the right to it passes with the reversion.

At common law, a reversion could not be alienated without the attornment

---

§1006.1

[1]See *infra*, §1009.2.

[2]Co. Litt. 46a; *Earl of Derby v. Taylor* (1801), 1 East. 502, 102 E.R. 193; *Re Russell Road Purchase-Moneys* (1871), L.R. 12 Eq. 78 at p. 84, *per* Malins, V.C.

[3]Challis, p. 100.

[4]Co. Litt. 54a.

[5]Challis, p. 22.

[6]18 Edw. 1, cc. 1, 2 (1290).

[7]*Ibid.*, c. 3.

[8]*Doe d. Cameron v. Robinson* (1850), 7 U.C.Q.B. 335.

[9]*Doe d. Burnham v. Bower* (1851), 8 U.C.Q.B. 607.

[10]*Hope v. White* (1869), 19 U.C.C.P. 479, and see *Hopkins v. Hopkins* (1883), 3 O.R. 223 at p. 230.

of the tenant to the grantee but this necessity was abolished by the Imperial *Statute of Anne*,[11] which provides that every grant or conveyance of any rent or any reversion or remainder in land is good and effectual without any attorn-ment of the tenant of the land or of the particular tenant upon whose particular estate the reversion or remainder is expectant, but a tenant is not prejudiced by the payment of any rent to the grantor before notice to him of such grant. This provision was adopted in several of the Canadian provinces.[12]

Conversely, it was provided by Imperial statute[13] that every attornment by a tenant to a stranger claiming title to the estate of his landlord is absolutely null and void and possession by the landlord is not changed or affected by such attornment unless it is made pursuant to, or in consequence of, a judgment or order of the court or made with the privity and consent of the landlord, or is made to a mortgagee after the mortgage is forfeited. This provision was also adopted in some Canadian jurisdictions.[14]

Hence, where the title to certain land was in dispute and the defendant made a lease to the plaintiff's tenant in order to secure possession, it was held that the plaintiff was entitled to recover possession, the question of title being left open.[15]

1006.2 Other Future Interests Distinguished

A reversion is to be distinguished from a remainder and an executory interest which arise, not by operation of law, but by act of the parties.[1] A remainder and an executory interest, moreover, do not vest or remain in the creator of the interest, but are held by another person or persons.

Where a testator devises by will a lesser estate than he has to one person and in a subsequent clause in the will devises all the residue of his property to another, the residuary clause should be regarded as creating a remainder, not a reversion.[2] However, such a residuary clause is usually regarded as creating a reversion.[3]

---

[11]*Administration of Justice Act*, 4 & 5 Anne, c. 16 (1705), s. 9.

[12]*Landlord and Tenant Act*, R.S.O. 1980, c. 232, s. 62; R.S.M. 1970, c. L70, s. 56; R.S.S. 1978, c. L-6, s. 60; R.S.N.B. 1973, c. L-1, s. 46; R.S.P.E.I. 1974, c. L-7, s. 22; *Commercial Tenancy Act*, R.S.B.C. 1979, c. 54, s. 14.

[13]*Distress for Rent Act*, 11 Geo. 2, c. 19 (1737).

[14]*Landlord and Tenant Act, supra*, footnote 12, Ont. Act, s. 61; Man. Act, s. 55; Sask. Act, s. 59; N.B. Act, s. 45; P.E.I. Act, s. 21.

[15]*Mulholland v. Harman* (1884), 6 O.R. 546 (H.C.J.).

§1006.2

[1]Williams, p. 362.

[2]A.L.P., §4.17.

[3]*Egerton v. Massey* (1857), 3 C.B. (N.S.) 338, 140 E.R. 771, devise "to A for life, remainder to her children in such shares as she should appoint, or in default of appoint-ment, or if A should die without issue, to B in fee", residuary devise "to A in fee". A died without issue but conveyed her interest to C. It was held that her residuary interest was a reversion and that her life estate and her reversion merged so as to destroy the contingent remainders. If A's reversionary interest were construed as a vested remainder, the interests of the children and of B would have been alternative executory interests, not subject to destruction: Gulliver, *Cases and Materials on the Law of Future Interests* (St. Paul, West Pub. Co., 1959), p. 255. See §1009, *infra*.

377

A reversion is also distinct from a possibility of reverter and from a right of entry for condition broken. While the latter do remain in the grantor, they are not vested estates, but possibilities which are contingent. They are created when a grantor or testator transfers a determinable estate in fee simple or an estate upon condition subsequent.

1006.3 Circumstances in which Reversions Arise

The simplest situation in which a reversion arises is where the testator fails to dispose of the entire interest that he has, as in a grant "to A for life".

A reversion may also arise where the grantor or testator believes that he has transferred his entire interest. This happens, for example, where he has created a contingent remainder in fee. Thus, in a grant "to A for life, remainder to B when he marries", the grantor retains a reversion which is defeasible and will be defeated if B marries in A's lifetime.[1] If he does not, the reversion vests absolutely.

A reversion also exists where there are alternative contingent remainders, as in a grant "to A for life, remainder to his children in fee if he has any, and if he dies without issue, to B in fee", for, if the remainders are destroyed, the estate reverts to the grantor.[2] Even in jurisdictions which have abolished artificial destruction of contingent remainders,[3] the grantor would still have a reversion. Indeed, even if natural destruction has been abolished,[4] it would seem that a reversion remains in the grantor until one or other of the remainders vests, even though, in the example given above, the reversion would then never fall into possession, for either A's children will take a vested remainder on A's death, or in default of issue, B will do so.[5]

The same result obtains in the following devise, "to A for life and after her death to her children who attain the age of 21, or for want of such issue, to B", where A dies survived by issue under 21.[6] Assuming the possibility of natural destruction, both alternative contingent remainders fail and the testator's

---

§1006.3

[1] At one time, it was thought that whenever a fee simple was created, it must at once depart out of the feoffor, so that the latter could not retain an interest. The fee was thus thought to be *in gremio legis* or *in nubibus*: Co. Litt. 342b. The modern law is as stated in the text: 1 Fearne, pp. 361-2; Williams, p. 389.

[2] *Loddington v. Kime* (1695), 1 Salk. 224, 91 E.R. 198. The case actually involved a devise, but the interests created were treated as contingent remainders and not as executory interests under the rule in *Purefoy v. Rogers* (1681), 2 Wm. Saund. 380, 85 E.R. 1181; see, *infra*, §1010.3. The remainders were destroyed artificially when the life tenant suffered a common recovery before he had a child.

[3] See §1009.5(c), *infra*.

[4] See §1009.5(d), *infra*.

[5] But see, *contra*, Simes and Smith, §85.

[6] *Festing v. Allen* (1843), 12 M. & W. 279, 152 E.R. 1204. A trust was employed in the will, but it was passive, so that the several interests were legal and fell under the rule in *Purefoy v. Rogers, supra*, footnote 2.

reversion vests absolutely. Where natural destruction has been abolished, it becomes possible to wait until a child of A reaches age 21. In the meantime, however, the testator has a reversion which should give any intermediate income to him.[7] If all of A's children die under 21, it is a question of construction whether B's interest will vest. In the above example it would not; B would only take a vested remainder if A died without children her surviving.

Where the grantor does not dispose of the entire estate that he has but gives another a power to appoint it, as in a grant "to A for life, remainder to such persons as A may appoint", the grantor has a reversion, defeasible if, and to the extent that, A appoints.

The grantor or the testator also has a reversion if a limitation fails to take effect, as where the devisee predeceases the testator so that there is a lapse, or if it is void, for example, for perpetuity.

A reversion also arises where an executory interest is created. Thus, in a devise "to A when he attains the age of 21", the testator's estate will have a reversion in fee simple until A reaches the age of 21 when it divests.[8]

A conveyance which creates a determinable life estate or a life estate upon condition subsequent, leaves a right of entry in the grantor in the latter case, as well as a reversion in both cases.

1006.4   Concealed Reversions: Remainders to the Grantor's or Testator's Heirs; The Doctrine of Worthier Title

At common law it was impossible for a person to limit a remainder to his heirs, either by deed[1] or by will.[2] The limitation would simply be disregarded and treated as a reversion in the grantor or testator. The rule operates so as to prefer a title derived by descent, rather than by purchase or devise for, since the estate reverts to the creator of the interest, it will then pass to his heir on his intestacy. At any rate, this is so where the interest was created by will. Clearly, where the interest was created *inter vivos*, the grantor could subsequently defeat his heir by disposing of the reversion. Because title by descent was preferred, the rule is often referred to as the "doctrine of worthier title". In fact, that somewhat pompous description applied only to the testamentary branch of the rule, although it is usual to refer to both the testamentary and the *inter vivos* branches of the rule as the doctrine of worthier title.

The reasons for the doctrine, which are similar to those applicable to the rule in *Shelley's Case*,[3] are obscure. However, it is probable that it was necessary in feudal society to prevent an avoidance of the lord's tenurial incidents.

---

[7]Megarry and Wade, p. 197.
[8]*Restatement, Property*, §154, comment a.
§1006.4
[1]*Bingham's Case* (1600), 2 Co. Rep. 91 a, 76 E.R. 611.
[2]*Chaplin v. Leroux* (1816), 5 M. & S. 14 at p. 20, 105 E.R. 957.
[3](1581), 1 Co. Rep. 93 b, 76 E.R. 206; see §1009.6, *infra*.

Those incidents, such as wardship, relief and marriage, could be exacted only if the property passed by descent, not if the heir took by devise or by purchase.[4] Moreover, land that passed by descent to the heir was available for the deceased's creditors, whereas land that passed by devise was not.

In a will, the rule would operate whether the purported remainder was to the testator's heirs, or to a named person who was in fact the heir of the testator. In a deed, however, the doctrine only applied if the purported remainder was to the heirs of the grantor. It could not apply to a named person, for a living person can have no heir.[5]

Today, land can no longer descend on the death of the parent to his heir, but passes to the deceased's personal representative in trust for the persons beneficially entitled to it, that is, either the devisee or the several heirs on an intestacy and, in either case, it is subject to the deceased's debts.[6] Moreover, the feudal reasons for the doctrine are now irrelevant. Hence the basis for the testamentary branch of the doctrine is gone. Furthermore, there seems to be no reason today to continue the *inter vivos* branch. For this reason, indeed, well before modern intestacy legislation was enacted, the doctrine in both its branches was abolished in England.[7] This legislation was followed in some of the Canadian provinces,[8] but not in others,[9] where the doctrine thus remains in effect.

Where the doctrine remains in effect, the testamentary branch may be regarded as otiose, for the reasons given above. This is also the view of the compilers of the Restatement.[10] The *inter vivos* branch remains in full force

---

[4]Co. Litt. 22b; 2 Fearne, §390; *Owen v. Gibbons*, [1902] 1 Ch. 636 at p. 638, *per* Farwell, J.

[5]Co. Litt. 8b.

[6]*Estate Administration Act*, R.S.B.C. 1979, c. 114, s. 90; *Devolution of Real Property Act*, R.S.A. 1980, c. D-34, s. 2; R.S.S. 1978, c. D-27, ss. 4, 5; *Devolution of Estates Act*, R.S.M. 1970, c. D70, s. 18; R.S.N.B. 1973, c. D-9, s. 3; *Estates Administration Act*, R.S.O. 1980, c. 143, s. 2(1); *Chattels Real Act*, R.S.N. 1970, c. 36, s. 2; *Real Property Act*, R.S.N.S. 1967, c. 261, s. 6(1); *Probate Act*, R.S.P.E.I. 1974, c. P-19, s. 108(1); *Devolution of Real Property Ordinance*, R.O.N.W.T. 1974, c. D-5, s. 3(1); R.O.Y.T. 1971, c. D-4, s. 3(1).

[7]By the *Inheritance Act*, 3 & 4 Will. 4, c. 106 (1833), s. 3.

[8]Ont.: *Real Property Act*, S.U.C. 1834, c. 1, s. 2, subsequently consolidated in the *Devolution of Estates Act*, R.S.O. 1897, c. 127, s. 26. That section was not carried forward in the *Devolution of Estates Act*, S.O. 1910, c. 56, and it stands unrepealed and unconsolidated in subsequent revisions. P.E.I.: *Probate Act*, R.S.P.E.I. 1974, c. P-19, s. 104. Nfld.: The doctrine does not apply in this province by reason of the *Chattels Real Act*, R.S.N. 1970, c. 36, which converts all interests in land into chattels real. All other provinces, except New Brunswick and Nova Scotia, date their reception of English law subsequent to the *Inheritance Act, 1833*. See ch. 3, *supra*. Hence, they never received the doctrine.

[9]N.B.: Law Ref. Div., Dept. of Justice, N.B., *Survey of the Law of Real Property* (n.d., by A.M. Sinclair and D.G. Rouse, Q.C., working report — Dept. of Justice, May, 1976), pp. 26-9. N.S.: The doctrine does not appear to have been dealt with legislatively or judicially in Nova Scotia.

[10]*Restatement, Property*, §314(2). There are some American cases which continue to accept the testamentary branch of the doctrine, however. See Simes and Smith, §1601.

in some of the United States. However, it is now usually regarded, not as a rule of law, but as a rule of construction which raises a presumption that the grantor intended to keep a reversion, and which may be ousted by evidence of a contrary intention.[11] Moreover, the rule has been extended to conveyances of personal property,[12] whether they be to the grantor's heirs or next of kin.[13] The rule has been abolished by statute in some jurisdictions and judicially in others.[14]

To the extent that the doctrine remains in force, it may have important consequences in respect of death taxes, since the grantor retains a reversion which passes on his death; in respect of the creditors of the grantor or his heirs, since the former will be able to reach the property, while the latter cannot, and in respect of the heirs themselves, since they cannot take the property unless the grantor subsequently conveys or devises it to them, or it passes the property to them on his intestacy if it is still in the estate.

1007. POSSIBILITIES OF REVERTER

A possibility of reverter is the interest that remains in the grantor, or in the heirs of the testator, who has conveyed or devised a determinable fee simple.[1] It is a possibility that the grantor or the testator's heirs will reacquire the fee, that is, a vested interest, in the future. Thus, it is a mere possibility and not an estate or interest in land.[2]

1007.1 Characteristics

A possibility of reverter is, in a sense, a hybrid interest. In one sense it is vested, because it remains in the creator of the interest, but in another sense it is contingent in that the reacquisition of the fee may or may not occur.[1] For this reason, there was doubt for a long time as to whether a possibility of reverter was subject to the rule against perpetuities. An English case held that

---

[11]*Doctor v. Hughes*, 225 N.Y. 305, 122 N.E. 221 (1919), and see 1 A.L.P., §§4.19 *et seq.* Simes and Smith, §§1603 *et seq.*

[12]See, *e.g., Beach v. Busey*, 156 F. 2d 496 (1946, 6th C.C.A.). For a case applying the testamentary branch to a bequest of personalty, see *Re Warren's Estate* (1931), 211 Iowa 940, 234 N.W. 835.

[13]See, *e.g., Scholtz v. Central Hanover Bank & Trust Co.*, 295 N.Y. 488, 68 N.E. 2d 503 (1946).

[14]See Simes and Smith, §1612; 1 A.L.P., §4.23.

§1007
[1]The determinable fee simple is discussed in §505.3, *supra.*
[2]1 Fearne, p. 381; Challis, p. 83.

§1007.1
[1]Perhaps for this reason, the *Restatement, Property*, in §154(2), defines a possibility of reverter as a reversionary interest subject to a condition precedent. In *Re McKellar*, [1972] 3 O.R. 16, 27 D.L.R. (3d) 289 (H.C.J.), affd [1973] 3 O.R. 178n, 36 D.L.R. (3d) 202n (C.A.), the interest was held to be vested.

it was,[2] while other English and Canadian cases held that it was not.[3] Modern perpetuities legislation resolves the difficulty by making the possibility of reverter and similar interests under a trust subject to the rule in the same way as the comparable interest, the right of entry for condition broken,[4] which was always held to be subject to the rule.[5]

It is apparent from such legislation that resulting trusts are treated as analogous to possibilities of reverter, and indeed they are, for a resulting trust arises where the settlor has failed to dispose of the entire beneficial interest under the trust or where an interest fails for perpetuity or other reasons.[6]

Apart from a trust, a possibility of reverter may be created out of legal or equitable estates. Moreover, it is possible to create interests analogous to possibilities of reverter in personal property.[7]

While determinable interests may be created in estates other than a fee simple, such as a life estate or a term of years, the interest remaining in the grantor does not then appear to be called a possibility of reverter.[8] This does not seem to make much difference in practice, however, as the grantor has a reversion in any event, or alternatively, the estate may pass by remainder, as in the following examples:

(1) A grant "to A for life or so long as he remains unmarried".

(2) A grant "to A for life or so long as she remains a widow".

The reversion in such a case would be the dominant interest and, since it is vested, the perpetuity rule is not offended. Even if the grantor is regarded as having an interest analogous to a possibility of reverter after a determinable life estate, the modern perpetuity statutes would not apply to it as they are restricted to possibilities of reverter on the determination of a determinable

---

[2]*Hopper v. Corp. of Liverpool* (1944), 88 Sol. Jo. 213.

[3]*Re Chardon; Johnston v. Davies*, [1928] Ch. 464; *Re Cooper's Conveyance Trusts*, [1956] 1 W.L.R. 1096; *Re Tilbury West Public School Board and Hastie*, [1966] 2 O.R. 20, 55 D.L.R. (2d) 407 (H.C.J.).

[4]*Perpetuities and Accumulations Act, 1964*, c. 55, s. 12; *Perpetuities Act*, R.S.O. 1980, c. 374, s. 15; S.A. 1972, c. 121, s. 19; *Perpetuity Act*, R.S.B.C. 1979, c. 321, s. 20; *Perpetuities Ordinance*, R.O.N.W.T. 1974, c. P-3, s. 16; O.Y.T. 1980 (1st), c. 23, s. 20.

[5]*Re Da Costa; Clarke v. Church of England Collegiate School of St. Peter*, [1912] 1 Ch. 337; *Re St. Patrick's Market* (1909), 1 O.W.N. 92 (H.C.); *Matheson v. Town of Mitchell* (1919), 46 O.L.R. 546, 51 D.L.R. 477 (C.A.); *Re Trustees of Hollis' Hospital and Hague's Contract*, [1899] 2 Ch. 540; *Re North Gower Twp. Public School Board and Todd*, [1968] 1 O.R. 63, 65 D.L.R. (2d) 421 (C.A.).

[6]*Cf.* Simes and Smith, §2.88.

[7]*Re Talbot; Jubb v. Sheard*, [1933] Ch. 895; *Re Randell; Randell v. Dixon* (1888), 38 Ch. D. 213; *Re Blunt's Trusts; Wigan v. Clinch*, [1904] 2 Ch. 767; *Re Chardon, supra*, footnote 3; *Re Chambers' Will Trusts; Official Trustees of Charitable Funds v. British Union for Abolition of Vivisection*, [1950] Ch. 267.

[8]See 1 A.L.P., §4.12; 1 Simes and Smith, §281; Megarry and Wade, pp. 74, 244 *et seq.*; Cheshire, pp. 362 *et seq.*; Morris and Leach, p. 209.

fee simple and a possibility of any determinable interest in real or personal property.[9]

At one time it was thought that a possibility of reverter could not be created because the Statute *Quia Emptores*[10] forbade it. This theory, which has already been adverted to in previous chapters,[11] has been laid to rest by modern cases which recognize the interest.[12]

Although it is a reversionary interest, the possibility of reverter is distinguishable from a reversion in that a possibility of reverter arises when a person conveys an estate of the same quantum as he owns, albeit a qualified estate; a reversion is created when a person conveys a lesser estate than he has.

A possibility of reverter is distinguishable from a right of entry for condition broken in the language used to create these interests and in the fact that the possibility of reverter revests the estate in the grantor or his heirs automatically upon the event specified in the limitation. A right of entry, on the other hand, merely entitles the grantor or his heirs to re-enter to determine the existing estate,[13] and it is thus a right of forfeiture.[14]

Moreover, in the case of a determinable fee, the determining event forms part of the limitation, or is an alternative limitation to the words "and his heirs", or "in fee simple".[15] In a fee simple upon condition subsequent, the condition is a superadded clause which operates to defeat the fee already granted. Thus, in a grant "to A in fee simple so long as the land is used for school purposes", the words "in fee simple so long as the land is used for school purposes" are words of limitation, while in a grant "to B in fee provided that the land is used solely for residential purposes", the words "in fee" are the words of limitation and what follows is a condition subsequent apt to defeat the estate granted if the lands are no longer so used.

It should be noted that certain limitations which appear to create a determinable fee and, hence, a possibility of reverter, do not in fact do so if the determining event is certain or bound to occur, such as the death of a person, or a fixed term of years. In that event the interest created is not a fee, which in theory should be able to last forever, but a lesser interest.[16]

Finally, if the specified event can no longer occur, as in a grant "to A in fee so long as B resides in England", and B continues to reside in England and

---

[9]Only those statutes which place a maximum limit on the period could apply to such interest in any event, as the life tenant would be a life in being and the interest would have to fall into possession during his lifetime, if at all. See *Perpetuities Act*, R.S.O. 1980, c. 374, s. 15.

[10]18 Edw. 1, cc. 1-3 (1290).

[11]§§209.1(d) and 505.3, *supra.*

[12]See the cases collected in footnotes 2 and 3, *supra.*

[13]Challis, pp. 208, 252, 261; Co. Litt. 214b.

[14]Megarry and Wade, p. 77.

[15]For this reason, the estate is sometimes called a fee upon a special limitation. See *Restatement, Property*, §44; 1 A.L.P., §2.6.

[16]Challis, p. 251.

dies there, the possibility of reverter is destroyed and the estate of the grantee becomes absolute.[17]

1007.2 Creation

As stated above,[1] a possibility of reverter is created when a person grants or devises a determinable fee simple. Language apt to create a determinable fee thus gives rise to a possibility of reverter. Typically, words of duration such as, "until", "while", "as long as" and "during" are required, as opposed to words of condition, which are apt to create a fee simple upon condition subsequent.[2] Nevertheless, it is a question of construction in each case to ascertain the grantor's or testator's intention and words which, being words of duration, would at first glance appear to create a determinable fee, may in their context be construed as creating a fee upon condition subsequent instead.[3]

Thus, for example, in *Re McKellar*[4] lands were granted to the Canadian National Railway Company. The deed recited that the fee should endure "only so long as the said Railway Company shall continue to occupy and use the . . . lands for [railway] purposes". After the description, however, the deed provided, ". . . but upon the express condition and understanding that so soon as the said Railway Company shall cease to occupy and use the lands [for railway purposes], then the fee simple . . . shall revert to [the grantor]", and in the *habendum* the grant was made subject to the above condition. It was held that the *habendum* annexed the condition to the grant so that it conveyed a fee simple upon condition subsequent and not a determinable fee.[5]

A determinable fee may also arise by implication as in a grant "to A and his heirs, tenants of the manor of Dale". In such a grant the words, "so long as they are", are implied.[6]

It would appear that, in case of doubt, the courts tend to construe a defeasible fee simple as one upon a condition subsequent, rather than as a determinable fee.[7] The reason is that if the determining event is void for public policy, uncertainty, restraint on alienation, or other reason, the entire gift fails in the case of a determinable fee, since it is improperly limited. By

---

[17]*Ibid.*, p. 254.

§1007.2

[1]§1007.

[2]*Hopper v. Corp. of Liverpool* (1944), 88 Sol. Jo. 213; *Re Tilbury West Public School Board and Hastie*, [1966] 2 O.R. 20, 55 D.L.R. (2d) 407 (H.C.J.); *Re North Gower Twp. Public School Board and Todd*, [1968] 1 O.R. 63, 65 D.L.R. (2d) 421 (C.A.); Megarry and Wade, p. 76; §§505.3 and 505.4, *supra*.

[3]See cases collected in footnote 2, *supra*.

[4][1972] 3 O.R. 16, 27 D.L.R. (3d) 289 (H.C.J.), affd [1973] 3 O.R. 178n, 36 D.L.R. (3d) 202n (C.A.).

[5]See also *Re Essex County Roman Catholic Separate School Board and Antaya* (1977), 17 O.R. (2d) 307, 80 D.L.R. (3d) 405 (H.C.J.).

[6]2 Bl. Comm. 109.

[7]See, *e.g.*, *Hopper v. Corp. of Liverpool, supra*, footnote 2.

contrast, in such a case a condition subsequent would merely be struck from a fee upon condition subsequent, thus making the gift absolute.[8] In order to allow the grantor's or testator's intention to be carried out, at least in part, therefore, a construction favouring a fee upon condition subsequent is appropriate, for the law disfavours forfeitures.[9]

It should be noted, however, that the rules regarding restraint on alienation, public policy and uncertainty are not applied as strictly to determinable fees, for the same reason. Thus, a conveyance of the fee "until bankruptcy"[10] has been held to create a valid determinable fee, and hence a possibility of reverter, whereas it might have been struck down if it had been a fee upon condition subsequent.[11]

It is not necessary that the grant or will specify that the estate shall revert to the grantor or the testator's heirs on the occurrence of the event specified, as the law implies it.[12]

On the other hand, it is not possible by common law conveyance to limit the possibility of reverter to a person other than the grantor, for by definition, it rests only in him. The interest could only descend to his heirs at common law, although by later statutes it was made assignable and devisable.[13] If the grantor did attempt to give the possibility of reverter to another by the same instrument, the gift would be void, leaving the interest in the grantor himself.[14] It was and is possible to give the possibility of reverter to another in the same instrument in the form of an executory interest under a use executed by the *Statute of Uses*,[15] under a trust, and under a will.[16]

Thus, in the following examples, the grantor retains a possibility of reverter in the first, but it is transferred to B by a legal executory interest in the second example, by an equitable executory interest in the third example and by an executory devise in the fourth example:

  (i) A grant "to A in fee so long as the land is farmed and then to B in fee".
  (ii) A grant "to X and his heirs to the use of A in fee so long as London Bridge stands and then to the use of B in fee".
  (iii) A grant "unto and to the use of X and his heirs in trust for A in fee until B graduates from law school and then in trust for B for life".
  (iv) A devise "to A in fee while B is travelling around the world and then to B in fee".

---

[8]Megarry and Wade, p. 81.
[9]*Restatement, Property*, §45, comment m.
[10]*Brandon v. Robinson* (1811), 18 Ves. Jun. 429, 34 E.R. 379; *Re Leach; Leach v. Leach*, [1912] 2 Ch. 422.
[11]See further ch. 9, *supra*, on this point.
[12]Simes and Smith, §286; 1 A.L.P., §4.13.
[13]See §1012, *infra*.
[14]Simes and Smith, §284.
[15]27 Hen. 8, c. 10 (1535).
[16]See §§1008.2, 1009.2, *infra*.

As distinguished from the life estate upon condition subsequent, it is possible to limit an estate in remainder after a determinable life estate at common law, for when the determining event occurs, the life estate determines naturally, according to the limitation; it is not defeated by a condition.[17] As in the case of a vested remainder after a life estate absolute, therefore, the remainder can take effect in possession without a gap in the seisin, or a need for the seisin to revert to the grantor. It will pass directly to the remainderman.

1007.3 Reverter when a Corporation is Dissolved

When a corporation is dissolved and it fails to dispose of all its assets before dissolution, it is sometimes said that the undisposed-of property reverts to the grantor. This is based upon an erroneous statement by Lord Coke.[1] Although in error, the dictum was referred to in many cases[2] and followed in some.[3] It was expressly disapproved of in an English[4] and a Canadian case.[5] In the latter case, it was held that where one company amalgamates with another and its property is not transferred to the other company, the amalgamated company is a bare trustee for the second company and a trustee will be appointed to transfer the property.[6]

Some provincial statutes now provide that on dissolution of a corporation its undisposed-of assets are forfeit to the Crown.[7]

1008. RIGHTS OF ENTRY FOR CONDITION BROKEN

A right of entry for condition broken is the interest that remains in the grantor, or in the heirs of the testator, who has conveyed or devised an estate

---

[17]Megarry and Wade, p. 186.

§1007.3

[1]Co. Litt. 13b. See on this error Gray, pp. 49-55.

[2]See, e.g., *Mayor of Colchester v. Brooke* (1845), 7 Q.B. 339, 115 E.R. 518; *Hastings Corp. v. Letton* (1907), 77 L.J.K.B. 149; *Re Strathblaine Estates, Ltd.*, [1948] Ch. 228; *Re Woking Urban District Council (Basingstoke Canal) Act, 1911*, [1914] 1 Ch. 300 (C.A.); *Re Canadian Fertilizer Co. and Canadian Industries Ltd.*, [1938] O.W.N. 335, [1938] 3 D.L.R. 765 (H.C.J.).

[3]See, e.g., *Lindsay Petroleum Co. v. Pardee* (1875), 22 Gr. 18.

[4]*Re Sir Thomas Spencer Wells; Swinburne-Hanham v. Howard*, [1933] Ch. 29 at p. 54; folld in *Re Strathblaine Estates, Ltd.*, [1948] Ch. 228.

[5]*Re Stowell-MacGregor Corp. and John MacGregor Corp.*, [1942] 4 D.L.R. 120 (N.B.S.C.); folld in *Re Jolin and Lart Investments Ltd.* (1977), 18 O.R. (2d) 161 (Dist. Ct.).

[6]See further on this point: Hughes, "Reverter to the Donor of the Legal Fee Vested in a Dissolved Corporation", 51 L.Q. Rev. 347 (1935) and reply, 51 L.Q. Rev. 361 (1935); Laskin, pp. 343-4.

[7]*Corporations Act*, R.S.O. 1980, c. 95, s. 322; *Business Corporations Act*, R.S.O. 1980, c. 54, s. 245; *Property of Dissolved Corporations (Vesting) Act*, R.S.N. 1970, c. 310; *Dissolved Corporations Property Act*, R.S.N.S. 1967, c. 77. See further §502.3(b), *supra*.

upon condition subsequent.[1] The estate may be of the same quantum as the grantor or testator has, or of a lesser quantum.[2] Thus, a right of entry for condition broken exists after a fee simple, a fee tail, a life estate and a term of years, all of which are made subject to a condition subsequent. The right of entry does not return the estate automatically to the grantor or his heirs, but is an election to forfeit the estate that has been granted, which is exercisable either by an actual entry or by an action for possession. For this reason the interest is sometimes called a power of termination.[3]

1008.1 Characteristics

A right of entry for condition broken is a contingent interest in that the forfeiture may or may not occur as the grantor or his heirs choose. For this reason, it has always been held to be subject to the rule against perpetuities,[1] and continues to be so under modern perpetuities statutes.[2]

The right of entry is distinguishable from a reversion in that a reversion is the interest remaining in a person who has created an absolute estate of lesser quantum than he has and in that a reversion is a vested interest which becomes possessory automatically upon the termination of the lesser estate. It is distinguishable from the possibility of reverter in that it becomes an estate in possession automatically, and from remainders and executory interests in that these may exist in other persons while the right of entry may exist only in the grantor or in his or the testator's heirs.

1008.2 Creation

A right of entry is created by a superadded clause which operates so as to defeat a properly limited estate. Words importing a condition, such as "provided", "but if", "on condition that", and similar expressions are apt to

---

§1008
[1]The estate in fee simple upon condition subsequent is discussed in §505.4, *supra*. As to estates in fee tail and for life upon condition subsequent, see §§605.3 and 702(a), respectively, *supra*.
[2]Cheshire, pp. 367, 368.
[3]Restatement, *Property*, §§24, 155.
§1008.1
[1]*Re Trustees of Hollis' Hospital and Hague's Contract*, [1899] 2 Ch. 540; *Re Da Costa*; *Clarke v. Church of England Collegiate School of St. Peter*, [1912] 1 Ch. 337; *Re St. Patrick's Market* (1909), 1 O.W.N. 92 (H.C.); *Matheson v. Town of Mitchell* (1919), 46 O.L.R. 546, 51 D.L.R. 477 (C.A.); *Re North Gower Twp. Public School Board and Todd*, [1968] 1 O.R. 63, 65 D.L.R. (2d) 421 (C.A.); *Re McKellar*, [1973] 3 O.R. 178n, 36 D.L.R. (3d) 202n (C.A.); *Re Essex County Roman Catholic Separate School Board and Antaya* (1977), 17 O.R. (2d) 307, 80 D.L.R. (3d) 405 (H.C.J.).
[2]*Perpetuities and Accumulations Act, 1964*, c. 55, s. 12; *Perpetuities Act*, R.S.O. 1980, c. 374, s. 15; R.S.A. 1980, c. P-4, s. 19; *Perpetuity Act*, R.S.B.C. 1979, c. 321, s. 20; *Perpetuities Ordinance*, R.O.N.W.T. 1974, c. P-3, s. 16; O.Y.T. 1980 (1st), c. 23, s. 20.

create the interest.[1] It is principally on the basis of the language used that the right of entry is distinguishable, as a factual matter, from the possibility of reverter, which is created by using words of duration. Nevertheless, an instrument which apparently creates a possibility of reverter may, because of the context, be construed to create a right of entry.[2] Indeed, the courts tend to so construe it in cases of doubt because it will prevent a complete forfeiture of the estate if the determining event specified is void for public policy, uncertainty, or some other cause. The reason is that if the determining event is void in the case of a determinable fee, not only is the possibility of reverter void, but so is the grant of the fee itself, since the estate is created by one limitation. In the case of an estate upon condition subsequent, only the condition will be void and it can be struck off, making the estate absolute.[3]

Because conditions subsequent confer a right of forfeiture, the courts tend to construe them strictly and will readily strike them down for uncertainty, public policy, restraint on alienation and other reasons.[4] Moreover, the court may, in its equitable jurisdiction, grant relief from forfeiture. The law in this respect is not well-developed as to conditions subsequent generally, but is applied to conditions subsequent in leases and to mortgages, both of which incorporate estates upon condition subsequent enabling the lessor and mortgagee to enter for breach of the conditions.[5]

Furthermore, to avoid a forfeiture, the courts may in appropriate circumstances be able to construe a condition subsequent as a trust,[6] an equitable charge,[7] or a covenant.[8] The latter gives rise only to a cause of action for damages and the courts tend to construe a deed as creating a covenant rather than a condition, unless the language clearly imports a condition.[9]

It would seem also that in order to effect a forfeiture for breach of a con-

---

§1008.2

[1]Megarry and Wade, p. 76; Cheshire, p. 315; *Re North Gower Twp. Public School Board and Todd*, [1968] 1 O.R. 63, 65 D.L.R. (2d) 421 (C.A.); *Re McKellar*, [1973] 3 O.R. 178n, 36 D.L.R. (3d) 202n (C.A.); *Re Essex County Roman Catholic Separate School Board and Antaya* (1977), 17 O.R. (2d) 307, 80 D.L.R. (3d) 405 (H.C.J.).

[2]*Re North Gower Twp. Public School Board and Todd, supra; Re McKellar, supra; Re Essex County Roman Catholic Separate School Board and Antaya, supra*, and see §1007.2, *supra.*

[3]*Ibid.*

[4]See §§903-903.7 where these points are discussed.

[5]Megarry and Wade, p. 78; 1 Simes and Smith, §257.

[6]*Re Frame; Edwards v. Taylor*, [1939] Ch. 700.

[7]*Re Oliver* (1890), 62 L.T. 533.

[8]*Pearson v. Adams* (1912), 27 O.L.R. 87 at p. 92, 7 D.L.R. 139 at p. 144 (H.C.J.), *per* Riddell, J., revd 28 O.L.R. 154, 12 D.L.R. 227 (C.A.), restd 50 S.C.R. 204; *Paul v. Paul* (1921), 50 O.L.R. 211, 64 D.L.R. 269 (S.C. App. Div.); *Stephens v. Gulf Oil Canada Ltd.* (1975), 11 O.R. (2d) 129 at pp. 158-9, 65 D.L.R. (3d) 193 at pp. 222-3 (C.A.), *per* Howland, J.A.; *British Columbia Forest Products Ltd. v. Gay* (1976), 74 D.L.R. (3d) 660, 1 B.C.L.R. 265 (S.C.), *per* Toy, J., affd 89 D.L.R. (3d) 80, 7 B.C.L.R. 190 (C.A.).

[9]See the cases in footnote 8, *supra*. The distinction between a condition and covenant is discussed in §901.2(b).

dition the election to do so must be made within a reasonable time or else it may be held to have been waived.[10]

A right of entry consequent upon a common law condition subsequent cannot be followed by a remainder for, if the right of entry follows upon a fee simple upon condition subsequent, the remainder will offend the rule that a remainder cannot be limited after a fee simple. Having granted the largest estate known to the law, the grantor has nothing left to give and the remainder is void.[11]

A remainder following a life estate upon condition subsequent is also void, however, at least if the grantor elects to terminate it for breach of condition. If he does not, the life estate will continue until its natural end when the remainder will take effect.[12]

The reasons for the voidability of the remainder in this case are twofold. First, the remainder will have to take effect in possession as a result of an unnatural defeasance of the prior life estate,[13] which is regarded as improper.[14] Second, the forfeiture operates to return the seisin to the grantor and cannot pass to the remainderman except by a new livery of seisin.[15]

Thus, at common law only the grantor and his heirs, or the testator's heirs, could take the benefit of a right of entry. Subsequent statutes have, however, made the interest alienable and devisable.[16]

A right of entry, whether consequent upon a fee simple or a lesser estate upon condition subsequent, can be limited to another by way of executory limitation[17] in the same instrument under a use not executed by the *Statute of Uses*,[18] under a trust, and under a will. The interest so created is called an executory interest.[19]

1009.   REMAINDERS

A remainder is the interest created by a transferor in a person other than himself or his heir,[1] which follows after one or more estates of lesser quantum

---

[10]There is a paucity of law on this point in Canada except in the context of the landlord and tenant relationship. In the United States the doctrine of waiver appears to apply to rights of entry generally. See 1 Simes and Smith, §§258 *et seq.*

[11]Co. Litt. 214b, 379a; 1 Fearne, p. 372; *Re Melville* (1886), 11 O.R. 626 (H.C.J.), at p. 631.

[12]Megarry and Wade, pp. 186-7.

[13]That is, a defeasance before its natural end, the death of the life tenant.

[14]1 Fearne, p. 261; 1 Sanders, p. 158.

[15]1 A.L.P., §4.8; 1 Simes and Smith, §253.

[16]See §1012, *infra.*

[17]Or a collateral limitation, 1 Preston, p. 42; or a conditional limitation, 1 Fearne, p. 272.

[18]27 Hen. 8, c. 10 (1535).

[19]See §1007.2, *supra*, and §§1010-1010.2 and 1011, *infra.*

§1009

[1]The words "or his heirs" are significant only in jurisdictions in which the doctrine of worthier title is still in force. That doctrine prohibits the creation of a remainder in the transferor's heirs; instead, it treats the apparent remainder as a reversion in the transferor. See §1006.4, *supra*. An apparent remainder to the transferor himself is a reversion.

than that owned by the transferor, created by the same instrument in the same land, and which, viewed from the time of its inception, must take effect in possession upon the natural determination of the prior estate.[2]

Thus, where a grantor, who owns the fee simple, conveys:

(a) "To A for life, remainder to B for life, remainder to C in fee simple", or

(b) "To A for life, remainder to B and the heirs of his body, and then to C and his heirs",

the estates limited in favour of B and C are valid remainders.

Similarly, where a grantor conveys "to A for life or until he becomes bankrupt and then to B", the remainder to B is valid. A's life estate is determinable, so its natural determination occurs either when he dies or when be becomes bankrupt. However, a conveyance "to A for life, but if he becomes bankrupt, to B", does not give B a valid remainder since it cuts short or defeats A's life estate by a condition subsequent, unless the grantor, who is the only person who may exercise the right of entry for condition broken, fails to do so. In the latter event, A's estate would determine naturally and B's interest would be allowed to take effect as a remainder.[3] An interest which operates so as to cut short a prior estate can take effect as an executory interest in a deed to uses, in a will and under a trust.

Furthermore, it is impossible for a remainder to exist after a fee simple whether the original fee is qualified or not, except that a remainder can exist after a base fee. A fee simple is the largest estate that a person can create. Having given it, a transferor has no power to limit a further estate after it by way of a remainder. Hence, a grant "to A for life, remainder to B in fee so long as he farms the land and, if he ceases to do so, to C in fee", gives no interest to C at all. C's interest could, however, take effect as an executory interest under a deed to uses, in a will and under a trust.[4]

It is clear from the definition of a remainder, given above, that if a grantor retains a reversion and subsequently assigns it to another person, the latter does not take a remainder, but the reversion. However, where the entire interest is disposed of to different persons by one instrument, the result is not always clear. Thus, where a testator devises a life estate in Blackacre to A and in the residuary clause gives the rest of his estate to B, it would seem that B takes a remainder interest in Blackacre. The same result should follow if the residuary clause is contained in a codicil rather than in a will, for the will and the codicil are, in effect, one document and take effect at the same time. Similarly, where a life interest is given to A in one instrument and the fee, following upon A's life interest, to B, in another, both instruments being delivered at the same time, B's interest is a remainder, since the two instruments take effect at the same time.[5]

---

[2]Co. Litt. 49a; Challis, pp. 77-9; 1 A.L.P., §4.25; Restatement, *Property*, §156(1).
[3]Megarry and Wade, pp. 185-6.
[4]Restatement, *Property*, §90.
[5]1 Preston, p. 90.

The difficulty with the case of a specific devise of a life estate followed by a residuary clause in the will arises because of *Egerton v. Massey*.[6] In that case the interest created by the residuary clause was called a reversion. The reason for doing so, however, was that the residuary clause followed after a contingent remainder in fee and the rule in *Loddington v. Kime*[7] provides that a vested remainder cannot be limited after a limitation in fee. Despite this case, most American writers treat an interest given by a residuary clause as a remainder.[8]

No practical difference arises, however, whether such an interest is called a reversion or a vested remainder today, although historically there was a difference in that there was tenure between the reversioner and the owner of a particular estate, while no tenure existed between the owner of a particular estate and the remainderman.[9]

1009.1   Classification of Remainders

Remainders may be classified in a variety of ways. The following, however, appear to be the more relevant:

(a) Remainders are either legal or equitable. If they are legal, they are subject to the legal remainder rules and to destruction. These matters are discussed below.[1] They are subject, in addition, to the rule in *Shelley's Case*[2] and the rule against perpetuities.[3] Equitable remainders are subject only to the latter two rules.

Legal remainders arise under common law conveyances, including modern grants. Formerly, they also arose under wills, but it is probable that all remainders arising under wills are now equitable.[4] Equitable remainders arise under a trust, or out of interests in property that were equitable at the time of their creation, such as an equity of redemption.[5]

(b) Remainders are either vested or contingent. They are vested if they are presently ready to take effect in possession or enjoyment upon the natural determination of the preceding estate or estates. A remainder is contingent if it is limited to an unborn or unascertained person, or if it is subject to a condition precedent.

Vested remainders may be further subdivided into three types, *viz.*, (i) those that are vested absolutely, (ii) those that are vested subject to partial divest-

---

[6](1857), 3 C.B. (N.S.) 338, 140 E.R. 771.
[7](1695), 1 Salk. 224, 91 E.R. 198.
[8]See, *e.g.*, Restatement, *Property*, §156; 1 A.L.P., §4.29; 1 Simes and Smith, §108.
[9]See §1006.1, *supra*.
§1009.1
[1]§§1009.2 and 1009.5, respectively.
[2](1581), 1 Co. Rep. 93 b, 76 E.R. 206. See §1009.6, *infra*.
[3]Discussed in ch. 11.
[4]This point is discussed in §1011, *infra*.
[5]This point is also dealt with in §1011, *infra*.

ment, and (iii) those that are subject to complete divestment. These subclasses have already been dealt with.[6]

1009.2 The Legal Remainder Rules

The legal remainder rules are a carry-over from feudal land law and are based on the importance that the law attached to seisin. While they are long since out of tune with modern conditions, they remain in force in common law Canada. Vested remainders do not present much difficulty in this context. Contingent remainders do. Indeed, for a long time, contingent remainders were regarded as void. Even after they were permitted, the question remained as to where the fee resided until the remainder vested. It was thought to be in abeyance, *in nubibus*, or *in gremio legis* until that time.[1] However, it has long been settled that until the contingent remainder vests, the grantor retains the reversion.

Rule 1: The first legal remainder rule requires that a remainder must be supported by a prior particular estate of freehold created by the same instrument. It cannot be allowed to spring up in the future after an hiatus because the fee must at all times repose in someone. This is because, at common law, livery of seisin was necessary to grant any freehold estate and the freehold could never be in abeyance, for there had to be someone at all times to perform the feudal services and against whom actions could be brought. Therefore, although a lease could be granted to take effect in the future, a conveyance which divested the freehold from the grantor had to vest it in the grantee immediately and not at a future time. Although both the above reasons for the rule have disappeared, the rule is still absolute.[2]

By reason of the fact that, necessarily, there can be no true remainder unless there is a preceding particular estate, it is said that the particular estate supports the remainder. Consequently, it follows that, usually, a remainder is defeated and void if the particular estate which supports it was void from the beginning, as where the limitation is to an unborn person so as to leave the freehold in abeyance pending his birth, or where the limitation offends the rule against perpetuities, or if the particular estate is defeated, as where it was an estate upon condition upon breach of which the grantor re-enters and the estate is forfeited.

Examples of interests void under this rule are the following grants:

"To A in fee at age 21" (A not yet being 21).
"To A's first son" (A having no son at the time of the grant).
"To A for life one year from date."

---

[6] §1004.1, *supra.*
§1009.2
[1] Megarry and Wade, p. 182.
[2] *Savill Brothers, Ltd. v. Bethell*, [1902] 2 Ch. 523 (C.A.).

Similarly, a conveyance "to A for 10 years, remainder to B in fee at age 21" (B not yet being 21), is void as to the remainder, since it is contingent and not supported by an estate of freehold. Similarly, in a limitation "to A for twenty-five years, remainder to his heirs in fee", the remainder is void as it is contingent and not supported by an estate of freehold.[3] However, a vested freehold remainder after a term of years is valid, for it operates so as to convey the immediate freehold to the remainderman, the seisin passing to him, subject to the term of years.[4]

Furthermore, a demise "to A for ten years when he attains age 21", where A has not yet reached that age, does not offend the rule, for the interest created is a leasehold and the seisin remains in the lessor.[5]

Rule 2: Once a grantor has disposed of the fee simple, he has nothing further to give under the quantitative theory of estates. Hence, the second rule stipulates that a fee simple in remainder after a fee is void.[6] Thus, where property was conveyed "to A in fee simple, with remainder to B if A should die without leaving children", it was held that the remainder after the fee simple was void and that A took an absolute fee simple.[7]

As appears from the foregoing example, the rule applies not only to the fee simple absolute, but also to qualified fees. Hence, the remainders in both the following grants are void. The first creates a determinable fee, the second a fee upon condition subsequent:

"To A in fee simple so long as London Bridge stands and when it falls down, to B in fee."

"To A in fee simple provided that he uses the land solely for residential purposes and if he ceases to do so, to B in fee."

An additional reason why the remainders in these two examples are void is that they purport to give the possibility of reverter in the first example and the right of entry for condition broken in the second, to a stranger. At common law these interests could only be reserved to the grantor and his heirs or to the testator's heirs under a will. They can now be limited to strangers under a will,[8] or under a deed to uses,[9] although not as remainders, but as executory interests.

Rule 3: The third rule voids remainders which operate so as to defeat the prior particular estate. An estate determines naturally if its limitation is allowed to run its proper course. It is determined unnaturally by the operation of a condition subsequent. The latter is not permitted.

---

[3]*Goodright v. Cornish* (1694), 1 Salk. 226, 91 E.R. 200; *White v. Summers*, [1908] 2 Ch. 256 at p. 265.
[4]*Boraston's Case* (1587), 3 Co. Rep. 19 a, 76 E.R. 668.
[5]1 Fearne, p. 285.
[6]*Musgrave v. Brooke* (1884), 26 Ch. D. 792.
[7]*Re Chauvin* (1920), 18 O.W.N. 178 (H.C.).
[8]*Ibid.*
[9]*Re Bayliss and Balfe* (1917), 38 O.L.R. 437, 35 D.L.R. 350 (H.C.).

Hence, a grant "to A for life or so long as he does not remarry, and then to B", gives B a valid remainder. The limitation is alternative, being cast in determinable form, and A's estate will determine either when he dies or when he remarries.

If, however, in the same example, A's life estate was subject to end on the happening of a condition subsequent, such as "provided he does not remarry", the remainder to B would be voidable, for the condition is apt to cut short or defeat A's estate unnaturally. B's remainder is avoided if the grantor or his heirs, the right being solely theirs,[10] exercise the right of entry on A's remarriage. If they fail to do so, B's remainder will be allowed to take effect on A's death, the natural determination of his life estate.[11]

Rule 4: The fourth common law remainder rule requires that a remainder vest during the continuance of the prior particular estate or at the moment that it determines. The existence of a gap or an abeyance of seisin between the prior particular estate and the next successive estate was abhorred by the common law and was the usual cause of invalidity and failure of a contingent remainder.[12]

There will be no gap, of course, if the remainder vests at the moment the prior estate determines. Hence, in a grant "to A and B for life, remainder in fee to the survivor", the remainder is contingent until the first of A and B dies, but vests in the survivor at that moment and is valid.

The limitation may be so worded as to stipulate for a gap, in which case it is void, as in a grant "to A for life, remainder to B when he reaches age 21 *after* A's death". On the other hand, if the gap may or may not occur at the time of the determination of the prior estate, the law permits the remainderman to wait and see until that time. If the remainder is then vested, it is allowed to take effect; if it is not, it is void. Hence, in a grant "to A for life, remainder to B when he marries" (B being a bachelor), B's remainder will be valid if he has married when A dies; if he has not, it will fail.

If the remainder is to a class, as in a grant "to A for life, remainder to such of his children as attain the age of 21", the remainder will be good as to those of A's children who are 21 at A's death. Children who qualify thereafter cannot take, even though they would not be excluded under the class closing rules.[13] Moreover, the interests of children who become 21 after the creation of the interest but before A's death, do not take effect as executory interests,

---

[10]See §1008.1, *supra.*

[11]Challis, p. 82; Megarry and Wade, pp. 185-6.

[12]*Cunliffe v. Brancker* (1876), 3 Ch. D. 393 (C.A.); *White v. Summers, supra,* footnote 3, at p. 265. And see Fetters, "Destructibility of Contingent Remainders", 21 Ark. L. Rev. 145 (1967).

[13]*Festing v. Allen* (1843), 12 M. & W. 279, 152 E.R. 1204; *Rhodes v. Whitehead* (1865), 2 Dr. & Sm. 532, 62 E.R. 722; *Brackenbury v. Gibbons* (1876), 2 Ch. D. 417; *Re Lechmere and Lloyd* (1881), 18 Ch. D. 524 at pp. 528-9; *Miles v. Jarvis* (1883), 24 Ch. D. 633; *Re Bourne* (1887), 56 L.T. 388; *Dean v. Dean,* [1891] 3 Ch. D. 150; 1 Preston, p. 244; 1 Fearne, pp. 312-15; 2 Fearne, §§702-5.

but as remainders.[14] The interests of those who are 21 at the creation of the interest are vested subject to partial divestment in favour of those who qualify subsequently.[15]

Since a freehold cannot, at common law, be limited to commence in the future and a remainder must vest not later than the end of the preceding estate, there cannot, at common law, be desultory limitations, that is, limitations creating estates to arise at intervals, not continuously, but with gaps between them.[16]

1009.3 Vested Remainders

A remainder is vested if the person entitled to it will obtain possession of the land upon the happening of no other contingency than the natural expiration of the prior estate. Thus, where a testator devised land to his wife for life during widowhood and, after her death, to his son upon condition that the son pay certain sums within a stated period for the benefit of others, it was held that the condition was a condition subsequent and the son had a vested remainder, because he would be entitled to possession on the death or re-marriage of the widow, although it was subject to being divested upon non-fulfilment of the condition.[1]

In other words, a remainder limited to take effect automatically upon the expiration of the prior particular estate is a vested remainder because a present estate is conferred although it is not to be enjoyed until that future time. The estate granted by way of remainder does not depend for its existence upon any contingency, even though the time when it will come into possession may be uncertain when the estate is created. The remainder may actually end or be divested before the preceding estate ends and thus never come into possession, but that possibility does not prevent it from being vested. On the other hand, a contingent remainder is one limited to depend for its existence upon the happening of some event, or the performance of some condition, which may never happen, or be performed, until after the preceding estate ends.[2]

---

[14]*Re Lechmere and Lloyd, supra,* footnote 13; 1 Preston, p. 244. It has, however, been argued that the interests of those who qualify later should be regarded as executory interests. The reason for the argument is that as the rule against perpetuities does not generally apply to vested interests, but does apply to interests which are vested subject to partial divestment, *i.e.,* class gifts, it would be appropriate to call the interests of class members who qualify after the creation of the interests as executory to which, of course, the rule applies. See 1 A.L.P., §4.34; 1 Simes and Smith, §114.

[15]*Oates d. Hatterley v. Jackson* (1742), 2 Str. 1172, 93 E.R. 1107; *Doe d. Comberbach v. Perryn* (1789), 3 T.R. 484, 100 E.R. 690.

[16]*Corbet's Case* (1600), 1 Co. Rep. 83 b at p. 87 b, 76 E.R. 187; *The Prince's Case* (1606), 8 Co. Rep. 1 a at pp. 13 b, 17 a, 77 E.R. 481; *Atkins v. Mountague* (1671), 1 Chan. Cas. 214, 22 E.R. 768; Challis, p. 113.

§1009.3

[1]*Lundy v. Maloney* (1861), 11 U.C.C.P. 143.

[2]1 Fearne, p. 3.

The present capacity of taking effect in possession if the possession were to become vacant, and not the certainty that the possession will become vacant before the estate limited in remainder determines, universally distinguishes a vested remainder from one that is contingent.[3] The distinction is simply illustrated by several of the leading cases.

If the land is granted "to A for a term of years, remainder to B in fee simple", the remainder is vested because B is immediately seised of the freehold subject to the term,[4] the owner of a freehold being seised in deed when a lessee is in actual possession of the land, as the lessee's possession is credited to the freeholder and supports his seisin.[5]

Similarly, if land were granted "to A for a term of years, remainder to B for life, remainder to C in fee simple", both remainders would be vested, as B would be entitled to possession immediately upon the expiration of the term of years and C would be entitled to possession immediately upon the death of B and, if B died before the end of the term, C would be entitled to possession at the end of the term.

If, however, the limitation were "to A for a term of years if he so long lives and, after his death, remainder to B", the remainder is contingent because B would not be entitled to possession at the end of the term if A still lived.[6]

Again, if a life estate is limited to three persons in succession, the last would get an immediate life estate on the death of the first two and a postponed life estate on the death of the first before the second[7] but, if there is a devise to one person for life with remainder to the children of another person if he leaves any surviving him, the remainder is contingent during the latter's life.[8]

If an estate given in remainder by will is to take effect at the end of the preceding estate, it vests at the testator's death and, if the person entitled to it dies before he attains actual possession, his personal representatives are entitled to claim the remainder.

Thus, where, after the death of the testator's widow, land was devised to his daughter but, if she did not come to live on it, it was to be rented, and the rents paid to her, the land to go to her heirs afterwards, it was held that these words did not make the devise contingent and the daughter took a vested interest.[9] Similarly, where a testator gave to his widow the use of personalty, farm and buildings for her support and the maintenance of his children and provided that, after her death, the whole of his realty and personalty was to be

---

[3]*Ibid.*, p. 216.
[4]*De Grey v. Richardson* (1747), 3 Atk. 469, 26 E.R. 1069.
[5]*Bushby v. Dixon* (1824), 3 B. & C. 298, 107 E.R. 744.
[6]*Boraston's Case* (1587), 3 Co. Rep. 19 a at p. 20 a, 76 E.R. 668; *Beverley v. Beverley* (1689), 2 Vern. 131, 23 E.R. 692.
[7]*Denn d. Radclyffe v. Bagshaw* (1796), 6 T.R. 512, 101 E.R. 675; *Doe d. Gilman v. Elvey* (1803), 4 East 313, 102 E.R. 851; *Cole v. Sewell* (1848), 2 H.L.C. 186, 9 E.R. 1062.
[8]*Price v. Hall* (1868), L.R. 5 Eq. 399.
[9]*Hamilton v. McKellar* (1878), 26 Gr. 110.

equally divided among his six children, the children took a vested remainder.[10]

Where a testator gave to his widow a life estate, followed by a joint life estate to his son A and his daughter M and the survivor of them and provided that, after the death of the widow and such son and daughter, the real property was to be divided into three equal portions, one of which was to go to the "family" of his son J, another to the "family" of his son G and the third to the family of his daughter, it was held that "family" meant children only, that the children took *per capita* and that their estates were vested remainders subject to the life estates of the widow, the son A and the daughter M.[11] Similarly, where a testator gave to his widow the use of his farm until his son J attained the age of 21 years when he was to get the east half of the farm, but was to support the widow and his four sisters until they became of age or married and provided that the real estate was to belong to the "family" as long as any of them were alive and was to remain the property of his son's heirs, it was held that "family" meant children and that the five children of the testator took life estates as tenants in common with a vested remainder in J in fee simple under the rule in *Shelley's Case*.[12]

In *Re Branton*,[13] the testator devised land to his widow during her widowhood and, in the event of her remarrying, to his two daughters. It was held that the devise to the daughters was not dependent upon the contingency of the widow's remarriage, but took effect upon her death, because the devise to her had the same effect as if it were to her for life if she should so long remain a widow, so the daughters took a vested remainder to take effect in possession upon the death or remarriage of the widow. Similarly, in *Re Shattuck*,[14] the testator devised all his real and personal property to his wife so long as she remained his widow and provided that, on her death or remarriage, the realty and personalty were to be sold and the proceeds divided among his younger sons. It was held that the interests of the sons vested on the death of the testator so that the interest of one son who died in the lifetime of the widow passed by his will to his executors.

A devise after the death of the life tenant, subject to the condition that, if the value of the property exceeds a certain sum, the property is to be sold and the sum paid to the devisee, gives the devisee a vested remainder.[15] Similarly, where property was devised to trustees, the income to be paid to the widow during her life and after her death, to a daughter, the daughter's interest was vested on the death of the testator and was transmissible notwithstanding that she died during the life of the widow.[16]

---

[10]*Town v. Borden* (1882), 1 O.R. 327 (H.C.J.).
[11]*Harkness v. Harkness* (1905), 9 O.L.R. 705 (H.C.J.).
[12]*McKinnon v. Spence* (1909), 20 O.L.R. 57 (H.C.J.).
[13](1910), 20 O.L.R. 642 (H.C.J.).
[14](1912), 3 O.W.N. 593, 1 D.L.R. 258 (H.C.J.); *Re Uniacke*, [1934] 2 D.L.R. 413 (N.S.S.C.).
[15]*Yorkshire & Can. Trust Ltd. v. Morton*, [1926] 4 D.L.R. 887, [1926] 3 W.W.R. 370 (B.C.C.A.).
[16]*Fewster v. Clements* (1914), 7 W.W.R. 843 (B.C.S.C. in Chambers).

A remainder may be vested even though there is a contingent remainder between it and the particular estate, as where there is a limitation to A for life, remainder to an unborn person in tail, remainder to C in fee simple, in which case, C has a vested estate but, upon the birth of the tenant in tail, the latter has a vested remainder which is lawful because it is less than a fee simple.[17] If the contingent remainder is in fee simple, however, no subsequent interest can be vested, although there may be alternative contingent remainders after the particular estate.[18]

Where A conveyed to B in fee, but reserved a life interest to herself and provided that if B should predecease her, the land should revest in A, it was held that B's estate was a vested remainder subject to divestment, not contingent.[19]

1009.4 Contingent Remainders

A contingent remainder is not an estate, but merely an interest in land, for it is not yet vested, and may never vest. For this reason it was not assignable at common law. Modern legislation permits such interests to be assigned and devised however.[1]

A contingent remainder is one which is either limited to an unborn or unascertained person, or to an ascertained person on an uncertain event, that is, upon a condition precedent.[2]

Fearne classified contingent remainders into the following four classes:

(1) those depending entirely on a contingent determination of the preceding estate;

(2) those in which the contingency is independent of the determination of the preceding estate;

(3) those in which the contingency is certain to happen but may not happen until after the determination of the particular estate;

(4) those limited to a person who is not ascertained or is not in being.[3]

An illustration of the first class of remainders is a limitation to A until the happening of a specified event which is not certain to happen and, on the

---

[17]1 Fearne, p. 223.
[18]*Ibid.*, pp. 225, 229, 373; *Loddington v. Kime* (1695), 1 Salk. 224, 91 E.R. 198, in which case there was a devise to A for life with remainder in fee to his male issue if he have such issue but, if he have no male issue, remainder to B in fee, this second remainder not being subsequent to, but alternative to, the first; *Doe d. Davy v. Burnsall* (1794), 6 T.R. 30 at pp. 34, 35, 101 E.R. 419; *Burnsall v. Davy* (1798), 1 B. & P. 215, 126 E.R. 867; *Doe d. Planner v. Scudamore* (1800), 2 B. & P. 289, 126 E.R. 1287; *Doe d. Gilman v. Elvey* (1803), 4 East 313, 102 E.R. 851; *Re White and Hindle's Contract* (1877), 7 Ch. D. 201.
[19]*Hiltz v. Langille* (1959), 18 D.L.R. (2d) 464, 42 M.P.R. 333 (N.S.S.C.).
§1009.4
[1]See §1012, *infra.*
[2]2 Bl. Comm. 169.
[3]1 Fearne, p. 5.

happening of the event, to B in fee simple.[4] In that case, A has an estate until his death or the happening of the event, whichever first occurs, and B's remainder is contingent on the happening of the event during A's life. Obviously, a remainder of this class cannot vest during the existence of the particular estate because the contingent event which determines the particular estate immediately vests the remainder and it cannot vest at all unless the event happens. Remainders of the other three classes can vest during the existence of the particular estate.

In the second class of remainders, the remainder will not take effect until the happening of the contingency, whether or not the preceding estate comes to an end. An illustration of this class of remainders is a limitation "to A for life, remainder to B for life and, if B dies before A, remainder to C for life".[5] Here, the remainder of C is contingent on B dying before A, is independent of the determination of A's life estate and can never take effect if B survives A.[6] Again, if there is a devise "to A for life with remainder to the children of B if he leaves any surviving him", the remainder of the children is contingent during the life of B although A's life estate ends.[7]

A testator devised property in trust for his widow during her life or widowhood and, on her death or second marriage, his son Thomas "if he be then living" was to have a particular lot. He also devised other lands to other children in fee and directed that all devises were to take effect on the death or marriage of the widow and not sooner. He made other provisions and provided that, if any of the children died without issue before coming into his or her share, the share of such child was to go to the survivors and their issue. Thomas died unmarried before his mother. It was held that the interest devised to him was contingent upon his surviving his mother.[8]

If the determination of a life estate marks the event on which the remainder vests, it vests in interest and possession at the same time. Thus, if there is a limitation "to A for life with remainder to B in fee if he survives A", the remainder is contingent during their joint lives but, if A dies first, the remainder vests in interest and possession at once.[9] If there is a limitation to two persons as tenants in common for their joint lives with a remainder to the survivor, the latter's remainder vests in interest and possession on the death of the other.[10]

A similar illustration is provided by a residuary gift to be converted on a contingency. Where a testator provided that the residue of his estate was to be held by his trustees in trust for the joint benefit of his widow and son during their lives but, if the son predeceased his mother without leaving lawful issue,

---

[4]*Boraston's Case* (1587), 3 Co. Rep. 19 a at p. 20 a, 76 E.R. 668.
[5]*Ibid.*
[6]1 Fearne, pp. 6, 7.
[7]*Price v. Hall* (1868), L.R. 5 Eq. 399.
[8]*Merchants Bank of Canada v. Keefer* (1885), 13 S.C.R. 515.
[9]*Doe d. Planner v. Scudamore* (1800), 2 B. & P. 289, 126 E.R. 1287.
[10]*Whitby v. Von Luedecke*, [1906] 1 Ch. 783.

the estate was to be converted into cash upon the death of the widow and divided among certain legatees, it was held that, upon the death of the son before the mother without issue, the estate vested in possession in the widow and the contingent interest of the legatees became a vested remainder to be enjoyed upon the death of the widow.[11]

An illustration of the third class of remainders in which the contingency is certain to happen but may not happen until after the particular estate ends, is a limitation "to A for life and, after the death of B, remainder to C in fee simple". Here, B's death is certain, but it may not occur until after the death of A. Also, if the limitation is "to A for a term of years if he so long lives and, after his death, to B in fee", B's remainder is contingent because, if A survives the term, it is not ready to vest in possession.[12] In such a case, however, if the term of years were so long that A could not by any reasonable probability survive it, B's remainder is treated as vested, a term of at least eighty years being held to be sufficient for such purpose, but it must be at least eighty years regardless of the age of the tenant.[13]

The defect of this third class of remainders is that they may never take effect because although the contingency is certain to happen, it may happen too late, that is, after the determination of the particular estate which is necessary to support it.[14]

An illustration of the fourth class of remainders, in which the person to take the remainder is uncertain, is a limitation "to A for life, remainder to the heirs of B". Here, there can be no heirs of B until he dies, because no one can be the heir of a living person and consequently the remainder is contingent until B's death.[15] Again, if a remainder is limited to the first son of a living person who, as yet, has no son, the remainder is contingent.[16] It is common to speak of a contingent remainder in such a case, although it is not one, for until a son is born there can be no legal relations between the grantor and that son, and hence, there can be no future interest.

If there is a limitation to several persons for their lives with remainder in fee simple to the heirs of the survivor, the life tenants are joint tenants for their lives and the survivor has a contingent remainder in fee simple.[17]

Where there are two successive remainders in fee simple of which the second is limited in such a way as not to divest the first, but as an alternative limitation, the general rule is that both are contingent remainders. They are called

---

[11]*Chipman v. Ross; Re Estate of Dunlap* (1918), 52 N.S.R. 129.
[12]*Boraston's Case, supra,* footnote 4; *Beverley v. Beverley* (1689), 2 Vern. 131, 23 E.R. 692.
[13]1 Fearne, pp. 20, 21; *Weale v. Lower* (1672), Pollex. 54 at p. 67, 86 E.R. 509; *Beverley v. Beverley, supra,* footnote 12.
[14]1 Fearne, pp. 7, 8; Challis, pp. 128 *et seq.*
[15]*Challoners and Bowyer's Case* (1587), 2 Leon. 70, 74 E.R. 366; *Boraston's Case, supra,* footnote 4; *Archer's Case* (1597), 1 Co. Rep. 66 b, 76 E.R. 146.
[16]1 Fearne, p. 9.
[17]*Quarm v. Quarm,* [1892] 1 Q.B. 184.

alternative contingent remainders or contingent remainders upon a double aspect.

Thus, in a grant "to A for life, remainder to such of A's children as shall attain the age of 21, and for want of such issue, to B in fee", the remainders of A's children and B are contingent.[18] A's children's interest cannot be regarded as vested, for then B's contingent remainder in fee would operate so as to defeat a vested fee simple which the law does not permit;[19] moreover, it would be a fee upon a fee and would be struck down under the second common law remainder rule.[20]

In the case of wills, however, there is an exception to the general rule under what is known as the rule in *Phipps v. Ackers*,[21] or the rule in *Edwards v. Hammond*.[22] Under this rule, where the gift over is on death under age or some other contingency, such as failure to survive the life tenant,[23] the first gift will *prima facie* be construed as vested subject to divestment and the second will then take effect as an executory interest if the first is in fact divested. However, for this rule to operate, the form of the limitation must be so worded as to provide for a condition subsequent. Thus, if the gift is "to A for life, remainder to B, but if B fails to reach the age of 21, then to C", the rule will apply. On the other hand, if the gift is "to A for life, remainder to B if he reach the age of 21, and if he does not reach that age to C", the rule will not apply, for the condition as to age is a condition precedent, incorporated into the limitation to B.[24]

1009.5 Destructibility of Contingent Remainders

(a) Generally

Contingent remainders are vulnerable in two respects. First, if they do not vest before the end of the prior particular estate, they fail or are destroyed naturally. Secondly, they were and, in some situations, still are, subject to artificial destruction.

There is one exception to natural destruction, known as the rule in *Reeve v. Long*.[1] This rule states that if an estate be limited by will to a person for life with remainder to his child and he dies before the child is born but while it is *en ventre sa mère*, and it is subsequently born, such posthumous child is

---

18*Festing v. Allen* (1843), 12 M. & W. 279, 152 E.R. 1204.
19*Loddington v. Kime* (1695), 1 Salk. 224, 91 E.R. 198; *Doe d. Davy v. Burnsall* (1794), 6 T.R. 30 at pp. 34, 35, 101 E.R. 419; *Burnsall v. Davy* (1798), 1 B. & P. 215, 126 E.R. 867; *Doe d. Planner v. Scudamore, supra*, footnote 9; *Doe d. Gilman v. Elvey* (1803), 4 East 313, 102 E.R. 851; *Re White and Hindle's Contract* (1877), 7 Ch. D. 201.
20See §1009.2, *supra*.
21(1842), 9 Cl. & Fin. 583, 8 E.R. 539.
22(1695), 3 Lev. 132, 83 E.R. 614.
23*Finch v. Lane* (1870), L.R. 10 Eq. 501.
24On the rule in *Phipps v. Ackers*, see further §1004.3(d), *supra*.
§1009.5
1(1694), 1 Salk. 227, 91 E.R. 202.

treated as being born in the father's lifetime so as to make the remainder vest in time.

By the *Statute of Posthumous Children*[2] the above rule was extended to deeds. In Ontario, the *Conveyancing and Law of Property Act*[3] provides that, where any estate is, by marriage or other settlement, limited in remainder to, or to the use of, the first or other son or sons of the body of any person lawfully begotten, or to or for the use of a daughter lawfully begotten, with any remainder over to or to the use of any other person, any son or daughter lawfully begotten and born after the death of his or her father takes the estate limited in the same manner as if born during the lifetime of the father, although there may be no estate limited to trustees after the death of the father to preserve the contingent remainder until the son or daughter is born. Section 37 of the British Columbia *Infants Act*[4] contains a similar provision. In the other provinces, there does not appear to be a similar specific statutory provision, nor does there appear to be legislation inconsistent with the above-mentioned Imperial Act of 1699, which, therefore, may still apply.

Artificial destruction arises where the prior particular estate is determined by one of the following methods before its natural determination. When they occur, any contingent remainders dependent upon them are destroyed. Most of the following methods have been abolished by statute as will appear below.

(i) Forfeiture

Formerly, an estate could be forfeited in a variety of ways, including treason and tortious conveyances. Forfeiture for treason has been abolished in Canada.[5] Tortious feoffments, that is, those in which the owner of a lesser estate was able to convey a fee simple, have also been abolished.[6] Certain types of forfeiture remain, however, namely, forfeiture for mortmain, charitable uses, breach of condition and in respect of undisposed-of assets of a dissolved corporation.

(ii) Disseisin

At common law, if the owner of a life estate was dispossessed, he retained a right of entry as well as a right of action against the disseisor. The first-mentioned right would continue to support contingent remainders. However, when the dispossessed owner died, five or more years after being dispossessed, his right of entry was gone because the "descent cast", that is, the descent or casting of the land upon the heir of the trespasser, "tolled", that is, took away,

---

[2]10 & 11 Will. 3, c. 16 (1699).
[3]R.S.O. 1980, c. 90, s. 45.
[4]R.S.B.C. 1979, c. 196.
[5]*Criminal Code*, S.C. 1892, c. 29, s. 965; see now R.S.C. 1970, c. C-34, s. 5(1)(*b*).
[6]See, *e.g.*, *Real Property Act*, 8 & 9 Vict., c. 106, s. 4 (1845); *Conveyancing and Law of Property Act*, R.S.O. 1980, c. 90, s. 3; *Real Property Limitation Act*, 3 & 4 Will. 4, c. 27, ss. 4, 5, 39 (1833); *Real Property Act*, R.S.P.E.I. 1974, c. R-4, s. 9; *Property Act*, R.S.N.B. 1973, c. P-19, s. 11(2).

the right of entry. Thereafter, any contingent remainders dependent upon the life estate were destroyed. Descent cast has been abolished by statute.[7]

(iii) Surrender

The surrender by a life tenant of his estate to a vested remainderman, had the effect of ending the life estate since it would merge into the remainder. Accordingly, any intervening contingent remainder would be destroyed. Thus, in a grant "to A for life, remainder to B's first son for life, remainder to C in fee", where B had no son as yet, the surrender by A of his life estate to C would destroy the contingent remainder limited to B's first son.

(iv) Merger

While this operates in much the same way as a surrender, the difference between merger and surrender is that only the owner of a lesser estate can surrender it to the owner of a greater. Merger arises whenever two different estates vest in the same person in the same right. Thus, in a grant "to A for life, remainder to B's first son for life, remainder to C in fee", if C sold his interest to A, the two estates would merge and the intervening contingent remainder would be destroyed.

There were two exceptions to the rule. First, an estate tail could not merge into another fee tail or into a fee simple. *De Donis Conditionalibus*[8] was thought to prevent it in that it protected the rights of the issue of the tenant in tail.[9] However, although there was no merger, the tenant in tail could, of course, bar the entail to get around this problem.

Secondly, where the life estate and the next vested estate were created in the same person by the same instrument, they merged, but not so as to destroy contingent remainders, for otherwise, the grantor's intention would be completely and immediately nullified. Hence, where a testator devised "to A for life, then to B, if B marries, residue to A", B's contingent remainder was not destroyed. However, if A sold both his estates to C, his interest would be destroyed.[10]

(v) Disclaimer

This arises where land is conveyed or devised to a person who refuses it. When a person disclaims a vested estate, it passes to the person next entitled and thus a disclaimer will destroy any contingent remainders dependent upon the disclaimed gift.[11]

---

[7]*Limitations Act*, R.S.O. 1980, c. 240, s. 10; expected soon to be replaced by new legislation, see §3106.21. The other provincial statutes of limitation do not appear to deal with this point, but the English legislation would have been received in the Western provinces and the Territories.

[8]13 Edw. 1, cc. 1-3 (1285).

[9]*Cf. Conveyancing and Law of Property Act*, R.S.O. 1980, c. 90, s. 10.

[10]*Egerton v. Massey* (1857), 3 C.B. (N.S.) 338, 140 E.R. 771.

[11]*Re Sir Walter Scott; Scott v. Scott*, [1911] 2 Ch. 374.

(b) Trustees to preserve contingent remainders

In order to prevent artificial destruction of contingent remainders, it became the practice in making settlements to appoint trustees and vest in them the remainder to commence after the determination of the life estate otherwise than by death. This protected the contingent remainders because the balance of the life estate would vest in possession in the trustees as a particular estate. A contingent remainder was not thus subject to being defeated by forfeiture, surrender or merger if it was an equitable interest, as where the legal estate was vested in trustees,[12] or in a mortgagee.[13]

(c) Statutory abolition of certain types of artificial destruction

In addition to the statutory abolition of tortious feoffments and descent cast, referred to above,[14] artificial destruction by forfeiture, surrender or merger has been abolished in some jurisdictions following the English *Real Property Act*.[15]

In Ontario, the *Conveyancing and Law of Property Act*[16] provides that every contingent remainder shall be capable of taking effect notwithstanding the determination by forfeiture, surrender or merger of any preceding estate of freehold.

In New Brunswick the *Property Act*[17] makes a similar provision.

(d) Abolition of natural destruction

The English *Contingent Remainders Act*[18] purports to ensure against failure of contingent remainders by the natural determination of the particular estate before they could vest, by providing that every contingent remainder created by any instrument or will executed after August 2, 1877, which would have been valid as a springing or shifting use or executory devise or other limitation if it did not have a sufficient estate to support it as a contingent remainder shall, in the event of the particular estate determining before the contingent remainder vests, be capable of taking effect as a springing or shifting use or executory devise or other executory limitation.

In Prince Edward Island similar provision is made by the *Real Property Act*,[19] but no other provinces have similar legislation.

The effect of this legislation is not entirely clear. It clearly has the effect

---

[12]*Berry v. Berry* (1878), 7 Ch. D. 657; *Abbiss v. Burney*; *Re Finch* (1881), 17 Ch. D. 211 at p. 229 (C.A.); *Marshall v. Gingell* (1882), 21 Ch. D. 790; *Re Brooke*; *Brooke v. Brooke*, [1894] 1 Ch. 43.
[13]*Astley v. Micklethwait* (1880), 15 Ch. D. 59.
[14]Footnotes 5 and 6, *supra*.
[15]8 & 9 Vict., c. 106 (1845), s. 8.
[16]R.S.O. 1980, c. 90, s. 35.
[17]R.S.N.B. 1973, c. P-19, s. 9. The English Act would have been received in the Western provinces and the Territories.
[18]40 & 41 Vict., c. 33 (1877).
[19]R.S.P.E.I. 1974, c. R-4, s. 13.

of reversing the rule in *Purefoy v. Rogers*,[20] which is dealt with below.[21] It does not, on its face, however, apply to a conveyance which does not employ a use. Nor does it specifically apply to class gifts in respect of the interests of members of a class who qualify after the determination of the particular estate.[22] Nevertheless, it has generally been assumed that the Act abolishes natural destruction in all cases.[23] These difficulties have lost their relevance in England since the *Law of Property Act*[24] converted all legal remainders into equitable interests, which are not capable of destruction.

The legislation does not save a contingent remainder which would be void for any other reason, such as perpetuity. Nor does it accelerate the vesting of contingent remainders. It merely allows them to take effect in accordance with their terms and until they in fact vest, the grantor or testator has a reversion.[25]

In jurisdictions in which the Act has not been enacted, it is thus necessary to convey land in trust for persons whose interests are subject to a contingency to prevent their natural destruction. Indeed, trustees to preserve contingent remainders are still necessary to prevent artificial destruction by disclaimer. Since a disclaimer occurs so rarely, however, that device has fallen into disuse.

1009.6 The Rule in Shelley's Case

(a) Generally

As the foregoing sections indicate, the particular estate and the remainders which follow it are separate estates, the person entitled to each estate or interest taking it directly under the limitation to him. A person thus taking an estate or interest by direct limitation in remainder is said to take it by purchase, the word signifying any method of acquiring an interest other than by inheritance. By a classic rule, however, known as the rule in *Shelley's Case*,[1] if a freehold estate is granted or devised to a person and, by the same instrument, an estate is limited by way of remainder to his heirs or the heirs of his body, whether the remainder immediately follows his estate or follows an intermediate remainder, the word "heirs" is construed as a word of limitation and not of purchase and he takes an estate in fee simple or in fee tail according to the description of the heirs. Thus, if a life estate is limited to him with remainder to his heirs or the heirs of his body, the remainder does not go directly to the

---

20(1671), 2 Wms. Saund. 380, 85 E.R. 1181.
21See §1010.3, *infra*.
22*Re Robson; Douglass v. Douglass*, [1916] 1 Ch. 116 at pp. 121-2.
23Cheshire, p. 308; Megarry and Wade, p. 197.
2415 & 16 Geo. 5, c. 20 (1925), s. 1.
25*Re Sir Walter Scott; Scott v. Scott*, [1911] 2 Ch. 374. As to the acceleration of contingent remainders generally, see Prichard, "Acceleration and Contingent Remainders", 32 Can. L.J. 246 (1973).
§1009.6
1(1581), 1 Co. Rep. 93 b, 76 E.R. 206.

heirs but is joined to his life estate to give him one enlarged estate of inheritance in fee simple or in fee tail, as the case may be, just as if the estate were limited to him and his heirs or the heirs of his body.

If a life estate limited to a person is immediately followed by a remainder to his heirs or the heirs of his body, the life estate and the remainder immediately join to give him an estate of inheritance in possession and an estate in fee simple or fee tail is said to be executed in him. If a vested remainder is interposed by the instrument between his life estate and the remainder to his heirs, the latter does not go to the heirs, but does not join with the life estate to give him one estate either; he has two separate estates, one for life in possession and an ultimate estate of inheritance in remainder following the intermediate vested remainder.[2]

If the intermediate remainder is a contingent remainder, his life estate and his ultimate remainder join for the time being, but they open up to let in the contingent remainder if and when it vests.[3]

If the remainder to which the holder of the particular estate is entitled is a contingent remainder, he holds two separate estates and the two do not join until the contingent remainder vests.[4]

(b) Both estates must be legal or equitable

The rule applies to both deeds and wills and to both legal and equitable estates or interests,[5] but the estate of the ancestor and that of his heirs must either be both legal or both equitable.[6]

The facts in *Re Romanes and Smith*[7] sufficiently illustrate the distinction. In that case, a testator devised land:

> ... to hold the same in trust for the use and benefit of my son William during his lifetime, and after the death of my son William in trust for his heirs, issue of his body, until the youngest of said heirs shall become of age, and then to convey it to said heirs, the children of my said son William taking equal shares, and the child or children of any deceased child of my said son to take their parent's share in equal proportions.

---

[2]*Coulson v. Coulson* (1740), 2 Str. 1125, 93 E.R. 1074; *Van Grutten v. Foxwell*, [1897] A.C. 658 at p. 677 (H.L.).

[3]1 Fearne, p. 37; *Bowles's (Lewis) Case* (1616), 11 Co. Rep. 79 b at p. 80 a, 77 E.R. 1252.

[4]Co. Litt., 378b; 1 Fearne, p. 33; see *Curtis v. Price* (1805), 12 Ves. Jun. 89, 33 E.R. 35.

[5]*Van Grutten v. Foxwell, supra,* footnote 2; *Re Romanes and Smith* (1880), 8 P.R. (Ont.) 323; *Re Hooper* (1914), 7 O.W.N. 104 (H.C.).

[6]*Tipping v. Cozens* (1695), 1 Raym. Ld. 33, 91 E.R. 918; *Jones v. Lord Say and Seal* (1728), 1 Eq. Cas. Abr. 383, 21 E.R. 1119; *Venables v. Morris* (1797), 7 T.R. 342, 101 E.R. 1009; *Ireson v. Pearman* (1825), 3 B. & C. 799, 107 E.R. 930; *Adams v. Adams* (1845), 6 Q.B. 860, 115 E.R. 324; *Cooke v. Blake* (1847), 1 Exch. 220, 154 E.R. 93; *Collier v. McBean* (1865), L.R. 1 Ch. 81; *Richardson v. Harrison* (1885), 16 Q.B.D. 85 (C.A.), at p. 104; *Re Fanning*, [1934] O.W.N. 397 (C.A.); Anderson "The Application of the Rule in Shelley's Case to Trusts", 15 S.C.L.R. 800 (1963).

[7]*Supra*, footnote 5, at p. 323.

It was held by Proudfoot, V.C., that the rule in *Shelley's Case* did not apply because the trustees had no active duties to perform during the son's lifetime so that, under the *Statute of Uses*,[8] the son acquired the legal estate and the interest of his heirs was merely equitable. If the trustees had had active duties in the son's lifetime, the *Statute of Uses* would not have operated. The trustees would have had the legal estate, both the son and his heirs would have had equitable interests, and the rule in *Shelley's Case* would have operated to give the son an equitable estate in fee simple.[9]

(c) An estate of freehold

The ancestor's estate must be an estate of freehold, so that the rule does not apply if the estate of the ancestor is merely a term of years.[10] It does apply where the estate is an estate *pur autre vie*,[11] or where the estate is not expressly limited but merely arises by implication, as on the construction of a will.[12]

The rule applies even if the estate limited to the ancestor may be determinable in his lifetime, so that he can have no heir on such determination because there can be no heirs of a living person.[13]

Furthermore, both the life estate and the remainder must be gifts of real property. If the life estate is real property, but the remainder is a gift of the proceeds of sale of the real property, the rule does not apply.[14]

(d) The estates must arise under the same instrument

The rule does not apply unless the estate of the ancestor and the remainder to his heirs both arise under the same instrument because, otherwise, the limitation to the heirs would not be a remainder; however, a will and a codicil are treated as the same instrument for the purpose of the rule.[15] An estate subsequently limited in the exercise of a power of appointment contained in the instrument is said to be treated as arising under the instrument.[16] If the ancestor is given a power of appointment in the instrument and he is under

---

[8]27 Hen. 8, c. 10 (1535).

[9]*Cf.* to the same effect *Re Rynard* (1979), 27 O.R. (2d) 619, 107 D.L.R. (3d) 443, 6 E.T.R. 115 (H.C.J.), affd on other grounds 31 O.R. (2d) 257, 118 D.L.R. (3d) 530 (C.A.).

[10]*Tipping v. Piggot* (1713), 1 Eq. Ca. Abr. 385, 21 E.R. 1120; *Harris v. Barnes* (1768), 4 Burr. 2157, 98 E.R. 125.

[11]*Low v. Burron* (1734), 3 P. Wms. 262, 24 E.R. 1055; *Forster v. Forster* (1741), 2 Atk. 259, 26 E.R. 560.

[12]*Hayes d. Foorde v. Foorde* (1770), 2 Bl. W. 698, 96 E.R. 410; 1 Fearne, pp. 41 *et seq.*

[13]*Merrel v. Rumsey* (1677), Raym. T. 126, 83 E.R. 68; *Curtis v. Price* (1805), 12 Ves. Jun. 89 at p. 99, 33 E.R. 35.

[14]*Re Rynard, supra*, footnote 9.

[15]*Hayes d. Foorde v. Foorde, supra*, footnote 12.

[16]1 Fearne, p. 74; *Venables v. Morris, supra*, footnote 6, at p. 348.

no obligation to exercise it, the existence of the power does not exclude the rule.[17]

It is immaterial whether the testator used the expression "on the determination of the life estate", or "on the determination of that estate", or "on the determination of the life" or "on the death of the tenant for life".[18]

(e) The rule is a rule of law

The rule is a rule of law and not a rule laid down to give effect to the grantor's or testator's express or presumed intention,[19] but the premises for the application of the rule must exist and it is always a question whether the language of the gift after the life estate, properly construed, is such as to embrace the whole line of heirs or heirs of the body or issue, and that question must be determined apart from the rule, according to the ordinary rules of construction.[20]

(f) Matters of construction

In *Van Grutten v. Foxwell*,[21] Lord Macnaghten said:

> ... the question now in every case must be whether the expression requiring exposition, be it "heirs" or "heirs of the body," or any other expression which may have the like meaning, is used as the designation of a particular individual or a particular class of objects, or whether, on the other hand, it includes the whole line of succession capable of inheriting.

Lord Davey said:

> Wherever, therefore, the Court comes to the conclusion that the gift over includes the whole line of heirs, general or special, the rule at once applies, and an estate of inheritance is executed in the ancestor or tenant for life, even though the testator

---

[17]*Re Hawkins* (1920), 19 O.W.N. 18 (H.C.), in which case a conveyance was made to Peter Hawkins, his heirs and assigns, to have and to hold unto the grantee for life and, on his death, to have and to hold unto such of his children as he might by will appoint and, in default of such appointment, to have and to hold to such of his heirs as would be entitled to the same by operation of law, it being held that he immediately took a fee simple; *Re Hooper* (1914), 7 O.W.N. 104 (H.C.); *Re Gracey* (1931), 41 O.W.N. 1 (C.A.).

[18]*Tunis v. Passmore* (1872), 32 U.C.Q.B. 419: "In every such case there is the limitation of the freehold and the limitation to the heirs, or heirs of the body, in the same instrument, to the same person, and that is all that is necessary to constitute the one enlarged estate, by reason of the two limitations", *per* Wilson, J., at p. 422; *Re Hawkins, supra,* footnote 17.

[19]*Van Grutten v. Foxwell*, [1897] A.C. 658 (H.L.); *Tunis v. Passmore, supra,* footnote 18; *Re Romanes & Smith* (1880), 8 P.R. (Ont.) 323; *Re Casner* (1884), 6 O.R. 282 (H.C.J.); *King v. Evans* (1895), 24 S.C.R. 356; *Re Nicholson* (1928), 34 O.W.N. 111 (H.C.).

[20]*Van Grutten v. Foxwell, supra,* footnote 19, at p. 677; *King v. Evans, supra,* footnote 19; *Re Rynard, supra,* footnote 9.

[21]*Supra,* footnote 19, at p. 677.

has expressly declared that the ancestor shall take for life and no longer, or has endeavoured to graft upon the words of gift to the heirs, or heirs of the body, additions, conditions, or limitations which are repugnant to an estate of inheritance, and such as the law cannot give effect to. The rule, I repeat, is not one of construction, and, indeed, usually overrides and defeats the expressed intention of the testator.

Again, he said:

The testator may conceivably shew by the context that he has used the words "heirs," or "heirs of the body," or "issue" in some limited or restricted sense of his own which is not the legal meaning of the words — e.g., he may have used the words in the sense of children, or as designating some individual person who would be heir of the body at the time of the death of the tenant for life, or at some other particular time. If the Court is judicially satisfied that the words are so used, I conceive that the premises for the application of the rule in *Shelley's Case* (1) are wanting, and the rule is foreign to the case.[22]

Again, in *Re Estate of Charles Tuck*,[23] Britton, J., said:

The simplest way in which this "rule in *Shelley's* case" has ever been put, it seems to me, is when Lord Thurlow stated (3 Juriscon. Ex 360), he did not "remember the time when he thought the application of the rule in *Shelley's* case could depend upon anything else but the question whether the word 'heirs' was the designation of some particular person, or included successively all who might pretend to inheritable blood".

If the words of a will, therefore, indicate that the testator's intention was that a gift over was to be taken by the life tenant's whole line of heirs or heirs of the body, the rule applies so that an estate in fee simple or fee tail, respectively, passes to him and subsequent words repugnant to such an estate are rejected. Thus, since the rule is a rule of law and not of construction, the rule applies notwithstanding words indicating an intent that the life estate is to have its ordinary limitation,[24] such as that the life tenant is to be without impeachment for waste,[25] or is to have the power of leasing,[26] or is to hold expressly for life only,[27] or is not to dispose of the estate for longer than his lifetime.[28]

For the same reason, the rule applies notwithstanding that words are added that the heirs are to take by purchase rather than by descent,[29] or that the

---

[22]*Supra*, footnote 19, at p. 685, note omitted.

[23](1905), 10 O.L.R. 309 at pp. 316-17 (H.C.J.).

[24]*Jesson v. Doe d. Wright* (1820), 2 Bligh 1, 4 E.R. 230 (H.L.); *Roddy v. Fitzgerald* (1858), 6 H.L.C. 823, 10 E.R. 1518; *Van Grutten v. Foxwell, supra*, footnote 19, at p. 672.

[25]*Papillon v. Voice* (1728), 2 P. Wms. 471, 24 E.R. 819; *Jones v. Morgan* (1783), 1 Bro. C.C. 206, 28 E.R. 1086; *Frank v. Stovin* (1803), 3 East 548, 102 E.R. 706; *Bennett v. Earl of Tankerville* (1811), 19 Ves. Jun. 170, 34 E.R. 482; *Tunis v. Passmore, supra*, footnote 18; *Re Hawkins, supra*, footnote 18.

[26]*Jones v. Morgan, supra*, footnote 25; *Frank v. Stovin, supra*, footnote 25.

[27]*Robinson v. Robinson* (1751), 2 Ves. Sen. 225, 28 E.R. 146, and 3 Bro. P.C. 180, 1 E.R. 1255 sub nom. *Robinson v. Hicks*; *Re Keane's Estate*, [1903] 1 I.R. 215.

[28]*Perrin v. Blake* (1770), 4 Burr. 2579, 98 E.R. 355.

[29]*Van Grutten v. Foxwell, supra*, footnote 19, at p. 663.

heirs are to have a life estate only,[30] or are to take as tenants in common,[31] or that words are added attempting to limit the fee given by the original limitation,[32] or that, after the death of the life tenant, the land was to go to and "be enjoyed by" his heirs.[33]

Thus, where a testator devised land to A for life and at his death unto A's heirs living at his death, "my desire being to have this property retained in the family name of 'Armstrong' ", the expression of desire was not sufficient to exclude the rule by limiting the remainder to children living at A's death, instead of his heirs generally.[34]

On the same principle, where a will provided that land was to be held by the testator's daughter who was to receive the rents and profits for her life and, after her death, the rents were to be invested for the benefit of her heirs on their coming of age, it was held that the rule applied and that the daughter took a fee simple in the land.[35]

The rule applies even though further words of limitation which do not change the course of descent are added to the original limitation to the heirs, such as where the limitation was to the heirs male of the body of the settlor and to the heirs male of the body of such heirs male,[36] or where the limitation to the heirs was words indicating that the estate was in fee simple or fee tail.[37] Thus, where a deed was to A for life, remainder to his heirs "and their heirs and assigns forever", it was held that A took an estate in fee simple,[38] and where a devise was to A for life with remainder to "his heirs, executors, administrators and assigns" it was held that A took a fee simple.[39]

The rule is excluded, however, if the added words of limitation change the course of descent inherent in the original limitation, as where the original limitation was to A for life with remainder to his heirs and the heirs male of

---

[30]*Doe d. Cotton v. Stenlake* (1810), 12 East 515, 104 E.R. 202; *Hugo v. Williams* (1872), L.R. 14 Eq. 224.

[31]*Doe d. Candler v. Smith* (1789), 7 T.R. 531, 101 E.R. 1116; *Pierson v. Vickers* (1804), 5 East 548, 102 E.R. 1180; *Bennett v. Earl of Tankerville, supra,* footnote 25; *Jesson v. Doe d. Wright, supra,* footnote 24; *Doe d. Bosnall v. Harvey* (1825), 4 B. & C. 610, 107 E.R. 1187; *Roddy v. Fitzgerald, supra,* footnote 24, at p. 881; *Van Grutten v. Foxwell,* [1897] A.C. 658 (H.L.) at p. 674.

[32]*Denn d. Webb v. Puckey* (1793), 5 T.R. 299 at p. 306, 101 E.R. 168; *Kinch v. Ward* (1825), 2 Sim. & St. 409, 57 E.R. 402; *Measure v. Gee* (1822), 5 B. & A. 910, 106 E.R. 1424; *Nash v. Coates* (1832), 3 B. & Ad. 839, 110 E.R. 308.

[33]*Atkinson v. Purdy* (1908), 43 N.S.R. 274 (S.C.).

[34]*Re Armstrong,* [1943] O.W.N. 43 (H.C.J.).

[35]*Re Thomas* (1901), 2 O.L.R. 660 (H.C.J.).

[36]*Shelley's Case* (1581), 1 Co. Rep. 93 b, 76 E.R. 206; *Legate v. Sewell* (1706), 1 P. Wms. 87, 24 E.R. 306; *Fetherston v. Fetherston* (1835), 3 Cl. & Fin. 67, 6 E.R. 1363.

[37]*Doe d. Dodson v. Grew* (1767), 2 Wils. K.B. 322, 95 E.R. 835; *Denn d. Webb v. Puckey* (1793), 5 T.R. 299, 101 E.R. 168; *Frank v. Stovin* (1803), 3 East 548, 102 E.R. 706; *Griffiths v. Evan* (1842), 5 Beav. 241, 49 E.R. 570.

[38]*Brown v. O'Dwyer* (1874), 35 U.C.Q.B. 354.

[39]*Re Hays* (1917), 13 O.W.N. 25 (H.C.).

their bodies,[40] or to A for life with remainder to her heirs "as if she had died sole and unmarried".[41]

The rule applies even though words of distribution are added to the limitation to the heirs,[42] such as the words "share and share alike", or "equally to be divided among them".[43]

A testator may use the word "heir" in a plural sense, as a collective name for "heirs", in which case the rule operates. Thus, where a testator devised land to a person and on his death to his "male heir forever", it was held that he took an estate tail.[44]

Conversely, the word "heir" may be used to denote a particular person and the rule is excluded where the limitation is to the "heir", in which case the life tenant is given a life estate only.[45]

In a deed, a limitation must be in the proper words to give an estate in fee simple or fee tail, as the case may be. Thus, a grant "to A for life and on his death to his 'heir' ", will convey to A only a life estate.[46]

In a will, however, the same strictness does not apply and the word "heir" attracts the rule if it is not followed by words of limitation,[47] but words of limitation make it a word of purchase.[48] A testator may clearly show that, in using the word "heir" or "heirs", he meant child or children, so that the rule does not apply.[49] Thus, where a testator devised land to his son for life and, if he should have a lawful heir or heirs, the land was to be equally divided among them "at the death of their father", it was held that the use of the word "father" indicated that "heirs" meant children.[50]

The context of a will may show that the words "heirs of the body" are used to

---

[40]*Doe d. Bosnall v. Harvey, supra*, footnote 31.

[41]*Brookman v. Smith* (1871), L.R. 6 Ex. 291 at p. 305, affd L.R. 7 Ex. 271 (Ex. Ch.); *Re Hall; Hall v. Hall*, [1893] W.N. 24 (C.A.).

[42]*Anderson v. Anderson* (1861), 30 Beav. 209, 54 E.R. 868; *Mills v. Seward* (1861), 1 J. & H. 733, 70 E.R. 938; *Grimson v. Downing* (1857), 4 Drewry 125, 62 E.R. 49.

[43]*Van Grutten v. Foxwell*, [1897] A.C. 658 (H.L.); *Re McTavish* (1923), 25 O.W.N. 362 (H.C.).

[44]*Silcocks v. Silcocks*, [1916] 2 Ch. 161; see also *Grant v. Squire* (1901), 2 O.L.R. 131 (H.C.J.). In the latter case the devise was to a son for life and, after his death, to his heir-at-law, if any, and, if not, to the testator's brother. It was held that by the operation of the rule in *Shelley's Case* the son took a defeasible fee simple or fee tail, subject to being defeated by the executory devise over if he died without such an heir.

[45]*White v. Collins* (1718), 1 Com. 289, 92 E.R. 1076; *Peddar v. Hunt* (1887), 18 Q.B.D. 565.

[46]See *Re Davison's Settlement; Cattermole Davison v. Munby*, [1913] 2 Ch. 498.

[47]*Blackburn v. Stables* (1814), 2 Ves. & Bea. 367, 35 E.R. 358; *Fuller v. Chamier* (1866), L.R. 2 Eq. 682.

[48]*Archer's Case* (1597), 1 Co. Rep. 66 b, 76 E.R. 146; *Willis v. Hiscox* (1839), 4 My. & Cr. 197, 41 E.R. 78; *Greaves v. Simpson* (1864), 10 Jur. N.S. 609, 33 L.J. Ch. 641; *Evans v. Evans*, [1892] 2 Ch. 173 (C.A.).

[49]*Re Smith and Ready* (1927), 60 O.L.R. 617, [1927] 3 D.L.R. 991 (S.C. App. Div.).

[50]*Smith v. Smith* (1885), 8 O.R. 677 (H.C.J.).

mean children, in which case the rule is excluded and they take by purchase.[51]

A testator may use the word "heirs" as meaning "heirs of the body", so as to pass a fee tail instead of a fee simple. Thus, where a testator devised land to a son for life and, after his death, to his heirs, with a gift over if he died without leaving a child or children, it was held that he took an estate tail because the reference to children showed that the testator, by "heirs", meant heirs of the body.[52]

The word "issue" is primarily a word of limitation and not of purchase, being equivalent to heirs of the body, and will be given that meaning so as to create an estate tail unless the context of the will clearly shows that children are meant.[53] Thus, where there was a devise to a person for life and, after his death, to his issue "and their heirs", the addition of these words was held not to change the primary meaning of the word "issue", so that under the rule the devisee took an estate tail.[54]

The word "issue" is a word of flexible meaning, however, and will be interpreted as meaning "children" when the context of the will shows that children were meant.[55] In *King v. Evans*,[56] Strong, C.J., said:

> The same may indeed be said of the more technical expression "heirs of the body," which may be read as children, if the testator has sufficiently expressed his intention that that shall be done. The word "issue" is, however, said to be a more flexible expression than "heirs of the body" and will more readily be diverted by force of a context or superadded limitations from its *primâ facie* meaning than the term "heirs of the body".

In that case, the testator, by the third clause of his will, devised land:

> ...to my son James for the full term of his natural life, and from and after his decease to the lawful issue of my said son James, to hold in fee simple, but in default of such issue him surviving then to my said daughter Sarah Jane for the term of her natural life, and upon the death of my daughter Sarah Jane then to the lawful issue of my said daughter Sarah Jane to hold in fee simple, but in default of such issue of my said daughter Sarah Jane then to my brothers and sisters and their heirs in equal shares.

---

[51]*Goodtitle d. Sweet v. Herring* (1801), 1 East 264, 102 E.R. 102; *North v. Martin* (1833), 6 Sim. 266, 58 E.R. 593; *Gummoe v. Howes* (1857), 23 Beav. 184, 53 E.R. 72; *Fetherston v. Fetherston* (1835), 3 Cl. & Fin. 67, 6 E.R. 1363; *East v. Twyford* (1853), 4 H.L.C. 517, 10 E.R. 564; *Van Grutten v. Foxwell, supra*, footnote 43.

[52]*Re Cole and Clarkson* (1921), 21 O.W.N. 88 (H.C.).

[53]*Roddy v. Fitzgerald* (1858), 6 H.L.C. 823, 10 E.R. 1518; *Van Grutten v. Foxwell, supra*, footnote 43; *Pelham Clinton v. Duke of Newcastle*, [1903] A.C. 111 (H.L.); *Shaw v. Thomas* (1872), 19 Gr. 489; *King v. Evans* (1895), 24 S.C.R. 356; *Re Davidson* (1926), 59 O.L.R. 643 (S.C. App. Div.).

[54]*Parker v. Clarke* (1855), 6 De G. M. & G. 104, 43 E.R. 1169.

[55]*Morgan v. Thomas* (1882), 9 Q.B.D. 643 (C.A.), at p. 645, in which case the wording of a gift over showed that "issue" meant children.

[56]*Supra*, footnote 53, at p. 359.

By a later clause, he added:

> It is my intention that upon the decease of either of my children without issue if my other child be then dead, the issue of such latter child (if any) shall at once take the fee simple of the devise mentioned in the second and third clauses of this my will.

It was held, that the clauses must be read together and that, by reason of the clause and the direction that the issue of James were to take in fee simple, which could not be construed as fee tail, there was a sufficiently clear expression of intention that James was to have a life estate only, so as to exclude the rule in *Shelley's Case*.

Similarly, where there was a devise to the testator's daughters for their lives as tenants in common, with remainder to "their respective issues in fee so that the child or children of each will take his her or their mother's share", it was held that by "issues" the testator meant "children", so that the rule did not apply and the daughters took only a life estate.[57]

Where the word "issue" has its primary meaning, the addition of words of distribution does not prevent the operation of the rule,[58] and ordinarily the addition of words of limitation in fee simple or fee tail does not exclude the operation of the rule if the course of descent is not altered by them,[59] nor is a gift over in default of issue essential for the rule to apply.[60]

On the other hand, where the course of descent is altered by the added words of limitation, the rule will not apply. Thus, in the case of a gift to A for life and after his death to his issue "to hold in fee simple", "issue" is given its secondary meaning as "children" and A takes a life estate and his children a fee simple. In *King v. Evans*,[61] Strong, C.J., said:

> It is however a very different thing from holding that the general word "heirs" may be restricted to "heirs of the body" in order to conciliate it with the previous limitation to say that the words "to hold in fee simple" should, without any context, be translated as meaning "to hold in fee tail" or be altogether rejected . . . We have here not a word like "heirs," but in the words "to hold in fee simple" an expression of "known legal import" which can admit of no secondary or alternative meaning.

Similarly, where there was a devise to A for life with remainder to "his

---

[57]*Re Taylor* (1916), 36 O.L.R. 116, 28 D.L.R. 488 (S.C. App. Div.); see also *Montreuil v. Walker* (1911), 3 O.W.N. 166 (H.C.J.); *Re Russell* (1915), 8 O.W.N. 248 (H.C.).
[58]*Doe d. Blandford v. Applin* (1790), 4 T.R. 82, 100 E.R. 906; *Doe d. Cock v. Cooper* (1801), 1 East 229, 102 E.R. 89; *Harrison v. Harrison* (1844), 7 Man. & G. 938, 135 E.R. 381; *Kavanagh v. Morland* (1853), Kay 16 at p. 27, 69 E.R. 7; *Woodhouse v. Herrick* (1855), 1 K. & J. 352, 69 E.R. 494; *Roddy v. Fitzgerald, supra*, footnote 53 at p. 872; *Re McTavish* (1923), 23 O.W.N. 362 (S.C. App. Div.).
[59]*Doe d. Dodson v. Grew* (1767), 2 Wils. (K.B.) 322, 95 E.R. 835; *Denn d. Webb v. Puckey* (1793), 5 T.R. 299, 101 E.R. 168; *Frank v. Stovin* (1803), 3 East 548, 102 E.R. 706; *Griffiths v. Evan* (1842), 5 Beav. 241, 49 E.R. 570; *Parker v. Clarke, supra*, footnote 54; *King v. Evans, supra*, footnote 53, at p. 363.
[60]*Fetherston v. Fetherston, supra*, footnote 51; *Williams v. Williams* (1884), 51 L.T. 779.
[61]*Supra*, footnote 53, at pp. 363-4.

lawful issue and to their heirs and assigns forever", it was held that A took a life estate and his children a fee simple.[62]

Where words both of limitation and of distribution are added to the word "issue", the rule is excluded,[63] and this is so whether there is an express gift to issue or a power to appoint to them.[64]

The word "descendants" primarily means heirs of the body and, where a testator uses it in its primary sense and devises land to a person for life with remainder to his descendants, the rule applies and the devisee takes an estate tail.[65]

On the other hand, the word "children" primarily means the immediate offspring and will be so interpreted unless the context of the will indicates that the testator used it in the broader sense of heirs or heirs of the body. Thus, where a testator devises to a person for life and to her children if any at her death, the rule does not apply and the devisee takes only a life estate.[66]

If there is a gift to a person for life with remainder on his death to his children with words of division or inheritance annexed to the remainder, the rule does not apply and the children take as purchasers.[67] In *Re Simpson*,[68] in which land was devised to a person for life "and after her death to her children in equal shares *per stirpes*", it was held that the rule did not apply. Duff, J., said:[69]

The precise question is this: Are the words "to her children in equal shares *per*

---

[62]*Re Addison* (1920), 19 O.W.N. 142 (H.C.).

[63]*Lees v. Mosley* (1836), 1 Y. & C. Ex. 589, 160 E.R. 241; *Crozier v. Crozier* (1843), 3 Dr. & War. 353; *Greenwood v. Rothwell* (1843), 5 Man. & G. 628, 134 E.R. 711; *Slater v. Dangerfield* (1846), 15 M. & W. 263, 153 E.R. 848.

[64]*Bradley v. Cartwright* (1867), L.R. 2 C.P. 511.

[65]*Re Sutherland* (1911), 2 O.W.N. 1386 (H.C.J.); *Pelham Clinton v. Duke of Newcastle*, [1903] A.C. 111 (H.L.), "to issue male and their male descendants, and see *Re Hooper* (1914), 7 O.W.N. 104 (H.C.), holding that, in the case of a gift to a person for life, remainder to such persons as would be entitled to his interest if it was absolute and he was to die intestate, the rule applied to give him a fee simple.

[66]*Grant v. Fuller* (1902), 33 S.C.R. 34; *Chandler v. Gibson* (1901), 2 O.L.R. 442 (C.A.). In the latter case there was a devise to a person for life "and then to go to his children, if he has any, but should he have no issue then to be equally divided among all my grandsons". It was held that the devisee took a life estate only. Moss, J.A., quoting from *Jarman on Wills*, 5th ed., p. 1307, said at p. 446: "That the words 'in default of issue,' or expressions of a similar import following a devise to children in fee simple, mean 'in default of children' . . . is free from all doubt." And see *Jeffrey v. Scott* (1879), 27 Gr. 314; *Sweet v. Platt* (1886), 12 O.R. 229 (H.C.J.); *McPhail v. McIntosh* (1887), 14 O.R. 312 (H.C.J.); *Peterborough Real Estate Co. v. Patterson* (1888), 15 O.A.R. 751; *Young v. Denike* (1901), 2 O.L.R. 723 (H.C.J.); *Purcell v. Tully* (1906), 12 O.L.R. 5 (H.C.J.); *Re Sharon and Stuart* (1906), 12 O.L.R. 605 (H.C.J.); *Re Anderson* (1911), 18 O.W.R. 924 (H.C.J.); *Re Robertson* (1916), 10 O.W.N. 365 (H.C.); *Re Haig* (1925), 57 O.L.R. 129 (S.C. App. Div.); *Re Beckstead* (1928), 62 O.L.R. 690, [1928] 4 D.L.R. 666 (H.C.).

[67]*Bowen v. Lewis* (1884), 9 App. Cas. 890 (H.L.), at p. 905; *Re Robertson, supra,* footnote 66; *Re Thompson and Robbins* (1917), 11 O.W.N. 344 (H.C.).

[68][1928] 3 D.L.R. 773, [1928] S.C.R. 329.

[69]*Ibid.*, at p. 774 D.L.R., p. 331 S.C.R.

stirpes," words of designation or words of limitation; do these words, "include the whole line of succession capable of inheriting?" . . . *Prima facie,* the word "Children," in such a context, denotes persons of the first degree of descent, and therefore, is a word of designation.

In the case of a devise to a person for life with remainder to his "sons and daughters", the rule does not apply unless the context of the will clearly shows that the testator meant the whole line of descendants capable of inheriting.[70] The word "son" or "sons" may be construed as a word of limitation or collective name in order to give effect to the limitations apparently intended by the testator.[71]

In the case of a devise to a person for life with remainder to his "family", ordinarily the word "family" means "children" and the rule does not apply, so that the devisee takes a life estate and his children the fee simple.[72]

As noted above, the rule only applies if the word "heirs" signifies the whole line of succession capable of inheriting. Modern wills statutes generally contain a limited definition of the word "heir", however. Thus, section 27 of the Ontario *Succession Law Reform Act*[73] provides that in a devise of real property to a person's heir or heirs, the words "heir" or "heirs" shall be construed to mean the person or persons to whom the real estate would descend on an intestacy. The definition does not, therefore, include the whole line of succession. However, the rule in *Shelley's Case* is not thereby impliedly repealed in the case of wills. The legislation merely abolishes the principle of primogeniture.[74]

(g) The rule does not apply to personalty

The rule by its terms speaks of an estate of freehold. Hence, it cannot apply to personal property.[75] Despite this, it was held to apply to personalty in an Ontario[76] and a New Brunswick[77] case. The cases are clearly wrong for, even if

---

[70]*Re Chandler* (1889), 18 O.R. 105 (H.C.J.); *Re Simpson, supra,* footnote 68, in which case Duff, J., said at p. 775 D.L.R., p. 332 S.C.R.: "Whatever may be said about the word 'Children,' it would require a very demonstrative context—a context having the force and value of an interpretation clause—to impart to the phrase 'sons and daughters' a meaning embracing the whole line of descendants capable of inheriting."

[71]*Mellish v. Mellish* (1824), 2 B. & C. 520, 107 E.R. 477, "son"; *Re Buckton; Buckton v. Buckton,* [1907] 2 Ch. 406, "sons and their sons in succession".

[72]*McKinnon v. Spence* (1909), 20 O.L.R. 57 (H.C.J.), in which case, Clute, J., said at p. 63: "The word 'family' may, however, be controlled by the context"; *Re Quebec* (1929), 37 O.W.N. 271 (H.C.), in which case Jeffrey, J., said at p. 272: "In the absence of manifest intention to the contrary, a gift to the 'family' of a specified person will be construed to mean the children of such person and does not include the parent."

[73]R.S.O. 1980, c. 488, formerly the *Wills Act,* R.S.O. 1970, c. 499, s. 31.

[74]*Re Rynard* (1980), 31 O.R. (2d) 257, 118 D.L.R. (3d) 530 (C.A.).

[75]*Re Woodward,* [1945] 2 D.L.R. 497, [1945] 1 W.W.R. 722 (B.C.S.C.); *Re Rynard* (1979), 27 O.R. (2d) 619, 107 D.L.R. (3d) 443, 6 E.T.R. 115 (H.C.J.), affd on other grounds 31 O.R. (2d) 257, 118 D.L.R. (3d) 530 (C.A.).

[76]*Re Woods,* [1946] O.R. 290, [1946] 3 D.L.R. 394 (H.C.J.).

[77]*Re Lloyd; Powell v. Richardson* (1929), 54 N.B.R. 336 (S.C.).

the rule could be extended by analogy, modern conditions preclude such an extension of a feudal rule.

(h) Abolition of the rule

The rule in *Shelley's Case* was abolished in England by the *Law of Property Act*.[78] It was held in an Alberta case that, since it was based on feudal conditions which did not apply in the Northwest Territories, the rule was never received there. Hence, it does not form part of the law of Alberta, where, in any event, it was displaced by the Torrens system of land registration.[79]

1010. LEGAL EXECUTORY INTERESTS

Legal executory interests are future interests which arise either under a use executed by the *Statute of Uses*[1] or, formerly, under a will.[2] Executory interests arising under wills today are probably equitable, however, by reason of the statutory trust in favour of the personal representative created by devolution of estates legislation.[3] Since this point was never firmly settled, they are first dealt with here as though they were legal executory interests.

Executory interests are interests that are so limited that they cannot comply with the common law remainder rules. This does not mean, however, that remainders, including contingent remainders, cannot be created under a use or by will. Both remainders and executory interests can be so created. If the limitation starts out, or can take effect, as a remainder, it will not be allowed to take effect as an executory limitation.[4]

Executory interests differ from remainders in several fundamental respects as follows:

(i) As has been seen,[5] a remainder never defeats the preceding estate, called the particular estate. Therefore, it must have a particular estate to support it,

---

[78]15 & 16 Geo. 5, c. 20 (1925), s. 131.

[79]*Re Simpson*, [1927] 4 D.L.R. 817, [1927] 3 W.W.R. 534 (Alta. S.C., App. Div.). On appeal to the Supreme Court of Canada, [1928] 3 D.L.R. 773, [1928] S.C.R. 329, the point was not in issue. To the same effect is *Re Budd* (1958), 12 D.L.R. (2d) 783, 24 W.W.R. 383 (Alta. S.C.). The rule appears to be in force in Sask.: *Re Ruse*, [1924] 1 D.L.R. 437, [1924] 1 W.W.R. 119, 18 Sask. L.R. 62, although it was ousted in that case by a contrary intention.

§1010

[1]27 Hen. 8, c. 10 (1535).

[2]1 Fearne, p. 386; Challis, p. 172.

[3]This point is dealt with in §1011, *infra*.

[4]*Purefoy v. Rogers* (1671), 2 Wms. Saund. 380 at p. 388, 85 E.R. 1181; *Goodright v. Cornish* (1694), 4 Mod. 255 at p. 259, 87 E.R. 380; *Carwardine v. Carwardine* (1758), 1 Eden 27 at p. 34, 28 E.R. 594; *Doe d. Mussell v. Morgan* (1790), 3 T.R. 763, 100 E.R. 846; *Brackenbury v. Gibbons* (1876), 2 Ch. D. 417 at p. 419; *Re Wrightson; Battie-Wrightson v. Thomas*, [1904] 2 Ch. 95 (C.A.); *White v. Summers*, [1908] 2 Ch. 256 at p. 263.

[5]§1009.2, *supra*.

and cannot be limited so as to take effect at any time later than the end of the preceding estate. The existence of a gap between the particular estate and the remainder is the usual cause of the invalidity and failure of a contingent remainder. By contrast, an executory interest is an interest that cannot take effect as a remainder, being one that is so limited that it does not wait for the end of the preceding estate, or is so limited that it cannot take effect at the end of the preceding estate. Instead, it may be limited to take effect before or after the preceding estate would otherwise end, or it may be limited to take effect and vest in possession at any time, provided that it does not offend the rule against perpetuities. It is a fundamental rule that if an interest is so limited that it can take effect during or at the end of the preceding estate, it is a remainder and is not allowed to take effect as an executory interest.[6] To make it a remainder, it is sufficient that it be so limited that it can take effect during the preceding estate or at the moment that it ends, and the improbability that it will actually do so does not change it from a remainder to an executory interest.[7]

(ii) As has been shown,[8] a remainder cannot be limited to take effect after a fee simple, because nothing remains after a fee simple. An executory interest can be limited to divest a fee simple on the happening of a specified event and to give it to another person, however.

(iii) At common law, land could not be conveyed to a person for a term of years for his life with a remainder for the balance of the term after his death, because a life estate was regarded as larger than any term of years and thus comprised the whole term. There can be an executory interest for the balance of the term after the death of the life tenant, however.

1010.1 Legal Executory Interests Arising by Deed

The *Statute of Uses*[1] provides that where a person stands seised of land to the use of another, that other henceforth shall stand seised of the land in such like estate as he had in use. The effect of the statute is that it executes the use, that is, it removes the feoffee to uses, who formerly had the seisin, and gives the legal interest to the *cestui que use*, who formerly had the equitable interest. Moreover, because the statute gives the *cestui que use* the same interest at law as he formerly had in equity, it was held that, if the *cestui que use* formerly had an equitable executory interest, the executory interest was also valid at law, even though it would have offended one of the common law remainder rules if it had been contained in a common law conveyance.[2]

6See cases collected under footnote 4, *supra*, and see §1010.3, *infra*.
71 Fearne, p. 395.
8§1009.2, *supra*.
§1010.1
127 Hen. 8, c. 10 (1535).
2*Woodliff v. Drury* (1596), Cro. Eliz. 439, 78 E.R. 679; *Mutton's Case* (1568), 3 Dy. 274 b, 73 E.R. 613.

As a result, resulting, springing and shifting uses became possible.

Of course, a use may be limited to take effect in the future by way of remainder rather than by way of executory interest, for the use is said to be as "clay . . . in the hands of the potter"[3] and the grantor or settlor may mould it as he wishes, except that a use limited as a remainder cannot take effect as an executory interest.[4] If a conveyance expressly or impliedly disposes of the uses of the entire fee simple by way of a particular estate and a remainder or reversion, each estate, if effectually limited, takes effect as a legal estate under the *Statute of Uses*[5] and is subject to the rules of common law which apply to those estates. Therefore, the uses in remainder or reversion, in order to be executed by the statute, must be so limited as to represent the estates necessary to prevent the freehold from being in abeyance because no seisin remains in the grantee to uses to fill any gap for that purpose, as the statute leaves nothing.[6]

(a) Resulting uses

When an owner conveys lands to uses and expressly or impliedly declares part of the use only and does not effectively dispose of the whole use, then at common law, so much of the use as the owner does not dispose of remains in him. This is known as a resulting use.[7] It is said to be based upon the principle that, in a conveyance without valuable consideration, so much of the use as is undisposed of by one seised of land remains in the grantor.[8] Even if a valuable consideration is paid, so much of the use as is undisposed of remains in or results to the grantor, for the extent of the express limitation is the measure of the consideration. But when in a conveyance of the fee simple to a purchaser for valuable consideration, it recites a contract for the purchase of the fee simple, any part of the use that is not limited by the conveyance vests in the purchaser and there can be no resulting use to the grantor or vendor.[9] The result is that a subsequent purchaser without notice is protected.[10]

At common law, a use which is not declared in such cases results to the grantor and remains part of his original estate.[11] If there are several grantors, it remains part of their respective estates.[12] In the case of a conveyance by a

---

[3]*Brent's Case* (1583), 2 Leo. 14 at p. 16, 74 E.R. 319, *per* Manwood, J.
[4]Gilbert, p. 304.
[5]27 Hen. 8, c. 10 (1535).
[6]*Brent's Case, supra*, footnote 3; Gilbert, p. 165.
[7]Cruise, *A Digest of the Laws of England Respecting Real Property*, 4th ed. by H.H. White (London, Saunders and Benning, 1835), tit. xi, c. 4, s. 21.
[8]Co. Litt. 23a, 271b; 1 Sanders, p. 101. And see Simpson, "The Equitable Doctrine of Consideration and the Law of Uses", 16 U. of T. L.J. 1 (1965).
[9]1 Sanders, pp. 102-3.
[10]*Cf. Conveyancing and Law of Property Act*, R.S.O. 1980, c. 90, s. 7 rep. & sub. 1984, c. 32, s. 17.
[11]1 Sanders, p. 97; *Dowman's Case* (1586), 9 Co. Rep. 7 b, 77 E.R. 743; *Beckwith's Case* (1589), 2 Co. Rep. 56 b at p. 58 a, 76 E.R. 541; *Clere's Case* (1599), 6 Co. Rep. 17 b, 77 E.R. 279; *Armstrong d. Neve v. Wolsey* (1755), 2 Wils. K.B. 19, 95 E.R. 662; *Doe d. Dyke v. Whittingham* (1811), 4 Taunt. 20, 128 E.R. 234.
[12]1 Sanders, p. 99; Gilbert, pp. 89 *et seq.*

tenant in tail, it results to him in fee simple.[13] If the conveyance, however, limits a use to the grantor, such as for life, and an undisposed of remainder results to him so as to cause the life estate to merge in it and thus defeat the limitation for life, the use undisposed of vests in the grantee.[14]

The operation of resulting uses was explained by Ruggles, C.J., in the case of *Van der Volgen v. Yates*[15] as follows:

> Before the statute of uses, and while uses were subjects of chancery jurisdiction exclusively, a use could not be raised by deed, without a sufficient consideration; a doctrine taken from the maxim of the civil law, *ex nudo pacto non oritur actio*. In consequence of this rule, the court of chancery would not compel the execution of a use, unless it had been raised for a good or valuable consideration; for that would be to enforce *donum gratuitum*. (1 Cruise, tit. 11, c. 2, §22.) And where a man made a feoffment to another, without any consideration, equity presumed that he meant it to the use of himself; unless he expressly declared it to be the use of another, and then nothing was presumed, contrary to his own expressions. (2 Bl. Com. 330.) If a person had conveyed his lands to another, without consideration, or declaration of uses, the grantor became entitled to the use or pernancy of the profits of the lands thus conveyed.
>
> This doctrine was not altered by the statute of uses. Therefore, it became an established principle, that where the legal seisin or possession of lands is transferred by any common-law conveyance or assurance, and no use is expressly declared, nor any consideration or evidence of intent to direct the use, such use shall result back to the original owner of the estate; for where there is neither consideration nor declaration of uses, nor any circumstances to show the intention of the parties, it cannot be supposed that the estate was intended to be given away. (1 Cruise, tit. 2, c. 4, §20.)
>
> But if a valuable consideration appears, equity will immediately raise a use correspondent to such consideration. (2 Bl. Com. 330.) And if in such case, no use is expressly declared, the person to whom the legal estate is conveyed, and from whom the consideration moved, will be entitled to the use. The payment of the consideration leads the use, unless it be expressly declared to some other person. The use results to the original owner, where no consideration appears, because, it cannot be supposed, that the estate was intended to be given away; and by the same rule, it will not result, where a consideration has been paid, because, in such case, it cannot be supposed, that the parties intended the land should go back to him who had been paid for it.
>
> The statute of uses made no change in the equitable principles which previously governed resulting uses. It united the legal and equitable estates, so that after the statute, a conveyance of the use was a conveyance of the land: and the land will not result or revert to the original owner, except where the use would have done so before the statute was passed. (Cruise, tit. x, c. 4, §20.)
>
> It is still, now, as it was before the statute, "the intention of the parties, to be collected from the face of the deed, that gives effect to resulting uses." (1 Sanders on Uses 104, ed. of 1830.)
>
> As a general rule, it is true, that where the owner, for a pecuniary consideration, conveys lands to uses, expressly declaring a part of the use, but making no disposition of the residue, so much of the use as the owner does not dispose of remains in him. (Cruise, tit. 11, c. 4, §21.) For example, if an estate be conveyed, for valuable consideration, to feoffees and their heirs, to the use of them for their lives, the

---

[13]*Dowman's Case, supra,* footnote 11; *Martin d. Tregonwell v. Strachan* (1743), 5 T.R. 107 at p. 110, 101 E.R. 61; *Tanner v. Radford* (1833). 6 Sim. 21 at p. 30, 58 E.R. 503.
[14]1 Sanders, pp. 103-4.
[15](1853), 9 N.Y. 219 at pp. 222-5.

remainder of the use will result to the grantor. In such case, the intent of the grantor to create a life-estate only, and to withhold the residue of the use, is apparent on the face of the deed; the words of inheritance in the conveyance being effectual only for the purpose of serving the declared use. The consideration expressed in the conveyance is, therefore, deemed an equivalent only for the life estate; the residue of the use remains in or results to the grantor, because there was no grant of it, nor any intention to grant it, and because it has never been paid for.

But the general rule above stated is clearly inapplicable to a case, in which the intention of the grantor, apparent on the face of the deed, is, to dispose of the entire use, or in other words, of his whole estate in the land ...

A use never results, against the intent of the parties. "Where there is any circumstance to show the intent of the parties to have been, that the use should not result, it will remain in the persons to whom the legal estate is limited." (1 Cruise, tit. 11, Use, c. 4, §41.)

... upon a feoffment to a void use, upon a pecuniary consideration, however small, the title vests in the feoffee for his own benefit.[16]

Thus, where a grantor conveys "to X and his heirs, to the use of A in fee at age 21", A not yet being 21, there is resulting use in favour of the grantor which is executed together with the express use. In the result, the grantor will hold the fee until A is 21, after which it passes to A. Similarly, where the grantor conveys "to X and his heirs to the use of A and his heirs after my death", there is a resulting use in favour of the grantor for the duration of the gap, that is, from the time of the conveyance until the property is conveyed to A. The uses in favour of A in both cases are examples of springing uses.

(b) Springing uses

A springing use is one which is not limited as a remainder and which arises as limited without defeating a preceding estate. It may arise either because the grantor did not create a preceding estate or because there is a gap between the end of the preceding estate and the vesting of the executory interest.

If a use is limited as a remainder, it must take effect as one and be supported by a preceding estate of freehold. Where a husband and wife limited land to the use of the heirs of their bodies by each other with remainder to the right heirs of the husband, it was held that the remainder was void as it was a future use with no preceding life estate limited by the conveyance to support it.[17] Again, in a lease by A to trustees and their heirs "to the use of A for ninety-nine years, remainder to the use of the trustees for twenty-five years, remainder to the heirs male of A's body", it was held that the remainder to his heirs was void for lack of the freehold to support it.[18]

A springing use is valid even though, at common law, it would be void as leaving the freehold in abeyance, so where it is the first use limited and is to arise at a future time, or where it arises after an interval following the end of the preceding estate, the use is valid. This validity is due to the doctrine

---

[16]See also *The Queen v. Porter* (1592), 1 Co. Rep. 22 b, 76 E.R. 50.
[17]*Davis v. Speed* (1692), 4 Mod. 153, 87 E.R. 318.
[18]*Adams v. Savage* (1703), 2 Salk. 679, 91 E.R. 577.

of resulting uses because, until the springing use takes effect, the resulting freehold is in the grantor, so that the freehold is not in abeyance. Consequently, springing uses are not really inconsistent with the rule against leaving the freehold in abeyance but are consistent with it.[19] Thus, a deed which may take effect as a covenant to stand seised to a use is valid, even though the use is to arise at a time which may be long after the death of the covenantor, and he does not dispose of the freehold meanwhile; this is because the use meanwhile results to the covenantor.[20] Similarly, where a father gave a deed to his son under which the son was to have possession on a day later in the year, it was held that, after that day had passed, supposing the deed to be void as a grant of the freehold in the future, the son was nevertheless entitled to possession as the deed amounted to a covenant to stand seised to his use, the seisin meanwhile remaining in the father.[21] Further examples of springing uses may be found above.[22]

(c) Shifting uses

A shifting use is one which, when it arises, defeats the preceding estate. Thus, it divests the preceding estate and shifts the property to the owner of the executory interest. It may be created by words of limitation or words of condition.[23]

A shifting use is valid even though it is contrary to the rules of common law which hold that an executory interest which defeats a prior estate cannot be created by deed and that no fee simple can be limited to defeat or take effect after a fee simple. Thus, in one of the leading cases, it was held that, if land is conveyed to A for life but, if B pays a certain sum to the grantor, then to B for life, this is a valid shifting use.[24] Again, in an old conveyance by way of fine to the use of the grantor "for life, with remainder to A. until B. returned from sea, and came of age or died, which ever shall first happen, and then to B.", the shifting remainder to B was held valid and vested in B immediately on his return, even though he was not then of age.[25] A shifting use may be validly created to defeat a fee simple and take effect upon the happening of a specified condition.[26] Thus, where a grantor conveyed land to the grantee and his heirs to hold to the use of the grantee and his heirs until his proposed marriage and then to hold to the use of the intended wife and her heirs, it was held that, on her marriage, the wife acquired an estate in fee simple.[27] In the absence of the device of inserting a use, however, a fee simple cannot be limited

---

[19]See 1 L.Q. Rev. (1885), p. 412.
[20]*Doe d. Dyke v. Whittingham, supra*, footnote 11.
[21]*Doe d. Starling v. Prince* (1851), 20 L.J.C.P. 223.
[22]In §1010.1(a).
[23]1 Sanders, p. 158.
[24]*Brent's Case* (1583), 2 Leo. 14, 74 E.R. 319; and see 1 Sanders, p. 156.
[25]*Lord Vaux's Case* (1592), Cro. Eliz. 269, 78 E.R. 525.
[26]1 Sanders, p. 150; *Gilbert*, pp. 217-18.
[27]*Re Bayliss and Balfe* (1917), 38 O.L.R. 437, 35 D.L.R. 350 (H.C.).

to take effect after a fee simple,[28] although that can be done by executory devise. If lands are conveyed "to A and his heirs to such uses as B may appoint and, until appointment, to the use of A and his heirs", A takes an estate in fee simple until the power of appointment is exercised and the use is then shifted from A.[29] Similarly, if the grantor conveys to such uses as he may appoint by will, the use vests in him until he exercises the power by declaring uses which then take effect as limited by force of the grant.[30] It was held in *Thuresson v. Thuresson*[31] that, where land is conveyed to A in fee simple to such uses as B may appoint, A's estate may be extinguished under the *Limitations Act*[32] by possession by a stranger and that thereafter any appointment by B would have no effect. Maclennan, J.A., who delivered the majority opinion, said:[33]

> The title of the grantees consisted of two things: the seizin and the use. A power when exercised operates on the use, and the Statute of Uses operates on the seizin and attracts it to the use. But when the title is extinguished there is neither seizin nor use to be operated upon either by the power or by the statute ... Indeed it seems to me an absurdity to say that when the title in fee simple is extinguished it nevertheless still continues to exist, for the purpose of being transferred by appointment to a new owner.

Since the seisin and the power to appoint to uses may exist in the same person, if land is conveyed to a husband in fee simple to such uses as he may appoint and, in default of and until appointment, to his use in fee simple, his wife has an inchoate right of dower in the land subject to its being divested upon his exercise of the power.[34]

(d) The vesting of interests under uses

Since the *Statute of Uses*[35] provides that, where the use is in fee simple or a lesser estate or is in remainder or reversion, the *cestui que use* is seised of such estate, the effect is that, if uses are for a particular estate, such as for life, with a vested remainder, both uses are executed by the statute, so that both life tenant and remainderman are seised of legal estates. When the use is of a contingent remainder or is otherwise executory, however, it cannot be executed until it vests and it cannot vest unless it has a particular estate of freehold to support it. For that reason, the Ontario *Conveyancing and Law of Property*

[28]*Re Chauvin* (1920), 18 O.W.N. 178 (H.C.).

[29]*Thuresson v. Thuresson* (1901), 2 O.L.R. 637 (C.A.).

[30]*Clere's Case* (1599), 6 Co. Rep. 17 b, 77 E.R. 279.

[31]*Supra*, footnote 29.

[32]R.S.O. 1897, c. 133.

[33]*Supra*, footnote 29, at p. 643.

[34]*Re Hazell* (1925), 57 O.L.R. 290, [1925] 3 D.L.R. 661 (S.C. App. Div.). *Re Kuntz and Hodgins* (1927), 61 O.L.R. 298, [1927] 4 D.L.R. 1009 (H.C.). *Lawlor v. Lawlor* (1882), 10 S.C.R. 194.

[35]27 Hen. 8, c. 10 (1535).

Act[36] provides that, where by any deed, will or other instrument, any land is limited to uses, all uses thereunder, expressed or implied, immediate or future, contingent, executory or to be declared under any power contained in the instrument, shall take effect as they arise by force of the seisin originally vested in the person seised to uses, and the continued existence in him or elsewhere of any seisin to uses or *scintilla juris* shall not be necessary to support or give effect to the future, contingent or executory uses, nor shall such seisin to uses or *scintilla juris* be deemed to be suspended or to remain or subsist in him or elsewhere.

The reference to *scintilla juris* is due to the fact that, before the *Statute of Uses*,[37] the seisin of the grantee to uses supported contingent uses in remainder but, upon passage of the Act, no estate was left in the grantee to uses, so the courts adopted the fiction that nevertheless a possibility of seisin, *scintilla juris*, or little spark of the law, remained in the grantee, which was sufficient to give effect, whenever necessary, to contingent and other executory uses.

This legislation thus overcomes the difficulty created by the *Statute of Uses* when it stripped the grantee to uses of all seisin, leaving him nothing to support contingent uses. The effect of the foregoing provision of the Ontario Act was thus stated by Maclennan, J.A., in *Thuresson v. Thuresson*:[38]

> That purpose was to remove the objection, which had been mooted, and much discussed, in the case of shifting or springing or contingent uses, that where the legal seizin was exhausted for the purpose of one or more such uses the other uses limited by the same instruments could not take effect for want of seizin to support them. As in the present case ... the grant is to the two grantees and their heirs, to the use of them and their heirs. until appointment by Eyre Thuresson, etc., the seizin in the grantees is in fee, and the use limited to them is also in fee, and co-extensive with the seizin, and so there is no seizin left to support any uses which Eyre Thuresson might appoint. What the statute says is that the *seizin originally vested* in the person seized *to the uses* shall be sufficient for all the estates limited, and that is all. It was intended to remove, and all it does is to remove, the doubt which existed upon the construction and effect of conveyances to uses. It merely *declares* that the *seizin* of the person seized to uses in such a deed shall have a certain effect.

Where letters patent of the Crown conveyed land to a father in fee simple in trust for his son, a lunatic, his heirs and assigns, it was held that the letters patent were an assurance within the statute and created a use which could not vest in the son by reason of his disability, but which was executed in his heir on his death, so that the heir's deed was valid as against the deed of the grantee in the letters patent.[39]

1010.2 Executory Devises

Executory interests arising under wills operate in the same way as executory

---

[36]R.S.O. 1980, c. 90, s. 34. To the same effect is the *Property Act*, R.S.N.B. 1973, c. P-19, s. 18.
[37]27 Hen. 8, c. 10 (1535).
[38]*Supra*, footnote 29, at p. 643.
[39]*Doe d. Snyder v. Masters* (1851), 8 U.C.Q.B. 55.

interests arising under a use. However, it is not necessary that they employ a use.[1] This is because the *Statute of Wills*[2] permitted a person to devise his land "at his free will and pleasure". That language was construed as permitting a testator to create legal executory interests by will which sprang up or shifted in the future despite the fact that they involved a gap in the seisin or defeated a prior estate. Executory devises are, therefore, of two kinds, namely, springing and shifting executory devises.

(a) Springing devises

A springing devise is one so limited that it has no preceding estate to support it, either because the testator did not create a preceding estate, or because there is a gap between the end of the preceding estate and the vesting in possession of the executory devise which may be limited to take effect at a time certain or upon the happening of a contingency.[3]

The following are examples of executory devises which are springing because no preceding estate was created by the testator: a devise to a person to take effect six months after the testator's death;[4] a devise to the heir of a person after that person's death and if he survives the testator;[5] a devise to the son of a person and the latter has no son at the testator's death;[6] and a devise to a specified son of the testator when he attains the age of 21 years and he has not attained that age at the testator's death.[7]

An example of a devise which is springing because there is a gap between the preceding estate and the vesting of the devise, is a devise to a person for life and, at a specified time after his death, to the eldest son of another person.[8]

In all such cases while the executory devise is in suspense after the testator's death or during the gap between the preceding estate and the vesting of the executory devise, the effect is that the testator, intentionally or otherwise, has left the freehold to descend, formerly, to the heir-at-law and, today, to the residuary devisee or the heirs general, who are entitled to the rents and profits

---

§1010.2

[1]The *Statute of Uses*, 27 Hen. 8, c. 10 (1535), does not apply to wills: *Re Tanqueray-Willaume and Landau* (1882), 20 Ch. D. 465 at p. 478, *per* Jessel, M.R. However, if a testator uses expressions in his will that are appropriate to a conveyance to uses, it is presumed that he intended them to be so construed and effect will be given to his presumed intention: 1 Sanders, p. 253; Gilbert, p. 356; Challis, p. 387; Co. Litt. 272a; *Baker v. White* (1875), L.R. 20 Eq. 166 at p. 170.

[2]32 Hen. 8, c. 1 (1540), ss. 1, 2.

[3]1 Fearne, pp. 395, 398, 400, 401.

[4]*Clarke v. Smith* (1699), 1 Lut. 793 at p. 798, 125 E.R. 416; *Pay's Case* (1602), Cro. Eliz. 878, 78 E.R. 1103.

[5]*Goodright v. Cornish* (1694), 1 Salk. 226, 91 E.R. 200; *Harris v. Barnes* (1768), 4 Burr. 2157, 98 E.R. 125.

[6]*Gore d. Gore* (1722), 2 P. Wms. 28, 24 E.R. 629; *Bullock v. Stones* (1754), 2 Ves. Sen. 521, 28 E.R. 333.

[7]*Doe d. Andrew v. Hutton* (1804), 3 Bos. & Pul. 643, 127 E.R. 347.

[8]See *White v. Summers*, [1908] 2 Ch. 256, and *Abbiss v. Burney*; *Re Finch* (1881), 17 Ch. D. 211 (C.A.).

of the land until the executory devise vests in the devisee, and the freehold is thus not left in abeyance.[9]

There may be a springing devise to a class. If land is devised to a person for life and, after his death, to his children who attain the age of 21 years before or after his death, the inclusion of children who attain that age after his death indicates that the testator contemplated a gap between the life estate and the vesting of the future devises and, since the interests of children attaining the required age after the death of their father could not take effect as remainders, the interests of all the children are regarded as executory devises.[10] The same thing is true where, after a life estate, the land is devised to another person's children born before or after the death of the life tenant.[11] In either case, the devise is to a class the members of which cannot be ascertained until after the end of the preceding estate.[12]

(b) Shifting devises

A shifting devise is one which is so limited that it does not wait for the natural determination of the preceding estate to take effect but takes effect upon the happening of an event which determines the preceding estate. It thus divests the preceding estate and shifts the property to the executory devisee. For example, if the devise of a life estate is subject to forfeiture on the happening of a specified event, so that the next interest devised is thereby accelerated, the latter does not take effect as a contingent remainder but as a shifting executory devise.

A testator devised land to his son for life, and after his death to all the son's children who should attain the age of 21 years in equal shares as tenants in common and, by a subsequent clause, provided that, if his son should attempt to dispose of his life estate or become bankrupt or insolvent, or if the life estate should be taken in execution by any creditor, the son's life estate should thenceforth absolutely vest in and belong to the next persons entitled thereto. A judgment creditor obtained the appointment of a receiver of the son's estate, at which time the son had two children, one of age and the other an infant, and afterwards had other children. It was held that, as the limitations to the children did not take effect on the natural determination of the prior life estate, they were not contingent remainders but executory devises and took effect in favour of all children that attained 21 whenever born.[13]

Even a fee simple may be thus divested and shifted to another person by

---

[9]*Pay's Case*, supra, footnote 4; *Clarke v. Smith*, supra, footnote 4; *Gore v. Gore*, supra, footnote 6; *Hopkins v. Hopkins* (1749), 1 Ves. Sen. 268, 27 E.R. 1024; *Bullock v. Stones*, supra, footnote 6; *Harris v. Barnes*, supra, footnote 5.

[10]*Re Lechmere and Lloyd* (1881), 18 Ch. D. 524; *Dean v. Dean*, [1891] 3 Ch. 150; *Re Bourne*; *Rymer v. Harpley* (1887), 56 L.J. Ch. 566, and see *Re Wrightson*; *Battie-Wrightson v. Thomas*, [1904] 2 Ch. 95 at p. 104 (C.A.).

[11]*Miles v. Jarvis* (1883), 24 Ch. D. 633.

[12]*White v. Summers*, supra, footnote 8.

[13]*Blackman v. Fysh*, [1892] 3 Ch. 209 (C.A.).

executory devise. For instance, a testator devised land to trustees in trust to pay the income to his nephew until he should assign, charge or otherwise dispose of it or become bankrupt, whichever should first happen and, if the trust thereby determined in the lifetime of the nephew, to accumulate the income for the benefit of the nephew's male heir of his body until he attained the age of 21 years, and if the nephew should die without leaving a male heir, the trustees were to apply the income to the nephew's brothers and the respective male heirs of their bodies, with remainders to the nephew's sisters as tenants in common. On proceedings for construction of the will, it was held that the nephew took an equitable estate in fee simple determinable on the happening of any of the specified events, which estate would, on his death without any such event happening, become an absolute estate in fee simple subject to the executory devise over if he should die without leaving a male heir, which meant failure of issue at his death and not an indefinite failure of issue.[14]

At common law before the Wills Act, if land were devised to a person or to a person and his heirs with a gift over if he died without issue or without having issue or without leaving issue, the gift over was construed as meaning an indefinite failure of issue at any time and the devisee took an estate tail.[15] Under the Ontario *Wills Act*,[16] the words are to be construed to mean a want or failure of issue in the devisee's lifetime or at his death and not an indefinite failure of issue, unless a contrary intention appears in the will by reason of such person having a prior estate tail or by reason of a preceding gift, being, without any implication arising from such words, a limitation of an estate tail to him or his issue or otherwise. The Act provides that it does not extend to cases where the words import if no issue described in a preceding gift be born, or if there be no issue who live to attain the age or otherwise answer the description required to obtain a vested estate by a preceding gift to such issue. The result of that is that, where the statutory rule of construction applies, a devise, instead of giving an estate tail, creates an estate in fee simple with an executory devise over on the death of the devisee without issue then living.[17]

The following are further examples of devises which are shifting:

Where a testator devised land to his son A and his heirs but, in the event of A dying without issue during B's lifetime, then to B and his heirs, it was held that A had a vested estate in fee simple which, upon his dying without issue during B's lifetime, would be divested and pass to B under B's shifting devise.[18]

If there is a devise to A for life, remainder to his first child in fee simple but, if the child dies before attaining the age of 21 years, then to B in fee simple,

---

[14]*Re Leach*; *Leach v. Leach*, [1912] 2 Ch. 422.
[15]See §605.2, *supra*.
[16]R.S.O. 1970, c. 499, s. 32, now *Succession Law Reform Act*, R.S.O. 1980, c. 488, s. 28.
[17]*Nason v. Armstrong* (1894), 21 O.A.R. 183, revd on other grounds 25 S.C.R. 263; *Re Pettigrew* (1929), 36 O.W.N. 182 (H.C.); *Re Toll and Mills* (1919), 16 O.W.N. 215 (H.C.).
[18]*Pells v. Brown* (1620), Cro. Jac. 590, 79 E.R. 504.

the contingent remainder of the child becomes vested upon his birth subject to being divested by the executory devise in favour of B if he does not attain the required age.[19]

Where a testator devised land to his widow for life and after his death, to his son P in fee simple, devised other land to another son, and provided that if either of his sons died leaving no children, the property of the son so dying was to be equally divided among all of his children, it was held that P's remainder was subject to being divested by his so dying, in which case the executory devise would take effect, so that P and the widow had no title which could be forced upon an unwilling purchaser.[20]

Where a testator devised land to his son A for life and, after his death, to his heir-at-law should he have any and, if none, to his brother J, it was held that under the rule in *Shelley's Case*,[21] A had a fee which, upon his dying without an heir, was divested by the executory devise to J.[22]

A testator devised land to his widow for life and, after her death, to his daughter for life and directed that after her death all realty and personalty was to be divided among such of her children as she might appoint and, in default of appointment, among all of her children, but provided that, if his son Thomas returned to Toronto within five years from the testator's death, the executors were to hold the lands for the son in trust for his life and after his death to divide them among his children, and the son did so return, entered into receipt of the rents and profits and died intestate and unmarried. It was held that the contention that the prior devises were only divested to the extent of Thomas' life estate was of no avail. The executory devise to Thomas was of the entirety; it took effect upon his satisfying the contingency of his return, and after his death, although the executory devise to his children failed, the lands did not revest in the first devisees but passed to the daughter under a residuary devise.[23]

Where a testator devised his realty to his widow for life and directed that, after her death, it was to be divided equally among his two brothers, the children of a deceased brother, and his sister and provided that, if either of the two brothers or the sister predeceased his widow, one-quarter was to go to his or her heirs, executors and administrators, and the sister predeceased the widow leaving a son, it was held that the sister took a vested remainder which was divested upon her death before the widow, so that her heirs took under the executory devise to them as a class and the son took his share as a purchaser.[24]

---

[19]See *Gulliver v. Wickett* (1745), 1 Wils. K.B. 105, 95 E.R. 517.

[20]*Vanluven v. Allison* (1901), 2 O.L.R. 198 (H.C.J.).

[21](1581), 1 Co. Rep. 93 b, 76 E.R. 206.

[22]*Grant v. Squire* (1901), 2 O.L.R. 131 (H.C.J.).

[23]*Walsh v. Fleming* (1905), 10 O.L.R. 226 (H.C.J.).

[24]*Glendenning v. Dickinson* (1910), 14 W.L.R. 419, 15 B.C.R. 354 (C.A.). See also the following cases: *Re Hildreth* (1923), 54 O.L.R. 139 (S.C. App. Div.), devise to son with executory devise over if he died without issue; *Re Dickinson* (1920), 17 O.W.N. 364 (H.C.), life estate, remainder to children of brother, executory devise over if

Any estate may be the subject of an executory devise. Thus, there may be an executory devise of an estate *pur autre vie*,[25] or of an estate tail. An executory devise which divests an estate tail and shifts it to another person is barred by a disentailing deed.[26]

A shifting devise may wholly defeat a preceding estate in fee simple, or only interrupt it to the extent necessary to give effect to the devise. If the preceding estate is a fee simple and the executory devise is only of a life estate, the preceding estate is only interrupted for the duration of the life estate.[27] If the devise of the life estate fails because there is no one who can take it, the preceding estate continues uninterrupted.[28] On the other hand, if the executory devise wholly defeats the preceding estate in fee simple, it remains defeated even if the executory devise fails to take effect.[29]

An executory devise only takes effect on the happening of the prescribed event. If the preceding estate fails in some manner other than being defeated by the executory devise, that event does not accelerate the executory devise, but the property passes instead to the heir-at-law or residuary devisee. Thus, in the case of a devise "to A but, if he dies under the age of 21 years, then to B", the latter takes only if A fails to attain the required age and, if A attains it but dies in the lifetime of the testator so that his devise lapses, B's devise does not take effect because of the form of its limitation.[30] If, however, a life estate is limited so as to be determinable and an executory devise is limited to take effect on such determination during the life, it may take effect on the death of the life tenant.[31]

(c) Relationship between executory devises and remainders

Ordinarily, if the limitation of a devise is executory, all subsequent interests are also necessarily executory because, if the division of the fee simple into a particular estate and remainders is interrupted by an executory devise, the interruption affects all subsequent interests.[32] If, however, after a will is made,

---

children die without issue; *Re Martin*, [1933] O.W.N. 114 (H.C.J.), devise in fee simple, executory devise over on death without issue. As to the construction of shifting provisions generally, see *Shuttleworth v. Murray*, [1901] 1 Ch. 819 (C.A.), affd, [1902] A.C. 263 *sub nom. Law Union and Crown Ins. Co. v. Hill* (H.L.); *Collingwood v. Stanhope* (1869), L.R. 4 H.L. 43.

[25]*Re Barber's Settled Estates* (1881), 18 Ch. D. 624; *Re Michell; Moore v. Moore*, [1892] 2 Ch. 87.

[26]*Doe d. Lumley v. Earl of Scarborough* (1835), 3 Ad. & E. 2, 897, 111 E.R. 313, 653 (Ex. Ch.); *Milbank v. Vane*, [1893] 3 Ch. 79 (C.A.).

[27]*Gatenby v. Morgan* (1876), 1 Q.B.D. 685.

[28]*Jackson v. Noble* (1838), 2 Keen 590, 48 E.R. 755.

[29]*Doe d. Blomfield v. Eyre* (1848), 5 C.B. 713, 136 E.R. 1058 (Ex. Ch.); *Robinson v. Wood* (1858), 27 L.J. Ch. 726; *Hurst v. Hurst* (1882), 21 Ch. D. 278 at p. 293; *Walsh v. Fleming* (1905), 10 O.L.R. 226 (H.C.J.).

[30]*Tarbuck v. Tarbuck* (1835), 4 L.J. Ch. 129; *Brookman v. Smith* (1872), L.R. 7 Ex. 271 (Ex. Ch.).

[31]*Re Seaton; Ellis v. Seaton*, [1913] 2 Ch. 614.

[32]1 Fearne, p. 503; *Reev v. Long* (1694), Carth. 309, 90 E.R. 782.

but during the life of the testator, an event happens which makes it impossible for an executory devise to take effect and the next subsequent interest is so limited that, in such event, it is to immediately follow the particular estate, it takes effect at the testator's death as a remainder, vested or contingent according to its limitation.[33] An executory devise may also take effect as a remainder by reason of the happening of an event after the testator's death,[34] although the reason seems to be simply that, if the event which shifts the estate happens and the executory devise is a future interest which is to follow the particular estate, it takes effect as a remainder.[35]

The same thing is not wholly true of remainders. A devise which fails as a remainder by reason of an event happening in the lifetime of the testator may take effect at his death as an executory devise. Thus, where a devisee for life dies before the testator, a devise which was limited as a contingent remainder may take effect at the testator's death as an executory devise in order to give effect to the testator's intention.[36] At common law, however, a remainder cannot be changed to an executory devise by an event after the testator's death.[37]

A future interest need not be created definitely as a remainder or an executory devise. It may be so devised as to leave it uncertain whether it is a remainder or an executory devise, in which case the happening of the specified event will determine which it is. Thus, if an estate tail is devised to A if he attains the age of 21 years or has issue but, if he dies before attaining that age or without issue, the fee simple is devised to B, no estate vests in A if he dies before age 21 without issue and B takes under an executory devise, but, if A attains age 21, the estate vests in him and the future interest of B is a remainder to the estate tail if A dies without issue.[38]

A future interest may be so devised as to depend upon two distinct events, the happening of one of which will make it a remainder and the happening of the other will make it an executory devise. In such a case, the invalidity of one contingency will not affect the other and the devise may take effect upon the happening of the latter accordingly.[39]

1010.3   The Rule in Purefoy v. Rogers

The rule in *Purefoy v. Rogers*,[1] which has already been adverted to in the previous paragraphs, is a rule of law which prevents certain types of future

---

[33]*Doe d. Harris v. Howell* (1829), 10 B. & C. 191 at p. 200, 109 E.R. 422.
[34]*Ibid.*
[35]*See Hopkins v. Hopkins* (1738), 1 Atk. 581 at p. 589, 26 E.R. 365.
[36]*Ibid.*; *Doe d. Scott v. Roach* (1816), 5 M. & S. 482 at p. 492, 105 E.R. 1127.
[37]*Mogg v. Mogg* (1815), 1 Mer. 654 at p. 704, 35 E.R. 811.
[38]*Brownsword v. Edwards* (1751), 2 Ves. Sen. 243, 28 E.R. 157; *Doe d. Herbert v. Selby* (1824), 2 B. & C. 926, 107 E.R. 626; *White v. Summers*, [1908] 2 Ch. 256 at p. 266.
[39]*Evers v. Challis* (1859), 7 H.L.C. 531, 11 E.R. 212.
§1010.3
[1](1671), 2 Wms. Saund. 380, 85 E.R. 1181.

interests from taking effect as executory interests and requires them to take effect as contingent remainders.

The rule states that if it is possible for a limitation to take effect as a contingent remainder at the time of its creation, it shall be construed as a contingent remainder and not as a legal executory interest.

The rule clearly cannot apply to executory interests which spring up in the future after a gap, or which defeat a preceding estate. It can and does apply, however, to limitations which, in a common law conveyance, permitted a contingent remainderman to wait and see if his interest would vest prior to the determination of the preceding estate, for they can take effect as contingent remainders.

Thus, in the following conveyances and devises the apparent executory interests are construed as contingent remainders:

(i) A grant "to X and his heirs to the use of A for life and then to the use of B at age 21".

(ii) A devise "to A for life, remainder to his children who shall attain age 21".[2]

The result in both examples would be that B's interest and A's children's interest would be destroyed if they were not 21 years old at A's death.

On the other hand, if the limitations in both examples had added "after A's death", or "either before or after A's death" they would have taken effect as executory interests since the limitations could then not have taken effect as contingent remainders, the words "after A's death" being construed to mean "any time after A's death", thus leaving a gap.

The effect of the rule is that it renders the interests to which it applies just as capable of natural and artificial destruction as contingent remainders created under a common law conveyance.

The rule has been reversed in England[3] and in Prince Edward Island,[4] but it remains in force in the other provinces.

The rule applies only to legal interests so that, if the limitation arises under a trust or in respect of any other equitable interest, it will take effect as an executory interest.[5]

1011. EQUITABLE REMAINDERS AND EQUITABLE EXECUTORY INTERESTS

As has been shown, the *Statute of Uses*[1] did not execute all uses, but only those that fell strictly within its terms.[2] Interests arising under unexecuted uses, therefore, remained equitable and in due course came to be called trusts. Such interests may be either remainders, in that they take effect at the

---

[2]*Cf. Festing v. Allen* (1843), 12 M. & W. 279, 152 E.R. 1204.
[3]*Contingent Remainders Act*, 40 & 41 Vict., c. 33 (1877). See §1009.5(d), *supra*.
[4]*Real Property Act*, R.S.P.E.I. 1974, c. R-4, s. 13. See §1009.5(d), *supra*.
[5]See §1011, *infra*.
§1011
[1]27 Hen. 8, c. 10 (1535).
[2]*Supra*, §1010.1.

moment of the determination of the preceding estates, or executory interests, They are not subject to the legal remainder rules, nor to the rule in *Purefoy v. Rogers.*[3]

Hence, in a conveyance "to X and his heirs, to the use of Y and his heirs, to the use of Z and his heirs when Z marries", the first use is executed, giving Y the legal estate and Z an equitable executory interest. The same result obtains if the limitation is syncopated as follows: "unto and to the use of Y and his heirs to the use of Z and his heirs when Z marries". Similarly, in a grant to a corporation, in which the use is not executed, such as, "to XYZ Ltd. in trust for (or, to the use of) A when he attains the age of 21", A would receive an equitable executory interest.

If the limitation is made in respect of an equitable interest, such as an equity of redemption, it is also protected. Thus, where a testator devised a freehold, which was subject to a mortgage, to the use of his son for life and then to the use of the son's children who should attain the age of 21 or die under that age leaving issue, it was held that the interests were equitable and thus the son's children's interest was not subject to destruction.[4] Malins, V.C., who had been counsel for the losing side in *Festing v. Allen,*[5] itself an application of the rule in *Purefoy v. Rogers,*[6] said in *Astley v. Micklethwait:*[7] "Why am I to go out of my way to destroy the will instead of preserving it? Anything that would enable the Court to get out of the monstrous doctrine of *Festing v. Allen . . .* ought to be adopted."

Moreover, if the executory limitation starts out as equitable in those circumstances, it is not subject to destruction, even though it later becomes legal when the mortgage is paid off.[8]

Where the legal estate is held by personal representatives in trust for the beneficiaries under the will, the same result obtains. Moreover, modern devolution of estates legislation creates a statutory trust in favour of the beneficiaries, constituting the personal representative the trustee. Thus, section 2(1) of the *Estates Administration Act*[9] provides:

> 2(1) All real and personal property that is vested in a person without a right in any other person to take by survivorship, on his death, whether testate or intestate and notwithstanding any testamentary disposition, devolves to and becomes vested in his personal representative from time to time as trustee for the persons by law beneficially entitled thereto . . .[10]

---

[3](1671), 2 Wms. Saund. 380, 85 E.R. 1181. See §1010.3, *supra.*
[4]*Astley v. Micklethwait* (1880), 15 Ch. D. 59.
[5](1843), 12 M. & W. 279, 152 E.R. 1204.
[6]*Supra*, footnote 3.
[7]*Supra*, footnote 4, at p. 63.
[8]*Re Freme; Freme v. Logan*, [1891] 3 Ch. 167.
[9]R.S.O. 1980, c. 143. While this section was first enacted in 1886, the statutory trust was not imposed until 1910, by S.O. 1910, c. 56.
[10]For similar legislation see: *Devolution of Real Property Act*, R.S.A. 1980, c. D-34, s. 3; R.S.S. 1978, c. D-27, ss. 4, 5; *Estate Administration Act*, R.S.B.C. 1979, c. 114, s. 90; *Devolution of Estates Act*, R.S.M. 1970, c. D70, s. 18; R.S.N.B. 1973, c. D-9, s. 3; *Chattels Real Act*, R.S.N. 1970, c. 36, s. 2; *Real Property Act*, R.S.N.S. 1967, c. 261, s. 6(1); *Probate Act*, R.S.P.E.I. 1974, c. P-19, s. 108(1); *Devolution of Real Property Ordinance*, R.O.N.W.T. 1974, c. D-5, s. 4; R.O.Y.T. 1971, c. D-4, s. 4.

The comparable section in the English *Land Transfer Act*[11] was held in *Re Robson; Douglass v. Douglass*[12] to have the effect of thus converting all legal interests under wills, that is, those which were not already subject to a trust, or which were not created out of equitable estates, into equitable interests, so as to protect executory interests from destruction under the rule in *Purefoy v. Rogers*.[13] Moreover, they did not become subject to destruction when the personal representative conveyed the interests to the beneficiaries, at which time they became legal.[14]

The *Robson* case has not been referred to subsequently and the matter is now academic in England and Manitoba where all future interests are now equitable.[15] The issue seems not to have been dealt with by the Canadian courts. However, if it should arise, *Re Robson*[16] should, it is submitted, be followed, both on principle and because the destructibility rule, being a rule of feudal law, is inappropriate to modern conditions in this country.

The principle of *Re Robson* seems to have been enacted by statute in Newfoundland and extended to deeds *inter vivos* in which no trust is employed.[17] This seems unnecessary since the *Chattels Real Act*[18] in that province treats real property as chattels real with the result that executory interests ought to be indestructible under the common law remainder rules and the rule in *Purefoy v. Rogers*.[19]

1012. ASSIGNABILITY OF FUTURE INTERESTS

At common law, no possibility or right of action was assignable because it might have led to litigation.[1] Contingent remainders and executory interests were treated as possibilities,[2] although they could be released[3] and contracts to convey them were enforced in equity if made for valuable consideration.[4]

Statutes based on the English *Real Property Act*[5] now provide that such interests are alienable *inter vivos*. Thus, the Ontario *Conveyancing and Law of Property Act*[6] provides in s. 10:

---

[11]60 & 61 Vict., c. 65 (1897), s. 1.
[12][1916] 1 Ch. 116.
[13](1671), 2 Wms. Saund. 380, 85 E.R. 1181.
[14]*Re Robson, supra,* footnote 12; *Re Freme, supra,* footnote 8.
[15]By the *Law of Property Act, 1925*, 15 & 16 Geo. 5, c. 20, s. 1; *Perpetuities and Accumulations Act,* S.M. 1982-83, c. 43, s. 4.
[16]*Supra,* footnote 12.
[17]*Chattels Real Act,* R.S.N. 1970, c. 36, s. 5, added by S.N. 1972, no. 13, s. 2.
[18]*Ibid.,* s. 2.
[19]*Supra,* footnote 13.

§1012
[1]*Lampet's Case* (1612), 10 Co. Rep. 46 b at p. 48 a, 77 E.R. 994.
[2]*Fulwood's Case* (1591), 4 Co. Rep. 64 b at 66 b, 76 E.R. 1031.
[3]*Lampet's Case, supra,* at p. 48 b.
[4]*Wright v. Wright* (1750), 1 Ves. Sen. 409, 27 E.R. 1111.
[5]8 & 9 Vict., c. 106 (1845), s. 6.
[6]R.S.O. 1980, c. 90.

10. A contingent, an executory, and a future interest, and a possibility coupled with an interest in land, whether the object of the gift or limitation of such interest or possibility is or is not ascertained, also a right of entry, whether immediate or future, and whether vested or contingent, into or upon land, may be disposed of by deed, but no such disposition, by force only of this Act, defeats or enlarges an estate tail.[7]

Wills statutes similarly provide for the devisability of contingent and executory interests. Thus, the Ontario *Succession Law Reform Act*[8] provides in s. 2:

2. A person may by will devise, bequeath or dispose of all property (whether acquired before or after making his will) to which at the time of his death he is entitled either at law or in equity, including,

. . . .

(b) contingent, executory or other future interests in property, whether the testator is or is not ascertained as the person or one of the persons in whom those interests may respectively become vested, and whether he is entitled to them under the instrument by which they were respectively created or under a disposition of them by deed or will; and

(c) rights of entry, whether for conditions broken or otherwise.[9]

In this respect the Nova Scotia statute is clearer in that it provides that a person may devise all his real property "which if not so devised . . . would devolve upon his heirs-at-law . . .".[10]

Moreover, under devolution of estates legislation the real property of a deceased person descends to his personal representative in trust for the persons beneficially entitled thereto.[11] Some of these statutes speak of real property that "is vested" in the deceased, however,[12] while others refer to real property to which a deceased person was entitled for an interest not ceasing at his death.[13]

The effect of these three types of statutes is generally assumed to be that contingent remainders, executory interests, possibilities of reverter and rights of entry for condition broken are alienable *inter vivos*, devisable and transmissible on death. There would appear to be no difficulty with the alienability and devisability of contingent remainders since the statutes specifically deal

---

[7]To the same effect are: *Property Act*, R.S.N.B. 1973, c. P-19, s. 15; *Real Property Act*, R.S.N.S. 1967, c. 261, s. 26; R.S.P.E.I. 1974, c. R-4, s. 11; *Property Law Act*, R.S.B.C. 1979, c. 340, s. 8.

[8]R.S.O. 1980, c. 488.

[9]To the same effect are: *Wills Act*, R.S.B.C. 1979, c. 434, s. 2; R.S.M. 1970, c. W150, s. 3; R.S.S. 1978, c. W-14, s. 3; R.S.N.B. 1973, c. W-9, s. 2; R.S.A. 1980, c. W-11, s. 3; *Wills Ordinance*, R.O.N.W.T. 1974, c. W-3, s. 4; R.O.Y.T. 1971, c. W-3, s. 4.

[10]*Wills Act*, R.S.N.S. 1967, c. 340, s. 2(1).

[11]*Devolution of Real Property Act*, R.S.A. 1980, c. D-34, s. 3; R.S.S. 1978, c. D-27, ss. 4, 5; *Estate Administration Act*, R.S.B.C. 1979, c. 114, s. 90; *Devolution of Estates Act*, R.S.M. 1970, c. D70, s. 18; R.S.N.B. 1973, c. D-9, s. 3; *Estates Administration Act*, R.S.O. 1980, c. 143, s. 2; *Chattels Real Act*, R.S.N. 1970, c. 36; *Real Property Act*, R.S.N.S. 1967, c. 261, s. 6(1); *Probate Act*, R.S.P.E.I. 1974, c. P-19, s. 108(1); *Devolution of Real Property Ordinance*, R.O.N.W.T. 1974, c. D-5, s. 4; R.O.Y.T. 1971, c. D-4, s. 4.

[12]The Ont., N.S., B.C., Man. and N.B. statutes referred to in footnote 11, *supra*.

[13]The Alta., Sask., N.W.T., Yukon and P.E.I. statutes referred to in footnote 11, *supra*.

with them. Whether such interests pass to the personal representatives under devolution of estates legislation which speaks of property which is vested is, however, another matter, for such interests are clearly not vested. That is also true of possibilities of reverter and rights of entry for condition broken, which are mere possibilities *not* coupled with an interest in land.

Rights of entry for condition broken are dealt with specifically in the several Wills Acts referred to above, so that these are clearly devisable. However, the reference to rights of entry in the conveyancing statutes can mean either a right of entry for condition broken or a right of entry to recover land that has been disseised. The latter meaning was adopted in a number of cases.[14] Except for the specific provisions in the Wills Acts, however, there would seem to be no reason to construe this term so restrictively.

Possibilities of reverter would appear to be devisable under the several Wills Acts since they are future interests in property to which the testator was entitled at his death.[15] However, since they are not possibilities coupled with an interest in land, it is arguable that they may not be assignable *inter vivos*. On the other hand, it appears to have been clearly the intent of the legislature to deal with such interests and to make them assignable. The point was dealt with, but was not definitely decided in *Re Tilbury West Public School Board and Hastie.*[16]

If these interests are not alienable, devisable or transmissible on death to the personal representatives, they will remain in the grantor or his heirs. And the heirs in this case are not the heirs general under modern intestacy legislation, but either the heir at law under the primogeniture rule, or else the heirs as determined under a statute preceding the modern intestacy legislation.[17]

Interests which are limited to a person on a contingency not personal to himself are transmissible on death, as where a fee simple is given to the children of a life tenant when they attain the age of 21, with a gift over to another person if the life tenant dies without issue him surviving. The contingent remainder under the gift over would be devisable, so that, if the devisee predeceases the life tenant, who later dies without issue, the interest passes under his will.[18] If the devisee himself had to attain the age of 21 and failed to do so, the interest would not have passed.[19]

---

[14]*Hunt v. Bishop* (1853), 8 Ex. 675, 155 E.R. 1523; *Hunt v. Remnant* (1854), 9 Ex. 635, 156 E.R. 271; *Baldwin v. Wanzer*; *Baldwin v. Canadian Pacific Ry. Co.* (1892), 22 O.R. 612 (H.C.J.), at p. 641.

[15]Possibilities of reverter held to be devisable in *Re Melville* (1886), 11 O.R. 626 (H.C.J.).

[16][1966] 2 O.R. 20, 55 D.L.R. (2d) 407 (H.C.J.), vard O.R. *loc. cit.* 511, 57 D.L.R. (2d) 519 (H.C.J.).

[17]See Armour, *Real Property*, pp. 404-7, 416-21; Armour, *Title*, pp. 4-7.

[18]*Re Stewart*, [1939] O.R. 153, [1939] D.L.R. 185 (H.C.J.).

[19]On the matter of assignability of rights of entry for condition broken and possibilities of reverter generally, see: Marsh, "Devolution of a Possibility of Reverter in Colorado", 41 Denver L.J. 396 (1964); Yee, "Devolution of a Possibility of Reverter in Colorado Revisited, 52 Denver L.J. 541 (1975); Fratcher, "Exorcise the Curse of Reversionary Possibilities", 28 J. of Mo. Bar 34 (1972); "Note", 2 Willamette L.J. 479 (1963); "Note", 13 Mercer L. Rev. 279 (1961); "Note", 45 Cornell L.Q. 373 (1960).

CHAPTER 11

PERPETUITIES

PART III   CONDITIONS AND FUTURE INTERESTS

1101. SCOPE OF THIS CHAPTER

The word "perpetuity" has had a variety of meanings during the course of the law. At different times it has encompassed restraints on alienation, unbarrable entails, perpetual trusts, accumulations and perpetuities. This chapter deals primarily with the modern law of perpetuities, although the different historical meanings of the word "perpetuity" will also be traced.[1]

The first part of the chapter will deal with the modern rule against perpetuities at common law,[2] followed by discussions of the rule in *Whitby v.*

---

§1101
[1]*Infra*, §1102.
[2]§§1102-1104.24.

Mitchell,[3] and the rule against indefinite duration.[4] The second part of the chapter[5] deals with modern statutory changes to the rule. It should be noted that modern perpetuities statutes do not abolish the common law rule.[5a] Nor do the statutes necessarily cover all the situations to which the common law rule applies. Moreover, they are not retroactive. For this reason it is necessary to discuss the common law rule in some detail before dealing with recent statutory reforms. The third part of the chapter discusses the law of accumulations.[6]

The subjects of unbarrable entails and restraints on alienation will not be dealt with beyond a brief survey in the next section. They are not today regarded as belonging to the law of perpetuities and are dealt with elsewhere.[7]

1102. HISTORICAL BACKGROUND

The following is a brief survey of the development of the concept of perpetuities. For further detail reference should be made to the standard texts.[1]

The law of perpetuities in its broadest sense is ancient in origin. It derives from the bias of the common law in favour of the free alienability of land. This bias was expressed in the early common law by the perception that the tenant's heir did not have an interest in the land, so that the tenant could freely dispose of it, and by statutes such as *Quia Emptores*[2] and the Statutes of Mortmain, which permitted free alienation and restricted conveyances to religious houses and corporations, respectively. Subsequently, decisions permitting warranties, fines and common recoveries made it possible to bar entails.[3] These several decisions and statutes were all designed to limit the right of a person to tie up his land for an indefinite period after his death. In other words, they were designed to prevent perpetuities.

Indeed, the earliest use of the word "perpetuity" is with respect to unbarrable entails, that is, those estates tail which provided that if the tenant in tail attempted to bar the entail, the estate would go over in remainder.[4] Such perpetuities were declared void by the end of the 16th century.[5]

3(1890), 44 Ch. D. 85 (C.A.). See §§1105-1105.1
4§§1106-1106.3.
5§§1107-1107.18.
5aExcept in Manitoba where the *Perpetuities and Accumulations Act*, S.M. 1982-83, c. 43, ss. 2, 3 repeal the entire law of perpetuities and accumulations.
6§§1108-1108.6.
7§§221, 221.8, 503.1(a) and (b), 903.7 (restraints on alienation); §§221, 221.4, 602, 604.1 (estates tail).
§1102
1Holdsworth, vol. 7, pp. 81-144, 193-238; Gray, §§123-200.1; Simes and Smith, §§1211-21; 6 A.L.P., §24.4; Morris and Leach, pp. 3-13; Fratcher, *Perpetuities and Other Restraints* (Ann Arbor, Univ. of Mich. Law School, 1954), pp. 259-70.
218 Edw. 1, cc. 1, 2 (1290).
3See generally §§221 *et seq.*
4*Chudleigh's Case; Dillon v. Freine* (1595), 1 Co. Rep. 120 a, 76 E.R. 270.
5*Corbet's Case; Corbet v. Corbet* (1600), 1 Co. Rep. 83 b, 76 E.R. 187.

Attempts by landowners to avoid these strictures by conveying their land to their issue in a series of life estates were curtailed by the rule which later became known as the rule in *Whitby v. Mitchell*.[6] This rule, which renders a remainder to the issue of an unborn person after a limitation for life to that person void, will be dealt with later.[7]

Even as late as 1682 in the *Duke of Norfolk's Case*,[8] the origin of the modern rule against perpetuities, Lord Nottingham described perpetuities in terms of unbarrable entails as follows:

> A Perpetuity is the Settlement of an Estate or an Interest in Tail, with such Remainders expectant upon it, as are in no Sort in the Power of the Tenant in Tail in Possession, to dock by any Recovery or Assignment, but such Remainders must continue as perpetual Clogs upon the Estate; such do fight against God, for they pretend to such a Stability in human Affairs, as the Nature of them admits not of, and they are against the Reason and the Policy of the Law, and therefore not to be endured.[9]

The modern rule against perpetuities became necessary when new executory interests were developed in the 16th century which were not subject to destruction under the rules of the common law. The early common law future interests presented no perpetuity problem, for even when contingent remainders were allowed about the middle of the 15th century, they were only permitted to take effect if they became vested during the continuance of a prior particular estate. The rule in *Purefoy v. Rogers*[10] further controlled executory interests created under uses and by will since it required that a limitation which could take effect as a contingent remainder should be so construed.

Other executory interests, which became possible as a result of the *Statute of Uses*[11] and the *Statute of Wills*,[12] were not controlled in this manner, however. Thus, in *Pells v. Brown*[13] a testator devised "to A and his heirs, but if A should die without issue in B's lifetime, then to B and his heirs". B's executory devise was held valid. Executory devises of long terms of years also tended to perpetuity and both types of future interest were regarded with suspicion by the courts since they could be used to avoid the well-established prohibitions against unbarrable entails.[14]

The problem with these new interests was not their indefinite duration,

---

6(1890), 44 Ch. D. 85 (C.A.).
7*Infra*, §1105.
8(1682), 3 Chan. Cas. 1, 22 E.R. 931.
9*Ibid.*, at p. 31. *Cf. The Use of the Law* (1629), 7 Bacon's Works, 491 (Spedding's Ed. 1870).
10(1671), 2 Wms. Saund. 380, 85 E.R. 1181.
1127 Hen. 8, c. 10 (1535).
1232 Hen. 8, c. 1 (1540). See §§1003-1003.3 and 1010-11, *supra*, for a discussion of these interests.
13(1620), Cro. Jac. 590, 79 E.R. 504.
14Thus, *e.g.*, in *Child v. Baylie* (1622), Cro. Jac. 459, 79 E.R. 393, an executory devise over of a term upon the death of the first devisee without issue living at his death, was held void.

however, but the fact that they might vest at too remote a time in the future and it is here that the modern law of perpetuities has its origin.

The development of the law of perpetuities was categorized as follows by Farwell, L.J., in *Re Nash*; *Cook v. Frederick*:[15]

> Our Courts have from the earliest times set their face against the suspense or abeyance of the inheritance and have from time to time laid down various rules to prevent perpetuity. One of those is the rule that a preceding estate of freehold is indispensably necessary to support a contingent remainder: Co. Litt. 342 b, Butler's note; another is the rule laid down in 1669 in *Purefoy v. Rogers* (1669), 2 Wms. Saund. (Ed. 1871), 768, 781-9 that no limitation shall be construed as an executory or shifting use which can by possibility take effect by way of remainder; and another (and probably the oldest) was the rule in question forbidding the raising of successive estates by purchase to unborn children, i.e., to the unborn child of an unborn child. The most modern rule, arising out of the development of executory limitations and shifting uses, is what is now usually called the rule against perpetuities, namely, that all estates and interests must vest indefeasibly within a life in being and twenty-one years after. But this is an addition to, not a substitution for, the former rules.

To summarize, the term "perpetuity" has had at least three meanings in the common law, namely, (1) an unbarrable entail, (2) an inalienable or indestructible interest, and (3) a remote executory interest. In the first sense it is no longer referred to in this chapter, except if and to the extent that the rule in *Whitby v. Mitchell*[16] derives from it, a question which has never been satisfactorily settled.[17] In the second sense the term applies to restraints on alienation and to perpetual non-charitable trusts. Only the latter are dealt with in this chapter under the heading "The Rule Against Indefinite Duration".[18] The third sense of the word is the modern one and it is in that sense that the term is used in this chapter. The modern rule against perpetuities might more properly have been called the rule against remoteness of vesting, as argued by Professor Gray and others.[19] However, by reason of long-established practice, the former term is used here.

The modern rule against perpetuities was first defined in the *Duke of Norfolk's Case*.[20] The facts were as follows: The Duke of Arundel conveyed land to trustees for 200 years upon trust for his second son, Henry, in tail male and, if his first son, Thomas, should die without issue in Henry's lifetime (Thomas being *non compos mentis*) then to his third son, Charles, in tail. The contingency stipulated happened and the earldom passed to Henry. The question then was whether the executory limitation in favour of Charles was valid. The Chancellor, Lord Nottingham, held that it was, despite the unanimous contrary opinion of the chief justices of the common law courts whom he had asked to advise him. In his view, if the executory interest is bound to

---

15[1910] 1 Ch. 1 at p. 7.
16(1890), 44 Ch. D. 85 (C.A.).
17The controversy is discussed in §1105, *infra*.
18See §§1106-1106.3, *infra*.
19Gray, §2. *Cf. Lewis*, p. 164.
20(1682), 3 Chan. Cas. 1, 22 E.R. 931.

vest during the lifetime of lives in being at the creation of the interest, it is valid. The decision was reversed by his successor, Lord Keeper North[21] but was restored by the House of Lords.[22]

Lord Nottingham did not place a specific limit upon the perpetuity period, but left that for future determination. Indeed, it was not for another century and a half that the rule as it is known today was fully defined. In the meantime, the perpetuity period was extended to allow for the birth of posthumous children and the minority of a person unborn at the creation of the interest, who could be either the devisee[23] or another.[24] Finally, in *Cadell v. Palmer*[25] it was held that it was not necessary to restrict the extension to the minority of a person, but that it could extend to a period in gross of twenty-one years after lives in being together with a period of gestation if necessary.

The origin of the twenty-one-year period is somewhat dubious. It is probable that it came about by accident because of the law respecting the discontinuance of an estate tail. Lord Brougham explains the extension as follows:

> The Judges held that that is now the law, whatever may have been its origin. It most clearly arises from a mistake. The law never meant to give a further term of twenty-one years, much less any period of gestation. The law never meant to say that there shall be twenty-one years added to the life or lives in being, and that within those limits you may entail the estate, but what the law meant to say was this: until the heir of the last of the lives in being attains twenty-one, by law a recovery cannot be suffered, and consequently the discontinuance of the estate cannot be effected, and for that reason, says the law, you shall have the twenty-one years added, because that is the fact and not the law, namely, that till a person reached the age of twenty-one he could not cut off the entail. For that reason and in that way it has crept in by degrees; *Communis error facit jus* . . .[26]

In addition, after the *Duke of Norfolk's Case* it was held that it was possible to use more than the one life in being employed in that case. Thus in *Scatterwood v. Edge*[27] the court noted, "let the lives be never so many, there must be a survivor, and so it is but the length of that life; [for Twisden used to say, the candles were all lighted at once,]". Moreover, the lives selected need not be beneficiaries, but can be anyone who is alive at the creation of the interest.[28]

The modern rule can thus be formulated as follows, in the words of Professor Gray:[29] "No interest is good unless it must vest, if at all, not later than twenty-one years after some life in being at the creation of the interest."

---

[21](1683), 3 Chan. Cas. 53, 22 E.R. 963.
[22](1685), 3 Chan. Cas. 54, 22 E.R. 963.
[23]*Stephens v. Stephens* (1736), Cases T. Talbot 228, 25 E.R. 751.
[24]*Massingberd v. Ash* (1684), 2 Ch. R. 275, 21 E.R. 677.
[25](1833), 1 Cl. & Fin. 372, 6 E.R. 956 (H.L.).
[26]*Cole v. Sewell* (1848), 2 H.L.C. 186 at p. 233, 9 E.R. 1062. *Cf. Long v. Blackall* (1797), 7 T. R. 100 at p. 102, 101 E.R. 875, *per* Lord Kenyon, C.J.
[27](1697), 1 Salkeld 229 at p. 229, 91 E.R. 203. The reference is to a remark by Twisden, J., in *Love v. Wyndham* (1670), 1 Mod. 50 at p. 54, 86 E.R. 724. *Cf. Gooch v. Gooch* (1853), 3 De G. M. & G. 366 at p. 384, 43 E.R. 143, *per* Lord Cranworth, L.C.
[28]*Thellusson v. Woodford* (1799), 4 Ves. Jun. 227, 31 E.R. 117, affd 11 Ves. Jun. 112, 32 E.R. 1030 (H.L.); *Cadell v. Palmer, supra*, footnote 25.
[29]§201.

The definition is defective in a number of ways. For example, it fails to take account of the fact that class gifts may be void for perpetuity even though they are vested, that contingent gifts to charities are not always subject to the rule and that the perpetuity period does not always commence to run at the creation of the interest. However, the definition is a convenient shorthand statement of the rule, which has often received judicial recognition. Its ramifications will be explored in detail in this chapter.

The rule against perpetuities started out in life as a flexible one. Lord Nottingham, in the *Duke of Norfolk's Case*,[30] expressly refused to impose limits upon it but stated that he would draw the line in future cases "wherever any visible Inconvenience doth appear". However, the rule soon became very rigid. The courts demanded absolute or mathematical certainty under the rule. Moreover, they insisted that all limitations be construed strictly without regard to the rule. In other words, the courts would first construe a limitation according to its strict grammatical meaning and only then would they consider the application of the rule to the limitation. It was not thought permissible to construe the limitation in such a way as to have regard to the effect of the rule.[31]

It is difficult today to appreciate the reasons for this development. However, it must be remembered that there was a long tradition in the common law which favoured free alienability of land. That tradition was threatened by the new executory interests, held to be indestructible in *Pells v. Brown*.[32] That decision "went down with the Judges like chopped hay".[33] Moreover, the courts seem to have repented of the indestructibility of executory interests[34] and, although that decision was irreversible, they took out their frustrations on the new perpetuity rule.

The rule was originally applicable only to interests in land, but was soon applied to future interests in personalty as well, even though the rationale for its application to land is different from that of its application to personalty.[35]

Because of the rigidity of the rule and its tendency to defeat the intentions of unwary testators, several jurisdictions in the United States passed legislation at an early stage modifying or replacing the rule. These statutes were not very effective and most were subsequently repealed.[36] As a result of the writings of the late Professor Leach and others, however, many jurisdictions in the United States and elsewhere have enacted modern perpetuities legislation. Generally, these statutes replace the mathematical certainty requirement of the rule with the principle of "wait and see", under which actual events determine

---

[30](1682), 3 Chan. Cas. 1 at p. 49, 22 E.R. 931, revd 3 Chan. Cas. 53, 22 E.R. 963, restd 3 Chan. Cas. 54, 22 E.R. 963 (H.L.).
[31]See, *e.g.*, *Pearks v. Moseley* (1880), 5 App. Cas. 714 (H.L.), at p. 719, *per* Lord Selborne, L.C.; *Re Hume*; *Public Trustee v. Mabey*, [1912] 1 Ch. 693 at p. 698, *per* Parker, J.
[32](1620), Cro. Jac. 590, 79 E.R. 504.
[33]*Scattergood v. Edge* (1699), 12 Mod. 278 at p. 281, 88 E.R. 1320.
[34]*Ibid.*
[35]Morris and Leach, p. 12.
[36]*Ibid.*, p. 13; 6 A.L.P., §24.4.

whether an interest is valid or void. In addition they usually correct the more blatant excesses of the rule. The Canadian statutes will be discussed in the second part of this chapter. It should be noted, however, that most of these statutes do not abolish the common law rule (which was received in all the Canadian provinces) but merely modify it. The *Perpetuities Act* of Prince Edward Island[37] is an exception. It supplants the common law rule and provides instead that an interest must vest within sixty years after a life or lives in being at the creation of the interest. The rules against perpetuities have been abolished in their entirety in Manitoba.[38]

1103. RATIONALE OF AND NEED FOR A RULE AGAINST PERPETUITIES

It has been seen in the preceding section that the modern rule against perpetuities was rendered necessary in order that future interests arising under the *Statute of Uses*[1] and the *Statute of Wills*,[2] which were indestructible under the common law remainder rules and the rules against unbarrable entails, might be controlled. The control was exercised by requiring that such interests must vest within a specified time. Although not itself concerned with inalienability, the rule was born out of the same concern for free alienability of land that produced the rules against unbarrable entails. Inalienability was considered harmful because it stagnated land, the primary source of economic wealth in earlier times. This arose because the various devices which tended to perpetuity created only limited interests in land, interests which either might be defeated or which might not arise until some future time. The owners of such interests had difficulty selling them and at the same time were loath to expend moneys to improve the land. This was thought to be inappropriate since it impoverished the nation's resources and diminished its wealth. The rule against perpetuities did not, of course, prohibit the creation of limited interests, but did have the effect of reducing the consequences of such interests by requiring that they must become vested within a life in being plus twenty-one years from the creation of the interest.[3]

The question should be asked, however, whether the rule is still relevant today when the nation's wealth consists primarily of personal property, not land, and when, moreover, there are other devices for preventing economic stagnation. The most noticeable example of the latter is modern income and death taxes which prevent an undue concentration of wealth in the hands of a few since they purport to redistribute wealth through a graduated income and a generational tax. Similarly, modern dependants' support legislation adequately protects dependants from capricious testators by enabling the

---

[37]R.S.P.E.I. 1974, c. P-3.
[38]By the *Perpetuities and Accumulations Act*, S.M. 1982-83, c. 43, s. 3.
§1103
[1]27 Hen. 8, c. 10 (1535).
[2]32 Hen. 8, c. 1 (1540).
[3]Morris and Leach, p. 15.

court to make provision out of the estates for dependants who have not been adequately provided for. The rule need not be retained for these reasons, therefore. It is appropriate, however, that there be some restrictions on testamentary freedom in addition to these devices, for in our society it does not seem proper to permit a person to control his property from the grave for an inordinate period of time. Thus, a gift to one's first great-great-grandson at age 30 would appear to most persons to be improper.[4] Indeed, judging by the many jurisdictions which have enacted modern perpetuities statutes, it may be assumed that the legislatures deem a perpetuity rule to be necessary. Thus, in this respect it may be said that "the Rule against Perpetuities strikes a fair balance between the desires of members of the present generation, and similar desires of succeeding generations, to do what they wish with the property which they enjoy".[5]

One can, of course, argue about the permissible perpetuity period. However, there is no *a priori* answer to the question of what period is appropriate. It may be that a fixed period of years might be appropriate although that alternative creates problems of its own. Therefore, in the absence of compelling reasons to change the period from the one to which the profession has become accustomed, it should be retained.[6]

At the same time, it is evident that the common law rule works great hardship and needs to be reformed. Modern perpetuities legislation has gone a long way to correct defects in the rule, although, as will be seen, the statutes are not without problems themselves.

1104. THE RULE AGAINST PERPETUITIES AT COMMON LAW

As indicated above, the rule against perpetuities, sometimes called the modern rule against perpetuities, might more appropriately be called the rule against remoteness of vesting since it strikes down interests which vest too remotely.[1] The rule applies in all the common law provinces and Territories of Canada except for Prince Edward Island. In that province an interest must vest within sixty years after a life or lives in being, but remainder interests are exempt from this limitation.[2] The rule continues to apply in those provinces and Territories which have enacted modern perpetuities legislation, for all these statutes provide that except as stipulated in them the common law rule

---

[4]The example is taken from Maudsley, p. 222. For a different view see Manitoba Law Reform Commission Report on *The Rules Against Accumulations and Perpetuities* (1982), pp. 28-46, 49-54.

[5]Simes, *Public Policy and the Dead Hand* (Ann Arbor, Univ. of Mich. Law School, 1955), p. 58.

[6]See Maudsley, pp. 223-4, who comes to this conclusion after discussing possible alternatives.

§1104

[1]§1102, *supra.*

[2]*Perpetuities Act*, R.S.P.E.I. 1974, c. P-3. Hereafter in this chapter referred to as the "P.E.I. Act".

continues to have full effect.³ In the second part of this chapter the argument will be made that the retention of the common law rule is unnecessary and redundant. However, because the rule is retained and because the statutes are not retroactive, the common law rule must first be considered in some detail.

1104.1 Statement of the Rule

The rule against perpetuities has been variously defined in the cases. The following definition, taken from the judgment of Cresswell, J., in *Lord Dungannon v. Smith*,¹ is representative:

> ... an executory devise to be valid must be so framed that the estate devised *must* vest, if at all, within a life or lives in being and twenty-one years after; it is not sufficient that it *may* vest within that period; it must be good in its creation; and unless it is created in such terms that it cannot vest after the expiration of a life or lives in being, and twenty-one years, and the period allowed for gestation, it is not valid, and subsequent events cannot make it so.

Another definition, taken from the same case, is similar:

> ... if at the time of its creation, the limitation is so framed, as not, *ex necessitate*, to take effect within the prescribed period, that is, if it is bad in its inception, it will not become valid by reason of the happenng of subsequent events which may bring the time of its actual vesting and taking effect within the period prescribed by law.²

It has been said that it is better to omit the reference to the period of gestation and to say instead "for the purposes of this rule, a child en ventre sa mère is considered as a life in being".³

Lewis phrased the rule as follows:

> A perpetuity is a future limitation, whether executory or by way of remainder, and of either real or personal property, which is not to vest until after the expiration of, or will not necessarily vest within, the period fixed and prescribed by law for the creation of future estates and interests; and which is not destructible by the persons for the time being entitled to the property subject to the future limitation, except with the concurrence of the individual interested under that limitation.⁴

---

³*Perpetuities Act*, R.S.A. 1980, c. P-4; R.S.O. 1980, c. 374; *Perpetuity Act*, R.S.B.C. 1979, c. 321; *Perpetuities Ordinance*, R.O.N.W.T. 1974, c. P-3; O.Y.T. 1980 (1st) c. 23. The *Perpetuities and Accumulations Act*, R.S.N. 1970, c. 291, merely provides that the rules of law and statutory enactments relating to perpetuities and accumulations do not apply to employee benefit trusts. The several statutes are hereafter in this chapter referred to as the "Alta. Act", the "N.W.T. Ord.", *etc.*

§1104.1
¹(1846), 12 Cl. & Fin. 546 at p. 563, 8 E.R. 1523 (H.L.), adopted by Lord Davey in *Hancock v. Watson*, [1902] A.C. 14 (H.L.), at p. 17.
²*Lord Dungannon v. Smith, supra,* at p. 613, *per* Tindal, C.J. *Cf. Ferguson v. Ferguson* (1876), 39 U.C.Q.B. 232, revd 1 O.A.R. 452, restd 2 S.C.R. 497; *Meyers v. Hamilton Provident and Loan Co.* (1890), 19 O.R. 358 (H.C.J.).
³*Re Wilmer's Trusts; Moore v. Wingfield,* [1903] 2 Ch. 411 (C.A.), at p. 422.
⁴Lewis, p. 164.

This definition has been followed by Farwell, J., in *Re Ashforth*; *Sibley v. Ashforth*,[5] and in other cases.[6]

Probably the best-known modern definition is that of Professor Gray, which has been adopted by many modern writers and has often been quoted in the cases. It is as follows: "No interest is good unless it must vest, if at all, not later than twenty-one years after some life in being at the creation of the interest."[7]

It should be noted that while this definition is perhaps the most convenient because of its brevity, it is defective in a number of ways. It fails to state, for example, that for the purpose of the rule against perpetuities a class gift is not vested unless the exact membership of the class has been ascertained. Nor does it suggest that the period does not always commence at the creation of the interest, for example, in respect of powers of appointment. However, if one remembers that save for such exceptional situations the rule is accurate, it becomes a useful working tool.

1104.2 The Perpetuity Period

The perpetuity period during which an interest must vest is a life in being, plus twenty-one years. In addition, actual periods of gestation, both at the beginning and at the end of the period may extend the period. In other words, a child *en ventre sa mère* may be a life in being for the purposes of the rule. Similarly, a child conceived but not yet born when the period ends is allowed to take, if he is in fact born. The following example illustrates this point:

A bequest, "to my children for life, remainder to my grandchildren who attain the age of 21".

If the testator had a child, C1, at his death, and one posthumous child, C2, both can be lives in being and, of course, take a life estate. If, C2 survived C, and C2 left a posthumous child, GC1, GC1 can take, even though his interest vests more than twenty-one years after the death of C2, the last life in being.[1]

It should be noted, however, that an additional period in gross of nine months is not permitted.[2] There must be an actual period of gestation and an actual birth.

5[1905] 1 Ch. 535 at p. 541.

6*Ferguson v. Ferguson*, *supra*, footnote 2. See also *Meyers v. Hamilton Provident and Loan Co.*, *supra*, footnote 2; *Re Miller*, [1938] O.W.N. 118, [1938] 2 D.L.R. 765 (H.C.J.).

7Gray, §201.

§1104.2

1*Cf. Thellusson v. Woodford* (1805), 11 Ves. Jun. 112, 32 E.R. 1030 (H.L.); *Re Wilmer's Trusts*; *Moore v. Wingfield*, [1903] 2 Ch. 411 (C.A.).

2*Cadell v. Palmer* (1833), 1 Cl. & Fin. 372, 6 E.R. 956 (H.L.); *Re Stern*; *Bartlett v. Stern*, [1962] Ch. 732 at p. 737.

(a) Commencement of the period

Although the rule against perpetuities is usually phrased in such a way that the period appears to commence at the creation of the interest,[3] it would be more accurate to say that the period commences when one person is no longer the sole beneficial owner of the interest, or can no longer make himself the sole beneficial owner whenever he chooses.[4]

The general rule is that the period commences on the date on which the instrument creating the estate or interest takes effect. In the case of a will, this is the date of the testator's death and, in the case of a deed or other non-testamentary instrument, it is the date of delivery.[5]

The following example illustrates the different results that may flow from the different date of commencement that applies to deeds and wills:

A gift, "to A in trust for such of my grandchildren as attain the age of 21 years".

If this is a testamentary gift, it will be valid, for at the testator's death all his children must perforce be alive and they are the lives in being. Hence all grandchildren, if they reach the age of 21 at all, must do so within a period of twenty-one years after the death of the survivor of the testator's children.

If the gift in the above example were *inter vivos*, however, it would fail. Since the deed takes effect from its delivery and not from the settlor's death, it is possible that he may have further children after the delivery of the deed. Those children cannot be lives in being since they were not living at the creation of the interest. Hence any children they may have could possibly take more than twenty-one years after the death of the last surviving life in being, namely, the settlor, or one of his children living at the date of the deed. It is of course possible that all of the grandchildren will in fact take vested interests during the lifetime of a life in being. However, the rule strikes the gift down, because it is mathematically possible that the gift will vest outside the period.

The general rule stated above yields in a number of situations. Thus, where a revocable trust is created by deed, the period begins to run when the power of revocation ends, namely, when the settlor dies or releases his power.[6]

Where a general power is created, the perpetuity period as regards the validity of an appointment begins to run when the power is exercised.[7] As regards the validity of a gift over in default of appointment under a general power, the period begins to run when the power can no longer be exercised.[8] The reason is that a general power to appoint enables the donee to appoint

---

[3]See §1104.1, *supra*.
[4]Morris and Leach, p. 57.
[5]*Long v. Blackall* (1797), 7 T. R. 100, 101 E.R. 875; *Thellusson v. Woodford, supra*, footnote 1, at p. 138; *Cadell v. Palmer, supra*, footnote 2.
[6]Gray, §524.1.
[7]*Ibid*., §524. It should be noted that in the United States, general powers to appoint by will only are treated as special powers: Gray, §§526-526.3; Simes and Smith, §1275.
[8]Morris and Leach, p. 57.

to himself. Therefore, when he appoints, it is as though he were disposing of his own property.

Where a special power is created, the period as regards the validity of an appointment and of a gift over in default of appointment begins to run when the power is created,[9] the appointment being "read back" into the instrument creating the power.

The validity of powers of appointment themselves, as well as the validity of appointments thereunder is dealt with elsewhere.[10]

No matter when the period commences to run, the only facts and circumstances that are relevant for the purposes of the rule are those that then exist.[11] For example, if a testator devises land,

To X's grandchildren when they attain the age of 21,

the fact that X was alive when the will was made is irrelevant. The fact that X is alive or dead at the testator's death is relevant, however. If X is then dead, his children must necessarily all be living (or have predeceased him), in which case they (or their issue if they are dead) are the lives in being and the gift will vest in time. If X is still alive, however, the gift will fail since he may have further children who cannot be lives in being and their children may reach the stipulated age more than twenty-one years after the death of the last life in being.

(b) Lives in being

The question of who are or may be the lives in being at common law has exercised the commentators perhaps more than any other aspect of the rule against perpetuities. In this respect the common law is simpler than some of the reforming statutes, however. At common law any living person may be a life in being for the purpose of a limitation.[12] On the other hand, he will not be regarded as such unless it is mathematically certain that the interest disposed of by the limitation must vest, if at all, during the life of that person plus twenty-one years.[13]

Thus, if it cannot be said that there is a person within whose lifetime plus twenty-one years an interest must vest, if it vest at all, there are no lives in being, for lives in being at common law are those which validate a gift.[14] Morris and Wade are of a different view. They hold that those persons are

---

[9]Gray, ss. 514-22; *Re Legh's Settlement Trusts; Public Trustee v. Legh,* [1938] Ch. 39 (C.A.); *Re Pratt's Settlement Trusts; McCullum v. Phipps-Hornby,* [1943] Ch. 356; *Re Johnson's Settlement Trusts; McClure v. Johnson,* [1943] Ch. 341; *Re Goodhue Trusts* (1920), 47 O.L.R. 178 (H.C.J.).

[10]See §1104.7, *infra.*

[11]*Lord Dungannon v. Smith* (1846), 12 Cl. & Fin. 546, 8 E.R. 1523 (H.L.); *Cattlin v. Brown* (1853), 11 Hare 372 at p. 382, 68 E.R. 1319.

[12]Maudsley, p. 42.

[13]*Ibid.,* p. 43.

[14]*Ibid.,* pp. 5, 88 *et seq.,* 94.

lives in being at common law whose lives, "as a matter of causality . . . restrict the vesting period". Not all those persons can save a gift for the rule against perpetuities, however, but only those which "restrict [the vesting period] sufficiently to satisfy the Rule".[15] They, therefore, recognize two categories of lives in being, a wide group which has some causal connection with the gift and another, a narrower group, whose members validate a gift. It has been convincingly demonstrated by Maudsley that the cases do not recognize the larger category.[16] Moreover, Morris and Wade's theory is not generally accepted by other commentators.[17]

In order to ascertain the life (or lives) in being for the purpose of a particular limitation, one can only effectively use those persons within whose lives (plus twenty-one years) it is possible to postulate that the interest will vest, if at all. In other words, there must be a relatively close connection between the life in being and the intended beneficiary. Again, the reason is not that any number of complete strangers on the other side of the world cannot be lives in being, but that one must be able to say of them that the interest will vest, if it vest at all, during their lives plus twenty-one years. Therefore, in a gift

To the children of X who attain the age of 21,

the lives of A, B, C and D, who dwell in Australia, are irrelevant. X, however, is relevant and, indeed, is the only life in being, for it can be said with certainty that the interests of his children must vest, if they vest at all, during X's lifetime or within twenty-one years (plus any actual period of gestation) thereafter.[18]

The question that should be asked in order to ascertain the life or lives in being is:

Can I point to some person or persons now living and say that this interest will by the very terms of its creation be vested in an identified individual within twenty-one years after that person dies?[19]

The persons whose lives make up the period are those indicated and ascer-

---

[15]Morris and Wade, "Perpetuities Reform at Last" (1964), 80 L.Q. Rev. 486 at p. 497. Cf. Morris and Leach, p. 62; Megarry and Wade, p. 221.

[16]Maudsley, pp. 96 et seq.

[17]See, e.g., Simes, "Is the Rule Against Perpetuities Doomed? The 'Wait and See' Doctrine", 52 Mich. L. Rev. 179 (1953-54), at p. 186; Allan, "Perpetuities: Who Are the Lives in Being?", 81 L.Q. Rev. 106 (1965), at p. 108; Fetters, "Perpetuities: The Wait-and-See Disaster — A Brief Reply to Professor Maudsley, with a Few Asides to Professors Leach, Simes, Wade, Dr. Morris, et al.", 60 Cornell L. Rev. 380 (1974-75), at p. 388. And see further, Maudsley, at pp. 94-5.

[18]It is, of course, possible today, through the utilization of sperm banks, that X may have a child many years after his death. For obvious reasons, the common law rule took no cognizance of this possibility. For an interesting article dealing with this problem, see Schuyler, "The New Biology and the Rule Against Perpetuities", 15 U.C.L.A. L. Rev. 420 (1967-68).

[19]Sparks, "Perpetuities Problems of the General Practitioner", 8 U. of Fla. L. Rev. 465 (1955), at p. 470.

tained by the instrument creating the estate or interest and it is not necessary that they take any interest in the property or be connected with any person having an interest.[20] Moreover, they may be expressly named in the instrument or they may be implied.

(i) Express lives

The testator or settlor may expressly select the lives in being, as in the following example:

> To my trustee, in trust to accumulate the rents and profits during the lives of my sons, grandsons and great-grandsons living at my death, and on the death of the survivor, to divide the corpus into three equal parts and to transfer each part to the eldest lineal male descendant of each of my three sons then living.[21]

A more simple example would be:

> To such of my grandchildren as attain the age of 21 within twenty-one years of the death of the survivor of A, B, C and D.

There is no limit to the number of lives selected, provided they be in existence and ascertainable at the creation of the interest.[22] If the number of the lives chosen is so large that it becomes virtually impracticable to ascertain them, the limitation is void for uncertainty and will fail, even though it is otherwise restricted to the perpetuity period.[23]

In *Re Viscount Exmouth; Viscount Exmouth v. Praed*,[24] the testator, a peer, bequeathed heirlooms to trustees in trust to permit them to be enjoyed for life by any person who should acquire the title, if such person was in existence at the testator's death, or born in due time afterwards. However, no person was to have an absolute interest until the expiration of twenty-one years after the death of all such persons as should be in existence at the testator's death and afterwards attain the title. It was held that the latter clause was void for uncertainty and that the first person born after the death of the testator and

---

[20]*Cadell v. Palmer* (1833), 1 Cl. & Fin. 372, 6 E.R. 956 (H.L.); *Hopkins v. Hopkins* (1738), 1 Atk. 581, 26 E.R. 365.

[21]The example is based upon *Thellusson v. Woodford* (1799), 4 Ves. Jun. 227, 31 E.R. 117, affd 11 Ves. Jun. 112, 32 E.R. 1030 (H.L.).

[22]*Cadell v. Palmer, supra*, footnote 20, in which the number was twenty-eight; *Thellusson v. Woodford* (1805), 11 Ves. Jun. 112 at p. 145, 32 E.R. 1030 (H.L.), in which Lord Eldon, L.C., said: "... it is competent to a testator to give a life-estate, to be appointed by the survivor of 1000 persons"; *Robinson v. Hardcastle* (1786), 2 Bro. C.C. 22 at p. 30, 29 E.R. 11, in which Lord Thurlow, L.C., said: "A man may appoint 100 or 1000 trustees, and that the survivor of them shall appoint a life-estate". That the question of impracticability must be decided at the date when the instrument takes effect was confirmed by *Re Leverhulme; Cooper v. Leverhulme*, [1943] 2 All E.R. 274 (Ch.), and *Re Warren's Will Trusts; Baker-Carr v. Warren* (1961), 105 Sol. Jo. 511.

[23]*Thellusson v. Woodford, supra*, footnote 22, at p. 145, *per* Eldon, L.C.

[24](1883), 23 Ch. D. 158.

attaining the title acquired an absolute interest in the heirlooms, notwithstanding that there was still living a person who was alive at the testator's death and who was capable of inheriting the title:

> ... from the death of the first of the class of persons indicated by the will down to the expiration of twenty-one years from the death of the last of the persons who may possibly attain the title the whole question of the possession of these chattels would be in uncertainty. In my judgment that is such an uncertainty in this condition or defeasance as prevents it from being clear and certain, and renders it inoperative.[25]

Similarly in *Re Moore*; *Prior v. Moore*,[26] a bequest in trust to keep in repair a tomb "for the longest period allowed by law, that is to say, until the period of twenty-one years from the death of the last survivor of all persons who shall be living at my death" was held void for uncertainty.

It became common in England during the 20th century to employ royal lives as express lives in being and this practice was followed to a lesser extent in Canada, but there do not appear to be any reported Canadian cases on "royal lives" clauses. Such clauses may cause difficulty because it may be impracticable to ascertain the lives. This was particularly true of those royal lives clauses drafted with reference to the descendants of Queen Victoria. The following clause is representative:

> A trust for distribution among described family members living "at the expiration of 20 years from the day of the death of the last survivor of all the lineal descendants of Her Late Majesty Queen Victoria who shall be living at the time of my death".[27]

The above clause was held valid in *Re Villar*.[28] The testator in that case died in 1926. At that time there were approximately 120 living descendants of Queen Victoria, spread all over Europe and elsewhere. Moreover, because of the recent upheavals caused by the war and the Russian revolution, including the massacre at Jekaterinburg, it could not be said with certainty that some were alive or dead. Nevertheless, the clause was upheld, although reluctantly.

In *Re Leverhulme*; *Cooper v. Leverhulme*,[29] a similar clause was upheld, the testator having died in 1925, although the case itself was not decided until 1943. The court warned that the formula should no longer be used.[30] Even as late as 1944, however, it was upheld, when there were 194 descendants of Queen Victoria.[31]

Presumably today one would be unwise to employ a Queen Victoria clause, but a George V or VI clause would probably be regarded as valid.

---

[25]*Ibid.*, at p. 166, *per* Fry, J.
[26][1901] 1 Ch. 936 at pp. 936-7.
[27]See *Re Villar*; *Public Trustee v. Villar*, [1928] Ch. 471 at p. 471, affd [1929] 1 Ch. 243 (C.A.).
[28]*Ibid.*
[29][1943] 2 All E.R. 274 (Ch.).
[30]*Ibid.*, at p. 281.
[31]*Re Warren's Will Trusts*, *supra*, footnote 22. The testatrix in that case made her will in 1943 and died in 1944.

Although the point is inherent in the statement of the rule against perpetuities, it should be noted that the lives in being can only be human lives, not those of animals or other living things, such as trees.[32]

(ii) Implied lives

Where the testator or settlor has not expressly selected the lives in being, they may be implied. The following examples will illustrate this point.

(1) A bequest, "to my grandchildren who attain the age of 21".
(2) An *inter vivos* trust, "to my grandchildren who marry".
(3) A bequest, "to the first of my lineal descendants to tour Europe with A".
(4) A bequest, "to the children of A who attain the age of 21".
(5) A bequest, "to the first grandchild of A to marry".

In the first example, the gift to the grandchildren will vest in time, for the lives in being are the testator's children who are all alive at his death or, if any be then dead, their children are themselves lives in being.

The gift in the second example is void because it is possible that the settlor may have further children who will not, of course, be lives in being. Thus, it is possible that their children's interest will vest more than twenty-one years after the death of the last life in being.

The gift in the third example is valid for it must vest, if at all, during the lifetime of A, a living person.

The gift in the fourth example is also valid, for A's children must clearly attain the age of 21 within twenty-one years of his death, A being the life in being.

By parity of reasoning, the gift in the last example is void unless one of A's grandchildren is already married at the testator's death. There is no life in being in this example, just as in the second example, because there is no person of whom it can be said with certainty that the gift will vest within twenty-one years of his death. Those persons who might be considered as lives in being, such as A, A's living children and their wives, and any living grandchildren, may all die more than twenty-one years before A's first grandchild marries.

It should be noted that one can draw a distinction between example (3) on the one hand and examples (1) and (4) on the other. In example (3) the gift must vest, if at all, during the lifetime of a living person named or referred to in the gift. That person is the implied life in being. In examples (1) and (4) the lives are also implied. However, in these cases, they automatically validate the gifts. Moreover, it is not necessary in these cases to refer to the life or death of the life in being; he is a life in being because he is biologically involved in the outcome. Maudsley puts them into a separate category of "automatic

---

[32]*Re Kelly; Cleary v. James*, [1932] I.R. 255. Contrast *Re Dean; Cooper-Dean v. Stevens* (1889), 41 Ch. D. 552, a trust to maintain the testator's horses and dogs for fifty years if they so long lived, held valid. The case was criticized in Jarman, 8th ed., vol. 1 (London, Sweet & Maxwell, 1951), p. 305, note (r).

lives" because they are included in the statutory list of measuring lives contained in the English *Perpetuities and Accumulations Act, 1964*,[33] whereas other implied lives, a category he calls "impliedly selected lives", are not.[34] This point is relevant also under the Alberta, British Columbia and Yukon statutes and will be dealt with again later in this chapter.[35]

(iii) Person en ventre sa mère

A child who is *en ventre sa mère* at the time of the creation of the interest is capable of being a life in being for the period of suspense allowed by the rule and may take the interest if it is given to him and he is born alive.[36] Consequently, where there was a devise to a child *en ventre sa mère*, for life in case it should be a son, remainder to the issue male or descendants of such child as at the time of his death would be his heirs-at-law and, in case at the time of his death there should be no such issue male or descendants or in case the child should not be a son, remainder over, the limitation over was held not to be too remote to take effect.[37] Also, where there was a devise to A for life with remainder to his child or children for their lives in equal shares, the share of any child dying to go to his child or children and their heirs as tenants in common, it was held that the limitation was not void for remoteness to the children of A's children as might be living at the death of the testator, a child *en ventre sa mère* being regarded as *in esse* for the purposes of the rule. The limitation was void to children of children unborn at the testator's death, the gifts of shares to the children of children being separate and independent, those capable of taking effect within the limits allowed by law being good and those incapable of taking effect within such limits being bad.[38]

The established rule that a child who is *en ventre sa mère* at the time of the testator's death and who is subsequently born must be treated as having been alive at the testator's death is not to be departed from merely because it may be in the interest of the child to contend that the gift is void as infringing the rule against perpetuities and the rule is applied whether or not it is to the advantage of the unborn child.[39] There is no fixed rule of construction, however, which compels a court to hold that a child was "born" in the lifetime of the testator because it was *en ventre sa mère* at his death; that peculiar rule of construction of the word "born" being limited to cases where that construction is necessary for the benefit of the unborn child.[40]

[33]C. 55 (1964, U.K.).
[34]Maudsley, pp. 92-4, 156-7.
[35]*Infra*, §1107.4(a)(iii).
[36]*Thellusson v. Woodford* (1805), 11 Ves. Jun. 112, 32 E.R. 1030 (H.L.); *Lord Dungannon v. Smith* (1846), 12 Cl. & Fin. 546, 8 E.R. 1523 (H.L.); *Villar v. Gilbey*, [1907] A.C. 139 (H.L.), in which Lord Atkinson said that the period of gestation may be added at both ends of the period of twenty-one years mentioned in the rule.
[37]*Long v. Blackall* (1797), 7 T. R. 100, 101 E.R. 875.
[38]*Knapping v. Tomlinson* (1864), 34 L.J. Ch. 3.
[39]*Re Wilmer's Trusts*; *Moore v. Wingfield*, [1903] 2 Ch. 411 (C.A.).
[40]*Blasson v. Blasson* (1864), 2 De G. J. & S. 665, 46 E.R. 534.

In *Blasson v. Blasson*[41] a testatrix declared a trust for accumulation until the youngest of the children of her three nephews and nieces who should be "born and living" at her death should attain age 21, after which the accumulation was to be divided among the children of the nephews and nieces as should then be living. It was held that the words "born and living" were used to ascertain a period of time and were not a description of children as objects of the bequest, so that children *in utero* were not included in the perpetuity period. Hence the trust for accumulation ceased when the youngest of the children actually born at the death of the testatrix attained his majority, at which time the fund became divisible among the children born after the death of the testatrix but before the period of division.[42]

The perpetuity period is not extended by a period of gestation except where gestation actually exists.[43] There may be more than one period of gestation,[44] such as the period of gestation of the life in being and that of his child who is the beneficiary. The question has arisen, but has not been decided, as to whether there might be three periods of gestation, that of the life in being, that of his child who is to attain age 21 and that of the ultimate beneficiaries.[45]

(c) A period in gross

The period of twenty-one years comprises the full perpetuity period if the instrument creating a limitation does not indicate any life or lives for the purpose of the period. Consequently, a limitation which purports to vest an interest in property in a person who may be unborn by the end of a specified period more than twenty-one years after the instrument creating the limitation takes effect is invalid.[46]

In *Speakman v. Speakman*,[47] the testator directed payment of the surplus income from his estate for the maintenance of his children during their minority and, after the youngest child attained the age of 21, directed division of the surplus equally among his children or their heirs every three years during his widow's life or widowhood and, after her death or marriage, every year, for fifty years, when the executors were to sell the estate and divide the money among the children or their heirs, the share of any child dying without issue to go to the survivors. It was held that "heirs" meant issue, and that the effect was a continuing direction to the trustees to pay the income from time to time, during the whole period of fifty years, to the children or, in case of their deaths, to such of their lineal descendants as might come *in esse*. It was further held that the limitations at the end of the fifty-year period were void for remoteness.

---

[41]*Supra*, footnote 40.
[42]See also *Villar v. Gilbey*, [1907] A.C. 139 (H.L.).
[43]*Cadell v. Palmer* (1833), 1 Cl. & Fin. 372, 6 E.R. 956 (H.L.); *Ferguson v. Ferguson* (1876), 39 U.C.Q.B. 232, revd 1 O.A.R. 452, restd 2 S.C.R. 497.
[44]*Villar v. Gilbey, supra*, footnote 42.
[45]*Smith v. Farr* (1838), 3 Y. & C. Ex. 328, 160 E.R. 728; and see Lewis, p. 726 and Supplement p. 22, and Gray, §222.
[46]*Palmer v. Holford* (1828), 4 Russ. 403, 38 E.R. 857.
[47](1850), 8 Hare, 180, 68 E.R. 323.

Similarly, a bequest to take effect on a contingency thirty years after the testator's death is too remote.[48]

In *Re Lord Stratheden and Campbell; Alt v. Lord Stratheden*,[49] a bequest of an annuity to a volunteer corps "on the appointment of the next lieutenant-colonel" was held void for the remoteness because he need not necessarily be appointed within the legal period after the death or retirement of the existing commander.[50] Similarly, a bequest "to my future nephews; if in the opinion of my said executor their parents are too poor to give them a proper education", was held void for remoteness.[51]

However, where a settlement conveyed real property to trustees to apply the rents and profits as directed for twenty-one years and, "at the expiration of the said term of twenty-one years", upon trust for sale, it was held that the trust for sale was not void for remoteness for exceeding a term of twenty-one years, because the end of the term and the commencement of the trust for sale arose at the same moment. It was also held that the term was to be reckoned from the beginning of the day of the date of the settlement.[52]

1104.3 Vesting for the Purposes of the Rule

(a) Generally

The rules as to vesting are set out in detail in the preceding chapter and need not be repeated here.[1] A brief recapitulation will not be out of place, however.

The term "vested" has two possible meanings, namely, the *prima facie* meaning, "vested in interest", and a secondary one, "vested in possession". The rule against perpetuities is concerned only with the former.

Hence, if an estate or interest limited to a person or class of persons must vest within the perpetuity period, if it vest at all, it is not rendered invalid by a provision merely postponing its possession or enjoyment until a time beyond the perpetuity period.[2] Accordingly, an estate or interest may be limited by a will to an unborn person to come into possession at an age or other event later than twenty-one years after the death of the testator.[3] It is to be observed that a person to whom an interest is limited with a proviso that he is not to enjoy it until he attains an age greater than the age of majority

---

[48]*Crooke v. De Vandes* (1805), 11 Ves. Jun. 330, 32 E.R. 1115.

[49][1894] 3 Ch. 265.

[50]See also *Baker v. Stuart* (1897), 28 O.R. 439 (H.C.J.).

[51]*Re MacMurray*, [1949] O.W.N. 701, [1950] 1 D.L.R. 280 (H.C.J.).

[52]*English v. Cliff*, [1914] 2 Ch. 376.

§1104.3

[1]§§1004-1004.3, *supra*.

[2]*Mann, Crossman & Paulin, Ltd. v. Registrar of Land Registry*, [1918] 1 Ch. 202, holding valid a lease to commence after the end of an existing lease which had more than twenty-one years to run.

[3]*Gosling v. Gosling* (1859), Johns. 265, 70 E.R. 423; *Re Edmondson's Estate* (1868), L.R. 5 Eq. 389; *Re Bevan's Trusts* (1887), 34 Ch. D. 716; *Re Coppard's Estate*; *Howlett v. Hodson* (1887), 35 Ch. D. 350.

is nevertheless entitled to enjoy it at the age of majority unless, during the interval, the property is given for the benefit of another or is so clearly taken away from him until he attains the required age as to induce the court to hold that, as to the previous rents and profits, there is an intestacy.[4]

Where there is no immediate gift to an unborn person, but only a direction that he shall be entitled to possession of an estate or interest upon attaining an age greater than 21 or upon the happening of some other event which is too remote, the direction itself constitutes the only gift and is a condition precedent to the vesting of the gift, so that it is void under the rule.[5]

In *Leake v. Robinson*[6] there was a gift of real and personal estate to trustees upon trust to apply the rents and dividends, or so much thereof as they might think fit, to the maintenance of W until he should attain the age of 25, then to permit him to receive them during his life and, after his death, to apply them to the maintenance of his children until they should attain the age of 25 respectively and then to assign and transfer them to such children as attained that age. There was a gift over if W should die without issue living at his death or with issue dying under that age, followed by a gift of the residue. It was held that the only gift was in the direction to pay and the interests could not vest until age 25. That age was too remote, there being no antecedent gift the enjoyment of which was merely postponed.

Where an interest, limited to a person by will, is vested within the perpetuity period, but a provision postpones its enjoyment until attainment by him of an age which is beyond the perpetuity period and there is an executory gift over on his failure to attain that age, the gift over is construed as a limitation divesting the vested gift, so that only the gift over is void for remoteness. Thus, in *Taylor v. Frobisher*[7] the testatrix devised her estates to her son charged with a sum payable to trustees upon trust to pay the interest to her daughter for life and, after her death, upon trust to dispose of it to or among the child or children of the daughter, to become a vested interest or vested interests on their respectively attaining the age of 30. There was a gift over of the share of any child dying under that age without issue to the survivor or survivors. It was held that the word "vested" was used in the sense of "not subject to be divested" or "indefeasible", so that the shares vested and only the gift over was void for remoteness. "The conclusion appears to me irresistible that the testatrix intended the child so dying and leaving issue to retain his share as an interest transmissible to his representatives, and considered that he would do so by force of the original gift."[8]

---

[4]*Gosling v. Gosling, supra,* footnote 3, at p. 272, cited by Anglin, J., in *Re Canadian Home Circles*; *Smith Case* (1907), 14 O.L.R. 322 (H.C.J.), at pp. 323-4; *Arkell v. Roach* (1884), 5 O.R. 699 (H.C.J.).

[5]*Leake v. Robinson* (1817), 2 Mer. 363 at p. 386, 35 E.R. 979.

[6]*Supra,* footnote 5.

[7](1852), 5 De G. & Sm. 191, 64 E.R. 1076.

[8]*Ibid.,* at p. 199, *per* Parker, V.C. And see *Doe d. Dolley v. Ward* (1839), 9 Ad. & E. 582, 112 E.R. 1332; *Re Townsend* (1969), 7 D.L.R. (3d) 270, 69 W.W.R. 630 (Alta. S.C.), in which a divesting clause was held void in part only.

Thus, while in a will, the word "vested" *prima facie* means vested in interest, by force of the context it may have a different meaning, such as "vested in possession", or "indefeasibly vested", or "payable".[9]

"Vest" may, if the context of the will permits that construction, be read as importing only that the interest previously vested is at a specified time to become absolute and indefeasible.[10]

A testatrix bequeathed the residue of her estate upon trust, as to one-fifth, for one of her great-nephews for life and, after his death, for all of his children equally, and, as to four-fifths, for her great-nieces and other great-nephews and their children. She directed that none of the shares of the children were to be "so paid to or become vested interests in" them until they attained the age of 25, and empowered the trustees to apply any of the income meanwhile to their maintenance. It was held that "vested" must be construed as "indefeasible", so that the remainders vested in all children that were alive at the death of the testatrix or were born afterwards.[11]

Where a testator devised freeholds to uses in strict settlement and by a codicil directed that no devisee should have a vested interest in or be entitled to possession until attaining the age of 24, notwithstanding anything in his will or any law to the contrary, the ordinary meaning of "vested" was inescapable, it being held that the effect of the codicil was to make the limitations in the will executory devises which were void for remoteness.[12]

Where property is limited to a person on his attaining an age which would otherwise be too remote, a provision applying rents for his maintenance during his minority may cause the limitation to be construed as not postponing vesting until the prescribed age.[13]

Similarly, where payment of a legacy to a child is postponed until attainment of an age beyond the perpetuity period but the income is directed to be applied to his maintenance during his minority, the vesting of the child's interest is

---

[9]*Re Stevens; Clark v. Stevens* (1896), 40 Sol. Jo. 296, *per* Stirling, J.; or "not subject to be divested" or "indefeasible" *Taylor v. Frobisher, supra,* footnote 7; *Re Baxter's Trusts* (1864), 10 Jur. (N.S.) 845.

[10]*Armytage v. Wilkinson* (1878), 3 App. Cas. 355 (P.C.), holding that, where a testator directed the trustees to hold a fund in trust for his child, if only one, or for all of his children equally if more than one, so that the interest of a son should be absolutely vested at age 21 and of a daughter at that age or marriage, the shares of the children were vested in interest on the death of the testator, although subject to be divested.

[11]*Re Edmondson's Estate* (1868), L.R. 5 Eq. 389.

[12]*Re Wrightson; Battie-Wrightson v. Thomas,* [1904] 2 Ch. 95 (C.A.). The same result obtains where the testator does not specify the time of vesting, but postpones distribution of the property for a period of twenty-five years from his death and includes after-born persons in the class of beneficiaries: *Re Fownes Estate* (1974), 10 N.B.R. (2d) 226 (Q.B.).

[13]*Jackson v. Marjoribanks* (1841), 12 Sim. 93, 59 E.R. 1066, gift to son for life, remainder to first grandson at age 25, with provision for grandson's maintenance during his minority, held vested.

not postponed until attainment of the prescribed age.[14] This principle is not applied to a gift to such members of a class as attain a specified age, for only those who qualify can take vested interests.

> In my opinion, when a legacy is payable at a certain age, but is, in terms, contingent, the legacy becomes vested when there is a direction to pay the interest in the meantime to the person to whom the legacy is given; and not the less so when there is superadded a direction that the trustees "shall pay the whole or such part of the interest as they shall think fit." But I am not aware of any case where, the gift being of an entire fund payable to a class of persons equally on their attaining a certain age, a direction to apply the income of the whole fund in the meantime for their maintenance has been held to create a vested interest in a member of the class who does not attain that age.[15]

(b) The criteria for vesting under the rule

At common law an interest is said to be vested if it is limited to a person who is ascertained and it is not subject to a condition precedent that remains unsatisfied.

For the purposes of the rule against perpetuities a third requirement must be added, namely, if the limitation is in favour of a class, the interest is vested when the exact membership of the class and the exact amount to which each member is entitled are determined.[16]

Moreover, since a gift to a class is treated as a single gift, if one member of the class could by possibility take outside the period, the entire gift is void under the common law rule.[17]

(c) Factors and evidence to be considered

In applying the rule, the facts or circumstances to be considered are those existing on the date from which the perpetuity period is reckoned, being the death of the testator in the case of a limitation by will and the date of the instrument in the case of a limitation by a non-testamentary instrument.[18]

In *Lord Dungannon v. Smith*[19] the testator gave leasehold premises to

---

[14]*Davies v. Fisher* (1842), 5 Beav. 201, 49 E.R. 554, a gift of personalty to trustees in trust for A for his life and, after his death, for his children as they severally attained the age of 25, the income to be applied for their maintenance during their minority, with a gift over in case no child of A should live until the age of 25; *Bell v. Cade* (1861), 2 J. & H. 122, 70 E.R. 996, a gift in trust for B during her life and, after her death, to divide the principal among her children on attaining the age of 24, the dividends to be applied meanwhile for their benefit; *Tatham v. Vernon* (1861), 29 Beav. 604, 54 E.R. 762, a gift to daughters for life and then to their children at the age of 25, the interest being applied to their maintenance during their minority.

[15]*Re Parker; Barker v. Barker* (1880), 16 Ch. D. 44 at pp. 45-6, *per* Jessel, M.R., and see *Re Thatcher's Trusts* (1859), 26 Beav. 365, 53 E.R. 939; *Re Ricketts* (1910), 103 L.T. 278; *Re Hume; Public Trustee v. Mabey*, [1912] 1 Ch. 693.

[16]Morris and Leach, p. 38; Maudsley, pp. 10-11.

[17]Class gifts are dealt with in detail in §1104.6, *infra*.

[18]*Vanderplank v. King* (1843), 3 Hare 1 at p. 17, 67 E.R. 273.

[19](1846), 12 Cl. & Fin. 546, 8 E.R. 1523 (H.L.).

trustees upon trust to permit his grandson, B, to take the profits for life and, after his death, to permit the heir male of the body of B for the time being to take the profits until he attained the age of 21, when the premises were to be conveyed to him. If no such person attained age 21, the trustees were to permit the successive heirs male of the father of B to take the profits until one of them attained age 21 when the premises were to be conveyed to him. At the death of B, his son, A, had attained the age of 21, but it was held that he had no title because the gift to the heir male of the grandson was void for remoteness in its inception.

Where, however, there is a gift to such of the children of a named person as shall attain an age greater than 21 years and that person dies in the lifetime of the testator and the class is ascertained at his death, the gift is valid. Hence a limitation to the unborn children of the testator's children for their lives is not void for remoteness merely because it was a gift to persons who might be unborn at the death of the testator.[20]

Similarly, where a limitation is made by will or other instrument in exercise of a power of appointment, the time for ascertaining the facts in applying the rule is the time of exercise of the power and not the time of its creation.

In *Peard v. Kekewich*[21] the testator devised to B for life with remainder to such of B's children as B should by deed or will appoint. B, by his will, appointed to trustees upon trust for his son, C, directing a conveyance to him in fee simple on his attaining the age of 23 and an accumulation of rents and profits to be paid to him at that age, with a gift over to other sons in case C were to die under age 21. It was held that the exercise of the power was good, that C took an estate in fee simple upon the death of B, liable to be divested if he died under age 21, and the trust for accumulation until C attained the age of 23, was good because, although C was unborn at the date of the will, he was three years of age when the testator died. Hence the vesting would occur within twenty-one years after the death of the testator, the creator of the special power.[22]

In *Wilkinson v. Duncan*[23] the testator gave property in trust for his nephew, A, for life, with power to A to appoint it among his children. A directed the trustees to pay certain parts to each of his daughters as and when they respectively attained the age of 24. It was held that the appointment was valid as to such of the daughters as were three years of age at his death, but void for remoteness as to the others because, when individual shares of members of a class can be ascertained within the proper period, the gift is valid as to those within the rule.

---

[20]*Williams v. Teale* (1847), 6 Hare 239, 67 E.R. 1155, and see *Faulkner v. Daniel* (1843), 3 Hare 199 at p. 216, 67 E.R. 355; *Re Mervin*; *Mervin v. Crossman*, [1891] 3 Ch. 197 at p. 204; *Re Smith*, [1942] O.W.N. 455 (C.A.).

[21](1852), 21 L.J. Ch. 456.

[22]To the same effect, see *Von Brockdorff v. Malcolm* (1885), 30 Ch. D. 172; *Re Thompson*; *Thompson v. Thompson*, [1906] 2 Ch. 199; *Re Eliot* (1913), 24 O.W.R. 494, 11 D.L.R. 34 (S.C. App. Div.).

[23](1861), 30 Beav. 111, 54 E.R. 831.

By contrast, when there is a gift to a class some of the members of which are within the rule while others are not and the class itself and the shares of each cannot be ascertained within the proper period, the whole gift is void.[24]

If, on the date from which the perpetuity period is reckoned, the limitations are such that events might have so turned out that the rule against remoteness would have been infringed, then the limitations fail, although in the events which actually did happen the period was not exceeded.[25] When a gift is infected with the vice that it may by possibility exceed the prescribed limit, it is at once and altogether void both at law and in equity. Even if, in its actual event, it should fall well within such limit, yet it is absolutely void, just as if the event had occurred beyond the limit.[26] Unless the limitation is created in such terms that it cannot vest after the expiration of a life or lives in being plus twenty-one years and the period allowed for gestation, it is not valid and subsequent events cannot make it so.[27] However, for the purposes of the rule, a child *en ventre sa mère* is, upon birth, treated retrospectively as a life in being.[28]

In determining the validity of limitations, the court can look at evidence of facts existing when the instrument making the limitation took effect but not at evidence of subsequent events or of opinion or probability. In *Re Wood*; *Tullett v. Colville*,[29] the testator directed his trustees to carry on his business of gravel contractor until his freehold gravel pits were worked out and then to sell them and hold the proceeds in trust for such child or children then living and such living issue of any deceased child, as should, being a son, attained age 21 or, being a daughter, attain that age or marry. It was held that both the trust for sale and the trust of the proceeds were void for remoteness. "It might have been in the highest degree probable at the time of the testator's death that the gravel pits would be worked out within the legal period; but, as I understand the law, the Court cannot look at evidence of that kind."[30] Similarly, in *Re Bewick*; *Ryle v. Ryle*,[31] a will created a trust of the proceeds of sale of realty which was subject to mortgage charges, taxes and outgoings for the payment of which rents and income were first liable, the trust being in favour of a class to be ascertained as soon as all charges on the realty were paid. It was held that the trust was too remote, notwithstanding a legal obligation to pay the charges within twenty-one years from the testator's death, as the court is not at liberty to speculate about probabilities.

---

[24]*Ibid*.

[25]*Re Wilmer's Trusts*; *Moore v. Wingfield*, [1903] 2 Ch. 411 (C.A.), at p. 422, *per* Stirling, L.J.

[26]*Meyers v. Hamilton Provident and Loan Co.* (1890), 19 O.R. 358 (H.C.J.), *per* MacMahon, J.

[27]*Lord Dungannon v. Smith* (1846), 12 Cl. & Fin. 546 at p. 563, 8 E.R. 1523 (H.L.), *per* Cresswell, J.

[28]*Re Wilmer's Trusts*, *supra*, footnote 25.

[29][1894] 3 Ch. 381 (C.A.).

[30]*Ibid*., at p. 387, *per* Davey, L.J.

[31][1911] 1 Ch. 116.

The court does admit evidence showing that a person mentioned in the will predeceased the testator, as well as evidence showing that the death of the person occurred at such a time before the testator's death as renders the gift valid.[32] Hence, evidence is allowed to show that, at the testator's death, all of a class of issue were then ascertained,[33] or that a line of issue had failed,[34] or that a person was *en ventre sa mère* at the testator's death.[35]

Since the court does not speculate about probabilities, no evidence can be given that a woman is past child-bearing and the court does not draw such an inference, whatever her age, for the purpose of determining whether a gift is void for perpetuity or not.[36] In Ireland such evidence has been admitted.[37]

(d) Some common traps for the unwary

Because of the common law's insistence on the required certainty of vesting, a limitation may fail in circumstances which are inexplicable to the layman and which are, indeed, traps for the unwary solicitor. Some of the more common situations are outlined below.[38]

(i) The "Fertile Octogenarian"

For the purposes of the rule a person is conclusively presumed to be able to

---

[32]*Re Dawson; Johnston v. Hill* (1888), 39 Ch. D. 155 at p. 159, *per* Chitty, J.

[33]*Southern v. Wollaston* (1852), 16 Beav. 276, 51 E.R. 785, in which case it was held that the gift of a legacy to A for life and, after his death, to his children who should attain the age of 25 would not be too remote if, by the death of the testator, all the children must necessarily attain age 25 within twenty-one years after the testator's death; *Re Thompson; Thompson v. Thompson*, [1906] 2 Ch. 199, in which case a testator gave his residuary estate upon trust for his wife for life and, after her death, for the benefit of his brother, C, and his present and future issue as his wife should appoint. She by will appointed the property in trust for C for life and, after his death, for all of his children who should attain the age of 25, if born in her lifetime, or the age of 21 if born after her death. The appointment was held good as the evidence showed that C had nine children, all born in the lifetime of the original testator and all of whom had attained the age of 25 before the death of the appointor, so that when her will took effect all the persons to take were ascertained and their shares vested and fixed.

[34]*Faulkner v. Daniel* (1843), 3 Hare 199, 67 E.R. 355.

[35]*Thellusson v. Woodford* (1805), 11 Ves. Jun. 112, 32 E.R. 1030 (H.L.); *Blackburn v. Stables* (1814), 2 V. & B. 367, 35 E.R. 358; *Storrs v. Benbow* (1853), 3 De G. M. & G. 390, 43 E.R. 153.

[36]*Jee v. Audley* (1787), 1 Cox. 324, 29 E.R. 1186, married couple aged 70; *Re Sayer's Trusts* (1868), L.R. 6 Eq. 319, woman of 62; *Re Dawson; Johnston v. Hill* (1888), 39 Ch. D. 155, woman of over 60; *Ward v. Van der Loeff; Burnyeat v. Van der Loeff*, [1924] A.C. 653 (H.L.); *Re Deloitte; Griffiths v. Deloitte*, [1926] Ch. 56, woman of 65.

[37]*Exham v. Beamish*, [1939] 1 I.R. 336, and see *Berry v. Geen*, [1938] A.C. 575 (H.L.), at p. 584.

[38]The titles for these traps were devised by the late Professor W. Barton Leach. See his "Perpetuities in a Nutshell", 51 Harv. L. Rev. 638 (1938), at pp. 643 *et seq.*, and "Perpetuities: The Nutshell Revisited", 78 Harv. L. Rev. 973 (1964-65), at p. 992. See also Morris and Leach, pp. 72 *et seq.*

procreate regardless of age or physiology.[39] The following example illustrates the results of this presumption:

A bequest, "to A for life, then to A's children for their lives, remainder to A's grandchildren".
A was a woman of 70 when the testator died.

The presumption of fertility avoids the remainder, because A is conclusively presumed to be able to bear children until her death. Such children would not be lives in being and the gift to the grandchildren might, therefore, not vest until more than twenty-one years after the death of the children living at the testator's death.

For the same reason, the gift of the principal fails in the following example:

A bequest, "to my wife for life or until her remarriage, remainder to the children of my brothers and sisters as shall attain the age of 21".
The testator's father and mother were 66 years old when he died.[40]

The gift of the principal fails because the testator's parents are conclusively presumed to be able to have further children. They would not be lives in being and, therefore, the gift to the testator's nephews and nieces might not vest until more than twenty-one years after the death of the brothers and sisters of the testator who were living at his death.

Such gifts can be saved by careful draughtsmanship. If the draughtsman had made it clear in the first example that only children of such children of A as were living at the testator's death were intended as beneficiaries, there would have been no problem. Similarly, in the second example the gift could, by appropriate language, have been restricted to children of such of the testator's brothers and sisters as were alive at his death.

That that was the intention of the testator in both cases seems obvious since he would not have thought it possible that A, in the first example, and his parents, in the second, could have further children. Indeed, it would be medically impossible. Nevertheless, the English and Canadian courts have applied the presumption of lifelong fecundity relentlessly and have refused to construe such gifts as being restricted to the children of living persons. American courts appear to be more ready to allow a benevolent construction.[41] Apart from reforming statutes, it would appear that the only certain way to avoid traps such as this is careful draughting.

To the category of the "Fertile Octogenarian" may now be added that of the "Fertile Decedent"[42] to describe the case of a man who deposits his sperm

---

[39]*Jee v. Audley*, *supra*, footnote 36. *Re Dawson, supra*, footnote 36; *Ward v. Van der Loeff, supra*, footnote 36; *Re Fasken* (1959), 19 D.L.R. (2d) 182 (Ont. C.A.).

[40]The example is based on *Ward v. Van der Loeff, supra*, footnote 36.

[41]Morris and Leach, p. 79; A.L.P. Suppl., §§24.21, 24.22.

[42]The term is that of Professor Leach, "Perpetuities in the Atomic Age: The Sperm Bank and the Fertile Decedent", 48 A.B.A.J. 942 (1962), and see A.L.P. Suppl., s. 24.22, p. 872.

in a sperm bank where it will remain fertile for many years. Such sperm may in due course fertilize the donor's wife or, it may be, another woman. The fact that the children would be illegitimate in the latter case, would not disentitle them from inheriting in jurisdictions which have abolished the status of illegitimacy. What the courts will do with the "fertile decedent" for the purposes of the rule remains to be seen. New biological developments, such as test-tube babies, have created fertile fields for speculation about the rule in the space age.[43]

(ii) The "Precocious Toddler"

This is the converse of the fertile octogenarian situation and concerns the minimum age at which a person is able to procreate. The trap derives from the case *Re Gaite's Will Trusts*; *Banks v. Gaite*.[44] The following example is based on this case:

A bequest, "to X for life, remainder to such of her grandchildren living at my death or born within five years thereafter who shall attain the age of 21".
X was a widow, 65 years of age at the testator's death, with two children and a grandchild.

The example incorporates a fertile octogenarian problem as well. However, the real difficulty is the clause "or born within five years thereafter". These words make it possible that X might remarry and have another child who might have a child, all within five years of the testator's death. Clearly this is virtually impossible[45] and, therefore, the clause should not be held to invalidate the gift.

In fact, the gift in *Re Gaite's Will Trusts*[46] was saved because a marriage between persons either of whom is under 16 was void under the *Age of Marriage Act*,[47] so that a grandchild born within five years of the testator's death would be illegitimate and would be excluded on that ground. Such a solution would not assist if the testator showed an intention to benefit illegitimate persons. Nor does it apply any more in jurisdictions which have abolished the status of illegitimate children.[48]

---

[43]See, *e.g.*, Schuyler, "The New Biology and the Rule Against Perpetuities", 15 U.C.L.A. L. Rev. 420 (1967-68); Leach, "Perpetuities in the Atomic Age: The Sperm Bank and the Fertile Decedent", *supra*, foootnote 42; Lynn, "Raising the Perpetuities Question: Conception, Adoption, 'Wait and See', and Cy Pres", 17 Vand. L. Rev. 1391 (1963-64).
[44][1949] 1 All E.R. 459 (Ch.).
[45]Although not, apparently, outside the realm of possibility. Morris and Leach, at p. 85, note 27, give an account of an authenticated birth to a five-year-old girl.
[46]*Supra*, footnote 44.
[47]19 & 20 Geo. 5, c. 36 (1929, U.K.).
[48]As in Ontario and New Brunswick. See the *Children's Law Reform Act*, R.S.O. 1980, c. 68; *Child and Family Services and Family Relations Act*, S.N.B. 1980, c. C-2.1, Part VI.

(iii) The "Unborn Widow"

This trap occurs when a settlor or testator wishes to make provision successively for his son (or daughter), then for his (or her) spouse, with remainder to their children. An example is the following:

> An *inter vivos* trust, "to pay the income to S for life; after his death to pay the income to S's widow for life, and then to pay the principal to S's children then living".

The problem with a gift in this form is that even if S were married at the time of the deed, his wife might die or the marriage might be dissolved and he might remarry a person unborn at the time of the deed. If this person outlived S by twenty-one years, the gift to the children would be void, although the gift to the widow would be valid.[49]

The gift may be saved if, from the context of the instrument, it appears clear that S's present wife was intended as beneficiary. From a drafting point of view, it would be better to name the wife. Alternatively, the words "then living" may be deleted, for the children's interest would then be vested when the instrument takes effect.

(iv) The "Magic Gravel Pit"

This trap takes its name from *Re Wood*; *Tullett v. Colville*,[50] a simplified version of which is as follows:

> The testator owned certain gravel pits. He devised them to his trustees "in trust to work my gravel pits until they are exhausted, and then to sell them and to divide the proceeds among my issue then living".
> The pits would, if worked at the rate the testator did, have been exhausted in four years. In fact, they were exhausted in six.

The gift fails because it is possible at the testator's death that the gravel pits might not be exhausted for more than twenty-one years,[51] in which case the gift will vest too remotely. The way to cure such a gift is to say, "to work the said pits for twenty-one years or until they are exhausted, whichever happens first", to change "issue" to "children" (who would be lives in being), or to name express lives in being.

Similarly, a gift to pay off a mortgage out of the rents of a certain property and then to divide the proceeds among the testator's issue then living,[52] and a gift to an armed forces unit "on the appointment of the next lieutenant-colonel",[53] are void.

---

[49]See, *e.g.*, *Re Frost*; *Frost v. Frost* (1889), 43 Ch. D. 246; *Re Curryer's Will Trusts*; *Wyly v. Curryer*, [1938] Ch. 952.
[50][1894] 3 Ch. 381 (C.A.).
[51]There being no lives in being, the perpetuity period is twenty-one years.
[52]*Re Bewick*; *Ryle v. Ryle*, [1911] 1 Ch. 116.
[53]*Re Lord Stratheden and Campbell*; *Alt v. Lord Stratheden*, [1894] 3 Ch. 265.

On the other hand, a covenant to reconvey land if the purchaser fails to construct a building on the land was held not to offend the rule. The covenant was construed to run until construction of the building, which was intended to occur within a reasonable time.[54]

It is submitted that the latter approach is the correct one also in the case of "magic gravel pit" types of situations. Indeed, this approach is sometimes followed in "administrative contingency" cases, as where a gift is made contingent on "the payment of my debts", "when my estate is realized", "when my will is probated", and the like. Such contingencies are often construed as meaning the date upon which the contingency specified occurs or the expiration of the executor's year, whichever first happens.[55]

1104.4 Duration of Interests

The rule is not concerned with how long limitations last. The remoteness against which the rule for the prevention of perpetuities is directed is remoteness in the commencement, or first taking effect, of limitations and not in the cesser or determination of them.[1]

Provided that the limitation must vest, if it vests at all, within the perpetuity period, even though it may last longer than the period, property may be limited to an unborn person for life,[2] or until marriage,[3] or other contingency,[4] or to a number of unborn persons for life as tenants in common.[5] However, if the unborn person is only entitled to receive such income as the trustees may in their discretion decide, his interest and, indeed, the trust itself is void.[6] Similarly, if the income is given to an unborn person for life, but the trustees are directed to encroach on the capital in his favour if the income falls below a stated amount, the direction is void.[7]

A life estate may be limited to the future husband or wife of a living person, although such husband or wife may possibly be unborn at the date of the gift, because it must vest during the life of the living person.[8]

---

[54]*Halifax v. Vaughan Construction Co.* (1957), 9 D.L.R. (2d) 431 (N.S.S.C.), revd on other grounds 12 D.L.R. (2d) 159, 41 M.P.R. 19 (N.S.S.C.).

[55]*Re Petrie; Lloyds Bank Ltd. v. Royal Nat'l Institute for Blind,* [1961] 3 W.L.R. 1348 (C.A.).

§1104.4

[1]Lewis, p. 173, adopted in *Wainwright v. Miller,* [1897] 2 Ch. 255 at p. 261.

[2]*Williams v. Teale* (1847), 6 Hare 239 at p. 250, 67 E.R. 1155; *Hampton v. Holman* (1877), 5 Ch. D. 183; *Re Ashforth; Sibley v. Ashforth,* [1905] 1 Ch. 535 at p. 540; *Re Crichton Estate* (1913), 13 D.L.R. 169, 4 W.W.R. 1184 (Man. K.B.).

[3]*Re Gage; Hill v. Gage,* [1898] 1 Ch. 498.

[4]*Wainwright v. Miller, supra,* footnote 1, becoming a member of the Roman Catholic Church or of any sisterhood.

[5]*Williams v. Teale, supra,* footnote 2.

[6]*Re Allan; Curtis v. Nalder,* [1958] 1 W.L.R. 220 (Ch.).

[7]*Re Johnson's Settlement Trusts; McClure v. Johnson,* [1943] Ch. 341.

[8]*Re Merricks' Trusts* (1866), L.R. 1 Eq. 551; *Re Harvey; Peek v. Savory* (1888), 39 Ch. D. 289 (C.A.); *Re Crichton Estate, supra,* footnote 2; *Re Brown Estate* (1919), 50 D.L.R. 550, [1920] 1 W.W.R. 264 (Sask. C.A.).

As the survivor of a number of unborn persons might not be ascertainable within the perpetuity period, no power of appointment may be given to such survivor,[9] and no estate or interest may be directly limited or appointed to such survivor.[10] Similarly, an appointment may not be made by will to the survivor of several persons because the survivor might not be ascertained within twenty-one years after the appointor's death.[11]

1104.5 Construction of Instruments

The validity of a limitation in an instrument depends on the time of its vesting, which is determined by construing the language of the instrument by the ordinary rules of construction. The traditional English approach as regards interests which may be void under the rule against perpetuities is one of remorseless construction. Lord Selborne explained this approach as follows in *Pearks v. Moseley*:[1]

> You do not import the law of remoteness into the construction of the instrument, by which you investigate the expressed intention of the testator. You take his words, and endeavour to arrive at their meaning, exactly in the same manner as if there had been no such law, and as if the whole intention expressed by the words could lawfully take effect. I do not mean, that, in dealing with words which are obscure and ambiguous, weight, even in a question of remoteness, may not sometimes be given to the consideration that it is better to effectuate than to destroy the intention; but I do say, that, if the construction of the words is one about which a Court would have no doubt, though there was no law of remoteness, that construction cannot be altered, or wrested to something different, for the purpose of escaping from the consequences of that law.[2]

---

[9]*Re Hargreaves; Midgley v. Tatley* (1890), 43 Ch. D. 401 (C.A.).

[10]*Courtier v. Oram* (1855), 21 Beav. 91, 52 E.R. 793, gift over, on the death of a grandchild of testator, to surviving grandchildren held void; *Garland v. Brown* (1864), 10 L.T. 292, remainder in fee simple to the survivor of the children of the testator's surviving child held void; *Re Hargreaves, supra*, footnote 9, devise upon trust for two sisters of the testatrix and their children for life successively and, after the deaths of all, upon such trusts as the survivor of the sisters and their children should appoint by deed or will, both the power and an appointment under it being held void; *Re Ashforth*; *Sibley v. Ashforth*, [1905] 1 Ch. 535, estate tail to the survivor of unborn persons held void; *Re Legh's Settlement Trusts*; *Public Trustee v. Legh*, [1938] Ch. 39 (C.A.); *Re Johnson's Settlement Trusts*; *McClure v. Johnson*, [1943] Ch. 341.

[11]*Whitby v. Von Luedecke*, [1906] 1 Ch. 783, appointment to survivor of two daughters held to be contingent, not vested, and therefore void; *Re Crichton's Settlement*; *Sweetman v. Batty* (1912), 106 L.T. 588, appointment to survivor of two daughters if the other died without issue held void.

§1104.5

[1](1880), 5 App. Cas. 714 at p. 719 (H.L.).

[2]*Cf.* to the same effect, *Re Hume; Public Trustee v. Mabey*, [1912] 1 Ch. 693 at p. 698, *per* Parker, J.; *Ward v. Van der Loeff*; *Burnyeat v. Van der Loeff*, [1924] A.C. 653 (H.L.), at p. 660, *per* Viscount Haldane, L.C., and at p. 662, *per* Viscount Cave; *Hewson v. Black* (1917), 36 D.L.R. 185 at pp. 189-90, 51 N.S.R. 81 at p. 92 (S.C.); *Re Goodhue Trusts* (1920), 47 O.L.R. 178 (S.C. App. Div.), at p. 184.

The result of this approach in *Pearks v. Moseley*[3] was that the courts felt constrained to construe the words "heirs" as "issue", not "children", thereby rendering the gift void for remoteness. Similarly, in *Ward v. Van der Loeff*[4] a gift in remainder to "the children of my brothers and sisters at age 21" was held void because the testator's parents were still alive and, although aged 66, were presumed to be capable of having further children, who would be brothers and sisters of the testator. Clearly, in the circumstances, the testator was referring only to his brothers and sisters living at his death.

A limitation void for remoteness may affect the construction of the rest of the instrument. Void dispositions are part of a will and must be resorted to as part of the context for all purposes of construction. If a clause in a will offends against the rule, it cannot be disregarded in construing the will but must be read as the expression of the testator's intention as though no such rule existed.[5]

Conversely, the meaning of words in one clause, apparently creating a limitation void for remoteness, may be controlled by other parts of the instrument, so that the instrument as a whole may show the limitation to be valid. Thus, where a testator gave the residue to trustees upon trust for his daughter for life and, after her death, for her children and their children who attained the age of 21, with a limitation over in case his daughter should have no child, or no child of hers should attain age 21 or leave issue attaining that age, it was held that the intent of the limitation over was to take effect only on failure of grandchildren who should survive the daughter and not attain age 21, so that it was not too remote.[6] Similarly, a limitation over, apparently on general failure of issue so as to be too remote, may be shown to mean only failure of particular issue referred to earlier in the will, so as to be valid.[7]

The rule of remorseless construction applies only where the language of the will is unambiguous. Where there is ambiguity, the courts may be inclined to consider evidence of surrounding circumstances and construe the will in light of such circumstances, thereby saving the gift. The rule of construction which holds that it must not be presumed that the testator intended to die intestate or to make an invalid gift then becomes relevant,[8] for a will is to be read with an inclination to believe that the testator did not intend to transgress the law, if that can be reasonably supposed.[9] Moreover, the courts will, if possible, avoid a combination leading to a perpetuity and a void

---

[3]*Supra*.
[4]*Supra*, footnote 2.
[5]*Cattlin v. Brown* (1853), 11 Hare 372 at pp. 375-6, 68 E.R. 1319; *Lord Dungannon v. Smith* (1846), 12 Cl. & Fin. 546 at p. 570, 8 E.R. 1523 (H.L.); *Heasman v. Pearse* (1871), L.R. 7 Ch. 275 at p. 283; *Re Goodhue Trusts, supra*, footnote 2, at p. 184.
[6]*Trickey v. Trickey* (1832), 3 My. & K. 560, 40 E.R. 213.
[7]*Morse v. Lord Ormonde* (1826), 1 Russ. 382, 38 E.R. 148; *Eno v. Eno* (1847), 6 Hare 171, 67 E.R. 1127; *Lewis v. Templer* (1864), 33 Beav. 625, 55 E.R. 511.
[8]*Gosling v. Gosling* (1859), Johns. 265, 70 E.R. 423.
[9]*Leach v. Leach* (1843), 2 Y. & C.C.C. 495, 63 E.R. 222, *per* Knight Bruce, V.C.

devise,[10] at least if that result can be achieved in accordance with the general intent of the will.[11]

It is also not improper to take into consideration that in the whole of the will the testator has carefully provided that the limitations of his estates shall not be open to the objection of being contrary to the law against remoteness and, if the clause in question is capable of two constructions, one of which would render it void upon a ground which the testator throughout his will seems to have been anxiously guarding against, and the other of which is reconcilable with all of his previously expressed intentions, there can be no doubt which of these ought to be adopted, namely, the latter.[12]

Where property is directed to be settled for a designated line of succession "so far as the rules of law admit" or words of like effect, an executory trust may be created to be executed, not to the further limit allowed by the rule, but to the limit which will enable the primary purpose of the instrument to be carried out.[13] Where there is no executory trust, however, but a direct limitation which offends the rule, the inclusion of words such as "so far as the rules of law admit", do not control the construction and make the limitation valid.[14] Where a testator, under a special power of appointment, appointed property to the uses and trusts of the prior instrument or such of them as were "capable of taking effect", it was held that this expression could be construed as meaning what the law allowed to take effect and need not be confined to what could still take effect by reason of the death of persons and other circumstances, so that, where some of the uses and trusts failed because the beneficiaries were not objects of the power or because they infringed the rule against perpetuities, they could be treated as excluded from the appointment.[15]

The rule of construction which disfavours finding an intestacy was probably applied in the context of the rule against perpetuities in two early cases, *Leach v. Leach*[16] and *Elliott v. Elliott*,[17] although the effect of the rule was not the basis of the decisions. For this reason they are not usually referred to in this context.[18] In *Re Powell; Crosland v. Holliday*,[19] however, the court

---

[10]*Exel v. Wallace* (1751), 2 Ves. Sen. 117, 28 E.R. 77, affd 2 Ves. Sen. 318, 28 E.R. 205.

[11]*Martelli v. Holloway* (1872), L.R. 5 H.L. 532 at p. 548; *Re Mortimer; Gray v. Gray,* [1905] 2 Ch. 502 (C.A.), at p. 506; *Re Earl of Stamford and Warrington; Payne v. Grey,* [1912] 1 Ch. 343 (C.A.), at p. 365.

[12]*Martelli v. Holloway, supra,* footnote 11, at p. 548, *per* Lord Chelmsford.

[13]*Countess of Lincoln v. Duke of Newcastle* (1806), 12 Ves. Jun. 217, at p. 236, 33 E.R. 83 (H.L.), in which case a covenant in a marriage settlement to settle leaseholds in trust for the same persons and for the estates, so far as the law would allow, as had been declared regarding realty limited to the first and other sons in tail male with remainder, was executed by giving the absolute interest in the leaseholds to the first tenant in tail attaining 21. See also *Williams v. Teale* (1847), 6 Hare 239, 67 E.R. 1155.

[14]*Christie v. Gosling* (1866), L.R. 1 H.L. 279 at p. 290.

[15]*Re Finch and Chew's Contract,* [1903] 2 Ch. 486.

[16](1843), 2 Y. & C.C.C. 495, 63 E.R. 222.

[17](1841), 12 Sim. 276, 59 E.R. 1137.

[18]See also *Re Coppard's Estate; Howlett v. Hodson* (1887), 35 Ch. D. 350, commented upon by Chitty, J., in *Re Wenmoth's Estate; Wenmoth v. Wenmoth* (1887), 37 Ch. D. 266.

[19][1898] 1 Ch. 227.

consciously chose that construction which prevented the gift from failing for perpetuity. In that case the testator gave the residue of his estate "to the children of X for life", with remainder to other children. X was a woman more than 80 years old when the will was made and when it took effect, to the testator's knowledge. In view of that fact, the court construed the phrase "the children of X" as meaning only those who were living at the testator's death.

Similarly, in *Re Deeley's Settlement; Batchelor v. Russell*[20] a settlor directed his trustees to hold separate shares of the trust fund in trust for each of three named beneficiaries "for his life and thereafter for [his] issue . . . as and when they attain the age of twenty one years". Although the word "issue" could not be construed as "children", in order to thereby save the gift, the court concluded that the settlor could not have intended all the issue born at any time to take, but rather only those born before the death of the life tenant. Moreover, the court stated that where the instrument is ambiguous in such a way that one construction will avoid the gift, whereas the other will save it, the latter construction should be adopted.

This sensible approach may, and, it is submitted, ought to become more common. Modern Canadian cases on the construction of wills are moving away from the 19th century strict constructionist approach which insisted that, if the language of the will was clear and unambiguous, no evidence of surrounding circumstances was admissible. The modern approach is to construe the testator's language in the context and from the vantage point of the circumstances surrounding the making of the will.[21]

In the United States a more lenient approach to construction generally prevails. The courts there tend to favour a construction which will save the gift under the rule.[22] This is also the approach of the Restatement.[23]

1104.6 The Rule Against Perpetuities and Class Gifts

Although the general principles of the rule against perpetuities apply to limitations to a class or to members of a class, there are some special features relating to such gifts that need particular mention.

(a) Definition of class gifts

A gift is said to be to a class of persons, when it is to all those who shall come within a certain category or description defined by a general or collective formula, and who, if they take at all, are to take one divisible subject in certain

---

20[1973] 3 All E.R. 1127 (Ch.), at p. 1127. And see *Re Roberts* (1978), 18 O.R. (2d) 387, 82 D.L.R. (3d) 591 (H.C.J.).

21See, *e.g.*, *Haidl v. Sacher* (1979), 106 D.L.R. (3d) 360, [1980] 1 W.W.R. 293, 2 Sask. R. 93, 7 E.T.R. 1 (C.A.); *Re Burke*, [1960] O.R. 26, 20 D.L.R. (2d) 396 (C.A.); *Marks v. Marks* (1908), 40 S.C.R. 210.

226 A.L.P., §24.45; A.L.P. Suppl., §24.45.

23Restatement, *Property*, §§242, 375, 377.

proportionate shares.[1] A gift to a class must be a gift to them as a class of persons having some common attribute, and not a gift to them as individuals.[2] Common examples of gifts to a class are gifts to a testator's grandchildren, or to his nephews and nieces, or to the children of a certain person or persons, or to the brothers and sisters of a certain person or persons, whatever may be the number of persons comprising the class. A gift may be a gift to a class although some of the individuals of the class are named, for example, a gift "to A and all other my nephews and nieces", and, although a gift "to A and all the children of B" is *prima facie* not a class gift, it may be if the context shows that the testator intended it to be so.[3] It has been held that a gift to grandchildren, except a specified one, is a gift to a class.[4]

On the other hand, a gift "to my three daughters, A, B and C" is not a class gift but a gift *nominatum*.[5] If the beneficiaries are designated by number and not by name, as in a gift "to the three children of X", it will normally also be construed as a gift to the children as *personae designatae*.[6] If there is an error in the number, the error is rejected and all of the children of X will take unless a contrary intention appears.[7]

(b) The applicability of the class closing rules

A class gift is treated as a single gift. Hence, it must be valid in its entirety for the purpose of the rule against perpetuities. If it is possible that the interests of some members may vest outside the perpetuity period, the whole gift will fail.[8] The class closing rules or rules of administrative convenience may operate, however, to save the gift by closing the class at a time when it is certain that the interests of those members of the class who are included must vest in time. The rules are designed to prevent inconvenience in the distribution of the estate. Hence they let in all persons who fit the description of the class and who are born before the period of distribution. They are rules of construction only and may, therefore, be excluded. However, in order to do so,

---

§1104.6

[1]*Pearks v. Moseley* (1880), 5 App. Cas. 714 (H.L.), at p. 723, *per* Lord Selborne, L.C.
[2]*Re Chaplin's Trusts* (1863), 12 W.R. 147, *per* Page Wood, V.C.
[3]*Kingsbury v. Walter*, [1901] A.C. 187 (H.L.), at pp. 192-3, *per* Lord Davey; *Re Jackson*; *Shiers v. Ashworth* (1883), 25 Ch. D. 162.
[4]*Illingworth v. Cooke* (1851), 9 Hare 37, 68 E.R. 404.
[5]*Re Brush*, [1942] O.R. 647, [1943] 1 D.L.R. 74 (H.C.J.); *Re Whiston*; *Whiston v. Woolley*, [1924] 1 Ch. 122 (C.A.).
[6]*Re Smith's Trusts* (1878), 9 Ch. D. 117; *Newman v. Piercey* (1876), 4 Ch. D. 41. But see *Re Burgess* (1968), 67 D.L.R. (2d) 526, 64 W.W.R. 44 (B.C.S.C.).
[7]*Newman v. Piercey, supra*, footnote 6; *Re Burgess, supra*, footnote 6.
[8]*Jee v. Audley* (1787), 1 Cox 324, 29 E.R. 1186; *Leake v. Robinson* (1817), 2 Mer. 363, 35 E.R. 979. In *Re Flavel's Will Trusts*; *Coleman v. Flavel*, [1969] 2 All E.R. 232 (Ch.), a superannuation fund for employees of a company was therefore void, since it included future employees.

the language of the instrument must be clear and unambiguous.[9] Nevertheless, two cases have held that where the gift is in the following form, "to A for life, remainder to such of his issue as attain the age of 21", the rules are excluded because the testator could not have intended to benefit all his issue no matter when born.[10] In both cases, therefore, the courts deduced that only such issue as were alive at the death of the life tenant were intended to take. This construction saved the gifts from being invalidated by the rule against perpetuities. If the class closing rules had been followed, the class would have closed at the later of the death of the life tenant and when the first remainderman reached the specified age and, in that event, the gift would have failed since the life tenant was the only possible life in being and a remainderman might possibly reach age 21 more than twenty-one years after the life tenant's death.

The rules, which apply to settlements as well as to wills,[11] are as follows:[12]

A. *Compound Gifts*

1. *An Immediate Gift to a Class*

An example would be a gift, "to the children of A equally".

The class closes on the testator's death and only those children then living

---

[9]Morris and Leach, pp. 124-5. In *Re Roberts* (1978), 18 O.R. (2d) 387, 82 D.L.R. (3d) 591 (H.C.J.), it was held that where a testator provides for the payment of annuities to named persons, living at his death, for twenty years or the death of the survivor whichever first occurs, with the income from the residue thereafter payable to his grandchildren for twenty-one years, after which the capital was to be distributed among his grandchildren then living, the *prima facie* rule that the class closes at the testator's death is ousted. In the circumstances it closed at the end of the twenty-one-year period. The gift of capital was valid because the annuitants were lives in being.

In *Re Manning* (1978), 19 O.R. (2d) 257, 84 D.L.R. (3d) 715 (C.A.), the testator bequeathed the income from part of his estate successively to his wife, his son, and named nephews and nieces "or their descendants", with power in the latter to appoint the capital to their children. It was held that the class of income beneficiaries closed at the son's death, when the gift vested and was valid. The gift of the capital was also valid because the power vested in the donees at the testator's death, so that the appointees would take directly under the testator's will. As to the latter point, see §1104.7, *infra*.

[10]*Re Cockle's Will Trusts*, [1967] Ch. 690; *Re Deeley's Settlement*; *Batchelor v. Russell*, [1973] 3 All E.R. 1127 (Ch.).

[11]*Re Knapp's Settlement*; *Knapp v. Vassall*, [1895] 1 Ch. 91; *Re Wernher's Settlement Trusts*; *Lloyds Bank Ltd. v. Mountbatten*, [1961] 1 W.L.R. 136 (Ch.).

[12]The rules are set out in summary form. For further detail reference should be had to the standard texts, *e.g.*, Jarman, pp. 1659-1702; Bailey, *The Law of Wills*, 7th ed. (London, I. Pitman, 1973), pp. 178 *et seq.*; *Hawkins and Ryder on the Construction of Wills* (London, Sweet & Maxwell, 1965), by Ryder, p. 106. Morris and Leach, pp. 109 *et seq.*; Maudsley, pp. 17 *et seq.* The rules are summarized in *Re Chartres*; *Farman v. Barrett*, [1927] 1 Ch. 466 at pp. 471-2, and in *Re Bleckly*; *Bleckly v. Bleckly*, [1951] Ch. 740 (C.A.), at pp. 748-50. See also Trautman, "Class Gifts of Future Interests: When is Survival Required?", 20 Vand. L. Rev. 1 (1966-67); Morris, "The Rule Against Perpetuities and the Rule in *Andrews v. Partington*", 70 L.Q. Rev. 61 (1954); Leach, "The Rule Against Perpetuities and Gifts to Classes", 51 Harv. L. Rev. 1329 (1937-38).

share in the gift.[13] However, if there are no children living at that time, the class remains open until it closes naturally, that is, by the death of A.[14]

2. A Postponed Gift to a Class

An example would be a gift, "to X for life, remainder to the children of A equally".

The class closes at the death of the life tenant and only those children then living, or the personal representatives of those who survived the testator but predeceased X, can take. But if there are no children living at that time, the class remains open to let in all afterborn children of A.[15]

3. An Immediate Gift to a Class Coupled With a Condition

An example would be a gift, "to the children of A when they attain age 21".

In this case the class closes on the testator's death, or as soon thereafter as one member of the class has satisfied the condition. Children alive at the time who have not yet satisfied the condition may take when they become 21, but all unborn children are excluded.[16]

4. A Postponed Gift to a Class, Coupled With a Condition

An example would be a gift, "to X for life, remainder to the children of A who attain age 21".

In this case the class closes at the later of the determination of the life estate and fulfilment of the contingency by a child of A. Other living children are potential members, but unborn children are excluded. The estates of children of A who survived the testator and attained the age of 21 but predeceased X, can take.[17]

B. Separate Gifts

1. An Immediate Gift to a Class, Whether or Not it is Coupled With a Condition

An example is a gift of "$1,000 to each of the children of A" (or, "who attain age 21").

The class closes at the testator's death, whether or not any takers or potential takers are in existence. Children who are born, but who have not yet satisfied the condition in the alternative example may take when they become 21.[18]

2. A Postponed Gift to a Class, Whether or Not it is Coupled With a Condition

An example is a gift, "to X for life, and then to pay $100 to each of the children of A" (or, "who become 21").

---

[13]*Viner v. Francis* (1789), 2 Cox 190, 30 E.R. 88.

[14]*Shepherd v. Ingram* (1764), Amb. 448, 27 E.R. 296.

[15]*Devisme v. Mello* (1782), 1 Bro. C.C. 537, 28 E.R. 1285; *Re Dawes' Trusts* (1876), 4 Ch. D. 210.

[16]*Andrews v. Partington* (1791), 3 Bro. C.C. 401, 29 E.R. 610.

[17]*Re Canney's Trusts; Mayers v. Strover* (1910), 101 L.T. 905; *Re Bleckly, supra,* footnote 12.

[18]*Rogers v. Mutch* (1878), 10 Ch. D. 25.

The class closes at the termination of the prior interest and only those persons who are then living, or the personal representatives of those who survived the testator and whose interest vested during the life tenancy can take, or are potential takers.[19]

The class closing rules probably do not apply to gifts of income, so that class members will be able to share in payments of income after they are born.[20]

(c) The application of the rule against perpetuities

(i) Generally

For the purpose of the rule against perpetuities, a class gift must be either wholly good or wholly bad. Not only must all the members of the class be ascertained within the period, but the amount of their shares, both minimum and maximum, must also be ascertainable within the period. If some members are ascertainable within the period, but others are not, the whole gift fails: ". . . the vice of remoteness affects the class as a whole, if it may affect an unascertained number of its members".[21]

In the leading case, *Leake v. Robinson*,[22] a class gift was void because the maximum size of the members' shares was not ascertainable within the period. The testator devised property "in trust for A for life and, after his death, to his issue, but if he should die without issue, then to such of A's brothers and sisters as attain age 25 or marry". A died without issue. When the testator died, A had five living brothers and sisters. Two more were born before A's death and one thereafter. It was held that the whole gift was void, for it was possible at the time of the testator's death that further brothers and sisters might be born who might attain the age of 25 beyond the perpetuity period, that is, more than twenty-one years after the death of persons living at the testator's death, for the class would not close in these circumstances until the first member of the class attained the age of 25. Afterborn brothers and sisters would have reduced the size of the shares of brothers and sisters living at the testator's death.

A gift to a class and an individual has peculiarities of its own. Thus, if the testator gives property "to A and all the children of B when they attain the age of 25", B being alive at the testator's death, the gift is capable of two constructions. *Prima facie*, A and the several children of B will take *per capita*, but if there is language in the will which suggests a *per stirpes* distribution

---

19*Ibid.*

20*Re Wenmoth's Estate*; *Wenmoth v. Wenmoth* (1887), 37 Ch. D. 266, but see *contra*, *Re Powell*; *Crosland v. Holliday*, [1898] 1 Ch. 227. On this point see Morris and Leach, pp. 121-2.

21*Pearks v. Moseley* (1880), 5 App. Cas. 714 (H.L.), at p. 723, *per* Lord Selborne, L.C.; *Jee v. Audley* (1787), 1 Cox 324, 29 E.R. 1186; *Cattlin v. Brown* (1853), 11 Hare 372 at p. 377, 68 E.R. 1319, *per* Page Wood, V.C.

22(1817), 2 Mer. 363, 35 E.R. 979.

among B's children, that construction will be adopted.[23] In the latter case, A's interest will be valid, since it is fixed and independent of the number of B's children. If a *per capita* construction is adopted, A's interest will be void as well as that of B's children, since it will vary with the number of children.[24]

(ii) Composite classes

It may also happen that the minimum size of the members' shares cannot be ascertained within the period. Typically this occurs where the testator gives property to a class with a substitutional gift to the issue of those members who die before distribution. If a member dies without issue, the shares of the other members would increase and, if this may by possibility occur beyond the period, the whole gift is void.

This happened in *Hale v. Hale*,[25] where the testator gave property to his widow during widowhood, with remainder to his children then living, the issue of any deceased child taking their parent's share at age 24. The problem in this situation is that if a child dies after the testator and before the dropping of the life estate, leaving a two-year-old child, it will not be known for another twenty-two years whether that grandchild will take and that may be more than twenty-one years after the death of the lives in being. The shares of the testator's children would thus have been increased beyond the period if the grandchild failed to attain the age of 24.

The gift in *Hale v. Hale* is an example of a gift to a composite class. The leading case, *Pearks v. Moseley*,[26] also falls into this category. In that case the testator bequeathed a sum of money to his daughter and her husband for life, "with remainder to all the daughter's children as shall attain the age of 21 years, the share of any child dying under that age to go to his issue who attain the age of 21 or die under that age leaving issue". The whole gift was held void, for while the gift to the children would have been valid by itself, the gift to the issue would be void and, since it was a gift to one class, although a composite class, it was void in its entirety.

A gift to a composite class is also created when the contingencies applicable to different members vary, as where there is a gift "to A for life, remainder to his children equally, if sons, at age 25 and, if daughters, at age 21 or when they marry". In that case also the gift is wholly void, although the gift to the daughters if it stood alone would be valid.[27]

The above principles apply only if the gift to the class, including the persons who enter because of the death of their parent, is an original gift. If the gift to the latter persons can be construed as substitutional, it may be saved in whole or in part. In order to do so, the gift to the parents must be given upon

[23]Jarman, pp. 1707 *et seq.*

[24]*Porter v. Fox* (1834), 6 Sim. 485, 58 E.R. 676.

[25](1876), 3 Ch. D. 643.

[26]*Supra*, footnote 21.

[27]*Re Slark's Trust* (1872), 21 W.R. 165. And see *Hewson v. Black* (1917), 36 D.L.R. 185, 51 N.S.R. 81 (S.C.).

a condition subsequent so as to divest their interest if they die under the specified age. Hence, instead of saying, "to A's children at age 21, the share of each child dying under that age to go to his issue at age 21" as in *Pearks v. Moseley*, the testator could say, "to children of A at age 21, but if any die under that age leaving children who attain age 21, such children will take their parent's share". Although the difference is only one of words, the effect is that in the latter case the children's interest is construed as vested subject to divestment[28] and their children will take by substitution. The result is that the interest of the children of those children of A who were living at the testator's death is valid, while the interest of those whose parents were afterborn is void, leaving their parents' interests indefeasibly vested.[29]

Whether the gift to the grandchildren is original or substitutional is a matter of construction and depends upon the language used in the will.[30]

(iii) Gifts to sub-classes

Where the gift is not to a composite class but to sub-classes, it can be split and will be valid for those persons whose interests must vest within the perpetuity period. The following example illustrates the point:

> A devise, "to A for life, remainder to all his children for their lives, remainder as to the share of each child so dying, to his children". A had six children who were living at the testator's death and several who were born afterwards.

In *Cattlin v. Brown*,[31] upon which the foregoing example is based, the court held that the interests of the children of A's children who were living at the testator's death were valid, while those of the children of afterborn children were void. The reason is that the gift to the children in each stock is independent of the gift to the children in the other stock and clearly, the gift to the children of A's children who were living at the testator's death would have to vest within the lives of their parents.

(iv) Gifts to each member of a class

Where there is a gift of a specified sum to each member of a class, the same result obtains as in *Cattlin v. Brown*, because the gifts are independent of each other. Thus, in *Storrs v. Benbow*[32] the testator bequeathed the sum of £500 "to each child that may be born to either of the children of either of my brothers" when they attained the age of 21. The class in this case would

---

[28]See §1004.3(d) on this rule of construction.

[29]*Goodier v. Johnson* (1881), 18 Ch. D. 441 (C.A.); *Re Turney; Turney v. Turney*, [1899] 2 Ch. 739 (C.A.).

[30]See further *Re Lord's Settlement; Martins Bank, Ltd. v. Lord*, [1947] 2 All E.R. 685 (Ch.), where a gift to grandchildren was held to be original. And see generally Morris and Leach, pp. 105-6.

[31](1853), 11 Hare 372, 68 E.R. 1319.

[32](1853), 3 De G. M. & G. 390, 43 E.R. 153.

close at the testator's death and the court so held, thereby saving the gift. However, in the alternative it was held that the gift would be valid as to any grandchildren of the brothers living at the testator's death. Accordingly, a grandchild conceived before and born after the testator's death was entitled to take.

If the class does not close at the testator's death, either because the class closing rule is expressly excluded or because there is a preceding life interest, the same result obtains. Thus, where a testator bequeaths a sum of money "to A for life, remainder to such of his children as he shall appoint" and A appoints £2,000 to each of his daughters at the age of 24, the appointments to such daughters as are three years of age or older at A's death, are valid.[33] The reason for this is that the power is special so that, while the period commences to run at the testator's death, regard can be had to the state of facts existing at the donee's death.[34]

1104.7 Powers of Appointment

(a) Generally

The rule against perpetuities applies to powers of appointment and similar powers such as powers of advancement, maintenance, encroachment and discretionary trusts in several ways. In the first place, the power may itself be invalid in that it may be exercisable beyond the perpetuity period. Secondly, even if the power is valid, an appointment made under it may be invalid for perpetuity. Thirdly, a gift in default of appointment may be invalid under the rule.

Powers of appointment and analogous powers are sometimes called dispositive powers. There are other powers, often referred to as administrative powers, such as the power to sell in order to pay debts, which may also be void for perpetuity. These are dealt with below.[1]

A power of appointment is an authority given by one person, the donor of the power, to another, the donee of the power (also called the appointor), to determine who shall receive the property that is the subject-matter of the power. The property is usually owned by the donor of the power. The recipient is called the appointee, while the persons to or among whom the donee may appoint are called the objects of the power.[2]

For the purpose of the rule against perpetuities it is necessary to distinguish between general and special powers of appointment. The definitions of these powers differ from those applicable generally. Indeed, the law of powers further recognizes a hybrid power, a concept which is irrelevant for perpetuities.[3]

---

[33]*Wilkinson v. Duncan* (1861), 30 Beav. 111, 54 E.R. 831.
[34]See §1104.7(c)(ii), *infra.*
§1104.7
[1]§1104.22. *infra.*
[2]See §1401. *infra.*
[3]See §1402, *infra.*

For the purposes of the rule, a general power is regarded as equivalent to absolute ownership in that the donee may appoint to himself. It may be defined as a power to appoint by deed or will (but not a power to appoint by will only) to anyone including the donee. Thus, even if the donee is a member of a class of objects, or is empowered to appoint to anyone except a named person,[4] the power is general.

For the purposes of the rule, a special power is one where the donee cannot, or cannot by himself alone, make the property his own. Thus, a power to appoint to anyone except the donee, and a power to appoint to anyone with the consent of,[5] or jointly with,[6] a named person, are special powers.

The above definitions apply not only to the validity of the power, but also to the validity of an appointment under it, with one exception. A power to appoint to anyone exercisable by will only is treated as a special power as regards the validity of the power,[7] but as a general power as regards the validity of an appointment made under it.[8] In the United States such a power is treated as special for both purposes.[9]

(b) Validity of the power

(i) General powers

To be valid a general power must become exercisable within the perpetuity period, although it does not in fact have to be exercised within the period.[10] This means that the donee must be ascertainable within the perpetuity period. If a general power of appointment be given to a person alive at the date of the instrument creating it, it must, of course, if exercised at all, be exercised during the lifetime of such person and is, therefore, valid. If a power can be exercised only in favour of a person living at the date of the instrument creating it, it must, if exercised at all, be exercised during the lifetime of such person and is, therefore, unobjectionable.[11]

The donee of a general power may be the survivor of any number of living persons.[12] He may even be unborn when the power is created so long as he is ascertainable within the perpetuity period, as where he is the child of a living person, and he may exercise the power by deed or will.[13] If the donee is the

---

[4] *Re Penrose; Penrose v. Penrose,* [1933] Ch. 793.

[5] *Re Watts; Coffey v. Watts,* [1931] 2 Ch. 302; *Webb v. Sadler* (1873), 8 Ch. App. 419.

[6] *Re Churston Settled Estates,* [1954] Ch. 334; *Re Earl of Coventry's Indentures; Smith v. Earl of Coventry,* [1974] Ch. 77.

[7] *Morgan v. Gronow* (1873), L.R. 16 Eq. 1.

[8] *Rous v. Jackson* (1885), 29 Ch. D. 521; *Re Flower; Edmonds v. Edmonds* (1885), 55 L.J. Ch. 200; *Re Fasken,* [1961] O.R. 891, 30 D.L.R. (2d) 193 (H.C.J.).

[9] Restatement, *Property,* §392; Gray, §526.2.

[10] *Morgan v. Gronow, supra,* footnote 7; *Re Meredith's Trusts* (1876), 3 Ch. D. 757; *Re Fasken, supra,* footnote 8.

[11] *Re De Sommery; Coelenbier v. De Sommery,* [1912] 2 Ch. 622.

[12] *Robinson v. Hardcastle* (1786), 2 Bro. C.C. 22, 29 E.R. 11; *Thellusson v. Woodford* (1805), 11 Ves. Jun. 112, 32 E.R. 1030 (H.L.).

[13] *Bray v. Hammersley* (1830), 3 Sim. 513, 57 E.R. 1090, affd 2 Cl. & Fin. 453, 6 E.R. 1225 sub nom. *Bray v. Bree* (C.A.).

survivor of a class of unborn children of living persons, he is not necessarily ascertainable within the period, so that the power is void.[14] Similarly, whenever the general power is exercisable after the occurrence of an event which may not happen until after the period, as where a general power is given to a person when he marries, it is void.[15]

(ii) Special powers

A special power must also be exercisable within the perpetuity period in order to be valid. If it is exercisable beyond the period, it is void.[16] Hence, if the power is given to a living person, or is exercisable only in favour of living persons, it is valid,[17] but a power given to the trustees of a will, which may be exercisable in favour of unborn persons, is void, for the trustees include not only the present, but also successor trustees.[18]

It has been argued that a power of advancement which is exercisable beyond the perpetuity period is not void, provided that the trusts to which the power is annexed are not too remote. The reason is that the exercise of such a power merely accelerates the time when a share of the capital vests, which is not within the mischief of the rule.[19]

(iii) Construction

Powers given to various persons may be severable, thereby rendering them valid in part. Thus, although a power vested in the trustees for the time being of a settlement has apparently been uniformly looked on as a single and indivisible power, it may be otherwise if the power be limited to A and B or other of the trustees of the settlement for the time being. The court may treat the settlor as having created one power vested in A and B while trustees and a distinct power vested in their successors, in which case the power vested in A and B would be open to no objection on the ground of remoteness.[20]

Where a testator gave a power of appointment to A or other of his trustees, and appointed A his sole executor with power to appoint new trustees, it was held that the power was divisible and was to be considered as two powers, one to be exercised by A and the other by succeeding trustees in default of A

---

[14]*Re Hargreaves; Midgley v. Tatley* (1890), 43 Ch. D. 401 (C.A.).

[15]*Morgan v. Gronow, supra,* footnote 7.

[16]*Re Watson's Settlement Trusts; Dawson v. Reid,* [1959] 2 All E.R. 676 (Ch.); *Re Coleman; Public Trustee v. Coleman,* [1936] Ch. 528, a discretionary trust; *Wollaston v. King* (1869), L.R. 8 Eq. 165, a power exercisable by will only; *Re Abrahams' Will Trusts; Caplan v. Abrahams,* [1967] 2 All E.R. 1175 (Ch.), a special power given to an unborn person.

[17]*Re De Sommery, supra,* footnote 11, at p. 631; *Re Albery,* [1964] 1 O.R. 342, 42 D.L.R. (2d) 201 (H.C.J.).

[18]*Re De Sommery, supra,* footnote 11; *Re Symm's Will Trusts; Public Trustee v. Shaw,* [1936] 3 All E.R. 236 (Ch.).

[19]Morris and Leach, p. 144. But see *Pilkington v. Inland Revenue Com'rs,* [1962] 3 All E.R. 622 (H.L.).

[20]*Re De Sommery, supra,* footnote 11.

exercising his power. The former power was valid whatever might be said of the latter.[21] Moreover, if a power be given to a living person and his heirs or assigns, it can at least be exercised by the living person.[22]

If the instrument creating the power does not specify when it must be exercised, the court will infer that it must be exercised within a reasonable time, that is, within the perpetuity period.[23]

Language which purports to limit appointments to the perpetuity period is not effective to save the appointments if they in fact exceed the period.[24]

(iv) Void powers

If a power of appointment is void, any appointment under it is void as well,[25] but not a gift over in default of appointment,[26] nor any subsequent limitations,[27] unless they would be void in themselves. However, a power is not void merely because an appointment under it would be void for perpetuity.[28]

(c) Validity of the appointment

(i) General powers

Since a general power is regarded as conferring ownership upon the donee of the power, an appointment under it is treated as though it were a gift by the donee. For this reason the perpetuity period only begins to run from the date of the appointment.[29] It will be recalled that a general power, as regards the validity of an appointment under it, includes an unrestricted power to appoint by will only.[30]

(ii) Special powers

In order to be valid, an appointment under a special power must be able to take effect within the perpetuity period, which runs from the date the power was created, the appointment being read back into the instrument creating the

---

[21]*Attenborough v. Attenborough* (1855), 1 K. & J. 296, 69 E.R. 470. See also *Re Abbott; Peacock v. Frigout*, [1893] 1 Ch. 54.

[22]*Earl of Bandon v. Moreland*, [1910] 1 I.R. 220.

[23]*Re Leek; Darwen v. Leek*, [1968] 1 All E.R. 793 (C.A.); *Re Gooderham*, [1971] 2 O.R. 369, 18 D.L.R. (3d) 36 (H.C.J.).

[24]*Inland Revenue Com'rs v. Williams*, [1969] 3 All E.R. 614 (Ch.); *Re Earl of Coventry's Indentures; Smith v. Earl of Coventry*, [1974] Ch. 77.

[25]*Morgan v. Gronow* (1873), L.R. 16 Eq. 1; *Re Hargreaves; Midgley v. Tatley* (1890), 43 Ch. D. 401 (C.A.); *Re Fasken*, [1961] O.R. 891, 30 D.L.R. (2d) 193 (H.C.J.).

[26]*Re Abbott, supra*, footnote 21.

[27]*Re Coleman; Public Trustee v. Coleman*, [1936] Ch. 528. *Re Allan; Curtis v. Nalder*, [1958] 1 W.L.R. 220 (Ch.).

[28]*Re Fane; Fane v. Fane*, [1913] 1 Ch. 404 (C.A.).

[29]*Re Thompson; Thompson v. Thompson*, [1906] 2 Ch. 199 at p. 202; *Re Fasken, supra*, footnote 25.

[30]See sub-subpara. (a) at footnote 8, *supra*.

power for this purpose.[31] If the class of objects is to be ascertained on a contingency, the contingency must necessarily occur within the period if the appointment is to be valid.[32] Thus, where the sister of a testatrix had power to appoint the proceeds of sale of property by will among grandchildren of the testatrix living at the time of the sale and the sale was directed to take place after the perpetuity period, the power was void.[33] The limitations made under the power must necessarily take effect within the perpetuity period.[34]

The rule requires not only that the objects of the power be ascertainable within the perpetuity period, but the very persons who are to take, "because the rule is aimed at the practical object of telling who can deal with the property, and if you cannot tell who are entitled to the property, but only who may become entitled to the property, the property is practically tied up".[35] If the class of objects designated by the donor of the power is such that at least some of the class, if it exists at all, must necessarily be ascertained within the perpetuity period, as where the power is to appoint to the issue generally of a living person, the power is valid and the only question that can arise is whether any particular disposition by the donee of the power is too remote.[36]

Limitations made by the donee of the special power must be such as would be valid if made by the donor of the power. They are read into the will or other instrument creating the power and, to the extent that they do not transgress the rule, the limitations are good. At the date of the instrument creating the power, the limitations are not known. However, in this case the rule permits a "second look", that is, it permits the taking into account of facts existing at the date the appointment is made. It may be that the donee of the power will so exercise it as to transgress the rule, in which case the limitations will fail, but it may be that he will so exercise it as not to transgress the rule, in which case the limitations hold good. At the date of the instrument creating the power, it is impossible to say whether the rule will be transgressed or not, but this uncertainty does not render a good limitation bad.[37]

> The fact that within the terms of the power an appointment could be made which would be too remote is of no moment; you must wait and see how in fact the power has been executed, and in order to test the validity of the appointment you must treat the appointment as if written in the original instrument creating the power.[38]

---

[31]Leach, "Perpetuities in a Nutshell", 51 Harv. L. Rev. 638 (1937-38), at p. 653; *Re Abrahams' Will Trusts*; *Caplan v. Abrahams*, [1967] 2 All E.R. 1175 (Ch.); *Re Manning* (1978), 19 O.R. (2d) 257, 84 D.L.R. (3d) 715, 2 E.T.R. 195 (C.A.).

[32]*Blight v. Hartnoll* (1881), 19 Ch. D. 294.

[33]*Ibid.*

[34]*Re Norton*; *Norton v. Norton*, [1911] 2 Ch. 27.

[35]*Blight v. Hartnoll, supra*, footnote 32, at pp. 300-1, *per* Fry, J.

[36]*Griffith v. Pownall* (1843), 13 Sim. 393 at p. 396, 60 E.R. 152; *Slark v. Dakyns* (1874), L.R. 10 Ch. 35; *Re Warren's Trusts* (1884), 26 Ch. D. 208.

[37]*Re Goodhue Trusts* (1920), 47 O.L.R. 178 (H.C.); *Re Fane*; *Fane v. Fane*, [1913] 1 Ch. 404 (C.A.).

[38]*Re Fane, supra*, footnote 37, at p. 411, *per* Cozens-Hardy, M.R. See also *Re Thompson*, *supra*, footnote 29; *Re Eliot* (1913), 24 O.W.R. 494, 11 D.L.R. 34 (S.C.); *Re Paul*; *Public Trustee v. Pearce*, [1921] 2 Ch. 1; *Re Fasken*, [1961] O.R. 891, 30 D.L.R. (2d) 193 (H.C.J.).

Thus, if a testator gives property to his nephew, A, for life, remainder to such of A's issue as A shall appoint and A appoints to his children when they attain the age of 24, the appointment is valid if the children were at least three years old when A exercised the power.[39]

A settlement created by an advancement made under a power of advancement attracts the rule against perpetuities in the same way as any special power.[40]

(d) Validity of gift in default of appointment

Where the donee of the power fails to appoint or releases the power, the gift in default of appointment is treated as though it were made by the donee at the moment that the power expires.[41] Hence, in the case of a general power, the period begins to run when the power expires, for it is at that moment that the donee is regarded as in effect making a gift from himself to those entitled to take in default of appointment.[42] Although a general power is normally exercised by will because the Wills Acts so provide,[43] the same principle applies to an unlimited power to encroach.[44]

In the case of a special power, the perpetuity period commences when the power is created, but the "second look" doctrine is applicable so that facts existing when the power expires may be taken into account.

In *Re Edwards*[45] the testator gave part of the residue of his estate in trust for his son, S, for life, remainder to such of S's children as he should by deed or will appoint and, in default of appointment, one half to S's children living when the youngest child attained the age of 21 and the other half to such of S's children living when the youngest attained the age of 35. When S died without exercising the power, he was survived by four children, the youngest of whom was 25. The gift in default of appointment was held valid, for the youngest child would have to attain the age of 35 within the perpetuity period.

---

[39]*Wilkinson v. Duncan* (1861), 30 Beav. 111, 54 E.R. 831. See also *Re Farncombe's Trusts* (1878), 9 Ch. D. 652, a gift to sub-classes, some of which were valid and others void. As to such gifts see §1104.6(c)(iii), *supra*.

[40]*Pilkington v. Inland Revenue Com'rs*, [1964] A.C. 612 (H.L.); *Re Hastings-Bass*; *Hastings-Bass v. Inland Revenue Com'rs*, [1975] Ch. 25 (C.A.).

[41]Morris and Leach, p. 159; *Re Edwards*, [1959] O.W.N. 313, 20 D.L.R. (2d) 755 (H.C.J.).

[42]*Re Fasken*, *supra*, footnote 38.

[43]*Wills Act*, R.S.A. 1980, c. W-11, s. 25; R.S.B.C. 1979, c. 434, s. 23; R.S.M. 1970, c. W150, s. 25; R.S.S. 1978, c. W-14, s. 24; R.S.N.B. 1973, c. W-9, s. 24; R.S.N.S. 1967, c. 340, s. 25; R.S.N. 1970, c. 401, s. 16; *Succession Law Reform Act*, R.S.O. 1980, c. 488, s. 25; *Probate Act*, R.S.P.E.I. 1974, c. P-19, s. 78; *Wills Ordinance*, R.O.N.W.T. 1974, c. W-3, s. 19; R.O.Y.T. 1971, c. W-3, s. 18.

[44]Morris and Leach, p. 160.

[45]*Supra*, footnote 41.

1104.8 Violation of the Rule Against Perpetuities

(a) Effect generally

The general rule is that an instrument containing any void limitation takes effect as if the void limitation and all limitations dependent on it were omitted from the instrument.[1] If a gift over in defeasance of a prior limitation is void, the prior limitation takes free from it and may thus become indefeasible,[2] and the person entitled under the prior limitation may be entitled to a conveyance of the property absolutely. Thus, in *Re Da Costa; Clarke v. Church of England Collegiate School of St. Peter*,[3] the testator devised real property in South Australia to trustees upon trust, during the lives of successive tenants for life, to apply the income in a specified manner and, after the last life tenancy, to convey it to the council of a school upon the condition that the council publish annually a statement of its receipts and disbursements and, in case of default in publication for six months, the disposition to the school was to cease and go to such public purpose as the Governor-in-Chief of South Australia should direct. It was held that the gift over and the condition were both bad, the former as not being a good charitable gift and the latter as being a common law condition subsequent, working a forfeiture in an event which was void for remoteness. The council of the school was, therefore, entitled to an absolute conveyance without reference to the condition or gift over.

Similarly, in *Re Brown and Sibly's Contract*,[4] the testator had power to appoint to his issue. He appointed to his son absolutely, but if the son should have no child who should attain the age of 25, then he appointed to a named grandson absolutely. The son and the grandson were unborn when the power was created. This meant that the gift to the grandson was too remote, with the result that the son took absolutely.[5]

Except where a limitation is a gift over in defeasance of a prior limitation, the estate or interest given by a limitation void for remoteness devolves in the same manner as if it were void for any other reason. Thus, if it is in a settlement or conveyance it reverts to the settlor or grantor or his representatives,[6] and, if it is in a will, it passes to the residuary devisee[7] or, if it is the residue itself or if there is no residuary devise, it passes to those entitled on

---

§1104.8

[1]Lewis, p. 657.

[2]*Taylor v. Frobisher* (1852), 5 De G. & Sm. 191, 64 E.R. 1076; *Courtier v. Oram* (1855), 21 Beav. 91, 52 E.R. 793; *Webster v. Parr* (1858), 26 Beav. 236, 53 E.R. 888; *Hodgson v. Halford* (1879), 11 Ch. D. 959; *Goodier v. Johnson* (1881), 18 Ch. D. 441 (C.A.).

[3][1912] 1 Ch. 337.

[4](1876), 3 Ch. D. 156.

[5]See also *Re Pratt's Settlement Trusts; McCullum v. Phipps-Hornby*, [1943] Ch. 356.

[6]*Re Morse's Settlement* (1855), 21 Beav. 174, 52 E.R. 825; *Re Slark's Trusts* (1872), 21 W.R. 165.

[7]*Leake v. Robinson* (1817), 2 Mer. 363 at p. 392, 35 E.R. 979; *Bentinck v. Duke of Portland* (1877), 7 Ch. D. 693 at p. 700.

an intestacy.[8] The estate or interest comprised in a void appointment under a power of appointment passes to those entitled in default of appointment.[9]

Where an estate or interest devolves by reason of a void limitation in a will, it devolves subject to such directions as were validly imposed by the testator. Thus, a direction to trustees to purchase land is good, even though the trusts of the land to be purchased result to the testator's heir-at-law because the limitation to specified beneficiaries is too remote.[10] Similarly, where a will creates a valid trust for the sale of real property, but the trusts of the proceeds of sale are void for remoteness, the trustees, under the doctrine of reconversion, hold the legal estate in trust for the person entitled to undisposed of realty who, if there is no other valid disposition, was formerly the testator's heir-at-law.[11]

Where the trust for sale is too remote and the persons to take the proceeds cannot be ascertained within the perpetuity period, both the trust for sale and the trusts of the proceeds are void for remoteness.[12]

However, where the trust for sale of real property is too remote, but the trusts of the proceeds are valid, or the trust for sale is merely the machinery to carry out a valid disposition of the proceeds, the trust for sale is void, but the beneficiaries take the property as realty.[13] Thus, where a testator devised his real estate upon trust for sale in an event which was beyond the perpetuity period, and gave the proceeds of sale to persons ascertainable within the perpetuity period, making no gift to them of the income until sale, it was held that, although the trust for sale was void for remoteness, it was mere machinery for the purpose of division and could be disregarded and that the beneficiaries of the proceeds took the property as real estate.[14]

The fact that a gift of the capital of a settled fund is void does not render the gift of the income invalid if it does not itself offend the rule.[15]

(b) Void restriction on valid limitation

In general, where there is a valid limitation, a restriction or condition that fetters the property beyond the perpetuity period is void and the limitation

---

[8]*Proctor v. Bishop of Bath and Wells* (1794), 2 H. Bl. 358, 126 E.R. 594; *Stuart v. Cockerell* (1870), L.R. 5 Ch. 713; *Bentinck v. Duke of Portland, supra,* footnote 7; *Ferguson v. Ferguson* (1878), 2 S.C.R. 497.

[9]*Routledge v. Dorril* (1794), 2 Ves. Jun. 357, 30 E.R. 671; *Chance v. Chance* (1853), 16 Beav. 572, 51 E.R. 901; *Ratcliffe v. Hampson* (1855), 1 Jur. N.S. 1104; *Wollaston v. King* (1869), L.R. 8 Eq. 165; *Whitby v. Mitchell* (1889), 42 Ch. D. 494, affd 44 Ch. D. 85 (C.A.); *Re Boyd; Nield v. Boyd* (1890), 63 L.T. 92.

[10]*Tregonwell v. Sydenham* (1815), 3 Dow. 194, 3 E.R. 1035.

[11]*Newman v. Newman* (1839), 10 Sim. 51, 59 E.R. 531; *Whitehead v. Bennett* (1853), 1 Eq. Rep. 560, 22 L.J. Ch. 1020; *Hale v. Pew* (1858), 25 Beav. 335, 53 E.R. 665.

[12]*Re Wood; Tullett v. Colville,* [1894] 3 Ch. 381 (C.A.).

[13]*Goodier v. Edmunds,* [1893] 3 Ch. 455.

[14]*Re Appleby; Walker v. Lever,* [1903] 1 Ch. 565 (C.A.). And see *Re Daveron; Bowen v. Churchill,* [1893] 3 Ch. 421.

[15]*Re White Trust,* [1952] O.W.N. 748, [1952] 4 D.L.R. 711 (H.C.J.).

stands without it. Thus, in *Re Staveley; Dyke v. Staveley*,[16] the testatrix, under a power of appointment, appointed a fund to one son, C, for life with remainder to his eldest son, provided that, in the event of their refusal to comply with a request by another son, A, to release their interests in other property, their interests were to go over to A absolutely. It was held that the appointment was unobjectionable but the condition was void as being contrary to the rule against perpetuities.

Similarly, if a restraint on anticipation is imposed upon the interest of an unborn person, so that it could possibly fetter the interest beyond the perpetuity period, it is void.[17]

If a limitation by will is to a class, a restraint on anticipation may be valid as to those members of the class existing at the testator's death, although void as to those born afterwards.[18]

Where there is an absolute gift to a person, followed by an attempt to limit it by a direction to settle it on issue who are too remote, the direction is rejected and the absolute gift is free from it under the rule in *Hancock v. Watson*.[19] Where, however, a gift is not absolute in the first instance and a restriction on its enjoyment is imposed which is void for remoteness, the gift is void.[20]

(c) Effect on subsequent limitations

If a limitation is void for remoteness, subsequent limitations that are expectant or dependent upon it, or are to take effect in defeasance of it, are not accelerated but are void also.[21]

---

[16](1920), 90 L.J. Ch. 111.

[17]*Fry v. Capper* (1853), Kay 163, 69 E.R. 70; *Armitage v. Coates* (1865), 35 Beav. 1, 55 E.R. 794; *Re Teague's Settlement* (1870), L.R. 10 Eq. 564; *Re Cunynghame's Settlement* (1871), L.R. 11 Eq. 324; *Re Errington; Bawtree v. Errington*, [1887] W.N. 23 (H.C.J.); *Shute v. Hogge* (1888), 58 L.T. 546; *Whitby v. Mitchell* (1889), 42 Ch. D. 494, not appealed on this point in 44 Ch. D. 85 (C.A.).

[18]*Wilson v. Wilson* (1858), 4 Jur. N.S. 1076; *Herbert v. Webster* (1880), 15 Ch. D. 610; *Re Russell; Dorrell v. Dorrell*, [1895] 2 Ch. 698 (C.A.); *Re Ferneley's Trusts*, [1902] 1 Ch. 543; *Re Millward; Steedman v. Hobday* (1902), 87 L.T. 476; *Re Game; Game v. Tennent*, [1907] 1 Ch. 276.

[19][1902] A.C. 14 (H.L.). See sub-subpara. (d) at footnote 40, *infra*. And see *Stephens v. Gadsden* (1855), 20 Beav. 463, 52 E.R. 682; *Cooke v. Cooke* (1887), 38 Ch. D. 202; *Re Boyd*, *supra*, footnote 9; *Re Johnson's Settlement Trusts*; *McClure v. Johnson*, [1943] Ch. 341; *Re Eliot* (1913), 24 O.W.R. 494, 11 D.L.R. 34 (S.C. App. Div.); *Re Goodhue Trusts* (1920), 47 O.L.R. 178 (S.C. App. Div.); *Re Jones*; *Re Watson*, [1947] O.W.N. 749 (H.C.J.).

[20]*Lassence v. Tierney* (1849), 1 Mac. & G. 551, 41 E.R. 1379.

[21]*Robinson v. Hardcastle* (1788), 2 T.R. 241, 380, 781, 100 E.R. 131, 205, 421; *Routledge v. Dorril* (1794), 2 Ves. Jun. 357 at p. 363, 30 E.R. 671; *Brudenell v. Elwes* (1801), 1 East 442 at p. 454, 102 E.R. 171; *Beard v. Westcott* (1822), 5 B. & Ald. 801, 106 E.R. 1383; *Palmer v. Holford* (1828), 4 Russ. 403, 38 E.R. 857; *Re Phillips* (1913), 28 O.L.R. 94, 11 D.L.R. 500 (H.C.J.); *Re Buckton's Declaration of Trust*; *Public Trustee v. Midland Bank Executor and Trustee Co., Ltd.*, [1964] 2 All E.R. 487 (Ch.).

It is settled that any limitation depending or expectant upon a prior limitation which is void for remoteness is invalid. The reason appears to be that the persons entitled under the subsequent limitation are not intended to take unless and until the prior limitation is exhausted; and as the prior limitation which is void for remoteness can never come into operation, much less be exhausted, it is impossible to give effect to the intentions of the settlor in favour of the beneficiaries under the subsequent limitation.[22]

This is so even if the subsequent limitation is to a person in being when the limitation is made and who otherwise would take a vested interest and even if such person only takes a life estate under it.[23] Moreover, if a prior limitation is to a living person for life and subsequent remainders for estates less than the fee simple are void for remoteness, the ultimate remainder to that person in fee simple is void.[24]

If the prior and subsequent limitations are both to take effect on the happening of the same event which is too remote, both limitations are necessarily void for remoteness.[25]

The statement by Stirling, J., quoted above, has been criticized as being too doctrinaire.[26] Indeed, it appears that an ulterior limitation fails only if it is itself void for perpetuity, or if it is dependent upon the prior interest, as where it commences with language such as, "in default of . . .". If it commences with words such as, "and then . . .", it is not dependent upon the first limitation.

In every case, it is a question of construction whether a subsequent limitation is dependent upon the contingency on which the prior limitation is to take effect, that is, whether the subsequent limitation is dependent upon the prior limitation taking effect.[27] If the subsequent limitation is dependent on the prior limitation taking effect and the latter is void for remoteness, the subsequent limitation is void also. If, however, the subsequent limitation can be construed as taking effect in an alternative event, which is not too remote, it will be valid. Thus, a trust which is to take effect "on the failure of" a trust which is void for remoteness may take effect as an alternative trust.[28]

As indicated above, a subsequent limitation which is void for remoteness does not defeat a prior vested interest.[29] Consequently, if an instrument creating a power of appointment makes a valid limitation in default of appointment, an appointment made under the power which is void for remoteness does

---

[22]*Re Abbott*; *Peacock v. Frigout*, [1893] 1 Ch. 54 at p. 57, per Stirling, J.

[23]*Beard v. Westcott, supra*, footnote 21; *Monypenny v. Dering* (1852), 2 De G. M. & G. 145 at p. 181, 42 E.R. 826; *Re Hewett's Settlement*; *Hewett v. Eldridge*, [1915] 1 Ch. 810.

[24]*Re Mortimer*; *Gray v. Gray*, [1905] 2 Ch. 502 (C.A.).

[25]*Proctor v. Bishop of Bath and Wells* (1794), 2 H. Bl. 358, 126 E.R. 594.

[26]Morris and Leach, pp. 179-81; Maudsley, p. 65.

[27]*Brudenell v. Elwes, supra*, footnote 21; *Re Abbott, supra*, footnote 22; *Re Hubbard's Will Trusts*; *Marston v. Angiers*, [1962] 2 All E.R. 917 (Ch.).

[28]*Willson v. Cobley*, [1870] W.N. 46. And see sub-subpara. (d), *infra*.

[29]See *Blease v. Burgh* (1840), 2 Beav. 221, 48 E.R. 1164; *Taylor v. Frobisher* (1852), 5 De G. & Sm. 191, 64 E.R. 1076; *Gooding v. Read* (1853), 4 De G. M. & G. 510, 43 E.R. 606; *Goodier v. Johnson* (1881), 18 Ch. D. 441 (C.A.).

not affect the limitation made in default of appointment[30] and a valid limitation made in default of appointment is not affected by the fact that the power of appointment is itself void for remoteness.[31] The reason is that, until a power of appointment is exercised, the property remains vested in those entitled to it in default of appointment.[32]

(d) Alternative limitations

If a limitation is made to take effect on the happening of either of two alternative events, one of which is too remote but the other is not, the limitation will take effect if the latter event actually happens, although it would otherwise be void. This is one of only two situations in which one could wait and see to let actual events determine the validity of the gift under the common law rule.[33] Thus, in *Longhead v. Phelps*,[34] a trust of a term was to arise on the contingency either that (a) A and B should die without leaving male issue, or (b) such male issue should die without issue. The trust was held to be good under the first branch of the contingency, since A and B had a son who died without issue during the lifetime of the survivor. The second branch of the contingency did not have to be considered since the son had not survived both A and B.

Similarly, in *Re Bullock's Will Trusts; Bullock v. Bullock*[35] the testator directed his trustees to pay a third of the rents and profits of his realty to his niece, B, a spinster, for life and, after her death, to any husband whom she might marry for his life and, after the death of both, to sell and hold the proceeds of one-third in trust for the children of B attaining the age of 21 and, if she should die without leaving a child or should have no child, then in trust for the children of S. It was held that the gift in favour of the children of B was not void as infringing the rule against limiting an estate to an unborn person (the potential husband who might be unborn when the limitation was created) with a remainder to his issue as purchasers but, even if it were, the gift to the children of S was good as an alternative and was a severable gift.[36]

Such a limitation on the happening of either of two alternative events is called a limitation upon a double aspect or a contingency with a double aspect,[37] but is said to really comprise alternative independent limitations.[38]

---

[30]*Wollaston v. King* (1869), L.R. 8 Eq. 165; *Webb v. Sadler* (1873), L.R. 8 Ch. 419; *Re Coulman; Munby v. Ross* (1885), 30 Ch. D. 186.

[31]*Re Abbott, supra.* footnote 22.

[32]*Lambert v. Thwaites* (1866), L.R. 2 Eq. 151.

[33]The other is the "second-look" doctrine in respect of appointments under special powers. See §1104.7(c)(ii), (d), *supra*.

[34](1770), 2 Black. W. 704, 96 E.R. 414.

[35][1915] 1 Ch. 493.

[36]And see *Miles v. Harford* (1879), 12 Ch. D. 691; *Re Davies and Kent's Contract*, [1910] 2 Ch. 35 (C.A.); *Minter v. Wraith* (1842), 13 Sim. 52, 60 E.R. 21; *Evers v. Challis* (1859), 7 H.L.C. 531, 11 E.R. 212.

[37]*Porter v. Bradley* (1789), 3 T.R. 143, 100 E.R. 500.

[38]*Monypenny v. Dering* (1852), 2 De G. M. & G. 145 at p. 183, 42 E.R. 826; *Re Davies and Kent's Contract, supra,* footnote 36, at p. 46.

In order to achieve this result the alternative contingencies must be express. If they are merely implied, the court will not split them.

In *Proctor v. Bishop of Bath and Wells*[39] the testator devised an advowson to the first or other son of B who should be bred a clergyman and be in holy orders but, if B should have no such son, then to C in fee. B died without having had a son. It was held that the devise to the son of B was void as depending on too remote a contingency and the devise over to C was void as depending on the same event and the words of the will would not admit of the contingency being divided so as to entitle C to the gift in the event of B having no son at all.

In *Re Harvey*; *Peek v. Savory*[40] the testatrix, after making provision for her two daughters, their husbands and issue, made an ultimate gift of her real estate in case both her daughters should die without leaving any child or the issue of any child living at the death of the survivor of their then or future husbands. Both daughters died leaving their husbands surviving, but without issue. It was held that the gift over was void for remoteness because it was not in the alternative on the happening of either of two distinct events, but a gift in one event involving two things and, as the testatrix had not severed the gift, the court could not do so.

In *Hancock v. Watson*,[41] the testator gave his residuary estate to trustees in trust for his wife for life and, after her death, to be divided into five parts, two of which were allotted by the testator to a married woman, S, with a direction that the two-fifths allotted to S remain in trust for her for life and, after her death, for her children on attaining age 25 if sons, or attaining age 21 or marrying if daughters, but, "in default of any such issue", to be divided among the children of C on remoter terms. S died without ever having had a child. It was held that the gift over was void for remoteness as it could not be split into two contingencies so as to allow it to take effect in the event of S dying without ever having had a child. Her two-fifths passed to her representatives, and there was no intestacy, however, because the gift to her was absolute and, when a trust engrafted upon an absolute gift fails for invalidity or any other reason, the absolute gift takes effect to the exclusion of the residuary legatee or next of kin as the case may be.

There is one exception to the rule that the court will not split alternative contingencies if one is merely implied, namely, that a devise which can take effect as a contingent remainder instead of an executory devise shall do so, so that, if it can take effect as a contingent remainder if one alternative event happens, it is allowed to take effect, although it would be void as an executory devise if dependent on the happening of the other event, which is too remote.[42]

In *Evers v. Challis*[43] the testator devised to A for life and, after her death,

---

[39](1794), 2 H. Bl. 358, 126 E.R. 594.
[40](1888), 39 Ch. D. 289 (C.A.).
[41][1902] A.C. 14 (H.L.).
[42]*Evers v. Challis* (1859), 7 H.L.C. 531, 11 E.R. 212.
[43]*Ibid.*

to her child or children attaining the age of 23 if a son, or 21 if a daughter and, in the event of her children dying under that age, or of her dying without issue, a devise over to the children of J attaining those ages. It was held that, as A died without having had a child and a daughter of J had then attained the age of 21, the devise over to such daughter took effect as a contingent remainder because no prior estate was divested but rather, in the determination of the particular estate, the life estate of A, the contingency on which the remainder was to take effect had occurred, although the devise would have been void for remoteness as an executory devise if it were dependent on the other specified event.

The rule in *Evers v. Challis* does not apply to equitable executory interests[44] or personalty.[45] It is probable that interests arising under wills are now all equitable by reason of statute[46] so that the rule no longer applies to testamentary gifts.

1104.9 Application of the Rule Against Perpetuities to Various Types of Interests

Thus far, the content of the rule against perpetuities has been examined in some detail, as well as its application to class gifts and powers of appointment, and the effects of violation of the rule. It remains now to examine the applicability of the rule to various types of interests. In the next several sections the application of the rule to various legal and equitable interests in property, to gifts to charity, contracts and other relationships, and to administrative powers and trusts, will be dealt with.

1104.10 Present Interests

Since the rule against perpetuities is a rule against remoteness of vesting and has no concern with how long an estate or interest lasts, present interests which are vested in some person are not objectionable on any ground of perpetuity regardless of the fact that they may last for an indefinite time. Consequently, the rule does not apply to vested interests, including easements and *profits à prendre*,[1] rent charges, and similar interests lasting indefinitely,[2]

---

[44]*Re Bence*; *Smith v. Bence*, [1891] 3 Ch. 242 (C.A.).

[45]*Re Hancock*; *Watson v. Watson*, [1901] 1 Ch. 482 (C.A.), affd [1902] A.C. 14.

[46]*Re Robson*; *Douglass v. Douglass*, [1916] 1 Ch. 116. See *Devolution of Real Property Act*, R.S.A. 1980, c. D-34, s. 3; R.S.S. 1978, c. D-27, ss. 4, 5; *Estate Administration Act*, R.S.B.C. 1979, c. 114, s. 90; *Devolution of Estates Act*, R.S.M. 1970, c. D70, s. 18(3); R.S.N.B. 1973, c. D-9, s. 3; *Estates Administration Act*, R.S.O. 1980, c. 143, s. 2; *Chattels Real Act*, R.S.N. 1970, c. 36, s. 2; *Real Property Act*, R.S.N.S. 1967, c. 261, s. 6(1); *Probate Act*, R.S.P.E.I. 1974, c. P-19, s. 108(1); *Devolution of Real Property Ordinance*, R.O.N.W.T. 1974, c. D-5, s. 4; R.O.Y.T. 1971, c. D-4, s. 4. And see §1011, *supra*.

§1104.10

[1]*London and South Western Ry. Co. v. Gomm* (1882), 20 Ch. D. 562 (C.A.), at p. 583.
[2]*Keppell v. Bailey* (1834), 2 My. & K. 517 at pp. 528-9, 39 E.R. 1042.

and restrictive covenants and conditions running with the land,[3] for they are so annexed to the land as to create something in the nature of an interest in the land.[4]

The rule also does not apply to an absolute immediate gift to a charity.[5]

A trust which is determinable by the beneficiaries because their interests are vested within the perpetuity period is not void under the rule merely because the trust may continue for an indefinite period.[6] The fact that a person to whom an interest is limited is under a disability is ignored in questions of perpetuity.[7]

Since the court acts on the principle that the rule is applied when there is no other sufficient protection against a perpetuity, the rule does not apply to the interests of corporations, the law of mortmain being a sufficient protection. Hence, where a testator gave the residue of his estate after the death of his wife to a limited company formed to promote a principle having an anti-religious tendency, it was held that no question of perpetuity arose as the donee was a limited company.[8]

1104.11 Limitation After an Estate Tail

The rule does not apply to a limitation to take effect on the determination of an estate tail, or in defeasance of an estate tail, because the tenant in tail has the power to destroy such limitation by barring the entail.[1]

No limitation after estates tail is ... too remote; and it appears to us clear that, whether the limitation be directly to a class of issue to be ascertained at the determination of the estate tail, or a gift to a trustee for such class, or upon trust to convey to such class, or to sell and to divide the produce amongst such class, is wholly immaterial, if the legal and beneficial interests should be both ascertainable at the moment of the determination of the estate tail.[2]

---

[3]*Mackenzie v. Childers* (1889), 43 Ch. D. 265; *Muller v. Trafford*, [1901] 1 Ch. 54.

[4]See also *Coles and Sims* (1854), 5 De G. M. & G. 1, 43 E.R. 768; *Elliston v. Reacher*, [1908] 2 Ch. 665 (C.A.); *Tulk v. Moxhay* (1848), 2 Ph. 774, 41 E.R. 1143.

[5]*Goodman v. Mayor of Saltash* (1882), 7 App. Cas. 633 (H.L.), at pp. 642, 650, 665; *Re Christchurch Inclosure Act* (1888), 38 Ch. D. 520 (C.A.), at pp. 530-2; *Re Mountain* (1912), 26 O.L.R. 163, 4 D.L.R. 737 (C.A.). And see §1104.17, *infra*.

[6]*Silvester v. Bradley* (1842), 13 Sim. 75, 60 E.R. 29, trust respecting timber; *Oddie v. Brown* (1859), 4 De G. & J. 179, 45 E.R. 70 (C.A.), trust for accumulation; *Re Tweedie and Miles* (1884), 27 Ch. D. 315, trust for sale in a settlement; *Re Douglas and Powell's Contract*, [1902] 2 Ch. 296, trust for sale in a will, the beneficiaries all being alive at its date.

[7]*Re Earl of Stamford and Warrington; Payne v. Grey*, [1912] 1 Ch. 343 (C.A.), at p. 355, per Cozens-Hardy, M.R.; *Ferrand v. Wilson* (1845), 4 Hare 344 at p. 374, 67 E.R. 680, per Wigram, V.C.

[8]*Re Bowman; Secular Society, Ltd. v. Bowman*, [1915] 2 Ch. 447, affd [1917] A.C. 406 (H.L.).

§1104.11

[1]*Nicolls v. Sheffield* (1787), 2 Bro. C.C. 215, 29 E.R. 121; *Heasman v. Pearse* (1871), L.R. 7 Ch. 275; *Van Grutten v. Foxwell*, [1897] A.C. 658 (H.L.), at p. 679; *Re Haygarth; Wickham v. Holmes*, [1912] 1 Ch. 510; *Re Mountgarret; Mountgarret v. Ingilby*, [1919] 2 Ch. 294.

[2]*Heasman v. Pearse, supra*, at pp. 282-3, per James, L.J.

Consequently, interests to take effect upon the contingency of failure of issue, if limited to persons ascertainable on or before the failure of issue, are valid.[3] Thus, where a testator directed trustees to convey the fee simple in equal shares to tenants in tail in possession in each line on their marriage or at their majority, the direction was held to be valid.[4]

Similarly, a limitation in defeasance of an estate tail, such as a shifting clause in the event of succession to family estates, need not be limited as to time, because of necessity it must take effect during the continuance of the estate tail.[5]

For the same reason, a power to trustees to enter into possession or receipt of rents and profits during the minority of a tenant in tail and to keep up the property and maintain the infant is valid.[6] Similarly, other powers not expressly limited as to time are good if they are exercisable during the continuance of an estate tail or successive estates tail, because they may be destroyed by a bar of the entail. Examples of such powers are, a power of sale,[7] a power to grant leases,[8] and a power to cut timber and apply the proceeds to discharge encumbrances.[9]

Limitations which are not barrable by the tenant in tail, such as estates or interests prior to the estate tail or those not taking effect on the determination of the estate tail or in defeasance of an estate tail, may be void for remoteness. Thus, where land was made subject to trusts to take effect on the failure of issue of the tenant in tail prior to a limitation of an estate tail, it was held that the trusts could not be barred by the tenant in tail and that they were too remote.[10]

A limitation after an estate tail, on general failure of issue, is void unless it can take effect as a legal contingent remainder. In *Bristow v. Boothby*[11] property was settled on a husband and wife for their lives, remainder to their sons in tail male, remainder to their daughters in tail, remainder to the survivor of the husband and wife in fee simple, with power to the wife to raise a charge if all the children died without issue. The husband survived and the power was held void for remoteness.

Most of the cases on this point have been cases in which a testator, having under a marriage settlement or other instrument a reversion after an estate tail,

---

[3]*Cole v. Sewell* (1848), 2 H.L.C. 186, 9 E.R. 1062.

[4]*Van Grutten v. Foxwell, supra,* footnote 1.

[5]*Nicolls v. Sheffield, supra,* footnote 1; *Carr v. Earl of Errol* (1805), 6 East 58, 102 E.R. 1209; *Harrison v. Round* (1852), 2 De G. M. & G. 190, 42 E.R. 844; *Bennett v. Bennett* (1864), 2 Dr. & Sm. 266, 62 E.R. 623.

[6]*Re Earl of Stamford and Warrington; Payne v. Grey,* [1912] 1 Ch. 343 (C.A.).

[7]*Biddle v. Perkins* (1829), 4 Sim. 135, 58 E.R. 52; *Waring v. Coventry* (1833), 1 My. & K. 249, 39 E.R. 675; *Lantsbery v. Collier* (1856), 2 K. & J. 709, 69 E.R. 967.

[8]*Wallis v. Freestone* (1839), 10 Sim. 225, 59 E.R. 599.

[9]*Briggs v. Earl of Oxford* (1852), 1 De G. M. & G. 363, 42 E.R. 592.

[10]*Case v. Drosier* (1839), 5 My. & Cr. 246, 41 E.R. 364. And see *Scarisbrick v. Skelmersdale* (1850), 17 Sim. 187, 60 E.R. 1100; *Floyer v. Bankes* (1869), L.R. 8 Eq. 115; *Sykes v. Sykes* (1871), L.R. 13 Eq. 56.

[11](1826), 2 Sim. & St. 465, 57 E.R. 424.

devised the property in the event of failure of issue, the devise being void for remoteness unless, upon its construction, the issue referred to are the issue who would inherit in tail, a construction to which the court leans, and not issue in general.[12]

In all provinces, except Manitoba, estates tail have been abolished and an estate which would otherwise be an estate tail is now regarded as an estate in fee simple. The limitations following what would formerly have been an estate tail are now interpreted as an executory devise over in default of heirs of the body of a person to whom the estate was first limited.[13] Such an executory devise is void under the rule against perpetuities, because the devise is limited to take effect upon a failure of issue at an indefinite time.[14]

1104.12   Contingent Remainders

It is sometimes said that contingent remainders, which operate at law, are not subject to the rule against perpetuities, although they are subject to the older and independent rule in *Whitby v. Mitchell* which renders void a remainder to the issue of an unborn person after a limitation for life to that person.[1] The reason given for this assertion is that the law of contingent remainders was well settled before the rule against perpetuities was developed and that the rule that a contingent remainder must vest during the continuance of the prior particular estate sufficiently controls such interests.

Thus, where A conveys "to B for life, remainder to C's eldest son", C having no son as yet, the contingent remainder limited to C's eldest son, if it is to be valid, must vest while B is still living, otherwise it will fail. The rule against perpetuities can have no application here, for it would allow a further period of twenty-one years from B's or C's death. If it did apply, it would render valid an interest that might be invalid under the common law remainder rules.

On the other hand, if the grant were "to B for life, remainder to his first son to marry", and B has no son as yet, the remainder might be valid under the

---

[12]In the following cases, the devise was held to be good as the issue referred to meant the issue who would inherit in tail: *Badger v. Lloyd* (1700), 1 Ld. Raym. 523, 91 E.R. 1249; *Lytton v. Lytton* (1793), 4 Bro. C.C. 441, 29 E.R. 979; *Egerton v. Jones* (1830), 3 Sim. 409, 57 E.R. 1051; *Eno v. Eno* (1847), 6 Hare 171, 67 E.R. 1127; *Lewis v. Templer* (1864), 33 Beav. 625, 55 E.R. 511.
In the following cases, the devise was held to be void for remoteness because the issue referred to in the devise were not the same as the issue who would inherit in tail: *Lady Lanesborough v. Fox* (1733), 3 Bro. P.C. 130, 1 E.R. 1223 (H.L.); *Jones v. Morgan* (1774), 3 Bro. P.C. 323, 1 E.R. 1346; *Bankes v. Holme* (1821), 1 Russ. 407, 38 E.R. 156 (H.L.).
[13]See §§607-607.1, *supra.*
[14]*Ernst v. Zwicker* (1897), 27 S.C.R. 594 at p. 626.
§1104.12
[1](1890), 44 Ch. D. 85 (C.A.). See *Fearne*, p. 565; Armour, *Real Property*, pp. 260 *et seq.* And see Challis, pp. 197, 206, 214-17.

common law remainder rules, but would, on the face of it, offend the rule against perpetuities. In this situation the rule was not thought to be applicable, however. Nor should it be, for the remainder will vest, if at all, during the continuance of the life estate.[2]

There are, however, situations in which the rule does become operative. Where a settlor conveys "to A for life, then to any wife he may marry for life, with remainder to his children then living", A being a bachelor, the remainder limited to A's children will vest, if at all, during the continuance of the prior life estate. However, the rule against perpetuities is also infringed since the remainder may not vest for more than twenty-one years after A's death. This is so because any wife he may marry may be unborn at the time of the grant and cannot, therefore, be counted as a life in being.[3]

For this reason, Gray argued, correctly it is submitted, that the rule does and should apply to contingent remainders.[4] However, it should only apply to contingent remainders limited after contingent remainders, as in the above example, not to contingent remainders limited after a vested life estate, since the policy of the rule is not infringed in such a case.

It should be noted that contingent remainders can only arise today under a deed. They can no longer arise under a will because of a statutory trust in favour of the personal representatives[5] and, therefore, such interests are equitable executory interests to which the rule does apply.[6] Even if the interest is created by deed, but arises out of an equitable estate, it is equitable[7] and the rule applies to such interests as well as to comparable interests in personalty.

1104.13 Legal Executory Interests

Legal executory interests are those which arise under uses executed by the *Statute of Uses*.[1] Executory devises were also legal executory interests[2] before the imposition of a statutory trust on the personal representatives.[3]

The rule applies to such interests. Indeed, it was developed to control

---

[2]Morris and Leach, p. 203.

[3]*Re Frost*; *Frost v. Frost* (1889), 43 Ch. D. 246; *Re Ashforth*; *Sibley v. Ashforth*, [1905] 1 Ch. 535; *Whitby v. Von Luedecke*, [1906] 1 Ch. 783.

[4]§§284-298.2. *Cf.* Lewis, p. 408.

[5]*Devolution of Real Property Act*, R.S.A. 1980, c. D-34, s. 3, R.S.S. 1978, c. D-27, ss. 4, 5; *Estate Administration Act*, R.S.B.C. 1979, c. 114, s. 90; *Devolution of Estates Act*, R.S.M. 1970, c. D70, s. 18(3); R.S.N.B. 1973, c. D-9, s. 3; *Estates Administration Act*, R.S.O. 1980, c. 143, s. 2; *Chattels Real Act*, R.S.N. 1970, c. 36, s. 2; *Real Property Act*, R.S.N.S. 1967, c. 261, s. 6(1); *Probate Act*, R.S.P.E.I. 1974, c. P-19, s. 108(1); *Devolution of Real Property Ordinance*, R.O.N.W.T. 1974, c. D-5, s. 4; R.O.Y.T. 1971, c. D-4, s. 4. And see §1011, *supra*.

[6]See §1104.14, *infra*.

[7]*Abbiss v. Burney*; *Re Finch* (1881), 17 Ch. D. 211 (C.A.); *Astley v. Micklethwait* (1880), 15 Ch. D. 59; *Re Freme*; *Freme v. Logan*, [1891] 3 Ch. 167.

§1104.13

[1]27 Hen. 8, c. 10 (1535).

[2]See §§1010-1010.2, *supra*.

[3]See §1104.12, footnote 5, *supra*.

them.[4] Within the perpetuity period, however, there may be any number of springing and shifting uses.[5]

In *Savill Bothers Ltd. v. Bethell*,[6] a freehold estate was conveyed to and to the use of a purchaser in fee simple, excepting and reserving a forty-foot strip commencing at a specified point and terminating at a road to be made by the purchaser, so as to give access to the road from other lands of the vendor. It was held that the strip had not been effectually excepted from the conveyance. If it operated at common law, it was in the nature of a limitation of a freehold to commence in the future and therefore bad and, if it operated under the *Statute of Uses*,[7] the exception was void under the rule against perpetuities because the road need not necessarily be constructed within the period prescribed by the rule.

A shifting clause by which the estate of one person is to shift to another on a certain event is void for remoteness, unless the event must necessarily take effect within the prescribed period. However, this does not apply to a shifting clause attached to an estate tail because the power to bar the entail is a sufficient protection against a perpetuity.[8]

1104.14 Equitable Executory Interests and Trusts

Equitable interests of all kinds are subject to the rule.[1] The mode in which the estate or interest is created, whether by devise, gift *inter vivos*, or contract, is immaterial.[2] The limits prescribed to the creation of future estates and interests are the same both at law and in equity. The law against perpetuity is of equal force, and its provisions are administered with equal strictness in both jurisdictions.[3]

Hence, equitable executory interests are subject to the rule, for "the Courts have acted upon the principle that the rule against perpetuities is to be applied where no other sufficient protection against remoteness is attainable. Thus, inasmuch as equitable executory interests never failed for want of a particular estate, it was held that the rule must apply to them."[4]

---

[4]*Carwardine v. Carwardine* (1758), 1 Eden 27, 28 E.R. 594; *Whitby v. Mitchell* (1890), 44 Ch. D. 85 (C.A.); *Lord Dungannon v. Smith* (1846), 12 Cl. & Fin. 546 at p. 563, 8 E.R. 1523 (H.L.); *Hancock v. Watson*, [1902] A.C. 14 (H.L.), at p. 17; *Meyers v. Hamilton Provident and Loan Co.* (1890), 19 O.R. 358 (H.C.J.).
[5]*Blandford v. Thackerell* (1793), 2 Ves. Jun. 238, 30 E.R. 612.
[6][1902] 2 Ch. 523 (C.A.).
[7]27 Hen. 8, c. 10 (1535).
[8]*Bennett v. Bennett* (1864), 2 Dr. & Sm. 266, 62 E.R. 623.
§1104.14
[1]*Duke of Norfolk's Case* (1682), 3 Chan. Cas. 1, 22 E.R. 931 (H.L.); *Lord Dungannon v. Smith* (1846), 12 Cl. & Fin. 546, 8 E.R. 1523 (H.L.).
[2]*London and South Western Ry. Co. v. Gomm* (1882), 20 Ch. D. 562 (C.A.), at p. 581, per Jessel, M.R.
[3]*Ferguson v. Ferguson* (1876), 39 U.C.Q.B. 232 at p. 238, per Harrison, C.J., revd 1 O.A.R. 452, restd 2 S.C.R. 497.
[4]*Re Ashforth; Sibley v. Ashforth*, [1905] 1 Ch. 535 at p. 545, per Farwell, J.

In *Abbiss v. Burney; Re Finch*,[5] the testator devised and bequeathed realty and personalty to trustees "upon trust to pay the income to the testator's wife for life and, after her death, if H was then living, to retain the rents of the realty for their own use during his life and pay him the income of the personalty for his life and, after his death, upon trust to convey and transfer the realty and personalty to such son of M as should first attain the age of 25 years". It was held that the limitation to such son was contingent upon his attaining that age and, assuming it to be an equitable remainder, it was void for remoteness.[6] In *Massenburgh v. Ash*[7] a trust of a term of years was limited "to H for life, remainder to his first son and, if the son die leaving issue, then to such issue but, if the son die in the lifetime of A without issue, then to the second son". The executory interest was held to be good as the contingency was to happen within twenty-one years.

Executory trusts, in common with other trusts, are subject to the rule.[8] An executory trust, however, can be executed by the court in such a way as to preclude the objection arising from the rule and can be moulded so as to carry out the intentions of the testator as far as the rules of law admit.[9] In so doing, a provision which offends against the rule is, if possible, omitted, or modified so as to confine it within the perpetuity period.[10]

Provisions are not altered, however, contrary to the general intent of the testator, which is to govern. In order to ascertain the general intent, the court is not confined to the language of the will, but may refer to the motives which led to the will, its general object and purpose to be collected from other instruments to which it refers and also to any circumstances which may have influenced the testator's mind towards the provisions.[11]

Where land or any interest in land which would descend to the heir-at-law is devised for purposes which the law will not permit, such as a trust for an unborn person with remainder to his issue, the trust is not altered and the heir-at-law takes the interest as undisposed of, regardless of the testator's intention.[12]

A trust for sale is, like other trusts, subject to the rule and, if it is to arise at a time beyond the perpetuity period, it is invalid.[13] Thus, a gift is not saved by creating a trust, instead of a power for sale.

---

[5](1881), 17 Ch. D. 211 (C.A.).

[6]See also *Re Wilmer's Trusts; Moore v. Wingfield*, [1903] 1 Ch. 874, affd [1903] 2 Ch. 411 (C.A.); *Re Ashforth, supra*, footnote 4.

[7](1684), 1 Vern. 234, 304, 23 E.R. 437, 485.

[8]*Gower v. Grosvenor* (1740), 5 Madd. 337, 56 E.R. 924; *Duke of Marlborough v. Earl Godolphin* (1759), 1 Eden 404 at p. 422, 28 E.R. 741; *Blackburn v. Stables* (1814), 2 V. & B. 367, 35 E.R. 358.

[9]*Christie v. Gosling* (1866), L.R. 1 H.L. 279 at p. 290.

[10]*Miles v. Harford* (1879), 12 Ch. D. 691; *Lyddon v. Ellison* (1854), 19 Beav. 565, 52 E.R. 470; *Lord Dorchester v. Earl of Effingham* (1813), 3 Beav. 180, n, 49 E.R. 71; *Bankes v. Le Despencer* (1840), 10 Sim. 576, 59 E.R. 739.

[11]*Sackville-West v. Viscount Holmesdale* (1870), L.R. 4 H.L. 543, *per* Lord Chelmsford.

[12]*Tregonwell v. Sydenham* (1815), 3 Dow. 194, 3 E.R. 1035.

[13]*Hale v. Pew* (1858), 25 Beav. 335, 53 E.R. 665; *Re Wood; Tullett v. Colville*, [1894] 3 Ch. 381 (C.A.); *Re Davies and Kent's Contract*, [1910] 2 Ch. 35 (C.A.); *Re Bewick; Ryle v. Ryle*, [1911] 1 Ch. 116.

There is, however, no substantial difference, for the purpose of the rule against perpetuities, between a trust for sale and a power of sale, where the sale is intended to be completed by a conveyance to the purchaser of the legal estate vested in the trustees. A testator or settlor cannot (as I think) impose an obligation to sell where he cannot lawfully confer a power to do so; or escape from the rule against perpetuities by vesting in his trustees an imperative instead of a discretionary power of sale.[14]

Where a trust for sale, however, is mere machinery to facilitate division between persons whose equitable interests vest during the perpetuity period, effect will be given to the equitable interests notwithstanding the invalidity of the trust for sale, as if the trust for sale were omitted.[15]

Thus, in *Re Appleby; Walker v. Lever*[16] the testator devised his real estate in certain events upon trust for sale and gave the proceeds of sale to classes of persons who were ascertainable without offending the rule. It was held that, although the trust for sale was void as not being required to take effect within the perpetuity period, it was mere machinery for the purpose of division and could be disregarded and that the beneficiaries took the property as real estate.

Where, however, the equitable interests may not vest within the perpetuity period, as where the gift is to a class living or to be ascertained at the time of sale, the equitable interests are invalid.[17]

In *Re Bewick; Ryle v. Ryle*[18] the testator bequeathed the proceeds of sale of certain real estate which was subject to a mortgage. The rents and income were made first liable for the payment of the mortgage, taxes and other outgoings. The trust was in favour of a class to be ascertained as soon as the charges on the real estate were cleared, which would be many years after the testator's death. The trust was held to be too remote, notwithstanding the legal obligation to pay the charges within twenty-one years after the testator's death.

Where a testator devised land to his son for life and after his death to his heirs and assigns forever and directed that the land be sold after the son's death if the son's youngest child was then twenty-one, the proceeds to be equally divided among the son's children at the time of sale, it was held that, under the rule in *Shelley's Case*,[19] the son took a fee simple, so that there was no trust for his children and that the executory devise in favour of the son's children was void as offending the rule against perpetuities.[20]

Not only are equitable interests which vest within the perpetuity period not rendered invalid by failure of a trust for sale, but conversely, an estate in

---

[14]*Goodier v. Edmunds*, [1893] 3 Ch. 455 at p. 461, *per* Stirling, J.
[15]*Ibid.*; *Re Daveron; Bowen v. Churchill*, [1893] 3 Ch. 421; *Goodier v. Johnson* (1881), 18 Ch. D. 441 (C.A.).
[16][1903] 1 Ch. 565 (C.A.).
[17]*Read v. Gooding* (1856), 21 Beav. 478, 52 E.R. 944; *Blight v. Hartnoll* (1881), 19 Ch. D. 294.
[18][1911] 1 Ch. 116.
[19](1581), 1 Co. Rep. 93 b, 76 E.R. 206.
[20]*Meyers v. Hamilton Provident and Loan Co.* (1890), 19 O.R. 358 (H.C.J.).

trustees may be validly created although the equitable interests be void for remoteness.[21]

A trust which may continue for an indefinite period is subject to the rule if the equitable interests may not vest within the perpetuity period.[22]

1104.15 Rights of Entry for Condition Broken

A right of entry (or re-entry) for condition broken is the interest left in the grantor who conveys, or in the heirs of the testator who devises, an estate upon condition subsequent.

Where the right of entry is reserved to a lessor, it is valid and the rule against perpetuities does not apply to it.[1] The reason is that the right of entry in this case is merely an incident of the lessor's fee simple in reversion, a vested interest, whereas, in the case of a right of entry arising out of a freehold estate upon condition subsequent, the grantor or the testator's heirs will recover the fee which they did not have theretofore.[2]

A right of entry arising under a fee simple upon condition subsequent is subject to the rule against perpetuities.

In the leading case, *Re Trustees of Hollis' Hospital and Hague's Contract*,[3] certain premises were assured by indentures of lease and release to J, his heirs and assigns, to hold to the use of T and of named trustees of a charity known as Hollis' Hospital, upon certain trusts for the maintenance and management of the hospital. The assurance was subject to a proviso "that if at any time hereafter the premises hereby conveyed or any part thereof, or the rents, issues, and profits of the same or of any part thereof, shall be employed or converted to or for any other use, or uses, intents, or purposes than as are hereinbefore mentioned and specified, then and from thenceforth all and every the buildings, lands, and premises hereinbefore conveyed to the uses and upon the trusts hereinbefore mentioned shall revert to the right heirs of T". E had entered into a contract with an agent acting for a majority of the trustees of the charity for the purchase of a portion of the freehold property. E was willing to accept the title when one of the trustees, who was heir-at-law of T, wrote to the solicitors for the charity that as such heir he had not concurred in the sale and drawing attention to the above proviso. E then took proceedings asking for a declaration that a good title had not been shown. It was held

---

[21]*Goodier v. Edmunds, supra,* footnote 14; *Re Appleby, supra,* footnote 16.

[22]*Mainwaring v. Baxter* (1800), 5 Ves. Jun. 458, 31 E.R. 681; *Thomson v. Shakespear* (1860), 1 De G. F. & J. 399, 45 E.R. 413 (C.A.).

§1104.15

[1]*Re Tyrrell's Estate,* [1907] 1 I.R. 292 (C.A.), at p. 298, *per* Walker, C. It has been suggested in an early case, however, that "if such a proviso as this were inserted in very long leases, it would be tying up property for a considerable length of time, and would be open to the objection of creating a perpetuity": *Roe d. Hunter v. Galliers* (1787), 2 T.R. 133 at p. 140, 100 E.R. 72, *per* Buller, J.

[2]Morris and Leach, p. 210, note 61.

[3][1899] 2 Ch. 540.

that the proviso was a common law condition subsequent to which the rule against perpetuities applied, but that the title was not one which should be forced on a purchaser. The court further held that if the clause in question ought to be construed as a limitation, or as creating a shifting or a springing use, it would also be void as infringing the rule against perpetuities.[4]

In *Re St. Patrick's Market*[5] land was conveyed to the corporation of the City of Toronto for use as a market. The deed provided that, if the corporation should thereafter alienate the land or use it for any other purpose than as a public market, the conveyance should be void and the land revert to the heirs of the donor. It was held that this proviso for re-entry was void under the rule against perpetuities. The court opined that it would be otherwise if it were possible to treat the conveyance as granting the land to the corporation as long as it should be used as a public market, but that such was not the form or effect of the conveyance.

It has been held that a proviso for re-entry upon non-payment of an assessment is void under the rule,[6] as is a proviso for reversion to the grantor if the land is no longer required or used for public school purposes.[7]

In *Matheson v. Town of Mitchell*[8] the testator devised land to a town corporation to be used as a public park, with a proviso that, if the corporation neglected or refused to keep the land and its surrounding fences in repair, the gift was to be void and the land would revert to the estate of the testator. It was held that the proviso was a common law condition subsequent which offended the rule against perpetuities. The devise might have been worded as a determinable fee, in which case it would have been valid.

> If the land had been granted to the town corporation so long as it should be used and maintained and kept in proper order and repair and as a public park should be kept, the result might have been different, but it has been granted for ever, and the proviso is wholly inoperative for the reason above stated.[9]

---

[4]See further *Re Da Costa; Clarke v. Church of England Collegiate School of St. Peter*, [1912] 1 Ch. 337; *Re St. Patrick's Market* (1909), 14 O.W.R. 794 (H.C.J.); *Matheson v. Town of Mitchell* (1919), 46 O.L.R. 546, 51 D.L.R. 477 (S.C. App. Div.); *Pardee v. Humberstone Summer Resort Co. of Ontario Ltd.*, [1933] O.R. 580, [1933] 3 D.L.R. 277 (H.C.J.); *Fitzmaurice v. Board of School Trustees of Monck Township*, [1949] O.W.N. 786, [1950] 1 D.L.R. 239 (H.C.J.), which all followed the *Hollis' Hospital* case.
[5](1909), 14 O.W.R. 794 (H.C.J.).
[6]*Pardee v. Humberstone Summer Resort Co.*, supra, footnote 4.
[7]*Fitzmaurice v. Board of School Trustees of Monck Township*, supra, footnote 4. To the same effect see *Re Essex County Roman Catholic Separate School Board and Antaya* (1977), 17 O.R. (2d) 307, 80 D.L.R. (3d) 405 (H.C.J.); *Re North Gower Township Public School Board and Todd*, [1968] 1 O.R. 63, 65 D.L.R. (2d) 421 (C.A.); *Imperial Tobacco Co. (of Great Britain and Ireland), Ltd. v. Wilmott*, [1964] 2 All E.R. 510 (Ch.), in which case the proviso for re-entry was erroneously called a reverter; *Re Ogilvy*, [1966] 2 O.R. 755, 58 D.L.R. (2d) 385 (H.C.J.), where the beneficiaries under a settlement were required to retransfer certain shares to the settlor at a fixed price if they desired to sell them.
[8](1919), 46 O.L.R. 546, 51 D.L.R. 477 (S.C. App. Div.).
[9]*Ibid.*, at p. 548 O.L.R., p. 479 D.L.R., *per* Maclaren, J.A.

497

It is permissible to convey land to a municipality and to specify the intended use of the land. The municipality will not be bound thereby, but the deed will be valid so long as there is no condition providing for re-entry.[10]

Where a deed contains a right of re-entry which is not restricted to the perpetuity period, the condition will be struck off, rendering the deed absolute.[11]

In Ireland and some of the United States, the rule does not apply to rights of re-entry,[12] however, most modern commentators agree that the rule should apply to such interests.

1104.16 Possibilities of Reverter

A possibility of reverter is the interest left in the grantor who conveys, or in the heirs of the testator who devises, a determinable fee simple. Apart from one English case,[1] most English and Canadian cases have held that the rule does not apply to possibilities of reverter,[2] nor to analogous interests in personalty.[3]

It is arguable that there ought to be no distinction between rights of entry for condition broken and possibilities of reverter for the purposes of the rule. The difference between these two interests is merely one of language. Moreover, the possibility that some persons may acquire an interest in the property at a remote future date is the same in both cases. That this may indeed occur in the case of possibilities of reverter is illustrated by *Re Tilbury West Public School Board and Hastie*,[4] where land was conveyed to trustees of a school section in 1890 "so long as it should be used for school purposes". The lands were used for a school until 1961. It was held that the deed created a determinable fee simple, that the rule against perpetuities did not apply to possibilities of reverter and that the land, therefore, reverted to the grantor's heirs.

A similar case, involving an even longer period of time is *Brown v.*

---

[10]*MacLeod v. Town of Amherst* (1973), 39 D.L.R. (3d) 146, 8 N.S.R. (2d) 504 (S.C.T.D.), affd 44 D.L.R. (3d) 723, N.S.R. *loc. cit.* p. 491 (S.C. App. Div.). And see *Re McKellar*, [1972] 3 O.R. 16 (H.C.J.).

[11]*Missionary Church, Canada East v. Twp. of Nottawasaga* (1980), 32 O.R. (2d) 88, 120 D.L.R. (3d) 489 (H.C.J.).

[12]*Attorney-General v. Cummins*, [1906] 1 I.R. 406; *Walsh v. Wightman*, [1927] N.I. 1 (C.A.); Gray, ss. 304-10.

§1104.16

[1]*Hopper v. Liverpool Corp.* (1943), 88 Sol. Jo. 213 (Lancaster, V.C.).

[2]*Attorney-General v. Pyle* (1738), 1 Atk. 435, 26 E.R. 278; *Re Cooper's Conveyance Trusts*; *Crewdson v. Bagot*, [1956] 1 W.L.R. 1096 (Ch.); *Re Tilbury West School Board and Hastie*, [1966] 2 O.R. 20, 55 D.L.R. (2d) 407 (H.C.J.), vard *loc. cit.* O.R. 511, 57 D.L.R. (2d) 519 (H.C.J.); *Re Chambers' Will Trusts*; *Official Trustees of Charitable Funds v. British Union for Abolition of Vivisection*, [1950] Ch. 267.

[3]*Re Randell*; *Randell v. Dixon* (1888), 38 Ch. D. 213; *Re Blunt's Trusts*; *Wigan v. Clinch*, [1904] 2 Ch. 767; *Re Chardon*; *Johnston v. Davies*, [1928] Ch. 464; *Re Chambers' Will Trusts, supra*, footnote 2.

[4]*Supra*, footnote 2.

Independent Baptist Church of Woburn.[5] In that case a testatrix devised land to the defendant church in 1849, "so long as they shall maintain and promulgate their present religious belief and faith and shall continue as a Church", with a gift over to ten named persons when it ceased to do so. The residuary clause gave the residue of the estate to the same ten persons. The church ceased operations in 1939. It was held that, while the gift over was void under the rule that one cannot reserve a possibility of reverter to anyone other than the grantor or the heirs of the testator, the possibility of reverter passed under the residuary clause and was not affected by the rule against perpetuities.

Modern perpetuities legislation makes the possibility of reverter subject to the rule.[6]

1104.17 Gifts to Charity

It is sometimes said that the rule against perpetuities does not apply to charities.[1] This is incorrect. The rule against perpetual trusts does not apply to trusts for charity, but only to non-charitable purpose trusts. However, the rule against perpetuities, which strikes down gifts which may vest too remotely, does apply to charitable gifts, albeit with some exceptions.

(a) Future gift to charity

Where there is a gift to a charity upon a future contingent event which may be too remote, the gift is void. Hence gifts to a regiment on the appointment of the next lieutenant-colonel,[2] and for the training for the priesthood of a person from a named church when a candidate comes forward,[3] are void.

If, however, the gift can be construed as indicating a general charitable intention to apply the property to charity absolutely and immediately, the gift will be valid and will be administered *cy-près* until the particular application of the property selected by the donor can be carried out.[4]

(b) Gift over from non-charity to charity

Where there is a gift to a non-charity, such as named individuals, followed by a gift over to a charity on a future event which may be too remote, the

---

[5]91 N.E. 2d 922 (1950, Mass. S.J.C.).

[6]See §1107.12, *infra*.

§1104.17

[1]See, *e.g.*, *Goodman v. Mayor of Saltash* (1882), 7 App. Cas. 633 (H.L.), at p. 642, *per* Lord Selborne; *Attorney-General v. National Provincial and Union Bank of England*, [1924] A.C. 262 (H.L.), at p. 266, *per* Lord Haldane.

[2]*Re Lord Stratheden and Campbell; Alt v. Lord Stratheden*, [1894] 3 Ch. 265.

[3]*Re Mander; Westminster Bank, Ltd. v. Mander*, [1950] Ch. 547. And see *Re Odelberg Estate* (1970), 72 W.W.R. 567 (Sask. Surr. Ct.), a gift to a church when a home for the aged is built.

[4]*Chamberlayne v. Brockett* (1872), L.R. 8 Ch. 206; *Jewish Home for Aged of British Columbia v. Toronto General Trusts Corp.* (1961), 28 D.L.R. (2d) 48, [1961] S.C.R. 465, 34 W.W.R. 638; *Re Mountain* (1912), 26 O.L.R. 163, 4 D.L.R. 737 (C.A.); *Re Pearse; Genn v. Pearse*, [1955] 1 D.L.R. 801 (B.C.S.C.).

gift over is void. Thus, a gift to a charity if a prior gift to unborn grandchildren at age 21 should fail, is too remote.[5]

(c) Gift over from charity to non-charity

Where there is a gift over from a charity to a non-charity, such as a named individual, on a future event which may be too remote, the gift over is void and the gift to the charity may become absolute and is distributed *cy-près*. Hence, in a gift in trust to establish certain schools, but if the government should thereafter establish a general system of education, to the residuary legatees, the gift over is void.[6] The money was given to charity in perpetuity and cannot, therefore, result.

If the property is not given in perpetuity, however, it is allowed to result to the testator's estate under a resulting trust, by analogy to the possibility of reverter. Thus, a gift in trust to pay the income to the incumbent of a church so long as he permits the pews to be occupied rent free and if he does charge rent, to the residuary legatees, is valid.[7]

On the other hand, a gift over following a determinable fee or similar interest in personal property is void if it may not vest until the perpetuity period ends.[8]

(d) Gift over from charity to charity

Where there is a gift over from one charity to another on a future uncertain event, the policy of the rule is not offended, since in either case the property is being used for purposes beneficial to the public. Thus, where property was given to a municipality in trust for its poor inhabitants with a gift over to another municipality in trust for a hospital if the first municipality should fail to carry out the trust, the gift over was valid.[9]

This exception to the general rule was applied in *Re Tyler; Tyler v. Tyler*,[10] where property was given to a charity and the limitation required the charity to keep the family tomb in good repair, with a gift over to another charity if it failed to do so. The gift over was held valid.[11] If the gift to the charity is

---

[5]*Re Mill's Declaration of Trust; Midland Bank Executor and Trustee Co., Ltd. v. Mill*, [1950] 2 All E.R. 292 (C.A.); *Re Johnson's Trusts* (1866), L.R. 2 Eq. 716.

[6]*Re Bowen; Lloyd Phillips v. Davis*, [1893] 2 Ch. 491. *Cf. Re Davies; Lloyd v. Cardigan County Council*, [1915] 1 Ch. 543; *Royal College of Surgeons of England v. National Provincial Bank Ltd.*, [1952] A.C. 631 (H.L.).

[7]*Re Randell; Randell v. Dixon* (1888), 38 Ch. D. 213. *Cf. Re Blunt's Trusts; Wigan v. Clinch*, [1904] 2 Ch. 767.

[8]*Re Chardon; Johnston v. Davies*, [1928] Ch. 464.

[9]*Christ's Hospital v. Grainger* (1849), 1 Mac. & G. 460, 41 E.R. 1343. *Cf. Royal College of Surgeons of England v. National Provincial Bank Ltd.*, supra, footnote 6; *Re Mountain*, supra, footnote 4.

[10][1891] 3 Ch. 252 (C.A.).

[11]To the same effect see *Re Lopes; Bence-Jones v. Zoological Society of London*, [1931] 2 Ch. 130.

conditional upon it applying the moneys themselves for the repair of a tomb, however, the gift will not be charitable.[12]

1104.18 Contracts and Options

(a) Personal contracts

The rule against perpetuities, being a rule of the law of property, has no application to contracts, unless the contract involves an interest in property. A mere personal contract calling for payment of money on some future contingent event, is not subject to the rule,[1] nor is a covenant to pay a sum of money if a person should die without issue,[2] nor a provision in a company's articles of association that a shareholder must, at any time during the company's existence, transfer his shares to specified persons at a specified price.[3]

A contract, although connected with land, such as a contract for sale, which is unlimited as to time, may nevertheless be construed as a mere personal contract unaffected by the rule. Thus, in *South Eastern Ry. Co. v. Associated Portland Cement Manufacturers (1900), Ltd.*,[4] a railway company, in buying land for its line, agreed that the landowner, his heirs and assigns, might at any time tunnel under the line to join the lands severed by it and also agreed to make a certain level crossing. It was held that this was a mere personal contract, even though connected with land, and therefore not obnoxious to the rule.[5] Similarly, in *Re Canadian Pacific R. Co. Caveat and Land Titles Act*,[6] a transfer of land under which the vendor reserved strips for a right of way wherever a certain railway line should be located on or within a certain distance of the land and for irrigation works that might be located by the vendor on the land was held not to infringe the rule against perpetuities.

The correctness of the decision in the *Portland Cement* case was doubted by the Supreme Court of Canada in *Harris v. Minister of National Revenue*,[7] the court stating[8] that a contract cannot at the same time be merely personal and one creating an interest in land.[9] However, the *Portland Cement* case and

---

[12]*Re Dalziel; Midland Bank Executor and Trustee Co., Ltd. v. St. Bartholomew's Hospital*, [1943] Ch. 277. *Cf. Re Martin; Barclays Bank Ltd. v. Board of Governors of St. Bartholomew's Hospital*, [1952] W.N. 339 (Ch.).

§1104.18
[1]*Walsh v. Secretary of State for India* (1863), 10 H.L.C. 367, 11 E.R. 1068.
[2]*Pinbury v. Elkin* (1719), 1 P. Wms. 563 at p. 566, 24 E.R. 518; *Pleydell v. Pleydell* (1721), 1 P. Wms. 748 at p. 750, 24 E.R. 597.
[3]*Borland's Trustee v. Steel Brothers & Co., Ltd.*, [1901] 1 Ch. 279.
[4][1910] 1 Ch. 12 (C.A.), at p. 33.
[5]The case was followed in *Hutton v. Watling*, [1948] Ch. 26; *Prudential Trust Co. Ltd. v. Forseth* (1959), 21 D.L.R. (2d) 587, [1960] S.C.R. 210, and *Re Kennedy & Beaucage Mines Ltd.*, [1959] O.R. 625, 20 D.L.R. (2d) 1 (H.C.J.).
[6](1917), 36 D.L.R. 317, [1917] 3 W.W.R. 170 (S.C.).
[7](1966), 57 D.L.R. (2d) 403, [1966] S.C.R. 489.
[8]*Ibid.*, at p. 416 D.L.R., p. 504 S.C.R.
[9]The court distinguished the *Forseth* case, *supra*, footnote 5, overruled the *Kennedy* case, *supra*, footnote 5, and opined that *Hutton v. Watling*, *supra*, footnote 5, was incorrectly decided.

those following it were applied in a subsequent Canadian case, *Radbourne v. Radbourne*[10] in which it was held that the rule cannot be raised as a defence to an action for specific performance brought against an original contracting party by the other party. This was the point that was considered incorrect in the *Harris* case, however, and therefore the case must be considered wrongly decided. The Supreme Court reaffirmed its stand in *Politzer v. Metropolitan Homes Ltd.*[11]

(b) Options and similar interests

An option creates an equitable interest in property and, if it may be exercised beyond the perpetuity period, it is void.[12] A right of first refusal, however, does not create an interest in land and the rule against perpetuities, therefore, does not apply to it.[13]

The leading case on options is *London and South Western Ry. Co. v. Gomm*.[14] The railway company in that case conveyed certain lands to Gomm's predecessor in title who covenanted that he would reconvey it for the same price if the company should demand it. Fifteen years later the railway sought to enforce the covenant. It was held that it could not do so because the option was exercisable at a remote future time. Jessel, M.R., said:[15]

---

[10](1977), 2 E.T.R. 85 (Sask. Q.B.).

[11](1975), 54 D.L.R. (3d) 376, [1976] 1 S.C.R. 363.

[12]*London and South Western Ry. Co. v. Gomm* (1882), 20 Ch. D. 562 (C.A.); *Trevelyan v. Trevelyan* (1885), 53 L.T. 853; *Re Button's Lease*; *Inman v. Button*, [1963] 3 All E.R. 708 (Ch.); *Tormey v. The King*, [1930] Ex. C.R. 178; *Re Albay Realty Ltd. and Dufferin-Lawrence Development Ltd.*, [1956] O.W.N. 302, 2 D.L.R. (2d) 604 (H.C.J.); *Stephens v. Gulf Oil Canada Ltd.* (1975), 11 O.R. (2d) 129 at pp. 150 *et seq.*, 65 D.L.R. (3d) 193 at pp. 214 *et seq.* (C.A.); *Laurin v. Iron Ore Co. of Canada* (1977), 82 D.L.R. (3d) 634 at p. 645, 19 Nfld. & P.E.I.R. 111 at p. 129 (S.C.T.D.); *Re McKee and National Trust Co. Ltd.* (1975), 7 O.R. (2d) 614, 56 D.L.R. (3d) 190 (C.A.); *British Columbia Forest Products Ltd. v. Gay* (1976), 74 D.L.R. (3d) 660 at p. 666, 1 B.C.L.R. 265 at p. 272 (S.C.), affd 89 D.L.R. (3d) 80, 7 B.C.L.R. 190 (C.A.); *Politzer v. Metropolitan Homes Ltd.*, *supra*, footnote 11; *Frobisher Ltd. v. Canadian Pipelines & Petroleums Ltd.* (1959), 21 D.L.R. (2d) 497, [1960] S.C.R. 126; *Yates Investment Co. Ltd. v. Willoughby* (1964), 46 W.W.R. 499 (Sask. Q.B.); *Re Pongracic*, [1962] O.R. 1132, 35 D.L.R. (2d) 478 (H.C.J.); *R. v. Cory-Park Mobile City Ltd.*, [1977] 6 W.W.R. 104, 2 R.P.R. 242 (Sask. Q.B.); *Re Ogilvy*, [1966] 2 O.R. 755, 58 D.L.R. (2d) 385 (H.C.J.), in which case the settlor had a right to buy shares back at a fixed price.

[13]*Canadian Long Island Petroleums Ltd. v. Irving Industries (Irving Wire Products Division) Ltd.* (1974), 50 D.L.R. (3d) 265, [1975] 2 S.C.R. 715. But see *Property Law Act*, R.S.B.C. 1979, c. 340, s. 9, which declares that a right of first refusal to land, also known as a right of refusal or a right of pre-emption, is an equitable interest in land. In England it has also been held that a right of pre-emption does not create an interest in land: *Pritchard v. Briggs*, [1980] 1 All E.R. 294 (C.A.). A right of first refusal is, however, converted into an option once the optioner has received an offer which is acceptable to him. At that point the optionee's personal and contractual right is converted by operation of law into an equitable interest in land. As such, a right of first refusal is caveatable: *Powers v. Walter* (1981), 124 D.L.R. (3d) 417, [1981] 5 W.W.R. 169 (Sask. C.A.).

[14](1882), 20 Ch. D. 562 (C.A.).

[15]*Ibid.*, at pp. 580-1.

It appears to me therefore plain ... that the option is unlimited in point of time. If then the rule as to remoteness applies to a covenant of this nature, this covenant clearly is bad as extending beyond the period allowed by the rule. Whether the rule applies or not depends upon this as it appears to me, does or does not the covenant give an interest in the land? If it is a bare or mere personal contract it is of course not obnoxious to the rule ... But if it binds the land it creates an equitable interest in the land. The right to call for a conveyance of the land is an equitable interest or equitable estate. In the ordinary case of a contract for purchase there is no doubt about this, and an option for repurchase is not different in its nature ...

It was suggested that the rule has no application to any case of contract, but in my opinion the mode in which the interest is created is immaterial. Whether it is by devise or voluntary gift or contract can make no difference.

Similarly, in *Politzer v. Metropolitan Homes Ltd.*,[16] an agreement of purchase and sale, which was construed to be an option since it did not bind the purchaser to complete and which required him to pay a substantial sum of money within thirty days of the execution of a subdivision agreement between the purchaser and the municipality, was held void, since it was not certain when, or if, the subdivision agreement would be signed.

Where the rules of a club provided that members might not sell their shares without the consent of the remaining members, it was held that this rule was invalid. By refusing consent, retention of the lands of the club, or the undivided interest therein, might be compelled for a period much longer than that limited by law.[17]

The rule also applies to options in a lessee to purchase the reversion.[18] However, where the lessor retains the right, either expressly or by operation of law, to terminate the lease and the option at any time, without the concurrence of the lessee, the rule is not infringed.[19]

If the option to purchase the reversion can be construed as several discrete options exercisable during the original term of the lease and during each renewal term, the option will be valid, provided that each term is less than the perpetuity period, even though the total number of years of the several terms exceeds the period.[20]

Any option, whether held by a lessee or not, is valid if it must be exercised, if at all, within the period.[21] This will be so where the interest vests within twenty-one years after the death of a designated person.[22]

Even though the option may, in terms, be unrestricted as to time, it may be construed as being limited so as not to offend the rule. Thus, in *Stocker v.*

---

[16]*Supra*, footnote 11.

[17]*Rutherford v. Rispin* (1926), 59 O.L.R. 506, [1926] 4 D.L.R. 822 (H.C.J.).

[18]*Woodall v. Clifton*, [1905] 2 Ch. 257 (C.A.); *Tormey v. The King*, [1930] Ex. C.R. 178; *United Fuel Supply Co. v. Volcanic Oil & Gas Co.* (1911), 20 O.W.R. 78 (H.C.J.); *Trevelyan v. Trevelyan* (1885), 53 L.T. 853. The rule is otherwise in the United States. There such an option is valid: 6 A.L.P., §24.57.

[19]*Auld v. Scales*, [1947] 4 D.L.R. 721 at p. 736, [1947] S.C.R. 543 at p. 561, *per* Estey, J.

[20]*Roberts v. Hanson* (1981), 120 D.L.R. (3d) 299, 28 A.R. 271 (C.A.).

[21]*Pan American Petroleum Corp. v. Potapchuk* (1964), 51 W.W.R. 700 (Alta. S.C. App. Div.), affd *loc. cit.* p. 767, [1965] S.C.R. vi.

[22]*Laurin v. Iron Ore Co. of Canada*, *supra*, footnote 12.

Dean[23] a right of pre-emption exercisable "at all times hereafter", given to the plaintiff, his trustees and assigns, was held to be a personal contract giving a right limited to the life of the owner of the property. Romilly, M.R., said: "I should require much more argument to convince me that a contract which gives a right of pre-emption, 'at all times hereafter,' is one which could be enforced after the death of the owner of the property." Similarly, in *Re Cousins*; *Alexander v. Cross*,[24] a testator devised his estate, including an hotel, to trustees upon certain trusts, giving to his son the option to purchase the hotel. It was held that this option was personal to the son and could not be exercised after his death by his executors. Again, where the owner of land leased a house and lot for three years, giving to the lessee an option to purchase the property, no time being set for its exercise, it was held that the option must be exercised within the three years and was, therefore, not void under the rule.[25]

Although an option may be void for perpetuity, it has been held in England that the optionee and his assigns can successfully sue the optionor and his estate for damages[26] and for specific performance.[27] The reason for these decisions is that the contract is regarded as involving not only an interest in property, but also a personal obligation, and the latter is enforceable, at least against the optionor. However, the Supreme Court of Canada has held these cases to be wrongly decided and the rule is therefore otherwise in Canada. In this respect the Canadian position accords with the view held in the United States.[28]

In *Harris v. Minister of National Revenue*[29] the appellant held a lease on a service station for 200 years, with an option to purchase at the end of the term. The option was held to offend the rule against perpetuities. Moreover, the court stated that a simple contract cannot be regarded as creating an interest in land, which is void for perpetuity, while at the same time containing a personal obligation which remains enforceable.[30]

Even where an option can only be exercised during the perpetuity period, it is void if it amounts to an absolute restraint on alienation. In *Re Rosher*; *Rosher v. Rosher*,[31] a testator devised land to his son in fee simple with a

---

23(1852), 16 Beav. 161 at p. 165, 51 E.R. 739.
24(1885), 30 Ch. D. 203 (C.A.).
25*Bennett v. Stodgell* (1916), 36 O.L.R. 45, 28 D.L.R. 639 (S.C. App. Div.).
26*Worthing Corp. v. Heather*, [1906] 2 Ch. 532, folld in *Bennett v. Stodgell, supra*, footnote 25, at p. 642; *McClement v. Lovatt* (1954), 13 W.W.R. (N.S.) 695 (Man. Q.B.), vard 15 W.W.R. 426 (Man. C.A.).
27*South Eastern Ry. Co. v. Associated Portland Cement Manufacturers (1900), Ltd.*, [1910] 1 Ch. 12 (C.A.), followed in *Hutton v. Watling*, [1948] Ch. 26; *Prudential Trust Co. Ltd. v. Forseth* (1959), 21 D.L.R. (2d) 587, [1960] S.C.R. 210; *Re Kennedy & Beaucage Mines Ltd.*, [1959] O.R. 625, 20 D.L.R. (2d) 1 (H.C.J.).
28As to the United States' position see Morris and Leach, p. 221.
29(1966), 57 D.L.R. (2d) 403, [1966] S.C.R. 489.
30To the same effect, see *Politzer v. Metropolitan Homes Ltd.* (1975), 54 D.L.R. (3d) 376, [1976] 1 S.C.R. 363, and *Frobisher v. Canadian Pipelines & Petroleums Ltd.* (1959), 21 D.L.R. (2d) 497, [1960] S.C.R. 126, to the same effect.
31(1884), 26 Ch. D. 801.

proviso that if the son, his heirs, or any person claiming through him, should desire to sell the estate or any part of it in the lifetime of the testator's wife, she should have the option to purchase it at a specified sum for the whole (being one-fifth of its real selling value) and a proportionate sum for a part and that it should be first offered to her accordingly. It was held that the proviso amounted to an absolute restraint on alienation during her life, that it was accordingly void and that the son was entitled to sell the estate as he pleased without first offering it to the widow.[32]

(c) Covenants and options to grant and renew leases

The rule applies to covenants or contracts to grant leases. Thus, where an instrument under seal gave "the first right or option of leasing the last-mentioned lands for oil or gas purposes", it was held that the option created a remote interest in the land and was invalid under the rule.[33]

In *Hope v. Corp. of Gloucester*,[34] a grantor granted to the defendants, for charitable purposes, an estate which was subject to a lease to P, the defendants covenanting with the grantor that, if any heir of the body of M should request a new lease at the end of the term, they would grant him a fresh lease for thirty-one years at the same rent and so continue from time to time forever if any such request were made at the end of any term. The defendants granted leases from time to time to heirs of the body of M and then refused to renew. It was held that the covenant did not create an estate tail or any interest in the nature of an estate tail and that it was void under the rule against perpetuities.[35]

The rule also applies to covenants to renew leases if they do not run with the land. In *Muller v. Trafford*[36] a sub-lessee leased the demised premises to F for the residue of his term and covenanted for himself, his executors, administrators and assigns that if he obtained an extension of his term he would grant to F a new lease for a term that would include the residue of the existing term and the extended term. It was held that the covenant was not strictly a covenant for renewal and did not on that account run with the land but, assuming that it ran with the land, the doctrine of perpetuity had no application because the doctrine has no application to covenants which run with the land, as they are so annexed to the land as to create something in the nature of an interest in the land.

Similarly, the rule does not apply to a covenant for perpetual renewal of a

---

[32]See further on this point *Stephens v. Gulf Oil Canada Ltd.* (1975), 11 O.R. (2d) 129, 65 D.L.R. (3d) 193 (C.A.); *Laurin v. Iron Ore Co. of Canada* (1977), 82 D.L.R. (3d) 634, 19 Nfld. & P.E.I.R. 111 (S.C.T.D.); *British Columbia Forest Products Ltd. v. Gay* (1976), 74 D.L.R. (3d) 660, 1 B.C.L.R. 265 (S.C.), affd 89 D.L.R. (3d) 80, 7 B.C.L.R. 190 (C.A.). And see §503.1(a), *supra.*
[33]*United Fuel Supply Co. v. Volcanic Oil & Gas Co.* (1911), 20 O.W.R. 78 (H.C.J.).
[34](1855), 7 De G. M. & G. 647, 44 E.R. 252 (C.A.).
[35]And see *Attorney-General v. Greenhill* (1863), 33 Beav. 193, 55 E.R. 341, and *Attorney-General v. Catherine Hall, Cambridge* (1820), Jacob 381, 37 E.R. 894.
[36][1901] 1 Ch. 54.

lease if the covenant runs with the land and is clearly expressed.[37] It has been suggested that the reason for this exception is that the option to renew is a present interest in the lessee and, as such, does not offend the policy of the rule.[38]

In *Muller v. Trafford*[39] Farwell, J., opined that the rule has no application to covenants which run with the land because they are so annexed to the land as to create something in the nature of an interest in the land. However, the covenant must bind the property from its inception, as otherwise it would create an executory interest arising in the future and would therefore be obnoxious to the rule. It has been pointed out, however, that in the case of a covenant giving an option to purchase, it is just because such a covenant does not create a future executory interest that it is obnoxious to the rule, and that it is illogical to hold that an option given to the lessee in a lease to buy the fee at any time is void under the rule, but an option to him in the same lease to take a renewal or renewals forever is valid.[40]

Although it is anomalous to hold that a covenant for perpetual renewal of a lease when running with the land is not subject to the rule, it is as Romer, L.J., said, "an anomaly, which it is too late now to question, though it is difficult to justify".[41] Consequently, although the courts lean against a construction that a perpetual right of renewal is given, unless clearly intended, they will give effect to it if clearly expressed.[42]

Where land was to be used for the purpose of a public reservoir and the defendants constructed the works, relying on a defective lease for twenty-one years perpetually renewable, the rule against perpetuities was not referred to, but the court, consisting of Wilson, C.J., Armour and O'Connor, JJ. held that the defendants were entitled to a lease for twenty-one years containing provision for its renewal from time to time for a further time of twenty-one years forever.[43]

In *Re Principal Investments Ltd. and Gibson*[44] a twenty-one-year lease required the lessor, his heirs and assigns, at the end of the term "and of every

---

[37]*Llanelly Ry. and Dock Co. v. London and North Western Ry. Co.* (1875), L.R. 7 H.L. 550; *Baynham v. Guy's Hospital* (1796), 3 Ves. Jun. 295, 30 E.R. 1019; *Hare v. Burges* (1857), 4 K. & J. 45, 70 E.R. 19; *London and South Western Ry. Co. v. Gomm* (1882), 20 Ch. D. 562 (C.A.); *Swinburne v. Milburn* (1884), 9 App. Cas. 844 (H.L.); *Woodall v. Clifton*, [1905] 2 Ch. 257 (C.A.); *Clinch v. Pernette* (1895), 24 S.C.R. 385, affg 26 N.S.R. 410 (S.C.); *Alexander v. Herman* (1912), 21 O.W.R. 461, 2 D.L.R. 239 (H.C.J.); *Davis v. Lewis* (1885), 8 O.R. 1 (H.C.J.).

[38]Gray, §§230-230.2; *Guardian Realty Co. v. John Stark & Co.* (1922), 70 D.L.R. 333 at p. 342, 64 S.C.R. 207 at pp. 211-12, *per* Duff, J.

[39]*Supra*, footnote 34.

[40]Armour, *Real Property*, p. 268.

[41]*Woodall v. Clifton*, *supra*, footnote 37, at p. 279.

[42]*Baynham v. Guy's Hospital*, *supra*, footnote 37; *Alexander v. Herman*, *supra*, footnote 37.

[43]*Davis v. Lewis* (1885), 8 O.R. 1 (H.C.J.).

[44][1963] 2 O.R. 507, 40 D.L.R. (2d) 264 (C.A.), affd 44 D.L.R. (2d) 673, [1964] S.C.R. 424. And see *Gooderham & Worts Ltd. v. Canadian Broadcasting Corp.*, [1947] 1 D.L.R. 417, [1947] A.C. 66 (P.C.).

subsequent term of 21 years granted by these presents", to give a further lease to the lessee, its successors and assigns, "containing the same covenants and stipulations including covenant for renewal" as contained in the original lease, with the rent for each successive term to be subject to arbitration. It was held that the lease was not a perpetual lease in that there was no immediate vesting in the lessee of an estate in perpetuity, but rather an agreement for successive leases *ad infinitum*, each complete in itself. Hence, the lessee's right to a new lease did not arise until the existing lease expired. Accordingly the lease was not void for perpetuity.

It should be noted that in England perpetually renewable leases have been abolished and converted into leases for 2,000 years.[45]

(d) Agreements for the sale of land

An agreement for the sale of land creates an immediate equitable interest in the purchaser and does not offend the rule against perpetuities. This is so even where the completion date is indefinite, as where a contract is to be completed "90 days after Planning Board approval".[46] If no time is fixed for completion, a reasonable time for completion within the perpetuity period will be inferred.[47]

1104.19 Mortgages

The rule against perpetuities does not apply to the proviso for redemption in a mortgage. Thus, even though a mortgage is not to be paid off in accordance with its terms until 100 years or more from its commencement, the right of redemption is valid.[1]

1104.20 Future Easements, Profits à Prendre and Restrictive Covenants

The rule has been held to apply to easements and *profits à prendre* which are to arise in the future. Thus, where a strip of land was conveyed for a tramway, the deed reserving to the vendors the right to cross the line at two points to be selected by them and containing a covenant by the purchasers to make and provide crossings at the two points selected, the reservation was held to be void:

> The effect of the reservation is said to be that it reserves to the vendors, their heirs and assigns the right of passage over the tramway at two points to be selected, but

---

[45]*Law of Property Act, 1922*, 12 & 13 Geo. 5, c. 16, s. 145, 15th Sched., para. 5. See *Re Hopkin's Lease*; *Caerphilly Concrete Products Ltd. v. Owen*, [1972] 1 All E.R. 248 (C.A.).
[46]*Aldercrest Developments Ltd. v. Hunter*, [1970] 2 O.R. 562, 11 D.L.R. (3d) 439 (C.A.).
[47]*Ibid.*, at p. 564 O.R., p. 441 D.L.R.; *Re Atkins's Will Trusts*; *National Westminster Bank Ltd. v. Atkins*, [1974] 2 All E.R. 1 (Ch.).
§1104.19
[1]*Knightsbridge Estates Trust, Ltd. v. Byrne*, [1940] A.C. 613 (H.L.), at p. 625.

there is no specified time within which the selection is to be made. Until the selection is made there is no easement; the reservation is of an easement *in futuro*, which may come into force at a time beyond the period allowed by the rule against perpetuities. The reservation, therefore, is bad.[1]

Where a testator provided that, if the minerals under devised property "should be worked", they were to be divided between his son and daughters in equal shares, it was held that the gift was void because, not being a present one under which the minerals would pass immediately, but a conditional one depending on the working and sale of the minerals, the condition might not happen within the perpetuity period.[2] Again, where a testator devised land to his two sons, directing them to make certain payments to his daughters for life and then to the children of each daughter and their heirs out of the royalties or rent payable out of coal under the land when worked or let, it was held that the testator thereby intended to create executory limitations in land to arise at some future, indefinite time on a contingency which might not happen. That direction was, therefore, void for remoteness so far as it concerned the grandchildren.[3]

Of course, if the easement or profit takes effect immediately, it is valid and is not rendered void merely because it may last indefinitely, or may terminate on a remote contingency.[4]

Similarly, a rent charge reserved on a sale of land until the happening of a certain event is valid, even though the amount due under the rent charge varies from time to time with the gross rateable value of the land.[5]

Restrictive covenants between a vendor and purchaser do not offend the rule.[6]

1104.21 Forfeiture of Leases

The right of a landlord to terminate a lease under a forfeiture clause does not offend the rule, even though it may occur at a future uncertain event. The right is regarded as incidental to the lease and, thus, as not infringing the policy of the rule.[1]

1104.22 Administrative Powers and Trusts

Administrative powers and trusts are those which do not purport to dispose of property to beneficiaries, but which are incidental to dispositive powers.

---

§1104.20
[1]*Sharpe v. Durrant* (1911), 55 Sol. Jo. 423, affd [1911] W.N. 158 (C.A.). And see *Savill Brothers Ltd. v. Bethell,* [1902] 2 Ch. 523 (C.A.), and *Dunn v. Blackdown Properties, Ltd.,* [1961] Ch. 433, to the same effect.
[2]*Thomas v. Thomas* (1902), 87 L.T. 58 (C.A.).
[3]*Edwards v. Edwards,* [1909] A.C. 275 (H.L.).
[4]*Re Winters and McLaren,* [1960] O.R. 479, 25 D.L.R. (2d) 131 (H.C.J.).
[5]*Beachway Management Ltd. v. Wisewell,* [1971] 1 All E.R. 1 (Ch.).
[6]*Mackenzie v. Childers* (1889), 43 Ch. D. 265 at p. 279.
§1104.21
[1]*Re Tyrrell's Estate,* [1907] 1 I.R. 292 (C.A.), at p. 298, *per* Walker, L.C.; Maudsley, p. 76.

Powers of sale and of lease fall into this category. Such powers are void if they are exercisable beyond the period.[1] However, if the trusts to which the power is annexed must come to an end or can be destroyed within the period, the power will be held valid.[2] Moreover, even if the power is unlimited as to time, it is often construed as being exercisable only until the shares of the beneficiaries fall into possession and within a reasonable time, that is, twenty-one years thereafter. Thus, if there is a devise "to X for life, remainder to his children in fee", with a power to the trustees to sell at any time, and the trustees sell within a year of X's death, the power is valid.[3] The power must, however, be exercisable during the lifetime of a life in being. If it is not, the administrative power is void, even though the beneficial interests themselves will vest in time.[4]

An administrative trust or power which arises on a contingent event which may be too remote, is void.[5] However, only the power will be void, not the gift of the beneficial interest if it must vest within the period, as where there is a power of sale which is too remote and the proceeds of sale are directed to be divided among a class of beneficiaries who are ascertainable within the period. In such a case the beneficiaries will receive the unconverted property.[6]

Trusts to pay debts do not offend the rule, even though they may be exercisable beyond the period, for they are not regarded as gifts, but as the discharge of obligations of the testator or of others.[7]

1104.23 Interests Arising by Operation of Law

Interests arising by operation of law are not subject to the rule, such as resulting uses and trusts[1] and rights of reverter conferred by law.[2]

§1104.22

[1]*Ware v. Polhill* (1805), 11 Ves. Jun. 257, 32 E.R. 1087.

[2]*Wolley v. Jenkins* (1856), 23 Beav. 53, 53 E.R. 21; *Lantsbery v. Collier* (1856), 2 K. & J. 709, 69 E.R. 967.

[3]*Re Lord Sudeley and Baines & Co.,* [1894] 1 Ch. 334. And see *Re Dyson and Fowke,* [1896] 2 Ch. 720; *Re Holmes and Cosmopolitan Press, Ltd.'s Contract,* [1944] Ch. 53; *Re Atkins's Will Trusts; National Westminster Bank Ltd. v. Atkins,* [1974] 2 All E.R. 1 (Ch.).

[4]*Re Allott; Hanmer v. Allott,* [1924] 2 Ch. 498 (C.A.), a devise in trust for X for life, remainder to his widow (possibly unborn) for life, remainder to X's children at 21 in fee, with power in the trustees to lease at any time.

[5]*Goodier v. Edmunds,* [1893] 3 Ch. 455; *Re Wood; Tullett v. Colville,* [1894] 3 Ch. 381 (C.A.); *Re Bewick; Ryle v. Ryle,* [1911] 1 Ch. 116; *Meyers v. Hamilton Provident and Loan Co.* (1890), 19 O.R. 358 (H.C.J.).

[6]*Goodier v. Edmunds, supra,* footnote 5.

[7]*Re Earl of Stamford and Warrington; Payne v. Grey,* [1912] 1 Ch. 343 (C.A.), at p. 368, *per* Farwell, L.J.

§1104.23

[1]*Re Randell; Randell v. Dixon* (1888), 38 Ch. D. 213; *Re Blunt's Trusts; Wigan v. Clinch,* [1904] 2 Ch. 767.

[2]*Attorney-General v. Cummins,* [1906] 1 I.R. 406; *Attorney-General v. Shadwell,* [1910] 1 Ch. 92.

1104.24 Crown Property

The question whether the Crown is bound by the rule against perpetuities cannot be said to be settled. In *Thellusson v. Woodford*[1] there was a trust in a will that in the event of the failure of certain issue the trustees were to sell the trust property and pay the proceeds to the Crown. It was not disputed that the Crown was bound by the rule against perpetuities, but it was not necessary to settle the point as the trusts of the will were affirmed.

In *Cooper v. Stuart*[2] there was a grant in 1823 of Crown land in New South Wales with a reservation of such parts as might be required for highways or public purposes. This reservation was held to operate in defeasance when put into force, which might not be within the perpetuity period. This raised the question of its validity under the rule, but was held that, if the rule against perpetuities is applicable to the Crown in England, it was not applicable in 1823 to the Crown in that colony.

In *Flower v. Hartopp*[3] dealing with a grant by Charles II in fee simple subject to a free-farm rent, with a proviso for re-entry in case a decree for repair should be made at the suit of the King and the property should remain out of repair for a year, the proviso for re-entry was assumed to be valid, but was held not to be exercisable because the Crown had assigned the rent, so that the decision is not conclusive on the point.

It has been said that the King cannot make a grant in derogation of the common law.[4] It has been held, for example, that he cannot grant peerages in such manner as to descend contrary to the common law,[5] or to shift in certain events to minors not entitled in descent. The question of remoteness of the event did not arise, however, the limitation merely being held void as unknown to the law.[6] On the other hand, it has been said that the King, unlike an ordinary person, can annex to his grant a condition against alienation[7] and, in an Irish case, *Fowler v. Fowler*,[8] such a condition was held to be a valid exercise of the royal prerogative.

As Armour states,[9] if full effect is to be given to this authority that the Crown can restrain alienation, it means that the Crown has the prerogative right to grant an inalienable estate, which is a perpetuity. To his remarks, it may be added that, if the Crown can create a perpetuity by that means contrary to the common law, it would seem to follow that the Crown could offend the common law rule against perpetuities. In keeping with the foregoing cases

---

§1104.24

[1] (1805), 11 Ves. Jun. 112, 32 E.R. 1030 (H.L.).

[2] (1889), 14 App. Cas. 286 (P.C.).

[3] (1843), 6 Beav. 476, 49 E.R. 910.

[4] Chitty, *Prerogatives of the Crown* (London, Butterworths; Dublin, J. Cooke, 1820; Farnborough, Gregg, 1968), pp. 386, 388.

[5] *Wiltes Claim of Peerage* (1869), L.R. 4 H.L. 126.

[6] *Buckhurst Peerage* (1876), 2 App. Cas. 1 (H.L.).

[7] Brooke's *Abridgement*, Prerogative le Roy (London, Tottyl, 1576), pp. 53, 102; Chitty, *op. cit.*, footnote 4, p. 388.

[8] (1865), 16 Ir. Ch. R. 507.

[9] *Real Property*, p. 267.

holding that the Crown cannot alter the common law course of descent, the true answer may be that the Crown is bound by the rule against perpetuities and that the view that the Crown can restrain alienation contrary to the common law is erroneous.

A Canadian case, *R. v. Cory-Park Mobile City Ltd.*,[10] has held that the rule against perpetuities does apply to the Crown, so that an option in the Crown to purchase land exercisable beyond the period, is void.

1105. THE RULE IN WHITBY v. MITCHELL

In addition to the rule against perpetuities or the rule against remoteness of vesting there is another rule, known variously as the old rule against perpetuities, the rule against double possibilities and, more commonly, as the rule in *Whitby v. Mitchell*.[1] This rule provides that if an instrument limits a life estate in real property to a person who is unborn when the instrument takes effect and limits a remainder to his issue as purchasers, the remainder is void, subject to the *cy-près* doctrine discussed in the next section.

The origin of this rule is obscure. It does not derive from the rule against double possibilities. That rule was a judicial invention for which there existed no basis. It was rejected by Lord Nottingham in the *Duke of Norfolk's Case*[2] and by the Court of Appeal in *Re Nash; Cook v. Frederick*.[3] It may be that the rule derived from the common law principle against unbarrable entails, discussed above.[4] Indeed, it appears to have been applied in that sense on a number of occasions before it resurfaced in modern times.

Thus, in *Duke of Marlborough v. Earl Godolphin*[5] limitations in a will were to trustees to the use of several persons for life with remainder to their first and other sons in tail male successively. The trustees were directed, on the birth of each son, to revoke the uses and limit the property to the son for life with remainder to the sons of such sons in tail male. This was held to create a perpetuity by means of the clause of revocation and resettlement, which would leave the property with the testator's issue forever without power of alienation for more than a life estate. The clause of revocation and resettlement was held void. Lord Northington said:[6]

> ... though by the rules of law an estate may be limited by way of contingent remainder to a person not *in esse* for life, or as an inheritance; yet a remainder to the issue of such contingent remainder-man as a purchaser, is a limitation unheard of in law, nor ever attempted, as far as I have been able to discover.[7]

10[1977] 6 W.W.R. 104, 2 R.P.R. 242 (Sask. Q.B.).
§1105
1(1889), 42 Ch. D. 494, affd 44 Ch. D. 85 (C.A.).
2(1682), 3 Chan. Cas. 1, 22 E.R. 931.
3[1910] 1 Ch. 1 (C.A.), at pp. 9-10.
4See §1102, *supra.*
5(1759), 1 Eden 404, 28 E.R. 741, affd 3 Bro. P.C. 232, 1 E.R. 1289 *sub nom. Lord Spencer v. Duke of Marlborough* (H.L.).
6*Ibid.*, 1 Eden at pp. 415-16.
7And see *Hay v. Earl of Coventry* (1789), 3 T.R. 83, 100 E.R. 468; *Monypenny v. Dering* (1852), 2 De G. M. & G. 145 at p. 170, 42 E.R. 826, *per* Lord St. Leonards, L.C.

Others believe that the rule ought not to have been resurrected.[8] It is indeed a redundant rule, for the rule against remoteness of vesting is adequate to prevent the tying-up of property in perpetuity. The rule was abolished in England by the *Law of Property Act, 1925*.[9] It was never followed in the United States,[10] nor does it appear to have been expressly followed in Canada, although a number of cases have referred to it with approval.[11] Modern Canadian perpetuities statutes have abolished it.[12]

The rule applies to legal[13] and equitable[14] contingent remainders in land. It does not apply to personalty[15] nor to interests in land devised upon a trust for sale.[16]

The following example illustrates the operation of the rule:

A devise "to A (a bachelor) for life, remainder to his issue for life, remainder to the issue of such issue in fee provided they are born within a life or lives now in being and twenty-one years afterwards".

The rule is infringed because the final remainder is limited to the unborn issue of the preceding unborn life tenant. The rule against perpetuities is not infringed, however, because of the proviso.

It should be noted that the rule does not strike down all limitations to the unborn issue of an unborn person, but only those that are preceded by a life estate to that unborn person. Hence, a devise "to the grandchildren of A who are living at his death" is valid if A is living but has as yet no children. So also if the limitation were preceded by a life estate to A. Moreover, the rule is not infringed where there is a preceding life estate to one parent who may be unborn, as in a devise "to A (a bachelor) for life, remainder to his widow, if any, for life, remainder to their children at age 21". The fact that A's widow may be unborn at the testator's death is irrelevant.[17]

In the case of appointments under special power of appointment, the rule

---

[8]The following sources are representative of the controversy: Sweet, "Perpetuities" 15 L.Q. Rev. 71 (1899); Sweet, "The Rule in *Whitby v. Mitchell*", 25 L.Q. Rev. 385 (1907); Sweet, "Limitations of Land to Unborn Generations", 29 L.Q. Rev. 304 (1913); Williams, "Contingent Remainders and the Rule Against Perpetuities — A Criticism of the Case of Whitby v. Mitchell", 14 L.Q. Rev. 234 (1898); Gray, "*Whitby v. Mitchell* Once More", 29 L.Q. Rev. 26 (1913).

[9]15 & 16 Geo. 5, c. 20, s. 161 (1925).

[10]Simes and Smith, §1219.

[11]*Re Phillips* (1913), 28 O.L.R. 94 at p. 99, 11 D.L.R. 500 at p. 504 (S.C.); *Stuart v. Taylor* (1916), 33 O.L.R. 20, 22 D.L.R. 282 (S.C. App. Div.).

[12]See §1107.14, *infra*.

[13]*Whitby v. Mitchell* (1889), 42 Ch. D. 494, affd 44 Ch. D. 85 (C.A.).

[14]*Re Nash*; *Cook v. Frederick*, [1910] 1 Ch. 1 (C.A.); *Re Clarke's Settlement Trust*; *Wanklyn v. Streatfield*, [1916] 1 Ch. 467.

[15]*Re Bowles*; *Amedroz v. Bowles*, [1902] 2 Ch. 650.

[16]*Fonseca v. Jones* (1911), 14 W.L.R. 148 at p. 162, 21 Man. R. 168 at p. 184 (C.A.).

[17]*Re Garnham*; *Taylor v. Baker*, [1916] 2 Ch. 413. *Re Park's Settlement*; *Foran v. Bruce*, [1914] 1 Ch. 595, and *Stuart v. Taylor* (1916), 33 O.L.R. 20, 22 D.L.R. 282 (S.C. App. Div.), which followed it, and which hold otherwise, must be regarded as wrongly decided.

is applied as of the date on which the instrument creating the power took effect, because the actual appointment is in law a disposition under the instrument creating the power and, apparently, if the appointed persons were unborn on that date, it is immaterial that they were alive at the date of the appointment.[18]

If the limitation to an unborn person and his issue is so worded that the rule in *Shelley's Case*[19] applies, so as to give him an estate in fee tail or fee simple, as the case may be, the rule in *Whitby v. Mitchell* does not apply.

1105.1   The Rule in Whitby v. Mitchell and Cy-près

Cy-près is a Norman French expression which may be said to mean "as near as possible" with reference to an indicated general intent.

The *cy-près* doctrine is a rule of construction of wills. It is used to give effect to the intention of a testator who devises land beyond the limits permitted by the rule in *Whitby v. Mitchell*,[1] by construing the limitation as an estate tail.[2]

The doctrine was described in the following terms by Lord Romilly, M.R.:

> ... this doctrine is a rule of construction, and ... when the Court finds that the object expressed by the testator is to give to *A.* an estate for life, to *A.*'s eldest son another estate for life, and to his eldest son a third estate for life, and so on, the Court will carry that intention into effect as nearly as it can, by giving to *A.* an estate for life, and to his eldest son, if unborn at the death of the testator, an estate in tail male, or, if he be alive at the death of the testator, an estate for life, with a remainder to his eldest son in tail male.[3]

In most cases where the rule applies, the testator's general intention is effected by sacrificing the particular intention so far as may be necessary to carry out the former according to law. However, in *Monypenny v. Dering*[4] Lord St. Leonards, L.C., describes the working of the doctrine as follows:

> In the first place, it is said that I am to effectuate this intention by means of the doctrine of *cy pres*. This doctrine, as I understand it, is nothing more than that which prevails in other cases of giving effect to the general intent, but with this difference, that it is not, as in them, carried into effect at the expense of the particular intent. In the common case there is a valid particular intent and there is a valid general intent, and the particular intent not in the view of the Court effectuating all the intentions which they presume the testator to have had, they look to his general intent, and they effect his general intent at the expense of his particular intent. In applying, however, the doctrine of *cy pres* nothing is sacrificed; for example, in the case of limitations under powers, where there is a good gift of a limited estate to a

---

[18]*Whitby v. Mitchell, supra*, footnote 13; *Re Nash, supra*, footnote 14; *Whitting v. Whitting* (1908), 53 Sol. Jo. 100.
[19](1581), 1 Co. Rep. 93 b, 76 E.R. 206.
§1105.1
[1](1890), 44 Ch. D. 85 (C.A.).
[2]*Hampton v. Holman* (1877), 5 Ch. D. 183; *Humberston v. Humberston* (1716), 1 P. Wms. 332, 24 E.R. 412.
[3]*Parfitt v. Hember* (1867), L.R. 4 Eq. 443 at p. 446.
[4](1852), 2 De G. M. & G. 145 at pp. 172-3, 42 E.R. 826.

person, an object of the power and then a gift over to his children who are not objects of the power, effect may be given to the whole intention by giving to the parent an estate of inheritance by means of which the estate will descend to his children. In such a case, no doubt, the general intent is effectuated, but it is done at no expense of the particular intent, because there is no valid particular intent to which effect can be given. So in the case, more closely applying to that now before the Court, of a limitation to an unborn son for life, with remainder to his unborn children in tail, where, as effect cannot be given to the expressed intention, because successive estates cannot be limited to an unborn person and to his issue, an estate tail is given to the party to whom the limitation was made for life; here again, the particular intent is not sacrificed, but effect is given to it as a general intent.

The doctrine also applies to direct devises. Thus, where estates for life are given to the children of a living person as a class with estates tail to the children of each member of the class, the limitations are valid in regard to members of the class born in the testator's lifetime and the *cy-près* doctrine is applied to a member unborn in the testator's lifetime.[5]

The doctrine is not applied where its application would benefit persons not intended to be benefited.[6] Thus, it is not applied where successive life estates are given only to a definite number of generations of issue.[7] Again, where successive life estates are given to a larger class of persons than would take under an estate tail, the doctrine is not applied.[8]

The doctrine is not applied where an estate tail would not represent the estate to be taken by the issue or the intended course of descent, as where children of an unborn person are to take in such shares as he may appoint,[9] or are to take successive estates for years determinable on lives,[10] or are to take a fee simple estate.[11] In *Pitt v. Jackson*[12] the doctrine was applied, however, where the children of an unborn person were to take as tenants in common in tail and, although that case was described as going to the verge of the law, it was considered as correct.[13]

The *cy-près* doctrine is not to be extended and does not apply to deeds,[14] or to gifts of personal property.[15]

---

[5]*Vanderplank v. King* (1843), 3 Hare 1, 67 E.R. 273. See also *Pitt v. Jackson* (1786), 2 Bro. C.C. 51, 29 E.R. 27; *Hampton v. Holman, supra,* footnote 2; *East v. Twyford* (1853), 4 H.L.C. 517 at p. 556, 10 E.R. 564.

[6]*Re Mortimer*; *Gray v. Gray*, [1905] 2 Ch. 502 (C.A.); *Re Rising*; *Rising v. Rising*, [1904] 1 Ch. 533.

[7]*Seaward v. Willock* (1804), 5 East 198, 102 E.R. 1046.

[8]*Re Richardson*; *Parry v. Holmes*, [1904] 1 Ch. 332.

[9]*Bristowe v. Warde* (1794), 2 Ves. Jun. 336, 30 E.R. 660.

[10]*Somerville v. Lethbridge* (1795), 6 T.R. 213, 101 E.R. 517; *Beard v. Westcott* (1822), 5 B. & Ald. 801, 106 E.R. 1383.

[11]*Hale v. Pew* (1858), 25 Beav. 335, 53 E.R. 665.

[12](1786), 2 Bro. C.C. 51, 29 E.R. 27.

[13]*Brudenell v. Elwes* (1801), 1 East 442 at p. 451, 102 E.R. 171; *Monypenny v. Dering* (1847), 16 M. & W. 418 at pp. 431-6, 153 E.R. 1252, (1852) 2 De G. M. & G. 145 at p. 175, 42 E.R. 826; *Re Mortimer, supra,* footnote 6, at p. 515.

[14]*Brudenell v. Elwes, supra,* footnote 13.

[15]*Routledge v. Dorril* (1794), 2 Ves. Jun. 357, 30 E.R. 671; *Harvey v. Towell* (1847), 7 Hare 231 at p. 234, 68 E.R. 94; *Raphael v. Boehm*; *Cockburn v. Raphael* (1852), 22 L.J. Ch. 299.

It is doubtful that the doctrine can be used in any of the Canadian provinces except Manitoba since, except for the latter, the estate tail has been abolished and a limitation that would have created an estate tail is construed as a fee simple or the greatest estate that the grantor or testator had.[16]

1106. THE RULE AGAINST INDEFINITE DURATION

It has been seen that the rule against perpetuities applies, although not in all its strictness, to charitable trusts.[1] There is no objection to such trusts lasting indefinitely, for the trust property is being devoted to purposes beneficial to the community. The rule against perpetuities also applies to trusts for non-charitable purposes. These must vest within the perpetuity period in order to be valid. There is, however, an additional rule, the rule against indefinite duration, which prohibits such trusts from lasting longer than the perpetuity period. The reason for this rule is that such trusts are, by definition, not beneficial to the public in such a way as the law regards charitable and, indeed, the purpose may be capricious.[2] Hence it is inappropriate to let the property comprised in them be withdrawn from commerce in perpetuity. Thus, the following gifts have been held void: a devise of land to trustees of a library;[3] a gift to a society upon trust to preserve angling in a certain river;[4] a direction to trustees to buy the family homestead and to hold it in the testator's estate for a family memorial forever;[5] a gift in trust to use the income to provide annually forever a cup to be given to the most successful yacht of the season;[6] and a devise of land upon which to build a home dedicated to the performance of religious services in memory of the testatrix and her husband.[7]

Even if the trust is restricted to the perpetuity period, however, it has often been said that it is invalid because it has no beneficiaries in whose favour the court can direct performance, or because it is uncertain.[8] This difficulty, while it continues to exist, has often been disregarded or has been overcome by construing the trust as one in favour of individuals and not for purposes. This is dealt with in the following sections.

---

[16]See §607, *supra*.

§1106

[1]See §1104.17, *supra*.

[2]As in *Brown v. Burdett* (1882), 21 Ch. D. 667, in which case a home was directed to be boarded up for twenty years.

[3]*Carne v. Long* (1860), 2 De G. F. & J. 75, 45 E.R. 550.

[4]*Re Clifford; Mallam v. McFie* (1911), 81 L.J. Ch. 220.

[5]*Re McLellan* (1914), 7 O.W.N. 447 (H.C.J.).

[6]*Re Nottage; Jones v. Palmer*, [1895] 2 Ch. 649 (C.A.).

[7]*Neo v. Neo* (1875), L.R. 6 P.C. 381.

[8]*Morice v. Bishop of Durham* (1804), 9 Ves. Jun. 399, 32 E.R. 656, affd 10 Ves. Jun. 522, 32 E.R. 947; *Re Astor's Settlement Trusts; Astor v. Scholfield*, [1952] Ch. 534; *Re Endacott; Corpe v. Endacott*, [1960] Ch. 232 (C.A.); *Re Shaw; Public Trustee v. Day*, [1957] 1 W.L.R. 729 (Ch.), compromised on appeal [1958] 1 All E.R. 245 (C.A.); *Re Albery*, [1964] 1 O.R. 342, 42 D.L.R. (2d) 201 (H.C.J.).

1106.1 Exceptions to the Rule Against Indefinite Duration

A number of exceptions to the rule against indefinite duration have been allowed, chiefly testamentary trusts for the maintenance of the testator's animals[1] or of monuments or tombs,[2] provided they are restricted to the perpetuity period.[3] Such exceptions are nowadays regarded as anomalous and not to be extended, however.[4]

On the other hand, it is possible to overcome the rule that a non-charitable trust is not enforceable. Thus, a gift to a charity, upon condition that it keep the family tomb in good repair, with a gift over to another charity upon the same condition if the first charity fails to do so, was held to be valid.[5] This device only works if the gift can be construed as primarily for the charitable purpose. If the gift is primarily for the upkeep of the tomb, with what is left over to go to the charity, it is void.[6]

In *Re Chardon*; *Johnston v. Davies*,[7] Romer, J., upheld a gift in trust to pay the income to a cemetery company during such time as it should continue to maintain two graves, with a gift over to the residue if it failed to do so. His Lordship held that the rule against indefinite duration, which he called the rule against inalienability, was not offended.[8]

An outright gift to a corporation does not offend the rule against indefinite duration, even though the corporation and, hence, its purposes, may last forever, for it is a legal person.[9]

1106.2 Unincorporated Associations

A gift to the trustees of an unincorporated society for its purposes is void

---

§1106.1

[1]*Re Dean*; *Cooper-Dean v. Stevens* (1889), 41 Ch. D. 552, a trust to pay a sum of money to trustees for fifty years, if the testator's horses and hounds should so long live, to provide for their upkeep; *Re Kelly*; *Cleary v. James*, [1932] I.R. 255, a gift to maintain the testator's dogs, limited to twenty-one years.

[2]*Trimmer v. Danby* (1856), 25 L.J. Ch. 424; *Mussett v. Bingle*, [1876] W.N. 170 (H.C.J.); *Lloyd v. Lloyd* (1852), 2 Sim. (N.S.) 255, 61 E.R. 338; *Re Hooper*; *Parker v. Ward*, [1932] 1 Ch. 38; *Estate of Crocker v. Senior* (1971), 2 Nfld. & P.E.I.R. 179 (Nfld. S.C.), a bequest of $2,000 to be invested "for life" to maintain certain graves, held to be equivalent to "so long as the law permits", thus validating the gift for twenty-one years.

[3]*Lloyd v. Lloyd, supra.* The point seems to have been overlooked in *Re Dean, supra.*

[4]*Re Astor's Settlement Trusts*; *Astor v. Scholfield*, [1952] Ch. 534 at p. 547; *Re Endacott*; *Corpe v. Endacott*, [1960] Ch. 232 (C.A.), at p. 251.

[5]*Re Tyler*; *Tyler v. Tyler*, [1891] 3 Ch. 252 (C.A.).

[6]*Re Dalziel*; *Midland Bank Executor and Trustee Co., Ltd. v. St. Bartholomew's Hospital*, [1943] Ch. 277.

[7][1928] Ch. 464.

[8]The problem of providing for perpetual care of graves was solved in Ontario by s. 23(1) of the *Cemeteries Act*, R.S.O. 1980, c. 59. Under that section a cemetery owner may take grants, bequests and devises on condition that he maintain a tomb or monument in perpetuity.

[9]*Bowman v. Secular Society, Ltd.*, [1917] A.C. 406 (H.L.).

as tending to perpetuity. Thus, a gift in trust to a community of nuns,[1] a trust to maintain a library,[2] a gift "to the Communist Party of Australia for its sole use and benefit",[3] a trust in favour of a friendly society,[4] a trust for a mechanics' institution,[5] and a trust in favour of a trade union,[6] have been held void, because they were purpose trusts which were not charitable and which lasted beyond the perpetuity period.

If, however, the gift can be construed in such a way as to permit the society to expend the capital as well as the income, the gift is immediate and valid.[7]

Alternatively, it may be possible to construe the gift as one not for the purposes of the society, but for the present members of the society, in which case it will be valid. Thus, in *Cocks v. Manners*,[8] a gift of residue to a Dominican convent, payable to the superior, was so construed. A trust for the maintenance of recreational grounds for the employees of a company was upheld on the same basis in *Re Denley's Trust Deed*; *Holman v. H.H. Martyn & Co. Ltd.*[9] On the other hand, if the gift is construed as a gift to present and future members, the gift will fail, not because of indefinite duration, but because of remoteness of vesting.[10]

In the further alternative, a gift to a society is sometimes construed as valid because the members are free to dispose of the property as they wish,[11] or to terminate the trust for their own benefit.[12]

Finally, where the unincorporated association is a members' club, such as a golf club, its property is held subject to its rules, which are regarded as a contract between the members. Since the rule against perpetuities does not apply to such contracts, a trust in favour of such a club is valid.[13]

---

§1106.2

[1]*Gilmour v. Coats*, [1949] A.C. 426 (H.L.); *Leahy v. A.-G. N.S.W.*, [1959] A.C. 457 (P.C.).

[2]*Carne v. Long* (1860), 2 De G. F. & J. 75, 45 E.R. 550.

[3]*Bacon v. Pianta* (1966), 114 C.L.R. 634 (H.C.). And see *Re Grant's Will Trusts*, [1979] 3 All E.R. 359 (Ch.), a gift to "the Labour Party Property Committee for the benefit of the Chertsey Headquarters".

[4]*Re Swain*; *Phillips v. Poole* (1908), 99 L.T. 604 (Ch.).

[5]*Re Dutton* (1878), 4 Ex. D. 54.

[6]*Re Amos*; *Carrier v. Price*, [1891] 3 Ch. 159.

[7]*Re Price*; *Midland Bank Executor and Trustee Co.. Ltd. v. Harwood*, [1943] Ch. 422; *Re Macaulay's Estate*; *Macaulay v. O'Donnell*, [1943] Ch. 435; *Re Drummond*; *Ashworth v. Drummond*, [1914] 2 Ch. 90.

[8](1871), L.R. 12 Eq. 574. And see *Re Smith*; *Johnnon v. Bright-Smith*, [1914] 1 Ch. 937.

[9][1969] 1 Ch. 373.

[10]*Neville Estates Ltd. v. Madden*, [1962] Ch. 832; *Re Flavel's Will Trusts*; *Coleman v. Flavel*, [1969] 2 All E.R. 232 (Ch.).

[11]*Re Clarke*; *Clarke v. Clarke*, [1901] 2 Ch. 110, a gift to the committee of the Corps of Commissionaires, "to aid in the purchase of their barracks, or in any other way beneficial to that corps".

[12]*Re Lipinski's Will Trusts*; *Gosschalk v. Levy*, [1976] Ch. 235, a gift to a Jewish organization to be used "solely in the work of constructing the new buildings of the association".

[13]*Re Recher's Will Trusts*; *National Westminster Bank Ltd. v. National Anti-Vivisection Society Ltd.*, [1972] Ch. 526.

1106.3 Statutory Trusts

A trust created by statute cannot be held invalid on the ground of perpetuity or on any other ground.[1] Hence, property interests of a fluctuating body which may last indefinitely may be valid if the interests are statutory. Thus, in an action by some, on behalf of all freemen or a borough to establish the right of all individual freemen to share for their private benefit the net proceeds of certain properties vested in the corporation, it was held that the effect of the saving of rights in a statute was to legalize the beneficial interests therein mentioned and to obviate any objection which might otherwise arise in respect of the tendency towards a perpetuity of any such beneficial interests.[2]

1107. PERPETUITY REFORM

The common law rule against perpetuities is often a trap for the unwary. Its requirement of mathematical certainty of vesting within the perpetuity period and the remorseless construction approach of the courts tended to defeat the intention of persons disposing of their property by will and *inter vivos*. Many an inattentive solicitor, thinking that he had avoided the strictness of the rule, discovered to his horror that he had stumbled into one of its pitfalls. Although there has been much agitation for reform of the rule, changes came slowly and not all of them were successful. Early legislation in the United States which proved unworkable has nearly all been repealed.[1] It is largely as a result of the writings of the late Professor Leach and others that the modern perpetuity statutes have come about.

The modern statutes almost invariably replace the mathematical certainty required by the common law rule with the principle of "wait and see". This principle permits actual events to determine whether an interest will be valid or void. In addition, the modern statutes correct some of the more serious pitfalls of the common law rule.

The Canadian statutes, with the exception of the Prince Edward Island Act, derive, in whole or in part, from the English *Perpetuities and Accumulations Act, 1964.*[2] Statutes have been enacted in Alberta,[3] British Columbia,[4]

---

§1106.3

[1]*Re Christchurch Inclosure Act* (1888), 38 Ch. D. 520 (C.A.), at p. 530, *per* Lindley, L.J. As to the right of Parliament to create perpetual interests, *cf. Wotherspoon v. Canadian Pacific Ltd.*; *Pope v. Canadian Pacific Ltd.* (1978), 22 O.R. (2d) 385, 92 D.L.R. (3d) 545 (H.C.J.), revd on other grounds 35 O.R. (2d) 449, 129 D.L.R. (3d) 1 (C.A.) involving a perpetual lease.

[2]*Prestney v. Mayor and Corp. of Colchester and Attorney-General* (1882), 21 Ch. D. 111.

§1107

[1]6 A.L.P., §24.4; Morris and Leach, p. 13.

[2]C. 55 (1964, U.K.), hereafter referred to as the "English Act".

[3]*Perpetuities Act*, R.S.A. 1980, c. P-4, hereafter called the "Alta. Act". The Act was first enacted in 1972.

[4]*Perpetuity Act*, R.S.B.C. 1979, c. 321, hereafter called the "B.C. Act". The Act was first enacted by S.B.C. 1975, c. 53.

Ontario,[5] the Northwest Territories,[6] Yukon Territory,[7] and Prince Edward Island.[8] The latter is the oldest, having been first enacted in 1931.[9] The Northwest Territories Ordinance is a virtual copy of the Ontario Act. The Alberta and British Columbia Acts and the Yukon Ordinance are based upon the *Uniform Perpetuities Act*.[10] The Newfoundland Act[11] deals only with the application of the rule to employee benefit trusts, a matter dealt with in several other provinces as well.[12]

In the succeeding sections the manner in which these several statutes reform the common law rule will be dealt with in detail.

The several rules against perpetuities have been abolished in Manitoba.[13]

1107.1 Retention of the Common Law Rule

All of the Canadian statutes, like the English Act, retain the common law rule as modified by the statutes and, except for the Prince Edward Island Act, so provide.[1] The Prince Edward Island Act, without expressly so stating, retains the rule, but modifies the period of the rule.[2] The retention of the common law rule is to be deplored. It serves no valid reforming purpose, but rather has the effect of requiring the retention of much obsolete learning.

The reason why the common law rule should have been abolished is simple. It is contained within the principle of wait and see. The common law rule states that an interest is valid if it must vest within the perpetuity period.[3] The wait and see principle states that an interest is valid if it vests in fact within the period. An interest which must vest within the period, if it vest at all, will clearly be valid under a system of wait and see, for actual facts will determine, even if logic does not, that under such a system, the interest is good if it vest

---

[5]*Perpetuities Act*, R.S.O. 1980, c. 374, hereafter called the "Ont. Act". The Act was first enacted by S.O. 1966, c. 113.

[6]*Perpetuities Ordinance*, R.O.N.W.T. 1974, c. P-3, hereafter called the "N.W.T. Ord.". The Ordinance was first enacted by O.N.W.T. 1968 (2nd Sess.), c. 15.

[7]*Perpetuities Ordinance*, O.Y.T. 1980 (1st), c. 23, hereafter called the "Yukon Ord.". The Ordinance was first enacted in substantially different form by O.Y.T. 1968 (2nd Sess.), c. 2.

[8]*Perpetuities Act*, R.S.P.E.I. 1974, c. P-3, hereafter called the "P.E.I. Act".

[9]By S.P.E.I. 1931, c. 15, repealed and re-enacted by S.P.E.I. 1940, c. 46, s. 5.

[10]Uniform Acts of the Uniform Law Conference of Canada (Toronto, Queen's Park, 1978), p. 34-1. This Act was promulgated in 1972.

[11]*Perpetuities and Accumulations Act*, R.S.N. 1970, c. 291.

[12]The expression "All the Canadian statutes" used hereafter in this chapter encompasses all the statutes referred to, except those of Newfoundland and Prince Edward Island, which are limited in scope, unless they are expressly referred to.

[13]By the *Perpetuities and Accumulations Act*, S.M. 1982-83, c. 43, s. 3. Hereafter, whenever reference is made to the Canadian statutes collectively, the Manitoba statute is not included.

§1107.1

[1]Alta. Act, s. 2; B.C. Act, s. 2(1); Ont. Act, s. 2; N.W.T. Ord., s. 3; Yukon Ord., s. 3.

[2]P.E.I. Act, s. 1.

[3]Not, it should be noted, that it will in fact vest; for that one must wait and see!

at all.[4] This is so only if the statute which introduces wait and see employs measuring lives which include all those that validated gifts under the common law rule, however.[5] Whether the Canadian statutes do so will be examined below.[6]

In addition to validating gifts valid under the common law rule, a system of wait and see may also, indeed almost invariably will, validate gifts that would have been void under the common law rule, because such a system no longer requires that the validity must be determined on the basis of facts known at the creation of the interest, but rather that actual facts shall determine the validity of the interest.

It must be said that, where the statute contains a relatively complete list of measuring lives, the common law rule can safely be disregarded for most purposes. The common law rule only becomes important in situations where it would validate a gift that is not validated by the statute and this only occurs if the list of measuring lives is defective in that it fails to include all those which validate gifts at common law.

It may, in certain circumstances, be advantageous to be able to determine at the outset that an interest can or cannot vest within the period. However, one does not need to retain the common rule for that purpose. The following examples will illustrate this point:

(1) A devise "to the descendants of A living 50 years after his death".

(2) A devise "to such of A's children as are alive 21 years after his death".

Assuming that the measurement of the perpetuity period is the same under the Act as it was under the common law rule, it is clear that the first gift will be void at the outset, there being no measuring lives, and that the second gift will be valid, since it must vest within twenty-one years of A's death. A system of wait and see would not save the first gift. It would confirm the validity of the second.

1107.2 The Introduction of Wait and See

All of the statutes, except the Prince Edward Island Act, introduce the wait and see principle. This is done in two stages. First, it is provided that a limitation or disposition creating a contingent interest in real or personal property shall not be treated as void for perpetuity merely because the interest may by possibility vest beyond the perpetuity period.[1] Secondly, the statutes provide that a contingent interest that is capable of vesting within or beyond the perpetuity period is presumptively valid until actual events establish either that it is incapable of vesting within the period, in which case it is void, or that it is incapable of vesting beyond the period, in which case it is valid.[2]

---

[4]Maudsley, pp. 6, 109.

[5]*Ibid.*

[6]*Infra*, §1107.4.

§1107.2

[1]Alta. Act, s. 3; B.C. Act, s. 4; Ont. Act, s. 3; N.W.T. Ord., s. 4; Yukon Ord., s. 4.

[2]Alta. Act, s. 4(1); B.C. Act, s. 5(1); Ont. Act, s. 4(1); N.W.T. Ord., s. 5(1); Yukon Ord., s. 5(1).

The second alternative is really redundant and, probably for that reason, the British Columbia Act omits it.

The first stage of the two-stage process is also not necessary, it is submitted, for it is contained in the second step.

Wait and see, therefore, may render a gift valid which was void under the common law rule, because at common law the validity had to be determined at the creation of the interest, whereas a system of wait and see allows actual events to determine validity or invalidity. The following examples will illustrate the operation of the principle:

(1) A devise "to the first of A's daughters to marry". A has no children when the testator dies.

At common law this gift would be void, for A's daughters may not marry until more than twenty-one years after A's death, and he is the only life in being. Under the wait and see principle, the gift will be valid if one of A's daughters marries within twenty-one years of his death.

(2) A devise in trust of the testator's gravel pits, directing the trustees "to work the same until they are exhausted and then to sell them and divide the proceeds among my issue then living".

This gift involves the so-called "magic gravel pit".[3] It was void at common law because the pits might not be exhausted for more than twenty-one years after the testator's death (there being no lives in being), even though it was expected that they would be worked out in a few years, as they were in fact. Under wait and see, the devise is good if the pits are exhausted within twenty-one years of the testator's death.

(3) A contract for the purchase and sale of land which provides that the purchaser "will close the transaction within 15 days after Building Permits become available".

The contract is valid. The condition precedent does not offend the rule against perpetuities, because the parties are permitted to wait and see whether it will be completed within the period.[4]

The wait and see principle, indeed, applies except where the statutes preclude it, in virtually all situations, outlined in the first part of this chapter, in which a gift would be void at common law because it might vest beyond the perpetuity period. It is not always necessary to rely on the principle, however, because of the specific remedies enacted by the statutes, such as the capacity to bear children, age reduction and class splitting. These will be dealt with below.[5]

Because of the unique way in which the rule applies to powers of appoint-

---

[3]The example is based on *Re Wood*; *Tullett v. Colville*, [1894] 2 Ch. 310, affd [1894] 3 Ch. 381 (C.A.). See §1104.3(d)(iv), *supra*.
[4]*Chain Gate Developments Ltd. v. Elder* (1977), 1 R.P.R. 285 (H.C.J.), at p. 298.
[5]§1107.5, *infra*.

ment, the statutes specifically provide for the application of the principle of wait and see to powers. This will be dealt with below.[6]

1107.3 The Perpetuity Period

Apart from a unique enactment in Prince Edward Island and the provision of an eighty-year alternative period in British Columbia, as well as special periods for certain kinds of interests, such as possibilities of reverter and rights of entry, the perpetuity period is not varied by the statutes.

(a) The Prince Edward Island Act

The Prince Edward Island Act does not make a change in the computation of the period as regards the measuring lives, but instead of the usual twenty-one years following the dropping of the last life, it permits sixty years, thereby substantially extending the period. The enactment is badly drafted. It provides in part:

> 1. ... the period during which the existence of a future estate or interest ... may be suspended ... may extend to, but must not exceed the life of a person or of the survivor of several persons born or *en ventre sa mere* at the time of the creation of the future estate or interest and ascertained for that purpose by the instrument creating the same, and sixty years to be computed from the dropping of such life or lives and ascertained for that purpose by such instrument.[1]

Presumably this means that a *contingent* interest *must vest* within the period specified, and that the measuring lives must be stipulated in or be ascertained from the instrument. Whether the sixty-year period must also be stipulated, is unclear.

The Act further provides that a remainder shall not be deemed to be a future interest within the meaning of the Act.[2] At common law a remainder was probably subject to the rule.[3]

(b) A fixed period of years

The British Columbia Act is the only Canadian statute which makes provision for a fixed period of years as an alternative to the normal perpetuity period. The Act provides:

> 3(1) Subject to subsection (2), an interest in property which either
> (a) according to the express terms of the disposition creating it; or
> (b) by necessary implication from the terms of the disposition creating it,
> must vest, if at all, not later than 80 years after the creation of the interest does not violate the rule against perpetuities.[4]

---

[6]§1107.8, *infra*.
§1107.3
[1]P.E.I. Act, s. 1.
[2]*Ibid.*, s. 3.
[3]See §1104.12, *supra*.
[4]Subsection (2) deals with special powers of appointment, which will be discussed in §1107.8, *infra*.

This provision derives from the English Act,[5] which in turn derives from the Western Australian Act.[6] Its purpose, according to the draftsman of the latter Act is "to woo draftsmen away from 'royal lives' clauses".[7] As such, it is a useful device but, as presently worded, it has its drawbacks.

The Brtish Columbia section, unlike the English, allows for the eighty-year period where it is implied, as well as where it is expressly provided for. Thus, a bequest "to such of my descendants as shall be living eighty years after my death", which is not possible in England, is effective in British Columbia.

It is, however, necessary under this enactment to relate the vesting of the interests to the eighty-year period (or such shorter period as may be selected). The following example will make this clear:

A devise "to the first of A's children to travel around the world. The perpetuity period applicable to this devise is eighty years from my death".

It is arguable that by necessary implication the gift must vest, if at all, within the period specified, and is thus valid. However, this is not at all clear. If that implication does not arise, then the gift, which would be void under the common law rule if A is still alive, can only be saved by wait and see, for which the period is not eighty years, but the period of the statutory measuring lives plus twenty-one years. Presumably, only if one of A's children travels around the world within the shorter of that period or eighty years, can he take.

What the testator should have done is to say:

To the first of A's children to travel around the world within eighty years of my death, that period being the perpetuity period for the purpose of this gift.

In that case, the gift would be valid if a child of A travels around the world within eighty years of A's death. In this respect a kind of "wait and see" is involved. Not the wait and see provided for by the statute, that is, the principle that permits actual facts to validate a gift for the purpose of perpetuities, but the "wait and see" necessary in all cases of contingent gifts to determine whether the contingency will in fact occur.

The reason for the requirement that the vesting of the interests must relate to the eighty-year period is that the Act retains the common law rule and fails to apply wait and see to the eighty-year period. Thus, the eighty-year period applies only to gifts that are valid at common law. If they are invalid, the "wait and see" principle using the statutory measuring lives is automatically invoked. It would have been preferable, therefore, that the statute repealed

---

[5]English Act, s. 1(1).
[6]*Law Reform (Property, Perpetuities and Succession) Act*, S.W.A. 1962, No. 83, s. 5.
[7]Allan, "The Rule against Perpetuities Restated", 6 U. of W.A.L. Rev. 27 (1963-64) at p. 39.

the common law rule and extended the wait and see principle to the eighty-year period.[8]

(c) Measuring lives plus twenty-one years

This is the normal period, familiar from the common law rule of "a life or lives in being plus twenty-one years". This is the period adopted by the statutes, except in Prince Edward Island,[9] for although none of them expressly so provide, it follows from the fact that they retain the common law rule. Under the statutes, however, the measuring lives are stipulated[10] or are ascertainable by a formula.[11] The provisions respecting the measuring lives will be dealt with below.[12]

(d) Where no lives are specified or implied

Where no lives were specified or implied by the instrument, the perpetuity period at common law was a period in gross of twenty-one years. This period was codified in some of the statutes.[13] The British Columbia Act equates this period, rather sensibly, with that of its fixed period, namely, eighty years.[14] The Prince Edward Island Act does not make a provision for a period in gross and it is, therefore, debatable whether the common law period of twenty-one years applies, or whether, by analogy to the development of this period at common law, it is sixty years, since the Act provides for a normal period of lives in being plus sixty years.[15]

In all jurisdictions except Prince Edward Island, which has not adopted the principle, wait and see governs the period in gross.

The following examples illustrate the operation of this provision, using a twenty-one-year period:

(1) A devise, "to the first person to circumnavigate the Americas."

If a person performed the act specified within twenty-one years of the testator's death, the gift would be valid. Otherwise it would fail.

(2) A Ltd. conveys Blackacre, "to B Ltd. in trust for C Ltd. when the latter becomes a public company."

If C Ltd. becomes a public company within twenty-one years of the conveyance, the gift is valid. Otherwise it fails.

---

[8]For a discussion of this point, see Maudsley, pp. 111-14, 155-6, 223-4.
[9]See sub-subpara. (a), *supra*.
[10]Alta. Act, s. 5; B.C. Act, s. 6; Yukon Ord., s. 6.
[11]Ont. Act, s. 6; N.W.T. Ord., s. 7.
[12]§1107.4, *infra*.
[13]Alta. Act, s. 5(1)(*b*); Ont. Act, s. 6(3); N.W.T. Ord., s. 7(3); Yukon Ord., s. 6(1)(*b*).
[14]B.C. Act, s. 6(1)(*b*).
[15]P.E.I. Act, s. 1.

(e) Commencement of the period

None of the statutes, except the British Columbia and Prince Edward Island Acts, deals with this point. In the context of its provision for a fixed period of years, the British Columbia Act provides that, for the purpose of that provision only, an interest created under the exercise of a special power of appointment is deemed to have been created when the power was created.[16]

The Prince Edward Island Act provides that the time of the testator's death shall be deemed to be the time of the creation of an interest created by will and that the time of the execution of the power shall be deemed to be the time of the creation of an interest created by the execution of a general power.[17]

1107.4 The Measuring Lives

While there has been much controversy over who may be lives in being under the common law rule, the orthodox view is that they are those lives which validate the gift and none other.[1] In theory the difficulty can easily be removed by statute, namely, by providing a statutory list of measuring lives. Given such a list, it becomes exceedingly simple for a trustee to determine whether a gift vests within the period under wait and see. All he has to do is to write out the names of the measuring lives on a sheet of paper, cross them off as they drop and wait a further twenty-one years after the last person on the list dies. If the interests have then vested they are valid; if not, they are void. Of course, if all the interests vest earlier, he can discard the piece of paper.[2]

Unfortunately, only the Alberta, British Columbia and Yukon statutes contain such a list. The Prince Edward Island statute does not introduce wait and see but merely alters the length of the period. Hence resort must be had in that province to the common law. Ontario and the Northwest Territories use a formula instead of a list of lives, which is likely to cause difficulties in ascertaining who may be used as measuring lives.

(a) The statutory list

The British Columbia Act provides as follows:

> 6(1) Where section 5 applies to a disposition and the duration of the perpetuity period is not determined by virtue of section 3, 18 or 19, the perpetuity period shall be determined as follows:
> (a) where any persons falling within subsection (2) are persons in being and ascertainable at the commencement of the perpetuity period, the duration of the period, to the extent it is determined by a life in being, shall be determined by reference to their lives and no others but so that the lives of any description of persons falling within subsection (2)(b) or (c) shall

---

[16]B.C. Act, s. 3(2).
[17]P.E.I. Act, s. 2.
§1107.4
[1]This point was dealt with in some detail in §1104.2(b), *supra*, and is not repeated here.
[2]Maudsley, p. 150.

be disregarded if the number of persons of that description is such as to render it impractical to ascertain the date of death of the survivor;

. . . . . .

(2) The persons referred to in subsection (1) are as follows:

(a) the person by whom the disposition is made;

(b) a person to whom or in whose favour the disposition was made, that is to say,

(i) in the case of a disposition to a class of persons, a member or potential member of the class;

(ii) in the case of an individual disposition to a person taking only on certain conditions being satisfied, a person as to whom some of the conditions are satisfied and the remainder may in time be satisfied;

(iii) in the case of a special power of appointment exercisable in favour of members of a class, a member or potential member of the class;

(iv) where, in the case of a special power of appointment exercisable in favour of one person only, the object of the power is not ascertained at the commencement of the perpetuity period, a person as to whom all of the conditions are satisfied, or some of the conditions are satisfied and the remainder may in time be satisfied; and

(v) in the case of a power of appointment, the person on whom the power is conferred;

(c) a person having a child or grandchild within paragraph (b)(i) to (iv), or a person any of whose children or grandchildren, if subsequently born, would by virtue of his descent, fall within paragraphs (b)(i) to (iv);

(d) a person who takes a prior interest in the property disposed of and a person on whose death a gift over takes effect;

(e) where

(i) a disposition is made in favour of any spouse of a person who is in being and ascertainable at the commencement of the perpetuity period;

(ii) an interest is created by reference to an event occurring during the lifetime of the spouse of a person who is in being and ascertainable at the commencement of the perpetuity period or during the lifetime of the survivor of them; or

(iii) an interest is created by reference to the death of the spouse of a person who is in being and ascertainable at the commencement of the perpetuity period or the death of the survivor of them,

the same spouse whether or not that spouse was in being or ascertainable at the commencement of the period.[3]

These measuring lives can be summarized as follows:

(1) The settlor of an *inter vivos* disposition: section 6(2)(a).

(2) The beneficiaries or potential beneficiaries: section 6(2)(b)(i) and (ii), their parents and grandparents and persons whose children or grandchildren if subsequently born would be beneficiaries or potential beneficiaries: section 6(2)(c).

(3) The objects of a special power of appointment: section 6(2)(b)(iii) and (iv), their parents and grandparents and persons whose children or grandchildren if subsequently born would be objects of the power: section 6(2)(c).

---

[3]The Alta. Act, s. 5, and the Yukon Ord., s. 6, are virtually the same. References in this subparagraph hereafter are to the B.C. Act, but apply *mutatis mutandis* to the Alta. Act and Yukon Ord. as well.

(4) The donee of a power of appointment: section $6(2)(b)(v)$.

(5) The holder of a prior interest: section $6(2)(d)$.

(6) A person on whose death a gift over takes effect: section $6(2)(d)$.

(7) An unborn spouse: section $6(2)(e)$.

(i) Some examples

(1) A bequest "to A for life, reminder to B's grandchildren when they attain the age of 21". At the testator's death, the following persons are alive: A; B and his wife, C, and their children, D and E; D's wife, F, and her parents, G and H; D's daughter, J, aged 22, and his son, K, aged 19; and K's wife, L, and her mother, M.

It will be seen that all of these persons, except L and M, are measuring lives. A is a measuring life by virtue of section $6(2)(d)$; B, C, D, E, F, G and H, by virtue of section $6(2)(c)$, and J and K by virtue of section $6(2)(b)(i)$.

On the foregoing facts there is no difficulty with the section. Suppose, however, that there are no grandchildren as yet. Does C qualify as a measuring life? Alternatively, suppose that E is also married, to N, but has no children. Do N and his parents, P and Q, qualify as measuring lives? The difficulty arises because of the phrase "by virtue of his descent". If these words mean by virtue of the grandchild's descent from N and his parents, then they cannot be measuring lives.[4] It is submitted, however, that the phrase refers back to B in the above example. If that is correct then, if a person when born is a grandchild of B, that person's parents and grandparents are included as measuring lives. Hence, C, N, P and Q would all be measuring lives from the outset.[5]

(2) A bequest "to the first daughter of A to marry". At the testator's death A and her husband, B, are alive, as is B's mother, C. A's daughters, D and E, are also living, both unmarried.

A, B and C are measuring lives by virtue of section $6(2)(c)$. D and E qualify under section $6(2)(b)(ii)$. Each is a person as to whom one of the conditions (that she is a daughter of A) is met and the other of which (that she be the first to marry) may in time be met.

(3) A bequest "to the eldest daughter of A to marry".

Assuming the same persons to be living as in the preceding example, E, the younger daughter, cannot be a measuring life, unless and until D dies unmarried, in which case E becomes A's eldest daughter.

This creates a practical difficulty, for the trustees will not have put her on their list of measuring lives and thus will not have kept track of her. It is perhaps arguable that in this situation all of A's living daughters should be

---

[4]See Prichard, "Two Petty Perpetuity Puzzles", 27 Camb. L.J. 284 (1969), at pp. 285-6.
[5]See Maudsley, pp. 131-3, and cf. id., "Measuring Lives Under a System of Wait-and-See", 86 L.Q. Rev. 357 (1970), at p. 377; Institute of Law Research and Reform, University of Alberta, Report on the Rule Against Perpetuities (Edmonton, 1971), p. 24.

treated as measuring lives, since they have satisfied the condition that they are A's daughters and may in time become the eldest daughter and marry.

(4) An *inter vivos* trust by X, empowering his trustees "to appoint to such of my issue as they see fit when they attain the age of 21". At the testator's death the trustees are A and B. Subsequently they retire and are replaced by D and E. The testator's children, F, G and H, who are 22, 20 and 18, respectively, and a grandchild, J, aged two, are also alive at the testator's death.

This is a special power, which would be void at common law, because it is exercisable beyond the perpetuity period in that it may be exercised by successor trustees who may not be lives in being. X is a measuring life under section 6(2)(a). F, G, H and J are undoubtedly measuring lives for the purpose of the validity of an appointment under section 6(2)(b)(iii). Whether A and B are also measuring lives under section 6(2)(b)(v) is debatable. If they are, they will continue to be so treated even after they retire. D and E are not measuring lives because they are not ascertainable at the commencement of the period.[6]

It has been argued, however, that A and B are not measuring lives for the purpose of the validity of an appointment, but only for the purpose of the validity of the power. This will be dealt with below.[7]

(5) A devise "to A for life, then to any wife he may marry for life, remainder to his issue then living".

This is an example of an "unborn spouse". The gift to the issue would be void at common law because A's wife might be unborn at the testator's death and live more than twenty-one years after A's death. A's wife is now regarded as a measuring life under section 6(2)(e), whether or not she was born or ascertainable when the period commenced. The location of this provision is awkward, since it does not fit in well with the other measuring lives who must be in being and ascertainable at the commencement of the period.[8] Other statutes have this provision elsewhere.[9]

(ii) Disregarding lives

Section 6(1)(a) provides that if the measuring lives prescribed by section 6(2)(b) and (c) are so numerous as to make the ascertainment of the death of the survivor impractical, as may very well happen in large discretionary trusts, they may be disregarded. Although section 6(a) is by no means clear, it would not seem appropriate automatically to disregard lives clause by clause, for then useful lives in clause (c), for example, would be lost. Rather, it is submitted. the class of beneficiaries should first be looked at to see if any of them ought to be disregarded. If within the class of beneficiaries there is a group of persons specially described who, together with the persons under

---

[6]Morris and Wade, "Perpetuities Reform at Last", 80 L.Q. Rev. 486 (1964), at p. 506.
[7]In §1107.8, *infra*.
[8]This point was recognized by the Alberta Institute, *Report*, *supra*, footnote 5, at p. 25.
[9]The "unborn widow" is dealt with further in §1107.5(d), *infra*.

clause (c) would be too numerous, that group of beneficiaries should be disregarded.

(iii) Lives omitted

The statute has not included all lives that might have been included. These are principally those who would validate a gift at common law. Wait and see does not apply to gifts which are valid at common law and one must refer back to the common law rule in these cases. The following is a list of persons omitted or situations not provided for:[10]

(1) Persons expressly selected by the grantor or testator himself, within whose lives plus twenty-one years the interest must vest are omitted. The Act does not apply in this case because by its terms, it is restricted to a situation that requires the wait and see remedy. The Act would apply if the vesting was not limited to the period selected by the testator.

(2) Similarly, implied lives are not included. Thus, a bequest, "to the first of my lineal descendants to go for a walk with X",[11] while perfectly valid at common law since it must vest within the lifetime of a living person, does not fit within the measuring lives of the statute, since X is not included. Moreover, it may be possible that the gift will not vest until more than twenty-one years after the death of the measuring lives prescribed by the statute. This does not present a problem, since the gift is valid anyway, but it does mean that one must again turn to the common law rule.

It should be noted that certain types of implied lives, called "automatic lives", do not cause this problem. Thus a gift "to the grandchildren of A at age 21", while void at common law if A is still alive, fits within the statute, since A and any living children and grandchildren as well as appropriate in-laws are included in the statutory list.[12]

(3) Where there is a gift over, the measuring lives specified by section 6(2)(d) are the owner of a prior interest and the person on whose death the gift over takes effect. However, where there is a bequest "to the children of A who marry and if there are none, to B", A is not a measuring life and neither are A's children, unless they were alive at the testator's death. Of course, B and his parents and grandparents are measuring lives under section 6(2)(b)(ii) and (c), but they may all die more than twenty-one years before the gift to B can vest. A should have been included as a measuring life.

(4) A special power exercisable in favour only of a living person is valid at common law. The statute, probably for this reason,[13] omits him from the list of statutory lives. The result is that for this purpose reference must be had to the common law rule again. If that rule were abolished, the donee of the power would have to be included in the list.

---

[10]The list is based on Maudsley, pp. 155 *et seq.*
[11]The example is Maudsley's, p. 156.
[12]*Ibid.*, p. 157.
[13]See Alta. *Report, supra,* footnote 5, at p. 22.

(5) The fact that wait and see does not apply to the fixed period of years has already been dealt with.[14]

(b) The statutory formula

Instead of a statutory list of measuring lives, Ontario and the Northwest Territories have adopted a formula by which they may be ascertained. The Ontario Act provides as follows:

> 6(1) Except as provided in section 9, subsection 13(3) and subsections 15(2) and (3), the perpetuity period shall be measured in the same way as if this Act had not been passed, but, in measuring that period by including a life in being when the interest was created, no life shall be included other than that of any person whose life, at the time the interest was created, limits or is a relevant factor that limits in some way the period within which the conditions for vesting of the interest may occur.
>
> (2) A life that is a relevant factor in limiting the time for vesting of any part of a gift to a class shall be a relevant life in relation to the entire class.[15]

There are two difficulties with this formula. In the first place, there is disagreement about who were to be regarded as lives in being at common law and it is those persons, subject to the proviso in the section, who will now become measuring lives. Secondly, it is not easy to determine what is meant by the phrase "whose life . . . limits or is a relevant factor that limits . . . the period".

The orthodox view of who are lives in being at common law is that anyone can be a potential life in being, but only those persons who validate the gift can qualify as actual lives in being. If there is no such person, the gift is void and there are no lives in being.[16] Thus, in a bequest, "to such of my grandchildren as attain the age of 21", the testator's children are the lives in being since the gift must vest within twenty-one years of their deaths. If the bequest had been "to A's grandchildren at age 21", however, and if A were alive, there would have been no lives in being, since there is no person of whom it can be said with certainty that the interest must vest within twenty-one years of his death.

Morris and Wade, on the other hand, say that lives in being at common law were those that as a matter of causality restrict the vesting period, although such lives are of no use at common law unless they save the gift.[17] Hence, in the above example of a bequest "to A's grandchildren at age 21", A being alive,

---

[14]*Supra*, §1107.3(b).

[15]The N.W.T. Ord., s. 7(1), (2) is virtually the same. References in this subparagraph hereafter are to the Ont. Act, but apply *mutatis mutandis* to the N.W.T. Ord. as well.

[16]Simes, "Reform of the Rule Against Perpetuities in Western Australia", 6 U. of W. A. L. Rev. 21 (1963-64), at pp. 22-5; *id.*, "Is the Rule Against Perpetuities Doomed? The 'Wait and See' Doctrine", 52 Mich. L. Rev. 179 (1953), at p. 186; Allan, "Perpetuities: Who Are the Lives in Being?", 81 L.Q. Rev. 106 (1965), at p. 108; Fetters, "Perpetuities: The Wait-and-See Disaster — A Brief Reply to Professor Maudsley, with a Few Asides to Professors Leach, Simes, Wade, Dr. Morris, et al.", 60 Cornell L. Rev. 380 (1974-75), at p. 388, Maudsley, pp. 94-6.

[17]Morris and Wade, "Perpetuities Reform at Last", 80 L.Q. Rev. 486 (1964). *Cf.* Morris and Leach, p. 62; Megarry and Wade, p. 221.

even though the limitation is void at common law, A is nevertheless a relevant life and becomes important under wait and see. It has been shown, however, that this theory is not supported by the cases.[18]

Turning then to the rule as modified by wait and see and in the absence of any restriction, Simes says that, since the measuring life need no longer be restricted to the time of vesting of a valid gift, anyone in the world can be a measuring life.[19]

Professor Allan basically agrees with Simes. However, in the alternative, he argues that if the statute states that the period is to be calculated in the same way as at common law, in other words, that the measuring lives are to be the same as the common law lives in being, then wait and see becomes irrelevant, since common law lives are only those which validate a gift and no others.[20]

Morris and Wade state that lives that were relevant at common law, but could not be used because they did not validate the gift, can now be used under wait and see. Hence in the above example of a bequest "to A's grandchildren at age 21", A being alive, they would say that A is a measuring life.[21]

Clearly, the Simes view is unworkable in practice unless it is restricted, the Allan alternative emasculates wait and see, and the Morris and Wade view is not supported by authority. The Ontario Act seems to be based on an amalgam of all three views. It apparently lets everyone who is alive in, but then restricts this impractical number to those persons whose lives, when the interest was created, limit or are relevant factors that limit in some way the period within which the vesting is to occur. That the draughtsman intended to include more than the common law lives, that is, those who validate a gift, is apparent from section 6(2). That provision lets in class members and their ancestors who would not have been lives in being at common law.

To determine who are probably measuring lives under the Act, it may be convenient to look at certain examples.

(i) Some examples

(1) A bequest, "to the grandchildren of A when they marry". At the testator's death A and his wife, B, are living. So are their children, C, D and E. C is married to F. They have one child, G. F's parents, H and J, are also alive.

At common law this gift would be void, for there is no person of whom it can be said that the interest must vest within twenty-one years of his death. Moreover, this is a class gift so that even though G's share would have to vest in time, that is, in his own lifetime, the gift is nevertheless void, for a class gift in order to be valid must be valid in its entirety. This difficulty has been removed by the statutes, as will be seen below.[22]

18Maudsley, pp. 96 *et seq.*
19Simes, "Reform of the Rule . . .", *loc. cit.*, footnote 16.
20Allan, *op. cit.*, *supra*, footnote 16, at p. 109.
21Morris and Wade, *op. cit.*, *supra*, footnote 17, at p. 498. The three views are admirably summarized in Gosse, *Ontario's Perpetuities Legislation* (Toronto, Carswell, 1967). pp. 23 *et seq.*
22§1107.5(c), *infra.*

Under the Ontario Act, wait and see becomes operative. The question is who are the measuring lives? It is probable that they include A and B. They are relevant factors that limit the vesting of their grandchildren's interest, because they are progenitors. On the other hand, they are hardly relevant as regards the time when the grandchildren will marry. The same may be said of C, D, E and F who are relevant factors in limiting the time for vesting of their own children's interests and thus are measuring lives under section 6(2), but they have very little to do with the time when they marry. As to H and J, it is doubtful that they can be measuring lives since they would not even have been considered at common law, as seems to be required by section 6(1). That leaves only G who is a measuring life under section 6(2).

It must be regarded as doubtful, however, that the section should be read so restrictively. Hence it is probable that all of A, B, C, D, E, F and G are to be regarded as measuring lives. But the matter is far from clear.[23]

(2) A devise, "to A for life, remainder to B's grandchildren living twenty-five years after the death of A's children". At the testator's death, A, B and his wife, C, and one child, D, are alive.

D, of course, cannot be used as a measuring life, even if he is included under section 6(2) since the interest does not vest for at least twenty-five years after his death. Is A a relevant factor? That is doubtful, because he does not limit the time of vesting at all.[24] B and C are relevant in that they are the progenitors of the grandchildren. On the other hand, they do not limit the time of vesting. Assuming, however, that they are intended to be measuring lives, the gift will be valid if they survive the death of A's children by four years. What happens, however, if only C does so? Is she a measuring life? If she was a measuring life originally, does she cease to be such when B dies? There are no *a priori* answers to these questions. Certainly, it would seem that if B were dead at the time of the testator's death, C could not be a measuring life, since she then has no relevance, in the terms of the gift, to the time of vesting.[25]

The foregoing examples illustrate the serious problems involved in applying a statutory formula such as that contained in section 6. Although a statutory list of measuring lives is not without difficulties, it is much to be preferred. The first draft of the Ontario Act as prepared by the Ontario Law Reform Commission did contain such a list,[26] but because of objections, it was replaced with the present formula.[27]

---

[23]See further on this point, Oosterhoff and Cudmore, "Problems in Ascertaining Lives in Being Under Ontario's Perpetuities Act (On Limiting Lives and Relevant Factors)", 4 E. & T. Q. 119 (1977).

[24]It would be otherwise if the gift were "to A for life, remainder to B's grandchildren born in A's lifetime and who attain the age of 21". A would then be a life in being at common law, the gift would be valid and there would be no need to wait and see.

[25]See further on this point, Oosterhoff and Cudmore, *op. cit.*, *supra*, footnote 23, pp. 127-8.

[26]Ontario Law Reform Commission, *Report No. 1* (Toronto, 1965), p. 47, App. A, s. 6(1).

[27]Ontario Law Reform Commission, *Report No. 1A* (Toronto, 1966), p. 2.

(ii) Lives omitted

There appears to be at least one situation in which the Ontario Act does not allow lives to be used which could be used at common law. Since the Act does not abolish the common law rule, however, one must turn to the common law to determine the validity of a gift in that situation. This is best illustrated by an example.

A bequest, "to the first daughter of X to marry someone born before the testator's death". At the time of the testator's death X is alive but has no daughters. A daughter, Y, is subsequently born and eventually marries Z. Z was born before the testator died.

The phrase "at the time the interest was created" in section 6(1) would exclude Z as a measuring life, since he was not ascertainable at the time a testator died.[28] At common law the gift is good, however, since it must vest, if at all, during the lifetime of a person living at the creation of the interest.[29]

1107.5 Specific Remedies

Although the principle of wait and see will be effective in most cases to save a gift that would be void at common law, the Canadian statutes go further and prescribe specific remedies for certain situations which caused the greatest difficulties at common law. These are dealt with in the next several sub-paragraphs.

(a) Capacity to have children

Because at common law a person was conclusively presumed to be able to have children at any age, many gifts were held void even though it was obvious that that capacity was lacking.[1] The statutes now provide that where a question concerning the capacity of a person to have a child at some future time arises in the context of the rule, it shall be presumed that a male is able to have a child at age 14 or over, but not under that age, and that a female is able to have a child at age 12 or over, but not under that age or over age 55. Moreover, evidence may now be introduced to show that a living person will or will not be able to have a child at a particular time.[2]

28Leal, "The Perpetuities Act — An Ontario Proposal", *Law Society of Upper Canada Special Lectures, Recent Developments in the Law* (Toronto, R. de Boo Ltd., 1966), p. 291, at pp. 304-5.
29Morris and Wade, *op. cit., supra,* footnote 17, pp. 498-9; Gosse, *op. cit., supra,* footnote 21, pp. 29-30.
§1107.5
1See §104.3(d)(i) and (ii), *supra.*
2Alta. Act, s. 9(1); B.C. Act, s. 10(1); Ont. Act, s. 7(1); N.W.T. Ord., s. 8(1); Yukon Ord., s. 10(1).

The following bequest illustrates the presumptions:

> To X for life, remainder to such of her grandchildren living at my death or born within five years thereafter as shall attain age 21.
> X is a widow, 65 years of age at the testator's death and has two children and one grandchild.

Leaving aside the question of legitimacy, the remainder would be void at common law. X might remarry and have another child, who might have a child, all within five years of the testator's death, and the latter child might attain the age of 21 more than twenty-one years after the death of the lives in being.[3]

Under the statutes, X is presumed to be incapable of having another child and, even if she were under 55, a child she might have would be presumed incapable of having a child. Hence the gift of the capital is valid.

In this situation there is, therefore, no need to wait and see. Where the measuring life, if female, is under age 55, one would wait and see until that age is reached, after which the presumption is applied.

It is also now possible at any time to lead evidence showing that a man is infertile, that a woman has had a hysterectomy, or other evidence showing that the person in question is incapable of having a child.

The statutes further provide that where it has been decided that a person is unable to have a child, he or she shall continue to be so treated even though he or she unexpectedly has a child later. If that happens, the court may make an order to protect the rights of such child and it may also do so where a child is subsequently adopted or legitimated, although the latter possibilities are to be disregarded in applying the presumptions.[4] Presumably the principal factor that the court would consider in deciding the matter is whether the estate has already been distributed so that such an order would be unfair to the beneficiaries to whom it has been distributed.

It should be noted that it is not necessary to make application to the court in order to apply the presumptions.

Questions about a person's capacity to have children have significance beyond the rule against perpetuities as well. The matter is relevant, for example, in the context of class closing and termination and variation of trusts. In essence, the reform made by the perpetuities statutes is a reform of a rule of evidence and it might have been better to insert a provision of this kind in a general statute reforming the law of property so as to make it applicable to all such situations.[5]

(b) Age reduction

Another situation in which many gifts failed was where vesting was post-

---

[3]See *Re Gaite's Will Trusts; Banks v. Gaite*, [1949] 1 All E.R. 459 (Ch.).

[4]Alta. Act, s. 9(2)-(4); B.C. Act, s. 10(2)-(4); Ont. Act, s. 7(2)-(4); N.W.T. Ord., s. 8(2)-(4); Yukon Ord., s. 10(2)-(4).

[5]*Cf.* Maudsley, p. 118; Ontario Law Reform Commission, Report No. 1 (Toronto, 1965), pp. 12-13.

poned to any age over 21. Some jurisdictions had made provision earlier to provide for age reduction.[6] The Canadian statutes also do so, by providing that where property is limited to a person at a specified age greater than 21 and actual events establish that the interest would be void for that reason, but that it would not be void if the specified age were 21 years, the limitation shall be read as if it had referred to the age nearest the age specified that would prevent it from being void.[7]

The statutes, therefore, first require the operation of wait and see and if the gifts would still fail, the age may then be reduced.

The following examples will illustrate the age reduction provision:

(1) A bequest, "to such of A's grandchildren as shall attain the age of 25". A, his two children, B and C, and a grandchild, D, five years old, are living at the testator's death.

At common law, since this is a class gift, it would be void. There is no person within twenty-one years of whose death it can be said that the gift to every member of the class must vest. Using wait and see under the several statutes, A, B, C and D are all lives in being. However, if three years after the testator's death all of them die, survived by two other grandchildren, E and F, aged two and one, respectively, wait and see will not assist them. The age reduction provision may then be used to reduce the specified age for both E and F to 22.[8]

(2) A bequest, "to the children of A, if sons at age 25 and if daughters at age 30". A and his wife, W, are living at the testator's death. One year later, A's daughter, B, is born and three years later his son, C, is born. A and W die together when C is one year old.

A and W could be used as the measuring lives for the purpose of wait and see, but on their death it becomes necessary to reduce the ages of B and C. This presents no problem in Alberta, British Columbia and the Yukon, which provide expressly that their ages shall be reduced separately, that is to 25 in B's case (21 plus four) and 22 in C's case (21 plus plus one).[9] Although the Ontario Act and the Northwest Territories Ordinance do not make express provisions for this situation, it is probable that the same result would obtain.

(3) A devise, "to the first grandchild of A to attain the age of 30". At the testator's death, A, his two children, B and C, and a grandchild, D, aged five, are living.

Although the age can readily be reduced for D if that should be necessary,[10]

---

[6]E.g., England: Law of Property Act, 1925, 15 & 16 Geo. 5, c. 20, s. 163.

[7]Alta. Act, s. 6(1); B.C. Act, s. 7(1); Ont. Act, s. 8(1); N.W.T. Ord., s. 9(1); Yukon Ord., s. 7(1).

[8]This age is conveniently calculated by adding twenty-one to the age of the youngest child when wait and see ceases to be effective: Gosse, Ontario's Perpetuities Legislation (Toronto, Carswell, 1967), p. 39.

[9]Alta. Act, s. 6(3); B.C. Act, s. 7(3); Yukon Ord., s. 7(3).

[10]In fact it is not in this example, since he is himself a measuring life.

what happens if D dies at age 27, survived only by two sisters, E and F, aged five and seven, A, B and C, having died two years earlier? Should one reduce D's age retrospectively to 23 so that his estate can take, or should one reduce E's age and, if E dies before she reaches the reduced age, then F's age, or should E's and F's ages be reduced together? The Ontario Act and the Northwest Territories Ordinance do not make provision for this situation. It is probable that a staged reduction is required under those enactments as to E and F. However, the solution is not at all apparent.[11] It should be noted further that under these enactments the potential beneficiaries would be measuring lives, but C and D would not, since this is not a class gift.[12] Hence, unless one were to reduce the age for D retrospectively, the age reduction, either staged or simultaneous, would have to occur at, or as of, the death of A and B.

The Alberta and British Columbia Acts and the Yukon Ordinance make specific provision for this situation. They provide that one age reduction to embrace all potential beneficiaries is to be made.[13] In the above example that would mean that the age reduction would take place at the death of D, a measuring life under those statutes, and it would be reduced to 26 for both E and F (21 plus five, the age of the youngest sister). The provision does not take into account the unfairness of this result to D, however, who reached an age greater than the reduced age, but whose estate cannot take simply because he was a measuring life.

Further examples of age reduction will be found in the next subparagraph.

(c) Class splitting

Under the common law rule, a class gift had to be able to vest within the perpetuity period in its entirety. If the interests of some members might vest outside the period, even though the interests of other members would vest in time, the gift was wholly void.[14] The statutes, however, provide that in such a situation the class may be split, by excluding those persons whose interests do not in fact vest in time.[15]

As at common law, the class closing rules are permitted to operate first and they may save the gift.[16] Under the statutes one then uses the wait and see principle and the age reduction provision. After that class splitting is permitted.

The following examples illustrate the use of this device:

---

[11] See further on this point Oosterhoff and Cudmore, "Problems in Ascertaining Lives in Being under Ontario's Perpetuities Act (On Limiting Lives and Relevant Factors)", 4 E. & T. Q. 119 (1977), at pp. 130 *et seq.*; Prichard, "Two Petty Perpetuity Puzzles", 27 Camb. L.J. 284 (1969), at pp. 287 *et seq.*

[12] See §1107.4(b), *supra.*

[13] Alta. Act, s. 6(2); B.C. Act, s. 7(2); Yukon Ord., s. 7(2).

[14] See §1104.6, *supra.*

[15] Alta. Act, s. 7; B.C. Act, s. 8; Ont. Act, s. 8(2)-(4); N.W.T. Ord., s. 9(2)-(4); Yukon Ord., s. 8.

[16] See §1104.6(b), *supra.*

(1) A devise, "to the grandchildren of A who marry".

At the testator's death, A, his children, B, C and D, and two grand-children, E and F, both unmarried, are living. Subsequently, three further grandchildren, X, Y and Z are born. Thereafter E marries.

The class will not close until the first grandchild marries. Hence the class closing rules will not save the gift. A, B, C, D, E and F are all measuring lives. Clearly, the gift to E and F will vest, if at all, during their lives. Whether the interests of X, Y and Z will be valid depends upon whether they marry within twenty-one years of the death of the last survivor of the measuring lives. Those who have not will be excluded.

(2) A bequest, "to A for life, remainder to A's children at age 25, and if any child of A dies under that age his share shall go to his issue who attain the age of 25".

A is alive at the testator's death, but has no children. When he dies, he has two children, B and C, aged 22 and three, respectively, and two grandchildren, X and Y, aged four and two.

This is a gift to a composite class. Using wait and see, only B's interest can vest in time. Using the age reduction provision at A's death, the age for the children and grandchildren is reduced to 23 (twenty-one plus two, the age of the youngest grandchild). Unborn children are excluded.

If, in the above example, B and C were three and one, respectively, at A's death, the age would be reduced to 22 (twenty-one plus one), and the grand-children, all unborn, would be excluded.

(d) The unborn spouse

Under the common law rule the remainder interest in the following gift would be void, because the widow might be unborn at the testator's death:

A devise, "to A for life, then to any wife he may marry for life, remainder to such of their children as are then living".

Statutes in different jurisdictions have provided different remedies for this situation. The Ontario Act and the Northwest Territories Ordinance deem the spouse to be a measuring life, but only after allowing the wait and see principle to operate.[17] The Alberta and British Columbia Acts and the Yukon Ordinance include the spouse as a measuring life in their statutory lists.[18] Both of these solutions are awkward, since they require the addition, after the fact, of a measuring life who is unascertained at the time the interest is created. This renders the operation of wait and see more difficult.

---

[17]Ont. Act, s. 9; N.W.T. Ord., s. 10. The Ontario Act defines "spouse" to include a person who cohabited with another person of the opposite sex immediately before that other person's death, continuously for not less than five years, or in a relationship of some permanence where a child is born to them.

[18]Alta. Act, s. 5(2)(e); B.C. Act, s. 6(2)(e); Yukon Ord., s. 6(2)(e). See §1107.4(a)(i). *supra*.

The English Act, on the other hand, does not add the spouse as a measuring life, but instead reforms the instrument by providing that, if the interests are not vested at the end of the perpetuity period in this situation, the disposition is to be treated as if it had been limited to vest at the end of the period. This is a preferable solution.[19] The same result could be achieved under the general *cy-près* provisions of the Alberta and British Columbia Acts and the Yukon Ordinance, discussed in the next subparagraph, without the addition of the unborn spouse as a measuring life.

(e) General cy-près

A number of jurisdictions have included in their statutes a general power, which becomes operative after wait and see and other specific remedies. Alberta, British Columbia and the Yukon are the Canadian jurisdictions in this category. The British Columbia Act provides:

> 9(1) Where it has become apparent that, apart from the provisions of this section, a disposition would be void solely on the ground that it infringes the rule against perpetuities, and where the general intention originally governing the disposition can be ascertained in accordance with the normal principles of interpretation of instruments and the rules of evidence, the disposition may, on application to the court by an interested person, be varied so as to give effect as far as possible to the general intention within the limits of the rule against perpetuities.
>
> (2) Subsection (1) does not apply where the disposition of the property has been the subject of a valid compromise.[20]

It is essential that this provision not become applicable (and the above by its terms does not) until after wait and see and other specific remedies, since the court would otherwise be given an unlimited discretion and choice. Because of these several remedies, it is unlikely that the general *cy-près* power will have to be relied upon often. However, there may be situations in which it is apposite. Thus, for example, where a testator gives a sum of money "upon trust to pay the income to the children of A for their lives and then upon trust for A's grandchildren who attain the age of 30", it might be possible to give the corpus to the life tenants absolutely if the gift to the grandchildren would fail under wait and see, age reduction and class splitting. This might be more appropriate than to let the property result to the estate, whence it would pass on an intestacy to the testator's remote next of kin.[21] On the other hand, if the gift is to the testator's descendants and fails for perpetuity, letting the property go on an intestacy would not be inappropriate.

(f) Order of applying remedies

The language of the statutes leaves no doubt as to the order in which the

---

[19]*Cf.* Maudsley, pp. 147-8.

[20]The Alta. Act, s. 8, and Yukon Ord., s. 20, are to the same effect, but do not provide expressly that the instrument is to be reformed by the court. That is undoubtedly intended, however.

[21]The example is based on Maudsley's, p. 231.

remedies should be applied. Out of an abundance of caution, however, the Alberta and British Columbia Acts and Yukon Ordinance make specific provision for it. The order under those statutes is: the capacity to have children, wait and see, age reduction, class splitting, and general *cy-près*.[22] The order under the Ontario Act and the Northwest Territories Ordinance is the same, except that the unborn spouse provision (included in the list of measuring lives in Alberta and British Columbia and the Yukon)[23] takes the place of the general *cy-près* provision, which the Ontario and Northwest Territories legislation do not have.[24]

1107.6 Interim Income

The problem of what to do with interim income from a valid contingent gift has not been adequately dealt with by the law. In certain circumstances it may be accumulated; in others it is treated as undisposed of. Of course, if the testator foresees the difficulty and disposes of the interim income there is no problem.

At common law, where an interest was limited to a minor, or was contingent, the trustees had no power to make advancements of capital to the beneficiary. Nor could they pay the interim income to him by way of maintenance. The court did exercise a very limited power to vary a trust by allowing maintenance payments. However, the power was sparingly exercised.

In *Re Wright*,[1] the testator left a large sum of money to a child, but postponed payment until age 30, for "reasons personal to the legatee". The court held that where the testator has provided for his family, but has postponed payment in such circumstances, it should be assumed that he did not intend that his children should be left unprovided for. Having given them such a large fortune, he must have intended that they should be enabled to receive an appropriate education to prepare them to manage their fortune, and in those circumstances, the court may direct that they be paid maintenance for that purpose.[2]

Because of the limited jurisdiction of the court in this respect, it is common to empower trustees of family trusts to apply the income from the trust for the maintenance of minors and to make advancements of capital to beneficiaries who have a contingent interest only. Where no power of maintenance is conferred, the interim income is undisposed of.

In some jurisdictions there are now statutory powers of maintenance and advancement, which operate in the absence of a contrary intention in the will.[3]

22Alta. Act, s. 11; B.C. Act, s. 12; Yukon Ord., s. 12.
23See §1107.4(a) and sub-subpara. (c), *supra*.
24See Gosse, *Ontario's Perpetuities Legislation* (Toronto, Carswell, 1967), p. 16.
§1107.6
1[1954] O.R. 755, [1955] 1 D.L.R. 213 (H.C.J.).
2See also *Chapman v. Chapman*, [1954] A.C. 429 (H.L.).
3*Trustee Act, 1925*, 15 & 16 Geo. 5, c. 19, ss. 31, 32; *Trustee Act*, R.S.P.E.I. 1974, c. T-9, ss. 39, 40; R.S.M. 1970, c. T160, s. 31 am. S.M. 1971, c. 82, s. 57, and s. 32.

In several of the Canadian provinces there is only a statutory power of maintenance, however.[4] Ontario does not have either power.[5]

The powers of maintenance and advancement, whether statutory or express, could not be exercised where the interest was void for perpetuity.[6] However, with the introduction of wait and see, the question of what to do with the intermediate income of a gift which is now presumptively valid until actual events show it to be invalid, became important. The several statutes provide that such income, if not otherwise disposed of, shall be treated as income arising from a valid contingent interest.[7]

This enactment presents difficulties, however. The question is what can be done with the income until the interest either vests or is destroyed? In jurisdictions in which there are wide powers of maintenance and advancement[8] the problem is somewhat less difficult in that the trustees there may make payments to or for the benefit of infant beneficiaries. Nor will there be a problem to the extent that the intermediate income has been disposed of, as where it is given to a prior life tenant. But where it has not been disposed of, or where there is surplus income, it must be dealt with otherwise.

It has been suggested that it must be accumulated.[9] A contingent gift does not, in all cases, carry the intermediate income, however, and where it does not, there can be no implied accumulation.[10] In those circumstances the income is, therefore, undisposed of and goes out on an intestacy. If the income or the surplus income is accumulated, then that can only be done for the period permitted by the statutory restrictions on accumulations in those jurisdictions in which there are such restrictions.[11] Subsequent income will be treated as undisposed of.

1107.7 Expectant Interests

At common law, limitations that are expectant or dependent upon a limitation that is void for remoteness are void.[1] Thus, the ultimate limitation in the

---

[4]*Trustee Act*, R.S.A. 1980, c. T-10, s. 33 and s. 36; R.S.B.C. 1979, c. 414, ss. 24-26; R.S.N. 1970, c. 380, s. 27 am. S.N. 1971, c. 4, s. 2; R.S.S. 1978, c. T-23, ss. 52-55; *Trustee Ordinance*, R.O.N.W.T. 1974, c. T-8, ss. 29, 30; R.O.Y.T. 1971, c. T-5, ss. 32, 33. The foregoing enactments are based on *Lord Cranworth's Act*, 23 & 24 Vict., c. 145, s. 26 (1860). The following are based on the *Conveyancing Act*, 44 & 45 Vict., c. 41, s. 43 (1881): *Trustees Act*, R.S.N.B. 1973, c. T-15, s. 14; *Trustee Act*, R.S.N.S. 1967, c. 317, s. 29.

[5]See further on this point, Waters, pp. 777 *et seq.*

[6]*Pilkington v. Inland Revenue Com'rs*, [1964] A.C. 612 (H.L.); *Re Hastings-Bass*; *Hastings-Bass v. Inland Revenue Com'rs*, [1975] Ch. 25 (C.A.).

[7]Alta. Act, s. 12; B.C. Act, s. 13; Ont. Act, s. 5(2); N.W.T. Ord., s. 6(2); Yukon Ord., s. 13.

[8]Many of the Canadian powers are defective in this respect. See Waters, *loc. cit.*, footnote 5.

[9]Sheard, "Perpetuities — the New Proposed Act", 14 Chitty's L.J. 3 (1966), at p. 5; Gosse, *Ontario's Perpetuities Legislation* (Toronto, Carswell, 1967), p. 20.

[10]See on this point §1108.1(b), *infra.*

[11]See §§1108 *et seq., infra.*

§1107.7

[1]See §1104.8(c), *supra.*

first of the following two examples would be void. The one in the second example might be valid if it could be argued that it was not dependent.

(1) A devise, "to X's grandchildren at age 25 and in default of such grand-children, to Y".

(2) A devise, "to X's grandchildren at age 25 for their lives, and then to Y".

Under the statutes, the gifts to X's grandchildren, while void at common law, may now be saved by wait and see, age reduction and class splitting. If none are born within twenty-one years of the death of the measuring lives, however, the gifts will fail.

The gifts to Y can now take effect, however. The statutes provide that if they are not themselves void for perpetuity, they can take effect. Moreover, the statutes permit the ultimate gifts to be accelerated.[2] They do not require acceleration. The reason is that, while in the above examples, Y's interest ought to be able to take effect retrospectively as of the testator's death as soon as it is determined that the prior limitations are void, Y's interest should not accelerate so long as it is contingent.[3]

1107.8 Powers of Appointment

It will be recalled that not only may an appointment under a power be void for perpetuity, the power itself may be void as well at common law.[1] For both purposes, the law draws a distinction between general and special powers. Because it is sometimes difficult to distinguish between them, the statutes have codified the classification.

Under the several statutes,[2] a power is general if it is exercisable by one person only and can be exercised by him at any time, when of full age and capacity, to immediately transfer to himself the whole of the interest governed by the power, without the consent of any other person or compliance with any condition other than a formal condition relating to the mode of execution of the power.

All other powers of appointment are special. However, for the purpose of determining whether an appointment under a power exercisable by will only is void for perpetuity, the power is treated as a general power. This is because the donee cannot appoint to himself. As regards the validity of such a power itself, however, the power is special. A discretionary trust contains a special power.[3]

Appointments under both types of power are presumptively valid under the

---

[2]Alta. Act, s. 13; B.C. Act, s. 14; Ont. Act, s. 10(2); N.W.T. Ord., s. 11(2); Yukon Ord., s. 14.

[3]See. *e.g.*, *Re Young's Settlement Trust*; *Royal Exchange Ass'ce v. Taylor-Young*, [1959] 1 W.L.R. 457 (Ch.); Morris and Leach, Suppl., p. 14.

§1107.8

[1]See §1104.7, *supra.*

[2]B.C. Act, s. 15; Alta. Act, s. 14; Ont. Act, s. 11; N.W.T. Ord., s. 12; Yukon Ord., s. 15.

[3]*McPhail v. Doulton*, [1971] A.C. 424 (H.L.).

wait and see provisions of the several statutes,[4] and the several specific statutory remedies already discussed[5] apply to such appointments as well.

It was necessary, however, to make specific provision for the validity of the powers themselves. The several statutes do so by providing that:

(a) a disposition conferring a general power of appointment, which would have been void at common law because it might be exercisable beyond the perpetuity period, is presumptively valid until actual events establish that it cannot be exercised in time; and

(b) a disposition conferring a special power of appointment which would have been void at common law because it might be exercised beyond the perpetuity period, is presumptively valid and becomes void only to the extent that it is not exercised within the period.[6]

Thus, the statutes apply wait and see to powers of appointment as well.

It should be noted that the Ontario and Northwest Territories statutes, when dealing with special powers, speak of "any power, option or other right, other than a general power of appointment".[7] This language was copied in part from the English Act.[8] It would appear that the words "option or other right" are unnecessary because these interests are dealt with elsewhere in those statutes.[9]

The following examples illustrate the operation of the legislation:

(1) A devise, "to A for life, remainder to A's eldest son for life, remainder as A's eldest son after his marriage may appoint".
    At the testator's death A is living, but has no son as yet.

At common law the general power in favour of A's eldest son was void, since the son might not marry for more than twenty-one years after A's death.

Under the statutes, the power will be presumed to be valid and only becomes void if A's eldest son has not exercised the power within the perpetuity period, that is, twenty-one years after A's death.

If A's eldest son does exercise the power within the period, the appointment is treated as a disposition made by him at that time, because he is regarded as the owner. This is because he can appoint to himself. Hence, for the purpose of the validity of the appointment, the perpetuity period begins to run when the son appoints.

---

[4]See §1107.2, *supra.*

[5]In §1107.5, *supra.*

[6]Alta. Act, s. 4(2), (3); B.C. Act, s. 5(2), (3); Ont. Act, s. 4(2), (3); N.W.T. Ord., s. 5(2), (3); Yukon Ord., s. 5(2), (3). For the application of the similar English provision to a power to distribute a fund among employees, see *Re Thomas Meadows & Co. Ltd. and Subsidiary Companies (1960) Staff Pension Scheme Rules*; *Fetherston v. Thomas Meadows & Co. Ltd.*, [1970] 3 W.L.R. 524 (Ch.).

[7]Ont. Act, s. 4(3); N.W.T. Ord., s. 5(3).

[8]Eng. Act, s. 3(3).

[9]Gosse, *Ontario's Perpetuities Legislation* (Toronto, Carswell, 1967), p. 18; Morris and Leach, Suppl., pp. 7-8.

(2) A devise, "to A for life, remainder to A's children for their lives, remainder as the survivor of A's children may appoint among the issue of A".

A is alive but has no children at the testator's death.

At common law the special power is void since it is exercisable beyond the perpetuity period, that is, twenty-one years after the death of A. Any appointment under the power would necessarily be void as well.

Under the statutes the power is presumptively valid. It will be void only to the extent that it is not exercised within the perpetuity period. Thus, if the survivor of A's children dies within twenty-one years of A's death and appoints to his issue at age 30, the power is valid.

As to the validity of the appointment, this must be read back into the testator's will, for under special powers, the period, as regards the validity of the appointment, runs from the date that this power is created.[10] It will be apparent that the above appointment is void, assuming that A is the only measuring life, except as to A's issue who reach age 30, or a reduced age under the section governing age reduction,[11] within twenty-one years of A's death.

Under the statutes it is not necessary to have regard to the common law "second look" doctrine, under which facts existing at the date of the appointment may be taken into account.[12] That doctrine is contained in the wait and see principle.[13]

It should be noted that the British Columbia Act has a special provision respecting special powers in connection with its eighty-year alternative perpetuity period. Under the Act, an interest created under an appointment made under a special power is deemed to have been created when the power was created for the purpose of the eighty-year period.[14]

1107.9 Administrative Powers

In most well-drawn trusts, the trustees are given powers of disposition, including powers of sale, exchange and lease. If the power is unrestricted as to time, it has been held that it is void, even though it is attached to a trust which is itself valid.

Thus, in *Re Allott; Hanmer v. Allott*,[1] the testator devised land in trust to A for life, then to her widower for life, remainder to A's children at age 21. He further gave the trustees the power to lease at any time. The remainder was valid at common law, but the trust to lease was held void, because it could

---

[10]See §1104.7(c)(ii), *supra*. The P.E.I. Act, s. 2, specifically so provides.
[11]See §1107.5(b), *supra*.
[12]See §1107.7(c)(ii), *supra*.
[13]Maudsley, p. 165.
[14]B.C. Act, s. 3(2).
§1107.9
[1][1924] 2 Ch. 498 (C.A.).

be exercised during the lifetime of A's widower, who might not be a life in being.

Since the purpose of such an administrative power is to facilitate the disposition of land, the policy of the rule is not infringed.[2] For this reason most modern statutes have provided that the rule does not apply to administrative powers. The Canadian statutes do so as well and provide, moreover, that the rule does not apply to an authorized payment to the trustees or other persons of reasonable remuneration for their services.[3] Furthermore, the statutes do not limit the provision to cases where the power is attached to a valid trust. Hence the rule does not, under the statutes, apply to administrative powers attached to a trust the beneficial interests of which are void, nor to a case where the power does not arise until a remote future event.

In all of the Canadian statutes this provision is made retroactive, so that it applies also to administrative powers under instruments taking effect before the statutes come into force.

1107.10 Contracts, Options and Commercial Transactions

In the discussion of this topic under the common law rule,[1] it was seen that:

(1) A mere personal contract, unconnected with property, is not subject to the rule.

(2) A contract connected with property, such as an option, is subject to the rule and, in Canada, although not in England, is unenforceable as between the contracting parties and their successors if it exceeds the perpetuity period.

(3) An option in a lessee to purchase the reversion is subject to the rule.

(4) An option to renew a lease, even if perpetual, held by the lessee, is not subject to the rule.

(5) A right of first refusal, a right of pre-emption and similar rights are not subject to the rule.

The Canadian statutes do not deal with the first point, nor was it necessary that they do so.

(a) Enforceability of contracts

As to the second point, the Canadian statutes all codify the Canadian rule. They do so in different ways, however. The Ontario Act, in its section dealing with options in gross of land, incorporates a provision that contracts connected with property are unenforceable as between the contracting parties and their successors if the contract is exercisable beyond the perpetuity period.[2] The

---

[2]Leach, "Powers of Sale in Trustees and the Rule Against Perpetuities", 47 Harv. L. Rev. 948 (1933-34).

[3]Alta. Act, s. 15; B.C. Act, s. 16; Ont. Act, s. 12; N.W.T. Ord., s. 13; Yukon Ord., s. 16.

§1107.10

[1]See §1104.18, *supra.*

[2]Ont. Act, s. 13(3). *Cf.* N.W.T. Ord., s. 14(3) to the same effect.

British Columbia Act does so as well, but its "options in gross" section is not in fact restricted to options but extends to other commercial transactions.[3] The Alberta Act and Yukon Ordinance rightly, it is submitted, deal with the point in a separate section.[4] The non-enforceability of such contracts is, or should be, the rule in respect of all commercial transactions which may be exercised too remotely.[5]

Presumably the rule regarding contracts other than options in gross of land in Ontario and the Northwest Territories is the same, but it is a common law rule, not a statutory one.

(b) Leases

All of the Canadian statutes reverse the rule stated in point (3) and codify the rule stated in point (4) above.[6] As to the reversal of the rule that an option in a lessee to purchase the reversion is subject to the rule, it should be noted that that tended to avoid the policy of the rule. It had the effect of making land unproductive and resulted in non-repair. The new statutory rule encourages a lessee who has an option, a right of first refusal or a right of pre-emption to purchase the reversion to make the land productive and to effect the necessary repairs.[7]

Under the statutes, the option to purchase must be exercisable only by the lessee or his successors in title and the option must not be exercisable more than one year after the termination of the lease.

The Alberta and British Columbia Acts and Yukon Ordinance specifically provide that the new rules extend to leases of real as well as of personal property. This would seem appropriate in view of the many forms of lease-purchase agreements with respect to personal property. The same result might be obtained under the other statutes, although it is doubtful that they were intended to extend to personal property. On the other hand, it may be that the general wait and see provision is applicable to leases of personal property.

(c) Rights of first refusal and similar rights

The Alberta, British Columbia and Yukon statutes reverse the rule stated in point (5) above.[8] The other statutes do not deal with it, except that in the context of special powers of appointment to which wait and see is applied, they speak of "any power, option or other right".[9] It is doubtful that this is

---

[3] B.C. Act, s. 18.
[4] Alta. Act, s. 16; Yukon Ord., s. 17.
[5] *Cf.* Institute of Law Research and Reform, University of Alberta, *Report on the Rule Against Perpetuities* (Edmonton, 1971), p. 47.
[6] Alta. Act, s. 17; B.C. Act, s. 17; Ont. Act, s. 13(1), (2), (4); N.W.T. Ord., s. 14(1), (2), (4); Yukon Ord., s. 18.
[7] Morris and Leach, p. 225.
[8] Alta. Act, s. 18(2); B.C. Act, s. 18(2); Yukon Ord., s. 19(2).
[9] Ont. Act, s. 4(3); N.W.T. Ord., s. 5(3). See further on this point, §1107.8, at footnotes 7 and 8, *supra*.

intended to refer to rights of first refusal and pre-emptive rights, because if that were the case, it is totally out of context.

(d) Options in gross

Options in gross are those not given to a lessee. The statutes all deal with these, but in quite different ways.

The Alberta, British Columbia and Yukon statutes deal with options in gross and other contractual rights, including contracts for a future sale or lease, rights of first refusal and of pre-emption, and future easements, *profits à prendre* and restrictive covenants in the same way.[10] In the first place, the contractual right of whatever type is made subject to the rule, whether the contract is with respect to land or personal property. The statutes are curiously drafted in that it is difficult to see how one may acquire an easement, restrictive covenant or profit in or over personal property. Nevertheless, the intention of the legislation is clear.

In the second place, in recognition of the fact that in commercial transactions measuring lives have no relevance, these three statutes draw a distinction between options and other rights that may be created by will or *inter vivos* trust and by contract. The sections only apply to the latter. The former are governed by the general provisions of the statutes and, therefore, measuring lives may be used in those cases or, if none are used, the perpetuity period is the period in gross specified by the statutes.

As to the applicable perpetuity period for contractual rights, these three statutes provide for an eighty-year period and apply wait and see to that period. If the contract specifies a period in excess of eighty years, the right is valid if it exercised within the eighty-year period.

It should be noted that the Alberta Act and Yukon Ordinance are inconsistent in their treatment of the perpetuity period as regards options. Those that are created by will to which no measuring lives are applicable must be exercised within twenty-one years.[11] Under the British Columbia Act the period is eighty years in both cases.[12] Furthermore, under the Alberta and Yukon legislation it is probable that only options created by will or *inter vivos* trust, not other, similar rights, are subject to the rule against perpetuities as modified by statute. In British Columbia such other rights, at least in land, are equated with options.[13]

The comparable sections in the other Canadian statutes are restricted to options in land only and the applicable perpetuity period is twenty-one years, which seems excessively short. Wait and see is applicable to the period and if the option is, by its terms, exercisable beyond the twenty-one-year period, it is valid if exercised within the twenty-one years.[14] No distinction is drawn in

---

[10]Alta. Act, s. 18; B.C. Act, s. 18; Yukon Ord., s. 19.
[11]Alta. Act, s. 5(1)(b); Yukon Ord., s. 6(1)(b).
[12]B.C. Act, s. 6(1)(b).
[13]*Property Law Act*, R.S.B.C. 1979, c. 340, s. 9.
[14]Ont. Act, s. 13(3); N.W.T. Ord., s. 14(3).

these statutes between options created by contract on the one hand and those created by will or *inter vivos* trust on the other. All of the Canadian statutes only apply, however, to options (and similar interests in Alberta, British Columbia and the Yukon) for valuable consideration. An option conferred by will may or may not require payment. All options in land for valuable consideration, therefore, can only be exercised within twenty-one years from the time the instrument creating them takes effect in Ontario and the Northwest Territories.[15]

It would seem that for all other options the period in these jurisdictions is that fixed elsewhere in the statutes, namely, measuring lives plus twenty-one years or, if there are no measuring lives, twenty-one years.

1107.11 Easements, Profits à Prendre and Restrictive Covenants

At common law the rule against perpetuities was held to apply to easements, *profits à prendre* and rent charges if they might arise at too remote a date in the future, although restrictive covenants were not within the rule.[1]

It is arguable that if contingent easements should be subject to the rule, restrictive covenants should be also.[2] The Alberta and British Columbia Acts provide accordingly that future *profits à prendre*, easements and restrictive covenants, if created by contract instead of by will or *inter vivos* trust, are subject to the rule.[3] The perpetuity period applicable to such interests is eighty years and wait and see is applicable to the period.

In addition, British Columbia makes a separate, but similar, provision for "the grant of an easement, profit-à-prendre or other similar interest" not referred to in the previous section. Presumably this can only refer to such interests if they are not for valuable consideration, because the previous section is restricted to the latter. The separate provision does not apply to such interests arising under a will or *inter vivos* trust. Whether restrictive covenants are included in the term "or other similar interest" is unclear.[4]

The statutes in the other provinces also apply the rule to an easement, profit, "or other similar interest", but impose a forty-year period instead.[5] Whether restrictive covenants are intended to be included is questionable.

---

[15]See *Marcrob Estates Ltd. v. Servedio* (1977), 1 R.P.R. 344 (Ont. C.A.), at p. 351.

§1107.11

[1]See §1104.20, *supra*.

[2]See Battersby, "Easements and the Rule Against Perpetuities", 25 Convey. (N.S.) 415 (1961).

[3]Alta. Act, s. 18(2), (3); B.C. Act, s. 18(2), (3); Yukon Ord., s. 19(2), (3).

[4]B.C. Act, s. 19.

[5]Ont. Act, s. 14; N.W.T. Ord., s. 15. The forty-year period appears to have been selected in Ontario because it coincides with the period for which a search of title must be conducted under the *Registry Act*, R.S.O. 1980, c. 445, Part III. See Leal, "The Perpetuities Act — An Ontario Proposal", *Law Society of Upper Canada Special Lectures, Recent Developments in the Law* (Toronto, R. de Boo Ltd., 1966), p. 291, at p. 311, note 41.

These statutes draw no distinction between the creation of such interests by contract or by will or *inter vivos* trust.

1107.12 Possibilities of Reverter and Rights of Entry for Conditions Broken

In the discussion of the common law rule, it was seen that that rule applied to rights of entry (or re-entry) for conditions broken, but did not apply to possibilities of reverter.[1] Neither concept is technically an interest in property, but a mere possibility. If they are considered to be interests in property, however, they can be regarded as vested and then the rule against perpetuities (that is, the rule against remoteness of vesting) ought to have no application to them. On the other hand, they do have the effect of tying up property for an indefinite period of time. It is, therefore, appropriate that that time be limited and that the same rule apply to both types of interest.[2]

Similar interests may be created in real and personal property under a trust. In the latter case, they are resulting trusts. By the same logic, such interests might arguably be subject to the rule, but this can cause some strange consequences as will be seen.

All of the Canadian statutes make similar provisions for these several interests. Thus all provide that a possibility of reverter and the possibility of a resulting trust on the determination of any determinable interest in real or personal property is subject to the rule as modified by the statutes in the same way as a right of entry or an equitable right in personal property is subject thereto. Wait and see is applicable and if the determining event occurs beyond the perpetuity period, the determinable interest becomes absolute and the determining event is disregarded, just as a condition subsequent would be disregarded.[3]

The perpetuity period in the several statutes applicable to such interests differs, however. Under the Alberta Act and Yukon Ordinance it is forty years for all such interests. Under the British Columbia Act it is the same period specified for contingent interests generally, namely, measuring lives plus twenty-one years, or eighty years if there are no applicable measuring lives.

The other statutes use a more complicated formula, namely, twenty-one years if no lives are relevant, or measuring lives plus twenty-one years to a maximum of forty years.

The following examples will illustrate the operation of the latter formula:

(1) A grant, "to A so long as the land is used for residential purposes".

This grant creates a determinable fee and the grantor retains a possibility

---

§1107.12

[1]See §§1104.15, 1104.16, *supra*.

[2]Ontario Law Reform Commission, *Report No. 1* (Toronto, 1965), pp. 31 *et seq.*; Institute of Law Research and Reform, University of Alberta, *Report on the Rule Against Perpetuities* (Edmonton, 1971), pp. 55 *et seq.*

[3]Alta. Act, s. 19; B.C. Act, s. 20; Ont. Act, s. 15; N.W.T. Ord., s. 16; Yukon Ord., s. 20.

of reverter. He may recover the land if it is used for other than residential purposes within twenty-one years. If that does not happen within twenty-one years, A's interest becomes absolute.

(2) A grant, "to A provided that the land is not used for commercial purposes during B's lifetime".

This grant creates a fee upon condition subsequent and the grantor retains a right of entry. He may re-enter if the land is used for commercial purposes within twenty-one years of B's death or forty years after the creation of the interest, whichever is shorter. If it does not happen within that time, A's interest becomes absolute.

(3) A bequest, "to my trustees to pay the income to the Forest Lawn Cemetery Company so long as it maintains my family mausoleum in perpetuity".

This bequest gives rise to a resulting trust if the company fails to do what is required. However, if it does not cease to do so for twenty-one years after the testator's death, it becomes entitled to the trust fund absolutely.

It is submitted that the reform breaks down in situations such as this. It is not indefensible to give the grantee under a private land use planning scheme, created by a determinable fee or a fee upon condition subsequent, or under a trust, an absolute interest after a certain period of time. The character of the neighbourhood may have changed by then. Similarly, it is not inappropriate to give the beneficiary under a trust "so long as he remains a Canadian resident" an absolute interest after a specified period. It is quite a different matter, however, to give the cemetery company in example (3) the absolute interest.

The gift in example (3) is, of course, one for a non-charitable purpose and the several statutes make special provision for those. In some circumstances they are allowed to take effect for twenty-one years, after which a statutory equivalent of a resulting trust arises.[4] Whether a gift such as that in example (3) will be dealt with under those provisions rather than under the sections dealing with possibilities of reverter and conditions subsequent, is debatable. It should be dealt with under the former.

Similar problems may occur where the purpose for which the property is given is charitable. The following example, again using the twenty-one–forty-year formula, illustrates the problem:

A bequest "to my trustees, to pay the income to Neighbourhood Improvements Ltd., provided that it uses the money to maintain the church where my family and I have been faithful members for many years".

The purpose of the gift is charitable. Yet, after twenty-one years the company would become entitled to the trust fund absolutely if it had maintained the church for twenty-one years. That this is inappropriate was recognized

---

[4]See §1107.13, *infra.*

in the Alberta, British Columbia and Yukon statutes, which provide that in such a case the money shall be applied *cy-près* to charitable purposes.[5]

Of course, under the other statutes, if the moneys are payable to a charity to be used for its purposes, there can be no objection to allowing the gift to become absolute.

It should be noted that none of the provisions respecting possibilities of reverter and rights of entry are concerned with situations in which there is a gift over upon the happening of the determinable event or condition. Those are governed by the other, general provisions of the statutes. It is, therefore, incongruous that the Alberta and British Columbia and Yukon statutes provide that the sections dealing with possibilities of reverter and rights of entry do not apply to a gift over from one charity to another.[6] Although this provision codifies the law, it is out of place.

1107.13 Specific Non-charitable Purpose Trusts

Save for certain anomalous exceptions, trusts for non-charitable purposes were void at common law, not under the rule against perpetuities, but under the rule against indefinite duration.[1] Although they are not charitable by definition and although they lack human beneficiaries to enforce them, the Canadian legislatures appear to have thought that such trusts are worthy of some protection. The Canadian statutes treat specific non-charitable purpose trusts as powers and allow them to be effective for twenty-one years, or such shorter period as the testator or settlor directs. The court is given power, however, to declare a perpetual non-charitable trust to be void if it is of the opinion that that would accord more closely with the testator's or settlor's intention. Unexpended income or capital at the end of the twenty-one years results to the estate.[2]

The reason why such trusts are treated as powers is to avoid the principles that a trust without a beneficiary is void[3] and that "a valid power is [not] to be spelt out of an invalid trust".[4]

The trust must be specific in order to avoid the problem that it may be struck down for uncertainty. That was the problem in *Re Astor's Settlement Trusts*,[5] which involved a trust for the maintaining of good understanding between nations, the preservation of the freedom and integrity of the press,

---

[5]Alta. Act, s. 19(3); B.C. Act, s. 20(2); Yukon Ord., s. 20(3).

[6]Alta. Act, s. 19(4); B.C. Act, s. 20(3); Yukon Ord., s. 20(4).

§1107.13

[1]See §§1106-1106.3, *supra*.

[2]Alta. Act, s. 20; B.C. Act, s. 21; Ont. Act, s. 16; N.W.T. Ord., s. 17; Yukon Ord., s. 21. The rule against indefinite duration has been abolished in Manitoba: *Perpetuities and Accumulations Act*, S.M. 1982-83, c. 43, ss. 1-3.

[3]*Re Astor's Settlement Trusts; Astor v. Scholfield*, [1952] Ch. 534.

[4]*Inland Revenue Com'rs v. Broadway Cottages Trust; Inland Revenue Com'rs v. Sunnylands Trust*, [1955] Ch. 20 at p. 36, *per* Jenkins, L.J.

[5]*Supra*, footnote 3, and *cf. Re Endacott; Corpe v. Endacott*, [1960] Ch. 232 (C.A.), trust "to provide some useful memorial to myself".

and similar purposes. Trusts to maintain the testator's animals, or his grave, are not uncertain. Hence, although logically the word "specific" should mean the opposite of "general", it is probable that the intended meaning is "certain" or "precise".[6]

This was the opinion expressed in *Re Russell; Wood v. The Queen,*[7] in which there was a bequest to the Edmonton Lodge of the Theosophical Society on trust for its "religious, literary and educational purpose". Applying the certainty test applicable to powers and discretionary trusts laid down in *McPhail v. Doulton*[8] by analogy, the court held those purposes to be uncertain and, hence, not specific.

Perhaps out of an abundance of caution the British Columbia statute provides that the section does not apply to any discretionary power to transfer a beneficial interest in property to a person by way of gift.[9] If this provision is designed to apply to a case such as *Re Denley's Trust Deed; Holman v. H.H. Martyn & Co. Ltd.,*[10] which involved a trust to maintain a sports ground for the employees of a company, with power in the trustees to permit others to use it, it does not seem appropriate for that purpose. Neither the employees nor such other persons are given a beneficial interest in the property. It is a purpose trust, but one which benefits certain persons indirectly. It was held valid because those persons could enforce it. Hence the rule that a purpose trust fails because it lacks beneficiaries to enforce it was circumvented.

1107.14   Abolition of the Rule in Whitby v. Mitchell

In the previous discussion of the rule in *Whitby v. Mitchell,*[1] it was seen that the rule is an unnecessary duplication and complication of the rule against perpetuities.[2] It was abolished elsewhere earlier and finally received its quietus in the several Canadian statutes as well.[3]

The Ontario section was amended to define "issue" for the purpose of the rule in *Whitby v. Mitchell* as including illegitimate offspring.[4] The amendment is inexplicable. The rule is not amended restrospectively to apply to such issue, but is abolished. It is, therefore, difficult to see what effect the amendment can have on a limitation to which the rule remains applicable, that is, one created before the abolition of the rule.

---

[6]*Re Endacott, supra,* footnote 5, at p. 247, *per* Lord Evershed, M.R.
[7](1977), 1 E.T.R. 285 (Alta. S.C.T.D.).
[8][1971] A.C. 424 (H.L.).
[9]B.C. Act, s. 21(3).
[10][1969] 1 Ch. 373.
§1107.14
[1](1889), 42 Ch. D. 494, affd 44 Ch. D. 85 (C.A.).
[2]See §§1105-1105.1, *supra.*
[3]Alta. Act, s. 21; B.C. Act, s. 2(2); Ont. Act, s. 17; N.W.T. Ord., s. 18; Yukon Ord., s. 22.
[4]By S.O. 1977, c. 40, s. 90(2), (3).

1107.15 Employee Benefit Trusts

Although the rule applies to all types of employee benefit trusts in England,[1] most of the Canadian provinces have enacted legislation based on a uniform act promulgated in 1954 by the Conference of Commissioners on Uniformity of Legislation in Canada designed to exempt such trusts from the rule, as well as from the statutory restraints on accumulations.[2] Many of these statutes were passed in the 1950s. They deem the rule and the restraints on accumulations never to have applied to such trusts.

The several jurisdictions which have since enacted perpetuities statutes have incorporated the enactment in those statutes.[3] The other provinces retain the provision in general legislation respecting property or trusts.[4] Prince Edward Island does not appear to have similar legislation.

The British Columbia Act extends the enactment to registered retirement savings plans and home ownership plans and to any property donated to a university or its foundation.[5] The latter would in most cases be charitable and thus would not be subject to the rule, unless it were subject to a gift over to a non-charity. In some cases, however, the gift might be for a non-charitable purpose and hence subject to the rule.

1107.16 Application to Crown

It is probable that the Crown was subject to the rule at common law, at least to a limited extent.[1] Only the Alberta, British Columbia and Yukon statutes specifically provide that the Crown is bound by the rule as modified by the Act. They make an important exception, however. The Crown is not bound in respect of dispositions of property.[2] This exception undoubtedly reflects the rule that Parliament can create interests which an individual cannot make and that the Crown has that power as an incident of its prerogative.[3]

---

§1107.15

[1] See, e.g., *Re Thomas Meadows & Co. Ltd. and Subsidiary Companies (1960) Staff Pension Scheme Rules*; *Fetherston v. Thomas Meadows & Co. Ltd.*, [1970] 3 W.L.R. 524 (Ch.).

[2] *Uniform Accumulations Act*, s. 5, Uniform Acts of the Uniform Law Conference of Canada (Toronto, Queen's Park, 1978), p. 1-2.

[3] Alta. Act, s. 22; B.C. Act, s. 22; Ont. Act, s. 18; N.W.T. Ord., s. 19; Yukon Ord., s. 23; Nfld. Act, s. 2.

[4] *Law of Property Act*, R.S.M. 1970, c. L90, s. 44, repealed by S.M. 1977, c. 57, s. 22; *Trustee Act*, R.S.N.S. 1967, c. 317, s. 65; *Queen's Bench Act*, R.S.S. 1978, c. Q-1, s. 45, para. 22; *Property Act*, R.S.N.B. 1973, c. P-19, s. 3.

[5] B.C. Act, s. 22(*b*), (*c*).

§1107.16

[1] See §1104.24, *supra*.

[2] Alta. Act, s. 23; B.C. Act, s. 23; Yukon Ord., s. 24.

[3] See further on this point, §§402.4, 405, *supra*.

1107.17 Applications to Court

Applications may be made to the court in respect of the applicability of the presumptions as to future parenthood.[1] The several statutes also contain a general section empowering an executor or trustee of property, or a person interested in the validity of an interest in the property, to make application to the court to determine the validity of an interest under the rule as modified by statute.[2] Whether such a section is necessary is doubtful. A similar right exists under the rules of the court to seek the opinion, advice and directions of the court.

1107.18 Application of Statutes

None of the statutes is retroactive,[1] except as regards administrative powers[2] and employee benefit trusts[3] and, in Alberta and British Columbia, as regards certain trusts for accumulation.[4] The common law rule and the rule in *Whitby v. Mitchell*,[5] therefore, continue to be relevant for instruments taking effect before the several statutes came into force.

This has relevance in the context of variation of trusts. The question may be asked whether a trust created before a statute takes effect, but which is varied thereafter, is subject to the common law rule, or the rule as modified by statute. It has been held in England that an arrangement to vary a trust, coupled with the court's order, constitutes an instrument as that term is defined in the English Act,[6] so that that Act would apply to it.[7] It is submitted that the same result would obtain under the Canadian statutes, although they do not speak of an "instrument", but of a "limitation"[8] or "disposition".[9]

1108. ACCUMULATIONS

An accumulation occurs when income is not distributed, but is added to the capital. Normally, an accumulation is, therefore, at compound interest. An accumulation also occurs, however, where income is directed to be added to

§1107.17
[1]See §1107.5(a), *supra*.
[2]Alta. Act, s. 10; B.C. Act, s. 11; Ont. Act, s. 5(1); N.W.T. Ord., s. 6(1); Yukon Ord., s. 11.
§1107.18
[1]Alta. Act, s. 25; B.C. Act, s. 25; Ont. Act, s. 19; N.W.T. Ord., s. 20; Yukon Ord., s. 25.
[2]See §1107.9, *supra*.
[3]See §1107.15, *supra*.
[4]*I.e.*, trusts for accumulation under which the interests have vested: Alta. Act, s. 24; B.C. Act, s. 24.
[5](1889), 42 Ch. D. 494, affd 44 Ch. D. 85 (C.A.).
[6]English Act, s. 15(5).
[7]*Re Holt's Settlement; Wilson v. Holt*, [1968] 1 All E.R. 470 (Ch.).
[8]Ont. Act, s. 1(*c*); N.W.T. Ord., s. 2(*b*).
[9]Alta. Act, s. 1(*b*); B.C. Act, s. 1; Yukon Ord., s. 2(1).

the capital, but the income from the income so added to the capital is distributed.[1] This is called a simple accumulation.

The various ways in which an accumulation may arise are discussed in the next section.

Express directions or powers to accumulate are usually included in discretionary trusts. They may also be used to generate capital to be passed on to a future generation.

The latter was the object of Peter Thellusson, a wealthy London banker. By his will he made more than adequate provision for his immediate family, but he gave the large residue of his estate on trust to invest and to accumulate the income during the lives of those of his sons, grandsons and great-grandsons who were living at his death or within the gestation period thereafter. After the death of the survivor, the fund was to be divided into three parts and settled on the eldest lineal male descendant then living of each of his three sons, provided they bore or took the name Thellusson. If there were no such descendants, the fund was to be given to the Crown to reduce the national debt.

The will caused a great outcry. It was thought to be unjust and heartless in that it tended to deprive the immediate family. In fact it did not do so. The will made ample provision for the family. It was also thought, however, that accumulation of income on this scale was improper in that it would tend to concentrate vast amounts of wealth in the hands of a few families. It was calculated, for example, that the accumulation of the original fund of six hundred thousand pounds might produce in seventy years (a rough guess of the duration of the accumulation) a sum exceeding twenty-three million pounds. In fact, it did nothing of the kind. As a result of mismanagement, the costs of litigation and petitions to Parliament to alter the will, only about fifty thousand pounds was realized when the fund became available for distribution in 1859.

The will was upheld by the courts in *Thellusson v. Woodford*.[2] The only restriction upon the creation of such a gift and direction, the courts held, was the rule against perpetuities. It will be observed that not only did the gift of the capital vest within the perpetuity period, but that the direction to accumulate also did not extend beyond that period. Hence it was valid.

As a result of the public outcry and the fears engendered by the will, Parliament passed the *Thellusson Act* in 1800.[3] This Act restricted the time during which accumulations could continue to one of four periods. These

---

§1108

[1] *Re Hawkins; White v. White*, [1916] 2 Ch. 570. *Cf. Re Fulford* (1926), 59 O.L.R. 440 (S.C. App. Div.).

[2] (1799), 4 Ves. Jun. 227, 31 E.R. 117, affd 11 Ves. Jun. 112, 32 E.R. 1030 (H.L.).

[3] *Accumulations Act*, 39 & 40 Geo. 3, c. 98 (1800). For a history of the will, the Act and the litigation, see Hargrave, *A Treatise on the Thellusson Act* (London, S. Sweet, 1842), esp. ch. 1. See also Barry, "Mr. Thellusson's Will", 22 Va. L. Rev. 416 (1935-36).

periods, which are substantially shorter than the perpetuity period, are discussed below.[4]

The Act was replaced in England by the equivalent provisions of section 165 of the *Law of Property Act, 1925*[5] and the latter were amended by the addition of two further accumulation periods by the *Perpetuities and Accumulations Act, 1964.*[6]

Under the rules for reception of English law in the Canadian provinces, the *Thellusson Act* was probably received in Newfoundland, Manitoba,[7] Alberta,[8] Saskatchewan,[9] British Columbia and the Territories. It would not have been received in the Maritime Provinces whose dates for reception predate the enactment of the Act.[10]

The *Thellusson Act* was re-enacted in British Columbia,[11] Ontario[12] and New Brunswick.[13] The English amendments of 1964 were enacted in British Columbia[14] and Ontario.[15] However, the legislation has since been repealed in British Columbia[16] and the *Thellusson Act* also no longer applies to Alberta[17] and Manitoba.[17a]

Prince Edward Island has a special rule which applies to accumulations. Its legislation provides that accumulations may continue for a period of lives in being plus sixty years. This is the same as its perpetuity period.[18]

It is doubtful that there are any restraints on accumulations in Nova Scotia. The *Thellusson Act* was not received in that province. However, it does have a statutory enactment which provides that the rule against perpetuities and the statutory enactments relating to accumulations do not apply to employee pension trusts.[19] It is submitted that, since this enactment is based on uniform legislation,[20] it does not introduce the *Thellusson Act* or any similar legislation by a side wind into that province.

---

[4]§1108.4, *infra.*

[5]15 & 16 Geo. 5, c. 20 (1925).

[6]C. 55, ss. 13, 14 (1964).

[7]*Fonseca v. Jones* (1911), 14 W.L.R. 148, 21 Man. R. 168 (C.A.); *Re Aikins Trusts* (1961), 35 W.W.R. 143 (Man. Q.B.).

[8]*Re Burns* (1960), 25 D.L.R. 427, 32 W.W.R. 689 (Alta. S.C. App. Div.).

[9]*Re Fossum Estate* (1960), 32 W.W.R. 372 (Sask. Q.B.).

[10]For the rules and the several dates of reception see ch. 3, *supra.*

[11]*Accumulations Restraint Act*, R.S.B.C. 1897, c. 2, re-enacted as the *Accumulations Act*, S.B.C. 1967, c. 2.

[12]*Accumulations Act*, R.S.O. 1897, c. 332.

[13]*Property Act*, C.S.N.B. 1903, c. 152, ss. 2, 3. See now *Property Act*, R.S.N.B. 1973, c. P-19, ss. 1, 2. Hereafter called "the N.B. Act".

[14]*Accumulations Act*, S.B.C. 1967, c. 2.

[15]*Accumulations Amendment Act*, S.O. 1966, c. 2. See now *Accumulations Act*, R.S.O. 1980, c. 5. The latter Act is hereafter called "the Ont. Act".

[16]*Perpetuities Act*, S.B.C. 1975, c. 53, s. 24(1). See now *Perpetuity Act*, R.S.B.C. 1979, c. 321, s. 24.

[17]*Perpetuities Act*, R.S.A. 1980, c. P-4, s. 24.

[17a]*Perpetuities and Accumulations Act*, S.M. 1982-83, c. 43, s. 2.

[18]*Perpetuities Act*, R.S.P.E.I. 1974, c. P-3, s. 1. Hereafter called "the P.E.I. Act".

[19]*Trustee Act*, R.S.N.S. 1967, c. 317, s. 65, first enacted by S.N.S. 1959, c. 43, s. 2.

[20]See §1107.15, *supra.*

1108.1 When an Accumulation Arises

(a) Trusts and powers to accumulate

An accumulation may be directed expressly and the statute will apply to such an accumulation. It was at one time questioned whether the statute also applies to a power to accumulate, but it was finally held that it does.[1] Certainly, from the point of view of the beneficiary, there is no difference in the result. Moreover, the statute does not regard the form of the disposition, but rather the result, so that if the income is accumulated beyond the permitted period, whether under a direction or a power, the disposition is to that extent unlawful.[2] Amendments to the statute in some jurisdictions now specifically provide that it applies to powers to accumulate.[3]

(b) Implied accumulations

An accumulation may also be implied. Such accumulations are also subject to the statute. Whether it is implied depends in the first instance upon a construction of the instrument. The problem normally arises where the testator or settlor has given annuities to certain persons which form a continuing charge on income, and the remainder is given to others after the death of the last annuitant, but the surplus income is not dealt with. The remainder interests may be vested absolutely or defeasibly, or they may be contingent. Moreover, the contingency may relate to the death of the surviving annuitant, or be unrelated to that event.

Some cases suggest that where the testator or settlor has not turned his mind to the possibility of any surplus income then it is undisposed of and, if the gift is of residue, goes out on an intestacy.[4] If the testator purports to dispose of the entire life interest and gives the remainder on a contingency, there can be no accumulation when the life tenants disclaim, because he has not turned his mind to that possibility. Thus, in *Re Scott; Widdows v. Friends of Clergy Corp.*[5] the testatrix bequeathed a fund to A and B for life and then to B's children at age 21, if male, or when they marry or at age 21, if female, and if there are no such children, to a charity. A and B disclaimed while B had no children. The income thus released was held undisposed of and could not be accumulated. The testatrix had not turned her mind to the problem. Moreover, because the two remainder interests were alternative contingent gifts, she had effectively denied the income to the charity until B's death without issue.

---

§1108.1

[1] *Re Robb; Marshall v. Marshall,* [1953] Ch. 459.
[2] *Baird v. Lord Advocate,* [1979] 2 W.L.R. 369 (H.L.).
[3] *Perpetuities and Accumulations Act,* 1964, c. 55 (U.K.), s. 13(2); *Accumulations Act,* S.B.C. 1967, c. 2, s. 4, repealed by S.B.C. 1975, c. 53, s. 24(1); Ont. Act, s. 1(2).
[4] See, *e.g., Re Baragar,* [1973] 1 O.R. 831, 32 D.L.R. (3d) 529 (H.C.J.); *Re Wragg; Hollingsworth v. Wragg,* [1959] 2 All E.R. 717 (C.A.); *Re Amodeo,* [1962] O.R. 548, 33 D.L.R. (2d) 24 (C.A.).
[5] [1975] 2 All E.R. 1033 (Ch.).

On the other hand, the language of the will, read in its context, may suggest an implied accumulation.[6] Moreover, other cases suggest that an implied accumulation arises whenever it is necessary, in order to carry out the purposes of the will, that there be an accumulation,[7] even though the testator never turned his mind to the possibility that there might be surplus income. Such a situation often arises where, because of the prevailing interest rates at the time the will is made, it is highly unlikely that there will be enough income for the annuitants, let alone any surplus income after the annuities are satisfied.[8]

An accumulation may only be implied if the interest carries the intermediate income. Whether it does or not depends upon the following *prima facie* rules, which may be ousted by a contrary intention:

(1) Neither a contingent nor a vested but deferred devise of real property carries the intermediate income whether the devise be specific or residuary. The reason is that an estate of freehold cannot be in abeyance.[9] The income, therefore, formerly went to the heir-at-law and now goes to the next of kin determined according to the statutory rules respecting distribution on an intestacy. If the gift is a blended contingent gift of residuary real and personal property, however, it carries the income.[10]

Today in England both contingent and deferred specific and residuary devises *prima facie* carry the intermediate income.[11]

(2) A contingent specific bequest does not carry the intermediate income unless it is separated from the estate and earmarked.[12] Similarly, a vested but deferred specific gift does not carry the intermediate income.[13]

In England both types of bequest now *prima facie* carry the intermediate income.[14]

(3) A residuary bequest which is vested absolutely, but is deferred until after the death of an annuitant, or a period of years, or for some other reason does not, in England, carry the intermediate income unless it is expressly given to the remainderman.[15] The same rule applies to a residuary bequest which is vested subject to divestment, as where there is a gift over in the event that the primary beneficiary is no longer living at the period of distribution.[16] Where

---

[6]*Re Geering; Gulliver v. Geering*, [1964] Ch. 136.
[7]*Tench v. Cheese* (1855), 6 De G. M. & G. 453 at pp. 461-2, 43 E.R. 1309, *per* Lord Cranworth, L.C.; *Moss's Trustees v. Bramwell*, [1935] S.C. 123, *per* Lord Thankerton; *Lord v. Colvin* (1860), 23 Dunl. (Ct. of Sess.) 111 at p. 136, *per* Lord Deas.
[8]*Re Struthers* (1980), 29 O.R. (2d) 616, 114 D.L.R. (3d) 492 (C.A.).
[9]*Countess of Bective v. Hodgson* (1864), 10 H.L.C. 656 at pp. 664-5, 11 E.R. 1181, *per* Lord Westbury, L.C.
[10]*Re Burton's Will; Banks v. Heaven*, [1892] 2 Ch. 38.
[11]*Law of Property Act, 1925*, 15 & 16 Geo. 5, c. 20, s. 175.
[12]*Re Woodin; Woodin v. Glass*, [1895] 2 Ch. 309 (C.A.).
[13]*Re McGeorge; Ratcliff v. McGeorge*, [1963] Ch. 544 at p. 551, *per* Cross, J.
[14]*Law of Property Act, 1925*, 15 & 16 Geo. 5, c. 20, s. 175.
[15]*Berry v. Geen*, [1938] A.C. 575 (H.L.); *Re Oliver; Watkins v. Fitton*, [1947] 2 All E.R. 162 (Ch.).
[16]*Re Gillett's Will Trusts; Barclays Bank Ltd. v. Gillett*, [1950] Ch. 102.

the residuary bequest is contingent and also deferred, the rule appears to be the same.[17]

It would appear that the rule in Canada, at any rate as regards residuary bequests which are vested subject to divestment, appears to be different. In *Re Hammond*[18] the Supreme Court of Canada held explicitly that such a bequest carried the intermediate income, so that an implied accumulation arose. This case was followed in a subsequent case by the court[19] and although it has been criticized, it appears to be good law. The criticisms were voiced in cases where the court was able to find an intention against an accumulation.[20]

(4) A contingent residuary bequest which is not deferred carries the intermediate income which must, therefore, be accumulated for the permitted period or until the bequest fails, unless there is a contrary intention. The rule is based on the probable intention of the testator that the income should follow the capital.[21]

(c) Accumulations required by law or by statute

At common law, where an infant has a vested interest in property any income not used for his maintenance will, in the absence of a contrary intention be directed by the court to be accumulated. The reason for such an order is that the infant cannot give a valid receipt. The statute does not apply to such an accumulation. The effect of this rule is that the testator may direct an accumulation, for example, for a period of twenty-one years from his death, after which the capital and accumulations are to be transferred to a specified person. If that person is then an infant (having been born after the testator's death), a further accumulation during his infancy will take place.[22]

The rule is otherwise if the beneficiary only had a contingent interest after a valid period of accumulations. Then an accumulation during his infancy cannot be made.[23]

In England, section 165 of the *Law of Property Act, 1925*[24] specifically provides that an accumulation of surplus income made during a minority under any statutory power or under the general law is not to be taken into account

---

[17]*Re Geering; Gulliver v. Geering*, [1964] Ch. 136, a bequest of an annuity, "to A for life, remainder on A's death to B, provided he attains age 21".

[18][1935] 4 D.L.R. 209, [1935] S.C.R. 550, and see also *Re Hammond*, [1934] 2 D.L.R. 580, [1934] S.C.R. 403.

[19]*Re Watson* (1964), 44 D.L.R. (2d) 346, [1964] S.C.R. 312 *sub nom. Watson v. Conant*. And see *Re Struthers* (1980), 29 O.R. (2d) 616, 114 D.L.R. (3d) 492 (C.A.).

[20]See, *e.g., Re Amodeo*, [1962] O.R. 548, 33 D.L.R. (2d) 24 (C.A.); *Re Baragar*, [1973] 1 O.R. 831, 32 D.L.R. (3d) 529 (H.C.J.).

[21]*Re Geering, supra,* footnote 17, at p. 144, *per* Cross, J. See generally as to these rules *Hawkins and Ryder on the Construction of Wills* (London, Sweet & Maxwell, 1965), by Ryder, pp. 74 *et seq.*; Theobald, *The Law of Wills*, §§547 *et seq.*

[22]*Mathews v. Keble* (1868), L.R. 3 Ch. 691 at p. 696; *Griffiths v. Vere* (1803), 9 Ves. Jun. 127 at p. 136, 32 E.R. 550.

[23]*Re Maber; Ward v. Maber*, [1928] Ch. 88.

[24]15 & 16 Geo. 5, c. 20 (1925).

in determining the permitted accumulation periods. The Canadian provinces have not enacted similar legislation, but the rule appears to be the same regardless, as noted above.[25]

Several Canadian provinces have enacted statutory powers of maintenance. These fall into three categories, namely, (1) those based on *Lord Cranworth's Act*,[26] (2) those based on the *Conveyancing Act*,[27] and (3) those based on the *Trustee Act, 1925*.[28]

Statutes in the first category,[29] with minor differences, provide that where property is held in trust for an infant, either absolutely, or contingently on his attaining the age of majority or the occurrence of an event before that time, the trustees can pay the income to the infant's guardians for his maintenance and education. Any income not so paid is to be accumulated. The accumulations can be resorted to for the infant's maintenance and education but, to the extent that they are not used, they are held for the persons ultimately entitled to the corpus.

There are several defects with these statutes. In the first place, the income can only be paid for the maintenance of an infant if he is "entitled" to it. Thus, it can only be paid for this purpose if the gift carries the intermediate income according to the rules discussed above.[30] Secondly, the statutes do not apply to vested interests which are defeasible, nor to contingencies which might not occur until after the infant attains his majority.[31]

Statutes based on the *Conveyancing Act*[32] permit payment of income for the benefit, maintenance and education of an infant in the same circumstances as under *Lord Cranworth's Act*,[33] as well as where a vested or contingent life interest is limited to an infant. These statutes do not expressly restrict payment to situations where the infant is "entitled" to the intermediate income, but they are so construed.[34]

The maintenance provisions of the English *Trustee Act*[35] were enacted in Manitoba[36] and Prince Edward Island.[37] These statutes, with minor differences, provide that the trustees may pay the income from property held for an infant to his parent or guardian for his maintenance, education or benefit if

---

[25] At footnote 22, *supra*.

[26] 23 & 24 Vict., c. 145 (1860), s. 26.

[27] 44 & 45 Vict., c. 41 (1881), s. 43.

[28] 15 & 16 Geo. 5, c. 19 (1925), s. 31.

[29] *Trustee Act*, R.S.A. 1980, c. T-10, s. 33; R.S.B.C. 1979, c. 414, ss. 24-26; R.S.N. 1970, c. 380, s. 27 am. 1971, No. 14, s. 2; No. 71, s. 47; R.S.S. 1978, c. T-23, ss. 52-55; *Trustee Ordinance*, R.O.N.W.T. 1974, c. T-8, ss. 29-30; R.O.Y.T. 1971, c. T-5, ss. 32-33.

[30] *Re George* (1877), 5 Ch. D. 837 (C.A.).

[31] Waters, p. 778.

[32] 44 & 45 Vict., s. 41 (1881), s. 43. Enacted in N.B. and N.S.: *Trustees Act*, R.S.N.B. 1973, c. T-15, s. 14; *Trustee Act*, R.S.N.S. 1967, c. 317, s. 29.

[33] 23 & 24 Vict., c. 145, s. 26 (1860).

[34] *Re Dickson; Hill v. Grant* (1885), 29 Ch. D. 331 (C.A.).

[35] 15 & 16 Geo. 5, c. 19 (1925), s. 31.

[36] *Trustee Act*, R.S.M. 1970, c. T160, s. 31 am. S.M. 1971, c. 82, s. 57.

[37] *Trustee Act*, R.S.P.E.I. 1974, c. T-9, s. 39.

the property carries the intermediate income. The interest of the infant may be vested, either absolutely or defeasibly, or contingent. Any income not paid out during the beneficiary's infancy is to be accumulated. After the beneficiary attains the age of majority the income from an interest that is not vested in possession is to be paid to him until it vests or the beneficiary dies or the interest fails, unless it is otherwise disposed of.[38] Income that has been accumulated is payable to the beneficiary either if his interest is vested and he attains his majority or marries before then, or if his interest vests in possession or interest when he attains his majority or marries before then and he does reach the age of majority or marry before that age. In all other cases, the accumulations pass to the person ultimately entitled to the capital.[39]

1108.2　The Policy of Restraints on Accumulations

The *Accumulations Act*[1] was passed with unseemly haste in a fearful reaction to the possible consequences of the vainglorious testamentary scheme of one man. Was it necessary? It is submitted that it was not, or if it was appropriate in the social and political climate of the time, it no longer serves a useful purpose.

The legislation does not foster the policy of keeping money in circulation, for an accumulation does not have the effect of tying it up in the dead hand as a perpetuity does. The income is not locked up, but is reinvested and is thus constantly in circulation.[2]

Accumulations were feared because they would have the effect of concentrating the wealth of the nation in the hands of the few. Even if it might have had that effect in 1800, it does not do so today because of the effect of generational taxation. In any event, in the many jurisdictions which do not have restrictions on accumulations, no such concentrations of wealth have materialized in the hands of individuals. The statute has no relevance to modern conditions and should never have been received in the Canadian provinces.[3]

An accumulation may have the effect of depriving the immediate family of the testator's bounty. However, the Thellusson will did not do so and if a will should have that effect today, the testator's dependants have the right to

---

[38]*E.g.*, by a direction to accumulate surplus income: *Re Turner's Will Trusts; District Bank, Ltd. v. Turner*, [1937] Ch. 15 (C.A.).

[39]See further Waters, pp. 779-81.

§1108.2

[1]39 & 40 Geo. 3, c. 98 (1800).

[2]*Thellusson v. Woodford* (1805), 11 Ves. Jun. 112 at p. 147, 32 E.R. 1030 (H.L.), *per* Lord Eldon, L.C.

[3]*Re Burns* (1960), 25 D.L.R. (2d) 427, 32 W.W.R. 689 (Alta. S.C. App. Div.), *per* Porter, J.A., dissenting.

make application under family disinheritance legislation in effect in all the provinces[4] for a share, or a larger share, of the estate.

The statute has proved difficult to apply in practice. Moreover, it is badly drafted and tends to defeat the intentions of the testator or settlor. Often remote next of kin receive a benefit under a partial intestacy when the testator did not wish to benefit them at all.

Although it can be argued that, as a matter of policy, compulsory saving at the direction of the dead hand, as distinct from voluntary saving by the living, should be subject to control, the rule against perpetuities already provides an adequate measure of control over the disposition of capital and a separate rule regarding the enjoyment of income is not necessary.

These arguments have been made on numerous occasions[5] and they were adopted by the legislatures of Alberta[6] and British Columbia,[7] which have abolished restrictions on accumulations. The restrictions have also been abolished elsewhere in the Commonwealth.[8] Statutes imposing restrictions on accumulations, some of which were modelled on the English Act of 1800, were enacted in about one-quarter of the United States. Most have since been repealed as unworkable.[9]

It is to be hoped that the Canadian jurisdictions which still retain the English Act or a re-enactment of it will repeal the legislation.

1108.3   Relationship Between Perpetuities and Accumulations

An accumulation which exceeds the permitted periods is not void absolutely, but only to the extent that it exceeds the appropriate period.[1] However, a direction or power to accumulate which enables the accumulation to extend beyond the perpetuity period is void.[2] This occurs where the persons among

---

[4]*Family Relief Act*, R.S.N. 1970, c. 124; R.S.A. 1980, c. F-2; *Testators' Family Maintenance Act*, R.S.N.S. 1967, c. 303; *Testator's Family Maintenance Act*, R.S.M. 1970, c. T50; R.S.N.B. 1973, c. T-4; *Dependants of a Deceased Person Relief Act*, R.S.P.E.I. 1974, c. D-6; *Dependant's Relief Act*, R.S.S. 1978, c. D-25; *Succession Law Reform Act*, R.S.O. 1980, c. 488, Part V; *Dependants' Relief Ordinance*, R.O.N.W.T. 1974, c. D-4; R.O.Y.T. 1971, c. D-3; *Wills Variation Act*, R.S.B.C. 1979, c. 435.

[5]Simes, *Public Policy and the Dead Hand* (Ann Arbor, Univ. of Mich. Law School, 1955), ch. 4; Morris and Leach, pp. 303 *et seq.*; Maudsley, pp. 200 *et seq.*; Allan, "The Rule Against Perpetuities Restated", 6 U. of W.A. L.R. 27 (1963-64), at pp. 70-2; Institute of Law Research and Reform, University of Alberta, *Report on the Rule Against Perpetuities* (Edmonton, 1971), pp. 74 *et seq.*

[6]*Perpetuities Act*, R.S.A. 1980, c. P-24, s. 24.

[7]*Perpetuity Act*, R.S.B.C. 1979, c. 321, s. 24.

[8]*Perpetuities and Accumulations Act*, S.V. 1968, No. 7750, s. 19; *Perpetuities Act*, S.N.Z. 1964, No. 47, s. 21; *Property Law Act*, S.W.A. 1969, No. 32, s. 113.

[9]For the position in the United States, see 6 A.L.P. §§25.100-25.118 and A.L.P. Supp., §§25.100-25.118.

§1108.3

[1]See §1108.4(b), *infra*.

[2]*Baker v. Stuart* (1897), 28 O.R. 439 (H.C.J.); *Re Miller*, [1938] O.W.N. 118, [1938] 2 D.L.R. 765 (H.C.J.).

whom the capital is to be distributed may not be ascertainable within the perpetuity period. The following example illustrates the point.

A testator gives a sum of money to his trustees to accumulate the income until the youngest of A's grandchildren shall attain the age of 30 and to divide the principal and the accumulated income among those of A's grandchildren who are then living.

The gift of the capital would be void for perpetuity at common law and the direction to accumulate would also be void. It is not reduced to one of the periods permitted by the statute. Under the wait and see principle introduced by the modern Perpetuities Acts, the gift itself would probably be saved. Actual events will determine that. Under some of the perpetuities statutes, however, the direction to accumulate may not be governed by wait and see, except perhaps by a strained construction.[3] The Ontario Act, for example, defines "limitation" as including "any provision whereby ... any right, power or authority over property, is ... created or conferred".[4] However, when that Act introduces wait and see, it says, "No limitation creating a contingent interest in ... property shall be treated as ... invalid ... by reason only of the fact that there is a possibility of such interest vesting beyond the perpetuity period".[5] Clearly, a direction or power to accumulate does not, of itself, create an interest in property. Under such statutes, therefore, one has the anomalous result that the disposition itself may be valid, but the direction to accumulate is void. The interim income is then undisposed of.

Clearly, the wait and see principle should apply also to a direction or power to accumulate. This was done in the Alberta and British Columbia statutes, which provide:

24(2) Where property is settled or disposed of in such manner that the income thereof may or must be accumulated wholly or in part, the power or direction to accumulate that income is valid if the disposition of the accumulated income is or may be valid but not otherwise.[6]

If such a provision is enacted, but restrictions on accumulations are retained, it will, or may be necessary to reduce the accumulation to the appropriate period.

There are several exceptions to the rule that an accumulation which may extend beyond the perpetuity period is void. If the accumulation is for the benefit of a charity and there is a general charitable intent, the direction to

---

[3]Megarry and Wade, p. 275.
[4]*Perpetuities Act*, R.S.O. 1980, c. 374, s. 1(c). *Cf. Perpetuities Ordinance*, R.O.N.W.T. 1974, c. P-3, s. 2(b); O.Y.T. 1980 (1st), c. 23, s. 2(1), which are even more restricted.
[5]*Perpetuities Act*, R.S.O. 1980, c. 374, s. 3. *Cf. Perpetuities Ordinance*, R.O.N.W.T. 1974, c. P-3, s. 4; O.Y.T. 1980 (1st), c. 23, s. 4(1), to the same effect.
[6]*Perpetuities Act*, R.S.A. 1980, c. P-24, s. 24(2); *Perpetuity Act*, R.S.B.C. 1979, c. 321, s. 24(1).

accumulate is disregarded and the income is distributed *cy-près*.[7] Similarly, if no one but the legatee for whose benefit the accumulation is directed has an interest in the property, he can terminate the accumulation under the rule in *Saunders v. Vautier*,[8] if his interest is vested and he is *sui juris*. An accumulation which is otherwise too remote is then valid.

Even though an accumulation is not directed to begin until after the perpetuity period, it is not void if the capital and the accumulated income must vest within the period, for example because it is given to a named person.

This occurred in *Re Arnold*.[9] In that case the testator gave the residue of his estate to his sister for life and after her death to her husband, if any, for life. Thereafter the income was to be accumulated for six years and added to the capital. Three-quarters of the income was then to be paid to a named cousin and the other quarter was to be accumulated for a further twenty-five years, after which the whole of the income was to be paid to the cousin for life. After further life interests the capital was then disposed of.

The sister was a spinster, 69 years old when the testator died. It was argued that she might, at age 90, marry a man aged 19 (hence a person unborn at the testator's death), who might outlive her by more than twenty-one years and that, therefore, the direction was void for perpetuity. It was held, however, that that is only so where the gift of the accumulated income may not vest beyond the perpetuity period. In this case, however, it had to vest, if at all, within the period. The period of accumulation was, of course, excessive and it was reduced to twenty-one years from the testator's death.

1108.4 The Accumulation Periods

(a) The periods allowed by statute

The Ontario Act permits an accumulation only during one of the following periods:

1. The life of the grantor.
2. Twenty-one years from the date of making an *inter vivos* disposition.
3. The duration of the minority or respective minorities of any person or persons living or *en ventre sa mere* at the date of making an *inter vivos* disposition.
4. Twenty-one years from the death of the grantor, settlor or testator.
5. The duration of the minority or respective minorities of any person or persons living or *en ventre sa mere* at the death of the grantor, settlor or testator.
6. The duration of the minority or respective minorities of any person or persons who, under the instrument directing the accumulations, would, for the time being, if of full age, be entitled to the income directed to be accumulated.[1]

---

[7] *Jewish Home for Aged of British Columbia v. Toronto General Trusts Corp.* (1961), 28 D.L.R. (2d) 48, [1961] S.C.R. 465; *Re Burns* (1960), 25 D.L.R. (2d) 427, 32 W.W.R. 689 (Alta. S.C. App. Div.).

[8] (1841), 4 Beav. 115, 49 E.R. 282, affd Cr. & Ph. 240, 41 E.R. 482.

[9] [1955] 4 D.L.R. 535, 16 W.W.R. 129 (B.C.S.C.).

§1108.4

[1] Ont. Act, s. 1(1).

Periods 1, 4, 5 and 6 are derived from the *Thellusson Act*.[2] Periods 2 and 3 are taken from the *Perpetuities and Accumulations Act, 1964*.[3] The same periods were adopted in British Columbia,[4] but the legislation has since been repealed in that province.[5] Legislation based on the *Thellusson Act* is in force in New Brunswick.[6] The Act remains in force in Manitoba and Saskatchewan and probably in Newfoundland, the Northwest Territories and Yukon Territory. The Act is probably not in force in Nova Scotia.[7] It no longer applies to Alberta.[8] In Prince Edward Island an accumulation is permitted for a period of a life or lives in being plus sixty years, the same as the perpetuity period in that province.[9]

It should be noted that an accumulation for the purchase of land only is permitted for any of the six periods set out above under the Ontario Act, but only for the sixth period under other statutes.[10]

(b) Selection of the period

Only one of the periods permitted by the statute may be selected.[11] Unfortunately, a testator or settlor often directs an accumulation for a period other than the ones prescribed. The court is then obliged to select a period which will most probably accord with his intentions and the accumulation will not be allowed longer than that. It should be noted that an accumulation for a period longer than allowed is not void, provided it does not infringe the perpetuity rule. Only the excessive accumulation beyond the permitted period is void.[12]

In the following examples some of the difficulties of construction are illustrated.

The Life of the Grantor

The following example illustrates this period:

A settlor directed an accumulation of part of the income under certain marriage settlements. He directed that the accumulations should not continue for a longer period than twenty-one years after his death. The trustees began the accumulation immediately.

---

[2]39 & 40 Geo. 3, c. 98 (1800).

[3]C. 55, s. 13(1) (1964, U.K.).

[4]*Accumulations Act*, S.B.C. 1967, c. 2.

[5]*Perpetuities Act*, S.B.C. 1975, c. 53, s. 24(1). See now *Perpetuity Act*, R.S.B.C. 1979, c. 321, s. 24.

[6]*Property Act*, R.S.N.B. 1973, c. P-19, s. 1.

[7]See §1108, *supra*, at footnotes 7-20.

[8]*Perpetuities Act*, R.S.A. 1980, c. P-24, s. 24.

[9]*Perpetuities Act*, R.S.P.E.I. 1974, c. P-3, s. 1.

[10]Ont. Act, s. 1(5); N.B. Act, s. 1(2); *Law of Property Act, 1925*, 15 & 16 Geo. 5, c. 20, s. 166(1).

[11]*Re Mulock Marriage Settlements*, [1957] O.W.N. 453 (H.C.J.).

[12]*Re Arnold*, [1955] 4 D.L.R. 535, 16 W.W.R. 129 (B.C.S.C.); *Harrison v. Harrison* (1904), 7 O.L.R. 297 (H.C.J.); *Fonseca v. Jones* (1911), 14 W.L.R. 148, 21 Man. R. 168 (C.A.).

Two periods were then possible, namely, the life of the grantor or twenty-one years from his death. The former was effectively selected and, thus, the accumulation ended at the settlor's death.[13]

Twenty-one Years from the Testator's Death

The following examples illustrate this period:

(1) A testator directs that surplus income not required to pay certain annuities shall be accumulated during the lives of the annuitants and the capital and accumulated income is to be divided amongst named persons on the death of the surviving annuitant.

A period of twenty-one years from the testator's death is the most appropriate period in the circumstances.[14]

(2) A testator gave the income from the residue to V for life. The income was then to be accumulated for six years. One-quarter of the income was then to be further accumulated for a further twenty-five years after which the income was to be paid to X for life. X also received the other three-quarters of the income. After further life interests the capital was disposed of. V died two years after the testator.

The period of twenty-one years from the testator's death was the most appropriate and, in view of the fact that the life tenant died two years after the testator's death, only nineteen years remained during which the accumulation might continue.[15]

During Minorities of Persons Living at the Testator's or Settlor's Death

The following examples illustrate these periods:

(1) A testator directs an accumulation during the minority of the children of his son. The children are to receive the principal and accumulations when they attain the age of 21.

The sixth period cannot be used because the testator has directed the accumulation of the whole income to continue even after some of the children who would be entitled to share in it have attained their majority. The fifth period is, therefore, the most appropriate. This period was breached, however, because the testator did not restrict the accumulation during the minority of children living at his death. The accumulation was, therefore, valid only during

---

[13]*Re Mulock Marriage Settlements, supra,* footnote 11. And see *Re Lady Rosslyn's Trust* (1848), 16 Sim. 391, 60 E.R. 925; *Baird v. Lord Advocate,* [1979] 2 All E.R. 28 (H.L.), power to pay income to children for life with power to accumulate surplus until death of children; *Re Erskine's Settlement Trusts; Hollis v. Pigott,* [1971] 1 All E.R. 572 (Ch.) direction to accumulate for life of settlor or until named beneficiary reaches age of 22.
[14]*Re Benor,* [1963] 2 O.R. 248, 39 D.L.R. (2d) 122 (H.C.J.); *Fasken, Jr. v. Fasken,* [1953] 3 D.L.R. 431, [1953] 2 S.C.R. 10; *Re Major,* [1970] 2 O.R. 121, 10 D.L.R. (3d) 107 (H.C.J.).
[15]*Re Arnold,* [1955] 4 D.L.R. 535, 16 W.W.R. 129 (B.C.S.C.).

the minority of any child of the testator's son who was living at the testator's death.[16]

The foregoing situation must be distinguished from the following:

(2) A testator directs an accumulation until the youngest child of X attains the age of 21. X only had one child, A, who reached the age of 21 sixteen years after the testator's death. There was, however, the possibility of further children.

In the circumstances the period of the minority of a living person was not appropriate since A was not necessarily the youngest child of X. The only other period that could apply was the period of twenty-one years after the testator's death.[17]

During Minorities of Persons Entitled to the Income if of Full Age

The following example will illustrate this period:

A testator gave certain annuities and directed that the surplus income be paid to his grandchildren at age 21. Until they reached that age the income on the shares appropriated for each grandchild was to be accumulated. One grandchild, A, was born five years after the testator's death. Another grandchild, B, was born thirty-two years after the testator's death.

In these circumstances an accumulation of the whole of the surplus income during A's minority was valid. Similarly, an accumulation of one-half of the surplus income during B's minority (the other half being paid to A) was valid.[18]

Under this period, therefore, the accumulation does not have to commence at the testator's death and successive accumulations are permitted.[19] The difference between this period and the preceding one is that the beneficiaries need not be living at the testator's death and the accumulation must end as to each beneficiary when he attains the age of majority. It cannot continue until all have reached that age.

If the testator directs that the accumulation shall commence at his death and continue until the intended beneficiaries, who are then unborn, attain the age of majority, the only period applicable is twenty-one years after the testator's death.

1108.5 Terminating an Accumulation

Under the rule in *Saunders v. Vautier*[1] a beneficiary who has an absolutely

---

[16]*Re Watt's Will Trusts; Watt v. Watt*, [1936] 2 All E.R. 1555 (Ch.).

[17]*Re Ransome; Moberly v. Ransome*, [1957] Ch. 348.

[18]*Re Cattell; Cattell v. Cattell*, [1914] 1 Ch. 177 (C.A.).

[19]See *Re Cattell; Cattell v. Cattell*, [1907] 1 Ch. 567, an earlier application in the same case.

§1108.5

[1](1841), 4 Beav. 115, 49 E.R. 282, affd Cr. & Ph. 240, 41 E.R. 482. The rule has been abolished in Alberta and Manitoba and replaced with a provincial discretion to vary or terminate: *Trustee Act*, R.S.A. 1980, c. T-10, s. 42; R.S.M. 1970, c. T160, s. 61, rep. & sub. 1982-83-84, c. 38, s. 4.

vested interest in the property and who is *sui juris* may demand that the property be paid or transferred to him even though under the terms of the gift payment is postponed until a later date. It follows from this rule that the beneficiary can, in such circumstances, terminate an accumulation which is directed to continue until the date of payment.

Thus, where a testator bequeaths a fund to a named person, but directs that until he reaches age 30 the income is to be accumulated and the capital and accumulated income is to be paid to him at that age, the beneficiary can stop the accumulation as soon as he reaches the age of majority.

Whether or not the beneficiary is solely interested in the property is a question of construction. In *Re Deloitte; Griffiths v. Deloitte*[2] the testator bequeathed a sum of money upon trust to pay an annuity to X for life and to accumulate the surplus income. The capital and the accumulations were given to X's children at age 21 after her death. X had no interest in the accumulations since the annuity was charged on current income. X was a woman past the age of child-bearing and her children were over 21. Since there is a conclusive presumption in law that a woman may bear children at any age, her children were not solely interested in the surplus income. They could not, therefore, stop the accumulations, with the result that twenty-one years after the testator's death, the end of the permitted period, the surplus income fell into residue.

It should be noted that the statutory changes in the common law presumption as to capacity to have children made by modern perpetuities statutes, have no application to this situation.[3] Clearly they ought to apply not only to the question of perpetuities, but to all situations in which the question may arise.

The question whether a beneficiary may terminate an accumulation most often arises where the property is given to a charity.

In *Wharton v. Masterman*[4] it was held that the right to terminate applies in such circumstances. In that case the testator provided for a number of annuities. He directed that any surplus income should be accumulated and after the death of the annuitants the capital and accumulations were to be divided among several charities. The important point was that the annuities were charged on the current income only. This meant that the charities were the only persons entitled to the surplus income and the capital. They were, therefore, entitled to call for payment of the capital to them immediately after setting aside sufficient sums to satisfy the annuities.[5]

The more normal situation, however, is for the annuities to be charged on the corpus as well. In that case the charities cannot terminate the accumulation because they are not solely interested in it and this is so even though it is highly

---

[2][1926] Ch. 56.
[3]See §1107.5(a), *supra*. The *Perpetuities and Accumulations Act, 1964*, c. 55, s. 14 (U.K.), provides otherwise, however.
[4][1895] A.C. 186 (H.L.).
[5]See also *Re Beresford Estate* (1966), 56 W.W.R. 248 (B.C.S.C.), to the same effect.

unlikely that it will ever be necessary for the annuitants to resort to the capital.[6]

The result in such a case is that, once the permitted accumulation period ends, the income thus released falls into residue or, if the gift was of residue, it goes out on an intestacy. In other words, it goes to persons the testator had no intention to benefit.[7]

On the other hand, it may be possible to distribute the released income for charitable purposes in any event. This can be done if the court finds that the testator had a general charitable intention. In those circumstances, no one is interested in the property except charity and the court can then distribute the surplus income *cy-près*.[8]

1108.6 Destination of Released Income After Accumulation Ends

Although the statutes say that a direction to accumulate beyond one of the permitted periods is null and void,[1] in fact the cases hold that except where the accumulation infringes the rule against perpetuities,[2] only the accumulation after the permitted period is void.[3] The statutes go on to provide that the released income shall go to those persons who would have been entitled thereto if there had been no direction to accumulate.[4] The question of who is entitled to the income may be difficult to determine.

In some cases the testator or settlor may have made his own provision, as in *Fasken, Jr. v. Fasken*,[5] in which the testator directed that on failure to appoint certain shares and the accumulated income thereon, the shares should go to his next of kin as on an intestacy.

The general rules as to wills are as follows: (a) if the income directed to be accumulated derives from a specific fund, then the surplus income after the permitted period falls into residue;[6] (b) if the income derives from the residue,

---

[6]*Berry v. Geen*, [1938] A.C. 575 (H.L.), followed in *Re Robertson*, [1939] O.W.N. 569, [1939] 4 D.L.R. 511 (H.C.J.); *Re Burns* (1960), 25 D.L.R. (2d) 427, 32 W.W.R. 689 (Alta. S.C. App. Div.), and *Re Owens*, [1968] 1 O.R. 318, 66 D.L.R. (2d) 328 (H.C.J.). And see *Re Birtwistle*, [1935] O.R. 433, [1935] 4 D.L.R. 137 (H.C.J.).

[7]On this point see the cases in the preceding footnote and §1108.6, *infra*.

[8]*Jewish Home for Aged v. Toronto General Trusts Corp.* (1961), 28 D.L.R. (2d) 48, [1961] S.C.R. 465; *Re Burns, supra*, footnote 6.

§1108.6

[1]Ont. Act, s. 1(6); N.B. Act, s. 1(3); *Accumulations Act*, 39 & 40 Geo. 3, c. 98 (1800), s. 1.

[2]As to which see §1108.3, *supra*.

[3]See §1108.4(b), footnote 11, *supra*.

[4]See the statutory references in footnote 1, *supra*.

[5][1953] 3 D.L.R. 431, [1953] 2 S.C.R. 10.

[6]*Re Mackey Trust*, [1944] 3 D.L.R. 298, [1944] O.W.N. 382 (C.A.); *Re Benor*, [1963] 2 O.R. 248, 39 D.L.R. (2d) 122 (H.C.J.); *Re Mercier* (1982), 132 D.L.R. (3d) 705, 11 E.T.R. 147 (Ont. H.C.J.).

the released income goes out on an intestacy.[7] These rules, of course, are ousted if the testator specifically disposes of the income otherwise.[8]

It sometimes happens that the testator provides for more than one residue. There will then be an ultimate residue, however, and released income from any other residue will fall into it.[9] Similarly, if there is one residue, but the testator excepts certain property from it and directs an invalid accumulation with respect to the excepted property, any released income will fall into the residue.[10]

If the accumulation arises under an *inter vivos* disposition, the surplus income will go on a resulting trust to the settlor or his estate.[11]

1108.7 Exceptions to the Statute

The legislation provides that it does not extend to any provision for the payment of debts of the grantor, settlor or other person, or for the raising of portions, or to a provision respecting the produce of timber or wood upon any lands.[1]

Save as to the provision respecting portions, these exceptions are self-explanatory. A "portion" in the sense of the statute means a part or a share for a child raised or set aside out of a fund or property given to others.[2] An accumulation directed for the maintenance, education and support of issue has been held to be within this exception.[3]

---

[7]*Re Amodeo*, [1962] O.R. 548, 33 D.L.R. (2d) 24 (C.A.); *Re Arnold*, [1955] 4 D.L.R. 535, 16 W.W.R. 129 (B.C.S.C.); *Re Baragar*, [1973] 1 O.R. 831, 32 D.L.R. (3d) 529 (H.C.J.); *Re Davidson* (1926), 58 O.L.R. 597 (H.C.J.), affd 59 O.L.R. 643 (S.C. App. Div.); *Re Davis*, [1946] O.W.N. 148, 2 D.L.R. 281 (H.C.J.); *Re Fairfoull* (1974), 41 D.L.R. (3d) 152 (B.C.S.C.), affd [1974] 6 W.W.R. 471, 18 R.F.L. 165 (B C.S.C.); *Re Hammond; Soldiers' Aid Com'n v. National Trust Co.*, [1935] 4 D.L.R. 209, [1935] S.C.R. 550; *Re Major*, [1970] 2 O.R. 121, 10 D.L.R. (3d) 107 (H.C.J.); *Re Martin* (1979), 24 O.R. (2d) 408, 98 D.L.R. (3d) 570 (C.A.); *Re Owens*, [1968] 1 O.R. 318, 66 D.L.R. (2d) 328 (H.C.J.); *Re Stevenson* (1976), 12 O.R. (2d) 614, 69 D.L.R. (3d) 630 (H.C.J.); *Re Tuckett*, [1954] O.R. 973, [1955] 1 D.L.R. 643 (H.C.J.); *Re Robertson*, [1939] O.W.N. 569, [1939] 4 D.L.R. 511 (H.C.J.); *Re Burns* (1960), 25 D.L.R. (2d) 427, 32 W.W.R. 689 (Alta. S.C. App. Div.); *Re Orford*, [1943] O.W.N. 714, [1944] 1 D.L.R. 277 (H.C.J.); *Re Watson* (1964), 44 D.L.R. (2d) 346, [1964] S.C.R. 312 *sub nom. Watson v. Conant*.

[8]*Re Fulford* (1926), 59 O.L.R. 440 (S.C. App. Div.); *Re Mulock Marriage Settlements*, [1957] O.W.N. 453 (H.C.J.).

[9]*Canada Permanent Trust Co. v. MacFarlane* (1927), 27 D.L.R. (3d) 480, [1972] 4 W.W.R. 593 *sub nom. Re Ryan Estate; Canada Permanent Trust Co. v. MacFarlane* (B.C.C.A.).

[10]*Re Herman*, [1961] O.R. 25, 25 D.L.R. (2d) 93 (C.A.); *Re Struthers* (1980), 29 O.R. (2d) 616, 114 D.L.R. (3d) 492 (C.A.).

[11]*Re O'Hagan; O'Hagan v. Lloyds Bank, Ltd.*, [1932] W.N. 188 (Ont. H.C.J.).

§1108.7

[1]Ont. Act, s. 2; N.B. Act, s. 2; *Accumulations Act*, 39 & 40 Geo. 3, c. 98 (1800), s. 2.

[2]*Edwards v. Tuck* (1853), 3 De G. M. & G. 40 at p. 58, 43 E.R. 17, *per* Lord Cranworth, L.C.

[3]*Re Davidson* (1926), 58 O.L.R. 597 (H.C.J.), affd 59 O.L.R. 643 (S.C. App. Div.).

Apart from the provisions of the legislation, the statute has been held not to apply to an accumulation directed to repair and maintain buildings on land since such improvements would have to be paid out of current income in any event.[4] An accumulation for the purpose of effecting a capital improvement is within the statute, however.[5]

Commercial transactions also fall outside the statute, such as an accumulation to pay the premiums on an insurance policy.[6] Similarly, an accumulation in a unit trust is not subject to the statute.[7]

Finally, the statute has recently been construed to apply only to individuals, not to corporate settlors.[8]

---

[4]*Re Mason; Mason v. Mason*, [1891] 3 Ch. 467; *Vine v. Raleigh*, [1891] 2 Ch. 13 (C.A.). And see *Re Hurlbatt; Hurlbatt v. Hurlbatt*, [1910] 2 Ch. 553.

[5]*Re Gardiner; Gardiner v. Smith*, [1901] 1 Ch. 697; *Vine v. Raleigh, supra*, footnote 4.

[6]*Bassil v. Lister* (1851), 9 Hare 177, 68 E.R. 464.

[7]*Re A.E.G. Unit Trust (Managers) Ltd.'s Deed; Midland Bank Executor & Trustee Co. Ltd. v. A.E.G. Unit Trust (Managers) Ltd.*, [1957] Ch. 415.

[8]*Re Dodwell Co. Ltd's Trust Deed*, [1978] 3 All E.R. 738.

PART IV

TRUSTS, SETTLEMENTS
AND POWERS

CONTENTS OF PART IV

CHAPTER 12

TRUSTS

1201. SCOPE OF THIS CHAPTER

In chapter 10 the development of the use was traced.[1] In this chapter, its direct successor, the trust, is discussed, followed in the next two chapters by the law of settlements and powers of appointment. These are all closely related and have some factors in common. They all involve the employment of a third person to accomplish the purposes of a grantor or testator in limiting an estate. An estate may be limited to a person to hold to the use of another person, specified or to be appointed, or it may be limited to a trustee to hold in trust for the beneficial enjoyment of another or others and in a settlement limiting a succession of estates, either or both of these devices may be used.

A work of this kind cannot deal with matters of procedure, many matters

---

§1201
[1] §1003.2, *supra.*

relating to the person of the trustee and beneficiary and numerous matters relating generally to trust property (which may consist of both realty and personalty), such as the appointment of trustees, their retirement from office, their general acts of administration, particular powers, their remuneration and other rights, the order in which property is liable for debts, the rights of creditors and other general matters. For all such aspects, the relevant legislation and the standard works and digests must be consulted.[2] This chapter relates only to real property held in trust, how the trust is created and the incidents of the estates that arise, with such other references as seem to be appropriate. Many of the cases cited deal with personalty, but they indicate the basic principles that govern all trusts.

1202.   TRUSTS GENERALLY

In the modern and confined sense of the word, a trust is a confidence or obligation enforceable in equity, reposed in a person (called a trustee) with respect to property of which he has possession, or over which he can exercise a power, to the intent that he may hold the property, or exercise the power, for the benefit of some other person or persons, of whom he may be one, or of an object (called the beneficiary or *cestui que trust*).[1]

The law of trusts in real property developed from the decisions of courts of common law and the Court of Chancery before the *Statute of Uses*[2] and from decisions construing that statute. Before the statute, when a grant was made to one person and his heirs to the use of another, at common law the addition of these latter words was regarded as void because they were repugnant to the limitation. The grantee was regarded as having the lawful seisin and legal estate in the land and the *cestui que use* had no estate, title or remedy at law. In the Court of Chancery which administered equity, however, the use was enforced as a trust or confidence, the effect being that the *cestui que use* was entitled to the profits and the legal owner should convey according to his directions. The *Statute of Uses* provided that, if any person were seised of any land, by con-

---

[2]Such as Waters, Scott, Lewin and Underhill. The relevant statutes are: *Trustee Act*, R.S.A. 1980, c. T-10; R.S.B.C. 1979, c. 414; R.S.M. 1970, c. T160; R.S.N.S. 1967, c. 317; R.S.N. 1970, c. 380; R.S.O. 1980, c. 512; R.S.P.E.I. 1974, c. T-9; R.S.S. 1978, c. T-23; *Trustees Act*, R.S.N.B. 1973, c. T-15; *Trustee Ordinance*, R.O.N.W.T. 1974, c. T-8; R.O.Y.T. 1971, c. T-5. These several statutes are hereafter in this chapter referred to as the "Trustee Act (Alta.)", *etc.*, without further citation.

§1202

[1]*Burgess v. Wheate; Attorney-General v. Wheate* (1759), 1 Eden 177 at p. 240, 28 E.R. 652, Henley, L.K.; *Wilson v. Lord Bury* (1880), 5 Q.B.D. 518 (C.A.), at p. 530, Brett, L.J.; *Dooby v. Watson* (1888), 39 Ch. D. 178 at pp. 181-2, Kekewich, J.; *Re Barney*; *Barney v. Barney*, [1892] 2 Ch. 265 at p. 272, Kekewich, J.; *Re Williams; Williams v. Williams*, [1897] 2 Ch. 12 (C.A.), at pp. 18-19, Lindley, L.J.; Underhill, p. 1; *Green v. Russell*, [1959] 2 Q.B. 226 (C.A.), at p. 241, Romer, L.J.; *Re Marshall's Will Trusts*, [1945] Ch. 217 at p. 219, Cohen, J.; *Tobin Tractor (1957) Ltd. v. Western Surety Co.* (1963), 40 D.L.R. (2d) 231 at p. 239, 42 W.W.R. 532 at p. 542 (Sask. Q.B.).

[2]27 Hen. 8, c. 10 (1535).

veyance, will or otherwise, to the use, confidence or trust of any other person, the latter was deemed to have the seisin and legal estate of the former, who was left with nothing. The courts of common law ruled, however, that the statute did not apply to a "use upon a use" so that, if a grant were made to A to the use of B to the use of, or in trust for, C, the statute did not apply to C who, as before the statute, held under a trust or confidence, enforceable only in equity. This ruling again gave the Court of Chancery the same jurisdiction over the second use or trust as it had formerly had over the first. Similarly, where the grantee to uses was not seised of the land, where the use was an active use, where a corporation was seised to uses, and where a person was seised to his own use, the statute did not operate.[3] From these exceptions the modern law of trusts developed, administered by one court since the courts of common law and of equity were merged, but on the basis that the rules of equity should prevail in the event of conflict.

The person holding property in trust is called the trustee, and the person for whom he holds it is called the *cestui que trust* or beneficiary. A trustee is a person holding the legal title to property under an express or implied agreement to apply it and the income arising from it to the use and benefit of another person.[4] All that is necessary to establish the relation of trustee and *cestui que trust* is to prove that the legal title is in one person and the equitable title in another.[5]

However, although the legal estate in property affected by a trust is usually in the trustee, that is not a necessity. A trustee may have merely an equitable estate in property, such as when he is trustee of property which is subject to an outstanding mortgage,[6] or of a term of years,[7] or is in receipt of rents, for "it is not ... necessary to constitute a trust that the person in receipt of the rents of the estate should have the legal estate, if so, no equitable owner could create a trust."[8] A trust does not need the immediate existence of a legal estate in the trustee to support it.[9] The fact that the creator of a trust does not transfer to the trustee the legal estate in the property which he subsequently gets in, is immaterial.[10]

The trust has been said to be the most important achievement of equity,[11] for it is a very convenient and flexible tool for making dispositions of property,

---

[3]See §1003.2(b), *supra*.

[4]*Per* Brett, L.J., in *Wilson v. Lord Bury, supra*, footnote 1, at pp. 530-1.

[5]*Hardoon v. Belilios*, [1901] A.C. 118 (P.C.), at p. 123.

[6]*Poole v. Pass* (1839), 1 Beav. 600, 48 E.R. 1074.

[7]*Head v. Lord Teynham* (1783), 1 Cox. 57, 29 E.R. 1061.

[8]*Knight v. Bowyer* (1857), 23 Beav. 609 at p. 635, 53 E.R. 239, *per* Romilly, M.R., affd 2 De G. & J. 421, 44 E.R. 1053.

[9]*Attorney-General v. Lady Downing* (1767), Wilm. 1 at p. 22, 97 E.R. 1. In this case Wilmot, C.J., stated that trust estates do not depend upon the legal estate for any existence but that a Court of Equity considers devises of trusts as distinct and substantive, standing on their own basis, independent of the legal estate.

[10]*Gilbert v. Overton* (1864), 2 H. & M. 110, 71 E.R. 402.

[11]Maitland, *Equity*, p. 21.

both real and personal, for all kinds of purposes. These include the transfer of property *inter vivos* and on death in a domestic setting to benefit persons in succession, to make provision for persons under a disability, to prevent wastrels from squandering their inheritance by means of a protective trust, to provide for persons without publicity under a secret trust, and to provide for charitable and non-charitable purposes such as the endowment of a university, or the caring for pet animals. One of the motives for using the trust may be to minimize the incidence of income tax and death taxes.

Furthermore, the trust may be used to great advantage in business, for example, to provide pensions for retired employees, or as a means of investment for the beneficiaries under the business or Massachusetts trust, or other investment trusts. Under an insurance trust, policies of insurance on the life of the settlor may be transferred to a trustee, either to provide for the settlor's dependants or to protect a business against the death of one of the proprietors or managers. Under a liquidation trust, the creditors of a business may enter into an agreement whereby a trustee continues to operate the business in order to pay off the debts. A trust to secure creditors, governed by a trust indenture, is normally entered into when a corporation wishes to float a loan by issuing bonds, debentures or notes to the public. The voting trust is a familiar device for securing the management or control of a corporation.

Finally, there are various types of statutory trust, such as the office of the personal representative, the office of the Public Trustee, solicitors in respect of their trust accounts, and the statutory trusts created under mechanics' lien statutes and under employment standards legislation for vacation pay.

1203. CLASSIFICATION OF TRUSTS

Trusts may be classified in a variety of ways. Thus one speaks of express and implied trusts, as well as of precatory trusts and of resulting and constructive trusts. Trusts may also be classified as executed and executory, completely and incompletely constituted, lawful and unlawful, private and public, and in a variety of other ways. These several distinctions are discussed below.

1203.1 Express and Implied Trusts

An express trust is one in which the intention of the person creating it clearly signifies that the property is to be held on trust. The term "implied trust" is much more difficult to define, for, historically, it has been given different meanings and it is still variously defined. One author, for example, uses the term to include resulting trusts and other trusts arising from the presumed intention of the settlor.[1]

----

§1203.1
[1]Lewin, p. 8.

In this work the term "implied trust" is used exclusively to describe a trust in which the language of the settlor has been judicially construed and it has been determined that, even though the settlor did not unequivocally state that he was creating a trust, he intended to do so. In this sense, therefore, an implied trust is merely a species of express trust.[2]

Related to the implied trust is the so-called *precatory trust*, that is, one created by precatory words, or words of prayer or request, or expressing a confidence or desire, that certain property be dealt with as indicated. The precatory words must be words that a court of equity can construe as imperative. It has been said, however, that the expression "precatory trust" is a roundabout way of saying that the court finds that there is a trust, although the trust is not expressed as such, but by words of prayer or suggestion.[3] It has also been said that the expression is misleading,[4] for if the settlor's intention to create a trust is not established, the precatory language is of no effect.[5]

1203.2 Resulting and Constructive Trusts

The terms "resulting trust" and "constructive trust" are also variously defined by different authors. For example, Underhill regards resulting trusts as express trusts to the extent that they arise from the intention of the parties, while he classifies trusts that arise by operation of law as constructive trusts.[1] Lewin treats resulting and constructive trusts as well as implied trusts as arising by operation of law.[2]

A more useful way to distinguish these two types of trust is to define in which situations they arise.[3] A constructive trust arises where the court, irrespective of the intent of the parties, raises a trust in order to enforce one person's obligation in equity to transfer property to another.[4] A constructive trust is raised, for example, to require a fiduciary to give up an advantage gained by him through his position or office.[5] The constructive trust is thus primarily a restitutionary device and is so regarded in the United States,[6] although in Anglo-Canadian jurisprudence it has often been treated more as a substantive trust.

A resulting trust arises where one person gratuitously transfers property

---

2*Cf.* Underhill, art. 3; Waters, p. 18.
3*Re Sanson; Sanson v. Turner* (1896), 12 T.L.R. 142.
4*Re Williams; Williams v. Williams*, [1897] 2 Ch. 12 (C.A.), at p. 27.
5See further §1205.1(a), *infra*.
§1203.2
1Underhill, art. 3.
2Lewin, p. 8.
3*Cf.* Waters, pp. 18 *et seq.*; Waters, "The Doctrine of Resulting Trusts in Common Law Canada", 16 McGill L.J. 187 (1970).
4Waters, p. 20.
5See, *e.g., Canadian Aero Service Ltd. v. O'Malley* (1973), 40 D.L.R. (3d) 371, [1974] S.C.R. 592.
64 Scott, §§461 *et seq.*

into the name of another, or the names of himself and another; or where he supplies the purchase money and has the title to the property vested in another, or himself and another; and where the purposes of an express trust fail to exhaust the trust property, because the settlor failed to specify the purposes completely, or because the purpose fails, or because the object of the trust is uncertain or is illegal. In all of these situations, the trust property reverts or results to the settlor on a resulting trust. It is possible to say that it does so on the basis of the presumed intent of the parties and it is for this reason that resulting trusts are sometimes regarded as implied trusts. On the other hand, it may be argued that the property results to the settlor by operation of law, that is, the court implies an obligation on the trustee to reconvey it to the settlor. Whatever rationale is chosen is immaterial to the outcome.[7]

1203.3 Completely and Incompletely Constituted Trusts

A trust is completely constituted or created when there is a clear intention to create it, when the property and the objects are certain and when the property has been transferred to the trustee. An incompletely constituted trust has the same characteristics, except that the trust property has not yet been transferred to the trustees and neither the trustees nor the beneficiaries are entitled to compel the settlor to transfer the property.[1] This type of trust, which, of course, is not a trust at all, often arises in connection with a covenant by the settlor to settle after-acquired property.[2]

1203.4 Executed and Executory Trusts

An executed trust is one in which the interests to be taken by the beneficiaries are clearly and finally set out in the trust instrument. In an executory trust the final terms are left for a subsequent determination.

Lord St. Leonards distinguished the two types as follows:

> All trusts are in a sense executory, because a trust cannot be executed except by conveyance, and, therefore, there is something always to be done. But that is not the sense which a Court of Equity puts upon the term "executory trust". A Court of Equity considers an executory trust as distinguished from a trust executing itself, and distinguishes the two in this manner:— Has the testator been what is called, and very properly called, his own conveyancer? Has he left it to the Court to make out from general expressions what his intention is, or has he so defined that intention that you have nothing to do but to take the limitations he has given to you, and to convert them into legal estates?[1]

---

[7]Waters, pp. 18 *et seq.*
§1203.3
[1]1 Scott, §31.1.
[2]See further §1206.1, *infra.*
§1203.4
[1]*Egerton v. Earl Brownlow* (1853), 4 H.L.C. 1 at p. 210, 10 E.R. 359.

The main effectual difference between the two types of trust arises in the construction of the trust instruments. An executory trust, in which the instrument declaring the trust does not define the terms of the trust with precision but directs the execution of a subsequent instrument defining them and creating the trust, is not, like an executed trust, construed according to the legal effect of the language used, but is construed so as to give effect to the apparent intention.[2] Where the assistance of trustees is necessary to complete the limitations expressed in the declaration of trust, the fact that the limitations were not completely declared by the disposer is sufficient evidence of his intention that they should be further moulded; but, where they have been completely declared by the disposer, there is no authority for interfering and making them different from what they would be at law.[3] If some further act of the creator of the trust or the trustee is necessary to give effect to the executory trust, a court of equity is not bound to construe technical expressions with legal strictness, but will mould the trusts according to the intent of those who created them.[4] In directing a settlement to carry out an executory trust, a court of equity, therefore, modifies any inapt provisions of the trust defined in it.[5] Consequently, if the disposer clearly contemplated a succession of estates or strict settlement, a court of equity directs life interests with remainders, even though the words used in the executory trust legally implied an immediate limitation to the first beneficiaries of an estate in fee, or an absolute interest.[6] Thus, for example, under an executory trust the court can avoid the effect of the rule in *Shelley's Case*[7] which requires that, in a limitation to a person with remainder to his heirs, the entire interest be given to the ancestor and that the heirs receive nothing. If the court can deduce the necessary intent, it can give the heirs a remainder interest.[8]

Similarly, where the limitation in an executory trust, if construed strictly, would offend the rule against perpetuities, a court of equity directs such a limitation as most closely approximates the expressed intention without offending the rule,[9] although in an executed trust the limitation would be void.[10]

---

[2]*Phillips v. James* (1865), 3 De G. J. & S. 72, 46 E.R. 565 (C.A.); *Sackville-West v. Viscount Holmesdale* (1870), L.R. 4 H.L. 543; *Cogan v. Duffield* (1876), 2 Ch. D. 44 (C.A.); *Hastie v. Hastie* (1876), 2 Ch. D. 304 (C.A.); *Re Parrott; Walter v. Parrott* (1886), 33 Ch. D. 274 (C.A.); *Nash v. Allen* (1889), 42 Ch. D. 54; *Re Ballance; Ballance v. Lanphier* (1889), 42 Ch. D. 62.

[3]Henley, L.K., in *Austen v. Taylor* (1759), 1 Eden 361 at pp. 368-9, 28 E.R. 725.

[4]*Adamson v. Adamson* (1889), 17 O.R. 407 (H.C.J.), at pp. 414-5 quoting *Lord Glenorchy v. Bosville* (1733), Cases T. Talbot 3, 25 E.R. 628.

[5]*Re Ballance; Ballance v. Lanphier, supra,* footnote 2.

[6]*White v. Briggs* (1848), 2 Ph. 583, 41 E.R. 1068; *Thompson v. Fisher* (1870), L.R. 10 Eq. 207; *Trevor v. Trevor* (1847), 1 H.L.C. 239, 9 E.R. 747; *Stonor v. Curwen* (1832), 5 Sim. 264, 58 E.R. 336.

[7](1851), 1 Co. Rep. 93 b, 76 E.R. 206. See §1009.6 for a discussion of this rule.

[8]Waters, pp. 21 *et seq.*

[9]*Lyddon v. Ellison* (1854), 19 Beav. 565, 52 E.R. 470; *Re Ballance; Ballance v. Lanphier, supra,* footnote 2; *Re Richardson; Parry v. Holmes,* [1904] 1 Ch. 332.

[10]*Blagrove v. Hancock* (1848), 16 Sim. 371, 60 E.R. 917; *Re Richardson; Parry v. Holmes, supra,* footnote 9.

The fact that the creator of a trust retains in his possession the document declaring it, which is otherwise complete, does not prevent it from being an executed trust.[11]

1203.5 Legal and Illegal Trusts

Trusts are valid or void on the same principles that apply to legal estates.[1] A trust for a purpose which is fraudulent, immoral or otherwise contrary to public policy is void and unenforceable, as where a conveyance of land is made to a grantee to hold for the grantor in fraud of the latter's creditors.[2] Moreover, a trust to defraud creditors is liable to be set aside at the suit of the creditors or the trustee in bankruptcy.[3] Similarly, the trust is void where the transaction involves a fraud on the purchaser,[4] or where property is transferred to a third person on trust to effect an immoral purpose,[5] or involves a gift on trust in favour of future illegitimate children,[6] or in favour of children before their parents' marriage is legalized.[7] The iniquity of such gifts to illegitimate children lies in the fact that it tends to encourage immorality. For

---

[11]*Toronto General Trusts Corp. v. Keyes* (1907), 15 O.L.R. 30 (H.C.J.), in which case Anglin, J., said at p. 35:

> If a deed constituting a trust, once delivered and executed, is effectual, though held by the settlor (*Fletcher v. Fletcher*) [(1844), 4 Hare 67 at p. 69, 67 E.R. 564, 14 L.J. Ch. 66], *à fortiori* a trust completely declared is operative, though the acknowledgment of the existence of the trust in documentary form be retained by the settlor. The property, the subject of the trust, had been delivered to the trustees, and the trustees had accepted it upon the trust. The trust was thus made complete and enforceable.

§1203.5

[1]*Burgess v. Wheate; Attorney-General v. Wheate* (1759), 1 Eden 177, 28 E.R. 652.

[2]*Johnson v. Cline* (1888), 16 O.R. 129 (H.C.J.); *McAuley v. McAuley* (1909), 10 W.L.R. 419, 18 Man. R. 544 (K.B.); *Scheuerman v. Scheuerman* (1916), 28 D.L.R. 223, 52 S.C.R. 625; *Chartered Trust and Executor Co. v. Wycott* (1920), 19 O.W.N. 240 (H.C.), affd 21 O.W.N. 65 (S.C. App. Div.); *Elford v. Elford* (1922), 69 D.L.R. 284, 64 S.C.R. 125, affg 61 D.L.R. 40, [1921] 2 W.W.R. 963 (Sask. C.A.); *Doty v. Marks* (1923), 55 O.L.R. 147, [1924] 3 D.L.R. 687 (S.C. App. Div.); *Harrington v. Harrington* (1925), 56 O.L.R. 568, [1925] 2 D.L.R. 849 (S.C. App. Div.); *Johnson v. Johnson* (1926), 31 O.W.N. 313 (H.C.); *Krys v. Krys*, [1929] 1 D.L.R. 289, [1929] S.C.R. 153; *Goodfriend v. Goodfriend* (1971), 22 D.L.R. (3d) 699, [1972] S.C.R. 640.

[3]Under the *Bankruptcy Act*, R.S.C. 1970, c. B-3, ss. 69-79; *Fraudulent Conveyances Act*, 13 Eliz. 1, c. 5 (1570); 27 Eliz. 1, c. 4 (1585), in force in some of the provinces as received English law; *Fraudulent Conveyances Act*, R.S.O. 1980, c. 176; *Fraudulent Conveyance Act*, R.S.B.C. 1979, c. 142; R.S.M. 1970, c. F160; *Assignments and Preferences Act*, R.S.O. 1980, c. 33; R.S.N.B. 1973, c. A-16; R.S.N.S. 1967, c. 16; *Fraudulent Preference Act*, R.S.B.C. 1979, c. 143; *Fraudulent Preferences Act*, R.S.A. 1980, c. F-18; R.S.S. 1978, c. F-21; *Marriage Settlement Act*, R.S.S. 1978, c. M-5; *Assignments Act*, R.S.M. 1970, c. A150; *Frauds on Creditors Act*, R.S.P.E.I. 1974, c. F-13.

[4]*National Bank v. Master* (1925), 28 O.W.N. 419 (H.C.).

[5]*Bakewell v. Mackenzie* (1905), 1 W.W.R. 68, 6 Terr. L.R. 257.

[6]*Re Springfield; Davies v. Springfield* (1922), 38 T.L.R. 263.

[7]*Thompson v. Thomas* (1891), 27 L.R. Ir. 457.

this reason, such gifts are void only to the extent that they provide for illegitimate children conceived after the trust takes effect. However, a gift to an illegitimate child *en ventre sa mère* when a will is executed is valid and a gift to an illegitimate child conceived between the date of the execution of the will and the date of the testator's death is probably valid as well.[8] Clearly, gifts to named illegitimate children are as valid as gifts to other named persons. It is probable that public policy in this respect is changing.[9] Indeed, this rule no longer applies in jurisdictions where the status of illegitimate children has been changed to conform to the status of legitimate children.[10]

A trust in favour of a wife within the prohibited degrees of marriage is also void as contrary to public policy.[11]

A trust may be made upon condition, either precedent or subsequent and the condition may offend public policy or be uncertain. If the condition is subsequent, the condition only is struck out, but if it is precedent, the trust itself is liable to be void. If the condition precedent is in respect of real property the trust is void. If it is in respect of personal property, however, the gift is void only if the condition is *malum in se*, that is, so fundamentally wrong that it would be rejected in any society. On the other hand, if the condition is *malum prohibitum*, and hence a minor wrong, only the condition is struck down.[12] Conditions which tend to remove children from parental control,[13] or that interfere with the duty of parents to teach their children religious and moral precepts, such as a gift to a child if he joins a particular faith, are void.[14] Apart from such cases, conditions in restraint of religion are

---

[8]*Occleston v. Fullalove* (1874), L.R. 9 Ch. App. 147.

[9]See, *e.g.*, *Re Nicholls*, [1973] 2 O.R. 33, 32 D.L.R. (3d) 683 (H.C.J.); *Re Stevenson* (1966), 66 D.L.R. (2d) 717 (B.C.S.C.); *Re Dunsmuir* (1968), 67 D.L.R. (2d) 227, 63 W.W.R. 321 (B.C.S.C.).

[10]As in Ontario and New Brunswick. See *Children's Law Reform Act*, R.S.O. 1980, c. 68, esp. ss. 1, 2; *Child and Family Services and Family Relations Act*, S.N.B. 1980, c. C-2.1, Pt. VI.

[11]*Phillips v. Probyn*, [1899] 1 Ch. 811, gift to deceased wife's sister before marriage was made valid.

[12]Thus a gift to a person on condition that she engage in prostitution would be *malum in se* whereas a condition that she is still living away from her spouse is *malum prohibitum*. See *Eastern Trust Co. v. McTague* (1963), 39 D.L.R. (2d) 743, 48 M.P.R. 134 *sub nom. Re Blanchard Estate* (P.E.I.C.A.). The distinction has been largely ignored in Canadian law, however. See, *e.g.*, *Re Gross*, [1937] O.W.N. 88 (C.A.); *Re Going*, [1951] O.R. 147, [1951] 2 D.L.R. 136 (C.A.). The recent case, *Re McBride* (1980), 6 E.T.R. 181 (Ont. H.C.J.), noted 5 E.T.Q. 97 (1980), which revives the distinction appears to be wrong.

[13]*Re Gross, supra*, footnote 12, gift to granddaughter if she has remained in custody of testator, his wife and his son subject to limited access rights in the mother, held to be a condition precedent and void.

[14]*Re Going, supra*, footnote 12. It has been held in England, however, that the time of choice for compliance or non-compliance with the condition must be postponed until the child reaches the age of majority and a reasonable time thereafter: *Re May*; *Eggar v. May*, [1917] 2 Ch. 126; *Re May*; *Eggar v. May*, [1932] 1 Ch. 99 (C.A.).

not void, however.[15] On the other hand, social discrimination cannot be made the subject of a condition.[16] Similarly, general restraints against marriage,[17] but not partial restraints,[18] and restraints against remarriage,[19] are void. However, if the gift is determinable on marriage,[20] or even where it is upon condition subsequent, but the court can find an intention that the testator intended to provide for the donee until marriage,[21] the condition will be held valid. Moreover, in the case of a condition subsequent against remarriage with a gift over, the gift over takes effect if the gift consists of realty or personalty, but if there is no gift over, where the gift is personalty, the condition is regarded as having been imposed *in terrorem* and is struck out.[22]

The rule that a limitation is void if it offends the rule against perpetuities because it will not necessarily vest within the required period, equally applies to equitable remainders the legal estate of which is vested in trustees,[23] so that a trust which offends the rule as modified by statue[24] is void.

A trust which is only void in part, however, may not be wholly void. In the case of a discretionary trust in favour of various objects or for various purposes in the alternative as the trustees may select, of which some are legal and others illegal, the trustees may exercise their discretion in favour of those which are legal, but cannot do so in regard to those which are illegal.[25] The cases cited dealt with trusts for charities but the principle is not confined to charities. Thus, where a testator conveyed land to trustees for the benefit of his creditors, to be disposed of by the trustees by lottery but, failing that plan, to sell as they might deem best, it was held that the trust, although void as to the provision for a lottery, was otherwise valid.[26]

Where a trust is for some legal and some illegal objects or purposes, the

---

[15]*Re Curran*, [1939] O.W.N. 191, [1939] 2 D.L.R. 803 (H.C.J.); *Blathwayt v. Baron Cawley*, [1975] 3 W.L.R. 684 (H.L.); *Re Tuck's Settlement Trusts*; *Public Trustee v. Tuck*, [1978] 2 W.L.R. 411 (C.A.).

[16]*Re Hurshman*; *Mindlin v. Hurshman* (1956), 6 D.L.R. (2d) 615 (B.C.S.C.), gift to daughter, provided she was not married to a Jew.

[17]*Re Cutter* (1916), 37 O.L.R. 42, 31 D.L.R. 382 (H.C.), a gift to testator's sister for life with gift over in the event of remarriage, held to be a general restraint under a condition subsequent.

[18]Such as a prohibition against marrying a person of a particular faith.

[19]*Re Muirhead Estate*, [1919] 2 W.W.R. 454, 12 S.L.R. 123 (K.B.).

[20]*Eastern Trust Co. v. McTague*, *supra*, footnote 12.

[21]*Re Haythornthwaite*, [1930] 3 D.L.R. 235, [1930] 1 W.W.R. 58 (Alta. S.C.); *Re Goodwin* (1969), 3 D.L.R. (3d) 281 (Alta. S.C.); *Re Gilbert*, [1959] O.W.N. 294 (H.C.J.); *Re McLean*, [1957] O.W.N. 11, 6 D.L.R. (2d) 519 (C.A.).

[22]On this and the preceding points, see generally Waters, pp. 230 *et seq*.

[23]*Re Finch*; *Abbiss v. Burney* (1881), 17 Ch. D. 211 (C.A.).

[24]*Perpetuities Act*, R.S.A. 1980, c. P-4; R.S.O. 1980, c. 374; R.S.P.E.I. 1974, c. P-3.

[25]*Sorresby v. Hollins* (1740), 9 Mod. 221, 88 E.R. 410; *Grimmett v. Grimmett* (1754), Amb. 210, 27 E.R. 140; *Faversham Corp. v. Ryder* (1854), 5 De G. M. & G. 350, 43 E.R. 905 (C.A.); *University of London v. Yarrow* (1857), 1 De G. & J. 72, 44 E.R. 649 (C.A.); *Carter v. Green* (1857), 3 K. & J. 591, 69 E.R. 1245; *Lewis v. Allenby* (1870), L.R. 10 Eq. 668; *Re Piercy*; *Whitwham v. Piercy*, [1898] 1 Ch. 565 (C.A.).

[26]*Goodeve v. Manners* (1855), 5 Gr. 114.

trust itself may be wholly valid, or wholly void, or partly valid and partly void, depending upon its form; and, if the part of the property applicable to illegal purposes is designated or ascertainable, the trust is valid for the legal purposes.[27] Consequently, if in form the trust is for a legal charitable purpose to consist of all that part of the property as is not applied to an illegal purpose, the whole of the property may be applied for the legal purpose,[28] and that is equally true of a trust for a legal purpose with an illegal purpose annexed to it;[29] but, if the parts of the property to be applied for legal and illegal purposes, respectively, are not designated or ascertainable, so that it is uncertain whether any residue would have remained for the legal purposes if the illegal purposes could have been fulfilled, the whole trust is void.[30] The same applies to cases where the trustees are given a discretion to apply trust property to "such charitable or benevolent purposes" as they shall select.[31]

On the other hand, where a conveyance of land was made and the grantees contemporaneously executed a declaration of trust in regard to it, under which the trustees were to sell the land, pay the annual revenue to the settlor for life and, after his death, to pay the annual revenue on a portion in the trustees' discretion to M for life, and the trustees sold the land but, at the settlor's death, it was alleged that the settlement was void because the disposition of the *corpus* was void under the *Statute of Mortmain*,[32] which it was, it was held that the trusts declared in favour of the settlor and M were valid and sufficient to support the sale.[33]

Similarly, the fact that one trust in a deed of settlement is void for remoteness does not make the whole deed void.[34] Thus, in one case land was devised to trustees in fee simple upon trust for A for life and, after his death, in trust for his children who should attain the age of 21 and the issue attaining age 21 of any child dying under age 21 but, in the event of their being no such child or

---

[27]*Chapman v. Brown* (1801), 6 Ves. Jun. 404 at pp. 410-11, 31 E.R. 1115; *Mitford v. Reynolds* (1842), 1 Ph. 185, 41 E.R. 602; *Re Rigley's Trusts* (1866), 15 W.R. 190; *Champney v. Davey* (1879), 11 Ch. D. 949; *Re Vaughan; Vaughan v. Thomas* (1866), 33 Ch. D. 187, all cases involving trusts for charities.

[28]*Fisk v. Attorney-General* (1867), L.R. 4 Eq. 521; *Re Williams* (1877), 5 Ch. D. 735; *Re Birkett* (1878), 9 Ch. D. 576.

[29]*Hunter v. Bullock* (1872), L.R. 14 Eq. 45; *Dawson v. Small* (1874), L.R. 18 Eq. 114.

[30]*Chapman v. Brown*, supra, footnote 27; *Limbrey v. Gurr* (1819), 6 Madd. 151, 56 E.R. 1049; *Attorney-General v. Hinxman* (1820), 2 Jac. & W. 270, 37 E.R. 630; *Cramp v. Playfoot* (1858), 4 K. & J. 479, 70 E.R. 200; *Re Taylor; Martin v. Freeman* (1888), 58 L.T. 538, 4 T.L.R. 302, being cases in which the first gift was contrary to the Mortmain Acts and uncertain in value; *Fowler v. Fowler* (1864), 33 Beav. 616, 55 E.R. 507, a case relating to a perpetuity in the maintenance of family graves.

[31]*Morice v. Bishop of Durham* (1804), 9 Ves. Jun. 399, 32 E.R. 656, affd 10 Ves. Jun. 522, 32 E.R. 947; *Chichester Diocesan Fund and Board of Finance (Inc.) v. Simpson*, [1944] A.C. 341 (H.L.); *Brewer v. McCauley*, [1955] 1 D.L.R. 415, [1954] S.C.R. 645; *Re Albery*, [1964] 1 O.R. 342, 42 D.L.R. (2d) 201 (H.C.J.).

[32]9 Geo. 2, c. 36 (1736).

[33]*McIsaac v. Heneberry* (1873), 20 Gr. 348. *Cf. Doe d. Vancott v. Reid* (1847), 3 U.C.Q.B. 244.

[34]*Fonseca v. Jones* (1911), 14 W.L.R. 148, 21 Man. R. 168 (C.A.).

issue attaining age 21, in trust for the children of B attaining age 21, with a provision for accumulation of the rents for twenty-one years after the testator's death in trust for such children of B. A died without ever having had a child and B had six children who attained age 21, the youngest being born after the eldest attained age 21 but before the end of the period of accumulation. It was held that the gift over to B's children was divisible into two alternative gifts; (a) a gift over in the event of A having no children, and (b) a gift over in the event of there being no child or issue of a child of A attaining age 21 and that, consequently, the first alternative gift over was valid, as it was not too remote and the event had happened.[35]

1203.6   Passive and Active Trusts

An active or special trust is one in which the trustee has active duties to perform that are imposed upon him by the settlor, or where the beneficiaries are not able to call for an end to the trust.[1]

A bare, naked, passive, or simple trust arises where the trustee holds property, in which he has no beneficial interest, in trust for the absolute benefit of persons of full age and otherwise *sui juris*, in regard to which he has no duties to perform, other than his legal duty to take reasonable care of the property by maintaining or investing it, and his duty to convey it to the beneficiaries, or at their direction, on demand.[2]

He is a bare trustee if he originally had no duties to perform, or if the duties which he had originally have ceased, so that, on the requisition of the *cestuis que trust* he would be compellable in equality to convey the estate to them or at their direction.[3] Thus, where a testator devised his real property to two married women, both of them having beneficial interests in the proceeds of sale, and part of the property was sold by them under a judgment in an action for the administration of the testator's estate, the purchaser paying his purchase money into court, it was held that the women were bare trustees of the property because they had no further interest in the property and no remaining duty to perform except to convey the property to the purchaser.[4] Where property was devised and bequeathed to a trustee for the benefit of another person and the trustee was "to take full control and disposal of the same in such manner as he may deem proper", it was held that such power of control and disposal were solely personal to such trustee and that, on his death, his executors succeeded to the trusteeship without such power and that they were

---

[35]*Watson v. Young* (1885), 28 Ch. D. 436.

§1203.6

[1]Underhill, art. 4.

[2]*Christie v. Ovington* (1875), 1 Ch. D. 279; *Morgan v. Swansea Urban Sanitary Authority* (1878), 9 Ch. D. 582; *Re Docwra; Docwra v. Faith* (1885), 29 Ch. D. 693; *Re Cunningham and Frayling*, [1891] 2 Ch. 567.

[3]*Christie v. Ovington, supra*, p. 281.

[4]*Re Docwra; Docwra v. Faith, supra*, footnote 2.

bare trustees with no duty but to preserve the legal estate of the *cestui que trust*.[5]

A person who has active duties to perform, although he has no beneficial interest in the trust property, is not a bare trustee.[6] In *Re Cunningham and Frayling*,[7] freeholds were conveyed to D and P upon certain trusts, the deed providing for appointment of new trustees, but the power to appoint being limited to named persons and, after the death of the survivor of them, to "the acting trustees or trustee for the time being, or the executors or administrators of the last acting trustee". D died; P died intestate leaving an heir, S; and S died intestate leaving his three daughters as heiresses. All of the persons having the power to appoint new trustees died without exercising it. By deed the three daughters appointed new trustees who contracted to sell the property under the trust for sale. It was held that S, having active duties to perform, had not been a bare trustee, that the legal estate descended to the heiresses who became acting trustees for the time being and that their appointment of new trustees was valid.

A person who has a beneficial interest of any kind in the trust property is in no circumstances a bare trustee of it.[8] In *Lysaght v. Edwards*,[9] the plaintiffs contracted to buy real property. After the title had been accepted but before completion of the transaction, the vendor died, devising all of his real estate to H and M upon trust for sale and devising to H alone all of the realty which, at the time of his death, might be vested in the vendor as trustee, which included the land so sold by him. H was not a bare trustee of it because the transaction was not completed. Jessell, M.R., said that the position of such a vendor is something between a naked or bare trustee and a mere trustee having no beneficial interest. He also held that a vendor of freeholds who let the purchaser into possession before payment of the purchase price and execution of a conveyance was not a bare trustee, as he had a lien on the property for the purchase price and was not bound to convey until payment had been made.[10]

After completion of a sale, however, the vendor has no beneficial interest left. Consequently, in British Columbia, it was held that a statute which purports to authorize so extraordinary a proceeding as the sale by an execution creditor of land which, although registered in the debtor's name, is merely held by him as bare trustee with no beneficial ownership in himself, must be very plain and clear; and a statute which gives a judgment creditor a lien on "all the lands of the judgment debtor" does not mean more than a lien on lands to the extent to which the debtor is beneficially interested therein.[11]

---

[5]*McKenzie v. McKenzie* (1924), 56 O.L.R. 247, [1925] 1 D.L.R. 373 (S.C.).

[6]*Re Cunningham and Frayling*, [1891] 2 Ch. 567.

[7]*Ibid.*

[8](1876), 2 Ch. D. 499 at p. 506, *per* Jessel, M.R.

[9]*Ibid.*

[10]*Cf. Morgan v. Swansea Urban Sanitary Authority*, *supra*, footnote 2.

[11]*Entwisle v. Lenz & Leiser* (1908), 14 B.C.R. 51, 9 W.L.R. 317 (Full Court), in which case execution creditors registered a judgment under the *Judgment Act*, S.B.C. 1908, c. 26, against the lands of the judgment debtor. He had previously sold a certain lot

Since a bare trustee's sole remaining function is to convey at the direction of the *cestui que trust*, he has no rights in the trust property. Hence, it was held that a bare trustee cannot settle an account on behalf of the *cestui que trust* without the latter's consent,[12] nor can he, without the consent of the *cestui que trust*, petition to have a debtor of the estate declared bankrupt.[13]

An estate of which a bankrupt is seised as bare trustee does not pass to the assignees,[14] and a bare trustee of an outstanding term cannot avail himself of it to establish a priority.[15] It has been held that the mortgagor, as owner of the beneficial estate, has the power to convey even if the legal estate is held by a bare trustee, and that he can compel the bare trustee to grant the legal estate, or to grant it to him so that he can convey it.[16] Since a bare trustee must convey to or at the direction of the *cestui que trust*, he cannot otherwise part with the legal estate so as to confer any benefit thereby.[17] He has no right to the legal estate when the trusts are at an end.

P devised a freehold house to trustees upon trust for certain persons during their lives and then for C in fee simple. C devised all of his real and personal property to trustees upon trust to pay to his wife or permit her to receive the produce thereof during her life or widowhood and, after her death or remarriage, whichever should first happen, upon trust for his natural son, G, his heirs, executors, administrators and assigns. The will empowered the trustees, during the life of the widow and minority of the son, to alter the investments and to sell realty or personalty and directed them to invest the proceeds; the widow died and G died intestate without issue. Upon their deaths and the death of the last life tenant under P's will, all trusts under both wills came to an end and the question arose whether the surviving trustee under P's will, or the surviving trustee under C's will, was entitled to the house. It was held that, as the trustees under C's will had no active duties to perform except during the life of C's widow and the minority of G, the surviving

---

to the plaintiff who neglected, through ignorance of the *Land Registry Act*, S.B.C. 1906, c. 23, to register his conveyance for some months. In an action to set aside the cloud on his title, it was held that the judgment creditors only had a right against lands possessed by the debtor and that, as he had conveyed the lot before the judgment of the execution creditors was obtained, he was a bare trustee of the land for the plaintiff. This case was followed in *Gregory v. Princeton Collieries; Re Execution Act* (1918), 40 D.L.R. 739, [1918] 1 W.W.R. 265 (B.C.S.C.), but was distinguished and to some extent questioned in *Bank of Hamilton v. Hartery* (1919), 45 D.L.R. 638, 58 S.C.R. 338, affg 43 D.L.R. 14, [1918] 3 W.W.R. 551 (C.A.), dealing with the *Land Registry Act* and holding that a judgment registered in the Land Registry Office on an application made after the date of execution of a mortgage, takes priority over the mortgage.

[12]*Per* Lord Hardwicke, L.C., in *Fell v. Lutwidge* (1740), Barn. C. 319 at p. 321, 27 E.R. 662.

[13]*Re Adams; Ex p. Cully* (1878), 9 Ch. D. 307 (C.A.); *Re Hastings; Ex p. Dearle* (1884), 14 Q.B.D. 184 (C.A.).

[14]*Re Elford; Ex p. Gennys* (1829), Mont. & M. 258.

[15]*Shaw v. Neale* (1858), 6 H.L.C. 581, 10 E.R. 1422.

[16]*Per* Jessel, M.R., in *General Finance, Mortgage and Discount Co. v. Liberator Permanent Benefit Building Society* (1878), 10 Ch. D. 15.

[17]See the comment of North, J., in *Garnham v. Skipper* (1885), 53 L.T. 940 (H.C.J.).

trustee under C's will was a bare trustee with no right to call for a conveyance of the legal estate.[18]

A trustee who has had active duties which have ceased so as to make him a bare trustee, however, is affected by the equitable rule against trustees purchasing the trust property.[19]

A bare trustee in respect of any estate held by him, cannot be the protector of a settlement of a fee tail under the Imperial *Fines and Recoveries Act*.[20] This Imperial Act is in force in Manitoba.[21]

1204. PARTIES TO AN EXPRESS TRUST

In the next three sections the capacity of the three parties to an express trust, the settlor, the trustee and the beneficiary, is discussed.

1204.1 The Settlor

Any person legally capable of alienating real property in his lifetime or by will is capable of creating a trust of it by disposing of it in trust in his lifetime or by will.[1] This includes aliens[2] and married women.[3] Minors, bankrupts and mental incompetents are limited in their right to convey real property, however.

Mentally ill persons are incapable of disposing of their property since they do not understand the nature of the transaction, although the test is likely to be more stringent in the case of disposition by will than *inter vivos*, for in the former they must not only be able to understand the nature of the act, but also be able to have regard to legitimate claims on their bounty.[4] If a person

---

[18]*Re Lashmar; Moody v. Penfold*, [1891] 1 Ch. 258 (C.A.), Fry, L.J., stating that, under the trust to pay to the wife or permit her to receive the annual produce during her life, the legal estate was not vested in the trustees but in the wife, according to the decision in *Doe d. Leicester v. Biggs* (1809), 2 Taunt. 109, 127 E.R. 1017. That decision was criticized by Lindley and Bowen, L.JJ., in *Re Lashmar, supra*, but appears to be correct.

[19]*Ex p. Bennett* (1805), 10 Ves. Jun. 381, 32 E.R. 893; as to this rule see §1212.2(a), *infra*.

[20]3 & 4 Wm. 4, c. 74 (1833).

[21]See *Law of Property Act*, R.S.M. 1970, c. L90, s. 30.

§1204.1

[1]*Rycroft v. Christy* (1840), 3 Beav. 238, 49 E.R. 93; *Knight v. Bowyer* (1857), 23 Beav. 609 at p. 635, 53 E.R. 239, Romilly, M.R., affd 2 De G. & J. 421, 44 E.R. 1053; *Gilbert v. Overton* (1864), 2 H. & M. 110, 71 E.R. 402.

[2]*Law of Property Act*, R.S.M. 1970, c. L90, ss. 2, 3; *Property Act*, R.S.N.B. 1973, c. P-19, s. 10; *Real Property Act*, R.S.N.S. 1967, c. 261, s. 1; *Aliens' Real Property Act*, R.S.O. 1980, c. 19; *Citizenship Act*, S.C. 1974-75-76, c. 108, s. 33. But note the restrictions on the quantity of land that can be held by aliens under the *Real Property Act*, R.S.P.E.I. 1974, c. R-4, s. 3.

[3]Pursuant to the several Married Women's Property statutes. See, *e.g.*, *Married Women's Deeds Act*, R.S.N.S. 1967, c. 175; *Family Law Reform Act*, R.S.O. 1980, c. 152, s. 65; S.P.E.I. 1978, c. 6, s. 60(2).

[4]For the different emphasis between the two types of disposition see Waters, p. 85.

is mentally ill the power to dispose of his property usually vests in some public official such as the Public Trustee and the creation of a trust of it in such a case is unlikely. The same applies to persons who are incapable of managing their affairs, whose dispositive powers are usually vested in his committee. The committee may be either a public official, a number of individuals or a trust company.

Minors are generally incapable of making a trust. However, they are permitted to make privileged wills, and hence a testamentary trust, if they are members of the armed forces or seamen while at sea or, in some cases, if they are married or are contemplating marriage.[5] An *inter vivos* settlement made by a minor is voidable at common law and has to be confirmed after he reaches the age of majority, but under statute in some provinces the court's consent to a disposition is necessary.[6] Minors are sometimes permitted to make marriage settlements, however, with the court's approval.[7]

1204.2 The Trustee

Any person capable of holding property in his own right may be a trustee, so a trustee may be an unmarried woman,[1] a married woman,[2] a minor[3], an alien,[4] or a trust company.[5] Minors or persons who are mentally incapacitated cannot effectively deal with trust property, however, and they can be removed and replaced under the provisions of the several Trustee Acts and mental incompetency legislation.[6]

A person may hold land as trustee for himself and other persons.[7] He may

---

[5]See, *e.g.*, *Succession Law Reform Act*, R.S.O. 1980, c. 488, s. 8.

[6]*Minors' Property Act*, R.S.A. 1980, c. M-16, s. 2; *Chancery Act*, R.S.P.E.I. 1951, c. 21, ss. 71, 72 (not consol. or rep. by R.S.P.E.I. 1974); *Minors Act*, R.S.O. 1980, c. 292, s. 4(1); *Infants Act*, R.S.S. 1978, c. I-9, s. 9(1).

[7]*Infants Act*, R.S.B.C. 1979, c. 196, s. 20; *Minors' Property Act*, R.S.A. 1980, c. M-16, s. 12. The comparable provisions in Ontario, *Infants Act*, R.S.O. 1970, c. 222, ss. 13-15, as amended by S.O. 1971, Vol. 2, c. 98, ss. 6, 16, Sched., para. 14, were repealed by the *Family Law Reform Act*, S.O. 1978, c. 2, s. 80(1). However, under that Act, a minor who has the capacity to contract marriage may enter into a marriage contract or separation agreement (but not a cohabitation agreement) with the approval of the court given before or after the contract is entered into. See generally on this point Waters, pp. 83-5.

§1204.2

[1]*Head v. Gould*, [1898] 2 Ch. 250 at p. 272; *Re Peake's Settled Estates*, [1894] 3 Ch. 520; *Re Dickinson's Trusts*, [1902] W.N. 104 (H.C.J.).

[2]*Lake v. De Lambert* (1799), 4 Ves. Jun. 592, 31 E.R. 305; *Drummond v. Tracy* (1860), Johns. 608, 70 E.R. 562; *Avery v. Griffin* (1868), L.R. 6 Eq. 606.

[3]*Re Tallatire*, [1885] W.N. 191 (H.C.J.).

[4]*Meinertzhagen v. Davis* (1844), 1 Coll. 335, 63 E.R. 444.

[5]Under the provisions of the several Trust Companies Acts and similar legislation. See Waters, pp. 91-94. As to the offices of the Public Trustee, judicial trustees and custodian trustees, see *ibid.*, pp. 88-91, 94-95.

[6]*Ibid.*, pp. 89-90.

[7]*Burges v. Lamb* (1809), 16 Ves. Jun. 174, 33 E.R. 950; *Ex p. Clutton* (1853), 17 Jur. 988; *Forster v. Abraham* (1874), L.R. 17 Eq. 351; *Re Courtier; Coles v. Courtier* (1886), 34 Ch. D. 136 (C.A.); *Head v. Gould, supra*, footnote 1. *Burn v. Gifford* (1879), 8 P.R. (Ont.) 44 (Ch. Ch.), at p. 47.

not be sole trustee and sole *cestui que trust* of the same estates,[8] as a man cannot be trustee for himself,[9] but he may be the legal owner of one estate and the equitable owner of a smaller estate which does not merge in the larger.[10] Although equitable estates in common will merge in a joint legal estate subsequently acquired by the tenants in common,[11] an equitable estate tail will not merge in a legal fee simple estate.[12] The creator of a trust may appoint himself as trustee to see to the fulfilment of the trust.[13]

Trusts do not fail by reason of the failure of trustees.[14] Consequently, a trust does not fail because no trustee is named in the instrument creating it, or because the named trustee declines to act, or is unable to act through death or otherwise.[15] If no trustee is effectively appointed, or all trustees appointed die before the trust takes effect, or refuse to act, the trust follows the legal estate in the property and the holder of that estate becomes a constructive trustee for the purposes of the trust.

1204.3 The Beneficiary

A trust can be created in favour of any person to whom, or to any object to which, a gift can lawfully be given directly.[1] By means of a trustee, a trust can be created in favour of persons not yet in existence and objects incapable of taking a benefit by direct gift,[2] such as a gift to maintain the testator's animals,[3] provided that it is not unlawful on grounds of public policy or as offending the rule against perpetuities. Land may be devised in trust in fee simple with an executory devise over in favour of another person on the

---

[8]*Habergham v. Vincent* (1793), 2 Ves. Jun. 204 at p. 210, 30 E.R. 595; *Brydges v. Brydges* (1796), 3 Ves. Jun. 120 at pp. 126-7, 30 E.R. 926; *Selby v. Alston* (1797), 3 Ves. Jun. 339 at p. 341, 30 E.R. 1042; *Re Douglas; Wood v. Douglas* (1884), 28 Ch. D. 327 at p. 331.

[9]*Goodright v. Wells* (1781), 2 Dougl. 771, 99 E.R. 491.

[10]*Robinson v. Cuming* (1739), 1 Atk. 473, 26 E.R. 302; *Brydges v. Brydges, supra,* footnote 8.

[11]*Re Selous; Thomson v. Selous,* [1901] 1 Ch. 921.

[12]*Merest v. James* (1821), 6 Madd. 118, 56 E.R. 1037, because the Statute *De Donis Conditionalibus*, 13 Edw. 1, c. 1 (1285), was thought to prohibit it. *Cf. Conveyancing and Law of Property Act,* R.S.O. 1980, c. 90, s. 10.

[13]*Re Helliwell's Trusts* (1874), 21 Gr. 346 at pp. 348-9.

[14]Lord Eldon, L.C., in *Ellison v. Ellison* (1802), 6 Ves. Jun. 656 at p. 663, 31 E.R. 1243; *Brown v. Higgs* (1803), 8 Ves. Jun. 561 at p. 570, 32 E.R. 473.

[15]*Dickenson v. Teasdale* (1862), 1 De G. J. & S. 52 at p. 59, 46 E.R. 21; *Siggers v. Evans* (1855), 5 El. & Bl. 367 at p. 374, 119 E.R. 518.

§1204.3

[1]*Burgess v. Wheate; Attorney-General v. Wheate* (1759), 1 Eden 177, at p. 195, 28 E.R. 652.

[2]*Re Bowles; Amedroz v. Bowles,* [1902] 2 Ch. 650.

[3]*Re Dean; Cooper-Dean v. Stevens* (1889), 41 Ch. D. 552 at p. 556.

happening of a specified contingency,[4] subject to the rule against perpetuities.[5]

In effect, therefore, any person, natural or corporate and whether under a disability or not, can be a beneficiary under a trust. However, persons under a disability cannot, themselves, dispose of their beneficial interest or call for a transfer of it to them, and certain persons such as mental incompetents and persons unborn are usually represented by others, such as the Public Trustee, a committee, or the Official Guardian, to protect their interests.

Unincorporated associations, not being persons, are incapable of being beneficiaries under a trust or of holding title to property except through trustees. Similarly, trusts for purposes, as opposed to persons, are severely restricted unless the purposes are charitable.[6] In Ontario, however, land conveyed or devised for a charitable purpose, that is, upon a charitable trust or to a charitable institution, is required to be sold within two years; if it is not, it vests in the Public Trustee who is required to sell it and pay the proceeds to the charity. There is provision for a charity to retain land required for its actual use and occupation with the sanction of the court.[7]

1205.   THE REQUISITES OF A TRUST

To create a trust, there must be words which are or can be construed as imperative. The property affected must be clearly described and the objects of the trust must be clearly designated and be lawful.[1] These "three certainties" are described in the following sections.

1205.1   Certainty of Intention

In creating a trust, the usual and technical words are "trust" and "trustee",

---

[4]*Spence v. Handford* (1858), 27 L.J. Ch. 767, 31 L.T. (O.S.) 244; *Re Finch*; *Abbiss v. Burney* (1881), 17 Ch. D. 211 (C.A.); *Re Morgan* (1883), 24 Ch. D. 114.

[5]*Leake v. Robinson* (1817), 2 Mer. 363, 35 E.R. 979; *Blagrove v. Hancock* (1848), 16 Sim. 371, 60 E.R. 917.

[6]This subject is not expanded upon here. For a discussion of non-charitable purpose trusts, see Waters, pp. 421-9, and of charities, see *ibid.*, ch. 14. Specific non-charitable purpose trusts are permitted to exist as powers of appointment for twenty-one years under perpetuities legislation: *Perpetuities Act*, R.S.O. 1980, c. 373, s. 16; R.S.A. 1980, c. P-4, s. 20.

[7]*Mortmain and Charitable Uses Act*, R.S.O. 1980, c. 297, ss. 6, 7, 10, 12. See generally Law Reform Com'n *Report on Mortmain, Charitable Uses and Religious Institutions* (Toronto, Ministry of the Attorney General, 1976); Oosterhoff, "The Law of Mortmain; An Historical and Comparative Review", 27 U. of T. L.J. 257 (1977). See also *Palmer v. Marmon* (1978), 32 O.R. (2d) 417 (H.C.J.), appeal dismissed, *ibid.*

§1205

[1]*Cruwys v. Colman* (1804), 9 Ves. Jun. 319 at p. 323, 32 E.R. 626; *Wright v. Atkyns* (1823), Turn. & R. 143 at p. 157, 37 E.R. 1051; *Knight v. Knight* (1840), 3 Beav. 148 at p. 172, 49 E.R. 58, affd 11 Cl. & Fin. 513, 8 E.R. 1195 *sub nom. Knight v. Boughton*; *Dooby v. Watson* (1888), 39 Ch. D. 178; *Hill v. Hill*, [1897] 1 Q.B. 483 (C.A.), at p. 493; *Re Williams*; *Williams v. Williams*, [1897] 2 Ch. 12 (C.A.), at p. 28; Williams, "The Three Certainties", 4 Mod. L. Rev. 20 (1940).

but it is not necessary to use those words and a trust may be created by the general effect of the instrument,[1] there being no magic in the word "trust".[2] A trust may be created by any words clear enough to show the intention of creating it.[3] Thus, where the words used were "on condition" that a person would pay a sum of money, it was held that the settlor used them in the same sense as he would have used the words "upon trust".[4]

(a) Precatory language

Words in a will expressing the testator's request, entreaty, wish, desire, confidence or hope that a devisee or legatee of property will apply it for the benefit of a specified person or to a specified object, often have been held in the past to create trusts, particularly where children would be the beneficiaries. The expression of intention must be definite, however, having regard to the context of the whole will.[5] A trust will not be regarded as created by precatory words if the general scope of the will leads to the inference that such was not intended, for the testator might, if he had so intended, have created an express trust by imperative words.[6]

It is clear that a precatory trust, once established, is just like any other trust.[7] In referring to precatory words, Rigby, L.J., said:

> As I understand the law of the Court, this phrase is nothing more than a misleading nickname. When a trust is once established, it is equally a trust, and has all the effects and incidents of a trust, whether declared in clearly imperative terms by a testator, or deduced upon a consideration of the whole will from language not amounting necessarily and in its prima facie meaning to an imperative trust.[8]

---

§1205.1

[1]*Ex p. Pye*; *Ex p. Dubost* (1811), 18 Ves. Jun. 140, 34 E.R. 271; *Kekewich v. Manning* (1851), 1 De G. M. & G. 176 at p. 194, 42 E.R. 519; *Re Flavell*; *Murray v. Flavell* (1883), 25 Ch. D. 89 (C.A.); *Tiffany v. Clarke* (1858), 6 Gr. 474; *Cameron v. Campbell* (1882), 7 O.A.R. 361.

[2]*Kinloch v. Secretary of State for India* (1882), 7 App. Cas. 619 (H.L.), at p. 630; *Elgin Loan and Savings Co. v. National Trust Co.* (1903), 7 O.L.R. 1 (H.C.J.), at p. 15.

[3]*Re Williams*; *Williams v. Williams*, [1897] 2 Ch. 12 (C.A.), at pp. 18-19; *Kendrick v. Barkey* (1907), 9 O.W.R. 356 (H.C.J.), at p. 361.

[4]*Mulholland v. Merriam* (1872), 19 Gr. 288, affd 20 Gr. 152.

[5]*Shaw v. Lawless* (1838), 5 Cl. & Fin. 129, 7 E.R. 353; *Knight v. Knight* (1840), 3 Beav. 148, 49 E.R. 58, affd 11 Cl. & Fin. 513, 8 E.R. 1195 *sub nom. Knight v. Boughton*; *Re Sanson*; *Sanson v. Turner* (1896), 12 T.L.R. 142; *Hill v. Hill*, [1897] 1 Q.B. 483 (C.A.).

[6]*Knight v. Boughton, supra*, footnote 5, at p. 553, *per* Lord Cottenham.

[7]Garrow, J.A., in *Re Rispin* (1912), 25 O.L.R. 633, 2 D.L.R. 644 (C.A.), affd 8 D.L.R. 756, 46 S.C.R. 649.

[8]*Re Williams*; *Williams v. Williams, supra*, footnote 3, at p. 27, quoted by Cameron, J.A., in *Perry v. Perry* (1918), 40 D.L.R. 628 at p. 637, [1918] 2 W.W.R. 485 at p. 493 (Man. C.A.).

Rigby, L.J., also said:

> No authoritative case ever laid it down that there could be any other ground for deducing a trust or condition than the intention of the testator as shewn by the will taken as a whole ... there could be no imperative obligation unless the subject-matter and the objects were both clearly ascertained.[9]

In another case, Cozens-Hardy, M.R., said:

> The Court ought to be very careful not to make words mandatory which are a mere indication of a wish or request. The whole will must be looked at, and the Court must come to a conclusion as best it can in construing, not one particular word, but the will as a whole, as to whether the alleged beneficiary is or is not a mere trustee or whether he takes beneficially with a mere superadded expression of a desire or a wish that he will do something in favour of a particular object, but without imposing any legal obligation.[10]

The tendency of modern decisions is against extending the doctrine of precatory trusts and, for words to operate as a precatory trust, they must be definite in the will as a whole and the subject of the trust must be sufficiently defined and certain.[11]

---

[9]*Re Williams*; *Williams v. Williams*, *supra*, footnote 3, at p. 28, quoted by Riddell, J., in *McKenzie v. McKenzie* (1924), 56 O.L.R. 247 at p. 251, [1925] 1 D.L.R. 373 at p. 376 (H.C.).

[10]*Re Atkinson*; *Atkinson v. Atkinson* (1911), 80 L.J. Ch. 370 (C.A.), at p. 373, quoted in *Johnson v. Farney* (1913), 29 O.L.R. 223 at p. 227, 14 D.L.R. 134 at p. 136 (S.C. App. Div.).

[11]*Mussoorie Bank Ltd. v. Raynor* (1882), 7 App. Cas. 321 (P.C.), at p. 331; and see *Shaw v. Lawless* (1838), 5 Cl. & Fin. 129 at p. 154, 7 E.R. 353 (H.L.); *Re Moore*; *Moore v. Roche* (1886), 55 L.J. Ch. 418 (H.C.J.); *McKenzie v. McKenzie, supra*, footnote 9; *Re Adams and Kensington Vestry* (1884), 27 Ch. D. 394 (C.A.), at pp. 406-10, *per* Cotton, L.J.
The following modern cases hold that a trust obligating the devisee or legatee to apply the property for the benefit of a specified person or object may be created by words expressing a "request": *Re Maddock*; *Llewelyn v. Washington*, [1902] 2 Ch. 220 (C.A.); or an entreaty, *Corbet v. Corbet* (1873), 7 I.R. Eq. 456, "I beg"; or a desire, *Stead v. Mellor* (1877), 5 Ch. D. 225 (but see *Re Conolly*; *Conolly v. Conolly*, [1910] 1 Ch. 219); or a reliance or confidence, *Re Williams*; *Williams v. Williams*, [1897] 2 Ch. 12 (C.A.), at p. 18 (but see *Re Lovett*; *Lovett v. Lovett* (1912), 132 L.T. Jo. 297). And see *Re Hamilton* (1912), 27 O.L.R. 445, 8 D.L.R. 529 (H.C.J.), affd 28 O.L.R. 534, 12 D.L.R. 861 (S.C. App. Div.); *Re Lowe* (1925), 28 O.W.N. 97 (H.C.); *Re Yost*, [1927] 2 D.L.R. 1001, [1927] 1 W.W.R. 925 (Alta. S.C.).
In the following cases the addition of words expressing a request, recommendation or similar precatory language was held not to create a trust: *Re Adams and Kensington Vestry, supra*, absolute gift of all property to widow in full confidence that she would do what was right as to disposal thereof between her children, either in her lifetime or by will at her decease; *Re Hamilton*; *Trench v. Hamilton*, [1895] 2 Ch. 370 (C.A.), a bequest to each of two legatees followed by the wish that they bequeath the same between the families of the testator's nephew and niece in such mode as they consider right; *Re Oldfield*; *Oldfield v. Oldfield*, [1904] 1 Ch. 549 (C.A.), a gift of all property equally to two daughters as tenants in common absolutely, with the added desire that "each of my said two daughters shall during the lifetime of my son pay to him one-third of the respective incomes of my said two daughters accruing from the moneys and

It often happens that the testator uses precatory words in combination with uncertainty of subject-matter. In that case the uncertainty of the one taints the other and vice versa. This is especially true of cases where the testator appears to make an absolute gift to a beneficiary and then attempts to cut down the gift by expressing a wish or a confidence that he will use "what remains" at his death for the benefit of others. Such gifts over are usually struck down because the property is uncertain and because the intention to create a trust is uncertain as well. In any event, the gift over is often regarded as repugnant to the interest already granted.[12]

In some cases, however, such gifts are construed as creating a life interest with a remainder. Thus, a testator gave all his property to his widow:

> ... absolutely in full confidence that she will make such use of it as I should have

---

investments" under the will; *Re Conolly*; *Conolly v. Conolly, supra*, absolute gift followed by expression of desire that the property be left by the donee to charitable purposes or to some other person; *Bank of Montreal v. Bower* (1889), 18 O.R. 226 (H.C.J.), gift of all property to widow absolutely followed by a wish and desire that she make a will dividing the realty and personalty among the children in such manner as she deemed just and equitable; *Nelles v. Elliot* (1878), 25 Gr. 329, devise of all estate to widow "for her own use and disposal, trusting that she will make such disposition thereof as shall be just and proper among my children"; *Keyes v. Grant*, [1928] 3 D.L.R. 558, [1928] 2 W.W.R. 295 (B.C.C.A.), gift followed by expressed wish subject to beneficiary's discretion; *Re Thomas*; *Ross v. Thomas*, [1932] 2 D.L.R. 334, 4 M.P.R. 431 (N.S.S.C.), gift of all estate to widow for her support and to bring up their son; *Re Puddington*, [1944] 2 D.L.R. 69, 17 M.P.R. 175 (N.B.S.C.), gift to executors in trust to pay one half of income to son to be used by him for educating his children; *Re Vance*, [1945] O.W.N. 323, [1945] 2 D.L.R. 593 (H.C.J.), gift of all estate to husband, requesting him "to keep an accounting of my estate separate from his own with the understanding that he is to will and bequeath the balance of the corpus of my estate to be equally divided between" two named charities; *Re Marshall*, [1945] O.W.N. 5, [1945] 1 D.L.R. 271 (H.C.J.), devise of house to trustees of a church "to be used as a manse for the minister from time to time"; *Re Trottier Estate*, [1945] 1 W.W.R. 90 (Alta. S.C.), absolute gift of all property to wife followed by the words, "However, if my wife should remarry after my death, then I wish the above farm and all I may die possessed of to be divided amongst my children, equally"; *Pahara v. Pahara*, [1946] 1 D.L.R. 433, [1946] S.C.R. 89, words indicating a mere expression of intention or a wish on the part of testators executing mutual wills that the survivor should dispose of the property in a certain way do not create a trust; and see *Re Richardson Estate*, [1949] 1 W.W.R. 1075 (Man. Surr. Ct.); *Re Levinger*, [1947] O.W.N. 349 (H.C.J.), gift of all property to three trustees on trust, one of which was "to hand over to [two named nephews] ... all the remainder of my estate ... and it is my wish ... that they should set up a trust fund to be used for the assistance of crippled and handicapped children in the City of Hamilton". See to the same effect *Johnson v. Farney* (1913), 29 O.L.R. 223, 9 D.L.R. 782 (H.C.), affd O.R. *loc. cit.*, 14 D.L.R. 134 (S.C. App. Div.); *Meagher v. Meagher* (1916), 30 D.L.R. 303, 53 S.C.R. 393; *Re Walker* (1925), 56 O.L.R. 517 (S.C. App. Div.); *Re Spry* (1929), 36 O.W.N. 343 (H.C.); *Hayman v. Nicoll*, [1944] 3 D.L.R. 551, [1944] S.C.R. 253; *Re McNally* (1979), 24 N. & P.E.I.R. 531, 65 A.P.R. 581 (P.E.I.S.C.).

[12]See, *e.g.*, *Re Walker, supra*, footnote 11; *Re Hornell*, [1945] O.R. 58, [1945] 1 D.L.R. 440 (C.A.); *Re Freedman* (1973), 41 D.L.R. (3d) 122, [1974] 1 W.W.R. 577 (Man. Q.B.), noted 1 E. & T. Q. 117 (1973-74); *Sprange v. Barnard* (1789), 2 Bro. C.C. 585, 29 E.R. 320; "Note", 28 Can. Bar Rev. 839 (1950).

made myself and that at her death she will devise it to such one or more of my nieces as she may think fit and in default of any disposition by her thereof by her will or testament I hereby direct that all my estate and property acquired by her under this my will shall at her death be equally divided among the surviving said nieces.

It was held that the meaning of the precatory words should be determined not by any rules of law or canons of construction but by looking at the words merely as they stand in the will and giving them their natural and ordinary meaning and that, upon a true construction of this will, there was an absolute gift of realty and personalty to the wife subject to an executory gift over of the same at her death to such of the testator's nieces as should survive her, equally if more than one, so far as his wife should not dispose by will of the estate in favour of such surviving nieces or any one or more of them.[13]

Conversely, since the intention is to be ascertained from the whole will, the use of the word "trust" or a declaration of trust may be construed as merely precatory or by way of recommendation, so as to create no enforceable equitable right or obligation.[14] In any instrument, a trust will not be imposed if the intention to impose a trust is expressly negatived.[15]

(b) Words of condition

If property is given to a person upon condition that he perform a specified act for the benefit of another person or object, the condition may be a trust if it is directed to be, or must be, satisfied out of the property, so as to impose upon him a fiduciary obligation in regard to the property.[16] It may be regarded as not imposing a trust, but merely a collateral duty, as where he was not to commit waste,[17] or was to provide a home for a lunatic at the latter's option.[18] A devise of land on condition that the devisee pay a sum of money, or an

---

[13]*Comiskey v. Bowring-Hanbury*, [1905] A.C. 84 (H.L.), revg [1904] 1 Ch. 415 *sub nom. Re Hanbury; Hanbury v. Fisher* (C.A.), in which the gift to the wife had been held to be absolute with no trust. *Cf. Re Shamas*, [1967] 2 O.R. 275, 63 D.L.R. (2d) 300 (C.A.).

[14]*Hughes v. Evans* (1843), 13 Sim. 496, 60 E.R. 192; *Williams v. Roberts* (1857), 27 L.J. Ch. 177, 30 L.T. (O.S.) 364; *Quayle v. Davidson* (1858), 12 Moore 268, 14 E.R. 913; *Clarke v. Hilton* (1866), L.R. 2 Eq. 810; *Irvine v. Sullivan* (1869), L.R. 8 Eq. 673; *Te Teira Te Paea v. Te Roera Tareha*, [1902] A.C. 56 (P.C.); *Re Rispin* (1912), 25 O.L.R. 633 at p. 642, 2 D.L.R. 644 at p. 652 (C.A.), affd 8 D.L.R. 756, 46 S.C.R. 649.

[15]*Re Pitt Rivers; Scott v. Pitt Rivers*, [1902] 1 Ch. 403 (C.A.).

[16]*Wright v. Wilkin* (1860), 2 B. & S. 232 at p. 259, 121 E.R. 1060; *Merchant Taylors' Co. v. Attorney-General* (1871), L.R. 6 Ch. App. 512; *Attorney-General v. Wax Chandlers' Co.* (1873), L.R. 6 H.L. 1; *Cunningham v. Foot* (1878), 3 App. Cas. 974 (H.L.), at p. 995; *Re Kirk; Kirk v. Kirk* (1882), 21 Ch. D. 431 (C.A.), at p. 436; *Re Richardson; Shuldham v. Royal Nat'l Lifeboat Inst.* (1887), 56 L.J. Ch. 784; *Re Richardson; Richardson v. Richardson*, [1904] 2 Ch. 777 at p. 780; *Re Frame; Edwards v. Taylor*, [1939] Ch. 700.

[17]*Kingham v. Lee* (1846), 15 Sim. 396, 60 E.R. 673.

[18]*Re Richardson; Richardson v. Richardson, supra*, footnote 16.

annuity does not create a trust, but may create a charge on the land.[19] The mere imposition of a charge does not create a trust.[20] A charge may, however, constitute a trust if the instrument shows that intent, or if it is coupled with some other trust.[21] On the other hand, an apparent trust may constitute a mere charge.[22]

1205.2 Certainty of Subject-matter

Anything may be the subject of a trust.[1] If the land in trust is situate in a foreign country, the court will enforce execution of the trust against a defendant within the jurisdiction.[2] To create a trust, the property affected must be so designated or defined that it can be ascertained and the shares that each beneficiary is to take must be described with certainty. If either of these elements is missing, the trust is void for uncertainty[3] and there is a resulting trust.

Thus, for example, a trust of "the bulk of my residuary estate" is void.[4] So was a trust in which a testator devised four houses to his trustees on trust to permit one daughter, M, to choose one for herself absolutely and to give the others to his other daughter, C. Since M predeceased the testator and was thus unable to choose, C received nothing.[5] It has been suggested, quite correctly, that such a case might more reasonably be construed as being a gift to C of four houses subject to a right in M to select one.[6]

Difficulties often arise in cases where a testator gives property to one person apparently absolutely, but then proceeds to cut down the gift by directing that what remains at the death of that person shall go to another. The

---

[19]*Hodge v. Churchward* (1847), 16 Sim. 71, 60 E.R. 799; *Cunningham v. Foot, supra,* footnote 16.

[20]*King v. Denison* (1813), 1 V. & B. 260, 35 E.R. 102; *Harrisson v. Duignan* (1842), 2 Dr. & War. 295 at p. 304 (Ir.), 1 Con. & Law. 376; *Hughes v. Kelly* (1843), 3 Dr. & War. 482, 2 Con. & Law. 223; *Francis v. Grover* (1845), 5 Hare 39 at p. 49, 67 E.R. 818; *Jacquet v. Jacquet* (1859), 27 Beav. 332, 54 E.R. 130; *Dickenson v. Teasdale* (1862), 1 De G. J. & S. 52, 46 E.R. 21 (C.A.).

[21]*Ball v. Harris* (1839), 4 My. & Cr. 264, 41 E.R. 103; *Jacquet v. Jacquet, supra,* footnote 20; *Saltmarsh v. Barrett* (1861), 3 De G. F. & J. 279, 45 E.R. 885 (C.A.); *Barrs v. Fewkes* (1864), 2 H. & M. 60 at p. 65, 71 E.R. 382.

[22]*Dawson v. Clarke* (1811), 18 Ves. Jun. 247 at p. 257, 34 E.R. 311; *Barrs v. Fewkes, supra,* footnote 21; *Re Oliver; Newbald v. Beckitt* (1890), 62 L.T. 533.

§1205.2

[1]*Dooby v. Watson* (1888), 39 Ch. D. 178.

[2]*Smith v. Henderson* (1870), 17 Gr. 6.

[3]*Stead v. Mellor* (1877), 5 Ch. D. 225; *Re Reis; Ex p. Clough,* [1904] 2 K.B. 769 (C.A.); *Re Moore; Prior v. Moore,* [1901] 1 Ch. 936.

[4]*Palmer v. Simmonds* (1854), 2 Drewry 221, 61 E.R. 704; and see *Bromley v. Tryon,* [1952] A.C. 265 (H.L.).

[5]*Boyce v. Boyce* (1849), 16 Sim. 476, 60 E.R. 959.

[6]Waters, p. 112.

remainder is usually held to be void not only because it is uncertain, but also because it is regarded as repugnant to the absolute interest already given. Moreover, if the remainder is expressed in terms of a wish or an entreaty that it be applied by the first person for the second, the original gift may fail for uncertainty of intention as well. Nevertheless, in some circumstances this type of gift may be construed as a life interest with a power to encroach in the first person followed by a valid remainder interest.[7]

A similar approach was taken in *Re Beardmore Trusts*,[8] in which a settlor, under a separation agreement, created an *inter vivos* trust as to three-fifths of his net estate on death for the benefit of his wife and children. The trust property was held to be uncertain since whatever property the testator might have had at the time of the creation of the trust might increase, decrease, or disappear by the time of his death.[9] It is therefore clear that certainty of subject-matter is required from the moment the trust is created and one cannot wait to see whether the property will be certain when the beneficial interests take effect. *Re Beardmore* has been criticized on the ground that there would seem to be no reason not to wait and see.[10] The trust was also held void because it was testamentary, however, and was not executed with the required formalities. Another difficulty with the case is that it is doubtful that a trust was created at all since no property was transferred to it at the time of the settlement. It was then an empty shell, and there was only a covenant by the settlor to settle after-acquired property which was uncertain. The covenant would have been enforceable by his wife as party to the agreement, but not by the children who were volunteers.[11]

The courts have been more lenient in respect of apparently uncertain discretionary trusts. Thus, in *Re Golay; Morris v. Bridgewater*,[12] the court held that a trust to permit the testator's wife to receive "a reasonable income" from certain properties was sufficiently certain, the term "reasonable income" being regarded as an objective yardstick. Similarly, a trust giving a beneficiary under an *inter vivos* trust the "full control" of an apartment building was held to be certain as to subject-matter.[13]

1205.3 Certainty of Objects

In order to be valid, the persons or objects must be designated with sufficient

---

[7]See cases collected in §1205.1(a), footnotes 12, 13.
[8][1951] O.W.N. 728, [1952] 1 D.L.R. 41 (H.C.J.).
[9]*Cf. Green v. The Queen in right of the Province of Ontario*, [1973] 2 O.R. 396, 34 D.L.R. (3d) 20 (H.C.J.), to the same effect.
[10]Waters, p. 110.
[11]On this point see further §1206, *infra*.
[12][1965] 2 All E.R. 660 (Ch.).
[13]*Re Parke* (1965), 49 D.L.R. (2d) 568 (B.C.S.C.).

certainty; otherwise, the trust is void for uncertainty[1] and there is a resulting trust.[2] In the case of non-discretionary trusts this requirement usually presents no difficulty as the beneficiaries will, in most cases, be named. However, if the objects are described as a class it must be shown that it is possible (1) to determine of any hypothetical person whether he is or is not a member of the class and (2) to make a list of the members of the class.[3] The reason for these requirements is that since a trust imposes a duty, the trustees are bound to distribute the property and if they cannot, or will not, the court will do it, if necessary, in the case of a discretionary trust, by distributing the property equally among all the members of the class on the basis of the maxim that equality is equity. For this reason the court must know all the members in the class.[4]

In this respect trusts were, until recently, distinguished from powers in respect of which only the first part of the test need be met.[5] However, in *McPhail v. Doulton*,[6] the House of Lords held that in respect of trust powers or powers in the nature of a trust, that is, trusts in which the trustees have a discretion to appoint the income or the capital in their discretion among a class of beneficiaries, although they must appoint all of it, the test of certainty is to be the same as that in respect of powers or mere powers, that is, a power (contained in a trust instrument) under which the trustees have not only a discretion to appoint among a named class, but also a discretion not to appoint at all if they see fit. Since *McPhail v. Doulton*, therefore, mere trusts, that is, those in which there is no discretion, must satisfy the twofold test, whereas trust powers and mere powers need satisfy only the first part of the test of certainty.

Mere powers are typically, although not exclusively, recognized by the fact that they are followed by a gift over in default of appointment. The subject is too extensive to be pursued here.[7]

McPhail v. Doulton has been followed in Canada in *Re Bethel*.[8] However,

---

§1205.3

[1]*Morice v. Bishop of Durham* (1805), 10 Ves. Jun. 522 at pp. 541-3, 32 E.R. 947; *Re Hetley; Hetley v. Hetley,* [1902] 2 Ch. 866; *Wright v. Atkyns* (1823), Turn. & R. 143 at pp. 158-9, 37 E.R. 1051; *Stead v. Mellor* (1877), 5 Ch. D. 225; *Buckle v. Bristow* (1864), 11 L.T. 265, 10 Jur. (N.S.) 1095; *Te Teira Te Paea v. Te Roera Tareha,* [1902] A.C. 56 (P.C.).

[2]*Morice v. Bishop of Durham, supra.*

[3]*Whishaw v. Stephens,* [1970] A.C. 508, [1968] 3 All E.R. 785, *sub nom. Re Gulbenkian's Settlement Trusts; Whishaw v. Stephens* (H.L.).

[4]*Ibid.*

[5]*Ibid.*

[6][1971] A.C. 424, [1970] 2 All E.R. 228 (H.L.), noted, 50 Can. Bar Rev. 539 (1972).

[7]See further §§1403.2(a), 1403.3, *infra.* And see Waters, pp. 65 *et seq.,* pp. 113 *et seq.;* Harris, "Trust, Power and Duty", 87 L.Q. Rev. 31 (1971); Hopkins, "Certain Uncertainties of Trusts and Powers", [1971] Camb. L.J. 68.

[8][1971] 2 O.R. 316, 17 D.L.R. (3d) 652 (C.A.), affd 35 D.L.R. (3d) 97, [1973] S.C.R. 635, *sub nom. Jones v. Executive Officers of The T. Eaton Co. Ltd.,* a trust for "any needy or deserving Toronto members of the Eaton Quarter Century Club".

that was a charitable trust in which the question of certainty was irrelevant.[9]
It has also been followed in a private trust.[9a]

Within the framework of the *McPhail v. Doulton* test, a trust for a person's
"family" or "relatives" is sufficiently definite,[10] but a trust for one's "friends",[11]
or even "close friends",[12] is not. The older cases in this respect should be read
subject to *McPhail v. Doulton*, however. This is particularly true of testamentary trusts in which evidence of the testator's relationships and other
extrinsic evidence may be admissible. A case such as *Re Connor*,[13] in which a
discretionary trust in favour of the testatrix's "close friends" was held to be
uncertain even though she had resided for many years in a small community,
would probably be decided otherwise today.

Trusts in which the objects are not set out, but the discretion to dispose of
the property is left entirely to the executors or trustees, are void.[14] The reason
is not only that the trust is uncertain as to objects but also, in the case of a
testamentary trust, that the testator has attempted to delegate his will-making
powers to another, which the law will not permit.[15]

Trusts for purposes are generally valid if they are charitable, for the law
has not required the same test of certainty for charitable trusts as it has for
other objects. Moreover, if the charitable objects are uncertain the court will
propound a scheme for distribution, although it will not do so if the testator
has delegated his power to make a will to his executors.[16] Thus, for example,
a trust for such charities and other public purposes as lawfully may be in a
named parish, is valid.[17] A trust, however, for such benevolent or other
purposes, not exclusively charitable, as the trustees may determine, is void
for uncertainty.[18] Indeed, all non-charitable purpose trusts, save for a number
of historic exceptions, such as those for the maintenance of tombs and the care
of specific animals, are void.[19] Not only do they lack certainty of objects, they

---

[9]See "Comment", 52 Can. Bar Rev. 114 (1974).
[9a]*Re Dickson and Richardson*; *Yau v. Richardson et al.* (1981), 121 D.L.R. (3d) 206,
   32 O.R. (2d) 158, 9 E.T.R. 66 (C.A.).
[10]*Grant v. Lynam* (1828), 4 Russ. 292, 38 E.R. 815.
[11]*Re Coates*; *Ramsden v. Coates*, [1955] Ch. 495. This case in fact concerned a mere
   power.
[12]*Re Connor* (1970), 10 D.L.R. (3d) 5, 72 W.W.R. 388 (Alta. S.C. App. Div.).
[13]*Ibid.*
[14]*Connell v. Connell* (1906), 37 S.C.R. 404; and see *Re Gilkinson* (1930), 38 O.W.N.
   26 (H.C.), affd 39 O.W.N. 115 (S.C. App. Div.); *Charteris v. Charteris* (1885), 10
   O.R. 738 (H.C.J.).
[15]*Grimond (or Macintyre) v. Grimond*, [1905] A.C. 124 (H.L.), at p. 126, *per* Lord
   Halsbury, L.C.
[16]*Ibid.*
[17]*Dolan v. Macdermot* (1868), L.R. 3 Ch. App. 676.
[18]*James v. Allen* (1817), 3 Mer. 17, 36 E.R. 7; *Ellis v. Selby* (1836), 1 My. & Cr. 286,
   40 E.R. 384 (C.A.); *Re Hewitt's Estate*; *Gateshead Corp. v. Hudspeth* (1883), 53 L.J.
   Ch. 132 (H.C.J.); *Blair v. Duncan*, [1902] A.C. 37 (H.L.); *Chichester Diocesan Fund
   and Board of Finance (Incorp.) v. Simpson*, [1944] A.C. 341 (H.L.).
[19]*Re Astor's Settlement Trusts*; *Astor v. Scholfield*, [1952] Ch. 534; *Re Endacott*; *Corpe
   v. Endacott*, [1960] 1 Ch. 232 (C.A.).

also lack beneficiaries who can call the trustees to account if need be and, in many cases, they offend the rule against perpetuities. In order to overcome these difficulties, specific non-charitable purpose trusts are now treated in some provinces as powers of appointment and may be valid for a period of twenty-one years.[20]

1206. CONSTITUTING THE TRUST

In order for a trust to be created, not only must it satisfy the three criteria of certainty but, in addition, the trust property must be vested in the trustee. A trust may, however, be completely constituted without its creation being communicated to the *cestui que trust*,[1] or to the trustee.[2]

A trust may be constituted (1) by a transfer of the trust property to the trustee, (2) by the settlor declaring himself a trustee, or (3) where the settlor is a beneficiary under a trust, by directing the trustees under that trust to hold the settlor's beneficial interest in trust for the persons designated by him. In the case of the second and third methods, no further transfer is necessary. A trust is not created by a declaratory judgment finding a trust, but comes into existence upon the agreement of the parties.[3]

Whichever method the transferor chooses to use, that is, one of the three methods listed, or an *inter vivos* gift, he must do everything which according to the nature of the property is necessary to be done in order to render the transaction binding, for the court will not perfect an imperfect gift, so that, for example, if the transaction was intended to take effect by transfer the court will not treat it as a declaration of trust.[4] In the case of land, in order to perfect a transaction, a deed is required; chattels may be delivered or given

---

[20]*Perpetuities Act*, R.S.A. 1980, c. P-4, s. 20; R.S.O. 1980, c. 374, s. 16; *Perpetuity Act*, R.S.B.C. 1979, c. 321, s. 21; *Perpetuities Ordinance*, R.O.N.W.T. 1974, c. P-3, s. 17; O.Y.T. 1980 (1st), c. 23, s. 21.

§1206

[1]*Purdom v. Northern Life Assurance Co. of Canada* (1928), 63 O.L.R. 12, [1928] 4 D.L.R. 679 (S.C. App. Div.), affd [1930] 1 D.L.R. 1003, [1930] S.C.R. 119, *sub nom. Fidelity Trust Co. of Ontario v. Purdom and Northern Life Assurance Co. of Canada*; *Dawson v. Dawson* (1911), 23 O.L.R. 1 (H.C.J.); *Re Commonwealth Savings Plan Ltd.* (1970), 17 D.L.R. (3d) 34, 14 C.B.R. (N.S.) 260 (B.C.S.C.).

[2]*Tate v. Leithead* (1854), Kay 658, 69 E.R. 279; *Armstrong v. Timperon* (1871), 24 L.T. 275; *Middleton v. Pollock*; *Ex p. Elliot* (1876), 2 Ch. D. 104; *Standing v. Bowring* (1885), 31 Ch. D. 282 (C.A.); *New, Prance & Garrard's Trustee v. Hunting*, [1897] 2 Q.B. 19 (C.A.); but see *Re Cozens*; *Green v. Brisley*, [1913] 2 Ch. 478, in regard to appropriation by an alleged defaulting trustee, and *Barclay's Bank Ltd. v. Quistclose Investments Ltd.*, [1968] 3 W.L.R. 1097 (H.L.).

[3]*Whonnock Lumber Co. Ltd. v. G. & F. Logging Co. Ltd.* (1968), 69 D.L.R. (2d) 561, 65 W.W.R. 147 (B.C.C.A.).

[4]*Milroy v. Lord* (1862), 4 De G. F. & J. 264, 45 E.R. 1185; *Richards v. Delbridge* (1874), L.R. 18 Eq. 11; *Carson v. Wilson*, [1961] O.R. 113, 26 D.L.R. (2d) 307 (C.A.); *Barnett v. Wise*, [1961] O.R. 97, 26 D.L.R. (2d) 321 (C.A.); *Re Mee* (1972), 23 D.L.R. (3d) 491, [1972] 2 W.W.R. 24 *sub nom. Public Trustee v. Mee* (B.C.C.A.); *Drummond v. Drummond* (1964), 50 W.W.R. 538 (B.C.S.C.); Taylor, "The Complete Constitution of Trusts and Gifts", 104 Sol. Jo. 573 (1960).

by deed; choses in action must be assigned. Moreover, in certain cases, such as shares and bonds, the transfer may have to be registered in order to be effective.

If the trust is properly constituted, the beneficiaries have a right as against the trustee to enforce it. If it is not properly constituted, they have a right to enforce it only if they have given consideration as they would under any contract, and for this purpose a marriage is treated as valuable consideration sufficient to enforce a marriage settlement at the suit of the marriage partners and their children and grandchildren.[5]

Apart from marriage settlements, volunteers, that is, persons who have not given consideration, cannot enforce an incompleted gift or unconstituted trust, for "equity will not assist a volunteer".

1206.1 Covenants to Settle Property

The principle that equity will not assist a volunteer has caused difficulties in connection with contracts or covenants to settle property on trust, particularly where a settlor covenants with the trustees of a trust which he has established, to settle after-acquired or future property on the trustees. The trustees, no doubt, have a right of action to compel performance of the contract, but the beneficiary is a volunteer under a contract and as such is precluded from suing on it in contract law unless a trust is established and as a volunteer he cannot sue for specific performance.[1]

In *Fletcher v. Fletcher*[2] the court held that equity will assist the volunteer by compelling the trustees to bring an action at law, or by permitting him to sue at law in their names. In that case the court acknowledged that it could not perfect an imperfect trust but held that the settlor's covenant that his executors would pay £60,000 to the trustees of the settlement one year after his death was already perfect.

In two subsequent cases, however, *Re Pryce*; *Neville v. Pryce*[3] and *Re Kay's Settlement*; *Broadbent v. Macnab*,[4] it was held that volunteers cannot do indirectly what they cannot do directly, so that, since they cannot obtain specific performance, they cannot force the trustees to sue at law, and trustees

---

[5]*Pullan v. Koe*, [1913] 1 Ch. 9. And see *A.-G. Ont. v. Perry*, [1934] 4 D.L.R. 65, [1934] A.C. 477 (P.C.).

§1206.1

[1]*Le Affréteurs Réunis Société Anonyme v. Leopold Walford (London) Ltd.*, [1919] A.C. 801 (H.L.); *Vandepitte v. Preferred Accident Insurance Corp. of New York*, [1933] A.C. 70 (P.C.); *Re Schebsman*; *Official Receiver v. Cargo Superintendents (London), Ltd.*, [1944] Ch. 83 (C.A.), at p. 104, *per* du Parq, L.J.; *Beswick v. Beswick*, [1968] A.C. 58 (H.L.).

[2](1844), 4 Hare 67, 67 E.R. 564, followed or approved in *Smith v. Stuart* (1866), 12 Gr. 246; *Toronto General Trusts Co. v. Keyes* (1907), 15 O.L.R. 30 (H.C.J.); *Zwicker v. Zwicker* (1899), 29 S.C.R. 527.

[3][1917] 1 Ch. 234.

[4][1939] Ch. 329.

can be directed not to sue on their behalf even if they are willing to do so. A more recent case, *Re Cook's Settlement Trusts; Royal Exchange Assurance v. Cook*,[5] followed this view and distinguished *Fletcher v. Fletcher* on the ground that that case involved a gift of specific property in existence at the time the covenant was made, whereas the covenant in *Re Cook's Settlement Trusts* was in respect of property which might or might not come into existence in the future.[6] The distinction between the cases, therefore, is that on the one hand there is a covenant to settle existing property in the future, whereas on the other the covenant is to settle in the future property that does not yet exist and may not come into existence. The latter cannot be the subject of an assignment at law and thus equity will not assist a volunteer to enforce it.

1206.2 Retention of Control by Settlor

The fact that the settlor has retained control of the property intended to be settled on trust often leads to the conclusion that the trust was not completely constituted, for in that case he has not done everything in his power to make the transaction binding.[1]

Thus, in *Carson v. Wilson*,[2] one Wilson executed deeds of land and assignments of mortgages in favour of named persons and gave them to his solicitor with instructions to deliver them to the grantees and assignees on Wilson's death. Wilson was able to recall the deeds at any time and he continued to manage the properties and to collect the mortgage payments. After his death it was held that he did not constitute a trust with either himself or his solicitor as the trustee, as he retained complete control of the property. In fact, he attempted to make a gift of the property which was not perfected because the deeds were not delivered.

This does not mean that a trust is not completely constituted if the settlor retains a life interest or a power of revocation, provided there is an unequivocal transfer to trustees or a declaration of trust. In the absence of evidence to that effect, the trust will not be regarded as constituted. Indeed, some cases appear

---

[5][1965] Ch. 902. See also Elliott, "The Power of Trustees to Enforce Covenants in Favour of Volunteers", L.R. Rev. 100 (1970); Hornby, "Covenants in Favour of Volunteers", 78 L.Q. Rev. 228 (1962); Scott, "The Power of Volunteers to Enforce Covenants in their Favour", 8 Malaya L.R. 153 (1966); Matheson, "The Enforceability of a Covenant to Create a Trust", 29 Mod. L. Rev. 397 (1966); Lee, "The Public Policy of Re Cook's Settlement Trusts", 85 L.Q. Rev. 213 (1969); Maudsley, "Incompletely Constituted Trusts", *Perspectives of Law* (Little, Brown & Co., Boston; Pound, Griswold, Sutherland, eds., 1964), p. 240.

[6]The covenant was to settle the sale price of certain paintings retained by the settlor on the trusts of the settlement if they were to be sold in the future.

1206.2

[1]*Milroy v. Lord* (1862), 4 De G. F. & J. 264, 45 E.R. 1185; *Re Rose; Rose v. Inland Revenue Com'rs*, [1952] Ch. 499 (C.A.).

[2][1961] O.R. 113, 26 D.L.R. (2d) 307 (C.A.).

to hold that the presence of a power to revoke is fatal to the trust.[3] This does not appear to be correct, however. Thus, in *Anderson v. Patton*,[4] the defendant received money from C and signed a receipt in the following terms: "Received from [C] sum of $5,000 which I am to hold in trust for the said [C], and which I am to pay out as instructed to [P] and [K], if anything should happen to the said [C]. The money will be returned if the said [C] should demand it." The trial judge and the majority in the Appellate Division construed the last sentence as a power to revoke and held the trust to be valid. Parlee, J.A., who dissented, was of the opinion that C retained full control over the money so that the trust was not constituted.

Another factor that arises out of both the *Anderson v. Patton* and the *Carson v. Wilson* cases is that the trust may not only not be properly constituted, it may also be testamentary in effect and be void for failure to observe the necessary formalities. The court so held in *Carson v. Wilson*,[5] but in *Anderson v. Patton* the courts were able to avoid the problem by holding that C retained a life interest (as well as a power to revoke), so that the trust took effect from its creation.[6]

1207. FORMAL REQUIREMENTS

Both the *Statute of Frauds*[1] and the several Wills Acts make certain stipulations as to the formalities required to create a trust and to transfer equitable interests under a trust. These are discussed below.

1207.1 The Statute of Frauds

The *Statute of Frauds*[1] provides that any contract for the sale of lands, and

---

[3]*Re Pfrimmer*, [1936] 2 D.L.R. 460, [1936] 1 W.W.R. 609 (Man. C.A.).

[4][1948] 1 D.L.R. 848, [1947] 2 W.W.R. 837 (Alta. S.C.T.D.), affd [1948] 2 D.L.R. 202, [1948] 1 W.W.R. 461 (S.C. App. Div.). *Cf.* dicta in *Copp v. Wood*, [1926] 2 D.L.R. 224, 53 N.B.R. 56 (S.C. App. Div.), and *Roy v. Investors Trust Co.* (1967), 60 W.W.R. 630 (Man. Q.B.).

[5]See to the same effect, *Re Beardmore Trusts*, [1951] O.W.N. 728, [1952] 1 D.L.R. 41 (H.C.J.); *Re Pfrimmer, supra*, footnote 3.

[6]*Cf. Cock v. Cooke* (1866), L.R. 1 P. & D. 241 at p. 243, *per* Sir J.P. Wilde; *Corlet v. Isle of Man Bank Ltd.*, [1937] 3 D.L.R. 163, [1937] 2 W.W.R. 209 (Alta. S.C. App. Div.); *Re Parke* (1965), 49 D.L.R. (2d) 568 (B.C.S.C.).

§1207
[1]29 Car. 2, c. 3 (1676). The statute is in force as received English law in Alberta, Saskatchewan, Manitoba, Newfoundland, Northwest Territories and the Yukon. It has been re-enacted in Ontario, R.S.O. 1980, c. 481; British Columbia, R.S.B.C. 1979, c. 393; New Brunswick, R.S.N.B. 1973, c. S-14; Nova Scotia, R.S.N.S. 1967, c. 290; and Prince Edward Island, R.S.P.E.I. 1974, c. S-6. The several provincial statutes are hereafter referred to as the "Ont. Act", etc.

§1207.1
[1]29 Car. 2, c. 3 (1676). For the several provincial re-enactments of this statute see §1207, footnote 1, *supra*.

hence, any contract to create a trust of land, must be in writing, otherwise it is unenforceable. The Ontario Act provides:

> 4. No action shall be brought ... upon any contract or sale of lands, tenements or hereditaments, or any interest in or concerning them ... unless the agreement upon which the action is brought, or some memorandum or note thereof is in writing and signed by the party to be charged therewith or some person thereunto by him lawfully authorized.[2]

Thus, for example, an agreement whereby one person agrees with another for value that he will settle land owned by him for the benefit of third persons, would appear to be caught by the section. However, a contract to sell land for another as distinguished from a contract of sale of land is not within the statute,[3] and neither is a contract for the division of the proceeds of the sale of land.[4] Neither contract deals with "a sale of land or some interest in land or concerning land".[5]

The statute further provides that all declarations of trust in real property must be proved by some writing signed by the person entitled to declare the trust or by his last will in writing, else they are void, except where a conveyance is made which gives rise to a trust or confidence by implication or construction of law.[6] Sections 9 and 10 of the Ontario Act provide:

> 9. Subject to section 10, all declarations or creations of trusts or confidences of any lands, tenements or hereditaments shall be manifested and proved by a writing signed by the party who is by law enabled to declare such trust, or by his last will in writing, or else they are utterly void and of no effect.
>
> 10. Where a conveyance is made of lands or tenements by which a trust or confidence arises or results by implication or construction of law, or is transferred or extinguished by act or operation of law, then and in every such case the trust or confidence is of the like force and effect as it would have been if this Act had not been passed.[7]

The writing need not actually declare the trust, it being sufficient if it is evidence of the fact of the trust,[8] but it must show the terms of the trust.[9] Hence, it may be quite informal, such as by letter or memorandum, if it clearly

---

[2]*Cf.* B.C. Act, s. 1(1); N.B. Act, s. 1; N.S. Act, s. 6; P.E.I. Act, s. 2.

[3]*Canadian General Securities Co. v. George* (1918), 42 O.L.R. 560, 43 D.L.R. 20 (C.A.), revd on other grounds 59 S.C.R. 641.

[4]*Harris v. Lindeborg*, [1931] 1 D.L.R. 945, [1931] S.C.R. 235.

[5]*Leslie v. Stevenson* (1915), 34 O.L.R. 473 (C.A.), at p. 483. See further on this point Waters, pp. 180-3.

[6]*Cole v. Deschambault* (1914), 26 O.W.R. 348 (H.C.); *Hutchinson v. Hutchinson* (1856), 6 Gr. 117 at p. 119; *Vaselenak v. Vaselenak* (1921), 57 D.L.R. 370, [1921] 1 W.W.R. 889 (Alta. S.C. App. Div.); *Houghton v. Foster* (1915), 9 W.W.R. 1150 (Alta. S.C.).

[7]*Cf.* B.C. Act, ss. 1(2), 4; N.B. Act, s. 9; N.S. Act, s. 4.

[8]*Per* Lord Loughborough, L.C., in *Forster v. Hale* (1800), 5 Ves. Jun. 308 at p. 315, 31 E.R. 603; *per* Grant, M.R., in *Randall v. Morgan* (1805), 12 Ves. Jun. 67 at p. 71, 33 E.R. 26; *Morton v. Tewart* (1842), 2 Y. & C.C.C. 67, 63 E.R. 29; *Dale v. Hamilton* (1846), 5 Hare 369, at p. 394, 67 E.R. 955.

[9]*Smith v. Matthews* (1861), 3 De G. F. & J. 139 at pp. 151-2, 45 E.R. 831 (C.A.); *Rochefoucauld v. Boustead*, [1897] 1 Ch. 196 (C.A.); *Harding v. Starr* (1888), 21 N.S.R. 121.

shows a gift to be in trust and sufficiently connects the trustee with the subject matter of the trust.[10] A trust may be proved by a subsequent acknowledgment by the trustee and, however late the proof, the trust will take effect from its creation.[11] It has been held that writing is not necessary to support a trust which is in the course of being executed.[12] It has also been held that a declaration of trust may, after a length of time, be presumed to have been made and lost.[13]

Finally, the statute requires that all grants and assignments of beneficial interests under a trust be made in writing. The Ontario Act provides:

> 11. All grants and assignments of a trust or confidence shall likewise be in writing signed by the party granting or assigning the same, or by such last will or devise, or else are likewise utterly void and of no effect.[14]

It should be noted that in this case the statute, except in British Columbia,[15] requires not merely that the assignment be evidenced in writing but that it be in writing. Moreover, the section applies to trusts of personalty as well as of land and, except in British Columbia,[16] it applies to trusts arising by operation of law as well as to express trusts. It would appear that a direction by a beneficiary to the trustee to hold the beneficial interest for another may not require a writing under this section, since it is the equivalent of a declaration of trust,[17] although, if it is in respect of land, it would presumably have to be in writing since it would create a trust. Similarly, if a sole beneficiary, who is *sui juris*, directs the trustee to convey his interest to a third party, no writing is required,[18] although it would be if the beneficiary surrendered his equitable interest to the trustee.

Equity, however, does not allow a statute to be made an instrument of fraud.[19] The *Statute of Frauds* does not prevent proof of a fraud, and it is fraud for a person to whom land is conveyed as a trustee and who knows that it was so conveyed, to deny the trust and claim the land as his own. Consequently, notwithstanding the statute, it is competent for a person claiming land conveyed to another to prove by parol evidence that it was so conveyed upon trust for the claimant, and that the grantee, knowing the facts, is denying the trust and relying upon the form of the conveyance and the statute in order

---

[10]*Mulholland v. Merriam* (1873), 20 Gr. 152 at p. 158; *McCue v. Smith* (1911), 17 W.L.R. 145 (Alta. S.C.T.D.).

[11]*Harper v. Paterson* (1864). 14 U.C.C.P. 538 at p. 545, quoting Lewin.

[12]*Harris v. Horwell* (1708), Gilb. Rep. 11, 25 E.R. 8.

[13]*Attorney-General v. Boultbee* (1794), 2 Ves. Jun. 380 at p. 385, 30 E.R. 683; *Re Bishop Gore's Charities* (1843), 2 Con. & Law. 411, 4 Dr. & War. 270.

[14]*Cf.* B.C. Act, s. 2; N.B. Act, s. 10; N.S. Act, s. 5.

[15]B.C. Act, s. 2.

[16]*Ibid.*, s. 3.

[17]*Grey v. Inland Revenue Com'rs*, [1958] Ch. 375, revd *loc. cit.* 690 (C.A.), affd [1960] A.C. 1 (H.L.). In the *Grey* case writing was required under the modern English legislation. *Law of Property Act, 1925*, 15 & 16 Geo. 5, c. 20, s. 53(1)(c) which speaks of "disposition" instead of "grant and assignment".

[18]*Vandervell v. Inland Revenue Com'rs*, [1967] 2 A.C. 291. See Waters, pp. 188-92.

[19]*Re Duke of Marlborough; Davis v. Whitehead*, [1894] 2 Ch. 133 at p. 141.

to keep the land himself.[20] A person who takes real property by instrument *inter vivos*, or real or personal property upon an intestacy or under a will, in either case in pursuance of a parol arrangement that the property shall be held by him upon trust, is not allowed to use the statute as a means of avoiding the trust. A court of equity does not set aside the statute, but it fastens on the individual who gets title under it, and imposes on him a personal obligation because he applies the statute as an instrument for accomplishing a fraud.[21] Consequently, a trust will be enforced upon satisfactory evidence of a verbal arrangement that the grantee in a voluntary conveyance was to reconvey in certain events,[22] or an arrangement that the grantee was to hold in trust for the grantor,[23] or for another person,[24] or an arrangement that land purchased by one person and conveyed to another was to be held in trust for the purchaser,[25] or an arrangement whereby a conveyance absolute in form was to operate as a mortgage.[26] Nevertheless, in all cases in which a trust is sought to be established by parol evidence, its existence must be brought within the range of reasonable certainty and not left within the shadowy region of conjecture.[27]

In most cases the trust that is enforced despite the statute is the express oral trust between the parties.[28] In some cases, however, an attempt is made to let the statute operate according to its terms, but to raise a constructive trust, which does not need to be in writing, to nullify the fraud.[29] In circum-

---

[20]*Per* Lindley, L.J., in *Rochefoucauld v. Boustead*, [1897] 1 Ch. 196 (C.A.), at p. 206; *Auger v. Auger* (1965), 50 D.L.R. (2d) 670 (Sask. C.A.); *Balaberda v. Mucha* (1960), 25 D.L.R. (2d) 760 (Sask. C.A.).

[21]*Per* Lord Westbury in *McCormick v. Grogan* (1869), L.R. 4 H.L. 82 at p. 97.

[22]*Hutchins v. Lee* (1737), 1 Atk. 447, 26 E.R. 284; *Davies v. Otty* (1865), 35 Beav. 208, 55 E.R. 875; *Haigh v. Kaye* (1872), L.R. 7 Ch. App. 469; *Re Duke of Marlborough*; *Davis v. Whitehead, supra*, footnote 19.

[23]*Booth v. Turte* (1873), L.R. 16 Eq. 182.

[24]*Rochefoucauld v. Boustead, supra*, footnote 20; *Brown v. Storoschuk*, [1947] 1 D.L.R. 227, [1946] 3 W.W.R. 641 (B.C.C.A.); *Bannister v. Bannister*, [1948] 2 All E.R. 133 (C.A.).

[25]*Davies v. Otty, supra*, footnote 22; *Haigh v. Kaye, supra*, footnote 22.

[26]*Lincoln v. Wright* (1859), 4 De G. & J. 16, 45 E.R. 6 (C.A.).

[27]*Per* Moss, J., in *McManus v. McManus* (1876), 24 Gr. 118 at p. 124. Trusts were held to be established by parol evidence despite the *Statute of Frauds* in *Barton v. McMillan* (1892), 20 S.C.R. 404; *McKibbon v. Welbanks* (1918), 15 O.W.N. 153 (H.C.), but in the following cases it was held that the *Statute of Frauds* prevented the establishment of a trust by parol evidence: *McNeil v. Corbett* (1907), 39 S.C.R. 608; *Fruchtenan v. Gurofsky* (1918), 14 O.W.N. 23 (H.C.); *McPherson v. L'Hirondelle*, [1927] 2 D.L.R. 1076, [1927] S.C.R. 429; *Drummond v. Drummond* (1964), 50 W.W.R. 538 (B.C.S.C.).

[28]See, *e.g.*, *Rochefoucauld v. Boustead, supra*, footnote 20, and *Brown v. Storoschuk, supra*, footnote 24.

[29]*Scheuerman v. Scheuerman* (1916), 28 D.L.R. 223 at pp. 230-1, 52 S.C.R. 625 at pp. 636-7, *per* Duff, J. In this case the constructive trust was not, in fact, permitted because of illegality in that the husband had transferred land to his wife under an oral agreement that she would hold for his benefit in fraud on his creditors. See also *Bannister v. Bannister, supra*, footnote 24, where a grantor transferred lands to another on the understanding that she would be permitted to continue to live on one property. The case might also have treated it as resulting trust since the consideration was minimal because of the agreement.

stances in which a resulting trust can be raised, as where one person supplies the purchase money but the land is conveyed to another, the resulting trust will also avoid the effects of the statute.[30]

1207.2 The Wills Acts

The several Wills Acts require that a will be in writing, signed by the testator or someone in his presence and at his direction, and be witnessed by two or more witnesses.[1] Reduced formalities apply to holograph wills[2] and privileged wills of soldiers and seamen and, in certain cases, of infants.[3]

These requirements are avoided under the law of secret trusts which, like the cases under the *Statute of Frauds*,[4] holds that a statute cannot be used as an instrument of fraud.

A secret trust is created where property is conveyed to a person or devised to him either absolutely or upon an indefinite trust and upon some parol or written undertaking or understanding that he will hold it in trust for some other person or object; in such cases, although the understanding is not clothed with the requisite formalities that are normally required to create a trust, it is enforced as a trust in equity on the ground that his failure to perform it would be an act of fraud.[5] A person is regarded as having accepted a secret trust if he silently acquiesced in it when it was communicated to him.[6] If a person, knowing that a testator, in making a disposition in his favour, intends it to be applied for purposes other than his own benefit, expressly promises or by silence implies that he will carry the testator's intention into effect and the property is left to him upon the faith of that promise or undertaking, he

---

[30]*Davies v. Otty, supra*, footnote 22; *Haigh v. Kaye, supra*, footnote 22.
§1207.2
[1]*Wills Act*, R.S.A. 1980, c. W-11, ss. 4, 5, 8; R.S.B.C. 1979, c. 434, ss. 3, 4, 7; R.S.M. 1970, c. W150, ss. 4, 5, 8; R.S.N.B. 1973, c. W-9, ss. 3, 4, 7; R.S.N.S. 1967, c. 340, ss. 5, 6; R.S.N. 1970, c. 401, s. 2; R.S.S. 1978, c. W-14, ss. 7, 8; *Succession Law Reform Act*, R.S.O. 1980, c. 488, ss. 3, 4, 7; *Probate Act*, R.S.P.E.I. 1974, c. P-19, s. 61; *Wills Ordinance*, R.O.N.W.T. 1974, c. W-3, ss. 6, 8; R.O.Y.T. 1971, c. W-3, ss. 6, 7. These several statutes are hereafter referred to as the "B.C. Act", the "N.W.T. Ord.", *etc.*
[2]Alta. Act, s. 7; Man. Act, s. 7; N.B. Act, s. 6; Sask. Act, s. 7(2); Nfld. Act, s. 2; Ont. Act, s. 6; N.W.T. Ord., s. 6(2); Yukon Ord., s. 6(2).
[3]Ont. Act, ss. 5, 8; Alta. Act, ss. 6, 9; B.C. Act, ss. 5, 7; Man. Act, ss. 6, 9; N.B. Act, ss. 5, 8; N.S. Act, s. 8; Nfld. Act, s. 2, and see also *Wills (Volunteers) Act*, R.S.N. 1970, c. 402; Sask. Act, ss. 5, 6; P.E.I. Act, s. 63; N.W.T. Ord., ss. 5, 7; Yukon Ord., s. 5.
[4]29 Car. 2, c. 3 (1677). See §1207.1, *supra*.
[5]*Carter v. Green* (1857), 3 K. & J. 591 at p. 602, 69 E.R. 1245; *Moss v. Cooper* (1861), 1 J. & H. 352, 70 E.R. 782; *Jones v. Badley* (1868), L.R. 3 Ch. App. 362; *McCormick v. Grogan* (1869), L.R. 4 H.L. 82; *Irvine v. Sullivan* (1869), L.R. 8 Eq. 673; *Re Fleetwood*; *Sidgreaves v. Brewer* (1880), 15 Ch. D. 594; *Re Stead*; *Witham v. Andrew*, [1900] 1 Ch. 237; *Re Maddock*; *Llewelyn v. Washington*, [1902] 2 Ch. 220 (C.A.); *Blackwell v. Blackwell*, [1929] A.C. 318 (H.L.).
[6]*Paine v. Hall* (1812), 18 Ves. Jun. 475, 34 E.R. 397; *Lomax v. Ripley* (1855), 3 Sm. & Giff. 48 at p. 73, 65 E.R. 558; *Tee v. Ferris* (1856), 2 K. & J. 357 at pp. 363-4, 69 E.R. 819; *Rowbotham v. Dunnett* (1878), 8 Ch. D. 430.

becomes a trustee.[7] Similarly, if an heir procures an intestacy by representing that he will carry out the intestate's wishes, he must do so to the extent that they are legal.[8]

If property is given to more than one person upon an undertaking or understanding with one of them that the property is to be held in trust for some particular person or object, all of them are bound by the trust if the undertaking or understanding was on behalf of all, although without the knowledge or consent of the others,[9] but, if the undertaking or understanding was entered into by only one of them after the gift was made, it does not bind the others,[10] and the fact that the gift is to them as tenants in common strengthens the case of the others that they are not bound.[11]

A secret trust for an illegal purpose is void and unenforceable,[12] an actual fraudulent intent not being necessary.[13]

Where land is held for sale under a secret trust, the trustee may convey it without notice to the equitable owner.[14]

Secret trusts are said to arise outside the will[15] so that, while they may depend upon the will for their vigour and effect in the sense that the trust fails if the will or the gift under it fails, the formalities required of a will are not avoided. There are two kinds, namely fully-secret trusts and semi-secret trusts.

Fully-secret trusts arise where there is an apparently absolute gift on the face of the will, or as a result of an intestacy, but the beneficiary has agreed with the deceased that he will hold the property in trust for others.[16] Semi-secret trusts are those in which there is a gift to someone named in the will but the trust objects are not set out and where the trustee has agreed to hold

---

[7]*Donovan v. Donovan* (1920), 18 O.W.N. 318 (H.C.), quoting *Jones v. Badley, supra,* footnote 5; *McDonald v. Moran* (1938), 12 M.P.R. 424 (P.E.I.S.C.); *MacMillan v. Kennedy,* [1942] 3 D.L.R. 170, [1942] 2 W.W.R. 497 (Alta. S.C. App. Div.).

[8]*McCormick v. Grogan, supra,* footnote 5, at p. 88; and see *Caton v. Caton* (1866), L.R. 1 Ch. App. 137 at p. 149, affd L.R. 2 H.L. 127; *French v. French,* [1902] 1 I.R. 172 (H.L.); *Sullivan v. Sullivan,* [1903] 1 I.R. 193 (H.C.J.).

[9]*Russell v. Jackson* (1852), 10 Hare 204, 68 E.R. 900; *Moss v. Cooper, supra,* footnote 5, at p. 367; *Re Stead; Witham v. Andrew, supra,* footnote 5, at p. 241.

[10]*Moss v. Cooper, supra,* footnote 5, p. 367; *Re Stead; Witham v. Andrew, supra,* footnote 5, at p. 241.

[11]*Tee v. Ferris, supra,* footnote 6, at p. 364; *Rowbotham v. Dunnett, supra,* footnote 6.

[12]*Muckleston v. Brown* (1801), 6 Ves. Jun. 52, 31 E.R. 934; *Stickland v. Aldridge* (1804), 9 Ves. Jun. 516, 32 E.R. 703; *Russell v. Jackson* (1852), 10 Hare 204, 68 E.R. 900; *Tee v. Ferris, supra,* footnote 6; *Springett v. Jenings* (1871), L.R. 6 Ch. App. 333; *Rowbotham v. Dunnett, supra,* footnote 6; *Emes v. Barber* (1869), 15 Gr. 679; *Day v. Day* (1889), 17 O.A.R. 157.

[13]*Buckland v. Rose* (1859), 7 Gr. 440.

[14]*Oland v. McNeil* (1902), 32 S.C.R. 23.

[15]*Re Gardner; Huey v. Cunningham,* [1923] 2 Ch. 230.

[16]*McCormick v. Grogan* (1869), L.R. 4 H.L. 82; *Re Boyes; Boyes v. Carritt* (1884), 26 Ch. D. 531; *Ottaway v. Norman,* [1972] 2 W.L.R. 50 (Ch. Div.); *Nicoll v. Hayman,* [1944] 2 D.L.R. 4, 17 M.P.R. 374 (N.S.S.C. App. Div.), revd [1944] 3 D.L.R. 551, [1944] S.C.R. 253.

the trust property for others.[17] The essential difference between the two is that, while there must be a communication of the trust and the objects to the intended trustee and an acceptance by him of the trust in both cases, for otherwise the conscience of the trustee is not bound, the cases hold that in a semi-secret trust the communication must be prior to or contemporaneous with the making of the will. A subsequent communication permits the testator to evade the Wills Acts by changing his will without complying with the formalities of those Acts and to introduce parol evidence to contradict the will.[18] In this respect the cases, which invariably involve a subsequent written communication, confuse the doctrine of secret trusts with the probate doctrine of incorporation by reference, which permits a document to be incorporated into a will provided that it predates the will and is clearly identified in the will.[19] In fact, semi-secret trusts are not treated as testamentary referential trusts for all purposes since cases have held that, since the trust arises outside the will, the fact that the trustee acted as a witness does not void the gift,[20] and the fact that the beneficiary under the secret trust predeceased the testator did not cause a lapse.[21]

Whether the trust is fully-secret or semi-secret, the communication and acceptance must take place before the testator's death, otherwise the intended trustee is not bound and he will take absolutely in the case of a fully-secret trust, whereas there will be a resulting trust in the case of a semi-secret trust.[22] There will also be a resulting trust where the fact of the trust, but not the objects, are communicated. However, an envelope containing a list of the objects given to the trustee by the testator,[23] or placed in a box the key to which is given to the trustee before the testator's death,[24] is regarded as a sufficient communication.

Much has been written about whether secret trusts are express or constructive, but the question has never been resolved. To the extent that they are imposed to prevent fraud, they might appear to be constructive and fully-secret trusts are usually so regarded. However, secret trusts are also

---

[17]*Blackwell v. Blackwell*, [1929] A.C. 318 (H.L.); *Johnson v. Ball* (1851), 5 De G. & Sm. 85, 64 E.R. 1029; *Re Keen; Evershed v. Griffiths*, [1937] Ch. 236 (C.A.); *Re Mihalopulos* (1956), 5 D.L.R. (2d) 628, 19 W.W.R. 118 (Alta. S.C.).

[18]*Ibid.*

[19]*In the Goods of Smart*, [1902] P. 238. See generally Holdsworth, "Secret Trusts", 53 L.Q. Rev. 501 (1937); Sheridan, "English and Irish Secret Trusts", 67 L.Q. Rev. 314 (1951); Fleming, "Secret Trusts", 12 Convey. (N.S.) 28 (1947); Andrews, "Creating Secret Trusts", 27 Convey. (N.S.) 92 (1963); Scamell, "Secret Trusts", 16 The Solicitor 224 (1949).

[20]*Re Young; Young v. Young*, [1951] Ch. 344; *Re Armstrong* (1969), 7 D.L.R. (3d) 36, [1965-69] 1 N.S.R. *sub nom. Re Armstrong's Estate v. Weisner* (S.C.T.D.).

[21]*Re Gardner; Huey v. Cunningham, supra*, footnote 15.

[22]*Re Mihalopulos, supra*, footnote 17; *Donovan v. Donovan* (1920), 18 O.W.N. 318 (H.C.).

[23]*Re Boyes; Boyes v. Carritt, supra*, footnote 16; *Re Keen; Evershed v. Griffiths, supra*, footnote 17.

[24]*McDonald v. Moran* (1938), 12 M.P.R. 424 (P.E.I.S.C.).

enforced where the trustee is perfectly willing to carry out his undertaking, so that the basis for a constructive trust would then not seem to arise. In any event, in the case of semi-secret trusts, the trust appears to be express on its face. This would mean, in the case of a trust of land, that it would have to be in writing under the *Statute of Frauds*,[25] although, as has been shown, the courts will not allow that statute to be used as an instrument of fraud and will enforce the trust despite the statute.[26] The question may be relevant under Statutes of Limitation, however, which impose a limitation period in respect of trusts arising by operation of law, but not on express trusts.[27]

1208. CONSTRUCTIVE TRUSTS

A constructive trust is a trust which arises by operation of law. Since the term "constructive" is commonly used as synonymous with "implied" and since resulting trusts and other trusts are also implied and arise by operation of law, there is much confusion and inconsistency of terminology in the cases, texts and digests when referring to constructive trusts, resulting trusts and other implied trusts. It is said that all trusts that are not express trusts are divisible into (a) constructive trusts, in which property not otherwise subject to a trust becomes trust property at law, (b) resulting trusts, in which the law imposes on trust property a trust that was not expressed when the trust was created and (c) other implied trusts arising from the contractual or other special relations of the parties concerned.[1] The latter are now usually referred to as constructive trusts as well. The term constructive trustee has also been applied to a person who, although not appointed as a trustee, is liable to be declared a trustee by a court of equity[2] and to a third party who, although not a trustee, interferes with an express trust and deals with the trust property so as to become a trustee by operation of law. However, such a person should more properly be regarded as an express trustee *de son tort*, and he is consequently dealt with herein under that sub-heading, because his legal position differs materially from that of other constructive trustees.

It has been said that, in its strict sense, a constructive trust is a trust that the law attaches to property which is not expressly subject to a trust but which has been acquired by a person by means of his holding other property in trust or in a fiduciary capacity.[3] But, in addition, a constructive trust is raised by

---

[25]29 Car. 2, c. 3 (1677).
[26]*Supra*, §1207.1.
[27]See §1217, *infra*.
§1208
   [1]See *Sands v. Thompson* (1883), 22 Ch. D. 614 at pp. 616 *et seq.*, and *Soar v. Ashwell*, [1893] 2 Q.B. 390 (C.A.), at pp. 393, 396, 400 and 405.
   [2]See *Taylor v. Davies* (1919), 51 D.L.R. 75 at p. 84, [1920] A.C. 636 at p. 651 (P.C.).
   [3]*Espinasse v. Lowe* (1764), 7 Bro. P.C. 345 at p. 355, 3 E.R. 223 (H.L.).

a court of equity whenever a person clothed with a fiduciary character gains some personal advantage by availing himself of his situation as trustee.[4]

In Anglo-Canadian jurisprudence, there are, therefore, two kinds of constructive trust which have been termed *institutional* or *substantive,* and *remedial.*[5] The first type arises in the operation of express trusts and makes property that would otherwise not be subject to an express trust subject thereto, or requires non-trustees to act as trustees. Remedial trusts are analogous to express trusts and require that property be held as if it were trust property, or that property be restored to others.[6] In American jurisprudence the remedial constructive trust is regarded exclusively as a restitutionary device to prevent unjust enrichment.[7] Anglo-Canadian jurisprudence did not, until recently, go this far.[8]

The principle of restitution was adopted in Canada in *Deglman v. Guaranty Trust Co.*[9] and subsequent cases,[10] but generally the courts have been hesitant in extending the doctrine and have not applied it unless a case falls squarely within the principle of the *Deglman* case.[11] Moreover, in these cases the constructive trust was not adopted as the necessary vehicle to achieve restitution. The cases usually involve oral contracts whereby one person agrees to make provision on his death for another if the latter performs certain services for the former during his lifetime without remuneration. Such contracts, not being in writing, are unenforceable, but the cases hold that the person performing the services can recover on a *quantum meruit* or *quasi*-contractual basis, which is an action at law.

Such a basis is clearly inapt where one person has title to property in which another claims a beneficial interest. American authorities hold that the latter will be entitled to such interest where the person having title would be unjustly enriched if he were allowed to rely on his title to exclude the

---

[4]*Taylor v. Davies* (1917), 41 O.L.R. 403 at p. 414, 41 D.L.R. 510 at p. 515 (S.C. App. Div.), affd 51 D.L.R. 75, [1920] A.C. 636 (P.C.); *Proctor v. Bentley*, [1930] 2 D.L.R. 6, [1929] 3 W.W.R. 711 (Sask. C.A.).

[5]Waters, pp. 335-6.

[6]*Ibid.*

[7]3 Scott, para. 461; *Restatement of the Law of Restitution* (St. Paul, Minn., Am. Law Inst., 1936), para. 160.

[8]See on this point, Waters, pp. 333-6. See also Waters, *The Constructive Trust* (1964), esp. the Introduction and ch. 1; Scott, "Constructive Trusts", 71 L.Q. Rev. 39 (1955); Waters, "The English Constructive Trust: A Look into the Future", 19 Vanderbilt L. Rev. 1215 (1965-66); Angus, "Restitution in Canada since the Deglman Case", 42 Can. Bar Rev. 529 (1964); "Comment", 32 U. of T. L. Rev. 83 (1974).

[9][1954] 3 D.L.R. 785, [1954] S.C.R. 725, per Cartwright, J., applying *Fibrosa Spolka Akcyjna v. Fairbairn Lawson Combe Barbour, Ltd.*, [1943] A.C. 32 (H.L.), at p. 61, per Lord Wright.

[10]*County of Carleton v. City of Ottawa* (1965), 52 D.L.R. (2d) 220, [1965] S.C.R. 663; *Arnett and Wensley Ltd. v. Good* (1967), 64 D.L.R. (2d) 181 (B.C.S.C.); *Re Gilroy*, [1971] 3 O.R. 330 (Co. Ct.).

[11]See, *e.g., Re Burgess* (1964), 52 D.L.R. (2d) 233, [1965-69] 4 N.S.R. 361 (S.C.); but see *Farrar v. MacPhee* (1970), 19 D.L.R. (3d) 720 (P.E.I.S.C.); and see Angus, "Restitution in Canada since the Deglman Case", *op. cit., supra,* footnote 8.

claimant.[12] There are different ways in which the desired result may be reached. In some cases an action at law may be sufficient, as where the title to a chattel, which is not unique, is acquired by fraud. The owner then has an action at law for conversion, although, if the defendant is insolvent, the plaintiff can recover the chattel under a constructive trust.[13]

The specifically equitable devices available to redress unjust enrichment are the constructive trust, the equitable lien and subrogation. An equitable lien is the appropriate remedy where, for example, a person makes improvements upon the property of another through fraud or mistake, where he acts on the representations of the owner.[14] Subrogation is appropriate where, for example, a person pays another's debt at the debtor's request. He is then entitled to be subrogated to the position of the creditor.[15] The constructive trust is typically available where a person obtains another's property by mistake or fraud or where he wrongfully sells another's property and purchases new property with the proceeds.[16] In some cases, too, where a constructive trust would be the appropriate remedy, the person who seeks redress may have an option whether to seek to recover the property under a constructive trust or to enforce his claim by way of an equitable lien. The former remedy would be more valuable if the property has increased in value. However, Scott is of the opinion that the plaintiff only has this option if the defendant is a conscious wrongdoer.[17]

The subject of this work precludes further discussion of remedies other than the constructive trust.

It should be reiterated that the remedial constructive trust now under discussion is not the only kind of constructive trust. Constructive trusts arising out of fiduciary relationships are other forms and these are dealt with in the following paragraphs .

The remedial constructive trust has been defined as "the formula through which the conscience of equity finds expression. When property has been acquired in such circumstances that the holder of the legal title may not in good conscience retain the beneficial interest, equity converts him into a trustee."[18] Furthermore, the *Restatement of the Law of Restitution*[19] defines the circumstances under which a remedial constructive trust arises as follows:

> Where a person holding title to property is subject to an equitable duty to convey it to another on the ground that he would be unjustly enriched if he were permitted to retain it, a constructive trust arises.

---

[12]5 Scott, *Trusts* (3d), §461.
[13]*Ibid.*, §462.3.
[14]*Ibid.*, §463.
[15]*Ibid.*, §464.
[16]*Ibid.*, §461.
[17]*Ibid.*, §463.
[18]*Beatty v. Guggenheim Exploration Co.*, 225 N.Y. 380 at p. 386, 122 N.E. 378 (1919, *per* Cardozo, J.).
[19](St. Paul, Minn., Am. Law Inst., 1936), para. 160.

It is this remedial constructive trust which has now finally been recognized in Canada as a vehicle for restitution.

In *Rathwell v. Rathwell*[20] the Supreme Court of Canada had occasion to consider the applicability of the constructive trust in a matrimonial property dispute. Traditionally such cases are dealt with on the basis of resulting trusts and the applicability of the presumptions of advancement and resulting trust.[21] However, the resulting trust is restricted in its operation in this context, as it operates only on the intention of the parties and it is often difficult, if not impossible to find a common intention on the part of the husband and wife to share their assets in a particular way.

Dickson, J., with whom Laskin, C.J.C., and Spence, J., concurred, in a well-reasoned judgment, concluded that the remedial constructive trust is available as a remedy to the spouse who does not have title, but who has contributed to the acquisition of the property in money, money's worth, family life, or otherwise. The court must find a causal connection between the contribution and the disputed asset and, if the contribution enabled the spouse having the title to acquire the asset, the latter will be held to be a constructive trustee for the other spouse. The respective interests of the parties will be determined by the court having regard to the contributions made by the parties. What is necessary in order to find a constructive trust is an enrichment of one party, a corresponding deprivation in the other, and the absence of any valid reason for the enrichment, such as a contract or a disposition of law.

Dickson, J., also held that the wife in the *Rathwell* case was entitled to succeed under a resulting trust since there was evidence of a common intention of the parties to share the property in question.

Martland, J., with whom Judson, Beetz and de Grandpré JJ. concurred, also agreed that there was a resulting trust but strongly dissented from the view that the constructive trust was applicable as a remedial device in cases of this kind. His Lordship was of the opinion that, rather than letting the court exercise an unlimited discretion in matrimonial property disputes to remedy what it considers to be unjust enrichment, these cases should be dealt with by legislation.

In his opinion, Dickson, J., referred with approval to the opinion of Lord Denning, M.R., in *Hussey v. Palmer*,[22] where he applied the remedial constructive trust in a property dispute. He further followed the opinion of Laskin, J., in his dissent in *Murdoch v. Murdoch*,[23] who there first propounded the applicability of the constructive trust in cases of this kind. The majority in that case held that the plaintiff was not entitled to an interest in her husband's

---

[20](1978), 83 D.L.R. (3d) 289, [1978] 2 S.C.R. 436. See Waters, "Comment", 53 Can. Bar Rev. 366 (1975); Oosterhoff, "Remedial Constructive Trusts — Matrimonial Property Disputes — Justice and Equity or 'Palm-Tree' Justice?", 57 Can. Bar Rev. 356 (1979).

[21]See § 1209.4(d), *infra.*

[22][1972] 1 W.L.R. 1286 (C.A.), at pp. 1289-90.

[23](1973), 41 D.L.R. (3d) 367, [1975] 1 S.C.R. 423.

farm under a resulting trust because her contribution consisted of labour on the farm and amounted to no more than might be expected of the average farmer's wife. Moreover, they held that the resulting trust does not apply to business property, a proposition with which Laskin, J., in his dissent, and Dickson, J., in the *Rathwell* case, disagreed.

The opinion of Dickson, J., in *Rathwell*, that the remedial constructive trust is applicable to matrimonial property disputes, was applied by the majority of the Supreme Court in *Pettkus v. Becker*.[24] The facts in that case were similar to those in *Rathwell*, except that the parties were not married but had lived together as husband and wife for many years and except that no evidence of an agreement or common intent to share the property was found at trial. The non-owner's only remedy, therefore, was under a constructive trust, and Dickson, J., who wrote the judgment for the majority held that she was entitled to a half interest in the property to which the appellant held title, but which was acquired by the efforts of both parties over the years, on that basis. His Lordship held further that the fact that the parties were not married, made no difference to the applicability of the remedy. The minority in the *Pettkus* case would have awarded the respondent a half interest in the property on the basis of an imputed resulting trust.

The belated recognition of the remedial constructive trust in Canadian jurisprudence is an exciting development which will not lead to "palm-tree" justice if the guide-lines set forth in the opinion of Dickson, J., and analyzed above, are followed. It may be expected that this new remedy will find application in areas other than matrimonial property disputes.[25]

A constructive trust arises from the circumstances which give rise to the restitutionary remedy. Hence, the person who has been wronged has a beneficial interest in the property from the time that the wrong occurred. The subsequent court decree, therefore, does not create, but merely enforces the duty to make restitution.[26]

1208.1 Profits Made by Express Trustees

Profits derived by a trustee from the trust property, or from his office of trustee, belong to the *cestui que trust*, it being a well-settled principle that, if

---

[24](1980), 117 D.L.R. (3d) 257, [1980] 2 S.C.R. 834. See also *Nuti v. Nuti* (1980), 28 O.R. (2d) 102, 108 D.L.R. (3d) 587 (H.C.J.), to the same effect, varied as to valuation of property only 32 O.R. (2d) 405n, 122 D.L.R. (3d) 384n (C.A.). But contrast *Brown v. Millett* (1979), 6 E.T.R. 88 (N.S.S.C.T.D.), in which a causal connection between acquisition of property and the common law spouse's contribution was not found to exist. *Pettkus v. Becker* was followed in *Pratt v. McLeod* (1981), 129 D.L.R. (3d) 123, 25 R.F.L. (2d) 27 (N.S.S.C.T.D.). And see *Murray v. Roty* (1982), 36 O.R. (2d) 641, 134 D.L.R. (3d) 507 (H.C.J.), affd 41 O.R. (2d) 705, 147 D.L.R. (3d) 438 (C.A.).

[25]See further on this development §1209.4(d), *infra*.

[26]5 Scott, *Trusts* (3d), §462.4, adopted in *Chase Manhattan Bank N.A. v. Israel-British Bank (London) Ltd.*, [1979] 3 All E.R. 1025 at p. 1036, *per* Goulding, J. See also *Re Sharpe*, [1980] 1 All E.R. 198, at p. 203, *per* Browne-Wilkinson, J.

a trustee make a profit out of his trusteeship, it shall enure to the benefit of his *cestui que trust*,[1] for a trustee can never benefit himself by any dealing with the trust property,[2] but is accountable for any profit to the beneficiaries. The following are some illustrations of the rule.[3]

Where trustees acquire a benefit as ostensible owners of trust property, that benefit cannot be retained by them, but must be surrendered to those who are beneficially interested; so, where trustees of land acquire from the Crown a right of salmon fishing in the adjacent sea, the acquisition enures to the benefit of the *cestui que trust*.[4] Where a testator gave real property to trustees in trust to invest in such securities as they might deem fit and they invested in debentures of a limited company, but one of them received a considerable commission without the knowledge of the other who later died, it was held that the surviving trustee, having received a bribe, could not have honestly seen fit to make the investment and, therefore, must refund the bribe to the trust estate and make good any loss sustained by the investment, but that the deceased trustee had made the investment honestly, so that his estate was not liable.[5] Thus no bribe can be retained by a trustee.[6]

If the trustee of an expiring leasehold renews the lease for his own benefit he is deemed to have renewed it for the benefit of the *cestui que trust*.[7] The rule is that, if a person holds in whole or in part as trustee, agent or in a fiduciary capacity for another person, a lease which is renewable by contract or custom and obtains a renewal of it, he holds the renewal for the benefit of that other person,[8] but not where, without fraud, he obtains the renewal or acquires the reversion of a lease which is not renewable by contract or by custom.[9] The renewal is held in trust notwithstanding the fact that the lessor refuses to renew for the benefit of the *cestui que trust*.

In *Keech v. Sandford*,[10] the *locus classicus* of constructive trusts, the leasehold of a market was devised to the trustee for an infant and the lessor,

---

§1208.1

[1]*Per* Stuart, V.C., in *Sugden v. Crossland* (1856), 3 Sm. & G. 192, 65 E.R. 620.

[2]Wigram, V.C., in *Dobson v. Land* (1850), 19 L.J. Ch. 484.

[3]As to the rule against a trustee purchasing trust property, see §1212.2, *infra*.

[4]*Aberdeen Town Council v. Aberdeen University* (1877), 2 App. Cas. 544 (H.L.).

[5]*Re Smith; Smith v. Thompson*, [1896] 1 Ch. 71.

[6]*Metropolitan Bank v. Heiron* (1880), 5 Ex. D. 319 (C.A.).

[7]*Toronto Hockey Club v. Arena Gardens* (1924), 55 O.L.R. 509 at p. 520, [1924] 4 D.L.R. 384 at p. 394 (S.C.).

[8]*Plowman v. Plowman* (1693), 2 Vern. 289, 23 E.R. 786; *Keech v. Sandford* (1726), Sel. Cas. T. King. 61, 25 E.R. 223; *Fitzgibbon v. Scanlan* (1813), 1 Dow. 261 at p. 269, 3 E.R. 694 (H.L.); *Mill v. Hill* (1852), 3 H.L.C. 828, 10 E.R. 330; *Clegg v. Edmondson* (1857), 8 De G. M. & G. 787, 44 E.R. 593 (C.A.); *Archbold v. Scully* (1861), 9 H.L.C. 360, 11 E.R. 769; *Re Anderson's Estate* (1869), 18 W.R. 248; *Isaac v. Wall* (1877), 6 Ch. D. 706; *Re Morgan; Pillgrem v. Pillgrem* (1881), 18 Ch. D. 93 (C.A.); *Re Lulham; Brinton v. Lulham* (1885), 53 L.T. 9 (C.A.); *Griffith v. Owen*, [1907] 1 Ch. 195.

[9]*Randall v. Russell* (1817), 3 Mer. 190, 36 E.R. 73; *Longton v. Wilsby* (1897), 76 L.T. 770; *Bevan v. Webb*, [1905] 1 Ch. 620.

[10]*Supra*, footnote 8.

before expiration of the lease, refused to renew it for the benefit of the infant, so the trustee took the renewal himself. King, L.C., said:

> I must consider this as a trust for the infant; for I very well see, if a trustee, on the refusal to renew, might have a lease to himself, few trust-estates would be renewed to *cestui que use*; though I do not say there is a fraud in this case, yet he should rather have let it run out, than to have had the lease to himself. This may seem hard, that the trustee is the only person of all mankind who might not have the lease: but it is very proper that rule should be strictly pursued, and not in the least relaxed; for it is very obvious what would be the consequence of letting trustees have the lease, on refusal to renew to *cestui que use*.[11]

It makes no difference that the renewed lease covers additional property and is at an increased rent,[12] although in *Acheson v. Fair*[13] it was held that the additional land was not a graft upon the old lease. If the creator of the trust takes a renewal of a lease, he holds it for the trust.[14] If the trustee acquires the reversion from the person from whom he could have claimed a renewal, he holds the reversion on the same trust as the lease,[15] but not if he purchased it from a person to whom it was assigned by the lessor and who is not obliged by contract or custom to renew.[16] Where a husband, whose title to a house was subject to a declaration of trust by him in favour of his wife for a three-fifths interest, agreed to sell the house and, upon default by the purchaser, took a quit claim deed from the latter and later exchanged the house for another property, it was held that the property thus acquired was subject to the same trust.[17]

In general, if an accretion or augmentation of any kind comes to property held in trust or in a fiduciary capacity, it becomes part of the trust property and the trustee is a constructive trustee of it for the *cestui que trust*.[18] If, however, a person is trustee of property only to the extent of a specific sum charged on it or payable out of it, he is personally entitled to the whole of

---

[11]See also *Fitzgibbon v. Scanlan, supra*, footnote 8, *per* Lord Eldon, L.C., at p. 269; *Re Knowles' Will Trusts*, [1948] 1 All E.R. 866 (C.A.); *National Trust v. Osadchuk*, [1943] 1 D.L.R. 689, [1943] S.C.R. 89.

[12]*Re Morgan; Pillgrem v. Pillgrem, supra*, footnote 8.

[13](1843), 3 Dr. & War. 512, 2 Con. & Law. 208.

[14]*Re Lulham; Brinton v. Lulham, supra*, footnote 8.

[15]*Re Lord Ranelagh's Will* (1884), 26 Ch. D. 590; *Phillips v. Phillips* (1885), 29 Ch. D. 673 (C.A.).

[16]*Randall v. Russell* (1817), 3 Mer. 190, 36 E.R. 73; *Bevan v. Webb*, [1905] 1 Ch. 620.

[17]*Spelman v. Spelman*, [1944] 2 D.L.R. 74, [1944] 1 W.W.R. 691 (B.C.C.A.).

[18]*Re Curteis' Trusts* (1872), L.R. 14 Eq. 217, an addition made by a *cestui que trust* to a trust fund held not to be a resulting trust to him for an augmentation of the trust fund; *Aberdeen Town Council v. Aberdeen University* (1877), 2 App. Cas. 544 (H L.), acquisition of fishing rights by trustees; *Re Payne's Settlement; Kibble v. Payne* (1886), 54 L.T. 840, a devise of rents of a leasehold to the mortgagees thereof who were trustees under a settlement and had taken the mortgage to secure advances, the trustees and beneficiaries being strangers to the testator, it being held that the trustees took the devised rents upon the trusts of the settlement.

any accretion to or augmentation of the property, being liable only for the specific sum.[19]

The rule that a trustee may not profit from his trust is normally applied strictly. However, in some modern cases the courts have been more lenient. Thus, in *Crocker and Croquip Ltd. v. Tornroos*,[20] there was a tripartite share purchase agreement entered into between the three controlling shareholders of a company. Of the three, T died, naming the other two, D and C, as his trustees. D died shortly thereafter and C then purchased D's shares from his estate in accordance with the agreement. T's estate was advised that it could not purchase one-half of D's shares as they were improper investments and the Supreme Court of Canada found that they could not have been purchased under the salvage rule either since T could have anticipated the potential sale and his trustees were not embarrassed by an emergency that would render it imperative that they purchase the shares for the protection of the estate. Moreover, the court held that C's purchase was pursuant to a contractual right personal to him which he was free to exercise without offending the rule that a trustee's duty and interest must not conflict.

Similarly, in *Holder v. Holder*,[21] a trustee who had renounced after performing minimal duties as an executor, was allowed to purchase the tenancies of certain farms from the estate. He had farmed the lands in question for some years under tenancy with the testator and his knowledge about the properties thus arose not out of his office as trustee, but independently. Accordingly, his interest did not conflict with his duty.

While cases such as these are rare, they indicate that in appropriate circumstances the strict rule of equity may be relaxed.

Wherever trust property becomes vested in a person who is not the trustee, because no person was effectively appointed trustee, or all trustees died before the instrument creating the trust came into operation, or declined to act, he becomes a constructive trustee of the property upon the same trusts.[22] The individuals named as trustees by the creator of a trust are only the nominal instruments to execute his intention that the trust shall be performed. If they fail, either by death, or by being under a disability, or by refusing to act, or if no trustees are appointed at all, and the defect cannot otherwise be supplied, the office is in the first instance assumed by a court of equity of competent jurisdiction which will take care that trustees are appointed to execute the trust.[23] New trustees may be appointed either under a power contained in the instrument creating the trust, or under statutory power, or

---

[19]*Re Campbell*; *Campbell v. Campbell*, [1893] 3 Ch. 468.
[20](1957), 7 D.L.R. (2d) 104, [1957] S.C.R. 151.
[21][1968] Ch. 353 (C.A.).
[22]*Sonley v. Clockmakers' Co.* (1780), 1 Bro. C.C. 80, 28 E.R. 998; *Attorney-General v. Hickman* (1732), 2 Eq. Ca. Abr. 193 at p. 194, 22 E.R. 166; *Attorney-General v. Lady Downing* (1767), Wilm. 1, 97 E.R. 1; *Moggridge v. Thackwell* (1792), 1 Ves. Jun. 464 at p. 475, 30 E.R. 440, affd 13 Ves. Jun. 416, 33 E.R. 350 (H.L.); *Re Davis' Trusts* (1871), L.R. 12 Eq. 214.
[23]*Per* Wilmot, L.C.J., in *Attorney-General v. Lady Downing* (1767), Wilm. 1, 97 E.R. 1.

under a court order. When necessary, the court will make the heir-at-law of the creator of the trust a trustee.[24]

1208.2 Strangers Intermeddling with the Trust

Trusts may be constituted not merely by direct declaration of trust, but also by the constructive operation of the consequences flowing from the acts of the parties, and equity enforces a trust not only against the trustees but against all persons who obtain possession of the trust property with notice of the trust.[1] A stranger to the trust who receives trust property with notice of the trust, or who knowingly assists the actual trustee in a fraudulent and dishonest disposition of the trust property, is a constructive trustee.[2]

In the case of strangers who knowingly, although not necessarily dishonestly, intermeddle with a trust, a distinction should be drawn between (1) those who receive trust moneys and deal with them in a manner inconsistent with the terms of the trust, and (2) those who are jointly engaged with the trustee in a fraudulent breach of trust, but do not in fact receive any trust moneys. The first are really express trustees and are called trustees *de son tort*. The latter are often called constructive trustees,[3] although they are not trustees since they have received no trust property. They are, however, normally liable to the beneficiaries of the trust. Trustees *de son tort* are also sometimes called constructive trustees[4] and this is correct, although they are treated on the same basis as express trustees for the purpose of limitations of actions.

A person whose acts are referable to his appointment as a trustee is not to be deemed to be a trustee *de son tort*, for he is not a stranger to the trust.[5]

Where a retiring trustee, expecting that a new trustee would be duly appointed, executed a transfer of trust funds into the name of the proposed new trustee who allowed a breach of trust to be committed, it was held that the retiring trustee was liable for the breach of trust and that the proposed trustee was liable as trustee *de son tort* in respect of trust funds which actually came into his hands.[6] Where money payable to a widow as trustee for her infant child was collected for her by M and, by arrangement between them, was retained by him and used in his business, he acknowledging in writing to

---

[24]*Ibid.*

§1208.2

[1]*Per* Romilly, M.R., in *Pooley v. Budd* (1851), 14 Beav. 34 at pp. 43-4, 51 E.R. 200; *Ankcorn v. Stewart* (1920), 47 O.L.R. 478, 54 D.L.R. 74 (S.C. App. Div.); *Bowler v. Redman* (1920), 18 O.W.N. 286 (S.C. App. Div.).

[2]Kay, L.J., in *Soar v. Ashwell*, [1893] 2 Q.B. 390 (C.A.); *Barnes v. Addy* (1874), L.R. 9 Ch. App. 244.

[3]*Selangor United Rubber Estates Ltd. v. Cradock*, [1968] 1 W.L.R. 1555 (Ch. Div.), at pp. 1578-91, *per* Ungoed-Thomas, J.; *Mara v. Browne*, [1896] 1 Ch. 199 (C.A.); *Soar v. Ashwell, supra*, at p. 394, *per* Lord Esher, M.R.

[4]*Soar v. Ashwell, supra*, footnote 2, at pp. 400, 405, *per* Kay, L.J.

[5]*Mara v. Browne, supra*, footnote 3, at p. 207, *per* Lord Herschell.

[6]*Pearce v. Pearce* (1856), 22 Beav. 248, 52 E.R. 1103.

the widow that he was holding the money to the credit of the infant with interest at six per cent per annum, it was held that he was a trustee *de son tort* and, as such, either as an express or a constructive trustee, liable to account to the infant and entitled under the *Trustee Relief Act*[7] to pay the money into court against the opposition of the widow who desired the money to be paid to her.[8]

The fact that such persons are express trustees, and not mere constructive trustees, with all the liabilities to which express trustees are subject, including the effect of the Statutes of Limitation, appears to be settled by the Privy Council. Viscount Cave, in referring to persons who, although not named as trustees, had assumed the position of trustees for others or had taken possession or control of trust property for them, said:

> These persons though not originally trustees had taken upon themselves the custody and administration of property on behalf of others; and though sometimes referred to as constructive trustees, they were, in fact, actual trustees, though not so named. It followed that their possession also was treated as the possession of the persons for whom they acted, and they, like express trustees, were disabled from taking advantage of the time bar. But the position in this respect of a constructive trustee in the usual sense of the words — that is to say, of a person who, though he had taken possession in his own right, was liable to be declared a trustee in a Court of Equity — was widely different, and it had long been settled that time ran in his favour from the moment of his so taking possession.[9]

When a person has assumed, with or without consent, to act as trustee of property, that is, to act in a fiduciary capacity with regard to it, and has in consequence been in possession of or has exercised command or control over it, he will be charged with all the liabilities of an express trustee and be classed with and called an express trustee of an express trust, and he must account to his *cestui que trust* without regard to lapse of time.[10] However, where the stranger can show that his receipt of trust property is inconsistent with the trust, there is no liability on him.[11]

A constructive trust may also be raised upon a resulting trust. Thus, where a wife transfers property to her husband on the faith of a misrepresentation, he holds upon a resulting trust and where he thereafter transfers the property to a corporation which he controls, the corporation is chargeable as a constructive trustee since it has constructive notice of the trust.[12] But that is not

---

[7] R.S.O. 1897, c. 336.
[8] *Re Preston* (1906), 13 O.L.R. 110 (H.C.J.).
[9] *Taylor v. Davies* (1919), 51 D.L.R. 75 at pp. 84-5, [1920] A.C. 636 at pp. 651 (P.C.), holding that a mortgagee of land which formed part of an estate assigned for the benefit of creditors was not an express trustee, nor in respect of the equity of redemption conveyed to him by the assignee, but was at most a constructive trustee and the *Limitations Act*, R.S.O. 1914, c. 75, ran in his favour, affg 41 O.L.R. 403, 41 D.L.R. 510 (S.C. App. Div.).
[10] *Mattice v. Mattice*, [1925] 1 D.L.R. 755, 2 W.W.R. 203 (B.C.S.C.); *Morrison v. Coast Finance Ltd.* (1965), 55 D.L.R. (2d) 710, 54 W.W.R. 257 (B.C.C.A.).
[11] *Constantine v. Ioan* (1969), 67 W.W.R. 615 (B.C.S.C.).
[12] *Moore v. Moore* (1970), 16 D.L.R. (3d) 174 (B.C.C.A.).

the case where the transferee is a *bona fide* purchaser for value without notice.[13]

A person does not become a constructive trustee merely by acting as solicitor or other agent of trustees in transactions within their powers, unless he receives and becomes chargeable with some part of the trust property or assists in what he knows to be a dishonest or fraudulent design on the part of the trustees,[14] but he may become a constructive trustee or trustee *de son tort*, by intermeddling with the performance of the trust,[15] or by dealing with the property in a manner not justified by the terms of his employment, or not consistent with performance of trusts of which he is aware.[16]

Although the general rule is that to make a person a constructive trustee of trust property which he takes as his own, he must have notice that it is being misapplied by being transferred to him or, in other words, he must be a party to the fraud or breach of trust,[17] nevertheless, a person may, in certain cases, become a constructive trustee even without notice of the trust. A person who, without notice of the trust and without valuable consideration, acquires the legal estate in trust property, takes the property as a trustee and subject to performance of the trust, because, where property is subject to a trust, the trust follows the legal estate wherever it goes, unless it comes into the hands of a purchaser for valuable consideration without notice.[18] Where a person receives trust property from the trustee as a volunteer, he takes the property burdened with the trust regardless of whether or not he had any knowledge thereof.[19] Similarly, he is a trustee if he acquires, gratuitously and without notice, an equitable interest in the property because, without consideration, he stands in no better position than the transferor and has no better title than the transferor.[20] Also, he becomes a trustee if he acquires, without notice of the trust, an equitable interest in the property without the right to call for the legal estate.[21] In such cases, however, he is entitled to protect himself from

---

[13]*Hawker v. Hawker* (1969), 3 D.L.R. (3d) 735 (Sask. Q.B.).

[14]*Barnes v. Addy* (1874), L.R. 9 Ch. App. 244.

[15]*Myler v. Fitzpatrick* (1822), 6 Madd. 360, 56 E.R. 1128; *Hardy v. Caley* (1864), 33 Beav. 365, 55 E.R. 408.

[16]*Morgan v. Stephens* (1861), 3 Giff. 226, 66 E.R. 392; *Lee v. Sankey* (1872), L.R. 15 Eq. 204.

[17]Per Lord Eldon, L.C., in *Colchester Corp. v. Lowten* (1813), 1 V. & B. 226 at p. 246, 35 E.R. 89; Jessel, M.R., in *Russell v. Wakefield Waterworks Co.* (1875), L.R. 20 Eq. 474 at p. 479; *Re Blundell; Blundell v. Blundell* (1888), 40 Ch. D. 370; *Moxham v. Grant*, [1900] 1 Q.B. 88 (C.A.).

[18]Per Wilmot, L.C.J., in *Attorney-General v. Lady Downing* (1767), Wilm. 1 at p. 21, 97 E.R. 1.

[19]*Swanson v. Smith*, [1945] 3 D.L.R. 431, [1945] 2 W.W.R. 469 (B.C.C.A.).

[20]Cotton, L.J., in *Taylor v. Blakelock* (1886), 32 Ch. D. 560 (C.A.), at pp. 568, 570.

[21]*Newton v. Newton* (1868), L.R. 6 Eq. 135, in which case a trustee of funds which were invested in a mortgage in his name deposited the title deeds in an equitable mortgage without notice of the trust in order to secure an advance to himself and it was held that the *cestui que trust* had priority over the equitable mortgagee and was entitled to delivery up of the deeds; *Maundrell v. Maundrell* (1805), 10 Ves. Jun. 246 at p. 260, 32 E.R. 839; *Mumford v. Stohwasser* (1874), L.R. 18 Eq. 556.

the trust by acquiring the legal estate from a person who can give it to him without breach of trust.

Thus, in *Taylor v. Russell*,[22] trustees under a settlement, with powers of sale and mortgage, made a legal mortgage of the land and later sold the lands to A and handed the title deeds to him without notice of the mortgage which was apparently forgotten. A obtained an equitable mortgage from the plaintiffs by deposit of forged title deeds, the plaintiffs believing that they thereby acquired a legal mortgage. A then obtained a second equitable mortgage from the defendant by deposit of the true title deeds, the defendant also believing he thereby acquired a legal mortgage. The defendant then discovered the existence of the plaintiffs' equitable mortgage and of the prior legal mortgage and arranged with the legal mortgagee to release the land from the mortgage and to reconvey the legal estate to the trustees upon condition that the trustees would then convey the legal estate to the defendant. This was done and the trustees, without knowledge of the first equitable mortgage, conveyed the legal estate to the defendant. The plaintiffs brought action to establish their priority as equitable mortgagees and it was held that there was nothing to show that the defendant had acted inequitably in getting in the legal estate and that there was no equity which prevented him from availing himself of its protection, so that he had priority over the first equitable mortgage.[23] A person cannot thus protect himself, however, by acquiring the legal estate from a person who is not, in equity, entitled to convey it to him. Thus, when a first mortgage is paid off, the first mortgagee, holding the legal estate, is trustee for all subsequent encumbrancers according to their priorities and must convey the legal estate to the subsequent encumbrancer who has the best right to it.[24]

A person who acquires the legal estate in trust property for valuable con-

---

[22][1892] A.C. 244 (H.L.).

[23]*Cf. Bailey v. Barnes*, [1894] 1 Ch. 25 (C.A.), in which case, J, as owner of four houses, mortgaged them to a mortgagee who later transferred the mortgages to B for the outstanding mortgage debt. Two days later, B sold the houses to H under power of sale for the exact sum he had paid and conveyed the houses to him free from the equity of redemption; H mortgaged the houses and, on her death, her successor in title, E, sold the equity of redemption to L. Judgment creditors of J, the original owner, then brought action against B and E on the ground that the sale to H was a fraudulent exercise of the power of sale and it was so declared by the court. L was not a party to this action but heard of it, paid off the mortgage and received from the mortgagees a conveyance of the legal estate. When he bought the equity of redemption, he was unaware of any impropriety in the sale to H, although he had seen a valuation which appeared to show that the sale had been at an undervalue, but he made no enquiries about the sale. It was held that he did not have constructive notice of the impropriety of the sale and that he was protected against the prior equitable interests of the plaintiffs by having acquired the legal estates. See also *Maundrell v. Maundrell, supra*, footnote 21; *Carter v. Carter* (1857), 3 K. & J. 617, 69 E.R. 1256; *Bates v. Johnson* (1859), Johns. 304, 70 E.R. 439; *Sharples v. Adams* (1863), 32 Beav. 213 at p. 216, 55 E.R. 84.

[24]*Sharples v. Adams, supra*, footnote 23; *Grugeon v. Gerrard* (1840), 4 Y. & C. Ex. 119, 160 E.R. 945.

sideration without notice of the trust takes it free from the trust.[25] A subsequent purchaser from him is not affected by notice of the trust, since the property was freed from it by the first purchase for valuable consideration without notice.[26] It is said that the only exception to the rule which protects a purchaser with notice who takes from a purchaser without notice is that which prevents a trustee who has sold trust property, or a person who acquired property by fraud, from saying that he sold it to a *bona fide* purchaser for value and repurchased it from him.[27]

A person who, for valuable consideration and without notice of the trust, acquires an equitable interest in trust property with the right to call for the legal estate, also takes free from the trust. In *Taylor v. London and County Banking Co.*; *London and County Banking Co. v. Nixon*,[28] T, a co-trustee under a settlement and the holder in his own right of a mortgage upon the security of a leasehold of which he held the deeds, transferred the mortgage debt to the trust fund to cover a misappropriation by him, no further action being taken by those interested after they became aware of the appropriation. Later, T, sole trustee of another estate known as the T settlement, informed N, upon the latter's appointment as co-trustee of that settlement, that the mortgage debt belonged to the T settlement, exhibiting the deeds and, at N's request, transferred the mortgage to N and himself as trustees. N had no knowledge of the other trust. Later, T, without N's knowledge, deposited the deeds with his bankers as security for a loan and then absconded. In proceedings to determine priorities, N as trustee was held entitled to the mortgage debts, legal estate and title deeds in priority to the other trust and bank, as his valuable consideration was forbearing to sue T for the debt to the trust. Stirling, L.J., stated that:[29]

> A purchaser for value without notice is entitled to the benefit of a legal title, not merely where he has actually got it in, but where he has a better title or right to call for it ... It has accordingly been held that if a purchaser for value takes an equitable title only, or omits to get in an outstanding legal estate, and a subsequent purchaser for value without notice procures, at the time of his purchase, the person in whom the legal title is vested to declare himself a trustee for him, or even to join as party in a conveyance of the equitable interest (although he may not formally convey or declare a trust of the legal estate), still the subsequent purchaser gains priority.[30]

---

[25]*Thorndike v. Hunt*; *Browne v. Butter* (1859), 3 De G. & J. 563, 44 E.R. 1386 (C.A.); *Pilcher v. Rawlins* (1872), L.R. 7 Ch. App. 259; *Heath v. Crealock* (1874) L.R. 10 Ch. App. 22; *Taylor v. Blakelock* (1886), 32 Ch. D. 560 (C.A.).

[26]*Per* Lord Eldon, L.C., in *M'Queen v. Farquhar* (1805), 11 Ves. Jun. 467 at p. 478, 32 E.R. 1168.

[27]*Per* Jessel, M.R., in *Re Stapleford Colliery Co.*; *Barrow's Case* (1880), 14 Ch. D. 432 (C.A.), at p. 445.

[28][1901] 2 Ch. 231 (C.A.).

[29]*Ibid.*, at pp. 262-3.

[30]See also *Wilkes v. Bodington* (1707), 2 Vern. 599, 23 E.R. 991; *Stanhope v. Earl Verney* (1761), 2 Eden 81, 28 E.R. 826; *Wilmot v. Pike* (1845), 5 Hare 14 at p. 22, 67 E.R. 808; *Rooper v. Harrison* (1855), 2 K. & J. 86, 69 E.R. 704.

1208.3 Trusts Arising from Relationships

Although no trust relationship exists between the parties, the courts have extended the constructive trust device by analogy to other fiduciary relationships. A fiduciary relationship arises where one person is in a position to exercise influence over or, because of his position, to take advantage of another[1] and, if a wrong arises, the same remedy exists against the wrongdoer as would exist against a trustee of an express trust.[2] Typical fiduciary relationships include solicitor and client, guardian and ward, doctor and patient and principal and agent. Similar relationships, sometimes called "confidential relationships" because they are less well-defined in law than fiduciary relationships,[3] may also give rise to a constructive trust because one party has exercised undue influence over another. An example of this type is the relationship between an elderly patient and the operator of a nursing home.[4] Moreover, a constructive trust may also be raised in a commercial transaction where one party has a decided economic advantage over the other and there has not been full disclosure, or where one party uses confidential information obtained through the other party to his own advantage.[5]

Accordingly, if under a contractual or other relationship between parties, one holds or deals with property of the other in a fiduciary capacity, he is regarded in equity as doing so upon a constructive trust, subject to the conditions which the relationship implies or involves.[6]

The following relationships have attracted a constructive trust where one party has gained an advantage at the expense of the other.

(a) Agents

A contract of agency does not, in itself, make an agent a trustee, but he may, under power of attorney or otherwise, hold or deal with property of his principal in such circumstances and manner as to constitute him a trustee for his principal.[7]

The general rule is that the court will not allow a trustee, agent, or other

---

§1208.3

[1]*Follis v. Township of Albemarle*, [1941] O.R. 1, [1941] 1 D.L.R. 178 (C.A.), per McTague, J.A.

[2]Fry, L.J., in *Re West of England and South Wales District Bank; Ex p. Dale & Co.* (1879), 11 Ch. D. 772 at p. 778.

[3]Scott, "The Fiduciary Principle", 37 Cal. L. Rev. 539 (1949); 1 Scott, paras. 4A-16A.

[4]*Public Trustee v. Skoretz* (1972), 32 D.L.R. (3d) 749, [1973] 2 W.W.R. 638 (B.C.S.C.).

[5]*Pre-Cam Exploration & Development Ltd. v. McTavish* (1966), 57 D.L.R. (2d) 557, [1966] S.C.R. 551.

[6]*Per* Lord O'Hagan in *Shaw v. Foster* (1872), L.R. 5 H.L. 321 at p. 349; Lord Westbury in *Knox v. Gye* (1872), L.R. 5 H.L. 656 at pp. 675-6; Jessel, M.R., in *Earl of Egmont v. Smith; Smith v. Earl of Egmont* (1877), 6 Ch. D. 469 at pp. 475-6.

[7]*Per* Lord Cottenham, L.C., in *Foley v. Hill* (1848), 2 H.L.C. 28 at pp. 35-6, 9 E.R. 1002; *Burdick v. Garrick* (1870), L.R. 5 Ch. App. 232 at p. 240; *North American Land and Timber Co. Ltd. v. Watkins*, [1904] 1 Ch. 242, affd [1904] 2 Ch. 233 (C.A.); *Reid-Newfoundland Co. v. Anglo-American Telegraph Co. Ltd.*, [1912] A.C. 555 (P.C.).

person holding an office or place of trust and confidence, to put himself in a position where his interest conflicts with his duty, or, without disclosure, to make a profit out of his agency.[8] The general rule, that an agent must not make a profit for himself out of his employment other than the amount payable to him by his principal, is one calculated to secure the observance of good faith between principal and agent and to prevent the agent sacrificing his principal's interest and obtaining gain and advantage for himself.[9]

A profit made by the agent without the knowledge of the principal may be recoverable by the latter from the agent.[10] Thus, where a purchaser of land entered into an agreement with the vendor's agent through whom he bought the land, that the agent was to have a share of profits on a resale, it was held that both the agent and the purchaser thereby became implied trustees of the vendor and were accountable to him for all of the profits.[11] If an agent is employed to negotiate the purchase of a particular parcel of real estate for his principal, he will be held a trustee of it for the principal if he buys the property with his own money in his own name.[12] When the purchase money is increased by a sum which, without the knowledge of the purchaser, is to be paid to the purchaser's agent, it is a bribe and can be recovered back by the purchaser either from his agent who was bribed, or from the vendor and agent jointly and severally.[13]

Members of a committee of managers appointed by mortgagees to sell mortgaged premises stand in a fiduciary relationship towards the mortgagees so that, if they sell the property at an undervaluation to a person not dealing at arm's length with them, they are accountable to the mortgagees.[14]

(b) Solicitors

Ordinarily, a solicitor is not a trustee for his client, even though money or

---

[8]*Cook v. Deeks* (1916), 27 D.L.R. 1, [1916] 1 A.C. 554 (P.C.); *Roxborough Gardens of Hamilton v. Davis* (1919), 46 O.L.R. 615, 52 D.L.R. 572 (S.C. App. Div.); *Millar v. Philip* (1916), 9 O.W.N. 469 (H.C.); *Foster v. Reaume*, [1924] 2 D.L.R. 951 (S.C.C.), revg 54 O.L.R. 245, [1923] 4 D.L.R. 51 (C.A.); *Radford v. Stannard* (1914), 19 D.L.R. 768, 7 W.W.R. 986 (Alta. S.C. App. Div.).

[9]*Per* Brodeur, J., in *Hitchcock v. Sykes* (1914), 23 D.L.R. 518 at p. 531, 49 S.C.R. 403 at p. 422.

[10]*Raeff v. Dimitroff* (1920), 18 O.W.N. 164 (H.C.); *Killeen v. Butler*, [1929] 1 D.L.R. 52 (N.S.S.C.).

[11]*Coy v. Pommerenke* (1911), 44 S.C.R. 543.

[12]*Archibald v. Goldstein* (1884), 1 Man. R. 45 (Q.B.). See also *Othen v. Crisp*, [1951] O.W.N. 459 (C.A.).

[13]*Peacock v. Crane* (1913), 29 O.L.R. 282, 14 D.L.R. 217 (S.C. App. Div.), citing *Grant v. Gold Exploration and Development Syndicate*, [1900] 1 Q.B. 233 (C.A.), and stating at p. 292 O.L.R., p. 220 D.L.R.: "The extent to which the Court will go in protecting a purchaser is well shewn in *Beck v. Kantorowicz* (1857), 3 K. & J. 230, [69 E.R. 1093], where the ultimate purchaser or transferee of the mine was held entitled to the shares set apart by way of secret commission by the vendors to one of a group of co-adventurers who bought and then sold to the company".

[14]*Krendel v. Frontwell Investments Ltd.*, [1967] 2 O.R. 579, 64 D.L.R. (2d) 471 (H.C.J.).

property of the client passes through his hands,[15] although, like any other agent, he may become a trustee by his acts.[16] It is said that to become a trustee, he must have duties to perform in regard to the disposition of the property, such as to invest or manage it.[17]

In *Boardman v. Phipps*[18] a solicitor was held accountable to trust beneficiaries, along with one of the beneficiaries. The solicitor had been acting for the trust and, in order to protect an investment of the trust, a large block of shares in a private company, he and a trustee-beneficiary represented themselves as agents of the trust and acquired the other outstanding shares of the company in their own names. The trust was not able to purchase the shares itself as they were not a proper trust investment. Nevertheless, even though the solicitor and the trustee acted without *mala fides*, and even though the trust benefited from their action, they were held accountable to the other beneficiaries for the profit subsequently made by them on their shares.

(c) Directors, officers and promoters

A constructive trust for the company, involving the obligation to account for personal profits made out of transactions affecting the company, attaches to a director,[19] to an officer,[20] and to a promoter of a company.[21]

The basis of liability in these cases is that the director or officer has made a profit out of information that comes to him in his capacity as director or officer and in the course of the execution of his office.[22] If those facts are established, the fact that the director acted *bona fide* and that the company itself could not have made a profit is irrelevant.[23]

In *Regal (Hastings), Ltd. v. Gulliver*,[24] R Co. negotiated the purchase of a lease to a subsidiary, A Co. It was a term of the assignment that R Co.'s directors guarantee the rent until the shares in A Co. were fully subscribed. R Co. could only afford to subscribe part of the shares in A Co. and, because one of the directors objected to the guarantee, the remaining shares were

---

[15]*Watson v. Woodman* (1875), L.R. 20 Eq. 721.

[16]*Harpham v. Schacklock* (1881), 19 Ch. D. 207 (C.A.); *Re Vernon, Ewens, & Co.* (1886), 33 Ch. D. 402 (C.A.).

[17]*Gray v. Bateman* (1872), 21 W.R. 137; *Dooby v. Watson* (1888), 39 Ch. D. 178.

[18][1966] 2 A.C. 46 (H.L.).

[19]*Re Iron Clay Brick Manufacturing Co.; Turner's Case* (1889), 19 O.R. 113 (H.C.J.); *Hyatt v. Allen* (1911), 18 O.W.R. 850 (H.C.J.); *Cape Breton Cold Storage Co. Ltd. v. Rowlings*, [1929] 3 D.L.R. 577, [1929] S.C.R. 505.

[20]*North American Exploration & Development Co. v. Green* (1913), 24 O.W.R. 843 (H.C.).

[21]*Erlanger v. New Sombrero Phosphate Co.* (1878), 3 App. Cas. 1218 (H.L.); *Lagunas Nitrate Co. v. Lagunas Syndicate*, [1899] 2 Ch. 392 (C.A.); *Gluckstein v. Barnes*, [1900] A.C. 240 (H.L.); *Re Hess Manufacturing Co.; Edgar v. Sloan* (1894), 23 S.C.R. 644; *Rumford v. Hinton* (1922), 52 O.L.R. 47, [1923] 2 D.L.R. 471 (S.C. App. Div.).

[22]*Regal (Hastings), Ltd. v. Gulliver*, [1942] 1 All E.R. 378 (H.L.), *per* Lord Russell of Killowen.

[23]*Ibid.*

[24]*Ibid.*

issued to the other directors and R Co.'s solicitor and others. Subsequently the shares in R Co. and A Co. were sold at a profit and the new management brought action against the directors and the solicitor to recover the profit. It was held that, despite the *bona fides* of the directors and the fact that R Co. was unable to subscribe the shares, they were liable to the company for the profit which they had gained by reason of their position as directors and as such were fiduciaries. The inevitable and unfortunate result of such cases is that the new shareholders reap a profit without having taken any risk.

In *Peso Silver Mines Ltd. (N.P.L.) v. Cropper*[25] the courts reached a different conclusion in very similar circumstances. In that case, C, a director of a company trading in mining claims, acquired a number of claims on his own behalf after they had been rejected by his company. The features which distinguish this case from *Regal (Hastings), Ltd. v. Gulliver* are that Peso Silver Mines Ltd. was in the business of buying mining claims and considered many offers on a regular basis. Moreover, the company was not in a position to buy the claims in question because of strained financial resources; besides, they were of speculative value. In addition, the courts found, rather surprisingly, that when C subsequently acquired the claims he had put the original offer out of his mind. C's purchase was thus not made because of information acquired because of his directorship and accordingly he was not accountable to the company.

It would appear that the *Peso* case was exceptional because of its peculiar facts and the Supreme Court of Canada has subsequently reasserted the conflict rule in *Canadian Aero Service Ltd. v. O'Malley*.[26] However, in that case Laskin, C.J.C., delivering the judgment of the court stated that the rule should not be applied rigidly, but that regard must be had to the facts of each case.[27]

(d) Employers and employees

By reason of the relationship between them, an employer may become a trustee for his employee. An employer purchased and paid for land in his own name at the request and on behalf of an employee, under an oral arrangement providing for repayment of the price by the employee and for the latter remaining as employee for three years. The employee left within the three years, because the employer repudiated the oral arrangement. The employee tendered the amount due to the employer before taking action, but it was

---

[25](1966), 58 D.L.R. (2d) 1, [1966] S.C.R. 673, affg 56 D.L.R. (2d) 117, 54 W.W.R. 329 (B.C.C.A.).

[26](1973), 40 D.L.R. (3d) 371, [1974] S.C.R. 592. See Roberts, "Corporate Opportunity and Confidential Information: Birds of a Feather that Flock together or Canaeros of a Different Colour?" (1976), 28 C.P.R. (2d) 68.

[27]*Cf. Industrial Development Consultants Ltd. v. Cooley*, [1972] 2 All E.R. 162, noted 50 Can. Bar Rev. 623 (1972). As to corporate opportunity generally, see further Beck, "The Saga of Peso Silver Mines: Corporate Opportunity Reconsidered", 49 Can. Bar Rev. 80 (1971); Jones, "Unjust Enrichment and the Fiduciary's Duty of Loyalty", 84 L.Q. Rev. 472 (1968).

refused. A trust was declared in favour of the employee, subject to a charge for the amount due to the employer.[28]

Employees may also become constructive trustees for their employers where they obtain trade secrets or "know-how" in the course of their employment. As this matter does not concern real property primarily, it is not further pursued here.[29]

(e) Personal representatives

In a loose sense, a personal representative is a trustee for the beneficiaries and creditors of the deceased, because he holds the real and personal estate of the deceased for their benefit and not for his own[30] and is also liable for breach of trust if he misapplies it,[31] because a personal representative, in accepting the office, accepts its duties and becomes a trustee in the sense that he is personally liable in equity for all breaches of the ordinary trusts which in courts of equity are considered to arise from his office.[32] In England, it was held that, in his capacity as executor, he is not strictly a trustee for a legatee,[33] or the next of kin of the testator,[34] and does not become a trustee by signing a residuary account,[35] but that, if property is bequeathed to him in trust, he becomes a trustee of it when he has paid the debts,[36] or in the case of a legacy, has assented to it,[37] or has severed it from the rest of the estate,[38] or has executed a declaration of trust.[39] A personal representative is also declared by Imperial statute[40] to be a trustee of all real property which devolves upon him for the persons beneficially entitled to it.

Similarly, in Ontario, it was held that, where a person is named as executor and as trustee of a legacy, he holds it in his character as trustee as soon as he

---

[28]*Brown v. Storoschuk*, [1947] 1 D.L.R. 227, [1946] 3 W.W.R. 641 (B.C.C.A.).

[29]See, *inter alia*, North, "Disclosure of Confidential Information", [1965] J. Bus. L. 307; [1966] J. Bus. L. 31; and "Further Disclosures of Confidential Information", [1968] J. Bus. L. 32; Baram, "Trade Secrets: What Price Loyalty", 48 Harv. Bus. Rev. 66 (1969); Goff and Jones, *The Law of Restitution*, 2nd ed. (1978), p. 521.

[30]*Per* Lindley, L.J., in *Re Davis (Jane)*; *Re Davis (T.H.)*; *Evans v. Moore*, [1891] 3 Ch. 119 (C.A.), at p. 124.

[31]*Per* Turner, V.C., in *Fordham v. Wallis* (1853), 10 Hare 217, 68 E.R. 905.

[32]*Per* Kay, J., in *Re Marsden*; *Bowden v. Layland*; *Gibbs v. Layland* (1884), 26 Ch. D. 783 at p. 790.

[33]*Re Barker*; *Buxton v. Campbell*, [1892] 2 Ch. 491; *Re Mackay*; *Mackay v. Gould*, [1906] 1 Ch. 25.

[34]*Re Lacy*; *Royal General Theatrical Fund Ass'n. v. Kydd*, [1899] 2 Ch. 149.

[35]*Attenborough & Son v. Solomon*, [1913] A.C. 76 (H.L.), at p. 81.

[36]*Charlton v. Earl of Durham* (1869), L.R. 4 Ch. App. 433; *Re Timmis*; *Nixon v. Smith*, [1902] 1 Ch. 176.

[37]*Re Timmis*; *Nixon v. Smith*, *supra*, footnote 36; *Attenborough v. Solomon*, *supra*, footnote 35, at pp. 83-4.

[38]*Ex p. Dover* (1834), 5 Sim. 500, 58 E.R. 425; *Phillipo v. Munnings* (1837), 2 My. & Cr. 309, 40 E.R. 658.

[39]*Re Rowe*; *Jacobs v. Hind* (1889), 58 L.J. Ch. 703 (C.A.).

[40]*Land Transfer Act, 1897*, 60 & 61 Vict., c. 65, s. 1.

has assented to it and set apart a sum of money to answer it.[41] Under the *Estates Administration Act*[42] all real and personal property of a testator or intestate devolves to and becomes vested in his personal representative as trustee for the persons beneficially entitled thereto (although, unless he registers a caution, it vests in the beneficiaries after three years), but it has been held that, after he has fulfilled his duties respecting the property, he is a trustee for the beneficiaries.[43] Apart from the Act, the legal estate in realty may, under the terms of a will, be expressly vested in the executors as trustees. It has also been held that realty may vest in executors as trustees where, although there is no express devise of realty to the executors, the whole tenor of the will, together with the fact that it appoints them as trustees, makes it clear that it is vested in them as trustees.[44] It appears that, after debts are paid and ten years have elapsed, there should be a presumption that one of several executor-trustees who is dealing with assets is dealing with them as trustee and not as executor and that the onus lies on a person seeking to uphold a transaction to show that he dealt with the other party as an executor.[45] Also, although the executors were not expressly called trustees, it was held that a trust was intended to be created as to all portions of the estate which could not be completely vested in possession until the death of either of two persons.[46]

A person who intrudes and intermeddles with the estate of a testator or intestate without having been appointed an executor, or without having obtained letters of administration from a competent court, becomes liable as an executor *de son tort* (there being no term "administrator *de son tort*"). The slightest intermeddling with the assets in such a way as to signify an assumption of authority, or an intention to assume the functions of an executor, may make a person an executor *de son tort*.[47]

(f) Guardians

A testamentary guardian is a trustee and, therefore, the Statutes of Limita-

---

[41]*Re Mulholland and Morris* (1909), 20 O.L.R. 27 (H.C.J.), at p. 29.

[42]R.S.O. 1980, c. 143, s. 2. *Cf. Devolution of Real Property Act*, R.S.A. 1980, c. D-34, s. 2(1); R.S.S. 1978, c. D-27, ss. 4, 5; *Estate Administration Act*, R.S.B.C. 1979, c. 114, s. 90; *Devolution of Estates Act*, R.S.M. 1970, c. D70, s. 18; R.S.N.B. 1973, c. D-9, s. 3; *Chattels Real Act*, R.S.N. 1970, c. 36, s. 2; *Real Property Act*, R.S.N.S. 1967, c. 261, s. 6(1); *Probate Act*, R.S.P.E.I. 1974, c. P-19, s. 108(1); *Devolution of Real Property Ordinance*, R.O.N.W.T. 1974, c. D-5, s. 3(1); R.O.Y.T. 1971, c. D-4, s. 3(1).

[43]*Re C.P.R. and National Club* (1893), 24 O.R. 205 (H.C.J.).

[44]*Banque Provinciale du Canada v. Capital Trust Corp.* (1927), 60 O.L.R. 452 at p. 456, [1927] 3 D.L.R. 199 at p. 202 (H.C.), affd 62 O.L.R. 458, [1928] 4 D.L.R. 390 (S.C. App. Div.).

[45]*Cumming v Landed Banking and Loan Co.* (1893), 22 S.C.R. 246 at p. 250; *Dover v. Denne* (1902), 3 O.L.R. 664 (C.A.), at p. 689.

[46]*Re Fisher* (1924), 26 O.W.N. 295 (H.C.).

[47]*Peters v. Leeder* (1878), 47 L.J. Q.B. 573; and see *Pickering v. Thompson* (1911), 24 O.L.R. 378 (H.C.J.). See also *Re O'Reilly (No. 2)* (1980), 28 O.R. (2d) 481, 111 D.L.R. (3d) 238 (H.C.J.), in which two of several beneficiaries under a will who remained in possession of land were held not to be executors *de son tort*.

tions do not apply to accounts between guardian and ward, but the court should be very strict in not allowing stale demands, especially where records have been lost so that payments may be unable to be proved.[48] In Ontario, it was held that, when a mother was appointed by the Surrogate Court as guardian of her son, she became an express trustee during his minority, so that she could not acquire title against him by possession, but that the guardianship and trust ceased when the son attained his majority and that, as thereafter the mother dealt with the land as her own for twenty-two years, she acquired good title to it by possession. It was suggested that, if she had continued to manage the property for his benefit after his majority, she would have been a constructive trustee, not an express one.[49] That case was followed in another case in which it was held that, although a guardian appointed by the court could not, during the ward's infancy, acquire title by possession, the possession after the ward's majority changes its character and becomes that of a stranger, so that the statute runs in favour of the guardian.[50] In another case, however, a husband conveyed land to his wife in consideration of "respect and of one dollar" and the two remained in possession until she died, when by her will she devised her real estate to their two daughters, aged 17 and 12, and the husband continued in possession until his death, leaving a will devising the land. An action was brought by the younger daughter and the son of the elder daughter to recover possession from the devisee. It was held that the statute did not apply to extinguish the right of the plaintiffs to recover, the presumption being that, after the husband conveyed to his wife, he was in possession and receipt of the rents and profits for and on behalf of his wife and that, after her death, he entered into possession for and on behalf of the infant children as their natural guardian, so that his possession and receipt of the rents and profits were the possession and receipt of the wife and, after her death, of the children and those claiming under them and that the statute never began to run.[51]

(g) Life tenants, lessees and other limited owners

In a broad sense, a life tenant or other limited owner is not a trustee for persons entitled in remainder.[52] By reason of his position, however, he is treated for some purposes as a fiduciary, or a trustee, for those entitled in remainder.[53] Thus, if he renews a renewable lease, he does so for their benefit

---

[48]Romilly, M.R., in *Mathew v. Brise* (1851), 14 Beav. 341, 51 E.R. 317; and as to claims by ward against guardian see *Sleeman v. Wilson* (1871), L.R. 13 Eq. 36.

[49]*Hickey v. Stover* (1886), 11 O.R. 106 (H.C.J.).

[50]*Clarke v. Macdonell* (1890), 20 O.R. 564 (H.C.J.).

[51]*Kent v. Kent* (1891), 20 O.R. 445 (H.C.J.), affd 19 O.A.R. 352.

[52]*Per* Stirling, J., in *Re Llewellin*; *Llewellin v. Williams* (1887), 37 Ch. D. 317 at p. 325, *per* Stirling, J.; *Perry v. Perry* (1918), 2 W.W.R. 485 (Man. C.A.), at p. 494, *per* Cameron, J.A.; *Re Chupryk* (1980), 110 D.L.R. (3d) 108, [1980] 4 W.W.R. 534 (Man. C.A.), *per* Matas, J.A.

[53]See *Re Biss*; *Biss v. Biss*, [1903] 2 Ch. 40 (C.A.), and cases there cited and, for the general relations between life tenant and remainderman, see *Dicconson v. Talbot* (1870), L.R. 6 Ch. App. 32; *Hickman v. Upsall* (1876), 4 Ch. D. 144 (C.A.).

as well as his own.[54] If he unduly cuts timber or works mines, he is liable to account and make good the loss.[55] Even if he is expressly unimpeachable for waste, he is not permitted to commit wanton acts of destruction, known as equitable waste, which waste is treated as a breach of trust for which he must account to the remaindermen and, after his death, his assets are liable to make it good.[56] The liability of a limited owner for waste, however, does not really arise under a trust but by virtue of law. Nevertheless, the circumstances are analogous.

While a lessee is not normally a fiduciary, he may be treated as one in special circumstances. Thus, where a perpetual lease of a railway, which received legislative sanction, imposed and conferred typical lessee obligations and rights, including the duty to work and maintain the railroad and to yield it up at the end of the lease, and the lease contained forfeiture provisions for breach of covenants, the lessee is a fiduciary towards the lessor and will be made accountable for the proceeds of disposition of any lands it has declared surplus for railway purposes and sold.[57]

(h) Mortgagees

Although there is ordinarily no relationship of trustee and *cestui que trust* between mortgagee and mortgagor, certain circumstances create duties that are treated as a trust, such as the mortgagee being trustee for rents and profits if he enters into possession or for surplus proceeds if he sells under power of sale.[58]

(i) Partners

Partnership does not in itself create a fiduciary relationship between partners so as to make one a trustee for the other or his representatives, but a trust may arise in special circumstances.[59] Thus, where two partners of a firm sell partnership lands without the consent of all partners, ostensibly to a stranger, but in reality in order that they or one of them might keep all of the profits on a rising market, such partners are both in a fiduciary relationship towards the remaining partners, so as to entitle the latter to a full accounting.[60]

---

[54]*Waters v. Bailey* (1843), 2 Y. & C.C.C. 219, 63 E.R. 96; *Trumper v. Trumper* (1873), L.R. 8 Ch. App. 870.

[55]*Bagot v. Bagot; Legge v. Legge* (1863), 32 Beav. 509, 55 E.R. 200.

[56]*Ormonde (Marquis of) v. Kynersley* (1820), 5 Madd. 369, 56 E.R. 936.

[57]*Wotherspoon v. Canadian Pacific Ltd.* (1982), 35 O.R. (2d) 449, 129 D.L.R. (3d) 1 (C.A.), *per* Arnup, J.A., at p. 59; *per* Goodman, J.A., at p. 76.

[58]See further ch. 34, "Mortgages".

[59]*Per* Lord Westbury in *Knox v. Gye* (1872), L.R. 5 H.L. 656 at pp. 675-6; *Cassels v. Stewart* (1881), 6 App. Cas. 64 (H.L.), *per* Lord Penzance at p. 77, and *per* Lord Blackburn at p. 79.

[60]*Gordon v. Holland; Holland v. Gordon* (1913), 10 D.L.R. 734, 4 W.W.R. 419 (P.C.).

(j) Co-owners

There is no fiduciary relationship between joint tenants or tenants in common so as to make them liable as constructive trustees.[61] This is so even if one co-tenant has been allowed to collect the rents and to manage the property, unless there are other factors which give that co-tenant an advantage over the other.[62] Such a person may be liable to account as a co-owner, however.[63]

(k) Joint venturers

Joint venturers may be held to be fiduciaries in appropriate circumstances, especially in oil and mineral exploration cases. Thus, in *McLeod v. Sweezey*,[64] a prospector agreed with others that he would stake and record certain asbestos mineral claims in a specific area, in consideration of special knowledge supplied as to their location and of a twenty-five per cent interest in the claims. The prospector reported back that there was no asbestos to be found, but subsequently, in concert with others, he staked the area and chrome was found. When he made a profit, his original "partners" brought action against him and the court found him to be a fiduciary and liable to his partners under a constructive trust. His partners had bargained with him, so the court found, not just for his ability to find asbestos, but for his mature judgment as a mineral prospector. In that context the prospector used information supplied to him for his own benefit.

On the other hand, where the joint venturers have specifically contracted to limit the area covered by their agreement, a fiduciary relationship may be precluded or restricted. In *Pine Pass Oil & Gas Ltd. v. Pacific Petroleums Ltd.*,[65] the defendant company held certain gas exploration permits in trust for the plaintiff company under an agreement which required the defendant to exploit the lands encompassed by the permits in return for an interest in the net revenues. The agreement specifically excluded any lands outside the permit areas. Hence, when the defendant purchased adjacent lands for gas and oil development, he could not be held accountable under a constructive trust, even though he acquired the lands as a result of information gained while he was a fiduciary.[66]

Any joint business venture may attract fiduciary duties. In *Hogar Estates Ltd. in Trust v. Shebron Holdings Ltd.*,[67] the defendant, S, held title to land in trust for the plaintiff and S, who intended to develop the land as a joint venture. S proposed to H that H sell its interest to S and informed H that

---

[61]*Kennedy v. De Trafford*, [1897] A.C. 180 (H.L.).

[62]*Fleet v. Fleet* (1925), 28 O.W.N. 193 (S.C. App. Div.).

[63]See §§1502.4 and 1503.9, *infra*.

[64][1944] 2 D.L.R. 145, [1944] S.C.R. 111.

[65](1968), 70 D.L.R. (2d) 196 (B.C.S.C.).

[66]*Cf. Midcon Oil & Gas Ltd. v. New British Dominion Oil Co. Ltd.* (1958), 12 D.L.R. (2d) 705, [1958] S.C.R. 314.

[67](1979), 25 O.R. (2d) 543, 101 D.L.R. (3d) 509 (H.C.J.).

development had been blocked by planning authorities. While this statement was true at the time, the situation changed before the agreement was entered into, to S's knowledge. S did not inform H, however. It was held that S owed a fiduciary duty to H to disclose all material facts and, having failed to do so, the agreement should be set aside.

(l) Franchisors

A franchise agreement may raise a fiduciary relationship as well, but only where there is a real disparity between the bargaining power of the parties amounting to a "serious disability" on the part of one of the parties to negotiate effectively and so to protect his interest. Thus, where the parties are both experienced in business and are both represented by counsel throughout their contractual negotiations, the express terms of the agreement should not be departed from by the addition of further protection resulting from classifying the relationship as fiduciary.[68]

(m) Creditors

It is beyond the scope of this work to deal with trusts imposed by or arising under the federal *Bankruptcy Act*[69] and other trusts for creditors. The reader is referred to the standard texts and articles on the subject.

1208.4 Other Circumstances in Which Constructive Trusts Arise

(a) Sale of land

An agreement for the sale of land, if capable of specific performance, operates as an alienation of the vendor's beneficial interest in the property to the purchaser[1] and the purchaser, as beneficial owner, may dispose of the property by sale, mortgage, or otherwise, and may devise it.[2] The vendor at once becomes a constructive trustee of the property for the purchaser.[3] He must take reasonable care of the property, so that it will not deteriorate until possession is delivered to the purchaser[4] to the same extent as any other

---

[68]*Jirna Ltd. v. Mister Donut of Canada Ltd.*, [1970] 3 O.R. 629, 13 D.L.R. (3d) 645 (H.C.J.), revd [1972] 1 O.R. 251, 22 D.L.R. (3d) 639 (C.A.), affd 40 D.L.R. (3d) 303, [1975] 1 S.C.R. 2.

[69]R.S.C. 1970, c. B-3.

§1208.4

[1]*Wall v. Bright* (1820), 1 Jac. & W. 494 at p. 500, 37 E.R. 456; *Rose v. Watson* (1864), 10 H.L.C. 672 at p. 678, 11 E.R. 1187.

[2]*Paine v. Meller* (1801), 6 Ves. Jun. 349 at p. 352, 31 E.R. 1088; *Shaw v. Foster* (1872), L.R. 5 H.L. 321 at pp. 333, 338.

[3]*Wall v. Bright, supra*; *Hadley v. London Bank of Scotland, Ltd.* (1865), 3 De G. J. & S. 63 at p. 70, 46 E.R. 562 (C.A.); *Shaw v. Foster, supra*, at p. 333.

[4]*Clarke v. Ramuz*, [1891] 2 Q.B. 456 (C.A.), at p. 462.

trustee,[5] the purchaser only being entitled to have the property handed over to him on completion in the same condition as when he entered into the contract.[6] The property is at the risk of the purchaser as to loss or deterioration,[7] but the purchaser is entitled to accessions to the value.[8] In the absence of a provision in the contract, the vendor is not bound to maintain insurance, or to inform the purchaser that it has lapsed.[9]

Although the vendor is considered in equity to be a constructive trustee of the estate for the purchaser and the latter to be a trustee of the purchase money for him, the vendor is not a mere trustee. He is in progress towards it and finally becomes such when the money is paid and he is bound to convey. In the meantime, he retains for certain purposes his old dominion over the estate.[10] Thus, he has a lien on the property for the purchase price,[11] the right to retain possession until he is paid,[12] the right to be indemnified by the purchaser against the liabilities of the property,[13] the right to protect his interest and to assert it if anything in derogation of his right occurs, the trusteeship being subject to that paramount right,[14] and the right to receive the rents and profits for his own benefit until the day fixed for completion,[15] after which they belong to the purchaser and, if the vendor receives them, he holds them in trust for the purchaser.[16] Until completion, the vendor is the proper person to enforce rights which depend upon possession of the legal estate, which remains in him. The purchaser, in general, is not entitled to enforce his equitable rights against third parties until he has completed his title by conveyance.[17]

Furthermore, the vendor has only a qualified trusteeship until the price is

---

[5]*Phillips v. Silvester* (1872), L.R. 8 Ch. App. 173 at p. 177; *Earl of Egmont v. Smith*; *Smith v. Earl of Egmont* (1877), 6 Ch. D. 469 at p. 475; *Royal Bristol Permanent Building Society v. Bomash* (1887), 35 Ch. D. 390 at p. 398.

[6]*Foster v. Deacon* (1818), 3 Madd. 394, 56 E.R. 550.

[7]*Paine v. Meller, supra,* footnote 2, loss by fire; *Harford v. Purrier* (1816), 1 Madd. 532, 56 E.R. 195, loss through tenant vacating due to misunderstanding with purchaser; *Poole v. Adams* (1864), 33 L.J. Ch. 639, 12 W.R. 683, in absence of provision in contract, purchaser not entitled to fire insurance proceeds paid to trustee-vendor or to deduct amount from purchase price; and see *Counter v. Macpherson* (1845), 5 Moore 83, 13 E.R. 421; *Raynor v. Preston* (1881), 18 Ch. D. 1 (C.A.).

[8]*Vesey v. Elwood* (1842), 3 Dr. & War. 74 at p. 79 (Ir.).

[9]*Paine v. Meller, supra,* footnote 2; *Poole v. Adams, supra,* footnote 7; *Dowson v. Solomon* (1859), 1 Dr. & Sm. 1 at p. 12, 62 E.R. 278.

[10]Per Plumer, M.R., in *Wall v. Bright* (1820), 1 Jac. & W. 494, 37 E.R. 456.

[11]*Lysaght v. Edwards* (1876), 2 Ch. D. 499; *Morgan v. Swansea Urban Sanitary Authority* (1876), 9 Ch. D. 582.

[12]*Lysaght v. Edwards, supra,* footnote 11.

[13]*Dodson v. Downey,* [1901] 2 Ch. 620 at p. 623.

[14]*Shaw v. Foster* (1872), L.R. 5 H.L. 321 at p. 338; *Rafferty v. Schofield,* [1897] 1 Ch. 937 at p. 943.

[15]*Cuddon v. Tite* (1858), 1 Giff. 395, 65 E.R. 971.

[16]*Paine v. Meller* (1801), 6 Ves. Jun. 349 at p. 352, 31 E.R. 1088; *Monro v. Taylor* (1850), 8 Hare 51 at p. 70, 68 E.R. 269; *Plews v. Samuel,* [1904] 1 Ch. 464 at p. 468.

[17]*Tasker v. Small* (1837), 3 My. & Cr. 63 at pp. 70, 71, 40 E.R. 848.

paid and nothing remains to be done by either party except to complete the transaction by conveyance but, when that stage is reached, the full relationship of trustee and *cestui que trust* is established and relates back to the formation of the contract.[18] Although it is often said that, after a contract for the sale of land, the vendor is a trustee for the purchaser, it must not be forgotten that in each case it is tacitly assumed that the contract would be enforced specifically. If for some reason equity would not decree specific performance, or if the right to specific performance has been lost by the subsequent conduct of the party in whose favour it might originally have been granted, the vendor either never was, or has ceased to be, a trustee in any sense at all.[19] It has been held that equitable interests arising under sale agreements will be recognized between the parties under a Torrens title system where specific performance could be obtained.[20]

When a vendor is in the position of being a trustee for the purchaser, he may not derogate from his own grant, or take advantage of circumstances caused by an unwarrantable act of default on his part. Thus, a grantor cannot take advantage of his own failure to pay taxes outstanding at the time of the grant by re-acquiring the land at a tax sale and, in such case, he is a trustee of the land for his grantee.[21] Where the owner of land registered under the *Land Titles Act*[22] sold it, neither the transfer nor several subsequent transfers being registered, and he later transferred the land to a subsequent transferee who procured a registered title to the exclusion of the original purchaser, the vendor was held liable to the latter in damages for breach of the implied covenant for quiet enjoyment and also for breach of trust.[23] Where a person assigned a lease and a renewal thereof but the lease contained no right of renewal and the assignor obtained a renewal in his own name before expiry of the assigned term, he was held to be an implied trustee for the assignee.[24]

Since the vendor is a trustee, any action by the purchaser is covered by the limitation periods applicable to trustees, not the limitation period applicable

---

[18]*Per* James, L.J., in *Raynor v. Preston* (1881), 18 Ch. D. 1 (C.A.), at p. 13; *Wall v. Bright* (1820), 1 Jac. & W. 494 at p. 503, 37 E.R. 456; *Shaw v. Foster* (1872), L.R. 5 H.L. 321 at p. 356, *per* Lord Hatherley, L.C.; *Ridout v. Fowler*, [1904] 1 Ch. 658 at p. 661; *Shebley v. Rural Mun. of Mervin No. 499* (1922), 63 D.L.R. 632, [1922] 1 W.W.R. 384 (Sask. C.A.).

[19]*Snider v. Carleton*; *Central Trust and Safe Deposit Co. v. Snider* (1915), 35 O.L.R. 246, 25 D.L.R. 410 at p. 414 (P.C.); *Howard v. Miller* (1914), 22 D.L.R. 75 at pp. 79-80, [1915] A.C. 318 at p. 326 (P.C.).

[20]*Church v. Hill*, [1923] 3 D.L.R. 1045, [1923] S.C.R. 642, revg on another point, [1923] 1 D.L.R. 203, [1922] 3 W.W.R. 1207, *sub nom. Re Church* (Alta. S.C. App. Div.), and see *McDougall v. MacKay* (1922), 68 D.L.R. 245, 64 S.C.R. 1, affg 63 D.L.R. 247, [1921] 3 W.W.R. 833 (Sask. C.A.).

[21]*Follis v. Township of Albemarle*, [1941] O.R. 1, [1941] 1 D.L.R. 178 (C.A.).

[22]R.S.O. 1927, c. 158.

[23]*Guest v. Cochlin* (1929), 64 O.L.R. 165, [1929] 3 D.L.R. 790 (S.C. App. Div.).

[24]*Pong v. Quong*, [1927] 3 D.L.R. 128, [1927] S.C.R. 271, affg 56 O.L.R. 616, [1925] 2 D.L.R. 1192 (C.A.).

to the sale of land,[25] but the vendor may nevertheless plead lapse of time to limit the purchaser's remedies.[26]

(b) Mutual wills

Mutual wills are wills made by two or more people, usually husband and wife, which are drawn *mutatis mutandis* in the same terms. For example, in the case of husband and wife, the husband in his will may leave a life interest to his wife if she survives him, with remainder to the children of the marriage or to strangers. The wife in her will then gives a life interest to her husband if he survives her, with remainder as in the husband's will. A joint will is one executed by two parties whereby they dispose of their property on death in much the same way as occurs in the case of mutual wills. The common law does not give any special effect to a joint will,[27] so that it is virtually identical to a case of mutual wills.

If it is shown, beyond the bare fact of the existence of the mutual wills or joint will, that the parties have made an agreement to dispose of their property in that fashion and intend it to be binding (and this is said to be more easily inferred in the case of a joint will),[28] their will or wills become irrevocable. They can, of course, be revoked in fact and in law, but if one party does revoke, the agreement is breached and certain remedies flow from that. It would seem that if one party revoked his will in the lifetime and to the knowledge of the other, the other party has an action for damages, or he may treat the agreement at an end. If, on the other hand, as most commonly occurs, the surviving party revokes his will after the death of the other, the only remedy is that of a trust. This was the conclusion reached in the leading case, *Dufour v. Pereira*,[29] and many cases which have followed it on the basis that otherwise there would be a fraud on the deceased. Typically, the trust would be a constructive trust, although the cases do not make this clear and much has been written on the subject of the type of trust and the date as of which it arises or is imposed.[30] If it takes effect on the date of the agreement, both parties are bound by it throughout their lives so that, if the survivor fails to live up to the agreement during the joint lives, he or his estate is bound.[31]

---

[25]*Limitation of Actions Act*, R.S.S. 1978, c. L-15, ss. 36, 43.
[26]*O'Dell v. Hastie* (1968), 67 D.L.R. (2d) 366, 63 W.W.R. 632 (Sask. Q.B.).
[27]*Per* Laskin, J.A., dissenting in *Re Gillespie*, [1969] 1 O.R. 585, 3 D.L.R. (3d) 317 (C.A.), affg [1968] 2 O.R. 369, 69 D.L.R. (2d) 368 (H.C.J.). For another case see *Pratt v. Johnson* (1958), 16 D.L.R. (2d) 385, [1959] S.C.R. 102.
[28]*Re Gillespie, supra*, footnote 27; *Re Grisor* (1979), 26 O.R. (2d) 57, 101 D.L.R. (3d) 728 (H.C.J.).
[29](1769), 1 Dick. 419, 21 E.R. 332.
[30]See, *e.g.*, Mitchell, "Some Aspects of Mutual Wills", 14 Mod. L. Rev. 136 (1951); Burgess, "A Fresh Look at Mutual Wills", 34 Convey. (N.S.) 230 (1970); Sheridan, "The Floating Trust: Mutual Wills", 15 Alta. L. Rev. 211 (1977); Youdan, "The Mutual Wills Doctrine", 29 U. of T. L.J. 390 (1979); Davis, "Contracts to Make Wills" (1975), 2 E. & T.Q. 322.
[31]*Re Fox*, [1951] O.R. 378, [1951] 3 D.L.R. 337 (H.C.J.).

It may also take effect on the death of the first party since there is then no longer any mutual right to change the agreement.[32] If the trust were only to take effect on the survivor's death, the death of a beneficiary during the survivor's lifetime would cause the gift to him to lapse. Nevertheless, that view has found support.[33] The issue has never been finally resolved.

A further difficulty may arise where the will does not specify what property shall be subject to the agreement, whether it be the parties' joint property at the time of the agreement or acquired during their lifetimes, or whether it shall also encompass property acquired by the survivor subsequently. The latter result was apparently the intention of the parties in *Pratt v. Johnson*.[34] However, unless the parties clearly describe the trust property, one would think that the courts would be loath to include after-acquired property, since the effect of such a finding may be that it deprives the survivor of the means to support a second family.

In *Re Ohorodnyk*[35] a husband and wife executed a joint will in which they gave their estates to the survivor "absolutely". However, the will further provided that upon the death of the survivor, the estates of the two testators were to be divided among five named beneficiaries. The husband died first and the wife then made a new will, leaving her entire estate, including that part derived from her husband, to another beneficiary. The court found that the parties had made an agreement not to revoke, but held that, as the husband gave his estate to his wife "absolutely", she was free to dispose of it as she wished. It is submitted that the case is wrongly decided. Read in its context, the parties clearly intended to benefit the survivor for life, followed by a remainder interest to the named beneficiaries.

In *Re Grisor*[36] a husband and wife executed a joint will by which they gave the survivor all property possessed by them at the death of either of them, to be used as the survivor saw fit. One property was a business, owned by the husband. It was directed to be continued by the survivor and on his or her death to pass equally to the parties' two children. The wife died first. The husband then sold the business and died. The children claimed the proceeds of sale. It was held that they were not entitled to the proceeds, for, while there was an agreement not to revoke, the constructive trust which thereby arose bound only the property of the deceased spouse, not that of the survivor, who could deal with it as he or she wished. It is submitted that this case was also wrongly decided. The authorities hold that the constructive trust binds all property that the parties intended to be bound thereby. Clearly the parties in this case intended their agreement to extend to the business.

---

[32]*Pratt v. Johnson, supra*, footnote 27.
[33]*Re Fiegehen*, [1942] O.W.N. 575 (H.C.J.).
[34]*Supra*, footnote 27.
[35](1979), 24 O.R. (2d) 228, 97 D.L.R. (3d) 502 (H.C.J.), affd 26 O.R. (2d) 704n, 102 D.L.R. (3d) 576n (C.A.).
[36]*Supra*, footnote 28.

(c) Licences

In recent years a number of cases involving contractual licences have been decided on the basis of constructive trusts. Thus, in *Bincius v. Evans*[37] the widow of an employee was allowed to reside in a cottage rent-free for her life under an agreement with her late husband's employer. The latter subsequently sold the property to a purchaser, who took with notice of the agreement. It was held that the widow was protected against the purchaser as a beneficiary under a constructive trust.

In *Re Sharpe*[38] Mr. Sharpe's aunt had loaned him a large sum of money to enable him to purchase and decorate a shop and attached living quarters. In consideration for the loan she was entitled to reside with Mr. and Mrs. Sharpe as long as she wished. Mr. Sharpe later went bankrupt and his trustee in bankruptcy agreed to sell the land. He brought proceedings to obtain vacant possession, but it was held that, although the aunt did not have an interest in property under a resulting trust since the agreement was one of loan, she was entitled to remain in possession so long as the loan was outstanding as against the trustee. Whether she had a similar right as against the purchaser was not decided.

In a slightly different context, it was held in *D.H.N. Foods Ltd. v. Tower Hamlets London Borough Council*[39] that a company in possession of land under an inevitable licence was entitled to compensation for disturbance in an expropriation. The licence gave it an interest under a constructive trust which was a sufficient proprietary interest to support the claim.

It has been argued forcefully that these cases misuse the constructive trust in order to do justice and that in the process the rights of third parties are disregarded.[40]

1209. RESULTING TRUSTS

As explained above,[1] resulting trusts have been defined either as implied trusts arising because of the presumed intention of the parties, or simply as trusts arising by operation of law. In either case the trust operates in favour of the disposer of the property. Resulting trusts arise in the following two situations: (1) where the trust is not exhausted or fails, and (2) where property is purchased in the name of another, or is voluntarily transferred to another. These are sometimes referred to respectively as automatic resulting

---

37[1972] Ch. 359 (C.A.).
38[1980] 1 All E.R. 198.
39[1976] 1 W.L.R. 852 (C.A.).
40See Hanbury and Maudsley, *Modern Equity* (11th ed., 1981), pp. 396-8, 731-2.
§1209
1§1203.2, *supra*, and see generally Waters, "The Doctrine of Resulting Trusts in Common Law Canada", 16 McGill L.J. 187 (1970).

trusts and presumed resulting trusts.[2] The two types are examined below. In these situations, to the extent that the beneficial interest in the property has not been disposed of, except where the failure of a declared trust arises from the illegality of the object, it results or reverts to the creator of the trust or, in the event of his previous death, to his representative.[3]

1209.1 Failure to Exhaust Trust

Where the settlor or testator has failed to dispose of the whole beneficial interest in the property, either because he has failed to name the beneficiaries, or because the purposes for which the trust was established do not exhaust the property, the undisposed of interest, or the remaining part, will result to him or his estate. The same applies where there is no declaration of trust with respect to some property assigned to the trustee.[1]

At common law, the resulting trust would, where the creator of the trust died, result to his heir-at-law if the property were realty, or to his next of kin if it were personalty. However, under modern devolution of estates legislation all property which is vested in any person on his death, notwithstanding any testamentary disposition, devolves to and becomes vested in his personal representative as trustee for the persons by law beneficially entitled thereto and so far as such property is not disposed of by deed, will, contract or other effectual disposition, the same is administered, dealt with and distributed as if it were personal property not so disposed of.[2]

Thus, where there was a devise upon a future contingency and no disposition of the rents and profits in the interim, it was held that the estate meanwhile resulted to the testator's heir.[3] Similarly, where a tenant *pur autre vie* disposed of the beneficial interest upon a contingency which did not happen, the interest was not effectually disposed of and there was a resulting trust in his favour,[4] and in a marriage settlement, where personal property of the wife is given to the husband after her death so long as he remains a widower, his life interest

---

[2]The two names were devised by Megarry, J., in *Re Vandervell's Trusts; White v. Vandervell Trustees Ltd.*, [1974] 1 All E.R. 47, revd [1974] Ch. 269, [1974] 3 All E.R. 205 (C.A.).

[3]*Lloyd v. Spillet* (1740), 2 Atk. 148, 26 E.R. 493.

§1209.1

[1]*Parnell v. Hingston* (1856), 3 Sm. & Giff. 337, 65 E.R. 684.

[2]*Devolution of Estates Act*, R.S.M. 1970, c. D70, s. 18; R.S.N.B. 1973, c. D-9, s. 3; *Estates Administration Act*, R.S.O. 1980, c. 143, s. 2(1); *Devolution of Real Property Act*, R.S.A. 1980, c. D-34, s. 2(1); R.S.S. 1978, c. D-27, ss. 4, 5; *Estate Administration Act*, R.S.B.C. 1979, c. 114, s. 90; *Chattels Real Act*, R.S.N. 1970, c. 36, s. 2; *Real Property Act*, R.S.N.S. 1967, c. 261, s. 6(1); *Probate Act*, R.S.P.E.I. 1974, c. P-19, s. 108(1); *Devolution of Real Property Ordinance*, R.O.N.W.T. 1974, c. D-5, s. 3(1); R.O.Y.T. 1971, c. D-4, s. 3(1).

[3]*Attorney-General v. Bowyer* (1798), 3 Ves. Jun. 714, 30 E.R. 1235; see also *Re Van Hagan*; *Sperling v. Rochfort* (1880), 16 Ch. D. 18; *Wade-Gery v. Handley* (1876), 1 Ch. D. 653; *Leslie v. Duke of Devonshire* (1787), 2 Bro. C.C. 187, 29 E.R. 107.

[4]*Northen v. Carnegie* (1859), 28 L.J. Ch. 930.

ceases on his remarriage and there is a resulting trust of it to the wife's estate.[5]

Where a settlor, by voluntary settlement, conveyed freeholds to trustees upon trust, together with a sum in stocks already transferred, for the settlor for life and, after his death, to his reputed son W, when and if he attained the age of 21 years, with a trust for W if he had not attained that age at the settlor's death, and with a limitation over if W died under 21 or in the settlor's lifetime without leaving issue living at his death, but there was no limitation in the trust for W in the event that he survived the settlor, attained age 21 and died, which in fact happened, it was held that W took only a life estate in the freeholds under the settlement and there was a resulting trust to the settlor.[6]

Where real property is settled by deed upon trust to sell for specified purposes and one of the purposes fails, the property, to the extent of such purpose, results to the settlor as personalty from the moment that the deed is executed, whether the trust for sale is to arise in the lifetime of the settlor, or not until after his death.[7] Where W conveyed estates in fee simple to trustees to sell and pay debts and to apply the residue to raise a sum and pay the interest to D until marriage, then to pay the principal to him within twelve months after marriage and divide the rest among the plaintiffs, but D died unmarried, it was held that the sum was held on a resulting trust to the settlor, but as personal estate which passed as part of the residue.[8]

The terms of a will, however, may indicate that, where a trust fails or an interest is not disposed of, or is disposed of ineffectually, the resulting trust of the beneficial interest will not be in favour of the testator's heir or next of kin but will, by lapse or otherwise, be in favour of the residuary devisee or legatee, as the case may be, for in such cases the testator's intention prevails (except in the case of a trust for sale).[9] Thus, where a testator devised a freehold to trustees for the benefit of E for her separate use and, after her death, upon trust for each of her sons who should attain age 21 and each of her daughters who should attain that age or marry, and E died leaving an infant daughter who did not marry before attaining age 21, it was held that the legal estate was in the trustees, the daughter took the property on attaining age 21, but the interim rents went to the testator's residuary devisee.[10]

A resulting trust cannot take effect where a contrary intention, to be gathered from the whole instrument, is indicated by the grantor. Thus, where a deed from father to son recited that the father was desirous of settling the property so as to make it a provision for himself during life and for his wife and children after her death and the deed released and assigned the property to the son upon declared trusts as to part of the property in favour of his wife, his daughter and a niece, but declared no trust as to the surplus, it was

---

[5]*Re Wyatt; Gowan v. Wyatt* (1889), 60 L.T. 920.
[6]*Middleton v. Barker* (1873), 29 L.T. 643.
[7]*Clarke v. Franklin* (1858), 4 K. & J. 257, 70 E.R. 107.
[8]*Hewitt v. Wright* (1780), 1 Bro. C.C. 86, 28 E.R. 1001.
[9]As to which see §1209.3, *infra.*
[10]*Re Eddels' Trusts* (1871), L.R. 11 Eq. 559.

held that the surplus did not result to the grantor but belonged to the son.[11] When once the conclusion is arrived at that a grantor intends to part with his whole legal and equitable interest in favour of another, there can be no resulting trust unless, in the view of a court of equity, there is no consideration to support the transaction, or the consideration, if any, fails.[12]

Similarly, where property is devised to a person upon trust, the trustee may be entitled to the beneficial interest in undisposed of property where there is an indication of intention in the instrument of disposition that the trustee was to take the residue for his own benefit. Ordinarily, if property is given to a person in trust, there is a presumption that it was given to him entirely as trustee and not beneficially.[13] This presumption, however, may be rebutted by an indication of intention in the will that, if a trust does not exhaust the entire beneficial interest in the trust property, the trustee is to have the residue for his own benefit. Thus in *Croome v. Croome*,[14] a testator gave to his brother, E, all of his real estate on trust to pay thereout debts and certain annuities to his other brother and sisters and appointed E as executor. It was held that E was not a bare trustee and took the beneficial interest and residue of the realty after satisfying the express trusts and there was no resulting trust to the heir-at-law. Similarly, in *Williams v. Roberts*,[15] a testator gave all of his residuary estate to his wife upon trust to pay thereout an annuity and certain legacies which did not exhaust the personal estate and referred to her as executrix, although he did not expressly appoint her as such. It was held that she was entitled beneficially to the surplus estate.[16] The question whether a trustee is to take a beneficial interest is one of intention to be ascertained from the words of the will itself,[17] but the intention must clearly appear.[18]

It should be noted that by *Lord Sugden's Act,* [19] adopted or in force in some

---

[11]*Cook v. Hutchinson* (1836), 1 Keen 42, 48 E.R. 222.

[12]*Per* Lord Parker in *Snider v. Carleton; Central Trust and Safe Deposit Co. v. Snider* (1915), 35 O.L.R. 246 at p. 260, 25 D.L.R. 410 at p. 413 (P.C.).

[13]*Burgess v. Wheate; Attorney-General v. Wheate* (1759), 1 Eden 177 at p. 251, 28 E.R. 652; *Middleton v. Spicer* (1783), 1 Bro. C.C. 201 at p. 205, 28 E.R. 1083; *Southouse v. Bate* (1814), 2 V. & B. 396, 35 E.R. 369; *Clarke v. Hilton* (1886), L.R. 2 Eq. 810 at p. 815; *Wainford v. Heyl* (1875), L.R. 20 Eq. 321; *Re West; George v. Grose*, [1900] 1 Ch. 84 at p. 87; *Re Barrett* (1914), 25 O.W.R. 735 (H.C.), affd 26 O.W.R. 305 (S.C. App. Div.); *Ballard v. Stover* (1887), 14 O.R. 153 (H.C.J.).

[14](1889), 61 L.T. 814 (H.L.).

[15](1857), 27 L.J. Ch. 177.

[16]See also *Rogers v. Rogers* (1733), 3 P. Wms. 193, 24 E.R. 1026; *Walton v. Walton* (1807), 14 Ves. Jun. 318, 33 E.R. 543; *Williams v. Arkle* (1875), L.R. 7 H.L. 606; *Attorney-General v. Jefferys*, [1908] A.C. 411 (H.L.).

[17]*Williams v. Arkle, supra,* footnote 16; *Briggs v. Newswander* (1902), 32 S.C.R. 405 at p. 412; *Re Aspel* (1918), 42 O.L.R. 191 (H.C.); *Re McCuaig* (1924), 25 O.W.N. 712 (H.C.); *Re Gracey* (1928), 63 O.L.R. 218, [1929] 1 D.L.R. 260 (S.C. App. Div.); *Re Melvin* (1972), 24 D.L.R. (3d) 240, [1972] 3 W.W.R. 55, *sub nom. Re Melvin Estate* (B.C.S.C.).

[18]*Meagher v. Meagher* (1916), 30 D.L.R. 303 at p. 310, 53 S.C.R. 393 at p. 403.

[19]*Executors Act, 1830,* 11 Geo. 4 & 1 Will. 4, c. 40.

of the provinces,[20] an executor is deemed to be a trustee of any residue not expressly disposed of in favour of those entitled to take on an intestacy, unless it appears by the will that the executor was intended to take beneficially.

If a gift is made to a person subject to that person carrying out certain purposes, even though they are described as trusts or charges, he is entitled to the property beneficially after carrying out the purposes, but where property is given to a trustee without anything to indicate that a beneficial interest is intended, there is a resulting trust. Thus, where a testator gave all his personal estate to his grandson, his executors, administrators and assigns, subject to payment of debts, legacies and specified trusts, and upon trust to convert and stand possessed of the trust moneys, but the trusts did not exhaust the funds, the grandson, who was one of three executors, took the surplus beneficially.[21] Similarly, where a testator devised all of his real and personal estate equally to four nephews and a grandnephew, appointing them executors, upon trust that they and the survivors of them would support his widow for life, but she predeceased the testator, it was held that the devisees took the beneficial interest in the entire estate.[22]

1209.2 Failure of Trust

A trust may fail in whole or in part because of mistake, fraud, duress or undue influence, because it is uncertain,[1] or because it is illegal or contrary to public policy.[2] In these cases there will generally be a resulting trust as well.

Thus, where a testator bequeathed a sum of money and his personal estate, directing it to be invested in the names of the vicar and churchwardens of a certain church upon trust, first, to maintain the testator's tomb out of the income and then to distribute the remainder among the poor of certain almshouses, it was held that, the gift to maintain the tomb being invalid, the whole income passed to the vicar and churchwardens on behalf of the almshouses.[3]

The same result obtains where the purpose of the trust fails because it is never executed or cannot be executed. Thus, in *Re Bank of Western Canada; Genevese v. York Lambton Corp. Ltd.*[4] certain securities were offered for sale on condition that the proceeds were to be used solely for investment in a

---

[20]*Trustee Act* (Man.), s. 50(1); (Ont.), s. 55.
[21]*Clarke v. Hilton, supra*, footnote 13.
[22]*Ballard v. Stover, supra*, footnote 13.
§1209.2
[1]*Fonseca v. Jones* (1911), 14 W.L.R. 148, 21 Man. R. 168 (C.A.).
[2]For example, because it offends the rule against perpetuities: *Re Nash's Settlement* (1882), 51 L.J. Ch. 511; or because it offends against the rule that a testator may not delegate his will-making power: *Fowler v. Garlike* (1830), 1 Russ. & M. 232, 39 E.R. 90.
[3]*Re Rogerson; Bird v. Lee*, [1901] 1 Ch. 715.
[4][1968] 2 O.R. 569, 70 D.L.R. (2d) 113 (H.C.J.), revd [1970] 1 O.R. 427, 8 D.L.R. (3d) 593 (C.A.), leave to appeal to S.C.C. refused [1969] S.C.R. xii.

proposed bank. The bank never in fact commenced business. It was held that the transaction created a trust and, as the object of the trust failed, the purchasers were entitled to the return of their moneys by way of resulting trust.

Where a person conveyed property to another on condition that the latter should "look after" the plaintiff until his death and the defendant failed to do so, it was held that the conveyance created a trust in favour of the plaintiff for a particular purpose. Since the purpose was thwarted by the defendant, there was a total failure of consideration and the court ordered a rescission of the original grant to return the property to the plaintiff.[5]

Where a trust is evidently intended to be created, but no trust is declared, or the trusts declared are too vague and uncertain to be executed, there is a resulting trust in favour of the settlor or his representatives. In *Briggs v. Newswander*,[6] B agreed to convey his interest in mining claims to N for a named price with a stipulation that, if the claims on development proved to be valuable, a company would be formed by N or his associates and the shares should be allotted to B as he should deem just. By a contemporaneous agreement, N agreed that a company should be immediately formed and that B should have a reasonable amount of stock according to its value. No company was formed by N and B brought an action to have it declared that he was entitled to an undivided half interest in the mining claims or that the agreement be specifically enforced. It was held that the dual agreements provided for a transfer of the interest in the mining claims at a nominal price in trust to enable N to capitalize the claims and form a company to work them on such allotment of stock as the parties should mutually agree upon and that, upon breach of such trust, B was entitled to a reconveyance of his interest in the claims with an accounting of moneys received, or that should have been received from the working of the claims in the meantime.[7]

Where property is conveyed to a person in form for his own use, but actually upon secret trust for a purpose which fails or is not carried out, there will also be a resulting trust for the grantor.[8]

Where a person conveys property upon a trust which fails because its purpose is illegal, but nothing has been done to carry the purpose into effect, he may be entitled to have it reconveyed;[9] but this principle was doubted in *Kearley v. Thomson*.[10] If the illegal purpose has been partly carried out, the court will grant no assistance to impose a resulting trust.[11]

---

[5]*Croft v. Humphrey* (1971), 18 D.L.R. (3d) 20, 4 N.S.R. (2d) 127 (S.C.T.D.); see also *Poirier v. Brulé* (1891), 20 S.C.R. 97, to the same effect.

[6](1902), 32 S.C.R. 405.

[7]See also *Fleming v. Royal Trust Co.* (1920), 18 O.W.N. 386 (H.C.), in which case there was a resulting trust where the property was conveyed to trustees without explanation as to the nature of the trust.

[8]*Childers v. Childers* (1857), 1 De G. & J. 482, 44 E.R. 810 (C.A.).

[9]*Symes v. Hughes* (1870), L.R. 9 Eq. 475; *Taylor v. Bowers* (1876), 1 Q.B.D. 291 (C.A.).

[10](1890), 24 Q.B.D. 742 (C.A.), at p. 746.

[11]*Brackenbury v. Brackenbury* (1820), 2 Jac. & W. 391, 37 E.R. 677.

The principle does not apply to a trust for an object which, although not unlawful in itself, is incapable by law of taking under the trust.[12] Thus, if the purposes of the trust are not illegal, but the intended trustee lacks the capacity to act, there will be a resulting trust.[13]

The court will not, on grounds of public policy, impose a resulting trust which would constitute a fraud on the court. Thus, where a person claimed to be entitled under a resulting trust on the ground that he transferred property to another in order to be able to testify as a disinterested party in court proceedings concerning the title to that property and he was accepted as a witness in testifying that he had no interest in property, he was not permitted to set up what was a fraud on the court and to invoke the aid of the court in establishing that he was a beneficial owner.[14]

1209.3 Effect of Conversion on Resulting Trusts

A different rule prevails in regard to property devised or conveyed upon an imperative trust for sale.[1] When there is an imperative direction that land be converted into money or money into land and not just a power to convert, the rule that "equity regards as done that which ought to have been done" is applied, and the property is theoretically converted at the time of the testator's death in the case of a will and at the time of delivery in the case of a deed. The consequence is that the proceeds of land thus theoretically converted, and not entirely or effectively disposed of, do not pass to the residuary legatee and, in similar circumstances, the proceeds of money theoretically converted into land do not pass to the residuary devisee, but in both cases are held on a resulting trust for those entitled to inherit. A resulting trust arises (a) where a will directing sale does not entirely dispose of the proceeds, (b) where the purposes for which conversion was directed by a will or deed fail wholly or partly, and (c) where a will directs money to be raised out of realty, but does not indicate how the money is to be applied.

Under the old rules of descent referred to in many cases, the resulting trust is in favour of either the heir-at-law or the next of kin, depending upon whether the interest affected is to descend as realty or devolve as personalty, but modern devolution of estates legislation provides that all property devolves upon the personal representative and is distributable as personalty.[2] The effect

---

[12]*Russell v. Jackson* (1852), 10 Hare 204, 68 E.R. 900.
[13]*Parkland Mortgage Corp. Ltd. v. Therevan Development Corp. Ltd.* (1981), 130 D.L.R. (3d) 682, [1982] 1 W.W.R. 587 (Alta. Q.B.).
[14]*Taylor v. Wallbridge* (1879), 2 S.C.R. 616.

§1209.3
[1]As to such trusts, see generally §1210, *infra*.
[2]*Devolution of Estates Act*, R.S.M. 1970, c. D70, s. 18; R.S.N.B. 1973, c. D-9, s. 3; *Estates Administration Act*, R.S.O. 1980, c. 143, s. 2(1); *Devolution of Real Property Act*, R.S.A. 1980, c. D-34, s. 2(1); R.S.S. 1978, c. D-27, ss. 4, 5; *Estate Administration Act*, R.S.B.C. 1979, c. 114, s. 90; *Chattels Real Act*, R.S.N. 1970, c. 36, s. 2; *Real Property Act*, R.S.N.S. 1967, c. 261, s. 6(1); *Probate Act*, R.S.P.E.I. 1974, c. P-19, s. 108(1); *Devolution of Real Property Ordinance*, R.O.N.W.T. 1974, c. D-5, s. 3(1); R.O.Y.T. 1971, c. D-4, s. 3(1).

of this change is not to transform realty into personalty for the purposes of descent, but to abolish the former distinction between the course of descent of realty and devolution of personalty, so that those entitled to share in personalty are in like manner entitled to succeed to realty.[3] Moreover, the several statutes do not affect the rule of law that, in the events which create a resulting trust, the property affected will not ordinarily fall into a residuary devise or residuary bequest, but will result to those entitled to inherit. The old rule remains important because the personal estate is still the primary fund for the payment of debts. Moreover, the legislation provides that where there is a residuary devise or bequest the real and personal property therein comprised bear the debts rateably unless a contrary intention appears from the will.[4] Consequently, in the context of this section, reference will be made to those entitled to inherit, and references in the cases cited referring to the heir and next of kin should be construed in the light of statutes which have abolished the distinction in regard to the course of descent and devolution.

In the case of a will devising real property upon trust for sale without entirely disposing of the proceeds of sale, there is a resulting trust in respect of the undisposed of surplus in favour of those entitled to inherit, notwithstanding that the testator directs that no part of such proceeds shall in any event lapse for the benefit of the heir-at-law, or that the proceeds shall form part of his personal estate, the direction being ineffective without an actual gift away from the heir.[5] The same rule applies to proceeds not disposed of because of lapse of a gift. Where, for example, a testatrix devised realty to trustees upon trust for sale, declared that the proceeds should be deemed to be part of the residual personal estate and be applied accordingly and bequeathed the residue of the personalty to the trustees upon trust for seven children equally, but one of them died in the lifetime of the testatrix, it was held that the lapsed share went to the heir-at-law of the testatrix. The court enunciated the following principles: (1) If a testator directs a sale of his real and personal estate, the proceeds to form a mixed fund, the heir-at-law, in the event of a portion of the mixed fund not taking effect, will be entitled to so much as was the proceeds of the real estate upon the principle that the heir-at-law cannot be disinherited unless the property were actually given away from him. (2) The court, where it has no direction from the testator to whom money arising from a sale of part of his real estate shall go, will give it to his heir-at-law. (3) The meaning of a direction to sell real estate and that the proceeds shall form part of the personal estate is that, so far as the intention of the testator can be carried out, the conversion takes effect

---

[3]*Re Smith.* [1938] O.R. 16, [1938] 1 D.L.R. 94 (C.A.); and see *Re Wagner* (1903), 6 O.L.R. 680 (H.C.J.).

[4]Ont. Act, s. 5, footnote 2, *supra.* The other provinces do not appear to have a similar provision but provide merely that real property is to be administered as personalty and is subject to payment of debts: Man. Act, s. 4; N.B. Act, s. 6; Alta. Act, s. 7; Sask. Act, s. 8; B.C. Act, s. 91(3); P.E.I. Act, s. 111; N.W.T. Ord., s. 7; Yukon Ord., s. 7; Ont. Act, s. 4.

[5]*Fitch v. Weber* (1848), 6 Hare 145, 67 E.R. 1117.

according to the direction of the will; but where the object fails, the direction does not take effect; in case of lapse, the personal estate does not go to the next of kin because the testator intended it, but because the law carried it to them. Hence, as to real estate, the law gives it to the heir and the law would do the same if the testator had said that his real estate should not go to his heir, but had omitted to make a valid devise of it.[6]

If the purposes for which conversion was directed wholly fail, the conversion is considered in equity not to have taken place. Thus, a testator devised his real estate to trustees to sell and to pay the proceeds equally to persons who, at the death of S and M, would be their heirs; one of the trustees was the testator's heir and the trustees sold part of the property. After the death of that trustee-heir, it was discovered that the heirs of S and M had all died in the testator's lifetime, so that the trusts in their favour failed. It was held (1) that the testator's realty was not absolutely converted by his will into personalty, but only for the purpose expressed therein and, that purpose having failed, it descended to his heir, and (2) the proceeds of that part of the property which was sold had been sold under the erroneous impression that one or more of the heirs of S and M might be in existence and, consequently, such part must be regarded as real estate for the heir.[7]

However, if the purposes for which conversion was directed only partly fail, the conversion operates so that, under the old rules, land directed to be sold goes to the heir as personalty,[8] even though it was not actually sold,[9] and money directed to be converted into land goes to the next of kin as land, whether or not land was purchased.[10] The same principles apply where the testator disposes of the proceeds of the sale of realty together with personalty as a mixed fund.[11] A gift of property to trustees on trust for sale, followed by the declaration of a trust which does not exhaust the whole of the property thus given, will be treated as creating a primary general trust of the whole of such property, so that there will be a resulting trust of the unexhausted residue in favour of the testator's heir and next of kin.[12]

If the purpose for which a testator directs a conversion partly fails, the heir-at-law takes the beneficial interest under the resulting trust as personalty,[13] even if the conversion has not taken place.[14]

There is also a resulting trust to the heir if the testator directs a sum of money to be raised out of his real estate and fails to dispose of it.[15] The

---

[6]*Taylor v. Taylor* (1853), 3 De G. M. & G. 190. 43 E.R. 76 (C.A.).

[7]*Davenport v. Coltman* (1842), 12 Sim. 588, 59 E.R. 1259.

[8]*Ibid.*

[9]*Re Richerson*; *Scales v. Heyhoe*, [1892] 1 Ch. 379.

[10]*Curteis v. Wormald* (1878), 10 Ch. D. 172 (C.A.).

[11]*Ackroyd v. Smithson* (1780), 1 Bro. C.C. 503, 28 E.R. 1262; *Jessop v. Watson* (1833), 1 My. & K. 665, 39 E.R. 832.

[12]*Re West*; *George v. Grose*, [1900] 1 Ch. 84.

[13]*Steed v. Preece* (1874), L.R. 18 Eq. 192.

[14]*Re Richerson*; *Scales v. Heyhoe, supra,* footnote 9.

[15]*Emblyn v. Freeman* (1720), Prec. Ch. 541, 24 E.R. 243; *Cruse v. Barley* (1727), 3 P. Wms. 19, 24 E.R. 952.

rule applies even if the testator directs the sum to be paid to his executors and it is not needed to pay debts.[16]

If a conversion is directed by deed and there is a total or partial failure of the purposes of conversion, the same principles apply as in the case of conversion under wills except that the theoretical conversion in equity takes place at the time of delivery of the deed and the resulting trust in any property as to which the trust fails is in favour of the settlor and not of his heir or next of kin.[17]

If there is total failure of the purpose, whether the conversion was for a particular purpose or was absolute, but the proceeds were to be applied for a particular purpose and the purpose fails, the intention fails and the court regards the grantor as not having directed the conversion, so the property results to him as realty.[18] If there is only partial failure of the purpose, the property results to the settlor as personalty.[19] Similarly, if money is directed to be laid out in land and there is a total failure of the purpose, the money results to the settlor as personalty but, if there is only a partial failure, it results to him as realty.[20]

1209.4   Purchase in the Name of Another and Voluntary Transfers

Where one person purchases property in the name of another, or in the name of himself and another or others, a rebuttable presumption of a resulting trust arises where the other person is a stranger, since equity presumes bargains, not gifts. However, if the transfer is to a child or, until recent family law reform legislation in most provinces, to a wife, there is a rebuttable presumption of advancement or gift instead. The same presumptions arise where there is a voluntary transfer by one person to another or others, or to the transferor and another or others. However, there is some doubt whether a resulting trust can arise in the latter case. This is discussed below.[1]

(a)   Purchase in the name of another

If property is purchased in the name of another without express declaration of trust, there is a resulting trust for the purchaser by presumption, unless

---

[16]*Hutcheson v. Hammond* (1790), 3 Bro. C.C. 128, 29 E.R. 449; *Collins v. Wakeman* (1795), 2 Ves. Jun. 683, 30 E.R. 841.

[17]*Griffith v. Ricketts; Griffith v. Lunell* (1849), 7 Hare 299 at p. 311, 68 E.R. 122.

[18]*Ripley v. Waterworth* (1802), 7 Ves. Jun. 425 at p. 435, 32 E.R. 172.

[19]*Hewitt v. Wright* (1780), 1 Bro. C.C. 86, 28 E.R. 1001; *Clarke v. Franklin* (1858), 4 K. & J. 257, 70 E.R. 107; *Biggs v. Andrews* (1832), 5 Sim. 424, 58 E.R. 396.

[20]*Wheldale v. Partridge* (1803), 8 Ves. Jun. 227 at p. 236, 32 E.R. 341; *Clarke v. Franklin, supra,* footnote 19.

§1209.4

[1]In §1209.4(b), *infra.* As to the changes made by modern family law reform statutes, see ch. 16.

it appears from their relationship or other circumstances that a gift was intended.

> The trust of a legal estate, whether freehold, copyhold, or leasehold; whether taken in the names of the purchaser and others jointly, or in the name of others without that of the purchaser; whether in one name or several; whether jointly or *successive*, results to the man who advances the purchase-money.[2]

A resulting trust is presumed to arise when property is purchased with the money of one person, but the conveyance is taken in the name of another, although there is no written evidence of the trust.[3]

In order to raise such a resulting trust, the party asserting it must be able to show that, at the time of the completion of the purchase, he either actually paid, or came under an absolute obligation to pay, the whole or some ascertained portion of the price. A trust thus *prima facie* resulting from the payment or an obligation to pay the purchase price may always be rebutted by parol evidence on the part of the nominal purchaser. On the other hand, this rebutting evidence may in turn be contradicted by the same sort of evidence on the part of the alleged beneficiary and the question to be decided may thus become a pure question of fact to be determined on the conflicting evidence alternately adduced for these purposes.[4] Where the plaintiff, to protect his property from legal process in an alimony action brought against him, conveyed it to his solicitor for a money consideration and subsequently the solicitor reconveyed it to the plaintiff, but retained the conveyance and later, at the plaintiff's request, struck out his name as grantee and inserted that of the plaintiff's sister, the consideration being paid by the plaintiff, it was held that this did not divest the plaintiff of his title under the reconveyance to him and that there was a resulting trust in his favour.[5]

The basic principle of a resulting trust is an intention, express or presumed by the law, on the part of the person paying the purchase money, that he should have the beneficial interest. Consequently, it would follow that, if there can be shown to have been in fact an intention on the part of a purchaser that the beneficial interest should go to the person to whom the property is conveyed, the presumption is entirely removed and no trust would result.[6]

---

[2]Eyre, C.B., in *Dyer v. Dyer* (1788), 2 Cox. 92 at p. 93, 30 E.R. 42.

[3]*Barton v. Muir* (1874), L.R. 6 P.C. 134; *Gordon v. Handford* (1906), 4 W.L.R. 241, 16 Man. R. 292 (Full Court); *Dudgeon v. Dudgeon* (1907), 6 W.L.R. 346, 13 B.C.R. 179; *Stagg v. Ward* (1921), 30 B.C.R. 385 (Co. Ct.); *Young v. Young* (1907), 6 W.L.R. 724 (Man.); *Joos v. Henschell* (1911), 18 W.L.R. 191 (Sask.); *Vaselenak v. Vaselenak* (1921), 57 D.L.R. 370, [1921] 1 W.W.R. 889 (Alta. S.C. App. Div.); *Re Lang Estate*; *Western Trust Co. v. Lang*, [1919] 1 W.W.R. 651, 12 Sask. L.R. 94 (K.B.).

[4]*Per* Strong, J., in *McKercher v. Sanderson* (1887), 15 S.C.R. 296 at p. 298.

[5]*Wilson v. Owens* (1878), 26 Gr. 27.

[6]*Per* Harvey, J., in *King v. Thompson* (1905), 6 Terr. L.R. 204, in which case it was held that, when it appears that the actual purchaser by whom the price is paid directs the conveyance to be made to a third party, intending the latter to have the beneficial interest in the land, no trust results to the actual purchaser, although no value is given by the third party.

Moreover, where land is purchased by one person in the name of another, the resulting trust may be rebutted as to part of the land, or part of the interest in the land.[7]

If land is purchased by two persons, or by one for two, and each pays part of the purchase price, but the conveyance is made to one only, there is a trust for the other to the extent of the proportion paid by him, provided that all or part of the whole consideration for the whole estate is paid and the proportion paid by the one alleging the trust can be ascertained.[8] The same rule applies where property is purchased by a number of persons and is put in the name of two for convenience; in which case, if the property is sold by the survivor, the proceeds must be apportioned as moneys held on trust.[9]

If the proportions paid towards the purchase by the parties cannot be ascertained with certainty the court will often find that the transferee holds the property on a resulting trust equally for the several contributors on the basis that equality is equity.[10]

At common law, where a conveyance is made jointly to both persons concerned and they contribute equal shares of the purchase money, they hold as joint tenants with the benefit of survivorship, unless there is evidence showing a contrary intention at the time of the purchase,[11] but, unless a contrary intent is shown, if they contribute unequal shares, they hold as tenants in common, because the court leans in favour of a tenancy in common.[12] By statute, where two or more persons, other than executors or trustees, acquire land, it is considered that such persons take as tenants in common and not as joint tenants, unless an intention sufficiently appears on the face of the letters patent, assurance or will, that they are to take as joint tenants.[13]

If the person alleging a trust merely lent the money to the transferee, no resulting trust can be raised in his favour.[14] Similarly, no resulting trust can arise out of a contractual relationship, as where A buys property for himself with his own money and agrees with B to transfer the property to B when B pays him the purchase price, but it is otherwise where the property was bought,

---

[7]*Per* Leach, M.R., in *Benbow v. Townsend* (1833), 1 My. & K. 506 at p. 510, 39 E.R. 772.

[8]*Taylor v. Wallbridge* (1879), 2 S.C.R. 616 at pp. 680-1, in which case, Henry, J., added "I can find no case of a beneficial interest having been declared in favour of one who did not himself *purchase,* but who only paid a part of the consideration money years after the purchase was made".

[9]*Wood v. Strange,* [1946] O.R. 139, [1946] 2 D.L.R. 76 (H.C.J.).

[10]*S. v. S.,* [1952] 5 W.W.R. (N.S.) 523 (Man. Q.B.).

[11]*Harrison v. Barton* (1860), 1 J. & H. 287, 70 E.R. 756.

[12]Lord Hardwicke, L.C., in *Rigden v. Vallier* (1751), 2 Ves. Sen. 252, 28 E.R. 163.

[13]*Law of Property Act,* R.S.A. 1980, c. L-8, s. 8; *Property Law Act,* R.S.B.C. 1979, c. 340, s. 11; *Law of Property Act,* R.S.M. 1970, c. L90, s. 15; *Property Act,* R.S.N.B. 1973, c. P-19, s. 20; *Real Property Act,* R.S.N.S. 1967, c. 261, s. 4; *Conveyancing and Law of Property Act,* R.S.O. 1980, c. 90, s. 13; *Land Titles Act,* R.S.S. 1978, c. L-5, s. 242; R.S.C. 1970. c. L-4, s. 169; *Tenants in Common Ordinance,* R.O.N.W.T. 1974, c. T-3; R.O.Y.T. 1971, c. T-1.

[14]*Rupar v. Rupar* (1964), 49 W.W.R. 226 (B.C.S.C.). But see *Chupak v. Cirka* (1982), 132 D.L.R. (3d) 251, 23 R.P.R. 1 (Ont. H.C.J.).

not on behalf of himself, but on behalf of B, for in that case A effectively lent the purchase price and the property will result to B, or be held on trust for B.[15]

(b) Voluntary transfers

An advancement is the transfer by a father or, prior to recent family law reform legislation in most provinces, a husband, of a portion of his assets to his wife or child before his death, thereby giving him or her an advance of that which they might expect to receive at his death. An advancement is essentially a share and not the whole of the transferor's estate.[16]

If a husband purchases property in the name of his wife or transfers property to her, the general rule, apart from statute, is that there is a rebuttable presumption that he intended it as an advancement or gift to her.[17] If a man purchases and pays for lands with his own money and causes them to be conveyed to a stranger, there is, for want of consideration, a resulting trust in the purchaser's favour; but, if he causes the conveyance to be made to his wife, the relationship implies a consideration and the law presumes that the conveyance was intended as an advancement. The existence of that intention, however, is a question of fact and, if it is disproved, the wife is a trustee for the husband. If the husband, at the time of the purchase and conveyance to the wife, does not intend a resulting trust, he cannot, by subsequent change of intention, deprive her of the beneficial ownership and make her a trustee.[18] The same is true of a conveyance by husband to wife. Where a husband conveys lands to his wife in absolute form, the relationship implies a consideration. The law presumes that the conveyance was intended as an advancement and not as a resulting trust and, unless he brings forward clear, distinct and precise testimony of a definite trust in his favour, there is no resulting trust.[19] Where the legal title is in the wife at the time of her death, the presumption is that there was no trust, but the presumption is rebuttable.[20] Thus, the *Statute of Frauds*[21] is no bar to the enforcement of an agreement between husband and wife that the survivor was to be owner of the land which he conveyed to her (and she had at the same time made a will in his favour to carry out the agreement); the arrangement is enforceable against her, despite her later will made contrary to the agreement.[22]

---

[15]*Brown v. Storoschuk*, [1947] 1 D.L.R. 227, [1946] 3 W.W.R. 641 (B.C.C.A.). *Cf. Vaselenak v. Vaselenak* (1921), 57 D.L.R. 370, [1921] 1 W.W.R. 889 (Alta. S.C. App. Div.).

[16]*Pahara v. Pahara*, [1946] 1 D.L.R. 433 at p. 438, [1946] S.C.R. 89 at p. 95, per Rand, J.

[17]*McLeod v. Curry* (1923), 54 O.L.R. 205, [1923] 4 D.L.R. 100 (S.C. App. Div.), revg 51 O.L.R. 68, 64 D.L.R. 684 (H.C.); *Hyman v. Hyman*, [1934] 4 D.L.R. 532 (S.C.C.); *Beemer v. Brownridge*, [1934] 1 W.W.R. 545 (Sask. C.A.); *Toronto General Trusts Corp. v. Estlin* (1911), 18 W.L.R. 11 (Man.).

[18]*McLeod v. Curry* (1921), 51 O.L.R. 68, 64 D.L.R. 684 (H.C.), reversed on facts but not on law, 54 O.L.R. 205, [1923] 4 D.L.R. 100 (S.C. App. Div.).

[19]*Hyman v. Hyman, supra*, footnote 17.

[20]*Fulton v. Mercantile Trust Co.* (1917), 12 O.W.N. 139 (H.C.).

[21]R.S.O. 1914, c. 102.

[22]*Breitenstein v. Munson* (1914), 16 D.L.R. 458, 6 W.W.R. 188 (B.C.S.C.).

It is the wife's privilege to declare the property to be in trust notwithstanding the presumption in her favour. Thus, it was held that a married woman, in an action brought against her upon the covenant in a mortgage made by her husband and herself, which contained no recital of ownership and was given to secure part of the purchase price of land purchased by the husband and conveyed to her, may show that the conveyance was taken by her merely as trustee for her husband and not for her benefit, although the mortgagee or those claiming under him had no knowledge of her position.[23]

The foregoing presumption, however, applied only to a wife. There was no presumption of a gift where a man bought real property in the name of a woman who was not his wife and with whom he was merely cohabiting. The bare fact that he paid the purchase price was sufficient to raise a presumption of resulting trust in his favour and this presumption was not rebutted by his admission that he put title in her name "to keep peace in the house". In such cases, where a gift was alleged, it had to be shown that the donor fully intended to make a gift and realized the legal effect of the transaction.[24] Similarly, there was no presumption of advancement in the case of a transfer by a man into the joint names of himself and a woman who was not his wife, even though they believed at the time that they were legally married. There was, instead, a presumption of a resulting trust to the man, rebuttable by clear evidence. Whether there was a gift depended on the man's intention at the time of the transfer and evidence by him on this point was admissible.[25] Also, where there was a housekeeping arrangement between a woman and an older illiterate man and a deed to the house was taken in her name on her instructions, there was a resulting trust in his favour.[26]

More recent cases have, however, held that the same principles apply whether the parties are merely living together as husband and wife, or whether they are legally married.[27] This view was adopted by the Supreme Court of Canada in *Pettkus v. Becker*.[28]

The presumption is the opposite when a wife conveys to her husband. The general rule is that, when a wife hands over to her husband property belonging to her separate use, whether real or personal, it is presumed that a gift was not intended and that he is a trustee of it for her, unless there is evidence of a contrary intention.[29] Consequently, where a former wife put her time, money and labour into the acquisition and improvement of a house, the title to which

---

[23]*Gordon v. Warren* (1897), 24 O.A.R. 44.

[24]*Stagg v. Ward* (1921), 30 B.C.R. 385 (Co. Ct.).

[25]*Clelland v. Clelland*, [1945] 3 D.L.R. 664, [1945] 2 W.W.R. 399 (B.C.C.A.), affg with variation [1944] 4 D.L.R. 703, [1944] 3 W.W.R. 234 (B.C.S.C.); *Derhak v. Dandenault* (1954), 11 W.W.R. 37, 62 Man. R. 13 (K.B.); *Copley v. Guaranty Trust Co. of Canada*, [1956] O.W.N. 621 (H.C.J.).

[26]*Paroschy v. Balan*, [1947] O.W.N. 778 (H.C.J.), affd [1948] O.W.N. 248 (C.A.).

[27]*Cooke v. Head*, [1972] 2 All E.R. 38 (C.A.); *Eves v. Eves*, [1975] 3 All E.R. 768 (C.A.).

[28](1980), 117 D.L.R. (3d) 257, [1980] 2 S.C.R. 834.

[29]*Green v. Carlill* (1877), 4 Ch. D. 882; *Re Flamank*; *Wood v. Cock* (1889), 40 Ch. D. 461; *Mercier v. Mercier*, [1903] 2 Ch. 98 (C.A.); *Briggs v. Willson* (1897), 24 O.A.R. 521; *Ward v. Ward* (1920), 17 O.W.N. 413 (H.C.); *Phinn v. Glover* (1922), 21 O.W.N.

was taken in the husband's name only, and it appeared that she did not intend to make a gift to her husband, but rather to devote her money and efforts to the acquisition and renovation of a house which would belong to both and be their home, it was held that a trust resulted in her favour.[30] It has been held that, while the spouses are living together, a husband is not liable to account for the income of property that he uses, as it is presumed that he applied it for their joint benefit.[31] Where the widow of an intestate claimed to be the sole beneficial owner of land which she bought with her own money and conveyed to him without consideration, it was held that parol evidence was admissible to show that a consideration of $100 expressed in the deed had not been paid, that the land was held in trust and that an amendment of the claim to set up fraud should be allowed.[32]

The same presumption of advancement arises where a father or a person standing *in loco parentis* purchases property in the name of a child or adopted child or transfers property to such child.[33] The law generally holds that there is no presumption of advancement where a mother is the purchaser or transferee,[34] although it is probable that where the mother is the only head of the family and the children are dependent upon her, little need be shown to rebut the presumption of resulting trust.[35]

There is the same rebuttable presumption that an advancement or gift was intended if a father purchases or transfers property in the joint names of a child and a third party.[36]

Where the purchase is in favour of a stranger the presumption is one of resulting trust.[37]

421, 63 D.L.R. 523 (S.C.); *Butler v. Standard Fire Ins. Co.* (1879), 4 O.A.R. 391; *Ellis v. Ellis* (1913), 5 O.W.N. 561, 15 D.L.R. 100 (S.C. App. Div.); *Hart v. Toronto General Trusts Corp.* (1920), 47 O.L.R. 387 (H.C.), release of an equity of redemption to husband; *Moore v. Moore* (1970), 16 D.L.R. (3d) 174 (B.C.C.A.), appeal to S.C.C. dismissed 49 D.L.R. (3d) 479n; transfer by wife to husband pursuant to his misrepresentation.

[30]*Sywack v. Sywack* (1943), 51 Man. R. 108 (K.B.).

[31]*Re Flamank*; *Wood v. Cock, supra*, footnote 29.

[32]*Re Lang Estate*; *Western Trust Co. v. Lang*, [1919] 1 W.W.R. 651, 12 Sask. L.R. 94 (K.B.).

[33]*Standing v. Bowring* (1885), 31 Ch. D. 282; *Eldridge v. Royal Trust Co.* (1922), 66 D.L.R. 674, [1922] 2 W.W.R. 1068 (Alta. S.C. App. Div.), affd [1923] 2 D.L.R. 689, [1923] 2 W.W.R. 67 (S.C.C.); *Northern Canadian Trust Co. v. Smith*, [1947] 3 D.L.R. 135, [1947] 1 W.W.R. 765 (Man. C.A.); *Young v. Young* (1958), 15 D.L.R. (2d) 138 (B.C.C.A.). An illegitimate child is included in the presumption: *Soar v. Foster* (1858), 4 K. & J. 152 at pp. 157 *et seq.*, 70 E.R. 64.

[34]*Edwards v. Bradley* (1957), 9 D.L.R. (2d) 673, [1957] S.C.R. 599.

[35]See *Main v. Main*, [1939] 1 D.L.R. 723, [1939] 1 W.W.R. 7 (Man. K.B.); *Rupar v. Rupar* (1964), 46 D.L.R. (2d) 553, 49 W.W.R. 226 (B.C.S.C.), where the court thought there was a presumption of advancement.

[36]*Crabb v. Crabb* (1834), 1 My. & K. 511, 39 E.R. 774.

[37]Jessel, M.R., in *Marshal v. Crutwell* (1875), L.R. 20 Eq. 328 at p. 329; *Hudson's Bay Co. v. Hosie*, [1926] 4 D.L.R. 489, [1926] 4 W.W.R. 730 (Sask. C.A.); *Re Kettle* (1965), 51 M.P.R. 1 (Nfld. S.C.), transfer to daughter-in-law; *Groves v. Christiansen* (1978), 86 D.L.R. (3d) 296, [1978] 4 W.W.R. 64 (B.C.S.C.).

Similarly, if a person transfers property into his own name jointly with another person who is not his child or adopted child, there is a *prima facie* resulting trust for the transferor, but the presumption may be rebutted by showing that, at the time, the transferor intended a benefit to the transferee.[38] The general principle was stated in the Privy Council by Lord Parker that, when once the conclusion is arrived at that a grantor intends to part with his whole legal and beneficial interest in favour of another, there can be no resulting trust unless, in the view of a court of equity, there is no consideration to support the transaction, or the consideration, if any, entirely fails.[39] A voluntary conveyance of real property from one person to another does not give rise to a resulting trust in favour of the grantor if it can be gathered from all the circumstances that it was intended to vest the beneficial as well as the legal title in the grantee.[40]

The foregoing cases concern personal property only, however. The question whether there would be a resulting trust where the transfer involved real property was never finally resolved in England. The resulting trust derives from the resulting use before the *Statute of Uses*.[41] Before that statute, if A conveyed to B without consideration, B was regarded as holding upon a resulting use for A. To avoid this presumption the conveyance had to be made "to B and his heirs, to the use of B and his heirs". The statute, however, executed the resulting use where none was expressed and vested the legal estate in the grantor. When trusts developed it became the practice to convey to another to uses, in other words, for A to convey "to B and his heirs to the use of B and his heirs" or, in syncopated form, "unto and to the use of B and his heirs", in order to vest the legal estate in B. The question then was whether, in the case of a voluntary grant, a resulting trust could be raised in favour of the grantor, by analogy to the earlier doctrine of resulting uses. This question was much disputed in England, but was never settled. Since the 1925 property reforms the matter has become academic there, for the *Law of Property Act, 1925*[42] provides that in a voluntary conveyance a resulting trust for the grantor is not to be implied merely because the property is not expressed to be conveyed to the use of the grantee. Thus, there was no longer a need to convey to uses.

In Canada the prevailing opinion appears to be, albeit expressed in dicta only, that a resulting trust would be presumptively raised in respect of land transferred by a voluntary conveyance.[43] However, the presumption does

---

[38]Per Cotton, L.J., in *Standing v. Bowring, supra,* footnote 33; *Vandervell v. Inland Revenue Comr's,* [1967] 2 A.C. 291 (H.L.).

[39]*Snider v. Carleton; Central Trust and Safe Deposit Co. v. Snider* (1915), 35 O.L.R. 246 at p. 260, 25 D.L.R. 410 at p. 413 (P.C.).

[40]*M.D. Donald Ltd. v. Brown,* [1933] 4 D.L.R. 145, [1933] S.C.R. 411, revg 46 B.C.R. 406 (C.A.).

[41]27 Hen. 8, c. 10 (1535).

[42]15 & 16 Geo. 5, c. 20, s. 60(3).

[43]*Niles v. Lake,* [1947] 2 D.L.R. 248 at pp. 253, 256, [1947] S.C.R. 291 at pp. 297-8, 302, *per* Kerwin and Taschereau, JJ.; *Neazor v. Hoyle* (1962), 32 D.L.R. (2d) 131, 37 W.W.R. 104 (Alta. S.C. App. Div.), *per* Macdonald, J.A.

not usually have to be resorted to, for the courts tend to prefer to consider the totality of the evidence and to rely on the presumption only if the evidence is so evenly weighted that only the presumption can decide the case.[44]

(c) Rebutting the presumptions of resulting trust and advancement

The onus of displacing either presumption rests on the party who desires to rebut it and clear evidence is required for that purpose.

Where a deed was taken in the name of two brothers and one of them later took proceedings to have his co-grantee declared a trustee of one-half of the property for him, but the evidence showed that the deed was intentionally drawn as it was, that receipts for instalments of the price were taken in both names and that a mortgage to secure the balance of the price was executed by both, it was held that, even if all of the purchase money was advanced by one, it was not sufficient to show that the purchase was made solely for his benefit.[45] The inference that a gift was intended is strengthened when the transaction is between brothers.[46] Where land was purchased with the money of a son but the deed was taken in the names of himself and his mother as tenants in common, it was held that there was a resulting trust in favour of the son and a conveyance by the mother of an undivided half interest was set aside.[47]

Where a partner purchases real property out of partnership funds, taking the deed in his own name, it will be presumed, in the absence of evidence to the contrary, that he holds the property in trust for the partnership.[48] Where real property is purchased by one partner with partnership funds and the conveyance is taken in the name of his wife because the other partner has a judgment against him and also because the vendor would have been reluctant to deal with him, there is a resulting trust in favour of the partnership. It is only when a party, in order to make out his case, must set up his own fraudulent act as a step in his claim that a court of equity refuses assistance. The fact that the creditors of the one partner might have impeached the transaction does not affect its validity as between the partners.[49]

Where there is a gift of property *inter vivos*, accompanied by the expression of a wish as to the mode of employing it and, at the same time, a declaration that no legal obligation is intended to be imposed, the clear intention is thereby shown that the dominion of the property is to remain in the grantee and evidence of want of consideration moving from the grantee cannot raise a resulting trust.[50]

---

[44]See, *e.g.*, *Neazor v. Hoyle, supra,* footnote 43.

[45]*Hutchinson v. Hutchinson* (1856), 6 Gr. 117.

[46]Strong, J., in *Taylor v. Wallbridge* (1879), 2 S.C.R. 616 at p. 660.

[47]*Mason v. Hayes* (1924), 51 N.B.R. 137 (S.C.).

[48]*Wright v. Kyle,* [1939] O.W.N. 464, [1939] 4 D.L.R. 727 (S.C.), citing *Fowkes v. Pascoe* (1875), L.R. 10 Ch. App. 343, and *Stock v. McAvoy* (1872), L.R. 15 Eq. 55; *McFadgen v. Stewart* (1865), 11 Gr. 272.

[49]*Moore v. Clark,* [1942] 4 D.L.R. 560, 16 M.P.R. 383 (N.B.S.C.).

[50]*Wheeler v. Smith* (1860), 29 L.J. Ch. 194.

Only such evidence as demonstrates the intention of the parties at the time of the original transaction may be led to rebut the presumptions. These include acts and declarations of the parties before, at the time of, or immediately after the transaction so that they constitute part of it. Subsequent declarations are admissible only against the party who made them.[51]

Thus, for example, in *Barr v. Barr*,[52] a mortgagee, when purchasing a prior mortgage, was advised by his solicitor to take an assignment in the name of a third person as trustee and took it accordingly in the name of his son, it being held that parol evidence was admissible to prove a trust and not a gift.

Although subsequent acts or declarations of the child may establish that a trust was intended,[53] subsequent acts or declarations by the parent will not change an advancement or gift into a trust.

Thus in *Allison v. Allison*,[54] a father conveyed all of his property to his son without consideration, independent advice, or power of revocation, and fifteen years later sought to set aside this improvident transaction. It was held that the conveyance must stand as the son was not guilty of fraud or other impropriety but that, on the evidence, he took the property on the distinct stipulation that he would support the family and take care of the mother who had barred her dower on this understanding, so that a trust to this effect must be declared and the father and mother declared to be entitled to a suitable allowance by the son for their maintenance. Similarly, in *Northern Canadian Trust Co. v. Smith*,[55] it was held that, where a person buys a house in his son's name and there is no evidence of an agreement by the son to hold it in trust, the presumption is that the father intended it to be an advancement, especially if the son is an infant. As a result there is no resulting trust and, although such presumption may be rebutted by evidence of a contrary intention, mere evidence that the father and his family occupied the premises rent free, that the father improved the property and that the mother spent money on decorating the house is not sufficient to rebut the presumption, since subsequent acts or declarations by the purchaser or transferor will not suffice to negative an advancement. The evidence of acts or declarations of the father to rebut the presumption of advancement must be those made before or contemporaneously with the transaction, or else immediately after it, so as in effect to form part of the transaction. The subsequent acts and declarations of a son can be used against him and those claiming under him by the father, where there is nothing showing the intention of the father at the time of the transaction sufficient to counteract the effect of those declarations.[56]

---

[51]*Shephard v. Cartwright*, [1955] A.C. 431 (H.L.), at p. 435, *per* Viscount Simonds; *Clemens v. Clemens Estate* (1956), 1 D.L.R. (2d) 625, [1956] S.C.R. 286, *per* Cartwright, J.

[52](1868), 15 Gr. 27.

[53]*Jeans v. Cooke* (1857), 24 Beav. 513 at p. 521, 53 E.R. 456.

[54][1943] 3 D.L.R. 637, [1943] 2 W.W.R. 628 (Man. C.A.).

[55][1947] 3 D.L.R. 135, [1947] 1 W.W.R. 765 (Man. C.A.).

[56]*Per* Proudfoot, V.C., in *Birdsell v. Johnson* (1876), 24 Gr. 202 at p. 206.

The particular circumstances of the transaction may raise a presumption that an advancement or gift was not intended.

Thus, in *Atkinson v. Atkinson*,[57] a father, believing that his recovery from a serious illness was doubtful, transferred lands into his son's name without the latter's knowledge but kept the title deeds and, after his recovery, disposed of part of the lands. It was held that he had satisfied the onus on him of showing that a gift was not intended.

A husband, by arrangement with his wife and two daughters by a former marriage, purchased land and built on it, paying for it out of money produced by the joint labour of himself, his wife and the daughters. The deed was taken in the name of the wife upon the understanding that she should hold the property for the benefit of herself and her husband during their lives and that, after their death, it was to go to the daughters. By his will, the husband declared that he had no real estate, but desired the wife to direct her executors to sell the property and to divide the proceeds between his two daughters and a daughter of his wife by her former husband. It was held that there was no advancement but a resulting trust in favour of the testator, although the trusts for the daughters were void as being by parol only, and thus insufficient to satisfy the *Statute of Frauds*.[58] Where a husband and wife, with the help of their children, accumulated considerable property over a period of years and the husband put the land in his wife's name, it being agreed between them that each would, by will, leave the property for the benefit of the survivor and the children, it was held that a disposition by the wife's will contrary to the agreement was ineffective, as the land was held in trust for the benefit of the surviving husband and children.[59]

As indicated previously, there must be clear and precise testimony of a definite trust to rebut the presumption that an advancement was intended.[60] Consequently, where a husband took a hotel property in the name of his wife, putting all of his property into the first payments and undertaking with her to pay the balance, both to work in the hotel as manager and cook, respectively, it was held that the presumption of a gift to her was not overcome merely by

---

[57](1944), 52 Man. R. 208 (K.B.); and see *Hawker v. Hawker* (1969), 3 D.L.R. (3d) 735 (Sask. Q.B.).

[58]29 Car. 2, c. 3 (1677); *Owen v. Kennedy* (1873), 20 Gr. 163.

[59]*Pahara v. Pahara*, [1945] 1 D.L.R. 763, [1945] 1 W.W.R. 134 (Alta. S.C. App. Div.), affd in this respect, although otherwise vard by [1946] 1 D.L.R. 433, [1946] S.C.R. 89. In the following cases, the presumption was rebutted and it was held that there was a resulting trust: *Nelson v. Nelson* (1911), 19 O.W.R. 225 (H.C.J.), purchase by husband in wife's name; *Macdonald (John) & Co. Ltd. v. Teasdale* (1913), 24 O.W.R. 534 (H.C.), conveyance by husband; *Hicks v. Rothermel*, [1949] 2 W.W.R. 705 (Sask. K.B.); *Downing v. Home Insurance Co. of New York*, [1934] 2 D.L.R. 617, 8 M.P.R. 1 (N.B.S.C. App. Div.); *Palmer v. Palmer* (1912), 42 N.B.R. 23 (S.C.); *Re Black* (1924), 26 O.W.N. 285 (H.C.); *Re Pond*, [1947] 1 W.W.R. 670 (Alta. S.C.); *Zebberman v. Zebberman*, [1948] 2 D.L.R. 269, 21 M.P.R. 1 (N.B.S.C.); *Dudgeon v. Dudgeon* (1907), 6 W.L.R. 346, 13 B.C.R. 179 (S.C.), money advanced to wife to enable her to purchase.

[60]*Hyman v. Hyman*, [1934] 4 D.L.R. 532 (S.C.C.).

the fact that such actions by him had the effect of depriving him of all of the fruits of years of enterprise. A document signed by the wife on their separation but not signed by him, agreeing to give him one-half of the property "he agreeing to pay half of all the debts against the above property up to date for the said half interest" was held to be merely an option to him and not a declaration of trust in his favour.[61]

The fact that a child has already been provided for does not necessarily rebut the presumption that an advancement or gift was intended[62] and, conversely, where the circumstances raise a presumption that a resulting trust was intended, a mere moral obligation to provide for a child is not sufficient to rebut that presumption.[63]

The presumption that an advancement or gift was intended, however, is not so strong in the case of a mother as in that of a father. In each case, it is a question of fact to be determined on the evidence.[64] In *Main v. Main*,[65] a mother made her will, naming two of her sons executors and, on the same day, transferred land to them with the object of avoiding succession duties, but she continued until her death to treat the land as her own, made leases and collected rents. It was held that the onus was on the sons to prove that a gift was intended and, having failed to do so, they were trustees of the land for the benefit of all of the beneficiaries of the testatrix.

(d) Fraudulent transfers

A person is not permitted to lead evidence of his own wrongful act in order to defeat the presumption of advancement. Thus, where a husband took a lease of land in his wife's name and built a house upon it with his own money, using her name with her knowledge because he was in debt and desired to protect the property from his creditors, it was held, in an action by him for a declaration that she held the property as trustee for him, that he could not be allowed to set up his own fraudulent design to rebut the presumption that the conveyance was intended as a gift to her use, and that she was entitled to retain the property for her own use, notwithstanding that she was a party to the fraud.[66] When both parties are dishonest, the court will not act, adopting the maxim "Let the estate lie where it falls". In *Scheuerman v.*

---

[61]*Reynolds v. Betson*, [1931] 2 D.L.R. 760, [1931] 1 W.W.R. 793 (Man. C.A.). In the following cases also, the presumption that an advancement was intended was not successfully rebutted: *Anning v. Anning* (1916), 38 O.L.R. 277, 34 D.L.R. 193 (S.C. App. Div.), conveyed by husband; *Slater v. Slater* (1918), 13 O.W.N. 429 (H.C.), purchase by husband; *Pillon v. Edwards* (1920), 19 O.W.N. 195 (H.C.), conveyance by husband; *Taylor v. Taylor* (1921), 20 O.W.N. 461 (H.C.), conveyance by husband; *Re Jay* (1925), 28 O.W.N. 214 (H.C.), purchase by husband, conveyance to himself and wife; *Re Mills*, [1937] 3 D.L.R. 464 (N.B.S.C.); *Johnson v. Johnson*, [1945] 1 D.L.R. 404, 18 M.P.R. 254 (N.S.S.C.), affd [1945] 3 D.L.R. 413, [1945] S.C.R. 455.
[62]*Hepworth v. Hepworth* (1870), L.R. 11 Eq. 10.
[63]*Soar v. Foster* (1858), 4 K. & J. 152 at p. 161, 70 E.R. 64.
[64]*Bennet v. Bennet* (1879), 10 Ch. D. 474 at pp. 479-80.
[65][1939] 1 D.L.R. 723, [1939] 1 W.W.R. 7 (Man. K.B.).
[66]*Gascoigne v. Gascoigne*, [1918] 1 K.B. 223.

Scheuerman[67] property was conveyed by a husband to his wife with intent to evade his creditors, the wife verbally agreeing to reconvey the land when the judgment was satisfied. It was held that he could not recover the property after satisfying the debt, because of his fraudulent intent, even though the land actually was exempt from execution. Thus the court will not declare a resulting trust when the reason for the conveyance was to defeat, delay or hinder creditors,[68] or to protect the property from, or evade payment of, an anticipated claim,[69] or possible claim, for damages,[70] even though he denies any fraudulent intent,[71] and a fraudulent intent is not really necessary to exclude him from setting up the claim.[72] Although a court will not assist a husband, who transfers property into his wife's name when he is in financial difficulties in order to delay and hinder creditors, by declaring that she holds the property as trustee for him, the court will not refuse a decree on mere suspicion of the purpose of the transfer.[73] It makes no difference, however, that the design to defeat creditors was never carried out and that they were paid, or that the wife was unaware of the transfer to her at the time or for ten years thereafter, as acceptance by her is not necessary to complete the gift to her. The gift vests in her subject to her right to repudiate or disclaim when becoming aware of the transfer.[74]

Another line of cases, however, suggests that evidence of wrongdoing may be led where the creditors were not in fact hindered or defrauded because the parties resiled from their fraudulent purpose.[75] This was also the view of the minority in *Goodfriend v. Goodfriend*,[76] but the majority were content to distinguish *Scheuerman v. Scheuerman*[77] on the ground that it was the wife who had misled the husband to make a gratuitous transfer to her because he might be sued successfully when, in fact, there was no valid cause of action against him.

Clearly, where a conveyance of property purchased by the husband is made to the wife with the object of protecting it from his creditors, she may convey it to him at any time and her creditors have no right to have the conveyance set aside.[78]

---

[67]*Scheuerman v. Scheuerman* (1916), 28 D.L.R. 223, 52 S.C.R. 625.

[68]*Johnson v. Johnson* (1926). 31 O.W.N. 313 (S.C. App. Div.); *Walsh v. Walsh*, [1948] O.R. 81, [1948] 1 D.L.R. 630 (H.C.J.), affd [1948] O.W.N. 668, [1948] 4 D.L.R. 876 (C.A.).

[69]*McAuley v. McAuley* (1909), 10 W.L.R. 419, 18 Man. R. 544 (K.B.); *Harrington v. Harrington* (1925), 56 O.L.R. 568, [1925] 2 D.L.R. 849 (S.C. App. Div.).

[70]*Fricke v. Fricke*, [1940] 1 D.L.R. 783, [1940] 1 W.W.R. 87 (Alta. S.C.).

[71]*Harrington v. Harrington*, *supra*, footnote 69; *Walsh v. Walsh*, *supra*, footnote 68.

[72]*Harrington v. Harrington*, *supra*, footnote 69. citing *Buckland v. Rose* (1859), 7 Gr. 440.

[73]*Cole v. Cole*, [1944] 2 D.L.R. 798, [1944] S.C.R. 166, affg [1944] 1 D.L.R. 37, [1943] 3 W.W.R. 532 (B.C.C.A.).

[74]*Walsh v. Walsh*, *supra*, footnote 68.

[75]*Krys v. Krys*, [1929] 1 D.L.R. 289, [1929] S.C.R. 153; *Re Szymczak and Szymczak*, [1970] 3 O.R. 202, 12 D.L.R. (3d) 582 (H.C.J.).

[76](1971), 22 D.L.R. (3d) 699, [1972] S.C.R. 640.

[77]*Supra*, footnote 67.

[78]*Gibbons v. Tomlinson* (1891), 21 O.R. 489 (H.C.J.).

(e) The resulting trust and matrimonial property

In recent years the presumptions of resulting trust and of advancement have played a large role in matrimonial property disputes. Typically, although not exclusively, these concern disputes on a breakdown of the marriage as to the contribution to the purchase price by the spouse who does not have title. If the parties have previously agreed to the beneficial ownership of the property no difficulties arise, but in most cases they have not directed their minds to the question at all. If they have not, the presumptions are invoked to decide the issue.[79]

Contribution may consist of different acts. Thus, for example, the wife may have contributed to the purchase price, or have helped to pay off the mortgage. Alternatively, she may have paid for the housekeeping, which enabled the husband to pay the mortgage. Again, she may have contributed to the building of the matrimonial home, or worked in her husband's business, thereby enabling him to build up an estate. Finally, she may have done none of these things, but simply have kept house and raised the family, while the husband earned the income to support the family and to acquire the assets in his name.

Traditionally, the courts have taken the view that only a contribution to the purchase price entitles a spouse to an interest in the property and while some forms of indirect contribution, such as payment of the housekeeping bills, have been acceptable for this purpose,[80] the rule was usually applied strictly. The difficulty for the non-contributing spouse was compounded by the fact that the courts have held that in applications under section 17 of the *Married Women's Property Act*[81] and comparable Canadian legislation[82] they were not empowered to allocate property between spouses, but only to declare their respective property rights as they exist.[83]

In order to avoid these strictures, some courts readily found an implied intention that the parties agreed to share the property equally. However, in many cases this amounted only to an agreement being imputed by the court on the basis of a deemed intent,[84] and this continued even after the Supreme Court and House of Lords decisions that rejected such an approach.[85]

---

[79]*Pettitt v. Pettitt*, [1970] A.C. 777 (H.L.); *Gissing v. Gissing*, [1971] A.C. 886 (H.L.); *Thompson v. Thompson* (1960), 26 D.L.R. (2d) 1, [1961] S.C.R. 3; *Murdoch v. Murdoch* (1973), 41 D.L.R. (3d) 367, [1975] 1 S.C.R. 423.

[80]*Gissing v. Gissing, supra*, footnote 79.

[81]45 & 46 Vict., c. 75 (1882).

[82]*E.g., Married Women's Property Act*, R.S.O. 1970, c. 262, s. 12, repealed by *Family Law Reform Act*, S.O. 1978, c. 2, s. 82.

[83]*Pettitt v. Pettitt, supra*, footnote 79; *Thompson v. Thompson, supra*, footnote 79.

[84]*Rimmer v. Rimmer*, [1953] 1 Q.B. 63 (C.A.).

[85]*Supra*, footnote 79. See, *e.g., Tinker v. Tinker*, [1970] P. 136 (C.A.); *Falconer v. Falconer*, [1970] 1 W.L.R. 1333 (C.A.); *Heseltine v. Heseltine*, [1971] 1 All E.R. 952 (C.A.); *Davis v. Vale*, [1971] 1 W.L.R. 1022 (C.A.); *Trueman v. Trueman* (1971), 18 D.L.R. (3d) 109, [1971] 2 W.W.R. 688 (Alta. S.C. App. Div.); *Wiley v. Wiley* (1971), 23 D.L.R. (3d) 484, 6 R.F.L. 36 (B.C.S.C.); *Humeniuk v. Humeniuk*, [1970] 3 O.R.

While most cases involve the title to the matrimonial home, the same principles are applicable to a business operated by, or contributed to, by both parties.[86]

In a recent Supreme Court case, *Murdoch v. Murdoch*,[87] the majority agreed with the trial judge that a wife was not entitled to a declaration of resulting trust with respect to an interest in her husband's ranch where she had not contributed financially or with her labours beyond what can be expected of a normal rancher's wife. Moreover, the court held that the resulting trust only extends to the matrimonial home and cannot encompass a husband's business. In his dissent Laskin, J., disagreed with the latter point. In any event, he would have raised a constructive trust in the circumstances of the case on the ground of unjust enrichment.

In a more recent case, *Rathwell v. Rathwell*,[88] the Supreme Court of Canada again had occasion to consider the applicability of the doctrines of resulting and constructive trusts to matrimonial property disputes. In this case a husband and wife pooled their resources in a joint bank account and, over a period of time, bought land with the money in the account and commenced a farming operation. Title was taken in the husband's name. The wife contributed to the business in much the same way as the wife in the *Murdoch* case, but in the *Rathwell* case the husband had at one time stated that the farming operation was a joint venture and that he and his wife were working together as a team in the farming business. When the parties separated, the wife brought an action for a declaration that she had an interest in one-half of all the real and personal property owned by her husband and for an accounting. Her action was dismissed at trial but she was successful on appeal.

In the Supreme Court of Canada, Dickson, J., with whom Laskin, C.J.C., and Spence, J., concurred, held that the wife should succeed either on the basis of a resulting or a constructive trust. In that there was positive evidence of a common intention that both parties should share in the joint venture, the husband held the property, which the court held to be family property and not business property, on a resulting trust as to a one-half interest for his wife.

521, 13 D.L.R. (3d) 417 (H.C.J.); *Moore v. Moore* (1970), 16 D.L.R. (3d) 174 (B.C.C.A.); *Re Taylor and Taylor*, [1971] 1 O.R. 715, 16 D.L.R. (3d) 481 (H.C.J.); *Calder v. Cleland*, [1971] 1 O.R. 667, 16 D.L.R. (3d) 369 (C.A.); *Beard v. Beard*, [1973] 1 O.R. 165, 30 D.L.R. (3d) 513 (H.C.J.); *Fiedler v. Fiedler* (1975), 55 D.L.R. (3d) 397, [1975] 3 W.W.R. 681 (Alta. S.C. App. Div.); *Re Whiteley and Whiteley* (1974), 4 O.R. (2d) 393, 48 D.L.R. (3d) 161 (C.A.); *Madisso v. Madisso* (1975), 11 O.R. (2d) 441, 66 D.L.R. (3d) 385 (C.A.); *Hazell v. Hazell*, [1972] 1 W.L.R. 301 (C.A.), at p. 304 *per* Lord Denning, M.R. See also Pollock, "Matrimonial Property and Trusts: The Situation from Murdoch to Rathwell", 16 Alta. L. Rev. 357 (1978).

[86]*Trueman v. Trueman*, *supra*, footnote 85; *Fiedler v. Fiedler*, *supra*, footnote 85; *Nixon v. Nixon*, [1969] 3 All E.R. 1133; *Re Cummins*, [1971] 3 All E.R. 782; *Murdoch v. Murdoch*, *supra*, footnote 79.

[87]*Supra*, footnote 79.

[88](1978), 83 D.L.R. (3d) 289, [1978] 2 S.C.R. 436. See Waters, "Comment", 53 Can. Bar Rev. 366 (1975); Oosterhoff, "Remedial Constructive Trusts–Matrimonial Property Disputes — Justice and Equity or 'Palm-Tree' Justice?", 57 Can. Bar Rev. 356 (1979).

At the same time, his Lordship held that the resulting trust is not restricted to the matrimonial home, but can apply also to business and personal property in appropriate circumstances.

He went on to hold, however, that the doctrine of constructive trusts may apply to matrimonial property disputes where no common intention that the property is to be shared can be found. The constructive trust can be raised where the court finds a causal connection between the contribution of the non-owning spouse and the disputed asset. If the contribution enabled the spouse with title to acquire the property, the court will, as in this case, raise a constructive trust and will make an equitable distribution between the parties on the basis of their respective contributions. In this case the wife was entitled to a share, not just in the homestead, but in the entire farm (save for some property given to the husband after the separation) since her contribution was to the entire farm.

In reaching this conclusion Dickson, J., was faced squarely with two Supreme Court decisions which followed a more traditional analysis. In *Thompson v. Thompson*[89] the court had held that where there is no financial contribution by the non-owning spouse and no agreement between the spouses, he or she is not entitled to an interest in the matrimonial home. In *Murdoch v. Murdoch*[90] the majority followed the *Thompson* case and again emphasized the necessity of a financial contribution or a common intent. Moreover, they restricted the applicability of a resulting trust to the matrimonial home. Dickson, J., was able to distinguish these cases in that there was a financial contribution by Mrs. Rathwell. In addition, the applicability of the constructive trust doctrine was not argued before the courts in the earlier cases, whereas it was in the *Rathwell* case. Finally, he concluded that, if the *Murdoch* case stands for the proposition that a wife's labour cannot amount to a contribution in money's worth so that the resulting trust does not apply, and that a constructive trust is inapplicable to such cases, he would decline to follow it.

Ritchie, J., with whom Pigeon, J., concurred, held the wife to be entitled under a resulting trust and felt it to be unnecessary to consider the applicability of the doctrine of constructive trusts.

While Martland, J., with whom Judson, Beetz and de Grandpré, JJ., concurred, agreed that the wife was entitled, on the facts, to a beneficial interest, though not an equal interest, in the property on the basis of a resulting trust, he strongly dissented from the view that, in matrimonial property disputes, a spouse might be entitled under the doctrine of constructive trusts as a means of preventing an unjust enrichment. In his view such a presumption of joint assets should not be created through the exercise of judicial discretion, but should be the subject of legislation.

Nevertheless, the *Rathwell* case thus became the first Canadian case[91] of

---

[89](1960), 26 D.L.R. (2d) 1, [1961] S.C.R. 3.

[90](1973), 41 D.L.R. (3d) 367, [1975] 1 S.C.R. 423.

[91]For an English case in which the constructive trust was applied to a similar property dispute, see *Hussey v. Palmer*, [1972] 1 W.L.R. 1286 at pp. 1289-90, *per* Lord Denning, M.R.

the highest authority to recognize the constructive trust as a remedial or restitutionary mechanism and, as such, a third head of obligation distinct from contract or tort.[92]

The opinion of Dickson, J., in the *Rathwell* case and the dissent of Laskin, J., in *Murdoch v. Murdoch* on the applicability of the constructive trust as a remedial device to matrimonial property, were followed by the Supreme Court of Canada in *Pettkus v. Becker*.[93] The facts in this case were similar to those in the *Rathwell* case, but no evidence of a common intention was found by the trial judge, so that a resulting trust could not be raised, unless the court opted for an imputed agreement under the guise of an implied agreement. That is what the minority did in the case. That the majority did not do so, but applied the doctrine of constructive trusts instead, is to be applauded.[93a] The court affirmed the view in the case that the remedy is available whether the parties are legally married, or are simply living together as husband and wife as was the case in *Pettkus v. Becker*.

The unsatisfactory state of the law of matrimonial property was changed completely by family law reform legislation enacted in the last several years in virtually all of the Canadian common law jurisdictions. This legislation is discussed in detail in chapter 16.[94]

1210. TRUSTS FOR SALE

In this section the 19th century English development of the trust for sale and the socio-political reasons for it will not be examined since the trust for sale in that sense has little relevance to Canadian real property law.[1] Nor will its distinction from the settlement be discussed.[2] Rather, the effects of a trust for sale will be dealt with; that is, the equitable or deemed conversion that arises when a trust for sale is created.[3]

The trustee's duty to sell and convert arising under the rule in *Howe v. Earl of Dartmouth*[4] and related rules is a specialized subject that is beyond the scope of this work; the standard trusts treatises should be consulted for a consideration of these rules. It should be noted, however, that the Supreme Court of Canada has recently affirmed the English position that the rules, that

---

[92]See further on this point §1208, *supra*.

[93](1980), 117 D.L.R. (3d) 257, [1980] 2 S.C.R. 834. And see *Nuti v. Nuti* (1980), 28 O.R. (2d) 102, 108 D.L.R. (3d) 587 (H.C.J.), to the same effect, varied as to valuation of property only 32 O.R. (2d) 405n, 122 D.L.R. (3d) 384n (C.A.). But contrast *Brown v. Millett* (1979), 6 E.T.R. 88 (N.S.S.C.T.D.).

[93a]See to the same effect *Murray v. Roi* (1982), 36 O.R. (2d) 641, 134 D.L.R. (3d) 507 (H.C.J.), affd 41 O.R. (2d) 705, 147 D.L.R. (3d) 438 (C.A.).

[94]See §§1605-1605.11, *infra*.

§1210

[1]For this development see §221.9, *supra*.

[2]Settled estates are discussed in ch. 13.

[3]As to situations where land is converted and not entirely or effectively disposed of, thus raising a resulting trust, see §1209.3, *supra*.

[4](1802), 7 Ves. Jun. 137, 32 E.R. 56.

is, the duty to convert and apportion, do not apply to a residuary devise of real property.[5]

A trust for sale arises whenever a settlor or testator transfers property to trustees and directs them to sell the property and distribute it, or to invest it in other property. Such a trust is common in wills particularly where it is desirable to require the trustees to convert hazardous or non-productive assets into proper trust investments. The trust is sometimes coupled with a power to postpone so as to enable the trustees to sell at an opportune time and in Manitoba there is a statutory power to that effect.[6]

An imperative trust for sale must, however, be distinguished from a mere power of sale and it is sometimes difficult to ascertain from the trust instrument whether the maker intended a trust or a power. This is dealt with further below.

The doctrine of conversion is an application of the rule that "equity considers that as done which ought to have been done".[7] The principle thus is that money directed to be employed in the purchase of land and land directed to be sold and converted into money are considered to be the type of property into which they are directed to be converted. The direction may be given by will, contract, settlement, or otherwise. Moreover, the money may be actually paid or only covenanted to be paid, and the land may be actually conveyed or only agreed to be conveyed.[8] Land is not changed into money, however, if it is directed to be sold and the sale proceeds are directed to be reinvested in other land.[9]

The theoretical conversion of realty into personalty or personalty into realty, when directed by a will, takes place at the time of the death of the testator[10] and, when directed by deed, takes place at the time of delivery of the deed,[11] unless the deed indicates that the property is to remain in its existing state until a future event.[12] This rule as to time applies notwithstanding that the directions are to sell within a specified time,[13] or to sell whenever it appears

---

[5]*Lottman v. Stanford* (1980), 107 D.L.R. (3d) 28, [1980] 1 S.C.R. 1065. See Oosterhoff, "The Application of the Rule in Howe v. Earl of Dartmouth to Residual Real Property", 5 E.T.Q. 127 (1980).

[6]*Trustee Act*, R.S.M. 1970, c. T160, s. 35.

[7]Jekyll, M.R., in *Lechmere v. Earl of Carlisle* (1733), 3 P. Wms. 211 at p. 215, 24 E.R. 1033, affd Cases T. Talbot 80, 25 E.R. 673 *sub nom. Lechmere v. Lady Lechmere*; Lord Hardwicke, L.C., in *Guidot v. Guidot* (1745), 3 Atk. 254 at p. 256, 26 E.R. 948; Lord Thurlow, L.C., in *Hutcheon v. Mannington* (1791), 1 Ves. Jun. 366, 30 E.R. 388; Parker, J., in *Re Walker; MacIntosh-Walker v. Walker*, [1908] 2 Ch. 705 at p. 712.

[8]*Fletcher v. Ashburner* (1779), 1 Bro. C.C. 497, 28 E.R. 1259.

[9]*Pearson v. Lane* (1809), 17 Ves. Jun. 101, 34 E.R. 39; and see *Attorney-General v. Londesborough* (1904), 73 L.J.K.B. 503 at p. 510.

[10]*Hutcheon v. Mannington, supra,* footnote 7; *Attorney-General v. Hubbuck* (1884), 13 Q.B.D. 275 (C.A.).

[11]*Griffith v. Ricketts; Griffith v. Lunell* (1849), 7 Hare 299 at p. 311, 68 E.R. 122; *Clarke v. Franklin* (1858), 4 K. & J. 257 at p. 263, 70 E.R. 107.

[12]*Wheldale v. Partridge* (1803), 8 Ves. Jun. 227 at p. 236, 32 E.R. 341.

[13]*Pearce v. Gardner* (1852), 10 Hare 287, 68 E.R. 935, direction in will for sale with all convenient speed and within five years.

advantageous,[14] or to sell "as soon as the trustees shall see necessary for the benefit of the children",[15] or to sell "whenever it shall appear to their satisfaction that such sale shall be for the benefit of" the children,[16] or that the sale is postponed until the happening of a specified event.[17]

If the specified future event is contingent, however, the conversion does not take place until it happens. Thus, a testator devised and bequeathed the residue of his realty and personalty to trustees upon trust to call in accounts receivable and, if there should be insufficient to satisfy an annuity given to his wife, upon trust to sell realty and personalty and out of the proceeds and the rents of realty until it was sold, to pay the annuity; the rents were not sufficient to pay the annuity, but none of the realty was sold until after the death of the widow, at which time a considerable sum was due to her for arrears. It was held that the trust for sale arose immediately upon it being ascertained that the rents were insufficient to pay the annuity and the residue must be regarded as personalty.[18]

The effect of the doctrine of conversion is that (a) land which has, in equity, been theoretically converted into money is personalty for the purposes of the estate of the *cestui que trust*, so that, under his will, if not otherwise disposed of, it will pass to his residuary legatee[19] and not under a devise[20] and, upon his intestacy, it passes as personalty,[21] and (b) conversely, money which has, in equity, been theoretically converted into land, is such for the purposes of the estate of the *cestui que trust*, so that, under his will, it will pass under a general devise of his real estate or, if not otherwise disposed of, to his residuary devisee,[22] and will not pass under a bequest of personalty.[23]

Where the proceeds of sale of lands in Staffordshire under power of sale were to be invested in realty in England or Wales and they could be invested

[14]*Robinson v. Robinson* (1854), 19 Beav. 494, 52 E.R. 442.
[15]*Doughty v. Bull* (1725), 2 P. Wms. 320, 24 E.R. 748.
[16]*Re Raw; Morris v. Griffiths* (1884), 26 Ch. D. 601.
[17]*Tily v. Smith* (1884), 1 Coll. 434, 63 E.R. 488, namely, when children attain the age of 21 years, at which time the proceeds were to be divided between the widow and as many children as she might have at the death of the testator, this indicating that there was to be an absolute conversion in the event of the wife and any child surviving him; *Clarke v. Franklin, supra*, footnote 11, deed of settlement of land to the use of the settlor for life, remainder to use of trustees upon trust to sell and pay certain sums to named persons or to such of them as might be living at his death, it being held that, although the trust was not to arise until after his death, the property was to be regarded as personalty immediately upon the execution of the deed.
[18]*Ward v. Arch* (1846), 15 Sim. 389, 60 E.R. 670.
[19]*Gover v. Davis* (1860), 29 Beav. 222, 54 E.R. 612.
[20]*Elliott v. Fisher* (1842), 12 Sim. 505, 59 E.R. 1226.
[21]*Ashby v. Palmer* (1816), 1 Mer. 296, 35 E.R. 684; *Biggs v. Andrews* (1832), 5 Sim. 424, 58 E.R. 396, estates actually unsold thus considered as personalty; *Griffith v. Ricketts; Griffith v. Lunell, supra*, footnote 11.
[22]*Chandler v. Pocock* (1880), 15 Ch. D. 491, affd 16 Ch. D. 648 (C.A.); *Re Greaves' Settlement Trusts* (1883), 23 Ch. D. 313; *Re Duke of Cleveland's Settled Estates*, [1893] 3 Ch. 244 (C.A.).
[23]*Gillies v. Longlands* (1851), 4 De G. & Sm. 372, 64 E.R. 875.

anywhere in those countries, it was held that the money thus theoretically converted into realty could not pass under a devise of lands in Staffordshire, but passed to the residuary devisee.[24]

Where a husband deposited bonds with a trustee under an ante-nuptial settlement for the purpose of buying a house after the marriage, to be held by the husband and wife as joint tenants, but where no property was purchased with the funds, the bonds belong to the wife after her husband's death and do not form part of his estate.[25]

The doctrine of conversion does not apply, however, unless there is an imperative duty to convert. To convert real or personal property, as between real and personal representatives, from the state in which it is found at the death, the character of land or money must, by the trust or covenant, be imperatively and definitely affixed to it; if there is a mere option, there is no conversion in equity.[26] The doctrine does not apply where there is merely a power of sale in a will,[27] or a mere power to invest in realty.[28]

In *Re Richardson*,[29] M, by her will, gave certain real property to her trustees to permit her daughter, X, to use it until her marriage, subject to a right in her son, Y, to lodge therein until Y's death or marriage, whereupon the property was to be sold and the proceeds paid into a trust fund created out of the residue in the will. The trust fund was to be established by converting specified assets into cash and investing it in trust investments, with the income to be paid to M's brother, A. On A's death the fund was to be converted into cash and divided between X and Y. The trust fund was never established as the residue was insufficient. X and Y lived on the real property until X's death. X never married and by her will purported to leave her interest in the realty to Y who then claimed to be the absolute owner. The court held, however, that M gave X no devisable interest, that she contemplated a complete distribution on A's death and that there was thus no equitable conversion of the real property. In the circumstances there was an intestacy as to the realty on X's death.

It is sufficient if an imperative duty to convert, although not in express terms, is indicated by the whole will. Thus, where the testator gave his executors "full power" to sell houses and other estates and convert his funded property, and then to pay certain legacies, after which the whole of the property was to be divided among his twelve first cousins, it was held that the real estate should be regarded as converted.[30]

---

[24]*Re Duke of Cleveland's Settled Estates, supra,* footnote 22.

[25]*Re Merikallio,* [1970] 1 O.R. 244, 8 D.L.R. (3d) 142 (H.C.J.).

[26]*Wheldale v. Partridge* (1800), 5 Ves. Jun. 388, 31 E.R. 643.

[27]*Re Hotchkys; Freke v. Calmady* (1886), 32 Ch. D. 408 (C.A.); *Re Ibbitson's Estate* (1869), L.R. 7 Eq. 226; *McDonell v. McDonell* (1894), 24 O.R. 468 (Q.B.), at p. 571.

[28]*Stamper v. Millar* (1744), 3 Atk. 212, 26 E.R. 923, in a settlement; *De Beauvoir v. De Beauvoir* (1852), 3 H.L.C. 524, 10 E.R. 206, in a will; *Atwell v. Atwell* (1871), L.R. 13 Eq. 23, in a settlement; *Re Bird; Pitman v. Pitman,* [1892] 1 Ch. 279, in a will.

[29][1951] O.R. 130, [1951] 2 D.L.R. 162 (C.A.).

[30]*Burrell v. Baskerfield* (1849), 11 Beav. 525, 50 E.R. 920.

Again, if trustees appear to be given an option or power to invest money either in personalty or realty, but the limitations expressed are applicable only to realty, the money is treated as converted into realty.[31] Also, if there is only an express power to sell the realty, but the terms of the trust make it necessary that the power be exercised, a conversion is regarded as being effected.[32]

Conversion cannot be brought about, however, merely by words of a testator as to the character certain property shall have. When land is settled subject to a power of sale and the power is exercised, it is converted into personalty from the time of the sale, unless the proceeds are reconverted into land or are stamped with a trust for reinvestment in land. A trust to reinvest the proceeds in land, or government, or real securities, with a direction superadded that these, when purchased, shall be and enure and be made liable to the same uses, trusts, estates, limitations and provisos as the land originally settled, does not amount to a trust for reinvestment in land, at least when the limitations of the land originally settled are applicable to personalty as well as realty. There was nothing compulsory in the clause allowing an investment in land.[33]

Although the Legislature can by a simple enactment to that effect make personalty devolve and pass to a series of persons successively for the same interests as if it had been realty, an individual can only do so by the creation of an imperative trust for the conversion of the personalty into realty and for the settlement of that realty to uses which will secure the devolution or create the estates desired to be created.

A mere declaration that personalty shall devolve or pass to persons successively as realty is in itself inoperative, for the whole doctrine of conversion turns on the maxim that Equity considers to have been done what ought to have been done pursuant to the trust; and a mere declaration such as I have mentioned creates no

---

[31]*Cowley v. Hartstonge* (1813), 1 Dow. 361, 3 E.R. 729, power to trustees to lay out residue, after payment of legacies, either in the purchase of lands of inheritance or at interest as they might deem proper, and to pay the rents and profits to H for life and, after his death, to convey and assign the whole in successive estates in tail male; *Earlom v. Saunders* (1754), Amb. 241, 27 E.R. 161, testator devised land to his wife for life, remainder over and final remainder to W and P in fee; he then left money to be laid out in the purchase of land or any other security the trustees might think fit, to be settled as his land was devised; *De Beauvoir v. De Beauvoir, supra,* footnote 28, devises of estates in tail with power to trustees to lay out personal estates in purchase of freeholds to be settled in same manner.

[32]*Ralph v. Carrick* (1877), 5 Ch. D. 984, testator gave all of his property to trustees in trust for payment of his debts with full power to sell all or any of his estates or to lease them, directing that the surplus be invested to secure an annuity to his wife, it being held that the intent was that all should be converted and kept together for the purpose of paying the annuity; *Grieveson v. Kirsopp* (1838), 2 Keen 653, 48 E.R. 780, in which case a testator empowered his widow to sell all of his estates "and the money arising from such sale, together with my personal estate, she my said wife *shall* and may divide and proportion among my said children", it being held that this was a direction to sell and operated as a conversion of realty.

[33]Romilly, M.R., in *Atwell v. Atwell, supra,* footnote 28.

obligation as to dealing with the property one way or another. It is true that such a declaration, in cases where the construction of an instrument is doubtful, may help the Court to construe the instrument as creating an imperative trust for conversion, and this, I think, is more especially the case where the express limitations contained in the instrument are limitations appropriate only to real estate; but, except on the question of construction, such a declaraion as that to which I am referring, is, I think, according to the decisions, absolutely nugatory.[34]

Similarly, a testator devised his realty and personalty to trustees upon trust, after payment of debts and an annuity, for all of his sons who should attain age 21 and his daughters who should attain that age or marry and added,

I give to my said trustees a power of sale over all or any part of the real and personal estate hereinbefore devised and bequeathed to them, and I declare that my residuary real estate so bequeathed in trust aforesaid shall for the purposes of transmission be impressed with the quality of personal estate from the time of my decease.

Four children became entitled and, in an administration action against the trustees, a decree was made directing the sale of the residuary estate. J, a younger son, was then an infant and, on attaining age 21, obtained leave to attend the proceedings under the decree, but he died intestate before the decree for sale of the realty was carried out. It was held that the words in the will were not sufficient to effect a conversion of the testator's residuary realty into personalty as of the time of his death, but that the decree operated as a conversion from its date and that the share of J in residuary realty remaining unsold at the time of his death must be treated as personalty.[35]

When the beneficial interest in property which is subject to a trust for conversion is vested in a person absolutely, he is entitled to elect to take the property in its existing state without conversion and such an election by him terminates the theoretical conversion of the property and it is theoretically reconverted to its existing state.[36] It is not necessary that he expressly state that he so elects, it being sufficient that his acts show his intention to take the property as it is, and it is immaterial whether or not he knows that, without an election by him, there would be conversion.[37]

---

[34]Parker, J., in *Re Walker; Macintosh-Walker v. Walker*, [1908] 2 Ch. 705 at pp. 712-13, holding that a bequest of personalty upon trust for sale and to hold the net proceeds upon the trusts and in the manner upon and in which the same would be held and applicable if they had arisen from a sale of freeholds devised by the will in settlement under the *Settled Land Act*, 45 & 46 Vict., c. 38 (1882), was not an imperative trust and that a person who had become entitled to an estate tail in them had become entitled to the personalty bequeathed without executing a disentailing assurance.

[35]*Hyett v. Mekin* (1884), 25 Ch. D. 735.

[36]*Cookson v. Cookson* (1845), 12 Cl. & Fin. 121 at p. 146, 8 E.R. 1344; *Pearson v. Lane* (1809), 17 Ves. Jun. 101 at p. 104, 34 E.R. 39; *Crawford v. Lundy* (1876), 23 Gr. 244 at pp. 250-1.

[37]*Harcourt v. Seymour* (1851), 2 Sim. (N.S.) 12 at p. 46, 61 E.R. 244, in which case Lord Cranworth, V.C., held that there was a superfluity of evidence that a person intended to take money that was to be converted into land, in that he included it in his statements of personalty, he executed a deed in which the money was treated as payable to him and made a will similarly treating the money.

When the absolute beneficial interest in land that is to be converted into money vests in several persons, there is a similar right of election, but all must concur, else the trust for conversion continues.[38]

A person entitled to a vested remainder may elect to take the property unconverted and such election will take effect if the property is still unconverted when he becomes entitled to possession.[39]

Similarly, a person entitled to a contingent remainder in the proceeds of sale of realty may, pending the contingency, elect to take the land and such election will become operative upon the contingency happening before or upon his death.[40]

In order to elect, a person must be *sui juris* and hence an infant cannot elect to take money instead of land,[41] or land instead of money,[42] but the court will, if it is in his interest, make the election for him.[43] Similarly, a lunatic cannot elect,[44] but the court may elect for him,[45] although it is the rule, so far as possible, not to alter the character of his property.[46]

1211. INTERESTS OF THE PARTIES

In this section the respective estates of the trustee and beneficiary are discussed, including the vesting of trust property in the trustee.

1211.1 Estate of the Trustee

The estate of the trustee consists of the title to the trust property. It may be either legal or equitable depending upon the nature of the property.

The possession by a trustee of an estate conveys to him the legal burdens and invests him with the legal privileges of that estate.[1] He must pay the

---

[38]*Holloway v. Radcliffe* (1857), 23 Beav. 163, 53 E.R. 64; *Biggs v. Peacock* (1882), 22 Ch. D. 284 (C.A.); *Re Tweedie and Miles* (1884), 27 Ch. D. 315; *Re Douglas and Powell's Contract*, [1902] 2 Ch. 296 at p. 312.

[39]*Crabtree v. Bramble* (1747), 3 Atk. 680, 26 E.R. 1191, in which case a lady entitled in remainder, after a life tenancy, to the proceeds of conversion was said to be entitled to demand conversion during the life tenancy, but had instead made leases after becoming entitled to possession, such leases being held to be sufficient election to take the land.

[40]*Meek v. Devenish* (1877), 6 Ch. D. 566, in which case the remainderman resided upon the land until he died and devised it in his will.

[41]*Re Harrop's Estate* (1857), 3 Drewry 726, 61 E.R. 1080.

[42]*Van v. Barnett* (1812), 19 Ves. Jun. 102 at p. 109, 34 E.R. 456.

[43]*Robinson v. Robinson* (1854), 19 Beav. 494, 52 E.R. 442.

[44]*Re Wharton* (1854), 5 De G. M. & G. 33, 43 E.R. 781 (C.A.); *Re Jump*; *Galloway v. Hope*, [1903] 1 Ch. 129.

[45]See *Re Douglas and Powell's Contract*, *supra*, footnote 38.

[46]*Attorney-General v. Marquis of Ailesbury* (1887), 12 App. Cas. 672 (H.L.).

§1211.1
[1]*Burgess v. Wheate*; *Attorney-General v. Wheate* (1759), 1 Eden 177 at p. 251, 28 E.R. 652.

taxes and rates on the property[2] or, if it is leasehold property, he must pay the rents and perform the covenants.[3] If an absolute equitable estate is vested in trustees and the legal estate is vested in a bare trustee, they have the right to require the bare trustee to convey the legal estate to them,[4] this being the right that any equitable owner has.[5]

The trust property vests in the trustees when they are appointed and the property is transferred to them. In the case of a testamentary trust this arises only after the estate has been administered by the personal representatives.[6] At that time, a conveyance by them to the trustees is, therefore, required. If, as is usual, the personal representatives and the trustees are the same persons, the question arises whether such a conveyance, called an "assent", is still required. With respect to personal property it has always been held in England that an assent may be made informally and may be inferred from the circumstances.[7] Canadian cases are to the same effect.[8] In England, it has been held, however, that where real property is vested in an executor, a written assent is required to transfer it from him as executor to himself as trustee under section 36(4) of the *Administration of Estates Act, 1925*,[9] despite section 40 of the *Trustee Act, 1925*,[10] which provides that a deed appointing a new trustee, if it contains a declaration to that effect, vests the estate in the trustee without a conveyance being necessary. There appears to be no legislation in Canada similar to section 36(4) of the *Administration of Estates Act, 1925*, although there is legislation comparable to section 40 of the *Trustee Act, 1925*. However, in view of the fact that a deed is required to transfer real property from one person to another and that there is enabling legislation permitting one person to convey to himself (in another capacity),[11] it is at least arguable that such an assent is required when an executor becomes a trustee in Canada as well. It is not, in fact, in common use.

---

[2]*R. v. Sterry* (1840), 12 Ad. & E. 84 at p. 93, 113 E.R. 743; *R. v. Stapleton* (1863), 4 B. & S. 629, 122 E.R. 595.

[3]*Walters v. Northern Coal Mining Co.* (1855), 5 De G. M. & G. 629, 43 E.R. 1015 (C.A.); *White v. Hunt* (1870), L.R. 6 Ex. 30; *Wright v. Pitt* (1870), L.R. 12 Eq. 408; *Ramage v. Womack*, [1900] 1 Q.B. 116.

[4]*Angier v. Stannard* (1834), 3 My. & K. 566, 40 E.R. 216; *Poole v. Pass* (1839), 1 Beav. 600, 48 E.R. 1074.

[5]See § 1203.6, *supra*.

[6]*Baker v. Archer-Shee*, [1927] A.C. 844 (H.L.); *Com'r of Stamp Duties (Queensland) v. Livingston*, [1965] A.C. 694 (P.C.).

[7]*Attenborough v. Solomon*, [1913] A.C. 76 (H.L.), assent inferred from executors' passing of accounts and subsequent lapse of several years. And see *Re Ponder; Ponder v. Ponder*, [1921] 2 Ch. 59; *Harvell v. Foster*, [1954] 2 Q.B. 367 (C.A.); *Re Cockburn's Will Trusts; Cockburn v. Lewis*, [1957] Ch. 438.

[8]*Ewart v. Gordon* (1867), 13 Gr. 40 at p. 47; *Cumming v. Landed Banking and Loan Co.* (1893), 22 S.C.R. 246 at p. 250; *Dover v. Denne* (1902), 3 O.L.R. 664 (C.A.), at p. 689, per MacLennan, J.A.; *Re Baty*, [1959] O.R. 13 at p. 17, 16 D.L.R. (2d) 164 at p. 168 (C.A.).

[9]15 & 16 Geo. 5, c. 23.

[10]15 & 16 Geo. 5, c. 19.

[11]See, *e.g.*, *Conveyancing and Law of Property Act*, R.S.O. 1980, c. 90, ss. 3, 41.

Most of the Canadian Trustee Acts contain a provision similar to section 40 of the English *Trustee Act, 1925*,[12] and provide that where an instrument by which a new trustee is appointed contains a declaration that any property subject to the trust shall vest in the appointee, the declaration vests the property in him without any conveyance.[13] Certain property, namely, mortgages held by trustees, securities transferable only on the books of the corporation or in a manner prescribed by legislation[14] and, sometimes, leaseholds,[15] are excepted from the operation of the declaration. In the case of leaseholds, this is to prevent an inadvertent forfeiture by reason of the assignment. In the case of the other two types of property, the reason is that the trust is usually not disclosed on the deed or register, or a special form of transfer is prescribed, rendering a separate vesting necessary. In any case where there is no declaration or the assistance of the court is otherwise required, the court may make an order vesting the trust property in the new trustees.[16]

1211.2   Estate of the Cestui Que Trust

Equitable estates are dealt with upon the principle that equity follows the law,[1] meaning that equity treats the common law as laying the foundation of all jurisprudence, and it does not unnecessarily depart from legal principles.[2] "The law is clear, and courts of equity ought to follow it in their judgments concerning titles to equitable estates; otherwise great uncertainty and confusion would ensue."[3] Consequently, an equitable estate or interest is construed in the same way and devolves in the same manner as a corresponding legal estate or interest.[4]

A *cestui que trust* has the same power of alienation or disposition of his equitable estate as the owner of a legal estate has. Courts of equity have given the same power to a *cestui que trust* as to alienation of his estate as if it were

---

[12]*Supra*, footnote 10.

[13]*Trustee Act* (Alta.), s. 17; (Man.), s. 15; (N.W.T.), s. 14; (Ont.), s. 9; (Sask.), s. 21; (Yukon), s. 17; legislation in three other provinces is similar, but requires that the declaration be by deed: (B.C.), s. 29; (Nfld.), s. 13; (N.S.), s. 17.

[14]*Ibid*. Mortgages securing debentures are not so excepted in Manitoba: *Trustee Act* (Man.), s. 15(4)(*a*).

[15]*Trustee Act* (Man.), s. 15(4)(*b*).

[16]This is specifically provided for in the following statutes: *Trustee Act* (B.C.), s. 33; (P.E.I.), s. 8; (Man.), s. 16; (Nfld.), s. 35; (Ont.), s. 13; (Sask.), ss. 30, 32; (N.B.), ss. 15, 23. The Manitoba Act deems a declaration to be implied where the instrument does not contain one: *Trustee Act* (Man.), s. 15(1)(*b*).

§1211.2

[1]*Coape v. Arnold* (1855), 4 De G. M. & G. 574 at p. 585, 43 E.R. 631.

[2]*Per* Clarke, M.R., in *Burgess v. Wheate*; *Attorney-General v. Wheate* (1759), 1 Eden 177 at p. 195, 28 E.R. 652.

[3]*Per* Jekyll, M.R., in *Cowper v. Earl Cowper* (1734), 2 P. Wms. 720 at pp. 753-4, 24 E.R. 930.

[4]*Per* Jekyll, M.R., in *Banks v. Sutton* (1732), 2 P. Wms. 700 at p. 713, 24 E.R. 922;

an executed use.[5] The court has determined that equitable estates are to be held perfectly distinct and separate from legal estates. They are to be enjoyed in the same condition, entitled to all the same benefits of ownership, disposable, devisable and barrable, exactly as if they were estates executed in the party.[6]

The *cestui que trust* exercises his disposing rights over his estate by the same instruments and subject to the same formalities that are applicable to legal estates. Thus, it was held that the formalities required by the *Statute of Frauds*[7] apply to both legal and equitable estates, so that a testator could not revoke a trust, any more than he could devise, without such formalities.[8] At a time when three witnesses to a will were required and a *cestui que trust* had a power of appointment, it was held that a devise of the land by him must be attested in the same manner as a devise of the legal estate, so that a devise by him in a will having only two witnesses was void and did not operate as an appointment.[9]

Notice of a disposition need not be given to the trustee. A voluntary assignment by deed of the interest of a *cestui que trust* is good without notice to the trustees,[10] the only value of a notice being to secure priority against a subsequent encumbrancer who may give notice to the trustee.[11]

1211.3 Remedies for Breach of Trust

Where the trustee improperly appropriates trust property for himself or transfers it to another, the beneficiary has a personal action against the trustee for damages for breach of trust. He may also, however, be able to follow or trace the property into the hands of a third party, even where it has been converted into a different form. The beneficiary's personal action is beyond the scope of this book. However, his proprietary remedy is relevant in so far as it concerns real property.

There are, in fact, two proprietary remedies, namely, the right to follow property at law and the right to trace in equity. The common law remedy permits a person to follow property into its product, for the product of, or substitute for, the original thing follows the nature of the thing itself as long as it can be ascertained as such, and the right only ceases when the means of

---

Cowper v. Earl Cowper, supra, footnote 3, at p. 736; *Burgess v. Wheate, supra*, footnote 2, at p. 195.

[5]*Per* Lord Hardwicke, L.C., in *Hopkins v. Hopkins* (1738), 1 Atk. 581, 26 E.R. 365.

[6]*Per* Arden, M.R., in *Brydges v. Brydges; Philips v. Brydges* (1796), 3 Ves. Jun. 120 at p. 127, 30 E.R. 926.

[7]29 Car. 2, c. 3 (1677).

[8]*Per* Lord Hardwicke, L.C., in *Addlington v. Cann* (1744), 3 Atk. 141 at p. 151, 26 E.R. 885.

[9]Lord Macclesfield, L.C., in *Wagstaff v. Wagstaff* (1724), 2 P. Wms. 258, 24 E.R. 721; *Jones v. Clough* (1751), 2 Ves. Sen. 365, 28 E.R. 234.

[10]*Donaldson v. Donaldson* (1854), Kay 711, 69 E.R. 303, stock; *Re Way's Trusts* (1864), 2 De G. J. & S. 365, 46 E.R. 416, reversion.

[11]Romilly, M.R., in *Re Lowes' Settlement* (1861), 30 Beav. 95, 54 E.R. 825.

ascertainment fail.[1] As soon as the trust funds are mixed with others, the right to follow disappears against the funds and against any property into which they are converted. Furthermore, the beneficiary of an express trust cannot avail himself of the common law remedy as he has no title that is recognized at law, unless he joins the trustee as co-plaintiff. If he is a beneficiary under a constructive or resulting trust, however, and has a title at law, he will be able to follow his property.[2]

The equitable tracing remedy is more flexible and is available to trust beneficiaries and other persons under a fiduciary relationship. It permits a person to follow his property into a mixed fund or into property into which it has been converted. However, the remedy fails against a *bona fide* purchaser for value who takes without notice. As between *cestui que trust* and trustee and all parties claiming under the trustee, otherwise than by purchase for valuable consideration without notice, all property belonging to the trust, however much it may be changed or altered in its nature or character, and all the fruits of such property, whether in its original or in its altered state, continue to be subject to or affected by the trust, provided the property can in some manner be ascertained.[3] Consequently, if a person, gratuitously or for valuable consideration, acquires property or an interest in property which is subject to a trust of which he has actual or constructive notice, he becomes the trustee of it for the purposes of the trust.[4] Therefore, if trust property has been sold, rightfully or wrongfully, the *cestui que trust* is entitled to the proceeds of sale if he can identify them and there is no distinction between rightful and wrongful disposition of the property as regards the right of the beneficial owner to follow the proceeds.[5] If the proceeds have been invested in the purchase of other property, the *cestui que trust* is only entitled to that property or a charge on it for the amount of the trust money but, if the trustee mixed other money with the proceeds, the *cestui que trust* is entitled to a charge on the property for the trust money in priority to any claim by the trustee.[6]

As to what constitutes constructive notice, the settled test in all cases is, did the party against whom notice of some fact is asserted have before him such knowledge as ought to have put him on inquiry and, if he had acted with

---

§1211.3

[1]Lord Ellenborough in *Taylor v. Plumer* (1815), 3 M. & S. 562, 105 E.R. 721.

[2]Waters, p. 890.

[3]*Per* Turner, L.J., in *Pennell v. Deffell* (1853), 4 De G. M. & G. 372 at p. 388, 43 E.R. 551 (C.A.); *Re Hallett's Estate*; *Knatchbull v. Hallett* (1880), 13 Ch. D. 696 (C.A.), at p. 733; *Sinclair v. Brougham*, [1914] A.C. 398 (H.L.); *Re Diplock*; *Diplock v. Wintle*, [1948] Ch. 465 (C.A.), affd [1951] A.C. 251 *sub nom. Ministry of Health v. Simpson* (H.L.).

[4]*Boursot v. Savage* (1866), L.R. 2 Eq. 134; *Mumford v. Stohwasser* (1874), L.R. 18 Eq. 556.

[5]*Re Halletts' Estate*; *Knatchbull v. Hallett, supra*, footnote 3.

[6]*Ibid.*; *Carter v. Long* (1896), 26 S.C.R. 430; *Weitzen Land and Agricultural Co. v. Winter* (1914), 17 D.L.R. 750, 6 W.W.R. 964 (Sask. S.C.).

reasonable business prudence, would he have learned of the fact?[7] Constructive notice was defined by Lord Chelmsford, L.C., as the knowledge which the court imputes to a person upon a presumption of the existence of the knowledge so strong that it cannot be allowed to be rebutted, either from his knowing something which ought to have put him upon some further inquiry or from his wilfully abstaining from inquiry to avoid notice.[8]

"The defence of purchase for value without notice is a defence which must be pleaded and proved affirmatively. It is a defence in respect of which the onus in the strict sense is on the party claiming the benefit of it. He must affirmatively establish absence of notice."[9] When the fact that property is in trust appears on the face of a transfer the grantee will not acquire a clear title unless he makes inquiry to see that the trustee has the right to give it and so deprive the *cestui que trust* of the property.[10]

The rules for continued identifiability of the property are more lenient in tracing than they are in the common law remedy of following property. Nevertheless, there are limits. In *Re Diplock; Diplock v. Wintle*[11] the Court of Appeal suggested that if the property is used to pay debts, is spent on comestibles (that is, food), or is used to finance alterations to the third party's building, the right to trace is lost.

The main drawback of the tracing remedy is that it is only available where

---

[7]*St. John and Quebec R. Co. v. Bank of British North America* (1921), 67 D.L.R. 650 at p. 653, 62 S.C.R. 346 at p. 351, affg 52 D.L.R. 557, 47 N.B.R. 367 (S.C. App. Div.).

[8]*Espin v. Pemberton* (1859), 3 De G. & J. 547 at p. 554, 44 E.R. 1380, in which case he held that notice to a solicitor is actual notice to his client, saying

> I should therefore prefer calling the knowledge which a person has, either by himself or through his agent, actual knowledge; or if it is necessary to make a distinction between the knowledge which a person possesses himself, and that which is known to his agent, the latter might be called imputed knowledge;

and see also *Cookson v. Lee* (1853), 23 L.J. Ch. 473 (C.A.). In *Selangor United Rubber Estates Ltd. v. Cradock (No. 3)*, [1968] 1 W.L.R. 1555, Ungoed-Thomas, J., formulated a wider test for constructive notice, namely, "knowledge of circumstances which would indicate to a reasonable man that [a dishonest and fraudulent] design was being committed or would put him on inquiry ... whether it was being committed". The test was followed in *Karak Rubber Co. Ltd. v. Burden (No. 2)*, [1972] 1 W.L.R. 602, but was doubted by Stephens, J., Barwick, C.J., concurring, in *Consul Development Pty. Ltd. v. D.P.C. Estates Pty. Ltd.*, [1975] 49 A.L.J.R. (H.C. of Aust.). By contrast, in *Carl Zeiss Stiftung v. Herbert Smith & Co. (No. 2)*, [1969] 2 Ch. 276 (C.A.), Sachs, L.J., stated at p. 296, that a stranger who is aware only of a doubtful equity of "a disputed claim the validity of which he cannot properly assess", does not thereby become a constructive trustee.

[9]*Per* Duff, J., in *McDougall v. MacKay* (1922), 68 D.L.R. 245, 64 S.C.R. 1 at p. 7, affg 63 D.L.R. 247, [1921] 3 W.W.R. 833 (Sask. C.A.).

[10]*Sweeny v. Bank of Montreal* (1885), 12 S.C.R. 661, affd 12 App. Cas. 617 (P.C.); *Raphael v. McFarlane* (1890), 18 S.C.R. 183. But this is not so under s. 67 of the *Registry Act*, R.S.O. 1980, c. 445. See: *Re McKinley and McCullough* (1919), 46 O.L.R. 535 (S.C. App. Div.); *Elevated Construction Ltd. v. Nixon*, [1970] 1 O.R. 650, 9 D.L.R. (3d) 232 (H.C.J.); *Re Cohen and McClintock* (1978), 19 O.R. (2d) 623, 86 D.L.R. (3d) 16 (H.C.J.).

[11]*Supra*, footnote 3.

the original wrongful conversion was made by a fiduciary.[12] However, this restriction appears to be disregarded or circumvented in recent cases. In *Goodbody v. Bank of Montreal*[13] a person who acquired share warrants fraudulently, or with knowledge that they were stolen from the plaintiff, was held to be a constructive trustee. The plaintiff was entitled to trace the proceeds of sale into a bank account into which they were deposited. Similarly, in *B.C. Teachers' Credit Union v. Betterly*[14] it was held that the plaintiff could trace moneys stolen by an employee into a house purchased by him in the name of the defendant with whom he lived.[15]

Where a trustee mixes trust funds with his own, the beneficiary is entitled to the whole of the resulting fund or property bought with it, except to the extent that the trustee can prove what part belongs to him, the onus of proof being on the trustee.[16] The same result obtains where the mixed fund is transferred to a volunteer, or where two trust funds are commingled, except that as between the beneficiaries of such trusts the funds will be divided equally where their respective shares cannot be determined.[17] If a beneficiary can identify an asset as having originated from his moneys, however, he is entitled to it,[18] but if the funds of two sets of beneficiaries remain commingled in an active current account, the rule in *Clayton's Case*[19] applies, which presumes that moneys first paid into such an account are the first to be withdrawn.[20]

1212. POWERS, DUTIES AND LIABILITIES OF TRUSTEES

A discussion of the general powers, duties and liabilities of a trustee and what may or must be done in regard to the legal or equitable estate in particular circumstances is beyond the scope of this work. The sections following particularly refer to incidents of trust estates in realty.

1212.1 Trustee's Duty of Care

The law requires of a trustee no higher degree of diligence than a man of ordinary prudence would exercise in the management of his own private

---

[12]*Carter v. Long* (1896), 26 S.C.R. 430; *Re Diplock, supra*, footnote 3.

[13](1974), 4 O.R. (2d) 147, 47 D.L.R. (3d) 355 (H.C.J.).

[14](1975), 61 D.L.R. (3d) 755 (B.C.S.C.).

[15]See also *Chase Manhattan Bank NA v. Israel-British Bank (London) Ltd.*, [1979] 3 All E.R. 1025, annotated 6 E.T.R. 72.

[16]*Re Hallett's Estate; Knatchbull v. Hallett* (1880), 13 Ch. D. 696 (C.A.).

[17]*Re Diplock; Diplock v. Wintle*, [1948] Ch. 465 (C.A.), affd [1951] A.C. 251 (H.L.); *Sinclair v. Brougham*, [1914] A.C. 398 (H.L.).

[18]*Re Diplock, supra,* footnote 17.

[19](1816), 1 Mer. 572, 35 E.R. 781.

[20]*Bailey v. Jellett* (1884), 9 O.A.R. 187; *Re C.A. Macdonald & Co.* (1958), 17 D.L.R. (2d) 416, 26 W.W.R. 116 (Alta. S.C.).

affairs, having regard, nevertheless, to the fact that he is a trustee for others and is not acting for himself; but beyond this he is not bound to adopt further precautions.[1] This duty is of general application to all the trustee's functions, but it is particularly acute in making trust investments. Most provinces, however, include a list of authorized investments in their Trustee Acts which a trustee may not deviate from unless the trust instrument permits otherwise, and in practice, if the trustee invests trust funds in securities on this "legal list" he is treated as having met his duty of care and prudence. In many of the United States the legal list has been replaced by a "prudent man" statute which codifies the common law rule.[2] Such a statute was promulgated by the Conference of Commissioners on Uniformity of Legislation in Canada[3] and has been adopted by New Brunswick and Manitoba.[4]

Arising out of the trustee's duty of care is his duty to be impartial, or the duty to hold an even hand between the parties interested under the trust and to look to the interests of all beneficiaries and not of any particular beneficiary or class of beneficiaries,[5] for trustees are not appointed for the remaindermen alone in disregard of the rights of the life tenant, or for the life tenant in disregard of the interests of the remaindermen. Trustees must preserve an even hand between these two conflicting interests. The duty towards the remainder-man is to preserve the capital intact. The duty towards the tenant for life is to obtain as large a yield as is consistent with safety and the observance of the law under the instrument of trust as to the class of investment made; and, furthermore, so to adjust the investments that the life tenant will receive annually his due proportion.[6] Failure of the trustee to observe the even-hand rule amounts to breach of trust which may render the trustee liable to a beneficiary and possibly to his removal.[7]

A discussion of the rule in *Howe v. Earl of Dartmouth*[8] and related rules,

---

§1212.1

[1] Lord Blackburn in *Speight v. Gaunt* (1883), 9 App. Cas. 1 (H.L.), at p. 19; Cotton, L.J., and Lindley, L.J., in *Re Whiteley; Whiteley v. Learoyd* (1886), 33 Ch. D. 347 (C.A.), at p. 355 and Lord Watson on appeal 12 App. Cas. 727 at p. 733 *sub nom. Learoyd v. Whiteley* (H.L.); *Knox v. Mackinnon* (1888), 13 App. Cas. 753 (H.L.), at p. 768; *Rae v. Meek* (1889), 14 App. Cas. 558 (H.L.), at p. 569; *Eaton v. Buchanan*, [1911] A.C. 253 (H.L.); *Davies v. Nelson* (1927), 61 O.L.R. 457 at p. 463, [1928] 1 D.L.R. 254 at p. 257 (S.C. App. Div.); *Fales v. Canada Permanent Trust Co.; Wohlleben v. Canada Permanent Trust Co.* (1976), 70 D.L.R. (3d) 257, [1976] 6 W.W.R. 10 (S.C.C.). This principle was codified in the *Trustee Act* (Man.), s. 77(*a*), rep. and sub. 1982-83, c. 38, s. 5.

[2] See Oosterhoff, "Trustees' Powers of Investment", Study for Ontario Law Reform Com'n (Toronto, Ontario Law Reform Com'n, 1970).

[3] (1970), 52 Conf. Comm. Unif. Legis. p. 117, App. E. Since 1974 the Conference has been known as the Uniform Law Conference of Canada.

[4] *An Act to Amend the Trustees Act*, S.N.B. 1971, c. 73, now *Trustees Act*, R.S.N.B. 1973, c. T-15, Pt. II; *Trustee Act* (Man.), s. 70(2), rep. and sub. 1982-83, c. 38, s. 5.

[5] *Per* Turner, L.J., in *Re Tempest* (1866), L.R. 1 Ch. App. 485 at pp. 487-8; *Re Jones Trusts* (1910), 20 O.L.R. 457 (H.C.J.), at p. 463.

[6] *Per* Middleton, J.A., in *Re Armstrong* (1924), 55 O.L.R. 639 (H.C.), at p. 641.

[7] *Re Smith*, [1971] 1 O.R. 584, 16 D.L.R. (3d) 130 (H.C.J.), affd with variations [1971] 2 O.R. 541, 18 D.L.R. (3d) 405 (C.A.).

[8] (1802), 7 Ves. Jun. 137, 32 E.R. 56.

which require the trustee to convert wasting, future or reversionary assets into authorized securities and to apportion income and capital, and which are designed to implement the even-hand rule, is beyond the scope of this work. It should be noted, however, that the Supreme Court of Canada has recently affirmed the English position that the rules, that is, the duty to convert and apportion, do not apply to a residuary devise of real property.[9]

1212.2   Conflict of Duty and Interest

It is a principle of law to be applied strictly that no one having duties of a fiduciary character should be allowed to put his duties in conflict with his interest.[1] From the rule that he is not allowed to put himself in the position where his interest and duty conflict, it follows that a person in a fiduciary position is not allowed, unless otherwise expressly provided, to make a profit out of his trust.[2] Benefits acquired by him as owner of the property cannot be retained, but must be surrendered for the benefit of those beneficially interested.[3] It is a settled rule of equity that no one having duties of a fiduciary nature shall be allowed to enter into engagements in which he has or can have a personal interest conflicting, or which possibly may conflict, with the interests of those whom he is bound to protect.[4] The application of these rules arises in the purchase and sale of trust assets by the trustee as discussed below.

(a) Purchase of trust property

A consequence of the rule that a trustee may not permit his duty and interest to come into conflict is that a trustee for sale or with power to sell property cannot be both vendor and purchaser and buy it from himself,[5] except under the express authority of the trust instrument or a court order and the court will only approve the sale to trustees if it is clearly for the beneficiaries' benefit.[6] One of several trustees cannot buy from the others.[7] To purchase

---

[9]*Lottman v. Stanford* (1980), 107 D.L.R. (3d) 28, [1980] 1 S.C.R. 1065. See Oosterhoff, "The Application of the Rule in Howe v. Earl of Dartmouth to Residuary Real Property", 5 E.T.Q. 127 (1980).

§1212.2

[1]*Davis v. Kerr* (1890), 17 S.C.R. 235 at p. 246; *Gastonguay v. Savoie* (1899), 29 S.C.R. 613 at p. 614.

[2]*Per* Lord Herschell in *Bray v. Ford*, [1896] A.C. 44 (H.L.), at p. 51.

[3]*Per* Lord Cairns, in *Aberdeen Town Council v. Aberdeen University* (1877), 2 App. Cas. 544 (H.L.), at p. 549; *Sugden v. Crosland* (1856), 25 L.J. Ch. 563; and see the cases cited in §§1208 *et seq.*, *supra*, dealing with constructive trusts.

[4]*Per* Lord Cranworth, L.C., in *Aberdeen R. Co. v. Blaikie Bros.* (1854), 1 Macq. 461, 23 L.T. (O.S.). 315 (H.L.).

[5]*Re Bloye's Trust* (1849), 1 Mac. & G. 488, 41 E.R. 1354 (C.A.), affd 3 H.L.C. 607, 10 E.R. 239 *sub nom. Lewis v. Hillman; Denton v. Donner* (1856), 23 Beav. 285, 53 E.R. 112; *Dyson v. Lum* (1866), 14 L.T. 588, 14 W.R. 788.

[6]*Tennant v. Trenchard* (1869), L.R. 4 Ch. App. 537 at p. 547; *Re Mitchell* (1970), 12 D.L.R. (3d) 66, 1 N.S.R. (2d) 922 (S.C. App. Div.).

[7]*Wright v. Morgan*, [1926] A.C. 788 (P.C.), purchase arranged before retiring as trustee.

trust property he must be discharged from his trusteeship[8] and even then, he must show that the transaction is unimpeachable and that he did not take advantage of knowledge he acquired as trustee.[9]

He cannot sell trust property to himself jointly with others, or to a trustee for himself,[10] or to any person for resale to himself.[11] After contracting to sell trust property, he cannot, while the contract is executory (so that he can enforce it or rescind or alter it), repurchase the property for his own benefit, but only for the benefit of his principal,[12] nor can one of several trustees do so.[13] The fact that a trustee sold property in the hope of being able to repurchase it for himself at a future time and not upon such an arrangement or understanding, is not of itself sufficient ground for setting aside the sale if the price was not inadequate or the sale improper in other respects. An actual repurchase after some time and a final resale at a large profit is immaterial if the trustee's sale was at the market value at that time.[14]

The agent of a trustee stands in the same position as a trustee in regard to sale of trust property.[15] If trustees for sale sell to their solicitors and the sale is set aside, a mortgage of the property by the solicitor to a mortgagee who had constructive notice of the trust is also set aside,[16] but not where the mortgagee is a *bona fide* purchaser for value without notice.[17] A trustee cannot act as agent for a purchaser.[18] A trustee cannot purchase trust property by retiring from the trust for the purpose.[19] The rule against purchases by trustees is not confined to trusts for sale, but extends to all trustees where the conflict between duty and interest arises.[20]

The rule of equity which prohibits parties placed in a situation of trust or

---

[8]*Ex p. Lacey* (1802), 6 Ves. Jun. 625 at p. 627, 31 E.R. 1228; *Ex p. James* (1803), 8 Ves. Jun. 337 at p. 348, 32 E.R. 385; *Downes v. Grazebrook* (1817), 3 Mer. 200 at p. 208, 36 E.R. 77; *Re Boles and British Land Co.'s Contract*, [1902] 1 Ch. 244.

[9]*Ex p. Lacey, supra*, footnote 8, at pp. 626-7; *Taylor v. Davies* (1917), 39 O.L.R. 205 at p. 221, revd on other grounds 41 O.L.R. 403, 41 D.L.R. 510, affd 51 D.L.R. 75, [1920] A.C. 636.

[10]*Downes v. Grazebrook, supra*, footnote 8; *Robertson v. Norris* (1858), 1 Giff. 421, 65 E.R. 983; *Farrar v. Farrars, Ltd.* (1888), 40 Ch. D. 395 (C.A.), at p. 409.

[11]*Cook v. Collingridge* (1823), Jacob 607, 37 E.R. 979.

[12]*Per* Mellish, L.J., in *Parker v. McKenna* (1874), L.R. 10 Ch. App. 96; *Williams v. Scott*, [1900] A.C. 499 (P.C.).

[13]*Delves v. Gray*, [1902] 2 Ch. 606.

[14]*Re Postlethwaite; Postlethwaite v. Rickman* (1888), 60 L.T. 514, 5 T.L.R. 76 (C.A.); *Baker v. Peck* (1861), 4 L.T. 3 (C.A.).

[15]*Re Bloye's Trust, supra*, footnote 5; *Spring v. Pride* (1864), 4 De G. J. & S. 395, 46 E.R. 971 (C.A.); *Farrar v. Farrars, Ltd., supra*, footnote 10. *Re Follis* (1874), 6 P.R. 160 (Ont.).

[16]*Cookson v. Lee* (1853), 23 L.J. Ch. 473 (C.A.).

[17]*Parker v. Thomas* (1893), 25 N.S.R. 398 (S.C.); and see *Ricker v. Ricker* (1882), 7 O.A.R. 282.

[18]*Stahl v. Miller* (1918), 40 D.L.R. 388, 56 S.C.R. 312, revg 37 D.L.R. 514, [1917] 3 W.W.R. 901 (B.C.C.A.).

[19]*Spring v. Pride, supra*, footnote 15; *Re Canada Woollen Mills Ltd.* (1905), 9 O.L.R. 367 (C.A.).

[20]*Parkes v. White* (1805), 11 Ves. Jun. 209 at pp. 232 *et seq.*, 32 E.R. 1068.

confidence from purchasing trust property is not confined to a particular class of persons, such as trustees, guardians or solicitors, but applies universally to all who come within its principle, which is that no party can be permitted to purchase an interest where he has a duty to perform that is inconsistent with the character of purchaser.[21] The rule extends to a trustee who has had active duties which have ceased so that he becomes a bare trustee,[22] but does not extend to a trustee to preserve contingent remainders who has had no active duties and whose function is merely passive,[23] nor does it extend to a person who was named as a trustee, but who disclaimed the office or never acted.[24] The rule does extend to constructive trustees and trustees *de son tort*, however.[25]

If a purchase of trust property is made by a trustee for sale or with power to sell while he is trustee and without the consent of the *cestui que trust*, it is invalid and the latter is entitled either to confirm it, or to have it set aside and take back the property.[26] It is not necessary to show that the purchase was to the trustee's advantage.[27] In cases in which the trustee has resold the property at a profit to a purchaser for value without notice, he is trustee of the profit,[28] or for the difference between the price paid by the trustee and the actual value of the property.[29]

The rule against a purchase by the trustee is not absolute. It was held that the rule in equity which invalidates a sale made by a trustee to himself is one which admits of some qualification and, if it can be shown that the trustee has acted fairly and openly and with the concurrence of all parties having a primary interest, the court will not set aside the transaction.[30] So also, the

---

[21]*Greenlaw v. King* (1840), 3 Beav. 49, 49 E.R. 19; *Aberdeen R. Co. v. Blaikie Bros.* (1854), 1 Macq. 461, 23 L.T. (O.S.) 315 (H.L.); *Erlanger v. New Sombrero Phosphate Co.* (1878), 3 App. Cas. 1218 (H.L.).

[22]*Ex p. Bennett* (1805), 10 Ves. Jun. 381, 32 E.R. 893.

[23]Dictum of Kindersley, V.C., in *Pooley v. Quilter* (1858), 4 Drewry 184, 62 E.R. 71.

[24]*Stacey v. Elph* (1833), 1 My. & K. 195, 39 E.R. 655; *Mackintosh v. Barber* (1822), 1 Bing. 50, 130 E.R. 21; *Clark v. Clark* (1844), 9 App. Cas. 733 (P.C.).

[25]*Plowright v. Lambert* (1885), 52 L.T. 646.

[26]*Fox v. Mackreth; Pitt v. Mackreth* (1788), 2 Bro. C.C. 400, 29 E.R. 224, affd 2 Cox. 320, 30 E.R. 148, affd 4 Bro. P.C. 258, 2 E.R. 175 (H.L.); *Lord Hardwicke v. Vernon* (1799), 4 Ves. Jun. 411, 31 E.R. 209; *Ex p. Lacey* (1802), 6 Ves. Jun. 625, 31 E.R. 1228; *Ex p. James* (1803), 8 Ves. Jun. 337 at p. 348, 32 E.R. 385; *Ex p. Bennett*, *supra*, footnote 22, at pp. 388, 394; *Randall v. Errington* (1805), 10 Ves. Jun. 423, 32 E.R. 909; *Hamilton v. Wright* (1842), 9 Cl. & Fin. 111, 8 E.R. 357 (H.L.); *Re Mitchell* (1970), 12 D.L.R. (3d) 66, 1 N.S.R. (2d) 572 (S.C. App. Div.).

[27]*Ex p. James*, *supra*, footnote 26; *Ex p. Bennett*, *supra*, footnote 22.

[28]See *Fox v. Mackreth*, *supra*, footnote 26; *Whichcote v. Lawrence* (1798), 3 Ves. Jun. 740, 30 E.R. 1248; *Ex p. Reynolds* (1800), 5 Ves. Jun. 707, 31 E.R. 816; *Baker v. Carter* (1835), 1 Y. & C. Ex. 250 at p. 252, 160 E.R. 102.

[29]*Mackreth v. Fox* (1791), 4 Bro. P.C. 258, 2 E.R. 175 (H.L.); *Lord Hardwicke v. Vernon*, *supra*, footnote 26.

[30]*Dover v. Buck* (1865), 5 Giff. 57, 66 E.R. 921; and see further *Clarke v. Swaile* (1762), 2 Eden 134, 28 E.R. 847; *Re Douglas and Powell's Contract*, [1902] 2 Ch. 296 at p. 313; *Re Leslie*, [1972] 3 O.R. 297, 28 D.L.R. (3d) 139 (H.C.J.).

transaction was allowed where the *cestui que trust* had full information and managed the sale and settled particulars, including prices,[31] and where the *cestui que trust* urged the trustee to purchase.[32]

Thus, where an executor performed only minor functions as executor before resigning his office and where his knowledge of the trust assets was acquired before the deceased's death, his purchase was permitted.[33] Similarly, where a trustee purchased shares under a contractual pre-emptive right in circumstances where the trust itself was unable to purchase the shares, the purchase was allowed.[34]

(b) Purchase of property from beneficiary

There is no absolute rule against a trustee purchasing from his *cestui que trust*.[35] A trustee may buy from the *cestui que trust*, provided there is a distinct and clear contract, ascertained to be such after a zealous and scrupulous examination of all the circumstances, that the *cestui que trust* intended the trustee to buy and there is no fraud, no concealment, and no advantage taken by the trustee of information acquired by him in the character of trustee.[36]

> If, notwithstanding the form of the conveyance, the trustee (or any person claiming under him) seeks to justify the transaction as being really a purchase from the cestui que trusts, [sic], it is important to remember upon whom the onus of proof falls. It ought not to be assumed, in the absence of evidence to the contrary, that the transaction was a proper one, and that the cestui que trusts [sic] were informed of all necessary matters. The burthen of proof that the transaction was a righteous one rests upon the trustee, who is bound to produce clear affirmative proof that the parties were at arm's length; that the cestui que trusts [sic] had the fullest information upon all material facts; and that, having his information, they agreed to and adopted what was done.[37]

---

[31]*Coles v. Trecothick* (1804), 9 Ves. Jun. 234, 32 E.R. 592.

[32]*Morse v. Royal* (1806), 12 Ves. Jun. 355 at p. 375, 33 E.R. 134.

[33]*Holder v. Holder*, [1968] Ch. 353 (C.A.); and see *Hollinger v. Heichel*, [1941] 1 W.W.R. 97 (Alta. S.C.).

[34]*Crocker and Croquip Ltd. v. Tornroos* (1957), 7 D.L.R. (2d) 104, [1957] S.C.R. 151; see *contra Regal (Hastings), Ltd. v. Gulliver*, [1942] 1 All E.R. 378 (H.L.); and *Boardman v. Phipps*, [1966] 2 A.C. 46 (H.L.).

[35]Arden, M.R., in *Campbell v. Walker* (1800), 5 Ves. Jun. 678 at p. 681, 31 E.R. 801; Lord Eldon, L.C., in *Gibson v. Jeyes* (1801), 6 Ves. Jun. 266 at p. 271, 31 E.R. 1044; *Ex p. Lacey, supra*, footnote 26 at p. 626; *Parkes v. White* (1805), 11 Ves. Jun. 209 at p. 226, 32 E.R. 1068; *Morse v. Royal, supra*, footnote 32; *Sanderson v. Walker* (1807), 13 Ves. Jun. 601, 33 E.R. 419; Lord Cottenham, L.C., in *Knight v. Marjoribanks* (1849), 2 Mac. & G. 10 at p. 12, 42 E.R. 4; Romilly, M.R., in *Denton v. Donner* (1856), 23 Beav. 285 at p. 290, 53 E.R. 112; Field, J., in *Plowright v. Lambert* (1885), 52 L.T. 646 at p. 652; Lord Cairns, L.C., in *Thomson v. Eastwood* (1877), 2 App. Cas. 215 (H.L.), at p. 236.

[36]Per Lord Eldon, L.C., in *Coles v. Trecothick, supra*, footnote 31; and see *Dougan v. Macpherson*, [1902] A.C. 197 (H.L.), at pp. 200-1, 204 *et seq.*; *Crighton v. Roman*; *Roman v. Toronto General Trusts Corp.* (1960), 25 D.L.R. (2d) 609 at p. 618, [1960] S.C.R. 858 at p. 868, *per* Cartwright, J.; *Field v. Banfield*, [1933] O.W.N. 39 (H.C.J.).

[37]Per Sir Ford North delivering the opinion of the Privy Council in *Williams v. Scott*, [1900] A.C. 499 (P.C.), at p. 508.

Thus the trustee must give full value.[38] Moreover, it has been held that the *cestui que trust* must have independent advice,[39] but it has also been held that independent legal advice is not essential.[40] It has been said that the trustees must affirmatively establish that they fully and fairly disclosed every fact and circumstance within their knowledge which would or might affect the action of their *cestui que trust*. They must not leave it to the court to speculate how much was concealed and how much revealed. They must make it clear that they concealed nothing and revealed all, or the sale cannot be upheld.[41]

Subject to the same principles as govern all trustees in purchasing from a *cestui que trust*, a trustee for sale or with power to sell may purchase the beneficial interest of his *cestui que trust*.[42]

If a trustee acquires the entirety, the relation of trustee and *cestui que trust* ceases,[43] for in purchases by a trustee from his *cestui que trust* an act is done which, although open to inquiry, puts an end to the relationship between them. If the purchase stands, he is no longer a trustee, since the *cestui que trust* has permitted him to become the beneficial owner.[44]

A purchase by a trustee will not be set aside if there has been long delay in impeaching it, or if there has been a subsequent dealing by the *cestui que trust* with the trustee, denoting acquiescence in the transaction, as acquiescence may have the same effect as original agreement.[45]

When the trustee's purchase is set aside, the *cestui que trust* has two options.

---

[38]*Morse v. Royal, supra*, footnote 32, at p. 373; *Luff v. Lord* (1864), 34 Beav. 220 at pp. 231, 233, 55 E.R. 619; *Thomson v. Eastwood* (1877), 2 App. Cas. 215 (H.L.); *Plowright v. Lambert, supra*, footnote 35; *Williams v. Scott, supra*, footnote 37; *Dougan v. Macpherson, supra*, footnote 36.

[39]*Luff v. Lord, supra*, footnote 38; *Plowright v. Lambert, supra*, footnote 35.

[40]*Per* Kekewich, J., in *Readdy v. Pendergast* (1886), 55 L.T. 767 at p. 768, affd on terms 56 L.T. 790 (C.A.).

[41]*Per* Lennox, J., in *Taylor v. Davies* (1917), 39 O.L.R. 205 (H.C.), at p. 221, revd on other grounds 41 O.L.R. 403, 41 D.L.R. 510 (S.C. App. Div.), affd [1920] A.C. 636, 51 D.L.R. 75 (P.C.); and see generally *Hope v. Beard* (1860), 8 Gr. 380; *Johnston v. Johnston* (1872), 19 Gr. 133; *Simpson v. Corbett* (1883), 5 O.R. 377 (H.C.J.); *Re Iron Clay Brick Manufacturing Co.; Turner's Case* (1889), 19 O.R. 113 (H.C.J.); *Thompson v. Clarkson* (1891), 21 O.R. 421 (H.C.J.); *Morrison v. Watts* (1892), 19 O.A.R. 622; *Segsworth v. Anderson* (1895), 24 S.C.R. 699; *Chatham National Bank v. McKeen* (1895), 24 S.C.R. 348; *Tyrrell v. Tyrrell* (1918), 43 O.L.R. 272 (S.C. App. Div.).

[42]*Randall v. Errington* (1805), 10 Ves. Jun. 423 at p. 427, 32 E.R. 909. *Cf. Re Hutton; Re Flynn, Swift Canadian Co. Ltd. v. Bull*, [1926] 4 D.L.R. 1080, [1926] 3 W.W.R. 609 (Alta. S.C.).

[43]*Per* Lord Eldon, L.C., in *Gibson v. Jeyes* (1801), 6 Ves. Jun. 266 at pp. 271, 277, 31 E.R. 1044; *per* Lord Erskine, L.C., in *Morse v. Royal* (1806), 12 Ves. Jun. 355 at p. 373, 33 E.R. 134.

[44]*Per* Plumer, M.R., in *Chalmer v. Bradley* (1819), 1 Jac. & W. 51 at p. 68, 37 E.R. 294.

[45]*Randall v. Errington* (1805), 10 Ves. Jun. 423 at p. 427, 32 E.R. 909; *Gregory v. Gregory* (1815), G. Coop. 201 at p. 205, 35 E.R. 530, affd Jacob 631, 37 E.R. 989, eighteen years delay; *Roberts v. Tunstall* (1845), 4 Hare 257, 67 E.R. 645, seventeen years; *Re Worssam; Hemery v. Worssam* (1882), 51 L.J. Ch. 669, nine years; *Hollinger v. Heichel*, [1941] 1 W.W.R. 97 (Alta. S.C.).

If he wishes, the property will be directed to be reconveyed to him upon repayment by him of the purchase money with interest at four per cent and sums expended by the trustee in repairs and permanent improvements, the trustee, or any purchaser from him with notice of the trust, accounting for all rents and profits and paying an occupation rent if he has been in occupation.[46] A trustee guilty of fraud is not given an allowance for improvements, however.[47] Alternatively, at his option, he may require the property to be resold, in which case it is put up at the price at which the trustee purchased it, together with the value of repairs and improvements made by the trustee. If a higher sum is offered, it is sold at that figure but, if not, the trustee is held to his purchase.[48]

(c) Lease to trustee

As a general rule, a trustee is not permitted to take, alone or jointly with others, a lease of the trust property from himself or his co-trustees.[49] L and S were appointed by the court as trustees for the plaintiff. Later L obtained from the plaintiff a lease of the property to himself. Some years later, the plaintiff took proceedings to set the lease aside on the grounds of inadequacy of rent and want of proper advice by L when the lease was executed. The court granted the relief, giving to L the option of accepting a new lease on terms to be settled by the Master, which decree was affirmed by the full court on a rehearing.[50]

(d) Sale or loan of trustee's assets to trust

The rule which prohibits a conflict of duty and interest also strikes down sales by the trustee of his own assets to the trust and loans by him to the trust. Thus in *National Trust Co. Ltd. v. Osadchuk*,[51] where a trust company purchased mortgages with its own funds and later assigned them to a trust under its administration, it was held that a subsequent loss was to be borne by the trustee. This is not so, however, where it can be shown that the trust's own assets were used to purchase the property.[52] Similarly, a loan by a trustee to

---

[46]*York Buildings Co. v. Mackenzie* (1795), 8 Bro. P.C. 42 at p. 71. 3 E.R. 432; *Campbell v. Walker* (1800), 5 Ves. Jun. 678, 31 E.R. 801; *Ex p. James* (1803), 8 Ves. Jun. 337 at p. 351, 32 E.R. 385; *Ex p. Bennett* (1805), 10 Ves. Jun. 381 at pp. 400-1, 32 E.R. 893; *Smedley v. Varley* (1857), 23 Beav. 358 at p. 359, 53 E.R. 141; *Silkstone and Haigh Moor Coal Co. v. Edey*, [1900] 1 Ch. 167. Cf. *Daly v. Brown* (1907), 39 S.C.R. 122; *Atkinson v. Casserley* (1910), 22 O.L.R. 527 (C.A.). Presumably the rate of interest today would be substantially higher.

[47]*Mill v. Hill* (1852), 3 H.L.C. 828 at p. 869, 10 E.R. 330.

[48]*Lister v. Lister* (1802), 6 Ves. Jun. 631. 31 E.R. 1231; *Ex p. Lacey* (1802), 6 Ves. Jun. 625, 31 E.R. 1228; *Robinson v. Ridley* (1821), 6 Madd. 2, 56 E.R. 988.

[49]Per Lord Eldon, L.C., in *Re Dumbell; Ex p. Hughes; Ex p. Lyon* (1802), 6 Ves. Jun. 617 at p. 622, 31 E.R. 1223.

[50]*Seaton v. Lunney* (1879), 27 Gr. 169.

[51][1943] 1 D.L.R. 689. [1943] S.C.R. 89.

[52]*Re Brown*, [1944] 4 D.L.R. 419, [1944] 3 W.W.R. 401 (Man. C.A.).

the trust is usually prohibited.[53] However, it has been held that if the terms of the trust authorize the raising of money on the security of the trust property, one of several trustees may lend money on the security of a mortgage and exercise all of the powers of a mortgagee against the property.[54] A trustee may also lend money to a beneficiary upon the security of a mortgage of the equitable interest of the beneficiary in the trust property.[55]

A loan by a trust to the trustee is also prohibited.[56]

1213. CO-TRUSTEES

Where there are several trustees, except where the trust instrument provides otherwise, and except in charitable trusts where majority rule is permitted,[1] all must concur in a transaction affecting a trust estate in order to bind the estate and one another. As it was put by Jessel, M.R., in a case in which there were three trustees, there is no law which enables the majority of trustees to bind the minority; the only power to bind is the act of the three, and consequently the act of two, even if it could bind them by reason of delay or acquiescence, could not bind the trust estate.[2]

Where absolute discretion is given to trustees in the exercise of their power, the court will not compel them to exercise it but, if they propose to exercise it, the court will see that they do not exercise it improperly or unreasonably. A testator gave his two trustees power at their absolute discretion to sell realty, declaring that the proceeds should be applied at their discretion in the purchase of other realty, and gave them power at their absolute discretion to raise money by mortgage for the purchase of realty. In a suit for the execution of the trusts of the will, some proceeds of the sale of realty were paid into court. One trustee proposed to purchase a large estate, apply the money in court in part payment and raise the rest of the price by mortgage on the estate to be purchased. The other trustee refused to concur in the purchase. It was held that the court could not control the dissenting trustee in the exercise of his discretion in refusing to make the purchase and to raise money by mortgage for the purpose.[3]

---

[53]*Ferrier v. Reid* (1966), 55 W.W.R. 299 (B.C.S.C.); *Re Pick Estate* (1965), 52 W.W.R. 136 (Sask. Surr. Ct.), trust company prohibited from investing trust funds in its own guaranteed investment certificates.

[54]*Attorney-General v. Hardy* (1851), 1 Sim. (N.S.) 338, 61 E.R. 131; *Re Mason's Orphanage and London and North Western R. Co.*, [1896] 1 Ch. 54 at p. 60, affd *loc. cit.* p. 596 (C.A.).

[55]*Phipps v. Lovegrove*; *Prosser v. Phipps* (1872), L.R. 16 Eq. 80 at p. 88; *Newman v. Newman* (1885), 28 Ch. D. 674.

[56]*Re Lerner*, [1952] 4 D.L.R. 605, 6 W.W.R. (N.S.) 187 (Man. Q.B.).

§1213

[1]*Re Whiteley*; *Bishop of London v. Whiteley*, [1910] 1 Ch. 600.

[2]*Luke v. South Kensington Hotel Co.* (1879), 11 Ch. D. 121 (C.A.), at pp. 125-6, holding that the trust estate was not bound or a mortgage released by the act of the two.

[3]*Tempest v. Lord Camoys* (1882), 21 Ch. D. 571 (C.A.), but contrast *Klug v. Klug*, [1918] 2 Ch. 67.

Similarly, it was held that, when land is vested in three trustees to sell at their discretion, the *cestui que trust* is entitled to the best judgment of all three and to have that judgment manifested by their signatures on the contract of sale.[4] Again, where an agreement for the sale of land was made by one of two trustees named in a will, it was held that it was not binding on the other and could not be specifically enforced, regardless of the fact that the trustee who made the sale died, directing in his will that the agreement should be carried out.[5]

When two of four trustees made an agreement to lease the trust property to the plaintiff without the knowledge or consent of the others, who took only a passive interest in the management of the estate, it was held that the agreement did not bind the estate and specific performance of it was refused.[6]

Where a mortgage is made to all of the executors and trustees under a will, there is no power in any less than all of them, if living, to give a valid discharge of the mortgage unless some special power has been conferred upon them to do so but, where the will confers upon a majority of the executors power to discharge mortgages which they are empowered to take, there is no reason in law why a mortgage should not be so discharged.[7] However, it was held that a discharge of a mortgage made in 1899, signed by one of three executors of the deceased mortgagee, was valid under the statutes then in force in Ontario.[8] Also, it was held that a discharge executed by one of two executors of the mortgagee's estate is, when registered, a valid reconveyance of the land.[9] But if the mortgage is made to two or more executors, all of the executors must execute the discharge unless the will permits otherwise.[10]

All trustees must join in a receipt for money[11] and a receipt by one of several does not operate as a discharge of the debt,[12] although Lord Eldon, L.C., said that *prima facie* there is a distinction between executors and trustees, in that one executor can, and one trustee cannot, give a discharge.[13] Thus, where a firm of solicitors, employed by two trustees under a will to receive the proceeds of the testator's realty that had been taken over by a railway company, paid the money to one of the trustees without the receipt or authority of the other and the money was lost to the estate due to the insolvency and death of the trustee who received the money, it was held that the receipt of one trustee only, although also an executor, was not a sufficient discharge to the solicitors for the money which they had received by the authority of the two and that

---

[4]*Gibb v. McMahon* (1905), 9 O.L.R. 522 (C.A.), affd 37 S.C.R. 362.
[5]*Chisholm v. Chisholm* (1915), 24 D.L.R. 679, 49 N.S.R. 174 (S.C.).
[6]*McKelvey v. Rourke* (1868), 15 Gr. 380.
[7]*Re Spellman and Litovitz* (1918), 44 O.L.R. 30 (H.C.).
[8]*Re Stair and Yolles* (1925), 57 O.L.R. 338, [1925] 3 D.L.R. 1201 (S.C.); *Ex p. Johnson* (1875), 6 P.R. (Ont.) 225.
[9]*Re A. and B.* (1927), 60 O.L.R. 647, [1927] 3 D.L.R. 1070 (S.C.).
[10]*Re Spellman and Litovitz, supra*, footnote 7.
[11]*Lee v. Sankey* (1872), L.R. 15 Eq. 204.
[12]*Hall v. Franck* (1849), 11 Beav. 519, 50 E.R. 918.
[13]*Walker v. Symonds* (1818), 3 Swans. 1, 36 E.R. 751.

they were personally liable to make good the loss which had resulted to the estate from such improper payment.[14] In accordance with the principle of uniformity, it was held that devisees upon trust for sale of real property must unite in receipts for the sale proceeds unless the will provides otherwise and that the case was not affected by the fact that the property was charged with debts and the power of sale was to them by name; and that, where a mortgage was taken and the mortgagees were described as executors and devisees in trust, payments to one only were not thereby authorized.[15]

The theory of every trust is that the trustees shall not allow the trust moneys to get into the hands of any one of them, but that all shall exercise control over them. If by their acts they enable one of themselves to receive the moneys, they are liable for the receipt of them just as much as if they all received them, because they enabled the one trustee to do that which, but for their special authority, he would not have been enabled to do.[16] Where there are two trustees and one of them places a fund so that it is under the sole control of the other, if the money is misapplied by that other, both are equally liable; the object of having two trustees is to double the control over trust properties and, when one trustee thinks fit to give the other the sole power of dealing with the trust property, he defeats that object and becomes himself responsible.[17]

It is not uncommon to hear one of several trustees spoken of as the acting trustee, but the court knows no such distinction. All who accept the trust are, in the eye of the law, active trustees. Great mistakes, and of very serious consequences, often occur from a trustee assuming that he may safely remain passive and leave the management of the trust estate to a co-trustee. A trustee can no more confide the management of a trust fund to a co-trustee than to a stranger.[18]

Where one or more of several trustees acts or act in getting in and dealing with trust funds, an inactive trustee is accountable, therefore, equally with the others if, having the means of knowledge by the exercise of ordinary diligence, he stands by and permits a breach of the trust to go on. Thus, in *McCarter v. McCarter*[19] three executors sold real estate of the testator; one of them who was entitled to the annual income of the sale proceeds took the most active part in the management of the estate because the others lived at a distance. He employed a solicitor who received several sums out of the sale proceeds some years apart and two years later absconded, causing a loss to

---

[14]*Lee v. Sankey, supra*, footnote 11.

[15]*Ewart v. Snyder* (1867), 13 Gr. 55.

[16]*Per* Kay, J., in *Re Flower (C.) M.P. and Metropolitan Board of Works; Re Flower (M.) and Same* (1884), 27 Ch. D. 592.

[17]*Per* Fry, J., in *Rodbard v. Cooke* (1877), 36 L.T. 504, 25 W.R. 555.

[18]*Per* Spragge, C., in *Mickleburgh v. Parker* (1870), 17 Gr. 503 at pp. 506-7. See also *Fales v. Canada Permanent Trust Co.; Wohlleben v. Canada Permanent Trust Co.* (1976), 70 D.L.R. (3d) 257, [1977] 2 S.C.R. 302; Waters, "Note", 55 Can. Bar Rev. 342 (1977); 4 Est. & Tr. Q. 134; *MacDonald v. Hauer* (1976), 72 D.L.R. (3d) 110, [1977] 1 W.W.R. 51 (Sask. C.A.); Waters, "Note", 4 E. & T. Q. 12 (1977).

[19](1884), 7 O.R. 243 (H.C.J.), at pp. 248-9.

the estate of nearly $2,000. The other executors knew that these sums were in his hands and, notwithstanding that the will provided that each of the executors should be responsible for his or her acts only and not responsible for any loss unless it arose through his or her own wilful neglect or default, it was held that all three executors were equally liable and must make good the loss to the estate.[20]

A testator empowered his executors to sell, if necessary, part of his land to pay debts and encumbrances against his estate and all of them in some degree acted as executors or trustees but, by tacit consent, one of them took the active management of the estate and received the moneys, including the proceeds of the sale which he misappropriated. It was held that an executrix, who had joined in the deed but did not receive any of the purchase money or know that her co-trustee had a balance after paying debts and encumbrances and was misapplying it, was not responsible to the estate for the misappropriation in all the circumstances and that even if she were liable for the principal misappropriated, she was not liable for the interest on it as the principal never came into her hands.[21]

Since all trustees must concur in the exercise of powers conferred on them with reference to the trust estate, an acknowledgment by one of two executors and devisees of real estate, against the wishes of the other, that more than six years' interest was due under a mortgage made by the testator, could not be treated as the valid act of the two and was not a good acknowledgment.[22] Similarly, it was held that an acknowledgment by one of two trustees will not prevent the *Statute of Limitations*[23] from running.[24] On the other hand, a notice of intention to renew a lease when given to one of two trustees, was held to be sufficiently given.[25]

Notwithstanding the general rule that trustees must act together, it appears to be established that, in regard to the exercise of a discretionary power, the act of one trustee may be approved and sanctioned by another. A testator directed in his will that it should be lawful for the trustees, if they considered it desirable to do so, to purchase out of a certain share of the trust funds an annuity in the name and for the benefit of A. Payments to A were made instead by the acting trustee, which A applied to his own purposes. Lord Romilly, M.R., said:

> I had some doubts at first whether, as the discretion was to be exercised by the two trustees and one only had acted, the discretion had been properly exercised;

---

[20]As to improvident investment in real estate through the activity of one trustee, see *Larkin v. Armstrong* (1862), 9 Gr. 390.

[21]*Re Crowter; Crowter v. Hinman* (1885), 10 O.R. 159 distinguishing *McCarter v. McCarter, supra,* footnote 19; *Rodbard v. Cooke, supra,* footnote 17, on the ground that, in those cases, the passive trustees deliberately, or with more knowledge, entered into or concurred with action of the active trustee.

[22]*Astbury v. Astbury,* [1898] 2 Ch. 111.

[23]3 & 4 Will. 5, c. 27 (1833).

[24]*Richardson v. Younge* (1871), L.R. 6 Ch. App. 478.

[25]*Nicholson v. Smith* (1882), 22 Ch. D. 640.

but I have come to the conclusion that as the other trustee approved and sanctioned what was done by the one who made the payments, no breach of trust was committed.[26]

It has been said, however, that such sanction must be strictly proved.[27]

In *Davis v. Lewis*[28] Wilson, C.J., said that, if one trustee refuses to act or is incapable of acting, the other trustee cannot proceed alone and that, in such cases, the administration devolves upon the court. The several Trustee Acts contain provisions for the removal of trustees and the Privy Council has held that all courts of equity have jurisdiction to remove trustees and substitute others, not only in cases of misconduct, but whenever it appears that the continuance of the trustees could prevent the trusts from being properly executed, the main guide to the court being the welfare of the beneficiaries. No more definite rule is laid down because the matter is so essentially dependent on details often of great nicety.[29] In cases of refusal to enforce proper mortgage remedies, Jessel, M.R., stated that, if some trustees should decline to foreclose or to agree to any other remedy, it might be a reason for removing them from office.[30]

1214. REVOCATION OF TRUST

There is a wealth of decisions that a lawful express trust which is completely constituted and does not contain a power of revocation is generally binding and cannot be revoked, whether it was declared for valuable consideration or was voluntary.[1] This principle holds even though the beneficiary has no notice

---

[26]*Messeena v. Carr* (1870), L.R. 9 Eq. 260.

[27]*Lee v. Sankey* (1872), L.R. 15 Eq. 204; and *Davis v. Lewis* (1885), 8 O.R. 1 (H.C.J.); which held that a particular lease made by one of several trustees was not binding on the co-trustees unless they could be shown to have agreed to it. As to control by the court of trustees' discretionary powers, see generally Cullity, "Judicial Control of Trustees' Discretions", 25 U. of T. L.J. 99 (1975); Sheard, "Limitations on Discretions given to an Executor or Trustee", 44 Can. Bar Rev. 660 (1966).

[28]*Supra*, footnote 27, at p. 16.

[29]*Letterstedt v. Broers* (1884), 9 App. Cas. 371 (P.C.), at pp. 386-7.

[30]*Luke v. South Kensington Hotel Co.* (1879), 11 Ch. D. 121 (C.A.).

§1214

[1]See *Kekewich v. Manning* (1851), 1 De G. M. & G. 176, 42 E.R. 519 (C.A.); Turner, V.C., in *Smith v. Hurst* (1852), 10 Hare 30 at p. 47, 68 E.R. 826; Romilly, M.R., in *Bridge v. Bridge* (1852), 16 Beav. 315 at pp. 321-2, 51 E.R. 800; Cranworth, L.C., in *Jones v. Lock* (1865), L.R. 1 Ch. App. 25 at p. 28; Cotton, L.J., in *Re Flavell*; *Murray v. Flavell* (1883), 25 Ch. D. 89 (C.A.), at pp. 102-3; *Re B.*; *Canada Trust Co. v. Gardiner* (1928), 33 O.W.N. 217 at p. 219, [1928] 1 D.L.R. 501 at p. 504 (S.C.), and see also the following cases: *Dodgson v. Dodgson* (1930), 37 O.W.N. 346 (H.C.), affd 39 O.W.N. 396 (S.C. App. Div.); *Toronto General Trusts Corp. v. Keyes* (1907), 15 O.L.R. 30 (H.C.J.); *Re Cummer Marriage Settlement* (1911), 2 O.W.N. 1486 (H.C.J.); *Horne v. Huston and Merchants Bank of Canada* (1919), 16 O.W.N. 173 (H.C.), affd 17 O.W.N. 2 (S.C. App. Div.); *Roy v. Investors Trust Co.* (1967), 60 W.W.R. 630 (Man. Q.B.).

of the trust and has neither affirmed nor repudiated it.[2]

The list of cases referred to deal mainly with trusts of personal property but the principle is the same for real property and is clearly stated by Lord Langdale, M.R., as being that a declaration of trust is considered in a court of equity as equivalent to the transfer of a legal interest in a court of law, and, if the transaction by which the trust is created is complete, it will not be disturbed for want of consideration.[3] Consequently, where real estate was granted by a voluntary settlement to and to the use of a trustee upon certain trusts, but the settlor did not reserve a power of revocation by the settlor and, a year later, the trustee executed a deed of disclaimer and the settlor also purported to put an end to the settlement, it was held that the settlement was not thereby rendered inoperative but that the trust was imposed on the settlor to whom, by operation of law, the trust had reverted.[4]

Again, an owner of land, "in consideration of natural love and affection and of one dollar", conveyed it to the defendants in fee simple, subject to a life estate in his own favour and to payment by the defendants of certain sums to the plaintiffs, the deed being voluntary as to them. The deed was executed by the grantor and the defendants who therein covenanted to make the payments. Seven months later, the grantor conveyed the same land to the defendants in fee simple for their own use absolutely, free from all encumbrances, but subject to a life estate to him. It was held that an irrevocable trust in favour of the plaintiffs had been created by the first deed, that it was enforceable by them and that the trust was not affected or released by the second deed.[5] When property is held in trust merely for the benefit of the settlor, however, he may revoke the trust at any time and require the trustee to reconvey it to him.[6]

Where the trust is for the benefit of the settlor's creditors generally, however (as opposed to specific, named, creditors), the trust remains revocable by the settlor until the trust is communicated to the creditors. Equity regards the supposed beneficiaries, that is, the creditors, as not having acquired an equitable interest. That interest remains in the debtor, the benefit to the debtor being that his debts are paid.[7] Trusts for specific creditors are irrevocable in the absence of a power of revocation and trusts for creditors generally become irrevocable when the existence of the trust is communicated to the creditors, when they join in the deed, or where they forbear to sue in reliance on the deed of trust.

---

[2]*Purdom v. Northern Life Assurance Co. of Canada* (1927), 63 O.L.R. 12, [1928] 4 D.L.R. 679 (S.C. App. Div.), affd [1930] 1 D.L.R. 1003, [1930] S.C.R. 119, *sub nom. Fidelity Trust Co. v. Purdom.*

[3]*Collinson v. Pattrick* (1838), 2 Keen 123, 48 E.R. 575.

[4]*Mallott v. Wilson*, [1903] 2 Ch. 494.

[5]*Edmison v. Couch* (1899), 26 O.A.R. 537.

[6]*Poirier v. Brulé* (1891), 20 S.C.R. 97 at p. 102; *Re Campbell Trusts* (1919), 17 O.W.N. 23 (H.C.).

[7]*Bill v. Cureton* (1835), 2 My. & K. 503, 39 E.R. 1036; *Industrial Incomes Ltd. v. Maralta Oil Co. Ltd.* (1968), 69 D.L.R. (2d) 348, [1968] S.C.R. 822.

1215. TERMINATION OF TRUST

If a person devises his estate to trustees to do something for another and that purpose is at an end, the estate ceases.[1] When a trust has terminated, those entitled to the trust property can require the trustee to convey the trust property at their expense to them, or at their direction, provided that they clearly show to the trustee that the trust has terminated.[2] If he trustee refuses to convey after adequate proof of the facts, he may be ordered to pay the costs of all unnecessary proceedings.[3] The necessity that the trustee convey at the direction of the beneficiary is due to his having become a bare trustee.[4]

Moreover, under the rule in *Saunders v. Vautier*,[5] a sole beneficiary who is *sui juris* and who is alone entitled to the entire beneficial interest, may terminate a trust and demand that the trust property be transferred to him. The rule applies to all beneficiaries under a trust, whether they are interested concurrently or successively, and whether their interests are vested or contingent, provided that they are among them solely entitled to the entire interest and agree among themselves to a division of the property.[6] Moreover, the rule applies to prevent an accumulation where it is in favour of capacitated beneficiaries who are solely entitled to the trust moneys[7] and it applies to charities as well where the gift is given to the charity absolutely but payment is postponed. It does not, however, apply so as to enable a charity to terminate a trust where the gift is of the annual income and there is no specific gift of the capital.[8]

The rule also applies where the beneficiaries have a general power of appointment enabling them to appoint the entire fund to themselves in their lifetime,[9] or on their death.[10]

The fact that the trustees have been given a discretion to appoint the trust property among the beneficiaries will not oust the operation of the rule, unless they have the discretion to withhold payment, so that there is a gift over in default of appointment.[11]

----

§1215

[1]*Per* Bayley, J., in *Morrant v. Gough* (1827), 7 B. & C. 206, 108 E.R. 700.

[2]*Willis v. Hiscox* (1839), 4 My. & Cr. 197, 41 E.R. 78; *Holford v. Phipps* (1841), 3 Beav. 434, 49 E.R. 170.

[3]*Jones v. Lewis* (1786), 1 Cox. 199, 29 E.R. 1127; *Holford v. Phipps, supra*; *Willis v. Hiscox, supra*; *Thorby v. Yeats* (1842), 1 Y. & C.C.C. 438, 62 E.R. 960.

[4]See §1203.6, *supra*.

[5](1841), 4 Beav. 115, 49 E.R. 282, affd 1 Cr. & Ph. 240, 41 E.R. 482.

[6]*Re McCrossan* (1961), 28 D.L.R. (2d) 461, 36 W.W.R. 209 (B.C.S.C.); *Re Smith*; *Public Trustee v. Aspinall*, [1928] 1 Ch. 915.

[7]*Saunders v. Vautier, supra*, footnote 5; *Wharton v. Masterman*, [1895] A.C. 186 (H.L.).

[8]*Halifax School for Blind v. Chipman*, [1937] 3 D.L.R. 9, [1937] S.C.R. 196.

[9]*Re Campbell-Renton & Cayley*, [1960] O.R. 550, 25 D.L.R. (2d) 512 (H.C.J.).

[10]*Re Johnston* (1964), 48 D.L.R. (2d) 573 (B.C.S.C.); *Re Canada Permanent Trust Co. and Bell* (1982), 131 D.L.R. (3d) 501, 10 E.T.R. 276 (N.S.S.C.T.D.).

[11]*Re Smith, supra*, footnote 6; *Re Johnston, supra*, footnote 10.

If the beneficiary's interest is contingent, he has no right to terminate the trust.[11a]

The rule has been abolished in Alberta and Manitoba and the court is given power to determine whether the trust should be terminated or varied under the variation of trusts provisions in the *Trustee Act*,[12] having regard to the intent of the donor and the interest of the donee.[13]

1216. VARIATION OF TRUST

Variation of trusts legislation in Canada, which is based on the English *Variation of Trusts Act, 1958*,[1] became necessary because of changed tax-planning priorities and because of limitations on the court's inherent power to vary trusts described by the House of Lords in *Chapman v. Chapman*.[2] Those limitations effectively prevented trust variations sought on behalf of incapacitated beneficiaries who could not take advantage of the right to terminate a trust under the rule in *Saunders v. Vautier*.[3]

The court has an inherent jurisdiction to vary trusts in four cases, *viz.*, under the conversion, compromise, maintenance and emergency powers.

Under the conversion power the court may change an infant's real property interest under a trust into personalty and vice versa, if it is shown to be for his benefit. The emergency or salvage jurisdiction permits the court to vary a trust to preserve the trust property where an emergency arises which was not foreseen by the settlor and not provided for by him, and which threatens the existence of the trust. Under its maintenance jurisdiction the court can direct that income, which the settlor has directed to be accumulated, shall be used for the benefit of beneficiaries who are in need, but who are not immediately entitled to it, whether because of the accumulation, or because their interests are contingent.[4]

The compromise jurisdiction permits the court to approve compromise settlements on behalf of infants and unborn beneficiaries where there is a dispute as to the quantum of their respective interests. In *Chapman v. Chapman*,[5] the House of Lords held, however, that unless there is a genuine

---

[11a]*Re Salterio* (1981), 130 D.L.R. (3d) 341, 14 Sask. R. 18 *sub nom. Little v. Salterio Estate* (C.A.).

[12](Alta.), ss. 42-43; (Man.), s. 61 rep. and sub. S.M. 1982-83, c. 38, s. 4.

[13]*Statute Law Amendment Act*, S.A. 1973, c. 13, s. 12.

§1216

[1]6 & 7 Eliz. 2, c. 53.

[2][1954] A.C. 429 (H.L.).

[3](1841), 4 Beav. 115, 49 E.R. 282, affd 1 Cr. & Ph. 240, 41 E.R. 482. See §1215, *supra*. As to the history of variation of trusts legislation, see Waters, pp. 899-904; and see generally McClean, "Variation of Trusts in England and Canada", 43 Can. Bar Rev. 181 (1965); Leal, "The Ontario Variation of Trusts Act, 1959" (1960), 13 U. of T. L.J. 284; Hull, "Mobility and Flexibility of Trusts under the Variation of Trusts Act", 16 Chitty's L.J. 88 (1968).

[4]See, *e.g., Re McCallum*, [1956] O.W.N. 321, 2 D.L.R. (2d) 618 (S.C.).

[5]*Supra*, footnote 2.

dispute or doubt, the court cannot vary the trust even though it would benefit the beneficiaries. In that case it undoubtedly would have benefited them since the proposed variation would have prevented the imposition of estate duty on the death of the testator, but as there was no dispute about the interests of the beneficiaries the court was powerless to intervene.

The several provincial statutes respecting variation of trusts[6] are very similar in language. The legislation permits the court, on behalf of infants and other incapacitated, unascertained or unborn persons, and persons who may become entitled to an interest in the trust on the happening of a future event or by reason of a discretionary power on the failure of an existing interest, to amend the trust, by approving any arrangement varying or revoking the trust or enlarging the trustees' administrative powers. However, the court may only do so if the variation appears to be for the benefit of those persons. The consent of capacitated beneficiaries is not required, but is invariably obtained.

The important criterion of the legislation is that it must benefit the persons on whose behalf the application is made, unless they are persons who may become entitled to an interest by reason of a discretionary power. However, in addition, the court will have regard to the over-all effect of the proposed variation on all beneficiaries. The benefit criterion has been liberally construed and is not restricted to financial benefit only. Thus, in *Duchess of Westminster v. Royal Trust Co.*,[7] a trust gave a life interest to two beneficiaries with remainder to their children. It was unlikely at their stage in life that the life tenants would have children, so they proposed to vary the trust so as to acquire the capital, but they were willing to take out insurance in the name of possible future children. The court held that unborn children would receive a benefit by acquiring an immediate vested interest on birth in the form of insurance, instead of at the death of their parents and by the fact that the parents would be better able to provide for them.[8]

Similarly, in *Re Zekelman*,[9] a trust in favour of the settlor's son, which was subject to his surviving the settlor and attaining the age of 25, was varied to include other children as well. The court agreed that, while the variation was not for the son's financial benefit, there was a benefit to him in that the variation would remove a possible source of family dissension and would accelerate the vesting age, while at the same time it could result in tax savings.[10]

---

[6]*Trust Variation Act*, R.S.B.C. 1979, c. 413; *Variation of Trusts Act*, R.S.P.E.I. 1974, c. V-1; R.S.N.S. 1967, c. 323; R.S.O. 1980, c. 519, R.S.S. 1978, c. V-1; *Variation of Trust Ordinance*, R.O.N.W.T. 1974, c. V-1; R.O.Y.T. 1971, c. V-1; *Trustee Act* (Alta.), ss. 42-43; (Man.), s. 61, rep. and sub. 1982-83, c. 38, s. 4; (N.B.), s. 26.

[7](1972), 32 D.L.R. (3d) 631 (N.S.S.C.).

[8]*Cf. Re T's Settlement Trusts*, [1964] Ch. 158, capital interest on majority varied to protective trust where beneficiary shown to be immature and spendthrift.

[9][1917] 3 O.R. 156, 19 D.L.R. (3d) 652 (H.C.J.).

[10]*Cf. Re Remmant's Settlement Trusts; Hooper v. Wenhaston*, [1970] Ch. 560, term of trust deleted which would divert gift to Roman Catholics and thus favour one group of children over others.

Variations for the purpose of tax savings are, indeed, one of the main reasons for applying under the legislation. The overriding consideration is, nevertheless, the benefit to the applicant. Thus, for example, the removal of a trust to a tax haven has been disapproved of, because it would not be of moral and social benefit to the infant beneficiaries to remove them from a metropolitan city to a small island community.[11]

The power to vary trustees' administrative powers has been used largely to secure more suitable investment powers. After some restrictive interpretations of that power,[12] the courts now seem ready to grant such powers in appropriate circumstances.[13]

It has been held that the legislation applies only to existing trusts, so that a court cannot create a trust under a will and then vary it.[14]

Where the trust comprises land, the application to vary is normally made under the variation of trusts legislation and, in provinces that have such legislation,[15] under settled estates legislation.

1217. LIMITATION OF ACTIONS

The several provincial Statutes of Limitation are a confusing amalgam of legislation, particularly as regards trusts. They are based largely on three English statutes[1] and raise serious difficulties as to the limitation periods applicable to express trusts, trusts arising by operation of law and statutory trusts, including the office of personal representative. Statutes based on the English *Limitation Act* of 1939[2] have been enacted in Manitoba[3] and British Columbia[4] and have removed these difficulties. Similar legislation has been introduced in Ontario.[5] The interpretational difficulties are discussed in the next sections.

1217.1 Trustee and Beneficiary

Until modern legislation ameliorated the equitable principle, there was no time limit upon the right of a beneficiary to recover land or rent from an express trustee.

---

[11]*Re Weston's Settlements; Weston v. Weston*, [1969] 1 Ch. 223 (C.A.). Contrast *Re Windeat's Will Trusts*, [1969] 1 W.L.R. 692 (Ch. D.), where the beneficiaries had already long since established a permanent home in Jersey. *Cf. Re Nathanson* (1981), 45 N.S.R. (2d) 151, 9 E.T.R. 256 (S.C.T.D.).

[12]*Re Mitchell*, [1969] 2 O.R. 272, 5 D.L.R. (3d) 123 (H.C.J.).

[13]*Re Kiely*, [1972] 1 O.R. 845, 24 D.L.R. (3d) 389 (H.C.J.).

[14]*Re Davies*, [1968] 1 O.R. 349, 66 D.L.R. (2d) 412 (H.C.J.).

[15]*Land (Settled Estates) Act*, R.S.B.C. 1979, c. 215; *Settled Estates Act*, R.S.O. 1980, c. 468; *Trustee Act* (N.B.), ss. 44-8.

§1217

[1]*Real Property Limitation Act, 1833*, 3 & 4 Will. 4, c. 27, s. 25; *Real Property Limitation Act, 1874*, 37 & 38 Vict., c. 57; *Trustee Act, 1888*, 51 & 52 Vict., c. 59. s. 8.

[2]2 & 3 Geo. 6, c. 21.

[3]*Limitation of Actions Act*, R.S.M. 1970, c. L150.

[4]*Limitation Act*, R.S.B.C. 1979, c. 236.

[5]Bill 160 (Ont. 1983). The Bill died upon prorogation of the Session, but is expected to be reintroduced in due course.

The English *Real Property Limitation Act, 1833*,[1] provides that, where any land or rent is vested in a trustee upon an express trust, the right of the *cestui que trust*, or any person claiming through him, to bring an action against the trustee, or any person claiming through him, to recover the land or rent, shall be deemed to have first accrued, within the meaning of the Act, at and not before the time when the land or rent was conveyed to a purchaser for valuable consideration and then shall be deemed to have accrued only as against such purchaser and any person claiming through him.[2] That provision was re-enacted in Ontario and is now section 44(1) of the *Limitations Act*.[3] Subsection (2) adds that, "Subject to section 43, no claim of a *cestui que trust* against his trustee for any property held on an express trust, or in respect of any breach of such trust, shall be held to be barred by any statute of limitations."[4]

The British Columbia Act[5] was completely recast in 1975 and does not contain a similar provision.[6]

The following cases indicate the application of the English Act of 1833 and of Canadian statutes based thereon.

A trustee who holds possession of land to which he has a valid legal title cannot, by any act of his own, make that possession adverse to his real *cestui que trust* and, so long as he is in possession, the *Statute of Limitations* will not run against the *cestui que trust*, even though the trustee should, through error or other cause, treat himself as trustee for other persons and account to them for the rents of the land.[7]

Where there was a devise of land upon trust for sale, the proceeds to form part of the personalty, and the trustees left part of the land unsold for fifty years, it was held that, since it was an express trust within the Act, the residuary legatee was entitled to a decree for execution of the trust.[8]

Where a trustee has taken possession of trust property in the character of trustee, he cannot hold it adversely to a *cestui que trust* after the legal estate

---

§1217.1

[1] 3 & 4 Will. 4, c. 27, s. 25.

[2] The *Real Property Limitation Act, 1874*, 37 & 38 Vict., c. 57, supplemented the Act of 1833 and, by s. 9, provided that the 1833 Act should continue in force.

[3] R.S.O. 1980, c. 240. Hereafter referred to as *Limitations Act* (Ont.), expected soon to be replaced by new legislation, see §3106.21.

[4] Taken from the *Supreme Court of Judicature Act, 1873*, 36 & 37 Vict., c. 66, s. 25(2). For similar legislation see *Limitation of Actions Act*, R.S.A. 1980, c. L-15, s. 42; R.S.M. 1970, c. L150, s. 52; R.S.S. 1978, c. L-15, ss. 42, 44; R.S.N.B. 1973, c. L-8, s. 58; R.S.N.S. 1967, c. 168, s. 27; *Limitation of Actions (Realty) Act*, R.S.N. 1970, c. 207, s. 21; *Statute of Limitations*, R.S.P.E.I. 1974, c. S-7, ss. 43, 45. These several statutes are hereafter referred to as "*Limitations Act*" (Alta.), *etc.* The territorial ordinances do not deal with trusts: *Limitation Ordinance*, R.O.N.W.T. 1974, c. L-6; R.O.Y.T. 1971, c. L-7.

[5] *Limitations Act*, S.B.C. 1975, c. 37. See now *Limitation Act*, R.S.B.C. 1979, c. 236. Hereafter referred to as "Limitation Act" (B.C.). Similar legislation has been proposed for Ontario: *Discussion Paper on Proposed Limitations Act* (Ministry of the Attorney General Ontario, Sept., 1977) and Bill 160 (Ont. 1983). Although the Bill died on the Order Paper it is expected to be reintroduced in due course.

[6] For a discussion of this Act see text at footnote 25, *infra*.

[7] *Lister v. Pickford* (1865), 34 Beav. 576, 55 E.R. 757.

[8] *Mutlow v. Bigg* (1874), L.R. 18 Eq. 246.

under which possession was taken has determined, and his continuance in possession is deemed to be that of the *cestui que trust*.[9]

If the *cestui que trust* is in possession of the trust property, he is the trustee's tenant at will and the estate of the trustee will not be barred.[10] In the case of an express trust, the *Statute of Limitations* is no bar to the demand of a *cestui que trust*, although for more than twenty years he has been excluded from the rents which were received from the trustee by the other *cestuis que trust*.[11] If, however, some *cestuis que trust* are in possession of the property to the exclusion of the trustee and the other *cestuis que trust*, they may acquire title.[12]

As indicated above,[13] a trustee *de son tort* is treated as a trustee upon an express trust for the purpose of limitations of actions. Hence, time does not run in his favour. Thus, where a trustee devised his real estate to G, subject to payment of a legacy, so that the trust estate did not pass, but G nevertheless acted as trustee, it was held that she must be deemed to be a trustee upon an express trust and that the *Statute of Limitations* was, therefore, no defence to a claim against her for breach of trust.[14]

Also as indicated above,[15] a person is affected by an express trust when he participates in any fraudulent conduct of the trustee to the injury of the *cestui que trust*, or by intermeddling with the performance of the trust, or dealing with the property inconsistently with performance of the trust. Hence, it was laid down in the leading case on this point as follows: first, the doctrine that time is no bar in the case of express trusts has been extended to cases where a person who is not a direct trustee nevertheless assumes to act as a trustee under the trust. Secondly, the rule has also been thought appropriate to cases where a stranger participates in the fraud of a trustee. Thirdly, a similar extension of the doctrine has been acted on in a case where a person received trust property and dealt with it in a manner inconsistent with trusts of which he was cognizant. Fourthly, a person occupying a fiduciary position, who has property deposited with him on the strength of such position, is to be dealt

---

[9] *Per* Turner, L.J., in *Stone v. Godfrey* (1854), 5 De G. M. & G. 76, 43 E.R. 798 (C.A.).
[10] *Garrard v. Tuck* (1849), 8 C.B. 231, 137 E.R. 498; *Knight v. Bowyer* (1858), 2 De G. & J. 421, 44 E.R. 1053 (C.A.).
[11] *Knight v. Bowyer, supra*, footnote 10.
[12] *Bolling v. Hobday* (1882), 31 W.R. 9, in which case a testatrix devised realty to trustees in trust for her daughter for life and, after her death, to sell and divide the proceeds among four persons; the life tenant occupied the property until her death in 1857 and then two of the four persons took and remained in possession until the death of one of them; the other remained in possession until his death in 1880. The trustees had never acted in any way so far as the realty was concerned and the possession by the two and then of the survivor of them was without interruption or acknowledgment. It was held that the title of the trustees had been extinguished by the expiration of twenty years from the death of the testatrix and, with it, the trust affecting it.
[13] *Supra*, §1208.2.
[14] *Life Ass'n of Scotland v. Siddal*; *Cooper v. Greene* (1861), 3 De G. F. & J. 58, 45 E.R. 800.
[15] *Supra*, §1208.2.

with as an express trustee and not merely as a constructive trustee of such property.[16]

> These persons though not originally trustees had taken upon themselves the custody and administration of property on behalf of others; and, though sometimes referred to as constructive trustees, they were, in fact, actual trustees, though not so named. It followed that their possession also was treated as the possession of the persons for whom they acted, and they, like express trustees, were disabled from taking advantage of the time bar.[17]

A trustee who had committed a breach of trust died in 1847, leaving real and personal property to his widow for life with remainder to his two sons. The widow proved the will, but refused to make good the breach of trust. On her death in 1865, the sons took out letters of administration and entered into possession of the property devised to them on remainder. On citation proceedings, it was held that they must make good the breach of trust out of their father's assets received by them and that the lapse of time was no defence.[18]

In general, a person who receives money or property in a fiduciary capacity is treated as an express trustee for the purposes of the Act. Thus, it was held that a testamentary guardian is a trustee and that the *Statute of Limitations* does not apply to accounts between him and his ward for rents of land received during the ward's minority.[19]

Time does not run against the heir entitled under a resulting trust in real property because it is treated as an express trust. Thus, where a testator devised a house and all of his other real estate to executors upon certain trusts, but the declaration of trust applied to the house only and he died seised of two other houses, possession of which was taken by the executors who received the rents for more than twelve years, it was held that there was an express trust for the heir-at-law in regard to the two houses and that his right was not barred.[20]

However, constructive and implied trustees do stand in a somewhat different position and time will even run in favour of express trustees in some respects. The English *Trustees Act, 1888*[21] defines "trustees" as including an executor, an administrator and a trustee whose trust arises by construction or operation of law, as well as an express trustee. The Act provides[22] that, in an action against a trustee or any person claiming through him, except where the claim is

---

[16]*Per* Bowen, L.J., in *Soar v. Ashwell*, [1893] 2 Q.B. 390, in which case Lord Esher, M.R., said at p. 394, that the stranger who by his conduct has been affected by an express trust is, more properly speaking, an express trustee *de son tort*.

[17]Viscount Cave in *Taylor v. Davies* (1919), 51 D.L.R. 75 at pp. 84-5, [1920] A.C. 636 at p. 651 (P.C.), affg 41 O.L.R. 403, 41 D.L.R. 510 (S.C. App. Div.).

[18]*Woodhouse v. Woodhouse* (1869), L.R. 8 Eq. 514.

[19]*Mathew v. Brise* (1851), 14 Beav. 341, 51 E.R. 317.

[20]*Patrick v. Simpson* (1889), 24 Q.B.D. 128; and see *Simmons v. Rudall* (1851), 1 Sim. (N.S.) 115, 61 E.R. 45, in which case an heir was held entitled to realty which was undisposed of and was, therefore, held by the trustees in trust for him.

[21]51 & 52 Vict., c. 59 (1889).

[22]*Ibid.*, s. 8.

founded upon fraud or fraudulent breach of trust to which the trustee was party or privy, or is to recover trust property, or the proceeds thereof still retained by the trustee or previously obtained by him and converted to his use, (a) he has the rights and privileges conferred by a statute of limitations to the same extent as if he were not a trustee, and (b) if the action is to recover money or property to which no existing statute of limitations applies, he may plead the lapse of time to the same extent as if it were an action of debt for money had and received, but the statute shall not begin to run against any beneficiary until the interest of the beneficiary becomes an interest in possession.

These provisions were adopted in most of the provinces.[23] The Manitoba legislation[24] is clearer however. Section 50(1) defines "trustee" almost exactly as does the English Act. Section 50(2), which provides that no limitation prescribed by the Act applies to an action by a beneficiary under a trust for fraud or fraudulent breach of trust to which the trustee was a party, or to recover from a trustee trust property or the proceeds thereof in the possession of the trustee or previously received by him and converted to his use. Section 50(3) provides that, subject to subsections (1) and (2), an action by a beneficiary to recover trust property or in respect of breach of trust, not being an action for which a period of limitation is prescribed by the Act, shall not be brought after six years from the date on which the right of action accrued, which right shall not be deemed to have accrued to a beneficiary having a future interest until the interest falls in possession.

The British Columbia Act[25] defines "trust" like the English Act, but provides a ten-year limitation period for actions against personal representatives and trustees, whether the trustee was guilty of fraud or fraudulent breach of trust or of conversion to his own use or not, as well as for tracing action.[26] In the case of fraud or conversion of trust property, however, the running of time is postponed until the beneficiary becomes fully aware of the trustee's action.[27]

It has been stated that the effect of the English *Trustee Act* is that, except in case of fraud by the trustee, retention of trust property by him, or receipt by him and conversion of it to his own use, a trustee who has committed a breach of trust is entitled to the protection of the *Statute of Limitations* as if actions or proceedings for breaches of trust were enumerated in them.[28] The Act was passed in order to remove what was thought to be a hardship on innocent trustees, that whatever might be the lapse of time since the com-

---

[23]*Limitations Act* (Alta.), s. 41; (Sask.), s. 43; (N.S.), s. 26; (N.B.) s. 56; (P.E.I.), s. 44; (Ont.), s. 43 (expected to be replaced by new legislation, see §3106.21); *Trustee Act*, R.S.N. 1970, c. 380, s. 31.

[24]*Limitations Act*, s. 50. *Cf.* proposed Ontario Act, *supra*, footnote 5, at p. 7, s. 3(2)(*b*)-(*e*). The Ontario legislation, if enacted, will be similar to the Manitoba legislation.

[25]*Limitation Act*, s. 1. *Cf.* proposed Ontario Act, *supra*, at p. 12, s. 6(1).

[26]*Ibid.*, B.C. Act, s. 3(2). *Cf.* proposed Ontario Act, *supra*, at p. 7, s. 3(2) (*b*)-(*e*).

[27]*Ibid.*, B.C. Act, s. 6(1). *Cf.* proposed Ontario Act, *supra*, at p. 12, s. 6(1).

[28]*How v. Earl of Winterton*, [1896] 2 Ch. 626 (C.A.). If the trustees retain trust property, however, time is not a bar: *Carpenter v. Registrar of Supreme Court of Newfoundland* (1979), 100 D.L.R. (3d) 501 (Nfld. S.C.T.D.).

mission of an innocent breach of trust, the trustee was unable to rely upon the *Statute of Limitations*.[29]

For the purpose of this legislation, a distinction is drawn between constructive trustees who receive property under an instrument of trust or other instrument and who thereafter retain it or convert it to their own use, and other constructive trustees, such as agents who make a profit out of their agency or other fiduciary relationship. The former fall within the express terms of the legislation and time is no bar in actions against them, while time is a bar in respect of the latter.[30]

In 1878, the trustees under a settlement committed an innocent breach of trust by investing trust money in a mortgage on property of insufficient value. The mortgagor paid the interest under the mortgage directly to the tenant for life. In 1892, the life tenant and the infant remainderman brought an action against the trustees to make good the amount of the investment. It was conceded that the trustees were liable to make good the loss to the estate in so far as the infant plaintiff was concerned, but it was held that the action of the life tenant was barred after six years from the time of the investment, and, although the payment by the mortgagor to the life tenant amounted in law to payment to the trustee, it was not an admission or acknowledgment that would take the case out of the statute.[31]

A mortgagee of land which formed part of an estate assigned for the benefit of creditors and to whom the assignee conveyed the equity of redemption is not an express trustee for such equity of redemption, but merely a constructive trustee, so that the *Statute of Limitations* ran in his favour and might be pleaded in an action to recover the equity of redemption.[32]

Personal representatives are constituted trustees for the persons beneficially entitled on the death of a deceased[33] and, in any case, they are so treated under

---

[29]*Re Richardson; Pole v. Pattenden*, [1920] 1 Ch. 423, in which case it was held that, since the action was to recover a legacy within the *Real Property Limitation Act, 1874*, 37 & 38 Vict., c. 57, and as there was thus an existing applicable *Statute of Limitations*, the *Trustee Act* did not apply and, since the twelve years limited by the *Real Property Limitation Act, 1874*, had not expired when the action was brought, that Act afforded no defence to the action. For similar legislation see *Limitations Act* (Ont.), ss. 17, 23, 24, expected soon to be replaced by new legislation, see §3106.21.

[30]*Wotherspoon et al. v. Canadian Pacific Ltd.; Pope et al. v. Canadian Pacific Ltd. et al.* (1978), 22 O.R. (2d) 385, 92 D.L.R. (3d) 545 (H.C.J.), revd on other grounds 35 O.R. (2d) 449, 129 D.L.R. (3d) 1 (C.A.), leave to appeal to S.C.C. granted 37 O.R. (2d) 73*n*, 44 N.R. 83*n*.

[31]*Re Somerset; Somerset v. Poulett*, [1894] 1 Ch. 231 (C.A.).

[32]*Taylor v. Davies* (1919), 51 D.L.R. 75, [1920] A.C. 636 (P.C.), in which case it was stated, at pp. 83-6 D.L.R., pp. 649-53 A.C., that the provisions in what is now s. 43 of the Ontario *Limitations Act* (expected soon to be replaced by new legislation, see §3106.21), taken from the Imperial *Trustee Act*, apply to an express trustee and a constructive or implied trustee who originally took possession upon trust for or on behalf of others, but do not alter for the worse the position of a person who, having taken possession in his own right, may subsequently be declared a constructive trustee by a court of equity, in which case time will run in his favour.

[33]*Devolution of Estates Act*, R.S.M. 1970, c. D70, s. 18; R.S.N.B. 1973, c. D-9, s. 3; *Estates Administration Act*, R.S.O. 1980, c. 143, s. 2(1); *Devolution of Real Property Act*, R.S.A. 1980, c. D-34, s. 2(1); R.S.S. 1978, c. D-27, ss. 4, 5; *Estate Administration*

the several Trustee Acts.[34] They are, therefore, treated as trustees for limitations of actions purposes.[35] Whether they are express trustees is another matter. They were not so regarded in some Ontario cases.[36] However, in *Re Wilson and Bradshaw*[37] they were thought to be express trustees by reason of section 2 of the *Devolution of Estates Act*.[38]

Actions of account against trustees are generally limited to six years from the time that the cause of action arose.[39] However, where the breach of trust is a continuing one, as where the fiduciary relationship arises under a perpetual lease, the covenants of which are breached by the lessee by a sale of surplus lands, a new cause of action arises so long as the breach continues.[40] As with all defences under a statute of limitations, the specific section of the statute relied upon must be pleaded.[41]

1217.2 Third Persons

As against third parties, a trustee and the *cestui que trust* are regarded in equity as one person, holding one entire estate, so that possession of trust property by the *cestui que trust* is possession by the trustee,[1] and, conversely, possession by the trustee is possession by the *cestui que trust*.[2] The possession of the *cestui que trust* gives the trustee the seisin of the estate which is not interrupted by the death of the *cestui que trust*, but immediately enures for the benefit of the person next entitled to the equitable interest.[3] If the *cestui que*

Act, R.S.B.C. 1979, c. 114, s. 90; *Chattels Real Act*, R.S.N. 1970, c. 36, s. 2; *Real Property Act*, R.S.N.S. 1967, c. 261, s. 6(1); *Probate Act*, R.S.P.E.I. 1974, c. P-19, s. 108(1); *Devolution of Real Property Ordinance*, R.O.N.W.T. 1974, c. D-5, s. 3(1); R.O.Y.T. 1971, c. D-4, s. 3(1).

[34]*Trustee Act* (Ont.), s. 1(*q*); (Alta.), s. 1(*a*); (B.C.), s. 1; (Man.), s. 2(*v*); (N.S.), s. 1(*p*); (N.B.), s. 1; (Nfld.), s. 2(*n*); (P.E.I.), s. 1(*p*); (Sask.), s. 2(1); (N.W.T.), s. 2; (Yukon), s. 2(1).

[35]See, *e.g.*, *Limitations Act* (Ont.), ss. 42, 43(1) (exected soon to be replaced by new legislation, see §3106.21).

[36]*Re Thompson*, [1955] O.W.N. 521 (H.C.J.); *Re Baty*, [1959] O.R. 13, 16 D.L.R. (2d) 164 (C.A.), but in these cases s. 2 of the *Estates Administration Act, supra*, footnote 33, was not referred to.

[37][1952] O.W.N. 101, [1952] 1 D.L.R. 764 (H.C.J.).

[38]R.S.O. 1970, c. 129, and see generally Ontario Law Reform Com'n, *Report on Limitation of Actions* (1969).

[39]See, *e.g.*, *Limitations Act* (Ont.), s. 46 (expected soon to be replaced by new legislation).

[40]*Wotherspoon v. Canadian Pacific Ltd.* (1978), 22 O.R. (2d) 385, 92 D.L.R. (3d) 545 (H.C.J.), revd on other grounds, 35 O.R. (2d) 449, 129 D.L.R. (3d) 1 (C.A.).

[41]*Ibid.*

§1217.2

[1]Per Lord Hardwicke, L.C., in *Earl Pomfret v. Windsor* (1752), 2 Ves. Sen. 472 at p. 481, 28 E.R. 302; Lord Ellenborough, C.J., in *Keene d. Lord Byron v. Deardon* (1807), 8 East 248 at p. 263, 103 E.R. 336; *per* Wigram, V.C., in *Parker v. Carter* (1845), 4 Hare 400 at p. 417, 67 E.R. 704.

[2]Per Grant, M.R., in *Lord Grenville v. Blyth* (1809), 16 Ves. Jun. 224, 33 E.R. 969; *Parker v. Carter, supra*, at pp. 413-4.

[3]*Parker v. Carter, supra.*

trust is in actual occupation with the consent or acquiescence of the trustees, he may be regarded as their tenant at will but, if he is merely allowed by the trustees to receive the rents or otherwise deal with the property which is actually occupied by tenants, he stands in the relation merely of an agent on behalf of the trustees who choose to allow him to act for them in the management of the estate. Hence, such tenants, by not paying rent or acknowledging title for the statutory period, may acquire title against the trustees as well as the *cestui que trust*.[4]

In the absence of acquiescence or laches on the part of the *cestui que trust*, time does not run against him if the trust property passes to the trustee's legal representatives,[5] or is conveyed to a person without valuable consideration.[6] If the trustee conveys the legal estate to a purchaser for value without notice of the trust, the latter is fully protected.[7] If the trustee conveys the property to a purchaser for value with notice of the trust, but without fraud or fraudulent breach of trust, time runs against the *cestui que trust* from the conveyance if he has an equitable estate in possession,[8] but it does not run against those entitled in remainder until the remainder becomes an estate in possession, or against those under disability until the disability ceases.[9]

If a trespasser, who has notice of the trust, acquires title by the length of possession as against the trustee, he holds subject to the equities and the *cestuis que trust* have an independent remedy against him. The time does not run against them until they become entitled in possession and are free from disability.[10]

1217.3 Acquiescence and Laches

A person whose claim is not statute-barred may be unable to enforce it by reason of his acquiescence or long delay.

The Imperial *Real Property Limitation Act, 1833*,[1] provides that nothing in the Act interferes with any rule of equity in refusing relief, on the ground of acquiescence or otherwise, to any person whose right to bring an action is not barred by the Act. This provision was re-enacted in the several provinces.[2]

The word "acquiescence" is commonly used in two senses, namely, one

---

[4]*Melling v. Leak* (1855), 16 C.B. 652, 139 E.R. 915.

[5]*Patrick v. Simpson* (1889), 24 Q.B.D. 128.

[6]See *Sturgis v. Morse* (1858), 3 De G. & J. 1, 44 E.R. 1169 (C.A.).

[7]*Pilcher v. Rawlins* (1872), L.R. 7 Ch. App. 259.

[8]See *Attorney-General v. Flint* (1844), 4 Hare 147, 67 E.R. 597.

[9]*St. Mary Magdalen College, Oxford v. Attorney-General* (1857), 6 H.L.C. 189 at p. 215, 10 E.R. 1267.

[10]*Scott v. Scott* (1854), 4 H.L.C. 1065, 10 E.R. 779.

§1217.3

[1]3 & 4 Will. 4, c. 27, s. 27 (1833).

[2]*Limitations Act* (Alta.), s. 3; (Man.), s. 61; (Sask.), s. 51; (N.B.), s. 65; (Nfld.), s. 23; (N.S.), s. 30; (Ont.), s. 2 (exjected soon to be replaced by new legislation, see §3106.21); (P.E.I.), s. 52; *Limitation Act*, R.S.B.C. 1979, c. 236, s. 2. S. 2 of the Ontario Act was applied in *Re O'Reilly* (1980), 28 O.R. (2d) 481, 111 D.L.R. (3d) 238 (H.C.J.).

denoting that a person makes no objection to a violation of his legal right while it is occurring, the other denoting that he refrains from seeking a remedy after a violation, unknown to him at the time, comes to his knowledge. The first is the proper sense of the term, acquiescence in the second sense being involved in laches. If a person having a right stands by and sees another dealing with the property in a manner inconsistent with that right and makes no objection while the act is in progress, he cannot afterwards complain; that is the proper sense of the word "acquiescence".[3]

Acquiescence by words or conduct in such circumstances as to infer an assent creates an estoppel.[4] In order that A may be estopped in equity from complaining of the violation of his rights by B, the general requirements of the rule are that A must know of his legal rights because the rule is founded on his conduct in the light of that knowledge; B must be mistaken as to his own legal rights because, if he is aware he is infringing A's rights, he takes the risk of A later asserting them; B must spend money or do some act to his prejudice because otherwise he would not suffer by A subsequently asserting his rights; and A must know of B's mistaken belief so as to make it inequitable for him to keep silent and allow B to proceed.[5] If an owner gives notice of his claim to property, however, that is sufficient to avoid the equitable doctrine of mistake by the party in possession, or of acquiescence on his own part being applied to him, and he does not need to repeat it.[6]

Laches is undue delay in prosecuting a claim. It is an old rule that a court of equity refuses its aid to stale demands where the plaintiff has slept upon his rights and acquiesced for a great length of time.[7] "Length of time where it does not operate as a statutory or positive bar operates, as I apprehend, simply as evidence of assent or acquiescence."[8] A person is not barred by laches, however, if there is a statutory bar, in which case he is entitled to the full statutory period before his claim becomes unenforceable.[9]

There can be no acquiescence by a person in the acts of others unless he is fully aware of his right to object to them.[10] Acquiescence imparts full

---

[3]*Per* Lord Cottenham, L.C., in *Duke of Leeds v. Earl of Amherst* (1846), 2 Ph. 117 at p. 124, 41 E.R. 886.

[4]*De Bussche v. Alt* (1878), 8 Ch. D. 286 (C.A.).

[5]See *Willmott v. Barber* (1880), 15 Ch. D. 96 (C.A.), at p. 105; *Dann v. Spurrier* (1802), 7 Ves. Jun. 231 at p. 235, 32 E.R. 94; *Archbold v. Scully* (1861), 9 H.L.C. 360 at p. 383, 11 E.R. 769; *Neesom v. Clarkson* (1845), 4 Hare 97, 67 E.R. 576; *Arsene v. Jacobs* (1963), 37 D.L.R. (2d) 254 (Alta. S.C.), affd 44 D.L.R. (2d) 487 (Alta. S.C. App. Div.); *Wawanesa Mutual Ins. Co. v. J.A. (Fred) Chalmers & Co. Ltd.* (1969), 7 D.L.R. (3d) 283, 69 W.W.R. 612 (Sask. Q.B.).

[6]*Clare Hall (Master, etc.) v. Harding* (1848), 6 Hare 273, 67 E.R. 1169.

[7]Lord Camden in *Smith v. Clay* (1767), 3 Bro. C.C. 646, 29 E.R. 743.

[8]*Per* Turner, L.J., in *Life Ass'n of Scotland v. Siddal; Cooper v. Greene* (1861), 3 De G. F. & J. 58 at p. 72, 45 E.R. 800 (C.A.).

[9]*Per* Lord Wensleydale in *Archbold v. Scully* (1861), 9 H.L.C. 360 at p. 383, 11 E.R. 769.

[10]*Marker v. Marker* (1851), 9 Hare 1 at p. 16, 68 E.R. 389; *Earl of Beauchamp v. Winn* (1873), L.R. 6 H.L. 223 at p. 249.

knowledge and a *cestui que trust* cannot be bound by acquiescence unless he has been fully informed of his rights and of all the material facts and circumstances of the case.[11]

Lapse of time can only commence to run from the discovery of the circumstances, or until such reasonable notice of what has happened has been given to the party injured, as to make it his duty, if he intends to seek redress, to make inquiry and to ascertain the circumstances of the case. No man can be supposed to acquiesce in that of which he was in entire ignorance.[12] In general, when the facts which give rise to a right are known, the right is presumed to be known.[13]

Although a remainderman may assent to a breach of trust before his interest comes into possession, ordinarily he is not bound to enforce his rights and delay does not prejudice his case until his interest comes into possession.[14]

A breach of trust cannot be held to have been acquiesced in by the mere knowledge and non-interference of the *cestui que trust* before his interest had come into possession and a *cestui que trust* cannot be bound by acquiescence unless he has been fully informed of his rights and all of the material facts and circumstances of the case.[15]

Furthermore, if a person is an infant or lunatic, he cannot acquiesce and, therefore, laches is not imputed to him while the disability continues.[16]

Delay by the *cestui que trust* due to statements made to her by the trustee which caused matters to be postponed cannot be taken advantage of by the trustee.[17]

Apart from acquiescence, a delay in enforcing a claim may be so great as to in itself constitute laches, so that the court will not enforce the claim.

[11]*Life Ass'n of Scotland v. Siddal, supra*, footnote 8.
[12]*Per* Ritchie, C.J., in *Taylor v. Wallbridge* (1879), 2 S.C.R. 616 at p. 656.
[13]*Stafford v. Stafford* (1857), 1 De G. & J. 193 at p. 202, 44 E.R. 697 (C.A.).
[14]*Life Ass'n of Scotland v. Siddal, supra*, footnote 8, at p. 73.
[15]*Inglis v. Beaty* (1878), 2 O.A.R. 453 at p. 460.
[16]*March v. Russell* (1837), 3 My. & Cr. 31, 40 E.R. 836; *Young v. Harris* (1891), 65 L.T. 45.
[17]*Mack v. Mack* (1894), 23 S.C.R. 146.

CHAPTER 13

SETTLED ESTATES

1301. SETTLEMENTS GENERALLY

A settlement is a deed, agreement, will, statute or other instrument, or any number of such instruments, under which any land or estate or interest in land is limited to or in trust for any persons in succession.[1]

The purpose of a settlement is to preserve property and provide for its enjoyment successively by persons specified by the settlor. It may be modest in scope, merely providing for a life estate and a remainder thereafter in fee simple, or its scope may be extensive, as in the case of settled estates in England, providing for several life estates, contingent remainders, possibly successive remainders in fee tail and an ultimate remainder in fee simple. Such extensive settlements were formerly common in marriage settlements the purpose of which is to secure, by means of trustees, a separate estate for the intended wife, free from the control and debts of her husband, as if she were a

---

§1301

[1]*Settled Estates Act, 1877*, 40 & 41 Vict., c. 18, s. 2; *Settled Estates Act*, R.S.O. 1980, c. 468, s. 1(1)(f); *Land (Settled Estate) Act*, R.S.B.C. 1979, c. 215, s. 1; *Re Symon; Public Trustee v. Symon*, [1944] S.A.S.R. 102 at p. 109, *per* Mayo, J.

feme sole, and to secure property to the issue of the marriage and their descendants.

Settlements originated in the social and political climate of 17th century England. They were designed for the purpose of maintaining the family estates as a unit and this was achieved by the device of the strict settlement whereby property was settled in favour of the settlor for life, remainder to his eldest son in tail, remainder to other sons and, possibly, daughters successively in tail, and with an ultimate remainder in fee simple. Provision would also be made for wives and widows by way of pin money and jointures and for other children by way of portions. When the eldest son reached his majority, the property would be resettled by agreement between father and son in such a way that in return for an immediate share in the estate, the son would take a life estate and vest the remainder in his eldest son in tail. By the use of the strict settlement and the resettlement, the property was retained in the family during each successive generation.[2]

There were serious drawbacks to the use of settlements, however. They tended to stagnate the economy and ultimately led to the destruction of the properties themselves. The reason was that all beneficiaries had only a limited interest and often were unable to raise money to maintain the properties. This was especially so if the life tenant was not given powers of management.[3] A series of statutes culminating in the *Settled Estates Act, 1877*[4] were designed to meliorate these problems. This Act permitted a life tenant to sell, exchange or partition land and to grant certain leases with the consent of the Chancery Division. Leases up to a period of twenty-one years could be made without the court's consent.

This Act was adopted in British Columbia,[5] Ontario[6] and, in part, in New Brunswick.[7] The Act was also held to be applicable in Nova Scotia by reason of the *Judicature Act*[8] which confers on the Supreme Court of that province all powers exercisable by the English High Court of Justice on October 1, 1884.[9]

In Saskatchewan, an earlier version of the English statute, the *Settled Estates Act, 1856*,[10] was held to be applicable under the rules of reception of English law, it being thought suitable to conditions in Saskatchewan.[11]

In Manitoba, where there is no settled estates legislation, it has been held

---

[2]The process is more fully described in §221.9, *supra*.
[3]*Ibid.*
[4]40 & 41 Vict., c. 18, hereafter referred to as the "English Act".
[5]*Land (Settled Estate) Act*, R.S.B.C. 1979, c. 215, hereafter referred to as the "B.C. Act".
[6]*Settled Estates Act*, R.S.O. 1980, c. 468, hereafter referred to as the "Ont. Act".
[7]*Trustees Act*, R.S.N.B. 1973, c. T-15, ss. 44-48, hereafter referred to as the "N.B. Act".
[8]S.N.S. 1919, c. 32, ss. 15, 16. This statute was re-enacted as the *Judicature Act, 1950*. See now *Judicature Act*, S.N.S. 1972, c. 2, s. 3.
[9]*Re Baugild and Baugild*, [1954] 3 D.L.R. 586, 34 M.P.R. 346 (N.S.S.C.).
[10]19 & 20 Vict., c. 120 (1856).
[11]*Re Moffat Estate* (1955), 16 W.W.R. 314 (Sask. Q.B.).

that the court does not have the inherent equitable jurisdiction to empower the life tenant to raise money for repairs on the security of a mortgage which is binding on the remainderman. In appropriate circumstances, however, the life tenant or the remainderman may seek or be compelled to suffer partition or sale under the *Law of Property Act*.[12]

A much more drastic reform in England was effected by the *Settled Land Act, 1882*.[13] This Act vested wide powers of management, including powers of sale, exchange and lease in the life tenant, and introduced the principle of overreaching whereby the interests of other beneficiaries were transferred to the purchase money when the purchaser paid it to two trustees or into court. This statute was never adopted in Canada.

A much more recent device than the settlement, the trust for sale, developed in England in the 19th century. Its purpose was not to keep land in the family but to make provision for its members. Land or other property would be conveyed to trustees upon trust for sale and to hold the proceeds in trust for the beneficiaries. Because of the equitable doctrine of conversion the beneficiaries were regarded as having only an interest in personalty if the subject-matter of the trust was land. This concept simplified conveyancing as a purchaser would not have to concern himself with the beneficial interests. While trusts for sale are recognized in Canada,[14] the trust for sale of land as it developed in England and is now regulated by the *Law of Property Act, 1925*[15] does not form part of the Canadian law of real property.

It should be noted that the Canadian settled estates legislation did not arise out of a similar social and political background as did the English Act and, therefore, the English cases must be read with caution.[16] Indeed, the Canadian legislation is no more than a type of variation of trusts legislation designed to avoid the necessity of having to obtain a private Act to vary a settlement.[17] With the advent of variation of trusts legislation in most of the Canadian provinces,[18] settled estates legislation might be regarded as otiose. However, the Settled Estates Acts do contain special powers in respect of land which continue to be useful. Moreover, in the absence of such legislation the court has no power to vary a settlement that is not part of a trust.[19] In provinces which have both types of legislation an application to vary a trust of land is usually brought under both.

While settlements of land are not nearly as common as they once were for social and tax reasons, it is likely that marriage settlements generally will

---

[12]R.S.M. 1970, c. L90. See *Re Chupryk* (1980), 110 D.L.R. (3d) 108, [1980] 4 W.W.R. 534 *sub nom. Chupryk v. Haykowski; Haykowski v. Chupryk* (Man. C.A.).

[13]45 & 46 Vict., c. 38 (1882); now the *Settled Land Act, 1925*, 15 & 16 Geo. 5, c. 18.

[14]See §1210, *supra*.

[15]15 & 16 Geo. 5, c. 20 (1925).

[16]*Re Fell*, [1940] O.R. 397, [1940] 4 D.L.R. 73 (C.A.).

[17]See the reference in section 22 of the Ont. Act to the former practice of obtaining private Acts.

[18]See §1216, *supra*.

[19]*Re Chupryk, supra*, footnote 12.

be used with more frequency as a result of modern matrimonial property legislation.[20]

1302. CREATION

A settlement may be created by deed or by will. It may also be the subject of a contract. The different forms are dealt with in the next two paragraphs.

1302.1 Contract for Settlement

The normal contract rule, that until the parties have reached a final, mutual agreement in writing, the contract does not exist, applies to contracts for settlements. Thus, where a life tenant and two remaindermen entered into negotiations to create a settlement and while correspondence between their solicitors showed substantial agreement on most points and an intention to execute a formal agreement, but where several points were still under negotiation, it was held that there was no contract, merely an agreement to enter into a contract.[1]

In order to be enforceable, the contract must be evidenced by a memorandum in writing signed by the party to be charged with it, or by some person authorized by the first to sign it.[2]

Most often a contract for settlement is one made in consideration of marriage. In Manitoba marriage settlements are specially regulated by statute.[3]

It follows from the statutory requirement that a verbal contract made before marriage is not enforceable,[4] nor is one evidenced only by an unsigned memorandum.[5] A verbal agreement before marriage may, however, be sufficiently evidenced by writing made after the marriage so as to satisfy the

---

[20]*Family Law Reform Act*, R.S.O. 1980, c. 152; S.P.E.I. 1978, c. 6; *Family Relations Act*, R.S.B.C. 1979, c. 121, s. 48; *Marital Property Act*, S.M. 1978, c. 24; S.N.B. 1980, c. M-1.1; *Matrimonial Property Act*, R.S.A. 1980, c. M-9, ss. 37, 38; S.N.S. 1980, c. 9; S.S. 1979, c. M-6.1; *Matrimonial Property Ordinance*, O.Y.T. 1979 (2nd), c. 11.

§1302.1

[1]*Re Lennox; Ronald v. Williams*, [1948] 3 D.L.R. 45, [1948] 1 W.W.R. 903 (Man. C.A.), vard on another point [1948] 4 D.L.R. 753, [1948] 2 W.W.R. 640 (Man. C.A.), vard [1949] 3 D.L.R. 9, [1949] S.C.R. 446.

[2]*Statute of Frauds*, 29 Car. 2, c. 3, s. 4 (1676), in force in Alberta, Saskatchewan, Manitoba, Newfoundland, Northwest Territories and the Yukon; R.S.O. 1980, c. 481, s. 4; R.S.B.C. 1979, c. 393, s. 1(1); R.S.N.B. 1973, c. S-14, s. 1; R.S.N.S. 1967, c. 290, s. 6; R.S.P.E.I. 1974, c. S-6, s. 2.

[3]*Marriage Settlement Act*, R.S.M. 1970, c. M60. And see the statutes collected in §1301, footnote 19, *supra*.

[4]*Viscountess Montacute v. Maxwell* (1720), 1 P. Wms. 618, 24 E.R. 541; *Spicer v. Spicer; Spicer v. Dawson* (1857), 24 Beav. 365, 53 E.R. 398.

[5]*Thynne (Lady) v. Earl of Glengall* (1848), 2 H.L.C. 131, 9 E.R. 1042; *Caton v. Caton* (1867), L.R. 2 H.L. 127.

Statute of Frauds[6] and be enforceable[7] and such writing may be a recital in a post-nuptial settlement,[8] or letters,[9] or an affidavit in legal proceedings.[10]

The absence of a memorandum in writing is not a bar to proof of a verbal agreement made before marriage, if there has been part performance of it by delivery of possession of the land after marriage,[11] because possession by another is such cogent evidence of a contract as to compel the court to admit evidence of its terms in order to do justice.[12]

Marriage in reliance upon a verbal contract to settle property is not part performance of the contract, however, so as to exclude operation of the *Statute of Frauds*.[13]

A contract for a marriage settlement need not be formal. An offer to make a settlement upon marriage, sufficient to make an enforceable contract when the marriage takes place, may be contained in letters which amount to a definite offer.[14]

A pre-nuptial agreement to settle property contained in letters will be enforced if the letters become lost through accident and the existence and substance of the letters can be clearly established by evidence[15] and, similarly, if the letters are destroyed without evil intent.[16]

---

[6]29 Car. 2, c. 3 (1676).

[7]*Re Holland*; *Gregg v. Holland*. [1902] 2 Ch. 360 (C.A.).

[8]*Ibid.*; *Dundas v. Dutens* (1790), 1 Ves. Jun. 196, 30 E.R. 298.

[9]*Hodgson v. Hutchenson* (1712), 5 Vin. Abr. 522.

[10]*Barkworth v. Young* (1856), 4 Drewry 1, 62 E.R. 1.

[11]*Surcome v. Pinniger*; *Ex p. Pinniger* (1853), 3 De G. M. & G. 571, 43 E.R. 224; *Ungley v. Ungley* (1877), 5 Ch. D. 887 (C.A.); *Sharman v. Sharman* (1892), 67 L.T. 833 (C.A.).

[12]*Ungley v. Ungley, supra,* footnote 11, in which case a father agreed verbally, in consideration of his daughter's marriage, to give her a house free from encumbrances. He gave her possession after her marriage, paid mortgage instalments during his life and, after his death, there remained a balance of mortgage debt which was held payable out of his estate.

[13]*Dundas v. Dutens, supra,* footnote 8; *Lassence v. Tierney* (1849), 1 Mac. & G. 551, 41 E.R. 1379; *Warden v. Jones* (1857), 2 De G. & J. 76, 44 E.R. 916; *Caton v. Caton, supra,* footnote 5.

[14]*Laver v. Fielder* (1862), 32 Beav. 1, 55 E.R. 1, in which a father wrote "I still adhere to my last proposition" — to allow the daughter a specified sum per year — "and at my decease she shall be entitled to her share of whatever property I may die possessed of", parol evidence being admitted to prove what was meant by "her share"; *Coverdale v. Eastwood* (1872), L.R. 15 Eq. 121, in which a father wrote that his daughter would come into what belonged to him at his death, that it was his intention, in the event of a marriage taking place, to settle his property on the daughter in strict settlement, and "agree" to allow the daughter and her husband a specified sum per year and added that he would take care that his property would be properly secured upon her and her children; *Viret v. Viret* (1881), 17 Ch. D. 365n, in which the intended husband, the day before the marriage, wrote the lady's solicitor agreeing that her fortune be settled on her subject to certain conditions respecting himself and the children, if any.

[15]*Gilchrist v. Herbert* (1872), 26 L.T. 381.

[16]*Stuart v. Thomson* (1893), 23 O.R. 503 (H.C.J.), in which case letters between the husband and wife, written before marriage, were destroyed after the marriage and performance of the agreement, the parties believing that the letters were no longer needed, it being held that the duty of the husband to convey to the wife pursuant to the letters negatived the intention to defeat creditors.

The expressions in the letters must amount to a definite offer, however, a mere expression of intention being insufficient to make a binding contract.[17]

In equity a person who makes a representation in order to induce another to act upon it and he does act upon it, will be held to the representation. Thus, if a parent or his agent holds out inducements to a suitor to celebrate a marriage and the suitor consents and celebrates the marriage accordingly, believing that it was intended that he should have the benefits held out to him, a court of equity will give effect to the proposals.[18] In *Heichman v. National Trust Co.*,[19] H, desiring to marry S, took her to his father who told them that he was giving certain land and chattels to H. On the faith of this representation S consented to the marriage. After H's death, his father purported to take back the chattels. In H's administrator's action for specific performance of the promise, it was held that he could enforce it, for the father was bound to make good his representations on the faith of which the marriage took place.

As is thus indicated, a contract resulting from marriage pursuant to an offer to settle, is enforced whether the offer is made by one of the marrying parties to the other, or is made by a third person to either and it is enforced against the estate of the person who made the offer.

If a settlement is executed prior to a marriage, however, there is a presumption that it contains the whole of the marriage contract respecting property, and prior promises left out of the settlement are not enforced, but the presumption is rebuttable by sufficient evidence.[20]

"Marriage articles" is a term commonly used to describe a contract made in consideration of marriage to settle property, setting forth terms to be embodied in a formal marriage settlement. Although articles may so completely declare the trusts that no further instrument is required, usually they are in

---

[17]*Re Fickus*; *Farina v. Fickus*, [1900] 1 Ch. 331, "[S]he will have a share of what I leave after the death of her mother"; *Moorhouse v. Colvin* (1851), 15 Beav. 341, 51 E.R. 570, "she is and shall be noticed in my will, but to what further amount I cannot say"; *Maunsell v. Hedges* (1854), 4 H.L.C. 1039, 10 E.R. 769,

> my will has been made for some time, and I am confident that I shall never alter it to your disadvantage. I have mentioned before, and I again repeat, that my county of [T] estate will come to you at my death, unless some unforeseen occurrence should take place. I have never settled anything on any of my nephews, and I should give cause for jealousy if I was to deviate in this instance from a resolution I have long made.

[18]*Hammersley v. De Biel* (1845), 12 Cl. & Fin. 45, 8 E.R. 1312 (H.L.).

[19](1920), 60 S.C.R. 428.

[20]*Loxley v. Heath* (1860), 1 De G. F. & J. 489, 45 E.R. 451, in which case a father, prior to marriage, wrote the husband that all of his property would be equally divided between his children at his death but, in the marriage settlement executed prior to the marriage, no such intent was expressed. It was held that all that was intended to be binding upon the father was embodied in the settlement; *Re Badcock*; *Kingdon v. Tagert* (1881), 17 Ch. D. 361, where a father wrote the husband that he and his wife had determined to settle on the intended wife, their daughter, a specified sum and that, in addition, she would have a further specified sum on her mother's death. A formal settlement referred to only one sum and did not refer to the latter. It was held that the settlement superseded the letter so that the husband could not claim both sums from the father's estate.

the nature of executory trusts and a court of equity directs a settlement in accordance with the intent disclosed by the articles rather than with the technical meaning of the words used.[21]

1302.2 Creation by Deed or Will

The normal rules of capacity applicable to the creation of a trust apply to the creation of a settlement, special rules being applicable to infants in respect of wills and marriage settlements.[1]

If a settlement is created by will, it is construed according to the general rules applicable to wills. If it is created by deed, it is construed according to the rules applicable to any deed. Although technical words are not necessary and, by legislation,[2] a conveyance passes all the estate or right which the grantor has or has power to convey in the property, nevertheless proper words of limitation should be used. This is especially so in jurisdictions in which the legislation makes no provision for conveyances without words of limitation. Thus, where land was conveyed to trustees of a settlement without words of limitation, it was held that they took only a life estate for their joint lives and the life of the survivor, the reversion after the life estate remaining in the settlor.[3]

Where the estate of the settlor and, after his death, that of his heirs are both equitable, the rule in *Shelley's Case*[4] applies so as to give the settlor an estate in fee simple.[5] Thus, a woman, in contemplation of marriage, conveyed land to her husband and another person in trust for her for life and, after her death, for her child or children in fee simple but, if she should die without issue before her husband or if he should predecease her and she should leave no children, in trust for her heirs absolutely. There were no children of the marriage and her husband predeceased her. Being 53, she asked the trustees for a reconveyance, but they asked the sanction of the court, as the reference to children was wide enough to include children of a second marriage. It was held that the rule in *Shelley's Case*[6] did not apply to the estate that children might have taken, as they would take by purchase, but that, as there

---

[21]*Webb v. Kelly* (1825), 3 L.J.O.S. 172; *Sackville-West v. Viscount Holmesdale* (1870), L.R. 4 H.L. 543. See further on this point §1203.4, *supra*.

§1302.2

[1]See §1204.1, *supra*.

[2]*Conveyancing and Law of Property Act*, R.S.O. 1980, c. 90, s. 5; *Property Law Act*, R.S.B.C. 1979, c. 340, s. 19; *Law of Property Act*, R.S.A. 1980, c. L-8, s. 7(1); *Law of Property Act*, R.S.M. 1970, c. L90, s. 4; *Property Act*, R.S.N.B. 1973, c. P-19, s. 12(3); *Conveyancing Act*, R.S.N.S. 1967, c. 56, ss. 2(2), 5; R.S.N. 1970, c. 63, s. 19.

[3]*Re Hudson; Kühne v. Hudson* (1895), 72 L.T. 892; *Re Irwin; Irwin v. Parkes*, [1904] 2 Ch. 752.

[4](1581), 1 Co. Rep. 93 b, 76 E.R. 206.

[5]*Richardson v. Harrison* (1885), 16 Q.B.D. 85; *Cooper v. Kynock* (1872), L.R. 7 Ch. 398; *Van Grutten v. Foxwell*, [1897] A.C. 658.

[6]*Supra*, footnote 4.

were no children and it must be assumed that she could never have any, the trust was for her and her right heirs who took by limitation and not by purchase, so that the rule applied and she had an equitable estate in fee simple and was entitled to a reconveyance.[7]

Similarly, where an owner of land in fee simple conveyed it to trustees upon trust to lease it and pay the rent to him for life and, after his death, to convey it to such persons as he might appoint by will and, in case of his death intestate, to hold it in trust for his right heirs according to the law of descent and he died intestate, it was held that, his estate and that of his right heirs both being equitable, he had an equitable estate in fee simple which passed to his administratrix.[8]

Recitals in a deed of settlement do not control the operative part,[9] but may explain it.[10] A recital may, however, amount to a covenant.[11]

The doctrine of repugnancy which strikes down subsequent words that contradict a preceding clear grant in a deed, applies to settlements created by deed and by will.[12] In the case of wills, however, it yields to the general rule that the testator's intention must be ascertained from the whole document.[13]

A settlement may be created by more than one deed, so that one deed may make the conveyance and another declare the trusts, or a number of instruments may otherwise constitute one settlement. This was common in England and was described as a "compound settlement".[14] Such a settlement may consist of a deed or will and a statute. Thus, where a father devised lands to his son, restraining him from selling or mortgaging them but giving him power to devise them among his children and the son obtained a special Act empowering him to sell them as they did not produce a substantial revenue and were subject to heavy taxation, the Act providing that the purchase money was to be paid to a trust company for investment, the annual revenue to be paid to the son

---

[7]*Farrell v. Cameron* (1881), 29 Gr. 313.

[8]*Re Bower Trusts* (1905), 9 O.L.R. 199 (H.C.J.).

[9]*Holliday v. Overton* (1852), 14 Beav. 467, 51 E.R. 366; *Dawes v. Tredwell* (1881), 18 Ch. D. 354 (C.A.).

[10]*Jenner v. Jenner* (1866), L.R. 1 Eq. 361, in which case a marriage settlement recited that, under certain instruments, certain hereditaments were limited as the settlor might appoint. The settlor was seised of a fee simple estate not comprised in the recited instruments. It was held that the general words were restricted by the recital so that such estate did not pass under the settlement.

[11]*Farrall v. Hilditch* (1859), 5 C.B. (N.S.) 840, 141 E.R. 337, in which case an indenture made between plaintiff and defendant recited that the plaintiff was seised of certain property, that the plaintiff was indebted to the defendant who had commenced action to recover it, that the plaintiff desired to stay the action and, in order to secure the defendant, had agreed to convey the property to the defendant upon certain trusts and that it had been agreed that the defendant might sign judgment, but was not to issue execution until this security had been realized. It was held that this recital amounted to a covenant by the defendant not to issue execution accordingly.

[12]*Re Walmsley* (1921), 19 O.W.N. 405 (H.C.).

[13]See generally, §502.2(c), *supra*.

[14]*Re Earl of Carnarvon's Chesterfield Settled Estates; Re Earl of Carnarvon's Highclere Settled Estates*, [1927] 1 Ch. 138.

for life, and empowering the son to dispose of the fund among his children, it was held that the fund did not form part of the son's estate but passed to those ultimately entitled by virtue of the son's power of appointment under the father's will which was the only right reserved to the son by the Act.[15]

In regard to the exercise of a power of appointment, there is no distinction between a general power to appoint by deed or will and a general power to appoint by will only.[16] If a life tenant has a power to appoint by deed or will, he need not wait to appoint until his death but, if he appoints by deed absolutely, he cannot again appoint by will. Thus, where the wife had power under a marriage settlement to appoint the trust property and appointed it to her son absolutely, subject to a life interest to herself, and the son died in her lifetime intestate without issue, but leaving a widow, it was held that the wife could not, by her will, appoint the property to her executors and administrators, but that the son's widow was entitled to half of the property, subject to the life interest of the son's mother, and his parents were entitled to the other half. "... the mother chose to give the property absolutely to her son, subject only to her own life estate. Applying also the familiar principle that where an appointment is made the appointment is to be read into the settlement, the situation then becomes perfectly plain".[17]

The Wills Acts[18] provide that a general devise is construed to include any property over which the testator had a general power of appointment and operates as an exercise of the power unless a contrary intention appears in the will. Hence, where a husband, making a marriage settlement, reserved to himself a power of appointment, it was held that he exercised it by a clause in his will, made a few days after the marriage, giving to his wife "all property and estate of which I die seised or possessed".[19]

1303. VOLUNTARY SETTLEMENTS

Settlements may be for valuable consideration or voluntary. Marriage itself, apart from any pecuniary benefit, constitutes valuable consideration for a settlement.[1] If the contemplated marriage is one which the parties cannot legally contract, the settlement is merely a voluntary settlement.[2] If a settle-

---

[15]*Re Northcote* (1921), 20 O.W.N. 175 (H.C.).

[16]*Re Campbell Trusts* (1919), 17 O.W.N. 23 (H.C.), at p. 24.

[17]*Re Plumb* (1915), 8 O.W.N. 284 (H.C.), at p. 286, *per* Middleton, J.

[18]*Wills Act*, R.S.A. 1980, c. W-11, s. 25; R.S.B.C. 1979, c. 434, s. 23; R.S.M. 1970, c. W150, s. 25; R.S.S. 1978, c. W-14, s. 24; R.S.N.B. 1973, c. W-9, s. 24; R.S.N.S. 1967, c. 340, s. 25; R.S.N. 1970, c. 401, s. 16; *Probate Act*, R.S.P.E.I. 1974, c. P-19, s. 78; *Wills Ordinance*, R.O.N.W.T. 1974, c. W-3, s. 19; R.O.Y.T. 1971, c. W-3, s. 18; *Succession Law Reform Act*, R.S.O. 1980, c. 488, s. 25.

[19]*Re Hammond* (1920), 18 O.W.N. 253 (H.C.), citing *Re Jones*; *Greene v. Gordon* (1886), 34 Ch. D. 65, and *Re Jacob*; *Mortimer v. Mortimer*, [1907] 1 Ch. 445.

§1303

[1]*Ex parte Marsh* (1744), 1 Atk. 158, 26 E.R. 102; *Churchman v. Harvey* (1757), Amb. 335, 27 E.R. 225; *Prebble v. Boghurst* (1818), 1 Swans. 309, 36 E.R. 402.

[2]*Seale v. Lowndes* (1868), 17 L.T. 555.

ment is effectually made by the settlor having done everything which makes it binding upon him, the court decrees performance of the trusts created by it, even though it is gratuitous and not for valuable consideration.

If a voluntary settlement is complete, *bona fide* and unaffected by any statutory disability, there is no distinction between such a deed and one executed for valuable consideration; the estates and limitations created in such a deed have the same operation and effect as in a deed executed for value and must be construed in the same manner; it carries with it all the same incidents and rights attached to the property conveyed as are carried by a deed executed for value, and the grantee in this respect stands exactly in the same situation as if he had paid value for the property conveyed.[3] In *Calvert v. Linley*,[4] a father intended by deed of gift to convey a life estate to his daughter with remainder to her issue but, by lack of skill of the person preparing the deed, the fee simple was conveyed to her and her interest was later sold under execution, the sheriff stating to the purchaser that the interest being sold was a life estate. The purchaser afterwards claimed the fee under the deed of gift and the conveyance by the sheriff. It was held that the children of the daughter, though volunteers, had such an interest as entitled them to rectification of the deed in accordance with the true intent of the grantor. Similarly, in *Whitehead v. Whitehead*,[5] at a time when a conveyance by husband to wife was ineffectual to pass the legal estate, a husband conveyed to his wife by deed of bargain and sale in consideration of natural love and affection and the sum of five dollars, it was held that the evident intent of the deed should be given effect to and an order was made vesting in the wife the estate and interest of her husband at the time of the deed.

In *A.-G. Ont. v. Perry*[6] Lord Blaneburgh distinguished two classes of marriage settlements, namely, (1) settlements made by a husband on his own marriage for the benefit of his wife and the issue of the marriage, and (2) settlements made by a third party in consideration of a marriage, for example, a settlement made by a father on the marriage of his daughter. The difference between the two is that the first is made for valuable consideration, that is, the marriage, while the second is voluntary.

A post-nuptial settlement is voluntary, unless made pursuant to a pre-nuptial agreement[7] and, in that respect, there is no distinction between a gift to wife and children and a gift to a stranger.[8]

If, however, the settlement is pursuant to a bargain between husband and wife, each of whom has an interest which is altered by the settlement, the

---

[3]*Per* Romilly, M.R., in *Dickinson v. Burrell; Stourton v. Burrell* (1866), L.R. 1 Eq. 337.
[4](1874), 21 Gr. 470.
[5](1887), 14 O.R. 621 (H.C.).
[6][1934] 4 D.L.R. 65, [1934] A.C. 477 (P.C.).
[7]*Goodright d. Humphreys v. Moses* (1775), 2 Black. W. 1019, 96 E.R. 599; *Evelyn v. Templar* (1787), 2 Bro. C.C. 148, 29 E.R. 85; *Currie v. Nind* (1836), 1 My. & Cr. 17, 40 E.R. 283; *Shurmur v. Sedgwick; Crossfield v. Shurmur* (1883), 24 Ch. D. 597.
[8]*Holloway v. Headington* (1837), 8 Sim. 324, 59 E.R. 128.

settlement is not without valuable consideration,[9] but valuable consideration between husband and wife does not extend to their children who are volunteers and they cannot enforce the settlement, unless they are parties to it, or there is an executed trust in their favour.[10]

Where a husband and wife purchased property in their joint names and both worked on the construction of the house on the property, and where the wife made substantial contributions to the family purse out of her own earnings, it was held that there was no evidence of a post-nuptial settlement.[11]

1303.1 Fraudulent Settlements

The *Fraudulent Conveyances Act*[1] provides that a conveyance of real property made with intent to defeat, hinder, delay or defraud creditors is void as against them, unless it was conveyed upon good consideration and *bona fide* to a purchaser who had no notice of the vendor's intent, and further, that a conveyance of real property, not made for good consideration and *bona fide*, with intent to defraud or deceive the purchaser is void as against him and his assigns. The Act also provides that if a person makes a conveyance of real property with a provision for revocation or alteration at his will and pleasure and thereafter sells or charges the property for money or other good consideration, the first conveyance is void as against the purchaser or chargee under the second instrument, or anyone claiming through him. The Act goes on to provide, however, that the provisions respecting purchasers shall not extend to a conveyance executed in good faith and registered before the execution of the second conveyance to a subsequent purchaser and before the creation of a binding contract for conveyance to him, nor shall a conveyance, merely by reason of absence of valuable consideration, be void as against such purchaser.[2]

In Alberta, section 2 of the *Fraudulent Preferences Act*[3] provides that a gift, conveyance or transfer of any real or personal property made by a person when he is in insolvent circumstances or unable to pay his debts in full, or who knows he is on the eve of insolvency, with intent to defeat, hinder, delay or prejudice his creditors, or any of them, is void.[4]

---

[9]*Teasdale v. Braithwaite* (1876), 4 Ch. D. 85, affd 5 Ch. D. 630 (C.A.); *Re Foster and Lister* (1877), 6 Ch. D. 87.

[10]*Green v. Paterson* (1886), 32 Ch. D. 95 (C.A.). As to the enforceability of covenants in favour of volunteers, see §1206.1, *supra*.

[11]*Burkmar v. Burkmar*, [1953] 2 D.L.R. 329, 8 W.W.R. (N.S.) 397 (B.C.S.C.).

§1303.1

[1]R.S.O. 1980, c. 176, ss. 2-7.

[2]*Ibid.*, s. 8.

[3]R.S.A. 1980, c. F-18.

[4]For similar legislation see the *Fraudulent Preference Act*, R.S.B.C. 1979, c. 143, s. 3; *Fraudulent Preferences Act*, R.S.S. 1978, c. F-21, s. 3; *Assignments and Preferences Act*, R.S.N.B. 1973, c. A-16, s. 2; *Frauds on Creditors Act*, R.S.P.E.I. 1974, c. F-13, s. 2; *Fraudulent Preferences and Conveyances Ordinance*, O.Y.T. 1973 (1st Sess.), c. 3, s. 3(1).

In Manitoba, section 3 of the *Fraudulent Conveyances Act*[5] provides that every conveyance of real property made or hereafter made with intent to defeat, hinder, delay or defraud creditors is null and void as against them.

In Nova Scotia, section 3 of the *Assignments and Preferences Act*[6] provides that any transfer of property made by an insolvent person with intent to defeat, hinder, delay or prejudice his creditors, or any one or more of them, is void as against the creditor or creditors defeated, hindered, delayed or prejudiced.

Some of these statutes apply to personalty as well as to realty. The same is true of the *Bankruptcy Act*.[7] Under section 69 of this Act a settlement made within one year of bankruptcy is void and one within five years is void if it is shown that the settlor was unable, at the time of the settlement, to pay all his debts without the aid of the property comprised in the settlement. However, the section does not apply to a settlement made in consideration of marriage, where it is made in good faith and for valuable consideration, or where it is made in favour of the settlor's wife or children in respect of property that accrued to him after marriage in right of his wife or children.

A marriage contract to settle after-acquired property is also void unless it is completed by the date of the bankruptcy,[8] and it may also be declared void if it was completed less than six months before the bankruptcy, or where the settlor was unable to pay his debts at the time of the transfer, or if the transfer was made in respect of property the settlor expected to receive on the death of a named person, within three months after the property came into the settlor's possession.[9]

A conveyance which gives a preference to a creditor is also void if made within three months of the bankruptcy.[10]

Transactions made in good faith, for valuable consideration and without notice of an act of bankruptcy on the part of the bankrupt, are protected.[11]

The provincial legislation applies to both future and existing creditors and, if it is made at a time when the settlor is insolvent and with the intent to defeat future creditors, it may be impeached by a creditor even though no actual debt was shown to have existed at the date of the settlement.[12] In *Buckland v. Rose*,[13] the evidence was that the husband made a settlement of real property on his wife and children at the request of his wife, having regard to the uncertainties of the husband's partnership business into which he had just entered. Spragge, V.-C., held that it was void against subsequent creditors, although there was no dishonesty or expectation that there would be debts, "but still the contingency of debts being contracted, and their not being satis-

---

[5]R.S.M. 1970, c. F160.
[6]R.S.N.S. 1967, c. 16.
[7]R.S.C. 1970, c. B-3.
[8]*Ibid.*, s. 70.
[9]*Ibid.*, s. 71.
[10]*Ibid.*, s. 73; twelve months if the creditor is related to the settlor, s. 74.
[11]*Ibid.*, s. 75.
[12]*Ferguson v. Kenny* (1889), 16 O.A.R. 276 at pp. 291-2.
[13](1859) ,7 Gr. 440 at p. 445.

fied by the partnership assets, was looked to; and the object of the settlement was to provide for that contingency".

A voluntary settlement made by a man on his wife on the eve of entering into a hazardous business for the purpose of putting his property out of the reach of creditors whom he may have, although he hopes that the business may be prosperous, cannot be supported. Nevertheless, this proposition must not be made too wide; the court must still judge the intent and object of the settlement.[14] However, where the result of a transaction is to defeat, hinder, delay or defraud creditors, the presumption is that it was done with intent.[15]

If the effect of a settlement is to withdraw from creditors assets which would otherwise have been available to them, it is a delaying of creditors within the meaning of the statute.[16] Thus, a conveyance by a husband to his wife in consideration of natural love and affection was set aside at the instance of a secured creditor because it prejudiced him in enforcing the husband's personal liability on the covenant in a mortgage.[17] Similarly, a voluntary settlement of land was held void as tending to hinder and delay creditors even though the vendor was solvent when he made it, because it resulted in denuding him of all his property and so rendered him insolvent thereafter.[18]

A voluntary conveyance or settlement, however, made by a person not indebted at the time and not engaged in or contemplating engagement in business and, therefore, not conceived in fraud of present or future creditors, is good against future creditors of the grantor or settlor.[19] Moreover, a transfer is not fraudulent where the creditor is unable to reach the property by legal process.[20]

To give validity to a deed made in consideration of marriage, the wife must be a party to the transaction, else it is merely voluntary. Where the wife did not sign the deed, was not present when it was executed, no negotiation for it had taken place and she did not know of it until some years after the marriage, it was held that the deed was voluntary and it was set aside as a fraud on the husband's creditors.[21]

Where it is sought to impeach a settlement made in alleged consideration of marriage the court will consider the following principles: (1) That it was either colourable or made with the intent of both parties to defeat creditors.

---

[14]*Per* Middleton, J., in *Wade v. Pedwell* (1920), 19 O.W.N. 190 (H.C.), at p. 191, upholding a voluntary settlement.

[15]*Atlantic Acceptance Corp. Ltd. v. Distributors Acceptance Corp. Ltd.*, [1963] 2 O.R. 18, 38 D.L.R. (2d) 307 (H.C.J.).

[16]*Goodwin v. Williams* (1856), 5 Gr. 539, in which case a person whose chattel property was insufficient to pay execution creditors for small amounts, settled his only real property in trust for his wife and children, it being held that the settlement was fraudulent and void.

[17]*Dixon v. Walsh*, [1937] 1 D.L.R. 585 (Ont. C.A.), and see *Hatch v. Hatch* (1957), 7 D.L.R. (2d) 430 (N.S.S.C.).

[18]*Sun Life Assurance Co. of Canada v. Elliott* (1900), 31 S.C.R. 91, and see *Campbell v. Chapman* (1879), 26 Gr. 240.

[19]*O'Doherty v. Ontario Bank* (1882), 32 U.C.C.P. 285.

[20]*Hopkinson v. Westerman* (1919), 45 O.L.R. 208, 48 D.L.R. 597 (C.A.).

[21]*Mulholland v. Williamson* (1865), 12 Gr. 91.

(2) Mere knowledge on the part of the grantee of the grantor's insolvency is not enough. (3) The fact that the result of the conveyance is to defeat creditors is not conclusive proof that the intention was fraudulent. (4) The fact of intent will be deduced from the whole of the circumstances surrounding the execution of the conveyance.[22]

A marriage celebrated in order to enable the husband to make a settlement on the wife to defeat his creditors is not sufficient consideration for the settlement.[23]

A voluntary post-nuptial settlement is void only as against creditors at that time.[24] A voluntary settlement in favour of children, with no evidence of intent to defeat subsequent creditors, is not void as against subsequent creditors or subsequent purchasers[25] and is not defeated by a subsequent sale by the settlor.[26] Post-nuptial settlements, like all other voluntary transactions, are valid and binding as between the parties and can only be impeached as fraudulent by others.[27]

The mere fact that some obligation attaches to the property conveyed, as where a husband conveys to his wife for natural love and affection and assumption by her of a mortgage, does not necessarily make the conveyance one for valuable consideration.[28] In order to set aside a settlement made for valuable consideration, not only must the intent to defraud be proved but the purchaser must be shown to have been privy to the intent.[29] The existence of valuable consideration dominates every circumstance which might be regarded as suspicious.[30]

1303.2 Setting Voluntary Settlement Aside

A settlement may be made for the protection of the settlor himself and in such case, it is desirable, though not necessary, that it contain a power of

---

[22]McKinnon v. Gillard (1907), 9 O.W.R. 77 (H.C.J.).

[23]Bulmer v. Hunter (1869), L.R. 8 Eq. 46, in which case a man married the woman with whom he had been cohabiting with intent to defraud his creditors. The court found that she was implicated in the fraud; Thompson v. Gore (1886), 12 O.R. 651 (H.C.J.), in which it was shown that husband and wife, before marriage, had been living on intimate terms, that she would have accepted a proposal of marriage without settlement and that he was insolvent, of which fact she must have been aware, so the settlement was set aside; Fallis v. Wilson (1907), 15 O.L.R. 55 (H.C.J.), in which case the settlement was upheld despite the husband's financial difficulties because the wife honestly refused to marry without the settlement.

[24]Ibid., citing Curtis v. Price (1805), 12 Ves. Jun. 89 at p. 103, 33 E.R. 35, and Kidney v. Coussmaker (1806), 12 Ves. Jun. 136 at p. 155, 33 E.R. 53.

[25]Newstead v. Searles (1737), 1 Atk. 265, 26 E.R. 169.

[26]McGregor v. Rapelje (1871), 18 Gr. 446, citing Newstead v. Searles, supra, footnote 25.

[27]Lavin v. Lavin (1882), 2 O.R. 187 (H.C.J.), citing Bill v. Cureton (1835), 2 My. & K. 503, 39 E.R. 1036; Doe d. Newman v. Rushan (1852), 17 Q.B. 723, 117 E.R. 1459.

[28]Ottawa Wine Vaults Co. v. McGuire (1911), 24 O.L.R. 591 (Div. Ct.), revd 27 O.L.R. 319, 8 D.L.R. 229 (C.A.), affd 13 D.L.R. 81, 48 S.C.R. 44.

[29]Fallis v. Wilson (1907), 15 O.L.R. 55 (H.C.J.), at p. 60, citing Re Johnson; Golden v. Gillam (1881), 20 Ch. D. 389.

[30]Per Osler, J.A., in Hickerson v. Parrington (1891), 18 O.A.R. 635.

revocation. Such a settlement may be set aside at the instance of the settlor. Where a woman made a settlement two months after attaining her majority, being told that it was prudent to make it, and ten years later filed a bill to set it aside because she had had no independent legal advice and it did not contain a power of revocation and was improvident, it was held that it must be set aside.[1]

If the settlor understands the deed, it will not be set aside merely because it contains provisions which are unusual and which the court thinks ought not to have been inserted. The court will not consider the impropriety of clauses except as evidence that the settlor did not understand what he was doing, the only question being whether he understood what he was doing and its effect on his position with regard to the property.[2] Those who prepare a deed and evidence its execution are bound to show that it is proper in all respects or, if it contains anything unusual, that the settlor understood and approved it.[3] If he did not understand it, it will be set aside.[4] Where a settlor had a general knowledge of what he was about to do, but refused a description of the provisions because he relied upon his solicitors with respect to them, the court refused to set aside a deed.[5] Where a settlor understood a settlement, but his attention had not been called to the omission of a power of disposition in default of issue, the settlement was rectified by insertion of the power.[6]

If a voluntary settlement is made for the purpose of benefiting another person, the relation between the settlor and such other person may be such as to give rise to a presumption that undue influence was exercised to obtain the settlement. The general rule is that influence which is undue is different in the case of gifts *inter vivos* from that which is required to set aside a will. In the case of gifts or other transactions *inter vivos*, it is considered by the courts of equity that the natural influence arising out of the relation of parent and child, husband and wife, doctor and patient, attorney and client, confessor and penitent, or guardian and ward, exerted by those who possess it to obtain a benefit for themselves, is an "undue" influence. Gifts or contracts brought about by it are, therefore, set aside unless the party benefited can show affirmatively that the other party to the transaction was placed in such a position as would enable him to form an absolutely free and unfettered judgment.[7] Thus, a voluntary settlement by a widow upon a clergyman and his family was set aside as obtained by undue influence and an abuse of the confidence reposed in the defendant as an agent undertaking the management of her

---

§1303.2

[1]*Everitt v. Everitt* (1870), L.R. 10 Eq. 405.

[2]*Dutton v. Thompson* (1883), 23 Ch. D. 278.

[3]*Phillips v. Mullings* (1871), L.R. 7 Ch. 244.

[4]*Prideaux v. Lonsdale* (1863), 1 De G. J. & S. 433, 46 E.R. 172 (C.A.); *Dutton v. Thompson, supra,* footnote 2.

[5]*Lovell v. Wallis (No. 2)* (1884), 50 L.T. 681.

[6]*James v. Couchman* (1885), 29 Ch. D. 212.

[7]*Parfitt v. Lawless* (1872), L.R. 2 P. & D. 462.

affairs.[8] Where no such relation exists, so that the presumption of undue influence does not arise, the person receiving a benefit must show that the donor voluntarily and deliberately did the act, knowing its nature and effect.[9]

A voluntary settlement executed by a settlor when he was *in extremis* was set aside on the ground it did not reserve to him, as it should have done, a power of revocation because, although the absence of such a power does not invalidate a voluntary settlement, it is a circumstance to be taken into consideration[10] and particularly if it appears that the propriety of reserving such power was not impressed upon the grantor.[11] Hence, a deed of voluntary settlement made by a woman in her 69th year at the instance of her relatives was set aside because it did not contain a power of revocation and she was under the impression that the deed had the effect of a will.[12] On the other hand, a woman advanced in years settled real estate upon herself for life and, after her death, to the use of her nephew in fee simple. She had instructed the family solicitor and he prepared the settlement in accordance with her wishes. At the time of its execution by her, the solicitor spent four hours explaining it to her. She had not had a previous copy, but appeared to understand it and it was in accord with her intention at the time. Although the settlement contained no power of revocation and the solicitor had not questioned her on that point, the court dismissed her bill to set it aside.[13]

A voluntary settlement, the nature of which is not fully understood by the donor, may be set aside after the donor's death at the suit of the heir or of those claiming under the donor's will. Thus, where a voluntary deed containing no power of revocation was executed by a woman over 70 years of age, depriving herself of all her property in favour of a niece with whom she was living and to whom she had the clear intention of leaving all her property, the deed was set aside at the instance of those claiming under a will made prior to the deed because the deed was neither explained to, nor understood by her and it appeared that she understood that, under the deed, she would be left with the enjoyment of an estate for life in the property.[14] Similarly, a young woman, an orphan, agreed before she attained her majority to make a voluntary settlement which she executed after attaining her majority, upon the recommendation of the family solicitor but without independent legal advice. By the settlement she assigned to her stepfather and an uncle as trustees the whole of her fortune upon trust for herself for life with remainder to her children or testamentary appointees and, in default of children, to her next

---

[8]*Huguenin v. Baseley* (1807), 14 Ves. Jun. 273, 33 E.R. 526.

[9]*Cooke v. Lamotte* (1851), 15 Beav. 234, 51 E.R. 527, in which case a nephew who was provided for in his aunt's will obtained a bond from her which made the will irrevocable and it was set aside because he did not prove that she understood that the bond had that effect.

[10]*Forshaw v. Welsby* (1860), 30 Beav. 243, 54 E.R. 882.

[11]*Mountford v. Keene* (1871), 24 L.T. 925; *Hall v. Hall* (1873), L.R. 8 Ch. 430.

[12]*Henshall v. Fereday* (1873), 29 L.T. 46.

[13]*Toker v. Toker* (1863), 3 De G. J. & S. 487, 46 E.R. 724.

[14]*Anderson v. Elsworth* (1861), 3 Giff. 154, 66 E.R. 363.

of kin. The settlement reserved to her the power to raise a comparatively small sum for herself, but contained no power of revocation and gave her no voice in investments or appointment of new trustees. It was held that, although the trustees and solicitor really acted with the intention of benefiting her, the settlement must be set aside as imprudent.[15] Where A made a voluntary settlement in favour of a relative who was his solicitor (the deed containing no power of revocation) and later made a will prepared by the same solicitor making a general devise of his property, but not revoking the settlement, the court considered that A intended to reserve a power of revocation, that it was the duty of the solicitor when preparing the will to have asked the testator whether he intended to revoke the deed, that it appeared to have been the intention of the testator that the estate should pass to his devisees and that, as against all persons claiming under the settlement, the estate was subject to the trusts of the general devise in the will.[16]

A marriage settlement may also be set aside as being contrary to public policy. Thus, where a husband and wife provided in their marriage settlement for the division of the property in the event of their future separation, it was held to be void.[17] It is clear that public policy has changed in this respect, however, and it is doubtful that such a settlement would be regarded as void today.[18] In another case, a power given to a life tenant to appoint in favour of any woman he might marry and as often as he should marry, was held to be valid even though it made provision for the event of a divorce.[19]

It is not contrary to public policy for persons, by a marriage contract, to contract out of statutory rights, such as dower, on their respective deaths.[20]

1304. REVOCATION AND TERMINATION

When property is in the hands of a trustee merely for the benefit of the settlor, the latter can revoke the trust at any time and require the trustee to reconvey to him. In *Poirier v. Brulé*,[1] a settlor conveyed property to trustees pursuant to an agreement between himself, the trustees and a beneficiary. If the beneficiary performed certain conditions precedent intended for the support and security of the settlor, the trustees were to convey the property to the beneficiary. When the latter failed to perform the conditions, the settlor brought an action to have the deed set aside. The court held that he was

---

[15]*Everitt v. Everitt* (1870), L.R. 10 Eq. 405.

[16]*Nanney v. Williams* (1856), 22 Beav. 452, 52 E.R. 1182.

[17]*Nelson v. Nelson* (1909), 12 W.L.R. 150 (B.C.S.C.).

[18]See, *e.g., Family Law Reform Act*, R.S.O. 1980, c. 152, and statutes collected in §1301, footnote 19, *supra*.

[19]*Duchess of Marlborough v. Duke of Marlborough*, [1901] 1 Ch. 165 (C.A.), at p. 171.

[20]*Stern v. Sheps*, [1968] S.C.R. 834.

§1304

[1](1891), 20 S.C.R. 97.

entitled to have it set aside since the beneficiary had no right to demand performance of the trust, having failed to perform the conditions and because the settlor was thus the sole person benefited by the trust, so that he could terminate it at any time.

In *Re Bartlett Trust*[2] the settlor was to receive the income from a trust fund for life and on her death the trustee was to dispose of the corpus as she should by will direct. It was held that, even though the settlor did not retain a power of revocation, she was entitled to terminate the agreement since the class of beneficiaries under the power was uncertain and since the settlor could not be compelled to make a will.

Apart from such cases, however, in a completely executed trust, there is no power of revocation unless the power is reserved.[3] The fact that a grantor retains custody of the deed is not evidence that he did so in order that he might revoke it if he is the proper custodian of it, as where it reserves a life estate to him.[4] A settlement made in consideration of marriage cannot, after the marriage, be revoked at the will of those who made it without the consent of all persons entitled under its trusts. Thus, where a mother and her son, who contemplated marriage, made a settlement providing for the son's wife and family and, after the marriage, a revocation of the settlement was made by them, but to which the son's wife was not a party, the revocation was set aside by the court at the instance of an infant child of the son. The son's wife "was not a party to the attempted revocation, nor could she by joining in it have deprived the issue of the marriage, whether born or unborn, of their rights thereunder. The attempted revocation, in so far as it purported to revoke the settlement, was utterly futile".[5] Similarly, where there was an executed trust under a settlement for husband and wife for life and in default of children, for the wife if she survived but, if the husband survived, as the wife might by will appoint and, in default of appointment, for her next of kin, it was held that the trusts for the next of kin could not be revoked, although there was no possibility of issue, the next of kin being *cestuis que trust* whose consent was necessary and the fact that they were volunteers was immaterial.[6]

1305. SETTLED ESTATES LEGISLATION

The statutes of the three provinces that have settled estates legislation are very similar (although the New Brunswick legislation is not as extensive), as they are all based on the English Act. The similarities and differences are discussed in the following sections.

---

[2][1939] 2 W.W.R. 19 (Man. K.B.); and see *Re McCrossan* (1961), 28 D.L.R. (2d) 461, 36 W.W.R. 209 (B.C.S.C.).

[3]*Edmison v. Couch* (1899), 26 O.A.R. 537 at p. 543; see also *Re Cummer Marriage Settlement* (1911), 2 O.W.N. 1486 (H.C.J.).

[4]*Edmison v. Couch, supra,* footnote 3, at p. 540.

[5]*Re Cope*; *Re Smart* (1929), 35 O.W.N. 338 (H.C.), at p. 339, *per* Orde, J.A.

[6]*Paul v. Paul* (1882), 20 Ch. D. 742 (C.A.).

1305.1 Definition

In Ontario, a settled estate means land and all estates or interests in land which are the subject of a settlement.[1] In British Columbia, settled estates are defined as being all interests in land which are the subject of a settlement.[2] In Ontario, "settlement" means a statute, deed, agreement, will or other instrument, or any number of such instruments, under or by virtue of which land or any estate or interest in land stands limited to or in trust for any persons in succession, including any such instruments affecting the estates of any one or more of such persons exclusively.[3] In British Columbia, the definition of settlement is substantially the same.[4] In British Columbia, where a person seised of, or entitled to land for an estate in fee simple or less estate, is an infant, the land is a settled estate under the Act.[5]

All estates or interests in remainder or reversion not disposed of by the settlement and reverting to a settlor or descending to the heir, or as upon an intestacy to the representative of a testator, are deemed to be estates coming to such settlor, heir or representative under or by virtue of the settlement.[6]

1305.2 Leases

The New Brunswick Act does not contain a power to lease but the Ontario and British Columbia Acts confer wide powers on the court to authorize leases and confer on specified persons the authority to make particular leases without application to the court.

The Ontario Act provides that any of the following persons may, without any application to the court, demise a settled estate or any part of it for any term not exceeding twenty-one years to take effect at or within one year after the making of the demise, unless a demise is expressly prohibited in the settlement: (a) a person entitled to the possession or the receipt of the rents and profits of a settled estate for an estate for life or for a term of years determinable with any life or lives, or for any greater estate and not holding merely under a lease at a rent; (b) a tenant in fee simple with an executory limitation, gift or disposition over on failure of his issue, or in any other event; (c) a tenant for years determinable on a life and not holding merely under a lease at a rent; (d) a tenant for the life of another and not holding merely under a lease at a rent; (e) a tenant for his own or any other life or for years determinable on a life whose estate is liable to cease in any event during that life, whether by expiration or conditional limitation, or be defeated by an executory limitation or disposition over, or is subject to a trust for accumulation

§1305.1
[1]Ont. Act, s. 1(1).
[2]B.C. Act, s. 1.
[3]Ont. Act, s. 1(1).
[4]B.C. Act, s. 2.
[5]*Ibid.*, s. 4.
[6]Ont. Act, s. 1(2); B.C. Act, s. 2.

718

of income for payment of debts or other purpose; and (f) a person entitled to the income of land during any life, or until sale of the land, or until forfeiture of his interest on bankruptcy or other event.[1] These powers could also be exercised by a person entitled to the possession or to the receipts of rents and profits of unsettled land as tenant by the curtesy or tenant in dower when those interests were still possible.[2] Any of the foregoing persons may make a lease for giving effect to a contract by a predecessor in title to make a lease which would have bound his successors in title, or for giving effect to a covenant for renewal which could be enforced against the owner for the time being of the settled estate, or for confirming a previous void or voidable lease which, when confirmed, could have been lawfully made originally.[3] Where two or more persons are entitled in possession to concurrent estates for life, or are concurrently entitled to possession or receipt of the rents and profits, they must act concurrently.[4] Every demise under the section must be by deed in duplicate and for the best rent reasonably obtainable.[5] It is not lawful to make the lease without impeachment for waste, or to authorize the cutting of timber, except in the ordinary course of husbandry and the lease must contain a covenant to pay rent half-yearly or more often and be subject to the right of re-entry for non-payment of rent conferred by the *Landlord and Tenant Act*.[6]

In order to be able to invoke these powers to the detriment of the remaindermen, the legislation should be complied with strictly and the onus is on the lessee to prove compliance.[7]

The British Columbia Act provides that it is lawful for any person entitled in possession or to receipt of the rents and profits of any settled estate for life, or for a term of years determinable with a life or lives, or for any greater estate (unless the settlement expressly declares that it shall not be lawful for such person to demise), or for any person entitled to possession or the rents and profits as tenant by the curtesy or in dower, without application to the court, to demise the estate or any part thereof from time to time for a term not exceeding twenty-one years to take effect in possession at or within one year after making it; such demise to be by deed, the best obtainable rent to be reserved, without fine or other benefit in the nature of a fine, which rent shall be an incident to the immediate reversion; the demise not to be without impeachment of waste and to contain a covenant for payment of rent and such other covenants as the lessor deems fit and to contain also a condition for

---

§1305.2
[1]Ont. Act, s. 32(1).
[2]*Ibid.*, s. 32(2).
[3]*Ibid.*, s. 32(3).
[4]*Ibid.*, s. 32(4).
[5]*Ibid.*, s. 32(5).
[6]R.S.O. 1980, c. 232, and see the *Residential Tenancies Act*, R.S.O. 1980, c. 452; Ont. Act, s. 32(6).
[7]*Hunter v. Doan*, [1942] O.W.N. 291 (H.C.J.); and see *Camston Ltd. v. Volkswagen Yonge Ltd.*, [1968] 2 O.R. 65 (Co. Ct.).

re-entry on non-payment of rent for twenty-eight days after it becomes due or a lesser period; and the lessee must execute a counterpart of the lease.[8]

Both Acts provide that every lease so authorized is valid against the person granting it and all persons entitled to estates subsequent to his estate under the same settlement.[9] Both Acts further provide that a person is deemed to be entitled to possession or to receipt of the rents and profits although his estate is charged or encumbered either by himself or by the settlor, but the estates or interests of the persons entitled to the charges or encumbrances are not affected by his acts unless they concur in them.[10]

A testator devised real estate to his executors upon trust to allow his wife, for so long as she remained his widow, the use and occupation and the rents and profits for her own use absolutely, and directed that, after his wife's remarriage or death, the property was to be sold and the proceeds divided equally among his children. In January, 1906, the widow leased the property to the defendant for five years with a right of renewal; she died in April and the lease was not registered until December. No confirming lease was executed by the executors, but they received the rent until the land was sold to the plaintiff's predecessor in title who had knowledge of the defendant's lease and his possession under it. It was contended that the land was not a settled estate within the meaning of the Act, that the widow did not have the statutory power to lease because she did not have an estate for life or greater estate and that the lease did not take effect until it was registered, after which the payment and acceptance of rent created a new monthly tenancy between the executors and the defendant, so that the lease did not bind persons subsequent to the estate of the lessor. It was held (1) that the land was a settled estate within the meaning of the Act; (2) that the widow had power under the Act to lease, as an estate during widowhood is an estate for life, and (3) that, after its registration, the lease operated from its execution.[11] Since the Act provides that a lease must not be made without impeachment for waste, it was held that a lease which exempted the lessee from liability for "fair wear and tear and damages by tempest" was void as not complying with that provision[12] and a lease which allowed the lessee to cut down timber trees of a diameter less than five inches, or of a greater diameter in certain circumstances, was also held void under the Act.[13]

[8]B.C. Act, s. 48.

[9]Ont. Act, s. 33(1); B.C. Act, s. 49.

[10]Ont. Act, s. 37; B.C. Act, s. 56.

[11]*National Trust Co. v. Shore* (1908), 16 O.L.R. 177 (H.C.J.), citing as to point (1) *Re Morgan's Settled Estates* (1870), L.R. 9 Eq. 587; *Carlyon v. Truscott* (1875), L.R. 20 Eq. 348, and *Re Cornell* (1905), 9 O.L.R. 128 (H.C.J.); citing as to point (2) Co. Litt. 42a, *Re Carne's Settled Estates*, [1899] 1 Ch. 324; and citing as to point (3) *Vaughan d. Atkins v. Atkins* (1771), 5 Burr. 2764 at p. 2787, 98 E.R. 451, and *Doe d. Spafford v. Brown* (1833), 3 U.C.Q.B. (O.S.) 90, adding, that in any event, this point was completely answered by section 24 of the *Real Property Act*, R.S.O. 1897, c. 330. See also *Williams v. Williams* (1861), 9 W.R. 888, holding that a widow having an estate for life or widowhood holds an estate for life within the meaning of the Act.

[12]*Davies v. Davies* (1888), 38 Ch. D. 499.

[13]*Monro v. Toronto Ry. Co.* (1904), 9 O.L.R. 299 (C.A.), citing *Davies v. Davies, supra,* footnote 12.

Under the Ontario Act, the court, having due regard for the interests of all persons entitled under the settlement, may authorize leases of any settled estate, or of any rights or privileges over or affecting any settled estate, if it regards the lease as beneficial to the inheritance, but the following conditions are to be observed: the lease may be for such term of years as the court directs, but must take effect in possession at or within one year from the making; it must provide for the best rent reasonably obtainable, payable half-yearly or more often (except in mining, repairing or building leases); it must not authorize the cutting of timber except in the ordinary course of husbandry or so far as the court deems necessary, and is not to be without impeachment for waste; it is to be by deed in duplicate, executed by the lessor and lessee and is to be subject to the right of re-entry for non-payment of rent conferred by the *Landlord and Tenant Act*.[14] Leases for the whole or any part of the settled estate may be authorized.[15] The court may exercise its power either by approving a particular lease or by ordering that the power to lease be vested in trustees,[16] who may be the existing trustees under the settlement or different trustees, and the exercise of the power by them is subject to such conditions as to consents or otherwise as the court may impose.[17] Where a particular lease or contract for a lease is approved by the court, it is to direct what person is to execute it as lessor and the lease or contract executed by such person takes effect as if he were absolutely entitled to the whole estate under the settlement.[18] Where the lease is for any earth, coal, stone or minerals, a portion of the rent is to be set aside and invested[19] and is to be applied to particular purposes.[20]

The English Act[21] permitted renewable ninety-nine-year building leases where it was the usual custom of the district in which the land was situate and it was held that as that Act was incorporated into the law of Ontario "usual custom" must be satisfied with something less than the immemorial custom of England. In Ontario the test will be satisfied if it is found that there is an approved and well-recognized method of framing building leases in a given locality which fixes the rule by long-continued usage. Thus, where it was shown to be the usual practice in Toronto to grant leases with extended rights of renewal beyond ninety-nine years, a petition for leave to lease a settled estate for such a term was granted, the lands being unproductive and the estate lacking the money to improve them.[22]

In British Columbia, the Act provides that any person entitled to possession or receipt of rents and profits of any settled estate for a term of years

---

[14]R.S.O. 1980, c. 232, and see the *Residential Tenancies Act*, R.S.O. 1980, c. 452; Ont. Act, s. 2.
[15]Ont. Act, s. 4.
[16]*Ibid.*, s. 7.
[17]*Ibid.*, s. 10.
[18]*Ibid.*, s. 9.
[19]*Ibid.*, s. 2(1), para. 3.
[20]*Ibid.*, s. 23.
[21]Ss. 4, 7.
[22]*Re Watson's Trusts* (1892), 21 O.R. 528 (H.C.J.).

determinable on his death, or for an estate for life or any greater estate, or his assignee, may apply to the court to exercise the powers conferred by the Act.[23] The court, having due regard for the interests of all parties entitled under the settlement, may authorize leases of any settled estates, or of any rights or privileges over or affecting settled estates, every lease to be made to take effect in possession at or within one year after it is made and to be for a term of years not exceeding a prescribed number, which differs according to whether it is an agricultural or occupation lease, a mining lease, a lease of water mills or easement, a repairing lease or a building lease, but the court may direct a longer term if it is satisfied that it is the local custom or is beneficial to the inheritance to lease for a longer term; the lease must reserve the best rent obtainable, to be payable half-yearly or more often, without taking any fine or other benefit in the nature of a fine but, in the case of a mining, repairing or building lease, a peppercorn rent or rent smaller than the rent ultimately payable may, if the court directs, be made payable during the first five years of the term; where the lease is of earth, coal, stone or mineral or is of timbered land or a timber limit, one-fourth of the whole rent or payment is to be set aside and invested when and so long as the person entitled to the receipt of the rent is a person who, by reason of his estate or a declaration in the settlement, is entitled to work the earth, coal, stone or mineral for his own benefit or to cut and market the timber, and otherwise three-fourths; no such lease, other than of timbered land or a limit, is to authorize the felling of trees except so far as is necessary to clear the ground for agricultural purposes or for any buildings, excavations or other works authorized by the lease; every lease is to be by deed, the lessee is to execute a counterpart and the lease is to contain a condition for re-entry on non-payment of the rent for twenty-eight days after it is due or for some lesser specified period.[24] Leases for the whole or any part of the settled estate may be authorized.[25] The court may exercise its powers either by approving a particular lease or by ordering that the power to lease be vested in trustees,[26] who may be the existing trustees under the settlement or different trustees, and the exercise of the power by them is subject to such conditions as to consents or otherwise as the court may impose.[27] Where a particular lease or contract for a lease is approved by the court, it is to direct what person is to execute it as lessor and the lease or contract executed by such person takes effect as if he were absolutely entitled to the whole estate under the settlement.[28]

The British Columbia Act further provides that nothing in the Act authorizes a lease beyond the term of twenty-one years when the reversion is in the Crown.[29]

---

[23] B.C. Act, s. 28.
[24] *Ibid.*, s. 6.
[25] *Ibid.*, s. 8.
[26] *Ibid.*, s. 11.
[27] *Ibid.*, s. 14.
[28] *Ibid.*, s. 13.
[29] *Ibid.*, s. 57.

1305.3 Sale and Mortgage

The Ontario Act provides that, if the court thinks it proper, having regard to the interests of all persons interested under the settlement, it may (a) authorize a mortgage of the whole or any part of the settled estate to raise money to repair, rebuild or alter a building, or to build upon or improve the estate, or to discharge all or part of an encumbrance; (b) authorize a sale of all or part of the settled estate, or of an easement or right, or of timber, and (c) sanction any action, defence or other proceeding for the protection of the settled estate and order that the expenses be raised by means of a sale or mortgage of or charge upon all or part of the estate, or be paid out of the rents and profits, or out of money or the income from money to be invested in the purchase of land to be settled in the same manner as the settled estate.[1]

The British Columbia Act provides that, when the court considers it necessary or expedient in the interest of the parties concerned to release the settled estate or any portion of it from any encumbrance, charge or lien on it, or to spend money on it to prevent its deterioration in value, or to increase its productive power, it may order from time to time that all or any part of the money required for any such purpose and for related costs and expenses be raised by means of a sale or mortgage of, or charge on, all or any part of the settled estate, or out of any moneys or investments liable to be laid out in the purchase of hereditaments to be settled in the same manner as the settled estate, or out of the income of such moneys or investments, or out of any accumulation of rents or income.[2]

Both Acts provide that, if land is sold for building purposes, the court may allow all or any part of the consideration to be a rent issuing out of the land which may be secured and settled as the court may direct.[3] Both Acts provide that the court may direct that any part of a settled estate be laid out for streets, roads, paths, squares, gardens, open spaces, sewers, drains or watercourses, to be dedicated to the public or not, and may direct that the parts so laid out remain vested in the trustees and may direct how the expenses are to be paid and how such parts are to be repaired or maintained.[4]

Both Acts provide that, on every sale, mortgage or dedication, the court may direct what person is to execute the deed or mortgage, which shall take effect as if he had the power under the settlement.[5]

The Acts provide for the application of money received on any sale.[6]

The British Columbia Act provides that nothing in the Act authorizes a sale of any settled estate where the reversion is in the Crown.[7]

---

§1305.3

[1]Ont. Act, s. 13(1).
[2]B.C. Act, s. 17.
[3]Ont. Act, s. 14; B.C. Act, s. 23.
[4]Ont. Act, s. 16(1), (2); B.C. Act, ss. 25, 26.
[5]Ont. Act, s. 17; B.C. Act, s. 27.
[6]Ont. Act, s. 23; B.C. Act, s. 38.
[7]B.C. Act, s. 57.

Under the New Brunswick Act the trustees of a settlement may, with the concurrence by deed of the person entitled to the immediate possession of the land, sell all or part of the land, or grant an easement, right or privilege over it, exchange the land for other land, or concur in making a partition of the land.[8] Before exercising these powers the trustees must obtain an order of the court approving the sale, exchange or partition.[9]

Every transaction must be made for the best consideration obtainable.[10]

The proceeds of sale, or land obtained under an exchange or partition, are to be held by the trustees upon the trusts of the settlement[11] and any moneys are to be invested in trust investments.[12]

It was held that, before making permanent improvements or purchasing fixtures, executors or trustees should obtain the sanction of the court, which will be granted in proper cases on proper terms.[13] The expense of improvements and repairs ought to be provided for in such a way as to throw the burden equitably on the tenant for life and remainderman and not entirely upon either.[14] Where the testator directs that repairs are to be paid for out of income, it means repairs arising after his death and not dilapidations existing prior to his death.[15]

A tenant for life was authorized, upon application under the Act, to borrow money upon the security of a mortgage on the estate for the purpose of paying for repairs, taxes and other expenses, provision for insurance being made a condition of authorizing the encumbrance.[16] The English Act, from which the provincial Acts were taken, in the main was intended to enable the court to authorize such powers to be exercised as were ordinarily contained in a well-drawn settlement and thus it has been held that it ought to be liberally construed.[17] Hence, where a settlement provided that trustees, with the approval of the settlors or the survivor of them, might sell, but not mortgage the property, it was held that the object of the provision was to give the trustees a power of sale which they would not otherwise possess, that the words "but not mortgage" meant only that the power of sale did not include a power to mortgage and did not amount to an express declaration that the

---

[8]N.B. Act, s. 44.

[9]*Ibid.*, s. 48.

[10]*Ibid.*, s. 45.

[11]*Ibid.*, s. 46.

[12]*Ibid.*, s. 47.

[13]*Re Elliot* (1917), 41 O.L.R. 276 at pp. 279-80, 40 D.L.R. 649 at pp. 651-2 (S.C.), citing *Re Freman*; *Dimond v. Newburn*, [1898] 1 Ch. 28 at p. 33, and *Re Hotchkys*; *Freke v. Calmady* (1886), 32 Ch. D. 408 (C.A.).

[14]*Re Elliot, supra*, footnote 13, citing *Re Hotchkys, supra*, footnote 13.

[15]*Re Elliot, supra*, footnote 13. *Re Smith*; *Bull v. Smith* (1901), 17 T.L.R. 588.

[16]*Re Darch* (1914), 6 O.W.N. 107, 16 D.L.R. 875 (H.C.), and see *Re Bridgman* (1910), 1 O.W.N. 468 (H.C.J.).

[17]*Re Hooper* (1896), 28 O.R. 179 (H.C.J.), at p. 181, citing *Lord Bruce v. Marquess of Ailesbury*, [1892] A.C. 356 at p. 364; *Re Shepheard's Settled Estate* (1869), L.R. 8 Eq. 571 at p. 573, and *Beioley v. Carter* (1869), L.R. 4 Ch. 230 at p. 240.

property should not be mortgaged and that, accordingly, the court could authorize a mortgage under the Act.[18]

The Acts only empower the court to authorize a mortgage and to direct who shall execute it. The court cannot compel the trustees to act upon the authority given them by the court. Hence, where two trustees cannot agree as to the arrangement to be made, it is not for the court to decide; if they cannot agree, they should either give up the trust, or apply to the court for advice.[19]

Unless the statute provides for it (as does the New Brunswick Act), the court cannot authorize an exchange of land.[20]

The court will authorize a sale where all present beneficiaries consent and where there is only a remote possibility of others ever becoming entitled,[21] but it is loath to exercise its powers where the main person interested is incapable of giving his consent.[22]

In *Re Cornell*,[23] the testator directed his executors to lease land until his youngest son came of age unless prior thereto, with the approval of the adult children, the executors could sell the property advantageously. The will directed that the property was to be valued when the youngest child came of age, certain options to purchase being given to the children and a power of sale being given to the executors for the purpose of distribution. Boyd, C., held that there was substantially a trust for sale, but not before the majority of the youngest child, unless the sale were sanctioned by adult children, that (with some hesitation) the case might be regarded as coming within the Act as being a limitation "by way of succession", and, as the petitioner had made a good case for realizing money from the sale of the whole property because of increased taxation, disrepair of the house and inability to make sufficient outlay from the funds of the estate, he directed a sale.

Where lands, settled upon trust for sale after the death of the life tenant, were sold under the Act during his lifetime, the proceeds of sale were directed to be paid to the trustees to be held upon the trusts of the settlement.[24] Where a sale was authorized under the Act, the proceeds were directed to be paid into court subject to the trusts of the will and a mortgage for the balance of the purchase price was directed to be made to the Accountant of the Supreme Court.[25]

The proceeds of sale cannot be used to purchase lands out of the jurisdiction, even on the same trusts.[26]

---

[18]*Re Currie and Watson's Trusts* (1904), 7 O.L.R. 701 (H.C.J.).

[19]*Shepard v. Shepard* (1911), 20 O.W.R. 810 (H.C.J.).

[20]*Re Bishoprick* (1874), 21 Gr. 589.

[21]*Re Graham* (1910), 1 O.W.N. 674 (H.C.J.).

[22]*Re Anderson*, [1951] O.W.N. 349 (H.C.J.).

[23](1905), 9 O.L.R. 128 (H.C.J.).

[24]*Re Morgan's Settled Estates* (1870), L.R. 9 Eq. 587.

[25]*Re Milligan Settled Estates* (1912), 21 O.W.R. 701, 2 D.L.R. 883 (H.C.J.).

[26]*Re Fell*, [1940] O.R. 397, [1940] 4 D.L.R. 73 (C.A.).

1305.4 Applicants

In Ontario, the Act provides that any of the persons authorized by section 32 to make a lease, or any person entitled to possession or receipt of the rents and profits of a greater estate than that mentioned in that section, or any tenant in common, joint tenant or coparcener, and the assigns of any such person, may apply to the court to exercise the powers conferred by the Act.[1]

The British Columbia Act permits any person entitled to possession, or to the receipt of the rents and profits under a life lease, a life estate, or a greater estate, or any assignee of such person, to apply to the court to exercise the powers conferred by the Act.[2]

It was held that a person entitled to the possession or the receipt of rents and profits of a settled estate does not necessarily mean beneficially entitled, so that, where there is no equitable owner, the trustees may apply.[3] The assignee of a tenant for life can petition the court for a sale.[4] Persons beneficially interested in the proceeds of sale of an estate directed to be sold after the death of the life tenant also have beneficial interests within the meaning of the provision,[5] but not unascertained contingent remaindermen.[6]

1305.5 Consents

Both the Ontario and British Columbia Acts provide that an application to the court under the Act must be with the concurrence or consent (a) of the tenant in tail, if any and of full age, and of all persons in existence having any prior estate or interest under the settlement and of all trustees having any prior estate or interest on behalf of an unborn child, or (b) in every other case, of the persons in existence having any beneficial estate or interest under the settlement and of trustees having any estate or interest on behalf of an unborn child, and provision is made for notices, dispensing with consent and preserving the rights of non-consenting parties.[1] The British Columbia Act also provides that, if an infant is tenant in tail under the settlement, the court may dispense with the concurrence or consent of the person or persons entitled beneficially or otherwise to any estate or interest subsequent to the estate tail of the infant.[2]

---

§1305.4
[1] Ont. Act, s. 18.
[2] B.C. Act, s. 28.
[3] *Vine v. Raleigh* (1883), 24 Ch. D. 238.
[4] *Re Ebsworth and Tidy's Contract* (1889), 42 Ch. D. 23 (C.A.).
[5] *Re Ives; Bailey v. Holmes* (1876), 3 Ch. D. 690.
[6] *Beioley v. Carter* (1869), L.R. 4 Ch. 230 at p. 233; *Re Strutt's Trusts* (1873), L.R. 16 Eq. 629.
§1305.5
[1] Ont. Act, s. 19, and see also ss. 34-36; B.C. Act, s. 29, and see also ss. 30-33 and 51-56.
[2] B.C. Act, s. 29.

The Ontario Act does provide, however, that a court order under the Act is not invalidated for lack of consent.[3]

Where there is doubt as to the mental capacity of a remainderman and no committee has been appointed for him the court will refuse to make an order under the Act.[4]

1305.6 Disabilities

Both the Ontario and British Columbia Acts provide for powers, applications, consents and notifications where mentally unsound persons, bankrupts, insolvents, debtors in liquidation or infants are concerned.[1] Both Acts provide that a married woman may make, consent to or oppose an application under the Act, whether or not she is of full age,[2] but, in British Columbia, special provision is made in regard to her examination apart from her husband in regard to her knowledge of the effect of the application.[3]

A husband and wife held land as joint tenants. Immediately after their divorce the husband executed a declaration of trust in favour of his infant son with respect to his interest. When the husband died the wife sought a declaration to have the property vested in her by right of survivorship. The Public Trustee appeared on behalf of the infant, as infants' lands are deemed to be settled estates under the British Columbia Act.[4] It was held that the husband's declaration of trust effected a severance of the joint tenancy and created a valid trust in favour of his son as to a half interest in the property.[5]

1305.7 Effect of Court Order

Under the Ontario Act an order of the court is not, as against a lessee, mortgagee or purchaser, invalidated because of want of jurisdiction, concurrence, consent, notice or service, whether he had notice of it or not.[1] The British Columbia Act makes a similar provision, except where a concurrence or consent was not obtained, or notice was not served upon a person entitled thereto, or an order dispensing with notice was not made.[2]

---

[3]Ont. Act, s. 30.
[4]*Re Anderson*, [1951] O.W.N. 349 (H.C.J.).
§1305.6
[1]Ont. Act, s. 34; B.C. Act, s. 51.
[2]Ont. Act, s. 35; B.C. Act, s. 54.
[3]B.C. Act, ss. 52, 53.
[4]*Ibid.*, s. 4.
[5]*Re Mee* (1972), 23 D.L.R. (3d) 491, [1972] 2 W.W.R. 424 *sub nom. Public Trustee v. Mee* (B.C.C.A.).
§1305.7
[1]Ont. Act, s. 30(1).
[2]B.C. Act, s. 44.

CHAPTER 14

POWERS

1401. DEFINITION

A power is an authority given by one person, the donor of the power, to another, the donee of the power, to deal with or dispose of property that is not owned, or not owned solely by the donee of the power.[1] Powers may be administrative in nature or dispositive. Administrative or executive powers are often conferred by statute, such as trustees' powers of sale,[2] lease,[3] investment[4] and appointment of new trustees,[5] but they may also be conferred or modified by instrument. Dispositive powers, normally conferred by instrument, include powers of advancement, maintenance, encroachment and powers to appoint. A power of appointment authorizes the donee of the power (also called the appointor), in his discretion, to determine who shall receive the property that is the subject-matter of the power. The recipient is called the appointee; the persons to or among whom the donee of the power may appoint

§1401
[1]Freme v. Clement (1881), 18 Ch. D. 499 at p. 504, per Jessel, M.R.; Waters, p. 65; Hanbury and Maudsley, p. 178; Farwell, p. 1.
[2]Trustee Act, R.S.O. 1980, c. 512, s. 17; R.S.A. 1980, c. T-10, ss. 18, 19; R.S.B C. 1979, c. 414, ss. 5, 6; R.S.M. 1970, c. T160, ss. 27-30; R.S.N.S. 1967, c. 317, ss. 18-19; R.S.N. 1970, c. 380, ss. 14, 15; R.S.S. 1978, c. T-23, ss. 37, 38: Trustees Act, R.S.N.B. 1973, c. T-15, s. 7; Trustee Ordinance, R.O.N.W.T. 1974, c. T-8, ss. 16, 17; R.O.Y.T. 1971, c. T-5, ss. 19, 20.
[3]Trustee Act, R.S.O. 1980, c. 512, s. 22: R.S.M. 1970, c. T160, ss. 29, 30, 40; R.S.N.S. 1967, c. 317, s. 20; R.S.N. 1970, c. 380, s. 20; Trustees Act, R.S.N.B. 1973, c. T-15, s. 11.
[4]Trustee Act, R.S.O. 1980, c. 512, ss. 26, 27; R.S.A. 1980, c. T-10, ss. 3-13; R.S.B.C. 1979, c. 414, ss. 15-22; R.S.M. 1970, c. T160, ss. 70-77; R.S.N.S. 1967, c. 317, ss. 2-14; R.S.N. 1970, c. 380, ss. 3-10: R.S.P.E.I. 1974, c. T-9, ss. 2, 3; R.S.S. 1978, c. T-23, ss. 3-12; Trustees Act, R.S.N.B. 1973, c. T-15, ss. 2-4; Trustee Ordinance, R.O.N.W.T. 1974, c. T-8, ss. 3-5; R.O.Y.T. 1971, c. T-5, ss. 3-8; as am. 1980 (1st), c. 33.
[5]Trustee Act, R.S.O. 1980, c. 512, ss. 3, 4; R.S.A. 1980, c. T-10, s. 14; R.S.B.C. 1979, c. 414, s. 27; R.S.M. 1970, c. T160, s. 10: R.S.N.S. 1967, c. 317, s. 15; R.S.N. 1970, c. 380, s. 11; R.S.S. 1978, c. T-23, s. 15; Trustee Ordinance, R.O.N.W.T. 1974, c. T-8, ss. 7, 8; R.O.Y.T. 1971, c. T-5, s. 11.

are called the objects of the power. This chapter deals primarily with powers of appointment.[6]

The advantage of powers of appointment is that it enables the testator or settlor to postpone the final decision as to who shall be the objects of his bounty. In many cases he will wish to delay this decision so that future events and the later circumstances of the intended beneficiaries may be taken into account. By giving a power to appoint, he may vest this power of final determination in the donee of the power. A typical power of this type is a gift by will to a life tenant who is given a power to appoint the remainder among the testator's issue in such shares as he shall see fit. Care must be taken, in this respect, to ensure that the testator does not completely delegate his will-making powers, for such a delegation would be void. It is rare, however, for a court to find such a delegation.[7] Thus, for example, a power enabling trustees to add to the class of objects of a power is not objectionable.[8]

A power of appointment must be distinguished from a property interest. If a person is given full dispositive powers over property he has the entire property in it and is not subject to the court's intervention for disposing of the property contrary to his power.

In *Re MacInnis and Townshend*[9] a testatrix devised her half interest in real property held in common with her executrix to the latter, "to be used and disposed of as she wishes during her lifetime and that any that is left after her death shall go to my niece". The executrix executed a deed in respect of this half interest to herself and the niece, conveying a life interest to herself with remainder to the niece. Thereafter she purported to convey the entire fee simple to a third party. It was held that the will gave the executrix the whole interest of the testatrix so that she could thereafter do with it as she liked. Having conveyed it in her representative capacity to herself and the niece, and being party to the deed in her personal capacity, that deed was valid and she could not, thereafter, convey the whole interest to another.

On the other hand, where a testator gives a usufruct to his son and his wife but, as to the bare ownership of the property, gives it to be disposed of by his wife in her will, the widow has an unqualified right to dispose of the property, although not *qua* owner, but under a general power of appointment.[10]

A power of appointment may also be used to permit the application of property to purposes, both charitable and non-charitable. As to charitable

---

[6]See generally Gallagher, "Powers of Appointment", Isaac Pitblado Lectures Series, 1974, p. 111; Baker, "Are Wills Draftsmen Misusing Discretionary Powers", 1 E. & T. Q. 172 (1973-74).

[7]For cases on this point see *Re Triffit's Settlement*; *Hall v. Hyde*, [1958] Ch. 852; *Tatham v. Huxtable* (1950), 81 C.L.R. 639 (H.C. Aust.); *Re McEwen*, [1955] N.Z.L.R. 575, and see Gordon, "Delegation of Will-making Power", 69 L.Q. Rev. 334 (1953).

[8]*Re Manisty's Settlement*; *Manisty v. Manisty*, [1974] Ch. 17.

[9](1973), 35 D.L.R. 459, 4 Nfld. & P.E.I.R. 211 *sub nom. Townshend v. McInnis* (P.E.I.S.C.).

[10]*Minister of National Revenue v. Lemieux-Fournier*, [1971] F.C. 39, [1971] C.T.C. 592 (T.D.).

purposes, the power will be valid whether it be a trust power or not, but in order for a non-charitable purpose trust to be valid its objects must be certain.[11] Moreover, such trusts are often held to be void because they lack human beneficiaries to enforce them and because they may be exercised beyond the perpetuity period. A power is not subject to those defects and, so long as the objects are specific,[12] it will be valid, provided it is exercised within the perpetuity period.[13] In *Re Ogilvy and Ogilvy*[14] a power in the life tenant, the testator's widow, to encroach on the principal to use for such charitable or other purposes as in her judgment her husband would have approved of, was held to constitute a power and not a trust and, as such, was valid.

1402. CLASSIFICATION

Powers may be classified in the several ways described below.

(a) Administrative powers and dispositive powers

This distinction has been dealt with in the previous paragraph. Administrative powers are those which confer a power to manage or otherwise deal with property and the power to appoint to office, such as the power to appoint new trustees. Dispositive powers are those which enable the donee of the power to give the property to specific persons by way of advancement, encroachment, maintenance or appointment.

(b) Statutory powers and powers conferred by instrument

This distinction was also dealt with in the previous paragraph and need not be elaborated upon further.

(c) Common law powers, powers under the Statute of Uses and equitable powers

A common law power enables the donee of the power to convey the legal estate even though it is not vested in him. Before land was made devisable by the *Statute of Wills*,[1] such powers were employed to obtain a degree of testation. The owner could give his executors a power to sell the land. They would receive no estate, for it was not devised to them, but they were thus

---

[11]As to the question of certainty of objects, see §1403.2(a), *infra*.

[12]As to non-specific objects, see *Re Astor's Settlement Trusts; Astor v. Scholfield*, [1952] Ch. 534; *Re Endacott; Corpe v. Endacott*, [1960] 1 Ch. 232 (C.A.).

[13]Trusts for specific non-charitable purposes are, for this reason, sometimes construed as powers. See *Perpetuities Act*, R.S.O. 1980, c. 374, s. 16; R.S.A. 1980, c. P-4, s. 20; *Perpetuity Act*, R.S.B.C. 1979, c. 321, s. 21; *Perpetuities Ordinance*, R.O.N.W.T. 1974, c. P-3, s. 17; O.Y.T. 1980 (1st), c. 23, s. 21, and see *Re Russell; Wood v. The Queen* (1977), 1 E.T.R. 285 (Alta. S.C.).

[14][1952] O.W.N. 625, [1953] 1 D.L.R. 44 (H.C.J.).

§1402

[1]32 Hen. 8, c. 1 (1540).

enabled to pass the legal estate to the purchaser. Until the power was exercised, therefore, the legal estate remained in the donor of the power or his heir-at-law.[2]

A power of attorney to convey land is the main modern example of a common law power. A further example is the mortgagee's power of sale where he holds the legal interest.

An equitable power is one which affects the equitable or beneficial estate only. It arises where the legal estate is in one person, while the power vests in another.[3] Thus, where A holds on trust, "for B for life, with remainder on such trusts as C may appoint", C has an equitable power. When C exercises the power, A may, in equity, be compelled to convey the legal estate to the appointee.[4]

A power under the *Statute of Uses*[5] is used to revoke existing, or declare future, uses. The power is vested in some person named in the deed.[6] A power operating under the *Statute of Uses* has the effect of calling future legal estates into existence, since the statute executes the use.

Thus, where X conveys "to Y and his heirs, to such uses as Z may appoint", there is a resulting use to X until the appointment and, when Z appoints, for example, to A, the use passes to A and is immediately executed, giving A the legal estate.[7] If a person limits his estate to such uses as he may appoint and, until appointment, to the use of himself and his heirs, the fee simple continues to be vested in him subject to being divested upon the exercise of his power of appointment.[8]

(d) Powers of ownership and powers collateral, in gross and appendant or appurtenant

Powers over real estate were formerly usually classified as (1) powers of ownership, (2) powers collateral and (3) powers relating to the estate which the donee of the power has in the land, being either powers appendant or powers in gross.[9]

A power of ownership is one which gives the donee of the power complete dominion over an estate, although he may have no interest in it, such as a limitation to such uses as he may appoint and, in default of appointment, to the use of another person.[10]

A collateral power is a bare authority to deal in some way with an estate no interest in which is vested in the donee of the power.[11] An example is a power of sale given to trustees to whom no estate is limited.

---

[2]Sugden, *Powers*, p. 45; Farwell, p. 2.
[3]Farwell, p. 3.
[4]*Re Brown; Dixon v. Brown* (1886), 32 Ch. D. 597 at p. 601.
[5]27 Hen. 8, c. 10 (1535).
[6]Farwell, p. 3.
[7]Megarry and Wade, p. 462.
[8]*Re Hazell* (1925), 57 O.L.R. 290 at p. 294, [1925] 3 D.L.R. 661 at p. 668 (C.A.); *Re Rowe*, [1957] O.R. 9, 10 D.L.R. (2d) 215 (H.C.J.).
[9]Farwell, p. 9.
[10]*Ibid.*
[11]*Per* Lord Westbury, L.C., in *Dickenson v. Teasdale* (1862), 1 De G. J. & S. 52, 46 E.R. 21.

A power appendant, or appurtenant, is one the exercise of which affects the estate of the donee of the power, as where a tenant for life has the power to lease, or has covenanted to stand seised to the use of another,[12] or where a person with power of appointment by will is a tenant for life for his separate use with remainder to his right heirs on default of appointment.[13] It is a power exercised by a person who has an interest in the property, which interest is capable of being affected, diminished, or disposed of to some extent by the exercise of the power.[14]

A power in gross is one the exercise of which does not affect the estate of the donee of the power, as where a tenant for life has the power to appoint the remainder among his own children or otherwise.[15] Thus, the power of a life tenant under a marriage settlement to appoint, by deed or will, a sum of money as portions for younger children is a power in gross.[16] This classification remains important in most of the Canadian provinces in that powers appendant and in gross may be released while powers collateral may not. This rule was formerly applicable in England, Ontario, Prince Edward Island and New Brunswick as well, but is now changed by statute.[17]

(e) General, special and hybrid powers of appointment

A general power of appointment is one which the donee of the power may exercise in favour of such persons as he chooses, including himself. As such, it is virtually the equivalent of ownership[18] and it is usually so treated for death tax purposes. A power to appoint by will only is none the less a general power if it permits the donee to dispose of the property as he sees fit, and it is so treated for the purpose of statutes respecting wills which include in a general devise of real property any property over which the testator had a general power of appointment.[19]

---

[12]*Edwards v. Sleater* (1665), Hardres 410, 145 E.R. 522.

[13]*Penne v. Peacock* (1734), Cases T. Talbot 42, 25 E.R. 652.

[14]*Re D'Angibau; Andrews v. Andrews* (1879), 15 Ch. D. 228, *per* Jessel, M.R., affd *loc. cit.*, at p. 236 (C.A.).

[15]Co. Litt. 342; *Edwards v. Sleater, supra*, footnote 12.

[16]*Nottidge v. Dering; Raban v. Dering*, [1909] 2 Ch. 647, affd [1910] 1 Ch. 297 (C.A.), and see *Cowan v. Besserer* (1883), 5 O.R. 624 (H.C.J.), at p. 630.

[17]See § 1410, *infra*.

[18]*Re Fasken*, [1961] O.R. 891, 30 D.L.R. (2d) 193 (H.C.). A power to encroach does not give a life tenant all rights of ownership however; *Re Stanners* (1978), 85 D.L.R. (3d) 368, [1978] 3 W.W.R. 70 (Sask. Q.B.).

[19]*Re Powell* (1870), 18 W.R. 228; *Wills Act*, R.S.A. 1980, c. T-10, s. 25; R.S.B.C. 1979, c. 434, s. 23; R.S.M. 1970, c. W150, s. 25; R.S.S. 1978, c. T-23, s. 24; R.S.N.B. 1973, c. W-9, s. 24; R.S.N.S. 1967, c. 340, s. 25; R.S.N. 1970, c. 401, s. 16; *Probate Act*, R.S.P.E.I. 1974, c. P-19, s. 78; *Succession Law Reform Act*, R.S.O. 1980, c. 488, s. 25; *Wills Ordinance*, R.O.N.W.T. 1974, c. W-3, s. 19; R.O.Y.T. 1971, c. W-3, s. 18.

In this respect, *Re Comstock*, [1949] O.R. 537, [1949] 3 D.L.R. 677 (H.C.J.), in which a gift in trust to the testator's daughters for life with remainder to go as they might by will appoint and with a gift over in default of appointment, was construed as creating a qualified or special power, is wrong. Such a power would be general. The case must be read in the context of the issue for which it was litigated, namely, whether the

Where trustees were given a power to administer the residue of an estate as they in their judgment considered best, with a further discretion to use an undefined portion for the benefit of certain relatives, it was held that no trust for any person was created and that the trustees had an absolute power of appointment which they could exercise in favour of themselves.[20]

A general power does not become special merely because the will contains a protective or spendthrift trust so long as the trustees are not required to retain or shift the payment of any moneys on the happening of any improvident events, but may in their discretion do so.[21]

A special power of appointment is one where the donee may appoint among a specified class of objects. A typical example of such a power is a power given to a life tenant to appoint the remainder among his issue. The power is none the less special even though the donee is himself a member of the class of objects.[22]

The donee of a general power may convert it into a special power by a partial release, thereby restricting the objects of the power.[23]

Hybrid powers are those where the donee of the power may appoint to anyone except named persons or a named class of persons, such as himself, or himself and his wife.[24] If, however, the objects are not limited, but the appointment may only be made with the consent of another, such as the settlor, the power is a general one.[25] A power in trustees to add to the class of beneficiaries is a hybrid power.[26]

Hybrid powers are treated as special powers for the purpose of the Wills Acts,[27] and for the purposes of perpetuities legislation.[28] It is, therefore, questionable whether this intermediate class has much utility. For this reason, it has been suggested that general and special powers should be qualified as limited or unlimited, depending upon whether consent is required, or whether the objects are restricted. If that is done, the hybrid class of powers can be eliminated.[29]

---

daughters had received the entire interest rather than a life interest coupled with a power to appoint because of earlier language in the will which appeared to create an absolute gift.

[20]*Higginson v. Kerr* (1898), 30 O.R. 62 (H.C.J.), at pp. 67-8. To the same effect is *Re Miles* (1917), 11 O.W.N. 292 (H.C.), where executors had power to dispose of the residue "in such manner as may in their discretion seem best".

[21]*Re Fasken, supra*, footnote 18.

[22]*Re Penrose; Penrose v. Penrose*, [1933] Ch. 793.

[23]*Re Fasken, supra*, footnote 18.

[24]Hanbury and Maudsley, p. 180.

[25]*Re Fasken, supra*, footnote 18.

[26]*Re Manisty's Settlement; Manisty v. Manisty*, [1974] Ch. 17.

[27]See the statutes collected in footnote 19, *supra*.

[28]*Perpetuities Act*, R.S.O. 1980, c. 374, s. 11; R.S.A. 1980, c. P-4, s. 14; *Perpetuity Act*, R.S.B.C. 1979, c. 321, s. 15; *Perpetuities Ordinance*, R.O.N.W.T. 1974, c. P-3, s. 12; O.Y.T. 1980 (1st), c. 23, s. 15. And see ch. 11, *supra*.

[29]See Fleming, "Hybrid Powers", 13 Conv. (N.S.) 20 (1948); Marshall, "Trusts and Powers", 35 Can. Bar Rev. 1060 (1957).

Where a power is contained in a will and it is unclear whether it is a special or a general power, affidavit evidence to show which was intended is admissible.[30]

(f) Bare powers, fiduciary powers, mere powers and trust powers

Bare powers are powers given to non-trustees who are under no duty to exercise them. Fiduciary powers are like bare powers, except that they are given to fiduciaries who, because they are fiduciaries, are required to consider whether and to what extent they should exercise them.

Mere powers are those in which the donee is under no duty to exercise them, whether they be vested in trustees or non-trustees, whereas trust powers are trusts for distribution coupled with powers of selection.

These several types are fully discussed in the next several sections.[31]

1403. DISTINCTION BETWEEN POWERS AND TRUSTS

Although powers partake of many of the attributes of trusts, there is a clear distinction between these two institutions. A power is discretionary, while a trust is imperative. Thus, the donee of a power is not required to exercise it, whereas a trustee is under a duty to carry out his trust. Powers may, however, be given to trustees as well as to persons who are not trustees. Moreover, even if a trust is found to exist, it may confer substantial discretion upon the trustee. Hence, the dividing line between trusts and powers is not always easily drawn. Whether a trust or a power is created depends upon the intention of its creator, ascertained from a proper construction of the instrument creating it. This will be dealt with below.[1]

1403.1 Types of Powers and Trusts

It will be useful at this point to distinguish between the various types of powers and trusts, which distinctions (although not necessarily the names attached to them) have become much clarified as a result of a recent line of English cases, culminating in *Re Gulbenkian's Settlements*[1] and *McPhail v. Doulton*.[2]

As a result of these cases, one may distinguish first of all between *bare powers* and *fiduciary powers* or *powers ex officio*. Neither of these are trusts. A bare power is one given to a person who is not a trustee. It may be contained in a trust and be given, for example, to a beneficiary, such as a power of

---

[30]*Re Hardy*, [1952] 2 D.L.R. 768, 29 M.P.R. 358 (N.S.S.C.).
[31]§§1403-1403.3, *infra*.
§1403
[1]§1403.3, *infra*.
§1403.1
[1][1970] A.C. 508 (H.L.).
[2][1971] A.C. 424 (H.L.).

appointment, or it may be given outside a trust, such as a power of attorney to convey land or a power of sale in a mortgage. A bare power may only be exercised by the donee of the power[3] or, if it is given to two or more persons jointly, by the donees acting together. The survivor cannot exercise it unless the instrument conferring the power permits it.[4] On the other hand, a fiduciary power, such as one given to trustees, may be exercised by the survivor,[5] or by their successors,[6] unless it is made clear that the power is to be exercised jointly only.[7] A power given *virtute officii* cannot be exercised in favour of the surviving trustee personally, even though, on its face, it appears to be unrestricted, where it is subject to a secret trust or agreement between the testator and the other, predeceased trustee.[8]

The main theoretical distinction between a bare power and a fiduciary power is that the donee of a bare power is not bound to exercise, or even consider whether he will exercise, the power and the court will not interfere if he does not. A fiduciary, on the other hand, because he is a fiduciary, must at least consider whether and to what extent he should exercise the power.[9] Although the court will not normally compel the fiduciary to exercise the power, since it is not a trust, it will intervene if he disregards the power by removing him.[10] The reason for such intervention is the fiduciary's breach of duty, not any property right of the objects of the power.[11]

The second distinction that may be made is between *mere powers* and *trust powers*, powers in the nature of a trust or powers coupled with a duty. Mere powers are powers of appointment which the donee is under no duty to exercise although, if he is a fiduciary, he cannot disregard the power. A trust power, on the other hand, is a form of trust which gives the trustees a power of selection among a defined class of beneficiaries. Since a trust power is a trust, the trustees are under a duty to exercise it, but they have a discretion as to the beneficiaries and the amounts each beneficiary shall receive. For this reason, a trust power is often called a discretionary trust.[12] However, a distinction can be drawn between discretionary trusts and trust powers. The

---

[3]*Re Harding*; *Harding v. Paterson*, [1923] 1 Ch. 182; *Re Lysaght*; *Hill v. Royal College of Surgeons*, [1966] Ch. 191.

[4]Farwell, p. 514; *Re Ward*, [1952] O.W.N. 1, [1952] 1 D.L.R. 463 (H.C.). See further §1405.9, *infra*.

[5]*Bersel Manufacturing Co. Ltd. v. Berry*, [1968] 2 All E.R. 552 (H.L.).

[6]*Re De Sommery*; *Coelenbier v. De Sommery*, [1912] 2 Ch. 622. See further §1405.9, *infra*.

[7]*Roach v. Roach*, [1931] 3 D.L.R. 374, [1931] S.C.R. 512.

[8]*Re Hardy*, [1952] 2 D.L.R. 768, 29 M.P.R. 358 (N.S.S.C.).

[9]*Re Gestetner Settlement*; *Barnett v. Blumka*, [1953] Ch. 672 at p. 688, *per* Harman, J.; *Re Abrahams' Will Trusts*; *Caplan v. Abrahams*, [1969] 1 Ch. 463 at p. 474; *Re Gulbenkian's Settlements, supra*, footnote 1, at p. 518, *per* Lord Reid; *McPhail v. Doulton, supra*, footnote 2, at p. 456, *per* Lord Wilberforce; *Re Manisty's Settlements*; *Manisty v. Manisty*, [1974] Ch. 17 at p. 25, *per* Templeman, J.

[10]*McPhail v. Doulton, supra*, footnote 2, at p. 456, *per* Lord Wilberforce.

[11]Hanbury and Maudsley, p. 184.

[12]*Re Baden's Deed Trusts (No. 2)*, [1973] Ch. 9 (C.A.), at p. 26, *per* Stamp, L.J.

former are only one example of the latter. Trust powers may, in fact, exist in three forms, namely, a power to appoint given to a non-trustee which must be exercised, so that the donee is, in effect, a trustee; a similar power given to a trustee; and a discretionary trust, that is, a trust for division coupled with a power of selection. The distinction between the first two types and the discretionary trust lies primarily in this, that powers of appointment, coupled with a duty to distribute, are typically employed for a single distribution, whereas discretionary trusts are used where the distribution is likely to take place over a period of time.[13]

A trust power, because it is a trust, is subject to intervention by the court for, while the individual beneficiaries of such a trust power have no proprietary interest in the trust property until the trustee has exercised his discretion in their favour,[14] the beneficiaries can require the trustee to exercise his discretion. If he fails to do so, the court can compel him and, if he refuses, the court can replace him or, if necessary, make the selection itself.[15]

The final distinction that may be drawn is between *mere trusts* or fixed trusts and trust powers. A mere trust confers no discretion upon the trustee in respect of distribution. The beneficiaries and the amounts they are to receive are fixed by the trust and the trustee is under a duty to distribute the property in accordance with the terms of the trust.[16]

1403.2 Importance of the Distinction

The question whether a trust or a power has been created is significant for several reasons, namely, as regards the certainty of objects and whether the beneficiaries as a class are entitled to the property either by terminating the trust, or under a trust in default of appointment.

(a) Certainty of objects

Prior to the decision in *McPhail v. Doulton*[1] a distinction was drawn in this respect between mere powers and trust powers. Before that case the same certainty was required of the objects of a trust power as of the objects of a fixed trust, that is, that they had to be described in such a way that the trustees could determine all of the beneficiaries. The reason is that since these are

---

[13]Waters, pp. 69-70.
[14]*Re Rispin; Canada Trust Co. v. Dairi* (1912), 25 O.L.R. 633, 2 D.L.R. 644 (C.A.), affd *sub nom. Canada Trust Co. v. Davis*, 46 S.C.R. 649, 23 O.W.R. 308, 8 D.L.R. 756; *Re Maw*, [1953] 1 D.L.R. 365, 6 W.W.R. (N.S.) 609 (Man. Q.B.); *Re Quinn and Executive Director and Director (Westman Region) of Social Services* (1981), 124 D.L.R. (3d) 715, [1918] 5 W.W.R. 565 (Man. C.A.). *Cf. Gartside v. I.R.C.*, [1968] A.C. 553 (H L.); *Sainsbury v. IR.C.*, [1970] Ch. 712.
[15]*McPhail v. Doulton*, [1971] A.C. 424 (H.L.).
[16]Waters, p. 67.
§1403.2
[1][1971] A.C. 424 (H.L.).

trusts, the trustees are required to make a division or, if they do not or cannot do so, the court will and thus they must be able to ascertain the objects.

On the other hand, the test for mere powers is less rigid. All the donee of the power must be able to do is to determine "whether any given postulant is a member of the specified class".[2] This test was further explained in *Re Gulbenkian's Settlements*[3] to mean not that a power will be valid so long as any individual can be found or postulated who will clearly fall within the description of the class, but that it will be valid only if the description of the class is sufficiently clear so that it can be said with certainty that any hypothetical postulant falls within it.[4] In the *Gulbenkian* case, the issue concerned the validity of a mere power to appoint in favour of Nubar Sarkis Gulbenkian, his wife, children or remoter issue, "and any person or persons in whose house or apartments or in whose company or under whose care or control or by or with whom the said Nubar Sarkis Gulbenkian may from time to time be employed or residing". The House of Lords held this class of objects to be certain. It is probable that the class would have been sufficiently certain if it were a trust power as well since the description of the class is such that a list could be made of all the possible members. That would not be so if the description were linguistically or semantically uncertain as, for example, a gift to a class of "my old friends"[5] or of "my close friends",[6] unless the terms were further defined or, in the case of testamentary gifts, evidence were admissible to remove any ambiguity.[7]

The certainty test for mere powers described above is sometimes referred to as the "individual ascertainability test", while the test for trust powers is called the "class ascertainability test".[8]

In 1971, however, the House of Lords in *McPhail v. Doulton*[9] held that, because it is often difficult to determine whether a mere power or a trust power has been created, the latter should not be held void merely because the entire class cannot be ascertained. Rather the certainty test applicable to mere powers should be applied to trust powers as well.

It should be noted that this does not otherwise remove the distinction between mere powers and trust powers. Trustees still have a duty to distribute and, for that reason, they must "make a wider and more systematic survey" of the class of beneficiaries than donees of a mere power, whether trustees or

---

[2]*Re Gestetner Settlement; Barnett v. Blumka*, [1953] Ch. 672 at p. 688, *per* Harman, J.
[3][1970] A.C. 508 (H.L.).
[4]See Hopkins, "Certain Uncertainties of Trusts and Powers", [1971] C.L.J. 68; "Comment", 50 Can. Bar Rev. 539 (1972). See also Harris, "Trust, Power and Duty", 87 L.Q. Rev. 31 (1971).
[5]*Re Gulbenkian's Settlements, supra*, footnote 3, at p. 524, *per* Lord Upjohn.
[6]*Re Connor* (1970), 10 D.L.R. (3d) 5, 72 W.W.R. 388 (Alta. S.C. App. Div.).
[7]*Re Gulbenkian's Settlements, supra*, footnote 3, at p. 524, *per* Lord Upjohn.
[8]"Comment", 50 Can. Bar Rev. 539 (1972), at p. 540.
[9]*Supra*, footnote 1. This case was applied in *Jones v. Executive Officers of T. Eaton Co. Ltd.* (1973), 35 D.L.R. (3d) 97, [1973] S.C.R. 635, but in the context of a charitable trust where the issue is irrelevant since, if the objects of a charitable trust are uncertain, they can be applied *cy-près*.

not.[10] But they are no longer required to prepare a complete list of all possible beneficiaries.[11]

Furthermore, the lack of a complete list does not prevent the court from executing the trust in the unlikely event that the trustees fail to do so and no other trustees can be found willing to execute it, for the court is not obliged to make an equal division.[12] Such a division was and is common in small family trusts on the basis that equality is equity, but it would clearly be inappropriate in large discretionary trusts for the benefit of numerous employees and their dependants. Instead, the court may distribute the fund in such a way as to give effect to the settlor's or testator's intention as closely as possible.[13]

The adoption of the certainty test previously applicable to mere powers did not resolve all the difficulties, however.

In the *McPhail* case the trustees were required to pay or apply the net income from the trust fund in their discretion to or for the benefit of "any of the officers and employees or ex-officers or ex-employees of [a] company or to any relatives or dependants of any such persons" in such amounts, at such times and upon such conditions as they thought fit. The House of Lords remitted the matter to the Chancery Division to determine whether this trust power was valid on the basis of the test adopted by the House. Brightman, J., held that the test was satisfied.[14] His decision was affirmed by the Court of Appeal.[15] However, the members of that court differed in their application of the test. Sachs, L.J., drew a distinction between conceptual or linguistic uncertainty and evidential uncertainty, and held that the test concerns only conceptual uncertainty. Thus, a class of persons to whom the settlor is "under a moral obligation" would be conceptually uncertain while a class of "first cousins" would not be, although it might be evidentially uncertain. However, such uncertainty can readily be resolved. The words "relatives or dependants" in the instant case were not conceptually uncertain in his view.

Megaw, L.J., held that the test was met since it could be said of at least a substantial number of objects that they fell within the trust.[16]

Stamp, L.J., construed the word "relatives" to mean "next of kin" which is certain. If that construction had not been possible he would have held the trust to be void, for it would then not have been possible to determine whether any individual was within or outside the class, the accent being on the word "any" since "it is not simply the individual whose claim you are considering who is spoken of".[17]

It is apparent, therefore, that the question of certainty is not by any means

---

[10]*McPhail v. Doulton, supra,* footnote 1, at p. 449, *per* Lord Wilberforce.

[11]*McPhail v. Doulton,* [1971] A.C. 424 (H.L.).

[12]*Ibid.,* at p. 450.

[13]*Ibid.,* at p. 458.

[14]*Re Baden's Deed Trusts (No. 2),* [1972] Ch. 607, affd [1973] Ch. 9 (C.A.).

[15][1973] Ch. 9 (C.A.).

[16]*Ibid.,* at p. 24.

[17]*Ibid.,* at p. 28.

resolved and trustees were wise to protect themselves in cases where they cannot give consideration to all possible claimants because they are not known by seeking the advice and directions of the court.

It is also possible to make an argument that where a trust is certain as to most of its objects but invalid as to some, the uncertain portion of the class should be struck out so as not to render the entire trust void.[18]

(b) Right to terminate the trust

The objects of a power have no proprietary interest in the subject-matter of the power until the donee has exercised it in their favour. Therefore, they cannot band together and call for distribution of the property. An individual beneficiary under a trust power does not have such a right either. However, all the beneficiaries of a trust, and hence of a trust power, if *sui juris*, may together terminate the trust and divide the trust fund among themselves, on the basis of the rule in *Saunders v. Vautier*.[19] Although such a right will be useful in trusts involving a small, homogeneous class of beneficiaries, it is clearly an illusory one where the class is large and diverse as in the *McPhail* case.

(c) Trusts in default of appointment

In some cases where a mere power is given, the settlor or testator will go on to provide that the fund shall be distributed among named persons or a defined class of persons if the donee of the power fails to appoint. Normally, the gift in default of appointment will be upon a fixed trust. In many instances, however, there is no such trust and the question has arisen in a number of cases whether a trust in favour of the class of objects can be implied. Such an implication will be made: "when there appears a general intention in favour of a class, and a particular intention in favour of individuals of a class to be selected by another person, and the particular intention fails, from that selection not being made", for then "the Court will carry into effect the general intention in favour of the class" by raising a trust for equal division in favour of the members of the class.[20] Such equal division is based on the principle that equality is equity.[21]

There is, thus, no inflexible rule that a trust in favour of the class will be raised on default of appointment. Rather, such a trust will be found only if it is possible to construe the gift as one to the class of objects, subject to the donee's power of selection among the members of the class.[22] The effect of

---

[18]Hanbury and Maudsley, p. 216.

[19](1841), 4 Beav. 115, 49 E.R. 282, affd 1 Cr. & Ph. 240, 41 E.R. 482. See *Re McCrossan* (1961), 28 D.L.R. (2d) 461, 36 W.W.R. 209 (B.C.S.C.); *Re Smith; Public Trustee v. Aspinall*, [1928] Ch. 915.

[20]*Burrough v. Philcox* (1840), 5 My. & Cr. 72 at p. 92, 41 E.R. 299, *per* Lord Cottenham, L.C.

[21]Hanbury and Maudsley, pp. 169-70.

[22]*Re Llewellyn's Settlement; Official Solicitor v. Evans*, [1921] 2 Ch. 281; *Re Arnold; Wainwright v. Howlett*, [1947] Ch. 131; *Re Weekes' Settlement*, [1897] 1 Ch. 289; *Re Combe; Combe v. Combe*, [1925] Ch. 210; *Re Perowne; Perowne v. Moss*, [1951] Ch. 785; *Roach v. Roach*, [1931] 3 D.L.R. 374, [1931] S.C.R. 512.

such a construction is to raise a trust in favour of the objects which is defeasible by the exercise of the appointment. In fact, many of the older cases speak in this context of a power in the nature of a trust or a power coupled with a trust.[23] This is confusing when compared to modern terminology for those terms are now often used interchangeably with the term "mere power". In any event the old usage is incorrect for under a mere power the objects do not have a proprietary interest until an appointment has been made in their favour.

It would appear, further, that an implied trust in default of appointment will not normally be raised unless the class of objects of the power is small and homogeneous.[24] Hence it would not be raised in cases such as *McPhail v. Doulton*[25] where the class was extremely large.

On the other hand, the class does not necessarily have to be described as a class but its members may be referred to by name. Thus, in *Re Lloyd*[26] the testatrix gave her husband, the life tenant, power to appoint the remainder among three named sisters and a named niece, the child of one of the sisters. Rose, C.J.H.C., was able to raise a trust in favour of the class in default of appointment, because the testatrix had carefully selected certain members of her family while excluding others.

If there is an express gift over in default of appointment, there is no room for an implied trust.[27]

(d) Capricious powers

In the context of certainty of objects, the right to terminate a trust and trusts in default of appointment, it is relevant to consider powers whose objects are so described that it is virtually impossible for the donee to exercise it properly. If that is the case, the power is void, for it "negatives a sensible consideration by the trustees of the exercise of the power".[28] In *McPhail v. Doulton*,[29] Lord Wilberforce suggested that a discretionary trust for "all the residents of Greater London" would be administratively unworkable because the objects do not form "anything like a class". In *Re Manisty's Settlement*,[30] Templeman, J., stated that such a power would be capricious and hence void:

If the settlor intended and expected the trustees would have regard to persons with some claim on his bounty or some interest in an institution favoured by the settlor, or if the settlor had any other sensible intention or expectation, he would not have

---

[23]*Re Weekes' Settlement, supra,* footnote 22; *Re Combe, supra,* footnote 22; *Re Perowne, supra,* footnote 22; *Re Lloyd,* [1938] O.R. 32, [1938] 1 D.L.R. 450 (H.C.J.).

[24]*Re Perowne, supra,* footnote 22, at p. 790.

[25][1971] A.C. 424 (H.L.).

[26]*Supra,* footnote 23. *Cf. Re Hislop* (1915), 8 O.W.N. 53, 22 D.L.R. 710 (S.C. App. Div.).

[27]*Re Weekes' Settlement, supra,* footnote 22; *Re Sprague* (1880), 43 L.T. 236.

[28]*Re Manisty's Settlement; Manisty v. Manisty,* [1974] Ch. 17 at p. 27, *per* Templeman, J.

[29]*Supra,* footnote 25, at p. 457.

[30]*Supra,* footnote 28.

required the trustees to consider only an accidental conglomeration of persons who have no discernible link with the settlor or with any institution.[31]

1403.3 Construction

Whether a mere power or a trust power be created depends upon a proper construction of the words used by the settlor or testator. It is axiomatic that, if the instrument provides for a gift over in default of appointment, a mere power only has been conferred. However, the absence of a gift over does not necessarily mean that a trust power exists.[1] The fact that in a will the testator has left the residue in favour of the members of the class does not, by itself, indicate a gift over in default of appointment of a specific gift, unless it is clear from the will that that is what the testator intended.[2]

The mere use of the words, "power" or "trust", is not conclusive,[3] nor is the use or absence of imperative language, or the conferring of a discretion on the trustees. It is instructive in this regard to compare the two leading cases, *Re Gulbenkian's Settlements*[4] and *McPhail v. Doulton*.[5]

In the *Gulbenkian* case an *inter vivos* settlement provided:

> 2. (i) The trustees shall during the life of ... Nubar Sarkis Gulbenkian at their absolute discretion pay all or any part of the income of the property hereby settled ... to or ... for the ... benefit of all or any one or more to the exclusion of the other or others of the following persons namely the said Nubar Sarkis Gulbenkian and any wife and his children or remoter issue for the time being ... and any person or persons in whose house or apartments or in whose company or under whose care or control or by or with whom the said Nubar Sarkis Gulbenkian may from time to time be employed or residing and the other persons or person other than the settlor ... entitled ... to ... the trust fund [established under subclause (ii)] in such proportions and manner as the trustees in their absolute discretion ... think proper.
>
> (ii) Subject to the discretionary *trust or power* hereinbefore contained the trustees shall during the life of the said Nubar Sarkis Gulbenkian hold the said income or so much thereof as shall not be paid or applied under such discretionary *trust or power* upon the trusts and for the purposes for which the said income would for the time being be held if the said Nubar Sarkis Gulbenkian were then dead.[6]

The validity of this settlement and a substantially similar one was litigated primarily on the question of certainty of the objects in clause 2(i). As has been seen, the courts held the class to be sufficiently certain despite the ungrammatical wording of the clause.[7] That question could be decided only after it had first been determined that the settlements created mere powers, as

---

[31]*Supra*, footnote 28, at p. 27, *per* Templeman, J.

§1403.3

[1]*Re Weekes' Settlement*, [1897] 1 Ch. 289; *Re Gulbenkian's Settlement*, [1970] A.C. 508 (H.L.).

[2]Waters, p. 70.

[3]Hanbury and Maudsley, p. 168.

[4]*Supra*, footnote 1.

[5][1971] A.C. 424 (H.L.).

[6]*Supra*, footnote 1, at p. 520, emphasis supplied.

[7]§1403.2(a), *supra*.

the courts held, and not trust powers. The reason that they were mere powers is that, despite the imperative language in clause 2(i) and the reference to a "trust" in clause 2(ii), referring back to clause 2(i), the trustees were not under a duty to exercise their discretion under clause 2(i), primarily because, if they failed to do so, the income would be subject to the trusts of clause 2(ii); in other words, it would be held upon a trust in default of appointment.

In the *McPhail* case the settlement contained the following provisions:

> 9. (a) The trustees shall apply the net income of the fund in making at their absolute discretion grants to or for the benefit of any of the officers and employees or ex-officers or ex-employees of [a] company or to any relatives or dependants of any such persons in such amounts at such times and on such conditions . . . as they think fit . . . (b) The trustees shall not be bound to exhaust the income of any year . . . and any income not so applied shall be [placed on deposit with a bank or invested]. (c) The trustees may realize any investments representing accumulations of income and apply the proceeds as though the same were income of the fund and may also (but only with the consent of all of the trustees) . . . realise any other part of the capital of the fund . . . in order to provide benefits for which the current income of the fund is insufficient.
> 10. All benefits being at the absolute discretion of the trustees, no person shall have any right title or interest in the fund otherwise than pursuant to the exercise of such discretion . . .[8]

Again, the question that was litigated was the certainty of the objects in clause 9(a) of the settlement. In the lower courts the clause was held valid as a power. These courts held it to be a power largely because if it were a trust, the class would be uncertain. In the House of Lords, however, the settlement was held to constitute a trust power, that is, a trust for distribution coupled with a power to withhold a portion and to accumulate or otherwise dispose of it. The reason for this conclusion was that the language of clause 9 was imperative, even though by clause 9(b) the trustees were not required to distribute all of the income in each year, but could, in effect, accumulate it. However, such accumulation (of income) could be released by a majority of the trustees, whereas accumulation of capital could only be released by a unanimous decision of the trustees. In the end result, therefore, there was no trust in default of appointment of any income. Presumably there would have been if any unused income was directed to be added to the capital of the fund which the trustees were directed to hold upon certain other trusts. As has been seen, the House then went on to hold that the certainty test for powers should be applied to trust powers of this sort as well.[9]

The dividing line between these two cases is obviously a fine one and that was the main reason why the House of Lords in the *McPhail* case held that the test for certainty should be the same for both mere powers and trust powers so as to avoid invalidity of the latter. Other important distinctions between the two institutions continue to exist, however, as has been seen,[10] and the question

---

[8]*Supra*, footnote 5, at p. 428.
[9]§1403.2(a), *supra*.
[10]§1403.2(b), (c), *supra*.

whether one is dealing with a mere power or a trust power will, therefore, remain and will depend in each case on a proper construction of the instrument creating it.

It would seem that, if the power be given to a trustee instead of to a non-trustee, the courts will more readily be inclined to find a trust power rather than a mere power.[11]

1404. CREATION OF POWERS

Powers not operating under the *Statute of Uses*[1] can be given in instruments of all kinds, but powers operating under the *Statute of Uses* can only affect the legal estate when given in instruments which transfer possession, such as declaration of uses or grants.[2] In the case of a devise to uses, however, the rules under the *Statute of Uses* are applied by analogy, since it is considered that such was the testator's intention.[3]

In *Re Brooke; Brooke v. Brooke*[4] a testatrix directed her debts to be paid by her executors, devised a freehold to her sons, H and W, and their heirs in trust to allow H to enjoy it for life and, after his death, in trust for such of his children as he might by deed or will appoint and, in default of appointment, in trust for his sons who attained 21 and his daughters who attained that age or married, and appointed H and W her executors. H died without exercising the power, leaving two infant, unmarried children. The question arose whether the remainder to the children was a legal contingent remainder which had failed for want of a freehold estate to support it or whether the legal estate was vested in the devisees and executors. It was held that the direction to pay debts indicated that the testatrix did not intend to avail herself of the machinery of the *Statute of Uses* in the devise to the sons and executors, or to make them mere conduit pipes of the legal estate, but intended the legal estate to pass to them, and not through them, "in trust" according to the modern significance of the term.

The mere possession of a power of appointment over property does not give the donee of the power an interest in the property although, if he may appoint in favour of himself, the exercise of the power would do so. As long as the power remains a power unexercised, it will remain a totally distinct thing from property.[5]

---

[11]Waters, p. 71.

§1404
[1]27 Hen. 8, c. 10 (1535).
[2]Sugden, *Powers*, p. 140.
[3]*Baker v. White* (1875), L.R. 20 Eq. 166 at p. 171; *Cunliffe v. Brancker* (1876), 3 Ch. D. 393 (C.A.); *Berry v. Berry* (1878), 7 Ch. D. 657.
[4][1894] 1 Ch. 43.
[5]*Townshend v. Harrowby* (1858), 27 L.J. Ch. 553, *per* Kindersley, V.-C., holding that a covenant to sell after-acquired property in accordance with a marriage settlement did not apply to property over which the wife's father subsequently gave her a power of appointment, which she exercised in her own favour; followed in *Tremayne v. Rashleigh*, [1908] 1 Ch. 681, not followed in *Re O'Connell; Mawle v. Jagoe*, [1903] 2 Ch. 574, and see *Bower v. Smith* (1871), L.R. 11 Eq. 279, followed in *Re Lord Gerard* (1888), 58 L.T. 800.

No two ideas can well be more distinct the one from the other than those of "property" and "power." This is a "power," and nothing but a "power." A "power" is an individual personal capacity of the donee of the power to do something. That it may result in the property becoming vested in him is immaterial; the general nature of the power does not make it property. The power of a person to appoint an estate to himself is, in my judgment, no more his "property" than the power to write a book or to sing a song. The exercise of any one of those three powers may result in property, but in no sense which the law recognizes are they "property".[6]

No technical words or even express words in a deed or will are necessary to create a power of appointment, it being sufficient that the intention to confer the power is indicated.[7] In *Bishop of Oxon v. Leighton*,[8] A, on his marriage, conveyed land to a trustee to the use of himself for life, remainder to his wife for life, remainder to the heirs of their two bodies, remainder to A in fee simple. A proviso was added that, in default of issue, the trustee was to convey to such uses as the survivor might appoint. A devised the land and died without issue. It was held that his wife had a valid power to dispose of the land by appointment.

Similarly, where a testatrix gave the residue of her estate to her trustee (her husband) with a direction to pay to himself any sum he might need for the purpose of living expenses, it was held that the gift conferred a general power of appointment on the husband, the word "need" being construed as "require" in the circumstances.[9]

The power may be implied from the language of the instrument, or from its disposition of estates. Thus, a proviso for forfeiture of an interest in case of alienation otherwise than for jointure or leases, implies powers of jointuring and leasing[10] and a gift over in the event that a married woman should die without disposing of her interest by will implies a power of appointment by will.[11]

The word "assigns" in a devise to a person and his assigns for life does not give the devisee a power of appointment.[12]

Where there was a devise "to my wife for life and by her to be disposed of to such of my children as she shall think fit", it was held that she took an estate for life with power to dispose of it in fee simple to any of the children.[13]

Similarly, it was held that a devise to the testator's wife for life and then to be at her disposal, provided that it be to any of his children, gave her a life estate with a power to dispose of the fee simple[14] and, where there was a devise to the testator's widow for life to be by her divided among such of the testator's children and their issue as should be surviving at her death, it was

---

[6]*Ex p. Gilchrist, Re Armstrong* (1886), 17 Q.B.D. 521 at p. 531, *per* Fry, L.J.
[7]Sugden, *Powers*, p. 140.
[8](1700), 2 Vern. 376, 23 E.R. 837.
[9]*Re Baskin; Canada Trust Co. v. Baskin*, [1954] 2 D.L.R. 748 (B.C.S.C.).
[10]*Read and Nashes Case* (1589), 1 Leon. 147, 74 E.R. 136.
[11]*Downes v. Timperon* (1828), 4 Russ. 334, 38 E.R. 831.
[12]*Brookman v. Smith* (1871), L.R. 6 Exch. 291; *Milman v. Lane*, [1901] 2 K.B. 745 (C.A.), but see, *contra, Quested v. Michell* (1855), 24 L.J. Ch. 722.
[13]*Liefe v. Saltingstone* (1674), 1 Mod. 189, 86 E.R. 819.
[14]*Tomlinson v. Dighton* (1712), 1 P. Wms. 149, 24 E.R. 335.

held that she had a power which was validly executed by a will appointing a share to each of his surviving children or, in case of their death, to their children and another share to the children of the deceased child.[15]

Where a testator gave his real and personal property to his brother J with full power to sell and dispose of some of it by deed, will or otherwise, appointed J as executor and gave such part as J should not dispose of to H for life with remainders over and appointed another executor, making several references in the will to the survivorship of himself and of J, it was held that, considering the whole will, the gift to J must be read as a gift to him for life with an absolute power of appointment.[16]

Where a testator gave all of his property to his wife for life and directed her to pay his debts and, at her decease, to make such a distribution and disposal of his then remaining property among his children as might seem just and equitable according to her discretion, it was held that this was a power, exercisable by will only, to appoint in favour of the testator's children living at her death.[17]

However, where a testator bequeathed to his wife "all my possessions to use and distribute to my relatives in a reasonable manner", it was held that the testator evinced an intention to give his wife the entire estate, subject to an obligation to give such amounts to relatives as she should think reasonable, rather than a life estate with a power to appoint.[18]

If there is a gift of a life estate with a power of appointment by deed or will added, the addition does not make the gift absolute. Thus, where a testatrix appointed real estate to her husband upon trust for his own use for life "with power to take and apply the whole or any part of the capital arising therefrom to and for his own benefit" and, after his death, "subject as aforesaid" over to other persons, it was held that he took a life estate only and, having died without exercising the power, the property went to those to whom it was given in remainder after his death.[19]

Where a testator gave all of his property to his widow for her life "to be disposed of as she may think proper for her own use and benefit according to the nature and quality thereof" and "in the event of her decease, should there be anything remaining of the property or any part thereof", he gave "said part or parts" to certain persons, it was held that the widow had no power to dispose of the property by will and, on her death, it went to those named in his will.[20]

A testator devised certain real estate to his sons in strict settlement and gave the residue of his real and personal estate to his widow absolutely, appointing her executrix and his sons executors after her death. By a codicil he revoked

---

[15]*Ex parte Williams* (1819), 1 Jac. & W. 89, 37 E.R. 309.
[16]*Re Stringer's Estate; Shaw v. Jones-Ford* (1877), 6 Ch. D. 1 (C.A.).
[17]*Freeland v. Pearson* (1867), L.R. 3 Eq. 658.
[18]*Re Gunnis-Wood* (1974), 4 O.R. (2d) 751, 49 D.L.R. 199 (H.C.J.).
[19]*Pennock v. Pennock* (1871), L.R. 13 Eq. 144.
[20]*Re Thomson's Estate; Herring v. Barrow* (1880), 14 Ch. D. 263 (C.A.).

746

the will and gave all of his property to his widow "so that she may have full possession of it and entire power and control over it, to deal with it or act with regard to it as she may think proper" but, in the event of her not surviving him or dying without having devised or appointed the whole or any part of the property, he declared that his will should take effect as if the codicil had not been made and he appointed his wife executrix of the codicil during her life. It was held that she took an estate for life only with a general power of appointment.[21]

The rule is the same even though the gift preceding the added power is in words of absolute gift. Thus, where a testator gave the residue of his property to his wife absolutely and by a codicil revoked this gift, made a specific gift and gave her the residue "for her own absolute use and benefit and disposal" but, without prejudice to the absolute power of disposal by her of all the residue, in case any part should "remain undisposed of" by her at her death, he gave it to two persons as tenants in common, it was held that the wife took a life interest only with a power of disposition *inter vivos*, but not by will.[22]

Where a testator gave to his wife

> the whole of my real and personal estate and property absolutely in full confidence that she will make such use of it as I should have made myself and that at her death she will devise it to such one or more of my nieces as she may think fit and in default of any disposition by her thereof by her will or testament I hereby direct that all my estate and property acquired by her under this my will shall at her death be equally divided among the surviving said nieces

it was held that, upon a true construction of the will, there was an absolute gift of his real and personal estate to the wife subject to an executory devise to the nieces at her death, equally if more than one, so far as she should not dispose of the estate by will in favour of the surviving nieces or any one or more of them.[23]

The effect of a will, however, may be that where there are words of absolute gift with power of disposal, the gift will vest absolutely and a gift over of what is not disposed of will fail as repugnant. Thus, a testator gave all of his property, subject to payment of debts, to his wife "for her absolute use and benefit, so that during her lifetime for the purpose of her maintenance and support she shall have the fullest power to sell and dispose of my estate absolutely" and went on to provide that, after her death, such parts of his estate "as she shall not have sold or disposed of as aforesaid" should be held upon trust for sale for the benefit of other persons and appointed her executrix. At her death a considerable portion of the property remained unsold and undisposed of. It was held that she took an absolute interest and the part

---

[21]*Re Sanford; Sanford v. Sanford*, [1901] 1 Ch. 939.

[22]*Re Pounder; Williams v. Pounder* (1886), 56 L.J. Ch. 113. *Cf.* to the same effect *Re Comstock*, [1949] O.R. 537, [1949] 3 D.L.R. 677 (H.C.J.), in which the beneficiaries were held to take a life interest with a testamentary power only.

[23]*Comiskey v. Bowring-Hanbury*, [1905] A.C. 84 (H.L.). See also *Re Stringer's Case. supra*, footnote 16.

undisposed of passed by her will.[24] Similarly, where a testator gave his residue to his wife "with power for her to dispose of the same" among his children or any of them for such interest, temporary or lasting, as she should see most fitting, it was held that she took absolutely.[25]

A power to appoint capital "operative on death", which is given to a life tenant, may be exercised in his own favour as soon as he reaches his majority and need not be exercised by will.[26]

If the existence of the power is subject to a condition precedent, as where a power is given to the testator's wife if another, named, person be dead at the testator's death, the widow cannot exercise the power if the named person is alive at that time since the condition goes to the very existence of the power. A gift over for failure to appoint would thus also be ineffective.[27]

Where property has vested absolutely in the beneficiaries, an apparent discretionary power in executors or trustees as to the mode of payment or transfer is repugnant and void.[28]

If there is a gift of real property to a person for life with power to appoint the remainder to his heirs, the rule in *Shelley's Case*[29] applies so that he has a fee simple. A testatrix devised a freehold to trustees, their heirs and assigns, upon trust for her daughter for her life and, after her death, upon trust for the lawful child or children of the daughter as she should by deed or will appoint and, in default of such appointment, in trust for the daughter's right heirs. After her mother's death, the daughter granted the property in fee simple and died unmarried. Her heir-at-law brought action to recover the freehold. It was held that it was devised to the trustees in fee simple, the limitation to the right heirs in default of appointment was a remainder and not an executory devise, both the life estate of the daughter and the remainder were equitable estates and, consequently, they coalesced under the rule in *Shelley's Case* so that the daughter could convey in fee simple. It was further held that a power given by will to a tenant for life to appoint to his children with an express limitation over in default of appointment cannot be construed as conferring upon the children any estate or interest in default of the exercise of the power of appointment, at least in the absence of provisions extending the operation of the power.[30]

Similarly, a devise to a person for life and, after his death, to the heirs of his body in such shares as he may by deed or will appoint and, in default

---

[24]*Re Jones; Richards v. Jones*, [1898] 1 Ch. 438, distinguishing *Re Pounder, supra,* footnote 22.

[25]*Howorth v. Dewell* (1860), 29 Beav. 18, 54 E.R. 531.

[26]*Re Jones*, [1949] 3 D.L.R. 604, [1949] 1 W.W.R. 1093 (Man. C.A.); *Robinson v. Royal Trust Co.; Re Mewburn*, [1939] 1 D.L.R. 257, [1939] S.C.R. 75, "upon his death his share shall go as he may by deed or will appoint".

[27]*Ryan v. Smith* (1971), 22 D.L.R. (3d) 1, [1972] S.C.R. 332.

[28]*Re Chodak* (1976), 8 O.R. (2d) 671, 59 D.L.R. 35 (H.C.J.).

[29](1581), 1 Co. Rep. 93 b, 76 E.R. 199.

[30]*Richardson v. Harrison* (1885), 16 Q.B.D. 85.

of appointment, to the heirs of his body as tenants in common and, in default of issue, to the heirs of the testator, gives the devisee an estate tail.[31]

In a will, the word "issue" *prima facie* means heirs of the body and is a word of limitation, but such *prima facie* construction will give way if there be on the face of the will sufficient to show that the word was intended to have had a less extensive meaning and to have applied generally to children, or to descendants of a particular class, or at a particular time.[32]

Where there is a gift over on general failure of issue, it is presumed that the word "issue" has been used by the testator as meaning heirs of the body; when the word is so employed, it is for the party seeking to give it a meaning other than that which it frequently bears to show clearly from the context of the will that the testator intended to give it a different meaning. The word "issue", besides having a technical sense, is used in common parlance. It has, however, been held that the word takes in all issue to the utmost of the family, as far as heirs of the body would do.[33]

Although the word "issue" is *prima facie* equivalent to heirs of the body, the court leans against so construing it when there are other expressions in the will to control that meaning. If words of limitation are added, as a gift to "issue and their heirs", the issue take as purchasers in fee simple and a gift over on a general failure of issue is ineffective.[34]

If there is a gift to a person for life and, after his death, to his issue in such shares as he may appoint by deed or will and, in default of appointment, to the issue equally or, if there be only one child, to such child, with a gift over in default of issue, the rule of interpretation of the word "issue" as meaning heirs of the body is applied, so that the gift over will not take effect until failure of the line of issue, in which case there is no need to imply an estate tail in the devisee and he takes a life estate with an added power of appointment.[35]

1405. EXERCISE OF POWER

In the several following paragraphs the formalities of executing a power will be described, followed by a discussion of the restrictions on the delegation of powers.

1405.1 Formalities of Execution

Subject to the provisions of statute and of the terms of the power, a power may be exercised in a way most suited to the particular circumstances. Technical words need not be employed so long as an intention to exercise the

---

[31]*Jesson v. Wright* (1820), 2 Bligh 1, 4 E.R. 230 (H.L.).
[32]*Slater v. Dangerfield* (1846), 15 M. & W. 263, 153 E.R. 848, *per* Parke, B.; *Pelham Clinton v. Duke of Newcastle*, [1902] 1 Ch. 34, affd [1903] A.C. 111 (H.L.).
[33]*Roddy v. Fitzgerald* (1858), 6 H.L.C. 823, 10 E.R. 1518, *per* Lord Cranworth.
[34]*Kavanagh v. Morland* (1853), 23 L.J. Ch. 41.
[35]*Roddy v. Fitzgerald, supra*, footnote 33.

power can be ascertained.[1] If the provisions of the statute or the conditions of the power are not observed, however, the exercise of the power, that is, the appointment, will be void.[2]

(a) Exercise by deed or will

Unless the power restricts the mode of exercise, it may be exercised either by deed or by will.

If a person is given a power to appoint property after his death, the reference to his death does not in itself limit his power to appointment by will only, commonly called a testamentary power. Thus, a gift to A for life, and "at" or "after" his decease to such persons as he shall appoint, gives A a life interest with a power of appointment either by instrument *inter vivos* or by will, there being no rule of construction under which a gift in such terms, unless controlled by the context, can be held to confer a testamentary power only.[3] Again, a devise and bequest to the testator's widow for the term of her life and to be distributed to the testator's family "at her decease as she might think proper" was held to give her a power of distribution either by deed or will.[4] Similarly, where there was a devise to the testator's wife for life and then to be at her disposal, provided it be to any of his children, it was held that her exercise of the power by conveyance was good.[5]

The wording of the power, however, may be inappropriate to its exercise by deed or may otherwise indicate the intention that it is to be exercised by will only. Thus, where a testator gave all his property to his wife for life, directed her to pay his debts and "at her decease to make such a distribution and disposal of his then remaining property among the children as might seem just and equitable according to her discretion", it was held that this was a power exercisable by will only, to appoint in favour of children living at her death.[6] And, where a testator devised all of his freehold estate to his wife during her life "and also at her disposal afterwards to leave it to whom she pleases", it was held that she could only leave it by will and that a conveyance in her lifetime was void.[7] Also, in the case of a devise to the testator's widow for life to be by her divided among such of the testator's children and their issue as should be surviving at her death, the power could only be exercised by will.[8]

---

§1405.1
[1]Farwell, p. 218.
[2]*Ibid.*, pp. 147 *et seq.*
[3]*Re Jackson's Will* (1879), 13 Ch. D. 189.
[4]*Humble v. Bowman* (1877), 47 L.J. Ch. 62. *Cf. Robinson v. Royal Trust Co.*; *Re Mewburn*, [1939] 1 D.L.R. 257, [1939] S.C.R. 75, "upon her death"; *Re Jones*, [1949] 3 D.L.R. 604, [1949] 1 W.W.R. 1093 (Man. C.A.), a power to appoint "operative on his death".
[5]*Tomlinson v. Dighton* (1712), 1 P. Wms. 149, 24 E.R. 335.
[6]*Freeland v. Pearson* (1867), L.R. 3 Eq. 658.
[7]*Doe d. Thorley v. Thorley* (1809), 10 East 438, 103 E.R. 842.
[8]*Ex parte Williams* (1819), 1 Jac. & W. 89, 37 E.R. 309.

A power to appoint by will only cannot be exercised in any other way.[9] In *Re Collard and Duckworth*[10] the testatrix devised land to trustees upon trust to hold one part to the use of her son, C.S.C., for his life and after his death to convey it to his children or such of the testatrix's other three sons or their children as C.S.C. by his last will might appoint, and the other part to the use of her son, W.D., in the same way; C.S.C. and W.D. each appointed his part to the other by will and each conveyed his life interest to the other and covenanted not to revoke the appointment made by will; they then contracted to sell both parts to a purchaser. It was held (1) that their powers of appointment could only be exercised by will; (2) that "the intention of the creator of such a power is taken to be that the donee of it shall not deprive himself until the time of his death of his right to select such of the objects of the power as he may deem proper";[11] (3) that notwithstanding the covenants not to revoke the appointments, a subsequent appointment by will to one of the objects of the power would be a good execution of it and the covenants would not affect the title of the subsequent appointee, for he could take the estate under the original testatrix and not under the devisee for life, and (4) that the statutory right to release or to contract not to exercise the power,[12] did not confer on the donees of the power the right to give the purchaser a good title.[13]

Since a will is essentially revocable, a power cannot be validly exercised in a revoked will, even if the donee of the power covenants not to revoke it. It is of the very nature of a will that it shall be revocable during the testator's life and any attempt of the donee to execute the power by an irrevocable instrument cannot bind the person taking under a later will.[14]

By contrast, it should be noted that, while a will is revoked by the marriage of the testator, there is no revocation where the will is made in exercise of a power of appointment of property which would not in default of the appointment pass to the heir, executor or administrator of the testator or to the persons entitled to the estate if the testator died intestate.[15] Only that part of the will which exercises the power remains unrevoked.[16]

Where a power is exercisable by will only, the court has no authority to authorize a donee of the power to exercise it in his lifetime because it is of

---

[9]*Reid v. Shergold* (1805), 10 Ves. Jun. 370, 32 E.R. 888.

[10](1899), 16 O.R. 735 (H.C.J.).

[11]*Ibid.*, at p. 736, *per* Street, J.

[12]*Law and Transfer of Property Act*, R.S.O. 1887, c. 100, s. 19.

[13]See also *Re Smith and King* (1917), 13 O.W.N. 54 (H.C.).

[14]*Re Collard and Duckworth, supra*, footnote 10, at p. 736, *per* Street, J.

[15]*Succession Law Reform Act*, R.S.O. 1980, c. 488, s. 16(c); *Wills Act*, R.S.A. 1980, c. T-10, s. 17(1)(b); R.S.B.C. 1979, c. 434, s. 15(b); R.S.M. 1970, c. W150, s. 17(b); R.S.S. 1978, c. W-14, s. 15(b); R.S.N.B. 1973, c. W-9, s. 16(b); R.S.N.S. 1967, c. 340, s. 16(c); R.S.N. 1970, c. 401, s. 9; *Probate Act*, R.S.P.E.I. 1974, c. P-19, s. 69(2)(b); *Wills Ordinance*, R.O.N.W.T. 1974, c. W-3, s. 12(3)(b); R.O.Y.T 1971, c. W-3, s. 11(3)(b).

[16]*Re Paul; Public Trustee v. Pearce*, [1921] 2 Ch. 1; *Re Gilligan*, [1950] P. 32.

the very essence of a power of appointment by will that it is revocable and to become operative only upon the death of the donee of the power.

Thus, where property was left to the testator's widow during her life and widowhood and, upon her death, to such of his children as she might appoint by will and, if she remarried, to such of the children as the executors might appoint, it was held that a child's share of the proceeds of land sold under the *Settled Estates Act*[17] could not be paid out to the child upon attaining majority even with the consent of the widow and other children of age.[18]

Conversely, a power which is to be exercised by deed only cannot be exercised by will,[19] even though the will is under seal.[20] It was held, however, that an instrument in the form of a deed, although really testamentary in effect, validly exercised a power exercisable by will only.[21]

(b) Formalities at common law

At common law, apart from statutory provisions as to execution, it is necessary that all of the terms of a power and the formalities required by it be strictly observed.[22] Hence, if the consent of a person to the exercise of the power is required, such as that of a wife to advances by trustees to her husband under a marriage settlement, advances made without her consent are invalid and her subsequent consent is ineffective and not retroactive in effect.[23]

(c) Statutory formalities

(i) Inter vivos

The *Law of Property Amendment Act*[24] made substantial changes in respect of formalities, which were re-enacted in Ontario. Section 25 of the *Conveyancing and Law of Property Act*[25] provides that a deed executed in the presence of and attested by two or more witnesses in the manner in which deeds are ordinarily executed and attested is a valid execution of an *inter vivos* power as regards execution and attestation, even though some additional or other form of execution or attestation or solemnity is required by the terms of the power. The section goes on to provide that the foregoing does not operate to defeat any direction in the instrument creating the power that the

---

[17]R.S.O. 1897, c. 71.

[18]*Re Newton* (1912), 3 O.W.N. 948, 2 D.L.R. 576 (H.C.).

[19]*Earl of Darlington v. Pulteney* (1775), 1 Cowp. 260, 98 E.R. 1075; *Countess of Cavan v. Doe d. Pulteney* (1795), 6 Bro. P.C. 175, 2 E.R. 1010 (H.L.); *Re Phillips*; *Robinson v. Burke* (1889), 41 Ch. D. 417 at p. 419.

[20]*Shore v. Shore* (1891), 21 O.R. 54 (H.C.J.), overruling *McDermott v. Keenan* (1887), 14 O.R. 687 (H.C.J.), to the contrary.

[21]*Marjoribanks v. Hovenden* (1852), Drury 11, 6 I.R. Eq. 238.

[22]*Ibid.*; *Rutland v. Doe d. Wythe* (1843), 10 Cl. & Fin. 419, 8 E.R. 801 (H.L.).

[23]*Bateman v. Davis* (1818), 3 Madd. 98, 56 E.R. 446; *Cocker v. Quayle* (1830), 1 Russ. & M. 535, 39 E.R. 206; *Wiles v. Gresham* (1854), 2 Drewry 258, 61 E.R. 718.

[24]22 & 23 Vict., c. 35, s. 12 (1859). See now *Law of Property Act, 1925*, 15 & 16 Geo. 5. c. 20, s. 159.

[25]R.S.O. 1980, c. 90.

consent of any particular person shall be necessary to the valid execution, or that any act shall be performed in order to give validity to any appointment, having no relation to the mode of executing and attesting the deed or instrument, and that nothing in the section prevents the donee of the power from executing it conformably to the power.

> The purpose of this legislation [is] only to give relief from burdensome and needless requirements in that respect sometimes contained in instruments creating such powers; not to make the manner of execution more burdensome in cases in which no burden had been imposed by the creator of the power.[26]

Hence, if the instrument creating the power does not prescribe the manner in which it is to be executed, the exercise of the power is valid if it complies with the *Statute of Frauds*,[27] it not being necessary to comply with the above section of the *Conveyancing and Law of Property Act*.[28]

Similar provision does not appear to have been made in the other provinces. It should be noted, however, that since deeds are not, today, normally attested by two witnesses, the above enactment has limited utility.

(ii) Testamentary

The several provincial statutes respecting wills do provide that a will made in accordance with the statute is a valid execution of a power of appointment by will, notwithstanding that it was expressly required that the will exercising the power be made in some other form.[29]

If a power to appoint by will is exercised by a person domiciled in a foreign country by a will which is made in accordance with the law of that country, although not in accordance with the *Wills Act*,[30] it is a valid exercise of the power.[31] A power exercisable by "an instrument in writing" may be exercised by a will because it is such an instrument,[32] but the *Wills Act* does not apply

---

[26]*Re Spellman and Litovitz* (1918), 44 O.L.R. 30 (H.C.), at p. 31, *per* Meredith, C.J.C.P.

[27]Thus, if the appointment is of land, it must be in writing, signed by the appointor: R.S.O. 1980, c. 481, ss. 1, 9; R.S.B.C. 1979, c. 393, s. 1; R.S.N.B. 1973, c. S-14, ss. 1, 9; R.S.N.S. 1967, c. 290, ss. 1, 4; R.S.P.E.I. 1974, c. S-6, s. 1. The English Act, 29 Car. 2, c. 3 (1677), ss. 1, 7, is in force as received English law in Alberta, Saskatchewan, Manitoba, Newfoundland, Northwest Territories and the Yukon.

[28]*Re Spellman and Litovitz, supra,* footnote 26.

[29]*Wills Act,* R.S.A. 1980, c. T-10, s. 10; R.S.B.C. 1979, c. 434, s. 8; R.S.M. 1970, c. W150, s. 10; R.S.S. 1978, c. W-14, s. 9; R.S.N.B. 1973, c. W-9, s. 9; R.S.N.S. 1967, c. 340, s. 7; R.S.N. 1970, c. 401, s. 4; *Probate Act,* R.S.P.E.I. 1974, c. P-19, s. 62; *Succession Law Reform Act,* R.S.O. 1980, c. 488, s. 9; *Wills Ordinance,* R.O.N.W.T. 1974, c. W-3, s. 9; R.O.Y.T. 1971, c. W-3, s. 8.

[30]7 Will. 4 & 1 Vict., c. 26 (1837), ss. 9, 10.

[31]*D'Huart v. Harkness* (1865), 34 Beav. 324, 55 E.R. 660; *Re Harman; Lloyd v. Tardy,* [1894] 3 Ch. 607; *Re Price; Tomlin v. Latter,* [1900] 1 Ch. 442; *Pouey v. Hordern,* [1900] 1 Ch. 492; *Re Simpson; Coutts & Co. v. Church Missionary Society,* [1916] 1 Ch. 502; *Re Wilkinson's Settlement; Butler v. Wilkinson,* [1917] 1 Ch. 620 at p. 627; *Re Spellman and Litovitz, supra,* footnote 26, at p. 31.

[32]*West v. Ray* (1854), Kay 385, 69 E.R. 163; *Orange v. Pickford* (1858), 4 Drewry 363, 62 E.R. 140; *Smith v. Adkins* (1872), L.R. 14 Eq. 402.

to a power to appoint "by an instrument in writing" and, therefore, any additional solemnities required by the instrument creating the power must be observed.[33]

1405.2 Illusory Appointments

Formerly, a non-exclusive power, that is, a power to appoint property among several objects in such a manner that some of the objects could be excluded from a share of the property, was void in equity, although valid at law, if some objects were excluded, or if an insubstantial or nominal share only were given to such objects. Such appointments are called illusory appointments.[1]

This rule created much inconvenience, especially since it could never be said with certainty how much a substantial share was. It was, therefore, enacted by the *Illusory Appointments Act*[2] that an appointment made in exercise of a power to appoint property amongst several objects shall be valid even though it appoints an insubstantial, illusory or nominal share only, or leaves such share to devolve upon one or more of the objects of the power.[3] The Act does not affect a power which declares the amount of the shares from which no object shall be excluded, nor does it give an appointment more validity than it would have had if it were non-illusory.

It was further enacted by the *Powers of Appointment Act*[4] that a non-exclusive power is valid in law and in equity even though an object of the power is excluded altogether by the exercise of the power or in default of appointment.[5] Again, a power declaring the amounts of the shares each object is to receive, was not affected by the Act.

Both statutes were enacted in British Columbia,[6] New Brunswick[7] and Manitoba,[8] while only the latter statute was enacted in Newfoundland.[9] There appears to be no similar legislation in the other provinces. However, the *Illusory Appointments Act*[10] is probably in force in Alberta, Saskatchewan and the Northwest and Yukon Territories as received English law.[11]

---

[33]*Taylor v. Meads* (1865), 4 De G. J. & S. 597, 46 E.R. 1050.
§1405.2
[1]Farwell, pp. 417 *et seq.*
[2]11 Geo. 4 & 1 Will. 4, c. 46 (1830).
[3]An object could, therefore, be "cut off with a shilling".
[4]37 & 38 Vict., c. 37 (1874). See now for both statutes, *Law of Property Act, 1925*, 15 & 16 Geo. 5, c. 20, s. 158.
[5]Hence, hereafter, a person could be "cut off without a shilling".
[6]*Power of Appointment Act*, R.S.B.C. 1979, c. 333.
[7]*Property Act*, R.S.N.B. 1973, c. P-19, ss. 52-54.
[8]*Law of Property Act*, R.S.M. 1970, c. L90, s. 8.
[9]*Appointment Under Powers Act*, R.S.N. 1970, c. 10.
[10]11 Geo. 4 & 1 Will. 4, c. 46 (1830).
[11]The date of reception for these areas being July 15, 1870. See §§310.2-310.5, *supra*.

1405.3 Contingent Powers

A power which is exercisable only when a future or contingent event happens or until some condition is fulfilled cannot be exercised until the event happens or the condition is fulfilled, because it has no existence meanwhile.[1]

Where a will gave a share of the estate to the testator's son but, if he should die before a specified "period of division", in trust for the son's issue as he might by will appoint, provided that if the son left a widow, he might leave the whole or any part of his share to her during any part of the remainder of her lifetime, it was held that the proviso gave the son a power to appoint to the widow whether or not he left issue. Moreover, he had power to appoint the whole of the income to her for her life from the date of his death.[2]

The same rule applies to a power of sale and distribution,[3] and to the passing of money.[4] Similarly, where property was devised to a tenant for life with power on death to divide it among the testator's children, it was held that a good title could not pass by a conveyance unless the life tenant and all children joined in the conveyance and were *sui juris*.[5]

1405.4 Loss of Power

Where there is a power to appoint among members of a class with a gift to the class in default of appointment and only one member remains before the power is exercised, such member must of necessity take the whole and the

§1405.3

[1]*Ryan v. Smith* (1971), 22 D.L.R. (3d) 1, [1972] S.C.R. 332, where the testator's widow was given a power to appoint if a named person was no longer living or employed by a company controlled by the testator when the testator died. Since the named person was then living, the widow did not have the power to appoint; *Earle v. Barker* (1865), 11 H.L.C. 280, 11 E.R. 1340, where residuary estate was given to the testator's executors upon trust to permit his nephew to receive the rents for life and, after his death, provided he left any child or children surviving him, the executors were to stand seised of the residuary estate upon trust for such persons and purposes as the nephew might by his will appoint but, if the nephew died without leaving child or children surviving and did not make any appointment prior to his death, the executors were to stand possessed of the residuary estate for other named persons. The nephew died without ever having had a child, leaving a will appointing the estate to two persons and it was held that, as he never had a child, the condition upon which his power was founded had not occurred, so that the power never came into existence and the appointment was invalid. See also *Re Abrahams' Will Trusts; Caplan v. Abrahams*, [1969] 1 Ch. 463.

[2]*Re Russell's Will Trusts*, [1954] O.W.N. 692, [1955] 1 D.L.R. 566 (C.A.), affd [1955] 2 D.L.R. 721 *sub nom. Re Russell; Andersen v. Evans* (S.C.C.).

[3]*Blacklow v. Laws* (1842), 2 Hare 40, 67 E.R. 17; *Johnstone v. Baber* (1845), 8 Beav. 233, 50 E.R. 91; *Mosley v. Hide* (1851), 17 Q.B. 91, 117 E.R. 1216; *Shaw v. Borrer* (1836), 1 Keen 559, 48 E.R. 422; *Want v. Stallibrass* (1873), L.R. 8 Exch. 175.

[4]*Wilkinson v. Thornhill* (1889), 61 L.T. 362.

[5]*Re Smith and King* (1917), 13 O.W.N. 54 (H.C.), and see *Re Rathbone and White* (1892), 22 O.R. 550 (H.C.J.), in which a will conferred a power to lease and to pay the proceeds to the widow for life in and, after her death, to sons. The widow and one son, being *sui juris*, joined in a conveyance of their interests.

person having the power loses the power.[1] The terms of the power may, however, permit it to be exercised where there is only one object left and that object takes in default of appointment, so that the interest passes by the appointment and not in default of it. Thus, in a devise of a life estate with the remainder to such children in such shares and to vest at such times as the life tenant might appoint by deed or will and, in default of appointment, the whole to the children equally or, if only one, to that one payable at age 21, the clause respecting vesting at age 21 applies only in case of default of appointment and, one of two children having died without issue after attaining age 21, the life tenant had the power to appoint the whole to the survivor.[2] Where there is a power to appoint to children of a marriage and there is only one child, the estate of that child cannot be defeated by an appointment to the child which fails for some reason, because the child must have the whole estate settled.[3] Where there was a power to appoint among children and, in default of appointment, the children were to take equally in tail, it was held that an appointment to a child for life, remainder to his children as he might appoint, was an excess of the power but that the appointment was void for the excess only and that what was ill-appointed went as in default of appointment.[4]

1405.5 Manner in Which Power is to be Exercised

(a) Generally

Whether a power is or is not exercised by the donee depends on his intention, which is ascertained in the usual manner by construing the instrument making the alleged appointment.[1] Generally, a special power is not exercised unless it specifically referred to.[2] Thus, the use of a stock phrase such as "all the rest of my property whatsoever and wheresoever belonging to me or over which I have control under any power of appointment or otherwise" in a residuary clause in a will, is not of itself conclusive that a special power is intended to be exercised.[3] When construing the instrument making the alleged appointment, extrinsic evidence tending to show the donee's intention is not admissible.[4]

On the other hand, the use of the word "appoint" is not necessary if the

§1405.4
[1]*Folkes v. Western* (1804), 9 Ves. Jun. 456, 32 E.R. 679.
[2]*Boyle v. Bishop of Peterborough* (1791), 1 Ves. Jun. 299, 30 E.R. 353.
[3]*Roe d. Buxton v. Dunt* (1767), 2 Wils. K.B. 336, 95 E.R. 843.
[4]*Bristow v. Warde* (1794), 2 Ves. Jun. 336, 30 E.R. 660.
§1405.5
[1]*Montreal Trust Co. v. Royal Exchange Ass'ce* (1956), 3 D.L.R. (2d) 455 (P.E.I.S.C.); *Re Dowsley* (1959), 15 D.L.R. (2d) 560 (Ont. H.C.J.); *Re Russell's Will Trusts*, [1954] O.W.N. 692, [1955] 1 D.L.R. 566 (C.A.), affd [1955] 2 D.L.R. 721 sub nom. *Re Russell*; *Andersen v. Evans* (S.C.C.).
[2]*Ibid.*
[3]*Montreal Trust Co. v. Royal Exchange Ass'ce, supra.*
[4]*Re Dowsley, supra,* footnote 1.

intention to exercise the power is clear,[5] but neither is the mere use of the word "appoint" conclusive.[6] If there is an express reference to the power, but it is given an inaccurate or incomplete description, the exercise of the power is valid, if the intention to exercise it is clear.[7]

Property over which a person has a general power of appointment will, however, pass by a general devise or bequest in that person's will, unless a contrary intention appears on the face of the will.[8] Hence, where a husband making a marriage settlement reserved to himself a power of appointment, it was held that he had exercised it by a clause in a will made a few days after the marriage giving to his wife "all property and estate of which I die seised or possessed".[9] An ineffectual exercise of a power of appointment is not an expression of a contrary intention within the meaning of the legislation, so that a residuary bequest will still operate as an execution of the power.[10]

Moreover, devolution of estates statutes, which generally provide that the real property of a deceased person vests in his personal representative as if it were personal property, go on to provide that a testator is deemed to have been entitled to an interest in real property passing under any gift in his will which operates as an appointment under a general power to appoint by will.[11]

A power of appointment may usually be exercised at different times by different instruments and it is not necessary that a partial exercise give each object a share.[12] Thus, where property was settled, subject to a life estate for the parents, to the use of the children of the marriage as the parents should by deed appoint and, in default of appointment, to the use of the children equally, and one-eighth was appointed to one child, while the remaining seven-eighths were subsequently appointed to the remaining four children, it was held that the appointment was good. The fact that the property was appointed by two deeds formed no objection to the due exercise of the power.[13] Where property was settled in trust for the children of a marriage

---

[5]*Re Russell's Will Trusts*, [1954] O.W.N. 692, [1955] 1 D.L.R. 566 (C.A.), affd [1955] 2 D.L.R. 721 *sub nom. Re Russell; Andersen v. Evans* (S.C.C.).

[6]*Ibid.*

[7]*Ibid.*

[8]*Wills Act*, R.S.A. 1980, c. T-10, s. 25; R.S.B.C. 1979, c. 434, s. 23; R.S.M. 1970, c. W150, s. 25; R.S.S. 1978, c. W-14, s. 24; R.S.N.B. 1973, c. W-9, s. 24; R.S.N.S. 1967, c. 340, s. 25; R.S.N. 1970, c. 401, s. 16; *Succession Law Reform Act*, R.S.O. 1980, c. 488, s. 25; *Probate Act*, R.S.P.E.I. 1974, c. P-19, s. 78; *Wills Ordinance*, R.O.N.W.T. 1974, c. W-3, s. 19; R.O.Y.T. 1971, c. W-3, s. 18.

[9]*Re Hammond* (1920), 18 O.W.N. 253 (H.C.), citing *Re Jones; Greene v. Gordon* (1886), 34 Ch. D. 65, and *Re Jacob; Mortimer v. Mortimer*, [1907] 1 Ch. 445.

[10]*Re White Trust*, [1952] O.W.N. 748, [1952] 4 D.L.R. 711 (H.C.J.).

[11]*Estates Administration Act*, R.S.O. 1980, c. 143, s. 2; *Devolution of Estates Act*, R.S.M. 1970, c. D70, s. 18; R.S.N.B. 1973, c. D-9, s. 3; *Devolution of Real Property Act*, R.S.A. 1980, c. D-34, s. 2; R.S.S. 1978, c. D-27, s. 4; *Estate Administration Act*, R.S.B.C. 1979, c. 114, s. 90; *Probate Act*, R.S.P.E.I. 1974, c. P-19, s. 108; *Devolution of Estates Ordinance*, R.O.N.W.T. 1974, c. D-5, s. 3; R.O.Y.T. 1971, c. D-4, s. 3.

[12]*Bristow v. Warde* (1794), 2 Ves. Jun. 336, 30 E.R. 660; *Wilson v. Piggott* (1794), 2 Ves. Jun. 351, 30 E.R. 668.

[13]*Colston v. Pemberton* (1836), Donnelly 19, 47 E.R. 199.

as the husband and wife should jointly appoint but, if either died before any appointment were made, then as the survivor should appoint, it was held that, notwithstanding a joint appointment of part of the property, a sole appointment might be made of the remainder by the survivor.[14] Similarly, a power to appoint a fee simple can be executed at different times, a life estate being appointed at one time and the fee subsequently.[15]

Where the trustees under a will have a discretion to pay the income from a business, which they had power to continue, to the daughter for life and on her death to her children, with further power to pay such part of the corpus to the daughter as they deemed advisable, the trustees could transfer the business to her in specie.[16]

Further, where a trustee and life tenant has a general power to encroach, she may pay the corpus over to herself.[17] Whether she has done so depends upon the circumstances. Where the proceeds of sale of estate assets are paid by her into her personal account and kept for her own use, the inference is that she has exercised the power.[18]

A power of appointment to be exercised by one instrument may be exercised by several deeds which, although each is insufficient in itself, will be treated as one disposition if that was the expressed intention of the parties in the first transaction.[19] Where a primary power of appointment is possessed by one person and, in default of appointment, a secondary power is possessed by another person, the partial exercise of the primary power does not exclude the exercise of the secondary power.

In *Mapleton v. Mapleton*[20] a husband had power to appoint among children and issue of children living at the wife's death and, in default of appointment, the wife had power to appoint among the children and issue of children living at the husband's death. The husband appointed among four children, but not to a fifth child who, with one child, was living at the husband's death. After his death, the fifth child died leaving three children, two born after the husband's death. The widow appointed to her four living children and to the eldest child of the deceased child. It was held that, although the other two grandchildren would have been objects of the husband's power, their exclusion by the exercise of both powers did not render the execution of either bad.

Where there is a general power of appointment, an appointment by way of mortgage reserving the right to redeem to persons other than those to whom the estate is limited in default of appointment is not in itself an appointment of the equity of redemption. The effect of an appointment by way of

---

[14]*Re Simpson's Settlement* (1851), 4 De G. & Sm. 521, 64 E.R. 940.
[15]*Bovey v. Smith* (1682), 1 Vern. 84, 23 E.R. 328, revd 1 Vern. 144, 23 E.R. 377, restd 15 Lords Journals 275 *sub nom. Boevey v. Smith* (H.L.).
[16]*Re Banko*, [1958] O.R. 213, 12 D.L.R. (2d) 515 (H.C.J.).
[17]*Re Box* (1957), 7 D.L.R. (2d) 478, 20 W.W.R. 636 (Man. C.A.).
[18]*Ibid.*
[19]*Lord Braybrooke v. Attorney-General* (1860), 9 H.L.C. 150 at p. 167, 11 E.R. 685, two deeds executed nine years apart treated as constituting one disposition.
[20](1859), 4 Drewry 515, 62 E.R. 198.

mortgage depends entirely on the intention indicated by the instrument as a whole, so that it may be regarded as creating a charge only, or as altering the limitations of the property.

In *Heather v. O'Neil*,[21] land of a wife was settled to such uses as she and her husband might appoint and, subject thereto, to the use of the husband for life, remainder to the wife for life, remainder to their children. The husband and wife then appointed the land to the use of trustees upon such trusts as the husband alone might appoint and, subject thereto, in trust for the husband for life or until his bankruptcy, remainder in trust for his wife for life and, after her death, upon the trusts in the former deed of settlement. Later, the husband executed a mortgage, therein reciting an agreement for a loan and appointing to the trustees upon trust for sale and securing payment of the mortgage debt and, subject thereto, upon trust for the husband and his heirs. It was held that the equity of redemption was thereby effectively resettled and belonged to the husband in fee simple. Similarly, in *Hipkin v. Wilson*[22] land was limited to a father for life, remainder as the father and son might appoint, remainder to the son in tail, remainder to the father in fee. Father and son appointed by way of mortgage with a proviso that, upon repayment, the mortgagees were to reconvey to the father and son, their heirs or assigns, or as they might direct, and it stipulated that the father during his life was to keep down interest. It was held that the course of limitation of the estate was not changed by this proviso.[23]

Consequently, a power of appointment may be fully exercised as to appointment of the legal estate without exhausting the power as to the equitable estate, so that, after mortgaging the fee, the equity of redemption may be appointed.[24] Although the appointment of the use by way of mortgage does not necessarily exhaust the power and the extent to which the appointment operates depends upon the intent to be gathered from the instrument taken as a whole,[25] where a person holds the fee simple to such uses as he may appoint and he appoints by way of mortgage, a discharge of the mortgage does not revest in him the original power of appointment, but only the legal estate in fee in the property.[26] On the other hand, it was held that the registration of a discharge of mortgage, which has the effect of reconveying the original estate of the mortgagor to the person best entitled thereto, does not defeat the uses created by a deed of the land registered prior to such discharge, so that it does not affect an appointment of the use.

---

[21](1858), 2 De G. & J. 399, 44 E.R. 1044 (C.A.).

[22](1850), 3 De G. & Sm. 738, 64 E.R. 684.

[23]See also *Whitbread v. Smith* (1854), 3 De G. M. & G. 727, 43 E.R. 286; *Re Byron's Settlement*; *Williams v. Mitchell*, [1891] 3 Ch. 474.

[24]See *Ruscombe v. Hare* (1828), 2 Bligh N.S. 192, 4 E.R. 1103 (H.L.).

[25]*Re Hazell* (1925), 57 O.L.R. 166, [1925] 3 D.L.R. 661, vard O.L.R. *loc. cit.*, p. 290, D.L.R. *loc. cit.* (S.C. App. Div.).

[26]*Ibid.*; *Re Dresser*, [1959] O.W.N. 103 (H.C.J.). The position is now otherwise in Ontario. The *Registry Act*, R.S.O. 1980, c. 445, s. 59, and the *Land Titles Act*, R.S.O. 1980, c. 230, s. 92, provide that the power may still be exercised after the mortgage is discharged.

This concept is important in jurisdictions in which dower was, until recently, retained. For example, it had been held that if land subject to a mortgage is conveyed to a husband to such uses as he may appoint and, until and in default of appointment, to himself in fee simple, his wife's inchoate right of dower would arise upon registration of a discharge of the mortgage, subject to being defeated by his exercise of the power, but he may appoint the use without bar of her dower being necessary.[27] Similarly, if land is conveyed to a husband to such uses as he may appoint and, in default of appointment, to himself in fee simple, his wife's inchoate right of dower attaches immediately, subject to being defeated on his exercise of the power.[28] That is because the common law seisin and a general power of appointment may exist in the same person.[29]

The power of a husband to appoint such uses created by a deed to uses may be exercised by his will and in that event the appointment will defeat his wife's dower.[30]

(b) Capricious exercise

It has been seen that the donee of a mere power is not under a duty to exercise it, so that, if he fails to exercise it, the court cannot and will not intervene at the behest of the objects.[31] The court can only intervene if the donee exceeds the power, or commits a fraud on the power.[32] However, if a mere power is given to a trustee, the trustee is under a duty to consider whether and to what extent he should appoint[33] and, if he disregards the power, the court can remove him.[34]

The court can also remove the donee-trustee if he acts capriciously, that is, "for reasons which [are] irrational, perverse or irrelevant to any sensible expectation of the settlor; for example, if [he chooses] a beneficiary by height or complexion or by the irrelevant fact that he was a resident of Greater London".[35]

The court can similarly remove a trustee who acts capriciously under a

---

[27]*Re Kuntz and Hodgins* (1927), 61 O.L.R. 298, [1927] 4 D.L.R. 1009 (S.C.), distinguishing *Re Hazell, supra,* footnote 25.

[28]*Re Hazell, supra,* footnote 25.

[29]This principle was once doubted, but may be regarded as settled by *Re Hazell, supra,* footnote 25. See D.L.R. Ann. Rev. (1911-28), p. 870; Gosse, *The Registry Act and The Land Titles Act of Ontario* (1967), p. 19.

[30]*Re Dresser,* [1959] O.W.N. 103 (H.C.J.).

[31]See §§1402-1403.1, *supra.*

[32]See §§1407-1408.6, *infra.*

[33]*Re Gestetner Settlement; Barnett v. Blumka,* [1953] Ch. 672 at p. 688, *per* Harman, J.; *Re Abrahams' Will Trusts; Caplan v. Abrahams,* [1969] 1 Ch. 463 at p. 474; *Re Gulbenkian's Settlements,* [1970] A.C. 508 at p. 518, *per* Lord Reid; *McPhail v. Doulton,* [1971] A.C. 424 at p. 456, *per* Lord Wilberforce; *Re Manisty's Settlement; Manisty v. Manisty,* [1974] Ch. 17 at p. 25, *per* Templeman, J.

[34]*McPhail v. Doulton, supra,* footnote 33, at p. 456, *per* Lord Wilberforce.

[35]*Re Manisty's Settlement, supra,* footnote 33, at p. 26, *per* Templeman, J.

trust power and it is at least arguable that the court should be able to declare a capricious appointment made under a bare power by a non-trustee void.

1405.6   Time of Exercise

If there is no specific time limit within which a power of appointment must be exercised, the donee of the power has his whole life during which to exercise it. In *Cowan v. Besserer*,[1] a testator devised land to his wife to be held and enjoyed by her as long as she lived and remained unmarried and, after her death or remarriage, to such son in fee simple as she might name by deed. She remarried without having exercised the power. It was held that the power did not cease upon her remarriage, but could be exercised during her life.

Where a power of appointment was to be made during a wife's coverture, it was held that its exercise after her husband's death was invalid.[2]

Further illustrations of the rule that the exercise must be within a specified time limit are supplied by cases of powers to appoint trust funds. In *Re Twiss's Settlement Trusts*,[3] a husband and wife had the power during their joint lives to revoke an appointment and appoint new trusts. The wife died before any revocation and thereafter the husband could not do so. In *Cooper v. Martin*,[4] a testator gave an estate upon trust for sale, the proceeds to be held upon such trusts as his wife might appoint by instrument before the testator's youngest child attained age 21. Her appointment by will, which was executed before such child attained that age, but which did not take effect until her death after that time limit, was not valid. In *Potts v. Britton*,[5] a fund under a settlement was held upon trust for such persons as G and B might jointly appoint with remainder to B for life and further remainder to such members of a class as B might appoint by deed or will but, if B committed any of certain acts, his life estate was to determine and pass as if he were dead. He did commit an act of forfeiture and died. It was held that an appointment in his will made before the forfeiture was ineffective.

On the other hand, where trustees under a marriage settlement were to hold funds upon such trusts as the wife might "during coverture by will or deed appoint", it was held that her will made during coverture was a valid execution of the power although she died after coverture.[6] Similarly, where funds under a marriage settlement were to be held upon trust for such persons as the wife "shall by will during the continuance of the intended coverture direct or appoint", it was held that her will made during coverture made an effective

---

§1405.6
[1](1884), 5 O.R. 624 (H.C.J.).
[2]*Halliday v. Overton* (1852), 20 L.T. (O.S.) 12.
[3](1867), 16 L.T. 139.
[4](1867), L.R. 3 Ch. 47.
[5](1871), L.R. 11 Eq. 433.
[6]*Re Illingworth; Bevir v. Armstrong*, [1909] 2 Ch. 297.

appointment of the funds although she survived her husband, there being no reason to imply a condition that she should not only make her will but die during coverture.[7]

1405.7 Effect of Non-appointment

If property is devised to a person for life with a general power of appointment and he dies without exercising the power, as where he dies intestate, the property passes to the next of kin of the testator.[1] The testator's next of kin is determined as of the date of his death and not at the date of the donee's death.[2]

If, however, there is a gift over in default of appointment, the property will pass to the persons specified to take in that event. Moreover, even though the gift over might otherwise be void for perpetuity, on the principle that, if at the moment the power expires by the death of the donee he had made an appointment that would have been valid under the rule against perpetuities to the objects of the power, then the gift over, if it is limited to the same objects, is also valid.[3]

Thus, in *Re Edwards*,[4] the testator directed his trustees to pay the income from part of the residue to his son X, for life, remainder as X might appoint among his children and, in default of appointment to distribute the corpus equally among X's children, as to one-half when the youngest became 21 and as to the other half when he or she became 35. X died without exercising the special power. He was survived by four children, all over 21. It was held that the gift over was valid, for it should be regarded as if X had elected to allow the gift in default to take effect and such a notional election is equivalent to an actual appointment. Although the perpetuity period begins to run when the power is created, in these circumstances the court can take a "second look" at the facts at the moment of the notional exercise. At that time X's youngest child would have to reach the age of 35, if at all, within twenty-one years of X's death and, therefore, the gift over was not void for perpetuity.[5]

1405.8 Exhausting the Power

Where there is a general power to appoint by deed or will and the donee of the power exercises it by deed, the power is exhausted and the donee cannot make another appointment by will. Thus, where the wife had power

---

[7]*Re Safford's Settlement; Davies v. Burgess,* [1915] 2 Ch. 211.
§1405.7
[1]*Re Gilkinson* (1930), 38 O.W.N. 26 (H.C.), affd 39 O.W.N. 115 (S.C. App. Div.); *Henderson v. Henderson* (1922), 52 O.L.R. 440 (H.C.).
[2]*Re Patterson,* [1957] O.W.N. 72, 7 D.L.R. (2d) 606 (H.C.J.).
[3]*Re Edwards,* [1959] O.W.N. 313, 20 D.L.R. (2d) 755 (H.C.J.).
[4]*Supra,* footnote 3.
[5]See further §1104.7(d), *supra.*

under a marriage settlement to appoint by deed or will and appointed the trust property to her son absolutely, subject to a life estate to herself, and the son died in her lifetime intestate without issue, but leaving a widow, it was held that his mother could not by her will appoint the property to her executors and administrators and that the son's widow was entitled to half of the property subject to the life estate, and the son's parents to the other half.[1]

1405.9 Who May Exercise the Power

The rule that the court will not allow a trust to fail for want of a trustee, but will appoint a new trustee, does not extend to mere powers. Hence, a bare power given to two or more persons by name and not annexed to an estate or office[1] cannot be exercised by the survivor,[2] but can only be exercised by the donee.[3] But if the power is annexed to an office, any person filling the office may exercise it.[4] Thus, a testator gave his residuary estate to two trustees upon trust for his children except J, who had misconducted himself, and appointed the trustees as executors and gave them and the survivor of them power to give a share to J if his conduct changed. He appointed a third executor by codicil; two of the three executors renounced, the third proved the will and appointed a share of the property to J whose conduct had been satisfactory. It was held that he had the power so to do.[5]

A power was given by and to the trustees or trustee for the time being, at their entire discretion, to pay rents to one or more of the children of a life tenant, with a power to the surviving or continuing trustee to appoint a new trustee. The trustees all died without appointing new trustees. A new trustee was appointed by the court and it was held that he had the discretionary power of the original trustees.[6]

Where a power is given to a trustee, there is a presumption that it is given as an incident to that office, so that the holder of the office, for the time being, may exercise it. Thus, if the named executor under a will becomes mentally incompetent and is replaced by an administrator with the will annexed, the latter may exercise the power.[7]

---

§1405.8
[1]*Re Plumb* (1915), 8 O.W.N. 284 (H.C.).
§1405.9
[1]See §1403.1, *supra.*
[2]*Re Harding*; *Harding v. Paterson*, [1923] 1 Ch. 182; *Re Roach* (1930), 38 O.W.N. 189, affd 39 O.W.N. 109, affd [1931] 3 D.L.R. 374, [1931] S.C.R. 512; *Re Ward*, [1951] O.W.N. 1, [1952] 1 D.L.R. 463 (H.C.J.); Farwell, p. 514.
[3]*Re Harding, supra*; *Re Lysaght*; *Hill v. Royal College of Surgeons*, [1966] Ch. 191.
[4]*Brassey v. Chalmers* (1852), 16 Beav. 223, 51 E.R. 763, affd 4 De G. M. & G. 528, 43 E.R. 613; *Bersel Manufacturing Co. Ltd. v. Berry*, [1968] 2 All E.R. 552 (H.L.); *Re De Sommery*; *Coelenbier v. De Sommery*, [1912] 2 Ch. 622. And see §1403.1, *supra.*
[5]*Eaton v. Smith* (1839), 2 Beav. 236, 48 E.R. 1171.
[6]*Bartley v. Bartley* (1855), 3 Drewry 384, 61 E.R. 949.
[7]*Re Gilliland* (1957), 10 D.L.R. (2d) 769, 39 M.P.R. 262 (N.S.S.C.).

If a power is annexed to an office, it can only be exercised by a person filling the office. A testatrix gave her residuary estate to such charitable purposes as might be thereafter specified or, in default, according to the best judgment of her sole executor. She died without specifying the charitable purposes. The sole executor renounced and it was held that, after renouncing, he could not specify the charities.[8] Similarly, it was held that, where land is devised to trustees upon trust with powers requiring the exercise of their judgment and discretion and they disclaim, the heir-at-law of the testator, as constructive trustee, cannot exercise such powers, although he may hold the property subject to the trusts of the will.[9]

A power given to the holder of an office, such as a trustee, cannot be exercised by him or by the survivor of several, in his own favour, even though on its face it appears to be unrestricted. Thus, where an apparently unrestricted power was given to the survivor of the two executors, A and B, but which was in fact the subject of a secret trust between the testator and A, who agreed to appoint in accordance with the testator's further instructions, which were never given, the survivor, B, who had no notice of the secret trust, could not appoint in his own favour.[10]

1405.10 Delegation of Powers

(a) Generally

The general rule relating to the delegation of powers is that a power which involves the exercise of a personal discretion by the donee of the power cannot be delegated by him to another person.[1] If A has a power of personal trust and confidence to exercise his judgment and discretion to appoint a fund, he cannot say that it shall be appointed at the discretion of B, for *delegatus non potest delegare*.[2] Thus, where a husband had power under a settlement to dispose of a reversionary interest among issue of the marriage in such proportions as he might think fit and he, by his will, delegated it to his wife to dispose of it in such shares between his son and daughters as she might think fit, it was held that the power, like a power of attorney, was not transmissible by him, but could be exercised by him only.[3]

A testator devised and bequeathed his real and personal estate upon trust for his wife for life, and, after her death, in trust for his children living at her death and their issue as she might appoint. By her will, she appointed two-fifths in trust for a son T and, after his death, in trust for his children as he might appoint, with certain conditions and other provisions. It was held

---

[8]*Attorney-General v. Fletcher* (1835), 5 L.J. Ch. 75.
[9]*Robson v. Flight* (1865), 4 De G. J. & S. 608, 46 E.R. 1054.
[10]*Re Hardy*, [1952] 2 D.L.R. 768, 29 M.P.R. 358 (N.S.S.C.).
§1405.10
[1]*De Bussche v. Alt* (1878), 8 Ch. D. 286 (C.A.), at p. 310.
[2]*Alexander v. Alexander* (1755), 2 Ves. Sen. 640, 28 E.R. 408.
[3]*Ingram v. Ingram* (1740), 2 Atk. 88, 26 E.R. 455.

that the limitation to the children of T as he might appoint was void as being a delegation of her power.[4]

Where the donee of a power to appoint among his children appointed to his son for life with remainder to such of the son's children as he might appoint and, in default of appointment, to the son absolutely, and the son died without exercising the power, it was held that the ultimate limitation to the son was valid and effective.[5]

Where a daughter had power under her father's will to appoint the principal of a trust fund among her children by deed or will and she appointed it among her sons who should attain age 21 and her daughters who should attain that age or marry, declaring that, during the period of twenty-one years after her death, the income of each child's share was to be paid to the child but, if any died within the period without issue, that child's share was to go by way of accruer to the other shares and by a proviso empowered the trustees under her father's will, in their absolute discretion, to pay to any of her sons who attained age 21 that son's share absolutely, it was held that this power in the proviso was an attempt to delegate to the trustees her own power and was therefore an invalid exercise of her power.[6]

On the other hand, where a widow had a special power to appoint a settled fund "in such manner and form in every respect" as she might appoint by deed or will and she appointed the fund by deed irrevocably to her two infant children equally and gave the trustees an ordinary power of advancement, it was held that, as she had appointed absolute interests, the power of advancement was not a delegation of her special power but was merely ancillary to the absolute appointment, so that it was valid.[7]

The donee of a special power over trust property may, so long as the instrument creating the power does not forbid it, appoint the property to trustees for the objects of the power, for it is of the essence of a power of appointment that the donee has the same discretion as the donor had except to the extent that it is limited by the instrument creating the power.[8]

(b) Delegation of power of consent

On the same principle, a person cannot delegate the power to consent to the exercise of a power of appointment. A settlor in a marriage settlement settled property upon himself for life and upon the children of the marriage in strict settlement, with a proviso that he might revoke old uses and declare new uses by deed to be enrolled with the consent of certain trustees. It was held that a deed of revocation executed by him and by all trustees except one who had given the settlor a prior power of attorney agreeing to any deed the

---

[4]*Stockbridge v. Story* (1871), 19 W.R. 1049.

[5]*Williamson v. Farwell* (1887), 35 Ch. D. 128.

[6]*Re Joicey; Joicey v. Elliot*, [1915] 2 Ch. 115 (C.A.).

[7]*Re May's Settlement; Public Trustee v. Meredith*, [1926] Ch. 136.

[8]*Re Moffat*, [1950] O.R. 606, [1950] 4 D.L.R. 630 (H.C.J.); *Re Abrahams' Will Trusts; Caplan v. Abrahams*, [1969] 1 Ch. 463.

settlor might make, under which power of attorney the settlor executed the deed in the name of such trustee, was void, and that a subsequent deed of revocation, properly executed and consented to but not enrolled until after the settlor's death, was also void, because everything required to be done in execution of a power must be strictly complied with and be completed within the lifetime of the person by whom it is executed.[9]

The right to delegate the power to consent, however, may be implied from the impossibility, obvious at the time of the instrument creating the power, of the donee always being able to act in person, such as where a trustee is in one country and the trust property in another. Hence, a trustee in England may appoint an attorney to act for him in matters of discretion in connection with trust property abroad.[10]

(c) Delegation of general power

In the case of a general power of appointment, which is equivalent to absolute ownership, the power may be delegated. Where A has an absolute power of appointment, he may exercise it by appointing to certain persons in such shares as another person nominates, because this implies an actual execution of the power by A.[11] Similarly, if a person has a general power to appoint the uses of property by his will or by instrument under his hand and seal, so as to indicate that the exercise of the power is personal to himself, he cannot by his will delegate the power but he can exercise it by appointing the property to another person to such uses as the latter may appoint.[12] In *Smith v. Chishome*,[13] land was conveyed under a marriage settlement to the use of the settlor (the mother of the intended husband) for life and, after her death, in trust to pay the rents to the intended wife and, in case she predeceased her husband, upon certain trusts in favour of the husband and children of the marriage but, if he died in her lifetime, then in favour of such persons as he by deed or will might appoint and, in default of appointment, to his right heirs. The husband had by his will delegated to his wife his general power of appointment. The delegation was valid. The husband

> merely attempted to transfer his power to his wife. That he could in his lifetime have executed an appointment by power of attorney, just as he could have conveyed the fee simple, need not be questioned. That would still have been *his* appointment. But if he could thus by his will delegate the execution of the power to his wife, I see not why she or any *delegatus* of hers might not do so, and so *ad infinitum*. If an appointment by her could take effect it would do so as an appointment by her under the settlement, not as a limitation under an appointment to her by the donee of the power to such uses as she should appoint. Such an execution of the power by him would have been effectual, for the power being a general one conferring on him

---

[9]*Hawkins v. Kemp* (1803), 3 East 410, 102 E.R. 655.
[10]*Stuart v. Norton* (1860), 14 Moore 17, 15 E.R. 212.
[11]*White v. Wilson* (1852), 1 Drewry 298, 61 E.R. 466; *Smith v. Chishome* (1888), 15 O.A.R. 738.
[12]*Smith v. Chishome, supra*, footnote 11.
[13]*Supra*, footnote 11.

the entire beneficial interest in the property subject to his wife's life estate, he might have disposed of it as he pleased, and subject to such restrictions and conditions as he thought proper. The difficulty is that he has *not* disposed of it.[14]

Where an estate is limited to such uses as A may appoint, his appointment to such uses as B may appoint passes the legal estate to B's appointee, because the *Statute of Uses*[15] does not operate until B's power is exercised, the seisin originally created awaiting such exercise and, when it is exercised, the statute transfers the legal estate.[16]

1406. DEFECTIVE EXECUTION OF A POWER

A power must be exercised in accordance with the terms of the instrument creating it. These include the observance of any condition, such as the obtaining of the consent of a third party, and of the formalities imposed by the instrument. The exercise of the power will be void unless this is done. However, in certain cases equity will validate a defective execution and by statute lesser formalities may be required. These are dealt with in the next two paragraphs.

1406.1 Equitable Jurisdiction to Validate Defective Execution

Equity will aid the defective execution of a power if the intended appointee is a purchaser from the donee of the power, or is the creditor, wife or child of the donee, or if the appointment is for a charitable purpose. Thus, in *Lucena v. Lucena*,[1] a testator gave his widow a power to appoint a fund among his children and she, by her will, which was not executed with the formalities required by the power, appointed the fund to the children equally, and the court supplied the formalities.[2]

The principle upon which the court acts is that, whenever a man having power over an estate, whether a power of ownership or not, in discharge of moral or natural obligations, shows an intention to execute such power, the court will operate upon the conscience of the heir or other person entitled in default of appointment to make him perfect this intention.[3] The intention to appoint, however, must be established. Thus, it was held that, where a testator refers to a power but does not legally execute it and other estates to which the

---

[14]*Smith v. Chishome, supra,* footnote 11, at p. 742, *per* Osler, J.A.

[15]27 Hen. 8, c. 10 (1535).

[16]Farwell, p. 505; Sugden, *Powers,* p. 196; *Re Hazell* (1925), 57 O.L.R. 166 at p. 170, [1925] 3 D.L.R. 661 at p. 664, vard on one point by O.L.R. *loc. cit.,* p. 290, D.L.R. *loc. cit.* (S.C. App. Div.).

§1406.1

[1](1842), 5 Beav. 249, 49 E.R. 573.

[2]See also *Harvey v. Harvey* (1739), 9 Mod. 253, 88 E.R. 433, 1 Atk. 561, 26 E.R. 352, *sub nom. Hervey v. Hervey; Re Walker; MacColl v. Bruce,* [1908] 1 Ch. 560.

[3]*Chapman v. Gibson* (1791), 3 Bro. C.C. 229, 29 E.R. 505, *per* Arden, M.R.

will can apply, the defects of execution cannot be supplied but, where he could not make the gift except in execution of the power, he is supposed to have intended to execute it and the defect will be supplied.[4] Where a woman, having power to appoint funds among her children by will attested in a specified manner, died intestate leaving an unattested memorandum reading, in part, "not having made a will, I leave this memorandum and hope my children will be guided by it, though it is not a legal document" and expressing a wish as to division of the funds, it was held that the memorandum showed no intention to execute the power and, consequently, the court could not remedy any defects in execution so as to give validity to it as an appointment.[5]

On the other hand, where a woman, having power to appoint a fund by deed attested in a certain way, signed an unattested memorandum stating her wish that, if she died suddenly, her eldest son should have the fund and that her intention was to make it over to him legally if her life were spared, but two months later she died, it was held that her intention to appoint the property was sufficiently clear and that the court would give effect to the memorandum as an execution of the power.[6]

Equity aids the defective execution of a power if it is for valuable consideration, and against a remainderman, or one not claiming under the power,[7] for where there is a covenant for valuable consideration for a thing to be done, the court ought to take it as done.[8] In the case of a power to appoint trust funds, it was held that, in order to constitute a person a purchaser in whose favour a defective execution of a power will be aided in equity, there must be consideration and an intention to purchase, either proved or to be presumed and that the maintenance of his household by a husband did not furnish such consideration to the wife having the power.[9]

In the case of a power to appoint land, it was held that, in order to aid a defective execution of the power in favour of a purchaser, there must be a binding contract. Land was settled to such uses as M and his son should jointly appoint by deed and, subject thereto, to M and his son for life successively, with remainder to the sons of the son in tail. A railway company had statutory power to take the land, M and his son contracted with the company for the sale of part of the land and the company was let into possession on an agreement under which the compensation was to be settled by arbitration or by a jury as M might choose. The company paid to M a sum on account of the compensation to be thus fixed, but M died before anything further was done. It was held that there was no contract specific performance of which the court could enforce or aid in carrying into effect

---

[4]*Lowson v. Lowson* (1791), 3 Bro. C.C. 272, 29 E.R. 532.
[5]*Garth v. Townsend* (1869), L.R. 7 Eq. 220.
[6]*Kennard v. Kennard* (1872), L.R. 8 Ch. 227.
[7]*Cotter v. Layer* (1731), 2 P. Wms. 623, 24 E.R. 887; *Wilkie v. Holme* (1752), 1 Dick. 165, 21 E.R. 232; *Sergeson v. Sealey* (1742), 2 Atk. 412, 26 E.R. 648.
[8]*Sergeson v. Sealey, supra,* footnote 7, *per* Lord Hardwicke, L.C.
[9]*Hughes v. Wells* (1852), 9 Hare 749, 68 E.R. 717.

as a defective execution of the power at the instance of the son and against those entitled in remainder.[10]

In contrast, lands under a settlement were limited to such uses as D by deed should appoint and, subject thereto, to the use of D and the heirs of his body with remainders over and D was also entitled to other land absolutely in fee simple. A railway company required part of the settled estates and of the land to which D was absolutely entitled. By agreement not under seal between D and two of the company's directors, reciting that the company required the land, that compensation had not been agreed upon and that it had been agreed that it be determined by named arbitrators and an umpire, the parties bound themselves to abide by such determination. An attached schedule of the lands required by the company did not distinguish between the titles under which they were held. A single sum was awarded to D as the purchase price of the entirety. D died before any conveyance was executed. It was held that the agreement operated in equity as an execution of the power in the settlement.[11]

The defective execution of a power without consideration will be aided in equity in favour of those to whom the person having the power is under a natural or moral obligation to provide,[12] so that the defective execution of a power without consideration will be aided if it is intended as a provision for wife or children.[13] Equity will not give aid in favour of a person to whom there is not an obligation to provide, such as a husband,[14] or grandchild,[15] or natural child,[16] or nephew or niece.[17] But although, on equitable principles, the court will aid the defective execution of a power for the benefit of children, it will not do so where the effect would be to take the property from children who would be entitled in default of appointment for the benefit of one child whose claim is under the defective appointment,[18] or from legitimate children entitled in default of appointment for the benefit of an illegitimate child,[19] at least in jurisdictions where the status of illegitimate children has not been changed.

---

[10]*Morgan v. Milman* (1853), 3 De G. M. & G. 24, 43 E.R. 10, and see *Re Battersea Park Acts; Re Arnold* (1863), 32 Beav. 591, 55 E.R. 232.

[11]*Re Dykes' Estate* (1869), L.R. 7 Eq. 337.

[12]*Chapman v. Gibson, supra,* footnote 3.

[13]*Harvey v. Harvey* (1739), 9 Mod. 253, 88 E.R. 433, 1 Atk. 561, 26 E.R. 352, *sub nom. Hervey v. Hervey.*

[14]*Moodie v. Reid* (1816), 1 Madd. 516, 56 E.R. 189.

[15]*Perry v. Whitehead* (1801), 6 Ves. Jun. 544, 31 E.R. 1187.

[16]*Bramhall v. Hall* (1764), 2 Eden 220, 28 E.R. 882.

[17]*Marston v. Gowan* (1790), 3 Bro. C.C. 170, 29 E.R. 471.

[18]*Shore v. Shore* (1891), 21 O.R. 54 (H.C.J.).

[19]*Ibid.* The rule would now be otherwise where the status of illegitimate children has been equated to that of legitimate children, as under the *Children's Law Reform Act,* R.S.O. 1980, c. 68, and the *Child and Family Services and Family Relations Act,* S.N.B. 1980, c. C-2.1, Pt. VI, and under wills and intestacy statutes permitting illegitimate persons to take on the same basis as legitimate persons.

1406.2 Statutory Provisions

The manner in which statutes have meliorated the formalities required for the execution of a power, both *inter vivos* and by will, has already been dealt with.[1]

1407. EXCESSIVE EXECUTION OF POWER

An appointment made beyond the terms of the power is one made in excess of the power. Such an appointment is void, either wholly or to the extent of the excess, depending upon the circumstances. The fundamental rule is that, where there is complete execution of a power and something improper is added, the execution is good and only the excess is void but, where there is not a complete execution of the power, or where the boundaries between the excess and the execution are not distinguishable, the execution is void.[1]

Thus, where a testator was given power under a trust to appoint the trust fund among his children or remoter issue, provided that the remoter issue should take a vested interest within twenty-one years of the testator's death, an appointment in favour of the same persons as were entitled under the residuary clause in the will was held valid, even though the remainder was limited to the testator's children for life with the remainder of each child's share to his issue. The testator intended to exercise the power in accordance with its terms and, therefore, he intended the trust fund to be distributed in the same manner as his residuary estate, but only so far as the terms of the power permitted. He did not, therefore, exceed the power, but even if he had intended to do so the appointment was still effective to the extent that it purported to benefit persons who were objects of the power.[2]

An appointment may be void because an excessive estate is given, because the property is appointed to a non-object, or because an unauthorized condition is added to the gift. These situations are dealt with in the next following paragraphs.

1407.1 Appointment of Excessive Estate

If the donee of the power appoints an estate larger than permitted by the power, the appointment is void.

Thus, in *Scane v. Hartwick*,[1] where a widow had the power to appoint an

---

§1406.2
[1]See §1405.1(c), *supra*.
§1407
[1]*Alexander v. Alexander* (1755), 2 Ves. Sen. 640, 28 E.R. 408, *per* Clarke, M.R.
[2]*Re Toronto General Trusts Corp. and Homer-Dixon*, [1967] 2 O.R. 602, 64 D.L.R. (2d) 591 (H.C.J.).
§1407.1
[1](1854), 11 U.C.Q.B. 550.

estate tail but appointed a fee simple, the appointment was void. Robinson, C.J., said:

> We are of opinion that the devise to the grandson in fee simple was a void execution of the power given to the widow by her husband's will; that in a court of law the estate can be to no extent and in no manner affected by it, and that the defendant cannot therefore be taken to have acquired a life interest or any interest under it. Where the deviation is on the other side, being rather an imperfect and defective than an excessive execution of the power, the disposition may be held good in equity, and perhaps in some cases at law, though certainly not as a general rule; but an excessive execution of the power is always held to be void at law, and is not allowed to operate even to such an extent as is within the power.[2]

Again, where a woman had power to appoint the use of land to any of the heirs of her body by deed or will and, by her will, devised and appointed the lands to her eldest son with instructions to dispose of it to her husband and children absolutely in the proportions mentioned in her will, it was held that this was an invalid exercise of the power and was inoperative.[3]

1407.2 Appointment to Non-object

An appointment to a person who is not an object of the power is in excess of the power and is void, but if the power is only partly in excess and that part is severable, the remaining part is valid. Thus, where a widow had power to divide her husband's estate among three named sons, but she appointed in favour of two of them and the infant son of the third son who was deceased, it was held that the appointment to this grandchild was void but, since it was severable from the appointment to the two sons, the appointment to them was valid.[1]

An invalid exercise of a power by appointing to a non-object, renders the appointment void, but does not destroy the power. The donee, at least where he has reserved the power to revoke, and logically also where he has not, can still make a subsequent valid appointment.[2]

If the legal estate is appointed by deed to a person who is not an object of the power with remainder to an object of the power, the whole appointment is void. Thus, where there was a power to appoint among children and an appointment was made to several children for life, remainder to grandchildren in tail, remainder to a daughter in fee simple, it was held that all appointments after the life estates were void and would pass as in default of appointment, the appointment to the grandchildren being in excess of the power.[3]

---

[2]*Ibid.*, at p. 553.

[3]*Archer v. Urquhart* (1893), 23 O.R. 214 (H.C.J.).

§1407.2

[1]*Re Matthews* (1924), 56 O.L.R. 406 (H.C.).

[2]*Re Fasken*, [1961] O.R. 891, 30 D.L.R. (2d) 193 (H.C.J.).

[3]*Brudenell v. Elwes* (1802), 7 Ves. Jun. 382, 32 E.R. 155; *Robinson v. Hardcastle* (1788), 2 T.R. 241, 100 E.R. 131; *Reid v. Reid* (1858), 25 Beav. 469, 53 E.R. 716.

If a particular estate is appointed by will, to a person who is not an object of the power, however, with remainder to an object of the power, the appointment of the particular estate fails, but the appointment of the remainder is good because, during the period of the void particular estate, the property goes to those entitled in default of appointment.[4] The remainder does not accelerate unless the instrument creating the power shows that that is intended.[5] Hence, where there is a proviso that the prior interest shall cease if it cannot take effect,[6] or where the prior interest is appointed to such trusts as are capable of taking effect,[7] in each case with a valid appointment in remainder, the remainder will accelerate.

If an estate be appointed to an object of the power with an executory limitation over on the happening of a certain event to a person who is not an object of the power, the executory limitation over is void but, if the event happens, it puts an end to the first estate,[8] unless the reason that the gift over cannot take effect is that it is void for perpetuity.[9]

Conversely, if there is an appointment to an object of the power, followed by an appointment to a person who is not an object of the power with an executory appointment over to an object of the power upon the happening of a certain event, the executory appointment takes effect if the event happens, but not otherwise.[10]

1407.3 Appointment Upon Unauthorized Condition

If an appointment is valid, but the donee has added a condition to the appointment which is not authorized by the power, the condition is void, but does not invalidate the appointment.[1]

In *MacLeod v. Town of Amherst*,[2] land was conveyed to a trustee in trust

---

[4]*Doe d. Duke of Devonshire v. Lord Cavendish* (1782), 3 Dougl. 48, 99 E.R. 532; *Robinson v. Hardcastle, supra,* footnote 3; *Reid v. Reid, supra,* footnote 3.

[5]*Craven v. Brady* (1867), L.R. 4 Eq. 209, affd L.R. 4 Ch. 296; *Line v. Hall* (1873), 43 L.J. Ch. 107.

[6]*Ibid.*

[7]*Re Finch and Chew's Contract,* [1903] 2 Ch. 486.

[8]*Doe d. Blomfield v. Eyre* (1848), 5 C.B. 713, 136 E.R. 1058, an appointment to a son, an object of the power, in fee simple, with a limitation over to a father-in-law, not an object of the power, if the son predeceased his father, which he did, his defeasible fee thereby ceasing; *Re Archer* (1907), 14 O.L.R. 374 (H.C.J.).

[9]*Re Pratt's Settlement Trust; McCullum v. Phipps Hornby,* [1943] Ch. 356, [1943] 2 All E.R. 458.

[10]*Alexander v. Alexander* (1755), 2 Ves. Sen. 640, 28 E.R. 408; *Robinson v. Hardcastle, supra,* footnote 3; *Long v. Ovenden* (1881), 16 Ch. D. 691, and see *Williamson v. Farwell* (1887), 35 Ch. D. 128.

§1407.3

[1]*Sadler v. Pratt* (1833), 5 Sim. 632, 58 E.R. 476; *Palsgrave v. Atkinson* (1844), 1 Coll. 190, 63 E.R. 378; *Watt v. Creyke* (1856), 3 Sm. & G. 362, 65 E.R. 695; *Blacket v. Lamb* (1851), 14 Beav. 482, 51 E.R. 371; *Rooke v. Rooke* (1862), 2 Dr. & Sm. 38, 62 E.R. 535; *Roach v. Trood* (1876), 3 Ch. D. 429 (C.A.).

[2](1974), 44 D.L.R. 723, 8 N.S.R. (2d) 491 (S.C. App. Div.).

for the Amherst Community Beach Association. The trustee had power to sell the land for such consideration as the association might direct. The property was sold to the municipality on condition that it be used for recreational purposes. Subsequently, the municipality sold the land in breach of the condition. In the trustee's action for a declaration that the town was in breach of the condition it was held that the trustee only had power to sell. He did not have power to add a condition. The condition was, therefore, void.

If the condition is inseparable from the appointment, however, the appointment is void.[3]

1408. FRAUD ON A POWER

The established rule is that a person having a special power must execute it in good faith for the end designed, otherwise it is corrupt and void.[1] If the power is not executed for the end designed, the execution is regarded as a fraud on the power. The use of the term "fraud" is not confined to cases involving moral turpitude, but extends to all cases in which the power is used for unauthorized purposes or in favour of unauthorized persons. The donee of the power must

> ... act with good faith and sincerity, and with an entire and single view to the real purpose and object of the power, and not for the purpose of accomplishing or carrying into effect any bye or sinister object (... sinister in the sense of its being beyond the purpose and intent of the power).[2]

The reason for this strict rule, even though a donee is not obliged to exercise the power, is that the property is vested in those persons who are entitled to take in default of appointment, subject to their interest being defeated by a valid appointment. Hence it would be a fraud on them if the power were exercised improperly.[3]

An appointment may be void because it benefits the donee, or a non-object, or because the donee has entered into a prior covenant or agreement as to the exercise of the power, or because the appointment is made for purposes or upon conditions foreign to the power. These matters are dealt with in the next several paragraphs.

1408.1 Benefiting a Non-object

If an appointment is made in favour of a non-object, it is fraudulent and void. Thus, where an estate was settled by a marriage settlement upon a

---

[3]*Webb v. Sadler* (1873), L.R. 8 Ch. 419; *Re Perkins; Perkins v. Bagot*, [1893] 1 Ch. 283; *Re Cohen; Brookes v. Cohen*, [1911] 1 Ch. 37.
§1408
[1]*Aleyn v. Belchier* (1758), 1 Eden 132, 28 E.R. 634, *per* Lord Northington, L.K.
[2]*Duke of Portland v. Lady Topham* (1864), 11 H.L.C. 32 at p. 54, 11 E.R. 1242, *per* Lord Westbury; and see *Topham v. Duke of Portland* (1869), L.R. 5 Ch. 39.
[3]*Ibid.*; Hanbury and Maudsley, pp. 188-9.

husband and wife for their lives, remainder to such child or children as the husband, with the consent of the trustees, should appoint and, in default of appointment, to the first and other sons in tail, and the husband appointed to his youngest son with the consent of the surviving trustee, which he obtained by misrepresentation, the appointment was set aside in proceedings by the eldest son.[1]

The appointment will be void even though, on its face it purports to benefit an object of the power, but the donee's intent is to benefit a non-object. Thus, where a testatrix appointed to her sister, an object of the power, but requested her, "without imposing any trust or legal obligation" to provide an annuity for the family with whom the testatrix resided and for whom she was unable to provide otherwise, it was held the appointment was fraudulent. Although the sister was not bound to carry out the testatrix's wishes she would, in the circumstances, feel morally obligated to do so, because the matter had been discussed with her.[2]

If, however, it can be established that the donee had a *bona fide* intention to benefit the appointee with a substantial appointment, the mere fact that he also requests the appointee to make provision for a non-object, would not be a fraud on the power.[3]

1408.2 Benefiting the Donee

An appointment which benefits the donee of the power directly or indirectly and whether financially or otherwise[1] will be void if it is shown that it was made with the intention to do so.

A testator, having a power under his father's will to appoint his share of his father's estate among his children or to his brothers or sister, appointed one-fourth of his estate to two of his children and the residue to his brother who was to pay the testator's debt to his father's estate and release from debt a policy of insurance which the testator had left to a stranger. It was held that the appointment to the children was good, but the appointment to the brother was void as being a fraudulent exercise of the power, so that there was an intestacy as to the residue.[2]

A father, being a tenant for life of an estate, with power of appointment to one or more of his children, appointed to his son in tail male. Three days later, father and son demised the estate in consideration of a sum to be applied in payment of the father's debts. Three years later, the son reconveyed to the

§1408.1
[1]*Scroggs v. Scroggs* (1755), Amb. 272, 27 E.R. 182.
[2]*Re Dick; Knight v. Dick,* [1953] Ch. 343 (C.A.). See also *Re Crawshay; Hore-Ruthven v. Public Trustee,* [1948] Ch. 123 (C.A.).
[3]Hanbury and Maudsley, pp. 148-9.
§1408.2
[1]*Cochrane v. Cochrane,* [1922] 2 Ch. 230.
[2]*Bell v. Lee* (1883), 8 O.A.R. 185.

father in consideration of debts of the son being paid by the father. It was held that these events raised such suspicions as to the validity of the appointment that it was necessary to inquire into the validity of it.[3]

If there is any indirect benefit to the donee intended to be effected by means of the appointment, it will not stand. In *Mackechnie v. Marjoribanks*,[4] the donee of a power to appoint a fund executed a deed by which she released her life interest in the subject-matter of the power and appointed the fund absolutely to one of her daughters who was an object of the power and about to be married. The daughter immediately directed the trustee of the fund to pay it into her mother's bank account, which the trustee did, with the exception of a sum paid to the daughter's husband. The rest of the fund was used by the mother for her private purposes. It was held that the appointment was a fraud on the power and the executors of the donee and trustees of the fund were liable to make good the fund out of their respective testators' effects in favour of those entitled to the fund in default of appointment.

If an appointment is otherwise unimpeachable, the fact that the appointor may ultimately benefit as next of kin does not necessarily make the appointment bad, for the court cannot determine an appointment to be improper upon the bare suggestion that a contingency might arise in which the appointment would ultimately turn out to be for the benefit of the appointor.[5] A husband and wife had power to appoint a fund to her children which, in default of appointment, was settled on such of her children as should attain age 21 and, in default of such children, on the wife's next of kin. The husband and wife had only one child of the age of three and in robust health, the wife being seriously ill. The husband and wife appointed the whole fund to that child who died three years later. The father became entitled to the property and the appointment was held to be valid.[6]

On the other hand, an appointment by a father to his son, who was in a state of mental and bodily disease from which he died a year later, was set aside. The court, having regard to the father's knowledge of the son's health, his pecuniary circumstances, the circumstances attending the execution of the appointment and the fact that it was not communicated to the person to whom it ought to have been communicated, held that the appointment was made by the father for his own benefit and not that of the son, which was a fraud upon the power.[7]

Although an appointment made with the object that the appointor may obtain an exclusive benefit for himself is bad, an appointment having the object of benefiting all of the objects of the power is not bad merely because the appointor may to some extent participate in the benefit. Thus, a tenant for life

---

[3]*Jackson v. Jackson* (1840), 7 Cl. & Fin. 977, 7 E.R. 1338.

[4](1870), 39 L.J. Ch. 604.

[5]*Pemberton v. Jackson* (1845), 5 L.T. (O.S.) 17.

[6]*Beere v. Hoffmister* (1856), 23 Beav. 101, 53 E.R. 40; *Henty v. Wrey* (1882), 21 Ch. D. 332 (C.A.).

[7]*Lady Wellesley v. Earl of Mornington* (1855), 2 K. & J. 143, 69 E.R. 728.

of real estate had a power under a marriage settlement to appoint the estate among the children of the marriage, of whom there were four. The settlement contained no power to grant building leases. An appointment was made to one of the children and subsequently the appointor and appointee joined in a conveyance to trustees upon trust to grant building leases, one-fourth upon trust for the appointee and three-fourths upon trusts corresponding with those in the original settlement. It was held that, although the object of the appointment was to enable building leases to be granted and the life tenant thereby gained a personal advantage, the transaction was valid as being for the benefit of all objects of the power.[8]

A father had power under a marriage settlement to appoint by deed or will a trust fund in favour of his children and, in default of appointment, the property was to go to the children equally. One of four children died intestate, the father being his personal representative. The father later, by deed, appointed to his surviving children, reserving a power of revocation. Subsequently he revoked the appointment, so that the property might stand limited as before. He proposed to execute a release of his power of appointment so that he could claim the interest of the deceased child. The defendants objected, claiming that he would thereby be obtaining a benefit for himself and the intention would be a fraud on the power. It was held that the donee of a power may deal with it as he pleases, that although by the death of his child, the father had accidentally derived a benefit by so doing, he could not be regarded as having committed a fraud on the power and, upon executing a proper release, he would be entitled to the share he claimed.[9]

1408.3   Covenants and Agreements Regarding Exercise of Power

An agreement or covenant between the donee and a prospective appointee concerning the exercise of a power is fraudulent and void.

Thus, for example, the donee of a special power to appoint by will among his children cannot, in anticipation of his last will, validly covenant that it shall be exercised in a particular way. Such a covenant is void as calculated to defeat the object of the creation of the power and cannot be enforced.[1] If the covenant is performed, however, the appointment is valid.[2] A covenant not to revoke a testamentary appointment is, in substance, a covenant to exercise the power of appointment in a particular way and is likewise void.[3] Although

---

[8]*Re Huish's Charity* (1870), L.R. 10 Eq. 5.
[9]*Shirley v. Fisher* (1882), 47 L.T. 109.
§1408.3
[1]*Re Bradshaw; Bradshaw v. Bradshaw,* [1902] 1 Ch. 436, and see *Coffin v. Cooper* (1865), 2 Dr. & Sm. 365, 62 E.R. 660; *Thacker v. Key* (1869), L.R. 8 Eq. 408; *Palmer v. Locke* (1880), 15 Ch. D. 294 (C.A.); *Re Cooke; Winckley v. Winterton,* [1922] 1 Ch. 292.
[2]*Coffin v. Cooper, supra.*
[3]*Re Cooke, supra.*

the court will not grant specific performance of a contract to leave property by will entered into by the donee of a testamentary power of appointment, there may be a remedy for damages for breach of the covenant.[4]

An appointment made pursuant to an agreement with the appointee to benefit the appointor personally is also void as being a fraudulent exercise of the power.[5]

The burden of proving invalidity is upon the person who alleges it and the whole matter and accompanying facts must be examined to ascertain the real nature of the transaction.[6]

An appointment made pursuant to an agreement with the appointee to benefit any other person who is not an object of the power is likewise void.[7]

The rule is the same even if the person having the power of appointment is the settlor of the property.

Thus, a settlor, desiring to settle property on the female descendants of C, settled part of it on named persons whom he thought were C's only female descendants. He reserved to himself a power to appoint the rest of the property among these named persons and further gave it to them in default of appointment. He discovered later that there were other female descendants of C and accordingly appointed part of the reserved fund to an object of the power, the object having executed a bond to pay it to the newly discovered persons. It was held that the appointment was void.[8]

An appointment to a child who is the object of a power and a contemporaneous independent settlement by the child of the appointed property is valid, however, unless it is shown that the settlement was pursuant to a bargain to include the appointed property.[9] The fact that the appointor knows that the appointee intends to settle the property in favour of a person who is not an object of the power does not invalidate the appointment, unless it is

---

[4]Re Parkin; Hill v. Schwarz, [1892] 3 Ch. 510, and see also Bulteel v. Plummer (1870), L.R. 6 Ch. 160; Re Bradshaw, supra, footnote 1.

[5]Farmer v. Martin (1828), 2 Sim. 502, 57 E.R. 876, agreement to pay appointor's debts; Arnold v. Hardwick (1835), 7 Sim. 343, 58 E.R. 869, agreement to lend money to the appointor; Jackson v. Jackson (1840), 7 Cl. & Fin. 977, 7 E.R. 1338 (H.L.), agreement respecting debts and reconveyance to appointor; Askham v. Barker (1853), 17 Beav. 37, 51 E.R. 945, agreement for exchange of appointed fund for estate of appointor; Cochrane v. Cochrane, [1922] 2 Ch. 230, increased appointment to wife divorced under a decree nisi so as to have it made absolute, enabling the donee to remarry.

[6]Askham v. Barker, supra, footnote 5.

[7]Daubeny v. Cockburn (1816), 1 Mer. 626, 35 E.R. 801, appointment to one child exclusively upon a secret understanding that the child will reassign part of the fund to a stranger; Wade v. Cox (1835), 4 L.J. Ch. 105, appointment on the eldest son on the understanding that he will release all claim to the trustees to whom the donor is indebted; Birley v. Birley (1858), 25 Beav. 299, 53 E.R. 651; Pryor v. Pryor (1864), 2 De G. J. & S. 205, 46 E.R. 353 (C.A.), appointments to children on the understanding that they would resettle the property partly on non-objects.

[8]Lee v. Fernie (1839), 1 Beav. 483, 48 E.R. 1027.

[9]Goldsmid v. Goldsmid (1842), 2 Hare 187, 67 E.R. 78; Daniel v. Arkwright (1864), 2 H. & M. 95, 71 E.R. 396; Re Turner's Settled Estates (1884), 28 Ch. D. 205 (C.A.).

shown that the appointment would not have been made without an agreement to that effect.[10]

In the case of a power to appoint to children, if an appointment is made for the absolute benefit of the appointee, it may be validly extended so as to appoint to the appointee's children with the consent of the appointee and the appointment and settlement on such grandchildren may be accomplished by the same instrument.[11] A reversionary interest may be thus appointed and settled on a daughter, her husband and children,[12] and, where there was only one object of the power, a married daughter, it was held that an appointment to her and, by arrangement with her, a resettlement giving an interest to her children and to a stranger to the power, was valid.[13] Similarly, an appointment to a son, an object of the power, for life and then to his wife who was not an object, the son joining in the deed of appointment, was held to be valid.[14]

Although the exercise of a power under an arrangement which benefits the appointor is generally invalid, if it is a family arrangement it will be upheld. Thus, in *Re Matthews*,[15] a widow appointed to her two sons who were the only objects of the power and they immediately conveyed their shares to her. The appointment was upheld.

1408.4 Appointment for Foreign Purposes

Whenever an appointment is made for purposes foreign to the power, it is void as a fraud on the power, as where it is made as an inducement to reside abroad,[1] or where it is made upon an unauthorized condition which is not severable from the appointment.[2] In *Re Cohen*; *Brookes v. Cohen*,[3] the donee of a special power to appoint his share under his father's will to his wife and children appointed an annuity to his wife and, in case his residuary estate was insufficient to pay his debts, he directed the trustees under his father's will to pay his wife an additional annuity on condition that she apply four-fifths of it in payment of his debts. If she fulfilled the condition, the trustees were to pay to her the remaining one-fifth for the rest of her life and, subject thereto, he appointed the trust fund to his children. It was held that the condition attached to the appointment of the additional annuities to the wife could not

---

[10]*Daniel v. Arkwright, supra*, footnote 9; *Pryor v. Pryor, supra*, footnote 7.

[11]*White v. St. Barbe* (1813), 1 V. & B. 399, 35 E.R. 155; *Re Gosset's Settlement* (1854), 19 Beav. 529, 52 E.R. 456; *Wright v. Goff* (1856), 22 Beav. 207, 52 E.R. 1087; *FitzRoy v. Duke of Richmond (No. 2)* (1859), 27 Beav. 190, 54 E.R. 74.

[12]*Re Gosset's Settlement, supra*, footnote 11.

[13]*Wright v. Goff, supra*, footnote 11.

[14]*Whitting v. Whitting* (1908), 53 Sol. Jo. 100.

[15](1924), 56 O.L.R. 406 (H.C.).

§**1408.4**

[1]*D'Abbadie v. Bizoin* (1871), 5 I.R. Eq. 205.

[2]*Re Perkins*; *Perkins v. Bagot*, [1893] 1 Ch. 283.

[3][1911] 1 Ch. 37.

be severed from the appointment which, being for a purpose wholly foreign to the power, was fraudulent and void.

Where a condition annexed to an appointment is inconsistent with the power and is severable from the appointment, the condition is void.[4]

1408.5 Severance of Invalid Appointment

Appointments cannot be severed so as to be good to the extent to which they are *bona fide* executions of the power, but bad as to the remainder, except where some consideration has been given which cannot be restored and it has, consequently, become impossible to rescind the transaction *in toto*, or where the court can sever the intentions of the appointor and distinguish the good from the fraudulent.[1]

In *Bell v. Lee*,[2] a testator, having a power under his father's will to appoint his share of his father's estate among his children or to his brother or sister, appointed one-fourth of his estate to two of his children and the residue to his brother who was to pay the testator's debt to his father's estate and release from debt a policy of insurance which the testator left to a stranger. It was held that the appointment to the children was good but the appointment to the brother was void as being a fraudulent exercise of the power, so that there was an intestacy as to the residue.

Where, however, the intentions cannot be thus severed, appointments will not be severed so as to be valid to the extent that they are a good exercise of the power and void as to the rest.[3]

1408.6 Effect of Fraud on Third Parties

An appointment under a common law power, or a power operating under the *Statute of Uses*[1] by which the legal estate has passed, is at most voidable and a purchaser for value of the legal estate without notice is not affected by the fraudulent exercise of the power for, although a person is not permitted to execute a power for his own benefit and the objection cannot be waived by a party participating in the benefit, nevertheless, as against other interests, the

---

[4]*Blacket v. Lamb* (1851), 14 Beav. 482, 51 E.R. 371, request to objects not to spend their shares but to leave them for the benefit of their children; *Palsgrave v. Atkinson* (1844), 1 Coll. 190, 63 E.R. 378.

§1408.5
[1]*Rowley v. Rowley* (1854), Kay 242, 69 E.R. 103; *Re Holland; Holland v. Clapton*, [1914] 2 Ch. 595; *Re Burton's Settlements; Scott v. National Provincial Bank Ltd.*, [1955] Ch. 82.

[2](1883), 8 O.A.R. 185.

[3]*Daubeny v. Cockburn* (1816), 1 Mer. 626, 35 E.R. 801; *Agassiz v. Squire* (1854), 18 Beav. 431, 52 E.R. 170; *Re Cohen; Brookes v. Cohen*, [1911] 1 Ch. 37.

§1408.6
[1]27 Hen. 8, c. 10 (1535).

court will not act against the title upon a suspicion that the transaction was of that nature.[2]

Thus, where a father executed a power of appointment in favour of his son, subject to a life estate to himself and his wife and all three joined in a sale at a fair value and received the money, it was held that it must be presumed to have been received according to their interests in the estate and that the purchaser was not bound to see to the application of the money.[3] The purchaser must be without notice, however. Thus, a conveyance to a purchaser for valuable consideration was set aside as proceeding upon an appointment by a father to his eldest son in fraud of the power, of which the purchaser had notice.[4]

An appointment in fraud of an equitable power, not operating so as to pass the legal estate or interest, is void and a purchaser for value without notice can only rely on such equitable defences as are open to purchasers for value without the legal title who are subsequent in time against prior equitable titles.[5] Hence, the claim of such a purchaser cannot prevail against those who, by reason of a fraudulent exercise of a power, are entitled in default of appointment.[6]

1409. ELECTION TO TAKE GIFT OR TO TAKE IN DEFAULT OF APPOINTMENT

The doctrine of election applies to appointments under powers of appointment. The general rule is that, where an appointment is directly made to a person who is not an object of the power and a gift is made to those who are entitled in default of appointment, the latter must elect between their gift and the interest unlawfully appointed.[1]

There is an obligation on the person who takes a benefit under a will or other instrument to give full effect to that instrument under which he takes a benefit. If it be found that that instrument purports to deal with something which it was beyond the power of the donor or settlor to dispose of, but to which effect can be given by the concurrence of the person who receives a benefit under the same instrument, the law will impose on him who takes the benefit the obligation of carrying the instrument into full and complete force and effect.[2]

A testatrix, life tenant of property which, in case of her death without issue, which happened, went over to her brothers and sisters, of whom J was one, by

---

[2]*Cloutte v. Storey*, [1911] 1 Ch. 18 (C.A.); *M'Queen v. Farquhar* (1805), 11 Ves. Jun. 467, 32 E.R. 1168.
[3]*M'Queen v. Farquhar, supra.*
[4]*Hall v. Montague* (1830), 8 L.J. O.S. Ch. 167.
[5]*Cloutte v. Storey, supra*, footnote 2.
[6]*Daubeny v. Cockburn* (1816), 1 Mer. 626, 35 E.R. 801; see also *Birley v. Birley* (1858), 25 Beav. 299, 53 E.R. 651; *Askham v. Barker* (1853), 17 Beav. 37, 51 E.R. 945; *Warde v. Dixon* (1858), 28 L.J. Ch. 315.
§1409
[1]*Whistler v. Webster* (1794), 2 Ves. Jun. 367, 30 E.R. 676.
[2]*Cooper v. Cooper* (1874), L.R. 7 H.L. 53.

her will exercised a power she erroneously thought she had and appointed property to a class of which J was not one, but a codicil gave J property which she was free to dispose of. It was held that J must elect to take under or against the will.[3] The necessity of electing only arises, however, when there is a direct appointment to a person who is not an object of the power and it does not arise in the case of a mere condition annexed to an appointment to an object.[4]

The rule as to election is applicable only as between a gift under a will and a claim outside the will and adverse to it, and not as between one clause in a will and another clause in the same will. The ordinary principle is clear that, if a testator, by design or by mistake, gives property which is not his to give and, at the same time, gives other property to the real owner of the property first mentioned, the real owner cannot take both. The principle has been applied where the first gift is made purportedly in execution of a power. Therefore, if under a power to appoint to children, the donee of the power appoints to grandchildren, which is void, and the children, who are entitled to claim by reason of the invalidity of the appointment, also take other property under the will, the grandchildren are entitled to put them to their election. But to this rule, so far as regards appointments, a notable exception is taken, namely, that when there is an appointment to an object of the power, with directions that the same shall be settled, or upon any trust, or subject to any condition, then the appointment is held to be a valid appointment, and the superadded direction, trust or condition is void and not only void, but inoperative to raise any case of election.[5]

There is no need to elect in regard to invalid modifications of an appointment. Where there is an absolute appointment by will in favour of a proper object of the power and that appointment is followed by attempts to modify the interest so appointed in a manner which the law will not allow, the court reads the will as if all the passages in which such attempts are made were swept out of it for all intents and purposes, not only so far as the attempt to regulate the *quantum* of the interest to be enjoyed by the appointee in the settled property, but also so far as the modifications might otherwise have been relied upon as raising a case of election.[6]

1410. EXTINGUISHMENT OF POWER

It may sometimes be advantageous for the donee of a power to release it. Thus, a trustee may have power to appoint to charitable and non-charitable objects and, in order to ensure that the gift is charitable, he can release the

---

[3]*Re Brooksbank; Beauclerk v. James* (1886), 34 Ch. D. 160; and see *White v. White* (1882), 22 Ch. D. 555; *Re Wells' Trusts; Hardisty v. Wells* (1889), 42 Ch. D. 646.
[4]*Carver v. Bowles* (1831), 2 Russ. & M. 301, 39 E.R. 409; *Blacket v. Lamb* (1851), 14 Beav. 482, 51 E.R. 371; *White v. White, supra*, footnote 3.
[5]*Wollaston v. King* (1869), L.R. 8 Eq. 165.
[6]*Woolridge v. Woolridge* (1859), Johns. 63, 70 E.R. 340; *Carver v. Bowles, supra*, footnote 4; *Blacket v. Lamb, supra*, footnote 4; *Langslow v. Langslow* (1856), 21 Beav. 552, 52 E.R. 973.

power to the extent that it permits appointment among non-charitable objects.[1] Similarly, he may release the power in order to make the interests of those who take in default of appointment indefeasible.[2] In addition, a power may be released so as to avoid tax,[3] or to vary a trust under variation of trusts legislation.[4] Although a trustee cannot normally release a power, an arrangement approved by the court under this legislation which effectively precludes the future exercise of the power or releases it, would appear to be valid.[5]

A power may be released by deed or by a contract in which the donee covenants not to exercise it. It is also released where the donee deals with the property in a manner inconsistent with its future exercise.[6]

In *Foakes v. Jackson*,[7] a husband and wife had a joint power and the survivor had a separate power to appoint property among certain objects. The husband, wife and the persons entitled in default of appointment executed a deed by which the wife, with the husband's consent, and those persons according to their respective estates and interests as beneficial owners, assigned the property to an object, the joint power not being referred to. The wife died and the husband then appointed the property to other objects. It was held that, whether or not the assignment operated as a joint appointment, which it apparently did, it released the surviving husband's separate power, so that his subsequent appointment was inoperative. Similarly, in *Re Hancock*; *Malcolm v. Burford-Hancock*,[8] a husband had power to appoint one-fourth of a fund to "his wife" and the rest to his children. He exercised the power; his wife died; he married again and purported to appoint one-fourth to his second wife. It was held that what he had previously done was inconsistent with any intent on his part to appoint to anyone else other than those for whom he was thus providing. He had exercised his power and exhausted it with intent to do so and, therefore, the subsequent appointment to the second wife was inoperative.

Not all powers can be released, however. Formerly the distinction drawn

---

§1410

[1] *Re Wills' Trust Deeds*; *Wills v. Godfrey*, [1964] Ch. 219.
[2] *Re Mills*; *Mills v. Lawrence*, [1930] 1 Ch. 654.
[3] *Re Montreal Trust Co. and Minister of Finance* (1974), 40 D.L.R. (3d) 751, [1974] 1 W.W.R. 231 (B.C.C.A.).
[4] *Trust Variation Act*, R.S.B.C. 1979, c. 413; *Variation of Trusts Act*, R.S.P.E.I. 1974, c. V-1; R.S.N.S. 1967, c. 323; R.S.O. 1980, c. 519; R.S.S. 1978, c. V-1; *Variation of Trusts Ordinance*, R.O.N.W.T. 1974, c. V-1; R.O.Y.T. 1971, c. V-1; *Trustee Act*, R.S.A. 1980, c. T-10, ss. 42, 43; R.S.M. 1970, c. T160, s. 61; *Trustees Act*, R.S.N.B. 1973, c. T-15, s. 26. See generally Cullity, "Renunciation of Dispositive Powers", 3 E. & T. Q. 12 (1976-77); Gallagher, "Powers of Appointment", Isaac Pitblado Lecture Series, 1964, p. 111; Bauman, "General Powers of Appointment under the Ontario Succession Duty Act and Related Death Tax Legislation", 32 U. of T. Fac. L. R. 159 (1974).
[5] *Re Courtauld's Settlement*; *Courtauld v. Farrer*, [1965] 2 All E.R. 544 (Ch.); *Re Ball's Settlement Trusts*; *Ball v. Ball*, [1968] 1 W.L.R. 899.
[6] *Blausten v. Inland Revenue Com'rs*, [1972] Ch. 256 (C.A.); *Muir v. Inland Revenue Com'rs*, [1966] 1 W.L.R. 251, revd *loc. cit.*, p. 1269.
[7] [1900] 1 Ch. 807.
[8] [1896] 2 Ch. 173 (C.A.).

between a power appendant, that is, one the exercise of which affects the estate of the donee; in gross, that is, one which does not do so, but where the donee does have an interest in the property; and collateral, that is, one in which the donee had no interest in the property,[9] was important in this respect. Powers appendant and in gross could be released, but powers collateral could not.[10]

By statute, in Ontario,[11] New Brunswick[12] and Prince Edward Island,[13] however, the donee of a power, whether coupled with an interest or not, may by deed disclaim, or release a power, or contract not to exercise. He may not thereafter exercise it, unless the instrument creating the power permits it, but any other donee or a surviving donee may.[14] No similar legislation was enacted in the other provinces.

This legislation does not confer on the donee of a power of appointment by will the right to give a purchaser a good title by covenanting that he will not exercise that power by will.[15] Where, however, land was devised to a widow for life and then to D for life with power to D to devise in fee simple, it was held that the widow, D, and the heirs of the testator ascertained at the time of his death, could make a good title in fee simple to a purchaser who should, however, be assured against exercise of D's power by D's covenant not to exercise it, and such covenant would operate as a release of the power.[16]

Where the donee of the power in fact holds under a trust so that he is under a duty to appoint, that is, where he has a trust power or a power of appointment coupled with a duty, the power cannot be released.[17] The reason is that if the donee-trustee fails to appoint, the court will divide the property equally between the objects,[18] unless the class of objects is so wide as to preclude equal division, in which case the court will divide it in some other manner most calculated to give effect to the donor's intention.[19]

A fiduciary power, that is, one given to a person *virtute officii*, cannot be released, unless the instrument creating the power permits it.[20]

If, however, the power is not a trust and is not a fiduciary one, but merely

---

[9]For the distinctions between these three types of powers, see §1402, *supra*.

[10]Farwell, pp. 12 *et seq.*

[11]*Conveyancing and Law of Property Act*, R.S.O. 1980, c. 90, s. 26.

[12]*Property Act*, R.S.N.B. 1973, c. P-19, s. 55.

[13]*Trustee Act*, R.S.P.E.I. 1974, c. T-9, ss. 35, 36.

[14]This enactment derives from the *Conveyancing Act, 1881*, 44 & 45 Vict., c. 41, s. 52, and the *Conveyancing Act, 1882*, 45 & 46 Vict., c. 39, s. 6. See now *Law of Property Act, 1925*, 15 & 16 Geo. 5, c. 20, s. 155.

[15]*Re Collard and Duckworth* (1889), 16 O.R. 735 (H.C.J.).

[16]*Re Drew and McGowan* (1901), 1 O.L.R. 575 (H.C.J.).

[17]*Re Eyre* (1883), 49 L.T. 259; *Re Montreal Trust Co. and Minister of Finance* (1974), 40 D.L.R. (3d) 751, [1974] 1 W.W.R. 231 (B.C.C.A.).

[18]*Re Weekes' Settlement*, [1897] 1 Ch. 289; *Re Combe; Combe v. Combe*, [1925] Ch. 210; *Re Perowne; Perowne v. Moss*, [1951] Ch. 785.

[19]*McPhail v. Doulton*, [1971] A.C. 424 (H.L.).

[20]*Muir v. Inland Revenue Com'rs*, [1966] 1 W.L.R. 251 (Ch.). As to this type of power, see §1402, *supra*.

a personal one, the donee may release it.[21] Moreover, he may release the power in whole or in part, not only in respect of the property which is the subject of the power, but also in respect of the class of appointees. Thus, the donee of a general power may execute a partial release in favour of a defined class of objects, thereby making the power special.[22]

Although a power of appointment given to the holder of a particular estate is extinguished if he acquires the fee simple, equity gives effect to a disposition he made in execution of the power.[23]

Dissolution of marriage does not extinguish a joint power held by husband and wife.[24]

---

[21]*Re Wills' Trust Deeds; Wills v. Godfrey*, [1964] Ch. 219.
[22]*Re Fasken*, [1961] O.R. 891, 30 D.L.R. (2d) 193 (H.C.J.).
[23]*Cross v. Hudson* (1789), 3 Bro. C.C. 30, 29 E.R. 390; *Mortlock v. Buller* (1804), 10 Ves. Jun. 292, 32 E.R. 857; *Sing v. Leslie* (1864), 2 H. & M. 68, 71 E.R. 385.
[24]*Fitzgerald v. Chapman* (1875), 1 Ch. D. 563; *Burton v. Sturgeon* (1876), 2 Ch. D. 318 (C.A.).

PART V

CONCURRENT INTERESTS

CONTENTS OF PART V

CHAPTER 15

CO-OWNERSHIP

1501. INTRODUCTORY

A person who is sole owner of an estate is said to hold it in *severalty* because he holds it in his own right with no one having any interest jointly with him.

There may be co-owners of any estate or interest in land, whether present or future. The two main classes of co-ownership are (a) *joint tenancy*, in which the co-owners, called joint tenants, have identical interests in that they take

787

undivided possession of the same property under the same instrument for the same interest which, unless the instrument is a conveyance under the *Statute of Uses*[1] or a will, vests in them at the same time and the survivor of them takes the entirety, and (b) *tenancy in common*, in which the co-owners, called tenants in common, have undivided possession of the property, but their interests need not otherwise be identical and the interest of each descends to his heirs. At common law, there was a third class of joint estate called *coparcenary*, in which several persons took property by the same title by descent, the common law rules regarding which have been altered by provincial legislation, and a fourth class called *tenancy by the entireties*, an estate together held by husband and wife during their coverture.

1502. JOINT TENANCY — GENERAL

A joint tenancy arises by the act of the person who creates the estate. It is distinguished by what are known as the four unities: (1) *unity of title*, that is, all joint tenants must take under the same instrument, (2) *unity of interest*, that is, the interest of each joint tenant must be identical in nature, extent and duration, (3) *unity of possession*, that is, each joint tenant is entitled to undivided seisin or possession of the whole of the property and none holds any part separately to the exclusion of the others and (4) *unity of time*, that is, at common law, the interest of each joint tenant must vest at the same time.

The interests of joint tenants may, however, vest at different times if the joint tenancy is created by conveyance under the *Statute of Uses*[1] or by devise by will.[2] However, a remainder which is to vest in members of a class only upon the attainment of a specified age cannot be a joint tenancy.[3]

Since the estate of each joint tenant must be the same in nature, there can be no joint tenancy between the holder of a freehold and the holder of a term of years or between the holder of a freehold in possession and the person entitled to a freehold in reversion.[4] Although the interests of joint tenants must be the same in duration, one of them may have an additional several estate. Thus, in the case of a grant to A and B for their lives, remainder to the heirs of A, A and B have a joint tenancy for their lives and A has the remainder in fee simple.

---

§1501
[1] 27 Hen. 8, c. 10 (1535).
§1502
[1] 27 Hen. 8, c. 10 (1535): *Earl of Sussex v. Temple* (1698), 1 Ld. Raym. 310, 91 E.R. 1102; *Stratton v. Best* (1787), 2 Bro. C.C. 233, 29 E.R. 130; *Hales v. Risley* (1673), Pollex. 369 at p. 373, 86 E.R. 578; *Doe d. Hallen v. Ironmonger* (1803), 3 East 533, 102 E.R. 701.
[2] *Oates d. Hatterley v. Jackson* (1742), 2 Strange 1172, 93 E.R. 1107; *Kenworthy v. Ward* (1853), 11 Hare 196, 68 E.R. 1245; *Morgan v. Britten* (1871), L.R. 13 Eq. 28; *Binning v. Binning*, [1895] W.N. 116 (C.A.).
[3] *Woodgate v. Unwin* (1831), 4 Sim. 129, 58 E.R. 50; *Hand v. North* (1863), 10 Jur. N.S. 7.
[4] Co. Litt. 188a.

In the case of a limitation to two persons and the survivor of them in fee simple, the reference to the survivor makes a joint tenancy for their lives with a contingent remainder in fee simple to the survivor of them.[5] Joint tenants were said by Littleton to be seised *per mie et per tout*, or in other words "each joint tenant holds the whole and holds nothing, that is, he holds the whole jointly and nothing separately".[6]

At common law, if land were granted or devised to two or more persons for the same estate, whether freehold or otherwise, without words indicating how they were to take, it was presumed that they took as joint tenants.[7] Thus, if the limitation to them was for their lives, they took as joint tenants for their joint lives, and if the limitation were to them in fee simple or for a term of years, they took as joint tenants in fee simple or as joint lessees. It did not matter, in the case of a will whether the gift was specific or residuary,[8] direct or by way of trust,[9] whether to next of kin,[10] relatives,[11] issue,[12] personal representatives,[13] children,[14] family[15] or to parents and children.[16] However, the common law rule that persons took as joint tenants, unless the contrary intention was shown, has been reversed by provincial statutes.

If it is desired to limit any estate as a joint tenancy by conveyance or devise, it should be specifically provided. In practice one frequently finds the expression "as joint tenants and not as tenants in common" but the latter negative words are superfluous.

In Ontario, the *Conveyancing and Law of Property Act*[17] provides that where, by any letters patent, assurance or will made or executed after July 1, 1834, land has been or is granted, conveyed or devised to two or more persons, other than executors or trustees, in fee simple or for any less estate, it shall be considered that they took or take as tenants in common and not as joint tenants, unless an intention sufficiently appears on the face of the letters patent,

---

[5]*Wiscot's Case*; *Giles v. Wiscot* (1599), 2 Co. Rep. 60 b, 76 E.R. 555, and see Co. Litt. 191a; *Van Grutten v. Foxwell*, [1897] A.C. 658 at p. 678.

[6]Co. Litt. 186a.

[7]*Morley v. Bird* (1798), 3 Ves. Jun. 628, 30 E.R. 1192.

[8]*Ibid.*; *Crooke v. De Vandes* (1803), 9 Ves. Jun. 197, 32 E.R. 577; *Walmsley v. Foxhall* (1863), 1 De G. J. & S. 451, 46 E.R. 179 (C.A.).

[9]*Aston v. Smallman* (1706), 2 Vern. 556, 23 E.R. 961; *Bustard v. Saunders* (1843), 7 Beav. 92, 49 E.R. 998.

[10]*Withy v. Mangles* (1843), 10 Cl. & Fin. 215, 8 E.R. 724; *Lucas v. Bandreth (No. 2)* (1860), 28 Beav. 274, 54 E.R. 371; *Baker v. Gibson* (1849), 12 Beav. 101, 50 E.R. 998.

[11]*Eagles v. Le Breton* (1873), L.R. 15 Eq. 148.

[12]*Hill v. Nalder* (1852), 17 Jur. 224; *Hobgen v. Neale* (1870), L.R. 11 Eq. 48.

[13]*Walker v. Marquis of Camden* (1848), 16 Sim. 329, 60 E.R. 900; *Stockdale v. Nicholson* (1867), L.R. 4 Eq. 359.

[14]*Oates d. Hatterley v. Jackson* (1742), 2 Strange 1172, 93 E.R. 1107; *Binning v. Binning*, *supra*, footnote 2.

[15]*Burt v. Hellyar* (1872), L.R. 14 Eq. 160; *Wood v. Wood* (1843), 3 Hare 65, 67 E.R. 298; *Gregory v. Smith* (1852), 9 Hare 708, 68 E.R. 698.

[16]*Mason v. Clarke* (1853), 17 Beav. 126, 51 E.R. 980; *Armstrong v. Armstrong* (1869), L.R. 7 Eq. 518.

[17]R.S.O. 1980, c. 90, s. 13.

assurance or will that they are to take as joint tenants, and it provides that the section shall apply notwithstanding that one of the persons is the wife of another of them.

The question whether an intention to take as joint tenants sufficiently appears on the face of the letters patent, assurance or will has caused much difficulty. Thus, where a testator devised land to A and B "jointly" it was held that a joint tenancy was created but where he devised land to C "and his family" it was held that C and his children took as tenants in common.[18] Yet in a subsequent case a devise to A and B "jointly and individually" was held not to create a joint tenancy.[19] A devise to A and B "jointly, and if they decide to sell the property, each of them is to have an equal share in the proceeds of the said sale" created a tenancy in common.[20] If the grantees are described as joint tenants they will take as joint tenants even where the only reference in the deed to joint tenancy is to be found in the description of the grantees.[21] Similarly, where the reference to joint tenancy was found in the *habendum*, a joint tenancy was created.[22]

It has been decided that an agreement of purchase and sale is not an assurance within the meaning of section 13 and thus the section is not applicable. Where the purchasers were husband and wife and the agreement was silent as to the capacity or interest that they were acquiring, the court concluded that the surviving wife took the entirety as the surviving tenant of the entirety.[23]

Provisions similar to the Ontario statute are found in other provinces.[24]

---

[18]*Re Quebec* (1929), 37 O.W.N. 271 (H.C.J.).

[19]*Re Dupont*, [1966] 2 O.R. 419, 57 D.L.R. (2d) 109 (H.C.J.).

[20]*McEwen v. Ewers*, [1946] O.W.N. 573, [1946] 3 D.L.R. 494 (H.C.J.).

[21]*Re Steeves and Haslam House* (1975), 8 O.R. (2d) 165, 57 D.L.R. (3d) 357 (H.C.J.).

[22]*Humeniuk v. Humeniuk*, [1970] 3 O.R. 521, 13 D.L.R. (3d) 417 (H.C.J.).

[23]*Campbell v. Sovereign Securities & Holding Co. Ltd.*, [1958] O.R. 441, 13 D.L.R. (2d) 195 (H.C.J.), affd [1958] O.R. 719, 16 D.L.R. (2d) 606 (C.A.). It is doubtful whether the conclusion, that a tenancy by the entirety can still exist in the face of the *Married Women's Property Act*, R.S.O. 1970, c. 262, is tenable in view of section 65(1)(2) of the *Family Law Reform Act*, R.S.O. 1980, c. 152, which provides:

> 65(1) For all purposes of the law of Ontario, a married man has a legal personality that is independent, separate and distinct from that of his wife and a married woman has a legal personality that is independent, separate and distinct from that of her husband.

> (2) A married person has and shall be accorded legal capacity for all purposes and in all respects as if such person were an unmarried person.

For a subsequent consideration of this case see *Re Demaiter and Link*, [1973] 3 O.R. 140, 36 D.L.R. (3d) 164 (H.C.J.). For an example of the opposite conclusion, *viz.*, that a tenancy by the entirety does not survive married women's property legislation, see *Registrar-General N.S.W. v. Wood* (1926), 39 C.L.R. 46 (H.C.). See also the *Transfer and Descent of Land Act*, R.S.A. 1980, c. L-8, s. 5.

[24]*Transfer and Descent of Land Act*, R.S.A. 1980, c. L-8, s. 8; *Property Act*, R.S.B.C. 1979, c. 340, s. 11; *Law of Property Act*, R.S.M. 1970, c. L90, s. 15; *Land Titles Act*, R.S.S. 1978, c. L-5, s. 242; *Property Act*, R.S.N.B. 1973, c. P-19, s. 20; *Real Property Act*, R.S.N.S. 1967, c. 261, s. 4; *Tenants in Common Ordinance*, R.O.N.W.T. 1974, c. T-3; R.O.Y.T. 1971, c. T-1.

It has also been decided in Ontario that lands held as partnership property are held in joint tenancy and are not affected by section 13.[25] It would appear that this position is unique to Ontario, and in principle is open to much criticism.[26] Equity raises a presumption, quite apart from section 13, in favour of tenancy in common with respect to partnership property as the right of survivorship has no place in business. However, in those jurisdictions where the equitable presumption operates it is still open for the partners to agree that lands will be held in joint tenancy.[27]

Although joint ownership can arise by way of promissory estoppel[28] or by application of the doctrines of resulting or constructive trusts,[29] in the face of section 13, one would presume that the form of joint ownership so arising would be tenancy in common as opposed to joint tenancy.

In Ontario, the *Estates Administration Act*[30] provides that, where real property becomes vested under the Act in two or more persons beneficially entitled under the Act, they take as tenants in common in proportion to their respective interests unless, in the case of a devise, they take otherwise under the provisions of the will of the deceased. The common law rule prevails, however, in the case of executors and trustees who hold as joint tenants because they are excluded from the foregoing provisions of section 13 of the *Conveyancing and Law of Property Act*.[31] The *Land Titles Act*[32] also provides that, where two or more persons are described as trustees, the property shall be held to be vested in them as joint tenants unless the contrary is expressly stated. Executors and trustees are left as joint tenants for the sake of convenience because, under the rule of survivorship that applies to joint tenancies, the trusts can thus be carried out by the survivors or last survivor and, in case of the death of the latter, a conveyance of the trust estate can be made by his heir or personal representative to new trustees.

No provision similar to the foregoing provision of the Ontario *Estates Administration Act* appears to have been made in the other provinces but it is provided in New Brunswick and Nova Scotia that every estate vested in trustees or executors as such is held by them in joint tenancy.[33] Also, the Trustee Acts of Alberta, British Columbia, Manitoba and of Saskatchewan

[25]*Harris v. Wood* (1915), 7 O.W.N. 611 (H.C.): followed reluctantly in *Hegeman v. Rogers*, [1971] 3 O.R. 600, 21 D.L.R. (3d) 272 (H.C.J.).

[26]Hanbury, *Modern Equity*, 7th ed. (London, Stevens, 1957), p. 53; Megarry & Wade, p. 403.

[27]*Re Sterenchuk Estate*; *Western Trust Co. v. Demchuk* (1958), 16 D.L.R. (2d) 505, 26 W.W.R. 728 (Alta. S.C. App. Div.).

[28]*Stanley v. Stanley* (1960), 23 D.L.R. (2d) 620, 30 W.W.R. 686 (Alta. S.C.), affd 36 D.L.R. (2d) 443, 39 W.W.R. 640 (Alta. S.C.).

[29]*Rathwell v. Rathwell* (1978), 83 D.L.R. (3d) 289, [1978] 2 S.C.R. 436, and see the discussion on matrimonial property, ch. 16, *infra*.

[30]R.S.O. 1980, c. 143, s. 14.

[31]R.S.O. 1980, c. 90.

[32]R.S.O. 1980, c. 230, s. 65(3).

[33]*Property Act*, R.S.N.B. 1973, c. P-19, s. 20; *Real Property Act*, R.S.N.S. 1967, c. 261, s. 4.

provide that, where an instrument under which a new trustee is appointed to perform a trust contains a declaration by the appointor to the effect that any estate or interest in land subject to the trust shall vest in the persons who by virtue of such instrument are the trustees for performing the trust, that declaration without a conveyance or assignment operates to vest the estate or interest in those persons as joint tenants for the purposes of the trust, and where an instrument under which a retiring trustee is discharged contains such a declaration by the retiring and continuing trustees, the declaration operates to vest the estate or interest in the continuing trustees as joint tenants for the purposes of the trust.[34]

At common law, if two or more persons having no title entered into possession of property in such circumstances as to give them a possessory title under the *Statute of Limitations*, they took as joint tenants[35] unless the circumstances showed they had separate interests, as where persons beneficially entitled as tenants in common acquired the legal estate by possession, in which case they took it as tenants in common,[36] although if some so entered into possession to the exclusion of the others, they acquired the legal estate in their own shares as tenants in common and in the shares of the others as joint tenants.[37] This acquisition of title by disseisin of the true owner applied where persons in possession under a lawful title remained in possession after the title came to an end, in which case they became joint tenants.[38] In Ontario, however, by section 13 of the *Conveyancing and Law of Property Act*, where two or more persons acquire land by possession, they are to be considered as holding as tenants in common and not as joint tenants. Similar provision does not appear to have been made in the other provinces.

There are special cases in which the court will declare an estate to be a tenancy in common, notwithstanding that documents do not provide for several interests. If purchasers of a property provide the purchase money in unequal shares, they may be declared to be tenants in common, notwithstanding the form of conveyance to them.[39] Parol evidence of the circumstances and subsequent dealings is admissible to prove the intent of the parties to hold as tenants in common,[40] although apparently statements of the parties are not admissible.[41] On the other hand, if the document indicates on its face the intent to hold as tenants in common, payment by them in equal shares does not change it to a joint tenancy.[42] Where a husband and wife purchased land,

---

[34]R.S.A. 1980, c. T-10, s. 17(1), (2); R.S.B.C. 1979, c. 414, s. 29(1), (2); R.S.M. 1970, c. T160, s. 15(1), (2); R.S.S. 1978, c. T23, s. 21(1), (2).

[35]*Ward v. Ward* (1871), 6 Ch. App. 789; *Bolling v. Holiday* (1882), 31 W.R. 9.

[36]*MacCormack v. Courtney*, [1895] 2 I.R. 97; *Marten v. Kearney* (1903), 36 I.L.T. 117.

[37]*Smith v. Savage*, [1906] 1 I.R. 469.

[38]*Myers v. Ruport* (1904), 8 O.L.R. 668 (C.A.).

[39]*Robinson v. Preston* (1858), 4 K. & J. 505, 70 E.R. 211.

[40]*Harrison v. Barton* (1860), 1 J. & H. 287, 70 E.R. 756; *Palmer v. Rich*, [1897] 1 Ch. 134 at p. 143.

[41]*Harrison v. Barton*, *supra*, footnote 40.

[42]*Fleming v. Fleming* (1855), 5 I. Ch. R. 129.

both signing the agreement and the wife as well as the husband binding herself to the covenants, including the covenant to pay, the husband paying the full purchase price, it was held that the husband, by making his wife a party to the purchase, must be presumed to have made her a gift by way of advancement, that there was no presumption of a resulting trust and that they took as tenants in common.[43] Provisions for children in marriage settlements are, if possible, construed as tenancies in common.[44]

1502.1 Right of Survivorship

The most important incident of a joint tenancy is the right of survivorship, called, since ancient times, the *jus accrescendi*, the right of surviving joint tenants to have their undivided interests progressively increased by the deaths of other joint tenants, although the survivors continue as joint tenants, the last survivor taking the entirety.[1] This feature of a joint tenancy is the natural consequence of the other incidents of complete unity of title, interest and possession, the interests of joint tenants not only being equal but being one and the same, their combined interests forming one estate. Although a joint tenancy can be severed and turned into a tenancy in common, while a joint tenancy continues all joint tenants have a concurrent interest, no one having a share separate from the others. Hence, if one dies, no person can claim his share by descent because, between such person and the surviving joint tenants, there could not be unity of title or unity of time of vesting and no one can have the right to a separate interest in any part of the property. When one joint tenant dies, there is no gap in the seisin or possession of the survivors or any partial divesting of their interests. The interest of the one who dies is simply extinguished and accrues to the survivors who thus have an increased share of the rents and profits of the property and an increased share on a severance of the joint tenancy. If no severance occurs, the last survivor takes the entire estate that was originally created as a joint tenancy, whatever the estate may be. It does not follow, however, that the right of survivorship is of equal value to joint tenants. If, for instance, a joint tenancy is limited to A and B for the life of A, A would take as survivor if B dies first, but if A dies first, nothing is left for B.[2] By reason of the rule of survivorship, the widow

---

[43]*Re Jay* (1925), 28 O.W.N. 214 (H.C.J.); *Kearney v. Kearney*, [1970] 2 O.R. 152, 10 D.L.R. (3d) 138 (C.A.). For an example of the presumption of advancement operating in such circumstances where the person claiming sole ownership stands *in loco parentis*, see *Young v. Young* (1959), 15 D.L.R. (2d) 138 (B.C.C.A.). In Ontario the presumption of advancement has been abolished between husband and wife but retained between parent and child.

[44]*Taggart v. Taggart* (1803), 1 Sch. & Lef. 84 at p. 88; *Rigden v. Vallier* (1751), 3 Atk. 731, 26 E.R. 1219; *Marryat v. Townly* (1748), 1 Ves. Sen. 102, 27 E.R. 918; *Re Bellasis' Trust* (1871), L.R. 12 Eq. 218; *Mayn v. Mayn* (1867), L.R. 5 Eq. 150; *Liddard v. Liddard* (1860), 28 Beav. 266, 54 E.R. 368.

§1502.1

[1]Co. Litt. 191a; 2 Bl. Comm. 183.

[2]Co. Litt. 181b.

of a joint tenant who was survived by another joint tenant had no dower in the property,[3] although a widow of a tenant in common was entitled to dower.[4]

At common law, there can be no joint tenancy between a corporation and an individual or between the Crown and a private person because neither the corporation nor the Crown can die, so that the individual could never take as survivor, and, also, a grant to a corporation is a grant to it and its successors, whereas a grant to an individual is a grant to him and his heirs, so that there can never be the blending of interest that is necessary to a joint tenancy and they consequently take as tenants in common.[5]

In England, however, by statute,[6] bodies corporate are put on the same footing as individuals. In Ontario, the *Conveyancing and Law of Property Act*[7] provides that a body corporate is capable of holding in joint tenancy as if it were an individual and, where a body corporate and an individual or two or more corporate bodies become entitled to property in circumstances which, had the body corporate been an individual, would have created a joint tenancy, they are entitled to hold the property as joint tenants, provided that the holding by the body corporate is subject to the same conditions and restrictions as attach to the holding of property by a body corporate in severalty, and, on the dissolution of the body corporate, the property devolves on the other joint tenant. Similar provision is made in Alberta,[8] British Columbia,[9] Manitoba[10] and Saskatchewan.[11]

A conflict of principles arises when one joint tenant murders his fellow joint tenant. On the one hand the principle of survivorship compels the conclusion that the victim's share held in joint tenancy devolves upon the murderer by survivorship while, on the other hand, the principle that a wrongdoer is not to benefit by his wrongful act compels the conclusion that the murderer is not to receive the beneficial interest of his victim. To resolve this conflict the court has decided that the victim's share does devolve upon the murderer by right of survivorship, but that a constructive trust immediately arises whereby the murderer holds the victim's share as trustee for his estate.[12] However, the murderer's undivided own interest is not forfeited to the victim's estate.[13]

In reaching this result, it is obvious that, in theory in any event, the murderer

---

[3]*Haskill v. Fraser* (1862), 12 C.P. 383.

[4]*Ham v. Ham* (1857), 14 U.C.Q.B. 497. Dower has been abolished in all the common law provinces, see §707, *supra.*

[5]*Law Guarantee and Trust Society, Ltd. v. Governor and Co. of Bank of England* (1890), 24 Q.B.D. 406.

[6]*Bodies Corporate (Joint Tenancy) Act* (1899), 62 & 63 Vict., c. 20.

[7]R.S.O. 1980, c. 90, s. 43.

[8]*Companies Act*, R.S.A. 1980, c. C-20, s. 9(2), (3), (4).

[9]*Company Act*, R.S.B.C. 1979, c. 59, s. 10.

[10]*Law of Property Act*, R.S.M. 1970, c. L90, s. 16.

[11]*Companies Act*, R.S.S. 1978, c. C-23, s. 34.

[12]*Schobelt v. Barber*, [1967] 1 O.R. 349, 60 D.L.R. (2d) 519 (H.C.J.); *Re Gore.* [1972] 1 O.R. 550, 23 D.L.R. (3d) 534 (H.C.J.); *Re Pechar; Re Grbic*, [1969] N.Z.L.R. 574.

[13]*Re Dreger* (1976), 12 O.R. (2d) 371, 69 D.L.R. (3d) 47 (H.C.J.).

has benefited to the extent that his own interest is no longer subject to the right of survivorship. In effect the imposition of the constructive trust "severs"[14] the joint tenancy. However, the courts have accepted this result on the basis that the imposition of the trust interferes less with the rights acquired by the parties and yet does not do violence to the rule of public policy.[15]

Complications arise in the application of the trust when one joint tenant murders one of several joint tenants. In that case it has been held that the beneficiary of the trust is the surviving and innocent joint tenant or tenants.[16]

It is important to note that if one joint tenant kills his fellow joint tenant but is found to be not guilty of murder by reason of insanity there is no conflict in the principles as set out above and therefore the living joint tenant takes the property by right of survivorship.[17]

1502.2   Release of Interest

Since each joint tenant is seised of the whole estate, the proper method to be followed by one who wishes to vest his interest in the others is for him to release his interest to the others[1] and not to grant it to them, although a grant will be construed as a release passing his interest.[2]

If a joint tenant releases his interest to the other joint tenant or tenants, the release does not operate to pass his estate but to extinguish it and it then rests exclusively in the other joint tenant or tenants so as to enlarge their interests which they continue to hold as joint tenants under their original title to the whole, but, if there are three joint tenants and one releases his interest to only one of the others, the release operates to pass his estate to the releasee,[3] giving the latter a fresh title to that undivided share, so that the release operates as a severance of that share which will then be held by the releasee and the other tenant as tenants in common, the other two undivided shares continuing to be held by them as joint tenants.[4]

In order for a release, or conveyance, to be effective it must be clear that the releasing joint tenant intends to release his interest. A release for a temporary purpose, with no intention to abandon the interest, will not result in abandonment.[5]

---

[14]*Kemp v. Public Curator of Queensland*, [1969] Qd. R. 145 (S.C.).

[15]*Schobelt v. Barber, supra*, footnote 12.

[16]*Rasmanis v. Jurewitsch*, [1970] 1 N.S.W.R. 650.

[17]*Re Public Trustee of Manitoba and Le Clerc* (1981), 123 D.L.R. (3d) 650, 8 Man. R. (2d) 267 (Q.B.).

§1502.2

[1]Co. Litt. 9b.

[2]*Eustace v. Scawen* (1624), Cro. Jac. 696, 79 E.R. 604; *Chester v. Willan* (1670), 2 Wms. Saund. 96, 85 E.R. 768.

[3]*Chester v. Willan, supra.*

[4]Littleton's Tenures, ss. 304, 312.

[5]*O'Bertos v. O'Bertos*, [1975] 2 W.W.R. 86, 20 R.F.L. 6 (Sask. Q.B.).

1502.3 No Fiduciary Relation Between Joint Tenants

There is no fiduciary relation between joint tenants or tenants in common as between themselves so as to make them subject to the disabilities or liabilities attaching to such a relation[1] and the mere fact that one co-tenant has been allowed to receive the rents, pay interest and taxes and manage the property generally does not create a fiduciary relation.[2]

1502.4 Accounting Between Joint Tenants

At common law, there could be no action of account by one joint tenant or tenant in common against another who had occupied the whole property unless he had appointed the latter as his bailiff, so as to make him liable to account in that capacity.[1] In a court of equity, however, one joint tenant or tenant in common was liable to account in an action by the other co-owners.[2]

By the Imperial statute of 1705,[3] a joint tenant or tenant in common was made liable to account to his co-tenants as bailiff if he received more than his just share but not otherwise. It was held that an action of account lay against him under the Act whether he was in sole occupation or was in receipt of the rents.[4] It was held that a joint tenant receives more than his just share within the meaning of the statute if he receives money or something else given or paid by another which the co-tenants are entitled to simply by being co-tenants and, if the amount which he so receives or keeps is more than his proportionate interest as such tenant; that he does not receive more than his just share within the meaning of the statute if he merely has the sole enjoyment of the property, even though by the employment of his own industry and capital he makes a profit by the enjoyment and takes the whole of such profit; and that, in an action of account, proof of such enjoyment and receipt of the whole profits is not evidence of the occupying co-tenant being bailiff within the meaning of the statute, nor presumptive evidence of his having received more than his just share.[5] It was also held that the account extends only to whatever was paid or given by the tenants or occupants of the common property to one co-owner in excess of his just share or proportion and that he does not receive more than his just share merely by having the whole enjoyment of the property where there was no exclusion or ouster of his co-tenants; and

---

§1502.3

[1]*Kennedy v. De Trafford*, [1897] A.C. 180 (H.L.).

[2]*Fleet v. Fleet* (1925), 28 O.W.N. 193 (S.C. App. Div.).

§1502.4

[1]Co. Litt. 186a, 200b; *Pulteney v. Warren* (1801), 2 Ves. Jun. 73, 31 E.R. 944; *Wheeler v. Horne* (1740), Willes 208, 125 E.R. 1135; *Gregory v. Connolly* (1850), 7 U.C.Q.B. 500.

[2]*Strelly v. Winson* (1685), 1 Vern. 297, 23 E.R. 480; *Leake v. Cordeaux* (1856), 4 W.R. 806 (Ch.).

[3]*Statute of Anne* (1705), 4 Anne, c. 16, s. 27.

[4]*Eason v. Henderson* (1848), 12 Q.B. 986, 116 E.R. 1140.

[5]*Henderson v. Eason* (1851), 17 Q.B. 701, 117 E.R. 1451.

that he was not answerable for any profit made out of the property by the use of his industry and capital by tilling and manuring the land, or by herding and grazing cattle, or for cutting down trees of suitable age and growth or other acts of waste, or for cutting and taking away a crop of hay, the produce of the property.[6] No liability arises because of one joint tenant's wilful default in failing to rent the premises.[7]

In Ontario, the *Courts of Justice Act, 1984*[8] provides that actions of account may be brought by one joint tenant or tenant in common, his heirs and administrators, against the other, his executors or administrators, as bailiff for receiving more than comes to his just share or proportion. Similar provision is made in Manitoba.[9] Similar express provision does not appear to have been made in the other provinces in which, therefore, the Imperial statute would seem to be in force.[10]

A joint tenant cannot compel the others to contribute to the cost of repairs.[11] In a partition action, however, he may be allowed sums properly spent on substantial repairs and improvements[12] and may be charged with excess rents and profits received by him[13] and if he has been in sole occupation, he may be charged with an occupation rent.[14] As each co-tenant is entitled to enter upon the whole property, one who has solely occupied the property is not liable to the others for occupation rent. If he does acts amounting to exclusion of the others, the court may appoint a receiver. If he actually receives rent, an account will be ordered. If a joint tenant or tenant in common has been in sole occupation and makes repairs or improvements, he is not entitled to be repaid for them unless he submits to an occupation rent and accounts for the profits he has received from his occupation.[15]

Many of the cases involving an accounting arise when husband and wife own the property as joint tenants. Because of the marital relationship, the applica-

---

[6]*Re Kirkpatrick*; *Kirkpatrick v. Stevenson* (1883), 10 P.R. (Ont.) 4 (H.C.J.), citing *Henderson v. Eason, supra,* footnote 5; *Nash v. McKay* (1868), 15 Gr. 247; *Martyn v. Knowllys* (1799), 8 T.R. 145, 101 E.R. 1313; *Rice v. George* (1873), 20 Gr. 221; *Griffies v. Griffies* (1863), 8 L.T. 758; *Jacobs v. Seward* (1869), L.R. 4 C.P. 328.
[7]*Osachuk v. Osachuk* (1971), 18 D.L.R. (3d) 413, [1971] 2 W.W.R. 481 (Man. C.A.).
[8]S.O. 1984, c. 11, s. 132(2).
[9]*Court of Queen's Bench Act*, R.S.M. 1970, c. C280, s. 77.
[10]See also provisions respecting the granting of equitable relief in *Judicature Act*, R.S.A. 1980, c. J-1, s. 17; *Queen's Bench Act*, R.S.S. 1978, c. Q-1, s. 44; *Judicature Act*, R.S.N.B. 1973, c. J-2, s. 26; *Judicature Act*, S.N.S. 1972, c. 2, s. 38, am. 1980, c. 55, s. 1; *Judicature Act*, R.S.N. 1970, c. 187, s. 21.
[11]*Leigh v. Dickeson* (1884), 15 Q.B.D. 60 (C.A.).
[12]*Ibid., Swan v. Swan* (1820), 8 Price 518, 146 E.R. 1281; *Pascoe v. Swan* (1859), 27 Beav. 508, 54 E.R. 201.
[13]*Hyde v. Hindly* (1794), 2 Cox. 408, 30 E.R. 188; *Lorimer v. Lorimer* (1820), 5 Madd. 363, 56 E.R. 934.
[14]*Turner v. Morgan* (1803), 8 Ves. Jun. 143 at p. 145, 32 E.R. 307; *Teasdale v. Sanderson* (1864), 33 Beav. 534, 55 E.R. 476.
[15]*Rice v. George* (1873), 20 Gr. 221 at pp. 222, 226; *Irvine v. Irvine* (1959), 67 Man. R. 238 (Q.B.). As to accounts in partition actions, see §§1502.12, 1502.13, 1503.12 and 1503.14, *infra.*

tion of the presumption of advancement, and the issue of existence of a gift, the cases must be read with some care.[16] However, certain general principles with respect to accounting for mortgage payments can be stated. First, joint tenants are equally responsible for mortgage payments, and apart from a special agreement each must accept responsibility for his share of the payments.[17] Secondly, if one joint tenant mortgages his interest in order to acquire the property, the mortgage only extends to his interest.[18] If the parties make some special agreement as to mortgage payments, that agreement in the normal course will be honoured.[19] Finally, where both joint tenants sign a mortgage, in the absence of a special agreement both are equally entitled to the proceeds of the mortgage.[20]

In British Columbia there is special legislation[21] which permits the court to order that a joint tenant or tenant in common, who pays more than this proportionate share of, *inter alia*, mortgage payments, taxes or insurance premiums, is to have a lien on the property.

1502.5 Trespass and Waste by Joint Tenants

Since each joint tenant has an equal right of entry on every part of the property, one cannot bring action against another for trespass but, if one joint tenant is ousted or denied the right of entry, he may take ejectment proceedings.[1]

In general, a co-tenant will be restrained by injunction from committing destructive waste, such as the improper cutting of trees.[2]

In Ontario, the *Conveyancing and Law of Property Act*[3] provides that joint tenants and tenants in common are liable to their co-tenants for waste or, in the event of partition, the part wasted away may be assigned to the tenant committing the waste at the value to be estimated as if no waste had been committed. Similar provision does not appear to have been made in the other provinces. Also, in Ontario, the *Judicature Act*[4] provides that the court may grant an injunction to prevent any threatened or apprehended waste or trespass, whether or not the person against whom it is sought is in possession under any

---

[16]See for example, *Morrison v. Guaranty Trust Co. of Canada*, [1972] 3 O.R. 448, 28 D.L.R. (3d) 458 (H.C.J.).

[17]*Irvine v. Irvine, supra*, footnote 15.

[18]*Re Vermette and Vermette* (1974), 45 D.L.R. (3d) 313, [1974] 4 W.W.R. 320 (Man. C.A.).

[19]*Shore v. Shore* (1975), 63 D.L.R. (3d) 354, [1976] W.W.D. 19 (B.C.S.C.).

[20]*Porter v. Porter* (1974), 14 R.F.L. 146 (Ont. H.C.J.).

[21]*Property Law Act*, R.S.B.C. 1979, c. 340, ss. 13, 14; *Re Brook and Brook* (1969), 6 D.L.R. (3d) 92 (B.C.S.C.).

§1502.5

[1]*Murray v. Hall* (1849), 7 C.B. 441, 137 E.R. 175.

[2]*Hole v. Thomas* (1802), 7 Ves. Jun. 589, 32 E.R. 237; *Arthur v. Lamb* (1865), 2 Dr. & Sm. 428, 62 E.R. 683; *Hersey v. Murphy* (1920), 48 N.B.R. 65 (S.C.).

[3]R.S.O. 1980, c. 90, s. 31.

[4]R.S.O. 1980, c. 223, ss. 19, 21, rep. & sub. by 1984, c. 11, s. 114.

claim of title or otherwise or, if out of possession does or does not claim a right to do the act sought to be restrained under a colour of title, and whether the estates claimed by both or either of the parties are legal or equitable and may award damages to the party injured either in addition to or in substitution for the injunction, or the court may grant such other relief as may be deemed just. Similar provisions exist in Alberta, Manitoba, Saskatchewan, New Brunswick, Newfoundland and Nova Scotia.[5]

1502.6   Acts Enuring to the Common Benefit of Joint Tenants

Since each joint tenant is seised *per mie et per tout*, the estate of joint tenants is one entire estate. Hence, every act done by one joint tenant for the benefit of himself and the others enures to the benefit of all and one cannot prejudice the estate of the others.[1] On this principle of complete unity, it follows that a payment of rent to one joint tenant is a payment to all and that, as regards third parties, delivery of possession to one joint tenant is delivery to all. At common law, possession by one co-owner was possession by all[2] but in regard to limitations of actions, by the Imperial *Real Property Limitation Act, 1833*,[3] possession by co-owners became separate, so that where a husband who was entitled to one moiety remained in uninterrupted possession of the entire property without acknowledging the title of the heir of his deceased wife who was entitled to the other moiety, the heir's claim was barred by the statute.[4]

In Ontario under the *Limitations Act*[5] if one or more of several persons entitled to land or rent as joint tenants, tenants in common or coparceners has or have been in possession or receipt of the entirety or of more than his or their undivided share or shares for his or their own benefit or the benefit of anybody other than those entitled to the other shares, such possession or receipt shall not be deemed to be possession or receipt by the latter. The effect of the statute is illustrated in a case where one of several tenants in common entered upon the land and dispossessed a trespasser. It was held that he was, in respect of his co-tenants, in possession simply as a stranger would be and his possession did not enure to the benefit of the co-tenants but, since he so acted by virtue of his legal estate, his act in that respect enured to the benefit of his co-tenants so as to give a fresh starting point for the statute to begin to

---

[5]*Law of Property Act*, R.S.A. 1980, c. L-8, s. 63; *Judicature Act*, R.S.A. 1980, c. J-1, s. 20; *Court of Queen's Bench Act*, R.S.M. 1970, c. C280, s. 59, am. 1970, c. 79, s. 1, and s. 60; *Queen's Bench Act*, R.S.S. 1978, c. Q-1, s. 45, paras. 8 and 9; *Judicature Act*, R.S.N.B. 1973, c. J-2, s. 33; R.S.N. 1970, c. 187, s. 21(*m*); S.N.S. 1972, c. 2, s. 39(9).

§1502.6
[1]*Tooker's Case*; *Rud v. Tooker* (1601), 2 Co. Rep. 66 b, 76 E.R. 567.
[2]*Ford v. Lord Grey* (1703), 6 Mod. 44, 87 E.R. 807; *Doe d. Thorn v. Phillips* (1832), 3 B. & Ad. 753, 110 E.R. 275.
[3]3 & 4 Will. 4, c. 27 (1833).
[4]*Ex parte Hasell*; *Re Manchester Gas Act* (1839), 3 Y. & C. Ex. 617, 160 E.R. 848.
[5]R.S.O. 1980, c. 240, s. 11, expected soon to be replaced by new legislation, see §3106.21; *Tolosnak v. Tolosnak*, [1957] O.W.N. 273, 10 D.L.R. (2d) 186 (H.C.J.).

run against them.[6] Similar provisions are found in New Brunswick, Newfoundland, Nova Scotia and Prince Edward Island.[7]

In Nova Scotia, it was held that, as between co-owners, the exclusive possession of one is to be regarded as adverse to the others and such possession for the period fixed by the *Statute of Limitations* is an absolute bar to the right of partition.[8]

It has been suggested[9] that in view of the four unities required for joint tenancy, it would be very difficult for one joint tenant to show acts of possession adverse to his remaining joint tenants and that adverse possession can be more easily established against a co-tenant. In view of the fact that unity of possession is required for a co-tenancy, and that this is the only unity involved in a claim of adverse possession, and in light of the statutes referred to above, this suggestion may be open to criticism. However, there is no doubt that as between spouses who hold as joint tenants, the court has been reluctant to find the necessary animus to support a claim of adverse possession.[10]

The *Limitation Act*[11] in British Columbia expressly precludes the adverse possessor from gaining any right or title to lands taken by adverse possession. Lands registered under Land Titles are not subject to the application of the concept of adverse possession.[12]

A co-owner who voluntarily makes improvements to common property may only recover compensation for money expended on a partition or sale in lieu of partition or on other judicial proceedings for a distribution of the common property among the co-owners.[13] The co-owner cannot recover while the property is held in common but the cost of improvements creates an equity which attaches to the land so that on partition the co-owner can recover his expenditure. The equity attaches to the land and passes with it to a purchaser of the co-owner's interest who may recover the expense of improvement made by his predecessor.[14] The equity may attach in the case of land held by tenants in common or by joint tenancy, but there may be a problem under joint tenancy

---

[6]*Harris v. Mudie* (1882), 7 O.A.R. 414; *Hartley v. Maycock* (1897), 28 O.R. 508 (H.C.J.).

[7]*Limitation of Actions Act*, R.S.N.B. 1973, c. L-8, s. 32; *Limitation of Actions (Realty) Act*, R.S.N. 1970, c. 207, s. 13; *Limitations of Actions Act*, R.S.N.S. 1967, c. 168, s. 14; *Statute of Limitations Act*, R.S.P.E.I. 1974, c. S-7, s. 34.

[8]*McDonald v. Rudderham* (1921), 56 D.L.R. 589, 54 N.S.R. 258 (S.C.).

[9]*Re Deal and Deal* (1974), 50 D.L.R. (3d) 564, [1975] W.W.D. 21 (Alta. S.C.T.D.).

[10]*Krause v. Happy*, [1960] O.R. 385, 24 D.L.R. (2d) 310 (C.A.); *Re Gibbins and Gibbins* (1977), 18 O.R. (2d) 45, 1 R.F.L. (2d) 352 (H.C.J.), affd 22 O.R. (2d) 116, 92 D.L.R. (3d) 285 (Div. Ct.); *Re Strong and Colby* (1978), 20 O.R. (2d) 356, 87 D.L.R. (3d) 589 (H.C.J.).

[11]R.S.B.C. 1979, c. 236, s. 12.

[12]For a discussion of this topic, see ch. 31, *infra*.

[13]*Leigh v. Dickeson* (1884), 15 Q.B.D. 60 (C.A.); *McMahon v. Public Curator of Queensland and McMahon*, [1952] St. R. Qd. 197 (S.C.); *Brickwood v. Young and Minister for Public Works of New South Wales*, [1905] 2 C.L.R. 387 (H.C.A.); *Ruptash v. Zawick* (1956), 2 D.L.R. (2d) 145, [1956] S.C.R. 347.

[14]*Brickwood v. Young, supra*, footnote 13.

where the tenant making the improvements dies prior to partition and his interest in the property dies.[15]

The compensation for improvements has been stated to be the amount of increase in the value of the property by the improvement[16] but it may be limited to a maximum of the actual cost of the improvement.[17]

1502.7 Actions Relating to Joint Tenancies

By reason of their complete unities, in actions relating to the joint estate, one joint tenant cannot sue without joining the others and one cannot be sued separately but all must be joined as defendants.[1]

1502.8 Powers of Leasing by Joint Tenants

If the whole property is leased by all joint tenants for a rent reserved to them jointly, the lease does not sever or suspend the joint tenancy.[1] All joint tenants should join in a lease to make it an effective lease of the entirety, because the lessee then holds the share of each joint tenant under each separately and holds the whole under all.[2] Upon the death of any joint tenant, the lessee holds the whole from the survivors.[3]

The question of severance or suspension of a joint tenancy by the granting of a lease is dealt with in detail subsequently.[4]

1502.9 Marriage of a Female Joint Tenant

As a matter of historical interest, the marriage of a female joint tenant did not sever the joint tenancy[1] and a subsequent lease by her husband and the other joint tenants did not sever the tenancy.[2]

1502.10 Land Purchased by Partners as to Profits

Under the *Partnerships Act* of Ontario,[1] where co-owners of an estate or interest in land, which is not partnership land, are partners as to profits made

---

[15]*Re Byrne* (1906), 6 S.R. N.S.W. 532.
[16]*Brickwood v. Young, supra,* footnote 13; *Noack v. Noack,* [1959] V.R. 137.
[17]*McMahon v. The Public Curator of Queensland, supra,* footnote 13.
§1502.7
[1]2 Bl. Comm. 182.
§1502.8
[1]*Palmer v. Rich,* [1897] 1 Ch. 134.
[2]*Doe d. Aslin v. Summersett* (1830), 1 B. & Ad. 135, 109 E.R. 738.
[3]*Henstead's Case* (1634), 5 Co. Rep. 10 a, 77 E.R. 63.
[4]See §1502.11, *infra.*
§1502.9
[1]Co. Litt. 185b; *Palmer v. Rich,* [1897] 1 Ch. 134; *Armstrong v. Armstrong* (1869), L.R. 7 Eq. 518; *Re Butler's Trusts*; *Hughes v. Anderson* (1888), 38 Ch. D. 286 (C.A.).
[2]*Palmer v. Rich, supra.*
§1502.10
[1]R.S.O. 1980, c. 370, s. 21(3).

by the use of the land and, out of the profits, purchase other land or estate to be used in like manner, the land or estate so purchased belongs to them, in the absence of agreement to the contrary, not as partners but as co-owners for the same respective estates and interests as they held in the other land or estate at the date of purchase. Similar provisions are found in the Partnership Acts of the other provinces and the Territories.[2]

1502.11 Severance of a Joint Tenancy

A joint tenancy depends on the continuance of the three unities of title, interest and possession and the destruction of any of such unities severs the joint tenancy and creates a tenancy in common or several tenancies.[1] It is the right of a joint tenant to thus sever the joint tenancy. The unity of time of vesting only applies to the original creation of the joint tenancy and cannot, therefore, be affected by any subsequent act.

The unity of title is destroyed if one joint tenant assigns his share to a third person[2] or mortgages his share to a third person.[3] If there were initially only two joint tenants such an act creates a tenancy in common between the assignee and the other joint tenant.[4] If there were more than two joint tenants it creates a tenancy in common between the assignee and the others, although the latter as between themselves continue as joint tenants.[5]

A severance may be effected by one joint tenant executing and registering a conveyance to himself.[6] It may also be effected by one joint tenant giving the property to a third person by a valid declaration of trust.[7] It is necessary, of course, that the trust be completely constituted thereby indicating an intention on the part of the joint tenant to divest himself of his interest.

It has been decided that a mere agreement for sale by one joint tenant to a third party does not, in itself, effect a severance. Thus, where one joint tenant who entered into an agreement of purchase and sale died before the actual sale took place, the remaining joint tenant took by survivorship and the agreement became a charge upon the property.[8] On the other hand, it has also

---

[2]R.S.A. 1980, c. P-2, s. 22(3); R.S.B.C. 1979, c. 312, s. 23(3); R.S.M. 1970, c. P30, s. 23(3); R.S.S. 1978, c. P-3, s. 22(2); R.S.N.B. 1973, c. P-4, s. 21(3); R.S.N. 1970, c. 287, s. 21(3); R.S.N.S. 1967, c. 224, s. 22(3); R.S.P.E.I. 1974, c. P-2, s. 23(2); R.O.Y.T. 1971, c. P-1, s. 22(3); R.O.N.W.T. 1974, c. P-1, s. 22(3).

§1502.11

[1]2 Bl. Comm. 195.

[2]*Partriche v. Powlet* (1740), 2 Atk. 54, 26 E.R. 430.

[3]*York v. Stone* (1709), 1 Salkeld 158, 91 E.R. 146; *Re Pollard's Estate and South-Eastern Ry. Co's Acts* (1863), 3 De G. J. & S. 541, 46 E.R. 746; *Re Sharer; Abbott v. Sharer* (1912), 57 Sol. Jo. 60.

[4]*Partriche v. Powlet, supra,* footnote 2.

[5]Littleton's Tenures, s. 294.

[6]*Re Murdoch and Barry* (1975), 10 O.R. (2d) 626, 64 D.L.R. (3d) 222 (H.C.J.).

[7]*Re Mee* (1971), 23 D.L.R. (3d) 491, [1972] 2 W.W.R. 424 (B.C.C.A.).

[8]*Re Foort and Chapman* (1973), 37 D.L.R. (3d) 730, [1973] 4 W.W.R. 461 (B.C.S.C.). But see *Brown v. Raindle* (1796), 3 Ves. Jun. 256, 30 E.R. 998; *Partriche v. Powlet, supra,* footnote 2.

been held that a severance is created once a conveyance is given. It is not necessary that the conveyance be registered to effect the severance even where the applicable recording statute required that the conveyance be registered to be effective "except as against the person making the same".[9]

The Torrens or land titles legislation[10] does not affect the normal common law incidences of a joint tenancy, one of which is the right to effect a severance by conveying one's share. A transfer under land titles legislation has the same effect as a deed under seal and does not have to be registered in order to sever the joint tenancy.[11] However, the legislation may have an effect on the right of a joint tenant to sever the joint tenancy by way of mortgage. The generally accepted view of a mortgage under the Torrens system is that it has effect only as security and does not operate as a transfer of the interest or estate charged. If that is the case, the unity of title is not destroyed by the giving of a mortgage.[12]

A conveyance by one joint tenant to the other of an undivided half of the property puts an end to the joint tenancy. The parties then become tenants in common so that the survivor could devise by will the half he had not conveyed.[13]

The filing of a writ of execution against the interest of one joint tenant does not in itself effect a severance. Although the joint tenant's estate is severable and his interest can be sold under execution something more by way of action such as actual seizure or advertisement is required.[14] It has been held that the registration of a judgment against the estate of one joint tenant does not sever the joint tenancy. The owner of the registered judgment has only a charge on the land but that does not constitute an enforceable contract to alienate which might operate as a severance.[15] Moreover, the filing of a writ of extent pursuant to section 171 of the *Land Registry Act*[16] against lands held in joint tenancy does not sever the joint tenancy. It merely binds the property in a limited sense. The four unities remain undisturbed until the lands are placed in execution by seizure with a view to sale.[17] However, where a joint tenant makes an authorized assignment in bankruptcy, the assignment severs the joint tenancy and turns it into a tenancy in common.[18]

---

[9]*Stonehouse v. A.-G. of British Columbia* (1961), 31 D.L.R. (2d) 118, [1962] S.C.R. 103 (S.C.C.). See also Raney, "Commentary", 41 Can. Bar Rev. 272 (1963).

[10]Such as, the *Land Titles Act*, R.S.O. 1980, c. 230.

[11]*Re Cameron*, [1957] O.R. 581, 11 D.L.R. 201 (H.C.J.).

[12]*Lyons v. Lyons*, [1967] V.R. 169 (S.C.).

[13]*Doe d. Eberts v. Montreuil* (1849), 6 U.C.Q.B. 515.

[14]*Sirois v. Breton*, [1967] 2 O.R. 73, 62 D.L.R. (2d) 366 (Co. Ct.).

[15]*Re Young* (1968), 70 D.L.R. (2d) 594, 66 W.W.R. 193 (B.C.C.A.).

[16]R.S.B.C. 1960, c. 208; now s. 200 of the *Land Title Act*, R.S.B.C. 1979, c. 219.

[17]*Re McDonald and The Queen* (1969), 8 D.L.R. (3d) 666, 71 W.W.R. 444 (B.C.S.C.). For an example of the step necessary to sever, see *Sunglo Lumber Ltd. v. McKenna* (1974), 48 D.L.R. (3d) 154, [1974] 5 W.W.R. 572 (B.C.S.C.).

[18]*Re White*, [1928] 1 D.L.R. 846, 33 O.W.N. 255 (S.C.); *Re Butler's Trusts; Hughes v. Anderson* (1888), 38 Ch. D. 286 (C.A.); *Re Chisick* (1968), 62 W.W.R. 586 (Man. C.A.).

A grant from one of two joint tenants in fee simple to a third person for life severs the joint tenancy as the freehold is in the third person and the other joint tenant under different titles. In that case, they hold as tenants in common.[19] However, the joint tenancy is only suspended, and, if the grantee dies during the joint lives, the joint tenancy revives.[20] If during the period of suspension the grantor or the other former joint tenant dies, the joint tenancy is permanently severed because there is no right of survivorship. For the right of survivorship to exist, the land must be held in joint tenancy at the time of the death of him who dies first.[21]

The effect of a lease, given by one joint tenant to a third party, on the joint tenancy, is not free from doubt. It has been suggested that a lease for years confers a right to possession which arises by separate title and that, thus, the lease effects a severance of the whole estate both before and after the lease.[22] On the other hand, it has been suggested that the lease does not sever the joint tenancy.[23] However, in *Clerk v. Clerk*,[24] the court concluded that if one of two joint tenants in fee simple leases his share for a term of years, the lease does sever the joint tenancy and the lease is binding on the other joint tenant after the death of the lessor, whether or not the lessee enters into possession during the life of the lessor. Again, it has been suggested that where one joint tenant leases his share to the other, the joint tenancy is severed.[25]

In an unusual case, three persons were joint tenants as devisees in trust with the power to lease to one of them. A lease was made under the power but it was held that the lease by a joint tenant to himself could not effect a severance. However, the lease by the remaining two would sever the joint tenancy during the term of the lease.[26]

Finally, where the joint tenancy is only for a term of years, a lease by one joint tenant for a term less than the residue severs the joint tenancy.[27]

A second accepted method of severing a joint tenancy is by mutual wills agreed to between the joint tenants. Thus, where two joint tenants agreed to dispose of leasehold property by will and trust for each other for life, and for their nieces after the death of the survivor, and the survivor later made a will disposing of the property in a different manner, it was held that the agreement between the joint tenants carried out by the making of the wills severed the joint tenancy and the property had to be administered as a tenancy in com-

---

[19]Co. Litt. 191b.

[20]*Ibid.*, 193a.

[21]*Ibid.*, 188a.

[22]Megarry & Wade, *The Law of Real Property*, p. 405.

[23]Co. Litt. 185a.

[24](1694), 2 Vern. 323, 23 E.R. 809; *Re Sorensen and Sorensen* (1976), 69 D.L.R. (3d) 326, [1976] 5 W.W.R. 140 (Alta. S.C.T.D.), revd on other grounds 90 D.L.R. (3d) 26, [1977] 2 W.W.R. 438 (S.C. App. Div.), leave to appeal to S.C.C. granted 6 A.R. 540.

[25]*Cowper v. Fletcher* (1865), 6 B. & S. 464 at p. 472, 122 E.R. 1267, but see *Re Sorensen and Sorensen, supra,* footnote 24, where it was concluded that a lease to one of the joint tenants did not sever the joint tenancy.

[26]*Napier v. Williams,* [1911] 1 Ch. 361.

[27]Co. Litt. 192a.

mon.[28] The execution of mutual wills by joint tenants whereby the tenants agree to dispose of their interest severs the joint tenancy and converts it into a tenancy in common.[29] A disposition by one joint tenant under his will would not effect the severance as no common intention could be shown. The will does not take effect until the joint tenant's death at which time the other joint tenant's vested right of survivorship takes effect.[30] However, the execution of mutual wills by agreement does effect a severance.

Underlying the proposition that a joint tenancy may be severed by mutual wills is the principle that a joint tenancy may be severed by mutual agreement or by the conduct of the joint tenants. If joint tenants enter into a mutual agreement to hold as tenants in common the joint tenancy is severed.[31] Thus, where joint tenants agree to sell the property and to divide the proceeds between them, the joint tenancy is severed and the property then is held as a tenancy in common.[32] Moreover, it is not necessary that the agreement to sell be carried through to the point of conveyance before the joint tenancy is severed.[33] Thus, where a husband and wife enter into a separation agreement whereby both parties agree that each is to have a one-half interest in any proceeds of the sale of the property held as joint tenants, and where the husband gives the wife an irrevocable option to buy his interest, the joint tenancy is severed from that moment. The subsequent purchase by the parties of a second parcel as joint tenants did not alter the severance of the first parcel.[34]

In order that a joint tenancy be severed by conduct, the acts of the joint tenants must be such as to preclude the survivor from claiming an interest by survivorship.[35] When joint tenants, by their conduct treat their interests as several, the joint tenancy is severed and it is not important that the joint tenants were unaware that their original interests were joint.[36] However, the mere fact that a trustee realizes part of an estate and pays the proceeds in certain proportions to the joint tenants does not sever the joint tenancy as to the rest of the estate that has not been received by the joint tenants.[37]

A more difficult issue to resolve is whether a joint tenancy can be severed by the unilateral intention of one joint tenant. In *Re Draper's Conveyance; Nihan v. Porter*,[38] the court concluded that the issuance of a writ to commence

---

[28]*Re Wilford's Estate; Taylor v. Taylor* (1879), 11 Ch. D. 267.
[29]*In Estate of Heys; Walker v. Gaskill* (1915), 111 L.T. 941 at p. 942; *Szabo v. Boros* (1967), 64 D.L.R. (2d) 48, 60 W.W.R. 754 (B.C.C.A.).
[30]2 Cruise's *Digest of the Laws of England Respecting Real Property* (London, Butterworths, 1804), tit. 18, c. 2, s. 19.
[31]*Frewen v. Relfe* (1787), 2 Bro. C.C. 220, 29 E.R. 123; *Williams v. Hensman* (1861), 1 J. & H. 546, 70 E.R. 862.
[32]*Schofield v. Graham* (1969), 6 D.L.R. (3d) 88, 69 W.W.R. 332 (Alta. S.C.).
[33]*Ibid.; Ginn v. Arsmstrong* (1969), 3 D.L.R. (3d) 285 (B.C.S.C.).
[34]*Re McKee and National Trust Co. Ltd.* (1975), 7 O.R. (2d) 614, 56 D.L.R. (3d) 190 (C.A.), revg 5 O.R. (2d) 185, 49 D.L.R. (3d) 689 (H.C.J.).
[35]*Re Wilks; Child v. Bulmer*, [1891] 3 Ch. 59.
[36]*Williams v. Hensman, supra*, footnote 31.
[37]*Leak v. Macdowall* (1862), 32 Beav. 28, 55 E.R. 11.
[38][1967] 3 All E.R. 853 (Ch.).

a partition application was sufficient to sever a joint tenancy. The issuance of the writ indicated a clear unilateral intention on the part of one joint tenant to sever the joint tenancy. However, in *Nielson-Jones v. Fedden*,[39] the court concluded that a unilateral declaration by one joint tenant of an intention to sever is incapable in law of effectively severing a joint tenancy. It also concluded that a course of negotiations not resulting in a final agreement between the joint tenants will never constitute a course of dealing capable of effecting a severance. However, that latter case was overruled in *Burgess v. Rawnsley*[40] where the court concluded that a course of dealing between two joint tenants whereby negotiations were carried on to sever the joint tenancy, even in the absence of any firm agreement, could result in a severance of the joint tenancy. In that case, it was sufficient if there were a course of dealing in which one of the parties made clear to the other the desire that the joint tenancy should be severed to result in a severance. Several recent Canadian cases illustrate this confusion. In *Rodrique v. Dufton*[41] the court concluded that a severance was not effected by the bringing of a partition application or by a unilateral declaration of an intent to sever. Similarly, in *Munroe v. Carlson*[42] the court concluded that the bringing of a Partition Act application that was discontinued does not effect a severance.

However, in *Re Walters and Walters*[43] the court concluded that there was a course of dealing between the joint tenants that amounted to voluntary partition. In that case, the matrimonial home was held in joint tenancy. The parties separated and the wife commenced a divorce action, together with a motion under the *Partition Act* and a motion under the *Married Women's Property Act*. Thereafter, the parties began negotiations on the basis that the wife was entitled to an undivided one-half interest in the matrimonial home. Mutual offers to purchase were presented between the joint tenants. Before the hearing of the partition application, the husband died and the wife claimed entitlement to the whole of the matrimonial home. The court concluded that the husband and wife established a course of dealing to sever the joint tenancy by mutual agreement. In reaching that conclusion the court expressly stated that it was not sufficient to rely on a unilateral intention. Thus, the position in Canada would appear to be that the intention to sever the joint tenancy must be a mutual, as opposed to a unilateral intention and this intention must be evidenced by some objective fact or facts.

The unity of interest is destroyed so as to sever the joint tenancy if one of

---

[39] [1974] 3 All E.R. 38.

[40] [1975] 3 All E.R. 142 (C.A.).

[41] (1976), 72 D.L.R. (3d) 16 (Ont. H.C.J.).

[42] (1975), 59 D.L.R. (3d) 763, [1976] 1 W.W.R. 248 (B.C.S.C.). See also *Re Sorensen and Sorensen* (1976), 69 D.L.R. 326, [1976] 5 W.W.R. 140 (Alta. S.C.T.D.), revd on other grounds 90 D.L.R. 26, [1977] 2 W.W.R. 438 (S.C. App. Div.), leave to appeal to S.C.C. granted 6 A.R. 540.

[43] (1977), 16 O.R. (2d) 702, 79 D.L.R. (3d) 122 (H.C.J.), affd 17 O.R. (2d) 592n, 84 D.L.R. (3d) 416n (C.A.).

several joint tenants for life acquires the fee simple by purchase or descent.[44] Similarly, there is a severance of the joint tenancy if there is a life estate to A with remainder in fee simple to B and C as joint tenants and thereafter A grants his life estate to B. In that case, B holds the one undivided share in fee simple and the other undivided share for the life of A with remainder to C in fee. However, it is otherwise if A merely surrenders his life estate to B because the surrender inures to the benefit of both B and C and as it merges with the fee they become joint tenants in fee simple and possession.[45] In a surrender, the smaller estate is given up to and merges in the greater estate.[46]

It seems well at this point to emphasize the distinction between the original limitation of a remainder in fee simple to one of several joint tenants for life and the subsequent acquisition of the fee by one to whom it was not originally limited. As indicated earlier,[47] one of several joint tenants may have an additional estate in severalty limited to him by the same instrument that created the joint tenancy, as in the case of a grant to A and B for their lives with the remainder to the heirs of A, in which case A and B have a joint tenancy for their lives and A has the remainder in fee simple.[48] It is only when the remainder or reversion in fee simple is not originally limited to a joint tenant for life but is otherwise subsequently acquired by him that his life estate is merged so as to sever the joint tenancy.

The unity of possession is destroyed and the joint tenancy severed if the property is partitioned by the joint tenants either by mutual agreement or by compulsion under statutory proceedings. At common law, they could only partition by mutual agreement and none could compel the others to partition.[49]

A statutory right to compel partition was conferred by the Imperial Statutes of Partition[50] under which the court had no power to refuse partition or to order sale in lieu of partition but, by the Partition Acts,[51] wide powers were conferred on the court to order sale in lieu of partition if the nature of the property and the interests of the parties make it desirable.

It is not possible in this work to deal with all of the voluminous references in provincial statutes to real property and this is particularly true of the references to powers of the courts under provincial rules of practice and statutes to deal with the property of persons who are not *sui juris* or are absentees or under disability of some nature. Therefore, with the exception of the following notations, further discussion of the topic of severance will be confined to partition by agreement and partition or sale by court order.

It is to be noted that under section 18(2) of the Ontario *Settled Estates*

---

[44]*Wiscot's Case; Giles v. Wiscot* (1599), 2 Co. Rep. 60 b, 76 E.R. 555; Co. Litt. 182b.
[45]Co. Litt. 182b, 183a.
[46]2 Bl. Comm. 326; Co. Litt. 336b, 50a.
[47]See §1102, *supra*.
[48]2 Bl. Comm. 181; *Wiscot's Case, supra*, footnote 44.
[49]Littleton's Tenures, ss. 290, 318.
[50]31 Hen. 8, c. 1 (1539); 32 Hen. 8, c. 32 (1540).
[51]31 & 32 Vict., c. 40 (1868); 39 & 40 Vict., c. 17 (1876).

Act[52] where two or more persons are entitled as joint tenants, tenants in common or coparceners, any of them may apply to the court to exercise the powers conferred by the Act.

It is also to be noted that where an application was made to the court on behalf of an infant, one of two joint tenants, to authorize a sale of the property and division of the proceeds between the infant and the adult joint tenant, the sale was sanctioned by Sutherland, J., he being of the opinion that a sale was in the interest of both parties but upon the terms that the proceeds were to be paid into court to remain until the infant attained majority.[53]

If land held by joint tenants is sold for taxes, any of them may redeem the property, it being unnecessary that all join in redeeming.[54] If one of several joint tenants purchases land at a tax sale without any prior agreement that the purchase is to be for their joint benefit and no fraud is involved, he is entitled to hold the land for his sole benefit[55] and the rule is the same if he is one of several tenants in common.[56]

1502.12 Joint Tenancy — Partition by Agreement

Parties who are *sui juris* may agree to partition the property and the agreement is mutually enforceable by and against them and persons deriving title under them in an action for specific performance.[1] Land of any tenure, including leaseholds,[2] and all corporeal hereditaments and estates therein, including reversions and remainders[3] and even mere expectancies,[4] may be partitioned by agreement. Easements may usually be exercised by the separate owners if the dominant tenement is partitioned[5] and, as against the servient tenement, the ordinary rule will apply that no greater right may be enjoyed than if there had been no division.[6] The division into parts may be made by the parties themselves or by some person nominated by them and, in either case, the allotment of the parts among the parties may be determined by their choice, or by lot or by the award of the nominated third party.[7] Where the division is by a nominated third party, he must be impartial and consider the interests

---

[52]R.S.O. 1980, c. 468.

[53]*Re Laws* (1912), 23 O.W.R. 408, 6 D.L.R. 912 (H.C.J.).

[54]*Ray v. Kilgour* (1907), 9 O.W.R. 641 (Div. Ct.).

[55]*Janisse v. Stewart* (1925), 28 O.W.N. 446 (H.C.J.).

[56]*Kennedy v. De Trafford* (1896), 1 Ch. 762 (C.A.), affd [1897] A.C. 180 (H.L.).

§1502.12

[1]*Knollys v. Alcock* (1800), 5 Ves. Jun. 648, 31 E.R. 785; *Pearson v. Lane* (1809), 17 Ves. Jun. 101, 34 E.R. 39; *Heaton v. Dearden* (1852), 16 Beav. 147, 51 E.R. 733; *Paine v. Ryder* (1857), 24 Beav. 151, 53 E.R. 314.

[2]*North v. Guinan* (1829), Beat. 342.

[3]*Oakley v. Smith* (1759), Amb. 368, 27 E.R. 245.

[4]*Beckley v. Newland* (1723), 2 P. Wms. 182, 24 E.R. 691; *Wethered v. Wethered* (1828), 2 Sim. 183, 57 E.R. 757.

[5]*Newcomen v. Coulson* (1877), 5 Ch. D. 133 (C.A.), at p. 141.

[6]*Menzies v. MacDonald* (1856), 2 Jur. N.S. 575 (H.L.).

[7]Littleton's Tenures, 243, 244, 246.

of all parties.[8] Where joint tenants in tail made an agreement for division of the property and thereafter enjoyed their allotments for thirty-six years, specific performance was ordered in an action then brought.[9]

In England, under the *Real Property Act* of 1845,[10] a deed is necessary to effectuate a partition. In Ontario, under the *Conveyancing and Law of Property Act*,[11] a partition of "land" (defined in section 1 to include messuages, tenements, corporeal or incorporeal hereditaments and any undivided share in land) is void at law unless made by deed. Similar provision is made in the *Property Act* of New Brunswick.[12] Equity will, however, enforce an agreement not made by deed if the agreement is capable of specific performance.[13]

1502.13 Joint Tenancy — Partition or Sale by Court Order

In Ontario, provision is made by the *Partition Act*[1] for the partition or sale of land. The provisions may be summarized as follows: Land is defined to include lands, tenements and hereditaments and all estate and interests therein. All joint tenants, tenants in common, coparceners and other persons interested in land may be compelled to make partition or sale of the land or any part thereof, whether the estate is legal and equitable or equitable only. Any person interested in land, or the guardian appointed by the Surrogate Court of a minor entitled to the immediate possession of an estate therein, may take proceedings for the partition of land or for its sale under directions of the Supreme Court if the court considers a sale to be more advantageous to the parties, but, if the land is held in joint tenancy, tenancy in common or coparcenary by reason of a devise or intestacy, no proceedings may be taken until one year after the death of the testator or intestate in whom the land was vested. If any person interested in the land has not been heard of for three or more years and it is uncertain whether he is living or dead, the court may, upon the application of anyone interested in the land, appoint a guardian to represent the absentee and those who, in the event of his death, would be entitled to his interest; the acts of such guardian are binding on all those represented by him, including minors, as if they were done by the absentee or those persons, and, if proof of absence affords reasonable ground for believing the absentee to be dead, the court may, on the application of the guardian or of anyone interested in the estate represented by him, deal with such estate or the proceeds thereof and order payment of the proceeds or the income thereof to the person who, if the absentee were dead, would be entitled thereto. In

---

[8]Co. Litt. 166b.
[9]*Graham v. Graham* (1858), 6 Gr. 372.
[10]8 & 9 Vict., c. 106, s. 3 (1845).
[11]R.S.O. 1980, c. 90, s. 9.
[12]R.S.N.B. 1973, c. P-19, s. 11.
[13]*Walsh v. Lonsdale* (1882), 21 Ch. D. 9 (C.A.).
§1502.13
[1]R.S.O. 1980, c. 369.

any action or proceeding for partition or sale in lieu of partition, if there is a life tenant who is a party, the court may determine whether the life estate should be sold or exempted from sale, having regard to the interests of all parties; if a sale including the life estate is ordered, all interest of the life tenant passes thereby and no conveyance or release by the life tenant to the purchaser is necessary and the purchaser is freed from all claims respecting the life estate, whether it be in an undivided share or in the whole or any part of the premises sold, and the court may, out of the purchase money, direct payment to the life tenant of a gross sum deemed, on the principles applicable to life annuities, as sufficient satisfaction for the life estate, or may direct payment of an annual sum or of the income as seems just and, for that purpose, order investment of the purchase money or any part thereof as may be necessary. Partition or sale by the court is as effectual for partitioning or conveying the estate or interest of a minor or mentally incompetent person who is a party as of a person competent to act for himself.

In British Columbia, the *Partition of Property Act*[2] provides that all joint tenants, tenants in common, coparceners and other persons interested in land may be compelled to make partition or sale of the land or any part thereof, whether the estate is legal or equitable or equitable only. The court may direct sale if half or more of the persons interested require a sale and distribution of the proceeds instead of division of the property.

The court may direct sale and distribution of the proceeds if it thinks this more beneficial to the parties interested by reason of the nature of the property, the number of parties interested, the disability of some or other circumstance. The court may direct sale and distribution of the proceeds if one party requires it and the others do not undertake to purchase his share and, in the case of the undertaking, the court may order valuation. Provision is made for request for sale or undertaking to purchase on behalf of persons under disability.

In Nova Scotia, the *Partition Act*[3] provides that all persons holding land as joint tenants, coparceners or tenants in common may be compelled to have the land partitioned or to have it sold and the proceeds distributed among the persons entitled. Any one or more of such persons may bring such an action but the action must be by a person having an estate in possession, not by a person entitled only to a remainder or reversion.

The action is maintainable by a tenant or tenants for years against co-tenants as if all were tenants of a freehold, but no tenant for a term of years, unless at least twenty years remain unexpired, may maintain the action against a tenant of the freehold.

Unless it appears to the court that a sale is necessary, the court may appoint three commissioners to partition. Where the land cannot be divided without prejudice to the owners, or where a particular part is of greater value than the share of any party and cannot be divided without prejudice to the owners, the whole or part so incapable of division may be set off to any of the parties who

---

[2]R.S.B.C. 1979, c. 311.
[3]R.S.N.S. 1967, c. 223.

will accept it upon payment by him to one or more of the others of such compensation as the commissioners determine.

The commissioners, instead of setting off the land or part may assign exclusive occupancy of the whole or part, as the case may be, to each of the parties alternately for specified times in proportion to their interests. Each such person is liable to the others for injury to the premises caused by his misconduct to the same extent as a tenant for years is liable to his landlord. Each such person may maintain an action for trespass as if he held under a lease for the term of his exclusive occupancy. Where the land or part cannot be divided or any party, by reason of infancy, insanity or absence from the province, cannot accept such land incapable of division, the court may order sale.

In Prince Edward Island, the *Real Property Act*[4] provides that all persons holding land as joint tenants, tenants in common or coparceners may be compelled to divide it. Any one or more may apply by petition to the court for partition, the petition being maintainable only by one having an estate in possession and not by one only entitled in remainder or reversion; no tenant for a term of years, unless at least twenty years remain unexpired, may petition but, when two or more hold jointly or in common for a term of years, either may have his share divided from the others as if they all had been tenants of the freehold. Where premises cannot be divided without damage to the owners, or a part is of greater value than another party's share and cannot be divided without damage to the owners, the whole or part incapable of division may be set off to a party who will accept it, paying such sums as the court awards to make the partition just and equal. The court, instead of setting off the premises or part, may assign exclusive occupancy of the whole or part to each of the parties alternately for specified times in proportion to their interests. Each of such parties is liable to the others for injury to the property caused by misconduct as a tenant for years is liable to his landlord. Each such person may bring an action for trespass as if he held under a lease for the term of exclusive occupancy.

In New Brunswick partition may be ordered under the Rules of the Supreme Court.[4a] The court may order sale in lieu of partition where the court considers a beneficial partition to be difficult.[4b]

In Newfoundland partition may be ordered under the *Judicature Act*[4c] and, again, sale may be ordered in lieu of partition.[4d]

In the Territories and Saskatchewan the court may order partition pursuant to the *Partition Act* of 1868.[5] Under this Act, and before the enactment of the *Partition and Sale Act*[5a] in Alberta it has been held that this Act gives a *prima*

---

[4]R.S.P.E.I. 1974, c. R-4, Pt. III.

[4a]N.B. 1969, O. 56, rr. 23-31.

[4b]*Ibid.*, r. 27.

[4c]R.S.N. 1970, c. 187, ss. 109-121.

[4d]*Ibid.*, ss. 116-118.

[5]31 & 32 Vict., c. 40 (1868).

[5a]S.A. 1979, c. 59; now *Law of Property Act*, R.S.A. 1980, c. L-8, Part 3.

facie right to partition, apart from the discretion to order sale instead of partition, and apart from the performance of certain acts required as conditions precedent in equity, *e.g.*, as required by the doctrine that he who seeks equity must do equity.[6] The right may be modified or waived by an agreement express or implied to postpone or waive partition or by an agreement as to the duration of the joint tenancy.[7]

In Manitoba it has been held that partition is a matter of right under the *Law of Property Act*[8] and that the court has no discretion to refuse a partition action brought by one co-tenant against another.[9] However, in subsequent cases[10] the court has concluded that it has discretion to refuse partition, and partition will be refused if the granting of the order would be vexatious or oppressive or if the applicant has not met the requirements of equity.[11]

In Ontario the court has a discretion to grant or refuse partition or sale of lands jointly owned.[12] The discretion will be exercised on the following principles: (1) A person who holds lands as a joint tenant, tenant in common or coparcener has a *prima facie* right to partition or sale of them at any time; (2) there is a corresponding obligation on joint tenants (and others) to permit partition or sale, and (3) the court should compel such partition or sale if no sufficient reason appears why such an order should not be made.[13] It has been held that if the application is vexatious or oppressive, sufficient reason is shown to refuse the order.[14] It has been held that the court can only refuse the order when the application is vexatious or oppressive.[15] Although the words "vexatious" and "oppressive" are very elastic, an attempt to fit subsequent decisions into these categories would be an exercise in sophistry. There is no doubt that subsequent cases referred to hereafter have greatly expanded the court's discretion. These decisions, arising in the context of matrimonial difficulties, are not uniform[16] and must be read in light of subsequent statutory changes.[17]

---

[6]*Clarke v. Clarke* (1974), 48 D.L.R. (3d) 707, [1974] 5 W.W.R. 274 (Alta. S.C. App. Div.).

[7]*Wilkstrand v. Cavanaugh*, [1936] 2 W.W.R. 69 (Alta. S.C. App. Div.), affg [1936] 1 W.W.R. 113 (S.C.T.D.). See also *Thomas v. Thomas* (1962), 29 D.L.R. (2d) 576, 36 W.W.R. 23 (Sask. C.A.); *Wagner v. Wagner* (1970), 73 W.W.R. 474 (Alta. S.C.).

[8]R.S.M. 1954, c. 138; now R.S.M. 1970, c. L90.

[9]*Szmando v. Szmando*, [1940] 1 D.L.R. 222, [1940] 1 W.W.R. 21 (Man. K.B.).

[10]*Steele v. Steele* (1960), 67 Man. R. 270 (Q.B.); *Shwabiuk v. Shwabiuk* (1965), 51 W.W.R. 549 (Man. Q.B.); *Fetterly v. Fetterly* (1965), 54 D.L.R. (2d) 435, 54 W.W.R. 218 (Man. Q.B.).

[11]*Steele v. Steele, supra*, footnote 10; *Shwabiuk v. Shwabiuk, supra*, footnote 10; *Fetterly v. Fetterly, supra*, footnote 10.

[12]*Re Hutcheson and Hutcheson*, [1950] O.R. 265, [1950] 2 D.L.R. 751 (C.A.); *Davis v. Davis*, [1954] O.R. 23, [1954] 1 D.L.R. 827 (C.A.).

[13]*Davis v. Davis, supra*, footnote 12.

[14]*Klakow v. Klakow* (1972), 7 R.F.L. 349 (H.C.J.); *Czarnick v. Zagora* (1972), 8 R.F.L. 259 (Ont. H.C.J.).

[15]*Re Roblin & Roblin*, [1960] O.R. 157 (H.C.J.).

[16]*Carton v. Carton* (1975), 21 R.F.L. 366 (Ont. S.C.).

[17]As for example, the *Family Law Reform Act*, S.O. 1978, c. 2.

In British Columbia the court has discretion to refuse partition.[18] Although there is a *prima facie* right to partition, partition will be refused if the application is vexatious, malicious, or oppressive.[19] The word "oppressive" has been interpreted as meaning "economic oppression" as opposed to inconvenience or even hardship in some cases.[20] However, other decisions have adopted a more liberal interpretation so as to include within it a shirking of family responsibilities.[21] In other instances the court has balanced equities to see if a sale would be oppressive in an objective sense,[22] and most recently has gone so far as to conclude that the earlier limited discretion has been significantly expanded so as to now include the test of relative hardship.[23]

As mentioned earlier, the court in Ontario has accepted a broader discretion when deciding whether to order partition. Although courts in other Canadian jurisdictions have also been willing to exercise more discretion in this area,[24] the issue appears to have come before the courts more often in Ontario and hence, reference to the Ontario cases may perhaps be more illustrative of any developing trend.[25] Again, it should be pointed out that the extension of discretion has come about in the context of matrimonial property held jointly by spouses and must be read subject to recent statutory changes. Moreover, an attempt to extend the principles enunciated in the decisions beyond the matrimonial context must be made with some caution.

When an attempt is made to set the parameters of the court's discretion a clear distinction must be made between those cases where one of the joint tenants is a deserted spouse and where there is no desertion. In *Re Maskewycz and Maskewycz*,[26] the Ontario Court of Appeal concluded that a deserted husband has a right to remain in possession of the matrimonial home, a right corresponding to the right of a deserted wife[27] and that where the right of a deserted spouse to remain in the home is in issue, a partition order will not be made on an application under the *Partition Act* unless and until the court

---

18*Lothrop v. Kline* (1957), 21 W.W.R. 333 (B.C.S.C.).

19*Korolew v. Korolew* (1972), 7 R.F.L. 162 (B.C.S.C.); *Reitsma v. Reitsma*, [1975] 3 W.W.R. 281, 17 R.F.L. 292 (B.C.S.C.).

20*Reitsma v. Reitsma, supra,* footnote 19; *Kaplan v. Kaplan* (1974), 15 R.F.L. 239 (B.C.S.C.); *Van Engel v. Van Engel* (1973), 11 R.F.L. 303 (B.C.S.C.).

21*Bergen v. Bergen* (1969), 68 W.W.R. 196 (B.C.S.C.).

22*Meadows v. Meadows* (1974), 17 R.F.L. 36 (B.C.S.C.).

23*Fernandes v. Fernandes* (1975), 65 D.L.R. (3d) 684, [1976] 3 W.W.R. 510 (B.C.S.C.).

24See for example, *Re Kornacki and Kornacki* (1975), 58 D.L.R. (3d) 159, 21 R.F.L. 400 (Alta. S.C. App. Div.); *Re Kronenberger and Kronenberger* (1977), 77 D.L.R. (3d) 571, 3 Alta. L.R. (2d) 121 (S.C.T.D.); *Melvin v. Melvin* (1975), 58 D.L.R. (3d) 98, 23 R.F.L. 19 (S.C. App. Div.); *Fernandes v. Fernandes, supra,* footnote 23.

25See particularly the review of Ontario decisions in *Melvin v. Melvin, supra,* footnote 24. It must be remembered that there is still a *prima facie* right to partition. See *Re Bisson et al. and Luciani et al.* (1982), 37 O.R. (2d) 257, 136 D.L.R. (3d) 287 (H.C.J.).

26(1973), 2 O.R. (2d) 713, 44 D.L.R. (3d) 180 (C.A.). This decision exhaustively reviews the law relating to matrimonial property prior to the passing of the *Family Law Reform Act*, S.O. 1978, c. 2.

27*Re Jollow and Jollow*, [1954] O.R. 895, [1955] 1 D.L.R. 601 (C.A.). See also *Re Hearty and Hearty*, [1970] 2 O.R. 344, 10 D.L.R. (3d) 732 (H.C.J.).

has decided upon the matters appropriate for consideration under section 12 of the *Married Women's Property Act*.[28]

The question of desertion is a question of fact that must be determined before an order of partition or sale will be made.[29] It has been held that desertion can occur even where both spouses continue to reside in the same house.[30] The right of the deserted spouse to remain in possession of the matrimonial home is a personal right that flows from the marriage. The right does not constitute an interest in the premises and comes to an end once a divorce decree is made absolute,[31] or where the obligation of support has come to an end because of circumstances disentitling the spouse to alimony.[32]

In Ontario the issue of the deserted spouse to remain in the matrimonial home has been rendered academic by the passing of the *Family Law Reform Act*.[33] Both husband and wife are given an equal right to possession that does not depend upon desertion and which is not affected by ownership by one or other, or indeed both of the spouses. Section 40 of the Act reads:

> 40(1) A spouse is equally entitled to any right of possession of the other spouse in a matrimonial home.
>
> (2) Subject to an order of the court under this or any other Act, and subject to a separation agreement that provides otherwise, a right of a spouse to possession by virtue of subsection (1) ceases upon the spouse ceasing to be a spouse.

However, the reasoning in those decisions rendered by the Ontario courts prior to the passing of the Act cannot be disregarded as it may have persuasive effect in other jurisdictions not having a similar statute.

Apart from desertion, it had been held as late as 1973 that on an application for partition or sale the court was bound to grant the order if the application was neither vexatious nor oppressive and if the applicant came to the court with clean hands.[34] However, several subsequent cases and even prior decisions clearly indicate that the court's discretion is somewhat wider. Serious hardship on the spouse, and particularly on the children of the marriage, which would result from partition has been accepted as a legitimate ground for refusal of the order.[35] It is incumbent upon the party resisting partition to establish serious hardship,[36] and the court will consider not only hardship to the one

---

[28]R.S.O. 1970, c. 262, rep. 1978, c. 2, s. 82; *Rush v. Rush* (1960), 24 D.L.R. (2d) 248 (Ont. C.A.). See also, *Green v. Green* (1971), 5 R.F.L. 361 (Ont. S.C.).

[29]*Re Cates and Cates*, [1968] 2 O.R. 447 (C.A.).

[30]*Knight v. Knight* (1975), 20 R.F.L. 381 (C.A.).

[31]*Re Perkins and Perkins*, [1973] 1 O.R. 598, 31 D.L.R. (3d) 694 (H.C.J.).

[32]*Fenik v. Fenik* (1974), 16 R.F.L. 14 (Ont. S.C.).

[33]S.O. 1978, c. 2, now R.S.O. 1980, c. 152. The effect of this statute on the respective rights of both spouses to real property *inter se* and vis-à-vis third parties is dealt with in detail in ch. 16, "Matrimonial Property".

[34]*Re Perkins and Perkins, supra*, footnote 31.

[35]*McFadden v. McFadden* (1972), 5 R.F.L. 299 (Ont. Co. Ct.); *Verzin v. Verzin* (1974), 16 R.F.L. 94 (Ont. H.C.J.); *Lindenblatt v. Lindenblatt* (1974), 4 O.R. (2d) 534, 48 D.L.R. (3d) 494 (H.C.J.); *MacDonald v. MacDonald* (1973), 13 R.F.L. 248 (Ont. C.A.).

[36]*Cmajdalka v. Cmajdalka* (1973), 11 R.F.L. 302 (Ont. C.A.).

side if partition is granted but also hardship to the other if it is refused.[37] The test of relative hardship has been applied not only as between spouses but also as between one spouse and creditors of the other.[38] Estoppel has also been used as an effective defence to an application for partition.[39]

Again, it should be remembered that, in Ontario, the *Family Law Reform Act*[40] has exhaustive provisions relating to the distribution of family assets on marriage breakdown and that these provisions apparently supersede any *prima facie* right to partition.

It is not possible to deal with the many cases that have arisen from time to time in regard to various fine points under the provisions of provincial rules of practice and statutes relating to partition. The task of determining which of them have continued application must be left to the readers in each province in the light of present rules. Several references, however, appear to be appropriate.

If only one of several co-tenants desires partition, a part may be allocated to such co-tenant and the residue held as before by the others jointly or in common.[41]

Four distinct parcels of land in different townships belonging to eighteen persons are not indivisible by nature like a home, mill or other property that cannot in its nature be divided.[42]

Although it was held that a life tenant is entitled to a partition and that, where there is a right to partition, there may be a right to a sale as the court may determine,[43] it was subsequently held that a sole life tenant had no status under the *Partition Act* of 1887 to apply for a sale of the estate and that, in the nature of things, no partition is possible as regards the life tenancy.[44]

The court will not decree the partition of lands, the title to which is vested in the Crown nor will it decree the sale of the lands at the instance of the representatives of the deceased locatee,[45] but, where a locatee of Crown lands was an absentee for over seven years so as to be presumed to be dead and, of his four children, one son and a daughter had occupied the property exclusively for fourteen years so as to obtain possessory title against the other two children, and where the son in possession had made improvements, it was held that the *Statute of Limitations* applied because the rights involved were merely private rights not affecting the pleasure or sovereignty of the Crown so that declaratory relief might be given which would work practically the same

---

[37]*Re MacDonald and MacDonald* (1976), 14 O.R. (2d) 249, 73 D.L.R. (3d) 341 (H.C.J.).

[38]*Re Yale and MacMaster* (1974), 3 O.R. (2d) 547, 46 D.L.R. (3d) 167 (H.C.J.).

[39]*Ibid.*

[40]R.S.O. 1980, c. 152. The provisions of the Act generally referred to above are dealt with in detail in ch. 16, "Matrimonial Property".

[41]*Devereux v. Kearns* (1886), 11 P.R. (Ont.) 452.

[42]*Re Dennie Applying for Partition* (1852), 10 U.C.Q.B. 104.

[43]*Lalor v. Lalor* (1883), 9 P.R. (Ont.) 455 (Ch. Div.).

[44]*Fisken v. Ife* (1897), 28 O.R. 595 (Div. Ct.).

[45]*Abell v. Weir* (1877), 24 Gr. 464.

as a partition, subject to the Crown being willing to act upon the judgment of the court and that the Crown in making partition should recognize the son's rights to improvements.[46]

An applicant for partition must be a person having a partitioning interest in land in the sense of being entitled to possession of his share, so that a person entitled to a legacy charged on land has no status to demand partition.[47] Partition will not be ordered until any honest dispute as to ownership is resolved.[48]

Although partition of an estate which is subject to a mortgage may be directed, if one of several co-tenants has mortgaged his undivided share, the mortgagee is a necessary party to partition proceedings in order to find the legal estate.[49]

A purchaser from a joint tenant is entitled *prima facie* to partition of the resulting tenancy in common. It has been held that if the purchaser has acted in good faith, without malice, inconvenience to the other co-tenant is not a sufficient ground to refuse partition.[50]

Sale as an alternative to partition will only be ordered where it is apparent that partition would not be advantageous to both parties.[51]

The general rule in accounting is that a joint tenant, unless ousted by his co-tenant, cannot sue him for use and occupation but, if the joint tenancy is terminated by court order for partition or sale, the court may make all allowances and should give such directions as will give complete equity to the parties.[52] What is equitable depends on the circumstances of each case. If the occupying tenant claims for upkeep and repairs, the court, as a term of allowing the claim, usually requires him to submit to an allowance for use and occupation. If one tenant has made improvements which increased the selling value, the other tenant cannot take advantage of the increase without submitting to an allowance for the improvements and, if one tenant paid more than his share of encumbrances, he is entitled to an allowance of the excess.[53] Thus, in an accounting on a partition application, the husband's share was turned over to his wife to satisfy maintenance arrears.[54] However, there is no

---

[46]*Pride v. Rodger* (1895), 27 O.R. 320 (H.C.J.).

[47]*Re Fidler and Seaman*, [1948] O.W.N. 454, [1948] 2 D.L.R. 771 (H.C.J.); *Morrison v. Morrison* (1917), 39 O.L.R. 163, 34 D.L.R. 677 (S.C. App. Div.).

[48]*Blackhall v. Jardine*, [1958] O.W.N. 457 (C.A.); *Noel v. Noel* (1903), 2 O.W.R. 628.

[49]*McDougall v. McDougall* (1868), 14 Gr. 267.

[50]*McGeer v. Green and Westminster Mortgage Corp. Ltd.* (1960), 22 D.L.R. (2d) 775 (B.C.S.C.).

[51]*Cook v. Johnston*, [1970] 2 O.R. 1 (H.C.J.).

[52]*Mastron v. Cotton* (1925), 58 O.L.R. 251, [1926] 1 D.L.R. 767 (S.C. App. Div.); *Shore v. Shore* (1975), 63 D.L.R. (3d) 354, [1976] W.W.D. 19 (B.C.S.C.). It is not necessary that there be an ouster when both joint tenants are spouses. The court has jurisdiction to charge occupation rent under the provisions of the *Family Law Reform Act*, R.S.O. 1980, c. 152. See *Diotallevi v. Diotallevi* (1982), 37 O.R. (2d) 106, 134 D.L.R. (3d) 477 (H.C.J.).

[53]*Mastron v. Cotton, supra*, footnote 52.

[54]*Re Crystal and Crystal* (1972), 32 D.L.R. (3d) 116, [1973] 1 W.W.R. 504 (Man. Q.B.), affd 38 D.L.R. (3d) 300, [1973] 5 W.W.R. 481 (Man. C.A.).

jurisdiction in the court to order the proceeds due one spouse to be paid into court to secure a future potential corollary relief order on divorce.[55] Moreover, there is no jurisdiction on an accounting, after the order of partition, to deny the interest of one of the joint tenants. The matter becomes *res judicata* after the partition order.[56]

When an account is taken, it is necessary to bear in mind the possibility of gift together with both the presumption of resulting trust and presumption of advancement where applicable. Thus, where the husband and wife purchased a house as joint tenants and the husband freely made subsequent mortgage payments, the subsequent payments were treated as gifts from him to her and were not to be accounted for.[57] Similarly, where a wife discharged a mortgage on property held jointly with her husband, with the intention that the money advanced was to benefit both, the mortgage payment was not included in the accounting.[58]

It is not possible in a book of this nature to discuss in detail the debit and credit items to be brought into account.[59] However, it should be mentioned that in Alberta it has been decided that where one joint tenant borrows money to purchase the property, he is entitled to repayment out of the proceeds of the sale of the property in priority to the other joint tenant.[60]

Although the general rule is that one joint tenant will not be restrained from committing waste at the instance of a co-tenant, the rule is different if a bill for partition of the estate has been filed.[61]

1503. TENANCY IN COMMON

The essential difference between a tenancy in common and a joint tenancy is that, in a tenancy in common, there is only one necessary unity — the unity of possession — it being unnecessary that there be unity of title, unity of interest or unity of time of vesting of the estates.[1] The occupation of tenants in common is undivided and none can claim a separate part except by partition.[2] "Only this property is common to both, namely, that their occupation is undivided, and neither of them knoweth his part in several."[3] It has been said:

> This tenancy happens, therefore, where there is a unity of possession merely, but perhaps an entire disunion of interest, of title, and of time. For if there be two tenants in common of lands, one may hold his part in fee-simple, the other in tail, or for

---

[55]*Hind v. Hind* (1975), 20 R.F.L. 331 (H.C.J.).

[56]*Davis v. Davis*, [1959] O.W.N. 41 (H.C.J.).

[57]*Andrews v. Andrews* (1969), 7 D.L.R. (3d) 744 (B.C.S.C.).

[58]*Morrison v. Guaranty Trust Co. of Canada*, [1972] 3 O.R. 448, 28 D.L.R. (3d) 458 (H.C.J.).

[59]For such a discussion, see *Spatafora v. Spatafora*, [1956] O.W.N. 628 (H.C.J.).

[60]*Brewin v. Ferguson* (1982), 134 D.L.R. (3d) 538 (Alta. Q.B.).

[61]*Lassert v. Salyerds* (1870), 17 Gr. 109.

§1503

[1]Littleton's Tenures, s. 292; Co. Litt. 189a; 2 Bl. Comm. 191.

[2]2 Bl. Comm. 194.

[3]Co. Litt. 189a.

life; so that there is no necessary unity of interest; one may hold by descent, the other by purchase; or the one by purchase from A., the other by purchase from B.; so that there is no unity of title; one's estate may have been vested fifty years, the other's but yesterday; so there is no unity of time. The only unity there is, is that of possession; and for this Littleton gives the true reason, because no man can certainly tell which part is his own; otherwise even this would be soon destroyed.[4]

A tenancy in common is created if the parties acquire the property without an express limitation that they are to take as joint tenants; by a limitation which vests the estates at different times; by severance of a joint tenancy without partition, or by acquiring title by possession.

There is no right of survivorship between tenants in common, the share of each passing according to its own limitation,[5] except where the right of survivorship is given expressly in the limitation.

1503.1 Tenancy in Common by Express Limitations

At common law there were only two ways of creating a tenancy in common by conveyance — either by limiting the estate to grantees expressly as tenants in common or by limiting to each grantee an undivided part.[1]

As discussed earlier,[2] the presumption at common law, when no express limitation was apparent, was in favour of joint tenancy but this presumption has been reversed by statute. Thus, the earlier cases which were concerned with a search to determine if the words used created a tenancy in common out of what would otherwise have been a joint tenancy are of little relevance, except in so far as those words which were held to have created a tenancy in common are illustrative of words that will not be sufficient to create a joint tenancy today under the reversed statutory presumption.

It has been held that the words "equally to be divided" in a deed to uses created a tenancy in common.[3]

In a will, words which signify that the devisees are to take divided rather than undivided interests create a tenancy in common. This may be because the property is to be held by them equally, or in parts, or by them and their respective heirs. Thus, a tenancy in common is created where, under the directions of the will, the property given to donees is "to be divided"[4] or "to be equally divided",[5] or "to be distributed in joint and equal proportions",[6] or that the donees are to "participate".[7] Similarly, the donees are tenants in

---

[4]Armour, *Real Property*, at p. 281.
[5]2 Bl. Comm. 194.

§1503.1
[1]*Stringer v. Philipps* (1730), 1 Eq. Ca. Abr. 291, 21 E.R. 1053.
[2]See §1102, *supra*, and cases cited therein.
[3]*Goodtitle d. Hood v. Stokes* (1753), 1 Wils. K.B. 341, 95 E.R. 651.
[4]*Ackerman v. Burrows* (1814), 3 V. & B. 54, 35 E.R. 400.
[5]*Davis v. Bennett* (1862), 4 De G. F. & J. 327, 45 E.R. 1209.
[6]*Ettricke v. Ettricke* (1767), Amb. 656, 27 E.R. 426.
[7]*Robertson v. Fraser* (1871), L.R. 6 Ch. 696.

common if the gift is to them "equally"[8] or "share and share alike",[9] or in "equal shares and proportions"[10] or "in moieties".[11] There is a tenancy in common if the gift to the donees is "amongst" them,[12] or "between" them,[13] or "between" them as a class,[14] or is given to them "respectively",[15] or is given to "each",[16] or to each "and their respective heirs".[17]

In general the effect of the language of a will is controlled by the apparent intent of the testator so that, wherever the words amount to a severance or distribution of the estate or indicate an intent to divide the property, they abrogate the idea of a joint tenancy and create a tenancy in common. Therefore, words otherwise indicating a joint tenancy may be controlled by other words indicating a tenancy in common: "pay, assign, and divide" as joint tenants conferred a tenancy in common;[18] "to be held jointly or divided equally at their pleasure" conferred a tenancy in common.[19]

On the other hand, words indicating a tenancy in common may be controlled by other words indicating the intent to be a joint tenancy.[20]

The right of survivorship is not the only incident that distinguishes a joint tenancy from a tenancy in common, so a tenancy in common may be created by will with the express right of survivorship between the tenants in common.[21] A tenancy in common with right of survivorship is a perfectly different and distinct estate from a joint tenancy which has different incidents and may be affected in a different manner. Thus, it may be severed in the one case but not in the other.[22]

A power to trustees to apply all or part of the income of property to which infants are entitled or presumptively entitled under a will to the maintenance or advancement of the infants indicates that a tenancy in common was intended.[23]

---

[8]*Denn d. Gaskin v. Gaskin* (1777), 2 Cowp. 657, 98 E.R. 1292.

[9]*Perry v. Woods* (1796), 3 Ves. Jun. 204, 30 E.R. 970.

[10]*Payne v. Webb* (1874), L.R. 19 Eq. 26.

[11]*Stewart v. Garnett* (1830), 3 Sim. 398, 57 E.R. 1047.

[12]*Richardson v. Richardson* (1845), 14 Sim. 526, 60 E.R. 462.

[13]*Lashbrook v. Cock* (1816), 2 Mer. 70, 35 E.R. 867.

[14]*Attorney-General v. Fletcher* (1871), L.R. 13 Eq. 128.

[15]*Re Moore's Settlement Trusts* (1862), 10 W.R. 315.

[16]*Hatton v. Finch* (1841), 4 Beav. 186, 49 E.R. 310.

[17]*Re Atkinson*; *Wilson v. Atkinson*, [1892] 3 Ch. 52.

[18]*Booth v. Alington* (1857), 27 L.J. Ch. 117.

[19]*Oakley v. Wood* (1867), 37 L.J. Ch. 28.

[20]*Armstrong v. Eldridge* (1791), 3 Bro. C.C. 215, 29 E.R. 497; *Cranswick v. Pearson*; *Pearson v. Cranswick* (1862), 31 Beav. 624, 54 E.R. 1281; *Begley v. Cook* (1856), 3 Drewry 662, 61 E.R. 1056.

[21]*Haddelsey v. Adams* (1856), 22 Beav. 266, 52 E.R. 1110; *Doe d. Borwell v. Abey* (1813), 1 M. & S. 428, 105 E.R. 160.

[22]*Haddelsey v. Adams, supra,* footnote 21.

[23]*Re Ward*; *Partridge v. Hoare-Ward*, [1920] 1 Ch. 334; *Bennett v. Houldsworth* (1911), 104 L.T. 304 (Ch.).

1503.2　Limitations Causing Vesting at Different Times

At common law if there is a grant or devise to two persons who cannot marry and the heirs of their bodies, they are joint tenants for life but, since the interests of the heirs vest at different times, the heirs take as tenants in common.[1] Thus, a devise to A and B and their "respective heirs" gives A and B a joint tenancy for life with several inheritances in fee simple[2] and similarly, where the residue was given to three nephews and their respective heirs, executors, administrators and assigns, the nephews were joint tenants for their lives and the life of the survivor with several remainders as tenants in common in fee simple.[3] Again, where there was a devise to grandchildren, their heirs male and the heirs male of the survivor or survivors of them forever, it was held this gave the grandchildren joint tenancies for life, with several inheritances in tail and cross-remainders in tail.[4]

Where no prior estate is limited and a grant is directly to the heirs of two living persons, they are regarded as having contingent remainders, or tenants in common, as their estates will vest at different times.[5]

1503.3　Tenancy in Common by Severance of Joint Tenancy

A tenancy in common arises when a joint tenancy or a tenancy in coparcenary is severed without partition of the property.[1]

1503.4　Tenancy in Common Arising out of Possessory Title

As indicated earlier,[1] at common law, if two or more persons having no title entered into possession of property in such circumstances as to give them a possessory title under the *Statute of Limitations*, they took as joint tenants.

1503.5　Incidents of Tenancy in Common

In matters other than undivided possession, the incidents of a tenancy in common are different from those of a joint tenancy. Tenants in common, not having unity of title, have several freeholds, while joint tenants and coparceners

---

§1503.2
[1]Littleton's Tenures, s. 283; 2 Bl. Comm. 192; *Hales v. Risley* (1673), Pollex 369 at p. 373, 86 E.R. 578; *Cook v. Cook* (1706), 2 Vern. 545, 23 E.R. 952; *Doe d. Littlewood v. Green* (1838), 4 M. & W. 229, 150 E.R. 1414.
[2]*Re Tiverton Market Act; Ex p. Tanner* (1855), 20 Beav. 374, 52 E.R. 647.
[3]*Re Atkinson; Wilson v. Atkinson*, [1892] 3 Ch. 52.
[4]*Tufnell v. Borrell* (1875), L.R. 20 Eq. 194.
[5]*Justice Windham's Case* (1589), 5 Co. Rep. 7 a, 77 E.R. 58.
§1503.3
[1]Littleton's Tenures, s. 292. As to such severance, see §1502.11, *supra*.
§1503.4
[1]See §1502, *supra*.

have only one.[1] Not having unity of interest, tenants in common may hold estates of unequal duration and in unequal shares which may be due to the original limitations or because other shares subsequently become vested somehow in one of the tenants in common, as each share is a separate freehold and may be the subject of a separate limitation.[2] Since they have separate interests, there is no right of survivorship between tenants in common, each share passing according to its own limitation,[3] although, as indicated earlier,[4] a tenancy in common with an express right of survivorship may be created by will.

1503.6 Leases by Tenants in Common

At common law, there is a subtle distinction between leases by joint tenants and leases by tenants in common. As joint tenants had the same interest in undivided shares, when they joined in a lease each demised his own share.[1] On the other hand, as tenants in common have no unity of interest, it was held that they could not make a joint lease,[2] and, on a joint lease, it was held that ejectment proceedings could not be maintained against the lessee for breach of covenant.[3] Nevertheless, it appears to be established that a lease by tenants in common, though joint in its terms, operates as a separate demise by each tenant in common of his undivided share[4] and a confirmation by each of his co-tenants, and the covenants may be construed as joint or several in respect of the covenantees according to their interest in the land apparent on the face of the document.[5]

Where two tenants in common make a joint lease reserving an entire rent, they may join in an action to recover it but, if the rent is reserved separately to each, each must bring a separate action to recover it. Where a lease reserving a rent was made by two tenants in common, rent was paid for a time to both of them and then one gave notice to the lessee to pay half of the rent to each tenant in common, it was held that it was a question of fact whether the parties

---

§1503.5
[1]Co. Litt. 189a.
[2]Challis, *Law of Real Property*, p. 370.
[3]2 Bl. Comm. 194.
[4]See §1503.1, *supra*.

§1503.6
[1]*Doe d. Aslin v. Summersett* (1830), 1 B. & Ad. 135, 109 E.R. 738, *per* Lord Tenterden, C.J.
[2]*Heatherley d. Worthington and Tunnadine v. Weston* (1764), 2 Wils. K.B. 232, 95 E.R. 783; *Doe d. McNab v. Sieker* (1837), 5 U.C.Q.B. (O.S.) 323.
[3]*Doe d. Campbell v. Hamilton* (1849), 13 Q.B. 977, 116 E.R. 1536; *Mantle v. Wollington* (1607), Cro. Jac. 166, 79 E.R. 145.
[4]*Burne v. Cambridge* (1836), 1 M. & Rob. 539, 174 E.R. 185.
[5]*Thompson v. Hakewill* (1865), 19 C.B. (N.S.) 713, 144 E.R. 966, *per* Byles, J.; *Gyles v. Kempe* (1677), 1 Freeman 235, 89 E.R. 168; *Craddock v. Jones* (1611), Brownl. & Golds. 134, 123 E.R. 712.

meant to make a new contract with a separate reservation of rent to each or a continuation of the former reservation of rent.[6]

If two tenants in common lease the property to a tenant, the latter cannot pay the whole rent to one tenant in common after the other has given him notice not to do so, and if he does so nevertheless, the other can distrain for his share.[7] It has been held that each tenant in common has a right to receive his share of rent, and payment of the whole rent to one, after notice of the joint interest, is not a good payment to the other or others who may distrain for his or their share.[8]

Where one of two tenants in common agreed to grant a lease of the mines under the land, it was held that the lessee was entitled to a decree of specific performance and for partition of the estate.[9] Where there were three tenants in common of land containing coal, it was held that two of them were entitled to work the coal by themselves or by a lessee, provided that they took no more than their proper share.[10]

1503.7 Mutual Rights of Tenants in Common

In matters relating to the unity of possession, the incidents of a tenancy in common are similar to those of a joint tenancy. Like joint tenants, they hold *per mie et per tout*,[1] that is, they hold the whole and nothing separately, their occupation being undivided.

1503.8 No Fiduciary Relation Between Tenants in Common

There is no fiduciary relation between tenants in common so as to make them subject to the disabilities and liabilities of that relation.[1]

1503.9 Accounting Between Tenants in Common

At common law there could be no action of account by one tenant in common against another who had occupied the whole property unless he had appointed the latter as his bailiff so as to make him liable to account in that capacity. In equity, however, a tenant in common is liable to account in an

---

[6]*Powis and Powis v. Smith* (1822), 2 B. Ald. 850, 106 E.R. 1402.

[7]*Harrison v. Barnby* (1793), 5 T.R. 246, 101 E.R. 138.

[8]*Bradburne v. Shanly* (1859), 7 Gr. 569.

[9]*Heaton v. Dearden* (1852), 16 Beav. 147, 51 E.R. 733.

[10]*Job v. Potton* (1875), L.R. 20 Eq. 84.

§1503.7

[1]*Gunn v. Burgess* (1884), 5 O.R. 685 (H.C.J.), at p. 688; *Lasby v. Crewson* (1891), 21 O.R. 255 (H.C.J.), at p. 260.

§1503.8

[1]*Kennedy v. De Trafford, Stourton and Dodson*, [1897] A.C. 180 (H.L.), and see §1105, *supra*.

action by the others and, by statute, a tenant in common who receives more than his share is made liable to account to co-tenants.[1]

Mere occupation of the property by one of several tenants in common, if unaccompanied by exclusion of the other co-tenants, does not make him liable to them for rent.[2]

As each tenant in common is entitled to enter upon the whole property, one tenant in common is not liable to another for occupation rent but, if his acts amount to an exclusion of the other, the court may appoint a receiver and, if he receives rents, an account will be ordered. He is not entitled to repayment in regard to repairs and improvements in the property, however, unless he submits to an occupation rent and accounts for the profits he has received.[3]

One tenant in common who expends moneys in ordinary repairs has no right of action against a co-tenant for contribution.[4] One tenant in common who has leased his interest to his co-tenant may recover from the latter use and occupation rent if the latter remains in occupation as tenant by sufferance after the expiration of the lease.[5]

A tenant in common in sole occupation is not entitled to be repaid for repairs and improvements unless he is charged an occupation rent[6] and similarly where he has been in occupation of part of the property[7] although, whether or not he is charged with an occupation rent, he is entitled to an inquiry as to expenditures properly made in permanent improvements to the property during co-ownership and the inquiry should be reciprocal.[8] If he is charged with occupation rent, he is entitled to contribution from his co-tenant for taxes and water rates paid by him.[9]

A tenant in common who holds possession of, manages and receives the rent of the common property which is subject to an encumbrance, is entitled when called to account by his co-tenant, to be allowed for advances properly and reasonably made by him for repairs, improvements and payments of principal and interest on the encumbrances, with interest from the time the advances are made. "There is a broad distinction between the cases of a co-tenant in actual sole occupation of the premises and one in receipt of the whole rents and profits."[10]

No tenant in common is entitled to execute repairs or improvements upon the property held in common, so long as it is enjoyed in common, and then

---

§1503.9
[1]See §1502.4, *supra*.
[2]*M'Mahon v. Burchell* (1846), 2 Ph. 127, 41 E.R. 889; *Griffies v. Griffies* (1863), 8 L.T. 758. See also *Bates v. Martin* (1866), 12 Gr. 490.
[3]*Rice v. George* (1873), 20 Gr. 221.
[4]*Leigh v. Dickeson* (1884), 15 Q.B.D. 60 (C.A.).
[5]*Ibid.*
[6]*Rice v. George, supra,* footnote 3.
[7]*Teasdale v. Sanderson* (1864), 33 Beav. 534, 55 E.R. 476.
[8]*Kenrick v. Mountsteven* (1899), 48 W.R. 141 (Ch.).
[9]*Wuychik v. Majewski* (1920), 19 O.W.N. 207 (H.C.).
[10]*Re Curry; Curry v. Curry* (1898), 25 O.A.R. 267, *per* Moss, J.A., at p. 286.

to charge his co-tenant with the cost, but, in a suit for partition, it is usual to have an inquiry as to those expenses of which nothing could be recovered so long as the parties enjoyed their property in common. When it is decided to put an end to that state of things, it is then necessary to consider what was expended on improvements or repairs: the property has been increased in value by the improvements and repairs; whether the property is divided or is sold by the decree of the court, one party cannot take the increase in value without making allowance for what has been expended in order to obtain that increased value. In fact, the execution of the repairs and improvements is adopted and sanctioned by accepting the increased value.[11]

In a partition action, however, the right of a tenant in common to be paid for improvements made by him is restricted to those made by him after his tenancy in common commenced. Thus, where a tenant in common in remainder, by an agreement with the life tenant, went into possession and expended large sums on improvements during the life tenancy at the life tenant's request, it was held that he was not entitled in a partition action to the value of those improvements.[12]

In a partition action in a court of equity, an allowance for the value of improvements was always made.[13]

A tenant in common who takes proceedings for partition and an account from his co-tenant is entitled to such account if he shows that the co-tenant received a greater share from the estate than that to which he was entitled. Thus, where one of several tenants in common had been in sole possession of a plaster bed and sold portions of the plaster, an account was ordered as to his receipts therefrom.[14]

A special note should be made of possession between parent and child. Where parent and child are tenants in common, usually possession of the parent is that of the child, but the presumption that the parent's possession was as bailiff or agent of the child's share is rebuttable. The relation of principal and agent may be dissolved by various circumstances but the attainment of majority by the child is not, in itself, sufficient to rebut the presumption referred to if there is no break in possession.[15]

1503.10 Trespass and Waste by Tenants in Common

Since each tenant in common has an equal right of entry on every part of the property, one cannot bring an action against the other for trespass but, if

---

[11]*Lasby v. Crewson* (1891), 21 O.R. 255 (H.C.J.), quoting Cotton, L.J., in *Leigh v. Dickeson* (1884), 15 Q.B.D. 60 (C.A.).

[12]*Ibid.*

[13]*Handley v. Archibald* (1899), 30 S.C.R. 130 at p. 141; *Griffies v. Griffies* (1863), 8 L.T. 758.

[14]*Curtis v. Coleman* (1875), 22 Gr. 561; see also §1502.13, *supra.*

[15]*Fry and Moore v. Speare* (1916), 36 O.L.R. 301, 30 D.L.R. 723 (S.C. App. Div.).

one is ousted or denied the right of entry, he may take ejectment proceedings.[1] A demand of possession by one tenant in common and a refusal by the other, stating that he claimed the whole, is evidence of an ouster.[2]

The court will not restrict a tenant in common in the legitimate enjoyment of the estate because an undivided occupation is of the very essence of a tenancy in common and to interfere with that right would be to deny an essential quality of title. Therefore, a tenant in common is not entitled to an injunction where his co-tenant is exercising his rights in a legitimate manner. If he desires relief, he must proceed by partition. Equitable waste will not be restrained but, if a tenant in common proceeds to destroy the common property, he will be restrained by injunction.[3] It has been said that, "It is clear that a tenant in common has not an *unlimited* power to do as he will with the estate; for though the court is slow to interfere between tenants in common, yet where one commits any act amounting to *destruction*, he will be restrained", and hence, the digging of earth for bricks was restrained.[4]

1503.11 Actions Relating to Tenants in Common

Unlike joint tenants, since the titles of tenants in common are not joint but several, it is not necessary that all join or be joined in an action except where some entirety is to be recovered. Where a stranger enters upon the land, a tenant in common who sues in ejectment for possession can recover from him, however, only the undivided share to which he is entitled and not the whole.[1] If a tenant in common separately demises his own portion, ejectment proceedings should be by him but, if all the tenants in common claim upon a joint right of re-entry reserved to them, they ought to join.[2] It has been held that tenants in common may join in an action of debt or covenant[3] but that,

---

§1503.10

[1]*Murray, Ash, and Kennedy v. Hall* (1849), 7 C.B. 441, 137 E.R. 175; *Elliott v. Smith* (1858), 3 N.S.R. 338 (S.C.); *Petrie v. Taylor* (1847), 3 U.C.Q.B. 457; *Wiggins v. White* (1836), 2 N.B.R. 179 (S.C.).

[2]*Doe d. Hellings v. Bird* (1809), 11 East 49, 103 E.R. 922; *Monro v. Toronto Ry. Co.* (1904), 9 O.L.R. 299 (C.A.).

[3]*Dougall v. Foster* (1853), 4 Gr. 319.

[4]*Ibid.*, per Spragge, V.-C., at p. 327; *Hole v. Thomas* (1802), 7 Ves. Jun. 589, 32 E.R. 237. For cases where a co-tenant has been restrained from committing waste, with respect to timber, see *Arthur v. Lamb* (1865), 2 Dr. & Sm. 428, 62 E.R. 683; *Pyat v. Winfield* (1730), Mosely 305, 25 E.R. 408; *Proudfoot v. Bush; Bush v. Proudfoot* (1859), 7 Gr. 518; *Christie v. Saunders* (1851), 2 Gr. 670; with respect to soil or quarries, see *Wilkinson v. Haygarth* (1847), 12 Q.B. 837, 116 E.R. 1085; *Goodenow v. Farquhar* (1873), 19 Gr. 614; with respect to crops, *Brady v. Arnold* (1868), 19 U.C.C.P. 42; *Jacobs v. Seward* (1872), L.R. 5 H.L. 464. For a review of the statutory provisions with respect to waste, see §1502.5, *supra.*

§1503.11

[1]*Barnier v. Barnier* (1892), 23 O.R. 280 (H.C.J.); *Lyster v. Kirkpatrick* (1866), 26 U.C.Q.B. 217; *Lyster v. Ramage* (1866), 26 U.C.Q.B. 233.

[2]*Doe d. Campbell and Portway v. Hamilton* (1849), 13 Q.B. 977, 116 E.R. 1536.

[3]*Midgley and Gilbert v. Lovelace* (1693), Carthew 289, 90 E.R. 771.

if one sues alone, he can only recover his portion.[4] In the case of a lease by tenants in common, the survivor may sue for the whole rent, although the reservation be to the lessors according to their respective interests. The action for rent by tenants in common is in its nature a joint action and consequently the survivors may sue for the whole.[5]

1503.12 Termination of Tenancy in Common

When one of several joint tenants destroys the unity of title or interest by disposing of his interest to another person, it severs the joint tenancy and such person becomes a tenant in common with the other former joint tenants.[1] In the case of a tenancy in common, there being no unity of title or interest but only unity of possession, the only ways in which it can be terminated are (a) by partition, so that each tenant in common becomes owner of a divided share in severalty, or (b) by one tenant in common acquiring ownership of the interests of the other tenants in common. When one tenant in common disposes of his interest to a stranger, the only effect is to make the latter a tenant in common with the other or others. If one of three or more tenants in common disposes of his interest to one of the others, the only effect is to give the latter a double undivided share. If, however, one of several tenants in common acquires the interests of the others by purchase, gift or descent, he owns the entirety in severalty. If property held as a tenancy in common is sold for taxes and one of several tenants in common purchases it without any prior agreement that the purchase is to be for their joint benefit and without fraud, he is entitled to hold the property for his own benefit.[2]

Partition may be by mutual agreement or by compulsion under statutory provisions.

1503.13 Tenancy in Common — Partition by Agreement

For a discussion of partition by agreement of the tenants in common, see §1502.12 where the law is discussed and is equally applicable to a tenancy in common. It is to be observed that partition must be by deed.

1503.14 Tenancy in Common — Partition or Sale by Court Order

For a discussion of partition or sale in lieu of partition by court order, see §1502.13. The statutory provisions equally apply to a tenancy in common. To the cases therein cited, however, the following, relating to a tenancy in common, may be added:

---

[4]*Blackborough v. Graves* (1673), 1 Mod. 102, 86 E.R. 765.
[5]*Wallace & Mortimer v. M'Laren* (1828), 1 Man. & Ry. K.B. 516.
§1503.12
[1]See §1502.11, *supra.*
[2]*Kennedy v. Trafford*, [1896] 1 Ch. 762 (C.A.), affd [1897] A.C. 180 (H.L.).

As to the status of a person to apply for partition or sale, it has been held that children who held a remainder as tenants in common are not entitled to partition or sale as against the life tenant, their mother, who objected,[1] as only a co-tenant in possession can compel partition.[2] It has been questioned whether the applicant whose only interest was that of mortgagee of an undivided part of the land has any status to bring a suit for partition.[3] It has been held that a trustee for sale is not in a position to ask for partition.[4]

If one of several co-tenants mortgages his interest and asks for partition, his mortgagee must be a party to the proceedings in order to bind the legal estate.[5] Where one of three tenants in common repudiates a lease to the defendants made when he was an infant and thereafter seeks partition against the defendants in respect of their possession under the lease, his co-tenants are necessary parties to the plaintiff's action.[6]

1504.   COPARCENARY

Although coparcenary has been abolished in all provinces of Canada, coparceners are still referred to in various provincial statutes, no doubt as a matter of precaution. For this reason, some short reference should be made to this estate.

An estate held in coparcenary arose where, upon the death of one man, lands of inheritance descended to two or more persons.[1] It arose either at common law or by special custom. At common law coparcenary would arise where a person seised of land in fee simple or fee tail died and the land descended upon two or more females as heirs general or heirs in tail. It also arose by custom when two or more males inherited land according to the custom in *gavelkind*.[2] Such persons were called coparceners and together constituted one heir. They had, like joint tenants, unity of title, interest and possession. However, in general their rights *inter se* resembled more those of tenants in common in that their estate was unaffected by the doctrine of survivorship. If one of two coparceners died his share would pass to his estate instead of to the survivor and the unity of possession would continue. Coparcenary could be put to an end by partition or by all shares becoming vested in one coparcener which would thereby convert it into separate ownership. If one parcener alienated her share to a stranger the estate would be con-

§1503.14
[1]*Murcar v. Bolton* (1884), 5 O.R. 164 (H.C.J.).
[2]*Bunting v. Servos*, [1931] O.R. 409, [1931] 4 D.L.R. 167 (S.C. App. Div.).
[3]*Laplante v. Scamen* (1882), 8 O.A.R. 557.
[4]*Keefer v. McKay* (1881), 29 Gr. 162, affd 9 O.A.R. 117.
[5]*McDougall v. McDougall* (1868), 14 Gr. 267.
[6]*Monro v. Toronto R.W. Co.* (1903), 5 O.L.R. 483 (C.A.).
§1504
[1]Littleton's Tenures, s. 254.
[2]*Ibid.*, s. 254; 2 Bl. Comm. 187.

verted into a tenancy at common. In England, by the 1925 *Law of Property Act*,[3] it is no longer possible to hold land in coparcenary.

In Ontario, it is provided that if real property becomes vested under the Act in two or more persons beneficially entitled under the Act, they take as tenants in common in proportion to their respective rights, unless in the case of a devise they take otherwise under the will of the deceased.[4]

Although coparcenary by common law was introduced into all of the common law provinces, there does not appear to have been enacted similar provisions to that in Ontario. However, in view of the statutory provisions regarding descent of land it is no longer possible for an estate in land to descend to two or more persons as coparceners.

1505. TENANCY BY THE ENTIRETIES

At common law, husband and wife were regarded as one person, the legal existence of the wife during marriage being regarded as incorporated or merged into that of the husband.[1] One result was that, if land were conveyed or devised to or devolved upon husband and wife during coverture in such manner that, if not married, they would have taken it as joint tenants, they took it as tenants by the entireties.[2] It was immaterial whether the estate was in possession, remainder or reversion.[3] Being regarded as one person, each was tenant of the whole and no less, *per tout et non per mie*, and they could not sever the tenancies and each have a share, nor could the husband alone alienate the land.[4] The husband was entitled to the rents and profits during their joint lives and the survivor of them was entitled to the whole.[5] They could even alienate it by a conveyance binding on the wife but otherwise the survivor of them took the whole of the land in severalty.[6]

At common law, if land were conveyed or devised to husband and wife and some third person, the husband and wife took one share as tenants by the entireties and the third person took the other share, so where there was a limitation to husband and wife and their daughter and their heirs, the husband and wife took one share and the daughter the other.[7] This rule as to respective shares was based on the doctrine of the unity of person of husband and wife.[8]

---

[3]15 Geo. 5, c. 20 (1925, U.K.).
[4]*Estates Administration Act*, R.S.O. 1980, c. 143, s. 14.
§1505
[1]1 Bl. Comm. 442.
[2]2 Bl. Comm. 182; Co. Litt. 187; *Purefoy v. Rogers* (1672), 2 Lev. 39, 83 E.R. 443; *Back v. Andrew* (1690), 2 Vern. 120, 23 E.R. 687; *Doe d. Freestone v. Parratt* (1794), 5 T.R. 652, 101 E.R. 363.
[3]Co. Litt. 187.
[4]Littleton's Tenures, s. 665; Co. Litt. 187b, 310a.
[5]Co. Litt. 187; *Doe d. Freestone v. Parratt, supra*, footnote 2.
[6]*Thornley v. Thornley*, [1893] 2 Ch. 229 at p. 233.
[7]*Back v. Andrew, supra*, footnote 2.
[8]*Dias v. De Livera* (1879), 5 App. Cas. 123.

Being a rule of construction in such cases, a slight expression of an intention to the contrary would exclude it, so that husband and wife might take two shares between them, although holding them as tenants by the entireties. The arrangement of the names was a material circumstance to be considered.[9]

By the Imperial *Married Women's Property Act*, 1882,[10] the common law doctrine as to the unity of the person of husband and wife was reversed and a married woman became entitled to acquire, hold and dispose of the legal or equitable estate or interest in real property of every kind in the same manner as if she were a *feme sole*, an unmarried woman. It applies to all women married on or after January 1, 1883, or, in the case of women married before that date, to property, the title of which accrued to her on or after that date. Under the Act, in regard to devises or other limitations of real property to husband and wife taking effect on or after that date, they take as joint tenants, the wife's share being her separate property, and tenancies by the entireties ceased to exist in the case of such limitations.

The Act, however, did not alter the common law rule regarding respective shares where the limitation is to husband and wife and some other person or persons. In that regard, husband and wife would still be entitled to only one share between them unless a contrary intention is shown in the instrument. In such a case, a tenancy in common and not a joint tenancy is created, as there can be no inequality of shares in a joint tenancy.[11]

A decree dissolving a marriage converts a tenancy by the entireties into a joint tenancy but does not sever a joint tenancy between husband and wife.[12]

In Ontario, a tenancy by the entireties virtually disappeared as the result of two statutes. By the *Married Women's Property Act*,[13] a statute first enacted in 1884 and being largely a re-enactment of the Imperial Act of 1882, a married woman is capable of acquiring, holding and disposing by will or otherwise of any real or personal property as her separate property as if she were a *feme sole* and without the intervention of a trustee, and every woman married on or after July 1, 1884, is also entitled to have, hold and dispose of as her separate property, all real and personal property belonging to her at the time of her marriage. By section 13 of the *Conveyancing and Law of Property Act*[14] where by any letters patent, assurance or will made and executed after July 1, 1834, land has been or is granted, conveyed or devised to two or more persons, other than as executors or trustees, in fee simple or for any less estate, it shall be considered that they took or take as tenants in common and not as joint tenants, unless an intention sufficiently appears on the face of such letters patent, assurance or will that they are to take as joint tenants, and by sub-

---

[9] *Warrington v. Warrington* (1842), 2 Hare 54, 67 E.R. 23.
[10] 45 & 46 Vict., c. 75 (1882).
[11] *Re Jupp; Jupp v. Buckwell* (1888), 39 Ch. D. 148. See also. *Re Dixon; Byram v. Tull* (1889), 42 Ch. D. 306; *Re March; Mander v. Harris* (1884), 27 Ch. D. 166 (C.A.).
[12] *Thornley v. Thornley, supra,* footnote 6.
[13] R.S.O. 1970, c. 262, s. 2, rep. 1975, c. 41, s. 6.
[14] R.S.O. 1980, c. 90.

section (2), the provision is to apply notwithstanding that one of such persons is the wife of another of them.[15] For similar provisions in other provinces see §1502.

In a most unusual case a husband and wife agreed to buy property. The agreement, on its face was silent as to the nature of the estate intended to be conferred on the purchaser. Before the date set for closing the husband died. The court concluded that the agreement was not an "assurance" within the meaning of section 13 of the *Devolution of Estates Act* and that section 2 of the *Married Women's Property Act* did not, in itself, oust the concept of a tenancy by the entirety.[16] However, it would now appear that the concept of tenancy by the entirety cannot exist, in any event, because of the provisions of the *Family Law Reform Act*[17] in Ontario and because of similar legislation in the other provinces.[18]

---

[15]This subsection being added in 1911 by 1 Geo. 5, c. 25, s. 13.

[16]*Campbell v. Sovereign Securities & Holding Co. Ltd.*, [1958] O.R. 441, 13 D.L.R. (2d) 195 (H.C.J.), affd O.R. *loc. cit.* 719, 16 D.L.R. (2d) 606 (C.A.).

[17]R.S.O. 1980, c. 152, s. 65.

[18]*Matrimonial Property Act*, R.S.A. 1980, c. L-8, s. 5(3); S.N. 1979, c. 32, am. S.N. 1980, c. 24, s. 11; S.N.S. 1980, c. 9; S.S. 1979, c. M-6.1; *Family Relations Act*, R.S.B.C. 1979, c. 121; *Marital Property Act*, S.M. 1978, c. 24, am. S.M. 1980-81, c. 26, s. 21; S.N.B. 1978, c. M-1.1; *Matrimonial Property Ordinance*, O.Y.T. 1979 (2nd), c. 11, am. O.Y.T. 1980 (2nd), c. 16, s. 10. The *Family Law Reform Act*, S.P.E.I. 1978, c. 6, s. 64(1), abolishes tenancies by the entireties specifically.

CHAPTER 16

MATRIMONIAL PROPERTY

PART V   CONCURRENT INTERESTS

1601. SCOPE OF THIS CHAPTER

The law of matrimonial property is vast, particularly so since the recent enactment of family law reform statutes in most of the Canadian jurisdictions. These statutes vary considerably from province to province. As a result it is impossible, in a book of this nature, to treat the subject exhaustively. Instead, a survey of the law will be presented which will pay particular attention to the real property aspects of family law, although by the nature of the subject, references to personal property cannot be avoided.

The chapter consists of three parts. The first part is a brief survey of matrimonial property law at common law, together with a discussion of the intervention of equity. The second part deals with the Married Women's Property Acts and the manner in which rights are determined under that legislation. Also included in the second part is a discussion of the deserted wife's right to possession of the matrimonial home and the related rights of common law spouses. The third, and major, part of the chapter deals with the modern legislation.

Some of the material covered in this chapter has been dealt with elsewhere. Thus, for example, dower and curtesy have been dealt with in chapter 7.[1] the doctrines of resulting and constructive trusts are covered in chapter 12[2] and co-ownership is discussed in chapter 15. Although a brief survey of these matters is included in this chapter, a more detailed discussion will be found in the others. Spousal rights of succession are discussed only incidentally in this chapter. These, including dependants' relief legislation, are dealt with more fully elsewhere.[3]

1602. MATRIMONIAL PROPERTY AT COMMON LAW

At common law, upon marriage, a husband and wife were regarded as one person and, as is often said, that one was the husband.[1] This is because the

---

§1601

[1] §§707-710.15, *supra.*
[2] See especially, §§1208. 1209.4(e), *supra.*
[3] §§503.1, *supra,* 2813-2813.7 and 2904.1, *infra.*

§1602

[1] Hahlo, "Matrimonial Property Regimes: Yesterday, Today and Tomorrow", 11 Osgoode Hall L.J. 455 (1973), at p. 463.

wife lost substantially all her property rights and these were acquired by the husband. Blackstone puts the position this way:

> By marriage, the husband and wife are one person in law: that is, the very being or legal existence of the woman is suspended during the marriage, or at least is incorporated and consolidated into that of the husband: under whose wing, protection, and *cover*, she performs every thing.[2]

The unity of the person had serious consequences for the wife. Not only did she lose most of her property rights, but many of her other legal rights as well. Thus, for example, she was incapable of entering into a contract except for necessaries and as to the latter, this was only on the basis that she was regarded as the husband's agent. She could not sue or be sued in her own name but her husband had to be joined as a party. She remained liable for any torts she committed, either before or during marriage but her husband was jointly liable with her. Furthermore, contracts, property transactions and torts between the spouses were impossible.[3]

With respect to the wife's property rights, these also passed to the husband or were suspended during the marriage. Upon marriage, the seisin of all freehold lands held by the wife or acquired by her during the marriage vested in the husband and he became solely entitled to the rents and profits from them. The wife had no power to sell them. In order to dispose of the lands, both spouses had to act together. However, while the lands vested in the husband, he did not acquire the fee simple in them but only an estate for the duration of the marriage.[4]

If the wife predeceased her husband, her freehold lands would pass to her husband for life as tenant by the curtesy. This life estate arose only if the wife would have been entitled to possession on her death and if a child were born alive who was capable of inheriting the lands. Thus, for example, if the wife were a tenant in tail female and a son were born to her, her husband would not be entitled to an estate by the curtesy. If the estate by the curtesy did not arise, the freeholds would descend to her heir-at-law. If the husband predeceased his wife, she regained sole control over the real property.[5]

Although the husband acquired substantial rights over his wife's real property, a wife acquired no similar rights over her husband's property. However, if she survived him, she became entitled to dower, that is, a life estate in one-third of all her husband's freehold estates of inheritance of which he was solely seised at any time during the marriage. This life estate only arose if the wife were capable of producing a child who was entitled to inherit the estate. Moreover, the husband could not dispose of his lands unless his wife barred her dower.[6]

---

[2] 1 Bl. Comm. 441.

[3] Kahn-Freund, "Matrimonial Property Law in England", in *Matrimonial Property Law* (Friedmann, ed., Toronto, Carswell, 1955), p. 267 at pp. 271-3.

[4] Bromley, *Family Law*, 4th ed. (London, Butterworths, 1971), pp. 347-8.

[5] See further on tenancy by the curtesy §§708-708.1, *supra*.

[6] The law of dower, including its extension by statute is discussed in detail in §§707-707.20, *supra*.

If land was conveyed to a husband and wife and their heirs, the doctrine of unity of the person demanded that they hold, not as joint tenants or as tenants in common, but as tenants by the entireties. This meant that both spouses had to join in a conveyance if they wished to dispose of the land. One party could not sever the tenancy so as to create a tenancy in common. When either party died, the survivor became entitled to the whole, just as in the case of a joint tenancy.[7]

Upon marriage, a wife's chattels real vested in her husband and he could dispose of them during the marriage and keep the proceeds of sale. If his wife predeceased him, he was entitled to retain the balance of the term. However, he could not dispose of the leaseholds by will and, if he predeceased his wife, the term reverted to her automatically.[8]

The wife's choses in possession vested in her husband absolutely upon the marriage and he could dispose of them as he saw fit. Even if he died intestate during the marriage, they would not revert to her. This was subject to one exception, namely, the wife's paraphernalia, that is, her clothing and personal ornaments suitable to her rank and station in life. These could not be disposed of by the wife during coverture, whereas the husband could do so. However, upon his death they became her property absolutely.[9]

The wife's choses in action also belonged to the husband absolutely if he recovered them, or reduced them into his possession. If he failed to do so, they would revert to his widow on his death. However, if he survived her, he could still recover them by taking out letters of administration of his wife's estate.[10]

The common law matrimonial property regime as outlined above was received in the common law provinces of Canada[11] and remained in effect until the enactment of the Married Women's Property Acts[12] in the second half of the 19th century.

1603. THE INTERVENTION OF EQUITY

The common law regime of matrimonial property became increasingly outdated with the advent of the mercantile class and the desire of the wealthy to convey property to their daughters without fear that it might be dissipated by fortune-seeking husbands. The equitable property regime developed by the Court of Chancery had as its motivation, not the desire to ensure a woman's legal rights but rather the desire to preserve family property for her next of kin. Thus arose the concept of a wife's separate property in equity.[1]

[7]See further as to tenancy by the entireties, §1505, *supra*.

[8]Bromley, *op. cit.*, *supra*, footnote 4, at p. 349.

[9]*Ibid.*

[10]*Ibid.*

[11]As to the rules and dates of reception of English law, see ch. 3, *supra*.

[12]See §1604, *infra*.

§1603

[1]Kahn-Freund, "Matrimonial Property Law in England", in *Matrimonial Property Law* (Friedmann, ed., Toronto, Carswell, 1955), p. 267 at p. 274.

By the end of the 16th century, it became possible to settle real or personal property in equity to the separate use of a married woman. The marriage settlement could be effected before or after the marriage had taken place and it kept the wife's property out of reach of her husband and his creditors. This was accomplished by giving the property to a trustee for the wife's "separate use". The wife, as *cestui que trust*, then had the power to dispose of her separate property by deed or will; she could enter into contracts with respect to it and she could order that it be conveyed to a third party or to herself.[2]

It was later held that it was not necessary for a third party to be the trustee. Thus, if property was conveyed or devised to a married woman to her separate use so that the legal estate vested in her husband, he was deemed to hold it on trust for her and was bound to deal with it upon the terms of the trust.[3]

There still remained the danger that the wife would assign her separate property, which was held in trust for her, to her husband, thereby defeating the interests of the next of kin as effectively as the common law system had done. To avoid this problem, equity developed the restraint on alienation. A restraint on alienation contained in a marriage settlement prevented the married woman from disposing of her property *inter vivos*, or anticipating and dealing with any income until it actually fell due. The restraint clause successfully kept the property safe for the next of kin. Its principal drawback was that, once attached, it was removable only by a private Act of Parliament.[4]

Equity thus increased a married woman's legal capacity considerably. With respect to her separate property she could contract, sue and be sued in her own name and dispose of her interest in it by will. However, equity never superseded the common law matrimonial property regime. Only the wealthy could take advantage of the doctrine of equity, for a married woman's separate property could only be created by formal transactions, such as wills and marriage settlements. Thus, until the late 19th century and the advent of the Married Women's Property Acts, there existed in England two matrimonial property regimes, namely, the common law for the poor and equity for the wealthy few.[5] Nevertheless, the equitable regime was important in that its offspring, the concept of a wife's separate property, was adopted in the subsequent legislation.

Both the common law and equitable regimes of matrimonial property law were received in the Canadian provinces.[6] It is doubtful that the equitable regime was in fact used to any great extent in Canada, however. The expense involved would render it unsuitable for the early pioneer communities in Canada. Moreover, there were few conveyancers and counsel skilled in Chancery practice in the early days of pioneer settlement.[7]

---

[2]Bromley, *Family Law*, 4th ed. (London, Butterworths, 1971), p. 351.
[3]*Ibid.*
[4]*Ibid.*, pp. 351-2; Dicey, *Lectures on the Relation between Law and Public Opinion in England During the Nineteenth Century* (London, Macmillan and Co., 1917), pp. 378-9.
[5]Dicey, *op. cit., supra*, footnote 4, at p. 383.
[6]See ch. 3, *supra*, for the rules of reception of English law.
[7]Auld, "Matrimonial Property Law in the Common Law Provinces of Canada", in Friedmann, *op. cit., supra*, footnote 1, p. 239 at p. 242.

1604. THE MARRIED WOMEN'S PROPERTY ACTS

By the middle of the 19th century, the common law system of unity of the person in matters of matrimonial property no longer reflected the position of women in society. Equity was of little assistance to most married women because separate property could only be created by a formal transaction, typically a will or marriage settlement, and the expenses involved in such formalities prevented access to that system to all but those who could afford the legal costs.[1] Thus, the majority of middle and lower class married women were subject to the common law, which did not meet the needs of increasing numbers of married women as wage earners to receive and control their earnings and their property free of their husbands' interference.[2]

In the second half of the 19th century a number of statutes were passed in England which sought to alleviate the disabilities of married women.[3] These culminated in and were replaced by the *Married Women's Property Act* of 1882.[4] This statute adopted the equitable concept of separate property and applied it to the legal title of property held by a married woman without the interposition of a trust. Thus, a married woman was thereafter entitled to retain the property which she owned at the time of the marriage as her separate property, and could acquire, hold and dispose of property during the marriage as if she were a *feme sole*.[5] Restraints on alienation and anticipation were not affected by the Act, however, so it was still possible to protect a woman's property from her husband by restraining her ability to convey it to him or to her creditors.[6] The Act applied to all property, personal and real, including wages, bank accounts and copyholds.[7] Moreover, the Act provided a means for settling disputes as to property rights between spouses in a summary fashion; to that extent, the bar on actions between spouses was removed.[8]

The common law provinces and territories of Canada adopted the principles of the English Act of 1882 through similar legislation.[9] The general effect of

---

§1604

[1] Bromley, *Family Law*, 4th ed. (London, Butterworths, 1971), p. 352.

[2] Dicey, *Lectures on the Relation Between Law and Public Opinion in England During the Nineteenth Century* (London, Macmillan and Co., 1917), pp. 385-6.

[3] *Matrimonial Causes Act* (1857), 20 & 21 Vict., c. 85; *Married Women's Property Act* (1870), 33 & 34 Vict., c. 93.

[4] 45 & 46 Vict., c. 75 (1882).

[5] *Ibid.*, s. 1.

[6] *Ibid.*, s. 19.

[7] *Ibid.*, ss. 1-8.

[8] *Ibid.*, ss. 12, 17.

[9] See now *Married Women's Act*, R.S.A. 1980, c. M-7; *Married Woman's Property Act*, R.S.B.C. 1979, c. 252; R.S.N.B. 1973, c. M-4, am. S.N.B. 1980, c. M-1.1. s. 50; *Married Women's Property Act*, R.S.M. 1970, c. M70, am. S.M. 1973, c. 12, s. 1; S.M. 1978, c. 27, s. 8; R.S.N. 1970, c. 227, am. S.N. 1974. No. 57, s. 38 (264(*u*)); R.S.N.S. 1967, c. 176, am. S.N.S. 1972, c. 2, s. 9; R.S.O. 1970, c. 262, rep. S.O. 1975, c. 41, s. 6 and S.O. 1978. c. 2, s. 82; R.S.P.E.I. 1974, c. M-6, rep. S.P.E.I. 1978, c. 6, s. 68; *Married Persons' Property Act*, R.S.S. 1978, c. M-6, am. S.S. 1979, c. M-6.1, s. 60; *Married Women's Property Ordinance*, R.O.N.W.T. 1974, c. M-6; R.O.Y.T. 1971, c. M-4. (These several statutes are hereafter referred to as the Alta. Act, N.W.T. Ord., *etc.*).

these statutes was to allow a married woman to acquire, hold and dispose of property as her separate property.[10] Restraints on alienation and anticipation were gradually abolished in most jurisdictions, usually through legislation which declared such restraints void except to the extent that a similar restraint could be placed upon the property of a man.[11] Alberta appears to be the only jurisdiction which still permits restraints on anticipation or alienation to be created against the property of married women.[12] It would seem that such restraints in any event have lost much of their utility today.[13]

More to the point for the purpose of this chapter is that the Acts removed the bar to an action by a married woman against her husband to protect her property rights and gave the courts jurisdiction to settle disputes involving questions of property rights summarily and to make such orders as might be fit or just in the circumstances.[14] This provision does not allow the court to reallocate the property of a husband and wife. It is procedural only and permits the court to determine what the respective property rights of the spouses are, but no more.[15] In order for a spouse to establish an interest in property the title to which is held by the other, it is necessary, under the Married Women's Property Acts regime of separate property, to resort to general principles of property and trust law.[16] These principles will be addressed in the next paragraph.

1604.1 Principles Applicable Under the Separate Property Regime

As noted in the previous section, the mere fact of marriage does not entitle the spouses to a share in each other's assets on the breakdown of the marriage or during it. The notion of separate property precludes that result. However, this often caused hardship to the non-titled spouse, usually the wife and, therefore, early cases readily reallocated the spouses' property on marriage breakdown on the basis of the court's jurisdiction, conferred by the Married

---

[10]Alta. Act, ss. 2, 4; B.C. Act, s. 2; Man. Act, ss. 3, 4(1); N.B. Act, s. 2; N.S. Act, ss. 3, 4; Nfld. Act, s. 3; Ont. Act, s. 2; P.E.I. Act, ss. 2, 3; Sask. Act, s. 3; N.W.T. Ord., ss. 3, 4; Yukon Ord., ss. 3(1), 4.

[11]B.C. Act, s. 14; Man. Act, s. 4(3); N.B. Act, s. 3; N.S. Act, s. 22; Nfld. Act, s. 3(2)-(4); Ont. Act, s. 10; P.E.I. Act, s. 15; Sask. Act, s. 23; N.W.T. Ord., s. 4; Yukon Ord., s. 4(2)-(4).

[12]Alta. Act, s. 5(2).

[13]Hahlo, "Matrimonial Property Regimes: Yesterday, Today and Tomorrow", 11 Osgoode Hall L.J. 455 (1973), at p. 466.

[14]B.C. Act, s. 26; Man. Act, s. 8(1); N.B. Act, s. 7(1); N.S. Act, s. 36(1); Nfld. Act, s. 16; Ont. Act, s. 12(1); P.E.I. Act, s. 13(1); Sask. Act, s. 22. The Alta. Act, s. 2, the N.W.T. Ord., s. 7, and the Yukon Ord., s. 7, merely removed the bar to the wife's action to protect her property rights against her husband.

[15]*Thompson v. Thompson* (1960), 26 D.L.R. (2d) 1, [1961] S.C.R. 3; and see *Pettit v. Pettitt*, [1970] A.C. 777 (H.L.), to the same effect.

[16]Cullity, "Property Rights During the Subsistence of Marriage", in *Studies in Canadian Family Law*, vol. 1 (Mendes da Costa, ed., Toronto, Butterworths, 1972), p. 179 at pp. 184-5.

Women's Property Acts,[1] to summarily settle questions of property rights between the spouses. An equal division of assets was usually the result, based on the maxim that equality is equity.[2] This approach, subsequently referred to as "palm-tree justice", was firmly rejected in Canada by the Supreme Court[3] and later in England by the House of Lords.[4] The jurisdiction conferred by the legislation was held to be procedural only. It merely allowed the court to ascertain and declare the respective property interests of the parties, but did not give it the right to make a division of their assets according to what the court might think just.

Under the separate property regime it is possible for a person to acquire property from his spouse even though the latter holds title to it. However, this can only be achieved by the application of well-recognized principles of property and trusts. These will be outlined briefly below.[5]

(a) Express agreement

If the spouses have entered into an express agreement, such as a marriage settlement, their property rights will be governed by it. Thus, even though one of the parties holds title to the property, he will be required to hold it in trust for the other to the extent provided by the agreement.[6] Express agreements or trusts have not been common in Canada, however. Moreover, if the agreement is with respect to land or is not to be performed within one year, the several Statutes of Fraud require that it be reduced to writing.[7]

Where there is no express agreement between the parties, the courts have had to resort to the doctrines of resulting trust and, more recently, constructive trust.

(b) The resulting trust and the presumption of advancement

A presumption of a resulting trust is raised in certain limited circumstances by equity, namely, where a person contributes to the acquisition of property the title to which is put in another's name or in both their names. The other person, or both persons, will then be regarded as holding the property on a resulting trust for the person or persons who, and in the proportions in which,

---

§1604.1

[1]The relevant sections in the Canadian statutes are set out in §1604, footnote 14, *supra*. The corresponding English provision is the *Married Women's Property Act* (1882), 45 & 46 Vict., c. 75, s. 12.

[2]See, *e.g.*, *Rimmer v. Rimmer*, [1953] 1 Q.B. 63 (C.A.); *Fribance v. Fribance*, [1956] P. 99; *Hine v. Hine*, [1962] 3 All E.R. 345 (C.A.).

[3]*Thompson v. Thompson* (1960), 26 D.L.R. (2d) 1, [1961] S.C.R. 3. See also *Rye v. Rye* (1974), 20 R.F.L. 118, 10 N.B.R. (2d) 97 (Q.B.).

[4]*Pettitt v. Pettitt*, [1970] A.C. 777 (H.L.).

[5]Further reference may be had to §§1208, 1209.4(e), *supra*.

[6]Cooper, "Matrimonial Property Law in Saskatchewan — The Embarrassment of Rathwell", 40 Sask. L. Rev. 185 (1976), at p. 200.

[7]*Statute of Frauds* (1677), 29 Car. 2, c. 3, ss. 4, 7, in force in Alberta, Manitoba, Saskatchewan, Newfoundland, the Northwest Territories and Yukon Territory: Waters, p. 179; R.S.B.C. 1979, c. 393, s. 1; R.S.N.B. 1973, c. S-14, ss. 1, 9; R.S.N.S. 1967, c. 290, ss. 6, 4; R.S.O. 1980, c. 481, ss. 4, 9; R.S.P.E.I. 1974, c. S-6, s. 2.

they contributed the money. There are other circumstances in which a resulting trust may arise, but the only one relevant to this discussion is the trust arising by contribution and its derivative, the trust arising by common intention.[8]

Where, however, a husband transferred property to his wife or purchased property which was put into his wife's name, a presumption of advancement, or gift, arose instead.[9] Both the presumption of advancement and resulting trust are rebuttable.[10]

Where title to the property is taken in the joint names of the spouses, the presumptions of resulting trust and advancement are applicable[11] but in most cases it has been assumed, in the absence of convincing evidence to the contrary, that the spouses have an equal interest in the property.[12]

As to the presumption of advancement, where the husband has transferred property to his wife or purchased property in his wife's name, the cases hold that the evidence to rebut it must be clear and cogent.[13] Hence, although it is not easy to rebut the presumption, it is possible to do so where the statements or conduct of the titled spouse, or the surrounding circumstances, clearly show that no gift was intended.[14]

---

[8]As to the other types of resulting trust, see §§1209-1209.4, *supra.*

[9]Waters, p. 290.

[10]See §1209.4(c), *supra,* and see *Morasch v. Morasch* (1962), 40 W.W.R. 50 (Alta. S.C.).

[11]*Tuomi v. Tuomi,* [1951] 4 D.L.R. 206 (B.C.S.C.); *Smith v. Smith* (1973), 12 R.F.L. 216 (B.C.S.C.); *Hillary v. Hillary* (1972), 9 R.F.L. 100 (Alta. S.C.); *Morrison v. Guaranty Trust Co. of Canada,* [1972] 3 O.R. 448, 28 D.L.R. (3d) 458 (H.C.J.); *Ingersoll v. Nettleton and Fonagy.* [1956] O.W.N. 738, 6 D.L.R. (2d) 28 (H.C.J.). The presumption of advancement does not apply where the parties have made an agreement as to the sharing of liabilities: *Shore v. Shore* (1975), 63 D.L.R. (3d) 354, [1976] W.W.D. 19 (B.C.S.C.).

[12]*Duncan v. Duncan,* [1950] 1 W.W.R. 545 (B.C.S.C.); *Szuba v. Szuba,* [1951] O.W.N. 61 (H.C.J.); *Spatafora v. Spatafora,* [1952] O.W.N. 757 (H.C.J.); *Klemkowich v. Klemkowich* (1954), 14 W.W.R. 418, 63 Man. R. 28 (Q.B.); *Lyon v. Lyon,* [1959] O.R. 305, 18 D.L.R. (2d) 753 (C.A.); *McWilliam v. McWilliam and Prudential Ins. Co. of America* (1961), 34 W.W.R. 476 (Alta. S.C. App. Div.); *Redgrove v. Unruh* (1962), 39 W.W.R. (N.S.) 317 (Alta. S.C. App. Div.); *Alexander v. Alexander and Caterline Cookies Ltd.* (1962), 33 D.L.R. (2d) 602 (B.C.S.C.); *Fetterly v. Fetterly* (1965), 54 D.L.R. (2d) 435, 54 W.W.R. 218 (Man. Q.B.); *Germain v. Germain* (1969), 70 W.W.R. 120 (Man. Q.B.); *Kearney v. Kearney,* [1970] 2 O.R. 152, 10 D.L.R. (3d) 138 (C.A.); *Eberle v. Eberle* (1973), 12 R.F.L. 268 (Sask. Q.B.); *Mancuso v. Mancuso* (1973), 12 R.F.L. 398 (Ont. C.A.); *Re Vermette and Vermette* (1974), 45 D.L.R. (3d) 313, [1974] 4 W.W.R. 320 (Man. C.A.); *Estensen v. Estensen* (1975), 21 R.F.L. 373 (B.C.S.C.); *Brody v. Brody* (1976), 1 A.R. 470 (S.C.T.D.); *Brokop v. Brokop* (1977), 3 A.R. 350 (S.C.T.D.).

[13]*Johnson v. Johnson,* [1945] 1 D.L.R. 404, 18 M.P.R. 254 (N.S.S.C.), affd [1945] 3 D.L.R. 413, [1945] S.C.R. 455; *Gagnon v. Gagnon* (1950), 28 M.P.R. 36 (N.B.S.C.); *Shepherd v. Shepherd* (1952), 34 M.P.R. 154 (N.B.S.C.); *Meek v. Meek* (1955), 17 W.W.R. 401, 63 Man. R. 283 (Q.B.); *Jackman v. Jackman* (1959), 19 D.L.R. (2d) 317, [1959] S.C.R. 702; *Demyen v. Demyen* (1974), 16 R.F.L. 381 (Sask. Q.B.); *Re Geller and Geller* (1975), 7 O.R. (2d) 454, 55 D.L.R. 486 (H.C.J.); *Gulf Oil Canada Ltd. v. O'Rourke* (1978), 21 O.R. (2d) 30, 89 D.L.R. (3d) 141 (C.A.).

[14]*Cole v. Cole,* [1944] 2 D.L.R. 798. [1944] S.C.R. 166, statements and conduct of wife sufficient to rebut presumption; *Pahara v. Pahara,* [1946] 1 D.L.R. 433, [1946] S.C.R.

Where the husband transfers property to his wife to defeat creditors, however, he cannot use the evidence of his own fraudulent intent to rebut the presumption of advancement, at least not if his creditors are actually defeated[15] and, probably more correctly, even if he merely has the intent to defeat possible future creditors.[16] Earlier cases which hold otherwise are now probably overruled.[17] On the other hand, where there was never any actual or apprehended creditor, the presumption may be rebutted by proving the true nature of the transaction.[18]

Where the wife transfers property to her husband to protect it from anticipated creditors, she need not rely on that evidence to recover the property, since she is not seeking to rebut a presumption of advancement, but to uphold the presumption of resulting trust.[19]

After the spouses have separated[20] or the marriage has been dissolved,[21] the presumption of advancement no longer applies.

89, husband transferring entire estate to wife, presumption rebutted; *Zebberman v. Zebberman*, [1948] 2 D.L.R. 269, 21 M.P.R. 1 (N.B.S.C.), presumption rebutted by wife's admissions; *Kaisla v. Kaisla*, [1953] O.W.N. 957 (C.A.), wife did not believe property was intended to be hers; *Sopow v. Sopow* (1958), 15 D.L.R. (2d) 57, 24 W.W.R. 625 (B.C.S.C.); *D'Ambrosio v. D'Ambrosio* (1959), 20 D.L.R. (2d) 177 (Ont. C.A.), husband unable to read or write English; *Winter v. Winter* (1974), 3 O.R. (2d) 425, 45 D.L.R. (3d) 641 (C.A.), spouses intending to take title jointly at time of purchase; *Spendlove v. Spendlove* (1976), 73 D.L.R. (3d) 659 (B.C.S.C.), wife acting as family bookkeeper had title put in her name unbeknownst to husband; *Greggain v. Greggain* (1970), 73 W.W.R. 677 (B.C.S.C.), husband quitclaiming joint interest to wife because of her inducements and pressing economic situation.

[15]*Scheuerman v. Scheuerman* (1915), 28 D.L.R. 223, 52 S.C.R. 625; *McGillan v. McGillan*, [1947] 4 D.L.R. 456, 20 M.P.R. 202 (N.B.S.C. App. Div.); *Walsh v. Walsh*, [1948] O.W.N. 668, [1948] 4 D.L.R. 876 (C.A.). See also *Fricke v. Fricke*, [1940] 1 D.L.R. 783, [1940] 1 W.W.R. 87 (Alta. S.C.); *Wolfe v. Wolfe* (1974), 16 R.F.L. 253 (Alta. S.C.); *Bank of Nova Scotia v. Brickell and Brickell* (1980), 22 B.C.L.R. 222, 36 C.B.R. (N.S.) 1 (S.C.).

[16]*Maysels v. Maysels* (1974), 3 O.R. (2d) 321, 45 D.L.R. (3d) 337 (C.A.), affd 64 D.L.R. (3d) 765n, [1975] 1 S.C.R. v; *Bingeman v. McLaughlin* (1976), 12 O.R. (2d) 65, 68 D.L.R. (3d) 17 (C.A.), affd 77 D.L.R. (3d) 25, [1978] 1 S.C.R. 548.

[17]See, *e.g.*, *Re Szymczak and Szymczak*, [1970] 3 O.R. 202, 12 D.L.R. (3d) 582 (H.C.J.), husband transferring house to wife because of threat of creditors of friend under cosigned note; *Bible v. Bible* (1974), 6 O.R. (2d) 213, 52 D.L.R. (3d) 341 (C.A.), no creditors defeated and no income tax evasion in fact; *Sepp v. Sepp* (1975), 22 R.F.L. 76 (Ont. C.A.), husband transferring house to wife because of anticipated business creditors, but never having any creditors; *Sinclair v. Sinclair* (1975), 17 R.F.L. 202 (Ont. H.C.J.), husband commencing business but no real chance of creditors, and see *Valta v. Valta* (1978), 95 D.L.R. (3d) 409, 8 R.F.L. (2d) 133 *sub nom. Valta v. Valta and Johansson* (B.C.C.A.).

[18]*Goodfriend v. Goodfriend* (1971), 22 D.L.R. (3d) 699, [1972] S.C.R. 640; *Kovacs v. Kovacs* (1973), 13 R.F.L. 255 (Ont. S.C.).

[19]*Marks v. Marks* (1974), 18 R.F.L. 323 (Ont. C.A.).

[20]*Bruce v. Bruce* (1976), 28 R.F.L. 190, 14 N.B.R. (2d) 422 (S.C. App. Div.).

[21]*Andrews v. Andrews* (1969), 7 D.L.R. (3d) 744 (B.C.S.C.); *Leippi v. Leippi*, [1977] 2 W.W.R. 497, 30 R.F.L. 342 (Man. C.A.); *Davis v. Cipryk* (1977), 21 N.S.R. (2d) 266 (S.C.).

(c) The resulting trust arising from contributions and common intention

The traditional basis for imposing a resulting trust is a financial contribution to the acquisition of the property. Thus, for example, if title to the property is placed in the name of the husband, but he pays only part of the purchase money, his wife paying the other part or, perhaps, the mortgage payments, the husband will hold on a resulting trust for his wife to the extent and in the proportion in which she has contributed, unless the presumption is rebutted.[22]

On this basis, a wife is not entitled to an interest in the property for indirect contributions such as labour, work in the house, contribution to housekeeping money, or raising the family, but only for direct or indirect financial contributions and the early cases so held.[23]

This approach, while technically correct, tended to work great hardship on wives and many courts began to recognize a resulting trust where the wife had made an indirect but substantial contribution to the acquisition or maintenance of the property, such as labour on a farm or construction of a house.[24]

---

[22]Cullity, "The Matrimonial Home — A Return to Palm-Tree Justice: Trust Doctrines Based on (a) Intent and (b) Unjust Enrichment", 4 E. & T.Q. 277 (1977-78), at pp. 282-3; *Murdoch v. Murdoch* (1973), 41 D.L.R. (3d) 367 at p. 387, [1975] 1 S.C.R. 423 at pp. 453-4, *per* Laskin, J.; *Thompson v. Thompson* (1960), 26 D.L.R. (2d) 1, [1961] S.C.R. 3; *Pettitt v. Pettitt*, [1970] A.C. 777 (H.L.), at p. 814, *per* Lord Upjohn; *Gissing v. Gissing*, [1971] A.C. 886 (H.L.), at p. 902, *per* Lord Pearson; *Grunert v. Grunert* (1960), 32 W.W.R. 509 (Sask. Q.B.); *Sywack v. Sywack* (1943), 51 Man. R. 108 (K.B.); *Rooney v. Rooney* (1969), 68 W.W.R. 641, 3 R.F.L. 222 (Sask. Q.B.); *Calder v. Cleland*, [1971] 1 O.R. 667, 16 D.L.R. (3d) 369 (C.A.); *More v. More* (1974), 17 R.F.L. 5 (B.C.S.C.); *Easton v. Easton* (1974), 6 O.R. (2d) 469, 53 D.L.R. (3d) 232 (H.C.J.); *Beard v. Beard*, [1973] 1 O.R. 165, 30 D.L.R. (3d) 513 (H.C.J.); *Ramer v. Ramer* (1975), 22 R.F.L. 232 (H.C.J.); *Calleja v. Calleja* (1975), 11 O.R. (2d) 342, 66 D.L.R. (3d) 84 (C.A.); *Lindenblatt v. Lindenblatt* (1974), 4 O.R. (2d) 534, 48 D.L.R. (3d) 494 (H.C.J.); *Ball v. Ball* (1976), 27 R.F.L. 271 (Ont. H.C.J.); *Affleck v. Affleck* (1976), 27 R.F.L. 119 (B.C.S.C.), and see *Dunne v. Dunne* (1977), 13 Nfld. & P.E.I.R. 234 (Nfld. Dist. Ct.); *Weston v. Weston* (1972), 8 R.F.L. 188 (B.C.S.C.); *Nemeth v. Nemeth* (1967), 64 D.L.R. (2d) 377 (B.C.S.C.).

[23]*Re Married Women's Property Act*; *Re Stajcer and Stajcer* (1961), 34 W.W.R. 424 (B.C.S.C.); *Lawson v. Lawson* (1966), 56 W.W.R. 576 (Man. C.A.); *Re Taylor and Taylor*, [1971] 1 O.R. 715, 16 D.L.R. (3d) 481 (H.C.J.); *Rooney v. Rooney* (1969), 68 W.W.R. 641, 3 R.F.L. 222 (Sask. Q.B.); *Moore v. Moore* (1975), 26 R.F.L. 346, 16 N.S.R. (2d) 220 (S.C.T.D.); *Sohkanen v. Sohkanen* (1976), 62 D.L.R. (3d) 765, [1976] W.W.D. 5 (B.C.C.A.); *Stevens v. Brown* (1969), 2 D.L.R. (3d) 687, [1965-69] 2 N.S.R. 301 (S.C.); *Weisgerber v. Weisgerber* (1969), 71 W.W.R. 461 (Sask. Q.B.); *Bussey v. Bussey* (1975), 8 Nfld. & P.E.I.R. 504 (Nfld. S.C.); *Murdoch v. Murdoch*, *supra*, footnote 22; *Gerk v. Gerk* (1975), 25 R.F.L. 32 (Alta. S.C.T.D.); *Re Soroka* (1975), 10 O.R. (2d) 638, 64 D.L.R. (3d) 234 (H.C.J.); *Lightfoot v. Early Morning Enterprises Ltd. and Gordon Lightfoot Ltd.* (1973), 14 R.F.L. 110 (Ont. H.C.J.); *Newton v. Newton* (1975), 19 R.F.L. 276 (Ont. H.C.J.); *Cook v. Cook* (1977), 2 R.F.L. (2d) 204 (Nfld. S.C.).

[24]*Trueman v. Trueman* (1971), 18 D.L.R. (3d) 109, [1971] 2 W.W.R. 688 (Alta. S.C. App. Div.); *Wiley v. Wiley* (1971), 23 D.L.R. (3d) 484, 6 R.F.L. 36 (B.C.S.C.); *Kowalchuk v. Kowalchuk* (1974), 45 D.L.R. (3d) 716 (Man. Q.B.), affd 51 D.L.R. (3d) 463, [1975] 2 W.W.R. 735 (Man. C.A.); *Beztilny v. Beztilny*, [1976] W.W.D. 105,

At the same time, a new element was introduced into the concept of resulting trusts, namely, that of a common understanding or intention. Strictly, a common intention on the part of spouses that they will have an equal or other interest in property even though title is taken in the name of one is irrelevant to the doctrine of resulting trusts. Only the intention of the contributor is relevant and it is presumed from his or her contribution. It would seem that there is a confusion in the cases between express trusts (which are unenforceable because they are not in writing) and resulting trusts based on contribution. The result is that often an express oral trust is enforced under the guise of a resulting trust.[25] Moreover, such a common intention is often inferred not just from one party's contributions, be they direct or indirect, but from the spouses' conduct, their stated or supposed expectations, whether they regarded their marriage and property as a joint venture and the respective efforts each party put into the venture either in money or money's-worth.[26]

Many of these cases were decided in reaction to the strict approach in *Thompson v. Thompson*,[27] which held that the summary proceeding provision of the Married Women's Property Acts could not be used to redistribute matrimonial property and in *Murdoch v. Murdoch*,[28] in which a rancher's wife who had done a lot of work on the ranch was denied a share in it because she was thought to have done no more than might be expected of a person in that position.

This search for a common intention of the spouses often involved, in effect, an imputation of common intent. This approach was rejected in England[29] and, therefore, the courts usually based their decisions on implied intent. However, it seems clear that they were forced to do so in order to do justice and equity between the spouses. Nevertheless, the fiction of a common intent appears to have led to the adoption of the constructive trust in matrimonial property disputes.

---

27 R.F.L. 393 (Alta. S.C.); *Borek v. Borek* (1976), 27 R.F.L. 352 (Alta. S.C.T.D.); *Re Whiteley and Whiteley* (1974), 4 O.R. (2d) 393, 48 D.L.R. (3d) 161 (C.A.); *Jensen v. Jensen* (1976), 29 R.F.L. 319 (B.C.S.C.); *Rathwell v. Rathwell* (1978), 83 D.L.R. (3d) 289, [1978] 2 S.C.R. 436.

25Cullity, *op. cit., supra*, footnote 22, at p. 284.

26*Mitchelson v. Mitchelson* (1953), 9 W.W.R. (N.S.) 316 (Man. Q.B.); *Atamanchuk v. Atamanchuk* (1955), 15 W.W.R. 301 (Man. Q.B.), revd in part 21 W.W.R. 335 (C.A.); *Cuthbert v. Cuthbert*, [1968] 2 O.R. 502, 69 D.L.R. (2d) 637 (C.A.); *Calder v. Cleland, supra*, footnote 22; *Re Whiteley and Whiteley, supra*, footnote 24; *Kowalchuk v. Kowalchuk, supra*, footnote 24; *Easton v. Easton, supra*, footnote 22; *Fiedler v. Fiedler* (1975), 55 D.L.R. (3d) 397, [1975] 3 W.W.R. 681 (Alta. S.C. App. Div.); *Calleja v. Calleja* (1974), 4 O.R. (2d) 754, 49 D.L.R. (3d) 202 (H.C.J.), vard 11 O.R. (2d) 342, 66 D.L.R. (3d) 84 (C.A.); *Gerk v. Gerk, supra*, footnote 23; *Ball v. Ball, supra*, footnote 22; *Borek v. Borek, supra*, footnote 24; *Madisso v. Madisso* (1975), 11 O.R. (2d) 441, 66 D.L.R. (3d) 385 (C.A.); *Rathwell v. Rathwell, supra*, footnote 24; *Armstrong v. Armstrong* (1978), 22 O.R. (2d) 223, 93 D.L.R. (3d) 128 (H.C.J.); *Tasker v. Tasker*, [1976] W.W.D. 176, 30 R.F.L. 79 (B.C.S.C.).

27*Supra*, footnote 22.

28*Supra*, footnote 22.

29*Pettitt v. Pettitt, supra*, footnote 22; *Gissing v. Gissing, supra*, footnote 22.

(d) The resulting trust in common law relationships

The traditional and historically correct view is that a presumption of advancement cannot arise in a common law relationship, because the female partner is a stranger in law to the male. Hence, the early cases held that where a man transfers property to a woman with whom he lives as husband and wife, a presumption of resulting trust arose.[30] The presumption can, of course, be rebutted by evidence of an intention to make a gift, which is often buttressed by the fact that the man has promised the woman that she will have a share in the property, because the property is taken in joint tenancy, or because of the length of the relationship, or contributions or labour by the woman or the man, from which the court can deduce a common intention that the parties have an equal or other share in the property.[31]

The search for an elusive common intention between common law spouses has also led to the adoption of the constructive trust in this area in recent years.

(e) The constructive trust

In some of the early cases the distinction between resulting and constructive trusts was not sharply drawn.[32] This led to confusion in some of the later cases. Often the courts would talk indiscriminately of doing equity on the basis of an implied, resulting or constructive trust.[33] Yet these trusts are distinct. The resulting trust arises only in certain well-defined circumstances.[34] The constructive trust, on the other hand, is a remedial device imposed by equity to avoid unjust enrichment. It was first proposed for use in matrimonial property disputes by Laskin, J., in his dissenting judgment in *Murdoch v. Murdoch*[35] and it has since been adopted by a minority of the Supreme Court in *Rathwell v. Rathwell*[36] and more recently by a majority in *Pettkus v. Becker*.[37] The

---

[30]*Clelland v. Clelland*, [1945] 3 D.L.R. 664, [1945] 2 W.W.R. 399 (B.C.C.A.); *Collins v. Sanders*, [1956] O.W.N. 505, 3 D.L.R. (2d) 607 (C.A.); *Blackhall v. Jardine*, [1958] O.W.N. 457 (C.A.); *Smith v. Barrie*, [1958] O.W.N. 284, 15 D.L.R. (2d) 435 (H.C.J.), and see *Tschcheidse v. Tschcheidse* (1963), 41 D.L.R. (2d) 138 (Sask. Q.B.); *Rowse v. Harris*, [1963] 2 O.R. 232, 39 D.L.R. (2d) 29 (H.C.J.).

[31]*Stanley v. Stanley* (1963), 36 D.L.R. (2d) 443, 39 W.W.R. 640 (Alta. S.C. App. Div.); *Barleben v. Barleben* (1964), 44 D.L.R. (2d) 332, 46 W.W.R. 683 (Alta. S.C. App. Div.); *Smith v. McLeod* (1972), 9 R.F.L. 39 (Ont. H.C.J.); *Smith v. Ahone* (1975), 56 D.L.R. (3d) 454, [1975] W.W.D. 101 (B.C.S.C.); *Douglas v. Guaranty Trust Co. of Canada* (1978), 8 R.F.L. (2d) 98, 4 E.T.R. 65 (Ont. H.C.J.); *Pettkus v. Becker* (1980), 117 D.L.R. (3d) 257, [1980] 2 S.C.R. 834, *per* Ritchie, Martland and Beetz, JJ.

[32]See, *e.g.*, *Gissing v. Gissing*, *supra*, footnote 22, *per* Lord Diplock.

[33]*Trueman v. Trueman*, *supra*, footnote 24; *Sikora v. Sikora*, [1977] 6 W.W.R. 580, 2 R.F.L. (2d) 48 (Alta. S.C.T.D.), affd [1980] 3 W.W.R. 142, 13 R.F.L. (2d) 391 (Alta. C.A.); *Cameron v. Armstrong* (1974), 47 D.L.R. (3d) 720, [1974] 5 W.W.R. 410 *sub nom. Cameron (Armstrong) v. Armstrong* (B.C.S.C.).

[34]See sub-subpara. (b), *supra*. As to implied trusts, see §1203.1, *supra*.

[35](1973), 41 D.L.R. (3d) 367, [1975] 1 S.C.R. 423.

[36](1978), 83 D.L.R. (3d) 289, [1978] 2 S.C.R. 436.

[37](1980), 117 D.L.R. (3d) 257, [1980] 2 S.C.R. 834, affg 20 O.R. (2d) 105, 87 D.L.R. (3d) 101 (C.A.).

doctrine has subsequently been applied in other cases.[38]

Both the *Rathwell* and *Pettkus* cases were very similar in their facts, except that in the former the parties were married, whereas in the latter they lived together as man and wife. In both cases the relationship had lasted for many years. Title to the property, a farming operation in both cases, was in the men, but the women made financial contributions and did a lot of work on the farms and in building up the businesses. In *Rathwell* the facts disclosed a common intention that the spouses should have an equal share in the property and the majority held in favour of the wife on the basis of a resulting trust. Dickson, J., who delivered the minority judgment, held in her favour either on the basis of a resulting or a constructive trust.

In *Pettkus* the Ontario Courts had found there to be no common intention, but Ritchie, J., who delivered the minority judgment in the Supreme Court found a common intention on the basis of the parties' conduct. Dickson, J., who delivered the majority judgment found in favour of the woman solely on the basis of a constructive trust.

Dickson, J., held in both cases that in order for a constructive trust to be raised there must be an unjust enrichment, a corresponding deprivation and the absence of any juristic reason for the enrichment.[39] Moreover, the court must assess the respective contributions, direct or indirect, financial or other and must find a causal connection between the contribution and the disputed asset.[40] Thus, where a man and woman have lived together for a number of years and have had a child, but where the woman has made no specific contribution to the matrimonial property, a constructive trust cannot be raised.[41]

In the end result, the type of inquiry required of the court under a resulting trust and constructive trust do not differ very much. However, the constructive trust is more flexible and avoids the search for an elusive common intent.[42]

---

[38]*Babrociak v. Babrociak* (1978), 1 R.F.L. (2d) 95 (Ont. C.A.); *Taylor v. Taylor* (1979), 10 R.F.L. (2d) 81 (Sask. Unified Fam. Ct.); *Boucher v. Boucher* (1980), 32 N.B.R. (2d) 647 (C.A.); *Pratt v. MacLeod et al.* (1981), 129 D.L.R. (3d) 23, 25 R.F.L. (2d) 27 (N.S.S.C.T.D.); *Murray v. Roty* (1983), 41 O.R. (2d) 705, 147 D.L.R. (3d) 438 (C.A.); *King v. King* (1980), 16 R.F.L. (2d) 117, 26 Nfld. & P.E.I.R. 121 (Nfld. S.C.T.D.), which refused to apply the constructive trust must be considered overruled after *Pettkus v. Becker, supra,* footnote 37, and see *Re Spears and Levy* (1974), 52 D.L.R. (3d) 146, 19 R.F.L. 101 (N.S.S.C. App. Div.), in which the doctrine was applied after the death of a common law husband. Neither the resulting nor constructive trust doctrines were held to be applicable under the *Married Person's Property Act,* R.S.S. 1978, c. M-6, s. 22, rep. S.S. 1979, c. M-6.1, s. 60, which conferred discretion on the court to do what it deemed "just and equitable" in a matrimonial property dispute: *Birkeland v. Birkeland* (1979), 10 R.F.L. (2d) 42, 3 Sask. R. 11 (C.A.).

[39]*Rathwell v. Rathwell, supra,* footnote 36, at p. 306 D.L.R., pp. 454-5 S.C.R.; *Pettkus v. Becker, supra,* footnote 37, at pp. 273-4 D.L.R., p. 848 S.C.R.

[40]*Ibid.* See further, Oosterhoff, "Comment", 57 Can. Bar Rev. 356 (1979).

[41]*Dwyer v. Love* (1975), 67 D.L.R. (3d) 550, 9 Nfld. & P.E.I.R. 325 (P.E.I.S.C.).

[42]Cullity, "The Matrimonial Home — A Return to Palm-Tree Justice: Trust Doctrines Based on (a) Intent and (b) Unjust Enrichment", 4 E. & T.Q. 277 (1977-78), at pp. 299 *et seq.*

(f) The continuing relevance of the trust doctrines

Although the trust doctrines discussed above have lost much of their relevance because of recent family law reform legislation, particularly on a breakdown of a marriage, they continue to be important for at least three reasons. In the first place, to the extent that these principles have been codified by the statutes, the earlier case-law provides a methodology and rationale for solving matrimonial property disputes. Secondly, it is often unclear whether the statutes provide a complete code in situations where there has not been a marriage breakdown.[43] And thirdly, the modern statutes do not apply, in their matrimonial property regimes, to common law relationships.

1604.2 Occupational Rights in the Matrimonial Home

(a) Generally

At common law a wife had a right to possession of the matrimonial home together with her husband. This arose from her right to her husband's consortium and his duty to maintain her.[1] More recently it was held that the husband enjoys a similar right, although in this case it is based solely on his right to consortium.[2]

In a series of English cases, beginning with *Bendall v. McWhirter*,[3] an attempt was made to confirm this right as an equity, the "deserted wife's equity" as it was called, enforceable against third parties. These cases were initially approved of in Canada.[4] Subsequently, however, the House of Lords in *National Provincial Bank v. Ainsworth*[5] reaffirmed the earlier law that the occupational right is personal only against the other spouse. The Canadian courts then followed the *Ainsworth* case.[6]

---

[43]Thus, in *Kiss v. Palachik* (1981), 34 O.R. (2d) 484, 130 D.L.R. (3d) 246 (C.A.), affd 146 D.L.R. (3d) 385, [1983] 1 S.C.R. 622, it was held that Part I of the *Family Law Reform Act*, R.S.O. 1980, c. 152, does not apply where one of the spouses has died, so that an application for an interest in the deceased spouse's property based on contributions thereto by the applicant does not lie under s. 8 of the Act, but must be made on the basis of a constructive trust.

§1604.2

[1]Cullity "Property Rights During the Subsistence of the Marriage" in *Studies in Canadian Family Law*, vol. 1 (Mendes da Costa, ed., Toronto, Butterworths, 1972), p. 208. The matrimonial home is the premises actually occupied by the spouses, such as a unit in an apartment building owned by the husband: *Re Chliwniak and Chliwniak*, [1972] 2 O.R. 840, 27 D.L.R. (3d) 19 (H.C.J.).

[2]*Re Maskewycz and Maskewycz* (1973), 2 O.R. (2d) 713, 44 D.L.R. (3d) 180 (C.A.).

[3][1952] 1 All E.R. 1307 (C.A.).

[4]See, *e.g.*, *Carnochan v. Carnochan*, [1953] O.R. 887, [1954] 1 D.L.R. 87 (H.C.J.), affd [1954] O.W.N. 543, [1954] 4 D.L.R. 448 (C.A.), affd [1955] 4 D.L.R. 81, [1955] S.C.R. 669; *Re Jollow and Jollow*, [1954] O.R. 895, [1955] 1 D.L.R. 601 (C.A.); *Rush v. Rush* (1960), 24 D.L.R. (2d) 248 (Ont. C.A.); *Richardson v. Richardson*, [1966] 2 O.R. 624 (S.C.).

[5][1965] 2 All E.R. 472 (H.L.).

[6]*Re Smyth and Smyth*, [1969] 1 O.R. 617, 3 D.L.R. (3d) 409 (H.C.J.); *Re Perkins and Perkins*, [1973] 1 O.R. 598, 31 D.L.R. (3d) 694 (H.C.J.); *Re Hearty and Hearty*, [1970] 2 O.R. 344, 10 D.L.R. (3d) 732 (H.C.J.); *Re Demaiter and Link*, [1973] 3 O.R. 140, 36 D.L.R. (3d) 164 (H.C.J.); *Re Maskewycz and Maskewycz, supra*, footnote 2; *Stevens v. Brown* (1969), 2 D.L.R. (3d) 687, [1965-69] 2 N.S.R. 301 (S.C.).

The right of possession ceased when the right to consortium was gone, namely, by adultery, desertion, dissolution of marriage, death, or court order.[7] As to desertion, it may be actual or constructive, as where one of the spouses forces the other to leave by his cruelty.[8]

Because of the husband's duty of maintenance towards his wife, he could not evict her from the matrimonial home (unless she disqualified herself by her conduct), except if he provided suitable alternative accommodation.[9]

Where one of the spouses is sole owner of the matrimonial home he or she would thus be entitled to exclusive possession if the right to consortium ceased.

Occupational rights in the matrimonial home are now governed by the matrimonial property law reform statutes enacted in most of the provinces.

(b) Co-ownership

The question was not that simple where the spouses were co-owners of the matrimonial home. Clearly, in this case the spouses have co-equal rights of occupation based on proprietary rather than mere personal rights. However, this right may be terminated when one of them applies for partition or sale. Legislation respecting partition is in force in all of the common law jurisdictions.[10] Most of these statutes give a discretion to the court to grant or refuse an application for partition or sale[11] but some confer a right to partition.[12]

In those jurisdictions in which the court is given a discretion, the application will generally be refused if the applicant has deserted his or her spouse and has acted vexatiously or oppressively.[13] It may also be refused if the parties are still living together in the matrimonial home with their children,[14] although it has been held that where the wife did not desert her husband, he could not

---

[7]See generally *Audras v. Audras*, [1970] 2 O.R. 46, 9 D.L.R. (3d) 675 (Dist. Ct.); *Re Maskewycz and Maskewycz, supra*, footnote 2; *Richardson v. Richardson, supra*, footnote 4.

[8]*Kay and Kay v. Kay* (1962), 36 D.L.R. (2d) 31 (N.B.S.C. App. Div.); *Krentz v. Krentz*, [1975] W.W.D. 116, 21 R.F.L. 87 (Sask. Dist. Ct.). A subsequent separation agreement ends the desertion and the rights that flow therefrom: *Makins v. Makins* (1978), 2 R.F.L. (2d) 104 (Ont. Unified Fam. Ct.).

[9]*Beauchamp v. Beauchamp* (1970), 6 R.F.L. 43 (Ont. H.C.J.).

[10]*Partition of Property Act*, R.S.B.C. 1979, c. 311; *Law of Property Act*, R.S.A. 1980, c. L-8; R.S.M. 1970, c. L90, ss. 19-26; *Rules of the Supreme Court* (N.B., 1969), O. 56, rr. 23-31; *Partition Act* (1868), 31 & 32 Vict., c. 40 (1868), in force in Saskatchewan, Northwest Territories and Yukon Territory; R.S.N.S. 1967, c. 223; R.S.O. 1980, c. 369; *Judicature Act*, R.S.N. 1970, c. 187, ss. 109-21; *Real Property Act*, R.S.P.E.I. 1974, c. R-4, ss. 21-54. (Hereafter referred to as the Alta. Act, Imp. Act, *etc.*)

[11]The B.C., Man., Ont. and P.E.I. statutes and the N.B. Rules of Court.

[12]The Imp. and Alta. statutes.

[13]*Re Hutcheson and Hutcheson*, [1950] 2 D.L.R. 751, [1950] O.R. 265 (C.A.); *Rayner v. Rayner* (1956), 3 D.L.R. (2d) 522 (B.C.S.C.); *Klakow v. Klakow* (1972), 7 R.F.L. 349 (Ont. H.C.J.).

[14]*Verzin v. Verzin* (1974), 16 R.F.L. 94 (Ont. H.C.J.).

obtain a stay of an order for sale obtained by her to permit him to continue to reside in the home.[15]

Although there is a discretion, the courts have stressed that it must be exercised judicially. Hence, even though the wife deserted her husband and treated him shabbily, partition will be granted if she does not act oppressively.[16] Similarly, where the husband deserted his wife but is paying her support and is bringing up the children of the marriage, partition will be granted.[17]

Thus, partition will be refused only if the applicant's actions are oppressive, malicious or vexatious.[18] "Oppressive" in this respect means oppressive in an economic sense as, for example, where a husband refused to honour his obligations to support his wife and children, or to provide alternative accommodation.[19] Mere inconvenience to the other spouse is insufficient to deny the application.[20]

On the other hand, where the housing market is difficult so that the wife would have difficulty finding another home, there is a chance of reconciliation, the husband acts maliciously and the order would vary a separation agreement, partition will be refused.[21] Similarly, where the husband deserts his wife and fails to pay support and to provide alternative accommodation,[22] or where there are young children living in the home and it is in their interest not to order a sale,[23] the application will be dismissed.

In Ontario it has long been held that where the question of desertion is involved and, in the case of the husband, his duty to provide alternative accommodation to his wife, an application should be made first under section 12 of the *Married Women's Property Act*[24] to determine the property rights of the spouses and then under the *Partition Act*, with the proceeds of sale

---

[15]*Duban v. Duban* (1975), 29 R.F.L. 129 (Ont. C.A.).

[16]*Lothrop v. Kline* (1957), 21 W.W.R. 333 (B.C.S.C.); *Shwabiuk v. Shwabiuk* (1965), 51 D.L.R. (2d) 361, 51 W.W.R. (N.S.) 549 (Man. Q.B.).

[17]*Richardson v. Richardson*, [1970] 3 O.R. 41, 12 D.L.R. (3d) 233 (H.C.J.).

[18]*Re Roblin and Roblin*, [1960] O.R. 157 (H.C.J.); *Czarnick v. Zagora* (1972), 8 R.F.L. 259 (Ont. H.C.J.).

[19]*Korolew v. Korolew* (1972), 7 R.F.L. 162 (B.C.S.C.); *Meadows v. Meadows* (1974), 17 R.F.L. 36 (B.C.S.C.).

[20]*Van Engel v. Van Engel* (1973), 11 R.F.L. 303 (B.C.S.C.); *Re Perkins and Perkins*, [1973] 1 O.R. 598, 31 D.L.R. (3d) 694 (H.C.J.); *Cmajdalka v. Cmajdalka* (1973), 11 R.F.L. 302 (Ont. C.A.); *Fenik v. Fenik* (1974), 16 R.F.L. 14 (Ont. S.C.); *Kaplan v. Kaplan* (1974), 15 R.F.L. 239 (B.C.S.C.); *Reitsma v. Reitsma*, [1975] 3 W.W.R. 281, 17 R.F.L. 292 (B.C.S.C.); *Bossert v. Bossert* (1976), 29 R.F.L. 387 (Ont. H.C.J.).

[21]*Steele v. Steele* (1960), 67 Man. R. 270 (Q.B.).

[22]*Bergen v. Bergen* (1969), 68 W.W.R. 196 (B.C.S.C.); *Knight v. Knight* (1975), 20 R.F.L. 381 (Ont. S.C.).

[23]*Buhlert v. Buhlert* (1975), 22 R.F.L. 215 (B.C.S.C.); *Carton v. Carton* (1975), 21 R.F.L. 366 (Ont. S.C.); *Fernandes v. Fernandes* (1975), 65 D.L.R. (3d) 684, [1976] 3 W.W.R. 510 (B.C.S.C.); *Clarke v. Clarke* (1975), 22 R.F.L. 102 (Ont. Co. Ct.); *Melvin v. Melvin* (1975), 58 D.L.R. (3d) 98, 23 R.F.L. 19 (N.B.S.C. App. Div.), affd R.F.L. *loc. cit.*, 11 N.B.R. (2d) 358 (S.C.Q.B. Div.); *McLennan v. McLennan* (1976), 29 R.F.L. 117 (B.C.S.C.).

[24]RS.O. 1970, c. 262, rep. S.O. 1975, c. 41, s. 6 and S.O. 1978, c. 2, s. 82.

being applied first to provide alternative accommodation, if necessary.[25] Hence, it became customary to make a combined application under both statutes.[26]

The Married Women's Property Acts have no application after the parties are divorced, but the courts continued to exercise their discretion under the Partition Acts in such cases and would refuse the application in appropriate circumstances. The test applied in more recent cases, both before and after divorce, was not solely whether the applicant had acted oppressively, maliciously or vexatiously. Rather, the courts tended to exercise their discretion on the basis of the relative hardship to the parties[27] and would refuse to make an order even as against the husband's trustee in bankruptcy where hardship to the wife would result.[28] Nevertheless, the right to partition is regarded as a primary right and should only be refused if there is real hardship.[29]

An application made by a purchaser of the interest of one of the spouses is also subject to the court's discretion but it will be granted if he acted in good faith and without malice.[30]

Even in those jurisdictions where partition is a matter of right, the courts will often exercise their discretion. Thus, in Alberta it has been held that while partition is a matter of right, a sale is discretionary and will be refused if the husband has failed to make provision for his wife[31] and where infant children reside in the home with the wife.[32]

Similarly in Saskatchewan where partition is a matter of right,[33] a husband was ordered to pay a lump sum to his wife in satisfaction of her interest in the matrimonial home.[34]

In appropriate circumstances the court will exercise its discretion to give

---

[25]*Rush v. Rush* (1960), 24 D.L.R. (2d) 248 (Ont. C.A.); *Re Cates and Cates*, [1968] 2 O.R. 447 (C.A.).

[26]*Re Hearty and Hearty*, [1970] 2 O.R. 344, 10 D.L.R. (3d) 732 (H.C.J.); *Green v. Green* (1971), 5 R.F.L. 361 (Ont. H.C.J.); *Neeson v. Neeson* (1971), 5 R.F.L. 348 (Ont. H.C.J.). *Cf.* to the same effect *Hammond v. Hammond* (1975), 22 R.F.L. 243 (B.C.S.C.), and see *Hamilton v. Hamilton*, [1976] W.W.D. 135, 28 R.F.L. 54 (B.C.S.C.); *Kaye v. Kaye* (1974), 6 O.R. (2d) 65, 52 D.L.R. (3d) 14 (H.C.J.).

[27]*McFadden v. McFadden* (1972), 5 R.F.L. 299 (Ont. Co. Ct.); *Re MacDonald and MacDonald* (1973), 13 R.F.L. 248 (Ont. C.A.); *Fernandes v. Fernandes, supra,* footnote 23.

[28]*Re Yale and MacMaster* (1974), 3 O.R. (2d) 547, 46 D.L.R. (3d) 167 (H.C.J.).

[29]*Re MacDonald and MacDonald* (1976), 14 O.R. (2d) 249, 73 D.L.R. (3d) 341 (H.C.J.).

[30]*McGeer v. Green and Westminster Mortgage Corp. Ltd.* (1960), 22 D.L.R. (2d) 775 (B.C.S.C.).

[31]*Clarke v. Clarke* (1974), 48 D.L.R. (3d) 707, [1974] 5 W.W.R. 274 (Alta. S.C. App. Div.); *Elligott v. Elligott* (1977), 3 R.F.L. (2d) 61, 6 A.R. 282 (S.C.), and see *Wagner v. Wagner* (1970), 73 W.W.R. (N.S.) 474 (Alta. S.C.). Mere inconvenience to the wife is not sufficient to deny the application, however: *Re Kronenberger and Kronenberger* (1977), 77 D.L.R. (3d) 571, 3 Alta. L.R. (2d) 121, 4 A.R. 546 and 6 A.R. 491 (S.C.T.D.).

[32]*Re Kornacki and Kornacki* (1975), 58 D.L.R. (3d) 159, 21 R.F.L. 400 (Alta. S.C. App. Div.).

[33]*Thomas v. Thomas* (1962). 29 D.L.R. (2d) 576, 36 W.W.R. 23 (Sask. C.A.).

[34]*Koshman v. Koshman* (1976), 27 R.F.L. 249 (Sask. Q.B.).

exclusive possession of the home to one of the spouses even though the property is jointly owned.[35]

Although property is held jointly, it is open to the parties to argue that they hold in unequal shares or that one has the entire beneficial interest. However, where both have made contributions to the acquisition of the property, although in unequal shares, the presumption is one of advancement even, it seems, as between common law spouses, and unless the presumption is rebutted the parties are entitled to partition or sale with an equal division of the proceeds.[36]

Partition and sale of the matrimonial home is now governed by the matrimonial property law reform statutes enacted in virtually all of the provinces.

1604.3 Property and Occupational Rights of Common Law Spouses

Although under the new family law reform legislation in the several Canadian jurisdictions common law spouses have been given rights of support in certain cases, they do not have a right to share in the family or other assets on a breakdown of the relationship as do spouses. Except where a common law spouse is a co-owner with the other, the only way in which he or she can assert a proprietary claim to the "matrimonial home" and other assets owned by the other party is under a resulting or constructive trust.[1]

In recent years the English courts have developed additional remedies for the non-titled common law spouse. These are the irrevocable contractual licence and the right to remain in possession of the property on the basis of proprietary estoppel.[2] Although these rights have been recognized in other contexts in Canada, they do not appear to have been extended to the common law spouse situation. Nevertheless they may prove useful in the future since they can often be applied where a trust cannot be raised.

(a) Contractual licence

If a licence is given for good consideration, which includes a term not to revoke the licence for a certain period, the licensor or promisor cannot revoke that right in breach of the contract. Such a licence may be inferred from the parties' conduct and the licensee is entitled to protect his legal, contractual

---

[35]*Krentz v. Krentz*, [1975] W.W.D. 116, 21 R.F.L. 87 (Sask. Dist. Ct.), husband forcing wife to leave by his cruelty.

[36]*Manley v. Schiller* (1980), 18 R.F.L. (2d) 109, 22 B.C.L.R. 61 (S.C.).

§1604.3

[1]See, *e.g., Pettkus v. Becker* (1980), 117 D.L.R. (3d) 257, [1980] 2 S.C.R. 834; *Cooke v. Head*, [1972] 2 All E.R. 38 (C.A.); *Eves v. Eves*, [1975] 3 All E.R. 768 (C.A.), and see §1604.1(d), (e), *supra*.

[2]For a discussion of these remedies see Anderson, "Of Licences, and Similar Mysteries", 42 Mod. L. Rev. 203 (1979); Ellis, "Contractual and Equitable Licences", 95 L.Q. Rev. 11 (1979); Oughton, "Proprietary Estoppel: A Principled Remedy" (1979), 129 New L.J. 1193; Richards, "The Mistress and the Family Home", 40 Conv. 351 (1976); Everton, "An Equity to Remain . . .", 40 Conv. 416 (1976); Zuckerman, "Formality and the Family — Reform and the Status Quo", 96 L.Q. Rev. 248 (1980), at pp. 251-71.

rights through the equitable remedy of an injunction and thereby keep possession of the premises for the promised period of time. He may also recover damages for wrongful eviction.[3]

In *Tanner v. Tanner*[4] the defendant woman gave up a rent-controlled flat to move in with the plaintiff man who provided a house for them, the title to which was put in his name. The plaintiff made it clear that he had no intention to marry the defendant, but they had children together and the defendant furnished the home with her own money. Subsequently the plaintiff married another woman and tried to turn the defendant out. The Court of Appeal held that in the circumstances a contract should be inferred whereby the plaintiff had granted the defendant an irrevocable licence to have accommodation in the house for herself and the children so long as they were of school age and the accommodation was reasonably required by them. The consideration for the licence was the giving up by the defendant of her former tenancy. The defendant having left, she was awarded judgment for £2,000 as damages for lost possession.[5]

The terms of the licence may, of course, vary depending on the circumstances. Thus, in *Chandler v. Kerley*[6] the defendant owned the matrimonial home jointly with her husband. When he moved out, the plaintiff commenced to live with the defendant. The three of them agreed that the plaintiff should purchase the house, which he did, but at a reduced price, on the understanding that the plaintiff would continue to provide a home for the defendant and her children. The defendant agreed to accept less than half of her share of the purchase price. Shortly thereafter the relationship ended and the plaintiff sought possession. The Court of Appeal held that in these circumstances an irrevocable licence could not be implied. In the absence of an express agreement by the plaintiff to provide a home for the defendant it would be wrong to infer that he had undertaken to assume the burden of housing another man's wife and children indefinitely. Hence, although the wife had a licence, it was held to be revocable on reasonable notice.

In order to establish a contractual licence it must be shown that there was an agreement to that effect. In *Horrocks v. Forray*[7] the deceased had lived with his mistress, the defendant, and their child in his house. After his death the defendant claimed that she had subordinated her life-style and choice of residence to those of the deceased in return for his undertaking to provide a home for her and their child. The court found that there had not been a meeting of the minds, nor reasonably clear proof of the terms of the agreement. Thus, it denied the defendant's claim to an irrevocable contractual licence.

---

[3]*Tanner v. Tanner*, [1975] 3 All E.R. 776 (C.A.).

[4]*Supra*, footnote 3.

[5]See also *Hardwick v. Johnson*, [1978] 2 All E.R. 935 (C.A.), and *Re Sharpe; Ex p. trustee of bankrupt v. Sharpe*, [1980] 1 All E.R. 198 (Ch.). These cases did not involve common law spouses but family members and irrevocable contractual licences were found to exist in circumstances similar to *Tanner v. Tanner, supra*, footnote 3.

[6][1978] 2 All E.R. 942 (C.A.).

[7][1976] 1 All E.R. 737 (C.A.).

The difficulty with this remedy is that it does not protect the common law spouse against a *bona fide* purchaser for value without notice, unless the licence can be and is in fact registered.

(b) Proprietary estoppel

Where A stands by and allows B to act to his detriment in reliance upon a representation by A that B has an interest in his property, equity will not allow A to deny that interest. He is estopped from denying it. Moreover, this proprietary estoppel may be used as a sword as well as a shield.[8]

Thus, in *Pascoe v. Turner*[9] a common law spouse allowed his partner to make improvements on the house owned by him after the relationship ended in reliance on his representation that the house and contents were hers. Some time later he sought to evict her. In the circumstances no constructive or resulting trust could be raised nor an irrevocable licence. However, the court refused to allow the plaintiff to evict the defendant because she had acted in detrimental reliance upon his representation. In order to afford the defendant adequate protection the court ordered that the property be transferred to the defendant in fee simple.[10]

The problem with this remedy is that it must be shown that there is in fact a reliance on some promise or standing by on the part of the owner and a substantial improvement by the other party before estoppel can be raised. Moreover, unless as in the *Pascoe* case the court directs a conveyance of the interest to the improver, the right would not be effective against a *bona fide* purchaser for value without notice.

(c) Other cases

Under the *Domestic Violence and Matrimonial Proceedings Act, 1976*[11] a spouse and a common law spouse can obtain an exclusion order against his partner in cases of domestic violence. It has been held that while the Act does not affect the property rights of the partner, the court can affect the enjoyment of those rights. Hence, even though a common law spouse owns the "matrimonial home" or has an interest in it, he may be excluded from it in cases of domestic violence.[12]

1604.4 Dower, Curtesy and Homestead Rights

(a) Dower

Dower is the wife's right to a life estate after her husband's death in one-third of all the real property of which her husband was solely seised during coverture

---

[8]*Crabb v. Arun District Council*, [1976] Ch. 179 (C.A.), at pp. 192-5, *per* Scarman, L.J.
[9][1979] 2 All E.R. 945 (C.A.).
[10]See also *Inwards v. Baker*, [1965] 2 Q.B. 29 (C.A.); *Williams v. Staite*, [1979] Ch. 291 (C.A.).
[11]C. 50 (1976, U.K.).
[12]*Davis v. Johnson*, [1978] 1 All E.R. 1132 (H.L.).

or to which he died beneficially entitled. Her right is destroyed if her husband disposes of the property with her consent.

Dower has been dealt with in detail in chapter 7[1] and will not be discussed further here. It has been abolished in Ontario and the maritime provinces by the recent family law reform legislation which will be discussed in the following paragraphs.

(b) Curtesy

The husband's right to curtesy, a life estate in all his wife's real property which she has not disposed of *inter vivos* or by will has already been discussed.[2] This right has not survived in recent family law reform legislation.

(c) Homestead rights

In the western provinces homestead legislation was enacted to take the place of dower and curtesy. It entitles the wife and, in some cases, the husband, to a life estate in the matrimonial home and surrounding land after the husband's or wife's death. These rights, which have been discussed in detail elsewhere,[3] have been continued under the new family law reform legislation in these provinces.

It should be noted that property may be a homestead even though it is jointly owned by the spouses.[4] Difficulties may arise in applications for partition or sale of the homestead where it is in co-ownership. The question is whether the spouse seeking partition must obtain the other spouse's consent or obtain a court order dispensing with consent before proceeding to partition. The law is unclear, there being cases which go both ways. Generally, it appears that the court will exercise its discretion in such circumstances.[5]

1605. MATRIMONIAL PROPERTY LAW REFORM

The reform of family law has been an issue in the Canadian common law provinces at least since 1965 when the Ontario Law Reform Commission began its research project on the topic. It was spurred on by court decisions such as *Murdoch v. Murdoch.*[1] That case, in particular, led to interim reforms in three

---

§1604.4

[1]See §§707-707.20, *supra.*

[2]See §§708-709, *supra.*

[3]See §§710-710.15, *supra.*

[4]*Wimmer v. Wimmer*, [1947] 4 D.L.R. 56, [1947] 2 W.W.R. 249 (Man. C.A.), but see, *contra, Evans v. Evans*, [1951] 2 D.L.R. 221, 1 W.W.R. (N.S.) 280 (B.C.C.A.).

[5]See Cullity, "Property Rights During the Subsistence of Marriage" in *Studies in Canadian Family Law*, vol. 1 (Mendes da Costa, ed., Toronto, Butterworths, 1972), p. 179, at pp. 232-48, and see *Wimmer v. Wimmer, supra,* footnote 4; *Robertson v. Robertson* (1951), 1 W.W.R. (N.S.) 183 (Alta. S.C.); *McWilliam v. McWilliam and Prudential Ins. Co. of America* (1960), 31 W.W.R. 480 (Alta. S.C.), affd 34 W.W.R. 476 (S.C. App. Div.).

§1605

[1](1973), 41 D.L.R. (3d) 367, [1975] 1 S.C.R. 423. See §1604.1(c), *supra.*

provinces, namely, British Columbia,[2] Ontario[3] and Saskatchewan.[4] Since then all the common law jurisdictions in Canada, except the Northwest Territories, have enacted comprehensive matrimonial property and other family law reform legislation.

The new legislation is discussed in detail in the following paragraphs. Although there is a great similarity among the several statutes, the differences are such that a province by province discussion is more appropriate. Some common features may be outlined, however.

All of the statutes provide for a deferred sharing of assets on a marriage breakdown, which is variously defined. In some provinces an application may also be brought after the death of one of the spouses. However, until an application is made for a division of assets, the separate property regime continues. That regime is modified by the reform legislation, but it is unclear to what extent the statutes have codified the common law principles applicable under it.

In recognition of the fact that the matrimonial home is the most important asset, all of the statutes make special provision for it, usually in the form of giving each spouse equal rights of possession with the other during marriage. The courts are empowered to confer exclusive rights of possession on one spouse. The Newfoundland Act[5] is exceptional in this respect in that it creates community of property with respect to the matrimonial home.

In respect of the right to share in the spouses' assets or the family assets and the rights in the family home, the statutes apply only to persons who are married to each other. They do not apply to cohabitees.

All of the statutes permit the parties to contract out of their provisions, with certain exceptions (typically with respect to the matrimonial home), but some of them also permit the court to set a domestic contract aside for inequity or unfairness. Although marriage contracts were uncommon in common law Canada heretofore, it is probable that they will become much more common as a result of the new legislation.

The statutes all contain provisions to overcome the effects of the *Murdoch* case.[6] The Nova Scotia provision is typical.[7] It provides as follows:

> 18. Where one spouse has contributed work, money or money's worth in respect of the acquisition, management, maintenance, operation or improvement of a business asset of the other spouse, the contributing spouse may apply to the court and the court shall by order
>> (*a*) direct the other spouse to pay such an amount on such terms and conditions as the court orders to compensate the contributing spouse therefore; or
>> (*b*) award a share of the interest of the other spouse in the business asset to the contributing spouse in accordance with the contribution,

---

2See §1605.2(a), *infra*.
3See §1605.7(a), *infra*.
4See §1605.9(a), *infra*.
5*Matrimonial Property Act*, S.N. 1979, c. 32, am. S.N. 1980, c. 24, s. 11.
6*Supra*, footnote 1.
7*Matrimonial Property Act*, S.N.S. 1980, c. 9, s. 18.

and the court shall determine and assess the contribution without regard to the relationship of husband and wife or the fact that the acts constituting the contribution are those of a reasonable spouse of that sex in the circumstances.

Most of the statutes also specifically abolish the presumption of advancement as between spouses. The New Brunswick statute[8] provides, for example:

> 15(1) The rule of law applying a presumption of advancement in questions of the ownership of property as between husband and wife is abolished and in place thereof the rule of law applying a presumption of a resulting trust shall be applied in the same manner as if they were not married, except that,
>
> > (a) the fact that property is placed or taken in the name of spouses as joint tenants is *prima facie* proof that each spouse is intended to have on a severance of the joint tenancy a one-half beneficial interest in the property; and
> >
> > (b) money on deposit in a chartered bank, savings office, credit union or trust company in the name of both spouses shall be deemed to be in the name of the spouses as joint tenants for the purposes of paragraph (a).
>
> (2) Subsection (1) applies notwithstanding that the event giving rise to the presumption occurred before the coming into force of this section.

Finally, the statutes contain a procedural provision permitting the court to determine property questions between spouses. The Ontario Act[9] is typical. It provides as follows:

> 7. Any person may apply to the court for the determination of any question between that person and his or her spouse or former spouse as to the ownership or right to possession of any particular property, except where an application or an order has been made respecting the property under section 4 or 6, and the court may,
>
> > (a) declare the ownership or right to possession;
> >
> > (b) where the property has been disposed of, order payment in compensation for the interest of either party;
> >
> > (c) order that the property be partitioned or sold for the purpose of realizing the interests therein; and
> >
> > (d) order that either or both spouses give security for the performance of any obligation imposed by the order, including a charge on property,
>
> and may make such other orders or directions as are ancillary thereto.

1605.1 Alberta

(a) Introduction

The *Matrimonial Property Act, 1978*[1] came into force on January 1, 1979. The Act does not abolish the separate property regime, but introduces a scheme for distribution of matrimonial property which may be invoked by spouses on the breakdown of their marriage. They need not avail themselves of it and, if they do not, or if there is no marriage breakdown, the separate

---

8*Marital Property Act*, S.N.B. 1980, c. M-1.1, s. 15.
9*Family Law Reform Act*, R.S.O. 1980, c. 152, s. 7.
§1605.1
1S.A. 1978, c. 22, now R.S.A. 1980, c. M-9 (hereafter referred to as the "Act").

property regime continues to apply. The Act further makes provision for possession of the matrimonial home.

(b) Application of Act

The Act may only be invoked by persons who are or were married to each other, even though the marriage is or was voidable or void.[2] The Act has, however, been interpreted as not being retroactive, so that it does not apply to persons who were divorced prior to its effective date.[3] The Act does not apply to common law spouses.

A person may seek an order under the Act in one of five circumstances, namely, (1) where the marriage has been terminated by divorce or annulment, (2) where there has been a judgment of judicial separation, (3) where there has been a marriage breakdown and the parties have lived separate and apart for at least one year or for less than one year if there is no possibility of reconciliation, (4) to prevent a gift or a transfer to a person who is not a *bona fide* purchaser for value with the intention of defeating a claim under the Act by the applicant where the spouses are living separate and apart and (5) to prevent dissipation of assets by one spouse to the detriment of the other, where they are living separate and apart.[4]

The application must be brought within two years of the decree *nisi* of divorce, declaration of nullity, or judgment of judicial separation and within two years of separation or, in the case of a transfer or gift, within two years after the transfer or gift.[5]

An application may be made after the death of one of the spouses but only if the application could have been commenced immediately before his death. Moreover, it must be commenced no later than six months after a grant of letters of probate or administration.[6] If the preconditions for making an order are met, the court must have regard to any benefits received by the applicant as a result of the death of the deceased spouse.[7] If the preconditions are not satisfied, however, the surviving spouse must rely on the general law respecting succession and, to the extent that there is a claim for a property interest in the estate apart from the law of succession, on the rules respecting the ascertainment of property interests under the separate property regime.

An order made under the Act takes precedence over the beneficiaries of a deceased spouse's estate.[8] However, the right to make application under the Act is personal to the spouses and does not survive their deaths.[9] The right of a spouse to make an application for support as a dependant under the *Family Relief Act*[10] is preserved.

---

[2]Act, ss. 1(*e*), 2.
[3]*Husted v. Husted* (1979), 108 D.L.R. (3d) 328, 13 R.F.L. (2d) 152 (Alta. C.A.).
[4]Act, s. 5(1).
[5]*Ibid.*, s. 6.
[6]*Ibid.*, s. 11.
[7]*Ibid.*, s. 11(3).
[8]*Ibid.*, s. 15.
[9]*Ibid.*, s. 16.
[10]R.S.A. 1980, c. F-2.

(c) Distribution of property

As distinguished from most of the other recent family law reform statutes, the Alberta Act does not distinguish between different assets on the basis of use but rather on the basis of ownership. It provides that all the property owned by both spouses and by each of them is distributable.[11] The Act recognizes three types of property, namely, exempt property, distributable property and divisible property.

Exempt property includes property acquired by a spouse by gift from a third person or by inheritance; property acquired by a spouse before marriage; and an award or settlement for damages in tort and the proceeds of an insurance policy which did not insure property, unless the award, settlement or proceeds are compensation for loss to both spouses. The market value of exempt property at the time of the marriage or its date of acquisition, whichever is later, is exempt from distribution.[12]

Distributable property includes the difference between the exempted value of exempt property and the market value at the time of trial of that property or property taken in exchange therefor, or the proceeds of sale thereof; property acquired during the marriage with income from exempt property; property acquired after a decree *nisi* of divorce, a declaration of nullity or a judgment of judicial separation; and interspousal gifts. Distributable property is to be divided between the spouses in such manner as the court considers just and equitable after taking into consideration the factors listed in section 8.[13]

Divisible property is property acquired by a spouse during marriage that is not exempt or distributable property. It is to be divided equally, unless it would not be just and equitable to do so, having regard to matters listed in section 8.[14]

The factors listed in section 8 which the court must consider include the contribution made by each spouse to the marriage; the contribution, whether direct or indirect, financial or other, made by a spouse to the acquisition, conservation, improvement, operation or management of a property or business; the financial resources and earning capacity of the spouses; the duration of the marriage; any agreement between the spouses; and the tax consequences of an order.

Whether property is exempt, such as, for example, a gift from a third party, depends upon the nature of the transaction. Thus, it has been held that where a husband and his parents agreed that the family farm would be transferred to the husband and his wife when she resumed cohabitation and it was transferred to the husband as a gift, it was not in fact a gift, but the fulfilment of an earlier arrangement. Hence, the farm was subject to equal division.[15]

---

[11]Act, s. 7(1).

[12]*Ibid.*, s. 7(2).

[13]*Ibid.*, s. 7(3). Funds obtained from a mortgage of inherited property are not exempt: *Baker v. Baker* (1981), 127 D.L.R. (3d) 247, 24 R.F.L. (2d) 21 (Alta. Q.B.).

[14]*Ibid.*, s. 7(4). Although shares in a corporation may be divisible, the assets of the corporation themselves are not: *Kenson Holdings Ltd. v. Kennedy* (1981), 20 R.F.L. (2d) 113 (Alta. Q.B.).

Moreover, where the property is partly exempt, it may be difficult to place a value on the exempt portion if, for example, it depends on a *quantum meruit* claim. For this purpose the factors listed in section 8 have to be taken into account.[16] Although the property may have increased in value after a separation as a result of improvements and inflation, it will nevertheless be valued at the time of the hearing.[17]

The wide discretion given to the court by sections 7 and 8 enable it to reallocate the spouses' property rather freely. Thus, although equal or near-equal division is sometimes indicated, as where both parties brought substantial assets into the marriage,[18] or even where the husband owned a farm and the wife did not really assist in the operation of the farm,[19] the courts do pay close regard to the factors listed in section 8 and will make an unequal division where, for example, the marriage was relatively short.[20] Moreover, where the husband owns several businesses, the valuation of exempt property is difficult and the liquidation of his holdings would be expensive and inappropriate for the children of the marriage, the court may make a lump sum maintenance award on the wife's petition for divorce, rather than make a distribution of property under the Act.[21]

The court is given wide powers under the Act to order a spouse to pay money or to transfer an interest in property to the other spouse, to order that property be sold and the proceeds be divided and to make an order providing for the recovery of property given or transferred to a third person for insufficient consideration.[22] It has been held, however, that despite the court's wide discretion, the Act is not designed as a vehicle for the redistribution of wealth but merely represents a recognition of rights in property arising from non-pecuniary contributions. A wife was, therefore, denied her application for a transfer of her husband's joint interest in the matrimonial home but merely received exclusive occupancy rights.[23]

(d) The matrimonial home

Part II of the Act empowers the court, on the application of a spouse, to make an order giving exclusive possession of the matrimonial home and

---

[15]*Mazurenko v. Mazurenko* (1980), 15 R.F.L. (2d) 148, 30 A.R. at p. 45 (Q.B.), revd on other grounds 124 D.L.R. (3d) 406, A.R., *loc. cit.* 34 (C.A.).

[16]*Foat v. Foat* (1980), 16 R.F.L. (2d) 153, 23 A.R. 168 (Q.B.).

[17]*McArthur v. McArthur* (1980), 15 R.F.L. (2d) 293, 26 A.R. 257 (Q.B.); *Nay v. Nay*, [1981] 3 W.W.R. 606, 20 R.F.L. (2d) 172 (Alta. Q.B.).

[18]*Visser v. Visser* (1980), 13 R.F.L. (2d) 361, 20 A.R. 434 (Q.B.), equal division.

[19]*Whiting v. Whiting* (1980), 14 R.F.L. (2d) 254 (Alta. Q.B.), 60% to husband, 40% to wife, and see *Fuhrman v. Fuhrman* (1980), 19 R.F.L. (2d) 404, 28 A.R. 152 (Q.B.), equal division.

[20]*Helstein v. Helstein* (1979), 12 R.F.L. (2d) 273, 11 Alta. L.R. (2d) 56 (Q.B.); *Augart v. Augart* (1979), 12 R.F.L. (2d) 327 (Alta. Q.B.).

[21]*Marquardson v. Marquardson* (1979), 10 Alta. L.R. (2d) 247, 19 A.R. 600 (S.C.T.D.).

[22]Act, ss. 9, 10.

[23]*Kamuchik v. Kamuchik* (1979), 9 R.F.L. (2d) 358 (Alta. S.C.T.D.).

exclusive use of the household goods to the applicant.[24] The order may be registered.[25] An application for exclusive possession of the matrimonial home may be refused where neither party can show a predominant reason for such an order.[26] The rights under Part II are in addition to the spouses' dower rights.[27]

(e) Contracting out

Spouses and persons contemplating marriage may enter into a written agreement which has the effect of ousting the distribution of property provisions of Part I of the Act.[28] The agreement is enforceable if each of the parties acknowledges in writing before his own lawyer that he is aware of the effect of the agreement and of the claims he is giving up and that he is executing it freely and voluntarily.[29]

(f) Presumption of advancement

The presumption of advancement is abolished for the purposes of the Act, but jointly owned property and money in joint bank accounts are *prima facie* owned equally by both spouses.[30]

1605.2 British Columbia

(a) Introduction

In 1972, as a result of a revision and consolidation of earlier legislation, the *Family Relations Act, 1972*[1] was enacted. This Act provided that the court could, on a marriage breakdown, "make any order that, in its opinion, should be made to provide for the application of all or part of the property [to which a spouse is entitled] for the benefit of either or both spouses or a child of a spouse or of the marriage".[2] Although early cases held that this section did not give the courts a broad equitable power to redistribute property regardless of proprietary interest,[3] the British Columbia Court of Appeal held subsequently that a prior proprietary interest was not necessary, but that the court had a very wide discretion to reallocate property under the section.[4] The Act

---

24Act, ss. 19, 25.
25*Ibid.*, ss. 22, 26.
26*Hickey v. Hickey and Beaverbrook Properties Ltd.* (1980), 18 R.F.L. (2d) 74, 13 Alta. L.R. (2d) 39 (Q.B.).
27Act, s. 28.
28*Ibid.*, s. 37.
29*Ibid.*, s. 38.
30*Ibid.*, s. 36.
§1605.2
1S.B.C. 1972, c. 20, rep. S.B.C. 1978, c. 20.
2*Ibid.*, s. 8.
3See, *e.g., Schell v. Schell*, [1976] W.W.D. 19, 29 R.F.L. 349 (B.C.S.C.).
4*Deleeuw v. Deleeuw* (1977), 82 D.L.R. (3d) 521, 3 R.F.L. (2d) 347 (B.C.C.A.).

did not supplant the common law, so that a finding of a resulting or constructive trust was possible, but the court could exercise its discretion under section 8 despite such a finding.[5]

In 1978 the entire subject of family law was completely revised by the *Family Relations Act, 1978*.[6] The Act deals with matters of jurisdiction; child custody, access and guardianship; matrimonial property; maintenance and support and various other family law matters. Only Part III of the Act which is concerned with matrimonial property is dealt with in this paragraph.

The Act retains the separate property regime but entitles spouses to claim an interest in their family assets on a breakdown of the marriage.

(b) Application of Act

Part III of the Act only applies to persons who were or are married to each other at the time it came into force.[7] It does not apply to common law spouses.[8] Nor does Part III apply after the death of one of the spouses.

An application to have an interest declared or enforced under Part III may be made as soon as the interest arises. An interest in family assets arises when a separation agreement, a declaratory judgment that there is no reasonable prospect of reconciliation, an order for dissolution of marriage or judicial separation, or an order declaring the marriage null and void, is made,[9] or pursuant to a marriage agreement.[10]

The definition of "spouse" in the Act as including a person who makes an application under the Act within two years of an order for dissolution of marriage, or a declaration that the marriage is null and void, appears to have the effect of requiring an application to be made within two years of one of those specified events.

(c) Operation of Act

Upon the occurrence of one of the events specified in section 43, the spouses are entitled to an undivided half-interest in the family assets as tenants in common.[11] Family assets are defined as property owned by one or both

---

[5]*Myers v. Myers* (1979), 12 B.C.L.R. 52 (C.A.).

[6]S.B.C. 1978, c. 20, am. S.B.C. 1979, c. 2. Now R.S.B.C. 1979, c. 121 (hereafter referred to as the "Act").

[7]See *Bandiera v. Bandiera* (1979), 13 B.C.L.R. 327 (S.C.). The 1972 Act applies where the decree *nisi* was pronounced before the 1978 Act came into force: *Vedovato v. Vedovato* (1981), 130 D.L.R. (3d) 283, [1982] 1 W.W.R. 752 (B.C.C.A.); if it is pronounced after the 1978 Act came into force, it applies: *Martelli v. Martelli* (1981), 130 D.L.R. (3d) 300 [1982] 2 W.W.R. 638 (B.C.C.A.).

[8]Act, s. 1, definition of "spouse".

[9]*Ibid.*, s. 43. The power of the court under section 44 to make a declaratory judgment that there is no reasonable prospect of reconciliation was held to be valid provincial legislation in *Farwell v. Farwell* (1979), 105 D.L.R. (3d) 364, [1980] 2 W.W.R. 518 (B.C.S.C.).

[10]Act, s. 50(1).

[11]*Ibid.*, s. 43(2).

spouses and ordinarily used by a spouse or a minor child of either spouse for a family purpose.[12] The definition specifically includes certain assets such as corporate shares, trust interests and money deposited in a bank account if those would otherwise be family assets, as well as rights under annuities, pensions, home ownership and retirement savings plans and shares in joint ventures to which money or money's-worth was contributed by the other spouse.[13]

Property owned by one spouse and used primarily for business purposes to which the non-titled spouse made no direct or indirect contribution (including savings through effective household management and child rearing responsibilities) is not a family asset.[14]

The court has a broad power to make an unequal division of family assets or to direct that other property be transferred to a spouse where equal division of the family assets would be unfair, having regard to certain criteria, including the duration of the marriage, the duration of any separation, and the extent to which the property was acquired by gift or inheritance.[15]

The definition of what is a family asset and its valuation has caused difficulties. Assets within the definition acquired before a separation are subject to equal division, but assets acquired thereafter are not normally family assets unless they fall within the extended definitions of section 45(3), such as a pension plan.[16]

While the user test imported by section 43 to determine what are family assets can usually be applied without too much difficulty,[17] the mere fact that one spouse brings assets into the marriage does not necessarily mean that they become family assets.[18]

A medical practice has been held to be a family asset under section 46 where the wife had made a substantial contribution to its acquisition and development. She was not precluded from acquiring an interest in it even though she

---

[12]*Ibid.*, s. 45(2). Thus, a jointly owned matrimonial home is a family asset: *Beynon v. Beynon* (1982), 135 D.L.R. (3d) 116, 37 B.C.L.R. 273 (C.A.).

[13]*Ibid.*, s. 45(3).

[14]*Ibid.*, s. 46.

[15]*Ibid.*, s. 51. *Margolese v. Margolese* (1981), 128 D.L.R. (3d) 705, [1981] 6 W.W.R. 585 (B.C.C.A.); *Zaurrini v. Zaurrini* (1981), 123 D.L.R. (3d) 744, 22 R.F.L. (2d) 161 (B.C.S.C.), unequal division because marriage of short duration and most of family assets contributed by husband. An equal division is the norm, however, and it is not correct to assume that a spouse earns an interest in the matrimonial home at a specified rate for each year of the marriage: *Baird v. Baird* (1981), 130 D.L.R. (3d) 128, [1982] 2 W.W.R. 8 (B.C.C.A.).

[16]*Goodman v. Goodman* (1980), 19 R.F.L. (2d) 415, 23 B.C.L.R. 175 (S.C.), and see *McLennan v. McLennan* (1980), 17 R.F.L. (2d) 44, 20 B.C.L.R. 193 (S.C.); *Vance v. Vance* (1981), 128 D.L.R. (3d) 109, [1981] 6 W.W.R. 431 (B.C.S.C.).

[17]See, *e.g., Rees v. Rees* (1980), 21 B.C.L.R. 188 (S.C.), in which the matrimonial home and a registered retirement savings plan were held to be family assets, but the husband's business assets and bonds used to support his mother were not: *Foy v. Foy* (1981), 125 D.L.R. (3d) 764, 22 R.F.L. (2d) 331 (B.C.C.A.), family home held to be family asset.

[18]Such as a painting: *Beynon v. Beynon* (1981), 23 B.C.L.R. 209 (S.C.).

was not licensed to practise medicine.[19] However, a wife was denied an interest in a law practice on the ground that she would thereby be entitled indirectly to practise law while not licensed to do so.[20] It is submitted that while a court should be reluctant to give a non-licensed spouse an interest in a professional practice it is possible to achieve the same result by giving him a right to share in the income or to make an unequal division of family or other assets under section 51.

Family assets are normally valued as of the date of dissolution of marriage[21] or, in appropriate circumstances, at the date of an earlier separation.[22] Problems may arise in connection with pension funds and savings plans in this respect. In one case the wife was awarded a half-interest in 6/23 of a pension fund, valued at the date of the separation, calculated on the basis that they had been married six years and the husband had contributed to the fund for twenty-three years.[23] In another case the husband's pension was determined as at the date of the separation and the wife was held to be entitled to one-half of the voluntary contribution plus accrued interest at separation and one-half of the voluntary contributions between separation and dissolution. The division of obligatory contributions was directed to be made on the basis of the numbers of years of contribution prior to separation.[24]

Although the *prima facie* right of the spouses on a breakdown of marriage is an equal interest in the family assets and the courts will so order where there are no extraordinary circumstances,[25] the courts do not appear to be at all reluctant to exercise their discretion to make a judicial reapportionment under section 51.[26]

---

[19]*Jackh v. Jackh* (1980), 113 D.L.R. (3d) 267, [1981] 1 W.W.R. 481 (B.C.S.C.). See also *McLennan v. McLennan, supra,* footnote 16.

[20]*Piters v. Piters*, [1981] 1 W.W.R. 285, 19 R.F.L. (2d) 217 (B.C.S.C.); *Re Ladner and Ladner* (1980), 116 D.L.R. (3d) 66 (B.C.S.C.).

[21]*Brayford v. Brayford* (1980), 17 R.F.L. (2d) 143 (B.C. Co. Ct.).

[22]*Dresen v. Dresen* (1980), 13 R.F.L. (2d) 97 (B.C.S.C.).

[23]*Parkes v. Parkes and Audette* (1980), 18 R.F.L. (2d) 7, 20 B.C.L.R. 289 (S.C.).

[24]*Rutherford v. Rutherford et al.* (1981), 127 D.L.R. (3d) 658, [1981] 6 W.W.R. 485 (B.C.C.A.).

[25]See, *e.g., Wood v. Wood* (1980), 17 R.F.L. (2d) 72, 20 B.C.L.R. 252 (S.C.); *Mills v. Mills* (1981), 20 R.F.L. (2d) 197 (B.C.S.C.).

[26]See, *e.g., Carlin v. Carlin* (1979), 10 R.F.L. (2d) 176 (B.C.S.C.), short marriage, wife bringing matrimonial home into marriage; *Beynon v. Beynon, supra,* footnote 12, short marriage, husband bringing assets into marriage; *Woff v. Woff* (1980), 20 R.F.L. (2d) 218 (B.C.S.C.), short marriage, husband contributing and maintaining property; *Bateman v. Bateman* (1979), 102 D.L.R. (3d) 375, 10 R.F.L. (2d) 63 (B.C.S.C.), wife's registered retirement savings plan received by gift from third party and never used for family purposes; *Brenner v. Brenner* (1979), 10 R.F.L. (2d) 208 (B.C.S.C.), wife making all payments on home, husband frequently leaving her; *Caskey v. Caskey* (1979), 10 R.F.L. (2d) 85, 14 B.C.L.R. 193 (S.C.), wife purchasing home with gift from parents, lack of capacity on part of wife to earn income, wife making contribution to family; *Stammler v. Stammler* (1979), 11 R.F.L. (2d) 83, 14 B.C.L.R. 57 (S.C.), short marriage, husband supplying home; *Treacher v. Treacher* (1979), 10 R.F.L. (2d) 216 (B.C.S.C.), husband's substantial business assets partly acquired during long separation used to reduce wife's share; *Murray v. Murray* (1979), 11 B.C.L.R. 338 (S.C.), short

As distinct from certain other jurisdictions, the presumption of advancement has not been abolished by the Act and may thus be used in the context of exempt business assets to establish an interest in the property.[27]

(d) Powers of the court

The court is given wide powers under the Act to determine ownership, right to possession and division of property, including the right to direct partition or sale.[28] Section 55 provides that Part III of the Act takes precedence over the *Partition of Property Act*.[29] However, it appears that the court has the same discretion under Part III as it would have under the *Partition of Property Act* to grant or refuse partition or sale, depending upon the circumstances.[30] In the context of the court's jurisdiction to determine ownership, it may award compensation to a spouse where the other spouse has dissipated the family assets.[31]

The court may also make orders for the preservation of property once a proceeding under Part III has been commenced.[32]

(e) The matrimonial home

Unlike most other statutes, the Act does not deal specifically with the ownership of the matrimonial home although it is, of course, a family asset. However, the court is empowered to make orders granting temporary exclusive occupancy of the family residence and preventing a person from entering it until the property rights of the parties are determined.[33] To the extent that these

---

marriage, wife economically independent, husband contributing funds to pension plan after separation; *Thompson v. Thompson* (1980), 20 B.C.L.R. 29 (S.C.), short marriage, husband supporting previous wife; *Middleton v. Middleton* (1980), 15 R.F.L. (2d) 174, 20 B.C.L.R. 285 (S.C.), wife making mortgage payments during long separation; *McPike v. Wiebe* (1980), 16 R.F.L. (2d) 102 (B.C.S.C.), husband paraplegic, purchasing joint home with damage award from accident; *Glover v. Glover* (1980), 17 R.F.L. (2d) 23 (B.C.S.C.), husband acquiring fishing boat by partial gift, wife helping in business, wife's interest reduced; *Thom v. Thom* (1980), 18 R.F.L. (2d) 175 (B.C.S.C.), wife paying down payment on home from previous marriage settlement, wife's share increased; *Calvert v. Calvert* (1980), 21 B.C.L.R. 226 (S.C.), husband bringing majority of assets into marriage, husband's share increased; *Ginn v. Ginn* (1980), 17 R.F.L. (2d) 223, 20 B.C.L.R. 205 (S.C.); *Heaps v. Heaps* (1980), 17 R.F.L. (2d) 119, 20 B.C.L.R. 382 (S.C.); *Robinson v. Robinson* (1980), 23 B.C.L.R. 193 (Co. Ct.); *Foy v. Foy*, *supra*, footnote 17, order permitting husband to retain family home and awarding wife half its value.

[27] *Murray v. Murray* (1979), 11 B.C.L.R. 338 (S.C.).

[28] Act, s. 52.

[29] R.S.B.C. 1979, c. 311.

[30] *Meneghetti v. Meneghetti* (1979), 11 R.F.L. (2d) 104 (B.C.S.C.), affd 18 R.F.L. (2d) 300, 25 B.C.L.R. 326 (C.A.).

[31] *Royer v. Royer* (1980), 20 R.F.L. (2d) 85, 24 B.C.L.R. 104 (S.C.).

[32] Act, s. 53. See *Craik v. Craik* (1979), 12 B.C.L.R. 226 (S.C.).

[33] Act, ss. 5, 6(1)(d), (e), 77-79.

powers are conferred upon the provincial court, they are unconstitutional.[34]

(f) Enforceability of interests against third parties

An interest arising under section 43, or under a marriage or separation agreement is not protected against third parties unless actual notice is given to them.[35] In the case of land this may be done by registration of a notice of the marriage or separation agreement, or of a *lis pendens,* or an order in proceedings taken under the Act.[36]

(g) Contracting out

The Act provides that the parties may enter into a written marriage agreement before or during their marriage to regulate the management of family assets or other property during marriage, or the ownership, or division of family assets or other property during marriage or after dissolution, nullity declaration, or judicial separation.[37] The Act prescribes certain formalities for such agreements. They need not be supported by valuable consideration.

Marriage agreements are, however, subject to variation under section 51 if their provisions are unfair, having regard to the criteria set out in that section.

It is unclear whether a separation agreement is a marriage agreement. However, any settlement that is not a marriage agreement may be varied by the court within two years of an order dissolving a marriage, or for judicial separation, or declaring a marriage null and void.[38]

1605.3 Manitoba

(a) Introduction

The *Marital Property Act, 1978*[1] came into force on October 15, 1978. It entitles spouses to share all assets acquired by them during the marriage, subject to certain exceptions.

(b) Application of Act

The Act applies only to spouses who were married before or after the Act came into force if their habitual residence or their last habitual residence is in

---

[34]*Polglase v. Polglase* (1979), 106 D.L.R. (3d) 601, [1980] 2 W.W.R. 393 (B.C.S.C.), and see *Reference re section 6 of the Family Relations Act* (1980), 116 D.L.R. (3d) 221, [1980] 6 W.W.R. 737 *sub nom. Reference re section 6 of the Family Relations Act, 1978* (B.C.C.A.).

[35]Act, s. 50.

[36]*Ibid.,* s. 49.

[37]*Ibid.,* s. 48.

[38]*Ibid.,* s. 54. See *Goodman v. Goodman* (1980), 19 R.F.L. (2d) 415, 23 B.C.L.R. 175 (S.C.), separation agreement giving sole occupation of matrimonial home to wife to provide home for children, parties failing to deal with occupancy after children grown.

§1605.3

[1]S.M. 1978, c. 24, am. S.M. 1980-81, c. 26, s. 21 (hereafter referred to as the "Act").

the province.[2] The Act also applies to voidable and void marriages, but in the latter case only so long as the parties believed the void marriage to be valid.[3] The Act does not apply to spouses who were living separate and apart on May 6, 1977, unless subsequent to that date they resume cohabitation for more than ninety days.[4]

The Act provides that spouses have a right to have their assets divided equally where they have entered into a separation agreement; where the court has made a separation order; where the parties have lived separate and apart for more than six months; where the marriage has been dissolved or a decree of nullity has been issued and where a spouse has committed an act amounting to dissipation.[5]

An action to enforce a right of division under the Act must be brought within sixty days after all appeals from a decree of divorce or nullity have been exhausted.[6]

The Act does not apply after the death of one of the spouses unless a right to a division of assets had already arisen by the date of death, in which case the action must be brought within six months of death.[7] However, if the surviving spouse has rights under the *Dower Act*,[8] the rights under the Act expire upon the death of the other spouse.[9] If the conditions precedent for a right to division have not arisen by the date of death, the surviving spouse must rely on the normal rules of succession. Moreover, the rights of spouses under the Act are in addition to their rights under the *Dower Act*,[10] which gives them rights of occupation while both spouses are living and a life estate to the survivor in the homestead.

The Act does not apply to persons who live together in a common law relationship. They must, therefore, rely on the trust doctrines in order to establish an interest in each other's property.

(c) Operation of Act

The Act provides for a deferred sharing of all assets of spouses on a marital breakdown, except articles of personal apparel.[11] Assets acquired before marriage are excluded unless they were obtained in contemplation of the marriage.[12] However, appreciation of such assets after marriage as well as any

---

[2]Act, s. 2(1).
[3]*Ibid.*, s. 2(2), (3).
[4]*Ibid.*, s. 2(4). See *Grewar v. Grewar* (1979), 10 R.F.L. (2d) 181 (Man. Q.B.).
[5]Act, s. 12.
[6]*Ibid.*, s. 18(2).
[7]*Ibid.*, s. 18(1).
[8]R.S.M. 1970, c. D100.
[9]Act, s. 24(2).
[10]*Ibid.*, s. 24(1).
[11]*Ibid.*, s. 1(a).
[12]*Ibid.*, s. 4(2). See *Simkin v. Simkin and Lenkowski* (1979), 12 R.F.L. (2d) 122, 1 Man. R. (2d) 44 (Q.B.), affd 17 R.F.L. (2d) 96, 3 Man. R. (2d) 205 (C.A.).

depreciation is taken into account.[13] Assets received by gift, under a trust, or by inheritance and any income therefrom or appreciation or depreciation in their value are excluded, unless they were intended to benefit both spouses.[14] However, income or appreciation from such assets used for a family asset is included.[15] On the other hand, assets that are already shared equally or that have been acquired from the other spouse pursuant to an equal sharing, such as a home owned jointly, are exempt from the scheme of the Act.[16] Damage awards for personal injury to one spouse are also excluded, but the proceeds of insurance claims for loss or damage to an asset are included.[17]

The Act draws a distinction between family assets and commercial assets. Family assets are defined as including the marital home, money in a bank account ordinarily used for family purposes and certain other assets over which a spouse has control and which would otherwise be family assets. Commercial assets are all other property owned by either or both spouses.[18] Both types of assets are subject to a *prima facie* right of equal division, unless or to the extent that they are exempt.[19]

The division of assets is based upon an accounting as of a closing and valuation date specified by the Act at which time the fair market value of each asset is determined and debts and liabilities are deducted.[20] The court is given a discretion to divide both the family assets and the commercial assets unequally if equal division would be unfair or inequitable, having regard to certain prescribed criteria.[21] Conduct of the spouses is irrelevant to an equal division of shareable assets.[22]

Where a spouse dissipates distributable assets, the value thereof is taken into account[23] and the other spouse may apply for a receiving order or other order to preserve the assets.[24]

(d) The matrimonial home

The Act provides that both spouses have an equal right of occupation of

---

[13]Act, s. 4(3).

[14]*Ibid.*, s. 7. See, *e.g., Tycholiz v. Tycholiz* (1980), 17 R.F.L. (2d) 81 (Man. Co. Ct.), affd 124 D.L.R. (3d) 699 (C.A.), term deposits given to wife by father; *Simkin v. Simkin, supra,* footnote 12, inheritance by husband.

[15]Act, s. 7(5). See *Smith v. Smith*, [1980] 6 W.W.R. 289, 18 R.F.L. (2d) 38 (Man. C.A.), proceeds of sale of inherited farm used to buy matrimonial home and invested and used for family purposes.

[16]Act, s. 9. See *Tycholiz v. Tycholiz, supra,* footnote 14.

[17]Act, s. 8.

[18]*Ibid.*, s. 1(*b*), (*d*).

[19]See *Roschuk v. Roschuk* (1979), 12 R.F.L. (2d) 34 (Man. Q.B.), vard 15 R.F.L. (2d) 196 (C.A.).

[20]Act, ss. 14, 15.

[21]*Ibid.*, s. 13.

[22]*Tycholiz v. Tycholiz, supra,* footnote 14.

[23]Act, s. 6(7).

[24]*Ibid.*, s. 20.

the marital home.[25] However, this right is subject, *inter alia*, to an order made under the *Family Maintenance Act*.[26] Under section 10 of that Act the court may award exclusive possession of the family residence to one of the spouses and may postpone the right of the other, or titled, spouse to partition or sell the residence.[27]

(e) Contracting out

Spouses may by a spousal agreement, that is, a marriage settlement, marriage contract, separation agreement or release, in writing, whether made before or after the Act came into force and before or during the marriage,[28] dispose of an asset otherwise subject to the Act, or may make the Act or any part of it inapplicable to their assets.[29]

1605.4 New Brunswick

(a) Introduction

The *Marital Property Act*[1] establishes a right in spouses to a deferred sharing of assets on marriage breakdown, similar to the statutes in the other provinces. Until a spouse decides to utilize the provisions of the Act the separate property regime is retained. The scheme of the Act is similar to that of Ontario, although there are important differences between the two Acts which will be discussed below.

The Act deals in Part I with the division of marital assets. Part II makes special provision for the marital home and household goods. Part III deals with domestic contracts and Part IV contains general and transitional provisions.

(b) Application of Act

The Act, in respect of its matrimonial property regime, only applies to spouses, not to cohabitees. It enables spouses in certain prescribed circumstances, described below, to bring an application for division of their marital assets.[2] This right is also extended to a surviving spouse on the death of the other.[3] The Act applies to marriages in effect when the Act came into force and to property that was acquired before that date.[4]

---

[25]*Ibid.*, s. 6(2).

[26]S.M. 1978, c. 25.

[27]See *Tycholiz v. Tycholiz* (1981), 124 D.L.R. (3d) 699, 23 R.F.L. (2d) 31 (Man. C.A.); *Thompson v. Thompson* (1979), 9 R.F.L. (2d) 193 (Man. Co. Ct.), for a definition of "family residence".

[28]Act, s. 1(*f*).

[29]*Ibid.*, s. 5. See *Bernan v. Bernan* (1979), 12 R.F.L. (2d) 165 (Man. Q.B.).

§1605.4

[1]S.N.B. 1980, c. M-1.1 (hereafter referred to as the "Act").

[2]Act, s. 3.

[3]*Ibid.*, s. 4.

[4]*Ibid.*, s. 43.

(c) Operation of Act

Where a decree *nisi* of divorce or a declaration of nullity is issued, or there is a breakdown of the marriage with no reasonable prospect of reconciliation, whether or not the parties are living separate and apart, each spouse may apply to the court to have the marital property divided into equal shares.[5] In the case of divorce or nullity, the application must be brought within sixty days of the termination of the marriage, but the court may extend this time.[6]

Marital property is defined as including family assets, property owned by one or both spouses that is not a family asset but which was acquired while the parties cohabited or in contemplation of marriage and property acquired by one spouse after cessation of cohabitation through the disposition of what would otherwise have been marital property. Property that is a business asset, that was an interspousal or third party gift or inheritance and the income thereon that represents the proceeds of disposition of a non-family asset and which was not acquired during cohabitation or in contemplation of marriage, including property purchased therewith or taken in exchange therefor, or that represents insurance proceeds with respect to loss of such property and property that is excluded by a domestic contract, is excluded from the definition.[7]

Family assets are defined on the basis of a user test as property, whether acquired before or after marriage, owned by one or both spouses and ordinarily used or enjoyed for family purposes. The definition includes a marital home and household goods, money in a bank account ordinarily used for family purposes and other property, such as shares in a corporation, which would otherwise be family assets.[8]

In addition to the division of the marital property, the Act also requires a fair and equitable division of marital debts.[9]

Although there is a *prima facie* right to equal division of marital property on marriage breakdown, the court is given a discretion to vary the proportion and to exclude certain assets. In the first place, the court may exclude a family asset from division where it was acquired before the spouses were married, or by way of interspousal or third party gift or inheritance, if in the court's opinion it would be unfair and unreasonable to include it, taking into account certain expressed criteria.[10]

Secondly, the court may make an unequal division of marital property if an equal division would be inequitable having regard to certain criteria, such as an agreement other than a domestic contract, the duration of cohabitation and separation and the date of acquisition of a gift.[11]

---

[5]*Ibid.*, s. 3(1).
[6]*Ibid.*, s. 3(2), (4).
[7]*Ibid.*, s. 1, definition of "marital property".
[8]*Ibid.*, s. 1, definition of "family assets".
[9]*Ibid.*, s. 9.
[10]*Ibid.*, s. 6.
[11]*Ibid.*, s. 7.

Thirdly, the court may make a division of non-marital property where a spouse has unreasonably impoverished the marital property or where the division of marital property would be inequitable in the circumstances.[12] It remains to be seen whether the court will prefer to make an unequal division of marital assets before turning to a division of other assets or not. That, it is submitted, is the appropriate course and one which is in accord with the scheme of the Act.

The court is given wide powers to give effect to a division such as directing that specified property be transferred to or vested in one spouse, directing a partition or sale, directing the giving of security and others.[13]

(d) The marital home

Each spouse is given an equal right of possession of the marital home and of the household goods together with the other, subject, however, to the provisions of a domestic contract.[14] On the other hand, the court may, notwithstanding a domestic contract, give one spouse exclusive possession of the marital home and of the household goods.[15]

The Act prohibits alienation of the marital home except with the consent of the other spouse or the fiat of the court and the court may set aside a disposition made in contravention of the Act except where it is made to a *bona fide* purchaser for value without notice.[16] The spouse who has a right of possession has the same right of redemption or relief against forfeiture in any proceedings to realize upon a lien, encumbrance or execution or to exercise a right of forfeiture as the other spouse has and notice must be given to him or her of the proceedings.[17]

As distinguished from the Ontario Act, a spouse is entitled to one-half of the net proceeds of sale or expropriation of the marital home during marriage and the court has power to make an unequal division if an equal division would be inequitable.[18] The Act provides that the proceeds of sale shall be held in trust for equal or unequal division, or in accordance with a domestic contract.[19] Strangely, the Act does not contain an overreaching provision to protect a purchaser from the wrongful application of the proceeds of sale. He must, therefore, protect himself by ensuring that the trust is properly executed.

The rights of the spouses with respect to the marital home and contents terminate when the marriage ends by death, divorce, or a declaration of nullity.[20]

---

[12]*Ibid.*, s. 8.
[13]*Ibid.*, s. 10.
[14]*Ibid.*, ss. 18, 26.
[15]*Ibid.*, ss. 23, 27(3).
[16]*Ibid.*, s. 19.
[17]*Ibid.*, s. 21.
[18]*Ibid.*, s. 20.
[19]*Ibid.*, s. 20(3).
[20]*Ibid.*, ss. 18(2), 20(4), 23(4), 26(2), 28.

(e) Contracting out

The Act makes extensive provisions in Part III for domestic contracts. Save for certain minor exceptions in respect of the marital home discussed above and in respect of agreements predating the commencement of the Act, the parties are at liberty to contract out of the provisions of the Act.[21]

(f) Effect on death

As distinct from the Ontario Act and other Acts, the right to a division of marital and other property survives the death of the first spouse, but the application must be brought within six months of that spouse's death.[22] Moreover, on the application the court must direct that the interest of the deceased spouse in the marital home vests in the survivor.[23] An application may be made by the survivor whether or not there has been a marriage breakdown. Moreover, an order made after death takes precedence over the deceased's will and over the provisions of the *Testator's Family Maintenance Act*,[24] but the court is required to have regard to the testator's wishes so far as practicable.[25]

An application brought after a marriage breakdown may be continued by or against the estate of a deceased spouse and an application brought after the death of one spouse may be continued by the estate of the survivor.[26]

(g) General provisions

In addition to the spouses' right to make application for a division of their property, they or any interested person may apply to the court for a determination of any question between spouses or former spouses as to the ownership or right of possession of any property and the court is given power to determine the question and to make orders accordingly. In determining such questions the court must have regard to contributions in money or money's-worth to the acquisition, management, maintenance, operation or improvement of the property, but without regard to the relationship of husband and wife. If there has been a substantial contribution by both spouses there is a presumption of equal contribution.[27] These provisions apply where an application has not been made, or can no longer be made for a division of marital property.

The presumption of advancement as between husband and wife has been abolished and replaced with a presumption of resulting trust, except that property held jointly or money in a joint account is *prima facie* deemed to be held equally.[28]

---

[21]*Ibid.*, ss. 40, 41.
[22]*Ibid.*, s. 4(1), (2).
[23]*Ibid.*, s. 4(1).
[24]R.S.N.B. 1973. c. T-4.
[25]Act, s. 4(4)-(6).
[26]*Ibid.*, s. 5(2), (3).
[27]*Ibid.*, s. 42. A creditor of a non-titled spouse is not entitled to apply for a declaration that that spouse has an interest in marital property: *Kuchuk et al. v. Bank of Montreal* (1982), 136 D.L.R. (3d) 355, 40 N.B.R. (2d) 203 (C.A.).
[28]*Ibid.*, s. 15.

Inasmuch as the right to an equal or other division under the Act only arises when the court so orders, the Act declares that such rights, as well as the rights to possession of the marital property and household goods, do not constitute an interest in property.[29]

Since the Act has made substantial property provision for spouses, the old dower right was rendered otiose and it has been abolished, except to the extent that a dower right was vested when the Act came into force.[30]

1605.5 Newfoundland

(a) Introduction

The *Matrimonial Property Act*[1] differs from those of all the other provinces in that it introduces community of property with respect to the matrimonial home. It is similar to those of the other provinces in that it provides for a deferred sharing of assets on marriage breakdown. Prior thereto the regime of separate property prevails.

(b) Application of Act

The Act only applies to persons who are married to each other. It does not apply to persons whose marriage was dissolved by decree absolute, or who have provided for a division of assets by a separation agreement prior to July 1, 1980.[2] "Spouse" is defined as either of a man and woman who are married to each other, whether the marriage is voidable or void, except that in the latter case they must have acted *bona fide* and have cohabited within the preceding year. The definition includes a surviving spouse.[3]

(c) The matrimonial home

A matrimonial home is the dwelling and real property occupied by the spouses as their family residence and owned by either or both of them. If the property is used also for other purposes, it includes only that portion reasonably necessary for the use and enjoyment of the family residence. There may be more than one matrimonial home[4] but the spouses may, in writing, designate one property as their matrimonial home, in which case all others cease to be so upon registration of the designation.[5]

Whether the matrimonial home was acquired by gift, inheritance or otherwise before the marriage and whether the marriage was entered into or the

---

[29]*Ibid.*, s. 47.
[30]*Ibid.*, s. 49.
§1605.5
[1]S.N. 1979, c. 32, am. S.N. 1980, c. 24, s. 11 (hereafter referred to as the "Act").
[2]Act, s. 2(3).
[3]*Ibid.*, s. 2(1)(e).
[4]*Ibid.*, s. 4.
[5]*Ibid.*, s. 7.

home was acquired before the Act came into force or not and even though only one of the spouses holds title to it, the Act confers a half-interest in the matrimonial home together with a right of possession on each spouse, to be held by them as joint tenants unless they took title as tenants in common.[6]

The Act prohibits the disposition or encumbrance of an interest in the matrimonial home except with the consent of the other spouse or the fiat of the court.[7] *Bona fide* purchasers and mortgagees for value without notice are protected, however.[8]

Both spouses are entitled to notice of any proceedings to realize upon a lien, mortgage or execution against the matrimonial home and have an equal right to redeem it. Moreover, each is entitled to one-half of the net proceeds of sale under such proceedings.[9]

The court has power to make an order giving exclusive possession to one spouse, or to a child where one of the spouses dies and the survivor does not reside in the matrimonial home.[10]

(d) Division of matrimonial assets

Apart from the provisions respecting the matrimonial home, the Act provides that when a petition for divorce is filed, the marriage is declared a nullity, the spouses have separated and there is no reasonable prospect of reconciliation, or where one of the spouses has died, each spouse (or the survivor) is entitled to apply to the court for an equal division of the matrimonial assets.[11] The latter are defined as all real and personal property acquired by the spouses during the marriage, including a matrimonial home, whether acquired before or after marriage but not gifts and inheritances from third parties (save for a matrimonial home), personal injury awards (except to the extent that they represent compensation for economic loss), personal effects, business assets, property exempted under a marriage contract or separation agreement, family heirlooms and property acquired after separation.[12] The market value of shares in a corporation the assets of which would otherwise be matrimonial assets are included.[13]

The court is given a wide discretion to make an unequal division of matrimonial assets if an equal division would be grossly unjust or unconscionable having regard to certain specific criteria other than misconduct.[14]

The court has ample power under the Act to effectuate a proper division. For example, it may direct that the title to property be transferred to or held in

[6]*Ibid.*, ss. 5, 6.
[7]*Ibid.*, s. 8.
[8]*Ibid.*, s. 9.
[9]*Ibid.*, s. 11.
[10]*Ibid.*, s. 13.
[11]*Ibid.*, s. 19.
[12]*Ibid.*, s. 16(1)(*b*).
[13]*Ibid.*, s. 16(3).
[14]*Ibid.*, ss. 20, 21.

trust for one spouse, it may order partition or sale and it may order that one spouse make a compensating payment to the other.[15]

The Act does not empower the court to make a division of non-matrimonial or business assets, except on the basis of contribution. This is dealt with in the next subsection.

(e) General provisions

Any spouse may make application to the court for an order determining the rights of the spouses to the ownership or possession of any property unless an application or order has been made under the Act with respect to that property and the court may make consequential orders for division of the property.[16]

The Act contains a provision typical of most matrimonial property statutes to overcome the effects of *Murdoch v. Murdoch*.[17] It provides that where a spouse has contributed work, money or money's-worth in respect of the acquisition, management, maintenance, operation or improvement of a business asset, the court shall assess the contribution without regard to the relationship of husband and wife and shall direct either a compensating payment, or award the contributor a share in the asset.[18]

The Act, in common with others, abolishes the presumption of advancement as between husband and wife and replaces it with the presumption of resulting trust, except as regards jointly held property or money in joint accounts.[19]

(f) Effect on death

If the matrimonial home is deemed to be held in joint tenancy,[20] it will pass to the survivor in accordance with the normal rules. Otherwise it will pass to the deceased's beneficiaries.

A spouse has a right to a division of the matrimonial property on the death of the other spouse whether or not there has been a breakdown of the marriage.[21] Moreover, his or her rights under the Act are in addition to the right to inherit from the deceased spouse.[22] However, the right of a surviving spouse under the Act is one of the factors to be taken into account in an application by him under the *Family Relief Act*.[23] The survivor may enter into an agreement with the personal representative of the deceased respecting ownership or division of the property.[24]

---

[15]*Ibid.*, s. 24.
[16]*Ibid.*, s. 25.
[17](1973), 41 D.L.R. (3d) 367, [1975] 1 S.C.R. 423. See §1604.1(c), *supra*.
[18]Act, s. 27.
[19]*Ibid.*, s. 29.
[20]*Ibid.*, s. 6(2), (3).
[21]*Ibid.*, s. 19(1)(d).
[22]*Ibid.*, s. 19(2).
[23]R.S.N. 1970, c. 124, as amended by Act, s. 43.
[24]Act, s. 40.

(g) Contracting out

The Act makes generous provisions for spouses to contract out of the Act. Such a contract must be in writing, signed by the parties and witnessed.[25] If it is validly executed, the agreement takes priority over the Act.[26] Moreover, it is enforceable against the estate of a deceased spouse notwithstanding that it does not comply with the formalities of the *Wills Act*.[27]

1605.6 Nova Scotia

(a) Introduction

The *Matrimonial Property Act*,[1] in common with most of the other family law reform statutes, introduces a deferred right to a division of assets on marriage breakdown and, in common with some of them, on death. Apart from this and certain consequential reforms, however, the separate property regime remains in effect.

(b) Application of Act

The Act applies only to spouses, defined as including persons who are married to each other under a valid, voidable, or void marriage. In the latter case they must have entered the marriage in good faith and have cohabited within the preceding year. The definition also includes a surviving spouse.[2] However, the Act does not apply to persons whose marriage was dissolved by decree absolute before the Act came into force.[3]

The Act is retroactive in that it applies to persons who were married before the Act came into force, to property acquired by a spouse before or after the Act came into force and to proceedings respecting matrimonial property rights commenced before the Act came into force.[4]

(c) Operation of Act

A spouse may apply for an order dividing the matrimonial assets into equal shares when a petition for divorce or an application for a declaration of nullity is filed, where the spouses are living separate and apart and there is no reasonable prospect of resumption of cohabitation, or where one of the spouses has died.[5]

Matrimonial assets are defined as the spouses' matrimonial home or homes

---

[25]*Ibid.*, s. 35.
[26]*Ibid.*, s. 41.
[27]R.S.N. 1970, c. 401, as amended; Act, s. 42.
§1605.6
[1]S.N.S. 1980, c. 9 (hereafter referred to as the "Act").
[2]Act, s. 2(*g*).
[3]*Ibid.*, s. 5(4).
[4]*Ibid.*, s. 5(1)-(3).
[5]*Ibid.*, s. 12(1).

and all property acquired by either or both of them before or during the marriage, except third party gifts and inheritances (save to the extent that they are used for the benefit of both spouses or their children), a damage award or settlement in favour of one spouse, the proceeds of insurance payable to one spouse, reasonable personal effects, business assets, property exempted under a marriage contract or separation agreement and property acquired after separation, unless there is a resumption of cohabitation.[6] A damage award or settlement and insurance proceeds paid in respect of matrimonial property are matrimonial assets.[7] Moreover, where property owned by a corporation would otherwise be a matrimonial asset, the market value of the spouse's shares is included.[8]

The term "matrimonial home" is defined as the dwelling and real property occupied by a person and his spouse as their family residence in which either or both have an interest other than a leasehold interest. Only that portion reasonably necessary for the use and enjoyment as a family residence falls within the definition where the residence is included in other property. However, it is possible to have more than one matrimonial home.[9]

"Business assets" are defined as property primarily used in connection with a commercial, business, investment or other income or profit producing purpose, except bank accounts ordinarily used for family purposes.[10]

It has been held that pension plans, including a registered retirement savings plan, are not matrimonial assets but business assets in the nature of a contractual right enforceable only on retirement.[11]

Although the *prima facie* right of the spouses is to seek an equal division of the matrimonial assets, the court is empowered to make an unequal division of them or to make a division of a non-matrimonial asset where equal division of the matrimonial assets would be unfair or unconscionable, taking into account certain listed factors, such as the unreasonable impoverishment of family assets by one spouse, a marriage contract or separation agreement, the length of cohabitation during the marriage and others.[12]

From the few cases so far decided under the Act it would appear that courts are willing to exercise their discretion to make an unequal division of matrimonial assets.[13] Moreover, it appears that they will take into account a spouse's

---

[6]*Ibid.*, s. 4(1).

[7]*Ibid.*, s. 4(2).

[8]*Ibid.*, s. 4(4).

[9]*Ibid.*, s. 3.

[10]*Ibid.*, s. 2(a).

[11]*Currie v. Currie* (1981), 119 D.L.R. (3d) 471, 21 R.F.L. (2d) 340 (N.S.S.C.T.D.); *Ryan v. Ryan* (1980), 43 N.S.R. (2d) 423 (S.C.T.D.).

[12]Act, s. 13.

[13]See, *e.g.*, *Currie v. Currie*, *supra*, footnote 11, husband having rights under non-divisible pension and entitled to retire at age 45, wife making substantial contribution to property. But see, *contra*, *Ryan v. Ryan*, *supra*, footnote 11, in which the husband had not acquired more business assets than the wife, except for a pension plan and a registered retirement savings plan.

contribution to the acquisition of matrimonial assets prior to the marriage while the parties cohabited.[14]

The court has wide powers under the Act to give effect to its orders, for example, by directing the transfer of property to one spouse, directing partition or sale, directing the giving of security and others.[15]

(d) The matrimonial home

The Act deals specifically with the matrimonial home, usually the spouses' major asset, by providing that the court may order that exclusive possession of the home be given to one of the spouses or, in certain limited circumstances, a child. The court is empowered to make consequential orders regarding the maintenance and disposition of the matrimonial home.[16]

(e) Effect on death

A surviving spouse may make application for a division of assets on the death of the other spouse.[17] The application must be brought within six months after letters probate or letters of administration have been issued but the court has power to extend the time.[18] The survivor's rights under the Act are in addition to his or her rights of inheritance from the deceased spouse.[19] However, the surviving spouse may make an agreement with the deceased's personal representative regarding the ownership or division of property under the Act.[20] Where an application is made for a division of assets on the death of one spouse, the order for division under the Act operates first and it determines what assets are left for the deceased to dispose of by his will.[21]

Since the Act confers substantial new rights on spouses, the common law rights of dower and curtesy were rendered otiose and are abolished, except in respect of a right to dower where the husband died before the Act came into force.[22]

(f) Contracting out

Spouses may contract out of their rights under the Act, including rights conferred by the Act on the death of a spouse, by a written marriage contract

---

[14] *Harwood v. Thomas* (1981), 21 R.F.L. (2d) 1, 43 N.S.R. (2d) 292 (S.C.T.D.), affd 22 R.F.L. (2d) 167, 45 N.S.R. (2d) 414 (S.C. App. Div.).
[15] Act, s. 15.
[16] *Ibid.*, s. 11.
[17] *Ibid.*, s. 12(1)(*d*), unless the death occurred before the Act came into force: *Pratt v. MacLeod* (1981), 129 D.L.R. (3d) 123, 25 R.F.L. (2d) 27 (N.S.S.C.T.D.).
[18] *Ibid.*, s. 12(2), (3).
[19] *Ibid.*, s. 12(4).
[20] *Ibid.*, s. 27.
[21] *Re Fraser* (1981), 130 D.L.R. (3d) 665, 25 R.F.L. (2d) 171 (N.S.S.C.T.D.). See also *Re Levy* (1981), 131 D.L.R. (3d) 15, 25 R.F.L. (2d) 149 (N.S.S.C.T.D.).
[22] Act, s. 33.

or separation agreement.[23] If such a contract purports to have effect on the death of one of the spouses, it is enforceable against the estate of the other.[24] The Act specifically reserves the court's right to vary a contract where it is unconscionable, unduly harsh on one party, or fraudulent.[25]

(g) General provisions

The Act contains certain general provisions, similar to those in other statutes which may be used where an application for division has not been made under the Act. These provisions are a power in the court to determine any question as to ownership or right to possession of property between spouses and to make consequential orders,[26] a power to determine and assess the contributions made to the acquisition, maintenance or improvement of business assets by one spouse[27] and the abolition of the presumption of advancement between spouses and its replacement by the presumption of a resulting trust.[28] As to the latter, where property is held by the spouses as joint tenants or is money held by them in a joint account, that is *prima facie* proof that they are entitled to a one-half share of the property on a severance.[29] It has been held, however, that the death of one of the spouses does not effect a severance. Hence, moneys in a joint account contributed solely by the deceased spouse will be held by the survivor upon a presumed resulting trust for the estate.[30]

1605.7 Ontario

(a) Introduction

Matrimonial property law reform of a limited nature took place in Ontario by the *Family Law Reform Act, 1975*.[1] That Act abolished the presumption of advancement prospectively[2] and gave a remedy to a spouse who had contributed money or money's-worth to the acquisition, maintenance and improvements of property owned by the other spouse. These provisions were carried forward, with amendments, into the new Act passed in 1978.

The *Family Law Reform Act, 1978*[3] introduced a full-scale reform of family

---

[23]*Ibid.*, ss. 23, 24.

[24]*Ibid.*, s. 28.

[25]*Ibid.*, s. 29. If the agreement was fairly bargained a wife's claim for an unequal division of property will be dismissed in the face of her release of all claims: *Cox v. Cox* (1982), 137 D.L.R. (3d) 546, 28 R.F.L. (2d) 98 (N.S.S.C. App. Div.).

[26]*Ibid.*, s. 16. The executors of a deceased spouse cannot make an application under this section, they must bring an action for a declaration: *Re Levy, supra*, footnote 21.

[27]*Ibid.*, s. 18.

[28]*Ibid.*, s. 21.

[29]*Ibid.* As to the evidence needed to rebut this presumption, see *Re Levy, supra*, footnote 21.

[30]*Re Levy, supra*, footnote 21.

§1605.7

[1]S.O. 1975, c. 41.

[2]See *Forbes v. Forbes* (1979), 22 O.R. (2d) 771, 94 D.L.R. (3d) 715 (H.C.J.).

[3]S.O. 1978, c. 2, now R.S.O. 1980, c. 152 (hereafter referred to as the "Act").

law, including matrimonial property law. The Act is divided into six Parts. Part I deals with family property; Part II defines support obligations; Part III confers certain rights in the matrimonial home; Part IV deals with domestic contracts; Part V provides for damage claims by dependants and Part VI makes various changes in the existing law. This section is concerned primarily with Parts I and III.

Part I introduces a deferred right to a division of assets on marriage breakdown. Apart from that, the separate property regime is maintained. However, by Part III spouses are given occupational rights in the matrimonial home regardless of the state of the marriage.

(b) Application of Act

Parts I and II of the Act apply only to spouses. That term is defined as persons who are married to each other under a valid or voidable marriage or who have in good faith gone through a form of marriage that is void and who have cohabited within the preceding year.[4] The Parts of the Act here considered, therefore, do not apply where a decree absolute of divorce has been granted,[5] nor to cohabitees. Nor do they apply after the death of the spouses. However, Part I is retroactive and extends to the proceeds of sale of family assets sold by one spouse after separation but before the Act came into force.[5a]

It has been held that the Act does not apply to Indian lands since Parliament has exclusive jurisdiction with respect to them.[6]

The Act is retroactive in the sense that proceedings commenced before it came into force are thereafter governed by the Act.[7]

(c) Definition of family assets

As noted above, the Act provides for a deferred sharing of assets on marriage breakdown. Where a decree *nisi* of divorce is pronounced, a marriage is declared a nullity, or where the spouses are separated and there is no reasonable prospect of a resumption of cohabitation, the spouses are entitled to have the family assets divided equally.[8]

---

[4]Act, s. 1(*f*).

[5]*Machuk v. Machuk* (1979), 10 R.F.L. (2d) 224 (Ont. Co. Ct.); *Forbes v. Forbes, supra*, footnote 2.

[5a]*Downes v. Downes* (1981), 129 D.L.R. (3d) 321 (Ont. H.C.J.).

[6]*Sandy v. Sandy* (1979), 25 O.R. (2d) 192, 100 D.L.R. (3d) 358 (H.C.J.), affd 27 O.R. (2d) 248, 107 D.L.R. (3d) 659 (C.A.), but see *Hopkins v. Hopkins* (1980), 29 O.R. (2d) 24, 111 D.L.R. (3d) 722 (Co. Ct.), which held that section 45 of the Act, which empowers the court to give exclusive possession to one spouse, did not conflict with the federal jurisdiction.

[7]See *Barzo v. Barzo* (1978), 23 O.R. (2d) 240, 7 R.F.L. (2d) 123 (S.C.); *Kuseta v. Kuseta* (1978), 8 R.F.L. (2d) 398 (Ont. H.C.J.). See also *Reicher v. Reicher and 291987 Ontario Ltd.* (1981), 20 R.F.L. (2d) 213, 19 C.P.C. 228 (Ont. Div. Ct.), fraudulent conveyance of matrimonial home before Act.

[8]Act, s. 4(1). The court will restrain a spouse from applying to make a decree *nisi* absolute in order to permit the other spouse to make application under the Act: *Barzo v. Barzo, supra*, footnote 7.

"Family assets" are defined as including the matrimonial home and property owned by one or both spouses and ordinarily used by both or their children while the spouses reside together for family purposes. They include bank accounts used for family purposes, the market value of corporate shares and trusts and partnership interests where property which would otherwise be a family asset is owned by a corporation, trust or partnership and property over which a spouse has control through a power of appointment and which would otherwise be a family asset.[9] The matrimonial home is property in which a person has an interest and that is or was occupied by him and his spouse as the family residence. If it is included in property normally used for other than residential purposes, the matrimonial home is only such part as is reasonably necessary to the use and enjoyment of the residence. Moreover, it is possible to have more than one matrimonial home.[10]

The question whether particular assets are family assets has been dealt with extensively by the courts. Thus, for example, bank accounts and bonds, even though owned by only one spouse, are family assets if they are used for family purposes, but a wife's doll collection is not where it is maintained purely as a financial venture.[11] Similarly, a husband's rug collection, to the extent that it was not on general display in the home, and a boat used exclusively by the husband, were held not to be family assets, but a painting owned by the husband's private company and hanging in the home for three years was.[12] In order for it to be a family asset it must be used for family purposes; occasional use by members of the family is not sufficient.[13]

Life insurance owned by one spouse is not regarded as a family asset,[14] nor are a spouse's pension rights,[15] although a husband's rights under a company share-purchase agreement may be.[16]

With respect to real property, clearly, the matrimonial home is a family asset.[17] In the case of a farm this would be the farmhouse and some contiguous land but not the entire farm.[18] The proceeds of sale of the matrimonial home are also a family asset if it was a family asset at the time the parties separated.[19]

---

[9]Act, s. 3(b).

[10]Ibid., s. 39. See Weir v. Weir (1978), 23 O.R. (2d) 765, 96 D.L.R. (3d) 725 (H.C.J.), home and cottage both matrimonial homes.

[11]Boydell v. Boydell (1978), 2 R.F.L. (2d) 121 (Ont. Unified Fam. Ct.), and see Grime v. Grime (1980), 16 R.F.L. (2d) 365 (Ont. H.C.J.), bonds and bank account in husband's name are family assets because they were intended to be used for the family.

[12]Bregman v. Bregman (1978), 21 O.R. (2d) 722, 91 D.L.R. (3d) 470 (Ont. H.C.J.).

[13]Re Brewer and Brewer (1980), 17 R.F.L. (2d) 215 (Ont. Unified Fam. Ct.), husband's boat not a family asset, but see Coburn v. Coburn (1978), 6 R.F.L. (2d) 235 (Ont. Unified Fam. Ct.), car driven almost exclusively by husband held to be family asset.

[14]Kastrau v. Kastrau (1978), 7 R.F.L. (2d) 318 (Ont. Unified Fam. Ct.).

[15]St. Germain v. St. Germain (1980), 14 R.F.L. (2d) 186 (Ont. C.A.); Re Leatherdale and Leatherdale (1980), 31 O.R. (2d) 141, 118 D.L.R. (3d) 72 (C.A.), husband's registered retirement savings plan not family asset.

[16]Couzens v. Couzens (1980), 18 R.F.L. (2d) 333 (Ont. Dist. Ct.).

[17]See Meszaros v. Meszaros (1978), 22 O.R. (2d) 695 (H.C.J.).

[18]Ling v. Ling (1980), 29 O.R. (2d) 717, 114 D.L.R. (3d) 261 (C.A.).

[19]Doroshenko v. Doroshenko (1979), 9 R.F.L. (2d) 61 (Ont. Co. Ct.).

On the other hand, a Florida condominium owned by the husband's company was held not to be a family asset, since it was never used by the family. A mere intention to use the property for recreational purposes is not sufficient to make it a family asset.[20] Similarly, property bought by the husband for the wife's parents' retirement home is not a family asset.[21] Moreover, where the matrimonial home is mortgaged, only the equity of redemption is a family asset.[22]

Property, such as the matrimonial home, which is conveyed to one spouse pursuant to a separation agreement ceases to be a family asset.[23]

Before any division of assets can take place, it is crucial for the court to determine whether they are family assets or not.[24] The onus of proving that any property is a family asset is on the spouse alleging it.[25]

(d) Division of assets

Although spouses have a *prima facie* right to an equal division of the family assets, the court may make an unequal division of family assets on the basis of section 4(4) which provides:

> 4(4) The court may make a division of family assets resulting in shares that are not equal where the court is of the opinion that a division of the family assets in equal shares would be inequitable, having regard to,
>
> (a) any agreement other than a domestic contract;
> (b) the duration of the period of cohabitation under the marriage;
> (c) the duration of the period during which the spouses have lived separate and apart;
> (d) the date when the property was acquired;
> (e) the extent to which property was acquired by one spouse by inheritance or by gift; or
> (f) any other circumstance relating to the acquisition, disposition, preservation, maintenance, improvement or use of property rendering it inequitable for the division of family assets to be in equal shares.

The court may also make a division of non-family assets under section 4(6), which provides as follows:

> 4(6) The court shall make a division of any property that is not a family asset where,
>
> (a) a spouse has unreasonably impoverished the family assets; or
> (b) the result of a division of the family assets would be inequitable in all the circumstances, having regard to,
>> (i) the considerations set out in clauses (4)(a) to (f), and

---

[20]*Taylor v. Taylor* (1978), 6 R.F.L. (2d) 341 (Ont. Unified Fam. Ct.).
[21]*Fisher v. Fisher* (1978), 21 O.R. (2d) 105, 89 D.L.R. (3d) 543 (H.C.J.).
[22]*Royal Bank of Canada v. Nicholson* (1980), 29 O.R. (2d) 141, 112 D.L.R. (3d) 364 (H.C.J.).
[23]Act, s. 3(b); *Mercer v. Mercer* (1978), 5 R.F.L. (2d) 224 (Ont. H.C.J.).
[24]*Re Leatherdale and Leatherdale, supra,* footnote 15.
[25]*Bregman v. Bregman* (1978), 21 O.R. (2d) 722, 91 D.L.R. (3d) 470 (H.C.J.); *Quick v. Quick* (1980), 16 R.F.L. (2d) 63 (Ont. H.C.J.), at p. 69.

(ii) the effect of the assumption by one spouse of any of the responsibilities set out in subsection (5) on the ability of the other spouse to acquire, manage, maintain, operate or improve property that is not a family asset.

In exercising its discretion under section 4, the court must have regard to section 4(5) which states that the purpose of the section is to recognize that child care, household management and financial provision are the spouses' joint responsibility and that there is a joint contribution inherent in the marital relationship which entitles them to a division of assets on a breakdown of the marriage.

Furthermore, the court is empowered to make orders directing the transfer of specified property to or in trust for one spouse, absolutely, for life, or for a term of years; for partition or sale; for payment out of the proceeds of sale to one or both spouses and similar orders providing for an appropriate division.[26]

If no application or order has been made under sections 4 or 6, the court may, on application, determine any question between spouses or former spouses as to ownership or right to possession of any property and make appropriate orders for vesting of the property or its division.[27]

The Act further contains a provision to overcome the effects of *Murdoch v. Murdoch*.[28] Secion 8 provides that where a spouse or former spouse has contributed money or money's-worth in respect of the acquisition, management, maintenance, operation or improvement of property other than family assets in which the other spouse has an interest, the court may direct a compensating payment to the contributor, or award him a share in the property. Moreover, the court is required to assess the contribution without regard to the relationship of husband and wife, or the fact that the acts of contribution are those of a reasonable spouse of that sex in the circumstances.

Finally, the Act abolishes the presumption of advancement as between husband and wife and substitutes the presumption of resulting trust. However,

---

[26]Act, s. 6. See, *e.g.*, *Weir v. Weir* (1978), 23 O.R. (2d) 765, 96 D.L.R. (3d) 725 (H.C.J.), and *Brown v. Brown* (1978), 20 O.R. (2d) 20, 86 D.L.R. (3d) 566 (S.C.), matrimonial home vested in wife; *Irrsack v. Irrsack* (1978), 22 O.R. (2d) 245, 93 D.L.R. (3d) 139 (H.C.J.), affd 27 O.R. (2d) 478*n*, 106 D.L.R. (3d) 705*n* (C.A.), and *King v. King* (1979), 24 O.R. (2d) 466, 9 R.F.L. (2d) 294 (S.C.), payment of compensating amount. The court will not direct partition or sale of the matrimonial home until it has determined that an order for exclusive possession should not be made: *Re Cipens and Cipens* (1978), 21 O.R. (2d) 134, 90 D.L.R. (3d) 461 (Unified Fam. Ct.). The court may also charge a spouse who has been in exclusive possession of the jointly owned matrimonial home with occupation rent: *Diotallevi v. Diotallevi* (1982), 37 O.R. (2d) 106, 134 D.L.R. (3d) 477 (H.C.J.). An order for sale of assets may be made in matrimonial proceedings without leave of the bankruptcy court where the husband goes bankrupt after a division of assets has been ordered: *Re Di Michele and Di Michele* (1981), 37 O.R. (2d) 314, 135 D.L.R. (3d) 306 (H.C.J.).

[27]Act, s. 7. An order vesting the jointly owned matrimonial home is subject to executions against the husband; *Re Maroukis and Maroukis* (1981), 125 D.L.R. (3d) 718 (Ont. C.A.).

[28](1973), 41 D.L.R. (3d) 367, [1975] 1 S.C.R. 423. See §1604.1(c), *supra*.

where property is held by the spouses as joint tenants there is a presumption that they each have a half-interest in it on severance. Moreover, money held in a bank account in the names of both spouses is deemed to be held by them as joint tenants.[29]

It should be noted that sections 7 and 8 apply regardless of whether there has been a marriage breakdown and, since they apply to former spouses as well, it might have been supposed that applications under these sections could be brought after divorce or death. However, it has been held that an application under section 8 lies only while both parties are living.[30]

Since the statute provides for a *prima facie* right of equal division of assets, but the courts have a discretion to make an unequal division, as well as to divide non-family assets, the basic principle which has been adopted is that the courts should not go beyond the *prima facie* right unless the result would be inequitable, having regard to the criteria set out in section 4(4).[31]

With respect to these criteria, in deciding whether the family assets should be divided unequally, the court will have regard, for example, to an agreement between the spouses which does not satisfy the requirement of a domestic contract under the Act, but which does deal with a division of assets on a breakdown of the marriage[32] but not if the parties did not direct their minds to the question.[33]

The short duration of the marriage may lead to an unequal division unless the assets were acquired in contemplation of the marriage[34] and the non-titled spouse tried to make the marriage work.[35]

The duration of separation is a relevant factor in that expenses to the family assets incurred by the titled spouse after separation are recoverable by him.[36] However, the assets are valued as at the date of the trial.[37]

---

[29] Act, s. 11. For the evidence needed to rebut this presumption see *Byzruki v. Byzruki* (1981), 131 D.L.R. (3d) 82 (Ont. H.C.J.).

[30] *Kiss v. Palachik* (1981), 34 O.R. (2d) 484, 24 R.F.L. (2d) 337 (C.A.), affd 146 D.L.R. (3d) 385, [1983] 1 S.C.R. 622. See also *Re Nevile and Beckstead* (1979), 27 O.R. (2d) 59, 11 R.F.L. (2d) 190 (Co. Ct.). But see McLeod, "Annotation" (1979), 11 R.F.L. (2d) 190; Hull, "Is a Deceased Spouse a Former Spouse under Sections 7 and 8 of the Family Law Reform Act?" (1980), 13 R.F.L. (2d) 174.

[31] *Silverstein v. Silverstein* (1978), 20 O.R. (2d) 185 at pp. 199-200, 87 D.L.R. (3d) 116 at p. 130 (H.C.J.), *per* Galligan, J. This principle has since been followed on numerous occasions. See, *e.g.*, *O'Reilly v. O'Reilly* (1979), 23 O.R. (2d) 776, 96 D.L.R. (3d) 742 (H.C.J.); *Ramboer v. Ramboer* (1979), 11 R.F.L. (2d) 320 (Ont. H.C.J.); *Calvert v. Calvert* (1979), 9 R.F.L. (2d) 162 (Ont. H.C.J.); *Fletcher v. Fletcher* (1980), 17 R.F.L. (2d) 325 (Ont. Unified Fam. Ct.); *Grime v. Grime* (1980), 16 R.F.L. (2d) 365 (Ont. H.C.J.).

[32] See, *e.g.*, *Wiebe v. Wiebe* (1980), 16 R.F.L. (2d) 286 (Ont. Co. Ct.); *Quick v. Quick, supra*, footnote 25; *Cushman v. Cushman* (1979), 10 R.F.L. (2d) 305 (Ont. H.C.J.).

[33] *Silverstein v. Silverstein, supra*, footnote 31.

[34] See, *e.g.*, *Woodbyrne v. Woodbyrne* (1980), 16 R.F.L. (2d) 180 (Ont. H.C.J.); *Tsanos v. Tsanos* (1980), 15 R.F.L. (2d) 368 (Ont. H.C.J.).

[35] *Irrsack v. Irrsack, supra*, footnote 26.

[36] *Mercer v. Mercer* (1978), 5 R.F.L. (2d) 224 (Ont. H.C.J.); *King v. King, supra*, footnote 26; *Quick v. Quick* (1980), 16 R.F.L. (2d) 63 (Ont. H.C.J.); *Grime v. Grime, supra*, footnote 31.

[37] *Re Young and Young* (1981), 32 O.R. (2d) 19, 120 D.L.R. (3d) 662 (C.A.).

Whether or not there is to be an unequal division because of the date when the asset was acquired seems to depend on the other factors listed in section 4(4), such as the length of the marriage.[38]

Property derived by gift or inheritance from a third party (but not from the other spouse)[39] may lead to an unequal sharing of family assets, unless the marriage was of long duration and the property had long formed part of the pool of family assets.[40]

The mere fact that one spouse made an unequal contribution to the marriage will not result in an unequal division under section 4(5), unless the spouse neglected his marital duties[41] but it is otherwise where he or she is incapacitated by illness.[42] Moreover, the fact that it is a childless marriage does not disentitle a wife to an equal division of family assets and she may also be entitled to a share of non-family assets which the husband was able to accumulate.[42a]

The court will make a division of non-family assets where, for example, a spouse has disposed of a family asset to evade the provisions of the Act, has committed acts of vandalism, or has otherwise improperly impoverished the family assets.[43] Alternatively, the other spouse may be awarded a larger share of the family assets.[44]

The mere fact that one spouse has assumed the duty of looking after the house and bringing up the children so as to enable the other to pursue business interests will not trigger an application of section 4(6). That is only one of the factors to be considered. In addition, the court must determine whether an equal division of the family assets would be inequitable in the circumstances and in that context, the efforts of the titled spouse in acquiring the assets are taken into account.[45]

---

[38]See, *e.g.*, *Meszaros v. Meszaros* (1978), 22 O.R. (2d) 695 (H.C.J.); *Irrsack v. Irrsack* (1978), 22 O.R. (2d) 245, 93 D.L.R. (3d) 139 (H.C.J.); *Woodbyrne v. Woodbyrne, supra,* footnote 34; *McLellan v. McLellan* (1980), 16 R.F.L. (2d) 323 (Ont. H.C.J.).

[39]*Silverstein v. Silverstein, supra,* footnote 31.

[40]*Calvert v. Calvert, supra,* footnote 31; *Weir v. Weir* (1978), 23 O.R. (2d) 765, 96 D.L.R. (3d) 725 (H.C.J.), but see, *contra, Gilbert v. Gilbert* (1979), 10 R.F.L. (2d) 385 (Ont. Co. Ct.); *Prytula v. Prytula* (1980), 30 O.R. (2d) 324, 116 D.L.R. (3d) 474 (H.C.J.).

[41]*Bregman v. Bregman* (1978), 21 O.R. (2d) 722, 91 D.L.R. (3d) 470 (H.C.J.); *King v. King* (1979), 24 O.R. (2d) 466, 9 R.F.L. (2d) 294 (S.C.); *Re Young and Young, supra,* footnote 37; *Whaley v. Whaley* (1981), 127 D.L.R. (3d) 63 (Ont. H.C.J.), aff'd 132 D.L.R. (3d) 322n (C.A.).

[42]*Grime v. Grime* (1980), 16 R.F.L. (2d) 365 (Ont. H.C.J.); *Bray v. Bray* (1979), 16 R.F.L. (2d) 78 (Ont. Co. Ct.).

[14a]*Whaley v. Whaley, supra,* footnote 41.

[43]See *Grime v. Grime, supra,* footnote 42; *Re Young and Young, supra,* footnote 37.

[44]See, *e.g., Woodbyrne v. Woodbyrne, supra,* footnote 34; *Simpson v. Simpson* (1980), 30 O.R. (2d) 497, 116 D.L.R. (3d) 127 (S.C.); *Szatori v. Szatori* (1979), 27 O.R. (2d) 595, 13 R.F.L. (2d) 233 (S.C.). See also *Tylman v. Tylman* (1980), 30 O.R. (2d) 721, 117 D.L.R. (3d) 730 (H.C.J.), wife awarded lump sum out of husband's matrimonial assets.

[45]*Re Young and Young, supra,* footnote 37; *Re Leatherdale and Leatherdale* (1980), 31 O.R. (2d) 141, 118 D.L.R. (3d) 72 (C.A.).

(e) Applications to determine property interests

As noted above,[46] section 7 permits a spouse to bring an application at any time during or after the marriage for a declaration that he has an interest in property owned by the other spouse, except where an application or order under section 4 has been made.[47]

The section is procedural only and does not create any new substantive rights.[48] However, the property rules applicable under the section are modified by section 11 which abolishes the presumption of advancement between spouses.[49]

Where the property is held jointly there is no need to rely on the presumption of a resulting trust raised by section 11 since section 11(1)(a) deems the parties to have a *prima facie* equal interest on severance.[50]

The principles applicable under resulting trusts are dealt with elsewhere.[51]

(f) Applications on the basis of contributions

Section 8 of the Act, described above,[52] introduces the doctrines of resulting and constructive trusts into the Act.[53] The section only applies to non-family assets, but an application under it may be made whether or not the parties' marriage continues.[54] It does not apply where the property is already held in co-ownership.[55]

It has now been established that before a spouse is entitled to an order under section 8, he or she must prove that there was a clear and direct connection between the contribution and the property in dispute.[56] The fact that a wife has assumed the role of wife and mother in order to enable the husband to work is not such a contribution, although those facts may be relevant under section 4.[57] On the other hand, actual and reasonably substantial work

---

[46]At footnote 30.

[47]*Re Cipens and Cipens* (1978), 21 O.R. (2d) 134, 90 D.L.R. (3d) 461 (Unified Fam. Ct.); *Ling v. Ling* (1980), 29 O.R. (2d) 717 at pp. 724-5, 114 D.L.R. (3d) 261 at p. 268 (C.A.).

[48]*Ling v. Ling, supra,* footnote 47; *Re De Freitas and De Freitas* (1979), 25 O.R. (2d) 174, 101 D.L.R. (3d) 173 (C.A.).

[49]See text at footnote 29, *supra.* And see *Re De Freitas and De Freitas, supra,* footnote 48; *Meszaros v. Meszaros* (1978), 22 O.R. (2d) 695 (H.C.J.); *Forbes v. Forbes* (1979), 22 O.R. (2d) 771, 94 D.L.R. (3d) 715 (H.C.J.).

[50]*Ling v. Ling, supra,* footnote 47. For the evidence needed to rebut this presumption see *Byzruki v. Byzruki, supra,* footnote 28.

[51]See §1209.4, *supra.*

[52]At footnote 28, *supra.*

[53]*Ling v. Ling, supra,* footnote 47, at pp. 724-5 O.R., p. 268 D.L.R., *per* Lacourcière, J.A. See McLeod, "Annotation" (1980), 19 R.F.L. (2d) 148.

[54]Although not in respect of former family assets, it seems: *Machuk v. Machuk* (1979), 10 R.F.L. (2d) 224 (Ont. Co. Ct).

[55]*Ling v. Ling, supra,* footnote 47.

[56]*Page v. Page* (1980), 31 O.R. (2d) 136, 118 D.L.R. (3d) 57 (C.A.); *Re Leatherdale and Leatherdale* (1980), 31 O.R. (2d) 141, 118 D.L.R. (3d) 72 (C.A.).

[57]*Ibid.*

by a spouse in the other spouse's business would suffice,[58] as will a contribution from a joint account[59] or a guarantee of a business loan.[60] Minor services or labour in the other spouse's business are insufficient to support an order under section 8.[61]

(g) Effect of Part I of the Act

Although the law is as yet unclear, it seems probable that Part I, including sections 4, 7, 8 and 11, is intended to be a complete codification of the common law. If this is so, the doctrines of resulting and constructive trusts as developed prior to the Act will no longer have any application to spouses and former spouses except by way of analogy;[62] and except after one spouse has died.[62a]

(h) Interim orders

Under section 9 of the Act the court may make temporary orders to prevent dissipation of property. It may be used by a spouse to prevent a threatened sale of a family asset.[63]

(i) The matrimonial home

Under Part III of the Act the spouses are given an equal right to possession of the matrimonial home[64] while they are married, unless a separation agreement or court order provides otherwise.[65]

The spouses may designate any property as the matrimonial home and upon registration of the designation any other property that might otherwise be a matrimonial home ceases to be one.[66]

In order to protect the non-titled spouse, the titled spouse is prohibited from alienating or encumbering the matrimonial home, except with his spouse's consent or court order. A conveyance or encumbrance to a person who is not a *bona fide* purchaser for value without notice may be set aside.[67] This does not

---

[58]See, *e.g.*, *Meszaros v. Meszaros, supra,* footnote 49; *Ramboer v. Ramboer* (1979), 11 R.F.L. (2d) 320 (Ont. H.C.J.); *McIntyre v. McIntyre* (1979), 9 R.F.L. (2d) 332 (Ont. H.C.J.).

[59]*Stere v. Stere* (1980), 15 R.F.L. (2d) 357 (Ont. H.C.J.).

[60]*Diamond v. Sugar* (1980), 30 O.R. (2d) 205, 115 D.L.R. (3d) 662 (H.C.J.).

[61]*Fisher v. Fisher* (1978), 21 O.R. (2d) 105, 89 D.L.R. (3d) 543 (H.C.J.); *Page v. Page, supra,* footnote 56; *Re Leatherdale and Leatherdale, supra,* footnote 56.

[62]See McLeod, "Annotation" (1980), 19 R.F.L. (2d) 165.

[62a]*Kiss v. Palachik, supra,* footnote 30.

[63]*Mageau v. Mageau* (1978), 22 O.R. (2d) 179, 92 D.L.R. (3d) 402 (H.C.J. Fam. Law Div.).

[64]Defined in section 39.

[65]Act, s. 40. See *Re Cotroneo and Cotroneo* (1978), 20 O.R. (2d) 252, 88 D.L.R. (3d) 764 (Co. Ct.), conveyance by wife of interest in matrimonial home to husband pursuant to separation agreement removes property from definition.

[66]Act, s. 41.

[67]*Ibid.,* s. 42, am. 1984, c. 32, s. 18(1), and s. 44. This is so even though the titled spouse has since died: *Re Van Dorp and Van Dorp* (1980), 30 O.R. (2d) 623 (Co. Ct.).

mean that the non-titled spouse has a property interest in the property, however. His interest is purely personal and cannot be reached by his creditors.[68]

If an encumbrancer commences proceedings to realize upon his security, the non-titled spouse is entitled to the same right of redemption as the titled spouse and must be served with notice of the proceeding. Section 43(2) provides that if notice is given by mail service shall be deemed to have been made on the fifth day after mailing. However, this does not require an additional five days of notice.[69]

The court is empowered to award interim or permanent exclusive possession to one of the spouses if other provision for shelter is inadequate, or if it is in the best interest of a child to do so.[70] It has been held that if these criteria are not met, the court has no discretion but must make an order for exclusive possession.[71]

Where both spouses have a property interest in the home, partition or sale may be refused on the basis of the criteria set out in section 45.[72]

(j) Contracting out

Part IV of the Act makes substantial provisions under which spouses and cohabitees may enter into domestic contracts, including marriage contracts and separation agreements, whereby they may exclude all or part of the Act. Thus, the operation of Part I of the Act may be excluded, but Part III may not be excluded in a marriage contract,[73] although the parties may do so in a separation agreement.[74]

In order to be valid the contract must be in writing, signed by the parties and witnessed.[75] It is subject to the law of contracts and may thus be set aside for any reason that vitiates any other contract, such as undue influence,[76] or withholding of information.[77]

---

[68]*Chalmers v. Copfer* (1978), 7 R.F.L. (2d) 393 (Ont. Co. Ct.).

[69]*Re Kinross Mortgage Corp. and Canada Mortgage & Housing Corp.* (1981), 128 D.L.R. (3d) 477 (Ont. H.C.J.). See also *Re United Dominions Investments Ltd. v. Cylwa* (1980), 29 O.R. (2d) 657, 114 D.L.R. (3d) 765 (Co. Ct.). Cf. *Re Bank of Nova Scotia and Canada Mortgage and Housing Corp.* (1980), 29 O.R. (2d) 667, 114 D.L.R. (3d) 713 (Co. Ct.).

[70]Act, s. 45, am. 1984, c. 32, s. 18(2). See, e.g., *Langtvet v. Langtvet* (1978), 7 R.F.L. (2d) 224 (Ont. H.C.J.), wife given exclusive possession until youngest child reaches age of 18.

[71]*Janssen v. Janssen* (1979), 25 O.R. (2d) 213, 11 R.F.L. (2d) 274 (Co. Ct.). Cf. *Miller v. Miller* (1978), 2 R.F.L. (2d) 129 (Ont. Prov. Ct. Fam. Div.), and as to interim possession: *Campbell v. Campbell* (1978), 6 R.F.L. (2d) 392 (Ont. H.C.J.); *Busse v. Busse* (1978), 2 R.F.L. (2d) 273 (Ont. Prov. Ct. Fam. Div.).

[72]*Cipens v. Cipens* (1978), 21 O.R. (2d) 134, 90 D.L.R. (3d) 461 (Unified Fam. Ct.); *Geers v. Geers* (1979), 10 R.F.L. (2d) 367 (Ont. Unified Fam. Ct.).

[73]Act, s. 51(2).

[74]*Ibid.*, s. 53.

[75]*Ibid.*, s. 54.

[76]*Youngblut v. Youngblut* (1979), 11 R.F.L. (2d) 249 (Ont. H.C.J.). Cf. *Richie v. Richie and Gow; Richie v. Richie and Hainge* (1981), 19 R.F.L. (2d) 199 (Ont. H.C.J.), in which no undue influence was shown.

[77]*Couzens v. Couzens* (1981), 34 O.R. (2d) 87, 126 D.L.R. (3d) 577 (C.A.).

The Act deems marriage contracts and separation agreements entered into before it came into force to be domestic contracts for the purposes of the Act.[78] Thus, releases contained in such agreements for claims against the other spouse may be valid.[79] If there has been a subsequent reconciliation, however, the prior separation agreement is not a bar.[80] On the other hand, where property has been transferred pursuant to an oral understanding or agreement between the parties before the Act came into force, the property is excluded from the Act.[81]

(k) Effect on death

Part I of the Act only applies to spouses. Hence, an application for division of assets cannot be commenced after one of the spouses has died, although it can be continued if it was commenced before his death.[82] Thus, if one of the spouses dies, the other must rely on the normal rules of succession. While these include a right to bring an application for relief under Part V of the *Succession Law Reform Act*,[83] such relief lies in the court's discretion and is not as of right as under Part I of the *Family Law Reform Act*. Since the Act makes substantial new provisions for spouses, the common law rights of dower and curtesy have been abolished.[84]

Applications under sections 7 and 8 can not be brought after the death of one of the spouses.[85]

Part III of the Act also applies only while both parties are living, for the right to equal possession ceases when a spouse ceases to be a spouse.[86] An order made before the death of one of the spouses giving the other exclusive possession for a specified period of time will, of course, survive the other's death.

Finally, the parties can arrange their affairs by domestic contract in such a way as to provide that their rights thereunder shall survive the death of one of them.[87]

---

[78]Act, s. 59.

[79]See, *e.g., Engel v. Engel* (1980), 30 O.R. (2d) 152, 116 D.L.R. (3d) 309 (H.C.J.); *Lotton v. Lotton* (1979), 25 O.R. (2d) 1, 99 D.L.R. (3d) 745 (C.A.); *Bebenek v. Bebenek* (1979), 24 O.R. (2d) 385, 98 D.L.R. (3d) 536 (C.A.); *Klein v. Klein* (1980), 30 O.R. (2d) 422, 17 R.F.L. (2d) 231 (S.C.), affd 32 O.R. (2d) 544n (C.A.), but see *Sinnett v. Sinnett* (1980), 15 R.F.L. (2d) 115 (Ont. Co. Ct.), in which a Quebec marriage contract was held not to be a bar to a claim under Part I because it sought to limit possessory rights in the matrimonial home.

[80]*Szabo v. Szabo* (1980), 15 R.F.L. (2d) 13 (Ont. Unified Fam. Ct.), and see *Diamond v. Sugar* (1980), 30 O.R. (2d) 205, 115 D.L.R. (3d) 662 (H.C.J.).

[81]*Moldovan v. Moldovan* (1980), 15 R.F.L. (2d) 42 (Ont. H.C.J.).

[82]Act, s. 4(3).

[83]R.S.O. 1980, c. 488.

[84]Act, s. 70 (dower); *Succession Law Reform Act*, s. 48 (curtesy).

[85]See footnote 30, *supra.*

[86]Act, s. 40(2).

[87]Act, ss. 51, 52.

1605.8　Prince Edward Island

(a) Introduction

The *Family Law Reform Act*[1] is virtually identical to the Ontario Act. Thus, it introduces a deferred right to a division of assets on marriage breakdown, with special provision being made for the matrimonial home. It is probable, therefore, that the Ontario decisions will be considered closely in the interpretation of the Act.

Rather than discussing the Act in detail, which would duplicate the material in the previous paragraph, the major differences between the two statutes will be outlined.

(b) Family assets

Whether or not an asset is a family asset depends on its present use, not when, or how, it was acquired.[2] However, contrary to some of the Ontario cases, the courts have held that there need not be an actual user of the asset as a family asset, so long as the parties intended that it be used for that purpose.[3]

The Act makes a specific provision respecting the onus of proof respecting family assets which is not found in the Ontario Act and is contrary to what the Ontario cases have decided. It provides that the onus is on the person alleging that an asset is not a family asset to prove the allegation.[4]

(c) Division of assets

The courts appear to be adopting a similar approach to those in Ontario in respect of applications for an unequal division of family assets and a division of non-family assets. There must be special circumstances, which meet the criteria set out in the Act, before such divisions will be made.[5]

(d) Ante-nuptial property

The Act contains an accounting provision which is not in the Ontario Act. It requires the court to deduct from the net value of any family asset acquired by a spouse before the marriage the value of that asset at the time of the marriage.[6] The purpose of this provision apparently is to prevent the break-up of family farms which might otherwise occur, especially after short marriages.[7] It should be noted that only the farmhouse and adjacent land is the matri-

---

§1605.8

[1] S.P.E.I. 1978, c. 6, am. S.P.E.I. 1980, c. 2, s. 3 (hereafter referred to as the "Act").
[2] Act, s. 4(*a*).
[3] *Gillis v. Gillis* (1980), 14 R.F.L. (2d) 147 (P.E.I.S.C.); *Ferguson v. Ferguson* (1980), 16 R.F.L. (2d) 207, 28 Nfld. & P.E.I.R. 498 (P.E.I.S.C.).
[4] Act, s. 6(2). See *Gillis v. Gillis*, *supra*, footnote 3.
[5] See *Gillis v. Gillis*, *supra*, footnote 3; *Dover v. Dover* (1979), 10 R.F.L. (2d) 50 (P.E.I.S.C.); *McCabe v. McCabe and Daley* (1979), 11 R.F.L. (2d) 260 (P.E.I.S.C.).
[6] Act, s. 5(4). See *Ferguson v. Ferguson*, *supra*, footnote 3.
[7] Dumont, "Prince Edward Island" in *Matrimonial Property Law in Canada* (Bissett-Johnson and Holland, eds., Calgary, Burroughs & Co., 1980), pp. PEI-9, 10.

monial home and, hence, a family asset available for division.[8] However, the rest of the farm is available for division as a non-family asset where the criteria of the Act for such a division are met.[9]

(e) Applications based on contributions

The Act contains a section to overcome the problems created by *Murdoch v. Murdoch*,[10] which is similar to that contained in the Ontario Act, but clearer, in that it specifically provides that the contribution is to be assessed on the basis that it creates a resulting trust.[11]

(f) Presumption of advancement

As in many of the other statutes, the presumption of advancement has been abolished as between a husband and wife and replaced with a presumption of resulting trust.[12] Thus, where a husband conveyed property to his wife at her request to keep it safe from a possible lawsuit which might arise out of his relationship with another woman, she held the property on a resulting trust for him and, since it was a family asset, it was available for equal division.[13]

(g) Effect on death

As under the Ontario Act, an application for division of assets cannot be made after one of the spouses has died, but can be continued if commenced before his death.[14] After the spouse has died, therefore, the survivor must rely on the normal rules of succession for a share in the deceased's estate.

Since the Act has made major new provisions for spouses the common law rights of dower and curtesy have been abolished.[15]

1605.9 Saskatchewan

(a) Introduction

In response to the problems posed by *Murdoch v. Murdoch*,[1] interim reform legislation was passed in Saskatchewan in the form of a repeal and re-enactment of section 22 of the *Married Women's Property Act*.[2] Section 22 enabled

---

[8]Act, ss. 4(*a*), 39(4).
[9]*Ibid.*, s. 5(6).
[10](1973), 41 D.L.R. (3d) 367, [1975] 1 S.C.R. 423. See §1604.1(c), *supra*.
[11]Act, s. 9.
[12]*Ibid.*, s. 12.
[13]*Henry v. Henry and Vincent* (1979), 10 R.F.L. (2d) 77 (P.E.I.S.C.).
[14]Act, s. 5(3).
[15]*Ibid.*, s. 62.
§1605.9
[1](1973), 41 D.L.R. (3d) 367, [1975] 1 S.C.R. 423. See §1604.1(c), *supra*.
[2]By S.S. 1974-75, c. 29, s. 1. The Act is now known as the *Married Person's Property Act*, R.S.S. 1978, c. M-6. However, section 22 was repealed and replaced by major reform legislation in 1979. See footnote 4, *infra*.

spouses to apply to the court for the determination of any question concerning property rights between them. The court then had to consider their respective contributions, whether in the form of money, services, prudent management, household and family duties, or other reasons, but subject to any written agreement between the spouses to the contrary. The court was empowered to make such orders dividing the property as it considered fair and equitable. The section thus conferred an extremely wide discretion upon the court, which was unfettered by any statutory criteria.[3] It was used extensively to redistribute assets between the spouses.

Section 22 was repealed by the *Matrimonial Property Act*[4] which introduced a comprehensive reform of the law of matrimonial property. The Act provides for a deferred right to a division of matrimonial property upon application of a spouse. However, if no application is made, the separate property regime remains in effect.[5] Part I of the Act makes special provision for occupation rights in the matrimonial home.

(b) Application of Act

The Act applies only to spouses under a valid or voidable marriage and under a void marriage if one of the parties entered into it *bona fide* and they have cohabited within the preceding year before making an application.[6] It also applies to a surviving spouse[7] and to spouses married before the Act came into force.[8] It does not apply to cohabitees or persons whose marriage has been dissolved.

The Act applies to property acquired before the Act came into force and to proceedings commenced before that date with respect to matrimonial property.[9]

(c) Distribution of matrimonial property

Part II of the Act provides for a *prima facie* equal distribution of the matrimonial property between the spouses in recognition of the fact that child care, household management and financial provision are joint and mutual responsibilities of the spouses.[10] Matrimonial property is defined as all property that is owned in whole or in part by one or both spouses and includes security,

---

[3]*Schneider v. Schneider* (1979), 10 R.F.L. (2d) 88 at p. 90, 1 Sask. R. 19 at p. 20 (C.A.); *Rusnak v. Rusnak*, [1976] 4 W.W.R. 515 at p. 520, 24 R.F.L. 24 at p. 29 (Sask. Q.B.); *Birkeland v. Birkeland* (1979), 10 R.F.L. (2d) 42 at p. 48, 3 Sask. R. 11 at p. 17 (C.A.); *Patron v. Patron* (1981), 120 D.L.R. (3d) 10, 7 Sask. R. 366 (Q.B.). The section did not completely replace the doctrine of constructive trust: *Thoreson v. Thoreson et al.; Re Thoreson and Thoreson* (1982), 137 D.L.R. (3d) 535, [1982] 5 W.W.R. 211 (Sask. C.A.).
[4]S.S. 1979, c. M-6.1, s. 60 (hereafter referred to as the "Act").
[5]Act, s. 43.
[6]*Ibid.*, s. 2(*k*).
[7]*Ibid.*
[8]*Ibid.*, s. 3(*a*).
[9]*Ibid.*, s. 3(*b*), (*c*).
[10]*Ibid.*, ss. 20, 21(1).

corporate, partnership and trust interests and property over which a spouse has control by a power of appointment or revocation.[11] Certain property is exempt from distribution, however, including the fair market value at the time of the marriage of property (other than the matrimonial home and household goods) acquired before marriage by third party gift or inheritance, unless given for the benefit of both spouses; the fair market value at the time of marriage of property owned by a spouse before the marriage; damage awards payable to one spouse, except those in respect of property;[12] property acquired in exchange for the foregoing[13] and property dealt with by the spouses in an interspousal contract unless the contract was, in the opinion of the court, unconscionable or grossly unfair.[14]

Despite the *prima facie* right to an equal division, the court is given a discretion to refuse to order a distribution, to vest all the matrimonial property in one spouse, or to make an unequal division if it is satisfied that it would be unfair and inequitable to make an equal division. Before exercising that discretion, however, the court must have regard to a long list of criteria, including a written agreement between the spouses, the duration of the cohabitation and separation, the tax consequences of an order and others but not to any immoral or improper conduct of a spouse unless it amounts to dissipation.[15] If the contributions by one spouse, the financial conduct of a spouse, or the facts relative to any of these criteria are minor, the court might order an equal division. An unequal division has been ordered, however, in favour of a husband who brought the farm, which provided the base of the family's capital, into the marriage,[16] because of third party contributions to the husband's assets[17] and because of the short duration of the marriage.[18]

The distribution of the matrimonial home is dealt with separately. It is defined as property owned by or leased to one or both spouses, or owned by a corporation in which one or both spouses have an interest, and which is or has been occupied as the family home or intended by them to be so occupied.[19] The matrimonial home must be divided equally, having regard only to any tax liability and debts and encumbrances pertaining to the home, unless it is unfair and inequitable, having regard only to extraordinary circumstances, or unless it is unfair and inequitable to the spouse who has custody of the children.

---

[11]*Ibid.*, s. 2(*h*).

[12]See *Wilson v. Wilson* (1980), 19 R.F.L. (2d) 321, 10 Sask. R. 21 (Q.B.), the cash surrender value of a life insurance policy is not exempt when determining the value of matrimonial property.

[13]Act, s. 23.

[14]*Ibid.*, s. 24.

[15]*Ibid.*, ss. 21(2), 25.

[16]*Evenson v. Evenson* (1980), 17 R.F.L. (2d) 389, 4 Sask. R. 47 (Q.B.), and see *Werner v. Werner* (1980), 16 R.F.L. (2d) 144, 1 Sask. R. 327 (Q.B.).

[17]*Wornath v. Wornath* (1980), 19 R.F.L. (2d) 289, 3 Sask. R. 266 (Q.B.); *Bains v. Bains*, [1980] 5 W.W.R. 7, 17 R.F.L. (2d) 193 (Sask. Q.B.).

[18]*Nister v. Nister* (1980), 16 R.F.L. (2d) 394, 8 Sask. R. 252 (Q.B.); *Rishel v. Rishel* (1980), 19 R.F.L. (2d) 221 (Sask. Q.B.).

[19]Act, s. 2(*g*).

In those cases only, the court may make similar orders to those it is empowered to make under section 21.[20] An equal division has been held to be unfair and inequitable where the husband had incurred substantial debts with respect to the home.[21] Similarly, where the wife refused to refinance the home to forestall foreclosure and had left her husband and children, the matrimonial home was ordered to be vested in the husband.[22]

With respect to exempt property, the court is empowered to distribute it, or make orders with respect thereto, where the court is satisfied that it would be unfair and inequitable to exempt the property, having regard to the criteria set out in section 21 and others.[23]

The court is given extensive powers to effect a distribution of matrimonial property,[24] including powers to set aside or retain gifts, transfers or sales of property to prevent dissipation of property and to restore dissipated property.[25] However, where a sale has been completed, a *bona fide* purchaser for value is protected.[26]

(d) The matrimonial home

Part I of the Act confers an equal right to possession of the matrimonial home upon both spouses, subject, however, to the provisions of an interspousal contract.[27] The right is also subject to section 43, which enables the titled spouse to alienate and encumber it at will.

The court may grant exclusive possession to one of the spouses and may make ancillary orders in connection therewith.[28] If such an order is made, it may be registered[29] and the titled spouse is then prohibited from dealing with property without the written consent of the other spouse.[30] A spouse who has an exclusive right of possession pursuant to a court order has the same right of notice and redemption that the titled spouse has against any encumbrancer.[31]

The rights under Part I are in addition to those conferred by the *Homesteads Act*.[32]

---

[20]*Ibid.*, s. 22.

[21]*Wilson v. Wilson, supra*, footnote 12.

[22]*Szeto v. Szeto*, [1981] 3 W.W.R. 124, 20 R.F.L. (2d) 99 (Sask. Dist. Ct.).

[23]Act, s. 23(4), (5).

[24]*Ibid.*, s. 26.

[25]*Ibid.*, ss. 28, 29.

[26]*Ibid.*, s. 28(2).

[27]*Ibid.*, s. 4.

[28]*Ibid.*, s. 5. This is so even where the parties are separated, hostile and in litigation and the court will not make such an order in favour of the spouse who has custody of the children: *Re Korolchuk and Korolchuk* (1982), 135 D.L.R. (3d) 184, 28 R.F.L. (2d) 216 (Sask. C.A.).

[29]*Ibid.*, s. 9.

[30]*Ibid.*, s. 12.

[31]*Ibid.*, s. 15.

[32]R.S.S. 1978, c. H-5. See Act, s. 16.

(e) Contracting out

Under Part V of the Act spouses may enter into interspousal contracts to regulate the ownership and possession of property and thereby to contract out of the provisions of the Act. The court may, however, distribute such property if it is of the opinion that the contract was unconscionable or grossly unfair.[33]

The court may also take agreements that do not satisfy the formalities of the Act into account in any application under it.[34] However, any agreement must in fact deal with the spouses' property rights, before it will exempt the property from distribution.[35]

(f) Effect on death

An application under the Act may be continued by a surviving spouse or by the estate of a deceased spouse. Moreover, a surviving spouse may bring an application within six months of the grant of probate or letters of administration.[36]

The rights of the surviving spouse are in addition to his rights on an intestacy,[37] to his rights under the *Dependants' Relief Act*[38] and, in the case of a widow, to her rights under the *Homesteads Act*.[39] Moreover, an order transferring property under the Act to a surviving spouse has the effect of excluding that property from the estate of the deceased unless the court directs otherwise with respect to creditors.[40]

(g) Presumption of advancement

In common with most of the other statutes, the Act abolishes the presumption of advancement as between spouses and replaces it with the presumption of resulting trust except where the property is held jointly and where it is money in a bank account in the names of both spouses.[41]

1605.10 Northwest Territories

(a) Introduction

The Northwest Territories is the only common law jurisdiction which does not have comprehensive matrimonial property law reform legislation. The

---

[33] Act, s. 24.
[34] *Ibid.*, s. 40. See *Beaudry v. Beaudry* (1981), 18 R.F.L. (2d) 384, 9 Sask. R. 38 (Q.B.).
[35] *Lee v. Lee* (1980), 19 R.F.L. (2d) 280, 3 Sask. R. 421 (Q.B.), release clause in separation agreement dealing only with maintenance.
[36] Act, s. 30.
[37] *Ibid.*, s. 30(3).
[38] R.S.S. 1978, c. D-25. See Act, s. 37.
[39] R.S.S. 1978, c. H-5. See Act, ss. 16, 52.
[40] Act, s. 35.
[41] *Ibid.*, s. 50.

Matrimonial Property Ordinance[1] is, in essence, legislation respecting homesteads and is dealt with as such elsewhere.[2] The Act does, however, contain a section respecting the resolution of property disputes between spouses, which is similar to those found in other provinces.

(b) Applications to settle property disputes

The Act provides that in any question between spouses as to the title to, or possession, ownership or disposition of property they, or any person who has an interest, may make a summary application to the court for the settlement of the question.[3] The court is empowered to make such order as it considers fair and equitable, taking into account the respective contributions of the spouses, whether in the form of money, services, prudent management, caring for the home, or otherwise.[4]

In order to give effect to its findings, the court may direct, *inter alia*, the sale of the property and a division of the proceeds, the partition of the property, or the vesting of the property in one or both spouses.[5]

1605.11 Yukon

(a) Introduction

The *Matrimonial Property Ordinance*[1] resembles the Ontario Act in that it introduces a deferred sharing of family assets coupled with a judicial discretion to make an unequal division or a division of non-family assets.

(b) Application of Ordinance

The Ordinance only applies to spouses upon a marriage breakdown, although the court may allow an application to be made after dissolution of marriage.[2] It does not apply after one spouse has died, except to the extent that an application was begun before death.[3] Marriage breakdown is defined as the pronouncement of a decree *nisi* of divorce or a declaration of nullity, separation without a reasonable prospect of resumption of cohabitation, or the making of an application under the Ordinance.[4]

§1605.10
[1]R.O.N.W.T. 1974, c. M-7, am. O.N.W.T. 1977 (3rd Sess.), c. 2, s. 13 (hereafter referred to as the "Ordinance").
[2]See §§710-710.15, *supra*.
[3]Ordinance, s. 28(1).
[4]*Ibid.*, s. 28(2), (4).
[5]*Ibid.*, s. 28(2).
§1605.11
[1]O.Y.T. 1979 (2nd Sess.), c. 11, am. O.Y.T. 1980 (2nd Sess.), c. 16, s. 10 (hereafter referred to as the "Ordinance").
[2]Ordinance, s. 16(2).
[3]*Ibid.*, s. 19(1).
[4]*Ibid.*, s. 7(2).

Unless an application is brought under the Ordinance, the separate property regime continues and after death the normal rules of succession apply.

(c) Operation of Ordinance

Upon a marriage breakdown each spouse is entitled to have the family assets divided equally between them.[5] Family assets are defined in virtually the same way as in the Ontario Act on the basis of a user test.[6]

The court is empowered to make an unequal division of family assets where an equal division would be inequitable having regard to a number of criteria, including the duration of cohabitation and separation, the date and manner of acquisition of the property and others.[7]

If a spouse has unreasonably impoverished the family assets or the result of a division of a family asset would be inequitable, the court may also make a division of any non-family assets.[8]

Contributions by a spouse to a non-family asset are to be assessed as if the spouses were unmarried.[9] Moreover, the presumption of advancement as between spouses has been abolished and replaced with a presumption of resulting trust, except where the property is jointly owned or is money in a joint account.[10]

The court is given wide powers to determine property rights between spouses and, to make appropriate orders to reallocate property between them.[11]

(d) The family home

The family home, that is, property in which a spouse has an interest and which has been occupied by him and his spouse as their residence,[12] is given special treatment under Part II of the Ordinance. Both spouses have an equal right of possession of it during marriage[13] but the court may award exclusive possession of the home to one of the spouses.[14]

The titled spouse is prohibited from alienating or encumbering the family home without the consent of the other spouse or a court order. Moreover, the spouses may register a designation of their family home.[15] The non-titled spouse has an equal right of redemption or relief against forfeiture as the titled spouse.[16]

---

[5]*Ibid.*, s. 7(1).
[6]*Ibid.*, s. 5.
[7]*Ibid.*, s. 14.
[8]*Ibid.*, s. 15.
[9]*Ibid.*, s. 8(1).
[10]*Ibid.*, s. 8(2).
[11]*Ibid.*, ss. 12, 13.
[12]*Ibid.*, s. 22.
[13]*Ibid.*, s. 23.
[14]*Ibid.*, s. 28(2).
[15]*Ibid.*, ss. 24, 25.
[16]*Ibid.*, s. 29.

(e) Contracting out

The spouses may, by domestic contract, oust the provisions of Part I of the Ordinance. They may also contract out of Part II by a separation agreement but not by a marriage contract.[17]

---

[17]*Ibid.*, s. 3.